CASTLES
~ OF THE ~
CLANS

THE STRONGHOLDS AND SEATS OF
750 SCOTTISH FAMILIES AND CLANS

~

MARTIN COVENTRY

GOBLINSHEAD

CASTLES
OF THE
CLANS

First published 2008
Reprinted Feb 2010
Copyright © Martin Coventry 2008

Published by

GOBLINSHEAD

130B Inveresk Road, Musselburgh EH21 7AY, Scotland
Tel: +44 (0)131 665 2894
Email: goblinshead@sol.co.uk

British Library Cataloguing in Publication Data
A catalogue record for this book is available from
the British Library.

ISBN 10: 1 899874 36 4
ISBN 13: 978 1 899874 36 1

Typeset by GOBLINSHEAD
from electronic Castles and Clans database
using Desktop Publishing
Printed and bound in Scotland by Scotprint

Front cover photograph by kind permission of (©) Graeme Wallace
(www.gwpublishing.com)

Disclaimer:
The information contained in this *Castles of the Clans* (the "Material") is believed to be accurate at the time of printing, but no representation or warranty is given (express or implied) as to its accuracy, completeness or correctness. The author and publisher do not accept any liability whatsoever for any direct, indirect or consequential loss or damage arising in any way from any use of or reliance on this Material for any purpose.

While every care has been taken to compile and check all the information in this book, in a work of this complexity and size it is possible that mistakes and omissions may have occurred. If you know of any corrections, alterations or improvements, please contact the author or the publishers at the address above.

CASTLES
OF THE
CLANS

Contents

Preface

Many years ago, round the time the first edition of *The Castles of Scotland* was published, I was unlucky enough to do some work for a clan internet site. Unlucky because although I did the work I got absolutely nothing in return (not even the introduction to suppliers in the USA that had been promised as an absolute minimum in recompense). The work had involved compiling a list of clan castles, identifying sites, locations and what, if anything, still remained of any building. At that time there were a hundred or so clans and families, some of whom had as many as half a dozen castles. It had been a fascinating project in itself, tracking down old family castles and whether they were still existed and, if they did, what state they were in, and who now owned them, and even if it was possible to visit them or stay at an ancestral pile. But other (paying) work then had to take priority. The list was left abandoned and over the years sank into an abyss of backups and discarded files. Yet one of the most frequently asked questions from customers was for more information on the families and clans who owned the castles of Scotland.

A few years later there was a second edition of the *Castles* book and then a third, and then I began doing research for a fourth edition.

The first three editions had been published by the morloks* at Goblinshead, while the fourth edition was going to that shining eloi* bastion that is Birlinn, but that new edition was (then) still some years away. About this time I dusted the discarded bytes from the skeletal list of clan and family castles and started working anew. Months passed and research and work continued, fleshing up entries and tracking down sites and then more sites, and then a few more again. Other books overtook *Castles of the Clans*, and the fourth edition of *The Castles of Scotland*** was published (it was also late...). More deadlines passed, one after and another. Finally, more than two years late, *Castles of the Clans* finally squeezed itself from the darkness, blinking a little on the desktop.

One hundred or so clans became more than 750 Scottish clans and families, all of whom who had held lands, properties or castles. This included not only 'official' clans, as recognised by the 'Authorities', but also all those other families and clans that populated the kingdom of Scots.

A few hundred castles became more than 3000 fortified houses, strongholds, mansions, historic houses and lands, many of which had previously been forgotten and did not even appear in my own new edition of *The Castles of Scotland*.

And a book that was originally planned to be a lean 400 pages became a positively muscular 640 pages.

Castles of the Clans had grown in the compiling and in complexity, and I would like to take this opportunity to apologise for its tardiness. The book was always envisaged as a substantial work, but it was not until it was typeset that I realised quite what a strapping monster it was. The index, alone, took three solid weeks of work to compile and another week to check; the selection and scanning of illustrations took many weeks; checking and proofreading the entries took many months – and began to feel like painting the Forth Bridge: as soon as a new set of proofs was produced it was necessary to go back to the beginning and start all over again.

The morloks at Goblinshead began to grunt angrily about the cost of the printing and postage and that the trees in the overworld were again beginning to shed their leaves.

Then, finally, almost unbelievably, the book was suddenly complete, or at least as finished as it could be. I immediately felt lost...

I am aware that, despite the many years spent in compiling this work on 750 families, many dedicated people spend decades researching just their own clan history. So, while (I believe) this is the most comprehensive book available, it can not be considered the 'definitive' work on the subject. If you know of any improvements, corrections, omissions or additions (or even like the book just a bit), please contact me at goblinshead@sol.co.uk, and I will try to include new material should there be a second edition.

As ever, I would like to take this opportunity to thank my partner in crime, Joyce Miller, without whose help this book would still be languishing with the morloks.

Martin Coventry
Musselburgh, October 2007

*Apologies to H.G. Wells
**The Castles of Scotland* Fourth Edition was published by Birlinn in September 2006 (ISBN 13: 1841584495/ ISBN 10: 1841584492). It is available from bookshops and internet retailers, including Amazon, or contact goblinshead@sol.co.uk for more information

Introduction

Castles of the Clans

Most, and probably all, Scottish lairds and landowners lived in castles or tower houses; it has been estimated that there was between 3,000 and 4,000 of these buildings in Scotland during the medieval and early modern period. Most of these were not the great fortresses of dukes and earls, but were the fortified houses of lesser landowners, strong enough to defend against a thieving neighbour or raiding parties but not against an invading army or a vengeful monarch. While many fine buildings survive as romantic ruins, family homes or hotels, many many others have gone, and there is no trace that they ever existed.

Clan and Family Names

More than 750 clans and families are listed, with some 500 cross references, along with the castles, properties and lands that they held. Names can be divided into four groups:

Territorial or Place

The name comes from the lands that the family held or from a place, country or burgh. This is the most common form of origin.

In many cases the name comes from the original family lands, and many surnames would have originally been prefixed with the French 'de', meaning 'of'; so 'de Pittillock' (a property in Fife) over time became the name 'Pittillock', and then 'Pattullo'; 'de Moray', which was shortened to Moray or Murray. Other famous families with this origin include the Douglases, the Gordons, the Guthries and the Forbeses.

Other families took the name of lands that they held or places in France or the Continent before coming via England to Scotland, including the Balliols, the Bruces, the Comyns, the Frasers, the Setons and the Sinclairs. Others took the names of properties held or from places in England, such as the Grahams (from 'Gray Home'), the Hamiltons (from Hambleton, possibly in Yorkshire), the Hepburns (from Hebburn in Northumberland), the Ramsays, (from Ramsey in Huntingdonshire) and (of course) the Coventrys (from the city in Warwickshire).

The name can come from the original country or nationality of origin of the progenitor, such as Fleming (from Flanders), Francis or French (from France), Inglis (from England) and Wallace.

Paternal

The name comes from the name, nickname or diminutive of the progenitor of the clan or family. MacDonald means 'son of Donald', this Donald being one of the grandsons of the renowned Somerled; MacDougall comes from Dougall, the eldest son of Somerled. This is the most common origin for clans, other examples being MacLeod (from 'Leod', a Norse personal name), MacEwan, MacFarlane (from 'Parlan', an old Irish personal name), MacGregor, MacInnes (from 'Angus'), MacKay (from the Gaelic for 'Hugh'), Mackenzie (from 'Kenneth'), and many more. The English equivalent is to add 'son' onto the end of a name: MacAdam in Gaelic is Adamson in English (it was not uncommon for this to occur, particularly in the seventeenth and eighteenth centuries, and an English-sounding name may still be from the Gaelic). Similarly a shortened form of Adam is Adie, so MacAdie or Addison. As mentioned elsewhere, spellings of names varied, and Mac was shortened to Mc or even M'; to avoid unnecessary repetition Mac has been used throughout the book.

Occupational

The name comes from the occupation or profession of an early member of the family. Examples include Brisbane (from 'bone breaker' or surgeon), Fletcher (an arrow maker), Smith (blacksmith), Falconer (an individual who looked after birds of prey), Clerk (cleric), and of course Stewart. This latter name comes from Steward (or from High Steward of Scotland, an office held by one branch of the family from the middle of the twelfth century). Originally the name would have been descriptive as in 'Adam the fletcher' or 'Walter the Steward'. Some clan names also have this origin, such as MacNab (son of the abbot), MacIntyre (son of the wright or carpenter), Mackintosh (son of the leader or chief), or Macpherson (son of the parson).

Descriptive

The name describes a physical characteristic of the progenitor of the clan. The most famous clan with this origin is probably Campbell, the name meaning 'crooked mouth' in Gaelic, and originally a nickname; Cameron means 'crooked nose'. Other examples include Laing (from 'long' in Scots), Bain (from 'fair' in Gaelic, describing either hair colour or complexion), Black, Cruickshank (from 'crooked shanks', meaning bow-legged), Duff (from 'black' in Gaelic), or Grant (from 'grande' meaning 'big' in French).

Spellings

The spelling of families down the century is problematic, and in medieval and early-modern documents there can be several different spellings of the same surname, even in family papers. In this book names have been standardised to that given in the heading; variations are listed in the clans and families section at the beginning, and at the end of each entry. Where it is known that existing branches of families spell their name in a different way, this is listed at the end of the entry (such as in Ogilvy instead of Ogilvie, or Montgomerie instead of Montgomery, or St Clair instead of Sinclair).

As mentioned elsewhere, spellings of names varied, and Mac was shortened to Mc or even M'; to avoid repetition Mac has been used throughout the book.

Maps

Thumbnail maps are given for each clan or family, the location of their castle and properties marked. Where many properties are found in the same area, only the more important ones are included, and locations on the maps may be very approximate. There is also a larger map of Scotland, showing many cities, towns, villages and islands, in the appendices, and National Grid References, if a more precise location is needed, are given for every site where this is known; some of these may also be approximate as exact locations are often impossible to determine.

Illustrations

There are more than 600 drawings and photos throughout the text, and there is an alphabetical listing of the illustrations at the beginning of the book. Although there are illustrations of the same castle in more than one clan or family section, illustrations are of different views or are by different artists. Many of the castles illustrated have been demolished or have deteriorated further, while others have been rebuilt or restored, and some, of course, are much the same as even 200 years ago.

Entries

Each entry begins with the name of the clan or family, a small map, and information about the family and their origins. Following this is a list of castles, houses and lands associated with the family, along with location, National Grid Reference, and whether the place is accessible to the public, or is now, for example, a hotel, a club house or a private residence. Websites and telephone numbers are listed. Each entry concludes with clan or family websites, the number of properties held, the ranking of this number against other clans or families (not surprisingly the Stewarts came out on top), and cross-referenced variations in names or spellings. The use of the word 'apparently' denotes where information is thought to be correct after consultation with *Burke's* but has not been verified or may have changed since the publication of that venerable tome. To reduce duplication, the websites for Historic Scotland and The National Trust for Scotland are not repeated in the text and are listed below.

Opening and Access

While many of the castles and sites are accessible to the public or are open as visitor attractions, many others are not. It should be assumed, unless otherwise stated, that sites are **not** open to the public. Although care has been taken to supply accurate opening and access, mistakes do happen and information changes (this book was compiled over many years). Please check opening locally or on websites before undertaking any visit.

Appendices

Other information in the appendices includes the development of the castle in Scotland, a glossary of castle terms, a glossary of titles and offices of state, and a map of Scotland, showing many cities, towns, villages and islands. Further reading concludes the book.

Index

There is a comprehensive index at the end of the book, listing castles, properties and lands mentioned in the main text. This has been cross-referenced with alternative spellings and names of sites as are listed in *The Castles of Scotland*, fourth edition. There are more than 4000 entries in the index.

Some Useful Websites

www.stirnet.com
www.burkes-peerage.net
www.thepeerage.com
www.baronage.co.uk
www.lyon-court.com
www.royal.gov.uk
www.historic-scotland.gov.uk
  (Historic Scotland)
www.nts.org.uk/www.scotlandforyou.co.uk
  (National Trust for Scotland)
www.rcahms.gov.uk
  (Royal Commission of Ancient and Historic Monuments of Scotland)
www.nls.uk
  (National Library of Scotland)
www.hha.org.uk
  (Historic Houses Association)
www.gardensofscotland.org
  (Scotland's Garden Scheme)
www.visitukheritage.gov.uk
  (some less known-about places to visit)

Websites for individual clans or families are listed in the entry for that family, and websites for individual castles and mansions are given in the text. The author/ publisher have no affinity nor any relationship with any of the websites listed nor have approved or even reviewed their content, nor have any of the websites with the author/publisher. Websites are only listed for interest or research purposes.

Families and Clans

Illustrations

Key

AA	Alasdair Anderson
AC	Anna Coventry
GC	Georgi Coventry
JM	Joyce Miller
JS	John Slezer
LF	Laura Ferguson
MC	Martin Coventry
M&R	MacGibbon and Ross
RWB	Robert W Billings
TP	Thomas Pennant

Some sites have an illustration in more than one family section, but these are either different views or are by a different artist.

Front cover photograph of Dunnottar Castle by (©) Graeme Wallace (www.gwpublishing.com).

Abercromby

The name is territorial and comes from lands held by the family one mile north-east of St Monans in Fife. William Abercromby was one of those to add his seal to the Ragman Roll of 1296. **Abercrombie Castle** [NO 518028], which stood near St Monans, has gone.

Another branch of the family was the Abercrombys of Birkenbog; **Birkenbog** [NJ 536651] is two miles south-east of Cullen in Aberdeenshire in the north-east of Scotland. The family was descended from the Abercrombys of Pitmedden, who are mentioned in 1457: **Pitmedden** [NJ 863149] was probably two miles north-west of Dyce, also in Aberdeenshire, although there is also a **Petmathen** [NJ 670262] six miles west and north of Inverurie.

Birkenbog House dates mostly from the eighteenth century, but incorporates a round tower from an earlier castle. The family acquired the lands in the fourteenth century, and were made Baronets of Nova Scotia in 1637. Alexander Abercromby was Grand Falconer in Scotland to Charles I, but the family then became Covenanters, and the Marquis of Montrose marshalled his forces at Birkenbog in 1645 in retaliation. The family abandoned Birkenbog in the eighteenth century and moved to **Glassaugh House** [NJ 558645], close by and two and a half miles south-west of Portsoy and a mile or so to the east. General James Abercrombie led the British forces at the poorly fought and costly Battle of Ticoderonga in 1758 against the French in Canada. Glassaugh was later sold and is now a ruin, having been used as a store for a farm. This branch of the family still flourishes, however, although they apparently live in the Canary Islands.

The Abercrombys also owned:
Airthrey Castle [NS 813967], near Bridge of Allan, Stirlingshire; altered castellated mansion.
 Built for the Haldanes from 1791 but passed to the Abercrombys in 1796 who held it until 1890. The building is now part of the University of Stirling.
Brucefield [NS 959916], near Clackmannan; large mansion.
 Held by the Bruces but was bought by the Abercrombys in the 1750s. Brucefield is now apparently a property of the Bruces, representatives of the line of Lord Balfour of Burleigh.
Carriden House [NT 026808], near Bo'ness, Falkirk; altered and extended tower house.
 Held by the Viponts and by the Cockburns, but passed to Abercrombys in 1541 and they sold the property to the Hamiltons of Letterick in 1601; it then passed to others. B&B accommodation is available and the house is suitable for weddings (01506 829811; www.carridenhouse.co.uk).
Colinton Castle [NT 216694], Edinburgh; ruinous tower house.
 Held by the Foulis family and then by the Forbeses, who built Colinton House. The property was later owned by James Abercromby, Lord Dunfermline, who was the Speaker of the House of Commons. He died at Colinton in 1858. The ruin of

the castle is located in the grounds of Merchiston Castle School (www.merchiston.co.uk), and Colinton House is now home to the science department of the school.
Drummuir [NJ 407448], near Keith, Moray; castle replaced by mansion.
 Held by the Leslies but passed to the Abercrombys. Two of the family are buried in Botriphnie kirkyard, but the property was sold to the Duffs in 1670. Drummuir is sometimes open to the public in the summer (01542 810225; www.drummuir estate.co.uk).
Fetternear [NJ 723171], near Inverurie, Aberdeenshire; site of castle and ruinous house.
 Held by the Leslies after the Reformation and then by the Abercrombys of Birkenbog from 1627. One of the family was Patrick Abercromby, personal physician to James VII after graduating from the University of St Andrews in 1685. The property returned to the Leslies in 1690, but the house was burned out in 1919 and is a ruin.
Forglen House [NJ 696517], near Turriff, Aberdeenshire; mansion incorporating castle.
 Held by the Ogilvies but passed by marriage to the Abercrombys. Still occupied.
Inchdrewer Castle [NJ 656607], near Banff, Aberdeenshire; restored L-plan tower house.
 Held by the Curror family and by the Ogilvies, but passed to the Abercrombys early in the nineteenth century, and then went to others. Partly restored but not apparently occupied.
Manor House [NS 827948], near Stirling; slight remains of castle.
 Held by the Callendars and by the Dundas family, but the property later went to the Haldanes and then to the Abercrombys in 1795. Manor was abandoned for Airthrey Castle.
Menstrie Castle [NS 852968], near Alloa, Clackmannan; castle.
 Held by the Alexanders and then by the Holbournes, but passed to the Abercrombys in 1719. This branch of the family was opposed to the Jacobites. Sir Ralph Abercromby, mentioned below, was born here. The building was rescued from demolition in the 1950s, and is open occasionally to the public in the summer (01259 213131 (Alloa Tower)).
Murthly Castle [NO 070399], near Dunkeld, Perthshire; fine extended castle.
 Held by the Ireland family but passed to the Abercrombys who held it from 1440 until 1615 when it passed to the Stewarts of Grandtully. Murthly can be used as a location for weddings and events (01738 494119; www.murthly-estate.com).
Tullibody House [NS 865945], near Alloa, Clackmannanshire; site of castle and mansion.
 Held by the Meldrums but passed to the Abercrombys in 1655, and they remodelled an older building in 1710. From this branch came Sir Ralph Abercromby, who was a successful general, being made commander-in-chief of forces fighting the French in the West Indies, and then of Scotland and of Ireland, and then in Egypt, where he died from his wounds after winning the Battle of Alexandria in 1801. His younger brother, Sir Robert, was commander of the British forces in India, and was governor of Edinburgh Castle for thirty years. This branch of the family became Lord Abercromby, but the line is now extinct. After the Abercrombys moved to Airthrey Castle in the 1790s, Tullibody House became derelict and was demolished in the 1960s.

No. of castles/sites: 17
Rank: 83=/764
Xref: Abercrombie

Abernethy

The origin of the name is not certain, but it is likely to have come from the place Abernethy in Perth and Kinross. There was an early Christian monastery here, of which an impressive round tower survives. The family were major landowners in the twelfth and thirteenth centuries.

Carpow [NO 204174], near Abernethy and two miles west of Newburgh in Fife, was held by the family in the thirteenth and fourteenth centuries, but was then given to the church. The nearby property of **Pitcairlie** [NO 236148] was also owned by the Abernethys, but passed by marriage to the Leslies in 1312. Pitcairlie House incorporates an old tower house, built by the Leslies, in the later mansion, and holiday accommodation is available (01337 827418; www.pitcairlie-leisure.co.uk). Sir William Abernethy was charged with the murder of Duncan, Earl of Fife, in 1288 and was sentenced to death.

Another William Abernethy was one of those who added his seal to the Declaration of Arbroath in 1320. The family held the lands of **Saltoun** [NT 461685] two miles east of Pencaitland in East Lothian, and one of the lairds was made Lord Saltoun in 1445. The lands had been sold by 1643 and the title passed to the Frasers by marriage in 1670, and this branch of the Frasers are now chiefs of that clan. There was a castle at Saltoun, some of which survives in the large baronial mansion. The building has been divided into separate private apartments, and is said to be haunted by a Grey Lady.

Hawthornden Castle [NT 287637], south of Loanhead in Midlothian, was also a property of the

Abernethys in the thirteenth century, but passed by marriage to the Douglases and then later to the Drummonds. It is a fine, partly ruinous building, and is now used as a retreat for writers.

Mount Lothian [NT 271693], which lies three miles south-east of Penicuik in Midlothian, may have been the site of a house of the Knights Templar. Prior Abernethy of Mount Lothian was instrumental in winning the Battle of Roslin, when a large English army was defeated by the Scots in 1303. Mount Lothian was held by the Murrays in the eighteenth century.

Rothiemay Castle [NJ 554484], five or so miles north of Huntly in Aberdeenshire in north-east Scotland, was originally built by the Abernethys, after they had been

Rothiemay Castle 1910?

given the lands by David II in the fourteenth century. Lord Saltoun gave a gift of pears from the castle orchard to James IV in 1496. The castle was extended down the centuries but was demolished in 1956 and very little remains today. The lands were sold to the Stewart Lord Ochiltree in 1612, and then to the Gordons five years later, and then went to others.

Nearby **Mains of Mayen** [NJ 576477] was held by the Abernethy family from the fourteenth century until 1612, when it too passed to the Gordons. An L-plan tower house stands here, which incorporates earlier work; the building was restored in the 1960s and is a private residence.

Dunlappie [NO 587679], one mile west of Edzell in Angus, was held by the family from the twelfth century until 1390. There may have been a castle here, also called Poolbrigs.

There was also a branch of the family, styled of Auchnacloich and Carskie. It is not clear where this was, although there is an **Auchnacloich** [NN 843393] in Perthshire, about ten miles north of Crieff.

Lour [NO 478462] or Methy Lour, three miles south of Forfar in Angus, was held by the Abernethys in 1264, but went to the Lindsays and then to other families. There was a castle, but it was replaced by a later house.

Cairnie [NO 635420], to the north of Arbroath also in Angus, may have been held by the family, but passed by marriage to the Leslies, and then went to the Aikmans. There was a castle or an old house.

No. of castles/sites: 10
Rank: 140=/764

Hawthornden Castle (M&R)

Adair

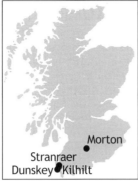

The first record of the name Adair appears to be one 'Edzaer' (or Edgar), a son of one of the leaders of the Scottish forces at the Battle of the Standard in 1138. Edzaer was the grandson of Donegal, who held **Morton Castle** [NX 891992], a stronghold two miles north and east of Thornhill in Nithsdale in Dumfries and Galloway. The castle is a picturesque ruin by Morton Loch, which mostly dates from the fifteenth century, and it is in the care of Historic Scotland and is open to the public. The lands had passed from the family by the beginning of the fourteenth century, and Morton was long associated with the Douglases.

The Adairs of Kilhilt became prominent in Galloway, and they had a castle at **Kilhilt** [NX 062564], two and a half miles south of Stranraer. Although this was once an important place, the last remains were cleared away in the 1930s. The family built (or rebuilt) the impressive **Dunskey Castle** [NW 994534] in 1510, which stands on cliffs above the sea to the south and east of Portpatrick, also in Galloway, although the Adairs held the lands in the fifteenth century. Dunskey is a fine ruin in a magnificent situation. The castle, or its predecessor, was torched in 1489 after William Adair of Dunskey had murdered one of the Hamiltons; and it was here that

Stranraer Castle (M&R)

the centre of Stranraer. The property had passed to the Kennedys by 1596. The castle now houses a museum telling the history of the building, including its use as a jail, and is open to the public in the summer (01776 705544; www.dumgal.gov.uk).

The Adairs of Kilhilt had another tower house at **Drummore** [NX 136364], sixteen miles south of Stranraer. Although still habitable in 1684, it became ruinous and was demolished in 1963.

www.adair.ca
No. of castles/sites: 5
Rank: 240=/764

Dunskey Castle 1920?

the Adairs tortured the last Abbot of Soulseat so that he would turn the abbey lands over to them. There is also a haunting associated with Dunskey: a nursemaid dropped a baby out of the windows and it was dashed on the rocks below. She is said to haunt the ruins. The castle is also said to have had a brownie, a helpful but cranky supernatural being. Dunskey was sold in the 1620s to the Montgomerys. It is accessible, although there are apparently plans afoot to restore it.

Around the same time as the building of Dunskey, the Adairs also constructed **Stranraer Castle** [NX 061608], also known as the **Castle of St John**, and in

Adam

Adam is a name of great antiquity in Scotland, and it is believed that Duncan Adam was one of the Scots who accompanied James Douglas and the heart of Robert the Bruce on pilgrimage to Granada in the fourteenth century. A shortened version of Adam is Addie or Adie. Also see MacAdam and Adamson.

The family came to especial prominence with William Adam, the famous architect. William married Mary Robertson of Gladney, and their son Robert, along with his brothers, James and John, became the most famous architectural dynasty in Britain, basing their designs on classical principals. William designed the splendid Duff House in north-east Scotland, and other notable buildings in Scotland by the Adams include Hopetoun House, Mellerstain House and Culzean Castle. All four of these buildings are open to the public. Robert Adam was architect to George III, and also MP for Kinross-shire in 1768.

William Adam bought the estate of Blair from the Colvilles of Cleish in 1733, renaming it **Blair Adam** [NT 129957], and built himself a new mansion. Blair Adam is about three miles south of Kinross; and is probably the least 'Adam' of any of his or his sons' buildings, consisting of a sprawling courtyard mansion of several styles. The Adams of Blair Adam still apparently live here. **Dowhill Castle** [NT 118973], a sixteenth-century tower house, stood three or so miles south of Kinross, but little remains. It was replaced by **Dowhill** [NT 119997], and the lands were long a property of the Lindsays before coming to Robert Adam, William's son, by 1740.

The Adam family also held **Chapelhouse** [NS 634279], some miles west of Muirkirk in Ayrshire, before it was sold to the MacAdam family in 1781. There was a small tower house, but little survives. **Denovan** [NS 820834], one mile north-east of Denny in Falkirk, dates from about 1750 and replaced a castle or old house. The lands were held by the Forresters, by the Johnstones of Alva and then by the Forbeses of Callander in 1830 before passing to the Adams. The house is still occupied.

No. of castles/sites: 4
Rank: 278=/764
Xrefs: Addie; Adie

Adamson

The name means 'son of Adam', and is conse-quently a common sur-name. Another form is Addison, from the diminu-tive for Adam, 'Addie'. The Gaelic form of the name is MacAdam (also see that section), and the name is on record from the middle of the thirteenth century. Patrick Adamson was Archbishop of St Andrews in 1575.

Craigcrook Castle [NT 211742], to the west of Edinburgh, is an impressive Z-plan tower house, dating from the sixteenth century but extended and remodelled down the centuries. Held by the Marjoribanks family,

Craigcrook Castle (M&R)

Craigcrook passed in the sixteenth century to the Adamsons, who built the original castle. William Adamson of Craigcrook was killed at the Battle of Pinkie in 1547. The lands were later held by Halls and by other families. The castle is still occupied, but is said to be haunted by the ghost of Lord Francis Jeffrey, who died here in 1850. The building is now used as the headquarters for Scottish Field (0131 312 4550; www.scottishfield.co.uk).

Careston Castle [NO 530599], four and a half miles west of Brechin in Angus, is a seventeenth-century Z-plan tower house, which incorporates older work. The castle was owned by several families before being acquired by the Adamsons of Careston in the nineteenth century, and they still apparently live here.

No. of castles/sites: 2
Rank: 396=/764
Xref: Addison; MacAdam

Agnew

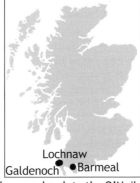

The origin of the name is probably from the Barony of d'Agneaux in France. The family, who are believed to have been Norman, first lived in England then became established in Scotland. Alternatively the name may originate in Ireland from O'Gnyw or O'Gnew, who were bards to the O'Neils of Antrim; the Agnews were also prominent in Ireland.

The family was given the original castle of **Lochnaw** [NW 994633], which stands on an island in a loch of the same name, in 1363. It lies four miles west and north of Stranraer, and David II made the Agnews keepers of the castle. The stronghold was captured and sacked in 1390 by Archibald the Grim, Earl of Douglas, and had been dismantled by 1426.

The Agnews built a new castle, also called **Lochnaw** [NW 991628] at the south end of the loch. The existing building is a sixteenth-century tower house, which was later extended by a wing, and then a mansion: although some of the later extensions have since been

Lochnaw Castle (LF)

demolished. Andrew Agnew of Lochnaw was killed at the Battle of Pinkie in 1547; another Andrew was made a Baronet of Nova Scotia in 1629. Sir Andrew Agnew commanded the Scots Fusiliers at the Battle of Dettingen in 1743. He then successfully held Blair Castle against the Jacobites in 1746. The Agnews held Lochnaw at the end of the nineteenth century, but it has since been sold. The castle is still occupied as a private residence. The Agnews were buried in the burial ground [NX 015637] of the old church at Leswalt. The line of the Agnews of Lochnaw continues, and they now apparently live in Edinburgh.

Galdenoch Castle [NW 974633], which is not far from Lochnaw, is a ruinous L-plan tower house, dating from the sixteenth century. It was built by Gilbert Agnew of Lochnaw, who was killed at the Battle of Pinkie in 1547. The family was ruined after they had been heavily fined for supporting the Covenanters. The castle is said to have been haunted at one time, probably in the

Galdenoch Castle (M&R)

seventeenth century, by an especially unpleasant, aggressive and violent ghost. The spirit would pick up old women bodily, and then deposit them in a nearby river. The ghost is said to have been the apparition of a local farmer, who had been shot dead by one of the Agnew lairds. The story goes that the ghost was exorcised by the singing of a priest, who presumably had an impressive voice if it could scare off this particular bogle.

Other castles of the Agnews are:
Barmeal Castle [NX 378412], near Whithorn, Galloway; site of a strong tower house.
  Held by the Agnews in the sixteenth century.
Croach [NX 064688], near Stranraer, Galloway; site of castle or old house.
  Held by the Agnews from the middle of sixteenth century or earlier. Colonel Andrew Agnew of Croach built Lochryan House in 1701. The same year the village of Cladahouse, now Cairnryan, was made into a Burgh of Barony for the Agnews. Lochryan House was still owned by the Agnews in the twentieth century and is still occupied. The gardens of the house are occasionally open to the public (www.gardensofscotland.org).
Cruggleton Castle [NX 484428], near Garlieston, Galloway; some remains of castle.
  Held by several families and then by the Agnews of Lochnaw after 1591. The castle was ruinous by the 1680s and excavated in 1978-82. Cruggleton Church is the most complete Romanesque church in the area and, although ruined before 1890, has been restored.
Cutreoch [NX 467357], near Whithorn, Galloway; site of castle.
  Held by the Houston family but passed to the Agnews in 1732.
Innermessan Castle [NX 084634], near Stranraer, Galloway; farm on site of castle.
  Held by the Agnews from 1429 until the end of the seventeenth century. The property was sold to the Dalrymples of Stair in 1723, and then used as a cavalry barracks. The castle was then demolished to built the farm.

No. of castles/sites: 8
Rank: 160=/764

Aikenhead

The name appears to come from the barony and lands of Aikenhead, which lie in Rutherglen to the south of Glasgow. The property was held by Gilbert Aikenhead according to the Ragman Roll of 1296. There was a castle at **Aikenhead** (now **Aitkenhead**) [NS 596603], but this had been replaced by a mansion by 1806. The lands had passed to the Stewarts by the fourteenth century, and then to the Maxwells and then to others. Aikenhead of that Ilk is on record, and James Aikenhead was granted arms in the 1670s. He was the son of David Aikenhead Provost of Edinburgh. Thomas Aikenhead, the son of an Edinburgh apothecary, was hanged for blasphemy in 1697 after making a joke at the doctrine of the Trinity. The Aikenheads held **Ranfurly Castle** [NS 384652], more usually associated with the Knoxs, which is just south of Bridge of Weir in Renfrewshire, for some years, although the building is now ruined. Ranfurly had been a property of the Cochrane Earls of Dundonald in 1865, and then of the Hamiltons, before being sold to the Aikenheads.

No. of castles/sites: 2 / Rank: 396=/764
Xref: Aitkenhead

Aikman

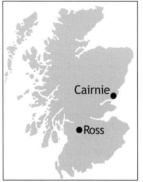

The derivation of the name is not certain, but one theory is that it is from 'oak man', 'aik' being the Scots pronunciation for 'oak'. The story goes that one of the captains fighting Macbeth at Dunsinane, suggested disguising his men by using oak branches from Birnam wood, hence Aikman. The family held the lands of **Cairnie** [NO 635420], just north of Arbroath in Angus, for many generations, and many of them are buried in Arbroath Abbey. There may have been a castle at Cairnie, but the property was sold in 1707 by William Aikman so that he could travel abroad to study in Italy. He went to London in 1723 and became a well-known and successful portrait painter and painter of historical scenes, and died in 1732. **Ross House** [NS 739558], a mile or so east of Hamilton in Lanarkshire, was held by the Aikmans of the Ross from 1704, having been purchased by Thomas Aikman, William's uncle, from the Hamiltons. The Aikman family line continues, but they now apparently live in England; Ross House is still occupied.

No. of castles/sites: 2 / Rank: 396=/764

Ainslie

The name apparently comes from the Saxon lords of Annesley in Nottinghamshire. They held much land in England, but were forced to flee after the invasion of William the Conqueror and the Normans in 1066. They were given refuge in Scotland by Malcolm Canmore, and eventually came to hold the lands of **Dolphingstone** (now **Dolphinston**) [NT 683150], four miles south-east of Jedburgh in the Borders. Robert Ainslie of Dolphingstone went on crusade with the Earl of Dunbar and March around 1250. There was a castle at Dolphinstone in the fourteenth century, although the Ainslies were forfeited by Robert the Bruce during the Wars of Independence, after opposing his bid for the throne, and the castle was then destroyed by the English about 1360. The Ainslies recovered the property in 1377, built a new stronghold, and held it until the sixteenth century when it passed by marriage to the Kerrs. There was a strong tower house at Dolphinston, but it has been demolished and the site is occupied by a farm. The castle had a brownie, a supernatural being who helped with household chores, but who was notoriously difficult to please. This one left in chagrin after being given an inappropriate present.

The Ainslies may also have held **Dolphingstone Castle** [NT 384729], which is one and a half miles west of Tranent in East Lothian, although this may be a confusion over names. Nothing of this stronghold survives.

John Ainslie of Crawford is also on record. This is a property near the village of Crawford in Lanarkshire; there was also a castle at **Crawford** [NS 954213], but little remains. In the nineteenth century the Ainslies also held **Delgatie Castle** [NJ 755506], which is near Turriff in Aberdeenshire. The castle has a long association with the Hays, and later returned to them after passing from the Ainslies. Delgatie is open to the public all year (01888 563479; www.delgatiecastle.com).

www.ainslie.org.uk
No. of castles/sites: 4
Rank: 278=/764

Airth

The name is territorial and comes from the lands of Airth, which are four miles north of Falkirk in central Scotland.

The family held the lands of Airth in 1309, or probably from earlier, as Hugh Airth was captured at the fall of Dunbar Castle in 1296. There was a castle at **Airth** [NS 900869], which saw action in the Wars of Independence. William Wallace is said to have rescued his uncle from here after he

Fordell Castle (M&R)

Fordell [NT 147854], one and a half miles north of Inverkeithing in Fife, was held by the Airth family until it passed by marriage to the Hendersons of Fordell in 1511. Fordell Castle is a fine Z-plan tower house, but the present castle probably dates from after it had passed from the Airth family.

No. of castles/sites: 4
Rank: 278=/764
Xref: Erth

Airth Castle (M&R)

had been imprisoned by the English, and the oldest part is now known as Wallace's Tower. The property passed by marriage to the Bruces in 1470 and then later to the Elphinstones. The castle was enlarged and altered down the years and is now a hotel (01324 831411; www.airth castlehotel.com).

Plean Castle [NS 850870], six miles south-east of Stirling, is a restored tower house and outbuildings ranged around a courtyard, and the building dates from the fifteenth century. The castle may have been first built by the Airths of Plean, although the lands passed by marriage to the Somervilles in 1449 and then to the Nicholsons of Carnock in 1643, and then to others. Accommodation is available in the castle (01786 480840; www.aboutscotland.co.uk/stirling/plane.html).

Two other properties were held by the Airths of Plean. **Bruce's Castle** [NS 857878], which was formerly known as **Carnock Tower**, stands five miles north and west of Falkirk. The building consists of a now ruinous keep, which dates from the fifteenth century and was built by the Airths. The property passed to the Hepburns in 1480 and later to the Bruces and then to the Drummonds.

Aitcheson

The name means 'son of Adam', and can be spelt Acheson, Aitcheson, Atchison and Atkinson. The name is on record in Scotland from the fourteenth century. The Gaelic form of this name is MacAdam and also see Adamson.

Thomas Atkinson of Bonkyll is on record in 1429. **Bonkyll** or **Bunkle** [NT 805596] lies two miles north and east of Preston in Berwickshire in the Borders, and there was a large castle here, dating from the twelfth century, although little now survives. It was to have several owners, including the Stewarts, the Douglases and the Homes.

Nothing at all remains of **Boadsbeck** or **Bodesbeck Castle** [NT 148093], a tower house which stood five miles north-east of Moffat in Dumfries and Galloway. It had been a property of the Moffats, but the Aitchesons of Bodisbek are on record in 1676. The property was eventually bought back by the Moffats.

Airdrie House [NS 749654] and **Rochsolloch** [NS 754649], which were both in Airdrie in central Scotland, were held by the Aitchisons in the eighteenth century, but both passed by marriage to the Alexanders. There were castles at both sites, and then later mansions, but both suffered the same fate and were demolished. Airdrie House was latterly used as the local maternity hospital before being demolished in 1964, while Rochsolloch was demolished in the nineteenth century and was replaced by a farm.

No. of castles/sites: 4
Rank: 278=/764
Xrefs: Acheson; Aitcheson; Atkinson; Attchison

Aitken

The name, which has several different spellings, is derived from a diminutive for Adam (also see that section).

Callands House [NT 155459], one mile south of Romanno Bridge in the Borders, was bought by the Aitkens in the middle of the eighteenth century. The house, remodelled in 1840, may stand on the site of a tower house; Callands, however, was sold in the same year to the Murrays.

Dalmoak Castle [NS 385768], one mile north-west of Dumbarton, was built for James Aitken in the late nineteenth century but apparently has no older origins.

No. of castles/sites: 2
Rank: 396=/764
Xrefs: Aiken; Atkins

Aldie

The name comes from the place Aldie, which is in Strathearn in Perth and Kinross. **Aldie Castle** [NT 052977], two miles south and east of Crook of Devon, is a sixteenth-century tower house, which was held by the Mercers and then by the Murrays; there is, however, no record that the lands were ever held by a family called Aldie. The castle later went to the Kinlochs, and was restored and is occupied after falling partly ruinous in the 1950s.

Whitehouse [NT 187766], in the Barnton area to the west of Edinburgh, is a fine mansion and incorporates a sixteenth-century L-plan tower house, which was extended in 1601. Whitehouse has had several owners down the centuries, including the Logans, the Primroses, the Corse family, the Menzies family, then the Aldies from 1719 until 1750, then the Strachans and then the Ramsays. The building is still occupied.

No. of castles/sites: 2
Rank: 396=/764

Alexander

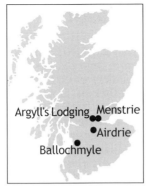

The name Alexander comes from Greek and means 'defender of man'; the most famous using the name was Alexander the Great. Three kings of Scots were called Alexander, the name having been intro-duced by the Saxon Queen Margaret, wife of Malcolm Canmore, in the eleventh century. The MacAlexanders were numerous on the west coast, being linked to the MacDonalds, although it does not appear that the sur-name 'Alexander', the 'Mac' having been dropped, was used until the fifteenth century.

Menstrie Castle [NS 852968], three miles north-west of Alloa in Clackmannanshire, is a sixteenth-century tower house, which was later extended, although most

Menstrie Castle (M&R)

of the subsidiary buildings have since been demolished. The property was held by the Alexanders from 1481. One of the family, Sir William Alexander, was born in 1575 and he was made Earl of Stirling in 1633. He was the founder of Nova Scotia, although he was later ruined and died bankrupt. The Alexander family supported the Campbells, and Menstrie was burned by the Marquis of Montrose in 1645. The Alexanders lost the lands four years later when Menstrie went to the Holbournes. The castle was going to be demolished in the 1950s, but it was saved and now houses a museum about Sir William Alexander and the Nova Scotia Baronetcies (01259 211701 (Alloa Tower); www.nts.org.uk).

Argyll's Lodging [NS 793938], at the top of Castle Wynd in Stirling, is more usually associated with the Campbells of Argyll, but it was actually first built by Sir William Alexander of Menstrie. It is the best example in Scotland of a seventeenth-century town house, and many of the rooms are refurbished as they would have been when first built. The Lodging is open all year (01786 431319).

Argyll's Lodging, Stirling (M&R)

Tillicoultry was purchased by the Alexanders of Menstrie in 1643, and is also in Clackmannan. There was a castle at **Tillicoultry** [NS 913975], which was replaced by Tillicoultry House, but this was itself demolished in 1938. The property had many other owners.

A different branch of the Alexander family became established on the west coast, and held lands in Renfrew and in Ayrshire, before purchasing the lands of **Ballochmyle** [NS 521264] from the Whitefoords in 1783. There was a tower house at Ballochmyle, which is one and a half miles east of Mauchline in Ayrshire, but this was replaced by a mansion of 1760, which was later extended and adapted. The Alexanders sold the property to the government in 1939, and a hospital was built with the house being used as offices and accommodation. The hospital was closed in 2000, and the house is to be redeveloped. The Hagart-Alexanders of Ballochmyle, Baronets, still flourish, and apparently live near Mauchline in Ayrshire.

Other properties held for some years by the Alexanders in modern times are **Airdrie House** [NS 749654] and **Rochsolloch** [NS 754649]. These had both passed by marriage from the Aikenheads, and both stood in different parts of Airdrie in Lanarkshire in central Scotland, although they have both been demolished. **Peffermill House** [NT 284717] in Edinburgh, an altered seventeenth-century tower house, has had several owners, including the Prestons of Craigmillar, the Edgars, the Osbornes, the Alexanders and the Gilmours. The house is still occupied.

No. of castles/sites: 7
Rank: 182=/764
Xrefs: MacAlexander; MacAlister

Allan

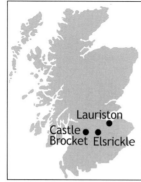

The name has two origins: one from the Gaelic, meaning 'rock'; the other as a personal name from Brittany in France. Allanson simply means the 'son of Allan'. Sir William Allan was a famous artist and traveller, a contemporary of Sir Walter Scott, and he painted many historical scenes as well as pictures from Scott's novels. The MacDonalds of Clanranald were sometimes known as Allanson.

Castle Brocket [NS 735420], also known as **Braidwood**, stood three and a half miles south-east of Strathaven in Lanarkshire, but there is nothing left of the building, and a farm occupies the site. The property was held by the Allans in the eighteenth century.

Elsrickle [NT 062435] is five miles east of Carnwath also in Lanarkshire, and there was a castle, although this has gone. The property was held by the Hepburns in the fifteenth century, but passed to the Allans, and then went by marriage to the Woddrops of Dalmarnock in the eighteenth century.

Lauriston Castle [NT 204762] at Davidsons Mains on the west side of Edinburgh is a fine castle and mansion, which dates from the sixteenth century but was extended in later centuries. Held by several families including by the Napiers of Merchiston, Lauriston went to the Allans in 1827. The property then passed to the Rutherfords, and then to others, and was given to the city of Edinburgh by the Reids. The castle stands in a public park and is open to the public by guided tours (0131 336 2060; www.cac.org.uk).

No. of castles/sites: 3
Rank: 328=/764
Xrefs: Alan; Allanson

Allardice

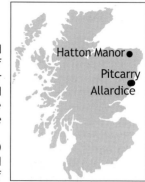

The name is territorial and comes from the lands of Allardice, which are near Inverbervie in the old county of Kincardine. The name is on record from the twelfth century.

Allardice Castle [NO 818739] is a handsome old building with ranges of buildings around a courtyard, and the family of the same name held the lands from the twelfth century, the grant confirmed by Robert the Bruce after he became king in 1306. Sir James Allardice was Clerk of the King's Treas-

Allardice Castle (M&R)

ury in the fifteenth century. The family held the lands until 1776, when they passed by marriage through Sarah Allan Allardice to the Barclays of Urie, who changed their name to Barclay Allardice. The line still flourishes, although they are now styled as Barclay of Mathers and Urie, and they apparently live in England. The castle was abandoned as a residence by the family and was then used as a farmhouse. Although burned out in the 1970s, it has been restored and is occupied as a private residence. Many of the Allardice family are buried at the fine St Ternan's Church at Arbuthnott [NO 801746], which is open to the public.

The family may also have held three other properties. There are slight remains of an old stronghold on a promontory above the sea at **Whistleberry** [NO 862753], which is near Allardice. They also held **Pitcarry** [NO 830740], but exchanged this property for **Hatton Manor** or **Auchterless** [NJ 709420] with the Meldrums in 1547. There are no remains of a stronghold which stood at Pitcarry, but it was located one mile north of Inverbervie in Kincardineshire. Part of a fortified building with a gunloop is built into a later house at Hatton Manor, which stands five miles south of Turriff in Aberdeenshire. This property was sold by the Allardice family to the Duffs in 1709.

www.allardice.org/www.allerdice.net
No. of castles/sites: 4 / Rank: 278=/764
Xrefs: Allardyce; Allerdice

Anderson

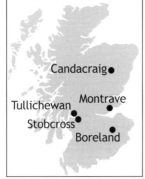

The name Anderson (or MacAndrew) means 'Andrew's son'. As Andrew was not an uncommon name, not least because Scotland's patron saint is St Andrew, there are many unrelated families with this name. MacAndrew can also be found in Ireland. Sir Robert Rowand Anderson, born in Edinburgh in 1835 and a well-known Scottish architect, designed what is now the National Portrait Gallery and the MacEwan Hall, both in Edinburgh, and Mount Stuart House on Bute.

Candacraig [NJ 339111], ten miles north of Ballater in Aberdeenshire, was built in 1835 but may incorporate some old work from a castle of the Andersons. They held the property from the sixteenth century until 1867 when Candacraig went to the Forbeses of Newe and then later the property passed to the Wallaces. A cottage on the estate can be rented (www.candacraig.com).

The Andersons, along with the Gibsons, also held **Boreland Tower** [NT 255480], a sixteenth-century tower house, the site of which is located five miles north of Peebles in the Borders. There are no remains.

Stobcross [NS 570655] stood two miles west of Glasgow Cathedral, and was an attractive old house, dating from the seventeenth century or earlier, and the building was probably fortified at one time. Stobcross

Stobcross (M&R)

was held by the Andersons until it was sold to the Orrs of Barrowfield in the 1730s or 40s. The building was demolished in the nineteenth century, and there are no remains. Nearby **Dowhill** [NS 596648] was another property owned by the Andersons in the sixteenth century.

The Andersons also held:
Curriehill Castle [NT 165678], near Currie, Edinburgh; site of castle and mansion.
    Held by a James Anderson at one time, but the property also had several other owners, including the Skenes, the Johnstones, the Scotts and the Marshall Lord Curriehill.

Montrave [NO 378067], near Leven, Fife; site of mansion and castle.
    Held by the Andersons in the eighteenth century, but passed to the Gilmours about 1800. The building has been demolished.
Tullichewan Castle [NS 380811], Alexandria, Dunbartonshire; site of mansion.
    Held by the Andersons of Tullichewan in the twentieth century after passing from the Campbells, but the property was sold in 1953 and the mansion was demolished the following year.

www.clananderson.net
showcase.netins.net/web/clanande/
freepages.genealogy.rootsweb.com/~andersonassociation/
No. of castles/sites: 6
Rank: 212=/764
Xref: MacAndrew

Annan

The name is territorial and comes from both Annan in Dumfries and Galloway, and the lands of Annand, which were in the old county of Forfarshire in Angus.

Sauchie Tower [NS 896957], two miles north of Alloa in Clackmannanshire, dates from the fifteenth century, but became ruinous and the courtyard buildings were demolished in the 1930s. Sauchie was given to the Annan family by Robert the Bruce in 1321; they held the property until 1420 when it passed by marriage to the Shaws, who were long in possession. The tower is to be (or has been) restored.

Robert the Bruce also gave the Annan family **Auchendrane** [NS 335152], five miles south of Ayr, which had been a property of the Browns but they were forfeited, having chosen the wrong side in the Wars of Independence. The lands soon went to the Mures who went on to hold Auchendrane for generations. There was a castle but this was cleared away when Blairstone House, dating from the eighteenth century, was built.

The lands of **Annand** [NO 510565] (also recorded as **Inyaney** and several other spellings) were held by a family of the same name from the thirteenth century until they were sold before 1546 to Cardinal David Beaton. The lands were located in the old county of Forfarshire, but a more precise location has not been determined.

No. of castles/sites: 3
Rank: 328=/764
Xref: Annand

Anstruther

The lands of Anstruther, which are to the south of Fife, were granted to a Norman, William Candela, in the twelfth century. In a few generations they changed their name to Anstruther as their territorial designation. The pretty fishing village of Anstruther stands on the coast, and is called 'Anster' by locals.

The family built a castle in **Anstruther Easter**, which was also known as **Dreel Castle** [NO 565035]. It was a tall and unusually narrow tower, but nothing survives except some walling in Wightman's Wynd (Castle Street) in the burgh. One of the family, Andrew Anstruther, fought at the Battle of Flodden in 1513, and was lucky enough to survive. James VI made John Anstruther the Hereditary Grand Carver in 1585, a position still held by the head of the family. Sir Philip Anstruther entertained Charles II at Dreel in 1651, and fought for the Royalist side at the Battle of Worcester the same year, although he was then taken prisoner. Cromwell seized the castle the same year. The family, however, flourished after the Restoration.

The family acquired the property of Airdrie in 1674, which is a few miles west of Crail, also in Fife. **Airdrie House** [NO 567084] is a sixteenth-century tower house, although it was later altered; the property had had several owners, including the Lumsdens and the Turnbulls, before it came to the Anstruthers. Sir James Anstruther of Airdrie was Principal Clerk of the Bills in the Court of Session. Airdrie was sold to the Erskine Earls of Kellie, and the building is occupied as a private residence.

Balcaskie House [NO 526035], one and a half miles north-west of Pittenweem also in Fife, is now a U-plan symmetrical mansion, but it incorporates a sixteenth-century L-plan tower house. It was extended in 1665 by Sir William Bruce, as well as in 1750 and again in 1830. Balcaskie was acquired by the Anstruthers in 1698, and they were made Baronets in 1700, and many of the family are buried at the nearby ruinous Abercrombie Church [NO 522034]. This branch of the family flourished, first inheriting the lands of the Carmichaels through marriage, and then as chiefs of the Anstruthers. They still apparently live at Balcaskie.

Newark Castle [NO 518012], two miles east and north of Elie in Fife, is a ruinous castle above the sea. It was held by the Anstruthers from 1694, having previously been a property of the Kinlochs, of the Sandilands of Cruivie and of the Leslie Lord Newark. For some years the Anstruthers used the title Lord Newark until this was relinquished in 1793. The property passed to the Bairds of Elie (www.inverie.com).

Newark Castle 1920?

Other properties owned by the Anstruthers:
Ardross Castle [NO 509006], near Elie, Fife; scant remains of a castle.
    Held by the Dishingtons and by the Scotts before passing to Sir William Anstruther at the end of the seventeenth century.
Barns [NO 597068], near Crail, Fife; site only.
    Held by the Cunninghams and then by the Lambies in the fourteenth century, and then by the Anstruthers, followed by the Drummonds.
Carmichael House [NS 938391], near Lanark; mansion on site of castle.
    The lands and mansion passed by marriage to the Anstruthers in 1817 after being held by the Carmichaels. The Anstruthers changed their name to Carmichael-Anstruther, then to Carmichael, and still apparently occupy the house.
Elie House [NO 496008], Elie, Fife; mansion incorporating tower house.
    Held by the Anstruthers from 1366 but by the seventeenth century was owned by the Scotts and then later went to the Bairds. The building was later used as a convent.

No. of castles/sites: 8
Rank: 160=/764

Arbuthnott

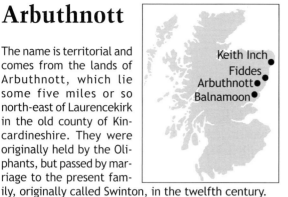

The name is territorial and comes from the lands of Arbuthnott, which lie some five miles or so north-east of Laurencekirk in the old county of Kincardineshire. They were originally held by the Oliphants, but passed by marriage to the present family, originally called Swinton, in the twelfth century.

The Arbuthnotts built a castle on a strong position between two rivers, on the site of which is **Arbuthnott House** [NO 795750]. This is now a large and imposing symmetrical mansion, but it incorporates a substantial part of a castle dating from the fifteenth century. There are some fine plaster ceilings.

In 1420 Hugh Arbuthnott was implicated for the murder of John Melville of Glenbervie by throwing him in a cauldron of boiling water, and then drinking the resultant broth. He was pardoned for his part in the murder. The family were made Viscounts in 1641. The two-storey Arbuthnott Aisle was added to St Ternan's Church [NO 801746] at Arbuthnott by Robert Arbuthnott around 1500. There is a medieval stone effigy in the church of one of the family, Hugh Arbuthnott, and the church is open to the public. The family still apparently live at Arbuthnott House, and the gardens are open all year, while the house is occasionally open to the public (01561 320417/361226; www.arbuthnott.co.uk).

Castle of Fiddes [NO 825813] lies four miles southwest of Stonehaven also in Kincardineshire, and is an attractive L-plan tower house with turrets and a watch-chamber. It was held by the Arbuthnotts but was sold to the Thomsons of Arduthie in the late seventeenth century. The building was restored in the 1960s, and is now used as a farmhouse.

Other properties owned by the family:

Arduthie [NO 868865], Stonehaven, Kincardineshire; site of castle or old house.
> Held by the Arbuthnotts from 1488 but passed to the Thomsons and then to the Barclays. The new town of Stonehaven was built on the lands.

Balglassie [NO 538576], near Brechin, Angus; site of castle or old house.
> Held by the Dishingtons and by the Turnbulls, but appears to then have been a property of the Arbuthnotts in the eighteenth century.

Balnamoon [NO 552638], near Brechin, Angus; altered castle and mansion.
> Held by the Collace family and then by the Carnegies, then Carnegy-Arbuthnotts of Balnamoon and Findrowie from 1745. Still occupied.

Fiddes [NJ 939244], near Ellon, Aberdeenshire; site of castle.
> May have been held by the Arbuthnotts.

Findrowie Castle [NO 554607], near Brechin, Angus; site of tower house.
> Held by the Arbuthnotts; date stones of 1584, 1638 and 1642 survive. The family married into the Carnegies of Balnamoon, and are now represented by the Carnegy-Arbuthnotts of Balnamoon.

Fordoun [NO 733770], near Laurencekirk, Kincardineshire; mansion on possible site of castle.
> Held by the Arbuthnotts in the eighteenth century and used as a dower house.

Keith Inch Tower [NK 138458], near Peterhead, Aberdeenshire; site of tower house and mansion.
> Held by the Keith Earls Marischal but was sold to the Arbuthnotts after 1715 when the Keiths were forfeited. The castle was demolished in 1813 when the Arbuthnotts built a new mansion.

Mains of Catterline [NO 865786], near Stonehaven; Aberdeenshire; site of castle?
> Held by the Oliphants, and then by the Arbuthnotts in the seventeenth and eighteenth centuries.

www.arbuthnot.org
www.arbuthnott.co.uk
members.lycos.co.uk/CAArbuthnots/
No. of castles/sites: 10
Rank: 140=/764

Castle of Fiddes (M&R)

Ardrossan

The name is territorial and comes from the lands of Ardrossan on the west coast of Ayrshire. The family were originally called Barclay, and held the lands from the twelfth century or earlier. They then became known as Ardrossan, one of whom swore fealty to Edward I at Brechin, and two of whom were prisoners in England in 1305. **Ardrossan Castle** [NS 233424] stands on a height above the sea, and is now a fragmentary ruin.

Ardrossan Castle was captured by William Wallace during the Wars of Independence. He had the English garrison slaughtered and thrown into the dungeon, the

Ardrossan Castle (M&R)

episode becoming known as 'Wallace's Larder'. Indeed, it is said that on stormy nights his ghost can be seen stalking the ruins. The castle was dismantled, but in the fourteenth century the property passed to the Montgomerys, who built a new stronghold. The Ardrossan family line died out.

No. of castles/sites: 1
Rank: 537=/764

Armstrong

The origin of the name is said to come from Siward Digry, who was the last Earl of Northumberland before the Norman invasion in 1066. Armstrong means 'sword strong arm'. Siward was the nephew of King Canute, and the Armstrongs are said to be related to both Duncan (of MacBeth fame), King of Scots, and William the Conqueror.

The name Armstrong was, and is, common on both side of the Scottish-English border. The Armstrongs became particularly prominent in Liddesdale, in Eskdale and in Ewesdale. They had many tower houses and it is said that they could raise 3000 men.

In the fifteenth century the chief of the Armstrongs built **Mangerton Tower** [NY 479853], which stood one mile south of Newcastleton near to the English border, and it was a strong tower house. The Armstrongs were an independent, unruly and war-like lot, renowned as reivers and cattle thieves; and often came into conflict with both the English and with the kings of Scots. Mangerton was burnt by the English in 1523, 1543, 1569 and 1601, and John 'Black Jock' Armstrong was hanged for reiving in 1530. The Armstrongs raided Tynedale in England in 1593, but James VI hoped to also become King of England and he did not want trouble on the Border. He dealt with the Armstrongs ruthlessly, harrying them relentlessly, and many were eventually hanged in 1610; others went to Ireland. Little remains of Mangerton Tower except part of the vaulted basement. Nearby, by the side of the B6357, is the Milnholm Cross, erected around 1320 to commemorate the murder of Alexander Armstrong in Hermitage Castle.

Whithaugh Tower [NY 489880], half a mile northeast of Newcastleton, was second in importance only to Mangerton. Again little survives except an unvaulted basement built into a later mansion. The tower was sacked in 1582 and 1599, and Simon Armstrong of Whithaugh was hanged in 1535.

Gilnockie Tower [NY 386782] lay in Eskdale, a couple of miles north of Canonbie in Dumfriesshire, and was apparently built in 1518, although there was probably an older stronghold on the site before this. The tower was burnt five years later by the English. Johnnie Armstrong of Gilnockie had acquired a reputation as a notorious reiver, and in 1530 James V invited him to join a hunting party along with fifty of his men. The king had other plans, however, and Johnnie and his followers were summarily hanged. A stone memorial marks the grave at Carlanrig [NT 403048]. Gilnockie was destroyed.

Nearby is **Hollows Tower** [NY 383787], which is also known as Gilnockie Tower. This has been reroofed and restored to house the Clan Armstrong Centre (01387 371876; www.armstrong-clan.co.uk). There is also the

Hollows Tower (LF)

Armstrong Clan Museum in Langholm, which is open April to October (01387 380610; www.armstrong-clan.co.uk), and the Liddesdale Heritage Centre in Newcastleton, which is open Easter to September (01387 375283).

The family also owned the following tower houses or castles, although none of these (apart from Kirkton) was probably of any great strength:

Arkleton Tower [NY 380914], near Langholm, Dumfries and Galloway; site of tower house.
  Held by the Maxwells, and then by the Armstrongs from 1537 but had passed to the Elliots by 1671. The tower was replaced by a mansion.

Barnglies [NY 329776], near Canonbie, Dumfries and Galloway; site of tower house.
  Christopher Armstrong of Barnglies was brother to Johnnie (mentioned above), and was hanged with him at Carlanrig in 1530. The site of the tower may be occupied by the farm.

Burnfoot [NY 390964], near Langholm, Dumfries and Galloway; site of tower house.
  Held by the Armstrongs.

Bush [NY 375923], near Langholm, Dumfries and Galloway; possible site of tower house.
  Held by the Armstrongs.

Byrsted Tower [NY 568999], near Newcastleton, Borders; site of tower house.
  Held by the Armstrongs or by the Elliots.

Calfield Tower [NY 341845], near Langholm, Dumfries and Galloway; site of tower house.
  Held by the Armstrongs.

Glendivan [NY 374907], near Langholm, Dumfries and Galloway; site of tower house.
  Probably held by the Armstrongs.

Glenvorann [NY 387965], near Langholm, Dumfries and Galloway; site of tower house.
  Held by Hobbie of Glenvore in 1590.

Greena Tower [NY 461807], near Newcastleton, Borders; site of tower house.
  Held by the Armstrongs.

Harelaw Tower [NY 436790], near Canonbie, Dumfries and Galloway; site of tower house.
  Held by Hector Armstrong in 1569.

Hill [by Calfield?], near Langholm, Dumfries and Galloway; site of tower house.
  Held by the Armstrongs.

Kirkton Tower [NY 368907], near Lockerbie, Dumfries and Galloway; site of tower house.
  Held by an important branch of the Armstrongs, and perhaps also by the Littles at one time.

Langholm Tower [NY 361849], Langholm, Dumfries and Galloway; slight remains of tower house.
  Possibly held by the Armstrongs but passed to the Maxwells.

Langholm Tower [NY 365855], Langholm, Dumfries and Galloway; some remains of tower house.
  Possibly held by the Armstrongs but passed to the Maxwells. The basement is built into the former Buccleuch Arms Hotel.

Nease [near Calfield?], near Langholm, Dumfries and Galloway; site of tower house.
  Held by the Armstrongs.

Muirburnhead [NY 444826], near Newcastleton, Borders; site of tower.
  Held by the Armstrongs.

Puddingburn Tower [NY 455858], near Newcastleton, Borders; site of tower house.
  Perhaps the stronghold of Jock Armstrong o' the Syde, although there was another tower at Syde (see below).

Roan Tower [NY 488895], near Newcastleton, Borders; site of tower house.
  Probably held by the Armstrongs.

Sark or **Kinmont Tower** [NY 333750], near Canonbie, Dumfries and Galloway; site of castle.
  Possibly held by the Carlyles in 1215 but passed to the Armstrongs. This was the property of William Armstrong of Kinmont in the 1590s, better known as 'Kinmont Willie', from the old ballad. It was from the tower that Scott of Buccleuch planned the daring rescue of Willie from imprisonment in Carlisle Castle.

Syde Tower [NY 473865], near Newcastleton, Borders; site of tower house.
  Probably the home of Jock o' the Syde, who features in Border ballads.

Thorniewhats [NY 389784], near Canonbie, Dumfries and Galloway; site of tower house.
  Probably held by the Armstrongs.

Westburnflat Tower [NY 497894], Newcastleton, Borders; site of tower house.
  Willie of Westburnflat was hanged for thieving cattle.

Whitlawside [NY 444800], near Canonbie, Dumfries and Galloway; site of tower house.
  Probably held by the Armstrongs.

Woodslee Tower [NY 389741], near Canonbie, Dumfries and Galloway; site of tower house.
  Held by the Armstrongs, and there may have been another tower to the north.

www.armstrong-clan-association.co.uk
www.armstrong.org
www.armstrong-clan.co.uk
www.armstrongclan.org.uk

No. of castles/sites: 26
Rank: 50=/764

Arnott

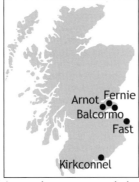

The name probably comes from the lands of Arnott, four miles north of Cardenden in the old county of Kinross-shire. The family are on record from the thirteenth century. **Arnot Tower** [NO 207016] is a now ruinous tower house, four storeys high and dating from the sixteenth century, and the lands were a property of the Arnotts from 1250 (or earlier) until 1705 when the property was sold to the Bruces because of debt. Sir Michael Arnott of that Ilk was made a Baronet in 1629 by Charles I. The gardens at Arnot are occasionally open to the public and can be hired for weddings or functions (01592 840115; www.arnot tower.co.uk/www.gardens ofscotland.org).

The Arnots of Balcormo were another important branch. The ruin of a large building at **Balcormo** [NO 516043] stood two miles to the north of St Monans in Fife, although nothing now remains. There was a castle, tower and fortalice here, and there is a date stone with 1388. Hugo Arnott of Balcormo was a lawyer and historian, and published a compilation of Scottish criminal trials in 1785. After a succession of owners, the Arnotts in 1586 bought **Fernie Castle** [NO 316147], four miles west of Cupar in Fife, from the Lovells but the property then soon passed by the marriage to the Balfours. The building is now a hotel (01337 810381; www.ferniecastle. demon.co.uk). The dramatically located **Fast Castle** [NT 862710], perched on cliffs near Coldingham in Berwickshire in the Borders, was also a property of the Arnotts for some years; as was **Mugdrum** [NO 228184], on the south coast of the Tay near Newburgh in Fife. This house dates from the eighteenth century, but includes older work, and it was held by the Arnotts in the seventeenth century. Other branches of the family are listed as Woodmiln (mentioned in 1750), Balkaithlie and Eastrynd. The Arnotts also held **Kirkconnel Hall** [NY 192752], to the north-west of Ecclefechan on the English border. One of the family was physician to Napoleon Bonaparte; the building is now used as a hotel (01576 300277; www.kirkconnel hall.co.uk)

No. of castles/sites: 6
Rank: 212=/764
Xref: Arnot

Arnot Tower (M&R)

Asloane

The name comes from the 'son of Sloan' (O'Sloan) and is Irish in origin. Sloan itself comes from a personal name 'Sluagadach', which means 'leader of a military expedition'. The family was also prominent in Ireland.

The Asloans or Sloans held lands at **Garroch** [NX 589823], three miles north-west of St John's Town of Dalry in Dumfries and Galloway, from the fifteenth century or earlier until at least the seventeenth century. George Asloane of Garroch, son of the then laird, was charged with taking Mass in 1613. The house, now known as **Old Garroch**, dates from the second half of the seventeenth century. Although it has no defensive features, it may stand on the site of a tower house as there is a date stone of 1633. The lands passed to the Maxwells and then to the Griersons and perhaps to the Carlyles. There was a newer mansion, but this was burnt out and then demolished in the first half of the twentieth century.

No. of castles/sites: 1
Rank: 537=/764
Xrefs: Asloan; Sloane

Assloss

The name is territorial and comes from lands Auchinloss, which are two miles north-east of Kilmarnock in Ayrshire. The name is on record from the fifteenth century. **Auchinloss** [NS 447401] was held by the Assloss or Auchinloss family from 1450 or earlier until around 1616, but the family has long been extinct. There was a sixteenth-century tower house at Auchinloss, but there are no remains. The lands passed to the Montgomerys and then to others, and are now part of Dean Castle Country Park (www.deancastle.com).

No. of castles/sites: 1
Rank: 537=/764
Xrefs: Auchinloss; Auchincloss

Auchinleck

The name appears to be territorial and is descriptive ('auchen' means 'higher ground', and 'lech' probably 'barren' in this context), but applies to both lands in Angus and in Ayrshire. It is likely that the two branches of the Auchinlecks or Afflecks are not related. The name is on record from the thirteenth century.

Affleck Castle [NO 493389], four miles north of Monifieth in Angus, is a hugely impressive L-plan tower of four storeys and an attic, and stands on high ground. The building is in good condition and had been taken into

Affleck Castle (M&R)

the care of Historic Scotland, but this has been relinquished because of access problems. The Auchinleck family are on record from 1306, and held the lands until the middle of the seventeenth century when they passed to the Reids.

They held two other castles in this part of Scotland. **Balmanno Castle** [NO 144156] is a sixteenth-century L-plan tower house, which was formerly surrounded by a moat. The lands, which are two miles south of Bridge of Earn in Perth and Kinross, were bought by the Auchinlecks about 1570, and they built the castle, although it passed from them to the Murrays later in the seventeenth century. The castle is in good condition, having been restored in 1916-21 after being used as a farmhouse, and is occupied as a private residence. There

Balmanno Castle (M&R)

may have also been a stronghold at **Balmanno** [NO 693666], four or so miles north-west of Montrose in Angus, although nothing of this castle apparently remains. There is a neat mansion on the site.

Glenbervie House [NO 769805], which lies seven miles south-west of Stonehaven in Kincardineshire, is a substantial mansion, dating from the eighteenth century, but with two round towers from a much earlier castle. It passed by marriage from the Melvilles to the Auchinleck family in 1468, then went by marriage to the Douglases in 1572, and then later passed to the Burnetts of Leys and then to the Nicholsons. The house is still occupied, and the gardens are occasionally open to the public (www.gardensofscotland.org).

There was a castle at **Auchinleck** [NS 501232], two miles south-west of Catrine in Ayrshire, which stood near to the present Auchinleck House. There are some remains of a fourteenth-century stronghold, which was held by this branch of the Auchinlecks until 1504 (or 1513), but then passed by marriage to the Boswells of Balmuto. The last laird, Sir John Auchinleck of that Ilk, was killed at the Battle of Flodden in 1513. The Boswells built a tower house on a new site, also called **Auchenleck** [NS 501232], itself now ruinous, and this was in turn was replaced by a classical mansion in the eighteenth century. Auchinleck House is in the care of the Landmark Trust, offers holiday accommodation and can be visited on Wednesday afternoons from Easter to the end of October by appointment only (01628 825925; www.landmark trust.org.uk).

Gillbank House [NS 706426], two miles south of Strathaven in Lanarkshire, was also held by the family. The laird of Auchinleck was active with William Wallace about 1300, and they reputedly raided Lanark from Gillbank. There was a tower house, but the last remains were cleared away in 1852.

No. of castles/sites: 6
Rank: 212=/764
Xref: Affleck; Auchenleck

Avenel

The name comes from Avenville, in the department of Orme in France. Robert Avenel was given lands in Eskdale by David I in the eleventh century, and held the barony of Westerker. His castle or seat may have been at what is now called **Bogle Walls, Enzieholm** [NY 292912], five and a half miles north-west of Langholm in Dumfries and Galloway. The earthworks of an Iron Age fort were reused in medieval times. The Avenel family prospered for a while, but when the last lord died around 1243 the lands passed by marriage to the Grahams.

The Avenels also held **Abercorn** [NT 083794], three miles west of South Queensferry in West Lothian. They had a castle, dating from the twelfth century, but this, along with the lands, also went to the Grahams and then to the Douglases and to others. All that remains of a later castle, which was besieged and destroyed in 1455, is a mound.

No. of castles/sites: 2
Rank: 396=/764

Ayton

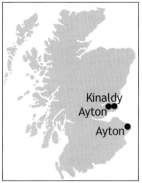

The name is probably territorial and comes from the lands of Ayton (pronounced Eye-ton, from the river) which are two miles south-west of Eyemouth in Berwickshire. The lands were held by the Ayton family from the eleventh century, and they were descended from a Norman knight called Gilbert. Sir Robert Ayton was secretary to Anne of Denmark, wife of James VI, and then Henrietta Maria, and he was also a accomplished poet in both English and Latin. He died in 1638.

There was an old castle at Ayton, but it passed along with the lands by marriage to the Homes. **Ayton Castle** [NT 929614] probably stands on the site of the old stronghold, but it is a modern castellated mansion,

Ayton Castle (Ayton)

designed by James Gillespie Graham and built in the 1840s. The building is open to the public in the summer (01890 781212/550; www.aytoncastle.co.uk).

The Aytons held lands in Fife in the sixteenth century. Andrew Ayton was Master of Works under James IV and supervised work on Stirling Castle. He was given lands, now known as **Ayton** [NO 302183], which lie some five miles north-west of Cupar in Fife, and he built a castle. There are no remains. The Aytons also held **Kinaldy** [NO 513104], three and a half miles south of St Andrews also in Fife, from 1539 or earlier until the eighteenth century. There was a tower house or castle, but this has also gone. Thomas the Rhymer prophesied that none of woman born would succeed to the lands of Kinaldy, save of Ayton blood. The property, however, later passed to the Monypennys.

Nearby are also **Drumcarro** [NO 453129] and **Feddinch** [NO 485135]. Drumcarro was held by the Aytons in 1681 and then by the Hays, and there was a castle or old house. Feddinch House is an elegant mansion and may stand on the site of an older residence. Feddinch was held by the Symsons until 1542, then by the Aytons and then by the Lindsays in the eighteenth century, and then by others. Accommodation is available at the house (01334 470888; www.feddinch-house.com).

No. of castles/sites: 5 / Rank: 240=/764
Xref: Aiton

Baikie

The name is territorial, and refers either to the lands of Baikie in Angus or to the lands of Beaquoy on Orkney. The family were certainly prominent on Orkney, and held **Tankerness House** [HY 446109] in Kirkwall. This is a fine sixteenth-century town house, which is dated 1574, and passed to the Baikies in the seventeenth century. The family were successful merchants, and Arthur Baikie was Provost of Kirkwall.

Tankerness House (M&R)

Tankerness House is now home to the excellent Museum of the Orkney, and the building is open to the public all year (01856 873191; www.orkneyheritage.com). There is information about the Baikies.

Hall of Tankerness [HY 524087], which is four miles east of Kirkwall, dates from 1550 and the old part of the house is a long two-storey range. The property was held by the Groats but passed to the Baikies in 1630. The Baikie family were buried and have a mausoleum nearby [HY 523088] in the remnant of St Andrew's chapel.

There was a **Baikie Castle** [NO 319492], four and a half miles east of Alyth in Angus, but there is no record of it being held by a family called Baikie. There are no remains of the castle, and the property was held by the Fentons in the thirteenth century before coming to the Lyons of Glamis around 1450.

No. of castles/sites: 2
Rank: 396=/764

Baillie

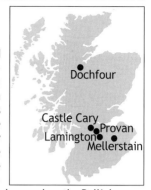

Baillie is probably derived from the French for 'bailiff' or 'steward', which was an important office in medieval times; Balliol is another derivation. The Baillies of Lamington may have been a branch of the Balliols, who changed the spelling of their name following the Wars of Independence when the Balliols were forfeited.

Not much now remains of **Lamington Tower** [NS 980320], which stands five miles south-west of Biggar in Lanarkshire. This is reputedly from where Marion Braidfute, wife of William Wallace, was seized by Hazelrig the sheriff and taken to Lanark. There she was slain, and in revenge William Wallace stormed the castle, killed Hazelrig and massacred the English garrison.

The lands were held by the Baillies from 1368, and Mary, Queen of Scots, visited Lamington in 1565, while William Baillie of Lamington was Master of the Wardrobe. The Baillies supported Mary, and fought for her at the Battle of Langside three years later. When she fled, they were forfeited, although they later recovered the lands. The tower at Lamington was occupied until 1750, but thirty years later was deliberately blown up so that the stone could be used to build field dykes. The Baillies became Lords Lamington in 1880, and built a small mansion nearby.

Alexander Baillie, son of the then laird of Lamington, fought bravely at the Battle of Brechin in 1452 and was given the lands of Dochfour and Dunain as a reward. **Dochfour House** [NH 604393] lies five miles south-west of Inverness, and there was a castle, which was replaced after the Jacobite Rising of 1745-46 by the present mansion. The lands are still apparently held by the Baillies, there are fine gardens, and the house can be rented for house parties, conferences and dinners (01463 861218; www.dochfour.co.uk). Nearby Dunain [NH 626423] may have also had an old stronghold, but the present baronial mansion dates from the nineteenth century.

Castle Cary [NS 786775], which stands two miles north and east of Cumbernauld in Lanarkshire, is a fine old castle with a strong tower and a later wing. Some of the masonry was reused from Roman times: the Antonine Wall passes close by. The property passed from the Livingstones to the Baillies in the first half of the seventeenth century, and William Baillie was general of the Covenanter forces that were defeated by the Marquis of Montrose at the battles of Alford and of Kilsyth, both in 1645. The castle was torched as a result, although it was rebuilt and reoccupied, but was burned again during the Jacobite Rising of 1715. It was restored, and then passed by marriage to the Dunbars in 1730. The castle is a private residence (www.castle-cary.org).

The castle is said to have two ghosts. One is reputed

Castle Cary (M&R)

to be Lizzie Baillie, who eloped with an unsuitable suitor, but died in remorse when she found out that the worry caused by her marriage had killed her father. The other is believed to be William Baillie (mentioned above), stricken that his actions had caused the castle to be burned.

Another branch, descended from the Lamington Baillies, bought Jerviswood, one mile north of Lanark, in 1636. **Jerviswood House** [NS 884455] is an altered L-plan tower, which dates from the sixteenth century.

Jerviswood House (M&R)

The house has been restored, receiving a Civic Trust commendation, and is still occupied. The family were Covenanters as mentioned above, and in 1684 Robert Baillie was hanged, drawn and quartered after being involved in a plot to shoot the king, parts of his body being displayed in Ayr, Edinburgh, Glasgow, Jedburgh and Lanark (although the folk of the latter burgh gave their part a decent burial). The family married into the Earls of Marchmont, when George Baillie of Jerviswood married Grizel, daughter of Sir Patrick Home, in 1692, and they moved to Mellerstain.

Mellerstain [NT 648392] is a magnificent castellated mansion with lovely gardens, and is located five miles east of Earlston in the Borders. It was designed by the

Mellerstain (MC)

father and son architects William and Robert Adam, and the present house dates from 1725. It is owned by the Baillie-Hamiltons, who are Earls of Haddington. The house is open to the public from May to September (01573 410225; www.mellerstain.com).

Provan Hall [NS 667663], near Coatbridge in central Scotland, is an interesting mansion with ranges of buildings and a wall with a gateway enclosing a central courtyard. It was first built by the Baillies, and William Baillie of Provand was Lord President of the Court of Session from 1565 until his death in 1595. Provan later passed by marriage to the Hamiltons, and later went to other families. A White Lady is said to haunt the building, the spirit of a woman who was murdered in a first-floor bedroom. The hall is open all year (0141 771 4399).

Other properties were held by the Baillies:

Carfin [NS 769575], near Carfin, Lanarkshire; no remains of a tower house.
  Held by the Baillies, but then by the Nisbets by 1710.

Carnbroe House [NS 735623], near Coatbridge, Lanarkshire; site of altered tower house.
  Held by the Baillies and then by the Hamiltons. Demolished around the 1950s.

Carphin [NO 319195], near Cupar, Fife; site only.
  Cuthbert Baillie of Carphin was Lord High Treasurer to James IV in 1512. Carphin later passed to the Haulkerstons and then to others.

Castlehill Tower [NT 214354], near Peebles, Borders; ruined tower house.
  Held by the Baillies of Jerviswood in 1672, and then by the Douglases.

Dunragit House [NX 150582], near Glenluce, Galloway; house incorporating a strong tower.
  Held by the Cunninghams, by the Baillies and later by the Dalrymple-Hays.

Edmonston Castle [NT 070422], near Biggar, Lanarkshire; ruined tower house.
  Held by the Baillies of Walston from 1650 until early in the eighteenth century.

Hills Tower [NT 049481], near Carnwath, Lanarkshire; site of tower house.
  Held by the Baillies of Lamington, then by the Hamiltons and by the Lockharts.

Jerviston [NS 757583], near Motherwell, Lanarkshire; L-plan tower house.
  Long held by the Baillies.

Mantle House [NT 589322], near Melrose, Borders; large mansion on older site.
  Home to Lady Grizel Baillie, and said to be haunted by a 'Grey Lady'. Now a hotel (01835 822261; www.dryburgh.co.uk).

Monkton House [NS 359271], near Prestwick, Ayrshire; site of castle.
  Held by the Hamiltons and by the Baillies of Monkton.

Jerviston (M&R) – see previous column

Penston [NT 444722], near Tranent, East Lothian; no remains.
  Held by the Balliols and then by the Baillies of Lamington. There were good seams of coal found here, and the village grew in size, although the miners were treated little better than slaves. The village was eventually abandoned; there is now only a farm and a few cottages.

Pittillock House [NO 278052], near Glenrothes, Fife; mansion incorporating a tower.
  Owned by several families including by the Baillies of Falkland.

Polkemmet House [NS 925650], near Whitburn, West Lothian; site of mansion.
  Held by the Cairns and by the Shaws, but was bought by the Baillies in 1820. The site is in the country park (01501 743905).

Red Castle [NH 584495], near Muir of Ord, Inverness-shire; altered ruinous mansion incorporating castle.
  Held by several families, including by the Baillies of Dochfour in the nineteenth century; they had the building remodelled in 1840.

Saughton House [NT 205713], Edinburgh; demolished tower house.
  Held by several families including by the Baillies; the site is in Saughton Park.

Todholes Castle [NT 038461], near Carnwath, Lanarkshire; demolished tower house.
  Held by the Douglases but had passed to the Baillies by 1649.

Torwood Castle [NS 836844], near Falkirk; ruined tower house.
  Long held by the Forresters but passed to the Baillies of Castlecary for some years.

Walston [NT 060455], near Carnwath, Lanarkshire; site of tower or old house.
  Held by the Baillies by 1650.

Whiteside Peel [NT 644384], Mellerstain, Borders; scant remains of tower house.
  Held by several families until coming to the Baillies of Jerviswood in 1642; Mellerstain is nearby.

Windgate House [NT 016271], near Biggar, Lanarkshire; some remains of a tower house.
  Held by the Baillies of Lamington, and said to be haunted by a couple in Victorian dress, who only appear when something of note or tragedy is going to happen to the family.

www.clanbailey.com
No. of castles/sites: 27
Rank: 47=/764
Xref: Bailey

Bain

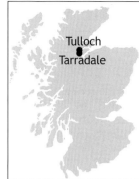
Tulloch
Tarradale

The name is from Gaelic and means 'fair', either hair or in colouring. A variation in spelling is Bean, and MacBain or MacBean means 'son of Bain' (also see that name). The name is on record from the fourteenth century.

The Bain family held lands north of Dingwall in the old county of Ross in the north of Scotland. **Tulloch Castle** [NH 547605], a mile or so north of Dingwall, incorporates a large keep or tower, probably dating from the sixteenth century but perhaps with work from as early as the twelfth century. To the castle was added a large extension in the seventeenth century. The lands were held by the Bains from 1526 and they were in possession until 1762 when

Tulloch Castle 1905?

the property was sold to the Davidsons. An underground passageway from the basement is believed to have led across the town to Dingwall Castle. It has collapsed but part of it can be seen from the middle of the front lawn. The castle is also said to have a Green Lady, which may have been active in recent times. The castle has been used as a hotel since 1996 (01349 861325; www.tulloch castle.co.uk).

The Bains of Tulloch held **Docharty** [NH 534603], also near Dingwall, which was in possession of the Munros but was sold to the Bains in 1553, and there was a tower house here; and **Tarradale** [NH 553488], two and a half miles north-east of Beauly. There was an old stronghold at Tarradale, although it was destroyed in 1308. The lands were held by the Mackenzies of Fairburn, but then passed to the Bains. The present Tarradale House is a field studies centre for Aberdeen University.

No. of castles/sites: 3
Rank: 328=/764
Xref: Bean

Baird

The name Baird appears to come from lands that they held near Biggar in Lanarkshire. According to tradition, they are said to have been given the property after saving William the Lion from a wild boar.

The first lands they held which are on record are the lands of **Kype** [NS 746407], three and a half miles south-east of Strathaven also in Lanarkshire, which the Bairds held from the thirteenth century, although by 1572 Kype had passed to the Dalziels and the property later went to the Hamiltons. There was a castle on the lands, although it is possible the site was at **Hall of Kype** [NS 708416].

The major branch of the family were the Bairds of Auchmeddan, a property nine miles west of Fraserburgh in the north-east of Scotland; the family held Auchmeddan from 1568 (or earlier) until the Bairds were forfeited for their part in the Jacobite Rising of 1745-46. **Auchmeddan Castle** [NJ 850647] dated from the sixteenth century, but was completely demolished at the end of the eighteenth. One of Thomas the Rhymer's prophecies related to the Bairds: 'there shall be an eagle in the craig while there is a Baird in Auchmeddan'. A pair of eagles which nested nearby are said to have left at the same time as the Bairds, but then returned when another branch of the family bought back the lands.

A branch of the Auchmeddan Bairds became lawyers and John Baird was a High Court Judge with the title Lord Newbyth. The original **Byth** [NJ 816565], seven miles north-east of Turriff, had been purchased by the Bairds, and James Baird of Byth was made Baron Deveron by Charles I, but died before he could assume the title. The Bairds then purchased a property in East Lothian, near North Berwick, called Foord and Whitekirk, and renamed the property **Newbyth** [NT 587805]. General Sir David Baird was a distinguished soldier, fighting both in India at the Battle of Seringapatam and during the Napoleonic Wars, and lost an arm at the Battle of Corunna in 1809. The Bairds built a grand new mansion at Newbyth, which was designed by William Adam but dates from the beginning of the nineteenth century. The house was damaged by fire in 1972, but was restored and is occupied. The Bairds of Newbyth now apparently live near Dalbeattie in Dumfries and Galloway.

Posso [NT 200332], six miles south and west of Peebles in the Borders, was long held by the family, and Sir Gilbert Baird of Posso was slain at the Battle of Flodden in 1513. There was a sixteenth-century tower house, but not much remains except the basement and the building was ruinous by 1775.

John Logie Baird, who was born in Helensburgh in 1886, was a pioneer of television technology and built the first working television system in 1929 (www.bairdtelevision.com).

Other properties held by the family include:

Broomhill House [NT 269674], near Edinburgh; site of castle.
Held by the Hendersons of Fordell but then went to the Bairds of Newbyth from 1709 to 1827 and then went to the Trotters of Mortonhall.

Cambusnethan [NS 788534], near Wishaw, Lanarkshire; scant remains of a tower house.
Held by the Bairds after being given to them by Robert the Bruce, but later passed to the Stewarts and then to the Somervilles and to the Lockharts. The castle is said to be haunted by a headless horsemen.

Closeburn Castle [NX 907921], near Thornhill, Dumfriesshire; massive keep with mansion.
Long held by the Kirkpatricks, but passed to the Bairds in 1852 and then to others.

Easter Braikie Castle [NO 637515], near Brechin, Angus; site of tower house.
Held by several families, including by the Gavins in 1752 and then passed by marriage to the Bairds, and then later went to the Campbells of Breadalbane.

Elie House [NO 496008], Elie, Fife; mansion incorporating tower house.
Held by the Anstruthers and by the Scotts, and then by the Bairds in the nineteenth century, and the Bairds, formerly of Elie, now apparently live in Edinburgh.

Kilhenzie Castle [NS 308082], near Maybole, Ayrshire; castle incorporated into a mansion.
Held by the Bairds before passing to the Kennedys in the seventeenth century.

Langhaugh Tower [NT 202310], near Peebles, Borders; ruined tower house.
Held by the Bairds of Posso although occupied by the Cockburns. This led to a dispute in 1561 between Janet Scott, widow of Baird of Posso, and a William Cockburn.

Lennoxlove [NT 515721], near Haddington, East Lothian; magnificent castle and mansion.
Long a property of the Maitlands and then the Stewarts but latterly held by the Bairds for some years, and then went in 1947 to the Duke of Hamilton. Open to the public Easter-October, Wednesday, Thursday and Sunday (01620 823720; www.lennoxlove.org)

Newark Castle [NO 518012], near St Monans, Fife; ruined castle.
Held by several families, including by the Leslies, then latterly by the Bairds of Elie (www.inverie.com).

Rickarton [NO 838886], near Stonehaven, Kincardineshire; mansion on site of castle or old house.
Latterly held by the Bairds of Urie (then Keiths from the 1930s), Viscounts Stonehaven from 1870.

Saughton House [NT 205713], Edinburgh; site of tower house.
Held by the Watsons, by the Ellis family and by the Baillies, and then went to the Bairds; Sir Robert Baird was made a

Saughton House (M&R)

Baronet of Nova Scotia in 1696. This branch of the family still flourishes as the Bairds of Saughton, Baronets. Saughton was used as a private lunatic asylum, before being bought by the local council, after which the grounds were turned into a park. The 1908 the Scottish National Exhibition took place in the grounds, but the house was burnt down in the 1950s and was demolished. The site is in Saughton Park.

Selvage [NT 125827], near Inverkeithing, Fife; seventeenth-century house.

Built by a John Bairdie in the 1630s or 40s.

Stichill House [NT 702392], near Kelso, Borders; site of castle and mansion.

Held by the Gordons and by the Pringles before being bought by the Bairds in the middle of the nineteenth century. They had made their money from coal and iron, and built a huge castellated mansion in 1866. Stichill later went to the Deuchars but the mansion was demolished in 1938.

Strathaven Castle [NS 703445], Strathaven, Lanarkshire; ruined castle.

Held by the Bairds for a time, and then by the Sinclairs, by

Strathaven Castle (M&R)

the Douglases, by the Stewarts and by the Hamiltons. Consolidated ruin and accessible to the public.

Strichen [NJ 944549], near Strichen, Aberdeenshire; ruined mansion on site of castle.

Held by the Frasers but passed to the Bairds in the nineteenth century.

Urie House [NO 860877], near Stonehaven; mansion incorporating tower house.

Held by several families, including by the Frasers, by the Keith Earls Marischal, by the Hays of Errol and by the Barclays and then went to the Bairds of Urie (Viscounts Stonehaven) in the nineteenth century.

Wellwood House [NS 665263], near Muirkirk; castle and mansion both demolished.

Held by the Campbells but passed to the Bairds in the nineteenth century.

Whitekirk [NT 595816], near North Berwick; restored tower house/ barn?

Held by the Sinclairs but went to the Bairds of Newbyth in the first quarter of the seventeenth century.

www.bairdnet.com
www3.nbnet.nb.ca/islands/clan.baird/
No. of castles/sites: 24
Rank: 56=/764

Balcanquhal

The name is territorial and comes from the lands of **Balcanquhal** [NO 163010], which are five miles west and south of Auchter-muchty in Fife. The family held the property the fourteenth century or earlier for at least 200 years. They had a tower house at Balcanquhal, mentioned in the sixteenth century, but nothing of the castle remains.

Walter Balcanquhal was minister of St Giles in Edinburgh in 1574, opposed the imposition of bishops, and went on to be minister of Trinity College Church. His son, another Walter, was chaplain to James VI, then later Dean of Durham, and was a supporter of Charles I.

No. of castles/sites: 1
Rank: 537=/764

Balcomie

The name is territorial in origin, and comes from the lands of Balcomie, which are some one and a half miles north of Crail in the south-east part of Fife.

The Balcomie family held the lands of **Balcomie** [NO 626099] from 1375 or earlier, but the property had passed to the Learmonths of Clatto by 1526, and then went to the Hopes in 1705, and then to others. Balcomie Castle is an L-plan tower house, dating from the sixteenth century, and has a small gatehouse and a walled garden. It is now used as a farmhouse.

A mile or so away is **Randerston** [NO 608108], another sixteenth-century L-plan tower house with turrets and gunloops. It was also held by the Balcomie family, but they were forfeited by James I in the fifteenth century after they had joined the English against him. They may have lost Balcomie at the same time. Randerston was given to the Myrtoun or Morton family, and then went to others, and the building is now a farmhouse.

No. of castles/sites: 2
Rank: 396=/764

Balfour

The name comes from the lands of Balfour (or 'Ba-lorr', meaning the 'settlement of the Orr': the Orr is a river which flows into the Firth of Forth), which are four miles east of Glenrothes in Fife. The lands are believed to have been held by the Balfours from as early as the eleventh century. It is likely that they had a castle at **Balfour** [NO 324003], but this was replaced in the sixteenth century by a tower house. This was then remodelled into a large baronial mansion, but the building was destroyed by being blown up in the 1960s. Nothing remains but a mound of rubble. Sir John Balfour, Sheriff of Fife, was slain at the sack of Berwick in 1296; several others of the family were also Sheriffs of Fife. Sir William Balfour was killed at a battle in 1298, fighting against the English on the side of William Wallace. The lands passed by marriage to the Beatons in 1360 and they held them until the end of the nineteenth century.

Other branches of the Balfour family, however, flourished and the Balfours became major landowners, especially in Fife.

The Balfours of **Denmylne** [NO 249175], which is a property one mile south-east of Newburgh in Fife, acquired the lands in 1452 and held them until 1710. They built a tower house in the sixteenth century, although this building is now ruinous. James Balfour of Denmylne died at the siege of Roxburgh Castle in 1460, while his son, John, died at the Battle of Flodden in 1513. Sir James Balfour of Denmylne and Kinnard, who was appointed Lyon King of Arms in 1639, compiled a collection of manuscripts, which form the basis of much

Denmylne Castle (M&R)

of authenticated Scottish history. He officiated at the coronations of Charles I and of Charles II, and died in 1657. His brother, Sir Andrew, founded the first botanical

garden in Edinburgh. The Balfours are buried in the ruinous parish church at Abdie [NO 260163].

Inchrye [NO 271169], two miles south-east of Newburgh, was held by the Balfours from 1501. There is a motte, and there was a much later Gothic mansion, dating from 1827, but this building was demolished in the 1960s. One story is that one of the lairds had a black wife, and treated the woman so badly that she died before her time. He passed away himself soon afterwards and had been laid out on his deathbed. Hearing a commotion, the servants entered the room to find that his corpse was now sitting up, and there was also a strong smell of brimstone. They believed that the Devil had come to take one of its own. The present Baron Balfour of Inchrye, a title which was created in 1945, apparently lives in Suffolk in England.

The Balfours acquired the property of Burleigh, which is one and a half miles north of Kinross in Perth and Kinross, in the middle of the fifteenth century, and probably built the now ruined **Burleigh Castle** [NO 130046]. The remains consist of a small tower house joined to a round tower by a curtain wall with a gate. Burleigh was visited by James IV. James Balfour was involved in the murder of Cardinal Beaton and was held as a French galley slave for two years. He was made

Burleigh Castle (M&R)

Lord President of the Court of Session, and was key in having James Douglas, fourth Earl of Morton, executed for his supposed part in the murder of Lord Darnley. In 1707, Robert Balfour, Master of Burleigh, fell in love with a local girl, but he was sent away as she was not a noble woman. When he returned, Balfour found the girl had married Henry Stenhouse, a schoolmaster, so Balfour shot and killed the poor man. Balfour was captured and sentenced to death, and only escaped execution by changing clothes with his sister and then fleeing to France. He fought on the Jacobite side in the 1715 Rising, and the family were forfeited. Balfour died unmarried in 1757. The castle is an attractive ruin, is in the care of Historic Scotland, and is open to the public: the key is available locally. The title Balfour of Burleigh is now held by the Bruces of Kennet, who apparently live in Clackmannanshire.

Fernie Castle [NO 316147], four miles west of Cupar also in Fife, is a sixteenth-century L-plan tower house, although there was probably an earlier stronghold on the site. Fernie was a property of the Balfours in the fifteenth century, and then again from 1586 after being held by the Fernies, by the Lovells and by the Arnotts. The Balfours were forfeited for their part in the Jacobite Rising of 1715, but recovered the lands in 1720. This is one of the many castles said to have a Green Lady, the ghost of a young girl who ran off with her lover. She fled to Fernie, but in the resultant melee fell from one of the upstairs windows. Her apparition has reputedly been seen and other manifestations witnessed. The building is now a hotel (01337 810381; www.ferniecastle. demon.co.uk).

Mountquhanie Castle [NO 347212], four and a half miles north and west of Cupar, is a ruinous sixteenth-century tower house, although one of the later wings is still occupied. Mountquhanie was held by the Balfours

Mountquhanie Castle (LF)

from 1459 until about 1600. One of the family, Sir Michael Balfour, a favourite of James IV, was killed at the Battle of Flodden in 1513, while others were involved in the murders of Cardinal David Beaton and Lord Darnley, Mary Queen of Scots's second husband, and Gilbert Balfour had to flee to Orkney. Mountquhanie was sold to the Lumsdens of Innergellie in about 1600.

The Balfours built Noltland Castle [HY 430487], a fantastic brooding ruin, rather incongruously located on the peaceful Isle of Westray, an island in Orkney. It is a Z-plan tower house and has many gunloops. The present castle was built (or rebuilt) by Gilbert Balfour, who was Master of the Household to Mary, Queen of Scots; he acquired the property by marriage. As mentioned above, Gilbert had been involved in the murders of Cardinal Beaton in 1546, for which he was imprisoned; and then Lord Darnley in 1567. He supported Mary after she fled to England, but when her cause became hopeless he fled Scotland, and served in the Swedish army until his death, being executed for treason against the Swedish king in 1576. The castle is said to have had a brownie, a helpful supernatural being who would do household chores. Another manifestation was reputedly the Boky Hound, which would be witnessed as a herald to the death in the family. Happier events

Noltland Castle 1920?

were announced by an eerie spectral light. Noltland was abandoned about 1760 after being damaged by fire in 1746, is in the care of Historic Scotland, and is open from July to September (01856 841815).

Forret [NO 385208] lies four and a half miles north of Cupar in Fife, and there was a castle or old house here. The property passed from the Forret family to the Balfours in the seventeenth century. James Balfour of Forret was knighted in 1674 and was made Lord Forret when he was raised to the Supreme Court.

Pilrig House [NT 265757], to the north of Edinburgh, is a restored seventeenth-century L-plan tower house, which has been reoccupied as private residences. It was held by the Balfours in 1718, many of whom are buried in South Leith graveyard. Robert Louis Stevenson was related to the family, originally being Robert Louis Balfour Stevenson. The house and grounds were given to the local council in 1941, but the building was later gutted by fire. Pilrig House was restored and divided, and now stands by a public park.

The Balfours held Balbirnie [NO 290018], two miles north-east of Glenrothes in Fife, from 1642 until the twentieth century. There was castle, but this was replaced by Balbirnie House, a mansion of 1777. It is now a hotel and stands in 400 acres of parkland and gardens (01592 610066; www.balbirnie.co.uk). The Balfours of Balbirnie still apparently live in Fife.

Whittinghame Castle [NT 602733] is a fine old castle and mansion, and stands two and a half miles south of East Linton in East Lothian. It has been held by the Balfours since 1818, previous owners including the Douglases, the Setons and the Hays. One of the family was Arthur James Balfour, Prime Minister of Great Britain from 1902-05, Foreign Secretary from 1916-19, and the first Earl Balfour and Viscount Traprain. The castle is still apparently occupied by the family.

Balfour Castle [HY 475165] on the Orkney island of Shapinsay is a castellated mansion and was built for the Balfours of Trenabie in 1847. The property was sold in 1961 and the building is now a small private hotel (01856 711282; www.balfourcastle.co.uk).

The Balfours also held other properties, mostly in Fife:
Balgarvie Castle [NO 354157], near Cupar, Fife; site of a strong castle and mansion.
The castle was destroyed by the English in the Wars of Independence in the fourteenth century. The lands were held by Balfours from the fifteenth century or earlier. There was a

later 'handsome' mansion at Balgarvie, but this was demolished around 1940.

Balgonie Castle [NO 313007], near Glenrothes, Fife; fine restored castle.

Held by the Sibbalds, by the Lundies and by the Leslies, before passing to the Balfours of Whittinghame in 1824, although it later passed to others. Recently restored and reoccupied and there are several ghost stories. Open to the public (01592 750119; www.balgonie-castle.com).

Bandon Tower [NO 276043], near Glenrothes, Fife; ruined tower house.

Held by the Balfours of Balbirnie from 1498 or earlier, then by

Bandon Tower (M&R)

the Beatons and then by the Balfours again from 1580 to 1630.

Cairneyflappet Castle [NO 220102], near Auchtermuchty, Fife; site of castle with moat.

Held by the Scotts and then by the Balfours of Burleigh from 1600 until the eighteenth century, and then went to the Skenes of Hallyards. The castle is said to have had a brownie, which is reputed to have stolen food from the stores.

Collairnie Castle [NO 307170], near Cupar, Fife; fine L-plan tower house.

Passed by marriage from the Barclays to the Balfours in 1789. Now part of a farm and still occupied.

Dawyck House [NT 168352], near Peebles, Borders; mansion on earlier site.

Held by the Veitch family and then by the Naesmiths, and later passed to the Balfours of Dawyck in the nineteenth century, and they apparently still live here. The botanic garden is nearby.

Isle of May [NT 655995], island in the Firth of Forth; fortified residence on site of priory.

The island was held by the Learmonths and then by Balfours of Mountquhanie for a time, before going to the Cunninghams of Barns in 1636, and then to others. The island can be visited from Anstruther in Fife (May-Sep).

Kinloch House [NO 280123], near Ladybank, Fife; site of castle or old house.

Held by the Kinlochs and then by the Balfours of Kinloch. One of the family, John Balfour, was involved in the murder of Archbishop Sharp on Magus Muir in 1679. He fled abroad and was forfeited in 1683, and died aboard ship in the entourage of William of Orange in 1689. The present house dates from about 1700, and was owned by the Kinnears in the nineteenth century.

Kinnaird House [NO 273174], near Newburgh, Fife; site only.

Held by the Balfours of Denmylne from 1630. Sir James Balfour of Denmylne and Kinnaird, Lord Lyon King of Arms, officiated at the coronations of Charles I and of Charles II, and was author of 'Annales of Scotland'.

Kirkforthar House [NO 297049], near Glenrothes, Fife; ruinous house.

Long held by the Lindsays but passed to the Balfours in the nineteenth century, who also own the Scourie estate.

Kirkton [NO 447260], near Leuchars, Fife; mansion incorporating castle.

Held by the Lockharts and then by the Balfours in the sixteenth century, but later went to the Youngs and then to the Gillespies. Partly restored.

Melville House [NO 298138], near Cupar, Fife; mansion on site of castle.

Held by the Balfours before 1592 but was sold to the Melvilles in that year and they built the mansion dating from 1692. Still occupied.

Monimail Tower [NO 299141], near Cupar, Fife; tower house.

Held by the church and then by the Balfours before 1592 but was then sold to the Melvilles and they built Melville House (see above). Monimail Tower may be visited (01337 810420).

Newton Don [NT 709372], near Kelso, Borders; mansion.

Held by several families, including by the Don family who eventually bankrupted themselves and sold the property to the Balfours of Whittinghame in 1847.

Pitcullo Castle [NO 413196], near Leuchars, Fife; restored tower house.

Held by the Sibbalds and then by the Balfours in the sixteenth century, and then later by the Trents. Restored and occupied.

Pittencrieff [NO 373159], near Cupar, Fife; site only.

Held by the Balfours but swopped for Mountquhanie with the Duff Earls of Fife and then went to the Turnbulls in 1602.

Pittillock House [NO 278052], near Glenrothes, Fife; mansion and tower house.

Held by the Balfours of Balbirnie at one time after being a property of the MacDuffs, of the Pattullos, and of the Lumsdens until 1651 when it went to the Baillies of Falkland. Remodelled about 1850.

Powis [NS 824956], near Stirling; mansion on site of castle?

Held by the Balfours in the sixteenth century.

Randerston [NO 608108], near Crail, Fife; farmhouse incorporating tower house.

Held by the Balcomie family, by the Morton family and by the Moncreiffes before being bought by the Balfours of Denmylne in 1663. Now a farmhouse.

Torrie Castle [NT 015867], near Dunfermline, Fife; site only.

Held by the Balfours at one time, as well as by the Wardlaws, by the Bruces and in the nineteenth century by the Erskine-Wemyss family.

Wormiston House [NO 612095], near Crail, Fife; restored tower house.

Held by the Spences and then by the Balfours from 1612 until 1621 when it went to the Lindsays. House rebuilt in the 1980s and the gardens are occasionally open to the public (www.gardensofscotland.org).

www.orkneybalfours.atfreeweb.com
No. of castles/sites: 33
Rank: 38/764

Ballindalloch

The name is territorial and comes from the lands of Ballindalloch, which lie some seven miles west of Charlestown of Aberlour in Moray. The name is on record from the four-teenth century.

The family built **Castle Stripe** [NJ 185361], the original Ballindalloch Castle, although all that survives now are some low walls. The lands had passed to the Grants by 1499, and they built a splendid new stronghold, **Ballindalloch Castle** [NJ 178365], at a different site. This is a large

Ballindalloch Castle (MC)

extended and altered Z-plan tower house with a fine interior and grounds, and is still owned by the descendants of the Grants. It is open to the public (01807 500206; www.ballindalloch castle.co.uk).

The Ballindallochs also held nearby **Tullochcarron** [NJ 180350], and there was a castle, built in the fifteenth century, but of which nothing survives. It also passed to the Grants.

There is another **Ballindalloch** [NS 535885], a property one mile west of Balfron in Stirlingshire. There was a castle here, which was replaced by a mansion, but this Ballindalloch does not appear to have been held by the Ballindallochs, being a property of the Cunninghams of Glencairn and then of others.

No. of castles/sites: 3
Rank: 328=/764

Balliol

The name is taken from Bailleul-en-Vimeu, a small village south of Abbeville in France, and is Picard in origin, not Norman. The first Balliol was mentioned in Scotland in the reign of David I in the twelfth century. The family gained extensive lands in the

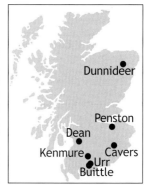

south of Scotland, and married into the royal family of Scotland. So it was that, with the death of Alexander III at the end of the thirteenth century, John Balliol had the senior claim to the throne of Scotland. His position was secured when he swore fealty to Edward I of England in 1292. His reign was to be brief and disastrous for his house. He abdicated in 1296 after the English had sacked Berwick and won the Battle of Dunbar. Robert the Bruce eventually came to the throne in 1306 and defeated the English at Bannockburn in 1314. The Balliols were stripped of their lands and titles. Edward Balliol, John's son, was put briefly on the throne in the 1330s by Edward III of England. His success was short lived and he had to flee back to England.

Buittle Castle [NX 819616] was built in the 1240s by John Balliol, father of King John, after he married Devorgilla, heiress of Alan, Lord of Galloway. Buittle is located north-west of Dalbeattie in Galloway in the south-west of Scotland. John Balliol (Toom Tabard) was born here in 1249. John, his father, established Balliol College (www.balliol.ox.ac.uk/history) in Oxford, and after his death, Devorgilla consolidated the establishment of Balliol College and founded Sweetheart Abbey [NX 964663], south of Dumfries, in memory of her husband, where his heart is buried; she kept it in a locket around her neck while she lived. She also established Greyfriars in Dundee, and when she died in 1290 she was interred at Sweetheart Abbey; her headless stone effigy survives, as does her reconstructed table tomb. The English occupied Buittle Castle in 1296, but it was captured by the Scots in 1313 and was slighted. The lands were given to the Douglases after the Balliols were forfeited, and there was a royal burgh in 1324. Buittle Old Parish Church [NX 807598], how a ruin, dates from 1234-96. A tower house [NX 817616] replaced the old castle in the sixteenth century, by which time Buittle was held by the Gordons.

Motte or Urr [NX 815647] is around a mile from Buittle, and is probably the best example of a motte and bailey castle in Scotland. It consists of a large 'pudding bowl' motte with a raised oval bailey, protected by another ditch. The castle probably dates from the twelfth century, when the lands were held by Lords of Galloway, but passed with Buittle to the Balliols.

Other properties held by the family:

Cavers [NT 540154], near Hawick, Borders; ruined tower house on
the site of an older castle.
  Held by the Balliols, who built a stone castle, but passed to
  the Douglases.
Dean Castle [NS 437394], Kilmarnock, Ayrshire; fine large castle.
  Briefly held by the Balliols in the fourteenth century but long
  a property of the Boyds; open to the public April to October
  (01563 522702; www.deancastle.com).
Dunnideer Castle [NJ 613282], near Inch, Aberdeenshire; slight
  remains of castle within the ramparts of Iron Age fort.
  Original castle probably built in the 1260s by the Balliols but
  it passed to the Tyries; open to the public by sign-posted
  footpath.
Heston Island [NX 839503], near Dalbeattie, Galloway; site of castle
  or manor.
  Held by the MacDowalls and burned by Edward Bruce, brother
  of Robert the Bruce, in 1308, and then used by Edward Balliol
  in the 1330s to 1340s.
Kenmure Castle [NX 635764], near New Galloway, Galloway; ruined
  tower house on older site.
  Held by the Balliols, who used a castle here, but passed to
  the Gordons of Lochinvar in 1297, who built the present castle
  and house, which was burnt out and then stripped in the 1950s.
Kirkcudbright Castle [NX 677508], Kirkcudbright, Galloway;
  earthworks of strong castle.
  Held by the Balliols. Edward I of England stayed in the castle
  for ten days in 1300. The lands passed to the Douglases, then
  to the Crown and was then given to the people of Kirkcudbright.
Lochinvar Castle [NX 656853], near St John's Tower of Dalry,
  Galloway; ruined castle.
  Held by the Balliols, but passed to the Gordons in 1297.
Penston [NT 444722], near Tranent, East Lothian; site of castle
  and mansion.
  Held by the Balliols in the thirteenth century but passed to
  the Baillies of Lamington.

No. of castles/sites: 11
Rank: 127=/764
Xref: Baliol

Balmakewan

The name is territorial and
comes from the lands of
Balmakewan, which are
five and a half miles north-
east of Brechin in Angus.
  Balmakewan Castle
[NO 667663] was held by
the Balmakewan family in
the fifteenth century, but
nothing remains except
one wall. The lands passed
to the Barclays, and the
castle was replaced by a
classical mansion, **Balmakewan House** [NO 668664], in
the 1820s.

No. of castles/sites: 1
Rank: 537=/764

Balmanno

The name is territorial,
and comes from the lands
of Balmanno two miles
south of Bridge of Earn in
Perth and Kinross. The
lands were held by the
Balmanno family, who pre-
sumably had a castle here,
until 1570 when the prop-
erty was sold to the
Auchinlecks. **Balmanno
Castle** [NO 144156] is a sixteenth-century L-plan tower
house with a tall tower in the re-entrant angle capped
by an ogee roof; there are later wings. This building,
however, was started by the Auchinlecks, and Balmanno
passed to the Murrays of Glendoick and then to others.
The castle was restored in 1916-21 and is still occupied.

No. of castles/sites: 1
Rank: 537=/764

Balnaves

The name is territorial in origin, and comes from the lands of Balneaves near Friockheim in Angus. The name Piper was common in Perthshire, but at the Reformation (because it had Catholic associations) several of the families called Piper changed their name to Balnaves. The Pipers held the lands of **Innerbundy** in 1457, although the location has not be determined except that the property was in Aberdeenshire.

The lands of **Balneaves**, probably later known as **Kinnell** [NO 599500], were held by the Balnaves family but passed to the Frasers in the fourteenth century and later to the Lyons of Glamis and then to others. There was a castle, which was already ruinous in the seventeenth century, but nothing remains.

The Balnaves family came to prominence through Henry Balnaves of Halhill, a Protestant reformer and lawyer in the reign of Mary, Queen of Scots; he was imprisoned in Blackness Castle and later in France where he was a galley slave after being associated with the murderers of Cardinal David Beaton in 1546. He died in 1579. **Halhill Tower** [NO 292132], some miles west of Cupar in Fife, was a sixteenth-century tower house, but nothing remains. The lands had passed to the Melvilles by the beginning of the seventeenth century.

No. of castles/sites: 2
Rank: 396=/764
Xrefs: Balneaves; Piper

Balwearie

The name is territorial and comes from the lands and barony of Balwearie, which are two or so miles south and west of Kirk-caldy in Fife. The name is on record from the middle of the thirteenth century.

Balwearie Castle [NT 251903] is a ruinous keep or tower with traces of a courtyard, and was held by the Balwearie family. The property passed by marriage to the Scotts before the end of the thirteenth century, and was held by them for nearly 400 years after which Balwearie went to the Melville Earls of Melville.

No. of castles/sites: 1
Rank: 537=/764

Bannatyne

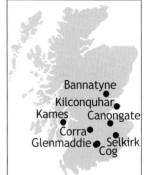

The name is probably territorial and comes from the lands of Ballenden near Selkirk in the Borders. The name is recorded with several different spellings: Bannatyne, Ballatyne or Bellenden being the most common, and being interchangeable even within the same branches of the family. James Ballantyne, who was born in 1772, was a school friend of Sir Walter Scott and went on to print Scott's novels, although the business became bankrupt in 1826.

Corra Castle [NS 882414], one and a half miles south of Lanark, is the scant ruin of a tower house in a pretty spot above the River Clyde. It was held by the Bannatynes from 1400 until 1695, and Mary, Queen of

Corra Castle 1924?

Scots, is said to have stayed here after defeat at the Battle of Langside in 1568. The property was sold in 1695 to the Somervilles of Cambusnethan. Corehouse [NS 882416] is a later mansion built for the Cranstouns and can be visited (01555 663126).

In 1499 the Bannatyne family were given Auchinoul or Auchnoule in Midlothian by the Earl of Morton, although the exact location has not been established. Sir Lewis Bannatyne (Bellenden) of Auchinoul was responsible for the building of **Canongate Tolbooth** [NT 265738] on Edinburgh's Royal Mile in 1592, his initials above the pend. Sir Lewis accompanied James VI on his trip to marry Anne of Denmark, and promoted his king's cause as the future King of England in the court of Elizabeth I. Several of the family were Justice Clerks and Lords of Session. The tolbooth houses the People's Story, a museum of the people of Edinburgh, and is open all year (0131 529 4057; www.cac.org.uk).

The Bannatynes obtained lands near Sanquhar in Dumfries and Galloway in the middle of the sixteenth century from the Crichtons. **Glenmaddie** [NS 742072] was held by the family, as was **Cog** [NS 815145], although John Bannatyne of Cog was forfeited in 1557 and declared outlaw.

Bannatyne House [NO 294410] is five and a half miles south-east of Alyth in Perthshire, and is a late sixteenth-century tower house, with newer additions. It was, as the name suggests, held by the family. George Bannatyne stayed here and compiled a unique collection of the works of Scottish authors, including by the poets Dunbar and Henryson. He began the collection in 1568 at Bannatyne, while avoiding the worst of the plague which was rife in Edinburgh. The building may now be occupied by MacGregors of MacGregor, Baronets.

Kilconquhar Castle [NO 494027], two miles north of Elie in Fife, was probably built by the Bannatynes in the sixteenth century after the property had been sold in 1528, previously belonging to the Kilconquhar family and to the Earls of Dunbar and March. The large mansion incorporates a tower house, and was remodelled in the nineteenth century. Kilconquhar was held by the Bannatynes from 1528 until 1640 when it was sold to the Carstairs family. The castle is now part of a holiday time-share development (01333 340501; www.kilcon quharcastle.co.uk).

A family of Bannatynes held **Kames Castle** [NS 064676], two and a half miles north-west of Rothesay on the island of Bute, from the fourteenth century or earlier. It is an impressive building with a large tower, and was formerly surrounded by moat. It later passed to the Stewarts of Bute.

Other properties owned by the family include:
Abbotsgrange, [NS 931811], Grangemouth, West Lothian; site of castle and mansion.
   Held by the Bannatynes of Auchinoul in 1611 after passing from the Livingstones and then from the Kerrs. Later went to the Drummonds.
Holylee [NT 392376], near Innerleithen, Borders; house on the site of tower.
   Held by Bannatynes from 1734 until 1827.
Kelly House [NS 198685], near Inverkip, Renfrewshire; site of mansion on older site.
   Held by the Bannatynes from the fifteenth century until 1792 when it was sold to the Wallaces. They built a new house but this was burned down in 1913, probably by suffragettes, and nothing remains.
Old Woodhouselee Castle [NT 258617], near Penicuik, Midlothian; not much remains of castle.
   Held by Sinclairs and then by the Hamiltons in the sixteenth century, then later passed to the Bannatynes. The old castle was taken down to build a new house called Fulford or Woodhouselee [NT 238645], but this has also been demolished.

No. of castles/sites: 12
Rank: 120=/764
Xrefs: Ballantyne; Bellenden

Kames Castle (M&R)

Bannerman

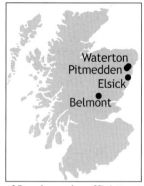

According to family traditions, the name alludes to the position of standard bearer, the standard of the Scottish kings being carried by the Bannermans in the tenth and eleventh centuries. This privilege had passed from them to the Scrymgeours by 1298, and is still held by the Earls of Dundee, who officiate at ceremonies.

The Bannerman family are first mentioned in 1366, when they held the lands of Waterton, one mile east of Ellon in Aberdeenshire. David Bannerman was physician to David II, and one of the family was Provost of Aberdeen. **Waterton Castle** [NJ 972305] is now very ruinous, but dated from the seventeenth century. This may have been built after the property passed to the Johnstones in 1611, and Waterton later went to the Forbes family.

Elsick was held by the family from 1387, having come from the Frasers. The lands are two and a half miles south-west of Portleithen in the old county of Kincardineshire. The Bannermans had a castle at **Elsick** [NO 891947], part of which may be built into the present Elsick House, which was rebuilt after a fire in 1754. This branch of the family were made Baronets in 1628. Sir Patrick Bannerman, son of the then laird, was imprisoned in Carlisle Castle for his part in the 1715 Jacobite Rising, but managed to escape and fled to France. The Bannermans were also accused of being involved in 1745-46 Rising after Sir Alexander Bannerman had fought at the Battle of Culloden. Bannerman hid in a secret closet at Elsick before escaping to the Continent. The family had to sell the property after being threatened with forfeiture. The house is in good condition, and is apparently now home to the Dukes of Fife, who are related to the Bannermans. The line of the Bannermans of Elsick continues, and they now apparently live in England.

Pitmedden House [NJ 885281], four miles west and south of Ellon in Aberdeenshire, dates from the seventeenth century, although it was remodelled in 1853 and 1954, and replaced a castle. The lands were held by the Pantons and then by the Setons before being confirmed to the Bannermans in the seventeenth century, but Pitmedden later passed to the Keiths. The house has a magnificent five-acre walled garden with formal flower beds and parterre, pavilions and fountains. The garden is open to the public from May to September, along with the Museum of Farming Life (01651 842352; www.nts.org.uk).

Belmont Castle [NO 286439], six and a half miles east of Blairgowrie in Perthshire, is a substantial baronial mansion but includes a tower house at its core. The castle was built by the Nairnes of Dunsinane, but later passed to Sir Henry Campbell-Bannerman, Prime Minister from 1905 to 1908 as leader of the Liberal Party. He was the son of a Glasgow draper, who became Lord Provost of Glasgow. He inherited a fortune from an uncle, was MP for Stirling burghs from 1868, and was knighted in 1895. The house was later made a Church of Scotland Eventide home.

No. of castles/sites: 4
Rank: 278=/764

Barbour

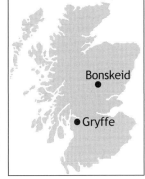

The name Barbour or Barber comes from the occupation of barber. The family are recorded in Scotland from the thirteenth century, and perhaps the most famous of all was John Barbour, who wrote *The Brus* around 1375, an account of the life and adventures of Robert the Bruce. Barbour was Archdeacon of Aberdeen, and he died in 1395.

Gryffe Castle [NS 385663], just north of Bridge of Weir in Renfrewshire, is a small mansion of 1841 standing on the site of a fifteenth-century stronghold. It was held by the Barbours in the nineteenth century.

Similarly **Bonskeid** [NN 885611], a later mansion standing three and a half miles north and west of Pitlochry in Perthshire, was also held by the family around the same time. Bonskeid had been in the possession of the Stewarts, but was sold to the Barbours, relations of the Stewarts, in the nineteenth century. Bonskeid was purchased by the YMCA in 1951.

No. of castles/sites: 2
Rank: 396=/764
Xref: Barber

Barclay

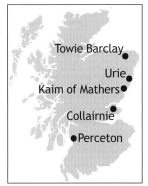

The Barclays, or the earlier form Berkeleys, originally came to England from France following the Norman conquest. They became Earls of Berkley, and it was in Berkley Castle that Edward II was murdered with a red-hot poker inserted into his bottom.

Some of the Barclays came to Scotland, and one was Chamberlain to William the Lion in 1165. The family were given extensive lands in the north-east of Scotland as well as in Fife and in Ayrshire. The family supported Robert the Bruce, and gained further properties as a result.

The lands of Towie, four miles south of Turriff in Aberdeenshire, were held by the Barclays from the twelfth century. **Towie Barclay Castle** [NJ 744439] is a

Towie Barclay Castle (AC)

tower house of the sixteenth-century, later altered with a new wing to L-plan. The walls are harled and pink-washed. The castle was attacked in 1639 by Royalists as the Barclays were Covenanters, the first action in the impending civil war. There is a fine memorial to one of the family, dated 1696, in the St Congan's kirkyard [NJ 722 498] in Turriff. One of descendants of the family was Prince Michael Barclay of Tolly, a Russian general during the Napoleonic Wars, and he is a character in Tolstoy's *War and Peace*. Barclay successfully repelled the French in 1812 by using a scorched-earth policy.

Some six miles north of Montrose in Kincardineshire are the shattered fragments of **Kaim of Mathers Castle** [NO 763649] on cliffs above the sea. The castle was built about 1420 on lands held by the Barclays of Mathers from 1351. One of the family, David Barclay, was involved in the murder of Sir John Melville, and used the castle as refuge, having been told by James I to live 'neither on land nor water'. Melville, an unpopular fellow in the area, had been murdered around 1420. He was boiled alive in a cauldron of boiling water by several local lairds, who then 'supped the broth'. Barclay was, however, pardoned. The lands were sold in 1611, and in 1648 the family bought Urie.

Perceton [NS 354406], or Pierston, lies two and a half miles east and north of Irvine in Ayrshire, and the Barclays held the lands from the 1440s until 1720; Perceton having earlier been held by the Morvilles, by the Stewarts and briefly by the Douglases. The Barclays probably had a castle, and there is an earlier moated site near the present eighteenth-century mansion. The Barclays were made Baronets of Nova Scotia in 1668. The family were later Jacobites and Sir Robert Barclay supported the Jacobites in the 1715 Rising. He went into exile and sold the property five years later to the Macredies and Perceton later went to the Maules.

Collairnie Castle [NO 307170] is a sixteenth-century L-plan tower house, dated 1581 and 1607. It stands four miles west of Cupar in Fife, and was held by the Barclays from the fourteenth century until it passed by marriage to the Balfours in 1789. Mary, Queen of Scots, visited in 1564 on her way to St Andrews to meet Lord Darnley. The house is still occupied and is now part of a farm.

Urie was bought by the Barclays of Mathers in 1648. There was already a castle at **Urie** [NO 860877], one mile north and west of Stonehaven, a Z-plan tower house of the sixteenth and seventeenth centuries. David Barclay of Urie had fought on the side of Gustave Adolphus in Sweden and then joined the Covenanters, then later became a Quaker. Although this faith had been persecuted and he had been imprisoned, Robert Barclay, David's son, became popular at court and Urie was made into a free barony in 1682. The lands were sold in the nineteenth century to the Bairds, and Urie House is now derelict after being abandoned in the 1940s. The line of the Barclays of Mathers and Urie continues, although they now apparently live in England.

The Barclays owned several other properties and castles:

Allardice Castle [NO 818739], near Inverbervie, Kincardineshire; restored altered castle.
Long held by Allardice family, but passed to the Barclays of Urie in 1776, and they took the name Allardice Barclay. The line died out in 1854.

Ardrossan Castle [NS 233424], Ardrossan, Ayrshire; ruinous castle.
Held originally by the Barclays but they changed their name to Ardrossan, and the property later passed to the Montgomerys.

Arduthie [NO 868865], Stonehaven, Kincardineshire; site of castle or old house.
The lands were held by the Arbuthnotts but passed to the Barclays of Urie in 1759. They built the new town of Stonehaven on the lands.

Balmakewan Castle [NO 667663], near Brechin, Angus; slight remains of castle.
Held by the Barclays in the seventeenth and eighteenth centuries after being a possession of the Balmakewan family. The castle was replaced by Balmakewan House [NO 668664],

a plain classical mansion of the 1820s. The Barclays of Balmakewan built a burial vault at the Old Kirkyard at Marykirk [NO 686656].

Balvaird Castle [NO 169118], near Bridge of Earn, Perth and Kinross; fine L-plan tower house.
Originally a property of the Barclays but passed by marriage to the Murrays of Tullibardine in 1500 (the Murrays built the castle), whose descendants moved to Scone Palace. The castle is open to the public some days (01786 431324) or may be viewed from the exterior.

Caddam Castle [NO 665682], near Brechin, Angus; site only.
Held by the Barclays.

Castle of Cullen of Buchan [NJ 732636], near Macduff, Aberdeenshire; site only.
Held by the Barclays. The last remains were cleared away in the nineteenth century.

Fawsyde [NO 845771], near Stonehaven, Kincardineshire; mansion on site of castle.
Held by the Barclays in 1478.

Gartly Castle [NJ 534335], near Huntly, Aberdeenshire; site only.
Held by the Barclays from the twelfth until the sixteenth century. Visited by Mary, Queen of Scots, in 1562. Last remnant cleared away in 1975.

Innergellie House [NO 575052], near Kilrenny, Fife; mansion on site of castle.
Held by the Barclays of Kippo for some years before 1642, having passed from the Beatons, and then went to the Lumsdens of Airdrie in 1642.

Kilbirnie House [NS 304541], near Kilbirnie, Ayrshire; ruined castle.
Held by the Barclays until 1470 when Kilbirnie passed by marriage to the Crawfords and later Kilbirnie went to the Lindsays.

Ladyland Castle [NS 324579], near Kilbirnie, Ayrshire; site only.
Property of the Barclays until 1689. The occupants were accused of 'adhering' to 'papastrie' during the Reformation. Hugh Barclay of Ladyland seized Ailsa Craig Castle in 1597 and held it for the Spanish. Ladyland went to the Montgomerys of Eglinton and then to the Cochranes, and then to others.

Maxton [NT 613302], near St Boswells, Borders; possible site of castle.
Held by the Maxtons and then by the Barclays by the end of the twelfth century and then by the Kerrs, who held Maxton in the sixteenth century.

Monboddo House [NO 744783], near Laurencekirk, Kincardineshire; mansion incorporating tower house.
Held by the Barclays from thirteenth century until by 1593 Monboddo had passed to the Strachans, then later went to the Irvines and to the Burnetts.

Mondynes Castle [NO 772795?], near Stonehaven, Kincardineshire; site only.
Held by the Barclays in the thirteenth century. The site may be at Castleton [NO 759788] rather than at Mains of Mondynes.

Pitcorthie [NO 570070], near Anstruther, Fife; site of castle or old house.
Held by the Strangs in the fourteenth century, but passed to the Barclays of Innergellie and then to the Hays of Kinglassie, who held Pitcorthie in the seventeenth century.

Red Castle [NO 687510], near Montrose, Angus; impressive shattered ruin.
Held by the Barclays but passed to the Earl of Ross in 1328 and later to the Stewarts of Innermeath; external access to ruin although castle is dangerously ruined.

www.clanbarclay.org
No. of castles/sites: 22
Rank: 58=/764
Xref: Berkeley

Barker

The name comes from the occupation of barker, a 'bark stripper' and a person who prepared the bark for tanning. The name became synonymous with 'tanner'.

Langshaw, four and a half miles north-east of Annan in the far south of Scotland, was held by the Barker family. **Langshaw House** [NY 243729] which dates from the eighteenth century with later modifications, replaced an earlier house or castle.

No. of castles/sites: 1
Rank: 537=/764

Barlas

The name is first on record in Scotland in the seventeenth century.

Craig Castle [NJ 472248], a couple of miles south-west of Rhynie in Aberdeenshire, is a fine sixteenth-century tower house, L-plan and of four storeys, with a modern mansion. The property was held by the Gordons, but they lost Craig in 1892 and the building is now apparently a property of the Barlas family of Craig.

No. of castles/sites: 1
Rank: 537=/764

Craig Castle 1920s

Barr

The name comes from the place called Barr, of which there are examples in both Renfrewshire and in Ayrshire, and the name is on record from the middle of the fourteenth century.

Harburn House [NT 044608] was built in 1804, and stands a couple of miles south-east of West Calder in West Lothian. It was built in 1804 for Alexander 'Paraffin Young', but later passed to the Barrs, and Charles X of France visited several times. There was a castle, which was garrisoned and repaired by Cromwell in the 1650s for use against mosstroopers in the area. Harburn House is now a hotel and conference centre (01506 461818; www.harburn house.com).

No. of castles/sites: 1
Rank: 537=/764

Barrie

The name may come from the place Barry to the west of Carnoustie in Angus, although there are other places in Angus with the name, and is recorded as early as the fourteenth century. Thomas Barrie, a unicorn pursuivant, was found guilty of forging the Regent's signature in 1570, and had his hand cut off before being banished from Scotland. The family were connected with the Gordons and the Farquharsons, and many of that name lived in Glen Muick and at Aboyne. The most famous with the surname was John Barrie, who was born in Kirriemuir in Angus in 1860, and went on to write the play 'Peter Pan'.

Two and a half miles west and south of Bankfoot in Perthshire, **Tullybelton House** [NO 034336], a nineteenth-century mansion, stands on or near the site of a castle or tower house. Tullybelton was a possession of the Graemes of Inchbrackie and then of the Robertsons and of the Richardsons before latterly being held by the Barries. The Barries were shipowners and merchants in Dundee, and briefly held the title Baron Abertay.

No. of castles/sites: 1
Rank: 537=/764

Barton

Barton appears to come from a name in Ayrshire, but another account has the family coming to Scotland from Yorkshire in the fourteenth century. The family are, however, on record in 1296, and Sir Andrew Barton, a ship's captain in the navies of James III and James IV, is mentioned in an old ballad.

Barton so harried English shipping as a Scottish privateer that a force was sent against him by Henry VIII in 1511, and during the subsequent battle Barton was fatally wounded and both his vessels were lost. Robert, Sir Andrew's brother, was also a merchant and privateer, and he served in the French navy. Robert was made Comptroller of Scotland in 1516 and then the associated office of Treasurer in 1529.

Kirkhill Castle [NX 146859], four and a half miles east and north of Ballantrae in Ayrshire, is a ruinous

Kirkhill Castle (M&R)

tower house, and it was replaced by the nearby mansion. In 1843 Kirkhill was sold by the Kennedys to Colonel Barton of Ballaird, a hero of the Battle of Waterloo in 1815, and he built the new house.

No. of castles/sites: 1 / Rank: 537=/764

Bason

Boquhan Castle [NS 661935], a mile or so south-east of Kippen in central Scotland, is recorded as being a property of the Bason family, as well as of the Graham family. The castle 'witnessed some sharp collisions of the clans'.

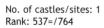

No. of castles/sites: 1
Rank: 537=/764

Baxter

The name comes from the occupation of baker or 'bakester' (most bakers were women and hence the feminine form of baker, 'bakester'), and the name is widespread throughout Scotland, although numerous in Argyll. The name is recog-

nised as a branch of the MacMillans. The story goes that one of the clan had fled from a murder and, seeking shelter in the kitchen of Inveraray Castle, swopped clothes with a cook. To avoid discovery, the man then began to work as a baker, and his descendants then earned the name MacBaxter. Jeffrey Baxter of Lissithe is recorded as taking an oath of fealty in 1296, but the family came to prominence in the nineteenth century.

Edward Baxter of Kincaldrum joined the British peerage, having made a fortune by being the first to bring power-weaving to Dundee. **Kincaldrum House** [NO 432448], three and a half miles south of Forfar, was the seat of the family, and they gave the lands to the burgh of Forfar, now Baxter Park, as well as endowing a college which eventually became the University of Dundee. The family now apparently live near Inverurie in Aberdeenshire. The family also built **Kilmaron Castle** [NO 357162], one mile north-west of Cupar in Fife, but this was demolished in the twentieth century.

The Baxters also owned **Balgavies** [NO 540516], two miles north and east of Letham in Angus, in the nineteenth century; and for some years owned the magnificent castle of **Earlshall** [NO 465211], near

Earlshall (AC)

Leuchars in Fife. The gardens of Earlshall are occasionally open to the public (www.gardens ofscotland.org).

www.clanmacmillan.org/Baxters.html
No. of castles/sites: 4
Rank: 278=/764
Xref: Baker

Beaton

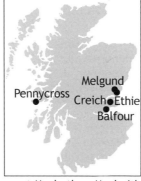

The name Beaton, often recorded as Bethune, is said to come from a place in France, but may also be derived from Macbeth, which means 'son of life' in Gaelic. A family of Beatons were famous physicians and lived on Mull at Pennycross, where there is a carved cross to them. Margaret Macbeth or Macbeith (probably a Beaton), was the wife of one of the Duries of Craigluscar in Fife, and was in demand for her knowledge of herbs and medicine. Margaret was in attendance at the births of royal children at Dunfermline Palace, and she is said to have been instrumental in saving the life of the future Charles I.

The lowland Beatons were first mentioned in Scotland in the twelfth century, and they became major landowners in Fife and in Angus. Alexander Beaton was knighted by Robert the Bruce but was killed at the Battle of Dupplin in 1332. Several of the Beatons were prominent churchmen, not least Cardinal David Beaton, mentioned below. James Beaton was Archbishop of Glasgow in 1509 under James IV, and was also Treasurer, and then Archbishop of St Andrews from 1522. He died in 1539. His nephew, another James Beaton (who was nephew of Cardinal David Beaton), was Archbishop of Glasgow in 1551 but he fled to France during the Reformation. He returned to Scotland and died in 1603.

The Beatons acquired the lands of Balfour, four miles east of Glenrothes in Fife, by marriage in 1360, and they held the property until the end of the nineteenth century or later. **Balfour House** [NO 324003] was a large castellated mansion, designed by David Bryce, and incorporated a sixteenth-century tower house. Nothing now survives but a mound of rubble after it was blown up in the 1960s. Mary, Queen of Scots, visited the castle with Lord Darnley, but the most famous or (to some) notorious of owners was Cardinal David Beaton, Archbishop of St Andrews after being abbot of Arbroath. Beaton was a staunch Catholic and was responsible for having George Wishart and other Protestant reformers burnt for heresy. Beaton was murdered at St Andrews Castle in 1546 and was hung naked from one of the windows. This is one of the places said to be haunted by his ghost.

The family acquired the lands of Creich, which are five miles north-west of Cupar also in Fife, in 1502. **Creich Castle** [NO 329212] dates from the sixteenth century and was an L-plan tower house, although it is now ruinous. Sir John Beaton was Lord High Treasurer of Scotland, and Elizabeth Beaton of Creich was a mistress of James V and cousin to Cardinal David Beaton. Robert Beaton of Creich accompanied Mary, Queen of Scots, to France in 1548, and later became Master of the Household. His daughter, Mary Beaton, niece of Cardinal David Beaton, was one of Mary Queen of Scots's

Creich Castle (M&R)

'Four Marys'; she married Alexander Ogilvie of Boyne in 1566 and died around 1597.

Ethie Castle [NO 688468] is a fine castle and mansion, dating from the fifteenth century but extended down the centuries into a grand house. It stands five miles north and east of Arbroath in Angus, and was a property of the Beatons. It was used by Cardinal David Beaton, and is another stronghold he is said to haunt;

Ethie Castle 1920s

the ghostly sound of his footsteps are said to have been heard climbing the stair. Stories have also been recorded of a Green Lady, whose appearance heralds a death in the family. The castle passed to the Carnegies in 1549, and Ethie is still occupied. Accommodation is available (01241 830434; www.ethiecastle.com).

Beaton's spirit is also said to haunt **Melgund Castle** [NO 546564], four and a half miles south-west of Brechin in Angus. It is believed that he built the castle for his mistress Marion Ogilvie (although he was probably

Melgund Castle (M&R)

married to her), with whom he had several children. This has been a large and impressive castle, but passed from the family in the seventeenth century. It became ruinous, but has been restored in recent years.

Incidentally, Cardinal David Beaton is also said to haunt the streets of St Andrews in a spectral coach.

Blebo Hole [NO 423134], three and a half miles east of Cupar, is a very ruinous castle or fortified house, and was held by the Beatons from 1649 until about 1900. They moved to **Blebo House** [NO 423134], and then to Mountquhanie. A spectral coach is also said to have been seen at Blebo, being driven furiously along the back drive of the house: perhaps another manifestation of Cardinal David Beaton.

Other castles owned by the Beatons include:
Annand [NO 510565], near Forfar, Angus; site of castle or old house (position approximate).
    Held by the Annand family but sold to Cardinal David Beaton before 1546.
Balfour Castle [NO 337546], near Kirriemuir, Angus; remains of a strong castle.
    Said to have been built by Cardinal Beaton for Marion Ogilvie, although the property was long held by the Ogilvies. Balfour later went to the Fotheringhams and then to the Farquharsons, and the reduced building is now used as a farmhouse.
Bandon Tower [NO 276043], near Glenrothes, Fife; ruined tower house.
    Held by the Balfours from 1498 or earlier, but then by Beatons, who held Bandon in the sixteenth and seventeenth centuries.
Boysack [NO 621491], near Friockheim, Angus; slight traces of castle.
    Held by the Beatons in the sixteenth century, but passed to the Carnegies in the seventeenth century.
Craigfoodie [NO 407180], near Cupar, Fife; old castle or house.
    Held by the Beatons in 1711 but passed to the Meldrums.
Dunbog Castle [NO 285181], near Newburgh, Fife; site of tower house and house.
    Said to have been built by Cardinal David Beaton and held by the Beatons of Creich, although later a property of the Dundas Marquises of Zetland.
Ethiebeaton [NO 479342], near Monifeith, Angus; site of castle.
    Held by the Beatons and said to have been associated with Cardinal David Beaton.
Guynd [NO 564418], near Arbroath; site of castle, possibly occupied by elegant mansion.
    Held by the Beatons in 1549 but later passed to the Ochterlony family, who held it in the seventeenth and eighteenth centuries.
Innergellie House [NO 575052], near Kilrenny, Fife; mansion on site of castle?
    Held by the Drummonds, but passed to the Beatons and then to the Barclays and to the Lumsdens.
Lahill House [NO 445038], near Lower Largo, Fife; site of castle or old house.
    Held by the Fotheringhams and by the Halketts. The later mansion is apparently the seat of the Lindesay-Bethune Earls of Lindsay.
Mountquhanie Castle [NO 347212], near Cupar, Fife; castle replaced by mansion.
    Long held by the Balfours, then by the Lumsdens and by the Crawfords. Mountquhanie House, dating from 1820, was held by the Beatons from 1900.
Naughton Castle [NO 373246], near Wormit, Fife; very ruined castle.
    Held by the Hays, by the Crichtons and by the Morrisons and then by the Beatons in the nineteenth century.

No. of castles/sites: 17 / Rank: 83=/764
Xref: Bethune

Beattie

The name comes from a diminutive form of Bartholomew, 'Batie' or 'Baty', and the family had connections with the Bains.

Beattie was relatively common in Ewesdale, in Eskdale and in Wauchopedale in the Borders. In 1569 Hew and John Beattie had to give pledges for themselves, and their sons, men and tenants with the name Beattie, presumably because they had been so unruly in this difficult area of the border.

The Beatties held several tower houses in the Borders:
Black Esk Tower [NY 231929], north-west of Langholm; site only.
    Held by the Beatties.
Enzieholm (Bogle Walls) [NY 292912], north-west of Langholm; possible site.
    Held by the Avenel family and by the Grahams, then later by the Beatties and then by the Scotts
Raeburnfoot [NY 252991], near Eskdalemuir; site, possibly within the earthworks of the Roman fort.
    Held by the Beatties.
Shiel [NY 283916], north-west of Langholm; site only.
    Held by the Beatties in the sixteenth century.
Tanlawhill Tower [NY 237910], north-west of Langholm; slight remains? and dated stone of 1659.
    Held by the Beatties of Tanlawhill at the end of the sixteenth century.
Westerkirk [NY 294916], north-west of Langholm; site only.
    Held by the Beatties.

No. of castles/sites: 6
Rank: 212=/764

Bell

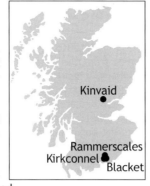

The Bells were a powerful Border family, and that branch of the family came from a Norman in the service of David I in the twelfth century. The name itself is probably from the French 'bel', meaning beautiful, fair or handsome. Consequently different branches may not be related by blood.

Alexander Graham Bell, born in Edinburgh in 1847, invented the first telephone in 1876.

The Bells held many tower houses in Annandale and the lands near the English Border.

The Bells of **Kirkconnel** [NY 253752], four and a half miles east of Ecclefechan in Dumfries and Galloway, held that property from the fifteenth century or earlier. Sir David Bell had been Clerk of the Wardrobe to Robert II. The Bells supported the Douglases in the troubles of the 1450s, and were forfeited, the lands going to the Irvines. There was a sixteenth-century tower house here.

The Bells of **Blacket House** [NY 243743], three miles east of Ecclefechan, flourished, and were the senior line. Their tower house was built in the sixteenth century, but was sacked by the English in 1547, and is now very ruinous. The Bells were warned about their unruly ways in a letter from James IV in 1517. One of the family was the suitor of Fair Helen of Kirkconnel Lea, but she rejected him in favour of Adam Fleming. Bell was enraged and tried to shoot Fleming, but Helen took the bullet and she died in her lover's arms. The lovers are said to be buried in Kirkconnel Church, and there are other fine memorials but little remains of the church. The events are recorded in the Border ballad, 'Fair Helen of Kirkconnel Lee'.

Like other Border families, the Bells suffered after the Union of the Crowns, and many of them went to Ireland, as well as to Australia and to New Zealand.

The Bells apparently also held lands at **Kinvaid** [NO 063300], north and west of Perth, although the exact location has not been determined. There was a castle, built in the fifteenth century, although the exact location has not been determined. This may have been the home of Bessie Bell, said to be the daughter of the laird of Kinvaid. She is the heroine of the tragic ballad called, 'The Twa Lassies' or 'Betsy Bell and Mary Gray'. The two girls were great friends but were both killed by the plague, given to them by a man they both favoured, sometime in the seventeenth century. Their remains were left unburied to bake in the sun.

Other tower houses and properties which were held by the Bells, mostly in the Border area are:

Albie [NY 247772], near Ecclefechan, Dumfries and Galloway; site of tower house.
Held by the Bells from 1300 or earlier.

Antermony Castle [NS 662765], near Milton of Campsie; site of castle and mansion.
Held by the Flemings and by the Lennox family and then by the Bells in modern times.

Clifton Hall [NT 109710], near Broxburn, West Lothian; mansion on site of castle.
Held by several families, including by the Douglases and by the Gibsons, before coming to the Bells in the nineteenth century. Robert Bell was a pioneer in the coal and shale oil industries.

Cowholm [NY 337721], near Gretna, Dumfries and Galloway; site of tower house.
Held by the Bells.

Crurie [NY 250950], near Langholm, Dumfries and Galloway; probable site of tower house, location not certain.
Held by the Bells.

Kirkpatrick Tower [NY 275701], near Gretna, Dumfries and Galloway; site of tower house.
Held by the Edgars and by the Flemings, and perhaps also by the Bells and by the Johnstones. This was the property held by Adam Fleming of Kirkpatrick whose love, Fair Helen of Kirkconnel Lea, was slain by one of the Bells of Blacket.

Middlebiehill [NY 214762], near Ecclefechan, Dumfries and Galloway; probable site of tower house.
Held by the Bells, although Carruthers of Mouswald had a charter of Middlebie in 1349.

Nucke [NY 204747], near Ecclefechan, Dumfries and Galloway; site of tower house.
Held by the Bells.

Poldean [NT 104001], near Moffat, Dumfries and Galloway; site of tower house.
Held by the Bells and by the Johnstones.

Rammerscales House [NY 081777], near Lockerbie, Dumfries and Galloway; mansion on probable site of tower house.
Held by the Bells, then by the Mounsey family in the eighteenth century and now by the Bell MacDonald family. The present house is a fine eighteenth-century mansion with attractive grounds and gardens. Sometimes open to the public (01387 810229; www.rammerscales.co.uk).

Redkirk [NY 300659], near Gretna, Dumfries and Galloway; site of tower house.
Held by the Bells in 1587.

Scatwell House [NH 399559], near Strathpeffer, Ross; mansion incorporating older house.
Held by the Mackenzies, but bought by the Bells in 1885.

Scotsbrig [NY 214769], near Ecclefechan, Dumfries and Galloway; site of tower house, location not certain.
Probably a property of the Bells but was held by the Carlyles in 1826.

Spottiswoode House [NT 603499], near Lauder, Borders; site of tower house and mansion.
Held by the Spottiswoode family and then by the Bells between 1620 and 1700; it then went back to the Spottiswoodes. The whole building was demolished in 1928.

Winterhopehead [NY 278833], near Lockerbie, Dumfries and Galloway; site of tower house.
Held by the Bells.

www.clanbell.org
No. of castles/sites: 18
Rank: 76=/764

Belshes

The name is probably territorial and comes from lands near Jedburgh, although it has also been suggested that it comes from Bellasis, a place near Seine-et-Marne in France, or from places in Northumberland or in Durham. The name is on record in Scotland from the thirteenth century.

The most prominent branch of the family, however, was in Perthshire. **Invermay** [NO 061163], which is five and a half miles south-west of Perth, was held by the Belshes family for many years. There is a sixteenth-century L-plan tower house, which was altered in the seventeenth century and there is also a later two-storey range. The family were buried at Mukkersie [NO 073157], where they have a burial aisle. **Balmanno Castle** [NO 144156], two miles south of Bridge of Earn also in Perthshire, was held by the Belshes of Invermay from 1752; and **Fettercairn House** [NO 656740], near Fettercairn in Kincardineshire, was also held by them in the eighteenth century.

The direct line of the family died out in the eighteenth century.

Tofts [NT 761447], now known as **Purves Hall** and which is three and a half miles south-east of Greenlaw in the Borders, was held by the Belshes family from 1610. One of the family was Sir Alexander Belshes of Tofts, who was a Senator in the College of Justice. Tofts passed to the Purves family and they changed the name to Purves Hall. The present mansion incorporates a much altered tower house, and it is a private residence.

No. of castles/sites: 4
Rank: 278=/764

Benham

The name is territorial and comes from the lands of Benholm, which are two miles south-west of Inverbervie in Kincardineshire. The name is on record from the beginning of the thirteenth century. Hugh Benholm was Bishop of Aberdeen but he was burned to death to at the bishop's palace at Loch Goul, near Dyce, in 1282.

Benholm Castle [NO 804705] dates from the fifteenth century, and consists of a large keep or tower and a later mansion. Benholm was a property of the

Benholm Castle (M&R)

Benham (or Benholm family) from the thirteenth century, but passed by marriage to the Lundie family around the end of the fourteenth century, and they built the castle. Benholm later went to the Ogilvies and then the Keith Earls Marischal. The castle became ruinous but restoration work is ongoing.

No. of castles/sites: 1
Rank: 537=/764
Xref: Benholm

Bennet

The name is a diminutive of Benedict, and the renown for St Benedict made the name popular in medieval times. The name is first recorded in the thirteenth century in Scotland, and it is more commonly only spelt with one 't' ('Bennet' rather than 'Bennett').

The Bennet family held lands in the old county of Roxburghshire in the Borders. The oldest branch may have been that which held **Grubbet** [NT 779248], just east of Morebattle near the Border with England. Nothing remains, but there was probably a tower house called Grubethous. William Bennet of Grubbet supported the Union of the Parliaments in 1707, and he led a force that protected Kelso from the Jacobites in the 1715 Rising. The lands passed to the Marquis of Tweeddale.

Whitton Tower [NT 759222], a couple of miles south of Grubbet, was held by the Bennets in 1523 when it was sacked by the English, and it was torched again in 1545. The property later passed to the Riddels, who rebuilt the tower, although it is now quite ruinous. **Chesters** [NT 628106], south and east of Bonchester Bridge also in Borders, was held by the family early in the sixteenth century, but nothing remains of a tower house which was located here. **Marlfield House** [NT 735255], five and a half miles south of Kelso and again in the Borders, is a three-storey mansion, but it incorporates a castle dating from the sixteenth century or earlier. It was held by the Bennets in the seventeenth century, but Marlfield passed to the Nisbets. The building is said to be haunted by a Green Lady, reported to have pushed past people in one of the passageways and to have been active in recent years. The house is a private residence.

No. of castles/sites: 4 / Rank: 278=/764
Xref: Bennett

Beresford

Macbiehill [NT 185514], a mansion of 1835 and designed by William Burn, replaced or incorporated a tower house, perhaps also known as Coldcoat or Coudcott. The house stood two miles east of West Linton in the Borders, and was demolished in the 1950s. The lands were held by the Montgomerys, but they had passed to the Beresfords before the end of the seventeenth century.

No. of castles/sites: 1 / Rank: 537=/764

Berry

The name is probably derived from Barrie (also see that name), and it is on record from the seventeenth century. The Berrys purchased the lands of Tayfield, in Newport-on-Tay in Fife, and other property from the Nairnes of Sandfurd in 1788. The Berrys built **Tayfield House** [NO 421275], which dates from 1788 but the building was enlarged and remodelled in 1829-30. The family were involved in developing the village as a ferry port for Dundee, and the Berrys of Tayfield still flourish.

No. of castles/sites: 1
Rank: 537=/764

Beveridge

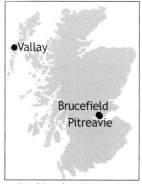

The name is believed to come from old English and means 'beaver island'. The family were prominent around Dunfermline in Fife, and held the lands of **Brucefield** [NT 101868] near the burgh in the nineteenth century, and then acquired **Pitreavie Castle** [NT 117847], to the south of Dunfermline, which had been held by the Wardlaws, by the Primrose Lord Rosebery and then by the Blackwood family. The Beveridges restored and remodelled the castle in 1885, but it was later used by the armed forces and it was put up for sale when the armed forces left.

According to *Burke's*, the family is styled Beveridge of St Leonard's Hill in Dunfermline, of Brucefield, and of Vallay in North Uist. The isle of Vallay is where they are said have their seat, although Vallay House is ruined. The family apparently live in England.

No. of castles/sites: 1
Rank: 537=/764

Biggar

The name is territorial, and comes from the lands and town of Biggar in Lanarkshire, and is on record from the twelfth century.

Biggar was held by Baldwin de Biggar, who was a Fleming (as in a native of Flanders), and the family eventually took the surname 'Fleming'. There was a strong and impressive castle at **Biggar** [NT 043378] in the thirteenth century. William Wallace won a battle against the English at Biggar in 1297, although the size of the English army – said to number 60,000 men, according to Blind Harry – seems a little large, even for Wallace to manage. The Flemings moved to Boghall, and the old castle became ruinous; the site is now occupied by a house.

Woolmet House [NT 309701], just north of Danderhall to the south-east of Edinburgh, was a large and attractive L-plan house, which was dated 1686, but probably incorporated older work. It was probably first

Woolmet House (M&R)

built by the Biggar family, but had passed to the Wallaces by 1686. The house was completely demolished except for the gateway in 1950 to allow mining work.

The Biggars also owned **Chapelton** [NX 798667], four miles north-east of Castle Douglas, in Dumfries and Galloway. The large farmhouse, dating from the middle of the nineteenth century, stands on the site of a castle or old house, earlier a possession of the Maxwells. The property passed to the Wilsons.

No. of castles/sites: 3
Rank: 328=/764

Binning

The name appears to be territorial in origin, coming from the lands of Binning or Binny in West Lothian, and it is on record from the middle of the thirteenth century.

Binny [NT 053734] is located two miles northwest of Broxburn in West Lothian, and was held by a family of that name. One of the Binnings is said to have been prominent in retaking Linlithgow Castle, during the Wars of Independence, by driving a cart full of men through the gates. Sir John Binning was the governor of the property in Scotland of the Knight Hospitallers in 1388. The lands of Binny passed to the Hamiltons and the Earls of Haddington still hold the title Lord Binning. There was a castle or old house at Binning.

Wallyford House [NT 370722], one and a half miles east of Musselburgh in East Lothian, dated from the seventeenth century or earlier, but the building has been demolished. The lands were held by the Binning family, one of whom, Sir William Binning of Wallyford, was Lord Provost of Edinburgh from 1675-77.

Pilmuir House [NT 486695], three and a half miles south-west of Haddington also in East Lothian, also appears to have been held by the family. Charles Binning of Pilmuir was an advocate in the eighteenth century, although Pilmuir was also owned by the Cairns family and by the Borthwicks in the middle of the seventeenth century. The gardens at Pilmuir House are occasionally open to the public (www.gardensofscotland.org).

No. of castles/sites: 3 / Rank: 328=/764
Xrefs: Binny; Binnie

Birnie

The name comes from the place near Elgin in Moray called Birnie, and is on record from the middle of the thirteenth century.

Broomhill Castle [NS 754508], just west of Larkhall in Lanarkshire, was once a large mansion and castle, but it was demolished after a fire in 1943, except for some cellars. The property was held by the Birnies in the twentieth century, having passed to them from the Hamiltons. The house was said to have been haunted by a Black Lady, the wife of one of the Hamiltons who had disappeared around 1900.

No. of castles/sites: 1 / Rank: 537=/764
Xref: Birney

Bishop's Palaces

The following castles, palaces and houses were held by the bishops of Scotland. Before the Reformation the church was by far the largest landowner in Scotland, and the bishops of the country held large possessions as part of their offices. Most of these palaces or residences were fortified and are castles rather than palaces; being a bishop was no protection from assault and murder, especially in the sixteenth and seventeenth centuries.

Spynie Palace [NJ 231658] is one of the finest castles in Scotland, standing two and a half miles north of Elgin in Moray, and it was the seat of the Bishops of Moray. There is a massive keep or tower, known as David's or Davey's Tower, and it rises to six storeys and has very

Spynie Palace (RWB)

thick walls. There are also the remains of a substantial courtyard, and the bishops were to have need of such a place. Spynie was the site of the cathedral of Moray, but it was moved to Elgin, where there is the magnificent although ruinous cathedral [NJ 222632], which is in the care of Historic Scotland and is also open to the public all year (01343 547171). The palace was probably built by Bishop Innes, just after Elgin Cathedral had been burnt by Alexander Stewart, the Wolf of Badenoch. Bishop David Stewart, who died in 1475, excommunicated the Gordon Earl of Huntly, and built the great keep to defend himself from retribution by Huntly. James IV visited the palace in 1493 and in 1505, as did Mary, Queen of Scots, in 1562. James Hepburn, fourth Earl of Bothwell and husband of Mary sheltered here after fleeing from Carberry in 1567, but soon rode north to Orkney and the Continent. After the Reformation, the lands were sold to the Lindsays, but the castle was subsequently used by Protestant Bishops. James VI stayed here in 1589. General Munro besieged the castle in 1640, and compelled Bishop Guthrie to

surrender it, and the Bishop was then imprisoned. The castle was held by Innes of Innes and Grant of Ballindalloch – who were Covenanters – against the Gordon Earl of Huntly, who besieged the palace unsuccessfully in 1645, while acting for the Marquis of Montrose. The last resident Bishop was Colin Falconer, who died here in 1686, and Bishop Hay, the last Bishop, was removed from office in 1688. There were stories of the bishops being in league with the Devil, and that every Halloween witches would be seen flying to the castle. Spynie is also reputedly haunted, and unexplained lights and unearthly music are said to have been witnessed here. There also stories of a phantom piper and a ghostly lion. The castle is now in the care of Historic Scotland and is open to the public (01343 546358).

St Andrews Castle [NO 513169] is in the fine old burgh of St Andrews, and stands by the sea, not far from the shattered ruins of St Andrews Cathedral [NO 516166], which is also in the care of Historic Scotland and open to the public (01334 472563). The old stronghold of the Bishops and Archbishops of St Andrews is ranged around a courtyard, and there is a bottle dungeon dug out of the rock. The first castle here was built by Bishop Roger, but this was dismantled by Robert the Bruce around 1310. It was rebuilt by the English in support of Edward Balliol in 1336, but was captured and slighted by Sir Andrew Moray the following year. Bishop Walter Trail rebuilt the castle, and Patrick Graham, first Archbishop, was deposed and imprisoned here in 1478. Archbishop Alexander Stewart, illegitimate son of James IV was killed at Flodden in 1513 along with his father. Cardinal David Beaton strengthened the castle by adding two round blockhouses, now destroyed. After George Wishart had been burned alive for heresy, a party of Protestants broke into the castle and murdered Beaton in 1546, and hung his naked body from one of the towers. Reinforced by others, including John Knox, they held the castle for a year. The besiegers tunnelled towards the walls, and the defenders countermined and captured their tunnel. Both tunnels still survive and can be entered. It was only with the arrival of a French fleet that the garrison surrendered and became galley slaves,

St Andrews Castle (M&R)

John Knox among them. Archbishop John Hamilton supported Mary, Queen of Scots, but was hanged in 1571, having been accused of being involved in the murders of Lord Darnley and the Regent Moray. The castle was annexed to the Crown in 1587, and given to the Home Earl of Dunbar in 1606, but was restored to the new Protestant bishops in 1612. However, the castle had lost its importance, and by 1654 the town council had stone removed from the castle to repair the harbour. Archbishop James Sharp was a Protestant bishop, but unpopular with Covenanters, and he was brutally murdered in front of his daughter at Magus Muir in 1679. The castle is said to be haunted by the ghost of Archbishop John Hamilton, or perhaps by Beaton himself, and a White Lady has been reported near the castle and on the beach. The castle is in the care of Historic Scotland and is open to the public (01334 477196).

Dornoch Palace [NH 797897] was the residence of the Bishops of Caithness, whose cathedral, now restored, is nearby in the middle of Dornoch in Sutherland. The palace is a strong castle, dating from the thirteenth or fourteenth century, rising to five storeys and with a round stair-tower. The property passed to the Earls of Sutherland after the Reformation, although the castle was besieged by the Sinclairs in 1567, who burnt the burgh and the cathedral. The building was later used as

Dornoch Palace (M&R)

a courthouse and jail, and is said to be haunted by a man convicted of stealing sheep. There are stories of an underground passageway linking the palace to the nearby cathedral (which is open to the public), into which all the bishop's wealth was placed following the Reformation. Should the treasure ever be found, the legend goes that this will herald the end of the Dukes of Sutherland. Dornoch Palace (or Castle) is now a hotel (01862 810216; www.dornochcastlehotel.com). Dornoch Cathedral [NH 797896], which was established in the thirteenth century but was restored in the nineteenth century, is open to the public (www.visitdornoch.com).

Bishop's Palace in Kirkwall [HY 449108] lies across from the magnificent St Magnus Cathedral [HY 449112] in the capital of Orkney, and consists of a long ruinous

Bishop's Palace, Kirkwall (M&R)

block with a tower at one end. The palace was the residence of the Bishops of Orkney from the twelfth century, when Orkney was held by the Norsemen. King Haakon Haakonson died here in 1263 after his defeat at the Battle of Largs. Robert Stewart, an illegitimate son of James V, acquired the lands of the Bishopric of Orkney in 1568, as well as the Earldom. He was followed by his son, Patrick Stewart, in 1593, who had the Bishop's Palace remodelled and built the adjacent Earl's Palace. The Stewarts were executed in 1615 after Robert had led a rising in the islands. The palace returned to the Bishops of Orkney, who occupied it until 1688. There are stories of an underground tunnel connecting the Bishop's Palace to the Cathedral, which is said to have a ghostly piper, sent to explore the passageway. He reputedly never returned, but at times the pipes are heard from beneath the ground. Both the Bishop's Palace and the magnificent Earl's Palace are in the care of Historic Scotland and are open to the public (01856 871918). St Magnus Cathedral [HY 449112], begun in the twelfth century, is also open to the public (01856 874894; www.orkneyheritage.com).

Glasgow Castle [NS 602655] stood near the magnificent Glasgow Cathedral [NS 602655], the only mainland cathedral to survive the Reformation more or less intact in Scotland and which is open to the public (0141 552 6891; www.glasgowcathedral.org.uk). Nothing remains of the castle and the site was cleared when the Royal Infirmary was built. The castle was the residence of the Bishops and Archbishops of Glasgow by the fourteenth century, and it had been recaptured from the English by William Wallace during the Wars of Independence. Bishop John Cameron built a large keep of five storeys in the fifteenth century, and the castle was further extended by the addition of a courtyard and a gatehouse with round towers. The castle changed hands six times in various conflicts between 1513 and the final defeat in 1571 of the Hamiltons and other families fighting for Mary, Queen of Scots. The castle was abandoned as a residence in the seventeenth century, but was then used as a prison. There are no remains and only a plaque marks the spot, although there are some fragments taken from the castle on display in the crypt of the cathedral.

The bishops also owned the following places:

Achadun Castle [NM 804392], Isle of Lismore, Argyll; picturesque ruinous castle on rock by sea.

Held by the Bishops of Argyll until about 1510 when they moved to Saddell in Kintyre. Part of their cathedral [NM 860434], now considerably altered and reduced in size but still a fine building, is still used as a parish church and can be visited. Achadun can also be visited.

Anderston [NS 582653], Glasgow; site of manor.

Held by the Bishops of Glasgow.

Birse Castle [NO 520905], near Aboyne, Aberdeenshire; mansion incorporating tower house.

Held by the Bishops of Aberdeen, but passed to the Gordons of Cluny. Rebuilt in the 1930s and still occupied.

Bishop Sinclair's Tower [NO 077457], near Dunkeld, Perthshire; site of castle.

Reputedly built by William Sinclair, who was Bishop of Dunkeld from 1309. He was active on behalf of Robert the Bruce, and is known as the 'fighting bishop' as he rallied the Scots against an English attack on Dunfermline in 1317. He crowned Edward Balliol in 1333, and died four years later.

Bishop's House, Elgin [NJ 221631], Moray; ruinous L-plan house.

First built a few years after the torching of the cathedral by the Wolf of Badenoch, and passed to the Setons after the Reformation. It was partly demolished in 1851 until the protests of local people stopped the destruction. The building is now in the care of Historic Scotland and can be viewed from the road. The L-plan North College was probably built as the Deanery in 1520, and South College probably incorporates part of the sixteenth-century Archdeacon's house. Also see Spynie Palace (above).

Bishop's House, Lochwood [NS 692666], near Coatbridge, Lanarkshire; site of hunting lodge.

Held by the Bishops of Glasgow. They are said to have joined the Molendinar burn, Hogganfield, Frankfield and Bishops lochs with a canal system so that they could sail here by barge from Glasgow Castle.

Bishop's Palace, Brechin [NO 597601], Angus; site of palace.

Held by the Bishops of Brechin, but nothing remains. The fine cathedral [NO 596601] is a cruciform church dating from the thirteenth century but was restored in 1900 and is open to the public (01356 629360; www.brechincathedral.org.uk). There is an unusual round tower.

Bishop's Palace, Dunblane [NN 782014], Stirlingshire; slight remains.

Held by the Bishops of Dunblane, and was ranged around a courtyard. The fine cathedral [NN 782015] dates from the thirteenth century but has an older tower. Margaret Drummond, who was poisoned along with her two sisters at Drummond Castle, is buried in the choir. The church is open to the public (01786 823338; www.dunblanecathedral.org.uk).

Bishop's Palace, Dunkeld [NO 013424], Perthshire; site of castle and palace.

Held by the Bishops of Dunkeld, and built by Bishop Cardeny in 1408. It consisted of a keep with a later wing and chapel, added by Bishop Brown. Dunkeld was besieged by Jacobites in 1689, and the palace may not have survived the burning of the town. The cathedral [NO 025426] is partly ruinous and the choir is used as the parish church. Points of interest include the stone effigy of Alexander Stewart, Wolf of Badenoch, and the tombs of Bishop Cardney and Bishop William Sinclair, the 'fighting bishop' who died in 1337. The cathedral is open to the public (01350 727688; www.dunkeldcathedral.org.uk).

Bishop's Palace, Loch Goul [NJ 911142], near Dyce, Aberdeenshire; slight remains of palace.

Held by the Bishops of Aberdeen. Bishop Hugh Benholm was burnt to death here in the palace in 1282. The palace may not have been reused after the Bishop's Palace, in Old Aberdeen, was built in the fourteenth century.

Bishop's Palace, Old Aberdeen [NJ 940088]; site of palace.

Held by the Bishops of Aberdeen, but destroyed in 1336, then rebuilt in the middle of the fifteenth century, and then demolished in the 1650s to build Cromwell's citadel in Aberdeen. The fine cathedral dedicated to St Machar [NJ 939088] is open to the public (01224 485988; www.stmachar.com).

Bishop's Palace, Penninghame [NX 409605], Galloway; site of castle or palace.

Held by the Bishops of Galloway, but passed to the Gordons after the Reformation.

Caisteal Bharraich [NC 581567], near Tongue, Sutherland; ruinous tower house.

Held by the Bishops of Caithness.

Castle Hill, Birnie [NJ 217580], near Elgin, Moray; site of castle.

Held by the Bishops of Moray in the twelfth century. The bishops moved from here to Kinneddar, then to Spynie.

Castle Hill, Whithorn [NX 448403], Galloway; site of castle.

Held by the Bishops of Galloway. Whithorn Priory is nearby and is open to the public.

Chanonry [NH 727567], Fortrose, Ross and Cromarty; site of tower.

Held by the Bishops of Ross, and part of the cathedral complex included a fortified tower, which was built by Bishop John Fraser around 1500. The lands passed to the Mackenzies of Kintail after the Reformation, and many of the buildings were demolished by Cromwell to built a fort at Inverness. The ruinous remains of the cathedral in the pretty village are open to the public.

Clachary [NX 424603], near Newton Stewart, Galloway; site of palace.

Held by the Bishops of Galloway, but passed to the Stewart Earls of Galloway, and it was at Clachary that Mary, Queen of Scots, lodged with the Master of Garlies in 1563.

Craigdhu [NX 401408], near Whithorn, Galloway; remains of motte and bailey castle.

Said to have been held by the Bishops of Galloway.

Easter Clune Castle [NO 612914], near Banchory, Aberdeenshire; slight remains of tower house.

Built by Archbishop James Stewart, who died in 1503, or by Archbishop Ross. It was replaced by Easter Clune House, which was owned by the Irvines.

Enrick [NX 614544], near Gatehouse of Fleet, Galloway; site of castle.

Held by the Abbots of Tongland but passed to the Bishops of Galloway.

Harrow Hope [NT 163393], near Peebles, Borders; site of old house.

Held by the Bishops of Glasgow, and mentioned in 1299.

Inchmurtach [NO 565132], near St Andrews; site of bishop's palace.

Built by William Lamberton, Bishop of St Andrews, about 1314. A parliament is believed to have been held here in the reign of David II. Some remains survived at the end of the eighteenth century.

Kinvaid Castle [NO 063300], near Perth; site of castle.

Built by Bishop Brown of Dunkeld, but appears to have been held by the Bells after the Reformation. The laird of Kinvaid was entreated to go to the cathedral at Dunkeld and there purge it of all statues, altars and monuments of idolatry in 1560.

Kinneddar Castle [NJ 224696], near Lossiemouth, Moray; site of castle.

Held by the Bishops of Moray from the twelfth century before they moved to Spynie. The parish church was also used as the cathedral for some years in the twelfth century, although little now remains.

Kirklands Tower [NT 025925], near Saline, Fife; site of castle.

Property of the Bishops of Dunkeld.

Maltan Walls [NT 632246], near Ancrum, Borders; site of castle or palace.

May have been held by the knights of Malta (and hence the name), but the lands were a property of the Bishops of Glasgow and they probably had a residence here.

Muckhart Castle [NO 003007], near Dollar, Clackmannan; site of castle.

Held by the Bishops of St Andrews. It was seized by the English during the Wars of Independence, but was recovered by the

Scots in 1311. William Lamberton, Bishop of St Andrews, is said to have stayed here around 1320. Some of the lands passed to the Campbells.

Saddell Castle [NR 789316], near Campbeltown, Argyll; keep or tower house.

Held by the Bishops of Argyll and built by Bishop David Hamilton in 1507. The property passed to the Campbells and then the Ralstons, and was attacked in 1559. It was replaced by Saddell House [NR 791318], but the old castle has been restored and can be rented as holiday accommodation (01628 825925; www.landmarktrust.org.uk).

Skaill House [HY 234186], near Stromness, Orkney, fine seventeenth-century house.

Built for George Graham, Bishop of Orkney, in the 1620s. The building is said to be haunted, and Skaill is open to the public in the summer (01856 841501; www.skaillhouse.com).

Stow [NT 460445], near Lauder, Borders; ruinous house.

Held by the Bishops and Archbishops of St Andrews, and dates from the fifteenth or sixteenth century. Ruins can be visited.

Woll [NT 465218], near Selkirk, Borders; site of house.

Held by the Bishops and Archbishops of Glasgow, and also known as Palace Walls.

No. of castles/sites: 36
Rank: 34=/764

Aboyne Castle (M&R) – see next column (Bisset)

Bisset

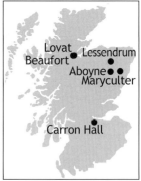

Bisset is thought to be Norman in origin, and some of the family came to Scotland in the twelfth century following the release of William the Lion from captivity in England. The family were major landowners in the north-east of Scotland at one time, and John Bisset, along with Alexander II, founded Beauly Priory [NH 527465], near Inverness. The buildings are now ruinous, but are in the care of Historic Scotland and are open to the public.

Aboyne Castle [NO 526995], just to the north of Aboyne in Aberdeenshire, is now a tall seventeenth-century tower house, but there was an earlier stronghold here held by the Bissets. Walter Bisset of Aboyne established a preceptory of the Knights Templar at Maryculter in 1225. On the site of this was built **Maryculter House** [NO 845999] seven miles to the south and west of Aberdeen. Maryculter was held by the Menzies family after the Reformation and is now a hotel (01224 732124; www.maryculterhousehotel.com). Walter Bisset of Aboyne was defeated by the Earl of Atholl in an tournament at Dalkeith in 1242. As a result and in a fit of violent anger, Bisset murdered the Earl and set fire to his lodging. This started a feud, many of the Bissets fled to Ireland, and Aboyne passed to the Knights Templar and then to other families.

The Bissets also held **Beaufort** [NH 507430] and **Lovat** [NH 539461], both near Beauly in Inverness-shire, and these passed by marriage to the great house of Fraser in the thirteenth century. **Red Castle** [NH 584495], three and a half miles east of Muir of Ord on the Beauly Firth dates from the twelfth century when it was a property of the Bissets. Most of the existing building is much later, and the lands were later owned by the Frasers and then by the Mackenzies. **Kilravock** [NH 814493], six miles south-west of Nairn also in Inverness-shire, was also a property of the Bissets, but passed by marriage to the Rose family in the thirteenth century. **Knock** [NO 352952], one and a half miles west of Ballater on Deeside, was also held by the Bissets in the thirteenth century, although this property went to the Gordons. These lands all have (or had) castles. Kilravock Castle is a magnificent building and may be visited (01667 493258; www.kilravockcastle.com).

The longest lasting branch of the family was that of **Lessendrum** [NJ 578415], a property three and a half miles east and north of Huntly in Aberdeenshire. The mansion, enlarged and altered in the nineteenth century, incorporates work from as early as 1470. It is now ruined and overgrown after a fire in 1928, when the Bissets still owned it.

The Bissets also held **Quarrell** [NS 891840], now known as **Carron Hall**, which is half a mile east of Stenhousemuir in central Scotland. There may have been a castle but this was replaced by a mansion. The property had been held by the Quarrels and then by the Redheughs, before passing to the Bissets who held it in the sixteenth century. It later passed to the Elphinstones and then to the Dundas family.

No. of castles/sites: 9
Rank: 149=/764

Black

The name may have at least two contradictory derivations: one is simply descriptive, as in dark haired or a dark complexion; but the other could be from old English and mean the opposite: bright, white or pale. The name is common in Scotland and is on record from the twelfth century. Many of the Lamont clan, however, changed their name to Black after being driven with much violence from Cowal in Argyll by the Campbells in 1646. Some MacGregors also changed their name to Black after that clan was proscribed by James VI at the turn of the seventeenth century.

Adam Black, who was born in 1784, was the publisher of the *Encyclopedia Britannica*, was Lord Provost of Edinburgh, and was MP for Edinburgh from 1856-65, standing for the Liberals.

Largo Castle [NO 418034], just north of Lower Largo in Fife, was a fifteenth-century castle with a keep with a later round tower. Around 1750 the castle was demolished to build Largo House, which was designed by John Adam, although this is now itself a ruined shell. Largo was held by the Blacks from 1618 until the property passed to the Gibsons of Durie in 1633.

The Blacks of **Wateridgemuir** [NJ 698087] are also on record from the sixteenth century, and many of the family were burgesses of Aberdeen. Wateridgemuir is three and a half miles north-west of Echt in Aberdeenshire, but it is not clear if there was a fortified building here.

Balgowan [NN 987237], seven miles west of Crieff in Perthshire, is the site of a castle and a mansion, but all that survives is a block dating from the eighteenth century which is itself derelict. The property was held by the Grahams but they sold Balgowan in 1859 and at the end of the nineteenth century the property was owned by the Blacks.

No. of castles/sites: 3
Rank: 328=/764
Xref: Blake

Blackadder

The name comes from a river in Berwickshire, the Blackadder. The 'adder' is from old English and means 'running water'. Robert Blackadder, Bishop of Glasgow from 1484 and then Archbishop from 1492, started the incomplete but magnificent Blackadder Aisle on the south side of Glasgow Cathedral (0141 552 6891; www.glasgowcathedral.org.uk) in the fifteenth century. He died on pilgrimage to the Holy Land in 1508, and is buried in Jedburgh Abbey [NT 650204], where there is a canopied tomb, although this has been reused as a later memorial. The ruins of the abbey are in the care of Historic Scotland and are open to the public (01835 863925). John Blackadder was a Covenanter after being minister of Troqueer, and he was outlawed in 1674. He fled abroad and when he returned he was imprisoned on the Bass Rock, where he died in 1681.

The Blackadder family held lands four miles east of Duns in Berwickshire in the Borders, and **Blackadder Castle** [NT 856540] was incorporated into a later house, but the building was completely demolished in the 1930s. The story goes that the Blackadders were robbed of the lands after the death of Andrew Blackadder at the Battle of Flodden in 1513. The Homes of Wedderburn seized the opportunity to acquire the property by murdering off any remaining heirs and marrying themselves to Beatrix and Margaret, the daughters of the last Blackadder laird. Indeed, the Homes besieged Blackadder Castle to gain possession of the girls. The remaining Blackadders fought to regain the lands, but after the murder of Patrick Blackadder of Tulliallan, again by the Homes, the matter was dropped, and the Homes of Blackadder were made Baronets in 1671. In the nineteenth century the lands had passed from the Homes, the building was unroofed after the First World War, and it was blown up to clear the site in the 1930s. Edrom Church [NT 827558] dates from 1732 but incorporates the much-altered Blackadder Aisle of 1499. It replaced an earlier church, the finely carved door of which had been reused in the Logan Burial aisle to the west of the church.

Tulliallan Castle [NS 927888], to the north of Kincardine in Fife, is an interesting and impressive ruined castle, consisting of a hall-house dating from the fourteenth century. It passed by marriage to the Blackadders in 1486, and they built much of the present building. Sir John Blackadder of Tulliallan was executed in 1531 for the murder of the Abbot of Culross. As mentioned above, Patrick Blackadder of Tulliallan was slain, reputedly by the Homes, and Tulliallan went to the Bruces of Carnock in 1605.

Blairhall [NS 997876], five miles west of Dunfermline also in Fife, was long a property of the Bruces but was

Tulliallan Castle, hall (M&R) – see previous page

apparently held by the Blackadder family in the seventeenth century, and there is a fine two-storey house.

No. of castles/sites: 3
Rank: 328=/764

Blackett

The name may derive from the lands of Blacket three miles east of Ecclefechan in Dumfries and Galloway, which were long a property of the Bell family, or it may come from the family of Blacket who held lands in Northumberland and in Durham in England. The Blacketts are first recorded in Scotland in the fifteenth century.

Arbigland House [NX 989574], two miles east of Kirkbean in Dumfriesshire, is a fine classical mansion built by William Craik in 1755. It passed to the Blacketts in 1852 after being held by several families. The grounds of Arbigland are said to be haunted by the daughter of one of the lairds, whose lover was cruelly slain.

No. of castles/sites: 1
Rank: 537=/764

Blackstock

Blackstock may be territorial in origin, and the name is on record from the sixteenth century. The Blackstocks held the lands of **Trailtrow** [NY 148718], four and a half miles north of Annan in Dumfries and Galloway. Members of the family are buried at Trailtrow burial ground [NY 155722], including Robert Blackstock of Trailtrow, who died in 1716.

No. of castles/sites: 1
Rank: 537=/764

Blackwood

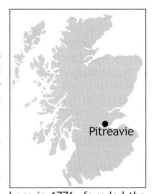

The name comes from the lands of Blackwood, and places of that name are found in Lanarkshire and in Dumfries and Galloway. The name is used in Scotland from the fourteenth century, and Adam Blackwood was a Privy Councillor to Mary, Queen of Scots. William Blackwood, born in 1776, founded the famous *Blackwood's Magazine* in Edinburgh in 1817, contributors including James Hogg and David Macbeth Moir. Different members of the Blackwood family remained editors of the magazine until 1976.

Pitreavie Castle [NT 117847], to the south of Dunfermline in Fife, has a seventeenth-century tower house at its core, although it was altered down the centuries. The tower was built by the Wardlaws of Balmule, but the property was owned by the Blackwoods from 1711, although by the 1850s the castle had been abandoned as a residence and by 1885 it was held by Beveridge family, who restored it. Pitreavie was used by the armed forces but when they left it was put up for sale.

No. of castles/sites: 1
Rank: 537=/764

Blair

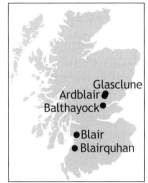

The name is from the descriptive 'blair' or 'blar', which means an 'open plain'. It is common place-name element in many parts of Scotland, and consequently families with the name Blair from different parts of the country are unlikely to be related by blood. James Blair, who was probably born in Edinburgh in 1656, emigrated to America in 1685 and was the Governor of Virginia from 1740-41.

One family with the name of Blair owned property in Perthshire. **Balthayock Castle** [NO 174230] stands a few miles east of Perth, and the building is located in a strong position above a ravine, and consists of a massive keep, dating from the fourteenth century. It was held by the Blair family, one of whom was Lord Provost of Perth, from the thirteenth century until about 1850. The castle is still occupied.

 This branch also held **Ardblair Castle** [NO 164445], to the west of Blairgowrie in Perthshire, which is an attractive L-plan tower house with a small courtyard, and dates from the sixteenth century. Patrick Blair of

Ardblair Castle (M&R)

Ardblair was implicated in the murder of George Drummond of Ledcrieff and his son in 1554, and was beheaded. The castle is reputedly haunted by a Green Lady, the spirit of Lady Jean Drummond, who fell in love with one of the Blairs here. The families feuded, a marriage was out of the question, and the poor woman died of a broken heart or committed suicide, according to different versions of the story (and also see Newton under the Drummond family). Ardblair can be visited (01250 873155).

 Also in Perthshire is **Glasclune Castle** [NO 154470], standing on a hillside two miles north-west of Blairgowrie. This has been a Z-plan tower house, dating from the sixteenth century, but it is quite ruinous. It had been held by the Herons of Drumlochy, but was purchased by the Blairs from the Crown. The Herons and the Blairs then feuded, presumably over ownership, and Drumlochy Castle was destroyed by the Blairs.

Glasclune Castle (M&R) – see previous column

Other properties held in the north by the Blairs were:
Aquhorthies [NJ 729200], near Inverurie, Aberdeenshire; castle or old house replaced by mansion.
 Held by the Leiths in the seventeenth century, but later by the Blairs. The mansion was used as a Roman Catholic seminary from 1799 to 1829
Ballathie House [NO 146367], near Blairgowrie, Perthshire; mansion on site of castle?
 Held by the Blairs at one time, as well as by the Drummonds and by the Richardsons and by the Coats of Paisley in 1910. The present mansion dates from the middle of the nineteenth century and is now used as a hotel (01250 883268; www.ballathiehousehotel.com).
Friarton Castle [NO 145305], near Perth; site of castle.
 Held by the Blairs
Kinfauns Castle [NO 151226], near Perth; mansion on site of castle.
 Long held by the Charteris family before passing to the Carnegies and then to the Blairs, and Kinfauns later went to the Grays and then to the Stewart Earls of Moray.
Rossie Ochil [NO 087130], near Perth; mansion on site of castle.
 Held by the Blairs until 1583 when sold to the Oliphants.
Williamston [NN 972220], near Perth; T-plan tower house from the seventeenth century
 Held by the Blairs of Kinfauns, but sold to the Oliphants and the present house was built for the Oliphants.

Another prominent branch lived in Ayrshire, some miles north of Kilwinning. **Blair Castle** [NS 305480] is an impressive mansion, remodelled in 1893, but incorporating a tower house with work from as early as the thirteenth century. The Blair family held the lands from 1165. Sir Bryce Blair is named in Blind Harry's epic poem *The Wallace* and in John Barbour's *The Brus*. He was a follower of the great William Wallace and was hanged as a patriot at Ayr along with Sir William

Blair Castle (M&R)

Wallace's uncle. Sir Roger Blair was knighted for his valiant part in the Battle of Bannockburn in 1314. The Blairs were accused of supporting the opponents of Mary, Queen of Scots, in 1545, and were required to find surety for their good behaviour. William Blair fought with the Covenanters, but was captured by John Graham of Claverhouse, although he later escaped. The line died out in 1732, and the property passed to the Scotts of Malleny, who took the name Blair. Robert Burns visited the castle in 1787. The castle is still owned by descendants of the family, and the castle may be rented (01381 610496; www.lhhscotland.com).

Blairquhan [NS 367055], which is some seven miles south-east of Maybole in Ayrshire, is a large castellated mansion, designed by William Burn, and built in the 1820s. It replaced a castle, and passed to the Hunter Blair family from the Whitefoords in 1790 and is still held by them. The house is open to the public in July and August (01655 770239; www.blairquhan.co.uk).

Other properties held by the Blairs were:
Bogton Castle [NS 575596], near Rutherglen, Renfrewshire; site of tower house and mansion.
  Held by the Blairs from 1543 and they built the castle.
Borgue Old House [NX 633483], near Kirkcudbright, Galloway; ruinous Y-plan mansion.
  Held by the Blairs.
Carberry Tower [NT 364697], near Musselburgh, East Lothian; fine sixteenth-century tower and later mansion.
  Held by the Riggs family and then by the Blairs of Lochwood from 1659 until 1689 when it went to the Dicksons of Inveresk and then to others. The building is now used as a residential Christian conference centre and accommodation is available (0131 665 3135; www.carberry tower.com).
Cowden Hall [NS 466571], near Neilston, Renfrewshire; ruinous mansion with fourteenth-century work.
  Held by the Spreulls and then by the Blairs from 1622 until 1725 when it passed to the Hamilton Marquis of Clydesdale and then to others. The Blairs married into the Cochrane Earls of Dundonald.
Dunimarle Castle [NS 977859], near Culross, Fife; fragments of castle by later mansion.
  Held by the Blairs until the nineteenth century, but then passed to the Erskines.
Dunskey Castle [NW 994534], near Portpatrick; imposing ruinous castle on cliffs
  Held by the Adairs and by the Montgomerys and then from the 1660s by John Blair, minister of Portpatrick. It was ruinous by 1684 and Dunskey House is a large baronial edifice of 1904 on the site of an earlier house.
Milton [NS 377054], near Dalmellington, Ayrshire; farm on probable site of castle.
  Held by the Blairs in the sixteenth century.
Parton Place [NX 710695], near Castle Douglas, Galloway; mansion on or near site of castle or old house.
  Held by the Glendinning family and then by the Murrays, before it became the residence of the Hunter Blairs.
Penninghame [NX 409605], near Newton Stewart, Galloway; castle replaced by mansion.
  Held by the Bishops of Galloway and then by the Gordons. Penninghame House [NX 384697] was a property of the Stopford-Blairs and dates from 1864.

www.clanblair.org / home.sprynet.com/~srblair/
No. of castles/sites: 20 / Rank: 70=/764

Blanerne

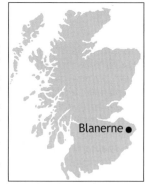

The name is territorial and comes from the lands of Blanerne, which are three miles east and north of Duns in Berwickshire in the Borders. The lands are mentioned in 1296.

Blanerne Castle [NT 832564] is a very ruinous stronghold, and the existing remains probably date from the sixteenth century, although there was an older stronghold here. The lands were held by the Blanerne family, but passed by marriage to the Lumsdens in 1329.

No. of castles/sites: 1 / Rank: 537=/764

Blyth

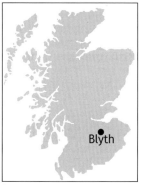

The name of the family is probably territorial, but may be from a Norman knight who lived at **Blyth** [NT 132458], which is four miles south of West Linton in Tweeddale in the Borders. There may have been a castle here. William Blythe is on the Ragman Roll of 1296, although he did homage for lands near Chirnside in the Borders.

No. of castles/sites: 1 / Rank: 537=/764

Bogle

The name probably comes from Bowgyhill or Boglehill, which is in the parish of Monkland near Glasgow, although 'bogle' is also a ghost or unfriendly spirit. The name was not uncommon in Glasgow, and is on record from the fifteenth century.

Daldowie House [NS 674619] was a large and impressive mansion, which dated from 1745 with later additions, and it stood five or so miles to the east of Glasgow by the banks of the Clyde. The property was held by the Stewarts and by others before coming to the Bogles in 1724. The Bogles also held Shettleston, and were successful Glasgow merchants. Daldowie later passed to the MacCalls, but the house has been demolished, nothing surviving except an old doocot; a crematorium may be on the site.

No. of castles/sites: 1 / Rank: 537=/764

Bonkyl

The name comes from the lands of the same name a couple of miles north of Preston in Berwickshire in the Borders. It is now spelt Bunkle, but other recorded forms include Bonkyl.

Bunkle Castle [NT 805596] dates from the twelfth century, but nothing survives except some fragments of masonry. It was held by the Bonkyl family until 1288 when it passed by marriage to the Stewarts.

No. of castles/sites: 1
Rank: 537=/764
Xref: Bunkle

Bonnar

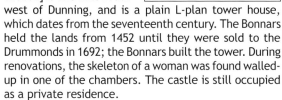

The names probably comes from the Old French 'bo-nair', meaning 'the gentle, courteous'. The name is recorded in Scotland from the thirteenth century, and the family held lands in Perthshire.

Keltie Castle [NO 008133] is one mile south-west of Dunning, and is a plain L-plan tower house, which dates from the seventeenth century. The Bonnars held the lands from 1452 until they were sold to the Drummonds in 1692; the Bonnars built the tower. During renovations, the skeleton of a woman was found walled-up in one of the chambers. The castle is still occupied as a private residence.

Five and a half miles south-west of Perth, **Invermay Tower** [NO 061163] dates from the sixteenth century, and is also an L-plan tower house. The property was held by the Bonnars, but later passed to the Stewarts, then to the Belshes of Invermay. The tower is apparently not currently occupied.

No. of castles/sites: 2
Rank: 396=/764
Xref: Bonar

Bontine

The name may come from Bunting, which is found as a surname in some parts of England. The family are on record from the thirteenth century, and variations in spelling include Bontine, Buntine, Bontin, Bontein and Buntain.

Ardoch [NS 412864], four miles north of Balloch in Dunbartonshire, was long held by the Bontines of Ardoch. There was probably a castle here, but the property passed by the beginning of the nineteenth century to the Buchanans, who remodelled Balloch Castle as their residence.

The Bontine family held other lands in the seventeenth century. **Law Castle** [NS 211484] is just north-east of West Kilbride in Ayrshire. It is a sturdy

Law Castle 1910?

keep, dating from the fifteenth century. It was probably built by the Boyds, but was sold in 1670 to the Bontines. The building has been restored and is now occupied as flats and can be rented (01505 703119; www.law castle.com).

Nothing but earthworks remain from **Balglass Castle** [NS 585876], four miles east of Killearn in Stirlingshire, formerly a strong castle dating from the thirteenth century. The lands were held by the Bontines, and in 1648 one of the family murdered Reverend John Collins, the Presbyterian minister of Campsie, on his way home from a presbytery meeting.

No. of castles/sites: 3
Rank: 328=/764
Xrefs: Bontein; Bontin; Buntane; Buntine

Borthwick

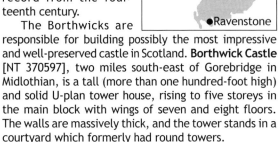

The name is territorial in origin, and probably comes from lands by the Borthwick Water, which is a river in the old county of Roxburghshire in the Borders. The name is on record from the fourteenth century.

The Borthwicks are responsible for building possibly the most impressive and well-preserved castle in Scotland. **Borthwick Castle** [NT 370597], two miles south-east of Gorebridge in Midlothian, is a tall (more than one hundred-foot high) and solid U-plan tower house, rising to five storeys in the main block with wings of seven and eight floors. The walls are massively thick, and the tower stands in a courtyard which formerly had round towers.

The castle was built by William Borthwick in 1430. He is buried, along with his wife, in the nearby parish church [NT 369597], where there are fabulously carved

Borthwick Castle (RWB)

stone effigies for the pair: the church is open to the public. One of the family had accompanied the heart of Robert the Bruce to Granada in Spain in the 1330s on crusade, along with the Black Douglas and other Scottish nobles. Although the crusade was a disaster for the Scots, and many were slain, Borthwick distinguished himself by killing a Moorish chief and sticking his severed head on a pike. The fourth Lord, another William, was keeper of Stirling Castle after the disastrous Battle of Flodden in 1513, and the infant James V was in his care. Mary, Queen of Scots, visited Borthwick with Bothwell in 1567, but fled disguised as a pageboy when confronted by an enemy force. Cromwell besieged the castle but it only took a few cannon balls for it to surrender: the damage done has never been repaired. The family abandoned the castle in the seventeenth century, although it was restored in 1890 and used to store records and paintings from the National Gallery during World War II. The castle is now used as a hotel (01875 820514; www.borthwick castlehotel.co.uk). The family line of Lord Borthwick

continues, and the family apparently still lives in Midlothian.

The castle is reputedly haunted by the ghost of a local girl, Ann Grant, who was made pregnant by one of the lairds. The story goes that he had the poor lass murdered, rather brutally, in what is now the Red Room. Various manifestations have been reported, including unexplained footsteps, scratchings and sobbing, doors opening and closing by themselves, and cold atmospheres. An older and more established story is that the apparition of Mary, Queen of Scots, disguised as a pageboy has repeatedly been witnessed.

There was another **Borthwick Castle** [NT 770544], one mile north-west of Duns in Berwickshire in the Borders, although all traces have gone except for a commemorative stone. It does not appear, however, that the property was held by the Borthwicks and was long a possession of the Cockburns.

The Borthwicks owned several other properties, mostly in the south and east of Scotland:

Catcune or Catclune Tower [NT 351605], near Gorebridge, Midlothian; site of tower.
>Held by the Borthwicks in the fifteenth century but passed to the Sinclairs, who probably built the tower.

Colmslie Tower [NT 513396], near Galashiels, Borders; very ruined tower.
>Held by the Borthwicks, but passed to the Cairncross family, who held it in the sixteenth century and probably built the tower, and then to the Pringles.

Crookston Old House [NT 425522], near Lauder, Borders; house incorporating castle.
>Held by the Borthwicks from 1446 or earlier until the end of the nineteenth century or later. The Old House was replaced by Crookston House [NT 426516], a large classical mansion of the nineteenth century, which was still owned by the Borthwicks at the end of the nineteenth century.

Dundarg Castle [NJ 895649], near Fraserburgh, Aberdeenshire; scant remains of castle.
>Held by the Comyns and by the Douglases but then by the Borthwicks about 1550 who had the site refortified by French engineers, but Dundarg was sold to the Cheynes of Esslemont.

Johnstounburn House [NT 460616], near Humbie, Midlothian; mansion dating from the seventeenth century.
>Held by the Johnstones and then by the Borthwick family in the seventeenth century or earlier, then passed to the Browns. The mansion was used as a hotel for many years but this closed. It is said to be haunted by the ghost of a lady.

Kaythe Castle [NT 431544], near Gorebridge, Midlothian; site of castle.
>Probably held by the Borthwicks.

Kingsmuir [NO 536084], near Anstruther, Fife; mansion.
>Held by the Borthwicks in the first half of the seventeenth century, but passed to the Hannays.

Langshaw Tower [NT 516397], near Galashiels, Borders; slight remains of tower.
>Held by the Borthwicks, then by the Murrays.

Newbyres Tower [NT 344614], Gorebridge, Midlothian; slight remains of a tower.
>Held by the Borthwicks in 1621, but later sold to the Dundases of Arniston.

Pilmuir House [NT 486695], near Haddington, East Lothian; fine T-plan house, dating from the seventeenth century.
>Held by Cairns family and then by the Borthwicks in the middle of the seventeenth century, and probably also the Binning family. The gardens are occasionally open to the public (www.gardensofscotland.org).

Langshaw Tower 1907? – see previous page

Pittarthie Castle [NO 522091], near Elie, Fife; L-plan tower house.
Held by the Monypennys and by the Murrays and then by the Logans in 1598 but had passed to the Borthwicks early in the seventeenth century until 1644, when Pittarthie was sold to the Bruces of Kinross.

Ravenstone Castle [NX 409441], near Whithorn, Galloway; extended but unroofed tower house.
Held by several families, including by the Stewarts in the middle of the seventeenth century, but was a property of Lord Borthwick in the nineteenth century; the castle was unroofed in 1948.

No. of castles/sites: 13
Rank: 113=/764

Newbyres Tower (M&R; reconstruction) – see previous page

Boswell

The origin of the name is from a place in France, perhaps Beuzevill, near Bolbec. A Norman called de Boville was one of the captains at the Battle of Hastings in 1066, and the family are on record in Scotland from the twelfth century. Walter Boswell was taken prisoner at the Battle of Dunbar in 1296.

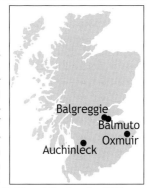

The family held lands at **Oxmuir** [NT 716418] near Hume in Berwickshire, but acquired the property of **Balgreggie** [NT 222963], four and a half miles north-east of Cowdenbeath in Fife, by marriage from the Wemyss family around the end of the fourteenth century. There was apparently a mansion, and probably a castle, but, if there was, these have gone. The Boswells went to Balmuto.

The family became prominent in Fife, and held **Balmuto** [NT 221898], two and a half miles north of Burntisland in Fife, from the fifteenth century after acquiring the property by marriage from the Glen family. They built a castle, consisting of a strong keep with later extensions, which has recently been restored. Sir Alexander Boswell of Balmuto was killed at the Battle of Flodden in 1513. The castle was destroyed in the 1560s or 70s, although it was later restored. One of the family, Sir John Boswell, was a favourite of James VI, and Sir Alexander Boswell died at Balmuto in 1822 following a duel (see below), and his ghost is said to haunt the building.

Pitteadie Castle [NT 257891], three miles to the north and east of Burntisland, was held by the Boswells of Balmuto for some years before 1671 when it was sold to the Calderwoods. The castle, which is now ruinous, had a large keep from the fifteenth century with a later stair-tower and courtyard. There are two fine gateways.

Auchinleck [NS 501232], which is south-west of Catrine in Ayrshire, passed by marriage from the Auchinlecks to the Boswells of Balmuto at the beginning of the sixteenth century. The castle, a sixteenth-century tower house with a moat and drawbridge, is now very

Auchinleck Castle (M&R)

ruinous. One of the family was the famous James Boswell, who accompanied Doctor Samuel Johnson on his tour of the Highlands in 1773 and wrote a biography of the good doctor in 1791; another was Alexander Boswell, Lord Auchinleck, a judge of the Court of Session; another was his son, Sir Alexander Boswell of Auchinleck, who was killed in a duel at Balmuto in 1822 by James Stewart of Dunearn after Boswell had caricatured Stewart. The castle had been abandoned in about 1760 with the building of Auchinleck House, now a classical mansion which was restored in the 1980s. The house is in the care of the Landmark Trust, offers holiday accommodation and can be visited on Wednesday afternoons from Easter to the end of October by appointment only (01628 825925; www.landmark trust.org.uk). The Boswells of Auchinleck still flourish, although they now apparently live in England.

Trabboch Castle [NS 458222], three and a half miles south of Mauchline in Ayrshire, was a strong castle but little remains. The lands were owned by the Boswells after coming from the Boyds and from the Douglases.

The Boswells also owned **Blackadder Castle** [NT 856540], four miles east of Duns in the Borders, in the nineteenth century, and **Ochiltree Castle** [NS 510212] in Ayrshire, in the 1850s; both of these buildings have been demolished. Blackadder had been a property of the Blackadders and then of the Homes, and Ochiltree had been owned by the Nisbets, by the Wallaces of Elderslie and then by several others.

No. of castles/sites: 8
Rank: 160=/764

Bowie

Bowie may come from the Gaelic 'buie' for yellow, probably meaning 'fair haired'. The name is re-corded in Scotland from the fifteenth century, and was common around Stir-ling and Dunblane in the seventeenth and eight-eenth centuries.

Keithock

Keithock [NO 603634], an estate two or so miles north of Brechin in Angus, was purchased by the Bowies in 1802 but they did not hold it for long. It had been owned by the Lindsays and then by the Edgars, and by the end of the nineteenth century it was held by the Mortons.

No. of castles/sites: 1
Rank: 537=/764

Boyd

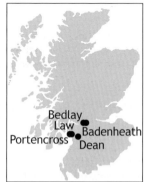

Bedlay
Law   Badenheath
Portencross
Dean

The origin of the name is thought to be descriptive and to come from the Gaelic 'buie', meaning 'yellow' or 'fair', or it may come from the island of Bute, which lies in the Firth of Clyde. The family are first recorded in Scotland at the beginning of the thirteenth century, and claim descent from Simon Stewart, son of Walter the High Steward. One of the family fought bravely at the Battle of Largs in 1263, Robert Boyd was one of William Wallace's companions, and Duncan Boyd was executed by the English in 1306.

The Boyds were given lands to the north-east of Kilmarnock in Ayrshire, which had formerly been held by the Balliols. The Boyds built a strong keep and castle, called Kilmarnock, or more usually **Dean Castle** [NS 437394]. Sir Robert Boyd had been one of Bruce's commanders at the Battle of Bannockburn in 1314, and

Dean Castle (M&R)

the castle may have been besieged during the Wars of Independence. Robert Boyd became Regent and Guardian of James III during his minority. He practically ruled Scotland from 1466-69, and his sister was married to the king. The Boyds fell from favour, and Robert had to flee to Denmark, while Sir Alexander, his brother, was executed for treason and James III divorced Boyd's sister. The Boyds had a bloody feud with the Montgomerys; and they supported Mary, Queen of Scots, and fought for her at the defeat of the Battle of Langside in 1568.

William, tenth Lord Boyd, was made Earl of Kilmarnock in 1661. While the third Earl, another William, opposed the Jacobites in the 1715 Rising, William, fourth Earl, was Privy Councillor to Bonnie Prince Charlie. Boyd fought, at and was captured after, the Battle of Culloden in 1746, and was then taken to London where he was executed by beheading. There is also a ghost story associated with the unlucky fourth

Earl. Before hostilities had broken out, his servants were terrified by an apparition of his severed head rolling about the floor in one of the chambers of the castle. Boyd told the Earl of Galloway about the manifestation, who predicted that Boyd would lose his head. He was proved to be right.

Although also a Jacobite, James Boyd recovered the lands in 1750, but eight years later sold them to the Hay Earls of Errol, who were relations. The family continues as the Boyd Barons Kilmarnock, and they apparently now live in England. Dean Castle was sold to the Cunninghams, passed through other families, and was eventually given to the people of Kilmarnock. Down the centuries it been developed into a large and imposing castle with a tower, palace block and a courtyard. Part of the castle was burnt out, but it was restored from 1905 and now houses a museum, surrounded by a public park, and is open to the public (01563 522702; www.deancastle.com).

Two miles west of West Kilbride in Ayrshire is **Portencross**, or Ardneil, Castle [NS 176488], which stands on a rock by the shore of the Firth of Clyde. The castle dates from the fourteenth century, and there is a keep with a later wing. The lands were given to the

Bedlay Castle (M&R) – see previous column

Moray as a result. The castle passed to the Coupers in the late seventeenth century, and was completely demolished in 1953.

Law Castle [NS 211484] stands in a prominent position overlooking the Clyde to the north-east of West Kilbride in Ayrshire, and is a sturdy fifteenth-century

Portencross Castle 1910?

Boyds of Kilmarnock by Robert the Bruce. Robert II and Robert III visited the castle on their way to Rothesay on Bute. The Boyds held the property until 1785 when it passed to the Fullertons of Overton. A gale had stripped off the roof in 1739, although the ruin is complete to the wallhead. There are moves afoot to restore Portencross. The castle was the subject of the BBC programme Restoration (www.portencrosscastle. org.uk).

Bedlay Castle [NS 692701], three miles south of Kirkintilloch in Lanarkshire, was built by the Boyds and is a sixteenth-century L-plan tower house with a later range. The Boyds held the lands from the Reformation until they were sold to the Robertsons in 1642 and Bedlay later went to the Campbells. The castle is occupied as a private residence, although it is said to be haunted by the spectre of a large bearded man as well as by a phantom coach.

Badenheath Castle [NS 713724] lay some three and a half miles south-west of Cumbernauld in Lanarkshire. Robert Boyd of Badenheath was one of Mary's bodyguard at Langside in 1568, and Boyd was exiled by Regent

Law Castle (M&R)

keep of four storeys and a garret. It was long held by the Boyds, but was sold in 1670 to the Bontines. The building has been restored and accommodation is available (01505 703119; www.lawcastle.com).

The Boyds owned several other properties:
Ballochtoul Castle [NX 192976], near Girvan, Ayrshire; site of castle.
  Held by the Grahams of Knockdolian but went to the Boyds of Penkill.
Barneil [NS 366085], near Maybole, Ayrshire; site of castle or old house.
  Held by the MacCrindles but passed to the Boyds of Trochague.
Brodick Castle [NS 016378], near Brodick, isle of Arran; fine castle and mansion.
  Although most usually associated with the Hamiltons, the castle and Earldom of Arran were held by the Boyds from 1467 until their fall from power in 1469. The castle is in the care of The National Trust for Scotland and open to the public (01770 302202; www.nts.org.uk).

Callendar House [NS 898794], Falkirk; grand mansion incorporating castle.

> Long a property of the Livingstones until 1715 when it was leased by William Boyd, fourth Earl of Kilmarnock. He was executed for treason and the property later went to the Forbeses. Open to the public and stands in a public park (01324 503770; www.falkirk.gov.uk/cultural/).

Duncow [NX 970833], near Dumfries; site of castle or old house.

> Held by the Comyns, but passed to the Boyds after the Wars of Independence, then later went to the Maxwells.

Grougar [NS 466388], near Kilmarnock, Ayrshire; possible site of castle.

> Held by the Logans, but passed to the Boyds and then to the Grahams about 1699.

Kipps Castle [NS 989739], near Linlithgow, West Lothian; ruinous tower house.

> Held by the Boyds, who are buried at Torphichen Preceptory [NS 972727], but later passed to the Sibbalds, who held it in the seventeenth century or earlier.

Merton Hall [NX 383640], near Newton Stewart, Galloway; mansion on site of castle?

> Held by the Gordons and then by the Boyds from 1785, now represented by the Lennox-Boyds, Viscount Boyds of Merton since 1960. The present house dates from 1767 but has two later semi-circular towers with conical roofs.

Penkill Castle [NX 232985], near Girvan, Ayrshire; restored tower house.

> Long held by the Boyds, who built the castle, but went to William Bell Scott, the pre-Raphaelite artist and poet, when he restored it in 1857.

Pitcon Castle [NS 299506], near Dalry, Ayrshire; mansion on site of castle.

> Held by the Pitcon family and then by the Boyds, but was sold to the MacRaes in the 1770s. The present house dates from the eighteenth century.

Pitkindie House [NO 248317], near Inchture, Perth and Kinross; fragments remain.

> Held by the Boyds in the fifteenth century, who reputedly fought with the Grays of Fowlis near Abernyte.

Trabboch Castle [NS 458222], near Mauchline, Ayrshire; slight remains of a castle.

> Held by the Boyds from the fourteenth century until about 1450 when Trabboch passed to the Douglases and then later went to the Boswells.

Trochrague or Trochrig [NS 213004], near Girvan, Ayrshire; house on site of castle.

> Held by the Boyds in the fifteenth century. Robert Boyd of Trochrig was principal of the University of Glasgow in 1615 and then of Edinburgh in 1622. Members of the family are buried in the kirkyard at Old Dailly.

www.clanboyd.org
www.clanboyd.info
No. of castles/sites: 18
Rank: 76=/764

Boyle

The name comes from the town of Beauville, near Caen in France, and the Boyles were a Norman family, although it has also been claimed that the name originates from Ireland. The Boyles are first on record in Scotland in the twelfth century, and they held lands at Kelburn from then or from the thirteenth century.

    Kelburn Castle [NS 217567], two miles south of Largs, is set in parkland with fine views and is a tall

Kelburn Castle (M&R)

sixteenth-century Z-plan tower house, rising to four storeys. The caste is dated 1581, but was altered and extended down the centuries.

    The Boyles fought at the Battle of Largs in 1263, and then at Bannockburn on the side of Robert the Bruce in 1314. John Boyle of Kelburn, a supporter of James III, was killed at the Battle of Sauchieburn in 1488, and another of the family was killed at Pinkie in 1547. The Boyles supported Mary, Queen of Scots, and were made Earls of Glasgow in 1703. The Boyles still occupy Kelburn, making it one of the longest occupied houses in Scotland. The castle is open in July and part of September and the grounds all year (01475 568685/204 (castle); www.kelburncastle.com).

Other lands and castles held by the Boyles:

Craigends House [NS 419662], near Kilbarchan, Renfrewshire; site of mansion and castle.

> Held by the Knoxs of Ranfurly and by the Cunninghams of Glencairn but was acquired by the Boyles in 1647 and then later returned to the Cunninghams. The mansion included old work but was demolished in 1957.

Dalduff Castle [NS 320070], near Maybole, Ayrshire; site of castle.

> Probably held by the Boyles and was a property of the Fergusons at one time.

Fairlie Castle [NS 213549], near Largs, Ayrshire; substantial ruined castle.

> Held by the Fairlies and then was bought by the Boyles in 1656.

Fairlie Castle (M&R) – see previous page

Hawkhead Castle [NS 501626], near Paisley, Renfrewshire; hospital on site of castle and mansion.
Long held by the Rosses of Hawkhead, but latterly passed to the Boyle Earls of Glasgow.

Kilbirnie House [NS 304541], Kilbirnie, Ayrshire; ruined castle and house.
Held by the Barclays, by the Crawfords and by the Lindsay Earls of Crawford before going to the Boyle Earls of Glasgow from 1833.

Rowallan Castle [NS 435424], near Kilmarnock, Ayrshire; fine courtyard castle.
Built by the Mures but passed by marriage to the Boyles in the 1700s then later went to the Campbells and to the Corbetts.

Rowallan Castle 1906?

Stanely Castle [NS 464616], near Paisley, Renfrewshire; ruined castle in waterworks.
Held by the Dennistouns, by the Maxwells of Newark, and by the Rosses of Hawkhead before passing by marriage to the Boyle Earls of Glasgow from around 1750. The basement of the ruin has been flooded since 1837.

No. of castles/sites: 8
Rank: 160=/764

Braid

The name is territorial and comes from the Braid Hills, which lie to the south of Edinburgh. The family held the Braids, Blackford Hill, Plewlands and Bavelaw, and are first mentioned in the twelfth century.

They probably had a castle at **Braid** [NT 251703], possibly at **Hermitage of Braid House**, although this is a poor defensive site. The Braids held the lands until 1426 when they passed to the Fairlies. The small mansion dates from the eighteenth century, and is now a countryside information centre, and the grounds have been a public park since 1888. **Bavelaw** [NT 168628], south of Balerno on the outskirts of Edinburgh, was also held by the Braids, but passed by marriage to the Forresters of Niddry and then went to others. Bavelaw Castle is an L-plan tower house, but it dates from the sixteenth century, after the Braids had lost possession.

No. of sites: 2
Rank: 396=/764

Brebner

The name comes from a native of Brabant in the Low Countries, and a 'braboner' was one of the weaving trade. The name is on record in Scotland from early in the fifteenth century, and it was common in parts of Aberdeenshire. There are many variations in spelling down the centuries, not least that of 'Bremner'.

Learney [NJ 633046] is a fine mansion with corbiestepped gables, and stands eight or so miles northwest of Banchory in Aberdeenshire. There was an older building, held by the Forbes family, but it passed to the Brebners in the eighteenth century, then later going by marriage to Innes of Raemoir.

No. of castles/sites: 1 / Rank: 537=/764
Xref: Bremner

Brisbane

The name is believed to derive from Anglo-French, and means 'bone breaker' from 'bris bane'. Brisbane is on record in Scotland from the end of the thirteenth century.

The family acquired the lands of Bishopton in 1332 or earlier, and they built the old part of **Bishopton House** [NS 422717], a tall, mostly seventeenth-century tower house. There is a later wing and other work, and the house lies three and a half miles north-east of Bridge of Weir in Renfrewshire. The Brisbanes held the property until around 1671, when it passed to the Walkinshaws. The house is now part of the Convent of the Gentle Shepherd.

The Brisbanes purchased the lands of **Killincraig** or **Kelsoland** (the property had been owned by the Kelso family) in 1671, and renamed the property Brisbane. They built **Brisbane House** [NS 209622], a four-storey

Brisbane House (M&R)

symmetrical mansion, stood on the site of a castle two miles north of Largs in Ayrshire, but the building was demolished after 1938. Sir Thomas Brisbane, who was born in the house, served as a soldier, but was very interested in astronomy. He built observatories at Makerstoun in Scotland, and near Sydney in Australia, where he was Governor of New South Wales from 1821-25. The Australian city of Brisbane is named after him. The Brisbanes held the lands into the twentieth century.

Ballanreoch Castle [NS 610794], one and a half miles north-west of Lennoxtown, was built by the Brisbanes, who acquired the lands in 1423. It was sold in 1625 to the MacFarlanes, and little or nothing remains of the castle. A later house, used as the Campsie Glen Hotel but burnt out in the 1980s and then restored for other uses, was built on the site.

No. of castles/sites: 3
Rank: 328=/764

Brodie

The name is territorial from the lands of Brodie, which are four miles west of Forres in Moray, and it is on record from the thirteenth century. It has been suggested that their name comes from 'brothaig', and means 'ditch'. Perhaps the most notorious of the name is William Brodie, who was a respectable Edinburgh cabinet maker and town councillor by day, but was a thief and burglar by night. He was eventually caught, tried and then hanged in 1788.

The lands of Brodie were held by the family from 1160 or earlier, and were confirmed by Robert the Bruce. Their early history has mostly been lost as the castle was sacked and torched by the Gordons in 1645. **Brodie Castle** [NH 980578] is a large and impressive building,

Brodie Castle (M&R)

mostly dating from after the sixteenth century but perhaps incorporating work from as early as the twelfth century. It was extended in the nineteenth century by the architect William Burn. It was possibly during this that the skeleton of child was found in one of the corner towers; the remains are on display in the charter room.

The Brodies were Covenanters, and Alexander Brodie had destroyed idolatrous images in Elgin Cathedral in 1640. The castle was torched by the Royalist Lord Lewis Gordon in 1645, although much of the internal work actually survived. The Brodies supported the Hanoverians in the Jacobite Risings. The building was renovated in 1980 after passing to The National Trust for Scotland, although the Brodie line continues in the twenty-fifth chief of Brodie.

The castle also has a ghost story, possibly regarding Lady Margaret Duff, who was the wife of James Brodie, the then chief. In 1786 she fell asleep in front of the fire and her clothes were set alight and she burned to death. An apparition of a woman was reported in the nursery room in 1992.

The castle is open to the public from April to September, while the grounds are open all year (01309 641371; www.nts.org.uk).

Lethen House [NH 937518], some four miles south-east of Nairn, dates from 1785, and is a three-storey mansion with later wings. It stands on the site of a castle and was torched in 1645 by Royalists, and then again in 1680. The mansion is still apparently occupied by the Brodies, now represented by the sixteenth Brodie of Lethen.

Other properties held by the Brodies:
Arnhall House [NO 613691], near Brechin, Angus; house on site of mansion.
   Held by the Carnegies but passed to the Brodies, who held Arnhall from 1796 until 1814 when it went to the Shands.
Asliesk Castle [NJ 108598], near Elgin, Moray; ruined tower house.
   Held by the Brodies and by the Innes family; Macbeth is said to have met the three witches on a nearby hillock.
Castle Hill, Pluscarden [NJ 154571], site of castle, the location not certain.
   The lands were held for some years by the Brodies of Lethen, as well as by the Setons, by the Mackenzies, by the Grants and by others. Pluscarden Abbey is an interesting partly-restored monastery, now a Benedictine establishment, and can be visited (01343 890257; www.pluscardenabbey.org).
Milton Brodie House [NJ 094627], near Forres; mansion on site of castle.
   Held by the Brodies.

No. of castles/sites: 6
Rank: 212=/764

Brotherton

The name is territorial and comes from the lands of Brotherton, which are some six miles south-east of Laurencekirk in Kincardineshire in north-east Scotland.

Brotherton Castle [NO 803676] was a courtyard castle, with ranges enclosing three of the sides. This was demolished and a huge baronial mansion, adorned with turrets, towers and

Brotherton Castle 1920?

gables, was built on the site in 1866. The lands were held by the Brotherton family and they built the old castle. The property passed to the Scotts of Logie in the seventeenth century and they held Brotherton until 1949; the building now houses Lathallan School.

No. of castles/sites: 1
Rank: 537=/764

Brown

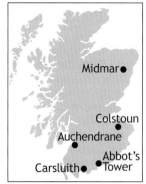

The name of Brown or Broun is very common in Scotland, and probably refers to colouring, either of face or of hair, although it was also a common personal name in Old English. The name is on record from the thirteenth century.

John Brown, who lived at Priestfield in Lanarkshire, was a well-known Covenanter and was shot by John Graham of Claverhouse in 1685 after weapons were found in Brown's house. Another John Brown was the servant of Queen Victoria at Balmoral Castle; he died in 1883 after serving her from 1849 or earlier.

Colstoun [NT 514712], which is two miles south of Haddington in East Lothian, came to the Browns in the thirteenth century or earlier, and they held the lands for more than 500 years. The Colstoun Pear is reputedly a magic fruit, given by Hugh of Yester, a reputed wizard, to his daughter as a dowry. So long as the family held the Colstoun Pear they would prosper, although some might see it as a very inexpensive marriage settlement. Sir William Brown of Colstoun defeated the English in a battle at Swordwellrig in Annandale in the fifteenth century. The family were made Baronets of Nova Scotia in 1686, and the property passed by marriage to the Ramsay Earls of Dalhousie in 1805. The title has, however, remained with the family, although they now apparently live in Australia. Some of the family earlier had settled in Elsinore in Denmark where they became successful merchants.

Three and a half miles south of Creetown in Galloway is **Carsluith Castle** [NX 495542], an L-plan tower house dating from the fifteenth century. The property passed from the Lindsays by marriage to the Browns early in

the sixteenth century. Gilbert Brown of Carsluith was the last abbot of Sweetheart Abbey, and adhered to Catholicism despite the tide of the Reformation flowing against him. He was imprisoned in Blackness Castle in 1603, and then exiled to France in 1608 (when he was already eighty years of age). He became rector of the Scots College in Paris, where he died in 1612. His son, John Brown, was heavily fined for failing to answer the charge of murdering MacCulloch of Barholm, and the family emigrated to India in 1748, abandoning the castle. The castle is in the care of Historic Scotland, and is apparently open to the public in the summer.

Abbot's Tower [NX 972667], near Sweetheart Abbey and just north of the village of New Abbey south of Dumfries, is a restored L-plan tower house, which dates from the sixteenth century. It was built by John Brown,

Abbot's Tower (M&R)

the last abbot. **Old House** [NX 962662] in New Abbey is a small two-storey house, and is said to also have been used by Browns.

The lands of Cunningar or Midmar, which are eight miles north of Banchory in Aberdeenshire, were held by the Browns from the thirteenth century until 1422 when they passed to the Gordons. They probably had a castle on the motte at **Midmar** [NJ 701060], although the story goes that this was abandoned in the sixteenth century because of plague. There is the impressive **Midmar Castle** [NJ 704053], but this was built in the sixteenth century after Midmar had passed from the Browns.

Bruntsfield in Edinburgh is said to come from 'Browne's Field', and is named after Richard Browne, King's Sergeant of the Muir, but had passed to the Lauders by 1380. **Bruntsfield House** [NT 252723] is a Z-plan tower house, but dates from the sixteenth century and is now part of James Gillespie's School.

Several other properties were held by the Browns:
Auchendrane Castle [NS 335152], near Ayr; castle replaced by mansion.
> Held by the Browns but they supported the wrong side in the Wars of Independence, and the property was given to the Annans by Robert the Bruce. Later went to the Mures, and then to others.

Auchlochan [NS 807375], near Lesmahagow, Lanarkshire; castle replaced by mansion.
> Held by the Browns of Auchlochan but now a nursing home. The mansion is said to be haunted by a Black Lady, the beautiful ghost of the black wife of one of the lairds.

Carsluith Castle (M&R)

Easter Fordel [NO 143124], near Perth; slight remains of castle.
　　Held by the Browns. Oliver Cromwell spent two nights here in 1651. The castle was replaced by a mansion in 1784.

Edmonston Castle [NT 070422], near Biggar, Lanarkshire; ruined castle.
　　Held by the Edmonstones, by the Douglases and by the Baillies of Walston but it passed to the Browns in the eighteenth century, and was then later sold to Woddrops of Elsrickle and Dalmarnock.

Greenhead Tower [NT 492295], near Selkirk, Borders; site of tower house.
　　Held by the Browns in the fourteenth century, but passed to the Kerrs in the sixteenth century who probably built the tower.

Hartree Tower [NT 046360], near Biggar, Lanarkshire; mansion on site of tower house.
　　Held by the Browns from 1434 or earlier until 1634 when sold to the Dicksons. The tower was inhabited until the 1780s but was then replaced by a mansion.

Houndwood House [NT 855630], near Granthouse, Borders; mansion with old work.
　　Held by several families before passing to the Browns in 1919.

Johnstounburn House [NT 460616], near Humbie, Midlothian; mansion with older core.
　　Held by the Johnstones and then by the Borthwicks before passing to the Browns in the eighteenth century. Johnstounburn had gone to the Ushers in 1884, was later used as a hotel but this has closed.

Knockbrex [NX 585497], near Gatehouse of Fleet, Galloway; mansion on site of castle.
　　Held by the Gordons but passed to the Browns in 1895 and they built the present house. The house can be rented as holiday accommodation (01381 610496; www.lhhscotland.com).

Marlee House [NO 149445], near Blairgowrie, Perthshire; mansion on site of castle.
　　Held by the Kinlochs but then by the Browns in the nineteenth century, and there is the extravagant tomb of John Brown of Marlee, dating from 1858.

Milnhead [NX 971811], near Dumfries; castle replaced by mansion.
　　Held by the Browns, possibly from the sixteenth to the nineteenth centuries.

Newhall Castle [NT 175566], near Penicuik, Midlothian; mansion with older work.
　　Held by several families before coming to the Browns in the eighteenth century. Newhall was the inspiration of 'The Gentle Shepherd' by Allan Ramsay when owned by the Browns. The garden is open to the public by appointment only (01968 660206; www.gardensofscotland.org).

www.clanbrown.com
No. of castles/sites: 19
Rank: 72=/764
Xref: Broun

Midmar Castle (AC) – see previous page

Bruce

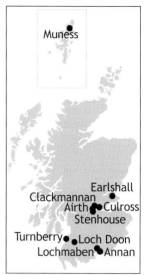

The name and the family originate from France, from Brix between Cherbourg and Valognes in Normandy. The Bruces came over to England with William the Conqueror, and held wide lands in Surrey and in Dorset. A Robert Bruce (many of the family were called Robert) came to Scotland as one of the Norman companions of David I in the twelfth century. The Bruces were given the Lordship of Annandale, although this led to division in loyalties in the family between their holdings in the two countries. Through marriage with one of the daughters of the brother of William the Lion, the Bruces had a good claim to the throne after the death of Alexander III. The crown was 'given' by Edward I of England to John Balliol, John I, but he was deposed in 1296. After the campaign of William Wallace and his execution, Robert the Bruce proclaimed himself king in 1306. Initially his cause went badly, and he was forced to flee as a hunted fugitive; but when he returned he led a brilliant campaign against the English which culminated in the crushing defeat of Edward II's forces at the Battle of Bannockburn in 1314. Robert I consolidated his hold on power in the following years, and England eventually recognised Scottish independence in 1328, a year before Robert the Bruce died. Bruce had a son David, who became David I. He died without legitimate heirs, and the crown passed through Bruce's daughter Marjorie to the Stewarts.

　　The Bruce family were also major landowners in many parts of Scotland.

The original **Lochmaben Castle** [NY 082822], just south of Lochmaben in Dumfries and Galloway, was the main stronghold of the Bruces when they were Lords of Annandale. Only a motte remains, and the castle was abandoned in 1298 when Edward I built a new fortress nearby at **Lochmaben** [NY 088812]. Robert the Bruce may have been born at the original castle.

　　Turnberry Castle [NS 196073] lies some seven miles west of Maybole in Ayrshire, and stands on a promontory by the sea. The building is very ruinous, but some vaults remains of a thirteenth-century fortress. It was held by the Earls of Carrick, and in 1271 Marjorie, the widowed countess, kidnapped Robert Bruce (Robert the Bruce's father) and forced him to marry her. Robert the Bruce may have been born here rather than at Lochmaben. Bruce landed at Turnberry in 1307 at the beginning of his campaign which led to Bannockburn seven years later. The castle was deliberately dismantled on his orders, and probably never rebuilt. The site is accessible.

Annan Castle [NY 192668], in the royal burgh of Annan in Dumfries and Galloway, was another castle of the Bruces, dating from about 1124. The castle may still have been in use in the sixteenth century but there are no remains.

Seven miles south of Dalmellington in Ayrshire, and moved from its original spot, **Loch Doon Castle** [NX 483950] is a ruinous thirteenth-century courtyard castle, polygonal in plan. There was a tower house, but this

Loch Doon Castle (M&R)

was not rebuilt when the original site was flooded by a hydroelectric scheme in the 1930s. Loch Doon was built by the Bruces of Carrick. It was captured by the English in 1306, and Sir Christopher Seton, Robert the Bruce's brother-in-law, was seized and hanged at Dumfries. The castle was retaken by the Scots by 1314. In 1333 it was one of the six strongholds which held out for David II against Edward Balliol.

Clackmannan Tower [NS 905920] is a prominent and impressive tower and castle, dating from the fourteenth century, but has been altered down the centuries. There

Clackmannan Tower (RWB)

was a later mansion, but this has been demolished; and the castle is on the west side of the town of Clackmannan in central Scotland. The lands were held by the Bruces from 1359 until 1796. The family had helped to organise

a rebellion against the English in Kyle in Ayrshire, and they were given Crown lands as a reward. Henry Bruce of Clackmannan fought for the Jacobites in the 1745 Rising. Henry Bruce's widow, Catherine, 'knighted' Robert Burns, with the sword of Robert the Bruce in 1787. The building was abandoned a few years later. The castle is can be viewed from the outside, and is now in care of Historic Scotland.

Airth Castle [NS 900869], four miles north of Falkirk in central Scotland, is now used as a hotel, but Wallace's Tower dates from the fourteenth century and there other parts from the sixteenth century. The castle was held by the Airth family, but passed by marriage to the Bruces of Clackmannan about 1470. The castle was torched in 1488 by James III before he went on to defeat and assassination at the Battle of Sauchieburn. It was soon rebuilt, and was held by the Bruces until 1642 when it passed by marriage to the Elphinstones and then later went to the Grahams. The castle is now a hotel (01324 831411; www.airthcastlehotel.com).

In the pretty village of the same name in Fife, **Culross Palace** [NS 986862] is a fine well-preserved town house

Culross Palace (M&R)

(not actually a palace in the modern sense of the word) which was built for Sir George Bruce of Carnock around 1600. He made his money from coal mining, constructing a mine which went out far under the Firth of Forth to an artificial island. This branch of the family were made Earls of Kincardine in 1647, but by 1700 Culross had passed to the Erskines. The building has been carefully restored by The National Trust for Scotland, has decorative paint work and original interiors, and is open to the public from April to September (01383 880359; www.nts.org.uk).

Also in Culross is **Culross Abbey House** [NS 989862], which dates from 1608 and was built for Edward Bruce, Lord Kinloss. Bruce had been commendator of Kinloss Abbey, was made a Lord of Session in 1597, and was later Master of the Rolls. Culross Abbey House was formerly an impressive building, but it became ruinous about 1800. It was altered in 1830, and again in 1955 when it was much reduced in size.

Also in the picturesque village are the ruins of the ancient abbey, the parish church, and the Town House and Study. Sir George Bruce, who died in 1625, has an elaborate burial monument with two stone effigies in the parish church [NS 989863], which was remodelled out of part of the church of Culross Abbey. Others of the family are buried here in the family mausoleum, and there is a plaque commemorating the heart burial of Edward, Lord Bruce, who died in 1613.

Broomhall [NT 077837], three miles south-west of Dunfermline in Fife, is a long classical mansion of the 1790s. It stands on the site of a castle, and was held by the Bruces from the beginning of the seventeenth century; they changed the name to Broomhall from Werty Gellet, perhaps understandably. Different branches of the Bruces were made Earls of Elgin in 1633, then Earls of Kincardine in 1647, and their descendants, who hold both titles, still occupied Broomhall until recently. The mansion was said to have housed the helmet and two-handed sword of Robert the Bruce, the latter having been used to 'knight' Robert Burns at Clackmannan Tower, as well as a bed slept in by Charles I. The building is now used as a hotel (01259 763360; www.broomhall castle.co.uk).

Stenhouse [NS 879829] stood a couple of miles north of Falkirk, and was a seventeenth-century L-plan tower house. It was held by the Bruces of Stenhouse from 1611, who built the tower, and they were made Baronets of

Stenhouse (M&R)

Nova Scotia in 1628. Sir William Bruce, took part in the Jacobite Risings of 1715 and 1719, while his grandson took part in the Rising of 1745-46. The house was demolished in the 1960s, and the site is now occupied by a housing estate. The line of the Bruces of Stenhouse continues, and they now apparently live in California.

Tulliallan Castle [NS 927888], to the north of Kincardine in Fife, is an impressive ruinous hall-house, which is enclosed by a ditch. It dates from the fourteenth century, and was probably built by the Blackadders. It passed to the Bruces of Carnock in 1605, and they lived here until about 1662. In 1619 five men were accused of imprisoning another man in the dungeon of Tulliallan and starving him to death. The property passed to the Erskines and then to others and a new mansion was

built half a mile away in 1822; it is now a police training college. The old castle is currently being restored for the Mitchell Trust.

Blairhall [NS 997876], five miles west of Dunfermline and north of Culross in Fife, is an attractive two-storey mansion, dating from the seventeenth century. It replaced a previous house or castle, and was held by the Bruces of Blairhall from 1541. Sir William Bruce, who built Kinross House, was from this branch, as are the Earls of Elgin. Blairhall may have been held by the Blackadders at one time.

Just east of Clackmannan is **Kennet** [NS 918908]. Kennet House replaced a castle and was an elegant mansion with a bow-front and was surrounded by gardens and plantations. Kennet was held by the Bruces from 1389 until the nineteenth century or later. Many of the family were distinguished soldiers, and Robert Bruce of Kennet was a judge of the Court of Session, having the title Lord Kennet. The family succeeded to the title Lord Balfour of Burleigh, but the mansion was demolished in 1955.

Brucefield [NS 959916], some three miles east of Clackmannan, is a substantial three-storey mansion, dating from the 1720s. It was built by the Bruces of Kennet, but was sold in the 1950s to the Abercrombys. It is now apparently held by the Bruces again, representatives of the line of Lord Balfour of Burleigh.

Near Leuchars on the east side of Fife is **Earlshall** [NO 465211], a fine and especially well-preserved sixteenth-century courtyard castle. The hall is a good chamber with panelled walls and a large carved

Earlshall (M&R)

fireplace, and there is a tempera painted ceiling of the 1620s. The castle was built by Sir William Bruce in 1546, who had fought at, and survived, the Battle of Flodden in 1513. Mary, Queen of Scots, visited in 1561; and one of the family was killed at the Battle of Worcester in 1651, fighting for Charles II. Sir Andrew Bruce of Earlshall is known as the 'Bloody Bruce' for his treatment of Covenanters. He and his men killed Richard Cameron, a noted Covenanter, at Airds Moss in 1680. Bruce then hacked off Cameron's head and hands, and took them back to Edinburgh, where he had them brought before the council. Indeed, Earlshall is said to be haunted by the ghost of Sir Andrew Bruce, and his footsteps have reportedly been heard on the stairs. The castle was ruinous when it was restored by Sir Robert Lorimer in 1892, although by then it had passed to the Mackenzies, and then to others. It is a private residence although the gardens are occasionally open to the public (www.gardensofscotland.org).

Fingask Castle [NO 228275], some seven and a half miles east of Perth, is a fine altered tower house, dating from 1594, with a later wing, making it T-plan. Fingask was held by the Bruces of Clackmannan from 1399 or earlier until 1672 when it was sold to the Threiplands. The castle was besieged in 1642 and was sacked and partly demolished in 1746. The building has been restored, and the gardens are occasionally open to the public (www.gardensofscotland.org).

Kinross House [NO 126020], to the east of Kinross near Loch Leven, is a magnificent symmetrical mansion, one of the finest examples of seventeenth-century architecture in Scotland. It was built by Sir William Bruce, who was Royal Architect to Charles II, as his own residence, but the property later passed to the Grahams. The gardens are open to the public from April to September (www.kinrosshouse.com). There was a tower house near the mansion, held by the Douglases, but this was demolished in 1723.

Lochleven Castle [NO 138018] was held by the Bruces at the same time, but also passed to the Grahams. The castle is in the care of Historic Scotland and is open to the public (07778 040483 (mobile))

Muness Castle [HP 629012] is the most northerly castle in Great Britain, and stands on the south-east side of the island of Unst in Shetland. It is a ruined Z-plan tower house, rising to three storeys, and is dated

Muness Castle (AC)

1598. Muness was built by Laurence Bruce of Cultmalindie, a Scottish incomer to Shetland, who moved to Muness after being involved in a murder. In 1573 he was appointed Chamberlain of the Lordship of Shetland, but his was a corrupt and repressive regime. The castle was burnt in 1627, possibly by French pirates, although it was later restored. It was abandoned about 1750, and unroofed by 1774. It is in the care of Historic Scotland and is open to the public (01856 841815).

Other properties owned by the Bruces are:
Alderstone House [NT 044662], near Livingston, West Lothian; tower house.
   Held by several families until it went to the Bruces in the nineteenth century, then to the Whitelaws in the twentieth.

Arkendeith Tower [NH 695561], near Fortrose, Ross and Cromarty; some remains of a tower house.
   Held by the Bruces of Kinloss in the seventeenth century.
Arnot Tower [NO 207016], near Cardenden, Perthshire; ruinous tower house.
   Held by the Arnots but acquired by Sir William Bruce in 1705 because of debt. The Bruces of Arnot built a small burial aisle at the East Burial Ground of Kinross. A garden has been laid out around Arnot Tower and it is occasionally open to the public or can be hired for weddings or functions (01592 840115; www.arnottower.co.uk/www.gardensofscotland.org).
Auchenbowie House [NS 798874], near Stirling; mansion incorporating tower house.
   Held by the Cunninghams of Polmaise but was bought by Robert

Auchenbowie House (M&R)

Bruce, who was Provost of Stirling in 1555. Captain William Bruce killed Charles Elphinstone in a duel at the end of the seventeenth century. Auchenbowie passed by marriage to the Munros in 1708, and the house is still occupied.
Balcaskie House [NO 526035], near Pittenweem, Fife; mansion incorporating tower house.
   Held by a succession of families until it went from the Moncreiffes to the Bruces in 1665. Much of Sir William Bruce's splendid interior survives, including painted ceilings and plasterwork. Balcaskie then passed to the Stewarts of Grandtully, then to the Nicholsons of Kemnay and then to the Anstruthers in 1698.
Bordie Castle [NS 956869], near Kincardine, Fife; ruined tower house.
   Held by the Bruces of Bordie.
Bruce's Castle or Carnock Tower [NS 857878], near Falkirk; ruined tower house.
   Held by the Bruces of Auchenbowie in the early sixteenth century but in 1608 passed to the Drummonds of Carnock. The Drummonds changed the name to distinguish it from Carnock House.
Carnock House [NS 865882], near Airth; site of tower house.
   Held by the Airths of Plean and then by the Hepburns but then went to the Bruces of Auchenbowie in the early sixteenth century. Carnock passed to the Drummonds in 1608. This branch of the Bruces were made Earls of Kincardine in 1647.
Castlemilk [NY 150775], near Annan, Dumfries and Galloway; motte and site of tower.
   Held by the Bruces but passed to the Stewarts at an early date and then to the Maxwells and to the Jardines. There is a large modern mansion nearby.
Ferrar [NO 484989], near Aboyne, Aberdeenshire; mansion on site of castle.
   Held by the Gordons and then by the Bruces in the nineteenth century. Peter Bruce of Ferrar was Principal of St Leonard's College in St Andrews.
Glen Tanar House [NO 476956], near Aboyne, Aberdeenshire; site of castle and large mansion.
   Held by the Gordons and by others before passing by marriage from the Coats of Paisley to the Bruce Earls of Elgin in the twentieth century.

Grangemuir [NO 539040], near Pittenweem, Fife; mansion on site of old house or castle.

Held by the Bruces in the eighteenth century and then later went to the Douglases. The old house was said to be haunted by the ghost of Buff Barefoot, who was murdered by her lover. The story goes that there were so many manifestations at the older house that it was demolished.

Hallguards Castle [NY 162728], near Ecclefechan, Dumfries and Galloway; site of castle.

Held by the Bruces in the fourteenth century, but passed to the Herries family and then to the Carruthers family.

Hartshaw Tower [NS 958915], near Clackmannan; site of tower.

Held by the Stewarts of Rosyth and then by the Bruces in the eighteenth century. They built Brucefield (see above).

Kinnaird House [NS 885849], near Stenhousemuir, Falkirk; mansion on site of castle.

Held by the Bruces from 1467 but passed to the Orrs. James Bruce, who was born here, was known as 'the Abyssinian Traveller'; and was a famous explorer, finding the source of the Blue Nile. He died when he fell down the stair of the house, and is buried at Larbert along with other members of his family. The house is a private residence.

Mannerston [NT 048790], near Linlithgow, West Lothian; mansion incorporating tower house.

Held by the Bruces of Airth at one time, as well as by the Hamiltons and by the Livingstones.

Myres Castle [NO 242110], near Auchtermuchty; Z-plan tower house.

Held by the Scrymgeours, by the Pattersons and by the Moncreiffes of Reidie before passing to the Bruces in the nineteenth century, and they extended and modified the building in 1828. It went to the Fairlies in 1887 and then to others. The gardens are occasionally open to the public and accommodation is available (01208 821341; www.myres.co.uk/ www.gardensofscotland.org).

Pittarthie Castle [NO 522091], near Elie, Fife; tower house.

Held by the Bruces of Kinross from 1664 to the eighteenth century when sold to the Cunninghams of Glencairn.

Pittillock House [NO 278052], near Glenrothes; tower house incorporated in mansion.

Held by several families and was sold by the Borthwicks to the Bruces in 1664. The Bruces remodelled the house in 1653 but in the eighteenth century the property went to the Cunninghams of Glencairn, now Hannay Cunninghams.

Powfoulis [NS 918856], near Stenhousemuir, Falkirk; house on site of castle.

Held by Bruces from the sixteenth century until 1729 when Powfoulis was sold to the Dundases. James Bruce of Powfoulis was killed at the Battle of Dunbar in 1650. The family built the Bruce Aisle of Old Airth Church, which is now a ruin. The house is now used as a hotel (01324 831267; www.powfoulis.co.uk).

Thomaston Castle [NS 240096], near Maybole, Ayrshire; ruined courtyard castle.

Original castle was probably built by Thomas, nephew of Robert the Bruce, but Thomaston had passed to the Corries of Kelwood by 1507 and then went to the MacIlvaines of Grimmet.

Torrie Castle [NT 015867], near Dunfermline, Fife; mansion on site of castle.

The lands may have been held by the Bruces at one time, as well as by the Wardlaws, by the Balfours and by the Erskine-Wemyss family.

Woodside or Glenbervie [NS 851845], near Larbert, Falkirk; mansion on site of castle.

Held by the Bruces in the seventeenth century but passed to the Stirlings, who renamed the property Glenbervie.

www.brucefamily.com
No. of castles/sites: 41
Rank: 25/764

Bryce

The name comes from a fifth-century French saint called Bricius, who was a nephew of St Martin of Tours. Bryce was a common first name in Scotland from the twelfth century, and then was used as a surname from the fourteenth century. David Bryce was a famous nineteenth-century architect and designed many country houses and other buildings in the Scots baronial style, including Fettes School in Edinburgh and the glowering Kinnaird Castle near Montrose in Angus.

Drumquhassle Castle [NS 483869] is gone but it dated from the sixteenth century and stood a mile or so south and east of Drymen in Stirlingshire. The property had several owners, apparently including the Bryces, who were an old Lennox family; it was also held by the Buchanans, by the Cunninghams and by the Grahams. In 1619 John Bryce of Drumquhassle helped the MacFarlanes in a feud against the Buchanans.

No. of castles/sites: 1
Rank: 537=/764

Buchan

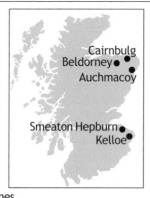

The name comes from the old lands and earldom of Buchan, which are in the far north-east of Aberdeenshire. The Earldom of Buchan may have been a Pictish province but it passed by marriage to the Comyns and then through several families, including the Stewarts, to the Erskines.

The principal family of that name were the Buchans of Auchmacoy. The property lies a couple of miles east of Ellon in Aberdeenshire, and **Auchmacoy House** [NJ 992308], a mansion dating from 1835, is built on the site of a castle. The family gained the lands in 1318, which were made into a barony in 1598. The family were Royalists; and one of them was General James Buchan, a Jacobite, who was defeated at the Battle of Cromdale in 1690 by the forces of William and Mary. Buchan was allowed to go into exile, returned and then fought at the indecisive Battle of Sheriffmuir in 1715, and died six years later. The Buchans' seat is still listed as Auchmacoy House (in *Burke's*), although their residence is given as London.

Beldorney Castle [NJ 424369], stands eight and a half miles south of Keith in Aberdeenshire, and is a substantial Z-plan tower house, dating from the sixteenth century. The castle was held by the Ogilvies, by the Gordons and by the Lyons, and then went to the Buchans after 1689, but they soon sold it to the Grants. The building has been restored.

Two and a half miles east of Fraserburgh, again in Aberdeenshire, is **Cairnbulg Castle** [NK 016640], an impressive building dating from as early as the fourteenth century. It was long associated with the

Kelloe Bastle [NT 828543], two and a half miles east of Duns in Berwickshire, was held by the Kelloe family and then by the Buchans in the eighteenth century. Nothing remains of the tower, and it was replaced by Kelloe, a mansion held by the Fordyce-Buchans in the nineteenth century.

The Buchans also hold the title Baron Tweedsmuir, after John Buchan the famous author of many books, including *The Thirty Nine Steps*, biographer and diplomat, was elevated to the peerage in 1935. His sister, Anna, was also an author, using the name O. Douglas, and their descendants apparently live in England.

Smeaton Hepburn [NT 593786], one mile north of East Linton in East Lothian, was long held by the Hepburns, but passed by marriage to the Buchans, who took the name Buchan-Hepburn. They were made Baronets in 1815, and the family flourishes, but now apparently lives in St Andrews. There was a castle or old house at Smeaton Hepburn, which was replaced by a mansion, but this later building has been partly demolished.

www-unix.oit.umass.edu/~buchan/
No. of castles/sites: 5
Rank: 240=/764

Cairnbulg Castle (M&R)

Frasers, but Cairnbulg was held by the Buchans around 1800, when the building was ruinous. It was bought back by the Frasers in 1934 after Philorth House had been burned down and Cairnbulg was restored and is still occupied.

Buchanan

The name may come from 'buth chanain', the 'house of canons' in Gaelic, or may be territorial in origin. The family is said to spring from one Absalon, whose descendants were known as MacAuslan, and he was given land by the shores of Loch Lomond in central Scotland in 1225. His descendants became known as the Buchanans. George Buchanan, born in Killean in 1506, was a Protestant reformer and was tried as a heretic, although he escaped execution. He opposed Mary, Queen of Scots, was principal of St Leonard's College in St Andrews, and died in 1582.

Buchanan Castle [NS 463886], which stands just west of Drymen in Stirlingshire, is a substantial castellated mansion with many turrets, dating from 1854 and designed by William Burn. At its core is a tower house, and the lands were long held by the Buchanans until sold in 1682 to the Grahams of Montrose because of

Buchanan Castle 1914?

debt. The castle is ruined but consolidated, and the grounds and gardens, designed by Capability Brown, are now a golf course. There was also an earlier castle known as **Buchanan Pele** [NS 457886], to the south of the present building. At one time this is was 'an old tower and a great many other buildings', but the last remains were demolished and cleared away before 1724.

Arnprior Castle [NS 613949], also in Stirlingshire and three miles east of Kippen, was held by the Buchanans in the sixteenth century but nothing now remains. The family were known as the 'Kings of Kippen' because of their lifestyle, which perhaps could not be matched by their wealth. The laird of the time was visited by James V and his men, after Buchanan had purloined a wagon of the king's goods. Buchanan was charming enough to be forgiven, and was invited back to Stirling. Buchanan of Arnprior, possibly the same fellow, was killed at the Battle of Pinkie in 1547.

Leny House [NN 613089], one and a half miles to the west and north of Callander in Stirlingshire, consists

of an L-plan tower house, to which has been added a large mansion of the nineteenth century. The property passed by marriage from the Leny family to the Buchanans, and descendants of the family held it until the twentieth century. Francis Buchanan was hanged in 1746 after Stewart of Glenbuckie, leader of Stewarts on their way to join the Jacobite army, was shot in the head at Leny. The building is now used as a hotel (01877 331078; www.lenyestate.com). Descendants of this branch of the family are now represented by the Carrick-Buchanans of Drumpellier and Corsewall, and they still apparently live in Scotland.

The Buchanans owned many properties down the centuries:

Ardoch [NS 412864], near Balloch, Dunbartonshire; site of castle.
   Held by the Bontines and perhaps by the Findlays before passing to the Buchanans of Ardoch in the nineteenth century, and they moved to Balloch.

Auchenreoch Castle [NS 678767], near Kilsyth, Dunbartonshire; site of tower.
   Held by the Kincaids, but passed to the Buchanans.

Auchleshie [NN 654072], near Callander, Stirlingshire; site only.
   Held by the Buchanans.

Balgair Castle [NS 607884], near Fintry, Stirlingshire; site of tower.
   Held by the Cunninghams of Glengarnock and by the Galbraiths of Culcreuch before passing to the Buchanans in 1605; Balgair may have also have been held by the Napiers of Gartness.

Balloch Castle [NS 386826], Balloch, Dunbartonshire; castle replaced by mansion.
   Held by the Stewarts of Lennox but then by the Buchanans of Ardoch in the nineteenth century. The present house dates from 1808 and now houses a visitor centre (01389 720620; www.lochlomond-trossachs.org).

Bardowie Castle [NS 580738], near Milngavie, Dunbartonshire; tower house.
   Held by the Galbraiths and by the Hamiltons, but passed by marriage to the Buchanans of Leny and Spittal in the eighteenth century or later.

Blairhenechan or **Blarhannachra Tower** [NS 338792], near Cardross, Dunbartonshire; mansion of Drumhead on site of tower.
   Held by the Buchanans from 1552, but passed by marriage to the Dunlops, who added Buchanan to their name. The family, now Buchanan-Dunlop of Drumhead still apparently lives here.

Blairvadach Castle [NS 263853], near Rhu and Gare Loch, Dunbartonshire; mansion and site of tower.
   Held by MacAulays of Ardincaple but was bought by Andrew Buchanan, a Glasgow merchant, around the end of the eighteenth century.

Boturich Castle [NS 387845], near Balloch, Dunbartonshire; mansion incorporating castle.
   Held by the Haldanes of Gleneagles and then by the Buchanans of Ardoch from 1792 until the 1850s. Holiday accommodation is available (www.scottscastles.com).

Carbeth House [NS 524876], near Killearn, Stirlingshire; mansion and site of castle.
   Held by the Buchanans from 1476, and they built a castle, but Carbeth passed to the Wilsons in the nineteenth century. The building was remodelled as a castellated mansion in 1840.

Carrick House [HY 567384], island of Eday, Orkney; fine seventeenth-century house.
   Held by John Stewart, Earl of Carrick (hence the name of the house) and Lord Kinclaven, but on his death passed to the Buchanans, then to the Feas, and then to the Laings and to the Hebdens. Open to the public June to September, Sundays: telephone or check website (01857 622260; www.eday.orkney. sch.uk/tourism/carricktour/index.htm) to confirm.

Catter Castle [NS 473871], near Drymen, Stirlingshire; site of castle on impressive motte.

Held by the Earls of Lennox and then by the Buchanans but passed to the Graham Dukes of Montrose. Catter House may incorporate part of an old building but mostly dates from the eighteenth century.

Craigend Castle [NS 545778], near Milngavie, Dunbartonshire; site of castle and mansion.

Long held by the Grahams, but passed to the Smiths, to the Inglis family, and then to the Buchanans in the nineteenth century, and then to the Wilsons. Described as a splendid edifice, the whole building was demolished in the twentieth century.

Craigievern Castle [NS 495902], near Drymen, Stirlingshire; site of castle and later house.

Held by the Buchanans.

Dalmarnock [NS 615628], Glasgow; castle or old house replaced by mansion.

Held by the Grays, but passed to the Buchanans of Ardoch, who built the mansion about 1800. It was later remodelled, and the property went to the Grahams. The Woddrops also held part of the lands.

Drumpellier House [NS 716650], near Coatbridge, Lanarkshire; site of castle or old house.

Held by the Hamiltons and then by the Colquhouns, before passing to the Buchanans in 1735. Andrew Buchanan, a Glasgow tobacco baron, was Lord Provost of Glasgow in 1740: Buchanan Street in Glasgow is named after him. Drumpellier passed to the Stirlings, but was bought back by the Buchanans, and there is a burial ground [NS 712647] for the family. The house was later demolished and the site is occupied by housing. The grounds are a country park after being given to the people of Airdrie by the Buchanans in 1919 (www.northlan.gov.uk).

Drumquhassle Castle [NS 483869], near Drymen, Stirlingshire; site of castle.

Held by the Dennistouns but passed by marriage to the Buchanans, and then went to the Cunninghams in the sixteenth century or before, and then to others.

Dunglass Castle [NS 436735], near Dumbarton; ruined castle.

Held by the Colquhouns of Luss and by the Edmonstones before passing to the Buchanans in 1812, and they remodelled and extended the building. May be in a dangerous condition.

Gartincaber House [NN 698001], near Doune, Stirlingshire; mansion incorporating tower.

Held by the Buchanans from the fifteenth to the eighteenth centuries, when Gartincaber went to the Macphersons and then to the Murdochs.

Grandhome House or Dilspro [NJ 899117], near Dyce, Aberdeenshire; mansion on site of castle.

Held by several families including by the Buchanans at one time, but passed to the Gordons and then to others. The mansion incorporates some old work.

Northbar or Oldbar [NS 481693], near Renfrew; castle replaced by mansion.

Held by the several families before coming from the Semples to the Buchanans in 1798; it was sold to the Stewarts in 1812.

Ross Priory [NS 415877], near Balloch, Dunbartonshire; mansion on site of castle.

Held by the Buchanans of Ross until 1925. Visited by Sir Walter Scott, and now owned by the University of Strathclyde. The descendants of this branch of the family are now Leith-Buchanans, Baronets, and they now apparently live in the United States. Accommodation is available at Ross Priory and the grounds are occasionally open to the public (0141 548 3565; www.rescat.strath.ac.uk/priory_accom.html/ www.gardensofscotland.org).

Scotscraig [NO 445283], near Tayport, Fife; castle replaced by mansion.

Held by several families, including by the Ramsays and then by the Buchanans at one time, then passed to the Erskines and to others.

Sound [HY 475165], Shapinsay, Orkney; site only.

A house of the Buchanans was burnt to the ground in 1746 by Hanoverian troops. A later mansion, Balfour Castle, was built after the property had passed to the Balfours, and can be visited (01856 711282; www.balfourcastle.co.uk).

www.buchanansociety.com
No. of castles/sites: 27
Rank: 47=/764
Xref: MacAuslan

Bulmer

The name may come from the parish of that name in North Yorkshire in England, and the family held land in Lanarkshire. The name is on record in Scotland from the twelfth century.

Glenochar Castle [NS 946139], two miles south of Elvanfoot, was a small tower house, dating from the middle of the sixteenth century and the building was occupied for about two hundred years. Glenochar was held by the Bulmer family, and a hoard of sixteenth-century coins was found near the buildings.

Glengonnar Castle [NS 899201], four miles north of Leadhills, was also held by the family. They made their living from mining lead and gold.

No. of castles/sites: 2
Rank: 396=/764

Burdon

The name probably comes from the place Burdon in County Durham, and the name is first on record in Scotland from the middle of the thirteenth century.

James, and his son John, Burden murdered Duncan MacGregor at Dundurn in 1549, for which they were respited, and John went on to acquire the lands of **Auchingarrich** [NN 788195], two miles south and east of Comrie in Perthshire. It is not clear if there was a castle here. The family were also in possession of **Easter Feddal** in 1647. **Feddal Castle** (or House) [NN 824089] is now ruinous, but it dated from the seventeenth century and stood a mile or so south-west of Braco in Perthshire. The stable and staff quarters have been renovated and can be rented as holiday accommodation (01764 663071; www.duchally.com).

No. of castles/sites: 2
Rank: 396=/764
Xref: Burden

Burnett

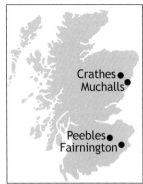

The name is derived from the Old English 'beaorn-heard', which means 'brave warrior'. The Bur-nard family were recorded in Scotland in the eleventh century, and they became major landowners in the Borders and in Aberdeen-shire.

Fairnington [NT 646280], three and a half miles north of Jedburgh in the old county of Roxburgh in the Borders, was held by the Burnetts from the twelfth century for about two hundred years. It passed to the Hepburns of Bothwell and they built the existing tower house which is built into Fairnington House; but the property later went to Frances Stewart, Earl of Bothwell, and then to the Rutherfords. This house is occupied as a private residence.

The family also held several properties and towers around Peebles in Tweeddale in the Borders:
Barns Tower [NT 215391]; tower house of three storeys.
    Held by the Burnetts and first built about 1498. One of John Buchan's early novels is called *John Burnet of Barns*. There is a later mansion nearby, built in 1773. The tower can be rented

Barns Tower (M&R)

as holiday accommodation and the gardens are occasionally open to the public (0845 090 0194; www.vivat.org.uk/ www.gardensofscotland.org).
Carlops [NT 161560]; site of tower.
    Held by the Burnetts in 1675.
Castlehill Tower [NT 214354]; ruined tower house, abandoned 1840.
    Held by several families including by the Douglas Earls of March but was sold to the Burnetts of Barns in 1729, who in 1838 sold the property to the Tweedies of Quarter.
Woodhouse Hill or Manor [NT 211370]; site only.
    Held by the Inglis family and then by the Pringles and then by the Burnetts of Barns in the late sixteenth century.
The Burnetts also held **Gadgirth House** [NS 409223]; near Ayr, in the nineteenth century. A mansion was built in the site of castle, but this house was completely demolished in 1968.

The Burnetts also held considerable estates in Kincardineshire and in Aberdeenshire. Alan Burnett was the Protestant Bishop of Aberdeen in 1663, and then Archbishop of Glasgow in 1664 and of St Andrews in 1679.

Pride of place has to go to the magnificent **Crathes Castle** [NO 734968], which is one of the finest surviving castles in Scotland. Crathes is a massive sixteenth-century tower house of four storeys and an attic, and it

Crathes Castle (RWB)

stands three miles east of Banchory in Aberdeenshire. The lower part of the tower is very plain while the upper works are a mass of corbels, turrets, chimneys and gables. There is a small wing and a beautiful walled garden. The interior of the castle is also very interesting with fine contemporary painted tempera ceilings and a magnificent fireplace in the hall.

The lands were held by the Burnetts of Leys from the fourteenth century. The Burnetts had an earlier stronghold on an island in the **Loch of Leys** [NO 700980]. This was used until 1543 when Alexander Burnett of Leys married Janet Hamilton, and with her came a sizeable dowry, the wealth needed to build Crathes. The old castle was reputedly haunted. Alexander Burnett originally fell in love with Bertha, a relative who was staying at Loch of Leys. His mother, Agnes, wanted a more advantageous match for her son and poisoned Bertha. Agnes was then apparently frightened to death by a spectre of Bertha, and a ghost is said to still appear on the anniversary of Bertha's death.

If that was not enough ghostly manifestations, Crathes Castle is also said to be haunted by a Green

Lady. The story goes back to the seventeenth century when a young woman found herself pregnant. She disappeared but then there were reports of an apparition being seen in what is now called the Green Lady's room. The ghost would be seen crossing the floor with a bundle in its arms, and was seen repeatedly, including in modern times. A further gruesome detail is that, when workmen were renovating the chamber, the small skeleton of a baby was found beneath the hearthstone of the fireplace. Some stories have the ghost appearing at times of misfortune or death in the family.

The family supported Robert the Bruce, and were given the jewelled ivory 'Horn of Leys', which is still on display at Crathes. The Burnetts were made Baronets of Nova Scotia in 1626, although this title is now dormant. The Burnetts held the castle and lands until they were given to The National Trust for Scotland in 1951. Crathes is open to the public from April until September (01330 844525; www.nts.org.uk).

Muchalls Castle [NO 892908], some four miles north and east of Stonehaven in Kincardineshire, is a well-

Muchalls Castle (RWB)

preserved and imposing courtyard castle, which dates from the seventeenth century. An L-plan block and wall enclose the courtyard, and there are fine plaster ceilings and a large fireplace dated 1624. The castle was built by the Burnetts. James VIII, the Old Pretender, stayed here in 1716 during the Jacobite Rising. It was used as a hotel for some years, then was put up for sale in 1997 for an asking price of offers over £650,000. Like Crathes, this castle is also said to be haunted by a Green Lady. There are stories that the old castle had a tunnel, which led about a mile to the sea at Gin Shore. The cave was used for smuggling, but one day, while a young woman awaited her lover, she fell into the water and was drowned. Her apparition has been reported on several occasions – or so the story goes.

Other properties held by the Burnetts in the north-east of Scotland:
Cobairdy [NJ 575438], near Huntly, Aberdeenshire; mansion on the site of a castle.
Built by the Murrays put passed to the Burnetts.

Countesswells [NJ 871043], near Aberdeen; mansion on site of castle.
Held by the Sandilands, then by the Burnetts and by the Gammills. The mansion dates from about 1700.
Craigmyle House [NJ 637019], near Banchory, Aberdeenshire; mansion and castle blown up by the owner in 1960.
Held by the Burnetts in the sixteenth and seventeenth centuries, but had passed to the Shaws Barons Craigmyle, who held it in the nineteenth century.
Ecclesgreig or St Cyrus [NO 738659], near Montrose, Angus; mansion on site of castle.
Held by the Burnetts from late in the seventeenth century, but the name was changed to Ecclesgreig by the Forsyth Grants (www.ecclesgreig.com).
Elrick House [NJ 883183], near New Machar, Aberdeenshire; castle replaced by mansion.
Held by the Innes family and then by the Burnetts, owners in the nineteenth century.
Glenbervie House [NO 769805], near Stonehaven, Kincardineshire; mansion incorporating castle.
Held by several families, including by the Melvilles, before coming to the Burnetts from 1675 until 1721 when Glenbervie was sold to the Nicholsons.
Kair House [NO 769765], near Arbuthnott, Kincardineshire; castle replaced by mansion.
Held by the Sibbalds and by the Guthries, and then by the Burnetts at one time, and then later by the Kinlochs.
Kemnay House [NJ 733154], near Inverurie, Aberdeenshire; mansion incorporating tower house.
Held by the Douglases and then by the Crombies, and then by the Burnetts in 1688. Thomas Burnett of Leys was a staunch Hanoverian, but while travelling through Paris his Jacobite enemies had him imprisoned in the Bastille.
Monboddo House [NO 744783], near Laurencekirk, Kincardineshire; mansion incorporating tower house.
Held by the Barclays, by the Strachans and by the Irvines, and then by the Burnetts after 1635. James Burnett, Lord Monboddo, wrote *The Origin and Progress of Man and Language*. He died in 1799. Dr Johnson and Boswell had visited Monboddo in 1773, as did Robert Burns some years later. The house was restored in the 1970s.
Old Kendal [NJ 838225], near Inverurie, Aberdeenshire; site only.
Held by the Burnetts.
Powis House [NJ 939081], Old Aberdeen; castle replaced by mansion.
Held by the Frasers and by the Lindsays, then by the Burnetts in 1781 and they held the property until 1866 or later. The house is now a community centre and a housing estate was built in the grounds in the 1930s.
Tillycairn Castle [NJ 664114], near Kemnay, Aberdeenshire; fine restored L-plan tower house.
Held by several families and then by the Burnetts after 1580, although it then later went to the Gordons. The castle was restored in the 1980s.

home.pacbell.net/roothub/
No. of castles/sites: 21
Rank: 63=/764
Xrefs: Burnett; Burnard

Burns

The name was originally Burness, and in Scotland probably comes from places such as Burnhouse or Burnside. The name is recorded from the sixteenth century. Robert Burns, Scotland's most renowned poet, was originally known as Burness, but when his family moved to Ayrshire the name was changed to Burns, to which Robert agreed in 1786. In the nineteenth century the Burns family held two properties in central Scotland. **Kilmahew Castle** [NS 352787], one mile north of Cardross in Dunbartonshire, is a ruined keep, dating from the fifteenth century, which was to be remodelled as a Gothic mansion, although the work was never completed. A new house was built close by. George and James Burns were pioneers of steam-powered vessels, and (along with Samuel Cunard) established the Cunard Shipping Company. The lands were held by James Burns in 1859, he built the new house and he died here. Kilmahew had previously been owned by the Napiers.

Not much remains of **Cumbernauld Castle** [NS 773759], in the town of Cumbernauld in central Scotland, and the old stronghold was replaced by Cumbernauld House. The mansion was owned for some years by the Burnses of Kilmahew, after the estate long being a possession of the Flemings and then of the Elphinstones; the building now houses offices.

No. of castles/sites: 2 / Rank: 396=/764
Xref: Burness

Burrell

The name probably originates from Burrill in North Yorkshire, and members of the Burrell family are found in the Borders from the twelfth century. Sir William Burrell, who died in 1958, was a Glasgow shipowner who acquired many works of art and other artefacts, which formed the basis of the Burrell Collection, which is open to the public all year (0141 287 2550; www.glasgow museums.com). **Eckford** [NT 709261], four miles south and west of Kelso and not far from the English border in the Borders, was a property of the Burrells, but passed to the Scotts in the fifteenth century. There was a tower house, nothing of which survives, but this was probably built after the property had passed to the Scotts. The tower was burnt by the English in 1554 and in 1570.

home.pacbell.net/roothub/
No. of castles/sites: 1 / Rank: 537=/764

Butter

It is possible that the name comes from 'bothar', the Gaelic for 'cattle road', although more prosaically it may be from places, such as Buttergask or Butterlaw. It may also be from 'bittern', a bird whose name in Scots is 'butter'. The family held lands in Perthshire from the twelfth century.

Faskally [NN 917601], two miles north of Pitlochry, was long held by the Butters, perhaps coming to them in the twelfth century, although it is recorded as also being held by the Robertsons. In 1598 Patrick Butter of Faskally was accused of besieging Ashintully Castle, and then imprisoning Andrew Spalding. The new house was built for Lieutenant Colonel Archibald Butter, who served in the British army in the Crimean War. Faskally House is an attractive mansion, dating from 1829 and was designed by William Burn. The property was sold in 1911, and it is now owned by the Scottish Executive and used as an outdoor centre.

Gormok [NO 144464] (or Gormack) is a couple of miles west and north of Blairgowrie, and there was a tower house or castle here, nothing of which apparently survives. One of the family, John Butter of Gormok, was outlawed for his part in the notorious murder of George Drummond of Ledcrieff in 1554.

The Butters bought the lands of Pitlochry from the Stewarts of Ballechin in 1600. This branch of the family still flourishes as the Butters of Pitlochry, and they still apparently live near the town.

No. of castles/sites: 2
Rank: 396=/764

Byres

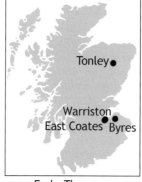

The name comes from the lands of Byres, a couple of miles north of Haddington in East Lothian, and is on record from the beginning of the fourteenth century. The property was held by the Byres family, but passed to the Lindsays of the Byres, and this branch of the Lindsays eventually became Earls. There are some remains of a castle [NT 495770] at **Byres**.

East Coates House [NT 241734], which now stands in the shadow of the impressive St Mary's Episcopal Cathedral in the centre of Edinburgh, is a pocket-sized L-plan tower house, dating from the seventeenth century. The house was built by Sir John Byres in 1615, who was Provost of Edinburgh and he was buried in

East Coates House (M&R)

Greyfriars Kirkyard. The house is in good condition, and is now the Episcopal Church's Theological Institute.

Warriston [NT 253757], to the north of Edinburgh, was held by the Kincaids, and then by the Byres family for some years, before passing to the Graingers. There was castle, replaced by a mansion, and a cemetery was laid out in the grounds.

The senior branch of the family became the Byres of Tonley. **Tonley House** [NJ 611135] is a large baronial mansion, which is now an impressive ruin. It stands three miles east of Alford in Aberdeenshire, and there was probably an old stronghold here. The Byreses of Tonley were Jacobites, and Major Patrick Byres had to flee to France after defeat at the Battle of Culloden in 1746. His son, James Byres, was a noted architect and antiquarian, and only returned to Tonley in 1790. The property passed to the Moirs by marriage, but they took the name Moir Byres. The lands were only sold by the family in 1947.

No. of castles/sites: 4
Rank: 278=/764

Caddell

The name is probably a variation of Calder, although there is a place Caddell, which is two or so miles south-west of Dalry in Ayrshire, so the name may be territorial. Francis C.B. Cadell is a well-known painter and one of the Scottish Colourists; he died in 1937.

Grange House [NT 015815], in Bo'ness in central Scotland, was an altered L-plan tower house of the sixteenth century when it was demolished in 1906, and

Grange House (M&R)

a stair-turret was built into the Grange at Linlithgow. The lands were held by the Hamiltons but were bought by the Caddells in 1788, now represented by the Cadells of Grange and Cockenzie, who apparently live at the Grange.

No. of castles/sites: 1 / Rank: 537=/764

Caird

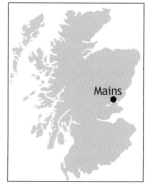

The name means an artist or craftsman, and later a travelling tinker; and the name is recorded in Scotland in the thirteenth century.

To the north of Dundee, **Mains Castle** [NO 410330], a courtyard castle dating from the fifteenth century, was held by the Caird family in the nineteenth century after having a succession of owners, including the Grahams who built the castle. The building was given to the city of Dundee and has been restored, while the grounds are a public park.

No. of castles/sites: 1 / Rank: 537=/764

Cairncross

The name is territorial and comes from Cairncross, the name of lands in Glenesk in Angus, although there is also a Cairncross near Coldingham in the Borders. The name is recorded in Scotland from the fourteenth century, and the family name Cairns may be a contraction of Cairncross. The family held lands in Glen Esk in Angus, and they may have had a castle or seat at or near **Cairncross** [NO 498795], twelve miles north and west of Brechin. They were in possession from 1230 or earlier until at least 1486. Thomas Cairncross and his wife may be buried in St Mary's Church in Dundee. **Balmashanner** [NO 461489], one mile south of Forfar also in Angus, was owned by the family from 1371 until 1491 or later. There was a castle, although apparently no remains survive; one of the family was Robert Cairncross, Abbot of Holyrood, Bishop of Ross, and Lord High Treasurer.

The Cairncrosses also had lands in the Borders, which may have been given to them by the Robert Cairncross mentioned above. **Colmslie Tower** [NT 513396], three miles north-east of Galashiels, is a very ruinous tower house, which was probably built by the family after Colmslie had passed to them from the Borthwicks. The Cairncrosses were apparently forfeited in 1571, perhaps because they supported Mary, Queen of Scots, and the lands later went to the Pringles. **Hillslap Tower** [NT 513394], only a short distance away, was also held by the family, and is an L-plan tower house and courtyard, and dates from the sixteenth century. The walls are pierced by gunloops; and it stands not far from Colmslie. Sir Walter Scott used Hillslap in his novel *The Monastery*, calling it 'Glendearg'. The tower was reroofed and restored in the 1980s. There was also a tower house at **Redpath** [NT 585358], two miles south of Earlston in the Borders, which was also known as Cairncross's Tower. There are no remains.

No. of castles/sites: 5
Rank: 240=/764
Xref: Cairns

Hillslap Tower (M&R)

Cairns

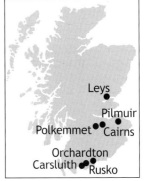

The name is most likely territorial and comes from the lands of Cairns, which are near Mid Calder to the west of Edinburgh. The name is first recorded in a charter of 1359, and the family held property in different parts of southern Scotland. Cairns may also be a contraction of Cairncross (and also see that name).

Cairns Tower [NT 091604] is some six and a half miles west and south of Balerno, and is a ruined fifteenth-century keep with a later wing. It was held by the family, but passed to the Crichtons, then to the Tennants in the middle of the sixteenth century. This castle may also have been known as East Cairns Castle, although this may refer to another stronghold nearby.

Pilmuir House [NT 486695], three and a half miles south-west of Haddington in East Lothian, is a fine seventeenth-century T-plan house with harled and whitewashed walls. There is a walled garden, and a doocot with more than 900 nesting boxes. Pilmuir was built by William Cairns and Agnes Brown, who are buried in Bolton Kirkyard. The property passed by marriage to the Borthwicks in the middle of the seventeenth century and perhaps also to the Binning family; the house is a private residence, although the gardens are occasionally open to the public (www.gardensofscotland.org).

One and a half miles west of Whitburn was **Polkemmet House** [NS 925650], a mansion which incorporated a house or castle dating from 1620 or earlier. The house has been completely demolished and the grounds are now a country park. The lands were held by the Cairns but passed to the Shaws and then to the Baillies.

The Cairns also held lands in the south-west of Scotland. **Carsluith Castle** [NX 495542], three and a half miles south of Creetown in Galloway, is an L-plan tower house which dates from the fifteenth century. The lands were held by the Cairnses, but passed to the Lindsays in 1460 and then went by marriage to the Browns. The castle is in the care of Historic Scotland and is apparently open to the public.

Orchardton Tower [NX 817551], four miles south of Dalbeattie in Galloway, is a unique free-standing round tower house, first built in the fifteenth century by the Cairns family. One of the family was present at the murder of MacLellan of Bombie, along with Gordon of Lochinvar, in the High Street of Edinburgh in 1527. Ordchardton passed by marriage to the Maxwells about 1550. The building is now ruinous, is in the care of Historic Scotland, and is open to the public all year. There was also castle or tower house nearby at **Glenshinnoch** [NX 811532], which had its own park, and was also held by the Cairns family. The old building was replaced by Orchardton House in the middle of the

Orchardton Tower (LF) – see previous page

eighteenth century, after the lands had passed to the Maxwells.

Rusko Castle [NX 584605], three miles north of Gatehouse of Fleet also in Galloway, is a fifteenth-

Rusko Castle (M&R)

century tower of three storeys, to which had been added a wing although this has been demolished. Rusko was held by the Cairns until it passed by marriage to the Gordons of Lochinvar early in the sixteenth century. The castle was restored in the 1970s and is still occupied.

At **Torr** [NX 814523], six miles south of Dalbeattie, was a tower or old house, which was replaced by a mansion in the eighteenth century, itself now mostly gone. This was in turn replaced by what is now **Torr House** [NX 801529]. Torr was a property of the Cairns family from the Reformation until 1817.

Leys [NO 262240], ten or so miles west of Dundee, was also a Cairns property, but it passed to the Hays of Leys around 1650.

No. of castles/sites: 9
Rank: 149=/764

72

Calder

The name is probably territorial in origin, although Calder is a common place name, and means 'little stream'. A family of that name are on record from the twelfth century.

Nairn Castle [NH 885566] dated from the twelfth century, and was built by William the Lion. The keepers of the castle were the Calders as Thanes of Cawdor, and this is another place where according to tradition Duncan was killed by Macbeth. The castle was garrisoned by the English in 1308 during the Wars of Independence. There are no remains and the site is in Constabulary Gardens in the burgh of Nairn in Inverness-shire.

One of the most splendid castles in Scotland, **Cawdor Castle** [NH 847499] lies some five miles south-west of Nairn. The Calders built much of the present building with a large but plain keep of four storeys, dating from the fourteenth century, and a courtyard enclosing ranges of buildings. The castle is reached across a ditch by a drawbridge.

The Calders had an earlier stronghold [NH 858512], but decided to build a splendid new castle. A site had to be chosen, and a donkey was allowed to roam at will until it came to a suitable spot. Cawdor is also built over a tree, the remains of which survive in the vaulted basement. It was long believed to be a hawthorn, but

Cawdor Castle (RWB)

in fact it proved to be a holly tree and it died in about 1372, when the castle was built.

The first Thane of Cawdor had taken the name of Calder/Cawdor when granted the lands by Alexander II in 1236, although one story is that the family were descended from a brother of Macbeth. Duncan, of course, was not murdered at Cawdor, as in Shakespeare's Scottish play. The castle is not nearly old enough, and Duncan was actually killed after a battle near Spynie. The third Thane of Cawdor, however, was murdered by Sir Alexander Rait of nearby Rait Castle.

The Calders were not to enjoy their splendid castle for long. The Campbells obtained Cawdor by kidnapping the girl heiress, Muriel Calder, and marrying her at the age of twelve to the Earl of Argyll's son, Sir John Campbell, in 1511. Campbell of Inverliver led the kidnapping, and lost all six of his sons in the resultant chase as the Calders sought to recover the girl. The property is still held by the Campbells, and the castle is open to the public from May until mid-October (01667 404401; www.cawdorcastle.com).

Asloun Castle [NJ 543149], two miles south and west of Alford in Aberdeenshire, was a Z-plan tower house of the sixteenth century, but little remains. Asloun was built by the Calders, but passed to the Forbeses.

Aswanley House [NJ 445397], seven miles west of Huntly also in Aberdeenshire, was held by the Cruickshanks and then by the Gordons, then from 1440 by the Calders, but it had to be sold in 1768 to the Duffs of Braco because of debt. The house can be used as a venue for weddings and holiday accommodation is available (01466 700262; www.aswanley.com).

No. of castles/sites: 4
Rank: 278=/764
Xref: Codwell

Calderwood

The name is territorial in origin, and comes from the lands of Calderwood, which are one mile north-east of East Kilbride to the south of Glasgow. The name is on record from the end of the thirteenth century.

The lands of **Calderwood** [NS 658560] were held by the family from the thirteenth century or earlier, but passed to the Maxwells of Calderwood in 1363 and the Maxwells held Calderwood for 500 years or more. There was a castle, but most of this has been demolished, while some of the outbuildings were incorporated into a mansion.

Pitteadie Castle [NT 257891], three miles north and east of Burntisland in Fife, was held by the Calderwoods in 1671 after being owned by several families, including by the Boswells of Balmuto. There was a strong keep, dating from the fifteenth century but later altered, along with a courtyard, but the castle is now ruinous.

Kingswells House [NJ 862064] is a couple of miles east of Westhill to the west of Aberdeen, and the present mansion dates from the middle of the seventeenth century. It was held by the Jaffreys from 1587 and then by the Edmonds, but later passed to the Calderwoods. The house was recently put up for sale for offers over £650,000.

No. of castles/sites: 3
Rank: 328=/764

Caldwell

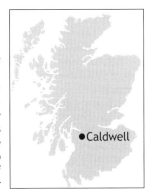

The name comes from the old English 'cealdwielle', which means (perhaps unsurprisingly) 'cold stream, spring or well'. There are many places with this name in Scotland, but the family name is likely to come from the lands of Caldwell, which are four miles west of Neilston in Renfrewshire in western Scotland.

Caldwell Tower [NS 422551] is a small three-storey tower house, mostly dating from the sixteenth century, although it probably incorporates earlier work. It was held by the Caldwells in 1342, but passed to the Mures after 1419 who held it, apart from one brief interlude, for hundreds of years and even into the twentieth century.

No. of castles/sites: 1
Rank: 537=/764

Callendar

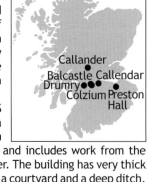

The name is territorial and comes from the lands of Callendar or Callander in Stirlingshire. The family are mentioned in the middle of the thirteenth century.

Callendar House [NS 898794], in Falkirk, is a massive ornate mansion with towers and turrets, and includes work from the fifteenth century or earlier. The building has very thick walls, and there was once a courtyard and a deep ditch. The property was held by the Callendar family from 1244 or earlier, but the family supported Edward Balliol and were forfeited in 1345. The lands were given to the Livingstones, who secured their position further by marrying the daughter of the last lord. The mansion is in the care of the local council and is open to the public (01324 503770; www.falkirk. gov.uk/cultural/).

Several other properties were held by the Callendars and also passed to the Livingstones. **Balcastle** [NS 702782], a mile or so west of Kilsyth in central Scotland, consisted of a castle on a motte; while **Drumry Castle** [NS 515710], two miles east and south of Duntocher, was a tower house but this has been demolished. **Colzium Castle** [NS 729788], also near Kilsyth, is very ruinous but there are some remains of an L-plan tower house dating from the sixteenth century. The castle was replaced by a nearby mansion, and the gardens at Colzium are open to the public (01236 624031; www.northlan.gov.uk).

Two miles east of Stirling is **Manor Castle** [NS 827948], although again little survives of a T-plan tower house. It was held by the Callendars from 1479 but had passed to the Dundas family by 1729.

Preston Hall [NT 394658], three and a half miles east of Dalkeith in Midlothian, is an imposing but elegant classical mansion with a main block and pavilions. It dates from 1790 but was remodelled in 1832. The lands were purchased from the Gordons by Alexander Callander in 1789, a descendant of the Callanders of Westertown, who had made a fortune in India. His descendants still apparently live at the mansion, the Burn-Callanders of Preston Hall.

No. of castles/sites: 6
Rank: 212=/764
Xref: Callander

Cambo

The name is territorial and comes from the lands of Cambo, one mile south of Kingsbarns in the far east of Fife. The family are on record from the thirteenth century.

Cambo House [NO 604115] is a classical mansion which was rebuilt after a fire in 1878, but it stands on or near the site of a castle. It was held by the Cambo family from 1225 or earlier. Walter Cambo was warden of the county of Fife in 1294 and Sir John Cambo was summarily executed by the English at Newcastle in 1306. The lands had passed to the Morton or Myrton family by 1364 and then much later went to the Erskines. The gardens of Cambo are sometimes open to the public (01333 450313; www.cambo estate.com).

Baledgarno (which is pronounced 'Balegarnie') Castle [NO 276304], two and a half miles west of Longforgan in Perthshire, was built in the twelfth century by Edgar King of Scots, but it was held by the Cambo (or by the Cameron) family until 1365 or later. Baledgarno was visited by Edward I of England in 1296. The site of the castle may be at Castlehill, a farmhouse which may incorporate some of the sixteenth- or seventeenth-century Edgar House. The property was held by the Grays in the fifteenth century and then later by the Fotheringhams.

No. of castles/sites: 2
Rank: 396=/764
Xref: Cambous

Cameron

The name has two origins, one derived from place names, found in Edinburgh, in Fife and in the Lennox. The Highland derivation is from the Gaelic 'cam-sron', which means 'wry or hooked nose' as members of the clan were reportedly blessed with such a deformed neb. Another legend is that they were descended from Camchron, a king of Denmark, although this is perhaps less likely.

John Cameron was Bishop of Glasgow and Chancellor of Scotland in 1426, and he rebuilt Glasgow Castle. His ghost is said to haunt Bedlay Castle, and the apparition of a large bearded man was reported at Bedlay in the 1970s. Richard Cameron is known as the 'Lion of the Covenant', and was an extreme Presbyterian reformer; his followers became known as the Cameronians. He repudiated the authority of the king with the Sanquhar Declaration in 1680, but was slain the same year at Airds Moss. His heads and hands were hacked off and then tried in Edinburgh in absence of the rest of his corpse.

The clan was a confederation of different families that was united as the Camerons around 1400. The clan held the lands of Lochiel, which lie to the north and east of Fort William in the west of the Highlands. The clan had a long and bitter feud with the Mackintoshes and Clan Chattan. The chiefs of the Camerons were descended from the Macgillonies and the Camerons of Baledgarno, and Donald Dubh married the heiress of the MacMartins of Letterfinlay, uniting the clan. **Baledgarno** (pronounced 'Balegarnie') **Castle** [NO 276304], is two and a half miles west of Longforgan in Angus, and was held by the Camerons or by the Cambo family in the thirteenth century. It later passed to the Grays and then to the Fotheringhams.

Ewan Cameron, thirteenth chief, was the first to be styled 'of Lochiel' in the 1490s. The Camerons had a castle or seat on **Eilean nan Craobh** [NN 090763], an island in Loch Eil, but their main stronghold became **Tor Castle** [NN 133786], which lies three miles northeast of Fort William in Lochaber in the Highlands. This is said to have been the stronghold of Banquo, of *Macbeth* fame. The lands were held by the Mackintoshes, but were seized by the Camerons, who built the massive tower house and courtyard, although there had been a castle here from the eleventh century. Ewan sided with the MacDonald Lord of the Isles in fighting with the Frasers in 1544, and he was later taken prisoner by the Earl of Huntly and was beheaded at Elgin. The castle was used as a refuge from the attacks of the MacDonalds of Keppoch.

In the seventeenth century, the main seat of the chiefs became **Achnacarry** [NN 175878], nine miles north-east of Fort William and near Spean Bridge. The seventeenth chief, Sir Ewan, was a committed Jacobite and fought at Killiecrankie in 1689, although an old man. He sounds a fearsome fellow: some thirty years earlier he had killed a man by tearing out his throat with his teeth. The next chief fought in the 1715 Jacobite Rising and was forfeited. Donald Cameron, nineteenth chief and known as the 'Gentle Lochiel', joined the Jacobite Rising of 1745-46, albeit reluctantly and later regretfully, and fought at the Battle of Culloden in 1746, where he was wounded. He escaped into exile but died in France a year later; his brother Archibald was executed in 1753 after being involved in Jacobite plotting. The lands of the Camerons were ravaged by the forces of Butcher Cumberland, and the house at Achnacarry was sacked and torched. The Camerons recovered the property in 1784, and in 1802 built a new house, which is still apparently occupied by Cameron of Lochiel, now the twenty-sixth chief. The house is not open to the public, but there is a museum in a converted cottage at Achnacarry, with information on the Camerons (01397 712090; www.clan-cameron.org).

Strome Castle [NG 862354], four miles south-west of Lochcarron in Ross and Cromarty, is now a shattered ruin, although it is in a lovely position guarding the former crossing and ferry. The Camerons of Lochiel held the stronghold for some years, but it was seized by the Earl of Huntly in 1503. Strome was blown up with gunpowder in 1602 after a long siege, although by then the castle was held by the MacDonalds of Glengarry. The site is now owned by The National Trust for Scotland (01599 566325) and the site is accessible.

www.clan-cameron.org

No. of castles/sites: 5
Rank: 240=/764

Campbell

The name is from Gaelic and is from 'Caimbeul', which means 'wry or crooked mouth', which could refer to a physical feature or perhaps a propensity to be less than honest. The name may originally have been a nickname and simply described the physical characteristic of an early progenitor of the clan. The Campbells are believed to have originally been known as Clan Duibhne or O'Duine from Diarmid O'Duine of Lochow (Lochawe), but the name Campbell comes on record from the middle of the thirteenth century. The clan were settled in Argyll in and around Loch Awe, where the MacDougalls of Lorn were pre-eminent. Neil Campbell supported Robert the Bruce, and married Bruce's sister, while the MacDougalls were on the side of John Balliol and the Comyn faction. When Bruce made himself undisputed king, the MacDougalls' power was greatly reduced and the Campbells benefited. While the Campbells prospered so did the MacDonalds, later Lords of the Isles, who also supported Bruce. When the Lords of the Isles was forfeited in 1493, more lands came into the hands of the Campbells until they held most of what is now Argyll, often at the expense of smaller and less-powerful clans.

Innis Chonnel Castle [NM 976119] stands on a wooded island in Loch Awe, some fourteen miles east of Kilmartin in Argyll. The building is an impressive ruin with a thick outer wall. Innis Chonnel was the original stronghold of the Campbells, perhaps from the eleventh century or earlier, and was the seat of Mac Cailean Mor, Sir Colin Campbell of Lochow, who was killed at the Red Ford of Lorn in 1296 fighting the MacDougalls. John MacDougall held the castle against Robert the Bruce in 1308, but Sir Neil Campbell, son of Colin, was a supporter and friend of the Bruce, and fought at Bannockburn in 1314. Campbell married Bruce's sister, Mary; and Sir Colin Campbell of Lochow fought in Ireland on the side of Edward Bruce. Sir Duncan Campbell was made Lord Campbell in 1445 and then his grandson, another Colin, was created Earl of Argyll in 1457. The first Earl was Lord High Chancellor of Scotland in 1483, and the clan acquired the Lordship of Lorn from the Stewarts by

Innis Chonnel Castle (M&R)

marriage. Innis Chonnel was abandoned as the Campbells' main residence for Inveraray in the fifteenth century, although it was still used as a prison. The young heir to the Lordship of the Isles, Donald, son of Angus, was imprisoned here after the Battle of Bloody Bay, off Mull, in 1484. He eventually escaped, but after invading Badenoch in 1503, he was again captured and imprisoned, this time in Edinburgh Castle, for forty years. Innis Chonnel was ruinous by the nineteenth century.

Inveraray Castle [NN 096093] stands to the north of the village of Inveraray on the east side of Loch Fyne in Argyll. There was a substantial castle, dating from the fifteenth century and rising to four storeys. This building was demolished after the present building, an imposing

Inveraray Castle 1920?

symmetrical mansion with towers and turrets, was built in 1743.

Archibald, second Earl of Argyll, was slain at the Battle of Flodden in 1513, and the fourth Earl, another Archibald, was at the forefront of the Reformation and took a prominent part in the Battle of Pinkie in 1547 and then in the siege of Haddington in 1548. James V had visited Inveraray in 1533, as did Mary, Queen of Scots, in 1563. Archibald, fifth Earl, led Mary's forces to defeat at the Battle of Langside in 1568, and was later Lord High Chancellor of Scotland. The seventh Earl, another Archibald, had several guardians when young, one of whom, John Campbell of Cawdor, was murdered by his kinsmen, and it is possible that this was an attempt to poison the young Earl. The seventh Earl went on to purchase Kintyre, which was formerly held by the MacDonalds, and the area was planted with lowlanders and much bloodshed. Archibald, eighth Earl, was made Marquis of Argyll in 1641. He led the armies that were defeated by the Marquis of Montrose at Inverlochy and at Kilsyth, both in 1645, and Inveraray Castle had been pillaged and burnt the previous year by Montrose. Montrose was defeated that year, and was then hanged, drawn and quartered in 1650, but the Earl went on to co-operate with the Cromwellian administration and was himself executed by beheading using the Maiden, an early guillotine, in 1661 after the Restoration of Charles II. Archibald, ninth Earl, was found guilty of treason and then later led an invasion of Scotland in 1685, but this failed and he was also beheaded (both the eight and the ninth Earls were buried at Kilmun – see below). Archibald, tenth Earl, was made Duke of Argyll in 1701. John, second Duke, led the Hanoverian forces at the indecisive Battle of Sheriffmuir in 1715 during the Jacobite Rising, and the Campbells continued to support the Hanoverian side. The old castle was demolished as part of Archibald, third Duke's, rebuilding of a new castle and village (which was moved from near the castle). Before succeeding to the Dukedom, Campbell had helped establish the Royal Bank of Scotland in 1727 and was its first Governor. Dr Johnson and Boswell visited Inveraray in 1773. The line of the Dukes of Argyll continues, now Sir Torquhil Ian Campbell, thirteenth Duke of Argyll and chief of the clan, and other titles held include Marquess of Kintyre and Lorne, Earl of Cowall, Viscount of Lochow and Gleyla, and many others. The Duke is also the hereditary Master of the Royal Household in Scotland.

Several ghost stories are recorded in various places about Inveraray, although these are refuted. The old castle was said to be haunted by a ghostly harper, one of Montrose's victims from the attack in 1644. The library is also reputedly haunted, and strange noises and crashes have reportedly been heard there. Other ghosts include a spectral birlinn, which is reputedly seen when one of the Campbells is near death, reportedly seen in 1913 on the death of Archibald Campbell, as well as gatherings of ravens. The ghost of a young servant, who was murdered by Jacobites, is said to haunt the MacArthur room.

The Clan Room features information of special interest to members of Clan Campbell. The castle is open to the public from April to October (01499 302203; www.inveraray-castle.com).

Kilmun was used as the burial place for many of the family (see below).

Dunstaffnage Castle [NM 882344], three and a half miles north-east of Oban, stands on a peninsula in the Firth of Lorn, also in Argyll. The castle consists of a massive curtain circling a rock and a later house within the walls. Dunstaffnage is an ancient site, and there was a stronghold here from the seventh century or earlier. It was held by the MacDougalls, but after it was seized by Robert the Bruce the Campbells of Argyll were made hereditary keepers of the castle. In 1455 the ninth Earl of Douglas fled here to seek help from the Lord of

the Isles after James II had destroyed the power of the Black Douglases. James IV visited twice, and Alexander Campbell, captain of the castle, was slain at Flodden in 1513. Archibald, ninth Earl of Argyll, burned the castle in 1685 during his rebellion, but he was captured and executed. In 1715 and 1746 government troops occupied the castle during the Jacobite Risings, and Flora MacDonald was briefly imprisoned here after helping Bonnie Prince Charlie. The castle is said to be haunted by a Green Lady, the 'Ell-maid of Dunstaffnage', and her appearance heralds events, both bad and good, in the lives of the Campbells. The Campbells moved to **Dunstaffnage House** [NM 900334], which is still apparently their residence. There is a fine ruined chapel [NM 881344] near the old castle in an atmospheric wooded setting. The chapel dates from the thirteenth century, but incorporates the Campbell burial aisle of 1740. The castle and the chapel are in the care of Historic Scotland and are open to the public (01631 562465).

Castle Campbell [NS 962994] is a picturesque partly-ruined stronghold perched up a hill half a mile north of Dollar in Clackmannan. The building is dominated by a strong keep or tower, rising to four storeys, and Castle Campbell is in one of the loveliest settings in Scotland.

Castle Campbell (RWB)

It was, however, originally known as Castle Gloom and is located by where the Burns of Care and Sorrow meet. The property was held by the Stewarts, but passed by marriage to Colin Campbell, first Earl of Argyll and Chancellor of Scotland, and he had the name changed to Castle Campbell by an Act of Parliament in 1489. John Knox stayed here in 1566. Cromwell's forces occupied the castle in 1653, and only part was restored

Dunstaffnage Castle (LF)

after a burning by General Monck in 1654. The Ogilvies are also said to have torched the castle in revenge for the burning of Airlie Castle. George, sixth Duke, sold the castle in the early nineteenth century to the Taits, who sold it in turn to the Orr family in 1859. In 1948 the castle was taken over by The National Trust for Scotland, but is administered by Historic Scotland. It is open to the public (01259 742408), and there is a fine walk up to the castle through Dollar Glen.

Argyll's Lodging [NS 793938], at the top of Castle Wynd in Stirling, is a fine fortified town house, which

Argyll's Lodging, Stirling (RWB)

dates from the seventeenth century. Gabled blocks with dormer windows surround a courtyard, and some rooms have been restored and furnished as they might have appeared when it was occupied by the Campbells. The lodging was built for the Alexanders of Menstrie, but it went to the Campbells of Argyll when the Alexanders became bankrupt; it was a useful base close to the court at Stirling Castle. The building is in the care of Historic Scotland and is open to the public (01786 431319).

Cawdor Castle [NH 847499], which is five miles south-west of Nairn in Inverness-shire, is a magnificent and stately castle with an impressive keep surrounded by a courtyard. The courtyard is defended by a ditch and drawbridge, and the castle dates from the fourteenth century. The property was long held by the Calders, but when it appeared the line was to end with the heiress Muriel Calder, the Campbells of Argyll decided to act. Campbell of Inverliver travelled from Argyll and he and his men kidnapped Muriel, although he lost all six of his sons. The girl, although treated well, was married at the age of twelve to Sir John Campbell, son of Archibald, the then Earl of Argyll, in 1511. The Campbells then acquired the property. John Campbell of Cawdor was one of the guardians of the young seventh Earl of Argyll, but he was murdered by his Campbell kinsmen in 1592. Sir James Campbell of Cawdor acquired Islay and part of Jura in 1615 and, although the MacDonalds fought to retain the lands, the Campbells eventually held both islands. The Campbells of Cawdor gave refuge to Simon, Lord Lovat, during his flight from Hanoverian troops in 1746 during the Jacobite Rising, and hid him in a secret room in the roof. Fraser was eventually caught and

Cawdor Castle (M&R)

executed. Bonnie Prince Charlie had visited the same year. The family were made Barons Cawdor in 1796 and then Earls Cawdor in 1827, and they still own the castle. A ghost in a blue velvet dress has reputedly been seen here, as has an apparition of John Campbell, first Lord Cawdor. The castle is open to the public (01667 404401; www.cawdorcastle.com).

Kilchurn Castle [NN 133276], which stands in a beautiful spot two miles west of Dalmally in Argyll, is one of the most photogenic of all Scottish castles. It is built on a peninsula (formerly an island) in Loch Awe and consists of a strong tower and a courtyard with ranges of buildings, ruinous but impressive. The lands were originally held by the MacGregors, but they went to the Campbells of Glenorchy, who were related to their kinsmen of Argyll, and they built (or perhaps rebuilt) the castle. Kilchurn was strengthened and improved after being damaged by the MacGregors at the end of the sixteenth century. The work was undertaken by Sir Duncan Campbell of Glenorchy, also known as Black Duncan of the Seven Castles, who was responsible for the construction of castles at Kilchurn, Achallader, Loch Dochart, Finlarig, Balloch (now called Taymouth) and

Kilchurn Castle (LF)

Edinample. The Campbells withstood a two-day siege in 1654 by General Middleton before Middleton retreated from Monk's Cromwellian forces. Sir John Campbell of Glenorchy acquired the extensive lands of the sixth Earl of Caithness, by foreclosing on his vast debts, and even claimed the title of Earl of Caithness. He led a bloody campaign in the north in 1680, and reportedly slew so many Sinclairs that the Campbells crossed the Wick River without getting their feet wet. This was when the song 'The Campbells are Coming' was composed. Although he failed to hold the Earldom of Caithness, he was made Earl of Breadalbane instead. Kilchurn Castle was inhabited by the Campbells until 1740 when they moved to Balloch, which is now called Taymouth. Kilchurn was, however, garrisoned by Hanoverian troops in 1745 but was unroofed by 1775. The castle was recently consolidated and repaired, is in the care of Historic Scotland and can be visited. There are regular sailings from Loch Awe pier (01866 833333); it can also be reached by foot although this is more problematic.

Taymouth Castle [NN 785466], located five miles west of Aberfeldy in Perthshire, is a large and dominating

Taymouth Castle 1922?

mansion, which was built between 1801 and 1842. It stands on the site of a stronghold then known as Balloch Castle, built by Sir Colin Campbell of Glenorchy around 1580, and the castle incorporates cellars from that building. As mentioned above, Sir John Campbell of Glenorchy was made Earl of Breadalbane in 1681, and the family were made Marquises in 1831. The castle was being used as a hotel in 1920, and in the 1980s was a school. The castle and estate were put up for sale in 1997 for offers over £5,500,000. The castle is reputedly haunted, and ghostly footsteps have been heard here. During the time it was used as a school, some students were so scared they would not stay in the building. Some accounts also have a harbinger of doom, which foretells events in the resident family.

Barcaldine Castle [NM 907405], which is four miles north of Connel in Argyll, is a well-preserved tower house, built on the L-plan in the sixteenth century. The Campbells acquired the lands in 1597, and the castle was built by Sir Duncan Campbell of Glenorchy. The castle was garrisoned in 1645 and in 1687. The Barcaldine family were involved in the murder of Sir Colin Campbell of Glenure, the Red Fox, in 1752 which features in Robert

Barcaldine Castle 1923?

Louis Stevenson's *Kidnapped*. John Campbell of Barcaldine, half brother of the Red Fox, tried James Stewart for the murder and had him hanged, although twelve of the fifteen members of the jury were Campbells. Barcaldine House [NM 965414] dates from 1707, and is a large mansion, extended down the years, and was built some distance away (hence the village of Barcaldine is not near the castle). The house is still occupied and B&B accommodation is available (01631 720219; www.barcaldinehouse.co.uk).

This branch of the Campbells were made Baronets in 1841, but by the following year the castle was already ruinous, and the property was sold. The old castle was bought back by the Campbells in 1896, and restored. The sister of the then owner, Harriet, died in the castle. Her apparition, a Blue Lady, has reputedly been seen, and it is said that on windy nights a piano can sometimes be heard. The castle is still occupied by the Campbells of Barcaldine and accommodation is available (01631 720598; www.barcaldinecastle.co.uk).

Loudoun Castle [NS 506378], one mile north of Galston in Ayrshire, is a huge ruined castellated mansion, which includes old work from a fifteenth-century castle; the mansion dated from the beginning of the nineteenth century. The property was held by the Crawfords, but passed by marriage to the Campbells in the fourteenth century, who sprung from Donald Campbell, second son of Colin Campbell of Lochaw. John Campbell, Chancellor of Scotland, was made Earl of Loudoun in 1641, and was from another branch of the family, the Campbells of Lawers in Perthshire. The castle was surrendered to General Monck for Cromwell in 1650 after a siege, during which part of the building was destroyed, but the Earl took part in an uprising in support of Charles II in 1653.

Loudoun Castle 1904?

The third Earl, Hugh, was Secretary of State for Queen Anne, and he fought for the Hanoverians at the Battle of Sheriffmuir in 1715; John, fourth Earl, was at Prestonpans in 1746. The property passed by marriage to Francis, Lord Hastings and later Viscount Loudoun, who built much of the mansion, although the family later ran out of money. The castle was used by Belgian troops during World War II, and in 1941 was accidentally torched and gutted. The castle is reputedly haunted by a Grey Lady, who was apparently seen often before the building was destroyed, and is said to have been witnessed since. The ghost of a hunting dog, with glowing eyes, is also said to roam the area. There are also tales of a ghostly piper and of a monk. The castle remains a large impressive ruin, and is now the centre piece of a theme park (01563 822296; www.loudouncastle.co.uk).

There was an older stronghold nearby at **Loudoun** [NS 516377], but it was destroyed by the Kennedy Earl of Cassillis towards the end of the fifteenth century, and the Campbells then moved to the present Loudoun Castle (see above).

The Campbells of Loudoun have a burial vault of 1622, built from the remains of the choir of Loudoun Kirk [NS 493374].

Inverawe House [NN 023316], a substantial harled and whitewashed building, incorporates a sixteenth-century tower house. It stands about one mile north-east of Taynuilt in Argyll, and was long held by the MacConnochie Campbells; Mary, Queen of Scots, is said to have visited. The house is thought to be haunted by a Green Lady, said to be the ghost of Mary Cameron of Callart (although she has been called Green Jean), who married the then laird, Diarmid Campbell. Campbell died in 1645 of wounds received at the Battle of Inverlochy, while fighting against the Marquis of Montrose, and is buried at Ardchattan Priory. Mary died after him, and her ghost is said to haunt the house. Another ghost is said to be that of Duncan Campbell, who died at the costly Battle of Ticonderoga in Canada in 1758. The house stands in a country park, and attractions include a smokery, fishing lochs and accommodation on the estate (01866 822446 (office 01866 822777); www.inverawe.co.uk).

Skipness Castle [NR 907577], seven miles south of Tarbert in Kintyre in Argyll, is a strong and imposing

building with a well-preserved tower house and a curtain wall which formerly enclosed ranges of buildings. The first stronghold was built by the MacSweens and it was later held by the MacDonald Lords of the Isles and then by the Forresters. In 1499 the property was granted to the Campbells, and it was besieged by Alasdair Colkitto MacDonald in the 1640s, although the castle held out. The building was abandoned around the end of the seventeenth century, and was used as a farm steading. Near the castle is **Skipness House** [NR 907578], built for the Graham family at the end of the nineteenth century, although it incorporates some of a much older house of the Campbells. The house is still occupied. Skipness is said to have a gruagaich, a 'Green Lady', described as being as small as a child but dressed in green and with golden hair. The castle was consolidated in 1898, and is now in the care of Historic Scotland and is open to the public.

Kilbrannan [NR 907577], a ruined chapel, lies to the south-east of the castle, and members of the Campbell family are buried here.

The Campbells also held:
Aberuchill Castle [NN 745212], near Comrie, Perthshire; fine L-plan tower house.
    Held by the MacGregors but passed to the Campbells in 1596, and they built the castle. The MacGregors, undeterred,

Aberuchill Castle (M&R)

continued to extract money from the Campbells. The castle was damaged by the Jacobites under Bonnie Dundee in 1689, but after the 1715 Jacobite Rising, when the MacGregors were on the losing side, the Campbell laird decided to stop paying blackmail. When Rob Roy MacGregor and his clansman surrounded the castle during a party the Campbells soon found the money. The house was occupied until gutted by a recent fire.
Achallader Castle [NN 322442], near Bridge of Orchy, Argyll; ruinous tower house.
    Held by the Fletchers, but the existing castle was built by Sir Duncan Campbell of Glenorchy. Campbell is said to have tricked the old laird into killing an English soldier so that Fletcher had to flee. The castle was burned in 1603 and again in 1689, and was not restored. It was the scene of a meeting in 1691 between the Campbell Earl of Breadalbane and Jacobite chiefs. They agreed to peace in exchange for Hanoverian gold.
Airds [NM 909450], near Benderloch, Argyll; castle replaced by mansion.
    Held by the Campbells. Black Sir Donald Campbell of Airds tricked the Livingstones of Bachuil out of most of their lands,

Skipness Castle (M&R)

although he seems to have see the error of his ways, rather too late, on his death bed. In about 1620 the Campbells of Airds acquired Castle Stalker, apparently as the outcome of a wager, fuelled by drink of course, with Duncan Stewart of Appin, the seventh chief. Airds had passed to the MacPhees by the end of the nineteenth century.

Ardchattan [NM 971349], near Connel, Argyll; later mansion by ruins of priory.

The priory was founded by the MacDougalls but the lands were given to the Campbells of Cawdor in 1602. The buildings were burnt in 1644 by Alasdair Colkitto MacDonald, and again in 1654 by Cromwell's forces. Colin Campbell of Glenure, murdered in 1752, is buried here; the events surrounding his death feature in the novel *Kidnapped* by Robert Louis Stevenson. Members of the Campbells family were buried in the Ardchattan Aisle, which dates from 1614. Ardchattan House was built out from the priory, and is still apparently occupied by the Campbells. The priory ruins are said to be haunted by the ghost of a nun. She is said to have been the lover of one of the monks. She hid beneath the floor so that she could visit her lover at night, but the prior found her and had her buried alive. The ruins of the priory are open to the public all year and the gardens of the house are open to the public from April to October (01631 750274).

Ardincaple Castle [NS 282830], near Helensburgh, Dunbartonshire; site of castle and mansion.

Held by the MacAulays, but sold to the Campbells in 1767, then later to the Colquhouns of Luss. Mostly demolished in 1957.

Ardkinglas House [NN 175104], near Inveraray, Argyll; site of castle.

Held by the Campbells. There is a monument to the Campbells of Ardkinglas in Lochgoilhead Kirk [NN 198015], and they had a burial aisle here, although this was demolished in 1850. The present house was built for the Nobles, and the woodland garden has a fine collection of rhododendrons and conifers, and is open to the public (01499 600261/263; www.ardkinglas.com).

Ardmaddy Castle [NM 788164], near Kilninver, Argyll; mansion on site of castle.

Held by the MacDougalls, who built the first castle, but passed to the Campbells. The castle was burnt down in 1620, but was enlarged by Neil Campbell, who was executed by Charles II in 1685. In 1692 Ardmaddy passed to the Campbell Earls, then Marquises, of Breadalbane. There is a fine walled garden, a water garden and woodland walks, which are open to the public (01852 300353; www.gardens-of-argyll.co.uk).

Ardpatrick Castle [NR 753593], near Tarbert, Argyll; mansion on site of castle.

Held by the Stewarts and by the MacAlisters, but then by the Campbells of Skipness. The mansion dates from the eighteenth century.

Aros Castle [NM 563450], near Tobermory, Isle of Mull; ruinous castle in lovely location.

Held by the MacDougalls, by the MacDonalds and then by the MacLeans of Duart, then later the lands passed to the Campbells. On the orders of James VI in 1608, Lord Ochiltree lured many unruly island chiefs onto his ship, where they were imprisoned and sent to Edinburgh for punishment. In 1674 the Campbell Earl of Argyll occupied Aros (and Duart) with 2000 men to punish the MacLeans of Duart, and there was much bloodshed.

Asgog Castle [NR 946705], near Tighnabruaich, Cowal, Argyll; ruinous castle.

Held by the Lamonts, but was torched and destroyed, with much treachery and murder, by the Campbells in 1646 after a long siege. The Lamonts were Royalists, and had been raiding Campbell lands, but had been promised that their people would go free if they surrendered the castle. The Campbell Marquis of Argyll had more than 200 men, women and children

slaughtered, although he himself was later executed in 1661 for treason.

Asknish House [NR 930913], near Lochgilphead, Argyll; castle replaced by mansion.

Held by the Campbells of Auchinbreck in 1583, but was sacked in 1685 because the family had supported the Earl of Argyll's rebellion of that year. The property was held by the Campbells until 1745. The castle was demolished about 1780, and replaced by Asknish House [NM 928915].

Auchenbreck Castle [NS 020813], Cowal, Argyll; slight remains of castle.

Held by the Campbells, but by 1870 had been demolished, and there are few remains. The present chief of the Campbells of Auchinbreck apparently lives in New Zealand. The family has a burial enclosure at Kilmodan Parish Church.

Ballimore [NR 922833], near Kilfinan, Cowal, Argyll; motte.

Held by the MacEwens, but passed to the Campbells in the fifteenth century, and the MacEwens became a broken clan. The summit of the mound has two burial enclosures of the Campbells of Otter, dating from the nineteenth century.

Balruddery [NO 315322], near Dundee; site of castle or old house.

Held by the Edwards and then by the Campbells of Balruddery, who had a town house on Overgate in Dundee. The laird of Balruddery is mentioned in Sir Walter Scott's *Guy Mannering*. Balruddery House was demolished in the 1960s.

Balvie [NS 535752], near Milngavie, Dunbartonshire; site of castle and mansion.

Held by several families including by the Campbells and then later by the Douglases. The mansion was demolished in the twentieth century to build Douglas Academy

Barbreck House [NM 831065], near Ardfern, Argyll; castle replaced by mansion.

Held by the Campbells from the fifteenth century, and now occupied by the Campbells of Strachur. A spot near the house is said to be haunted by the apparition of a young woman dressed and hooded in plaid and tartan, sitting on a rock. The apparition is said to disappear should anyone approach. There is also reputed to have been a battle near the house between the Vikings and the Scots, which ended with the killing of Olaf, a Norse prince. Barbreck's Bone, which is now in the Museum of Scotland, was believed to be able to cure madness. It is a piece of elephant ivory, but was thought to have fallen from heaven.

Barr Castle [NS 502365], Galston, Ayrshire; solid keep or tower of five storeys.

Held by the Lockharts, but was sold to the Campbells of Cessnock in 1670. The castle is apparently now a masonic hall.

Bedlay Castle [NS 692701], near Kirkintilloch, Dunbartonshire; L-plan tower house.

Held by the Boyds and by the Robertsons, before being bought by the Campbells of Petershill. The Campbells built a mausoleum in the garden, but there were then tales of spectral appearances in the grounds. In the eighteenth century, they had the mausoleum moved to Lambhill cemetery: the ghosts are said to have followed. The castle is still occupied.

Black Castle of Moulin [NN 946589], near Pitlochry, Perthshire; traces of a castle.

Built by the John Campbell of Lochow, nephew of Robert the Bruce, who was later made Earl of Atholl. The castle was occupied until the sixteenth century, but was then destroyed and torched because of plague.

Bolfracks [NN 822481], near Aberfeldy, Perthshire; site of castle or old house.

Held by the Stewarts and by the Menzies family, but passed to the Campbells of Breadalbane in the nineteenth century. The gardens at Bolfracks are open to the public (01887 820344; www.rannoch.net/Bolfracks-Garden/).

Caisteal Nighinn Ruaidh [NR 694778], Isle of Danna, near Tayvallich, Argyll; site of tower house on island.

Danna was a property of the Campbells in the sixteenth and

seventeenth centuries. The names means 'castle of red (-haired) girls'.

Caisteal na Nighinn Ruaidhe [NM 916137], near Kilmelford, Argyll; slight remains of castle.

Held by the Campbells.

Caisteal nan Con [NM 765136], Isle of Torsa, Argyll; small ruined castle.

Held by the Campbells, then by the MacDougalls of Rarey and by the MacLeans. The name means 'castle of the dogs'.

Camis Eskan [NS 321815], near Cardross, Dunbartonshire; mansion on site of castle.

Held by the Dennistouns of Colgrain, but passed to the Campbells of Breadalbane in 1836. The house was later used as a TB hospital, and had been divided into flats.

Carnasserie Castle [NM 837009], near Kilmartin, Argyll; fine impressive ruinous castle in a scenic spot.

Built by John Carswell, but passed to the Campbells. It was captured and sacked by the MacLeans and by the MacLachlans during the Earl of Argyll's rebellion of 1685. It is in the care of Historic Scotland and is open to the public.

Carnbane Castle [NN 677478], near Kenmore, Perthshire; some remains of castle.

Held by Red Duncan Campbell the Hospitable. The castle is said to have been destroyed by cattle thieves, who shot a lit arrow into the thatched roof.

Caroline Park House or **Royston Castle** [NT 227773], Edinburgh; mansion incorporating tower house.

Held by the Logans and by the Mackenzies of Tarbat before coming to the Campbell Duke of Argyll in 1639, who changed the name to Caroline Park (either after his daughter or George II's queen). It then passed by marriage to the Scotts of Buccleuch. There are fine interiors and the building is still in use, although it is said to be haunted by a Green Lady.

Carrick Castle [NS 194944], near Lochgoilhead, Argyll; restored keep or tower.

Held by the Lamonts, but passed in 1368 to the Campbell Earls of Argyll, and the current Duke of Argyll is still the

Carrick Castle 1910?

hereditary keeper of the castle. Mary, Queen of Scots stayed here in 1563. In 1685 the lands were pillaged and the castle burned during Argyll's rebellion. The property later passed to the Murray Earls of Dunmore and became ruinous but it has been restored in recent years.

Castle Coeffin [NM 853437], Isle of Lismore; ruinous and overgrown castle.

Held by the MacDougalls of Lorn, then by the Stewarts and by the Campbells.

Castle Ewen [NR 916796], near Kilfinan, Cowal, Argyll; slight remains of dun and castle.

Held by the MacEwens of Otter, but the lands passed to the Campbells and the MacEwens became a broken clan.

Castle Loch Heylipol [NL 986435], Isle of Tiree; mansion on site of castle.

Held by the MacLeans and then by the Campbell Earls of Argyll. The castle had been besieged by the Campbells in 1678-79.

The factor, called MacLaren, who had the house built is said to have died before he could enter it. His ghost reputedly haunts the house and there is also the phantom of a Green Lady.

Castle Stalker [NM 921473], near Connel, Appin, Argyll; dramatically sited restored keep or tower.

Held by the Stewarts of Appin, but the assassination of Campbell of Cawdor in 1592 started a feud between the family and the Campbells. The Stewarts of Appin fought at the Battle of Inverlochy, under the Marquis of Montrose, in 1645 against the Campbells. In 1620 the castle was sold to the Campbells, but the Stewarts retrieved it after a long siege in 1685. Open for some days in the summer (01883 622768; www.castlestalker.com).

Cessnock Castle [NS 511355], near Galston, Ayrshire; massive keep and mansion.

Held by the Campbells of Cessnock. Mary, Queen of Scots, came to Cessnock after her defeat at Langside in 1568; one of

Cessnock Castle 1920?

her ladies died here and is said to haunt the castle. The reformers George Wishart and John Knox (who is also said to haunt here) also visited, as did Robert Burns. The property later passed to other families.

Colonsay House [NR 395968], near Scalasaig, Isle of Colonsay; mansion.

The island had several owners, including the MacDuffies and the MacDonalds, before it went to the Campbell Duke of Argyll in 1701, the lands were exchanged for Crerar with the MacNeils, and Colonsay House dates from 1722. The gardens are open to the public some days (01951 200211; www.colonsay.org.uk).

Corranmore [NM 790029], near Ardfern, Argyll; site of castle.

Held by the Campbells of Corranmore.

Corsewall Castle [NW 991715], near Stranraer, Galloway; slight remains of castle.

Held by the Stewarts of Dreghorn, but passed to the Campbells of Loudoun in 1333, and then by marriage to the MacDowalls in 1547. The castle was replaced by the nearby house in the eighteenth century.

Craigie House [NS 352215], Ayr; mansion.

Built by the Wallaces of Craigie around 1730 but the property passed to the Campbells in 1782. Sold to the local council in 1942. The house is used as offices for Paisley University and the grounds are open to the public.

Craignish Castle [NM 773016], near Ardfern, Argyll; mansion on site of castle.

Held by the Campbells of Craignish. The castle withstood a six-week siege by Alaisdair Colkitto MacDonald in the 1640s. There are stories of a Green Lady haunting the castle, her apparition seen walking from the building to the place where her lover, a young French officer from Montrose's army, was executed by drowning. Still occupied.

Duart Castle [NM 749354], near Craignish, Isle of Mull; hugely impressive and interesting castle.

Long held by the MacLeans of Duart. Lachlan Cattanach, eleventh chief, became so unhappy with his Campbell wife that he had the poor woman chained to a rock in the Firth of Lorn to be drowned at high tide. However, she was rescued and taken to her father, the Campbell Earl of Argyll. As a result, MacLean was murdered in his bed in Edinburgh by Sir John Campbell of Cawdor. In 1674 the castle was acquired by the Campbell Earl of Argyll and was not used as a residence, although it was garrisoned. It was bought back by the MacLeans in 1911 and was restored from ruin, and is open to the public from May to mid-October (01680 812309/01577 830311; www.duartcastle.com).

Dun an Garbh-Sroine [NM 803089], near Kilmelford, Argyll; some remains of a castle.

Held by the MacIver Campbells from the thirteenth until the seventeenth century.

Dunderave Castle [NN 143096], near Inveraray, Argyll; restored L-plan tower house.

Held by the MacNaughtons. The last MacNaughton laird intended to wed the younger daughter of Sir James Campbell of Ardkinglas, but found himself married to the wrong girl. After fleeing to Ireland with his love, the younger daughter, Dunderave passed to the Campbells, probably around 1689; the MacNaughtons were also Jacobites and this may have been reason enough to go. The castle became ruinous but was restored in 1911-12 and was occupied by the Noble family.

Dundonald Castle [NR 700445], near Killean, Kintyre, Argyll; site of castle.

Held by the MacDonalds but passed to the Campbells. Killean House [NR 697443] is a large baronial mansion, dating from 1875, and accommodation is available at the house and on the estate (01257 266511; www.killeanestate.com).

Dunmaglas [NH 593223], near Inverfarigaig, Inverness-shire; site of castle or old house.

Held by the Campbells of Cawdor but passed to the MacGillivrays in the middle of the sixteenth century.

Dunmore House [NR 793619], near Tarbert, Argyll; ruinous house.

Held by the MacMillans but then by the Fraser-Campbells at the beginning of the nineteenth century. They have a mausoleum nearby, and the family now apparently live in Kilmacolm in Renfrewshire. The mansion was gutted by fire in 1985.

Duntrune Castle [NR 794956], near Lochgilphead, Argyll; fine castle and courtyard.

Held by the Campbells of Duntrune. The castle was besieged by a force led by Alasdair Colkitto MacDonald in 1644, after

Duntrune Castle 1920?

the Battle of Inverlochy, when the lands of the Campbells were ravaged by the Marquis of Montrose's army. It was burnt by the Earl of Argyll in 1685. In 1792 the lands were sold to the Malcolms of Poltalloch, who still own the castle. The castle is said to be haunted by a ghostly piper, who had had his finger chopped off. Holiday cottages available in grounds (01546 510283; www.duntrune.com).

Dunyvaig Castle [NR 406455], near Port Ellen, Isle of Islay; ruinous castle by the sea.

Long held by the MacDonalds, but passed to the Campbells of

Cawdor about 1677, and they demolished much of the building and moved to Islay House.

Easter Braikie Castle [NO 637515], near Brechin, Angus; site of tower house.

Held by several families before coming to the Campbells of Breadalbane. The castle was demolished in 1823 and replaced by a mansion.

Edinample Castle [NN 601226], near Lochearnhead, Stirlingshire; restored Z-plan tower house.

Held by the MacGregors, but passed to the Campbells. The castle is said to have been built by Sir Duncan Campbell of Glenorchy, Black Duncan of the Castles. The building is said

Edinample Castle (LF)

to be haunted by the mason who worked on the castle. The castle was supposed to have a parapet, and Campbell would not pay him. The mason tried to demonstrate that it was possible to walk around the roof, so Campbell pushed him off and the man fell to his death. His ghost is said to still sometimes scrabble about the roof. The castle was abandoned and derelict but has been restored and is occupied.

Eilean Dearg Castle [NS 008771], Cowal, Argyll; ruinous castle on island in Loch Ruel.

Held by the Stewarts but passed to the Campbells in the fourteenth century. This was once a strong tower, said to have been similar to Castle Stalker, and it was used by the Campbell Earl of Argyll during his rebellion of 1685. The castle was blown up with gunpowder the same year following naval action, and was not reused.

Eilean Ran Castle [NN 577334], near Killin, Stirlingshire; site of castle.

Held by the MacNabs, but the lands later passed to the Campbells.

Farnell Castle [NO 624555], near Brechin, Angus; altered tower house.

Held by the Campbells in 1566 after passing from the Bishops of Brechin (the Bishop was a member of the family), then by the Lindsays just two years later, then by the Carnegies of Kinnaird. Still occupied.

Fearnan [NN 725446], near Kenmore, Perthshire; site of castle.

Held by the Robertsons of Struan then by the Campbells.

Finlaggan [NR 388681], near Port Askaig, Isle of Islay; site of castle on island.

Held by the MacDonald Lord of the Isles, but the island passed to the Campbells. Finlaggan is open to the public (01496 810629; www.finlaggan.com).

Finlarig Castle [NN 575338], near Killin, Stirlingshire; ruinous tower house.

Held by the Menzies family, but the castle was built in 1621-29 by the Campbell 'Black Duncan of the Cowl' or 'Black Duncan of the Castles'. Parliament was summoned to appear here in 1651, but only three members turned up. Rob Roy MacGregor visited about 1713. There are the remains of a mausoleum close by. The ruin can be viewed from the exterior but is in a dangerously ruined condition.

Fordie [NN 799230], near Crieff, Perthshire; tower house replaced by mansion.

Fordie or Lawers was a property of the Campbells, and was later renamed Lawers from a property in Glenorchy. This branch of the family rose to inherit the Earldom of Loudoun in 1633. Campbell of Lawers was slain at the Battle of Inverlochy in 1645; and General James Campbell of Lawers was a distinguished soldier, and fought at the battles of Malplaquet in 1709, Dettingen in 1743 and then Fontenoy in 1745 where he died. The property later passed to the Robertsons, and the building is now used as a college of agriculture.

Fraoch Eilean Castle [NN 108251], near Dalmally, Argyll; slight remains of a castle on island.

Held by the MacNaughtons, but passed to the MacConnochie Campbells by 1485, and they acquired Inverawe. It was abandoned about the middle of the eighteenth century.

Gargunnock House [NS 715944], near Stirling; mansion on site of castle.

Held by the Grahams, by the Setons and by the Erskines, then by the Campbells in 1740 when it was held by Colonel Campbell of Ardkinglas (Glentirran?), Governor of Stirling Castle. Gargunnock went to the Stirlings at the end of the eighteenth century and the gardens are open to the public in the summer (01786 860392; www.gardensofscotland.org).

Garvie Castle [NS 035903], near Strachur, Argyll; site of castle.

Held by the MacAughtries and then by the Campbell Earls of Argyll.

Glendaruel [NR 998867], near Otter Ferry, Argyll; site of old house and mansion.

Held by the Campbells from the seventeenth century or earlier. The family were Jacobites, and Colin Campbell of Glendaruel led forces to attack Inveraray in 1715. The family were forfeited, and Glendaruel passed to another branch of the Campbells, who are still styled the Campbells of Glendaruel, although the property was sold in the middle of the nineteenth century. The mansion was gutted by fire in the 1970s and was then demolished.

Glenstrae Castle [NN 138296], near Dalmally, Argyll; site of castle.

Held by the MacGregors, but passed to the Campbells in 1604. The castle was burnt in 1611 by Sir Duncan Campbell.

Glentirran [NS 668944], near Kippen, Stirlingshire; site of castle and mansion.

Held by the Livingstones, but passed to the Campbells, who also held Gargunnock, in the eighteenth century.

Gorm Castle [NR 235655], near Bowmore, Isle of Islay; slight remains of castle on island.

Held by the MacDonalds, then the MacLeans, and then by the Campbells. The castle was refortified, or still in use, in 1615 when Sir James MacDonald fought against the Campbells on Islay and Kintyre. He was unsuccessful, and his forces had to surrender. The castle was garrisoned by the Campbells until the 1640s.

Granton Castle or **Royston House** [NT 225772], Edinburgh; site of castle.

Held by the Melvilles, by the Mackenzies and by the Hopes before coming to the Campbell Dukes of Argyll, who renamed the castle Royston House when the adjacent property of Royston was itself renamed 'Caroline Park' after the Duke's daughter – or alternatively after George II's queen. Granton Castle became ruinous, and was demolished in the 1920s.

Hundleshope [NT 230364], near Peebles, Borders; site of castle or old house.

Held by the Turnbulls, by the Murrays and by the Scotts before being held by the Campbells in the nineteenth century.

Inchinnan Castle [NS 482697], near Erskine, Renfrewshire; site of castle.

Held by different branches of the Stewarts before being bought by the Campbells of Blythwood. No remains.

Inverliever [NM 895055], near Kilmartin, Argyll; site of castle.

Held by the Campbells in the fifteenth and sixteenth centuries. It was Campbell of Inverliever who in 1511 seized Muriel Calder, heiress to the Cawdor estate near Inverness, and brought her to Argyll, although with the loss of all six of his sons. Muriel was married to the son of the Earl of Argyll, and the Campbells acquired Cawdor. There is, however, another Inverliever [NN 068359] on the south side of Loch Etive, some five miles east and north of Taynuilt.

Islay House [NR 334628], near Bowmore, Islay; large impressive mansion dating from 1677.

Built by the Campbells of Cawdor after they had acquired the island, but later went to the Campbells of Shawfield and Islay. Archibald Campbell, Lord (and then Earl of) Islay, helped set up the Royal Bank of Scotland in 1727 and was first Governor of the first bank; his portrait appears on bank notes. He later succeeded his father as the third Duke of Argyll, and he had Inveraray Castle built. Islay House is still occupied as a private residence.

Keithick [NO 203385], near Coupar Angus, Perthshire; castle replaced by mansion.

Held by the Campbells. One of the family was Nicholas Campbell who, although apparently illegitimate, was Dean of Lismore Cathedral; he also collected many histories and stories of the area. He died in 1587, and his carved gravestone is at the west end of Bendochy Parish Church [NO 218415]. Keithick House dates from the nineteenth century.

Kenmore Castle [NN 766454], near Aberfeldy, Perthshire; site of castle.

Built by the Campbells in the 1560s. The island was besieged by the Marquis of Montrose in 1645, and occupied by General Monck's forces during Cromwell's occupation of the 1650s.

Kilberry Castle [NR 709642], near Tarbert, Argyll ; mansion on site of castle.

Held by the Campbells, who built the castle about 1497. It was burnt by an English pirate, Captain Proby, in 1513, but was rebuilt and is still apparently occupied by the Campbells of Kilberry. There is an elaborately carved monument to Dugald Campbell on the mausoleum of 1733.

Kilbryde Castle [NN 756036], near Dunblane, Stirlingshire; L-plan tower house.

Held by the Grahams but passed to the Campbells of Aberuchill in 1669. Sir Colin, Lord Aberuchill of Session, was prominent in his activities against Rob Roy MacGregor, but still had to pay blackmail to be left alone by the MacGregors. One story is that the castle and the grounds near the old chapel were

Kilbryde Castle (M&R)

haunted by a White Lady. The gardens are open to the public by appointment only (01786 824505).

Kilkerran Castle [NR 729194], Campbeltown, Kintyre, Argyll; slight remains of castle.

Held by the MacDonald Lord of the Isles, but passed to the Campbells, and many lowlanders were settled here with considerable bloodshed.

Killellan [NR 680159], near Campbeltown, Kintyre, Argyll; site of castle or old house.

Held by the MacEarchans and passed to the Campbells, although the MacEarchans recovered the property in 1659.

Kilmartin Castle [NR 836991], Kilmartin, Argyll; restored Z-plan tower house.

Held by John Carswell, but passed to the Campbells by 1674, although the lands were pillaged in 1685. The Campbells held the property until 1922 and the castle became ruinous, but it was restored and is a private residence.

Kilmory Castle [NR 870868], near Lochgilphead, Argyll; mansion on site of castle.

Held briefly by the Lamonts before passing to the Campbells in 1575 and they held the property until 1828 when it passed by marriage to the Ordes. Now used as offices for the local council, and the fine gardens are open to the public (01546 604360; www.argyll-bute.gov.uk/content/leisure/heritage/kilmory).

Kilmun Church [NS 166821], near Dunoon, Cowal, Argyll; church with fortified tower.

The church stands on the site of a tenth-century monastery and still surviving is the strong tower of the 15th-century collegiate church, endowed by Duncan Campbell of Lochow in 1442; it may also have been used as a residence by the Campbells. On the site is the domed mausoleum of the Campbell Earls and Dukes of Argyll (both the eight and the ninth Earl are buried here). The later church is open to the public from April to September (01369 840342).

Kilpunt or **Kinpont** [NT 098718], near Broxburn, West Lothian; site of castle or old house.

Long held by the Grahams but apparently later went to the Campbells.

Kingencleugh Castle [NS 503256], near Mauchline, Ayrshire; slight remains of castle.

Held by the Campbells of Loudoun. John Knox is said to have preached at the tower, and the Campbells of Kingencleugh held the property until at least end of the eighteenth century. There is a later house, dating from 1765.

Kinnell House [NN 578329], near Killin, Stirlingshire; mansion incorporating castle.

Held by the MacNabs in 1580 but later passed to the Campbells.

Kinsteary [NH 927543], near Nairn; site of castle.

Held by the Sutherlands but also by the Campbells of Cawdor at one time. Kinsteary House is a later mansion.

Knockamillie Castle [NS 152711], near Dunoon, Cowal, Argyll; slight remains of a castle.

Held by the Lamonts, but passed to the Campbells about 1646. There was a later house but this has mostly gone.

Langton Castle [NT 756534], near Duns, Borders; site of castle and mansion.

Held by several families before coming to the Campbell Marquis of Breadalbane, who in 1862 built a mansion, but this was demolished in the 1950s.

Lawers [NN 684395], near Killin, Perthshire; site of tower house.

Held by the MacMillans and then by the Campbells from 1370, who went on to inherit the Earldom of Loudoun, and they moved east to Fordie, near Crieff. There was a village with a church and mill, some remains of which survive.

Lerags [NM 843245], near Oban, Argyll; castle or old house replaced by mansion.

Held by the Campbells from 1470 or so. Archibald Campbell of Lerags had a carved cross erected in 1515 after surviving the Battle of Flodden in 1513 when so many of his countrymen

had been slain. This was moved to its present site [NM 858259] in recent times. The family line died out in the seventeenth century. The present Lerags House dates from the nineteenth century and accommodation is available (01631 563381; www.leragshouse.com).

Loch Dochart Castle [NN 407257], near Killin, Stirlingshire; ruinous tower house.

Built by Sir Duncan Campbell of Glenorchy, Black Duncan of the Castles, between 1585 and 1631, but was burnt out in 1646. The ruins have been cleared and consolidated, and the site is traditionally associated with Rob Roy MacGregor.

Loch an Sgoltaire Castle [NR 386972], near Scalasaig, Isle of Colonsay; remains of castle.

Held by the MacDuffies, by the MacDonalds, then in the seventeenth century by the Campbell Earls of Argyll, then by the MacNeills. The 'big house' on Colonsay is said to have had a brownie (fairy or gruagach), which also acted as a herdsman.

Lochhead Castle [NR 718202], Campbeltown, Kintyre, Argyll; site of castle.

Held by Archibald Campbell, seventh Earl of Argyll, and built in 1609 after the Campbells had been given Kintyre.

Lochindorb Castle [NH 974364], near Grantown-on-Spey, Moray; ruinous castle on island.

Held by the Comyns, Stewarts and then the Campbells of Cawdor from 1606, who sold it to the Ogilvie Earl of Seafield in 1750. The castle can be seen from the shore.

Lochnell House [NM 887390], near Oban, Argyll; mansion incorporating old work.

Held by the Campbells, but passed to the Douglas Blair Cochrane Earls of Dundonald. The house is said to have had a brownie, and ghostly music has reportedly been heard here. At Ardchattan Priory [NM 971349], near Oban, is the Lochnell Aisle, which dates from 1620 and is where many of the Campbells were buried, including Alexander, sixth of Lochnell, who died in 1714. The ruins are open to the public.

Lochranza Castle [NR 933507], Lochranza, Isle of Arran; fine ruinous castle.

Held by the Campbells at one time as well as by the Stewarts, by the Montgomerys and by the Hamiltons.

Loudoun Hall [NS 337221], Ayr; fine town house.

Built by the Taits but passed to the Campbells of Loudoun in 1530 and then to the Chalmers family of Gadgirth in 1632. Saved from slum clearance and restored in 1948.

Lunga House [NM 795064], near Arduaine, Argyll; mansion dating from the seventeenth century.

Held by the Campbells of Craignish but passed to the MacDougalls of Lunga in the 1780s. Self-catering and B&B accommodation available (01852 500237; www.lunga.com).

Mains Castle [NN 668360], near Killin, Stirlingshire; site of tower house.

Held by the Campbells.

Mauchline Castle [NS 496273], Mauchline, Ayrshire; altered keep with wing.

Held by the Campbells of Loudoun after the Reformation and it was used as the factor's residence. Robert Burns paid his

Mauchline Castle (M&R)

rent here and was married in one of the blocks adjoining the keep

Meggernie Castle [NN 554460], near Killin, Perthshire; tall and attractive tower house.

Built by Colin Campbell of Glenlyon around 1585; he was responsible for the kidnapping of the Countess of Errol. The property passed to the Menzies family of Culdares and then to the Stewarts, and is said to be haunted by the upper and lower halves of a murdered lady. Still occupied.

Minard Castle or Knockbuie [NR 973943], near Lochgilphead, Argyll; mansion.

Held by the Campbells in the eighteenth century, but passed to the Lloyds (who were related to the Campbells) until the 1940s and then to the Gayres. Accommodation is available (01546 886272; www.minardcastle.com).

Mingary Castle [NM 502631], near Kilchoan, Ardnamurchan, Lochaber; ruinous courtyard castle.

Held by the Maclans of Ardnamurchan, but passed to the Campbells. It was captured by Alaisdair Colkitto MacDonald in 1644 for the Marquis of Montrose, but was recaptured by the Covenanter General David Leslie in 1646, then returned to the Argyll Campbells in 1651. The castle was garrisoned for the Government during the Jacobite Rising of 1745, and was probably still habitable around 1848.

Montcoffer House [NJ 685613], near Banff, Aberdeenshire; mansion with old work.

Held by the Campbells of Lundie and Montcoffer, but passed by marriage to the Russells, then was sold in 1750 to the Duff Dukes of Fife. Still occupied.

Monzie Castle [NN 873245], near Crieff, Perthshire; L-plan tower house.

Held by the Scotts and by the Grahams, but passed to the Campbells until 1869 when sold to the Johnstones of Lathrisk. The castle is open in the summer (01764 653110)

Muckhart Castle [NO 003007], near Dollar, Clackmannan; site of castle.

Some of the lands were held by the Campbells in the sixteenth century.

Mugdock Castle [NS 549772], near Milngavie, Dunbartonshire; ruinous courtyard castle.

Long a property of the Grahams, but was briefly held by the Campbells of Argyll in the 1650s, and then recovered by the Grahams in 1661. The ruin stands in the country park (0141 956 6100; www.mugdock-country-park.org.uk).

Newmilns Tower [NS 536374], Newmilns, Ayrshire; altered tower house.

Held by the Campbells of Loudoun, and was used as a prison for Covenanters. The castle was captured by a Covenanter

Newmilns Tower (M&R)

force, led by John Low, and the prisoners were rescued, although Low was killed in the fight.

Newton Castle [NN 731013], near Doune, Stirlingshire; L-plan tower house.

Held by the Edmonstones, but sold to John Campbell, a Glasgow merchant, in 1858. Still occupied.

Ormidale [NS 003817], near Tighnabruaich, Argyll; castle replaced by mansion.

Held by the Campbells from the middle of the fifteenth century. The mansion dates from the eighteenth century.

Ormsary [NR 740720], near Tarbert, Argyll; possible site of castle or old house.

Held by the Campbells from the middle of the seventeenth century or earlier, but passed to the Lithgow family, who still apparently live here.

Pinkerton [NT 703757], near Dunbar, East Lothian; site of castle or old house.

Held by the Pinkertons, by the Stewart Dukes of Albany and then by the Campbells of Argyll in 1483, and then later by the Homes. There is a beehive doocot.

Poltalloch [NR 814965], near Kilmartin, Argyll; ruined mansion on site of castle.

Held by the Campbells but passed to the Malcolms, who now live at Duntrune Castle.

Possil [NS 592705], Glasgow; site of castle and mansion.

Held by the Crawfords and then by several families before coming to the Campbells in the nineteenth century. The Carter-Campbells of Possil now apparently live near Penicuik in Midlothian. The mansion at Possil was demolished and the site is occupied by the Possilpark Trading Estate. The Campbells of Possil built Torosay Castle on Mull.

Rait Castle [NH 894525], near Nairn, Inverness-shire; fine ruinous hall-house and castle.

Held by the Raits, then by the Cummings and by the Mackintoshes, then by the Campbells of Cawdor. The Duke of Cumberland is said to have stayed here before victory at the Battle of Culloden against the Jacobites in 1746. Plans are afoot to have the castle consolidated (www.save raitcastle.org).

Rarey [NM 832206], near Oban, Argyll; site of castle.

Held by the MacDougalls but passed to the Campbells of Lochow in 1311, before returning to the MacDougalls. Replaced by a mansion at Rarey in the eighteenth century.

Renfield or Blythswood [NS 501684], near Renfrew; site of castle or old mansion.

Held by the Stewarts and by the Hays before coming to the Campbells of Blythswood, who changed the name. It later passed to the Elphinstones. Blythwood House, a large Greek Revival mansion, was demolished in 1935 and the site is occupied by a golf course.

Rosneath Castle [NS 272823], near Rosneath, Dunbartonshire; site of castle and mansion.

Held by the Campbells of Argyll from 1489 until 1939. After use as the administrative centre for the American Naval Base at Rosneath during World War II, the building was abandoned and then blown up in 1961. The site is now a caravan park.

Rowallan Castle [NS 435424], near Kilmarnock, Ayrshire; fine and large courtyard castle.

Held by the Comyns and by the Mures, then by the Boyle Earls of Glasgow at the beginning of the eighteenth century, then by the Campbell Earls of Loudoun, then by the Corbetts. In the care of Historic Scotland but not currently open to the public.

Saddell Castle [NR 789316], near Campbeltown, Kintyre, Argyll; keep or tower and courtyard.

Held by the Campbells of Argyll with the Ralston family as tenants, and the castle was replaced by Saddell House [NR 791318]. The castle is said to be haunted by a White Lady and a ghostly monk. Restored in the 1970s, and in the care of the Landmark Trust and can be rented as holiday accommodation (01628 825925; www.landmarktrust.org.uk).

Skeldon Castle [NS 378138], near Maybole, Ayrshire; some remains of castle.

Held by several families, including by the Campbells of Skeldon. David Campbell of Skeldon was outlawed for 'insolence' against the Jean Crawford, wife of MacDowall of Logan. Skeldon had passed to the Crawfords of Kerse by 1644 and then to others and there is an eighteenth-century house.

Sonochan [NN 038203], near Inveraray, Argyll; castle replaced by mansion.

Held by the Campbells of Lochawe, then by the MacPherdans from the fifteenth century or earlier, who had been given the lands for ferrying Robert the Bruce across the loch or for saving one of the Campbells from drowning. They were, however, driven from the area in 1706 by the Campbells. The Campbells have a burial enclosure [NN 042206], dating from 1760, near the later mansion.

Sorn Castle [NS 548269], near Mauchline, Ayrshire; altered and extended keep or tower.

Held by the Keiths of Galston, then by the Hamiltons of Cadzow and by the Setons of Winton before passing to the Campbell Earl of Loudoun around 1680, then Sorn went to the Somervilles at the end of the eighteenth century. Guided tours take place for some weeks in the summer (01290 551555).

Sornhill [NS 509342], near Galston, Ayrshire; L-plan tower house.

Held by the Nisbets, but sold to the Campbells in 1553. Later used as a farmhouse but apparently now derelict.

Stonefield Castle [NR 864717], near Tarbert, Argyll; mansion.

Held by the Campbells at the end of the nineteenth century. Now a hotel and the gardens are open to the public (01880 820836; www.stonefieldcastle.co.uk).

Strachur [NN 091016], Strachur, Argyll; castle or old house replaced by mansion.

Held by the Campbells from the end of the thirteenth century. This branch are still styled 'of Strachur', although they sold the property at the end of the nineteenth century and now apparently live further north at Barbreck House. The gardens of the house are occasionally open to the public (www.gardensofscotland.org).

Succoth [NN 296052], near Arrochar, Argyll; possible site of castle.

Held by the Campbells in 1616, who later also held the neighbouring lands of Ardgartan. Sir Ilay Campbell, Lord Succoth, was Lord-President of the Court of Session. The Campbells of Succoth now apparently live at Crarae.

Tangy Loch [NR 695279], near Campbeltown, Kintyre, Argyll; site of castle.

Held by the Campbells in 1576, although the MacEachan family are said to have lived here in the seventeenth century and the property later went to the Semples.

Tarbert Castle [NR 867687], Tarbert, Argyll; ruinous castle.

Held for the Crown by the MacAlisters, by the MacLeans and then by the Campbells of Argyll (and still a post held by the current Duke of Argyll). Walter Campbell of Skipness seized it from its hereditary keeper, Archibald Campbell, ninth Earl of Argyll, in 1685 during a rebellion by Argyll. The ruins are accessible.

Torosay Castle [NM 729353], near Craignure, Isle of Mull; impressive baronial mansion and gardens.

Built for the Campbells of Possil in 1858, and the gardens were laid out by Sir Robert Lorimer in 1899. The house is open to the public from April to Mid October (01680 812421; www.torosay.com).

Torran [NM 878048], near Kilmartin, Argyll; site of castle.

Held by the Campbells of Inverliever from 1529.

Toward Castle [NS 119678], near Dunoon, Cowal, Argyll; ruinous castle and courtyard.

Held by the Lamonts but passed to the Campbells after the Lamonts had been slaughtered and the lands and castle seized. A new mansion, Castle Toward, was built nearby and is now a private school. The old castle was excavated and consolidated in 1970, and is in the care of the Clan Lamont Society.

Treesbanks [NS 420346], near Kilmarnock, Ayrshire; site of castle and mansion.

Held by the Campbells of Cessnock. The present house dates from 1926.

Tullichewan Castle [NS 380811], near Alexandria, Dunbartonshire; site of mansion.

Held by the Campbells in the nineteenth century, then by the Andersons. The building was demolished in 1954.

Wellwood House [NS 665263], near Muirkirk, Ayrshire; site of castle and mansion.

Held by the Campbells, who built the castle. Said to have been haunted by a ghost called 'Beanie', the bogle of a young woman who is reputed to have been slain on the stairs. The later mansion of the Bairds, who bought the estate in 1863, incorporated a tower house but this was demolished in 1926.

www.ccsna.org
No. of castles/sites: 141 / Rank: 4/764
Xref: Duibhne

Cant

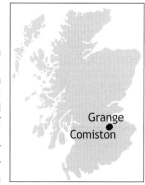

The name is mentioned in the fourteenth century, and may be from Flemish merchants with the surname. The Cants held lands on the south side of Edinburgh.

Grange House [NT 258718], an L-plan tower house of the sixteenth century, was a property of the Wardlaws but passed to the Cants for some years, and then to the Dicks in 1679 and then to the Lauders. The building was extended and altered down the years, but was demolished in 1936 and stood between Grange Loan, Lauder Place and Dick Place.

Comiston House [NT 240687] may occupy the site of a castle as there is a sixteenth-century tower or doocot, which is furnished with gunloops. Comiston was held by several families before passing by marriage from the Creichs to the Cants, but it then went by marriage to the Porterfields. The present mansion dates from 1815.

No. of castles/sites: 2
Rank: 396=/764

Grange House (M&R)

Carlyle

The name comes from the town of Carlisle in Cumbria in the north-west of England and near the Scottish border. The family were first recorded in Scotland in the middle of the twelfth century, and held lands around Annan in Dumfriesshire in the south-west of Scotland.

Torthorwald Kinmont
Hoddom

Thomas Carlyle, born at Ecclefechan in 1795, was a famed essayist, historian, and social reformer. He died in 1881. His birthplace in Ecclefechan is in the care of The National Trust for Scotland and is open to the public (01576 300666).

Hoddom Castle [NY 157730], five miles north-west of Annan, is a massive L-plan tower house of four storeys, but was built long after the lands had been held by the Carlyle family in the twelfth century. Hoddom was a property of the Herries family in the fourteenth and fifteenth centuries, then went to the Irvines and then to several other families. It now stands in a caravan park (01576 300251; www.hoddomcastle.co.uk).

Kinmont or Sark Tower [NY 333750], a few miles west and south of Canonbie, may have been held by the Carlyles in 1215, but it was long a property of the Armstrongs, although nothing survives of the tower. At Birrens [NY 219751] are the well-preserved ditches of a Roman fort, and within them was a small tower house of the Carlyles, dating from the fifteenth century but occupied by them for more than two hundred years. Birrens is six miles south-east of Lockerbie.

Torthorwald Castle [NY 033783], a few miles north-east of Dumfries, is a ruined fourteenth-century castle, which stands on a motte with earthworks and a ditch. It passed to the Carlyles in 1418, and in 1544 Lord Carlyle sacked the castle when it was held by his sister-in-law. The lands passed to the Douglases in the 1590s and the castle was occupied until about 1715.

The Carlyles held several other properties in Dumfries and Galloway:

Brydekirk Tower [NY 187711], near Annan; slight remains of a tower.
Held by the Carlyles in the sixteenth century.

Dornock [NY 231659], near Annan; site of tower house.
Probably held by the Carlyles of Torthorwald, although Dornock had passed to the Pulteney family by 1795.

Old Garroch [NX 589823], near St John's Town of Dalry; house on site of tower.
Held by the Asloan family, by the Maxwells and by the Griersons, as well as by the Carlyles at one time.

Scotsbrig [NY 214769], near Ecclefechan; site of tower house.
Held by the Bells and then by the Carlyles from 1826 or earlier.

No. of castles/sites: 8
Rank: 160=/764
Xref: Carlisle

Torthorwald Castle (M&R)

Carmichael

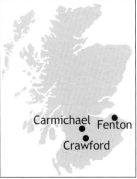

The name is territorial and comes from the lands of Carmichael in Lanarkshire, and the family is on record from the thirteenth century.

Carmichael House [NS 938391], which is five miles south-east of Lanark, is a mansion of 1734 but it stands on the site of a fourteenth-century castle. The Carmichaels held the lands from the 1370s or earlier. At the Battle of Baugé in 1421, Sir John Carmichael slew the Duke of Clarence, the brother of Henry V of England, breaking his spear and unhorsing him; hence the family's crest features a broken spear.

Peter Carmichael of Balmedie (this branch of the family held Ecclesiamagirdle House: see below) was one of those who was involved in the murder of Cardinal David Beaton at St Andrews Castle in 1546, and is believed to have repeatedly struck the Archbishop, presumably with a dagger. St Andrews Castle was besieged and eventually had to surrender, and Carmichael, along with others of the garrison, were made French galley slaves. He eventually escaped from imprisonment, disguised as a mendicant friar. Balmedie had passed by marriage from the Sibbalds of Balgonie to the Carmichaels, and may have been in Fife or in Aberdeenshire, but the location has not been determined.

The Carmichaels were made Baronets of Nova Scotia in 1628. The head of the family fought against Charles I at the Battle of Marston Moor in 1644, and against the Marquis of Montrose at the Battle of Philiphaugh in 1645, although two of his brothers were Royalists. In 1701 the Carmichaels were given the title Earls of Hyndford, and John Carmichael, third Earl, was a British envoy to Prussia and Russia, although this title became extinct in 1817. The Carmichaels were Hanoverians. The direct line of the family died out, and the lands and titles passed to the Anstruthers, who changed their name to Carmichael-Anstruther. Carmichael House is still apparently occupied by the family, and the Carmichael Heritage Centre [NS 948388] has information on the Carmichaels and other lowland families.

Crawford Castle [NS 954213], just north of the village also in Lanarkshire, is now very ruinous but stood on a mound surrounded by water. The lands were held by the Carmichaels, but passed to the Lindsays, although the Carmichaels of Meadowflat were keepers of the castle. William Wallace captured the stronghold from the English in 1297. Catherine, daughter of Sir John Carmichael of Meadowflat, was a mistress of James V. The king had **Boghouse Castle** [NS 878236] built by Sir James Hamilton of Finnart, so that he could entertain the lady without interruption; Catherine had a son.

Fenton Tower [NT 543822], two miles south of North Berwick in East Lothian, was held by the Carmichaels

Fenton Tower (M&R)

from 1587. Sir John Carmichael, the Scottish Warden of the Marches, argued with the English Warden, Sir John Foster, at a meeting at Carter's Bar in 1575. A battle resulted which the Scots eventually won, slaying many and taking captive several of the English leaders, embarrassing the Scottish leadership of the time. James VI sheltered at Fenton Tower in 1591 after escaping from a rebel army in Fife. In 1600 Sir John Carmichael was ambushed and murdered by the Armstrongs after he had tried to bring some of them to book for reportedly reiving. Carmichael of Edrom sought justice for his brother. Two of those who killed the Warden were taken to Edinburgh and were tried and found guilty. In 1601 they were hanged after having their right arms hacked off, and their corpses were then displayed in a gibbet on the Burghmuir. The tower became ruinous but has been restored, and Fenton was used in the BBC children's series Balamory. Luxury accommodation is available for up to twelve people (01620 890089; www.fenton tower.co.uk).

The family also held several other properties:
Aithernie Castle [NO 379035], near Leven, Fife; scant remains of tower house.
  Held by the Lundin family and then by the Carmichaels at one time, but passed to the Inglis family, then to the Riggs, who probably built the castle.
Blyth [NT 132458], near West Linton, Borders; site only.
  Held by several families before going to the Carmichaels of Skirling in 1752.
Eastend [NS 949374], near Lanark; mansion incorporating tower house.
  Held by the Carmichaels of Eastend for many years.
Ecclesiamagirdle House [NO 107164], near Perth; T-plan house, dating from seventeenth century.
  Held by the Halyburtons of Pitcur but passed to the Carmichaels of Balmedie from 1629, and they may have built or remodelled the house.
Edrom [NT 826559], near Duns, Borders; castle replaced by mansion.
  Held by the Homes but passed by marriage to the Carmichaels in 1635, then went to the Logans. Fragments of the old church stand nearby.

Harehead Castle [NT 692630], near Duns, Borders; site of castle. Held by the Carmichael Earls of Hyndford.

Holm or Holmhead Castle [NS 746474], near Stonehouse, Lanarkshire; site of castle.
Carmichael of Holmhead is mentioned in 1641, and other owners included the Hamiltons and then the Rae family in the nineteenth century.

Hyndford [NS 907417], near Lanark; site of castle or old house. Held by the Carmichaels, who were made Earls of Hyndford in 1701.

Nemphlar [NS 854447], near Lanark; sixteenth-century tower. Held by the Carmichaels in 1641.

Newbigging [NT 015460], near Carnwath, Lanarkshire; possible site of castle.
Held by the Newbigging family, but passed by marriage to the Carmichaels in the middle of the thirteenth century.

Skirling Castle [NT 072398], near Biggar, Lanarkshire; fragmentary ruin with moat.
Latterly held by the Cockburns and then by the Carmichaels of Skirling, before going to the Oswalds in 1683. The site had been excavated.

Waughton Castle [NT 567809], near East Linton, East Lothian; ruined castle and courtyard.
Held by the Hepburns and then by the Carmichaels in 1569 when it was raided by the dispossessed Robert Hepburn of Waughton.

Westraw [NS 947429], near Lanark; house which had fifteenth-century work.
Held by the Carmichaels and then by the Johnstones in the fifteenth and sixteenth centuries.

www.carmichael.co.uk
www.carmichael.org
No. of castles/sites: 16
Rank: 86=/764

Carnegie

The name is territorial and comes from the lands of Carnegie, which are some four miles north and west of Carnoustie in Angus. The family appear to originally have been called 'de Balinhard' from lands near Arbroath. **Carnegie Castle** [NO 535415] was owned by the family but there are no remains, and they held the lands from 1358 until the eighteenth century.

Their main seat was **Kinnaird Castle** [NO 634571], five and a half miles west of Montrose, also in Angus. This is now a large nineteenth century mansion, but it includes parts of a fifteenth-century stronghold, and

Kinnaird Castle 1901?

there was an earlier castle before this. Duthac Carnegie died at the Battle of Harlaw in 1411, and Walter Carnegie of Kinnaird fought at the Battle of Brechin in 1452 against the Earl of Crawford. The castle was later torched in revenge by the Lindsays. John Carnegie of Kinnaird was killed at the Battle of Flodden in 1513.

Sir Robert Carnegie was ambassador to France in 1550. The castle was visited by James VI, the family were made Earls of Southesk in 1633, and Charles I and Charles II both stayed here. The family were Jacobites, and were forfeited after the 1715 Jacobite Rising; but had recovered their estates and titles by 1858. The house is still apparently owned by the Earl of Southesk. The gardens are occasionally open to the public and accommodation is available (01674 810240; www.southesk.co.uk).

Ethie Castle [NO 688468], five miles north-east of Arbroath again in Angus, is a large castle, dating from the fifteenth century but extended down the centuries. It formerly had a courtyard defended by a moat. The castle was built by the Beatons, but passed to the Carnegies in 1549. The Carnegies were made Earls of Ethie in 1647, but exchanged this title for the Earldom of Northesk in 1662. William, seventh Earl, was a distinguished admiral, and third in command at the Battle of Trafalgar in 1805. Sir Walter Scott, a friend of the eighth Earl, often stayed at Ethie. He wrote *The*

Ethie Castle (M&R)

Antiquary here; Ethie is reputedly the Castle of Knockwhinnock. The building is reputedly haunted both by a Green Lady and by the ghost of Cardinal David Beaton. The property passed from the family in the twentieth century, and the Earls apparently now live in Hampshire in England. Accommodation is available at Ethie (01241 830434; www.ethiecastle.com).

Balnamoon [NO 552638] stands three and a half miles north-west of Brechin in Angus, and is an altered fifteenth-century castle to which a mansion was added in the 1830s. Balnamoon was held by the Carnegies from the beginning of the seventeenth century. Alexander Carnegie of Balnamoon was forfeited for his part in the Jacobite Rising of 1715, but recovered the property five years later. The next laird, James Carnegie, known as the 'Rebel Laird', fought in the 1745-46 Rising. The family married into the Arbuthnotts of Findrowie, and the name was changed to Carnegy-Arbuthnott in 1745. They still apparently live at Balnamoon.

Pittarrow Castle [NO 727751], some three miles north and east of Laurencekirk in Kincardineshire, was demolished in 1802 and all that remains is a date stone of 1599. It was built by the Wisharts, but passed to the Carnegies, who were made Baronets of Nova Scotia in 1663. This branch of the family eventually recovered the title of Earl of Southesk, lost after the Jacobite Rising of 1745-46.

Pittencrieff House [NT 087873], in Dunfermline, is a T-plan house, built in the seventeenth century with materials from the royal palace. In 1908 it was bought by Sir Andrew Carnegie, the famous industrialist and philanthropist, who gave it to the local authority and the grounds are now a public park (01383 722935/ 313838; www.fifedirect.org/museums). Carnegie was originally from Dunfermline, and had not been allowed to play in Pittencrieff when he was a boy; he emigrated to the USA in 1848.

Skibo Castle [NH 735891], four miles west of Dornoch, is a massive 19th-century castellated mansion, which was extended in 1899-1901. It had been purchased by Andrew Carnegie in 1895, but is now an exclusive country club (www.carnegieclubs.com).

Other properties held by the Carnegies include:
Arbigland House [NX 989574], near Kirkbean, Dumfriesshire; mansion on site of castle.
Held by the Carnegie Earls of Southesk for some years, but sold to the Craik family in 1679 and later went to the Blacketts. Still occupied.
Arnhall House [NO 613691], near Brechin, Angus; mansion on site of castle.
Held by the Carnegies but sold to the Brodies in 1796.
Balmachie [NO 545370], near Carnoustie, Angus; site of castle.
Held by the Carnegies in the 1590s.
Bolshan Castle [NO 617521], near Friockheim, Angus; site of castle and mansion.
Held by the Carnegies from 1635 until they were forfeited following the Jacobite Rising of 1715. Recovered by the Carnegies of Pittarrow in 1764. There was a mansion but this was demolished.
Boysack [NO 621491], near Friockheim, Angus; site of castle.
Held by the Carnegies of Boysack in the seventeenth century and they moved to Kinblethmont House in 1678.
Brandy Den [NO 478610], near Brechin, Angus; site of castle.
Held by the Mowats, by the Lindsays of Crawford and then by the Carnegies. By then the castle had been abandoned for Vayne.
Careston Castle [NO 530599], near Brechin, Angus; altered Z-plan tower house.
Held by the Dempsters and by the Lindsays before coming to the Carnegies of Balnamoon and they sold it to the Stewarts of Grandtully in 1707. Still occupied.
Colluthie House [NO 340193], near Cupar, Fife; mansion on site of castle.
Held by the Ramsays in 1356 but passed to the Carnegies of Colluthie. David Carnegie of Colluthie was a Privy Councillor in 1588, and his sons went on to be Earls of Southesk and Earls of Northesk. Colluthie had passed to the Inglis family by 1840.
Craig Castle [NO 254527], near Alyth, Angus; site of castle.
Held by the Carnegies of Kinnaird in the seventeenth century.
Craig House [NO 704563], near Montrose, Angus; courtyard castle with two ranges.
Held by the Rossies and by the Woods and then by the Carnegie Earls of Southesk from 1617. Lady Madelaine Carnegie, from this branch of the family, married James Graham, Marquis of Montrose. Still occupied.
Cruivie Castle [NO 419229], near Balmullo, Fife; ruined castle.
Held by the Kinlochs, by the Sandilands and by the Ramsays and then from 1583 by the Carnegies of Colluthie.
Elsick House [NO 891947], near Portlethen, Kincardineshire; mansion on site of castle.
Held by the Frasers and then long by the Bannermans, and now occupied by the Carnegie Dukes of Fife who are related to the Bannermans.
Farnell Castle [NO 624555], near Brechin, Angus; extended tower house.
Held by the Carnegies from the seventeenth century but lost in 1715 following the Jacobite Rising, then recovered in 1764.

Farnell Castle 1920?

Farnell was used to house farm labourers, then was abandoned; but the building has been restored and is occupied.

Finavon Castle [NO 497566], near Forfar, Angus; ruinous castle.
Held by the Lindsay Earls of Crawford, but then by the Carnegies for some years, before being sold to the Gordons of Aboyne in 1775 and then going to others.

Fithie [NO 635545], near Brechin, Angus; site of castle.
Held by the Fithie family and then by the Carnegies from the sixteenth or seventeenth century.

Fuirdstone or Balnabreich Castle [NO 542589], near Brechin, Angus; site of castle.
Held by the Ramsays but Robert Carnegie of Balnabreich is mentioned in 1593.

Glendye [NO 644864], near Banchory, Aberdeenshire; site of castle.
Held by the Carnegie Earls of Southesk but passed to the Gladstones of Fasque.

Hoddom Castle [NY 157730], near Annan, Dumfriesshire; large L-plan tower house.
Held by several families, then the Carnegie Earls of Southesk 1653 to 1690, then by the Sharps. The castle stands in a caravan park (01576 300251; www.hoddomcastle.co.uk).

Inglismaldie Castle [NO 644669], near Brechin, Angus; tower house and mansion.
Held by the Livingstones and then by the Carnegie Earls of Northesk from 1635 until 1693 when sold to the Falconers of Halkerton. Still occupied.

Invergowrie House [NO 363304], near Dundee; mansion and tower house.
Held by the Carnegies for some years before going to the Grays, and then to the Murrays and others. Divided into separate residences.

Kinblethmont [NO 638470], near Arbroath, Angus; little remains of a castle.
Held by the Melvilles and by the Lindsay Earls of Crawford, and then by the Carnegies, who built the castle.

Kinfauns Castle [NO 151226], near Perth; mansion on site of castle.
Held by the Charteris family and then by the Carnegies, by the Blairs and by others. Private residence.

Lour [NO 478462], near Forfar, Angus; site of castle.
Held by several families, including in 1639 by the Carnegies of Ethie, who also gained the title Lord Lour. They became Earls of Northesk and still held Lour at the end of the nineteenth century.

Panbride House [NO 572358], near Carnoustie, Angus; site of castle or old house.
Held by the Morhams and then by the Ramsays and by the Carnegies.

Rossie Castle [NO 702561], near Montrose, Angus; site of castle and mansion.
Held by the Rossie family and then by the Carnegies before passing to the Scotts of Logie by 1650 and then to others. Demolished in the 1950s.

Tarrie [NO 643449], near Arbroath, Angus; site of castle.
Held by the Strachans and by the Carnegies at one time.

Turin House [NO 545527], near Forfar, Angus; mansion on site of castle.
Held by the Turin family, by the Oliphants in the sixteenth century, and then by the Carnegies of Lour and Turin.

Vayne Castle [NO 493599], near Brechin, Angus; ruined Z-plan tower house.
Held by the Mowats, then by the Lindsay Earls of Crawford and then by the Carnegies from 1594 until 1766 when sold to the Mills. They built an elegant new house at Noranside [NO 472609]. The ruins of Vayne are said to be haunted.

No. of castles/sites: 36
Rank: 34=/764

Carruthers

The name is territorial and comes from the lands of Carruthers (apparently the name was locally pronounced 'Cridders') in the parish of Middlebie in Dumfriesshire. It is said to derive from 'Caer Rydderich', a fortress of the Britons; and the family came to prominence in the thirteenth century as stewards of Annandale. Nigel Carruthers was Chancellor to Robert, Steward of Scotland, in 1344, but he was killed at the Battle of Neville's Cross two years later.

Mouswald, nine miles west and north of Annan, was held by the Carruthers from 1320, after being given to them by Robert the Bruce. They built **Mouswald Tower** [NY 061739], but very little of that building now remains. Simon Carruthers of Mouswald was killed in a raid in 1548, leaving his two daughters as heiresses. They were placed into the wardenship of the Douglases. Marion, the elder daughter, did not want to marry Douglas of Drumlanrig. Even the Privy Council seemed to be against her and in 1563 ordered her into the wardenship of Borthwick Castle. Although she was sheltered in Comlongon Castle by the then laird, Sir William Murray, she was so distressed from the long dispute that she committed suicide by jumping from the lookout tower. An alternative version is that she was murdered by the Douglases who gained access to her room and threw her from the roof. Because she was thought to have committed suicide, she was not given a Christian burial. Her ghost, a Green Lady is said to haunt Comlongon Castle. Whatever the truth of it, Mouswald passed to the Douglases.

Dormont House [NY 112749], four and a half miles south and east of Lockerbie also in Dumfriesshire, was built in 1823 and replaced an old tower house. It was held by the Griersons in 1411, but was a property of the Carruthers of Holmains from the middle of the sixteenth century. The Carrutherses of Dormont still apparently live at Dormont.

The family owned several other towers:
Cornal Tower [NT 112044], near Moffat, Dumfriesshire; site of small tower house.
Held by the Carruthers of Mouswald in the fifteenth century, but passed to the Johnstones of Corehead and then to the Douglas Duke of Queensberry.

Denbie [NY 109729], near Lochmaben, Dumfriesshire; tower replaced by mansion.
Held by the Carruthers family from the seventeenth century or earlier. Denbie House [NY 111730], a two-storey mansion, dates from 1706.

Dornock [NY 231659], near Annan, Dumfriesshire; site of tower house.
Held by the Carruthers family or by the Carlyles of Torthorwald, and then by the Pulteney family in 1794.

Hallguards Castle [NY 162728], near Ecclefechan, Dumfriesshire; site of castle.

Held by the Bruces and by the Herries family, then later by the Carruthers family, but the castle was demolished under the terms of a Border treaty, and Hoddom became the main stronghold.

Hetlandhill [NY 091722], near Dumfries, Dumfriesshire; tower replaced by mansion?

Probably held by the Carruthers family. Hetland Hall dates from 1868 and is now used as a hotel (01387 840201; www.hetlandhallhotel.co.uk).

Hoddom Castle [NY 157730], near Annan; large L-plan tower house.

Held by the Carruthers family for some years, as well as by the Herrieses, by the Irvines, by the Maxwells and by others. The castle stands in a caravan park (01576 300251; www.hoddomcastle.co.uk).

Holmains Castle [NY 083767], near Lochmaben, Dumfriesshire; site of castle.

Held by the Carruthers family, although never a place of great strength. John Carruthers, and others, were accused in 1563 of assaulting Kirkpatrick of Closeburn and slaying several people. The lands had to be sold in 1772 because of debt.

Middlebie [NY 214762], near Ecclefechan, Dumfriesshire; possible site of castle.

Held by Carruthers of Mouswald in 1349, then probably by the Bells.

Raffles Tower [NY 086721], near Annan; site of tower house.

Held by the Raffles family and by the Carrutherses from 1361.

Warmanbie [NY 196689], near Annan, Dumfriesshire; mansion on site of tower.

Held by the Carruthers family at the end of the sixteenth century, but much later had passed to the Spencers. The mansion is said to be haunted and is now used as a hotel (01461 204015).

www.chebucto.ns.ca/Heritage/FSCNS/Scots_NS/Clans/ Carruthers.html

No. of castles/sites: 12
Rank: 120=/764

Carnasserie Castle (M&R) – see next column (Carsewell)

Carsewell

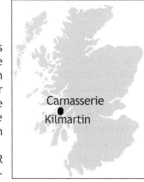

The name probably comes from the parish of the same name near Neilston in the west of Scotland, or from a place in Lanarkshire or in Roxburghshire. The family are mentioned in the thirteenth century.

Kilmartin Castle [NR 836991] is a small sixteenth-century Z-plan tower house, and stands above the small village of Kilmartin in Argyll. The castle was the residence of John Carsewell, who moved to Carnas-

Kilmartin Castle (M&R)

serie Castle when made Protestant Bishop of the Isles. Kilmartin Castle later became a property of the Campbells, and has recently been restored as a private residence.

Carnasserie Castle [NM 837009] stands above the road in an idyllic spot just a short distance north of Kilmartin. It is a ruined but mostly complete tower house and hall-block, which dates from the sixteenth century. The entrance, in one corner of the wing, is surmounted by a Gaelic inscription urging faith in God. The castle was built by John Carsewell (mentioned above), who published the first ever book in Gaelic in 1567, the Gaelic version of the Book of Common Order. He was minister of Kilmartin, then Chancellor of the Chapel-Royal at Stirling. He was made Bishop of the Isles in 1566 by Mary, Queen of Scots. On his death in 1572, he was buried at Ardchattan Priory [NM 971349], and the property passed to the Campbells of Auchinbreck. Carnasserie was captured and sacked by the MacLeans and MacLachlans during the Earl of Argyll's rebellion of 1685. The ruin is now in the care of Historic Scotland and is open to the public.

No. of castles/sites: 2
Rank: 396=/764
Xref: Carswell

Carstairs

The name is territorial in origin and comes from the lands of Carstairs, which are in Lanarkshire. The family are mentioned in charters from the middle of the thirteenth century.

Carstairs Castle [NS 939461] dated from the thirteenth century but nothing now remains; materials from the building were apparently used to built the parish church in 1794. The lands were held by the Bishops of Glasgow, and then by the Carstairs family, but passed to the Hamiltons in 1535.

Cassingray [NO 490070] lies some six or so miles south of St Andrews in Fife, and there may have been a castle or old house here. The property was held by the Carstairs family from the seventeenth century or earlier, but later passed to the Melvilles.

Kilconquhar Castle [NO 494027], a couple of miles north of Elie also in Fife, is a large mansion of the 1830s but incorporates a tall tower house dating from the sixteenth century. The castle was built by the Bannatynes, but was sold to Sir John Carstairs in 1640. It is now part of a holiday time share development (01333 340501; www.kilconquharcastle.co.uk).

No. of castles/sites: 3
Rank: 328=/764

Cathcart

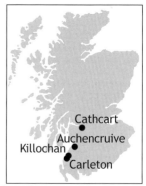

The name is territorial, and comes from the Cart River just south of Rutherglen near Glasgow. The family are recorded from the twelfth century, and they held the lands from this time.

Cathcart Castle [NS 586599] was built in about 1450, although there may have been an older fortress here. The building consisted of a strong tower enclosed by a rectangular courtyard with round corner towers.

Cathcart Castle 1910?

The Cathcarts had supported Robert the Bruce, and Sir Alan Cathcart was slain at Loudoun Hill in 1307. The property passed to the Semples in 1546, and the castle was abandoned and unroofed in the 1740s. The ruin was further reduced in 1980 and now only the base of the tower survives. It stands in Linn Park (0141 637 1147; www.glasgow.gov.uk).

The family acquired the lands of Auchencruive, three miles east and north of Ayr, from the Wallaces in 1374, and **Auchencruive Castle** [NS 387235] became their main seat. In 1447 the family were made Lords Cathcart and were made keepers of the royal castle of Dundonald. Several members of the family were killed at Flodden in 1513. Alan Cathcart, fourth Lord Cathcart, was a Protestant, and fought against Mary Queen of Scots at the Battle of Langside in 1568. The family were Hanoverians, and fought the Jacobites at Sheriffmuir in 1715 and at Culloden in 1746, where Charles Cathcart, eighth lord, was wounded. The family were made Earls of Cathcart in 1814 after William Cathcart, tenth lord, had had a successful military career. Auchencruive had passed to the Murrays in 1758, and the castle was replaced by what is now called Oswald Hall, an Adam mansion of 1767. It has been owned by the Scottish Agricultural College since 1927, and the grounds are accessible to the public. The line of the Earl of Cathcart continues, but they now apparently live Norfolk.

Killochan Castle [NS 227004] is one of the best and most impressive castles in Ayrshire, standing three miles north and east of Girvan. It is a tall L-plan tower house,

Killochan Castle (M&R)

dating from the sixteenth century, and replaced an older stronghold. The building is crowned by turrets and is dated 1586. Killochan was held by the Cathcarts from the fourteenth century. Robert Cathcart of Killochan was killed at the Battle of Flodden in 1513. In the feud between the Cassillis and Bargany branches of the Kennedys, the Cathcarts supported their neighbours of Bargany, and John Cathcart, builder of the castle, commanded the rearguard at a battle at Pennyglen, during which Bargany was mortally wounded. The Cathcarts occupied Killochan, although not continuously, until 1954.

Carleton Castle [NX 133895], some miles south of Girvan, is an atmospheric ruin, dating from the fifteenth

Carleton Castle (M&R)

century. It was held by Sir John Cathcart, who – the story goes – had had seven wives, but all of them had died or disappeared. He was then married to May Kennedy of Culzean, and one day they were walking on

cliffs at Games Loup. Cathcart tried to throw May to her death, but she was too quick for him and he ended up dead at the foot of the cliffs. Ghostly cries are said to have been heard from the vicinity of the old castle.

The Cathcarts also owned:

Auchendrane Castle [NS 335152], near Ayr; castle replaced by mansion.
  Held by the Kennedys, but passed by marriage to the Cathcarts in 1793 and was sold to the Coats in 1868. Blairstone House replaced the castle.

Camregan Castle [NX 215987], near Girvan, Ayrshire; slight remains of castle with ditch.
  Held by the Cathcarts from the thirteenth century.

Carnell [NS 467323], near Kilmarnock, Ayrshire; castle and mansion.
  Held by the Wallaces and then by the Cathcarts in the seventeenth century before returning to the Wallaces. The house is available to rent as holiday accommodation (01563 884236; www.carnellestates.com).

Dalmellington Castle [NS 482058], near Dalmellington, Ayrshire; motte and ditch.
  Held by the Cathcarts from the twelfth century and formerly a strong place. Also known as Dame Helen's Castle.

Easter Greenock Castle [NS 300755], near Greenock, Renfrewshire; site of large castle.
  Held by the Stewarts, by the Hamiltons, by the Shaws and then by the Cathcarts for some years, but returned to the Stewarts. Demolished in 1886 to allow the building of a railway.

Greenock Castle [NS 280765], Greenock, Renfrewshire; site of castle replaced by mansion.
  Held by the Cathcarts but passed to the Hamiltons and then the Shaws, later Shaw-Stewarts.

Kisimul Castle [NL 665979], Isle of Barra, Outer Hebrides; impressive castle on island in bay.
  Long held by the MacNeils, but the Cathcarts held Barra after the island had passed by marriage from the Gordons after 1840. The castle in the care of Historic Scotland and is open to the public from April to September (01871 810313).

Milncraig [NS 400208], near Ayr; site of castle or old house.
  Held by the Cathcarts of Corbieston, but passed by marriage to the Cunninghams of Milncraig around the end of the sixteenth century.

Pitcairlie House [NO 236148], near Auchtermuchty; mansion incorporating Z-plan tower.
  Held by the Abernethys and by the Leslies, and then by the Cathcarts from about 1750 until the twentieth century. Captain Robert Cathcart was captain of the Royal and Ancient Golf Course at St Andrews in 1901, and the building is said to have a Green Lady. Self-catering accommodation is available (01337 827418; www.pitcairlie-leisure.co.uk).

Sauchie Tower [NS 896957], near Alloa, Clackmannanshire; ruined tower being restored.
  Held by the Annans and then by the Shaws and then by the Cathcarts from 1752, one of whom William, was made Earl of Cathcart in 1814, and was ambassador to Russia during the Napoleonic Wars.

Sundrum Castle [NS 410213], near Ayr; mansion incorporating castle.
  Held by the Wallaces but passed to the Cathcarts, then to the Hamiltons by 1750. It has been divided into separate flats and was haunted by a Green Lady. Accommodation can be let (01530 244436; www.sundrumcastle.com).

Waterhead Castle or Little Rigend [NS 543115], near Dalmellington, Ayrshire; site of castle.
  Held by the MacAdams, but may have been a property of the Cathcarts at one time.

No. of castles/sites: 16
Rank: 86=/764

Cavens

The name is territorial and comes from the lands of Cavens, which are six miles south of New Abbey in Dumfries and Galloway. **Cavens Castle** [NX 958572] has gone and was replaced by a new mansion nearby at **Cavens** [NX 977584]. The lands passed to the Douglas Earls of Morton, and then to others, and Cavens House is now used as a hotel (01387 880234; www.cavens.com).

    Cruggleton Castle [NX 484428], which stands on cliffs two or so miles south of Garlieston in Galloway was once an important castle but is now very ruinous. It was held by several families including by the Comyns, by the Douglases and by others, including John Cavens in 1421.

No. of castles/sites: 2
Rank: 396=/764

Caverhill

The name is territorial and comes from the lands of Caverhill, which are a couple of miles south-west of Peebles in the Borders. The family are recorded at the beginning of the fifteenth century, and held **Caverhill** [NT 216383] until it passed to the Patersons of Caverhill in the sixteenth century. There was a tower house, but nothing now remains.

    There are also no remains of **Foulitch Tower** [NT 256436], a couple of miles north of Peebles. It was held by the Caverhills until 1559 or later, but eventually passed to the Williamsons.

No. of castles/sites: 2
Rank: 396=/764

Chalmers

The name comes from the office of chamberlain to the king or a chamber attendant, and can be spelt either Chalmers or Chambers. The name is recorded in Scotland from the twelfth century.

    Gadgirth Castle [NS 409223], some four and a half miles east of Ayr, was held by the Chalmers family from the twelfth century. Herbert was Great Chamberlain of Scotland from 1124 to 1153. James Chalmers of Gadgirth was a fervent Protestant, and earned the admiration of John Knox. Mary, Queen of Scots, is said to have visited, and John Knox to have preached, at Gadgirth. The property had passed to the Burnetts by the end of the nineteenth century. The castle, which dated from the fourteenth century, was replaced by Gadgirth House, built in 1801. Both castle and house were demolished in 1968 and the site was cleared.

    The Chalmers family owned two other properties in Ayrshire. **Kildonan** [NX 227831] is a large mansion on the site of a castle, just north-west of Barrhill. It was held by the Eccles family and then by the Chalmers family from the seventeenth century until 1830, when it was sold to the Hamiltons. Three miles north of Maybole was **Sauchrie Castle** [NS 303147], which was replaced by a small mansion in the late eighteenth century. It was a property of the Chalmers family in the seventeenth and eighteenth centuries but passed to the MacAdams.

A separate line came from the north-east of Scotland.

    Balbithan House [NJ 812189], three and a half miles south-east of Inverurie in Aberdeenshire, is a fine sixteenth-century L-plan tower house with turrets crowning the building. The lands were held by the Chalmers family from 1490, and they moved here from **Old Balbithan** [NJ 797174] because shots fired from the tower of Hallforest, a stronghold of the Keiths, landed in the courtyard of their old castle. Balbithan was sacked by Covenanters in 1640, and it provided refuge for

Balbithan House (M&R)

Jacobites after the Battle of Culloden in 1746. The property had passed to the Hays in 1690.

Two miles north-west of Torphins and also in Aberdeenshire is **Balnacraig** [NJ 604035], a mansion dating from the eighteenth century with three ranges around a courtyard. Balnacraig was held by the Chalmers family until 1735 when it passed to the Inneses.

The Chalmers family also held:

Aldbar Castle [NO 572577], near Brechin, Angus; site of large castle and mansion.
    Held by the Lyons and by others, but passed to Chalmers of Balnacraig, who held Aldbar in the twentieth century. The castle was demolished in 1965.
Cults [NJ 534313], near Huntly, Aberdeenshire; site of castle or old house.
    The Chalmers family held lands called Cults.
Drumlochy Castle [NO 158469], near Blairgowrie, Perthshire; little remains of a castle.
    Held by the Herons but possibly also by the Chalmers family. The castle was destroyed by the Blairs of Glasclune during a feud.
Loudoun Hall [NS 337221], Ayr; fine townhouse.
    Built by the Taits, but went to the Campbells of Loudoun around 1530, and then to Chalmers of Gadgirth in 1632. The building was restored in 1948.
Ormiston Tower [NT 315378], near Innerleithen, Borders; site of tower house and mansion.
    Held by the Stewarts of Traquair but bought by William Chambers, the well-known author and publisher, in 1849. William and his brother Robert established the company and published *Chamber's Encyclopedia*. William was Lord Provost of Edinburgh in 1865 and 1868, and he had St Giles Cathedral restored. Ormiston later went to the Thorburns.
Pitmedden House [NO 236117], Auchtermuchty, Fife; site of fortified house.
    The house was a property of James Chalmers, factor to James V. It was at the house that in 1517 Auchtermuchty was made a Royal Burgh, but the house was demolished in 1895.
Pittensear (now **Pittensair**) [NJ 282607], near Lhanbryde, Moray; site of old house.
    Held by the Chalmers family from early in the seventeenth century but the property later passed to the Ogilvies.
Polquhairn [NS 479158], near Drongan, Ayrshire; site of castle or old house.
    Held by the Cunninghams until the seventeenth century, then by the Chalmers family, and then by the Crawfords in the eighteenth century.
Rathven [NJ 444655], near Buckie, Aberdeenshire; site of castle.
    Held by the Chalmers family in the fourteenth century, then possibly by the Gordons of Letterfourie. Pronounced 'Raffen' or 'Raven'.
Tillery [NJ 915229], near Pitmedden, Aberdeenshire; ruin of mansion on site of castle.
    Held by the Udnys but in 1788 was purchased by John Chambers or Chalmers, who had been a plantation owner in the southern USA.

No. of castles/sites: 15
Rank: 94=/764
Xrefs: Chambers; Camera

Chancellor

The name comes from the office of 'chancellor', an important individual in either the church as a judge, or in the secular authorities as a recorder. The family held lands in Lanarkshire from 1432 or earlier. Lying three miles north-west of Biggar, **Shieldhill** [NT 008407] is a large mansion but incorporates a massive square keep dating from as early as 1199. The building was altered and extended down the centuries, and the keep is now the entrance hall to the rest of the house. Shieldhill was held by the Chancellor family, who supported Mary, Queen of Scots, and fought for her at the Battle of Langside in 1568. The castle is believed to be haunted by a Grey Lady, supposedly witnessed in recent years. Her apparition, wrapped in a grey cloak, has been seen in the old part of the building and in the burial ground. There are several versions of the story surrounding her, but she is said to be one of the daughters of a Chancellor laird who died tragically. The family left in the twentieth century, and the mansion is now a hotel (01899 220035; www.shieldhill.co.uk). The line of the family still flourishes and the Chancellors of Shieldhill now apparently live in Cambridgeshire in England.

Quothquan [NS 995395] stood nearby, some two and a half miles west and north of Biggar, and was also held by the Chancellors. Following their support for Mary, Queen of Scots at Langside in 1568, Quothquan Castle was razed by the Regent Moray and there are no remains.

No. of castles/sites: 2
Rank: 396=/764

Chaplin

The name comes from the religious office of 'chaplain', and members of the family are recorded in charters from the twelfth century. **Colliston Castle** [NO 612464], four miles north of Arbroath in Angus, is a fine Z-plan tower house with a main block and two round towers, one corbelled-out to square. The walls are harled and pink-washed. Colliston was held by the Guthries, who built Colliston, but in 1721 the property passed to the Chaplins, who held Colliston until 1920. The castle is still a private residence.

No. of castles/sites: 1
Rank: 537=/764

Charteris

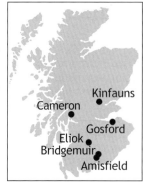

The name comes from the city of Chartres in France, which is famous for its cathedral. William of Chartres is believed to have come to England with William the Conqueror, and the family then came to Scotland in the retinue of David I in the twelfth century. Sir Thomas Charteris was High Chancellor of Scotland in 1280.

Amisfield Tower [NX 992838] is one of the best preserved and most interesting of all Border strongholds, and lies some five miles north of Dumfries in southern

Amisfield Tower (M&R)

Scotland. It is a sixteenth-century tower house, square in plan, of four storeys and a garret. The upper works of the building have a profusion of corbelling and turrets. The family supported Robert the Bruce, and William Charteris of Amisfield was with Bruce when the Red Comyn was stabbed to death in Dumfries in 1306. The Charteris family feuded with the Kilpatricks of Kirkmichael, and Roger Kilpatrick was murdered in 1526: several members of the Charteris family were charged with his murder. Sir Robert Charteris of Amisfield fought a duel with Sir James Douglas of Drumlanrig in 1530 in the presence of James V. **Amisfield House** [NX 992838] was built nearby in 1631, although it was much remodelled in the nineteenth century; the property had passed to the Dalziels of Newton in 1631. The tower is still a private residence, and the line of the Charteris family of Amisfield still continues and they apparently live in Dumfriesshire.

Bridgemuir [NY 093845], one and a half miles north-east of Lochmaben and also in Dumfriesshire, was held by the Charteris family at the end of the seventeenth century, but there are no remains of the tower that stood here.

Eliok House [NS 796074], two miles south-east of Sanquhar, more closely associated with the Crichtons, was held by the Charteris family in 1462, but then went back to the Crichtons. The house included part of a castle, and this part was burnt out in 1940 and remains ruinous.

Kinfauns [NO 151226] is a couple of miles east of Perth, and was held by the Charteris family. This branch claimed descent from Thomas de Longueville, 'The Red Rover'. He was a French knight who turned to piracy

Kinfauns Castle 1910?

after murdering a nobleman in the presence of Philip IV of France, and was known as the Red Rover from the colour of the sails of his ship. Around 1301, William Wallace captured him and managed to get Philip of France to pardon him. De Longueville then joined Wallace and after Wallace's death followed Robert the Bruce. In reward for his services in securing the capture of Perth from the English in 1313, he received a grant of lands and married the heiress of Charteris of Kinfauns, whose name he assumed. His two-handed sword was long preserved at Kinfauns Castle. This branch of the Charteris family feuded with the Ruthvens of Perth, and in 1552 John Charteris was murdered by the Ruthvens in Edinburgh's High Street. Kinfauns eventually passed to the Carnegies, and the building is now a private residence.

Cameron House [NS 376831], two miles north and west of Alexandria in Dunbartonshire, was held by the Lennox family, then by the Charterises, by the Dennistouns and by the Colquhouns, but was sold to the Smolletts in 1763. The mansion is now a hotel (01389 755565; www.cameronhouse.co.uk).

Gosford House [NT 453786], two miles north-east of Longniddry in East Lothian, is now home to the Charteris Earls of Wemyss and March (also see the Wemyss family). The house is a magnificent building, originally designed by Robert Adam but then rebuilt in the 1890s.

No. of castles/sites: 6
Rank: 212=/764

Cheape

The name is on record from the fifteenth century, and the Cheapes held the lands of **Mawhill** [NO 085035], which are a couple of miles west and north of Kinross. They may have had a castle, but Sir James Cheape bought the barony of Rossie in 1630, two miles to the east of Auchtermuchty in Fife. **Rossie House** [NO 265120] probably incorporated a tower house, which was mentioned in 1488 and 1541, but the old tower was removed when the house was extended in 1776. The property was held by the Cheapes until sold by the family in 1839.

Mugdrum [NO 228184], to the east of Newburgh also in Fife, was also held by the Cheapes in the seventeenth century. The house dates from the eighteenth century, but may incorporate older work; it later passed to the Murrays. This branch of the family is represented by the Cheapes of Strathtyrum and Fossoway, who still apparently hold Strathtyrum. **Strathtyrum House** [NO 491172], one mile to the north-west of St Andrews also in Fife, is a smart symmetrical mansion dating from the eighteenth century. The property passed to the Cheapes in 1782. Strathtyrum House is available for weddings and luxury accommodation on an exclusive basis (01334 473600; www.strathtyrumhouse.com).

Carse Gray [NO 464540], which is two miles north of Forfar in Angus, was held by the Grays from 1741, and the family is now Gray-Cheape.

No. of castles/sites: 5
Rank: 240=/764

Cheyne

The name is believed to come from Quesney, near Coutances in France, and means 'oak plantation', although this has sometimes wrongly been styled 'canis' meaning 'dog' ('chien' in French). The family are on record from the middle of the twelfth century, and are believed to have settled in Buckinghamshire in England before moving north. They held extensive lands in north-east Scotland and in Caithness.

Inverugie Castle [NK 102484], two and a half miles north-west of Peterhead in Aberdeenshire, was held by the Cheynes from the thirteenth century or earlier. Sir Reginald le Cheyne was Chamberlain of Scotland in the

Inverugie Castle (M&R)

1260s. The family were allied with the Comyns and so were enemies of Robert the Bruce, who destroyed their power, although another Reginald Cheyne added his seal to the Declaration of Arbroath in 1320. The lands passed by marriage to the Keiths. The castle is now quire ruinous, but was once an imposing place.

One and a half miles west and south of Ellon is **Castle of Esslemont** [NJ 932298], another Cheyne stronghold,

Castle of Esslemont (M&R)

99

and again little remains. Esslemont passed by marriage from the Marshalls and was held by the Cheynes until 1625 when it went to the Hays of Errol. The castle was sacked and torched in 1493 in the course of feud between the family and the Hays of Ardendracht.

Three miles north-west of Elgin in Moray is **Duffus Castle** [NJ 189672], a fine example of a motte and bailey castle, dating from the twelfth century. David I stayed here while supervising the construction of nearby Kinloss

Duffus Castle (MC)

Abbey. The castle was destroyed by the Scots during the Wars of Independence in 1297, but it was rebuilt in stone by the Cheynes in the late thirteenth or early fourteenth century, although this proved too much for the motte, and much of the tower has collapsed. Duffus passed by marriage to the Sutherland Lord Duffus in 1350 and the Sutherlands held Duffus until 1843. The castle is in the care of Historic Scotland and is open to the public all year.

Arnage Castle [NJ 936370], four and a half miles north of Ellon in Aberdeenshire, passed by marriage to the Cheyne family in the fourteenth century, who held

Arnage Castle (M&R)

it until it was sold to the Sibbalds in 1643. The building consists of a Z-plan tower house which has been extended by a mansion. The castle was restored in the 1930s and is still occupied.

Pitfichie Castle [NJ 677168] is a sixteenth-century tower house which has a large round tower projecting at one corner, and the building stands three and a half miles west of Kemnay, also in Aberdeenshire. Pitfichie was held by the Cheynes but passed to the Urie family. The castle was ruinous at one time, but has been restored as a private residence.

The Cheynes also owned other properties in the north-east and in Caithness:

Ackergill Tower [ND 352547], near Wick, Caithness; impressive tower and later mansion.
Held by the Cheynes but passed by marriage to the Keiths in 1350. The castle can be rented for exclusive use (01955 603556; www.ackergill-tower.co.uk).

Berriedale Castle [ND 121224], near Dunbeath, Caithness; very ruined castle.
Held by the Cheynes in the fourteenth century but passed by marriage to the Sutherlands, and then went to the Oliphants and then to the Sinclair Earls of Caithness. This is said to be the site of 'Beruvik' in the *Orkneyinga Saga*.

Brough Castle [ND 228741], near Castletown, Caithness; site of castle.
Held by the Cheynes at one time.

Caisteal Morar na Shein [ND 084461], near Watten, Caithness; site of castle.
Held by the Cheynes from around 1340 but ruinous by 1769.

Castle of Old Wick [ND 369488], near Wick, Caithness; picturesque ruin on cliffs.
Originally built by the Norseman, the castle was held by the Cheynes in the mid fourteenth century, but passed to the Sutherland Lord Duffus the same century, and then to other families. Held by Historic Scotland and open to the public but great care should be taken due to the location (01667 460232).

Dirlot Castle [ND 126486], near Watten, Caithness; site of castle.
Held by Cheynes but passed to the Gunns in the fifteenth century and then to others.

Dundarg Castle [NJ 895649], near Fraserburgh, Aberdeenshire; little remains of a castle.
Held by the Douglases and by the Borthwicks before passing to the Cheynes of Esslemont after 1550. It was probably abandoned a short time afterwards.

Forse Castle [ND 224338], near Dunbeath, Caithness; ruinous castle.
Held by the Cheynes but passed to the Keiths and then to the Sutherlands.

Ravenscraig Castle [NK 095488], near Peterhead, Aberdeenshire; ruined tower house with ditch.
Held by the Cheynes but passed by marriage to the Keiths in the fourteenth century and they built the castle.

Straloch House [NJ 860210], near New Machar, Aberdeenshire; castle replaced by mansion.
Held by the Cheynes but sold to the Gordons of Pitlurg in 1600.

No. of castles/sites: 15
Rank: 94=/764

Chiesly

The name is first recorded in Scotland in the 1530s.

Dalry House [NT 235728], which stands on Orwell Place in Edinburgh, was held by the Chiesly family in the seventeenth century. The fine building has hexagonal stair-towers and good plasterwork. John Chiesly of Dalry and his wife parted on acrimonious terms, and their dispute came to trial (there were eleven children to support). Sir George Lockhart of Carnwath, Lord President of the Court of Session, found against Chiesly in the divorce. Chiesly was outraged and in 1689 shot and killed Lockhart. Chiesly was caught and sentenced to be executed, and was mutilated, his arm being chopped off before he was hanged; the limb was displayed on a spike at the West Port. His one-armed apparition was reputedly often seen in and around Dalry House. When the house was renovated in the 1960s, the skeleton of a one-armed man was said to have been found, and his ghost has not apparently been witnessed since the remains were buried. The building is now an old people's day centre.

Chiesly's daughter, Rachel, a great beauty, was married to James Erskine, Lord Justice Clerk as Lord Grange and Lord of Justiciary; he was also the brother of John, sixth Earl of Mar, leader of the 1715 Jacobite Rising. Rachel (Lady Grange) and Erskine had several children, but the couple seem to have fallen out. When she discovered his Jacobite plotting in 1732, James had Rachel imprisoned, first in central Scotland and then in the Western Isles. After years of poor treatment, Rachel is thought to have died on Skye in 1745 and to be buried at Trumpan.

Cockburn House [NT 147651], which is a mile or so west and south of Balerno, is a late seventeenth-century mansion, L-plan in design and rising to two storeys and an attic. The lands were held by the Lindsays but in 1671 passed to William Chiesly, and he built the house, although he only held the property for a few years. The house is still occupied.

No. of castles/sites: 2 / Rank: 396=/764

Cockburn House (M&R)

Chirnside

The name is territorial and comes from the lands of Chirnside, which are four or so miles east of Duns in Berwickshire in the Borders. The property was presumably held by the family at one time, and there was a tower house at **Chirnside** [NT 870560], although this was apparently built by the Earl of Dunbar. The tower was demolished in the eighteenth century, but there is a sixteenth-century doocot near the church.

Balintore Castle [NO 290590], some five miles northwest of Kirriemuir in Angus, is a nineteenth-century mansion, designed by the architect David Bryce, and held by the Chirnside family in the nineteenth century. The building was abandoned in the 1960s.

No. of castles/sites: 2
Rank: 396=/764

Chisholm

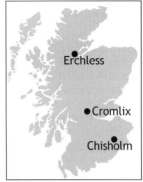

The name is territorial and comes from the lands and barony of Chisholm, which lie some six miles west and south of Hawick in the Borders. The family are first mentioned in the twelfth century, and may have had a castle or seat at **Chisholm** [NT 418122]. The present mansion of Chisholme dates from the eighteenth century, and is a private residence.

Erchless Castle [NH 410408], eight miles west and south of Beauly in Inverness-shire in the north of Scotland, became the main seat of the Chisholms in the fifteenth century, after passing by marriage to them from the Frasers. The present building is an altered L-plan tower house of four storeys and a higher stair-tower, which dates from the sixteenth century. In 1689 the castle was attacked by 500 Jacobites, led by Bonnie

Erchless Castle (M&R)

Dundee. The Chisholms, however, fought for the Jacobites at the Battle of Sheriffmuir in 1715; and in 1746 the chief's son and thirty of his men were killed at the Battle of Culloden. Sensibly, as it turned out, the chief and two other sons had not openly supported the Jacobites, and the family kept their lands. The castle is no longer owned by the Chisholms, but it is still occupied. The line of Chisholm of Chisholm continues, but they now apparently live in Suffolk. Self-catering accommodation is available at Erchless (01463 226990; www.scotland-holiday-homes.co.uk).

Cromlix Castle [NN 789064] stood three miles north of Dunblane in Stirlingshire, but little now survives, and the building was demolished in the nineteenth century and replaced by a new mansion. The lands were long a

property of the Chisholms of Cromlix, and three of the family (two Williams and a James) were Bishops of Dunblane, one of whom became Bishop of Vaison from 1570-85. Anne Chisholm, born at Cromlix in 1551, was in 1581 married to John Napier, the inventor of logarithms. The family opposed the Reformation and Sir James Chisholm of Cromlix was excommunicated by the General Assembly in 1593. The castle was unroofed in 1715, presumably because the Chisholms were Jacobites. One story is that Ann Chisholm of Cromlix was romantically involved with Sir Malaise Graham of nearby Kilbryde Castle. Graham appears to have tired of his love, and murdered her and hid her body in Kilbryde Glen. Her ghost, an apparition in a white blood-stained dress, is said to have been seen there and the story is that her bogle did not rest until her remains were found and properly buried.

The lands later passed to the Drummond Earls of Kinnoul.

Several other properties were held by the Chisholms:
Dores Castle [NO 253358], near Coupar Angus, Perthshire; site of castle.
    Possibly used by Macbeth in the eleventh century, but the lands were later held by the Chisholms of Pitcur.
Glassingall [NN 798045], near Dunblane, Perthshire; mansion on site of castle.
    Held by the Chisholms of Glassingall, and William Chisholm of Glassingall was prominent during the Reformation. The lands had passed to the Smiths by the nineteenth century.
Newhall, Kinrossie or **Thorngreen** [NO 186319], near Perth; site of castle.
    Kinrossie was held by the Chisholms.
Pitcur Castle [NO 252370], near Coupar Angus, Perthshire; massive but ruinous L-plan tower house.
    Held by the Chisholms from 1315 or earlier until 1432 when it passed by marriage to the Halyburtons of Dirleton and then much later to the Menzies family.
Stirches or **Stirkshaw** [NT 498162], near Hawick, Borders; altered tower house.
    Held by the Scotts but was bought by the Chisholms in 1650. The building is now apparently used as a Catholic Home for Ladies.

www.clanchisholmsociety.org
No. of castles/sites: 8
Rank: 160=/764

Christie

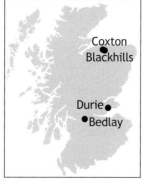

The name is a diminutive of Christian or Christopher, and was found widely in Fife. It is on record in Scotland from the fifteenth century.

Durie House [NO 372025], one mile northwest of Leven in Fife, is a classical mansion dating from 1762 although there was a castle here before the house was built. Durie was long associated with the Durie family, but the family was forfeited around 1614; the property passed to the Gibsons and then to the Christies in the eighteenth century. The house is still occupied.

A few miles south and east of Kirkintilloch in Lanarkshire is **Bedlay Castle** [NS 692701], an L-plan tower house of the sixteenth century with later modifications. Bedlay was held by the Boyds and by the Robertsons, but after 1805 passed by marriage from the Campbells of Petershill to the Christies. The castle is still occupied.

A later mansion which replaced **Cowden Castle** [NS 987997], two miles north-east of Dollar in Clackmannanshire, was held by the Christie family at the end of the nineteenth century. This mansion was, however, demolished in 1952.

Coxton Tower [NJ 262607], three miles east and south of Elgin in Moray, is a fine well-preserved tower house, which is said to have been built in 1644 although it appears to be considerably older. The lands were held by the Innes family and then by the Duffs of Fife but Coxton was later sold to the Christie family, who still apparently hold it.

Blackhills [NJ 270587] is nearby, some two miles south of Lhanbryde, and there was a small tower house and courtyard, although this has been replaced by a later mansion. The property has the same latter ownership as Coxton, and cottages can be rented on the estate and the gardens are occasionally open to the public (01343 842223; www.blackhills.co.uk).

No. of castles/sites: 5
Rank: 240=/764

Chrystal

The name is derived from a diminutive of Christopher, and it is recorded in Scotland from the middle of the sixteenth century. Thomas Chrystal, who died in 1535, was the abbot of Kinloss Abbey from 1499.

Auchendennan Castle or House [NS 368835], in a lovely spot on the shore of Loch Lomond two miles north-west of Balloch in Dunbartonshire, dates from the nineteenth century and has no older origins. It was owned by the Chrystal family, and is reputedly haunted by the ghost of girl known as Veronica and an apparition has been seen in one of the rooms. The building is now a youth hostel (0870 0041136; www.syha.org.uk).

No. of castles/sites: 1
Rank: 537=/764

Claverhouse

The name is territorial and comes from the lands of the same name, which are three and a half miles north of Dundee in Angus.

Claverhouse Castle [NO 405339] was held by a family of the same name, but the last remains of the stronghold were cleared away in 1792. There is another **Claverhouse** [NO 380442] at Milton of Ogilvie and also known as Hatton of Ogilvie, some seven and a half miles north of Dundee. This property was held by the Ogilvies ut had passed to the Grahams by the seventeenth century, and it is from here that John Graham of Claverhouse, Bonnie Dundee or Bloody Clavers, took his title.

No. of castles/sites: 1
Rank: 537=/764

Clayhills

The name comes from the lands of Clayhills, which are to the east of Blairgowrie in Perthshire. The family held two properties in Angus in the seventeenth century.

Baldovie [NO 324541], four and a half miles west of Kirriemuir, was owned by the Melvilles but passed to the Clayhills in the seventeenth century, and then later went to the Ogilvies. There was probably a castle or tower house.

Invergowrie House [NO 363304] stands two miles west of Dundee and the mansion incorporates a sixteenth-century tower house. The lands were bought from the Murrays by Robert Clayhills of Baldovie in 1615. The house was remodelled in 1837 but has since been divided into separate residences.

No. of castles/sites: 2
Rank: 396=/764

Clelland

The name is territorial and comes from the lands of Clelland or Kneland, which are one mile north and west of Wishaw in Lanarkshire in central Scotland. The name is on record from the thirteenth century. William Cleland was a Covenanter and fought at the battles of Bothwell Brig and then Drumclog in 1679 (when only eighteen years of age). He fled to Holland but was then made colonel of the Cameronians in the Jacobite Rising of 1689. He managed to hold Dunkeld against the Jacobites, but he was slain during the fighting.

Cleland Castle [NS 784577] was once a strong castle, but nothing remains. It was held by the family of the same name, who were hereditary foresters to the Earls of Douglas. Alexander Clelland is said to have been the husband of William Wallace's sister, and to have fought at the Battle of Bannockburn in 1314. A cave below Cleland Castle was reputedly used as a hiding place by William Wallace, although it is not as big as it once was as much of it has since collapsed. Alexander Clelland died at the Battle of Flodden in 1513; while another Alexander was accused of being involved in the murder of Henry Stewart, Lord Darnley, the husband of Mary, Queen of Scots.

Airdrie House [NS 749654] stood to the west of Airdrie town in Lanarkshire, and had been built on the site of a castle. The lands were held by the Clellands, and William Wallace is said to have marshalled his army near the old castle before the disastrous Battle of Falkirk in 1298. The Clelland lord of the time is thought to have been his brother-in-law (as mentioned above). The property passed to the Hamiltons in 1490, and the

Monkland House (M&R) – see next column

mansion was demolished in 1964 when Monklands General Hospital was built. A similar fate befell **Monkland House** [NS 730633], which lay one mile south of nearby Coatbridge. It was demolished in 1950 following a series of fires. It was a substantial building, which had been developed out of a tower house, and dated from the sixteenth century. The lands were acquired by Sir James Clelland of Monkland and he built the tower. A housing estate now occupies the site.

Faskine [NS 760631], a couple of miles south of Airdrie, was an old house or castle of two storeys, but was demolished in 1900 and a farm built on the site. The lands were held by the Clellands from the end of the fifteenth century, and the second laird was slain at the Battle of Flodden in 1513. The property passed to the Stirlings. **Knownoble** [NS 794589], three miles north of nearby Wishaw, was also held by the family, but this building has also gone.

www.clan-cleland.org
No. of castles/sites: 5 / Rank: 240=/764
Xref: Cleland

Clephane

The name is believed to originate from a family who held lands in England, their name Clephane being derived from Clapham in Sussex. The family were in Scotland from about 1200, and may have held property in Lauderdale.

Just west of Cupar in Fife, **Carslogie House** [NO 353144] was developed from a tower house dating from the fourteenth century, and was remodelled in the eighteenth century; but the building is now quite ruinous. The Clephane family held Carslogie from the late twelfth century until 1804. Alan Clephane of Carslogie fought on the side of Robert the Bruce at the Battle of Bannockburn in 1314, but his right hand was severed in a melee. He had a replacement hand constructed from steel, which was fitted with springs so he could still wield his sword. The hand was apparently preserved at Carslogie, and is now apparently in the possession of the Marquis of Northampton after a marriage into that family. The house was occupied until about 1870.

Strathendry Castle [NO 226020], four miles north of Cardenden also in Fife, is a somewhat dour rectangular tower of three storeys and has a courtyard with later ranges of buildings. It was held by several families, including by the Strathendrys and by the Forresters of Carden, but passed to the Clephanes of Carslogie in the nineteenth century. The castle is still occupied.

No. of castles/sites: 2
Rank: 396=/764

Clerk

The name comes originally from somebody in a religious order, then later a scholar or a keeper of books. As a family name, Clerk or Clark is recorded in Scotland from the twelfth century, and the name was, and is, common throughout the lowlands. Clarkson is from 'clerk's son'.

Pittencrieff House [NT 087873], which now stands in a popular public park in Dunfermline in Fife, is a T-plan house which dates from the seventeenth century. The lands had several owners after the Reformation before coming to the Clerks in the seventeenth century, but the property was sold in 1762 and then held by a Colonel Forbes. The house is open to the public (01383 722935/313838; www.fifedirect.org/museums).

Gladney House [NT 280908], which stood to the south of Kirkcaldy in Fife, was a fine mansion, dating from the seventeenth century but with classical fea-

Gladney House (M&R)

tures; it was demolished in the 1930s during slum clearance. The property was held by the Clerks in 1649, but later passed to the Robertsons.

Wrychtishousis or Wrightshouses [NT 247724], also known as Burgh Muir and Barganie House, was once described as a curious old pile, and the house dated from the fourteenth century. It was located off Gillespie Crescent in Edinburgh and was demolished in 1802: a school, James Gillespie's, was built on the site. This moved to Bruntsfield House, and for many years Wrychtishousis was used as the Blind Asylum. It was held by the Clerks in 1664, and is the scene of a gruesome ghost story. At the end of the eighteenth century a servant reported seeing the apparition of a decapitated woman, with an infant in its arms, rising from the hearth in his

Wrychtishousis (M&R)

chamber. When the building was later demolished, the skeleton of a woman and her child were found: her head had been removed to fit her corpse into the space. The story behind the murder is that James Clerk was killed in battle, and his younger brother murdered Clerk's wife and their infant so that he could inherit the property.

The Clerks of Penicuik made their fortune in France, and when they returned to Scotland in 1646 John Clerk purchased the lands and barony of Penicuik, which is in Midlothian. He built the magnificent **Penicuik House** [NT 217592], half a mile south of the town, from the 1760s, a large classical mansion of three storeys which had sumptuous interiors. The house was burnt out in 1899 and remains a shell. The family still apparently lives in Penicuik and the grounds of Penicuik House are occasionally open to the public (www.gardensof scotland.org). Nearby **Penicuik Tower** [NT 220596] may have been an old tower house, but this was demolished by the Clerks and replaced by a folly in the 1750s.

    Also near Penicuik are **Uttershill Castle** [NT 235594], a ruinous sixteenth-century building; and **Ravensneuk Castle** [NT 224590], another ruin, demolished to provide materials for a park wall. Both of these were held by the Clerks from the beginning of the eighteenth century, by when both had already been abandoned. There was a tower house at **Dumcrieff** [NT 102036], south of Moffat in Dumfries and Galloway, but this was replaced by a mansion in the eighteenth century. It was held by the Clerks of Penicuik for some years before passing in 1785 to John Loudoun Macadam. It is still a private residence.

    Cammo House [NT 174747], four and a half miles west of Edinburgh Castle, dated from 1693 and stood in landscaped grounds. The property was held by several families including by the Clerks before going to the Watsons of Saughton in 1741. The house was abandoned in 1975 and was vandalised before being demolished. The grounds are a country park.

    Dundas Castle [NT 116767], a mile or so south of South Queensferry in West Lothian, is a massive L-plan tower dating from the fifteenth century. It was long held by the Dundas family, but then by the Stewarts from 1875, now Stewart-Clarks. The castle is available for exclusive hire for weddings or corporate hospitality (0131 319 2039; www.dundascastle.co.uk).

No. of castles/sites: 10 / Rank: 140=/764
Xrefs: Clark; Clarkson; Clerkson

Clugston

The name is territorial and comes from the lands and barony of the same name, which were four and a half miles west of Wigtown in Galloway. The lands were held by the Clugston family from the thirteenth century or earlier, and there is an impressive motte at **Boreland** [NX 355574], near **Clugston**. Adam Clugston rendered homage in 1296, and John Clugston was captured at the siege of Berwick Castle the same year. The family still apparently held the lands in the fifteenth century, but the property had passed by marriage to the Dunbars of Mochrum some time in the sixteenth century or earlier.

www.cstone.net
No. of castles/sites: 1
Rank: 537=/764

Clyne

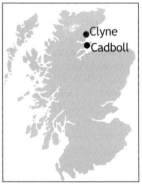

The name is territorial and comes from the lands of the same name two miles north of Brora in Suther-land in the far north of Scotland. There was a castle or old house at **Clyne** [NC 895060], although the location is not certain. It was held by the Clyne family until the middle of the sixteenth century. The laird died with only daughters as heirs and the lands passed by marriage to the Sutherlands of Clyne.

    Cadboll Castle [NH 879776], seven miles east and south of Tain in Ross and Cromarty, was held by the Clyne family in 1375, but passed to the MacLeods of Cadboll and then to the Sinclairs. The castle dates from the fourteenth century, and was modified into an L-plan tower house in following centuries; it is now a substantial ruin.

No. of castles/sites: 2
Rank: 396=/764

Coats

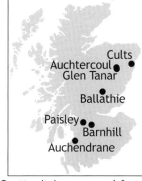

The name is apparently territorial and comes from the lands of Cults; there is more than one place from which this could come, including Cults to the south of Aberdeen. The surname was not uncommon in Upper Deeside, and could be spelt in several ways, including either Coats or Coutts. It is on record from the fourteenth century.

Auchtercoul or Ochtercoul [NJ 477023], four miles or so north-west of Aboyne in Aberdeenshire, was held by the family (Coutts) from 1433 or earlier, and they may have had a castle here. John and Donald Coutts had been outlawed in 1392 after being found guilty of the killing of Sir Walter Ogilvie, Sheriff of Angus, and of others. Sir James Coutts was in command of the king's ships in the reigns of both James IV and James V, and the family held the lands into the seventeenth century or later.

A branch of the family acquired Barnhill [NS 679574], which is near Blantyre three miles north-west of Hamilton, in the seventeenth century. The name was changed to Coats down the years, and James and Peter Coats founded J. and P. Coats in Paisley, a business producing thread and yarn, and the family were made Baronets in 1905. The family made many gifts to the burgh of Paisley, including parks and the Coats Observatory, which has displays on astronomy, meteorology and seismology, and is open to the public.

The family held Auchendrane [NS 335152], five miles south of Ayr, in the nineteenth century. There had been a castle here, long held by the Mures, but it was replaced by Blairstone House in the eighteenth century or earlier. Glen Tanar [NO 476956], three miles west and south of Aboyne in Aberdeenshire, was bought by the family in 1905, but the house has been greatly reduced to the ballroom; and Ballathie [NO 146367], seven miles south of Blairgowrie, in 1910. Ballathie House was converted to hotel in the 1970s (01250 883268; www.ballathie househotel.com).

No. of castles/sites: 5
Rank: 240=/764
Xrefs: Coates; Coutts

Cochrane

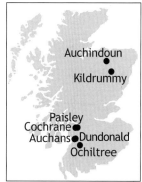

The name is territorial and comes from the lands of Cochrane, which are west of Johnstone in Renfrewshire. The story goes that the family are descended from a Norse incomer sometime before the end of the tenth century. The name Cochrane may be derived from the Gaelic for 'roar of battle', or from 'brave man', and it is said that one of the family slew three wild boars which were terrorising the area, hence the boars' heads on the chief's emblem.

The lands of that name were held by the Cochranes from the fourteenth century, but their stronghold Cochrane Castle [NS 418616] is gone. The site is commemorated by a small corbiestepped memorial which has a stone with the Cochrane arms and the date 1592. The lands were sold to the Johnstones in 1790. There was also a castle known as Easter Cochrane [NS 425623], now called Johnstone Castle. This is an altered sixteenth-century L-plan tower house, which had been extended by a mansion, and was held by the Cochranes until sold to the Houstons in 1733, who changed the name to Johnstone. The tower still survives but the mansion was demolished in 1950, and the surviving building stands in a housing scheme.

The Cochranes bought the lands and barony of Paisley in Renfrewshire from the Douglas Earls of Angus in 1653. Place of Paisley [NS 485639], by the abbey church, had been remodelled as a four-storey tower house on the site of the cloister ranges. In the eighteenth and nineteenth centuries the Place was used as dwellings and as a public house, but it was later restored to be used as the manse for the adjoining abbey church.

Dundonald Castle [NS 364345], three and a half miles north-east of Troon in Ayrshire, was long held by the Stewarts but was purchased by the Cochranes in 1636, although it was soon abandoned as a residence. Sir William Cochrane used materials from the old stronghold to rebuild nearby Auchans [NS 355346]. This

Dundonald Castle (M&R)

107

Auchans (RWB)

is now a ruinous L-plan tower house, which had been held by the Wallaces. Sir William Cochrane suffered financially during the Civil War of the 1650s because he supported the Royalists, but he was later rewarded by being made Earl of Dundonald in 1669. The property later passed to the Montgomery Earls of Eglinton. Dundonald Castle is open from the public (01563 851489; www.dundonald castle.org.uk).

Ochiltree Castle [NS 510212], ten miles east of Ayr, passed from the Stewarts to the Cochranes in 1675. There was a castle and then a later mansion, but these were completely demolished around 1950, and the site is occupied by a modern house. The direct line of the Earls of Dundonald failed, and the earldom passed to the Cochranes of Ochiltree. There was a succession of successful military men in the family, not least Thomas, tenth Earl, who in 1801 captured a Spanish frigate of thirty-two guns with only a brig and a crew of fifty-four men. After he had complained about the conditions in the Navy, he was convicted on trumped-up charges. He left Britain and in 1817 helped Chile with its own navy, and was instrumental in securing independence for that country and also for Peru, for Brazil and then for Greece. He was welcomed back to Britain in 1832, made a rear admiral, and was buried in Westminster Abbey. The family line continues, and the Earls of Dundonald now apparently have their seat at **Lochnell House** [NM 887390], six miles north of Oban in Argyll.

Auchindoun Castle [NJ 348374], which is two and a half miles south and east of Dufftown in Moray, is a substantial and picturesque ruinous L-plan tower house. It was held by Robert Cochrane, a master mason, who was one of James III's favourites. In 1482 he was hanged from Lauder Bridge by nobles led by Archibald 'Bell the Cat' Douglas, Earl of Angus. Auchindoun passed to the Ogilvies and then to the Gordons. The ruin is in the care of Historic Scotland and can be viewed from the exterior (01667 460232).

The Cochranes also owned several other properties:
Drumstinchall [NX 884580], near Dalbeattie, Galloway; site of castle.
 Held by the Murrays and then by the Cochranes after 1750, then passed to the Hanbury family.
Gallowhill [NS 499650], near Renfrew; site of castle and mansion.
 Held by the Hamiltons and then by the Cochrane Earls of Dundonald in the middle of the seventeenth century.

Kildrummy Castle [NJ 454164], near Kildrummy, Aberdeenshire; fantastic ruined castle.
 Held by the Cochranes before 1507, then passed to the

Kildrummy Castle (M&R)

 Elphinstones and then to others. In the care of Historic Scotland and open to the public April to September (01975 571331).
Kilmaronock Castle [NS 456877], near Drymen, Stirlingshire; ruined castle.
 Held by several families before coming to the Cochrane Earls of Dundonald, then passed to John McGoune in the eighteenth century.
Ladyland Castle [NS 324579], near Kilbirnie, Ayrshire; castle replaced by mansion.
 Held by the Barclays and by the Montgomerys before being bought by the Cochranes in 1717. The present house dates from 1817-21, and is apparently occupied by the Kennedy-Cochran-Patricks of Ladyland.
Lee Castle [NS 580590], near East Kilbride, Renfrewshire; site of castle.
 Held by Cochrane of The Lee in the fifteenth century, but passed to the Pollocks of Balgray. The foundations were cleared away in 1840.
Murieston Castle [NT 050636], near West Calder, West Lothian; ruined tower house, rebuilt as a folly.
 Held by the Cochranes at one time, as well as by the Sandilands, by the Steels in 1903 and perhaps by the Williamsons.
Ralston [NS 507642], near Paisley, Renfrewshire; site of mansion and castle.
 Held by the Ralstons but was sold to the Cochrane Earl of Dundonald in 1704, then later passed to the Hamiltons and then to the Orrs.
Ranfurly or **Ranforlie Castle** [NS 384652], near Bridge of Weir, Renfrewshire; ruined castle.
 Held by the Knoxs and then from 1665 by the Cochrane Earls of Dundonald, then was sold to the Hamiltons of Holmhead.
Rochsoles House [NS 756678], near Airdrie, Lanarkshire; site of castle and mansion.
 Held by the Cochranes but passed to the Gerard family, who held the property in the twentieth century.

www.clancochrane.org
No. of castles/sites: 19
Rank: 72=/764

Cockburn

The name is probably territorial and comes from the lands of Cockburn, one mile north-west of Preston in Berwickshire in the Borders. The derivation of the name may be from 'gowk's burn', 'gowk' being the Scottish term for the cuckoo: this may explain with it is usually pronounced 'Co'burn'; alternatively it may be from the English name 'Colbrand'.

The lands of Cockburn were held by the family of that name from the thirteenth century or earlier. Peres Cockburn appears on the Ragman Roll, when he did homage to Edward I of England in 1296. The family were made Baronets in 1671. They had a tower house at **Cockburn** [NT 770591] in the sixteenth century but there are no remains and the last vestige was removed in 1829.

Langton Castle [NT 756534], two miles west of Duns also in Berwickshire, dated from the fifteenth century and was later replaced by a mansion, which was itself demolished in the 1950s. The property was held by the Viponts but passed to the Cockburns after 1314, when the Vipont laird was killed at Bannockburn. The Cockburns were made hereditary ushers to the Kings of Scots. James IV had artillery brought here in September 1496 during the Raid of Ellem to try to keep the borderers in line. Sir William Cockburn and his son, Alexander, were both killed at the Battle of Flodden in 1513. Mary, Queen of Scots, visited the castle in 1566, and the castle was still occupied at the end of the seventeenth century. Langton was sold in 1758 to the Gavin family and then went to others. A new mansion was built in 1862, but this was demolished in the 1950s. The family line continues, now twelfth Baronet, and the Cockburns now apparently live in England.

Cockburn's Tower or **Henderland** [NT 230235], which is just west of Cappercleuch near St Mary's Loch in the Borders, was a sixteenth-century tower, although nothing survives but an overgrown mound. William Cockburn of Henderland, a noted Border reiver, was reportedly hanged from his own gates for treason by James V in 1530, although the execution probably took place in Edinburgh and was by beheading. The event is recorded in the tragic ballad 'The Border Widow's Lament'. After his execution, his wife tried to drown herself in a burn, at a place now called 'Lady's Seat'.

Two miles north-east of Biggar in Lanarkshire is **Skirling Castle** [NT 072398], once a substantial stronghold but little survives except the moat. It was a Cockburn property from the fourteenth century, and Skirling was visited by Mary, Queen of Scots, in 1563. The family supported their queen, and the castle was blown up with gunpowder on the orders of Regent Moray five years later. The lands passed to the Carmichaels and then to the Oswalds in 1683.

Ormiston Castle [NT 413677] stood four miles east of Dalkeith in Midlothian, but little is left of the original stronghold. It was a property of the Cockburns from the fourteenth century, and in 1545 George Wishart was held here before being taken to St Andrews where he was burned as a heretic. The Cockburns of Ormiston sided with, and the castle was garrisoned by, the dreaded English. The Earl of Arran besieged and seized Ormiston, torched the building, and even cut down the trees around it, in revenge for Cockburn's treachery. Adam Cockburn of Ormiston was made a Lord of Session in 1705 as Lord Ormiston, and was an agricultural improver. His son, John, was a member of the last Scottish Parliament and was a commissioner for the Union of 1707. His attempt in trying to improve the estate was less successful and the lands were sold in 1748 to the Hope Earls of Hopetoun.

Penkaet Castle [NT 427677], one mile south-west of Pencaitland in East Lothian, is a fine sixteenth-century tower house, which was extended in the seventeenth century and later. The east wing is dated 1628, and was probably built when it was held by the Cockburns in the

Penkaet Castle (M&R)

seventeenth century; it had passed to the Pringles in 1636 and then went to others. The building is said to be haunted by the spirit of John Cockburn, and the unexplained sounds of footsteps and the dragging of a heavy object have been reported, believed to relate to a murder. The ghost of Alexander Hamilton has also reputedly been witnessed in the grounds. He was denied hospitality and cursed the family, and the lady of the house and her daughter soon both died from a sudden illness. Hamilton was blamed for this, and other accusations included the use of witchcraft; and he was executed in 1630 by being throttled and then burned on Castle Hill in Edinburgh.

The Cockburns also held:
Bonaly Tower [NT 214678], near Edinburgh; mansion.
Held by the famous judge and author Henry Cockburn of Cockpen, Lord Cockburn, who died in 1854.
Borthwick Castle [NT 770544], near Duns, Borders; site of tower lost to quarrying.
Held by the Cockburns; a commemorative stone stands near the site.

Carriden House [NT 026808], near Bo'ness, West Lothian; altered tower house.
  Held by the Viponts but passed by marriage to the Cockburns, who held Carriden from 1358 or earlier until 1541 when the property went to the Abercrombys. B&B accommodation is available (01506 829811; www.carridenhouse.co.uk).

Cockpen [NT 325637], near Bonnyrigg, Midlothian; site of castle.
  Held by the Ramsays but passed to Henry Cockburn of Cockpen, Lord Cockburn, who died in 1854.

Duns Castle [NT 777544], Duns, Borders; impressive castle and mansion.
  Held by the Homes before passing to the Cockburns after 1645 and then went to the Hays, who still own it. Accommodation is available (01361 883211; www.dunscastle.co.uk) and the castle stands in country park.

Langhaugh Tower [NT 202310], near Peebles, Borders; site of tower house.
  Held by the Bairds with the Cockburns as tenants. In 1561 this led to a dispute between Janet Scott, widow of Baird of Posso, and William Cockburn.

Mayshiel [NT 622641], near Cranshaws, East Lothian; altered tower house.
  Held by the Stewarts and then by the Cockburns in the seventeenth century, then passed to the Maxwells and then to others. Occupied as a private residence.

Vogrie House [NT 375635], near Gorebridge, Midlothian; fine mansion.
  The lands were held by the Cockburns, but passed to the Dewars at the beginning of the eighteenth century and they built the mansion. The grounds are now a country park (01875 821990).

No. of castles/sites: 14
Rank: 104=/764

Collace

The name is territorial and comes from the lands and barony of Collace in Perthshire, seven or so miles north-east of Perth.

The Collace family are mentioned in the four-teenth century, and they may have had a castle, the site of which is possibly at **Dunsinnan House** [NO 167329]. The house was owned by the Nairnes from the fifteenth until the nineteenth century.

Balnamoon [NO 552638], three or so miles north-west of Brechin in Angus, consists of an altered fifteenth-century castle and a nineteenth-century mansion. The old castle was built by the Collaces. Collace of Balnamoon and his 300 men changed sides and probably turned the outcome of the Battle of Brechin in 1457, resulting in the defeat of the Earl of Crawford. The lands had gone to the Carnegies at the beginning of the seventeenth century. Balnamoon is apparently still occupied by their descendants, the Carnegy-Arbuthnott family.

No. of castles/sites: 2
Rank: 396=/764

Cockpool

The name is probably territorial and comes from the lands of Cockpool, which are seven or so miles west of Annan in Dumfries and Galloway in the far south of Scotland.

Cockpool [NY 070677] was held by the family of the same name, but had passed to the Murrays by 1320. Cockpool Castle was abandoned about 1450 when the Murrays built Comlongon Castle, and there are no remains at Cockpool.

Moss Castle [NY 126723], five miles north-west of Annan, was a medieval castle, most likely built in the remains of an Iron Age fort. A round ditch and bank survive. The lands were held by the Cockpools in the fifteenth century, but also probably passed to the Murrays. Nearby **Murraythwaite** [NY 127726], where there is a modern mansion, was long a property of the Murrays.

No. of castles/sites: 2
Rank: 396=/764

Collison

The name come from the 'son of Coille', 'Coille' being a diminutive for Nicholas. Collison was common in Aberdeenshire, and is on record from the fifteenth century.

The lands of **Auchlunies** [NO 890998] are some three miles north-west of Portleithen in Kincardineshire, and the house is an E-plan mansion of two storeys, but with work from the seventeenth century. There was probably a castle here, and the lands were held by the Collisons in the six-teenth and seventeenth centuries. Two of the family were provosts of Aberdeen, and members of the Col-lisons are buried in St Nicholas Church [NJ 940062] in Aberdeen, which is open to the public (01224 643494; www.kirk-of-st-nicholas.org.uk). Auchlunies passed from the family, but is still occupied, although as three sepa-rate dwellings.

No. of castles/sites: 1
Rank: 537=/764

Colquhoun

The name comes from the lands of Colquhoun, which are in Dunbartonshire, near Loch Lomond. The family were descended from a Humphrey of Kilpatrick, who was given the lands by one of the Earls of Lennox in the thirteenth century. They then began to use the designation of their lands, and became known as the Colquhouns. Around 1368 the clan acquired **Luss** [NS 360930], when Sir Robert Colquhoun married the 'Fair Maid of Luss', heiress of Godfrey, sixth laird. The family designation then became the Colquhouns of Luss.

Dunglass Castle [NS 436735], a couple miles east of Dumbarton, became their main stronghold for some years. The castle dated from the fourteenth century,

Dunglass Castle (M&R)

and this became a substantial place, but little now remains of the original castle. The Colquhouns were made keepers of Dumbarton Castle, but Dunglass passed from the clan in 1738 when it went to the Edmonstones; the site is now in an oil terminal.

Two miles south of Luss on the banks of Loch Lomond is **Rossdhu Castle** [NS 361896], which became the clan's main seat. The castle dates from the fifteenth century, but it is now very ruinous. It was replaced by nearby **Rossdhu House** [NS 362895], an attractive Adam-style mansion, which was built in 1772. The lands were held by the clan from the thirteenth century, but the lives of their chiefs were not destined to be peaceful. Sir John Colquhoun was assassinated on Inchmurrin, an island in Loch Lomond, in 1439; and another Sir John was killed by a cannon ball at the siege of Dunbar Castle in 1479. Sir Humphrey was slain at Bannachra (see below). Mary, Queen of Scots, visited Rossdhu, and the family were made Baronets of Nova Scotia in 1625. The new house was visited by Johnson and Boswell in 1773. Lady Helen, wife of Sir James Colquhoun, twenty-fifth laird of Luss, was none too enamoured of the good doctor when he waded through her new drawing room, water pouring from his boots, after returning from a boat trip on the loch. Indeed, Helen is believed to have been very house proud, and her ghost reputedly returns to the house

she loved; it has been most often reported in the staff quarters. Rossdhu House is now used as the clubhouse of the Loch Lomond golf club and accommodation is available (01463 655555; www.lochlomond.com). The ruinous chapel of St Mary [NS 361896] stands near the castle, and was probably first built in the twelfth century. Many of the Colquhouns were buried here.

Bannachra Castle [NS 343843], three miles east and north of Helensburgh in Dunbartonshire, was built by the Colquhouns in 1512, after the lands had passed to them from the Galbraiths. Sir Humphrey Colquhoun was murdered here by the MacGregors or by the MacFarlanes

Bannachra Castle (M&R)

in 1592. Sir Humphrey was shot by an arrow through a window, on his way to bed, having been illuminated and betrayed by a treacherous servant. Bannachra may have then been sacked, and does not appear to have been used afterwards. This and other events led to bad blood between the MacGregors and the Colquhouns, which came to battle at Glen Fruin in 1603. The Colquhouns were slaughtered, but the MacGregors were proscribed by James VI and their chief was executed.

Camstraddan Castle [NS 359922], also near Luss, was a property of the Colquhouns from 1395. The castle stood on an island in the bay, and was replaced by Camstradden House, which dates from 1739. One of the family fought at the Battle of Pinkie in 1547, and the Colquhouns of Luss now apparently live at Camstradden.

The Colquhouns also owned several other properties:
Ardincaple Castle [NS 282830], near Helensburgh, Dunbartonshire; castle and mansion, mostly demolished.
Held by the MacAulays and then by the Campbells before coming to the Colquhouns of Luss in 1890. The building was demolished in 1957.
Arrochar House [NN 297039], Arrochar, Dunbartonshire; castle or house replaced by hotel.
Long held by the MacFarlanes, but passed to the Colquhouns of Luss from 1767. The present building is a large hotel (01301 702238).
Balloch Castle [NS 386826], Balloch, Dunbartonshire; castle replaced by mansion.
Held by the Stewarts of Lennox and then by the Colquhouns of Luss from 1652, then to the Buchanans of Ardoch in the nineteenth century. The mansion is used as a visitor centre (01389 720620; www.lochlomond-trossachs.org).

Barnhill House [NS 425756], near Dumbarton; mansion incorporating part of castle.
   Held by the Colquhouns of Tresmass from 1543 or earlier.

Cameron House [NS 376831], near Alexandria, Dunbartonshire; mansion on site of castle.
   Held by the Lennox family, then by the Charteris family, by the Dennistouns and by the Colquhouns, but was sold to the Smolletts in 1763. The mansion is now an exclusive hotel (01389 755565; www.cameronhouse.co.uk).

Corston Tower [NO 208098], near Auchtermuchty, Fife; ruined castle.
   Held by the Ramsays and then by the Colquhouns from 1669.

Drumpellier House [NS 716650], near Coatbridge, Lanarkshire; site of castle or old house.
   Held by the Hamiltons and then by the Colquhouns, before passing to the Buchanans. The house has been demolished and the grounds are a country park (www.northlan.gov.uk).

Faslane Castle [NS 249903], near Faslane, Dunbartonshire; motte.
   Held by the Earls of Lennox and then by the MacAulays, then latterly by the Colquhouns of Luss.

Fincastle House [NN 870622], near Killiecrankie, Perthshire; mansion.
   Held by the Stewarts and then by the Colquhouns in the nineteenth century.

Garscadden Castle [NS 522710], near Bearsden, Dunbartonshire; site of castle and mansion.
   Held by the Flemings, by the Erskines and by the Galbraiths before going to the Colquhouns in 1664. Around the end of the eighteenth century, the laird of Garscadden was attending a drinking party at Law when another reveller mentioned how pale Garscadden appeared. Colquhoun of Kilmardinny told him that Garscadden had been dead for two hours, but he had not mentioned it for spoiling the party. This event is reportedly the origin of the phrase 'as gash as Garscadden', meaning deathly pale.

Glenmillan [NJ 593054], near Aboyne, Aberdeenshire; mansion on site of castle.
   Held by the Colquhouns at one time.

Inchgalbraith Castle [NS 369904], near Luss, Dunbartonshire; ruined castle on island.
   Held by the Galbraiths and then by the Colquhouns of Luss from the sixteenth century. The Colquhouns preferred Bannachra Castle, and Inchgalbraith was probably abandoned soon afterwards.

Kenmuir [NS 660622], near Rutherglen, Renfrewshire; site of castle.
   Held by the Colquhouns at one time, and also by the Corbetts.

Kilmardinny [NS 550727], Bearsden, Dunbartonshire; castle or old house replaced by mansion.
   The property was long held by the Colquhouns until the early eighteenth century when it went to the Grahams and then the Leitch family. The mansion houses the Kilmardinny Arts Centre. It was the laird of Kilmardinny who was so enjoying a night drinking and socialising with other local lairds that he decided not to mention that the laird of Garscadden had died (also see Garscadden above).

Overtoun Castle [NS 424761], near Dumbarton; mansion on site of castle.
   Held by the Colquhouns from fourteenth century until seventeenth century when Overtoun went to the Laings and then to others. The estate is open all year (www.overtoun house.com).

Tresmass [NS 428753], near Dumbarton; site of castle.
   Held by the Colquhouns of Tresmass, before they moved to Barnhills House in 1543, then later passed to the Lorane family.

www.clancolquhounsociety.co.uk
www.geocities.com/clancolquhoun_na
www.geocities.com/elachanuk
No. of castles/sites: 21
Rank: 63=/764

Colt

The name may be territorial and may come from a barony of Colt or Cult in Perthshire. The family is on record at the end of the thirteenth century.

Gartsherrie House [NS 726659], to the north of Coatbridge in central Scotland, stood on the site of castle, although this house has also been demolished. The lands were held by the Colts from the fourteenth century, but passed to the Whitelaws five hundred years later. The site of the house is apparently now occupied by a container base.

Inveresk House [NT 346721], to the north of Musselburgh in the picturesque village of Inveresk, was first built in 1597 and one range of the building dates from the seventeenth century. It stands near the site of a Roman fort and was built as a manse for nearby St Michael's Church. The property was held by the Colts from the sixteenth century until 1890. Oliver Cromwell stayed at the house for about two months in 1650 before going on to defeat the Scots at the Battle of Dunbar. The Duke of York, later James VII, dined at Inveresk House; and Bonnie Prince Charlie may have visited in 1745 before the Battle of Prestonpans. A tunnel was found in 1789 beneath the house, and in it were reputedly found the remains of a man in full armour with a barrel of gunpowder, perhaps a failed attempt to blow up Cromwell. B&B accommodation is available at the house (0131 665 5855; www.invereskhouse.com).

Auldhame [NT 602847], three or so miles east of North Berwick in East Lothian, is a small ruinous sixteenth-century tower house, and it stands in a picturesque spot above Seacliff sands. It was a property of the Otterburns, but was later held by the Colt family. There was a village and church at Auldhame but little survives above ground except the picturesque ruin of the castle.

No. of castles/sites: 3
Rank: 328=/764

Colville

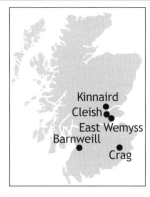

The name probably comes from the town of Colville, which lies in Normandy between Carn and Bayeux. The name means 'Col's farm or seat', and it is recorded in Scotland from the middle of the twelfth century. The family held lands in the Borders, in Ayrshire and in Perthshire.

Oxnam, a few miles east and south of Jedburgh, was held by the family from the twelfth century but passed to the Kerrs in 1502. There was a tower house called **Crag Tower** [NT 690190] but there are no remains.

Kinnaird Castle [NO 242291], nine miles east and north of Perth, is an impressive and tall tower, dating from the fifteenth century, and rising to four storeys

Kinnaird Castle (M&R)

and an attic. There is a later wing. The lands were held by the Colvilles from the thirteenth century and they built the castle. In 1449 Sir Robert Colville killed John Auchinleck, and the Douglas Earl of Angus besieged and sacked the castle and ravaged the lands. James VI visited Kinnaird in 1617 to hunt, during his only trip to Scotland after the Union of 1603. Kinnaird was sold to the Threiplands in 1674 and the building is still occupied.

Easter Wemyss or **MacDuff's Castle** [NT 344972] is just to the north of East Wemyss in Fife, and was probably first built by the MacDuffs. The castle is now ruinous, and there are remains of a tower, a gatehouse and a courtyard. The property was exchanged for Ochiltree with the Hamiltons; and the Colvilles held it from 1530 until 1630. Sir James Colville, third of Easter

MacDuff's Castle (M&R)

Wemyss, was a distinguished soldier, and was made Lord Colville of Culross in 1604 after acquiring lands there in 1589. The family were made Viscounts in 1885 and still flourish; Culross, however, passed to the Bruces.

Barnweill Castle [NS 407302], three miles north-west of Tarbolton in Ayrshire, was built on a motte, but only the mound survives. It was replaced by Barnweill House, which dates from the eighteenth century, and is now used as a farmhouse. The name 'Barnweill' is said to originate from William Wallace's torching of the Barns of Ayr, when he reputedly said 'the Barns of Ayr burn weel' (although there was also a family called Barnwell in Scotland before then). The lands were held by the Colvilles in the sixteenth and seventeenth centuries. The descendants of this branch of the family were made Barons Clydesmuir in 1948, and now apparently live near Biggar. The gardens at Barnweill are occasionally open to the public (www.gardensofscotland.org).

The Colvilles were also the holders of **Cleish Castle** [NT 083978], three and a half miles south-west of Kinross. The Colvilles held the property from 1530, and Mary, Queen of Scots, rested here after escaping from Lochleven Castle in 1568. The lands had passed from the family by 1840. The castle is a strong but altered sixteenth-century tower house, L-plan and of five storeys. It has a yew walk, which was first planted in the seventeenth century. The castle was ruinous but it was restored in the 1920s and altered in the 1960s, and is a private residence.

The Colvilles also held other lands and castles:
Balbedie [NT 198995], near Lochgelly, Fife; slight remains.
　　Held by the Colvilles but in 1612 passed to the Malcolms.
Blair (or **Blair Adam**) [NT 129957], near Kinross, Perth and Kinross; castle replaced by mansion.
　　Held by the Colvilles of Cleish but passed to the Adams.
Condie or **Newtown of Condie** [NO 076182], near Bridge of Earn, Perth and Kinross; site of castle and mansion.
　　Held by the Condie family and then by the Colvilles of Cleish but was sold to the Oliphants in 1601. There was another Condie Castle [NO 075117] some miles to the south.
Gascon Hall or **Gask** [NN 986175], near Auchterarder, Perthshire; castle replaced by old mansion.
　　Held by the Colvilles, but was bought by the Oliphants by the end of the thirteenth century.
Killernie Castle [NT 032924], near Cowdenbeath, Fife; very ruinous Z-plan tower.
　　Held by James Colville of Easter Wemyss in 1542, but he was forfeited and the property passed to the Duries.

Kinnaird House [NS 885849], near Stenhousemuir, Falkirk; mansion on site of castle.
 Held by the Colvilles in the thirteenth century but given to Newbattle Abbey and then was sold to the Bruces.
Ochiltree Castle [NS 510212], Ochiltree, Ayrshire; site of castle and mansion.
 Held by the Colvilles from the fourteenth century, but exchanged for Easter Wemyss with Sir James Hamilton of Finnart in 1530 and later went to the Stewarts.
Scotscraig [NO 445283], near Tayport, Fife; castle replaced by mansion.
 Held by several families but was latterly owned by the Colvilles, before passing to the Dalgleish family.
Tillicoultry Castle [NS 913975], near Tillicoultry, Clackmannanshire; site of castle and site of mansion.
 Held by the Erskines from 1236 but passed to the Colvilles of Culross in 1483, and they were made Lords Colville of Culross in 1609. Tillicoultry was sold to the Alexanders of Menstrie in 1634. The mansion was demolished in about 1938.

www.geocities.com/clancolville
No. of castles/sites: 16 / Rank: 86=/764

Comrie

The name is territorial and comes from the lands of Comrie, which are in Perthshire by the River Earn. The family is mentioned in records from the fifteenth century, although they owned the lands from 1297 until 1653 when they passed to the Drummond family and then later went to the Dundas Earl of Melville.

It is not clear whether the Comrie family had a seat or castle at the village of Comrie, but the family held **Dunira** [NN 738238], a couple of miles west of the village, where they had a tower house. This was replaced by an eighteenth-century house, then a baronial mansion, but this was mostly demolished in 1963 except for one wing.

After the MacGregors were proscribed, some of them settled near the village and changed their names to Comrie.

No. of castles/sites: 1
Rank: 537=/764

Comyn

The name comes from Comines, near Lisle, which is in northern France, and the Comyns claimed direct descent from the Emperor Charlemagne. The family came to England in the army of William the Conqueror in the eleventh century, and they held lands in Northumberland. David I invited the family to Scotland, and they became major landowners and probably the most powerful noble family in Scotland in the thirteenth century. They had a claim to the throne of Scotland when Richard Comyn married the granddaughter of the Scottish king Donaldbane, and William Comyn became Earl of Buchan when he married the heiress. He founded Deer Abbey [NJ 968482] in 1219, the ruins of which are open to the public. One branch were also Lords of Badenoch and then, for a (short) while, Earls of Menteith; William, Earl of Menteith, founded Inchmahome Priory [NN 574005] on an island in the Lake of Menteith (the priory can be visited). The Comyns supported John Balliol, as they were related to him, but this put them into conflict with Robert the Bruce. Bruce murdered the Red John Comyn, son of John Comyn, Lord of Badenoch, in a church in Dumfries in 1306, so starting a bitter fight between the two families and between their allies. Bruce was, of course, eventually victorious, and the power of the Comyns was smashed, and their lands and castles given to other families. John Comyn's son was killed at Bannockburn in 1314, fighting on the English side.

Some lines of the ancient family continued, most notably the Cummings (now Gordon Cummings) of Altyre, who are still represented today (see below).

Balvenie Castle [NJ 326409], just north of Dufftown in Moray, is a substantial courtyard castle with a large wall and ditch enclosing the stronghold. There are later ranges of buildings. The castle was held by the Comyns but was slighted by the forces of Robert the Bruce in 1308, and then passed to the Douglases and other families. It is an interesting ruin, is in the care of Historic

Balvenie Castle (M&R)

Scotland, and is open to the public from April to September (01340 820121).

Inverlochy Castle [NN 120754], a mile or so north-east of Fort William, is a ruinous courtyard castle and has a round tower at each corner, the largest of which

Inverlochy Castle (M&R)

is known as Comyn's Tower. The lands were held by the Comyns but passed to the Gordons of Huntly. The castle is in the care of Historic Scotland and can be viewed.

A few miles south of Forres is **Dunphail Castle** [NJ 007481], a very ruinous castle which was a property of the Comyns. The castle was besieged in 1330, and Alasdair Comyn of Dunphail and four of his men were captured after leaving to castle to find meal. They were beheaded and their heads flung over the walls, reputedly with the words, 'Here's beef for your bannocks'. The garrison tried to flee but were slaughtered. Five decapitated skeletons were reputedly found buried near the castle, and headless ghosts are said to haunt the old ruin; tales of the sound of fighting and groans have also been reported. The lands passed to the Dunbars, but nearby Dunphail House, built in 1828 and designed by William Playfair, was built for the Cummings.

The list of castles and lands the Comyns held is large, although (as stated above) most were lost during the Wars of Independence, except for the Cummings of Altyre (see below):
Auchry Castle [NJ 788507], near Turriff, Aberdeenshire; site of castle.
  Held by the Comyns
Banff Castle [NJ 689642], near Banff, Aberdeenshire; slight remains with large ditches.
  Held by the Comyn Earls of Buchan, and the castle was visited by Edward I in 1296. Garrisoned by the English and captured by the Scots about 1310. It was later sold to the Sharps.
Bedrule Castle [NT 598180], near Denholm, Borders; slight remains.
  Held by the Comyns, and visited by Edward I in 1298. Passed to the Douglases and then to the Turnbulls.
Blair Castle [NN 867662], near Pitlochry, Perthshire; massive mansion and castle.
  The Comyns had a castle, but Blair has long been held by the Earls, now Dukes, of Atholl. Edward III here stayed in 1336. Open to the public from April to October (01796 481207; www.blair-castle.co.uk).
Blervie Castle [NJ 071573], near Forres, Moray; ruined Z-plan tower house.
  An earlier castle was held by the Comyns, and later passed to the Dunbars.
Cadzow Castle [NS 734538], near Hamilton, Lanarkshire; ruined castle.
  Held by the Comyns but passed to the Hamiltons. The ruins are in Chatelherault park, and can be viewed from exterior (01698 426213).

Cairnbulg Castle [NK 016640], near Fraserburgh, Aberdeenshire; impressive castle.
  Held by the Comyns but passed to the Earl of Ross in 1316, then long held by the Frasers.
Castle Roy [NJ 007219], near Grantown-on-Spey, Strathspey; ruined castle.
  Held by the Comyns; the ruin is accessible.

Castle Roy (M&R)

Castle of King Edward or **Kinedar** [NJ 722562], near Turriff, Aberdeenshire; some remains of castle.
  Held by the Comyns but destroyed by the forces of Robert the Bruce in 1308. The property passed to the Ross family, and it was rebuilt.
Castle of Troup [NJ 838663], near Rosehearty, Aberdeenshire; some remains of castle in earthworks of an Iron Age fort.
  Held by the Comyns (or the Troup family) and probably destroyed in 1307-08; later passed to the Keith Earls Marischal and then to the Gardynes of Troup.
Castlemilk or **Carmunnock** [NS 608594], Rutherglen, Glasgow; some remains of large castle.
  Held by Comyns but passed to the Douglases, and later to the Hamiltons and to the Maxwells.
Cluggy Castle [NN 840234], near Crieff, Perthshire; ruined castle.
  Held by the Comyns and Malise, Earl of Strathearn, is said to have been besieged here by Robert the Bruce in 1306, but passed to Oliphants.
Comyn's Castle [NS 628563], near East Kilbride, Lanarkshire; motte.
  Held by the Comyns but passed to the Lindsays of Dunrod. One of the family, John Lindsay of Dunrod, along with Kirkpatrick of Closeburn, helped Robert the Bruce stab John Comyn to death in a church in Dumfries in 1306.
Craig Castle [NJ 472248], near Rhynie, Aberdeenshire; castle replaced by tower house and mansion.
  Held by the Comyns put passed to the Gordons of Craig.
Craig of Boyne Castle [NJ 615660], near Portsoy; ruinous castle.
  Held by the Comyns or by the Edmonstones, but later went to the Ogilvies.
Cruggleton Castle [NX 484428], near Garlieston, Galloway; foundations of castle.
  Held by the Comyns and captured by Edward I, then seized by William Wallace. The original castle was probably destroyed by Edward Bruce, Robert's brother, and the property went to the Douglases and then to others.
Cumbernauld Castle [NS 773759], Cumbernauld, Lanarkshire; slight remains.
  Held by the Comyns but passed to the Flemings in 1306.
Dalswinton Castle [NX 945841], near Dumfries; castle replaced by nearby mansion.
  Held by the Comyns and occupied by the English from 1309 until destroyed by the Scots in 1313. Passed to the Stewarts, but captured by the English in 1355 and destroyed in 1357. The gardens of Dalswinton House are occasionally open to the public (www.gardensofscotland.org).

Delgatie Castle [NJ 755506], near Turriff, Aberdeenshire; fine tower and mansion.
> Held by the Comyns but passed to the Hays. The castle is open to the public and accommodation is available (01888 563479; www.delgatiecastle.com).

Dores or **Durris Castle** [NO 779968], near Banchory, Aberdeenshire; site of castle.
> Held by the Comyns but passed to the Frasers.

Duncow [NX 970833], near Dumfries; site of castle or old house.
> Held by the Comyns, but passed to the Boyds after the Wars of Independence.

Dundarg Castle [NJ 895649], near Fraserburgh, Aberdeenshire; ruined castle.
> Held by the Comyns but destroyed by Robert the Bruce in 1308, then rebuilt in 1333 and held by the English, then destroyed using cannon by Regent Andrew Moray the next year. The property then passed to the Douglases.

Dunrod Castle [NS 224732], near Greenock, Renfrewshire; site of castle.
> Held by the Comyns but passed to the Lindsays after John Lindsay of Dunrod 'made sure' that the Red John Comyn was dead.

Ellon Castle [NJ 960307], Ellon, Aberdeenshire; ruined castle.
> Held by the Comyns and probably slighted in 1308, but passed to the Kennedys and then to others.

House of Tyrie [NJ 936632], near Fraserburgh, Aberdeenshire; site of castle.
> Motte held by the Comyns but this has gone. Later Tyrie went to the Frasers.

Inchtalla Castle [NN 572004], near Aberfoyle, Stirlingshire; ruins of castle on island.
> Held by the Comyns but passed to the Grahams and then to the Stewarts.

Kirkintilloch Peel [NS 651740], Kirkintilloch, Lanarkshire; earthworks only survive.
> Held by the Comyns from 1211 or so, but passed to the Flemings after the Wars of Independence.

Lochindorb Castle [NH 974364], near Grantown-on-Spey, Aberdeenshire; ruined castle on island.
> Held by the Comyns and occupied by the English and visited by Edward I in 1303. Held by the English in 1335 when Andrew Moray besieged it unsuccessfully, and he had to withdraw before a large army led by Edward III. Passed to the Stewarts.

Mains Castle [NS 627560], near East Kilbride, Glasgow; fifteenth-century castle.
> Held by the Comyns but had passed to the Lindsays of Dunrod by 1382.

Ochtertyre [NN 839236], near Crieff, Perthshire; site of castle and house.
> Held by the Comyns but passed to the Oliphants and then to the Murrays.

Old Slains Castle [NK 053300], near Cruden Bay, Aberdeenshire; slight remains of a strong castle.
> Held by the Comyns but passed to the Hays of Errol.

Quiech Castle [NO 426580], near Kirriemuir, Angus; site of castle.
> Held by the Comyns but passed to the Lindsays.

Raploch Castle [NS 763515], near Larkhall, Lanarkshire; site of castle.
> Held by the Comyns but passed to the Hamiltons in 1312.

Rattray Castle [NK 089580], near Fraserburgh, Aberdeenshire; earthworks of a castle.
> Held by the Comyns; destroyed by Robert the Bruce in 1308.

Rowallan Castle [NS 435424], near Kilmarnock, Ayrshire; fine large castle.
> Held by the Comyns but passed by marriage to the Mures.

Rough Hill [NS 607553], near East Kilbride, Glasgow; motte.
> Lands held by the Comyns but passed to the Douglases and then to the Hamiltons.

Ruthven [NJ 510468], near Huntly, Aberdeenshire; motte.
> Held by the Comyns but given to the Gordons by Robert the Bruce.

Ruthven [NN 764997], near Kingussie; ruinous barracks on site of castle.
> Held by the Comyns but passed to the Stewarts and then to the Gordons; in the care of Historic Scotland and open to the public (01667 460232).

Tarradale Castle [NH 553488], near Beauly, Inverness-shire; site of castle.
> Held by the Comyns but captured by Robert the Bruce in 1308 and probably razed. The lands passed to the Mackenzies of Fairburn.

Urquhart Castle [NH 531286], near Drumnadrochit, Inverness-shire; large ruin in picturesque spot.
> Built by the Durwards, but held by the Comyns. It was held in 1296 by the English, but after two attacks was taken by the Scots, only to be recaptured by the English in 1303 after a long siege. In 1308 it was seized by the Scots, led by Robert the Bruce. The castle held out for David II in 1333 against Edward Balliol and Edward III of England. The property passed to the Gordons and then to the Grants. The ruins are in the care of Historic Scotland and are open to the public (01456 450551).

The following properties, along with Altyre and Rait, were held by the Cummings after the Wars of Independence. The Cummings of Altyre were descended from Donald, the grandson of Red John Comyn, who married into the Mackintoshes. **Altyre House** [NJ 027550], a couple of miles south of Forres in Moray, replaced a castle. The lands were held by the Cummings from 1492 or earlier.

Rait Castle [NH 894525] is now a fine ruin, and stands a couple of miles south of Nairn. It was held by the Rait family but passed to the Cummings. The story (although there is more one version) goes that in 1524, when the

Rait Castle (M&R)

castle was held by the Cummings, they invited the Mackintoshes here for a feast, possibly a wedding banquet, but planned to murder their guests. The Mackintoshes apparently learned of the plan and came heavily armed, and managed to flee from Rait after killing many of their treacherous hosts. The Cumming laird was furious – he suspected his daughter had betrayed his plan as she was in love with one of the Mackintoshes – and he pursued the terrified girl through the building. She tried to escape out of an upstairs window, but her father hacked off her hands with his sword, as she hung from a window ledge, and she fell to her death. Her ghost, a handless phantom in a blood-stained dress, then began to haunt Rait. The Cumming laird and his followers were, themselves, apparently slain at Balblair in retribution. The lands passed to the Mackintoshes and then the Campbells of Cawdor. There are plans to clear and consolidate the ruin (www.save raitcastle.org).

The Cummings also held:
Couttie [NO 212409], near Coupar Angus, Perthshire; site only.
 Held by the Cummings of Couttie in 1606.
Craigmill [NJ 095542], near Forres, Moray; site only.
 Held by the Cummings.
Culter House [NJ 845013], Peterculter, Aberdeenshire, mansion on site of castle.
 Held by the Wauchopes but passed by marriage to the Cummings. They were made Baronets in 1695, and Archibald Cumming, second Baronet, was for a time the ruler of the Cherokee nation. The property passed to the Duffs and was then used as a boarding house for a girl's school.
Earnside Castle [NJ 109624], near Forres, Moray; site of castle replaced by later house.
 Held by the Cummings of Altyre in 1450, and replaced by Earnside House [NJ 107623].
Gordonstoun or **Plewlands** [NJ 184690], near Lossiemouth, Moray; mansion and castle.
 Held by the Ogstouns, by the Innes family, and by the Gordons but passed to the Cummings of Altyre in 1795. Gordonstoun has housed an exclusive school since 1934 and the gardens are occasionally open to the public (01343 837829; www.gordonstoun.org.uk).
Halhill Tower [NO 292132], near Cupar, Fife; site of tower house.
 Held by the Cummings of Inverallochy, but passed to the Balneave family in the sixteenth century.
Inverallochy Castle [NK 041630], near Fraserburgh, Aberdeenshire; slight remains of castle.
 Held by the Cummings of Inverallochy and then later by the Frasers of Lovat.
Kininmonth House [NK 033530], near Mintlaw, Aberdeenshire; castle replaced by mansion.
 Held by the Hays of Delgatie but sold to the Cummings around 1682.
Leask House [NK 026331], near Ellon, Aberdeenshire; ruinous mansion on site of castle.
 Held by the Leask family but had passed to the Cummings at the beginning of the eighteenth century, and then later went to the Gordons.
Logie House [NJ 006508], near Forres, Moray; mansion on site of castle.
 Held by the Cummings of Altyre, then by the Cunninghams.
Pittendrum [NJ 964670], near Fraserburgh, Aberdeenshire; castle or old house replaced by mansion.
 May have been held by the Cummings, but passed to the Keiths and then to the Grays.
Tom Pitlac [NH 947196], Boat of Garten, Strathspey; site of castle.
 Held by the Cummings. Associated with Matilda or Bigla Cumming, daughter of Gilbert Cumming, Lord of Glenchearnach. Matilda is a character in a number of stories, and other places associated with her are Bigla's Chair [NH 932204], where she is believed to have received the rents for her lands, and Bigla's Key Stone [NH 945225?] where she hid her keys before going to the church at Duthil.
Tor Castle [NJ 125530], near Elgin, Moray; site of castle.
 Held by the Cummings of Altyre, who built the castle in 1419. It was rebuilt by Robert Cochrane and occupied until the middle of the seventeenth century.

home.primus.ca/~rjb/cummings.htm
members.tripod.com/sassyoh_4/
    americanclancummingassociation/
No. of castles/sites: 58
Rank: 16=/764
Xrefs: Cunning; Cumming

Condie

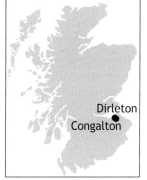

The name is territorial and comes from the lands of Condie, which are four or so miles south of Forgandenny in Perth and Kinross. The name is on record from the fifteenth century, and a Condie of that Ilk is mentioned.

Newton of Condie
Path of Condie

 There was a castle at **Newton of Condie** [NO 076182], known as **Condie Castle**, but this was later replaced by a mansion, itself burned out in 1866. The original castle, marked as 'Kondy', appears on Pont's sixteenth-century map to have been near **Path of Condie** [NO 075117], and this is likely to have been the Condie family's stronghold. The lands passed to the Colvilles of Cleish and then to the Spences in the sixteenth century and then to the Oliphants in 1601.

www.condie.net
No. of castles/sites: 2
Rank: 396=/764

Congilton

Dirleton
Congalton

The name is territorial and is from the lands and barony of Congalton in East Lothian. The family who held the lands may originally have come from Congalton in Cheshire in England, and they are on record from the twelfth century.
 Congalton [NT 544805], three miles south and west of North Berwick in East Lothian, was held by the family from around 1224, and there was a castle or hall-house, although there are no remains. Lauder of Congalton is, however, on record, and the Hepburns later held the lands.
 Dirleton Castle [NT 518840], a couple of miles west of North Berwick, is now a splendid and romantic ruin, but this has been a large and strong castle on a rock with the entrance defended by a deep ditch. The lands were held by the Congiltons in the twelfth century but passed to the Vaux family the following century, and they probably started the present castle; Dirleton then went by marriage to the Halyburtons, then to the Ruthvens, and then to others. There are fine gardens and the ruin is in the care of Historic Scotland and is open to the public all year (01620 850330).

No. of castles/sites: 2
Rank: 396=/764
Xref: Congalton

Coningsburgh

The name is probably territorial and comes from the south of the Border. The slight remains of **Barntalloch Tower** [NY 353878], two miles north of Langholm in Dumfries and Galloway, stand on a motte within a large bailey. The motte was constructed by the Coningsburgh family in the twelfth century, but the tower was built after the lands had passed to the Lindsays in 1285.

No. of castles/sites: 1
Rank: 537=/764

Constable

The name is not common in Scotland, and comes from the office of 'constable', originally a post of some power and dignity, and the constable of a castle was the next to in seniority to the lord, and could control, among other things, who was allowed to enter the castle. The Hays of Errol held the hereditary post of Constable to the kings of Scots, and were entrusted with the monarch's safety and security.

Craigcrook Castle (M&R) – see next column

The family name Constable, however, is more likely to come from the less high office of town constable or keeper of the peace. It is first recorded in Scotland in 1490.

Craigcrook Castle [NT 211742], to the west of Edinburgh, is a large sixteenth-century tower house, which was extended and modified down the years, and is still occupied. One of its several owners was Archibald Constable, who started the publishing firm and published Sir Walter Scott's Waverley novels. He lived here until 1814, although the business went bust twelve years later. His son, Thomas, refounded a publishing business, which from 1865 was Thomas and Archibald Constable. The castle is now home to Scottish Field magazine (0131 312 4550; www.scottishfield.co.uk).

No. of castles/sites: 1
Rank: 537=/764

Cook

The name is taken from the occupation of 'cook', and is a common name in Scotland, being found in records from the middle of the twelfth century.

Balcaskie House [NO 526035], a mile or so north-west of Pittenweem in Fife, is a U-plan symmetrical mansion, but it incorporates an L-plan tower house from the sixteenth century. The building may stand on the site of a much older stronghold. The lands were held by the Cooks in the thirteenth century, and they had a stronghold here, but passed by marriage to the Strangs of Balcaskie around 1362.

Abercrombie Castle [NO 518028], a mile north-east of St Monans also in Fife, dated from the twelfth century but there are no remains. The lands were held by the Cooks in 1260, but also by the Abercrombys (possibly the same family as the Cooks may have subsequently taken the name of their lands).

Some six miles north-west of Cupar again in Fife is **Carphin** [NO 319195], a modern mansion that replaced a castle or older house. The lands were latterly held by the Cooks, after being a property of the Baillies, of the Halkerston family and of the Raiths.

No. of castles/sites: 3
Rank: 328=/764
Xref: Cooke

Cooper

The name comes from two sources: the burgh of Cupar in Fife and from the profession of 'cooper', somebody who made barrels and kegs.

Castle Gogar [NT 164730], to the west of Edinburgh, is a fine and substantial L-plan tower house, which dates from the seventeenth century. The lands had been held by the Setons, by the Halyburtons

Castle Gogar (M&R)

and by the Logans of Restalrig, but the present castle was built by the Coopers (Coupers) in 1625 after they had bought the property in 1527. The castle is still occupied as a private residence.

Some three and a half miles south-west of Cumbernauld in Lanarkshire is the site of **Badenheath Castle** [NS 713724]. There was a large castle but the whole building was demolished in 1953. Badenheath had been held by the Boyds, but passed to the Coupers in the late seventeenth century, but was a property of the Keiths from 1708. The building was demolished in the 1950s, and the site is occupied by a sewerage works.

Ballindalloch Castle [NS 535885], one mile west of Balfron in Stirlingshire, is a large mansion dating from the nineteenth century, but this building replaced a castle. Ballindalloch was held by the Cunningham Earls of Glencairn and then by the Dunmores, and then by the Coopers in the nineteenth century. The gardens are open by appointment from May to June (01360 440202; www.gardensofscotland.org).

No. of castles/sites: 3
Rank: 328=/764
Xrefs: Cowper; Coupar

Corbett

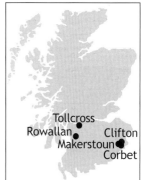

The name is a diminutive of the French 'corbeau', which means 'raven', and presumably also 'corbie' in Scots. It is thought the family had lands in Shropshire in England, and then came to the borders of Scotland, where they held property in the twelfth and thirteenth century, including at **Fogo** [NT 770490] in Berwickshire in the Borders, but also in other parts of the country. **Corbet Tower** [NT 776239], one mile south of Morebattle in the Borders, may have been held by

Corbet Tower 1905?

the Corbetts, but had passed by the sixteenth century to the Kerrs. The tower was burned by the English in 1522 and in 1544, but the building has been restored, extended and is still occupied.

Clifton [NT 816262] lies a mile or so south of Town Yetholm not far from the English border in Roxburghshire. The lands were held by the Corbetts in the thirteenth century, although they later passed to other families. There was a tower house, but this was destroyed by the English in 1545.

Makerstoun House [NT 672315] is three and a half miles to the west and south of Kelso, and is a mansion which incorporates a castle of the sixteenth century. Makerstoun was held by the Corbetts in the twelfth century, but then by the MacDougalls from 1373 until 1890, who presumably built the castle. The castle was sacked by the English in 1545.

Tollcross [NS 637637], a couple of miles east of Glasgow Cathedral, was held by the Corbetts from 1242 until 1810 when the property was sold to the Dunlops. The present mansion of 1848 replaced a castle, and is now converted to special needs housing. Four miles east of Rutherglen was Kenmuir [NS 660622], held by the Colquhouns and then by the Corbetts. There was a castle here but there are no remains, and the location is now by a land-fill site, a sewerage works and the M74.

Tom a' Chaisteal [NH 604449], Kirkton, is some miles west of Inverness, and was held by the Corbetts from

1220 until 1498. There was a stronghold on the summit of a rocky knoll, but nothing remains.

Rowallan [NS 435424], three miles north of Kilmarnock in Ayrshire, is a splendid courtyard castle,

Rowallan Castle 1917?

dating from the sixteenth century with a drum-towered gatehouse. It was held by the Corbetts in the twentieth century, but is now in the care of Historic Scotland although it is not open to the public. The line of the Corbett Barons Rowallan still continues, and they apparently live near Fenwick in Ayrshire.

No. of castles/sites: 7
Rank: 182=/764
Xref: Corbet

Cornwall

The name comes from Cornwall in the far south-west of England, and the family are on record from about 1180. They held lands in central Scotland.

Bonhard House [NT 020799], a mile or so south-east of Bo'ness in West Lothian, was a fine sixteenth-century tower house with an octagonal stair-turret in the re-entrant angle, but it was burned out and then demolished in the 1950s. The lands were long

Bonhard House (M&R)

held by the Cornwalls of Bonhard. John Cornwall of Bonhard was killed at the Battle of Flodden in 1513; while Nicholas Cornwall was Lord Provost of Linlithgow and died in 1607. The family line ended with an heiress, who died in 1763; and the property was later held by the Hamilton Dukes of Hamilton.

Carriden House [NT 026808] is nearby, and is a much-altered and extended sixteenth-century tower house, rising to five storeys. Carriden was held by several families, including by the Cockburns and by the Hamiltons, but was also a property of the Cornwalls of Bonhard for several years. It then passed to the Hope Johnstones, and it is still occupied as a private residence. B&B accommodation is available and Carriden is suitable for weddings (01506 829811; www.carridenhouse.co.uk).

No. of castles/sites: 2
Rank: 396=/764

Corrie

The name is territorial and comes from the lands of Corrie, which are three or so miles north-east of Lockerbie in Dumfries and Galloway in the far south of Scotland. The family are on record from the late twelfth century, and held several properties in Dumfriesshire, and then the lands of Thomaston in Ayrshire.

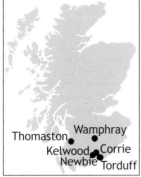

Corrie [NY 197843] was held by the family of the same name from the thirteenth century or earlier, and Nicholas Corrie was the Steward of Annandale in 1271. The Corries supported the Black Douglases in their dispute with the Crown, and lost lands and position after 1455 when the Douglases were forfeited. Corrie passed to the Johnstones of Corrie, who held the property in the sixteenth century. There was a tower house, but its exact location has not been established.

Torduff [NY 258646], three and a half miles east of Annan in Dumfriesshire, may have been held by the Corries from the twelfth century, but Torduff was also lost by the Corries in the fifteenth century, going to the Carruthers family and then to the Johnstones. Again there was a tower house, but there are no remains.

There are slight remains of **Newbie Castle** [NY 174647], a mile or so south-west of Annan. Thomas Corrie of Kelwood and Newbie died in 1513, probably at the Battle of Flodden. The property was sold to, and eventually held by, the Johnstones after a prolonged dispute.

Some four miles south of Dumfries is **Kelwood** [NY 015710], also held by the Corrie family. Thomas Corrie of Kelwood was respited for a murder in 1526, and this may be the same Thomas who was killed at the Battle of Fawsyde (or Pinkie) in 1547. The lands appear still have been held by the family in 1627.

Thomaston Castle [NS 240096], three or so miles west of Maybole in Ayrshire, consists of a ruinous L-plan tower house of the sixteenth century in a much earlier courtyard. The original castle was built by the Bruces, but had passed to the Corries of Kelwood by 1507, and they built the tower house. The property passed by marriage to the MacIlvaines of Grimmet around 1632, and Thomaston was occupied until 1800 or so.

The Corries (or Curries) also held:
Auchenfranco Castle [NX 893724], near Dumfries; site of strong castle.
  Held by the Douglases and by the Sinclairs and then by the Corries in the eighteenth century.
Dumcrieff [NT 102036], near Moffat, Dumfries and Galloway; castle replaced by mansion.
  Held by the Murrays and by the Clerks but was sold after 1785 to Dr James Currie, who wrote a biography of Robert Burns. Dumcrieff passed to the Rogersons, then to the Rollos.
Lunelly Tower [NY 197824], near Lockerbie, Dumfries and Galloway; slight remains of a tower house.
  Held by the Corries but passed to the Johnstones in 1516 and they built the tower.
Wamphray Tower [NY 128965], near Moffat, Dumfries and Galloway; site of a once strong castle.
  Held by the Corries but passed to the Kirkpatricks in 1357, then to the Johnstones in 1476 and they may have built the castle.

www.clancurrie.com
No. of castles/sites: 9
Rank: 149=/764
Xrefs: Corry; Currie

Corse

The name is derived from a Scottish rendering of 'cross', and the name is recorded in Scotland from the fifteenth century, and probably earlier.

Whitehouse [NT 187766] is a fine old L-plan tower house, dated 1615 and extended in 1901, and stands in the Cramond area to the west of Edinburgh on Whitehouse Road. It was held by the Logans and by the Primroses, before passing to the Corse family in 1676. Whitehouse later went to the Menzies family, and then to others. It is still a private residence.

No. of castles/sites: 1
Rank: 537=/764

Thomaston Castle (M&R)

Cospatrick

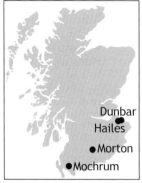

The name comes from the personal name 'Cospatrick' or 'Gospatrick', which was popular in the twelfth century. The family were Earls of Dunbar and were descended from the Earls of Northumberland as well as from the Scottish royal family. They also became Earls of March (meaning Berwickshire or the Merse), but the family were forfeited for treason in 1435. Also see Dunbar.

Dunbar Castle [NT 678794], by the harbour in Dunbar in East Lothian, was once one of the most important and strongest castles in Scotland, but it is now a

Dunbar Castle 1919?

fragmentary ruin perched on rocks. The Cospatricks held the stronghold, and it was captured by Edward I in 1296. Edward II sheltered here after defeat at Bannockburn in 1314. Black Agnes, Countess of Douglas, held the castle successfully for six weeks in 1338 against English armies, using a giant catapult against their mangonels. She reputedly said after the battle, as the English fled, 'behold of the litter of English pigs'. The site of castle can be visited, and the ruins and area are said to be haunted by an apparition known as Black Aggie, which is apparently only seen on clear nights.

Hailes Castle [NT 575758] is a fine ruin on a rocky ledge above the River Tyne, one and a half miles west and south of East Linton also in East Lothian. The castle dates from the thirteenth century, and consists of a series of towers; there are two pit-prisons. It was held by the Cospatricks, but passed to the Hepburns and then later to the Stewarts, to the Setons and to the Dalrymples. Hailes Castle is in the care of Historic Scotland and is open to the public.

The following castles or lands were also held by the family:
Black Bog Castle [NS 618137], near New Cumnock, Ayrshire; site of castle.
Held by the Cospatricks in the thirteenth century, but passed to the Dunbars of Cumnock.

Cockburnspath Castle [NT 785699], near Cockburnspath, Borders; ruinous castle.
Held by the Cospatricks but passed to the Homes, then to the Sinclairs and then to others.
Dolphinston Tower [NT 683150], near Jedburgh, Borders; farm on site of tower house.
The lands were held by Dolphin, son of Cospatrick, in the eleventh century and hence the name. Dolphinston had passed to the Ainslies by the thirteenth century or earlier and then to the Kerrs.
Lagg Tower [NX 880862], near Moniaive, Dumfries and Galloway; ruinous tower house.
Held by the Earls of Dunbar and March, but given in 1408 to the Griersons, who built the tower.
Longformacus [NT 685573], near Duns, Borders; site of castle.
Held by the Cospatricks but passed to the Sinclairs of Rosslyn.
Luffness House [NT 476804], near Aberlady, East Lothian; fine castle and mansion.
Held by the Cospatricks but passed by marriage to the Lindsays in the twelfth century and then later to the Hepburns and to the Hopes. Still a private home.
Morton Castle [NX 891992], near Thornhill, Dumfries and Galloway; ruin of castle.
Held by the Adairs and by Sir Thomas Randolph before coming to the Earls of March, who built the existing castle. The property passed to the Douglases, who were later made Earls of Morton. The castle is in the care of Historic Scotland and is open to the public.
Old Greenlaw Castle [NT 726448], near Greenlaw, Borders; site of castle.
Held by the Cospatricks in the twelfth century but passed to the Homes.
Old Place of Mochrum [NX 308541], near Glenluce, Galloway; large courtyard castle.
Held by the Dunbars, a branch of the Cospatricks, then later by the MacDowalls and then by the Stewarts of Bute.
Peelhill [NT 683572], near Longformacus, Borders; site of tower house.
Held by the Cospatricks but the tower was probably built after the property passed to the Sinclairs of Rosslyn.
Polwarth Castle [NT 749500], near Duns, Borders; site of castle.
Held by the Polwarth family, but passed to the Cospatricks, then to Sinclair of Herdmanston and then to the Homes.
Spott House [NT 679752], near Dunbar, East Lothian; mansion incorporating castle.
Held by the Cospatricks but passed to the Homes. George Home of Spott was made Earl of Dunbar in 1605 but the title became extinct on his death six years later.
Wedderburn Castle [NT 809529], near Duns, Borders; mansion incorporating tower house.
Held by the Wedderburns, then by the Earls of Dunbar, then on their forfeiture to the Douglases and then to the Homes. The castle can be hired for exclusive use (01361 882190; www.wedderburn-castle.co.uk).
Whittinghame Castle [NT 602733], near East Linton, East Lothian; large castle.
Held by the Cospatricks but passed to the Douglases in the fourteenth century. Still occupied, but now by the Balfours.

No. of castles/sites: 16 / Rank: 86=/764

Coulson

The name is probably from 'Cole's son', 'Col' or 'Cols' being a diminutive for Nicholas; alternatively it could be from the lands of Coulson in East Lothian.

Houndwood House [NT 855630], some three miles south-east of Grant-house in Berwickshire in the Borders, is a baronial mansion but it incorporates a sixteenth-century tower house. Houndwood was held by the Homes and by the Logans, but was a property of the Coulsons for some years in the eighteenth century or later, before passing to the Cooksons. It is still occupied, and is said to be haunted by a ghost known as 'Chappie'.

No. of castles/sites: 1
Rank: 537=/764
Xref: Colson

Coventry

The name comes from the city of Coventry in War-wickshire in England, and is recorded in Scotland from 1291. There were several churchmen with this name; one of the family was deacon of Aberdour in Fife in 1426.

The lands of **Mugdrum** [NO 228184], to the east of Newburgh in Fife, had a laird at one time called John of Covintre; but Mugdrum was later held by the Ormes, by the Arnotts and by others. Mugdrum House dates from the eighteenth century, although it may incorporate earlier work. Mugdrum was later held by the Hays and is still occupied.

No. of castles/sites: 1
Rank: 537=/764

Cowan

The name may be derived from 'Colquhoun', which can be pronounced 'Cohoon', or it may be from the Scot's word for a 'dry-stone dyker'. The name is common in many lowland areas of Scotland.

Steuarthall or **Wester Polmaise** [NS 826927], two miles east of Stirling, was a seventeenth-century tower house with a later wing, but the building has been demolished and the site was cleared in the 1980s. It was held by the Murrays of Touchadam, but was bought by the Cowans early in the seventeenth century, and they may have built the tower. The property later passed by marriage to the Stirlings of Garden.

The Cowans (or Cowanes) were successful merchants in Stirling, and had a town house **Cowane's House** [NS 793939] on St Mary's Wynd in the burgh, which dates from the sixteenth century. **Cowane's Hospital and Guildhall** [NS 792937] was built in 1639-49 and is a fine building. It was constructed using money left by John Cowane, who died in 1630, and was to house merchants

Cowane's Hospital, Stirling (M&R)

of the burgh who had fallen on hard times. The building was later used as a school and as an epidemic hospital, and now hosts ceilidhs, banquets and concerts, as well as housing the Family History Project and displays on the building's history (01786 473544; www.cowanes. org.uk).

Logan [NT 204630], a couple of miles north-west of Penicuik in Midlothian, is now very ruinous, but there was a stronghold here from 1230 or earlier. It was long held by the Sinclairs, but the property passed to the Cowan family in the nineteenth century.

No. of castles/sites: 3
Rank: 328=/764
Xref: Cowen

Cox

The name probably is simply a plural of 'cock', and it is recorded in Scotland from the thirteenth century.

The Cox family held properties in Scotland in the nineteenth century.

Clunie Castle [NO 114440], near Blairgowrie, Perthshire; ruined castle on island.

Held by the Crichtons and by the Ogilvies before coming to the Cox family of Lochlee in 1892.

Drumkilbo [NO 304449], near Coupar Angus, Perthshire; mansion incorporating castle.

Held by the Tyrie family and then others before going to the Cox family in 1900, who had made their money from jute in Dundee. It was sold to Lord Elphinstone in 1953 and the house is available to rent on an exclusive basis (01828 640445; www.drumkilbo.com).

Glendoick House [NO 208237], near Perth; mansion on site of castle.

Held by the Murrays and by the Craigies, but latterly held by the Coxes. The gardens open to the public from mid April to mid June (01738 860205; www.glendoick.com).

Snaigow House [NO 084430], near Dunkeld, Perthshire; house on site of mansion.

Held by the Keays but was sold to the Coxes of Snaigow, who still apparently live near Dunkeld.

No. of castles/sites: 4
Rank: 278=/764
Xref: Cocks

Coxwell

Robert Coxwell held the lands of **Myres** [NO 242110], just east of Auchtermuchty in Fife, in the fifteenth century. Coxwell was a favourite of James I and page to him when he was imprisoned in England. There was a castle, but this was replaced by the present Z-plan tower house, built after the property had passed by the marriage to the Scrymgeours, constables of Dundee and mace-bearers (Clavigers) to the king. The castle was put up for sale in 1997 with an asking price of more than £550,000. The gardens are occasionally open to the public and accommodation is available in castle (01208 821341; www.myres.co.uk/ www.gardensof scotland.org).

No. of castles/sites: 1
Rank: 537=/764

Craig

The name is local in origin and found all over Scotland, as there are many places called Craig or have it as an element in a place name. The surname is common throughout the lowlands of Scotland. James Craig, the son of an Edinburgh merchant, was the architect for the New Town of Edinburgh in 1767.

Craigston or **Craigfintray Castle** [NJ 762550], some four miles north-east of Turriff in north-east Scotland, is a tall tower house, rising to five storeys and a garret, and dates from the seventeenth century. It has two projecting wings, and the tower is dated 1607. Craigston was held by the Craig family for 250 years before passing to the Urquharts, whose descendants still apparently live here. The castle is open for some weeks in the spring and summer (01888 551640).

Nothing remains of a tower house at **Riccarton** [NT 183695], the site of which is near the Heriot Watt University Campus, some miles south-west of Edinburgh. Riccarton was a large building, dating from the fourteenth century, but was demolished in 1956. It was held by the Stewarts and then by the Craig family, one of whom was Sir Thomas Craig of Riccarton, an eminent sixteenth-century advocate. Riccarton passed by the marriage to the Gibsons in 1823.

www.certech.net/clancraig/
No. of castles/sites: 2
Rank: 396=/764

Myres Castle (M&R) – see next column (Coxwell)

Craigie

The name is territorial in origin, but there are lands with this name in Ayrshire, in West Lothian, in Angus and in Perthshire, and one branch was prominent in Orkney. The name is on record from the end of the thirteenth century.

Craigie Castle [NS 408317], four miles south of Kilmarnock in Ayrshire, may have been built by the Lindsays in the 1230s or 40s; but the property was held by the Craigies before passing by marriage to the Wallaces of Riccarton in 1371. The castle consists of a ruinous altered hall-house with later additions, and had two courtyards and was defended by ditches.

To the south and west of Edinburgh is **Merchiston Castle** [NT 243717], which now forms part of the complex of buildings of the campus of Napier University. The old tower, now L-plan, was somewhat brutally incorporated by slapping a corridor through the wing. The lands were held by the Craigies in 1367, but passed to the Napiers with whom Merchiston is more usually associated.

Dunbarney House [NO 111196], three miles south of Perth, dates from 1697 but stands on the site of a castle. The lands were held by the Mercers and by the Oliphants, but passed to the Craigies. One of the family, Robert Craigie, was Lord President of the Court of Session in 1754; and another was Lord Craigie, who died in 1834, and was also an eminent judge. The house is still a private residence.

Not very far away is **Glendoick House** [NO 208237], six miles east of Perth. This is a symmetrical mansion, dating from 1746, but may incorporate much older work from a tower house. There is fine panelling and plasterwork. The property passed from the Murrays to the Craigies in 1726, but is now apparently held by the Cox family. The gardens are open from mid April to mid June (01738 860205; www.glendoick.com).

Langskaill House [HY 435219], on the south-west side of the island of Gairsay in Orkney, is a courtyard castle, dating mostly from the sixteenth and seventeenth centuries. Only one range of buildings survives. The house stands on the site of the drinking hall of Svein Aliefson, as recorded in the *Orkneyinga Saga*. He was killed in Ireland. In the seventeenth century Langskaill was a property of the Craigies of Gairsay.

No. of castles/sites: 5
Rank: 240=/764

Craik

The name comes from Crayke, a village in Yorkshire in England, and the name is recorded in Scotland from the thirteenth century.

Arbigland House [NX 989574], two miles east of Kirkbean in Dumfries and Galloway, is a fine classical mansion of 1755, which replaced Arbigland Hall (the site now a sunken rose garden) and **McCulloch's Castle** [NX 997577], an old stronghold used until about 1500. The property was held by the MacCullochs, by the Murrays and by the Carnegies, but was sold to the Craiks in 1679 and they built the new house. Dr James Craik, who was born in 1731 at Arbigland, was physician-general of the United States Army after the American Revolution, and was a close friend of George Washington for some forty years, nursing Washington during his last illness. Arbigland passed to the Blacketts in 1852. The grounds of Arbigland are said to be haunted by the daughter of one of the Craik owners, the 'Ghost of the Three Crossroads'. She is said to have fallen for a groom, but her parents had her lover murdered. The groom's ghost, on a phantom horse, has also been reported near the main gates.

No. of castles/sites: 1
Rank: 537=/764
Xref: Crake

Cramond

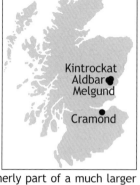

The name is territorial and comes from the lands and village of Cramond, which are to the west and north of Edinburgh. The name is on record from the thirteenth century.

Cramond Tower [NT 191770] is a tall and narrow sixteenth-century tower house, and was formerly part of a much larger building. It may have been held by the Cramond family at one time, but was long a property of the Bishops of Dunkeld, two of whom died here. The tower was later held by the Douglases and by the Inglis family, and became derelict. It was restored in 1983 and is a private residence.

Aldbar Castle [NO 572577], three miles west of Brechin in Angus, was a large mansion which included a

Aldbar Castle 1920?

sixteenth-century castle, but it was completely demolished in 1965. It was long a property of the Cramonds, but was sold in 1577 to the Lyon Lord Glamis, and then later passed to other families. The Cramond family also owned **Kintrockat** [NO 568592] and **Melgund** [NO 546564] in Angus.

Kintrockat is two or so miles west of Brechin, and there may have been a castle. The lands later passed to the Ochterlonys.

There is a fine castle at Melgund, four and a half miles south-west of Brechin. This was, however, built by the Beatons in the sixteenth century after the property had passed from the Cramond family.

No. of castles/sites: 4
Rank: 278=/764

Cranstoun

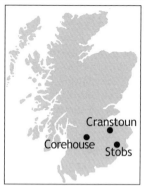

The name is territorial and comes from the lands and barony of Cranstoun, which are east and south of Dalkeith in Midlothian. The name is on record in the twelfth century, and the name may mean either the 'town or place of the crane' or 'Cran's or Cren's' (a Saxon forename) 'ton', meaning dwelling or seat.

The Cranstouns appear to have held Over Cranstoun, while the Riddells and the MacGills held the nearby property of Nether Cranstoun, which was also known as Cranstoun Riddell and as Oxenfoord, the latter the name the property is now known as.

Over Cranstoun or **Cranstoun** [NT 404651] is four or so miles west of Dalkeith, and there was a castle or fortified house here, nothing of which remains. The lands were long held by the Cranstoun family, possibly from the twelfth century. The family were apparently involved in the Gowrie Conspiracy of 1600, and Sir John Cranstoun of that Ilk was accused of harbouring his kinsmen, and his brother was executed in Perth. The family supported the Royalists, and the third Lord Cranstoun fought at the Battle of Worcester in 1651 and was imprisoned in the Tower of London. The property later passed to the Dalrymples, and Sir James Dalrymple of Upper Cranstoun and Cousland married Elizabeth Hamilton MacGill, the heiress of Oxenfoord (also known as Nether Cranstoun or Cranstoun Riddell) in 1760. The Cranstouns of that Ilk still flourish and now apparently live at Corehouse to the south of Lanark (see below).

Stobs Castle [NT 510084], four miles south of Hawick in the Borders, is a large castellated mansion dating from the 1790s, but this building replaced a castle which

Stobs Castle 1905?

was burnt out and gutted by fire in 1712. The lands were held by the Cranstouns from 1370 or earlier, but passed to the Elliots of Stobs, and they built the present building.

Two miles north-west of Jedburgh also in the Borders, is **Lanton Tower** [NT 618215], an altered sixteenth-century tower house which has been extended by a modern mansion. The tower was held by the Cranstouns in 1627, but had passed to Douglas of Cavers by 1687. The tower was restored in 1989 and is still occupied.

Corsbie Tower [NT 607438], two and a half miles west of Gordon also in the Borders, is a ruinous tower house, dating from the sixteenth century, and formerly rising to five storeys. Corsbie was sited in marshy ground and a causeway led to the castle. Corsbie was held by the Cranstouns, who were in possession in the middle of the seventeenth century.

The Cranstouns also held **Bold** [NT 374374], three miles east of Innerleithen, and **Dewar** [NT 349489], eight miles north-east of Peebles, both in the Borders.

Bold was held by the Sandilands and by the Stewarts of Traquair before coming to the Cranstouns, and there was a tower house here.

There was also a castle or old house at Dewar, which was held by a family of the same name before going to the Maxwells in the seventeenth century and then to the Cranstouns.

Corehouse [NS 882416], a mile or so to the south of Lanark, is a Tudor Revival mansion, designed by Sir Edward Blore. It was built in the 1820s for the Cranstouns, one of whom was raised to the bench as Lord Corehouse in 1826, and the mansion replaced the ancient **Corra Castle** [NS 882414].

Corehouse was visited by William and Dorothy Wordsworth, who described the mansion as 'a neat, white ladylike house'. The Cranstoun family still apparently live here, and the line is represented by Cranstoun of that Ilk and of Corehouse. The house is open for about one month in the spring and summer (01555 663126).

No. of castles/sites: 7
Rank: 182=/764
Xref: Cranstoun

Craw

Auchencrow

The name comes from the village of Auchencrow or Auchencraw, which is located a few miles north of Chirnside in Berwickshire near the English border. Auchencraw was reduced to Craw over time. Paul Craw (or Crawar or Cravar) was executed for heresy in 1432.

The family held two tower houses near the village of **Auchencrow**, one at **East Reston Tower** [NT 903612], four miles to the east; and the other at **Heugh Head** [NT 877625], two and a half miles to the north-east. There are no remains of either tower, and the Craws were forfeited for their part in the Jacobite Rising of 1715-16.

It is possible they also held **Ferneycastle** [NT 880602], two miles east of Auchencrow.

No. of castles/sites: 2
Rank: 396=/764
Xref: Auchencraw; Auchencrow

Crawford

The name is territorial and comes from the lands and barony of the same name. The family itself was probably Norman in origin, and the Crawfords came to Scotland in the retinue of David I in the twelfth century. Indeed Sir Gregan Crawford is said to have saved the king's life, along with some divine intervention, from the antlers of a stag in what is now Holyrood Park in Edinburgh (Archibald Crawford was Abbot of Holyrood in the fifteenth century). The Crawfords fought for William Wallace, and Wallace's mother may have even come from the family, and then they went on to support Robert the Bruce. Sir Reginald Crawford, Sheriff of Ayr, was murdered by the English in 1297, and his son, another Sir Reginald, was executed by the English in 1307. The family had a castle at **Crawfordjohn** [NS 879239], three and a half miles west of Abington in Lanarkshire, but this had passed to the Crown by 1359 and the family acquired other properties.

The two main branches of the family in Ayrshire were of Auchinames and of Crawfurdland.

Auchinames Castle [NS 395625] was a couple of miles south of Bridge of Weir in Renfrewshire, and dated from the fourteenth century. It had a large tower or keep, but it had been demolished by the end of the eighteenth century. The lands were given to the Crawfords in 1320 by Robert the Bruce. The then laird of Auchinames was killed at the Battle of Flodden in 1513; and another was slain at the Battle of Pinkie in 1547. The lands were only sold by the Crawfords in the twentieth century, and a branch of the family continues as Craufurd Baronets, and they now apparently live in Hampshire.

Two or so miles north-east of Kilmarnock in Ayrshire is **Craufurdland Castle** [NS 456408], a large baronial mansion, which incorporates an altered tower house

and seventeenth-century extensions. The King's Room has a fine plaster ceiling with the date 1668. An underground passage is said to have connected the castle with Dean Castle in Kilmarnock, some miles away. The Crawfords held the property from the early thirteenth century. John Crawford of Craufurdland was killed at the Battle of Flodden in 1513. In 1793 the property passed to the Howiesons or Houisons, and the castle was restored in the 1980s and is still occupied.

The Crawford owned many other properties, mostly in Ayrshire, in Renfrewshire, in Lanarkshire and in West Lothian:
Almond or Haining Castle [NS 956773], near Linlithgow, West Lothian; ruined castle.
　Held by the Crawfords from 1425, who built the castle about

Almond Castle (M&R)

　1470, but the property was owned by the Livingstones from 1540.
Ardmillan Castle [NX 169945], near Girvan, Ayrshire; ruined castle.
　Held by the Crawfords of Baidland from 1658 after passing by marriage from the Kennedys of Bargany. James Crawford of Ardmillan became Lord Ardmillan, the well-known Scottish

Ardmillan Castle (M&R)

　judge and Lord of Session, in 1855. The castle was burned out in the twentieth century and remains a shell.
Beoch Tower [NS 295145], near Maybole, Ayrshire; site of castle.
　Held by the Crawfords in the fifteenth and sixteenth centuries.

Craufurdland Castle (M&R)

Blackcraig Castle [NS 634082], near New Cumnock, Ayrshire; site of castle.

Held by the Crawfords but sold to the MacAdams in the second half of the sixteenth century. This has been suggested as the birthplace of William Wallace, and is reputed to have been used by him after the murder of the Sheriff of Ayr in 1297 and then before his capture at Robroyston in 1305.

Cartsdyke [NS 287756], near Greenock, Renfrewshire; site of castle.

Held by the Crawfords of Kilbirnie. Sir Patrick Crawford of Cartsdyke fought for Mary, Queen of Scots, at the Battle of Langside in 1568. Sir Thomas Crawford of Cartsdyke invested heavily in the new port in the seventeenth century, and lost heavily in the Darien Scheme.

Cloberhill [NS 532703], near Clydebank, Glasgow; site of castle.

Held by the Crawfords in 1567. Hew Crawford of Cloberhill was one of those involved with Crawford of Possil in attacking and capturing Corslie Castle in 1612.

Crosbie Castle [NS 217500], near West Kilbride, Ayrshire; mansion incorporating castle.

Held by the Crawfords of Auchinames. William Wallace sheltered here from the English in an earlier castle, and the treacherous murder of his uncle – who held the property – led to the torching of the Barns of Ayr

Crosbie House [NS 344301], near Troon, Ayrshire; ruined castle, remains later used as an icehouse.

Held by the Crawfords but passed to the Fullertons in the thirteenth century.

Douglaston House [NS 565742], near Milngavie, Dunbartonshire; site of castle and mansion.

Held by the Hamiltons, then by the Crawfords in 1796, but passed to the Kerrs.

Drongan Castle [NS 450179], near Drongan, Ayrshire; site of castle.

Held by the Crawfords.

Drumry Castle [NS 515710], near Duntocher, Glasgow; site of castle.

Held by several families, including by the Livingstones and by the Hamiltons, but passed to the Crawfords of Kilbirnie in 1528, who built the castle. The family were accused of treason, and the property went to the Semples in 1545. The castle was finally demolished in the 1950s.

Drumsoy Castle [NS 439175], near Drongan, Ayrshire; site of castle.

Held by the Crawfords in 1567.

Ednam [NT 737372], near Kelso, Borders; possible site of castle or old house.

May have been held by the Crawfords but was long a property of the Edmonstones from the fourteenth century.

Farme Castle [NS 620624], Rutherglen, Glasgow; site of castle and mansion.

Held by the Stewarts and by the Douglases, and then by the Crawfords from 1482 until 1599, then went to the Stewarts and to others. Demolished in 1960.

Fedderate Castle [NJ 897498], near New Deer, Aberdeenshire; site of castle.

Held by the Crawfords, who were in possession in 1519 and probably built the castle, but passed to the Gordons.

Gartlea [NS 765648], near Airdrie, Lanarkshire; site of castle.

Held by the Crawfords of Rochsolloch.

Glendevon Castle [NN 976055], near Dollar, Clackmannan; Z-plan tower house.

Held by the Douglases, then in the sixteenth century by the Crawfords, then by the Rutherfords in the eighteenth century. Used as a farmhouse.

Jordanhill [NS 538683], near Glasgow; site of castle.

Held by the Crawfords. Sir Thomas Crawford of Jordanhill fought at and survived the Battle of Pinkie in 1547, although he was captured by the English and ransomed. He did not support Mary, Queen of Scots, and after she had fled Scotland he captured Dumbarton Castle from her forces in 1570. In 1577 Crawford was made Provost of Glasgow, and he had Partick Bridge built. Jordanhill was sold to the Smiths in 1900.

Keirs Castle [NS 430081], near Dalmellington, Ayrshire; site of castle.

Held by the Crawfords of Keirs in 1512 but went to the Shaws by 1696.

Kerse Castle [NS 432144], near Dalrymple, Ayrshire; site of castle.

Held by the Crawfords from the thirteenth century.

Kilbirnie House [NS 304541], near Kilbirnie, Ayrshire; ruined castle.

Held by the Barclays, but passed by marriage to the Crawfords

Kilbirnie House (M&R)

in 1470, then to the Lindsay Earls of Crawford in 1661 and then later to the Boyle Earls of Glasgow. The building was burned out in 1757 and never restored. The Crawfords of Kilbirnie added the Crawfurd aisle to the Auld Kirk of Kilbirnie, and there is fine Renaissance-style carving. The church is open to the public in the summer (www.kilbirnieauldkirk.org.uk).

Laight Castle [NS 450089], near Dalmellington, Ayrshire; slight remains.

Held by the Crawfords.

Lauriston Castle [NT 204762], Edinburgh; fine castle and mansion.

Held by several families, including the Napiers of Merchiston, then much later by the Crawfords of Cartsburn, then by the Reids who gave the property to the City of Edinburgh, and now owned by the local council. Open to the public by public tour (0131 336 2060; www.cac.org.uk).

Lochcote Tower [NS 976737], near Linlithgow, West Lothian; slight remains of tower house.

Held by the Crawfords.

Loudoun Castle [NS 506378], near Galston, Ayrshire; ruined castle and mansion.

Held by the Crawfords before it passed by marriage to the Campbells in the fourteenth century and was long held by that family. Now the centre piece of a theme park (01563 822296; www.loudouncastle.co.uk).

Monorgan [NO 321285], near Dundee; site of castle.

Held by the Monorgan family, as well as the Grahams and by the Crawfords.

Mountquhanie Castle [NO 347212], near Cupar, Fife; ruined castle.

Held by the Balfours and by the Lumsdens, and then by the Crawfords from 1676. The castle is partly ruinous and was replaced by Mountquhanie House, which stands nearby and dates from 1820.

Newark Castle [NS 324173], near Ayr; tower house and later wing.

Held by the Kennedys, then by the by Crawfords of Camlarg by 1661, then by the Kennedy Earls of Cassillis in 1763. Still occupied.

Old Hall of Auchincross [NS 582141], near New Cumnock, Ayrshire; site of castle.

Held by the Crawfords, who were involved in feuds with other local families in the seventeenth century.

Polquhairn [NS 479158], near Drongan, Ayrshire; site of castle or old house.

Held by the Cunninghams and by the Chalmers family before coming to the Crawfords in the eighteenth century. James Boswell apparently visited Polquhairn in 1762.

Possil [NS 592705], Glasgow; site of castle.
  Held by the Crawfords. Crawford of Possil seized Corslie Castle in 1612 in an attempt to recover a debt, but all he managed to achieve was a term of imprisonment in Edinburgh Castle. The property passed into other hands. Possil House was a later house and stood to the south but this has been demolished.

Rochsoles House [NS 756678], near Airdrie, Lanarkshire; site of castle and mansion.
  Held by the Crawfords, but passed to the Cochranes then to the Gerard family, who held the property in the twentieth century.

Rochsolloch [NS 754649], near Airdrie, Lanarkshire; site of castle and mansion.
  Held by the Crawfords but went to the Hamiltons of Dalziel in 1647 and then to the Aitchisons in 1685 and then to the Alexanders.

Skeldon Castle [NS 378138], near Maybole, Ayrshire; cottage on site of castle.
  Held by the Campbells, but passed to the Crawfords of Kerse by 1644. William Crawford of Skeldon was one of the captains at the Battle of Marston Moor in 1645, fighting against Charles I. The lands later passed to the Fullartons.

Terringzean Castle [NS 556205], near Cumnock, Ayrshire; slight remains of castle.
  Held by the Loudoun family but passed to the Crawfords.

Ward of Lochnorris [NS 539205], near Cumnock, Ayrshire; site of castle.
  Held by the Crawfords in 1440 but passed to the Dalrymple Earls of Dumfries, who moved to Dumfries House [NS 541204], a classical mansion with a central block and pavilions. Dumfries House was recently put up for sale.

www.clancrawford.org
www.crawfordclan.org
No. of castles/sites: 39
Rank: 27=/764
Xrefs: Craufurd; Crawfurd

Creich

The name is from the lands of the same name, some five miles north-west of Cupar. The lands of Creich appear never to actually have been held by this family, being a property of the Liddels and then for hundreds of years of the Beatons. The name Creich is recorded in charters from the thirteenth century.

Comiston House [NT 240687], on the south side of Edinburgh, dates from no later than 1815, but a tower survives from the sixteenth century and it has gunloops. Comiston was held by several families before passing to the Creichs in 1608, and later passed by marriage to the Cants and to others.

No. of castles/sites: 1
Rank: 537=/764

Crichton

The name is territorial and comes from the lands of Crichton, which are a couple of miles east of Gorebridge in Midlothian. The lands are mentioned in charters dating from the twelfth century. Two of the family were Bishops of Dunkeld, although Bishop Robert Crichton supported Mary, Queen of Scots and was deprived of office in 1570. He was restored in his chair in 1584, but died the following year.

Located in a picturesque valley above the River Tyne, Crichton Castle [NT 380612] is a large, impressive and sophisticated stronghold, dating from the fourteenth century but modified down the centuries. Ranges of

Crichton Castle (LF)

buildings surround a small courtyard, and one side has a loggia with a diamond-faceted facade. The castle was long a property of the Crichtons, and the original castle was probably built in about 1370. Sir William Crichton, Chancellor of Scotland, entertained William, the young Earl of Douglas, and David, his brother, before having them murdered at the Black Dinner in Edinburgh Castle in 1440. John Forrester slighted the castle in retaliation. Crichton founded the nearby Collegiate Church [NT 381616], which is an impressive building in an interesting graveyard (and by the castle car park). The Crichtons were forfeited for treason in 1488 and the castle and lands passed to the Hepburns, later Earls of Bothwell. The castle is in the care of Historic Scotland and is open to the public from April to September (01875 320017); there is a short walk to the site.

Sanquhar Castle [NS 786092], just to the south of Sanquhar in Dumfries and Galloway, is a large and crumbling ruin of a thirteenth-century castle with later work, consisting of towers and ranges of buildings. It was held by the Edgars and by the Ross family before passing by marriage to the Crichtons in the fourteenth century. James VI visited in 1617. This branch of the family were made Earls of Dumfries in 1633, but six

Sanquhar Castle 1905?

years later sold the property to the Douglases of Drumlanrig. There are two ghost stories associated with the old stronghold. It is said to be haunted by a White Lady, the ghost of Marion of Dalpeddar, who was reputedly murdered at Sanquhar: the story goes that a skeleton was found here during work in the nineteenth century. The second ghost is supposed to be that of John Wilson, who got embroiled in a feud not of his own making and was unjustly executed by the Crichtons. The castle was is accessible with care.

Frendraught Castle [NJ 620418], six miles east of Huntly in Aberdeenshire, is a fine house and castle, and dates from 1656. Frendraught was a property of the Crichtons, and James V visited in 1535. The castle was torched in 1630 during a feud over land with the Gordons. Six Gordons, including John Gordon, Lord Rothiemay, and John Gordon, Lord Aboyne, were burned and killed in the castle, although James Crichton of Frendraught, the then laird, escaped with his folk. Crichton was tried and acquitted of their murders, although one of his servants was executed. The castle is said to be haunted by the ghost of Crichton's wife, Lady Elizabeth Gordon, daughter of the Earl of Sutherland, who may have been involved in the torching of the castle. Crichton's son, James, was made Viscount Frendraught in 1642 and, although a Covenanter, fought for the Marquis of Montrose in 1650. He was captured after being wounded, and died soon afterwards. The property passed to the Morrisons about 1690, and the house was restored in 1974 and is still occupied.

Blackness Castle [NT 056803] is a large and brooding stronghold by the sea, a few miles east of Bo'ness in central Scotland. It dates from the fifteenth century,

Blackness Castle (LF)

but was altered down the years and was used as a state prison. Before this it was held by the Crichtons, and was burned by an English fleet in 1481. It was also captured by General Monck for Cromwell in 1650, and was later the central ammunition depot for Scotland. It is now in the care of Historic Scotland, and is open to the public all year (01506 834807).

The Crichtons also held many other lands and castles:

Auchenskeoch Castle [NX 917588], near Dalbeattie, Galloway; slight remains of castle.
    Held by the Lindsays, but passed to the Crichtons, then later went to the Mackenzies.

Barnton Tower [NT 188758], near Edinburgh; site of castle.
    Held by Sir George Crichton, Admiral of Scotland and Sheriff of Linlithgow, but was destroyed in August 1444 by a force led by Sir John Forrester of Corstorphine on behalf of James II. The lands later passed to the Elphinstones.

Black Bog Castle [NS 618137], near New Cumnock, Ayrshire; site of castle.
    Held by the Dunbars, but passed to the Crichtons of Sanquhar in 1622.

Bothwell Castle [NS 688594], near Hamilton, Lanarkshire; splendid ruined castle.
    Held by the Douglases, but from 1455 by the Crichtons, until they were forfeited themselves, then by the Ramsays, by the Hepburns and by the Douglases again. The castle is in the care of Historic Scotland and is open to the public all year (01698 816894).

Braal Castle [ND 139601], near Thurso, Caithness; ruinous castle.
    Held by the Stewarts, and then by the Crichtons in the middle of the fifteenth century, but passed to the Sinclairs of Ulbster.

Brunstane Castle [NT 201582], near Penicuik, Midlothian; ruined castle.
    Held by the Crichtons. George Wishart was seized here in 1546 and the taken to St Andrews and burned there for heresy.

Brunstane Castle (M&R)

The laird of Brunstane was subsequently found guilty of plotting with the English, and the castle was torched in 1547. The property went to the Maitlands.

Brunstane House [NT 316725], east of Edinburgh; castle and mansion.
    Held by the Crichtons of Brunstane, but went to the Maitlands in 1632.

Cairns Tower [NT 091604], near Balerno, Edinburgh; ruined castle.
    Held by the Cairns, but passed to the Crichtons, then to the Tennants in the middle of the sixteenth century.

Carco Castle [NS 789141], near Sanquhar, Dumfries and Galloway; site of castle.
    Held by the Crichtons. One story has Abraham Crichton of Carco, an unpopular and apparently ruthless landowner, wishing to remove materials from the derelict church of Kilbride. A storm blew up and thunder frightened his horse, and Crichton tumbled from the saddle and was dragged along the ground all the way to Dalpeddar, dying an excruciating death. His ghost is then said to have haunted Sanquhar

churchyard, where he was buried, until exorcised by a priest. The family are said to have abandoned the castle at Carco towards the end of the sixteenth century, and moved to another building at **Orchard** [NS 781127].

Catslack Tower [NT 340260], near Selkirk, Borders; site of castle.
Held by the Crichtons.

Clunie Castle [NO 114440], near Blairgowrie, Perthshire; ruined castle on island.
Held by the Crichtons of Elliok from 1562. James Crichton, who spent much of his youth here, was known as the Admirable Crichton. He set out on his continental travels at the age of twenty, speaking twelve languages, as well as being skilled in swordsmanship, in riding and in music. He was tutor to the son of the Duke of Mantua, but was killed in a duel about the age of twenty-three in 1583. The lands passed to the Ogilvies.

Cluny Crichton Castle [NO 686997], near Banchory, Aberdeenshire; ruined castle.
Held by the Crichtons but later passed to the Douglases of Tilquhillie.

Cog [NS 805152], near Sanquhar, Borders; site of castle.
Held by the Bannatynes, but passed to the Crichtons in 1557.

Crawfordton Tower [NX 796905], near Moniaive, Dumfries and Galloway; site of castle.
Held by the Crichtons in the middle of the seventeenth century, but passed to the Hays.

Dunbeath Castle [ND 158282], near Dunbeath, Caithness; impressive cliff-top castle.
Held by the Crichtons from 1452 until 1507 when the property passed to the Inneses, then went to the Sinclairs. Still occupied and an impressive pile.

Eliock House [NS 796074], near Sanquhar, Dumfries and Galloway; mansion incorporating castle.
Held by the Dalziels in 1388 but passed to the Crichtons, then to the Charteris family in 1462. Eliok was probably built by the Crichtons after regaining the lands, and was held by Robert Crichton, Lord Advocate of Scotland to Mary, Queen of Scots, and James VI. He was the father of 'Admirable Crichton', who may have been born here, rather than Clunie Castle on its island. The property went to the Stewarts in 1593, and then to others. Part of the building was burnt out in 1940 and remains ruinous.

Friars Carse [NX 925850], near Dumfries; mansion on site of castle.
Held by the Kirkpatricks, by the Maxwells and by the Riddels, but passed to the Crichtons. Dr Crichton founded the Crichton Royal Institute, a hospital, in the nineteenth century. Friars Carse is now used as a hotel (01387 740388; www.classic-hotels.net).

Glenmaddie [NS 742072], near Sanquhar, Dumfries and Galloway; site of castle.
Held by the Bannatynes in 1548 but passed to the Crichtons of Sanquhar.

Innernytie [NO 129359], near Bankfoot, Perthshire; site of castle.
Held by the Crichtons, but passed to the Hays and then to the Stewarts by the 1670s.

Kinnairdy Castle [NJ 609498], near Aberchirder, Aberdeenshire; impressive castle with fine interior.
Held by the Inneses, but passed in 1629 to the Crichtons of Frendraught, then to the Gregorys in 1647. Accommodation is available (01463 780833; www.kinnairdy-castle.co.uk).

Monzie Castle [NN 873245], near Crieff, Perthshire; castle and mansion.
Held by several families, before going to the Crichtons after being restored by Sir Robert Lorimer in 1908. Open in the spring for about a month (01764 653110).

Naughton Castle [NO 373246], near Wormit, Fife; ruinous castle.
Held by the Hays, but passed by marriage to the Crichtons in 1494. Sir Peter Crichton was Master of the Wardrobe to James III. The lands passed back to the Hays, and then went to the Morrisons and then to the Beatons.

Newhall Castle [NT 175566], near Penicuik, Midlothian; mansion on site of castle.
Held by the Crichtons from 1529 or earlier, and its occupants were accused of 'adhering' to 'papastrie' around 1570. Newhall was sold to the Penicuik family in 1646, and the gardens are open to the public by appointment only (01968 660206; www.gardensofscotland.org).

Old Crawfordton [NX 815889], near Moniaive, Dumfries and Galloway; ruined castle, being restored?
Held by the Crichtons.

Ruthven Castle [NO 302479], near Alyth, Angus; slight remains of castle.
Held by the Lindsays Earls of Crawford, but had passed to the Crichtons by 1510, then was sold to the Ogilvies of Coul in 1744.

Ryehill Castle [NS 794086], near Sanquhar, Dumfriesshire; site of castle.
Held by the Crichtons in the sixteenth century.

Strathurd Castle [NO 074328], near Bankfoot, Perthshire; site of castle and mansion.
Held by the Crichtons in the fifteenth century. John Crichton of Strathurd was beheaded at Tulliemet along with the chief of the Robertsons after they had torched Blair Castle. The property passed to the Nairnes of Mukkersy and then to the Murray Dukes of Atholl.

Tilquhillie Castle [NO 722941], near Banchory, Aberdeenshire; Z-plan tower house.
Held by the Douglases but passed by marriage to the Crichtons in 1665. The castle has been restored and is occupied as a private residence.

No. of castles/sites: 32
Rank: 39/764

Crombie

The name comes from Crombie, a place in Auchterless parish in Aberdeenshire. The 'b' was silent, so most old records spell the name as Cromy or Cromie or similar variations. It is on recorded from the fifteenth century.

Phesdo [NO 676756], some four miles north-west of Laurencekirk in the old county of Kincardineshire, is a large two-storey mansion which dates from the nineteenth century. It replaced the Old House of Phesdo, which was demolished. The lands were held by the Keiths and by the Falconers, but were sold to the Crombies, then to the Gladstones of Fasque in the nineteenth century. Phesdo is still occupied.

Thornton Castle [NO 688718], a mile or so north-west of Laurencekirk, is a fine mansion and castle, which may date from the fourteenth century. The castle is dated 1531 and 1662. It was held by the Thorntons and by the Strachans, and by other families, before coming to the Crombies in the nineteenth century. Thornton was sold in 1893 to Sir Thomas Thornton, and the house is still apparently occupied by the Thornton-Kemsley family.

No. of castles/sites: 2 / Rank: 396=/764
Xrefs: Cromie; Cromy

Crosier

A 'crosier' is the top part of a bishop's staff, but it is not clear if this had anything to do with the origin of the surname. The Crosier family settled in Liddesdale from the fourteenth century, and many different spellings of the name are recorded. Like many other clans and families, they were an unruly lot, and in 1526 the Duke of Richmond complained about their exploits and they were in trouble again in 1569. William Crosier, however, was a professor of philosophy at the University of St Andrews when it was first founded in 1410. The following towers were held by the Crosiers in the Borders:

Adderston or Cleerie [NT 514092], near Hawick; site only.
Brighouse Tower [NY 526921], near Newcastleton; site only.
Brighousecleughhead? [NY 526933], near Newcastleton; site only
Hudshouse Tower [NY 576980], near Newcastleton; mound of rubble.
Rakestonleis? [NY 580988], near Newcastleton; site only. Held by Martin Crozier of Rakestonleis in 1590.
Riccarton Tower [NY 544958], near Newcastleton; slight remains built into a sheepfold. Perhaps an Elliot property.

No. of castles/sites: 4 (+2?) / Rank: 278=/764
Xref: Crosar

Cruickshank

The name is probably taken from a place, although a more colourful but doubtful origin is said to be from a descriptive term or nickname meaning 'crooked shanks' or 'bowleggedness'. The name is on record from the thirteenth century.

Aswanley House [NJ 445397], seven miles west of Huntly in Aberdeenshire, is a long low L-plan house, with yellow-washed walls and a round stair-tower. Aswanley was held by the Cruickshanks, but passed to the Gordons, to the Calders in 1440 and then much later to the Duffs of Braco. Holiday accommodation is available (01466 700262; www.aswanley.com).

Warthill House [NJ 710315], a couple of miles south of Rothienorman also in Aberdeenshire, is a L-plan house, dating from the seventeenth century and built on the site of an earlier castle. Warthill was held by the Cruickshanks, but passed by marriage to the Leslies around 1518; it is still apparently owned by their descendants.

No. of castles/sites: 2 / Rank: 396=/764
Xrefs: Crookshanks; Cruckshanks

Cunningham

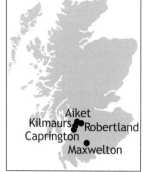

The name is territorial and comes from the area of the same name in the north of Ayrshire, and may come from 'cuinneag', meaning 'milk pail', and 'ham', meaning 'settlement or farm', from the Saxon. Cunningham is a common surname in lowland Scotland, and is first on record in the twelfth century.

The lands of Kilmaurs, two and a half miles north of Kilmarnock in Ayrshire, were held by the Cunninghams from the thirteenth century. The present **Kilmaurs Place** [NS 412411] dates from 1620 and is a T-plan house with corbiestepped gables and whitewashed walls. The family had fought against the Norsemen at the Battle of Largs in 1263, and may have had an older stronghold at **Jocksthorn** [NS 420408]. William Cunningham, Lord of Kilmaurs, endowed a collegiate church at Kilmaurs [NJ 415407] in 1413, and later the family built a mausoleum, known as the Glencairn Aisle, using the chancel of the old church. There is an elaborate monument to James, seventh Earl of Glencairn, and his wife in the aisle, and the building can be visited. Although made Earls of Glencairn in 1488, the first Earl was slain at Sauchieburn the same year. The lands of Kilmaurs were sold in 1786.

Maxwelton House [NX 822898], formerly known as **Glencairn Castle**, lies a couple of miles east of Moniaive in Dumfries and Galloway. The building is a fine seventeenth-century tower house of two storeys with a later mansion around a courtyard. The property was held by the Dennistouns, but passed by marriage to the Cunninghams of Kilmaurs in the fifteenth century. The family were made Earls of Glencairn in 1488, and Alexander Cunningham, fifth Earl, was opposed to Mary, Queen of Scots, being one of the commanders against her at Carberry Hill in 1568. William, ninth Earl, supported Charles II and led a rising against Cromwell's administration in 1653, although it was soon crushed. After the Restoration, he was made Lord Chancellor of Scotland. The title is now extinct, and Glencairn had been sold to the Laurie family in 1611, and the Lauries changed the name from Glencairn to Maxwelton.

Two miles south-west of Kilmarnock in Ayrshire is

Caprington Castle 1910?

133

Caprington Castle [NS 407363], which has a massive keep of the fifteenth century encased in a castellated mansion. Caprington was held by the Wallaces of Sundrum, but passed by marriage to the Cunninghams in 1425, who were afterwards styled 'of Caprington'. Sir John Cunningham of Caprington was an eminent lawyer, and was made a Baronet of Nova Scotia in 1669. This branch of the family continues as the Fergusson-Cunninghams of Caprington, and their seat is apparently at the castle.

Aiket Castle [NS 388488], four miles south-east of Beith also in Ayrshire, is an altered and extended tower house, dating from the sixteenth century. The lands were held by the Cunninghams from the fifteenth century, or earlier. Alexander Cunningham of Aiket took part in the

Aiket Castle (M&R)

murder of Hugh Montgomery, fourth Earl of Eglinton, in 1586. Cunningham was himself shot dead near Aiket soon afterwards by Montgomery's kinsmen. The property passed to the Dunlops at the beginning of the eighteenth century, and the building was later used to house farm labourers until burned down in the 1960s. The building was restored in 1979.

Robertland Castle [NS 441470] is one or so miles north-east of Stewarton again in Ayrshire, and was held by the Cunninghams from 1506. David Cunningham of Robertland, with others, murdered Hugh Montgomery, as mentioned above. Cunningham was hunted down and slain, but the feud between the families lasted at least another twenty years. This branch of the family were made Baronets of Nova Scotia in 1630. Sir William Cunningham of Robertland was a friend of Robert Burns. The family held the property until 1696 or later and still flourish, now as the Fairlie-Cunninghames of Robertland, but they now apparently live in Australia. The present mansion of Robertland dates from about 1804, but stands on the site of a sixteenth-century tower house.

The Cunninghams also owned several other properties:
Auchenbowie House [NS 798874], near Stirling; mansion incorporating castle.
> Held by the Cunninghams of Polmaise, but passed to Robert Bruce, who was Provost of Stirling in 1555, and then later to the Munros.

Auchenharvie Castle [NS 363443], near Irvine, Ayrshire; fifteenth-century castle.
> Held by the Cunninghams, and the family were industrialists and extracted coal from their lands as well as running a

Auchenharvie Castle (M&R)

brewery. The castle was abandoned when Seabank House, at Stevenson, was built

Balgair Castle [NS 607884], near Fintry, Stirlingshire; site of tower house.
> Held by the Cunninghams of Glengarnock from 1467 but passed to the Galbraiths of Culcreuch in 1563.

Ballindalloch Castle [NS 535885], near Balfron, Stirlingshire; mansion on site of castle.
> Held by the Cunningham Earls of Glencairn but had passed to the Dunmore family by the eighteenth century and later went to the Coopers. The gardens are open by appointment from May to June (01360 440202; www.gardensofscotland.org).

Barns [NO 597068], near Crail, Fife; site of castle.
> Held by the Cunninghams. William Drummond of Hawthornden stayed here in 1620. His fiancee, Mary Cunningham of Barns, was burned to death on the eve of their wedding, and Drummond never married and became a learned recluse.

Belton House [NT 644766], near Dunbar, East Lothian; ruined castle and mansion.
> Held by the Cunninghams of Belton, but passed by marriage to the Hays of Yester in 1468.

Bonnington House [NT 111691], near Ratho, Midlothian; mansion dated 1622.
> Held by several families including the Cunninghams at one time, but passed to the Wilkies of Ormiston.

Castle of Park [NX 189571], near Glenluce, Galloway; restored L-plan tower house.
> Held by the Hays from the Reformation and then by the Cunninghams from 1830. They abandoned the castle for Dunragit, using Park to house farm labourers. The castle has been restored and can be rented through the Landmark Trust (01628 825925; www.landmarktrust.org.uk).

Clonbeith Castle [NS 338455], near Kilwinning, Ayrshire; slight remains of castle.
> Held by the Cunninghams. John Cunningham of Clonbeith murdered the fourth Earl of Eglinton in 1586 during a feud. He was pursued by the Montgomerys and cut to pieces. The property was sold to the Montgomery Earl of Eglinton in 1717.

Coilsfield Castle [NS 444265], near Mauchline, Ayrshire; site of castle and mansion.
> Held by the Cunninghams of Caprington after the Reformation, but was sold to the Montgomerys in 1661.

Comiston House [NT 240687], Edinburgh; mansion on site of castle.
> Held by the Cunninghams of Kilmaurs after 1355 but passed to Foulis of Colinton in 1531 and then to others.

Corsehill Castle [NS 416465], near Stewarton, Ayrshire; slight remains of castle.
> Held by the Cunninghams of Kilmaurs. Patrick Cunningham of Corsehill was killed by the Montgomerys in 1588 as part of their continuing feud. This branch of the family were made

Baronets in 1672, and the line continues although they now apparently live in England.

Craigends House [NS 419662], near Kilbarchan, Renfrewshire; site of mansion and castle.

Held by the Cunninghams from the middle of the fifteenth century, but passed to the Boyles of Kelburn in 1647, before then returning to the Cunninghams. They built a mansion but this was demolished in 1957.

Dean Castle [NS 437394], near Kilmarnock, Ayrshire; fine restored castle.

Long held by the Boyds but passed to the Cunningham Earls of Glencairn after 1758, then passed to the Scotts of Balcomie and then to others. The castle is open to the public and stands in a park (01563 522702; www.deancastle.com).

Drumquhassle Castle [NS 483869], near Drymen, Stirlingshire; site of castle.

Held by the Dennistouns and by the Buchanans before going to the Cunninghams. Sir John Cunningham of Drumquhassle was keeper of Dumbarton Castle and in 1577 was Master of the King's Household. Drumquhassle passed to the Grahams and then to the Govans. There is a later mansion.

Dunragit House [NX 150582], near Glenluce, Galloway; mansion incorporating castle.

Held by the Cunninghams but passed to the Baillies and then to the Dalrymple-Hays.

Finlaystone House [NS 365737], near Port Glasgow, Renfrewshire; mansion on site of castle.

Held by the Cunninghams of Kilmaurs from 1404, and by the Earls of Glencairn from 1488. Alexander Cunningham, fifth Earl, supported the Reformation and had John Knox preach here in 1556. Robert Burns – whose patron was James, fourteenth Earl – visited the house, and scratched his name on a window pane with his diamond ring. He also wrote a lament for the earl, who had to sell his lands because of debt; and Burns called his son James Glencairn Burns. Finlaystone was sold in 1863 because of debt, and later passed to the McMillans. The grounds and garden are open to the public and there is a visitor centre (01475 540505; www.finlay stone.co.uk).

Gilbertfield Castle [NS 653588], near East Kilbride, Glasgow; ruinous tower house.

Probably held by the Cunninghams at one time but long a property of the Hamiltons.

Glengarnock Castle [NS 311574], near Kilbirnie, Ayrshire; ruinous castle.

Held by the Morvilles and by the Riddells before going to the Cunninghams from 1614 until early in the eighteenth century. The castle was then abandoned, stripped and part collapsed in a storm of 1839. The family added an aisle in 1597 to the Auld Kirk of Kilbirnie, a fine old church, which is open to the public in the summer (www.kilbirnieauldkirk.org.uk).

Hill of Beith [NS 360541], near Beith, Ayrshire; site of castle.

Held by the Cunninghams from after the Reformation.

Isle of May [NT 655995], island in Firth of Forth; site of fortified building.

Held by several families including by the Cunninghams of Barns at one time, then by the Scotts of Balcomie. The island can be visited from May to September (01333 310103/01333 451152).

Kerelaw Castle [NS 269428], near Kilwinning, Ayrshire; ruinous castle.

Held by the Lockharts in 1191 and the by the Cunninghams, later Earls of Glencairn, who built the castle. It was apparently destroyed in a feud in 1488, then sacked by the Montgomerys of Eglinton in 1528. Eglinton Castle was burned in retaliation. Kerelaw Castle was remodelled as a garden folly for the now demolished eighteenth-century Kerelaw or Grange House.

Kilmaronock Castle [NS 456877], near Drymen, Stirlingshire; ruinous castle.

Held by several families before coming to the Cunninghams from the end of the fourteenth century, but passed to the Cochrane Earls of Dundonald.

Kilmaronock Castle (M&R)

Kingsmuir [NO 536084], near Anstruther, Fife; mansion.

Held by the Borthwicks in the first half of the seventeenth century, but passed to the Hannays, later Hannay Cunninghams.

Kyle Castle [NS 647192], near Cumnock, Ayrshire; site of castle.

Held by the Cunninghams but passed to the Stewarts of Bute.

Lainshaw Castle [NS 410453], near Stewarton, Ayrshire; castle replaced by mansion.

Sold to the Cunninghams in 1779, one of Glasgow's 'tobacco lords'. The property was earlier held by the Stewarts and then by the Montgomerys from 1570. The building is said to have a Green Lady, reputed to be the apparition of Elizabeth Cunningham, wife of Montgomery of Lainshaw. She may have been involved in the plot which resulted in the murder of the Hugh Montgomery, fourth Earl of Eglinton, in 1586, and then the subsequent feud. The ghost is said to have been witnessed wearing a green dress and carrying a candle; the rustle of her dress is also reportedly been heard.

Livingston Peel [NT 040676], in Livingston, West Lothian; site of castle.

Held by the Livingstones and by the Murrays, but then by the Cunninghams at one time but passed to the Primrose Earl of Rosebery in 1812.

Logan House [NS 589207], near Cumnock, Ayrshire; mansion.

Held by the Logans before coming to the Cunninghams in 1802.

Logie House [NJ 006508], near Forres, Moray; castle replaced by mansion.

Held by the Cummings of Altyre but passed to the Cunninghams.

Mayshiel [NT 622641], near Cranshaws, East Lothian; altered tower house.

Held by several families before going to the Cunninghams in the eighteenth century but sold to the Houstons of Clerkington. Still occupied.

Milncraig [NS 400208], near Ayr; site of castle or old house.

Held by the Cathcarts, but passed by marriage to the Cunninghams of Milncraig around the end of the sixteenth century. Sir David Cunninghame of Milncraig was an eminent lawyer, and was a friend and supporter of Fletcher of Saltoun. He was made a Baronet of Nova Scotia in 1701-02. The family line continues in Cunynghame Baronets, but they now apparently live in England.

Monkredding House [NS 325454], near Kilwinning, Ayrshire; tower house and mansion.

Held by the Nevans and then by the Cunninghams of Clonbeith in 1698.

Montgreenan Castle [NS 342452], near Kilwinning, Ayrshire; mansion near site of castle.

Held by the Rosses and then by the Cunninghams of Montgreenan, but the family were forfeited in 1680. The mansion was built for the Glasgow family and is now a hotel (01294 850005; www.montgreenanhotel.com).

North Synton [NT 485237], near Selkirk, Borders; altered tower house.

Held by the Veitch family in 1407, but had passed to the Cunninghams by the end of the seventeenth century, then Hannay Cunninghams.

Pittarthie Castle [NO 522091], near Elie, Fife; large L-plan tower house.

The lands were held by several families before passing to the Bruces in 1644 but passed to the Cunningham Earls of Glencairn after 1715, then the Hannay Cunninghams. The building is being restored.

Place of Snade [NX 847857], near Moniaive, Dumfries and Galloway; site of castle.

Held by the Hays of Yester and then by the Cunninghams in 1472.

Polmaise Castle [NS 835924], near Stirling; site of castle and mansion.

Held by the Cunninghams at one time, but passed to the Murrays of Touchadam.

Polquhairn [NS 479158], near Drongan, Ayrshire; site of castle.

Held by the Cunninghams from 1388 until the seventeenth century when the property went to the Chalmers family and then to the Crawfords.

Prestonfield House [NT 278721], Edinburgh; fine and elegant mansion of 1687.

Held by the Hamiltons, but the present house was built for Sir James Dick of Braid. The family, later Dick-Cunyngham, held the property for some 300 years, and Dr Samuel Johnson visited in 1773. The house has been used as a hotel since 1958 and some of the grounds are used as Prestonfield Golf Course (0131 225 7800; www.prestonfield.com).

Seabegs [NS 824798], near Bonnybridge, Falkirk; motte.

David Cunningham of Seabegs is on record in the eighteenth century.

Skelmorlie Castle [NS 195658], near Largs, Ayrshire; restored castle.

Held by the Cunninghams of Kilmaurs from the fourteenth

Skelmorlie Castle (M&R)

century, but passed to the Montgomerys in 1461 and then in 1852 to the Grahams. Self-catering accommodation is available at Skelmorlie (01475 521616; www.aboutscotland.com/ayrshireskelmorlie.html).

Tarbolton Motte [NS 432273], near Prestwick, Ayrshire; motte and bailey castle. The lands were held by the Cunninghams of Enterkine in 1671.

www.clancunningham.us
www.clancunninghamusa.org
No. of castles/sites: 47 / Rank: 22=/764

Curror

The name is derived from the occupation of 'courier', and the name is on record in Scotland from 1296.

Some three miles south-west of Banff in the north-east of Scotland is **Inchdrewer Castle** [NJ 656607], which is an L-plan tower house of five storeys, and dates from the sixteenth century. It was later extended to T-plan. The lands belonged to the Curror family, but were sold to the Ogilvies of Dunlugas in the sixteenth century.

No. of castles/sites: 1
Rank: 537=/764
Xref: Courier

Cushnie

The name is territorial and comes from the lands of Cushnie, which are some six miles west and south of Alford in Aberdeenshire. The name is on record in charters from the twelfth century.

Cushnie Castle [NJ 525111] is a very ruinous tower house of the sixteenth century, and the existing building, Cushnie Lodge or House of Cushnie, dates from the seventeenth or eighteenth century. The lands were held by the Cushnie family from the twelfth century, but within 200 years had passed by marriage to the Leslies, then later went to the Lumsdens. House of Cushnie is still occupied.

No. of castles/sites: 1
Rank: 537=/764

Cutler

Orroland

The name means 'knife maker', and is on record in Scotland from 1296.

The family long held the lands of **Orroland** [NX 773466], which are two miles west of Moniaive in Dumfries and Galloway. The house incorporates part of a tower house from the sixteenth or seventeenth century with later modifications and extensions. The lands were a property of Dundrennan Abbey, but passed to the Cutlers in 1437. The story goes that the family came to the area to sharpen the tools of the mason employed in building the abbey. The Cutlers held Orroland until 1769 when it passed by marriage to the Fergussons of Craigdarroch.

No. of castles/sites: 1
Rank: 537=/764
Xref: Cutlar

Dacre

Hermitage

The name comes from a place near Penrith in Cumbria in the north of England.

Hermitage Castle [NY 494960], five miles north of Newcastleton in a windswept part of the Border, is one of the most impressive and oppressive of castles; and its legends of ghosts and witchcraft are not surprising. The Dacres held the property in the thirteenth century and they had a stronghold, which passed to the Soulis family, who rebuilt it. It went on to be owned by several of the great families of Scotland, including by the Douglases and by the Hepburns, and is now in the care of Historic Scotland. The castle is open to the public (01387 376222).

No. of castles/sites: 1
Rank: 537=/764

Dairsie

Dairsie

The name is territorial and comes from the lands of Dairsie, which are three miles east and north of Cupar in Fife. The name is on record from the first quarter of the fifteenth century.

Dairsie Castle [NO 414160] is a restored Z-plan tower house, which dates from the sixteenth century but was very ruinous

Dairsie Castle (AA)

when it was rebuilt in the 1990s. The lands were a property of the Bishops and Archbishops of St Andrews, but were held by the Dairsie family. The male line failed, and the heiress of the Dairsies married into the Learmonth family, and this became the Learmonths' main stronghold.

No. of castles/sites: 1 / Rank: 537=/764
Xref: Darie

Dalgleish

The name comes from the lands of Dalgleish, which are by the Tima Water some seven miles north of Eskdalemuir in the Borders. The lands were held by the Dalgleishs from the fifteenth century or earlier, and the family were apparently a turbulent lot. There was a tower house, possibly at **Over Dalgleish** [NT 260083], although it may have been at **Nether Dalgleish** [NT 274094]. The building was destroyed by the English in the 1540s or 50s, and the lands passed to the Scotts of Buccleuch in the seventeenth century.

On the west side of Edinburgh is the grand pile of **Lauriston Castle** [NT 204762], which dates from the sixteenth century but has a later Jacobean extension by the architect William Burn. The property was held

Lauriston Castle (M&R)

by the Napiers of Merchiston, but in 1657 passed to Robert Dalgleish, Charles II's solicitor, then in 1683 went to the Laws. The castle is now in the care of the local council and is open to the public by guided tour only (0131 336 2060; www.cac.org.uk).

Scotscraig [NO 445283], which is just west of Tayport in Fife, is a substantial mansion and replaced a castle. Scotscraig had several owners but was latterly held by the Dalgleishs, who built the present house in the nineteenth century, before Scotscraig passed to the Maitlands. The Dalgleishs of Scotscraig were descended from Dalgleish of that Ilk, and the line continues, although they no longer live in Scotland.

Other towers and castles were also held by the family.

Deuchar Tower [NT 360280], Yarrow, Borders; slight remains of tower house.
    Held by the Homes in 1502, but passed to the Dalgleishs, then to the Murrays of Deuchar by 1643.

Lempitlaw Tower [NT 787327], near Kelso, Borders; site of tower house.
    Held by the Dalgleish family: Dandy Dalgleish was slain by the English. The tower was destroyed in the 1540s or 50s.

Linton Tower [NT 774262], near Kelso, Borders; site of tower house.
    Held by the Somervilles in the twelfth century, then later probably by the Dalgleishs. The tower was torched in 1523 and destroyed in 1547 by the English.

Pitfirrane Castle [NT 060863], near Dunfermline, Fife; altered L-plan tower house.
    Long held by the Halketts, but in 1877 passed to the Dalgleish family. The building is now the clubhouse for a golf club.

Wideopen Tower [NT 767160], near Jedburgh, Borders; site of tower.
    Held by the Dalgleishs. John Dalgleish of Wideopen was in 1596 'slaughtered with Turkish barbarity, by Sir John Carey, in his own house'. The tower had also been sacked in the 1540s or 50s by the English.

No. of castles/sites: 8
Rank: 160=/764

Dallas

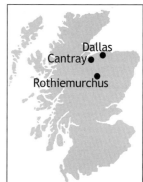

The name is territorial and comes from the lands and barony of Dallas, which are some eight or so miles south-west of Elgin in Moray. The family were descended from an Englishman William de Ripley, who held the lands in the twelfth century. George Dallas was the deputy Keeper of the Great Seal of Scotland, and he died in 1702. There was a castle at **Dallas** [NJ 125530], known as **Tor Castle**, but it was probably built after the lands had gone to the Cummings of Altyre; Tor Castle is now very ruinous.

There was a tower house at **Cantray** [NH 796479], which was probably on the site now occupied by Cantray House. There is a large and impressive, although rabbit-infested, motte at **Cantraydoune** [NH 789461], standing some sixty-foot high. The property was held by the Dallas family from the fifteenth century or before. William Dallas of Cantray was found guilty of certain crimes in 1494 and sentenced to be beheaded, but he was later pardoned. One of the family was killed at the Battle of Culloden in 1746, and the lands were sold to the Davidsons in 1768.

Rothiemurchus [NH 885098], two miles south of Aviemore in Strathspey, was a property of the Dallases but passed to the Gordons and then to the Grants in the sixteenth century. The house can be visited and the estate has a visitor centre (01479 812345; www.rothiemurchus.net).

No. of castles/sites: 3
Rank: 328=/764

Dalmahoy

The name is territorial, and comes from the lands of Dalmahoy, which are two miles north-west of Currie to the west of Edinburgh. The name is on record from the thirteenth century.

There was a castle at **Dalmahoy** [NT 145690], but this was replaced by an elegant classical mansion, built by the architect William Adam in the 1720s. The building has been greatly extended and modified down the centuries. The property was held by the Dalmahoys from the thirteenth century until it was sold to the Dalrymples in the eighteenth century, and then went to the Douglases. The building is now used as a hotel and leisure centre (0131 333 1845; www.marriott. com/edigs).

Liberton Tower [NT 265697] is a well-preserved but somewhat plain little tower house, dating from the

Liberton Tower (M&R)

fifteenth century, and with very thick walls. It stands to the south-east of Edinburgh, off Liberton Drive North. The lands were held by the Dalmahoys, but passed to William Little, Provost of Edinburgh, in 1587. He abandoned the tower and built nearby **Liberton House** [NT 267694]. The tower has been restored and can be let as holiday accommodation (0990 851133; www.cospt.fsnet.co.uk); the house can be visited but by appointment only (0131 467 7777; www.ngra.co.uk).

No. of castles/sites: 2
Rank: 396=/764

Dalrymple

The name is territorial, and comes from the lands of Dalrymple, which are a few miles north and east of Maybole in Ayrshire. The lands were held by the Dalrymple family from the fourteenth century or earlier.

Dalrymple or **Barbieston Castle** [NS 368142] is south-east of the village of Dalrymple, and there was a castle dating from the fourteenth century, which had been incorporated into a later mansion. The whole building was demolished in the nineteenth century. The property passed in the late fourteenth century to the Kennedys, who eventually became Earls of Cassillis.

Stair [NS 442239] is a fine and attractive L-plan tower house, which dates from the sixteenth century, and to which has been added later extensions. The lands were

Stair (M&R)

held by the Montgomerys then by the Kennedys of Dunure, but passed to the Dalrymples of Stair in 1429. The family supported the Reformation, and opposed the marriage of Mary, Queen of Scots, to Lord Darnley, and then fought against her at the Battle of Langside in 1568. James Dalrymple of Stair was an eminent lawyer, and became Lord President of the Court of Session. He had to flee Scotland after offending James VII, but returned with William of Orange and he was made Viscount Stair in 1690. His son, John Dalrymple, Master of Stair, was implicated in the organisation of the Massacre of Glencoe in 1692, but he was made Earl of Stair in 1703. John, second Earl, fought in the war against France and was made a Field Marshal. Stair passed from the family in the eighteenth century, but was then recovered in 1826. The house has been restored and is still occupied.

Two and a half miles east and north of Dalkeith in Midlothian was **Cousland Tower** [NT 377683], a sixteenth-century tower house, although little now remains. It was held by the MacGills of Cranstoun in the seventeenth century, but then passed to the Dalrymples, who were made Baronets of Nova Scotia in 1698. This branch of the family succeeded to the properties of the

MacGills of Oxenfoord, becoming Hamilton-Dalrymple-MacGill.

Oxenfoord Castle or **Nether Cranstoun Riddel** [NT 388656], three or so miles east and south of Dalkeith, is a magnificent Adam mansion built in the late eighteenth century and then extended by William Burn in 1842. The mansion encases a sixteenth-century L-plan tower house. The lands were held by the MacGills from the twelfth century, then in 1760 passed by marriage to the Dalrymples and this was a seat of the Earls of Stair. James Boswell stayed here in 1786. The castle was used as a girls' private boarding school from 1931, although this closed in 1984. The gardens are occasionally open to the public (www.gardensofscotland.org).

Castle Kennedy [NX 111609], three miles west of Stranraer in Galloway, is an impressive ruin of a late E-plan tower house. The lands were held by the Dalrymples

Carscreugh Castle (M&R)

Castle Kennedy (M&R)

of Stair from around 1677, and a fire gutted Castle Kennedy in 1716 and it was never reoccupied. The family moved to **Lochinch Castle** [NX 106618], about half a mile to the north, and the present mansion dates from 1864-67. It is a large, even graceful baronial house, with a flourish of turrets, spires, chimneys, battlements and crowsteps. It is still apparently the seat of the Dalrymple Earls of Stair, and the gardens around Castle Kennedy are open to the public (01776 702024; www.castlekennedygardens.co.uk).

The Dalrymples also owned:

Balneil [NX 179639], near Glenluce, Galloway; site of castle.
Held by the Kennedys, then by the Vauxs of Barnbarroch, then by the Rosses, then by the Dalrymples of Stair from 1643 and probably abandoned about twenty-five years later when the building at Carscreugh was completed.

Bargany Castle [NS 244003], near Girvan, Ayrshire; castle replaced by mansion.
Held by the Kennedys but also by the Dalrymples of Stair; gardens open from March to October (01465 871249).

Carscreugh Castle [NX 223599], near Glenluce, Galloway; ruined castle and mansion.
Held by the Vaux family and by the Rosses, then passed by marriage to the Dalrymples of Stair. Janet Dalrymple of Carscreugh was forced to marry Sir David Dunbar of Baldoon, although in love with another man. Janet died at Baldoon on

her wedding night, although the circumstances surrounding her death are unclear. Her ghost, in a bloodied wedding dress, is said to haunt the ruins of Baldoon.

Craigcaffie Tower [NX 089641], near Stranraer, Galloway; restored tower house.
Held by the Neilsons, but in 1791 passed to the Dalrymples of Stair. The building housed farm labourers at one time but it has been restored and reoccupied.

Cranston [NT 404651], near Dalkeith, Midlothian; site of castle.
Long held by the Cranstouns, but passed to the Dalrymples of Cousland. Sir James Dalrymple of Upper Cranston and Cousland, married Elizabeth Hamilton MacGill, the heiress of Oxenfoord in 1760.

Dalmahoy [NT 145690], near Currie, Midlothian; fine mansion on site of castle.
Held by the Dalmahoys but passed to the Dalrymples in 1725 then to the Douglases about 1750. Now a hotel (0131 333 1845; www.marriott.com/edigs).

Greenknowe Tower [NT 639428], near Gordon, Borders; well-preserved ruinous tower house.
Held by the Gordons, by the Setons and by the Pringles before passing to the Dalrymples; and occupied until about 1850. In the care of Historic Scotland and open to the public.

Hailes Castle [NT 575758], near East Linton, East Lothian; fine ruin in scenic setting.
Held by many families, including by the Hepburns, before passing to the Dalrymples in 1700, but they moved to Newhailes, near Musselburgh. The castle is in the care of Historic Scotland and is open to the public.

Innermessan Castle [NX 084634], near Stranraer, Galloway; farmhouse on site of castle.
Held by the Agnews of Lochnaw but sold to the Dalrymples of Stair in 1723. The castle was used as a cavalry barracks, but was demolished to build the farm.

Leuchie House [NT 572833], near North Berwick, East Lothian; mansion on site of older house.
Held by the Marjoribanks but sold to the Dalrymples in 1701. Sir Hew Dalrymple bought the Barony of North Berwick in 1694, and four years later he was made a Baronet of Nova Scotia. He bought Tantallon in 1699 and the Bass Rock in 1706. Leuchie House was a convent and then a home for the MS Society of Scotland (www.leuchie.com). The Hamilton-Dalrymples still apparently live in a house at Leuchie.

Newhailes or **Whitehill** [NT 325725], near Musselburgh, East Lothian; fine mansion.
Held by the Dalrymples from about 1700, and a plain and somewhat dour but impressive house with fine rococo interiors, including the library. Newhailes was visited by many leading figures of the Scottish Enlightenment. In the care of The National Trust for Scotland and open to the public (0131 665 1546; www.nts.org.uk).

Newliston [NT 110736], near Kirkliston, West Lothian; tower house replaced by mansion.

Held by the Dundas family but passed by marriage to the Dalrymples of Stair in 1699. It was home to Sir John Dalrymple, second Earl of Stair, a Field Marshal and British Ambassador to France. He died in 1747. The property was sold to the Hog family and they built the present mansion. Newliston is open to the public for some weeks in the spring (0131 333 3231).

Nunraw Castle [NT 597706], near East Linton, East Lothian; castle and mansion.

Held by the Hepburns after the Reformation, then by the Dalrymples and by the Hays. The castle is now part of a monastery, the Abbey of Sancta Maria. It is possible to stay in the abbey guest house (01620 830228 (guest house); liamdevlin.tripod.com/nunraw/).

Sinniness Castle [NX 215532], near Glenluce, Galloway; remains of castle.

Held by the Kennedys but passed to the Dalrymples of Stair.

Stranraer Castle or Castle of St John [NX 061608], Stranraer, Galloway; restored tower house.

Held by the Adairs and by the Kennedys, but passed to the Dalrymples of Stair in 1680. John Graham of Claverhouse stayed here while suppressing Covenanters in the 1680s. The castle now houses a museum and is open to the public (01776 705544; www.dumgal.gov.uk).

Tantallon Castle [NT 596851], near North Berwick, East Lothian; fantastic ruined castle.

Long held by the Douglases but was bought by the Dalrymples

Tantallon Castle 1910?

in 1699 but by then it had been abandoned as a residence. The castle is in the care of Historic Scotland and is open to the public (01620 892727).

Ward of Lochnorris [NS 539205], near Cumnock, Ayrshire; site of castle.

Held by the Crawfords in 1440, but passed to the Dalrymple Earls of Dumfries. They built Dumfries House [NS 541204] in 1757, the building being designed by John and Robert Adam for William Dalrymple, fourth Earl of Dumfries. The house is a classical mansion with a central block and pavilions. The property later passed to the Crichton-Stuart Marquesses of Bute, and was recently put up for sale and was expected to fetch around £20 million; the house and its contents were, however, saved from being broken up.

No. of castles/sites: 22
Rank: 58=/764

Dalziel

The name is territorial and comes from the lands and barony of Dalziel, which are south and east of Motherwell in central Scotland. There are a very many different ways of spelling the name, and the pronunciation is 'D-L'. The name is on record in Scotland from the middle of the thirteenth century.

Dalzell House [NS 756550] is a very fine castle with a strong tower, other ranges and a strong wall around a courtyard. The property was held by the Dalziels from

Dalzell House (M&R)

the thirteenth century, and they joined Robert the Bruce in the Wars of Independence. Sir William Dalziel lost an eye in the Battle of Otterburn in 1388. The family moved to Carnwath, and Dalzell was sold to the Hamiltons of the Boggs in 1649. The house has the distinction of having stories of four different ghostly females: Green, Grey, White and Brown ladies; and has been restored in recent times and divided into separate dwellings. Dalzell Park is open daily (0141 304 1907; www.northlan.gov.uk).

Carnwath House [NS 975465], at Carnwath in Lanarkshire, was a plain old mansion with work from a tower house, but it was demolished in 1970 and a golf clubhouse was built in the site. Carnwath had been held by the Somervilles and by the Lockharts, but passed to the Dalziels, who were made Earls of Carnwath in 1639. Robert Dalziel, second Earl, fought for Charles II at the Battle of Naseby in 1644 and died soon afterwards, and David, third Earl, was at the Battle of Worcester in 1651 but was captured after the fighting. The property was sold back to the Lockharts before 1674, although the family retained the title. Sir Robert, the sixth Earl, fought for the Jacobites in the Rising of 1715 and was captured after the Battle of Preston, and the family were forfeited and lost their titles and lands, although Robert was perhaps lucky not to also lose his head.

Three miles east and north of Linlithgow in West Lothian, **The Binns** [NT 051785] is a large castellated mansion, dating from the first half of the seventeenth century and painted in a delicate wash of pink. It has a fine interior including plaster ceilings, and stands on the site of a castle. The property was held by the Livingstones of Kilsyth, but was sold to the Dalziels in 1612. General Tom Dalziel of The Binns was a Royalist, and took a vow never to shave after Charles I was executed. He was taken prisoner in 1651 following the Battle of Worcester – when an army under Charles II was defeated by Cromwell – but escaped from the Tower of London, and joined the Royalist rising of 1653. He went into exile when this rising collapsed, and served in the Russian army with the Tsar's cossacks, when he is reputed to have roasted prisoners over open fires (and after which he reputedly introduced thumbscrews to Scotland – although they are on record as being used in Scotland from 1481 or earlier). Returning after the Restoration, Dalziel was made commander of forces in Scotland from 1666 to 1685. He led the force that defeated the Covenanters at the Battle of Rullion Green in 1666, although this was because of his supernatural powers (according to his enemies) which meant musket balls would bounce off him. He died in 1685 at the age of more than eighty. Perhaps not surprisingly, given his reputation in life, Dalziel's bogle is said to haunt the grounds of the Binns, at which times his boots disappear from the house. Tam also reputedly played cards with the devil, although being Tam, won. The hornéd one was so angry that it took the heavy marble table on which they had been playing and cast it into a nearby pond; which explains why the table was found in the Sergeant's Pond in about 1885. The line of Dalyell of the Binns continues, the latest having been another Tam, who was MP for Linlithgow for many years and was Father of the House. The Binns is in the care of The National Trust for Scotland and open to the public (01506 834255; www.nts.org.uk). The family have a burial aisle at Abercorn Church [NT 083792], which is a fine old building with an interesting burial ground and is open to the public.

There are several other properties held by the Dalziels:
Amisfield Tower [NX 992838], near Dumfries; very fine tower house.
    Held by the Charteris family, but passed to the Dalziels in 1636. The Dalziels were active Royalists during the Civil War, and Captain Alexander Dalziel was executed in 1650. The tower is still occupied,
Caldwell Tower [NS 422551], near Neilston, Renfrewshire; sixteenth-century tower house.
    Long held by the Mures. William Mure was involved with the Covenanters in the Pentland Rising, which ended in defeat in 1666 at Rullion Green. He fled abroad while his wife and daughters were imprisoned in Blackness Castle and his lands were forfeited and given to William Dalziel of The Binns. The Mure family regained the lands in 1690.
Carlowrie Castle [NT 142744], near Kirkliston, West Lothian; site of mansion.
    Held by the Dalziels of Carlowrie in the fifteenth century, but passed to the Marjoribanks family and to the Falconers, then to the Hutchinsons.

Eliock House [NS 796074], near Sanquhar, Dumfries and Galloway; mansion incorporating part of a castle.
    Held by the Crichtons, and by the Charteris family for some years, but passed to the Dalziels in the seventeenth century, then was sold to the Veitch family.
Glenae Tower [NX 984905], near Thornhill, Dumfries and Galloway; slight remains of a tower house.
    Held by the Dalziels.
Little Kype [NS 746407], near Strathaven, Lanarkshire; site of castle.
    Held by the Bairds, but then by the Dalziels in 1572, and then passed to the Hamiltons.

www.dalzell.org
No. of castles/sites: 9
Rank: 149=/764
Xrefs: Dalyell; Dalzell

Darleith

The name is territorial and comes from the lands and barony of Darleith, which are two miles north of Cardross in Dunbartonshire.

Darleith House [NS 345806] is a classical mansion but incorporates much of a sixteenth-century tower house. The property was held by the Darleiths from 1489 or earlier, when Arthur Darleith was granted remission for holding Dumbarton Castle against the king, either James III or James IV. The Darleiths sided with the MacFarlanes in a feud against the Buchanans in 1619, but the property was sold in 1670 to the Yuilles. The house was being used as a seminary in 1962 but is now ruinous.

No. of castles/sites: 1
Rank: 537=/764

Darling

The name may come from Old English, and is derived from a term to denote the young noble of a house, often the eldest and heir, but then became a family name. The name is on record from the fourteenth century.

Ladhope or **Appletreeleaves Tower** [NT 494366], just north of Galashiels in the Borders, is a now ruinous sixteenth-century tower house, but was long held by the Darling family.

The Stormonth Darlings, descended from this family, have held **Lednathie** [NO 340630] in Glen Prosen north of Kirriemuir, since 1683 and still apparently live here.

No. of castles/sites: 2
Rank: 396=/764

Darroch

The name is recorded in Scotland from 1406, and may be territorial as the name Darroch can be found in several places, including near Falkirk. The name is also said to come from 'Macdara', meaning 'son of the oak', perhaps a druidical reference. There was a branch of the family, who were numerous on Islay and Jura, and claimed descent from the MacDonalds.

Gourock was held by the Darrochs from 1784, after Duncan Darroch had made a fortune in Jamaica after being born on Jura. **Gourock Castle** [NS 244771], a plain mansion of 1747, replaced a small and reputedly unimportant castle of the Douglases and then of the Stewarts of Castlemilk. The fourth baron of Gourock acquired Torridon in Wester Ross, and the line of the Darrochs of Gourock continues, although they now apparently live in Surrey in England. Torridon is in the care of The National Trust for Scotland and is a particularly scenic and impressive part of the Scotland.

No. of castles/sites: 1
Rank: 537=/764
Xref: Macdara

Davidson

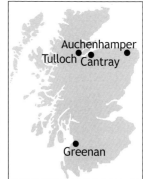

The name is from 'son of David' or 'son of Davie', and is recorded in Scotland from 1219. Variations include Davidson, Davison, Davis and Davie, as well as Dawson, Day and even Dean. The Davidsons were allied with the Mackintoshes and Clan Chattan, but many of them were killed at the Battle of Invernahaven in 1370. There had been a dispute over who should lead their army, resulting in the Davidsons being overwhelmed by the Camerons, before the Camerons in turn were finally defeated by the Macphersons. Robert Davidson, Provost of Aberdeen, was killed at the Battle of Harlaw in 1411, and there is a stone effigy of him dressed as a knight in the Kirk of St Nicholas in Aberdeen. The church is open to the public (01224 643494; www.kirk-of-st-nicholas.org.uk).

Tulloch Castle [NH 547605] stands about one mile north of Dingwall in the far north of Scotland. The building consists of an old keep or tower, possibly from as early as the twelfth century, with a later wing and other extensions. The lands were long held by the Bains, but were sold to the Davidsons in 1762 and they held Tulloch until 1945. There is a apparently tunnel from the basement which is believed to have led across the town to Dingwall Castle. It has collapsed but part of it can be seen from the middle of the front lawn. Tulloch is said to be haunted by a Green Lady. The story goes that a child surprised her father with another woman who was not the girl's mother. The girl was so startled that she fled the room and fell down a flight of stairs, killing herself. There have reputedly been manifestations in recent times. The building was used as a school, but has been a hotel since 1996 (01349 861325; www.tulloch castle.co.uk).

Cantray [NH 796479] is five or so miles east of the Culloden battlefield in Inverness-shire. It was a property of the Dallas family from the fifteenth century, but was sold to the Davidsons in 1768. There was a tower house, probably at the site of the present Cantray House, which now houses an agricultural college.

The Davidsons also held:
Auchenhamper [NJ 645458], near Turriff, Aberdeenshire; site of castle.
  Held by the Davidsons in the fifteenth and sixteenth centuries.
Greenan Castle [NS 312193], near Ayr; ruined tower house.
  Held by the Davidsons but was sold to the Kennedys in 1588. The castle has been suggested as the site of Arthur's Camelot.
Hatton House [NT 128687], near Balerno, Edinburgh; site of castle and mansion.
  Held by the Hattons, by the Lauders and by the Maitlands, but was sold in 1792 to the Davidsons of Muirhouse, then in 1870 to the Douglases.

Greenan Castle 1920? – see previous page

Inchmarlo [NO 670968], near Banchory, Aberdeenshire; castle replaced by mansion.

Held by the Douglases of Tilquhillie, but a possession of the Davidsons from 1838 until 1923 when the property was sold. The line continues but they now apparently live near Alnwick in Northumberland. The gardens of Inchmarlo are occasionally open to the public (www.gardensofscotland.org).

www.clandavidsonusa.com
No. of castles/sites: 6
Rank: 212=/764
Xrefs: Chattan; Davis; Davison; Dawson; Day

Dawson

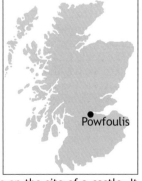

The name comes from 'Dawe's (a diminutive of 'David') son', and is mentioned in records in Scotland from the beginning of the fifteenth century (also see Davidson).

Powfoulis [NS 918856], a few miles east of Stenhousemuir in Falkirk, is an elegant mansion and stands on the site of a castle. It was held by the Bruces for many years, then by the Dundas family, but was sold to the Dawsons in 1855. They had been co-founders of the Carron Iron Works. The building is now a hotel (01324 831267; www.powfoulis.co.uk).

No. of castles/sites: 1
Rank: 537=/764

Delgarno

Garnieston Castle [NJ 734551], three miles north of Turriff in the north-east of Scotland, was held by the Delgarno family, but there are no remains.

No. of castles/sites: 1
Rank: 537=/764

Dempster

The name comes from the office of 'dempster' or 'judex', a position in the retinue of any lord, shire or parliament that was empowered to hold courts. The name is on record in Scotland from 1296. George Dempster was MP for Forfar and the Fife burghs from 1762 to 1790, and was a Director of the East India Company.

Four and a half miles west of Brechin in Angus, **Careston Castle** [NO 530599] is a Z-plan tower house, which rises to four storeys and dates from the seventeenth century. The building has been altered down the years, including in the eighteenth century. Careston was held by the Dempsters, and one of the family fought with the Bishop of Brechin over land, and stole cattle and horses and was involved in the kidnapping of monks. The property passed to the Lindsays, to the Carnegies, and then to others. It is still occupied.

Hatton Manor [NJ 709420], five miles south of Turriff in Aberdeenshire in the north-east of Scotland, was held by the Dempsters in the sixteenth century. Nothing of a castle remains except a fragment of masonry which may be built into a later house. The lands were also owned by the Allardice family and by the Meldrums.

Letham [NO 624457] was held by the Dempsters at the turn of the eighteenth century, and is located two miles north of Arbroath in Angus, but the property later passed to the Hays. There was a castle, although the precise location is not certain.

Skibo Castle [NH 735891], four miles west of Dornoch in Sutherland, was held by the Dempsters in 1786, but passed to the Sutherlands and then to Andrew Carnegie, and has had many other owners. The grand mansion stands on the site of castle and is now an exclusive country club (www.carnegieclubs.com).

No. of castles/sites: 4
Rank: 278=/764

Denholm

The name is territorial, and comes from either the lands and barony of that name five miles east and north of Hawick in the old county of Roxburghshire in the Borders, or from the parish in Dumfries and Galloway. The family is on record from the end of the thirteenth century. James Steuart Denham was a Jacobite in the 1745-46 Rising, and fled abroad. When he returned in 1763, he wrote the first treatise on economics in English.

Denholm [NT 568183] in Roxburghshire was held by the family of the same name, but later passed to the Douglases, who had a tower house, but there are no remains.

Westshield [NS 946494], five miles north-east of Lanark, was a mansion which incorporated a sixteenth-century tower house with slightly newer wings and then later additions. It was damaged by fire and was demolished in the 1980s. The lands were a property of the Denholms, but passed to the Lockharts of The Lee in the seventeenth century.

Some four miles east of Carnwath in Lanarkshire was **Hills Tower** [NT 049481], but again nothing survives. Hills was a property of the Denholms in 1299, but passed to the Baillies of Lamington, then to the Hamiltons and to the Lockharts.

No. of castles/sites: 3
Rank: 328=/764
Xref: Denham

Dennistoun

The name is territorial and comes from the lands of Danzielstoun or Dennistoun, which are two miles south of Kilmacolm in Renfrewshire in the west of Scotland. The origin is 'Daniel's town', presumed to have been from a Norman called Daniel. The family were important in the thirteenth and fourteenth centuries, and were related to the kings of Scots. Many of their lands passed through heiresses to the Maxwells and to the Cunninghams.

Dennistoun or **Danzielstoun Castle** [NS 364673] was held by the family, and used by them until at least the thirteenth century, even after they had moved to Colgrain. There are no remains.

Colgrain or **Camis Eskan** [NS 321815], three miles north-west of Cardross in Dunbartonshire, was held by the Dennistouns of Colgrain from the fourteenth century. John Dennistoun of Colgrain was a Royalist and fought for the king during the civil war and took part in Glencairn's Rising of 1653. The family held the lands until 1826 when they went to the Campbells of Breadalbane. There was a castle at Colgrain, but this was replaced by a later building of 1648, which was itself remodelled and extended in later years. It was used as a TB hospital, but has since been divided into luxury flats.

The family also owned:
Cameron House [NS 376831], near Alexandria, Dunbartonshire; mansion on site of castle.
Held by the Lennox family, then by the Charterises, by the Dennistouns and by the Colquhouns, but was sold to the Smolletts in 1763. The mansion is now a hotel (01389 755565; www.cameronhouse.co.uk).
Drumquhassle Castle [NS 483869], near Drymen, Stirlingshire; site of castle and house.
Held by the Dennistouns but passed by marriage to the Buchanans, then went to other families.
Finlaystone House [NS 365737], near Port Glasgow, Renfrewshire; fine mansion.
Held by the Dennistouns in the twelfth century, but passed to the Cunninghams of Kilmaurs in 1404. The Cunninghams, later Earls of Glencairn, held Finlaystone until 1863 when it was sold because of debt. A visitor centre and the ground are open to the public (01475 540505; www.finlaystone.co.uk).
Kilmaronock Castle [NS 456877], near Drymen, Stirlingshire; ruin of strong castle.
Held by the Flemings in 1329, then by the Dennistouns, then by the Cunninghams at the end of that century.
Maxwelton or **Glencairn House** [NX 822898], near Moniaive; fine castle and mansion.
Held by the Earls of Lennox, then by the Flemings and then passed by marriage to the Dennistouns in the fourteenth century, but went by marriage to the Cunninghams of Kilmaurs in the fifteenth century and later went to the Cochrane Earls of Dundonald and then to others. Still occupied.

Newark Castle (RWB)

Newark Castle [NS 331745], near Port Glasgow, Renfrewshire; fine
large tower house.
Held by the Dennistouns but passed by marriage to the
Maxwells of Calderwood in 1402. In the care of Historic
Scotland and open to the public from April to September (01475
741858).

Old Dalquhurn House [NS 390780], near Dumbarton; site of castle
or old house.
Held by the Earls of Lennox and then by the Spreulls, but was
bought by the Dennistouns in 1620. The property passed to
the Smolletts in 1692; the house has been demolished and a
church occupies the site.

Stanely Castle [NS 464616], near Paisley; ruined castle marooned
in water works.
Held by the Dennistouns in the fourteenth century, but passed
to the Maxwells of Newark, then later to the Rosses of
Hawkhead, and then to others.

No. of castles/sites: 10
Rank: 140=/764
Xrefs: Danielstoun; Danzielstoun

Denoon

The name is territorial and
comes from Denoon in
Angus, which is some
seven miles south-west of
Kirriemuir. A separate origin may be from Dunoon
in Cowal in Argyll. The
name is on record in Scotland from the beginning of
the fifteenth century.

The site of **Denoon Castle** [NO 348438] stands on
Denoon Hill but little or nothing remains. It is not clear
whether the lands were held by the Denoons, as they
were long a property of the Lyons. The predecessor of
Glamis was planned to be built at Denoon but this was
reputedly the realm of fairies and the foundations were
cast down every night; it was then decided to build
Glamis at its present site.

Two Campbell brothers were accused of certain
crimes and fleeing to Cromarty took the maiden name
of their mother, calling themselves Denoon. They
acquired the lands of **Davidston** [NH 769650], which
are three miles south-west of the village of Cromarty
on the Black Isle, and they may have had a castle or
tower house. They held the property from the fifteenth
century, and John Denoon of Davieston was respited for
staying at home and not joining the king's army in 1529.

No. of castles/sites: 1 / Rank: 537=/764
Xrefs: Dunoon; Denune

Deuchar

The name is territorial and
comes from the lands of
Deuchar, which are seven
miles north-west of Kirriemuir in the foothills of the
Angus hills. The family may
have been descended from
the Earls of Angus, and
they are believed to have
held the lands from 1230
or earlier until the property was sold in 1819. **Deuchar
House** [NO 467620] probably stands on the site of a
castle or old house. The Deuchars were long vassals of
the Lindsays. The Deuchar Sword, a massive weapon,
was kept at Deuchar until it was seized by the Jacobite
Lyon of Easter Ogil. It was returned to the family after
the Battle of Culloden in 1746 (the Deuchars were Hanoverian). Alexander Deuchar was a Lyon Herald at the
Court of the Lord Lyon and he was responsible for reviv-
ing the Knights Templars in Scotland, using the Deuchar
Sword to invest new knights, from 1805.

Deuchar Tower [NT 360280], at Yarrow in the Borders, does not appear to have been held by the family.

No. of castles/sites: 1 / Rank: 537=/764

Dewar

The name appears to have two origins: one is territorial and comes from the lands of Dewar, which are some eight miles north-east of Peebles, close to Heriot, near the border between Lothian and the Borders. The other is from the office of 'dewar', from the Gaelic 'deoradh', a keeper of a holy relic, such as the head of the crozier of St Fillan, which is now in the Museum of Scotland. The Dewars, a family from Glendochart in Perthshire, long looked after the relic, and are still represented by the Dewars of Glendochart, who apparently now live in Kirkintilloch.

Dewar [NT 349489], eight miles north-east of Peebles, was held by the family from the thirteenth century or earlier, one story being that they were given the land after killing a fearsome wolf. The lands were sold in the seventeenth century. **Deuchar Tower** [NT 360280], at Yarrow in the Borders, was a sixteenth-century tower house, but little survives. It was held by the Murrays of Deuchar in 1643, but later passed to the Dewars.

Vogrie House [NT 381632], two miles east of Gorebridge in Midlothian, dates from the second half of the nineteenth century, and is a large baronial mansion with Elizabethan and Arts and Crafts features. There was an older house, and the lands were held by the Cockburns before passing to the Dewars at the beginning of the eighteenth century. Vogrie House was built for James Dewar, who made his fortune from the Perth whisky company, John Dewar and Sons. The family line continues as the Dewars of that Ilk and Vogrie, and they now apparently live in Somerset. The house was used as the Royal Edinburgh Hospital for Mental and Nervous Disorders from 1924 until 1962, and is now the centrepiece of a country park (01875 821990; www.mid lothian.gov.uk) and brownie hostel.

Some two miles south-west of Perth is **Aberdalgie** [NO 081202], a classical mansion of about 1800 built on the site of an old castle. The lands were held by the Oliphants, but are now a property of the Dewars, Barons Forteviot from 1916 (see Vogrie).

Dupplin Castle [NO 056195], four miles south-west of Perth, is a Tudor mansion dating from the nineteenth century, but also stands on the site of an ancient castle. It was held by several families before coming to Dewars, Barons Forteviot, in 1911.

The Dewars also held the lands around Cambuskenneth, near Stirling, and this branch of the family now apparently lives near Ballantrae in Ayrshire.

No. of castles/sites: 5
Rank: 240=/764

Dick

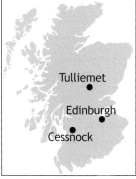

The name is from 'Dick', a diminutive of Richard, and is recorded in Scotland from the fifteenth century or earlier. William Dick, who died in 1866, was the founder of the (Dick) Veterinary College in 1823; James Dick, who had made his wealth from drive belts made from *gutta percha* (a sort of latex substance obtained from trees in south-east Asia), presented the Dick Institute Museum and Art Gallery (which is open to the public) to the people of Kilmarnock in 1901. His home, Elmbank House, had stood on the site of the institute.

Craighouse [NT 234709] is a fine restored tower house, much altered but dating from the sixteenth century, to the south and west of Edinburgh. The house is now part of the Napier University campus at Craighouse and is used as offices. The castle was built by the Symsons, but in the seventeenth century was owned by Sir William Dick of Braid, Provost of Edinburgh. He was one of the wealthiest men of his day, but he lost everything supporting Charles I. The property passed to the Elphinstones, and was later used as part of a psychiatric hospital. The building had a Green Lady at one time during its ownership by the Elphinstones.

Prestonfield House [NT 278721], to the south east of Edinburgh, is a fine and elegant mansion of 1687, which was designed by Sir William Bruce. The property has been held by the Hamiltons, but the present house was built for Sir James Dick of Braid. The family, later Dick-Cunyngham, held the property for some 300 years, and Dr Samuel Johnson visited in 1773. The house has been used as a hotel since 1958 and some of the grounds are used as Prestonfield Golf Course (0131 225 7800; www.prestonfield.com).

Grange House [NT 258718] also stood in Edinburgh, between Grange Loan, Lauder Place and Dick Place. It was a fine pile with turrets and battlements, and dated from the sixteenth century, but the house was completely demolished in 1936. It was held by the Dicks in 1679, and one of the ghosts was reportedly the spirit of a miser who is said to have rolled a barrel of gold through the house, perhaps a reference to Sir William Dick, mentioned above. Grange passed to the Lauders, and Bonnie Prince Charlie was entertained here in 1745.

Braid [NT 251703] is to the south of Edinburgh, and the Hermitage of Braid is now a picturesque public park. The lands were held by the Braid family, and then by the Fairlies and then by Sir William Dick. There may have been a castle, but the present house dates from 1785 and is now a countryside information centre.

Cessnock Castle [NS 511355] is an impressive castle one mile south-east of Galston in Ayrshire, and was long held by the Campbells, before coming to the Dicks, but then Cessnock then went to other families. Two miles

147

Cessnock Castle 1910? – see previous page

north of Broughty Ferry in Angus is **Pitkerro House** [NO 453337], a property of the Durhams, but which was later sold to the Dicks. The house is substantially a nineteenth-century mansion but it includes a small tower house, dating from the sixteenth century.

    Tulliemet House [NN 996540], a mile or so east of Ballinluig in Perthshire, dates from around 1800 and is a small classical mansion, perhaps on the site of a castle or older building. Tulliemet was a property of the Easons, but passed to Dr William Dick, who made a fortune from the East India Company, and he built the current house.

No. of castles/sites: 7
Rank: 182=/764

Dickson

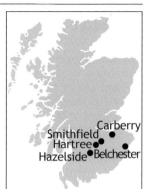

The name means 'son of Dick', from 'Dick', a diminutive of Richard, and was widely found in the Borders. Tom or Thomas Dickson was one of the followers of James Douglas, the friend and captain of Robert the Bruce, and is mentioned in Barbour's *The Brus* (also see Hazelside below).

    Maggie Dickson ('Half-Hangit Maggie') was a Musselburgh fishwife who was sentenced to death after her illegitimate child died following birth. Maggie was hanged in the Grassmarket of Edinburgh in 1728, but on the way back to Musselburgh for burial she was found to still be alive. Maggie was released from her coffin and went on to have several children and ran an alehouse and died after 1753; her husband had to remarry her as she was legally dead...

The Dickson family held lands in the Borders, in Lanarkshire and elsewhere in Scotland:
Belchester [NT 794433], near Coldstream, Borders; mansion incorporating tower house.
    Held by the Dicksons. John Dickson, whose father held Belchester, was convicted of the murder of his father in 1558. John was 'broken on ane rack' in Edinburgh and his remains put on display on the Burgh Moor.
Carberry Tower [NT 364697], near Dalkeith, East Lothian; altered tower house and mansion.
    Held by the Riggs and by the Blairs, but had passed to the Dicksons of Inveresk in 1689, then went to the Fullertons and others. The building is now used as a residential Christian conference centre (0131 665 3135; www.carberrytower.com).
Hartree Tower [NT 046360], near Biggar, Lanarkshire; mansion on site of tower house.
    Held by the Browns but sold to the Dicksons of Hartree in 1634, and they held the property at the end of the nineteenth century.
Hazelside Castle [NS 815289], near Douglas, Lanarkshire; site of castle.
    Held by the Dicksons. Thomas Dickson was one of those who captured Sanquhar Castle in 1295 when fighting with William Wallace – at least according to Blind Harry; he also helped capture Douglas Castle in 1307. He was given the lands of Hazelside as a reward. The property later passed to the Oliphants.
Kilbucho Place [NT 095352], near Biggar, Lanarkshire; altered tower house.
    Held by several families before coming to John Dickson, Lord Hartree, around 1650. It passed to the William family in the nineteenth century.
Ormiston Tower [NT 700279], near Kelso, Borders; site of tower house.
    Held by the Ormistons but passed to the Dicksons, who held Ormiston in the seventeenth century. It was burnt in 1523, and the barmkin was torched in 1544, both times by the English. The site is marked by a mound.
Ormiston Tower [NT 315378], near Innerleithen, Borders; site of tower house and mansion.
    Held by the Stewarts, and possibly the Dicksons, although this may be a confusion with the Ormiston near Innerleithen. It was later held by William Chambers.

Smithfield Castle [NT 253412], Peebles, Borders; castle replaced
by mansion.
  Held by the Dicksons and by the Hays of Smithfield. There is a
  hotel on the site (01721 730384; www.venlaw.co.uk).
Whitslade Tower [NT 112350], near Broughton, Borders; slight
remains of tower.
  Held by the Porteous family, by the Murrays of Stanhope and
  then by the Dicksons.
Winkston Tower [NT 245430], near Peebles, Borders; altered tower
house.
  Held by the Dicksons, one of whom, John Dickson of Winkston,
  was slain in 1572 while Provost of Peebles.

www.clankeith.org/fhaoilgeal/dixonheraldry.htm
No. of castles/sites: 10
Rank: 140=/764

Dingwall

The name comes from the
lands of Dingwall in Ross in
the north of Scotland.
There was a castle at
Dingwall [NH 553589], but
there is no evidence that
it was held by a family of
that name. William the
Lion held the castle in the
twelfth century, and it was
rebuilt in stone by the Earls of Ross. Little survives today. The Dingwalls are on record from the middle of
the fourteenth century.
  Dingwall Castle [NT 259739], the site now occupied
by Waverley Station in Edinburgh, consisted of a tower
house and courtyard with a round tower at each corner.
It was probably built for John Dingwall, who was provost
of Trinity College Church from 1525-32. John Knox,
perhaps not the most unbiased of critics when it came
to Catholic clergy, accused Dingwall of dallying with
the wife, and spending the money of, Alexander Furtour,
who at that time was imprisoned in the Tower of London.
Trinity College had been founded in 1462 by Mary of
Gueldres, but it was demolished and the site cleared
for the coming of the railway in 1848. Dingwall Castle
was later used as a prison, but was a ruin by 1647.

No. of castles/sites: 1 / Rank: 537=/764

Dishington

The name probably comes
from Dishington in North-
umberland in England, and
the family held lands in
Angus from the fourteenth
century and then also in
Fife. **Balglassie** [NO
538576], five miles west
and south of Brechin in
Angus, was held by the
Dishingtons in the fourteenth century, although the property later passed to the Turnbulls. Nearby **Flemington
Tower** [NO 527556], near Aberlemno, is a ruinous seventeenth-century tower house, L-plan and with two
stair-turrets. Flemington was held by the Dishingtons
at the beginning of the fifteenth century, but later
passed to the Ochterlonys.
  Ardross Castle [NO 509006], just north-east of Elie
in Fife, was a fourteenth- or fifteenth-century castle
but little now remains. The castle was built by the
Dishingtons, one of whom, Sir William Dishington, was
Sheriff of Fife in the fourteenth century; he was
responsible for the building of the fine St Monans Parish
Church [NO 523014], which is open to the public. Ardross
was sold to Sir William Scott of Elie in 1607.
No. of castles/sites: 3 / Rank: 328=/764

Doig

The name appears to come
from places associated
with St Cadoc, and to originate from 'ghille dog'
meaning 'St Cadoc's serv-
ant'. The family held lands
in Menteith. There are
many different spellings,
including Doig, Dog, Doag,
Doeg, Dogg and Doak.
Ballingrew [NS 692990], two or so miles south-west of
Doune in Stirling, was held by the Doigs in the fifteenth
and sixteenth centuries, but passed by marriage to the
MacFarlanes. **Gartincaber House** [NN 698001], which
is half a mile to the north-east, is a mansion dating
from the seventeenth century and earlier, but was altered down the years. The Doigs of Gartincaber are on
record in 1608. The property passed to the Macphersons, then later to the Murdochs. **Arnfinlay Castle** [NS
587955] is further to the west, some five miles south-
east of Aberfoyle; there was a castle, but nothing remains. Arnfinlay was also held by the Doigs, but by the
beginning of the nineteenth century had passed to the
Grahams. There was a manor place at **Knock** [NS
491662], to the south of Renfrew; in the 1590s the Doig
family were charged with repairing the manor as it was
becoming ruinous.
No. of castles/sites: 4 / Rank: 278=/764
Xref: Doag; Doak; Doeg; Dog

Don

The name may come from the Anglo-Saxon 'don' or 'dun', which means a 'strath' or 'open plain', and was once common in Aberdeenshire. Alternatively it could come from 'dun' or 'doune', a fortified place or hillock from Gaelic. The name is often spelt Dunn in old documents.

Newton Don [NT 709372], a couple of miles north of Kelso in the Borders, was held by several families before being purchased by the Don family in 1648. They renamed the property Newton Don. Alexander Don of Newton was a made a Baronet in 1667. The daughters of Sir Alexander, fifth Baronet, were drowned in 1795 while crossing the Eden Water near the house. The next Baronet bankrupted the estate by rebuilding the mansion, and the property was bought by the Balfours of Whittinghame in 1847, and they still apparently live here. The house was used in both World Wars as a hospital. The Baronetcy is now held by the Don-Wauchopes of Edmondstone, who live in South Africa.

Rutherford [NT 643303], which is three miles east of St Boswells also in the Borders, was held by the Rutherfords and by the Stewarts of Traquair, but was later held by the Dons. There may have been a tower or old house.

No. of castle/sites: 2
Rank: 396=/764
Xrefs: Daun; Dunn

Douglas

The name is territorial and comes from the lands of Douglas, which are by the Douglas Water in the south part of Lanarkshire. The name means 'black water', and the first of the family on record is William Douglas at the end of the twelfth century. A later William Douglas was governor of Berwick in 1296 when the burgh was overrun by the English and the townsfolk were slaughtered. The castle surrendered and he was taken prisoner, but he then supported William Wallace. Douglas was captured again, and died in England in 1302. Sir James Douglas, his son, was a friend and lieutenant of Robert the Bruce and helped the king win independence from the English. Douglas may have been born at Herbertshire [NS 804830], near Falkirk. When Bruce died, his heart was removed from his body and James Douglas took it on pilgrimage with other Scottish knights. They went to Granada in Spain and there fought the Moors, but Douglas was slain; although the casket containing the heart was returned to Scotland and buried at Melrose Abbey, as were many of the Douglases. Sir James, himself, was buried in St Bridget's Church in Douglas. In a few years the Douglases were to go from an unimportant family to probably the most powerful force in Scotland.

David Douglas, who was born in 1798 and came from Scone in Perthshire, was a traveller and botanist, and the Douglas Fir is named after him. He was gored and killed by a wild bull in the Sandwich Islands in 1834. O. Douglas was the pen-name for Anna Buchan, sister of the author John Buchan.

Douglas Castle [NS 843318] stood just north of the village of Douglas in the south of Lanarkshire. It was latterly a massive castellated mansion, rebuilt in 1757, but on the site of an old stronghold. The property was held by the Douglases, then minor landowners, but the castle was seized by the English. In 1307 James Douglas attacked the garrison while they were at their prayers.

Douglas Castle (M&R)

He had them slaughtered and stacked in the cellar before torching the building. The event became known as 'Douglas's Larder'. The castle was rebuilt, and William Douglas, nephew of James, was made Earl of Douglas in 1358, and the family gained wide estates from their support and friendship with Robert the Bruce. James, second Earl of Douglas, was slain at the Battle of Otterburn in 1388, although the Scots eventually won the battle; James is buried at Melrose Abbey with many of his kin. Archibald, third Earl, built Threave Castle (see below). Their good relations with the Scottish crown did not last, and Douglas Castle was sacked in 1455 after the defeat of the Black Douglases by James II who had murdered the eighth Earl (see Threave Castle below). The property was recovered, and the family were made Dukes of Douglas in 1707, although this title later became extinct. Douglas latterly passed to the Home Earls of Home, but the castle was mostly demolished in the 1930s and 1940s because of subsidence due to mining. All that survives is a corner tower and some vaulted cellars. One story about the old castle is that it was haunted by the spectre of a black dog.

Although there was a church at Douglas from early Christian times, the present fragmentary ruin of St Bride's Church [NS 835309] probably dates from 1330 and later. The church houses the stone effigy of the Good Sir James Douglas, who died in 1331. Other memorials include that of Archibald Douglas, fifth Earl of Douglas, who died in 1438; James, seventh Earl, who died in 1443, and his wife Beatrice Sinclair. The remains are in the care of Historic Scotland and are open to the public.

Tantallon Castle [NT 596851], three miles east of North Berwick in East Lothian, is one of the most impressive castles in Scotland, with a high pink wall of stone cutting off a promontory above sea cliffs. In front of the wall is a deep ditch; and there is a massive tower and gatehouse, and two ruinous corner towers. The lands were held by the Douglases from the fourteenth century. The castle was built by William Douglas, first Earl of Douglas, about 1350. William waylaid and slew his godfather, another William Douglas, the infamous 'Knight of Liddesdale'. George Douglas, the first Earl's son, became the first Earl of Angus, the first of the 'Red Douglases', and married Mary, second daughter of

Robert II. He was captured at the Battle of Homildon Hill in 1402, and died the following year. James, third Earl, used Tantallon to pursue a vendetta against the rival branch of the family, the Earls of Douglas or Black Douglases, who strongholds were at Threave, at Douglas and at Abercorn. His brother, George, later fourth Earl, and James II's army routed the Black Douglas forces at Arkinholm in 1455, and the third Earl was rewarded with the lordship of Douglas; he died in 1463.

Archibald, fifth Earl of Angus, better known as 'Bell-the-Cat', hanged James III's favourites, including the master-mason Robert Cochrane, from the bridge at Lauder in 1482. He entered into a treasonable pact with Henry VII of England, which led to James IV besieging Tantallon, although the castle held out. In 1513 Archibald died, and his two sons were killed at Flodden. Another of his sons was the renowned Gavin Douglas, who was Bishop of Dunkeld in 1515, a fine poet whose work included a translation into Scots of Vergil's *Aeneid*; he was accused of treason and died in London in 1522.

The fifth Earl's grandson, another Archibald, succeeded as the sixth Earl of Angus. In 1514 he married Margaret Tudor, widow of James IV and sister of Henry VIII. In 1528, after many dubious and possibly treasonous ventures in which Archibald was implicated, James V besieged the castle with artillery. After twenty days, the king was forced to abandon the attack. Douglas retired to England, and the castle passed into the hands of the Scottish king. When James V died in 1542, Archibald returned, and again took possession of Tantallon. By 1543, England and Scotland were at war, and Archibald offered to surrender the castle to the English. During the invasion, however, the English desecrated the Douglas tombs at Melrose Abbey, and Archibald changed sides and led the Scots to victory at the Battle of Ancrum Moor in 1545. He also led the Scots, along with the Earl of Hamilton, to defeat at the much more decisive Battle of Pinkie in 1547. Archibald died at the castle in 1556 .

Mary, Queen of Scots, visited in 1566. Archibald, eighth Earl, entered into more treasonable negotiations with the English, and had to go into exile in 1581. He died in England in 1588, as a result – it was said – of a spell cast by Agnes Simpson at North Berwick, who was later condemned as a witch and burnt. The ninth Earl died in 1591, and the tenth Earl, William, was a staunch Catholic, who was also forced into exile to die in France in 1611. His son, William, eleventh Earl also became Marquis of Douglas. Tantallon was seized by Covenanters in 1639. In 1650 moss troopers, based at the castle, did so much damage to Cromwell's lines of communication that in 1651 he sent an army to attack the castle. The bombardment lasted twelve days and the garrison surrendered. The castle was then abandoned as a fortress and residence, and in 1699 the property was sold to the Dalrymples and then to others. It is in the care of Historic Scotland and open to the public (01620 892727).

Tantallon Castle (RWB)

Threave Castle (M&R)

Threave Castle [NX 739623], a mile or so west of Castle Douglas in Galloway in the south-west of the country, is a fantastic ruin on an island in the River Dee. There is a massive keep which rises to five storeys, and the remains of a courtyard with a wall, ditch and corner towers, one of which survives. An earlier castle here was burnt by Edward Bruce in 1308. The present castle was started by Archibald the Grim – so named because his face was terrible to look upon in battle – third Earl of Douglas, and Lord of Galloway from 1369 until 1390; he also gained Bothwell by marriage. He established collegiate churches at Lincluden [NX 967779] (see below) and at Bothwell [NS 705586], near Hamilton in Lanarkshire, which he founded in 1398. Archibald died at Threave in 1400, and this branch of the family were known as the Black Douglases.

His son, Archibald, married James I's sister; he was captured by the English at the Battle of Homildon in 1402, and joined with the Percys against the king of England but was captured after the Battle of Shrewsbury the following year. He returned to Scotland in 1408, and was created Duke of Tourraine in France after winning the Battle of Baugé in 1421 against the English, although he was killed three years later at Verneuil in 1424. The fifth Earl, another Archibald, was also at Baugé, but then was at the defeat of Crevant in 1423; he was Lieutenant of Scotland during the early years of the reign of James II. He died in 1439.

It was from Threave that the young sixth Earl, William, and his brother, David, rode to Edinburgh Castle in 1440 for the Black Dinner, where they were taken out and summarily executed. They were succeeded by their great uncle, James 'the Gross', seventh Earl, who may have been complicit in their killing; he died three years later. The eighth Earl, another William, was murdered in 1452 by James II at Stirling, after being invited there as an act of reconciliation. James, ninth Earl, was rather hostile to the king after this act of murder and plotted with the English. In 1455, following the defeat of Douglas and his family the 'Black Douglases', James II besieged Threave with artillery, although not apparently with Mons Meg (a matter of dispute between 'authorities').

The king was helped by the MacLellans: Sir Patrick MacLellan of Bombie, had been murdered by beheading at Threave in 1452 by the Earl of Douglas. The garrison surrendered, but this seems to have been achieved as much by bribery as ordinance.

Threave then became a Royal fortress, and in 1513 the Maxwells were made keepers, and in 1525 the post was made hereditary. After being captured at the Battle of Solway Moss in 1542, the Maxwell keeper was obliged to turn the castle over to the English, but it was retrieved by the Earl of Arran in 1545. In 1640 the castle was besieged by an army of Covenanters for thirteen weeks until the Maxwell keeper, now Earl of Nithsdale, was forced to surrender it. The castle was slighted and partly dismantled. Threave was used as a prison for French troops during the Napoleonic wars, and was given to The National Trust of Scotland in 1948, although it is in the care of Historic Scotland and is open to the public (07711 223101 (mobile)).

Bothwell Castle [NS 688594] is one of the finest early stone castles in Scotland, and lies by the River Clyde near Uddingston in Lanarkshire. It consists of the remains of a magnificent round keep with its own moat, and a strong walled courtyard enclosing ranges of building with round towers at the corners. The castle saw action in the Wars of Independence. It was held by the English in 1298-99, but was besieged by Scots and

Bothwell Castle (LF)

eventually captured after fourteen months. In 1301 Edward I retook the castle, and it became the headquarters of Aymer de Valence, Earl of Pembroke, Edward I's Warden of Scotland. The stronghold was surrendered to the Scots in 1314, and the keep was partly demolished at this time. In 1336 the castle was taken and rebuilt by the English, and Edward III made Bothwell his headquarters; but it was slighted after recapture by the Scots around 1337. In 1362 it was acquired by Archibald the Grim, third Earl of Douglas and Lord of Galloway, and he rebuilt much of the castle. The property went to the Crichtons in 1455, but returned to the Douglases in 1492 after it was exchanged for

Hermitage Castle with Patrick Hepburn, Lord Hailes, later Earl of Bothwell. In the seventeenth century Archibald Douglas, first Earl of Forfar, built a classical mansion near the castle, which was itself demolished in 1926. The second Earl, another Archibald, was killed fighting for the Hanoverians at the Battle of Sheriffmuir in 1715. The Earldom of Forfar was joined with the Dukedom of Douglas, but both are now extinct. The ruins of Bothwell are in the care of Historic Scotland and open to the public (01698 816894). There are memorials to the Douglases in Bothwell Parish Church [NS 705586], and the church was made into a collegiate establishment (as mentioned above) by Archibald, third Earl of Douglas, in 1398; there is a laird's loft which was used by the Douglases. The church has an interesting burial ground, and is open to the public in the summer.

Aberdour Castle [NT 193854] is a partly ruinous but picturesque building in the attractive village of Aberdour in Fife. The first castle was an old keep or hall house, although this is the most ruinous part. The building was extended down the centuries into a comfortable residence, and there are fine chambers, one with a

Aberdour Castle (MC)

painted ceiling. The property was held by the Mortimers, but passed to the Douglases in 1342, and this branch of the family were made Earls of Morton about 1456. James Douglas, fourth Earl of Morton, was made Chancellor of Scotland in 1563, but was dismissed for his part in the murder of Rizzio, Mary's secretary. After Mary had fled Scotland, he was made Regent for the young James VI from 1572-78, but in 1581 he was executed, by being beheaded by the Maiden (a Scottish version of the guillotine) for his part in the murder of Darnley, the second husband of Mary, Queen of Scots. He often used the castle, but it was later abandoned for nearby Aberdour House, which dates from the eighteenth century. Part of castle was burnt out in 1715, although one range was used as a barracks, school room, masonic hall and dwelling until 1924. Aberdour House was occupied by the Douglases into the twentieth century, but was converted into flats and has houses built in its grounds. Aberdour Castle is in the care of Historic Scotland, has a fine walled garden, doocot and the beginnings of a restored terraced garden; and is open to the public (01383 860519).

Morton Castle [NX 891992], which is built on a strong site some miles north and east of Thornhill in Dumfries and Galloway, is a ruined fifteenth-century stronghold

Morton Castle (LF)

by the banks of Morton Loch. The property was held by the Adairs, but passed to the Douglases in 1459, and it was from the property that the Earls of Morton took their title. Sir James Douglas, first Earl of Morton and his wife Joanna, daughter of James I, are buried in the ruinous chancel of St Nicholas Buccleuch Parish Church [NT 330670], their tomb marked by weathered stone effigies. The church is open to the public (www.stnicholasbuccleuch.org.uk). When the third Earl died, the property went to James Douglas, then the fourth Earl, who was married to one of the third Earl's daughters. On the fourth Earl's execution, the Earldom went to the Maxwells in 1581, but the title returned to the Douglas Earl of Angus and then went to the Douglases of Lochleven. Morton Castle was abandoned about 1715, is in the care of Historic Scotland and is open to the public.

Drumlanrig Castle [NX 851992], which is a few miles north and west of Thornhill in Dumfries and Galloway, is a magnificent courtyard mansion which stands on the site of an old castle. The old castle dated from the fourteenth century, and was sacked in 1549 by the English, and then again in 1575 because the family had supported Mary, Queen of Scots. The castle was occupied by Cromwell in 1650. The present building is from the end of the seventeenth century, and was built by the

Drumlanrig Castle (AC)

architect William Wallace for William Douglas, third Earl of Queensberry, who was made Duke of Queensberry in 1684. The Duke spent only one night in his splendid new mansion, decided he did not like it, and moved back to Sanquhar Castle, where he died in 1695. His son, the second Duke, transferred his seat to Drumlanrig. Bonnie Prince Charlie stayed at Drumlanrig after his return from England, and his men ransacked the building. The property and title passed to the Scotts of Buccleuch in 1810, and Drumlanrig is still owned by the Dukes. The building was restored, and has a fine interior and collection of pictures, although one was infamously stolen from here. There are several stories of ghosts: the apparition of Lady Anne Douglas; a young woman in a flowing dress; and a monkey or other such creature in the Yellow Monkey Room. There is also a tale of a blood stain from a murder, which cannot be washed away. The castle is open to the public from late March to October (01848 331555; www.drumlanrig.com).

On an island one mile east of Kinross, **Lochleven Castle** [NO 138018] is a small ruinous castle in a lovely spot on a wooded island. It was a royal castle from 1257 and stormed by William Wallace, and was then besieged by the English in 1301. The stronghold was visited by Robert the Bruce, and held out against Edward Balliol and the English in 1335. The property later passed to the Douglases. Mary, Queen of Scots, was held prisoner here from 1567, her jailer being Margaret Erskine, wife of Robert Douglas of Lochleven (she had been the mistress of James V and their son was James Stewart, Earl of Moray, who was Mary's half-brother) until Mary escaped in 1568, during which time she signed her abdication; her ghost is said to haunt the castle. Mary was aided in her escape by George Douglas, younger brother of William Douglas of Lochleven. The castle passed to the Bruces, then to the Grahams, and to the Montgomerys. It is now in the care of Historic Scotland and is open to the public from April to October (07778 040483 (mobile)); the ferry leaves from Kinross.

Neidpath Castle [NT 236405] is a fine old keep or tower in a lovely spot above the River Tweed just west of Peebles in the Borders. The building dates from the fourteenth century, with later remodelling, and was held

Neidpath Castle 1902?

by the Frasers, by the Hays and then by the Douglases. Neidpath is reputedly haunted by the ghost of a young lass, the 'Maid of Neidpath', Jean Douglas, the youngest of the three daughters of Sir William Douglas, Earl of March. She died heartbroken after not being allowed to

marry her lover, and her apparition has reputedly been seen here, clad in a brown dress. The property passed to the Earls of Wemyss and March, and the castle is sometimes open to the public (01721 720333).

The Douglases owned many castles and properties:

Abercorn Castle [NT 083794], near South Queensferry, West Lothian; slight remains of castle.

The Douglas Earls of Douglas held the property from 1400, and James the Gross, sixth Earl, died here in 1443. The castle was destroyed, after a month-long siege, by James II in 1455, during his campaign against the Black Douglases, and many of the garrison were hanged. The lands passed to the Setons and then to the Hamiltons.

Auchen Castle [NT 063035], near Moffat, Dumfries and Galloway; slight remains of castle.

Held by the Douglases of Morton, before passing to the Maitlands in the fifteenth century.

Auchenfranco Castle [NX 893724], near Dumfries; site of castle.

Held by the Douglases but passed to the Sinclairs after 1455.

Baads Castle [NT 006614], near West Calder, West Lothian; site of castle.

Held by the Douglases in the sixteenth century and burned in 1736.

Balvenie Castle [NJ 326409], near Dufftown, Moray; fine ruinous courtyard castle.

Held by the Comyns, but passed to the Douglases, who held it until 1455, when it went to the Stewart Earl of Morays then to others. Open to the public April to September (01340 820121).

Balvie Castle [NS 535752], near Milngavie, Glasgow; site of castle.

Held by several families before being bought by the Douglases of Mains after 1819. They built a mansion but this was demolished in the twentieth century.

Barjarg Tower [NX 876901], near Thornhill, Dumfriesshire; L-plan tower house.

The lands were held by the Douglases of Morton in the sixteenth century, but the tower was built after the property had gone to the Griersons.

Bedrule Castle [NT 598180], near Denholm, Borders; slight remains of castle.

Held by the Comyns, but passed to the Douglases in the fourteenth century, then to the Turnbulls.

Belstane Castle [NS 850515], near Carluke, Lanarkshire; site of tower house.

Held by the Livingstones, by the Lindsays, by the Maxwells and by the Douglases.

Billie Castle [NT 851596], near Chirnside, Borders; very ruinous castle.

Held by the Earls of Dunbar, but passed to the Douglas Earls of Angus from 1435. Archibald Douglas, Earl of Angus, sheltered here in 1528 while James V was unsuccessfully besieging Tantallon Castle. The castle went to the Rentons.

Blackhouse Tower [NT 281273], near Cappercleuch, Borders; very ruined tower house.

Held by the Douglases from the thirteenth century, and an older castle may have been used by Sir James Douglas, friend and captain of Robert the Bruce. The tower is associated with the tragedy related in the old ballad 'The Dowie Dens of Yarrow'. Seven large stones near the tower are said to mark the spot where seven brothers of the lady in the ballad, Margaret, were slain by her lover, although he too was killed. The property passed to the Pringles in 1509.

Blacklaw Tower [NT 052067], near Moffat, Dumfries and Galloway; slight remains of tower.

Latterly held by the Douglases of Fingland, one of whom wrote 'Annie Laurie', concerning one of the Lauries of Maxwelton, around 1700

Blackmyre [NX 863973], near Thornhill, Dumfries and Galloway; site of castle.

Held by the Milligans in the seventeenth century but passed to the Douglases of Drumlanrig.

Blyth [NT 132458], near West Linton, Borders; site of castle.
Held by the Blyth family and then by the Douglases of Morton, before passing to the Lauders in the fifteenth century.

Buittle Castle [NX 819616], near Dalbeattie, Dumfries and Galloway; slight remains of castle.
Held by the Balliols, but the lands passed to the Douglases after the Wars of Independence, then to the Maxwells and to the Gordons. **Buittle Place** [NX 817616], a sixteenth-century tower house, replaced the old castle.

Bunkle Castle [NT 805596], near Preston, Borders; slight remains of castle.
Held by the Bonkyl family and the Stewarts, before passing the Douglas Earls of Angus, then went to the Homes.

Calder House [NT 073673], near Livingston, West Lothian; L-plan tower house.
Held by the Douglases but passed to the Sandilands in the fourteenth century.

Castlehill Tower [NT 214354], near Peebles, Borders; ruined tower house.
Held by several families including by William Douglas, Earl of March, from 1703 until 1729.

Castlemilk [NS 608594], near Rutherglen, Glasgow; remains of castle and mansion.
Held by the Comyns, then by the Douglases until 1455 when it went to the Hamiltons and then to the Stewarts.

Cathkin House [NS 627588], near Rutherglen, Glasgow; castle replaced by mansion.
Held by the Douglases, but passed to the Hamiltons and then to other families.

Cavens Castle [NX 958572], near New Abbey, Dumfries and Galloway; site of castle.
Held by the Douglases of Morton, but passed in 1581 to the Maxwells, then to others. Nearby is Cavens, a later mansion, which is now used as a hotel (01387 880234; www.cavens.com).

Cavers House [NT 540154], near Hawick, Borders; ruined tower house and mansion.
Held by the Balliols, but passed to the Douglases who held it from 1350 until 1878. The old part was built by Sir Archibald Douglas, younger son of the Earl of Douglas, who died at the Battle of Otterburn in 1388. The castle was burnt by Lord Dacre in 1523, by the English with the help of Scott of Branxholme in 1542, and then again by the Earl of Hertford in 1545. It was rebuilt, and in 1887 extended and remodelled after it had passed by marriage to the Palmers. It was unroofed and stripped in the 1960s.

Chesterhouse Tower [NT 772203], near Morebattle, Borders; slight remains of tower house.
Held by the Douglases.

Claypotts Castle [NO 452319], near Dundee; fine Z-plan tower house.
Held by the Strachans and by the Grahams as well as by the Douglas Earl of Angus after 1694, then by the Homes. In the care of Historic Scotland and open to the public (01786 431324).

Clifton Hall [NT 109710], near Broxburn; mansion on site of castle.
Held by the Grahams and by the Macalzeans, but passed to the Douglases in the seventeenth century. Archibald Douglas rode with General Tam Dalziel of The Binns in the Scots Greys. Later sold to the Gibsons of Pentland, then to the Bells. The mansion dates from 1850 and now houses a private school.

Cluny Crichton Castle [NO 686997], near Banchory, Aberdeenshire; ruined tower house.
Held by the Crichtons of Cluny but passed to the Douglases of Tilquhillie.

Cockburnspath House [NT 775710], Cockburnspath; tower house.
Held by the Douglases, although **Cockburnspath Castle** [NT 785699] was owned by several families, including by the Homes and by the Sinclairs.

Cornal Tower [NT 112044], near Moffat; site of tower house.
Held by the Douglas Dukes of Queensberry after 1633.

Coshogle Castle [NS 864052], near Sanquhar, Dumfries and Galloway; site of castle.
Held by the Douglases of Drumlanrig.

Craig Douglas Castle [NT 291249], near Cappercleuch, Borders; site of castle.
Held by the Black Douglases. The castle was seized by the English in the Wars of Independence, and was retaken by the Scots in 1307. It was attacked without warning and destroyed by James II in 1450, when the Earl of Douglas was on a pilgrimage to Rome. With the return of the Earl, his lands were restored, but after his murder in 1452, the Black Douglases rebelled, but were defeated at the Battle of Arkinholm three years later and had their lands forfeited. This is one of the several castles associated with 'The Douglas Tragedy', an old and bloody ballad.

Craignethan Castle [NS 816464], near Lanark; fabulous ruinous castle.
Originally held by the Black Douglases, but passed to the Hamiltons in 1455 and it was Sir James Hamilton of Finnart who built the castle. In the care of Historic Scotland and open to the public from April to September (01555 860364).

Cramond Tower [NT 191770], Edinburgh; restored tower house.
Held by the Bishops of Dunkeld, but passed to the Douglases, and then in 1622 to the Inglis family. The tower was replaced by Cramond House in 1680 and became ruinous but the tower was restored and reoccupied in 1983.

Cranshaws Castle [NT 681619], near Cranshaws, Borders; tower house.
Held by the Swintons until 1702 when it passed to the Douglases. The tower is said to have had a brownie, which did

Cranshaws Castle 1908?

all manners of chores but left after an ungrateful servant complained about the quality of its work.

Crawford Castle [NS 954213], near Crawford, Lanarkshire; slight remains of castle.
Held by several families including by the Lindsays, by the Carmichaels and by the Douglas Earls of Angus.

Crawfordjohn Castle [NS 879239], near Abington, Lanarkshire; site of castle.
Held by the Douglases from 1366 until 1455, when it passed to the Hamiltons and then to the Crawfords.

Cruggleton Castle [NX 484428], near Garlieston, Dumfries and Galloway; slight remains of castle.
Held by the Comyns, then by the Douglases until 1455, then by other families.

Dalkeith House [NT 333679], Dalkeith, Midlothian; mansion incorporating castle.
Held by the Douglases from 1350. Dalkeith was sacked in 1452 by the brother of the murdered sixth Earl of Douglas, but the

castle held out; and in 1458 the family were made Earls of Morton. Sir James Douglas, first Earl of Morton, and his wife, Joanna, daughter of James I, are buried in the ruinous chancel of St Nicholas Buccleuch Parish Church [NT 330670] in Dalkeith, their tomb marked by stone effigies. The church is open to the public (www.stnicholasbuccleuch.org.uk). James IV first met Margaret Tudor, his wife-to-be, at Dalkeith Palace in 1503. The castle was taken by the English after the Battle of Pinkie in 1547, and many Scots who had fled the fighting were captured. The fourth Earl of Morton – Chancellor for Mary, Queen of Scots, and later Regent for the young James VI – remodelled the castle and built a magnificent palace in 1575. James VI visited in 1581, after Morton had been executed. Charles I was entertained here in 1633, and the property was sold to the Scotts of Buccleuch in 1642, and is still owned by their descendants, the Dukes of Buccleuch and Queensberry. The castle is said to be haunted by one or more ghosts; and stands in a country park (0131 654 1666/0131 663 5684; www.dalkeithcountrypark.com).

Dalmahoy [NT 145690], near Currie, Midlothian; castle replaced by fine mansion.
Held by the Dalmahoys and by the Dalrymples, but passed to the Douglases of Morton about 1750. The building is reputedly haunted by a 'White Lady', the ghost of Lady Mary Douglas, a daughter of the first Earl of Morton to own the property and the wife of George Watson, founder of George Watson's College. Watson died in 1723. The ghost is said to be seen in both corridors and the bedrooms of the old part of the building, and to be a friendly ghost. The building is now used as a hotel (0131 333 1845; www.marriott.com/edigs).

Dalveen Castle [NS 884069], near Carron Bridge, Dumfries and Galloway; site of castle.
Held by the Douglases and there is a panel with the date 1622.

Darnaway Castle [NH 994550], near Forres, Moray; mansion incorporating castle.
Held by the Douglas Earls of Moray until 1455, when it passed to the Murrays and then to the Stewart Earls of Moray. Darnaway is still apparently occupied by their descendants.

Denholm [NT 568183], near Hawick, Borders; site of castle.
Held by the Denholm family and then by the Douglases. The tower was probably burnt by the Earl of Hertford in 1545.

Drochil Castle [NT 162434], near Peebles, Borders; fine overgrown ruinous castle.
Held by the Douglases and built by James Douglas, fourth Earl

Drochil Castle (RWB)

of Morton. Drochil was abandoned about 1630.

Drumlanrig's Tower [NT 502144], Hawick, Borders; restored and altered tower house.
Held by the Douglases of Drumlanrig, and was the only building untouched when the burgh was torched by the English in 1570.

The property passed to the Scotts, and the tower now houses an exhibition on local history (01450 373457; www.scotborders. gov.uk/outabout/museums).

Drumsargad Castle [NS 667597], near Hamilton, Lanarkshire; slight remains of castle.
Held by the Douglases from 1360 until 1455 when the property went to the Hamiltons.

Dundarg Castle [NJ 895649], near Fraserburgh, Aberdeenshire; slight remains of castle.
Held by the Comyns, but passed to the Black Douglases, who held the property until 1455. It then passed to the Borthwicks, then to the Cheynes.

Dunglass Castle [NT 766718], near Cockburnspath, Borders; site of castle.
Held by the Homes, but passed to the Douglases in 1516. The castle was sacked by the English in 1532 and again in 1547. James VI stayed here in 1603, but the castle was blown up in 1640. Apparently an English servant was so angered by insults directed against his countrymen that he ignited the castle's store of gunpowder, killing himself, the Earl of Haddington, and many of the Covenanting garrison. Dunglass House, successor of the castle, was demolished in 1947. Dunglass Collegiate Church, near the site of the castle, was founded by Alexander Home in 1423, and is open to the public.

Dunsyre Castle [NT 073482], near Carnwath, Lanarkshire; site of castle,
Held by the Douglases in 1368, then from 1492 by the Hepburns, then by the Lockharts.

Dupplin Castle [NO 056195], near Perth; mansion on site of castle.
Held by the Douglases of Morton from 1623 until the property passed to the Hay Earls of Kinnoul before 1688.

Edmonston Castle [NT 070422], near Biggar, Lanarkshire; ruined castle.
Held by the Edmonstones, but passed to the Douglases in 1322, who held it until sold in 1650 to the Baillies of Walston.

Enoch Castle [NS 879009], near Thornhill, Dumfries and Galloway; site of castle.
Held by the Menzies family, but sold to the Douglas Duke of Queensberry in 1703, then passed by marriage to the Scott Dukes of Buccleuch in 1810.

Evelaw Tower [NT 661526], near Westruther, Borders; ruined tower house.
Held by the Douglases from 1576, but passed by marriage to the Sinclairs of Longformacus.

Fala Luggie Tower [NT 425590], near Gorebridge, Midlothian; very ruinous tower house.
Held by the Douglases but passed to the Murrays in the fourteenth century.

Farme Castle [NS 620624], near Rutherglen, Glasgow; site of castle.
Held by the Stewarts and then by the Douglases until 1482 when it went to the Crawfords and then to others.

Fast Castle [NT 862710], near Coldingham, Borders; ruinous castle on cliffs.
Held by several families and then by the Douglases in 1602, but passed to the Homes and then to others.

Gelston Castle [NX 773577], near Castle Douglas, Dumfries and Galloway; ruined mansion.
Built for Sir William Douglas, who had made a fortune in trading with the Americas. His impressive mausoleum lies to the north of the parish church at Kelton.

Glenbervie House [NO 769805], near Stonehaven, Kincardineshire; mansion incorporating castle.
Held by the Auchinlecks in 1468, then by the Douglases but was sold to the Burnetts of Leys in 1675. The Douglases remodelled the chancel of the old parish church at Glenbervie [NO 767804] as a burial aisle, where there is a monument of 1680. The gardens of the house are occasionally open to the public (www.gardensofscotland.org).

Glendevon Castle [NN 976055], near Dollar, Clackmannan; altered Z-plan tower house.
Held by the Douglases, but passed to the Crawfords and then to the Rutherfords. Used as a farmhouse.

Glenshinnoch [NX 811532], near Dalbeattie, Dumfries and Galloway; site of castle.

Held by the Cairns family and then by the Maxwells, but was a property of the Douglases from 1785 until the twentieth century. Orchardton House replaced the old castle in the middle of the eighteenth century. This newer house was then incorporated into a large baronial mansion of 1881.

Gourock Castle [NS 244771], Gourock, Renfrewshire; site of castle.

Held by the Douglases until 1455 when the property passed to the Stewarts of Castlemilk.

Grange [NT 270886], near Kinghorn, Fife; mansion on site of castle.

Long associated with the Kirkcaldy family, but passed to the Douglases and to the Stewarts, before passing back to the Kirkcaldys.

Grangemuir [NO 539040], near Pittenweem, Fife; mansion in site of castle.

Held by the Scotts, but passed to the Bruces and then to the Douglases.

Grey Peel [NT 639179], near Jedburgh, Borders; site of tower house.

Held by the Douglases.

Hallbar Tower [NS 839471], near Carluke, Lanarkshire; restored tower house.

Held by the Douglases but passed to the Stewarts of Gogar in 1581, although Hallbar later returned to the Douglases. Holiday accommodation is available (0845 090 0194; www.vivat. org.uk).

Hatton House [NT 128687], near Balerno, Edinburgh; site of castle and mansion.

Held by several families before coming to the Douglases of Morton in 1870.

Hawthornden Castle [NT 287637], near Loanhead, Midlothian; attractive castle.

Held by the Abernethys but passed by marriage to the Douglases who sold it to the Drummonds about 1540. Now used as a retreat for writers.

Hermitage Castle [NY 494960], near Newcastleton, Borders; forbidding and impressive ruin.

Held by the Dacres, by the Soulis family, and then by the Grahams and then passed by marriage to the Douglases in the fourteenth century. William Douglas, 'The Knight of Liddesdale', was prominent in resisting Edward Balliol in 1330s. In a dispute over who had been given the Sheriffdom of Teviotdale, Douglas seized Sir Alexander Ramsay of Dalhousie while at his devotions in St Mary's Church in Hawick, and imprisoned him in a dungeon at the castle and starved him to death. Ramsay's spirit is said to be one of the ghosts that haunt the old ruin. In 1353 Douglas was murdered (he was buried at Melrose Abbey) by his godson, another William Douglas, after he had tried to block his claim to the lordship of Douglas. In 1492 Archibald, fifth Earl of Angus, exchanged (as in he was told to by James IV) Hermitage for Bothwell with Patrick Hepburn, Earl of Bothwell. The fine and foreboding ruin is in the care of Historic Scotland and is open to the public from April to September (01387 376222).

House of Mergie [NO 796887], near Stonehaven, Kincardineshire; tall T-plan tower house.

Held by the Douglases, but passed to Paul Symmer, an officer in Cromwell's army, and then to the Garrioch family and to the Duffs.

Inchmarlo [NO 670968], near Banchory, Aberdeenshire; mansion on site of castle,

Held by the Douglases of Tilquhillie before passing to the Davidsons in the nineteenth century. Now a nursing home.

Inveravon Castle [NS 953798], near Linlithgow, West Lothian; slight remains of castle.

Held by the Black Douglases but was besieged and slighted by James II in 1455.

Kelhead [NY 140687], near Annan, Dumfries and Galloway; castle replaced by mansion.

Held by the Douglases. The mansion was built for Charles Douglas, who became the Marquis of Queensberry, at a cost of £40,000, a princely sum in 1812.

Kemnay House [NJ 733154], near Inverurie, Aberdeenshire; L-plan tower house.

Held by the Douglases of Glenbervie, but passed to the Crombies in the seventeenth century and then to the Burnetts of Leys.

Kilbucho Place [NT 095352], near Biggar, Lanarkshire; L-plan tower house.

Held by Sir William Douglas, the Knight of Liddesdale, in the fourteenth century, but sold to the Stewarts of Traquair in 1631.

Killiechassie [NN 864503], near Aberfeldy, Perthshire; castle replaced by mansion.

Held by the Stewarts and by the Gordons but was bought by the Douglases in 1863.

Killiewarren [NX 796935], near Thornhill, Dumfries and Galloway; tower house.

Held by the Douglases.

Kilspindie Castle [NT 462801], near Aberlady, East Lothian; very slight remains of castle.

Held by the Spences but passed to the Douglases and then to the Hays.

Kinnordy [NO 367547], near Kirriemuir, Angus; site of castle.

Held by the Douglas Earls of Angus.

Kinross House [NO 126020], Kinross; fantastic early mansion.

The lands were held by the Douglases in the sixteenth century and they had a castle or residence. The present house was built by Sir William Bruce in the seventeenth century, but the property later passed to the Grahams. The gardens are open from April until September (www.kinrosshouse.com).

Kirkcudbright Castle [NX 677508], Kirkcudbright, Dumfries and Galloway; only ditches survive from castle.

Held by the Balliols, then by the Douglases until 1455 and the site was given to the burgh of Kirkcudbright in 1509.

Kirkhope or **Daer Tower** [NS 968065], near Elvanfoot, Lanarkshire; site of tower house.

Held by the Douglas Earl of Selkirk in 1646 but passed to the Duke of Hamilton in 1885.

Kirkhouse [NX 981592], near New Abbey, Dumfries and Galloway; site of castle or old house.

Held by the Douglases, and then by the Maxwells from 1581.

Knockdavie Castle [NT 213883], near Burntisland, Fife; slight remains of tower house.

Held by the Douglases in the seventeenth century, one of whom is said to have been a persecutor of Covenanters.

Langholm [NY 361849] and [NY 365855], Langholm, Dumfries and Galloway; remains of two towers.

Latterly held by the Douglases of Drumlanrig after being sold by the Maxwells. The Battle of Arkinholm was fought nearby, where the Black Douglases were defeated by the forces of James II in 1455.

Lanton Tower [NT 618215], near Jedburgh, Borders; altered restored tower house.

Held by the Cranstouns, but had passed to Douglas of Cavers by 1687 and later to the Reids of Ellon, Baronets.

Lincluden Collegiate Church [NX 967779], near Dumfries; ruins of a church and domestic buildings.

A nunnery was converted to a collegiate establishment in 1389 by Archibald the Grim, third Earl of Douglas, as he considered the nunnery had fallen into a state of disrepute, disgrace and disrepair. There is a fine stone effigy in a recessed tomb of Margaret, daughter of Robert III and wife of Archibald, fourth Earl of Douglas. The lands were given to the Stewarts after the Reformation, but passed to the Douglases of Drumlanrig, then to others, including to the Youngs of Lincluden. The ruins are in the care of Historic Scotland and are open to the public.

Lochindorb Castle [NH 974364], near Grantown-on-Spey, Speyside; ruined castle on island.

Held by the Stewarts, but passed to the Douglas Earls of Moray until 1455. It was then dismantled and not reused.

Longniddry House [NT 444762], Longniddry, East Lothian; site of castle and mansion.

Held by the Douglases of Longniddry, who were active in the Reformation. Hugh Douglas of Longniddry held Hailes Castle with fifty men for the English in 1548.

Lugton [NT 327677], near Dalkeith, Midlothian; site of castle.

Held by the Douglases, but passed to the Scott Dukes of Buccleuch.

MacLellan's Castle [NX 683511], Kirkcudbright, Dumfries and Galloway; fine ruinous tower house.

Held by the MacLellans and by the Maxwells of Orchardton but sold to the Douglas Earl of Selkirk in 1782. In the care of Historic Scotland and open to the public from April to September (01557 331856).

Mains Castle [NS 536743], near Milngavie, Dunbartonshire; site of castle and mansion.

Held by the Douglases of Dalkeith from 1373 until the twentieth century. In 1571 Matthew Douglas of Mains helped Crawford of Jordanhill in his 'Daring Raid' on Dumbarton Castle. Malcolm Douglas (Matthew's son), along with his father-in-law John Cunningham of Drumquhassle, were accused of taking part in the Raid of Ruthven, when the young James VI was taken prisoner and held in Ruthven Castle (Huntingtower). They were beheaded for treason in 1585. Malcolm's second son, Robert, was Page of Honour to Henry Stewart, Prince of Wales and, upon Henry's early death, was appointed Gentleman of the Bedchamber to James VI. The family acquired Balvie from the Logans, and moved there, renaming that property Mains.

Mains Castle [NO 410330], near Dundee; restored courtyard castle.

Held by the Douglas Earls of Angus from the fourteenth century until 1530 when it passed to the Grahams and then later to the Erskines and to the Cairds. The grounds are a public park.

Melrose Abbey [NT 550344], Melrose, Borders; ruins of abbey church and commendator's house.

Many of the Douglases were buried in the church, along with the heart of Robert the Bruce. After the Reformation, the lands were held by the Douglases, and the abbot's house was converted to a fortified dwelling in 1590. The ruins of the abbey are in the care of Historic Scotland and open to the public (01896 822562).

Mordington House [NT 951558], near Berwick-upon-Tweed, Borders; site of castle and mansion.

Held by the Douglases of Dalkeith, later Earls of Morton, from the fourteenth century until 1581, then by the Earls of Angus until 1741, then by the Hays and by the Rentons. The castle was replaced by a classical mansion in the eighteenth century but this was demolished in 1973.

Mouswald Tower [NY 061739], near Annan, Dumfries and Galloway; slight remains of tower house.

Held by the Carruthers family, but passed by marriage to the Douglases of Drumlanrig, although (if the ghost of Marion Carruthers of Mouswald at Comlongon is anything to go by) with a fair amount of foul play.

Newark Castle [NT 421294], near Selkirk, Borders; impressive ruined castle.

Held by the Douglases from 1423 until 1455, and replaced an 'auld wark' [NT 425286], east of the present castle and nothing of which remains. In the grounds of Bowhill and the ruin can be seen from the grounds (01750 22204; www.boughton house.org.uk).

Newton Don [NT 709372], near Kelso, Borders; castle replaced by mansion.

Held by the Douglases in the fourteenth century, but passed to the Don family in 1648 and then to the Balfours of Whittinghame in 1847.

Newton [NS 663613], near Cambuslang, Lanarkshire; site of castle and mansion.

Held by the Douglases before going to the Hamiltons of Silvertonhill in the fifteenth century and then later to the Montgomerys.

Old Gala House [NT 492357], Galashiels, Borders; mansion incorporating tower.

Held by the Douglases at one time, before passing to the Pringles and to the Scotts. The house has displays on the occupants and Galashiels and is open to the public from April to September (01896 752611).

Orchardton Tower [NX 817551], near Dalbeattie, Dumfries and Galloway; unique round tower house.

Held by the Cairns and then by the Maxwells, and then by the Douglases from 1785 until the twentieth century, and they lived at Ordchardton House [NX 811532], the site previously known as Glenshinnoch.

Ormond Castle [NH 696536], near Fortrose, Ross and Cromarty; slight remains of castle.

Held by the Murrays, but passed to the Douglases, who were briefly made Earls of Ormonde from 1445 until their forfeiture ten years later when Hugh Douglas, Earl of Ormond, was executed. The castle was retained by the Crown, and may have been dismantled in 1650.

Parisholm [NS 762280], near Muirkirk, Lanarkshire; site of tower house.

Held by the Douglases in the eighteenth century.

Parkhall [NS 863330], near Douglas, Lanarkshire; site of castle.

Held by the Douglases of Torthorwald (or Thorril).

Perceton House [NS 354406], near Irvine, Ayrshire; castle replaced by mansion.

Held by the Morvilles and by the Stewarts, and then by Douglases for a brief time, before passing to the Barclays in 1443, then later went to the Macreadies and then to the Mures.

Pittendreich [NJ 195613], near Elgin, Moray; site of castle.

Held by the Douglases from the middle of the fourteenth to the middle of the seventeenth century. James Douglas, fourth Earl of Morton, was styled 'of Pittendreich'.

Place of Paisley [NS 485639], Paisley, Renfrewshire; fortified house.

Held by the Hamiltons and then by the Douglas Earls of Angus for some years before it was sold to the Cochranes in 1653. Now the manse for the restored abbey church.

Poneil [NS 840343], near Douglas, Lanarkshire; site of tower house.

May have been held by the Douglases, but also by the Folkerton family until about 1495 and then by the Weirs.

Pumpherston Castle [NT 075686], near Livingston, West Lothian; site of castle.

Held by the Douglases in the sixteenth and seventeenth centuries. Sir Joseph Douglas of Pumpherston was drowned when the frigate *Gloucester* sank off Yarmouth: the Duke of York, later James VII, was on the same ship, but he was rescued.

Red Castle [NH 584495], near Muir of Ord, Ross and Cromarty; altered and extended tower house.

Held by several families including by the Douglas Earl of Ormond, who was executed in 1455.

Rough Hill [NS 607553], near East Kilbride, Lanarkshire; site of castle on motte.

Held by the Comyns, by the Douglases and then by the Hamiltons from 1455.

Sandilands [NS 892385], near Lanark; possible site of castle.

Held by the Douglases before going to the Sandilands family in about 1334.

Sanquhar Castle [NS 786092], near Sanquhar, Dumfries and Galloway; crumbling ruin of a large castle.

Sold by the Crichtons to Sir William Douglas of Drumlanrig in 1639, who was later made Duke of Queensberry. The Duke had Drumlanrig Castle built, but only spent one night in his new mansion, decided he did not like it, and moved back to Sanquhar. However, the family moved to Drumlanrig after his death, and Sanquhar was abandoned to become ruinous.

Snar Castle [NS 863200], near Crawfordjohn, Lanarkshire; slight remains of tower house.

Held by the Douglases of Snar, who made their living from mining lead and gold.

Spott House [NT 679752], near Dunbar, East Lothian; mansion incorporating castle.

Held by several families, including by the Homes and by the Douglases.

Sprouston [NT 755352], near Kelso, Borders; site of tower house.

Held by the Lempitlaw family and by the Francis family, and then was a property of the Douglases in the fifteenth century, but had passed to the Hamiltons in the sixteenth century.

Stoneypath Tower [NT 596713], near East Linton, East Lothian; L-plan tower house.

Held by the Lyles and then by the Hamiltons of Innerwick before passing to the Douglases of Whittinghame in 1616, then went to the Setons.

Strathaven Castle [NS 703445], Strathaven, Lanarkshire; ruinous castle.

Held by the Bairds and by the Sinclairs before coming to the Douglases. It was surrendered to James II in 1455 and probably sacked, before passing to the Stewart Lord Avondale in 1457, and then to the Hamiltons.

Strathendry Castle [NO 226020], near Cardenden, Fife; large castle with strong tower.

Held by the Strathendry family and by the Forresters before passing by marriage to the Douglases of Kirkness in 1700 before going to the Clephanes of Carslogie in 1882. The building had been altered and extended in 1824, and in 1845.

Tayport Castle [NO 457291], Tayport, Fife; site of strong castle.

Held by the Melvilles and by the Duries, then by the Douglases of Glenbervie.

The Peel, Busby [NS 594561], near East Kilbride, Lanarkshire; altered L-plan tower house.

Held by the Douglases but went to the Hamiltons in 1455, then passed to other families.

Thorril Castle [NS 864309], near Douglas, Lanarkshire; scant remains of tower house.

Probably held by the Douglases of Torthorwald.

Tibbers Castle [NX 863982], near Thornhill, Borders; slight remains of castle.

Held by the Dunbars and by the Maitlands before passing to the Douglases of Drumlanrig in 1592. In the grounds of Drumlanrig Castle.

Tilquhillie Castle [NO 722941], near Banchory, Aberdeenshire; impressive Z-plan tower house.

Held by the Ogstouns, then by the Douglases of Tilquhillie,

Tilquhillie Castle 1905?

who built the castle. The family supported the Gordon Earl of Huntly against Mary, Queen of Scots, at the Battle of Corrichie, but they were later pardoned. The lands passed to the Crichtons of Cluny in 1665. The castle is still occupied.

Timpendean Tower [NT 636226], near Jedburgh, Borders; ruinous tower house.

Held by the Douglases.

Tinwald Place [NY 006800], near Dumfries; site of castle.

Held by the Maxwells, by the Erskines, then by the Douglas Marquis of Queensberry, then in 1884 by the Jardines. The castle was replaced by Tinwald House, dating from 1740.

Todholes Castle [NT 038461], near Carnwath, Lanarkshire; site of tower house.

Held by the Douglases in 1572, but had passed to the Baillies by 1649.

Torthorwald Castle [NY 033783], near Dumfries; ruinous castle with motte and ditch.

Held by several families, then by the Douglases of Parkhead in 1609, then later by the Douglases of Drumlanrig. The castle was occupied until about 1715.

Trabboch Castle [NS 458222], near Mauchline, Ayrshire; slight remains of castle.

Held by the Boyds but passed to the Douglases around 1450, then to the Boswells.

Traquair House [NT 330354], near Innerleithen, Borders; fine castle and mansion.

Held by the Douglases, but had passed to the Stewart Earls of Buchan in 1478. Open to the public from Easter to October (01896 830323; www.traquair.co.uk).

Tulliallan Castle [NS 927888], near Kincardine, Fife; fine ruinous hall-house.

Held by the Douglases in the fourteenth century, but passed to the Edmonstones then to the Blackadders.

Wedderburn Castle [NO 435352], near Dundee; site of castle.

Held by the Douglas Earls of Angus, but passed to the Ogilvies and then to the Wedderburns.

Wedderburn Castle [NT 809529], near Duns, Borders; mansion incorporating tower house.

Held by the Wedderburns, then by the Earls of Dunbar, then on their forfeiture by the Douglases and then by the Homes. The castle can be hired for exclusive use (01361 882190; www.wedderburn-castle.co.uk).

Westhall Tower [NT 048473], near Carnwath, Lanarkshire; slight remains of tower house.

Held by the Grahams and by the Hepburns, before passing to the Douglases and then to the Lockharts.

Whittinghame Castle [NT 602733], near East Linton, East Lothian; castle and mansion.

Held by the Douglases in the fourteenth century. James Douglas, Regent Morton, held the castle during the reign of Mary, Queen of Scots. It is supposed to be where the plot to murder Lord Darnley, husband of Mary, was hatched with Morton, Maitland of Lethington and James Hepburn, fourth Earl of Bothwell, later Mary's third husband, although it may have been at Craigmillar Castle. The lands passed to the Seton and then to the Hays, before coming to the Balfours, who still apparently own the property.

Wreaths Tower [NX 953565], near New Abbey, Dumfries and Galloway; slight remains of castle.

Held by the Douglases until 1581, but passed to the Maxwells, then possibly back to the Douglases.

www.clandouglassociety.org

No. of castles/sites: 147

Rank: 3/764

Dow

The name probably comes from 'dubh', the Gaelic for the colour black, but pronounced 'Doo'; Duff comes from the same root. Alternatively, it may have originated from a diminutive for David or from the anglicisation of MacCalman.

Arnhall Castle [NS 764986], four miles north and west of Stirling, is a ruinous L-plan tower house of three storeys and a courtyard. It dates from the seventeenth century. The lands were held by the Dow family, but passed by marriage to the Stirlings of Keir.

No. of castles/sites: 1
Rank: 537=/764
Xrefs: Dove; Dowe

Dowall

The name is from the Gaelic 'dubh gall', meaning 'dark or black stranger', a term to mean a Danish Vikings (traditionally the Norwegian were blonde, fair or red-haired). The name is found in the form MacDougall, who held many properties in Argyll around the Firth of Lorn. The name is also found in the MacDowalls, meaning 'son of Dowall or Dougall'.

Skibo Castle [NH 735891], which is four miles west of Dornoch in the far north of Scotland, is now a magnificent castellated mansion, dating from the nineteenth century, but it is built on the site of an old stronghold. The property was held by the Mackays and by the Grays, before passing to the Dowalls, who held it for around ten years from 1776. It then passed to the Dempsters and then to the famous industrialist and philanthropist Andrew Carnegie, who had the present mansion built. Skibo Castle is now an exclusive country club (www.carnegieclubs.com).

No. of castles/sites: 1
Rank: 537=/764
Xrefs: Dougall; Dougald

Dowane

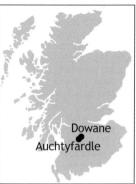

The name comes from the lands of Dowan or Dowane, which are a mile or so south-west of Lanark, and is on record from the fourteenth century.

Dowane [NS 857422] was held by Lesmahagow Priory, but was granted to the Dowanes around 1200. There may have been a castle, and the property later passed to the Weirs.

Just north-east of Lesmahagow is **Auchtyfardle** [NS 826409], which was held by the Dowanes from 1326. It too had been a property of the priory, and was exchanged for half of Dowane. There was a stronghold, but the lands again passed to the Weirs, and then to the Kennedys.

No. of castles/sites: 2
Rank: 396=/764

Dreghorn

The name is territorial and comes from the place and village of Dreghorn, east of Irvine in Ayrshire, although there was a **Dreghorn Castle** [NT 225684] to the south of Edinburgh, although it has been demolished and the site is occupied by an army barracks. Neither of these appear to have been held by this family.

Dreghorn of Rough Hill is mentioned in 1787, and there is a motte at **Rough Hill** [NS 607553], one mile north-west of East Kilbride to the south of Glasgow in western Scotland. There was a large tower on the motte, a vault from which was found in 1807.

No. of castles/sites: 1
Rank: 537=/764

Drummond

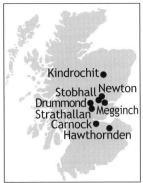

The name is territorial and comes from the lands and barony of Drummond, which covered the same territory as the parish of Drymen in Stirlingshire in central Scotland. The family may have been Hungarian in descent, and have come to Scotland in the retinue of Queen Margaret, wife of Malcolm Canmore, in the eleventh century. The name 'Drummond' probably comes from Gaelic, meaning 'ridge' or 'high ground'. The name comes on record in the thirteenth century, when the family were closely associated with the Earls of Lennox. The Drummonds fought in the Wars of Independence, and William Drummond probably died in English captivity in 1302.

Stobhall [NO 132344] is some seven miles north of Perth and is a sixteenth-century castle ranged around a courtyard, and is in a particularly picturesque spot.

Stobhall (M&R)

There is an L-plan block with a tower with a conical roof; and it houses a fourteenth-century chapel with a painted ceiling of 1630-40. The property was held by the Drummonds from 1360, and was the main Drummond stronghold until they moved to Drummond Castle (see below). Anabella, daughter of John Drummond of Stobhall, married the future Robert III in 1367. The family were forfeited for their part in the Jacobite Rising of 1745-46, but they recovered the property, and the current Earl of Perth has Stobhall as his seat. The gardens and chapel are occasionally open to the public (01821 640332; www.stobhall.com).

Drummond Castle [NN 844181] is a grand pile, two miles or so south and west of Crieff in Perthshire, and stands on a rocky outcrop. It dates from the fifteenth century, and there is a tower of five storeys, along with later and lower extensions. Sir Malcolm Drummond distinguished himself at the Battle of Bannockburn in 1314, and was given the lands here, which were originally known as Concraig. His daughter, Margaret, widow of Sir John Logie, married David II in 1364, although he divorced her six years later. The existing

Drummond Castle (M&R)

castle was begun in the fifteenth century by John, first Lord Drummond. Margaret Drummond, daughter of the builder, was a lover of James IV, and they were reputedly married and had a daughter. However, some of the nobles wanted James to marry Margaret Tudor, sister of Henry VIII, and form an alliance with England. To this end, and to 'free' James, Margaret, and two of her sisters, were murdered with poisoned sugared fruit, and are buried side by side in Dunblane Cathedral, where there is a memorial to them in the floor of the church. In 1490 William Drummond, her brother and second son of Lord Drummond, was executed after he torched Monzievaird Church, killing more than 150 Murrays, including women and children. Mary, Queen of Scots, visited the castle in 1566-67 with Bothwell; and the Drummonds were made Earls of Perth in 1605. The castle was badly damaged by Cromwell in the 1650s, after James, third Earl, had been active with the Marquis of Montrose, and James was captured following the Battle of Philiphaugh in 1645.

The castle was slighted after having been occupied by government troops during the Jacobite Rising of 1715. James, fifth Earl, had commanded the Jacobite cavalry at the Battle of Sheriffmuir that year, and the sixth, another James, commanded the left wing of the Jacobite army at the Battle of Culloden in 1746. He was wounded during the fighting, and although he managed to board a French ship, he died during the passage. The family had been made Dukes of Perth by James VII in 1689-90, but were forfeited after the Rising.

The Earldom of Perth was recovered in 1822, and the Drummond Earls of Perth now live at Stobhall. Their titles include Lord Drummond of Cargill and Stobhall, Lord Madderty and thirteenth Viscount Strathallan and Lord Drummond of Cromlix, as well as the Duke of Perth in the Jacobite peerage. Many of the Drummonds were buried on Inchmahome [NN 574005], an idyllic isle in the Lake of Menteith. There was a priory, which is now ruinous, but in the care of Historic Scotland and is open to the public (01877 385294). Drummond Castle has a magnificent formal garden, which is open to the public (01764 681433; www.drummondcastlegardens.co.uk).

Some eight miles east of Perth is **Megginch Castle** [NO 242246], which is an altered Z-plan tower house, dating from the fifteenth century but with a later wing. There are turrets and a watch-chamber crowned the building. Megginch was a property of the Hays, but was sold to the Drummonds of Lennoch in 1634. The third

Megginch Castle (M&R)

Drummond of Megginch was the first member of Parliament for Perthshire for the Union parliament of 1707. Rob Roy MacGregor was imprisoned in Perth Tolbooth by Drummond, and part of the film *Rob Roy* with Liam Neeson was made here. One story is that the old part of the castle is haunted by the unexplained whispering of two women. The Drummonds of Megginch, Barons Strange, apparently still live in the house, and the extensive and unusual gardens are open from April to October (01821 642222).

Newton Castle [NO 172453], just to the north-west of Blairgowrie in Perthshire, is a sixteenth-century Z-plan tower house, which is on the site of an older stronghold. Newton was a property of the Drummonds, who feuded with the Blairs of nearby Ardblair. The tower was sacked by the Marquis of Montrose in 1644, and torched by Cromwell in the 1650s, although the defenders of the tower are supposed to have survived in the vaults while the building burned around them. George Drummond, who was born around 1687, came from the family, and was Lord Provost of Edinburgh from 1725 to 1764. He was responsible for the first building

Newton Castle 1910?

of the New Town of Edinburgh. The castle is said to be haunted by the spirit of Lady Jean Drummond, a Green Lady, witnessed both in the castle, the grounds and also at Ardblair. Jean fell in love with one of the Blairs of Ardblair, but the families feuded or her lover tired of her, and Jean seems to have died of a broken heart, drowning herself in a local marsh (although there are other versions of the story behind her haunting involving witchcraft). Newton later passed to the Macphersons, is in good condition and is still occupied.

The Drummonds also held:

Abbotsgrange [NS 931811], near Grangemouth, West Lothian; site of castle and mansion.
  Held by the Drummonds at one time after being a property of the Livingstones, of the Kerrs and of the Bannatynes.

Auchterarder Castle [NN 936133], near Auchterarder, Perthshire; some remains of a castle.
  Held by the Grahams, but passed by marriage to the Drummonds.

Ballathie House [NO 146367], near Blairgowrie, Perthshire; castle replaced by mansion.
  Held by the Drummonds, later Earls of Perth, then by the Blairs and by the Richardsons of Tullybelton, then by the Coats of Paisley. The building is now used as a hotel (01250 883268; www.ballathiehousehotel.com).

Balhaldie [NN 812050], near Dunblane, Stirlingshire; site of castle or old house.
  Held by the MacGregors (Drummonds) until the nineteenth century. This branch of the MacGregors claimed the title of chief of the clan in 1714, but it went to others. They were Jacobites.

Balmoral Castle [NO 255952], near Ballater, Aberdeenshire; royal mansion and residence.
  Held by the Drummonds in 1390, but passed to the Gordons and to others, before being purchased by Prince Albert, husband of Queen Victoria, in 1852. The gardens, grounds and exhibitions are open to the public from around April to July (01339 742534; www.balmoralcastle.com).

Bruce's or **Carnock Castle** [NS 857878], near Falkirk; ruinous tower.
  Held by the Airths, by the Hepburns and by the Bruces, and then from 1608 by the Drummonds of Carnock, and they changed the name to distinguish the property from Carnock House.

Cargill [NO 157374], near Blairgowrie, Perthshire; site of castle on motte.
  Lands held by a Richard de Montifiquet but passed to the Drummonds in the fourteenth century.

Carnock House [NS 865882], near Airth, Falkirk; site of tower house.
  Held by the Somervilles and by the Bruces, but passed in 1608 to the Drummonds of Carnock, who built the house. Carnock went to the Nicholsons in 1634, then to the Shaws of Greenock.

Coldoch [NS 699982], near Doune, Stirlingshire; site of castle.
  Held by the Spittals, and then by the Drummonds in about 1450, but passed to the Stirlings and later to the Grahams, who built a mansion.

Colquhalzie [NN 914175], near Crieff, Perthshire; strong castle replaced by mansion.
  Held by the Drummonds in the seventeenth and eighteenth centuries, but had passed to the Hepburns by 1826.

Cultybraggan [NN 769197], near Comrie, Perthshire; site of castle, the location not certain.
  Held by the Redheughs in 1590 but also by the Drummonds.

Dunira [NN 738238], near Comrie, Perthshire; site of castle and then mansion.
  Held by the Comries, then by the Drummonds from 1653, then was sold to Henry Dundas, Viscount Melville.

Fornocht [NN 947248], near Crieff, Perthshire; site of small castle or tower.

Held by the Easons but was bought by the Drummonds in 1504.

Hawthornden Castle [NT 287637], near Loanhead, Midlothian; fine, partly ruinous castle.

Held by the Drummonds from 1540, and Mary, Queen of Scots, is believed to have visited. Hawthornden was the home of the poet William Drummond. His fiancee, Mary Cunningham of Barns, was burned to death on the eve of their wedding in 1615, and Drummond became a learned recluse. He was visited by the writer and playwright Ben Jonson in 1618-19, and Drummond died in 1649. He is buried in the restored burial aisle at the Old Parish churchyard at Lasswade [NT 302661]. Dr Johnson visited Hawthornden, as did Queen Victoria. The house is still occupied, and is now used as a retreat for writers.

Innergellie House [NO 575052], near Kilrenny, Fife; castle replaced by mansion.

The property was part of the dowry of Anabella Drummond, wife of Robert III, but passed to the Beatons, and then to the Barclays and to the Lumsdens.

Innerpeffray Castle [NN 904179], near Crieff, Perthshire; ruined L-plan tower house.

Held by the Drummond Lords Madderty after the Reformation, and they built or remodelled the building in 1610. Innerpeffray Chapel was raised to collegiate status, probably by John, first

Innerpeffray Castle (M&R)

Lord Drummond, and many of the Drummonds are buried here; the chapel is in the care of Historic Scotland and can be visited. Nearby is Innerpeffray Library [NN 902183], Scotland's oldest free-lending library. It was founded in 1691 by David Drummond, Lord Madderty, and is still open every day except Thursday. It is housed in a late eighteenth-century building, which is interesting in itself, and contains a notable collection of bibles and rare books (01764 652819).

Keltie Castle [NO 008133], near Dunning, Perthshire; L-plan tower house.

Held by the Bonnars, but sold to the Drummonds in 1692 and they held Keltie until 1812 when it went to the Ogilvies of Airlie. During renovations, the skeleton of a woman was found walled-up in one of the rooms. The castle is still occupied.

Kincardine Castle [NS 721986], near Doune, Perthshire; site of castle.

Held by the Drummonds from the beginning of the fourteenth century. Ruinous in 1714.

Kindrochit Castle [NO 152913], Braemar, Aberdeenshire; slight remains of a castle.

Held by Sir Malcolm Drummond in 1390, and he built a new stronghold. While supervising work on it, he was kidnapped and died in captivity about 1402, possibly at the hands of Alexander Stewart, son of the Wolf of Badenoch. Isabella, Countess of Mar, was forced to marry Stewart at Kildrummy

Castle in 1404. Stewart then acquired both the Earldom of Mar and the Lordship of Garioch.

Logie-Almond House [NO 014297], near Perth; site of castle and mansion.

Held by the Hays, but passed to the Drummonds, who held it in the sixteenth century, then later passed to the Murray Earls of Mansfield.

Lundin Tower [NO 399029], near Lower Largo, Fife; site of castle and mansion.

Originally held by the Lundin family and by the Maitlands, but had passed by marriage to the Drummonds in 1670. They were forfeited following the Jacobite Rising of 1745-46, and the property was later held by the Gilmours.

Midhope Castle [NT 073787], near Linlithgow, West Lothian; tower house and courtyard.

Held by the Drummonds in the sixteenth and seventeenth centuries, but passed to the Livingstone Earls of Linlithgow, then to the Hopes. It is being restored.

Muthill [NN 877164], near Crieff, Perthshire; site of castle.

Held by the Drummonds.

Strathallan Castle [NN 919155], near Auchterarder, Perthshire; mansion on site of castle.

Held by the Drummonds, who were made Viscounts Strathallan in 1686. The fourth Viscount was mortally wounded at the Battle of Culloden in 1746, during the Jacobite Rising, his last sacrament being whisky and an oatcake. The family was forfeited, but recovered their titles in 1824, and Viscount Strathallan is one of the titles of the Earl of Perth, who now lives at Stobhall.

www.angelfire.com/al/metaphysicsgalore/
Drummond.html
No. of castles/sites: 28
Rank: 44=/764

Duddingston

The name is territorial and comes from the lands and now picturesque village of Duddingston, which lies near Holyrood Park in Edinburgh; although there is also a property called **Duddingston** [NT 102776] near South Queensferry in West Lothian, but this was held by the Lindsays and then by the Dundas family. The name comes from

'Dodin's ton', 'Dodin' being a first name, and 'ton' meaning a 'settlement or seat'. The name Duddingston is recorded in charters from the twelfth century.

St Ford or **Sandford** [NO 482013], which is one mile north and west of Elie in Fife, was long held by the Duddingston family. Stephen Duddingston of Sandford was charged with 'abiding from the raid of Lauder' in 1558.

The Duddingstons also appear to have held **Kincaple** [NO 465182], which is two and a half miles north-west of St Andrews, again in Fife. The present mansion dates from the eighteenth century and was built by the Meldrums in the eighteenth century. **West Kincaple House** [NO 460183] dates from the seventeenth century.

No. of castles/sites: 2 / Rank: 396=/764

Duff

The name comes from 'dubh', pronounced 'doo' or 'doov', the Gaelic for 'black', probably referring to the colouring of complexion or of hair. It was used as a first name for centuries, and Dubh or Duff was a king of Scots in the tenth century. Duff is recorded as a surname from the thirteenth century. MacDuff, meaning 'son of Duff' was the name of the Earls of Fife from early times, and the Duffs, although holding lands in the north-east of Scotland, such as **Muldavit**, **Torriesoul** and **Dipple** (see below), were probably related. The Duffs were landowners who came to great prominence and wealth from the seventeenth century, taking advantage of the hard times when local nobles had lands but no money. William Duff of Braco, who was born in 1693, was the son of William Duff of Dipple. He was MP for Banffshire from 1727 until 1734, and was made Earl of Fife in 1754; the family were made Dukes in 1889. The title is now held by the Carnegie, Dukes of Fife and Earls of Southesk, and they apparently live at Kinnaird Castle in Angus.

Some three miles south-east of Turriff in the north-east of Scotland, **Hatton Castle** [NJ 758469] is a substantial castellated mansion with large round towers at the corners. It dates from 1814 but incorporates the ancient and strong castle of **Balquhollie**. The Duffs purchased **Hatton Manor** [NJ 709420] from the Meldrums in 1709, where they lived for some years; they then bought the nearby lands of Balquhollie from the Mowats in 1723, which they renamed Hatton when they moved there. They built the mansion, and still apparently live here. The walled garden is open by appointment only (01888 562279; www.gardensofscotland.org).

Duff House [NJ 692633] to the south of Banff also in the north-east of Scotland, is a fine classical mansion with colonnades and corner towers. It was designed by William Adam and dates from 1735, and was built for William Duff of Braco, later Earl of Fife. The architect and the earl got into a long and messy dispute about the cost of the building, which was eventually won by Adam, although at great cost to both parties. The house is now used to display works of art from the National Galleries of Scotland; and this is one of the many castles and houses that is said to be haunted by a Green Lady. Duff House is open to the public (01261 818181).

Drummuir [NJ 407448], four miles south-west of Keith in Moray, is an altered L-plan tower house, dating from the seventeenth century. The original castle was built by the Abercrombys, but the property was sold to the Duffs in 1670. The old stronghold was abandoned for Kirkton House, and then a new Drummuir Castle was built. This is a substantial castellated mansion, dating from the nineteenth century and recently restored. Alexander Duff of Drummuir seized Inverness for the Jacobites in 1715. The castle is now apparently occupied by the Gordon-Duff family of Drummuir and Park and has fine plasterwork, and there is a walled garden. The house and gardens are open to the public some days during the summer (01542 810225; www.drummuir estate.co.uk).

The Duffs also acquired many other properties:

Arnot Castle [NO 207016], near Cardenden, Fife; ruinous tower house.

Held by the Arnotts, then by the Duffs in the fifteenth century, before passing back to the Arnotts, then to the Bruces. The gardens are occasionally open to the public and the gardens can be hired for weddings or functions (01592 840115; www.arnottower.co.uk/www.gardensofscotland.org).

Aswanley House [NJ 445397], near Huntly, Aberdeenshire; mansion.

Held by the Gordons and by the Calders, but sold because of debt in 1768 to the Duffs. Holiday accommodation available and venue for weddings (01466 700262; www.aswanley.com).

Auchintoul [NJ 615524], near Aberchirder, Aberdeenshire; castle with main block and tower.

Held by the Gordons but then by the Duff Dukes of Fife in the 1890s.

Balnain House [NH 663445], Inverness; town house.

Built by the Duffs in 1722 and used as a hospital after the Battle of Culloden in 1746; now a regional office for The National Trust for Scotland.

Balvenie Castle [NJ 326409], near Dufftown, Moray; fine ruinous castle.

Held by the many families before being sold to the Duffs of Braco in 1687. The old castle was held by the Jacobites in 1689, but in 1715 was held against them by the Duffs. It was not occupied after William Duff committed suicide here in 1718, and was unroofed by 1724 – although a Hanoverian force, under the Duke of Cumberland, briefly held it in 1746. In the care of Historic Scotland and open to the public from April to September (01340 820121).

Ballintomb [NJ 213424], near Charlestown of Aberlour, Moray; possible site of castle or old house.

Held by the Grants in the seventeenth century, but passed by marriage to the Duffs.

Blackhills [NJ 270587], near Lhanbryde, Moray; castle replaced by mansion.

Held by the Innes family in the seventeenth and eighteenth centuries (see Coxton), and was sold to the Duffs of Fife and then to the Christie family. Holiday cottages are available on the estate and the gardens are occasionally open to the public (01343 842223; www.blackhills.co.uk).

Duff House (MC)

Blervie Castle [NJ 071573], near Forres, Moray; ruined Z-plan tower house.
> Held by the Dunbars and by the Mackintoshes before being sold to the Duffs of Braco.

Pluscarden [NJ 154571], near Elgin, Moray; abbey and castle.
> The lands were held by Pluscarden Abbey, but passed through several families until they came to the Duffs.

Corsindae House [NJ 686088], near Banchory, Aberdeenshire; L-plan tower house.
> Held by the Forbeses, but had passed to the Duffs of Braco by 1726.

Coxton Tower [NJ 262607], near Elgin, Moray; fine tower house.
> Held by the Innes family but was sold to the Duff Earl of Fife, who built a new house nearby. The tower house is in excellent condition and is still occupied (www.malcolm.christie.btinternet.co.uk).

Crombie Castle [NJ 591522], near Aberchirder, Aberdeenshire; altered L-plan tower house.
> Held by several families, including by the Innes family and by the Meldrums, before coming to the Duffs.

Delgatie Castle [NJ 755506], near Turriff, Aberdeenshire; imposing castle with fine interior.
> Long held by the Hays, but passed to the Duffs in 1798 and to others, before eventually returning to the Hays. Open to the public (01888 563479; www.delgatiecastle.com).

Dipple [NJ 329583], near Fochabers, Moray; mansion on older site.
> Held by the Duffs in the seventeenth century. William Duff of Dipple was the father of William Duff of Braco, and this branch of the family became the Earls, and then Dukes, of Fife.

Eden Castle [NJ 698588], near Banff, Aberdeenshire; ruinous Z-plan tower house.
> Held by the Leslies but sold to the Duff Earl of Fife in 1712.

Fetteresso Castle [NO 843855], near Stonehaven, Kincardineshire; mansion on site of castle.
> Held by the Strachans and by the Keiths before coming to the Duffs. The castle was ruinous at one time, but has been rebuilt and divided into seven dwellings.

Fisherie [NJ 765580], near Turriff, Aberdeenshire; site of castle.
> Held by the Duffs.

Gask House [NJ 730472], near Turriff, Aberdeenshire; site of castle.
> Held by the Forbeses, but passed to the Duff Earls of Fife in the nineteenth century.

Glassaugh House [NJ 558645], near Portsoy, Aberdeenshire; site of castle and ruins of mansion.
> Held by the Abercrombys, but passed to the Duffs of Glassaugh and Fetteresso. It was occupied into the twentieth century but is now a shell.

Glenbuchat Castle [NJ 397149], near Kildrummy, Aberdeenshire; impressive ruinous tower house.
> Held by the Gordons but sold to the Duff Earls of Fife in 1738, and replaced by **Glenbuchat House** [NJ 397148]. In the care of Historic Scotland and open to the public (01667 460232).

House of Mergie [NO 796887], near Stonehaven, Kincardineshire; T-plan tower house.
> Held by several families before coming to Colonel Duff of Fetteresso, who caught Robert Burns poaching on his estate. Now a farmhouse.

Innes House [NJ 278649], near Elgin, Moray; fine altered L-plan tower house.
> Long held by the Innes family, but sold to the Duff Earls of Fife in 1767.

Invermarkie Castle [NJ 429396], near Keith, Aberdeenshire; site of castle.
> Held by the Gordons, but was later replaced by a shooting lodge of the Duffs.

Keithmore [NJ 355391], near Dufftown, Moray; site of castle.
> Held by the Ogilvies but later passed to the Duffs, who moved to Hatton.

Lickleyhead Castle [NJ 627237], near Insch, Aberdeenshire; impressive tower house.
> Held by the Duffs at one time, as well as by the Leslies and by the Forbeses, and by others.

Mains of Mayen [NJ 576477], near Huntly, Aberdeenshire; L-plan tower house.
> Held by several families before coming to the Duffs after 1752, and they built nearby Mayen House in 1788.

Montcoffer House [NJ 685613], near Banff, Aberdeenshire; mansion with old work.
> Held by the Campbells of Lundie and Montcoffer, but passed by marriage to the Russells, then was sold in 1750 to the Duff Dukes of Fife. Still occupied.

Muldavit [NJ 504662], near Cullen, Aberdeenshire; possible site of castle or old house.
> Held by the Duffs from 1401 until sold in 1626, and passed to the Hays. In 1536, John Duff of Muldavit founded a chaplainry of St Anne at Cullen Church [NJ 507663], and St Anne's Aisle was completed three years later. His fine carved stone tomb survives in the church.

Park [NJ 587571], near Aberchirder, Aberdeenshire; Z-plan tower house.
> Long held by the Gordons, then by the Gordon-Duffs, now of Drummuir and Park, who apparently live at Drummuir. Accommodation available (01466 751667; www.castleofpark.net).

Rothiemay Castle [NJ 554484], near Huntly, Aberdeenshire; site of impressive castle and mansion.
> Held by the Gordons, but was in possession of the Duffs from 1741 until 1890 when it went to the Forbeses. The building was completely demolished in 1956.

Skene House [NJ 768097], near Westhill, Aberdeenshire; large mansion and castle.
> Long held by the Skenes, but owned by the Duffs from 1827 until 1880 when it was sold to the Hamiltons.

Torriesoul [NJ 540390], near Huntly, Aberdeenshire; site of castle.
> Held by the Duffs in the fifteenth and sixteenth centuries.

No. of castles/sites: 36
Rank: 34=/764

Duguid

The name was common in Aberdeenshire, and is on record at the beginning of the fourteenth century.

Auchenhove Castle [NJ 555024], three and a half miles north-east of Aboyne, is a very ruinous castle and courtyard, and was a property of the Duguid family from the middle of the fifteenth century. The castle was burned by the Duke of Cumberland's army during the Jacobite Rising of 1745-46, the wife and children of the house only just escaping. The Duguids supported the Jacobites, and had also been active in the 1715 Rising. Patrick Duguid of Auchenhove fought at the Battle of Culloden, and was hunted after the Rising although he was pardoned in 1775. Many of the family are buried in the Howff burial ground.

No. of castles/sites: 1
Rank: 537=/764

Dumbreck

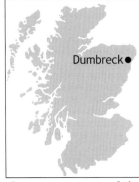

The name is territorial and comes from the lands of the same name, which are three or so miles west of Ellon in Aberdeenshire.

Dumbreck Castle [NJ 898289] was a sixteenth-century castle, but all that remains is a gunloop, built into one of the walls of Mains of Dumbreck. The lands were a property of the Dumbreck family, but passed to the Meldrums, who built the castle.

No. of castles/sites: 1
Rank: 537=/764

Dun

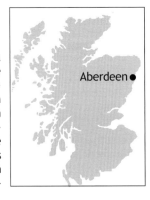

The name may be from a place of origin, and there are several possible candidates, such as Dun in Angus; although 'dun' in Gaelic means a hill or fortified place; or it may be from 'brown'. The name is recorded in Scotland from the middle of the thirteenth century.

Benholm's Lodging [NJ 936089], a fine town house dating from the early seventeenth century, originally stood near the Nethergate in Aberdeen, but it was demolished and rebuilt on its present site at Tillydrone, near St Machar's Cathedral, to make way for offices. The lodging was built by Sir Robert Keith of Benholm, brother to the fifth Earl Marischal, and the lodging was later occupied by Dr Patrick Dun, principal of Marischal College. The property later passed to the Hays and to other families, before coming into the ownership of the City of Aberdeen in 1918.

No. of castles/sites: 2
Rank: 396=/764
Xref: Dunn

Dunbar

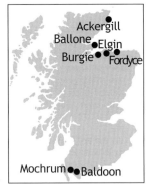

The name comes from the burgh and port of Dunbar in East Lothian on the south-east coast of Scotland, which was an important place, especially after the loss of Berwick-upon-Tweed to the English. Branches of the family were descended from the Cospatrick Earls of Dunbar, and then of March, who were forfeited in the fifteenth century by James I (also see Cospatrick). The family held lands in different parts of Scotland: from Caithness, in the far north, to Galloway, in the far south-west. William Dunbar was a fine poet in the reign of James IV, and celebrated the marriage of the king to Margaret Tudor in his work 'The Thistle and the Rose'; James, himself, seems to have been less enamoured of his bride. Dunbar died in 1514.

Old Place of Mochrum [NX 308541], seven miles east of Glenluce village in Galloway, is an attractive courtyard castle, which consists of two towers, dating from the fifteenth and the sixteenth centuries respectively. Ranges of buildings are built around the

Old Place of Mochrum 1904?

courtyard, and a passageway runs under the courtyard from one tower to the wing. The lands were long held by the Dunbars, one of whom was Gavin Dunbar, Archbishop of Glasgow and Chancellor of Scotland to James V. His uncle, another Gavin, was Bishop of Aberdeen from 1519, and rebuilt St Machar's Cathedral in Aberdeen, inserting a fine heraldic ceiling; his tomb recess can be seen in the south transept. The remaining part of the cathedral is open to the public all year (01224 485988; www.stmachar.com). Mochrum passed to the MacDowalls about 1694, and then to the Stewarts. The building was ruinous at one time but has been restored and is occupied. The line of the Dunbars of Mochrum continues, and they apparently live near Kirkcowan in Galloway.

Little now remains of **Baldoon Castle** [NX 426536], which was held by the Dunbars of Westfield from 1530 to about 1800. Baldoon is situated to the south and west of Wigtown in Galloway, and is the scene of a famous ghost story. In 1669 Janet Dalrymple of Carscreugh was in love with Archibald Rutherford, son of Lord Rutherford, but he was (relatively) poor and her parents were against their marriage. They chose Sir David Dunbar of Baldoon, and persuaded Janet to marry him, although she only agreed reluctantly. There are different versions of what happened next: Janet was either murdered on her wedding night, after having tried to slay her new husband; or died insane soon afterwards. Her ghost, in a blood-stained wedding dress, is said to be seen here on 12 September, the anniversary of her death; or at other times searching through the ruins. Sir Walter Scott's *Bride of Lammermuir* (and then Donizetti's opera) were inspired by the (reputed) events here. Dunbar went on to marry another girl.

Thunderton House [NJ 215615], on Thunderton Place in Elgin in Moray, may incorporate a fourteenth-century royal castle. It was held by the Sutherland Lord Duffus, but passed to the Dunbars of Thunderton. The building is said to be haunted by the ghost of Bonnie Prince Charlie, who stayed here for eleven days before going on to defeat at the Battle of Culloden in 1746. An alternative identity has been given as Lady Arradoul, his hostess. The building has been altered down the years and is now a public house (01343 554921; www.thundertonhouse.co.uk).

The Dunbars also held:

Ackergill Tower [ND 352547], near Wick, Caithness; fine tall tower house and mansion.
  Held by the Cheynes and by the Keiths, but passed to the Dunbars of Hempriggs in 1699, who held it until the 1980s. The castle is available to rent for totally exclusive use (01955 603556; www.ackergill-tower.co.uk).

Airyolland [NX 308475], near Port William, Galloway; slight remains of castle.
  Held by the Dunbars, but passed to the Vaux family in 1583.

Auchen Castle [NT 063035], near Moffat, Dumfries and Galloway; ruinous castle.
  Held by several families including by the Dunbar Earls of Moray in the fourteenth century. It was replaced by a modern mansion on a different site, also called Auchen Castle, which is now a hotel (01683 300407; www.auchencastle.com).

Auldearn Castle [NH 917557], near Nairn, Inverness-shire; motte.
  The lands were held by the Dunbars of Cumnock in 1511, and Boath House, a mansion of 1830, may be built on the site of, or incorporate part of, an older house or tower.

Ballone Castle [NH 929838], near Tain, Ross and Cromarty; fine Z-plan tower house.
  Held by the Earls of Ross, then by the Dunbars of Tarbat in 1507, then by the Mackenzies in 1623.

Ballone Castle (M&R)

Billie Castle [NT 851596], near Chirnside, Borders; little remains of a large castle.
  Held by the Dunbars from the beginning of the thirteenth century, then by the Douglases from 1435 and then by the Rentons around 1540.

Binsness [NJ 030629], near Forres, Moray; castle or old house replaced by mansion.
  Held by the Dunbars of Wester Moy in 1620.

Black Bog Castle [NS 618137], near New Cumnock, Ayrshire; site of castle.
  Held by the Dunbars of Cumnock but passed to the Crichtons of Sanquhar in 1622.

Blervie Castle [NJ 071573], near Forres, Moray; part of a Z-plan tower house.
  The castle was built by the Dunbars, but was sold to the Mackintoshes at the beginning of the eighteenth century, then went to the Duffs.

Burgie Castle [NJ 094593], near Forres; one tower survives from a Z-plan tower house.
  Held by the Dunbars from 1566, who built the tower. Dunbar

Burgie Castle (M&R)

of Burgie fought against the Marquis of Montrose in 1645, but bankrupted himself paying for supplies for Charles II's army in 1650, and had to sell the property to his kinsman Thomas Dunbar of Grange. Most of the castle was demolished in 1802 to build Burgie House, itself rebuilt in 1912 as a plain two-storey mansion.

Castle Cary [NS 786775], near Cumbernauld, Falkirk; fine castle with later wing.
  Long held by the Livingstones and by the Baillies, but passed to the Dunbars of Fingask by marriage in 1730 (www.castle-cary.org).

Castle Loch Castle [NX 294541], near Glenluce, Galloway; very ruinous courtyard castle.
  Held by the Dunbars of Kilconquhar, and one of the family was killed at the Battle of Flodden in 1513. The lands passed to the Vauxs in 1590. The site has been excavated.

Castle of Old Wick [ND 369488], near Wick, Caithness; ruinous castle on cliff tops.
  Held by several families, including by the Cheynes and by the Sinclairs, and then latterly by the Dunbars of Hempriggs, who were in possession in 1910. In the care of Historic Scotland and open to the public, although great care should be taken if visiting (01667 460232).

Clugston [NX 355574], near Wigtown, Galloway; motte.
  Held by the Clugston family, but passed by marriage to the Dunbars of Mochrum.

Conzie Castle [NJ 595450], near Huntly, Aberdeenshire; ruins of castle.
  Held by the Dunbars of Conzie in the fifteenth and sixteenth centuries.

Crailloch [NX 326526], near Culshabbin, Galloway; site of tower house.

Held by the Dunbars in 1539.

Cumstoun Castle [NX 683533], near Kirkcudbright, Galloway; slight remains of castle.

Held by several families including by the Dunbars before 1595, and then went to the Montgomerys and then to the Maitlands.

Darnaway Castle [NH 994550], near Forres, Moray; large mansion with some old work including a magnificent oak roof.

Held by the Earls of Moray, and Sir Thomas Randolph probably built the first castle. John, third Earl, died at the Battle of Neville's Cross in 1346 without any male heirs, and the Earldom went to Patrick Dunbar who was the husband of one of John's daughters. The male line of the Dunbars failed around 1430, and the Earldom went to the Douglases, then to the Murrays, and then to the Stewarts, with whose descendants it remains. The castle is still occupied.

Dunphail Castle [NJ 007481], near Forres, Moray; ruins of castle.

Held by the Comyns, then by the Cummings, but also by the Dunbars at one time.

Fordyce Castle [NJ 556638], near Portsoy, Aberdeenshire; L-plan tower house.

Held by the Dunbars in 1429, but passed by marriage to the Ogilvie Earls of Findlater, although the castle was built by Thomas Menzies of Dun, Provost of Aberdeen. Part of the castle can be rented as holiday accommodation (01261 843722; www.fordycecastle.co.uk).

Forres Castle [NJ 035588], Forres, Moray; site of castle.

May have been held by the Dunbars of Westfield at one time, as well as by the Murrays.

Girnigoe Castle [ND 379549], near Wick, Caithness; impressive ruins of a large castle.

Mostly associated with the Sinclairs, but latterly held by the Dunbars of Hempriggs, although it was sold back to the Sinclairs in 1950. There is a car park and faint path, but the ruins and cliffs are dangerous and great care should be taken if visiting (www.castle-sg.org/www.clansinclair.org).

Grangehill or **Dalvey Castle** [NJ 003585], near Forres, Moray; site of castle.

Held by the Dunbars, but passed to the Grants of Dalvey, who built a mansion on the site. This branch of the Dunbars became the Dunbars of Durn, who were made Baronets of Nova Scotia in 1697-98. The line continues, although they now apparently live in London.

Halhill Castle [NH 759519], near Inverness; site of castle.

Held by the Mackintoshes and then by the Dunbars and by the Ogilvies, and was sacked in 1502 and 1513 in a dispute over ownership.

Hempriggs Castle [NJ 103641], near Forres, Moray; site of castle.

Held by the Dunbars. Demolished to build a farm.

Hempriggs House [ND 359473], near Wick, Caithness; mansion on site of castle.

Held by the Sinclairs but passed to the Dunbars of Hempriggs, who held the property until the twentieth century. They were made Baronets of Nova Scotia in 1706, the line continues, and they still apparently live in Caithness. The house is now a residential home.

Inchbrayock House [NO 718562], near Montrose, Angus; castle replaced by house.

Held by the Dunbars of Inchbrayock in the seventeenth century.

Kilbulack Castle [NJ 095605], near Forres, Moray; site of castle.

Held by the Dunbars. Demolished to build a farm.

Knockshinnoch Tower [NS 609126], near New Cumnock, Ayrshire; site of castle.

Held by the Dunbars from the fifteenth century or earlier until the middle of the eighteenth century when the property passed to the Logans.

Machermore Castle [NX 416644], near Newton-Stewart, Galloway; mansion incorporating castle.

Held by the MacDowalls, but by 1866 the property was held by the Dunbars. Now used as a nursing home.

Mindork Castle [NX 322588], near Kirkcowan, Galloway; site of castle.

Held by the Dunbars.

Stevenson House [NT 544748], near Haddington, East Lothian; house incorporating part of castle.

Long held by the Sinclairs, but passed to the Dunbars in the twentieth century.

Tibbers Castle [NX 863982], near Thornhill, Borders; little remains of a castle.

The lands were held by the Dunbars, but passed to the Maitlands and then to the Douglases.

Westfield [NJ 163654], near Elgin, Moray; site of castle or old house.

Held by the Dunbars from 1450, and they were Sheriffs of Moray. It was from this family that many of the later branches were descended, including the Dunbars of Durn, the Dunbars of Northfield and the Hope-Dunbars of St Mary's Isle, all of whom were made Baronets and all of whom are still represented, although not in their original seats.

Whitmuir Hall [NT 503271], near Selkirk, Borders; mansion on site of castle.

Held by the Dunbars at the beginning of the eighteenth century.

www.dunbarfamilysociety.org.uk
No. of castles/sites: 38
Rank: 29=/764

Duncan

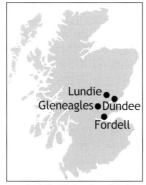

The name has its origins in a very early first name, and may come from 'donn cath', meaning 'brown warrior'; or 'dun cath' for 'fort warrior'. The name is very ancient, and 'Dunchad', eleventh abbot of Iona, died in 717. As a surname it is recorded from the twelfth century. Clan Dhonnchaidh (Robertson) takes its name from 'fat Duncan', who was chief in the early part of the fourteenth century. He was a follower of Robert the Bruce, and he is said to have made Duncan's Leap, on the River Ericht in Rannoch, when scouting out a camp of the MacDougalls.

Henry Duncan, who was born in Lochrutton in 1774, was the minister of Ruthwell near Dumfries, and he started the first savings bank in 1810 in an effort to relieve poverty. There is a museum in Ruthwell as well as the magnificent Ruthwell Cross, housed in the parish church, which Duncan helped to rebuild from its smashed fragments.

Lundie Castle [NO 309361] stood seven miles east and south of Coupar Angus in Angus, although there are now no remains. The castle was replaced by a house in the seventeenth century, itself demolished and replaced by the present mansion. The lands were held by the Duncans, and many of the family are buried in Lundie kirkyard [NO 291366]. One of the family, Adam Duncan, son of Alexander Duncan of Lundie, was a famous admiral, and defeated a Dutch fleet at Camperdown in 1797. Duncan was made Baron, and then Viscount Camperdown, and the family were later created Earls of Camperdown. The family built **Camperdown House** [NO 365327] in Dundee, a nineteenth-century mansion, set in nearly 400 acres of fine park land. The grounds are now a country park (01382 434296), and there are plans to have a museum about Admiral Duncan and the Battle of Camperdown established in the house.

To the north of Inverkeithing in Fife, **Fordell Castle** [NT 147854] is a fine Z-plan tower house, which dates from the sixteenth century, and there are turrets at the corners. The lands were held by the Airths, but is most associated with the Henderson of Fordell. The property passed in 1866 by marriage to Hon. Hew Adam Dalrymple Hamilton Haldane Duncan, second son of the Earl of Camperdown, who then added Mercer-Henderson to his name: addressing correspondence to him must have been time consuming. The castle is still occupied, although it has passed from the Duncans.

Gleneagles Castle [NN 929093], two and a half miles south and east of Auchterarder in Perthshire, is now a shattered ruin, and was abandoned when **Gleneagles House** [NN 931088] was built in 1624. This early house was integrated into a rebuilding in the middle of the

Fordell Castle (M&R) – see previous column

eighteenth century; and the present mansion is a large whitewashed edifice, which was remodelled in the nineteenth century. Gleneagles was held by the Haldanes from the twelfth century, but passed to Admiral Duncan in 1799. The lime avenue up to the house was planted to commemorate the Battle of Camperdown.

The line of the Earls of Camperdown is now extinct.

www.clan-duncan.co.uk
No. of castles/sites: 3
Rank: 328=/764

Dundas

The name is from the lands of Dundas, which are to the south of South Queensferry in West Lothian. The family were descended from Cospatrick, Earl of Northumberland, and were therefore related to the Earls of Dunbar and also to the Dunbar family. The name is on record from the twelfth century.

Dundas Castle [NT 116767] is a solid and strong keep of four storeys, which dates from the fifteenth century, but was later extended with a new wing to make it L-plan. The Dundases held the property from perhaps as early as 1124, and were in possession for 750 years; they built the castle in 1424. Dundas was besieged in 1449, and both Charles II and Oliver Cromwell stayed at the castle in 1651 (although not at the same time).

Dundas Castle (M&R)

George Dundas, twenty-third laird, was a captain in the East India Company, and was drowned in a shipwreck off Madagascar in 1792. A new mansion, designed in the Gothic style, was built nearby in 1818, and the castle was abandoned. The castle was converted for use as a distillery, and the property was sold to the Stewarts in 1875. The family line continues, although the Dundases now apparently live in South Africa, and the castle is available for exclusive hire for weddings or corporate hospitality (0131 319 2039; www.dundascastle.co.uk). Sir George Dundas founded a Carmelite friary or Whitefriars [NT 128785] in South Queensferry around 1330, the church of which survives, and there are memorials to the family in the building.

Arniston House [NT 326595], two miles south-west of Gorebridge in Midlothian, is a classical mansion, which was built for Robert Dundas of Arniston by William Adam in 1726 and replaced an earlier house or castle. There is fine plasterwork, although part of the house is undergoing restoration after the discovery of dry rot. Sir James Dundas of Arniston was knighted by James VI,

and many of the family were eminent lawyers and statesmen. The house can be visited (01875 830515; www.arniston-house.co.uk).

Melville Castle [NT 310669], a mile or so west of Dalkeith in Midlothian, also replaced an old castle, which had been visited by Mary, Queen of Scots. This was, in turn, replaced by a symmetrical castellated mansion of the eighteenth century, which was designed by James Playfair. Melville was held by the Rennies from 1705 before passing by marriage later that century to Henry Dundas, first Viscount Melville, who came from the Arniston branch of the family. He was a very powerful fellow, and there is a memorial crowning a column in St Andrew Square in Edinburgh, where he had his town house (now the headquarters of the Royal Bank of Scotland). He is buried in one of the burial aisles at the Old Parish churchyard at Lasswade [NT 302661]. His son, Robert, second Viscount, was Secretary for Ireland and First Lord of the Admiralty, and was then very influential in Scotland. The building has recently been renovated and is now used again as a hotel (0131 654 0088; www.melvillecastle.com). During renovations, an apparition of a woman was seen to walk through a wall, later found to be a blocked-up door. The ghost has been identified as the spirit of Elizabeth Rennie, Dundas's wife, although it is also said to be the ghost of Mary, Queen of Scots.

The Dundas family also owned:

Ballinbreich Castle [NO 271204], near Newburgh, Fife; impressive ruin of a castle.
   Long held by the Leslies, but was a property of the Dundases of Kerse in the nineteenth century, who were made Earls, then Marquises, of Zetland (Shetland).

Bavelaw Castle [NT 168628], near Balerno, Edinburgh; restored L-plan tower house.
   Held by several families before coming to the Dundas family in the sixteenth century, who may have built the castle. Mary, Queen of Scots, and James VI both visited. Bavelaw passed to the Scotts of Harperigg in 1628. It was ruinous at one time, but was restored in 1900 and is still occupied.

Blairlogie Castle [NS 827969], near Stirling; small L-plan tower house.
   Held by the Spittal family, but passed by marriage to the Dundases of Blair, and then to the Hares.

Duddingston [NT 102776], near South Queensferry, West Lothian; mansion incorporating older work.
   Held by the Lindsays, but passed by marriage to the Dundases at the end of the sixteenth century, and they held the property for 200 years or more.

Dunbog [NO 285181], near Newburgh, Fife; site of castle and ruined mansion.
   Held by the Dundas Marquis of Zetland; on the site of a house of Balmerino Abbey.

Dunira [NN 738238], near Comrie, Perthshire; tower house replaced by mansion, itself mostly demolished.
   Held by the Comrie family and by the Drummonds, and then was bought Henry Dundas, Viscount Melville; he was also made Baron Dunira. The gardens featured in the Channel 4 television series *Lost Gardens*.

Fingask Castle [NO 228275], near Perth; L-plan tower house.
   Held by the Dundases in the fourteenth century, but passed to the Bruces of Clackmannan and then to the Threipland family. The gardens are occasionally open to the public (www.gardensofscotland.org).

Inchgarvie [NT 137795], an island in the Firth of Forth; some remains of a castle.

Held by the Dundas family from 1491. It was fortified to protect the Forth from the American privateer John Paul Jones in the eighteenth century, then from German bombers trying to destroy the Forth Bridge in World War II.

Kerse House [NS 915817], Grangemouth, West Lothian; site of castle and house.

Held by several families before coming to the Dundas family. Laurence Dundas was made Marquis of Zetland and Earl of Ronaldsay in 1892.

Kersie [NS 872912], near Stirling; L-plan tower house, used as farmhouse.

May have been held by the Dundases of Kerse.

Manor Castle [NS 827948], near Stirling; slight remains of castle.

Held by the Callendars, then by the Dundas family from 1479 to 1729, and then by the Haldanes and then by the Abercrombies.

Newbyres Tower [NT 344614], near Gorebridge, Midlothian; slight remains of tower.

Held by the Borthwicks in 1621, but was later sold to the Dundases of Arniston.

Newliston [NT 110736], near Kirkliston, West Lothian; tower house replaced by mansion.

Held by the Dundas family, one of whom was Duncan Dundas, Lord Lyon King of Arms from 1452 to 1470, before passing by marriage to the Dalrymples of Stair in 1699, and then later to the Hog family. The mansion and grounds are open for some weeks in the spring/summer (0131 333 3231).

Powfoulis [NS 918856], near Stenhousemuir, Falkirk; mansion on site of castle.

Held by the Bruces, but sold to the Dundases in 1729 and they held Powfoulis until 1855 when it was sold to the Dawsons. Now a hotel (01324 831267; www.powfoulis.co.uk).

Quarrell or **Carron Hall** [NS 891840], near Stenhousemuir, Falkirk; castle or old house replaced by mansion.

Held by several families including by the Elphinstones before coming to the Dundas family, who held the property in the nineteenth century. They were involved in mining coal on their lands.

Shank House [NT 334611], near Gorebridge, Midlothian; ruinous house.

Long held by the Shank family and then possibly by George Mackenzie of Rosehaugh, but was purchased by the Dundases of Arniston in 1753 and was then absorbed into the Arniston estate.

www.dundas.co.za
No. of castles/sites: 19
Rank: 72=/764

Bavelaw Castle (M&R) – see previous page

Dunlop

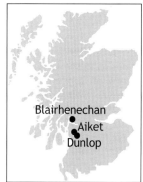

The name is territorial and comes from the lands of Dunlop, which are a couple of miles north of Stewarton in Ayrshire. The name may be derived from 'dun lub', which means the 'fort or hill of the bend'; or it may mean 'muddy hill'. The family is on record from the middle of the thirteenth century.

Dunlop House [NS 428493] in Ayrshire is a large Jacobean mansion of 1833, but stands on the site of an old castle. The lands were held by the Dunlops from about 1260, and they lived here until 1858 when the line failed. It is from here that the well-known 'Dunlop cheese' originates, created by Barbara Gilmour in the seventeenth century.

Aiket Castle [NS 388488] stands some miles southeast of Beith in the same parish. It is a sixteenth-century tower house of four storeys, extended and altered down the centuries. Aiket was held by the Cunninghams, but passed to the Dunlops at the beginning of the eighteenth century. The building later housed farm labourers, was gutted by fire in the 1960s, and was then restored and reoccupied in 1979.

Blairhenechan [NS 338792], now known as **Drumhead**, and a mile or so north-west of Cardross in Dunbartonshire, was held by the Buchanans. The property passed to the Dunlops, who changed their name to Buchanan-Dunlop. There was a castle, but this was replaced by the mansion of Drumhead, and the family still apparently live here.

The Dunlops also owned:

Bishopton House [NS 422717], near Bridge of Weir, Renfrewshire; tower house.

Held by the Brisbanes and by others including by the Dunlops. The castle was used as a farmhouse, but is now part of the Convent of the Good Shepherd.

Cathkin House [NS 627588], near Rutherglen, Glasgow; castle or old house replaced by mansion.

Held by several families, including by the Dunlops before passing to the MacLeas.

Corsock House [NX 760755], near Castle Douglas, Galloway; castle [NX 758748] replaced by mansion.

Held by the Neilsons but the modern house was a property of the Murray Dunlops about 1880. The gardens are open to the public by appointment only (01644 440250; www.gardensof scotland.org).

Tollcross [NS 637637], Glasgow; castle replaced by mansion.

Held by the Corbetts but was sold in 1810 to the Dunlops and then acquired by the city of Glasgow in 1896. The present mansion, dating from 1848, is now special needs housing.

www.angelfire.com/fl/ClanDunlop/
No. of castles/sites: 7
Rank: 182=/764
Xref: Dunlap

Dunmore

The name is territorial and comes from the lands and barony of Dundemore or Dunmore, which lie five miles north-west of Cupar in the north of Fife. The family are on record from the thirteenth century.

At **Dundemore** [NO 303189] are the remains of a seventeenth-century house, which have been altered for use as a barn and granary, among the farm buildings of Denmuir. The lands were held by the Dunmore family from the thirteenth century or earlier, and they fought in the Wars of Independence. The lands probably passed from the Dunmores in the fourteenth century, and were later held by the Pattersons.

Airdrie House [NO 567084] stands three miles west of Crail in Fife, and is an altered sixteenth-century tower house, which is dated 1586, and the lands were held by the Dunmores. One of the family was Regent during the minority of Alexander III, and the family fought for the Scots in the Wars of Independence. Airdrie passed to the Lumsdens in the fifteenth century, then to others, and is still occupied.

Ballindalloch Castle [NS 535885], a mile west of Balfron in Stirlingshire, has gone but a large nineteenth-century mansion stands on the site. The lands were held by the Cunningham Earls of Glencairn, but had passed to the Dunmore family by the eighteenth century, then to the Coopers in the next century. The gardens are occasionally open to the public by appointment only (01360 440202; www.gardensofscotland.org).

No. of castles/sites: 3
Rank: 328=/764
Xref: Dundemore

Dunnet

The name comes from the place in Caithness in the far north of Scotland, and the name is on record from the sixteenth century.

Hallgreen Castle [NO 832721], which is just east of the Kincardineshire village of Inverbervie, is a sixteenth-century L-plan tower house of three storeys and an attic. It has been altered down the years and there is a modern mansion.

Hallgreen Castle 1910?

The lands were held by the Dunnet family, and they built a castle, although the property passed to the Raits in the fifteenth century. Several ghosts are said to haunt Hallgreen, including that of a cloaked man, a woman who reputedly killed herself after the death of her child, and two servant girls. The building has been 'restored'.

No. of castles/sites: 1
Rank: 537=/764
Xref: Dinnet

Dunwoodie

The name is territorial and comes from the lands and barony of Dinwoodie, which are some five and a half miles north of Lochmaben in Dumfries and Galloway. There are as many as one hundred different ways of spelling the name in old documents.

The lands of **Dinwoodie** [NY 108907] were held by the family from the thirteenth century, and there was a castle or tower house here, although this has gone. Thomas Dunwoodie of that Ilk was slain by the Jardines in his own house in 1504, and another laird was killed in Edinburgh eight years later. The lands passed to the Maxwells in the sixteenth century, although Sir Robert Maxwell of Dinwoodie was murdered in 1605.

Applegarth [NY 105840], two miles north-west of Lockerbie also in Dumfries and Galloway, was also held by the Dunwoodies from the thirteenth century. There was a tower house, but the lands had passed to the Jardines by 1575.

freepages.genealogy.rootsweb.com/~jwar/
No. of castles/sites: 2
Rank: 396=/764
Xref: Dinwoodie

Pitkerro House (M&R) – see next column (Durham)

Durham

The name comes from the great city, cathedral and castle of Durham in the north-east of England. It is on record as a surname in Scotland from the middle of the fifteenth century.

Grange of Monifieth [NO 490330], just north-east of Monifieth in Angus, was held by the Durhams from 1322. There was a castle but it was demolished in 1829. In 1650 the Marquis of Montrose was held here on his way to Edinburgh to be executed. He nearly escaped by getting his guards drunk, but he was spotted and recaptured.

Largo Castle [NO 418034], half a mile north of Lower Largo in Fife, has all but been demolished except for a round tower. The property was held by the Blacks, then by the Gibsons of Durie, and then by the Durhams from 1633. Sir Alexander Durham of Largo was Lyon King of Arms in the seventeenth century. Around 1750 the old castle was mostly demolished to build Largo House, designed by John Adam, itself now a ruined shell. The Durham family held the lands until 1868.

The Durhams also owned:
Bonnington House [NT 111691], near Ratho, Midlothian; old house.
  Held by the Erskines, by the Foulis family and by the Durhams, and then by the Cunninghams and by the Wilkies.
Duntarvie Castle [NT 091765], near South Queensferry, West Lothian; ruined tower house.
  Held the Durhams in 1588, and they built the present castle,

Duntarvie Castle (M&R)

although there was apparently a stronghold here from the thirteenth century. The castle was abandoned about 1840 and has been 'being restored' for many years.
Duntervy Castle [NS 828401], near Lanark; site of castle.
  Held by the Durhams in the sixteenth century, and they built the Durham Aisle, part of the first post-Reformation church in Lesmahagow.
Pitkerro House [NO 453337], near Broughty Ferry, Angus; mansion and tower house.
  Held by the Durhams from 1534, and they built the tower house, but it was later sold to the Dick family. The house was restored in 1902 and is still occupied.

No. of castles/sites: 6 / Rank: 212=/764

Durie

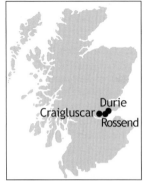

The name is territorial and comes from the lands of Durie, which are just north-west of Leven in the south of Fife. The derivation may be from 'du Roi', indicating that they were originally from France. One story is that the Duries came to Scotland in the retinue of Queen Margaret in the 1060s; she was married to Malcolm III, more commonly known as Canmore. Many of the family were eminent churchmen (also see below) and Andrew Durie (brother of George Durie, mentioned below) was Bishop of Galloway but died in 1558 apparently from shock at witnessing a riot by a Protestant mob. His son Robert was minister at Anstruther and then of the Scots kirk at Leyden in the Netherlands.

Durie House [NO 372025] is a three-storey classical mansion, and dates from 1762, although there was a castle on the site. The lands belonged to the Duries from the thirteenth century until the beginning of the sixteenth century. The property then passed to Sir Alexander Kemp, a favourite of James V, before passing back to the Duries. Mary, Queen of Scots, stayed here in 1565, but the Duries were later forfeited and the lands were sold to the Gibsons in 1614. The house is still occupied.

Rossend or **Burntisland Castle** [NT 225859] stands on a hill above the harbour in Burntisland also in Fife, and is an altered sixteenth-century tower house, which may have much earlier work. The lands were held by

Rossend Castle (M&R)

Dunfermline Abbey, but passed to the Duries. In 1563, while Mary, Queen of Scots, was staying in the castle, the French poet Chatelard secreted himself in the Queen's bedchamber. He had done the same at Holyrood and been pardoned, but this second attempt led to his execution by beheading at the Mercat Cross in

St Andrews. The property eventually passed to the Melvilles of Murdocairnie and to the Wemyss family before Rossend Castle was used as a boarding house. The building was restored from 1971 and is now occupied as offices.

Just a couple of miles north of Dunfermline, again in Fife, is **Craigluscar** [NT 066908], where the Duries had a castle or house. The lands were held by the Duries from the sixteenth century, and were owned by George Durie, Abbot of Dunfermline. The abbot was a friend of Mary, Queen of Scots, and it was he who made certain that most of the remains of St Margaret and Malcolm Canmore made their way abroad at the Reformation. His son, John, was educated in Paris and in Louvain, and returned to Scotland and was active in the south-west for the Catholics. Margaret Macbeth or Macbeith (perhaps a Beaton), was the wife of one of the lairds of Craigluscar, and was in demand for her knowledge of herbs and medicine. Margaret was in attendance at the births of royal babies at Dunfermline Palace. She is said to have been instrumental in saving the life of the future Charles I. The lands were held by the Duries until 1909, the line continues as the (Dewar) Duries of Durie, and the family apparently now lives in Stirlingshire.

The Duries also held:
Killernie Castle [NT 032924], near Cowdenbeath, Fife; ruins of Z-plan tower house.
    Held by the Colvilles in 1542 but passed to the Duries, then to the Scotts of Balwearie.
Scotscraig [NO 445283], near Tayport, Fife; mansion on site of castle.
    Held by many families, including by the Duries for some time.
Tayport Castle [NO 457291], Tayport, Fife; site of strong castle.
    Held by the Melvilles, but had passed to the Duries by 1599, then went to the Douglases. The castle was completely demolished by 1855.

No. of castles/sites: 6
Rank: 212=/764

Durward

The name comes from the important and powerful office of 'door-ward' to the king. It was held by the de Lundin family from the thirteenth century, and passed from father to son. The family held lands in Fife but the Lundins went to Aberdeenshire in pursuit of the Earldom of Mar and changed their name to Durward. They did not succeed to the earldom but they still became major landowners, although they were not to remain in prominence for long. Sir Alan Durward founded Blackfriars in Montrose in Angus in 1275, but there are no remains of this establishment. Also see the entry for the Lundin family.

Coull Castle [NJ 513023], two or so miles north of Aboyne in Aberdeenshire, was once a strong place consisting of a pentagonal courtyard with a twin-towered gatehouse and other towers. It dates from the thirteenth century, but is now very fragmentary. The lands were held by the Durwards from the thirteenth century. Alan Durward was Justiciar of Scotland before 1246, but he was accused of siding with the English and fled south in 1252. The castle was damaged in 1297, repaired soon afterwards, and was then garrisoned by the English. Coull was slighted during Robert the Bruce's campaign in 1307-08, and does not appear to have been reused. One story is that the bell of St Maddan of the nearby church of Coull would toll of its own accord when one of the Durwards was near death.

Peel Ring of Lumphanan [NJ 576037] is also near Aboyne, and was also held by the Durwards in the thirteenth century. All that remains is a large but low motte or mound defended by a wide ditch. The motte was enclosed by a strong stone wall, and there was a building called Hatton House on the site and, although occupied until 1782, this has gone. Lumphanan is associated with Macbeth, who was slain here in 1057; the lands had passed to the Irvines by the fifteenth century. The site is the care of Historic Scotland and open to the public (01667 460232).

Urquhart Castle [NH 531286] stands in a lovely position by the banks of Loch Ness, although perhaps not in the strongest of positions, and is a large but shattered ruin. It may have been built by the Durwards on a much older site: this is traditionally the stronghold the Pictish king Brude where St Columba confronted a water kelpie or monster in the loch (there have been many reported sightings of the big beastie from near Urquhart). The property passed to the Comyns, and saw much action in the Wars of Independence, and then went to the Gordons and to the Grants, before being deliberately slighted in 1691. The castle is now in the care of Historic Scotland and is open to the public all year (01456 450551).

Urquhart Castle 1907? – see previous column

The Durwards also held:

Castle Maud [NO 624995], near Banchory, Aberdeenshire; slight remains of castle.
    Held by the Durwards but was also used as a hunting lodge by the Bishops of Aberdeen.

Peel of Fichlie [NJ 460139], near Kildrummy village, Aberdeenshire; fine motte with traces of a wall.
    Held by the Earls of Mar in 1228, but passed to the Durwards, who probably built the castle.

Peel of Lintrathen [NO 263540], near Alyth, Angus; site of castle.
    Held by the Durwards, but passed to the Ogilvies. This is one of the places where they may have kept the Bell of St Madden.

Strachan [NO 657921], near Banchory, Aberdeenshire; remains of motte.
    Held by the Giffords in 1200 but then by the Durwards. The name is pronounced 'Straan'.

No. of castles/sites: 7
Rank: 182=/764
Xref: Dorward

Dyce

The name comes from the lands of Dyce to the north of Aberdeen, and there is now a town, really a suburb of the city, and airport of that name. The family were burgesses of Aberdeen and are mentioned from the middle of the fifteenth century.

Disblair House [NJ 862197], two mile west of New Machar in Aberdeenshire, dates from the nineteenth century, but there was a castle or old house here as there is a heraldic panel and an old doocot. The property was held by the Thompsons, by the Setons and by the Forbeses, before being a possession of the Dyce family about 1750.

No. of castles/sites: 1
Rank: 537=/764

Eadie

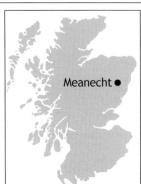

The name is from a nick-name for Adam, 'Adie', and spellings include Addie, Adie, Eadie and Eddy. The name is on record in Scotland from the first quarter of the sixteenth century. Addison is the 'son of Adie'.

The family held a property called **Moneaght**, probably now **Meanecht** [NJ 755062], five or so miles north-east of Banchory in Aberdeenshire. There may have been a castle or old house, and members of the family were burgesses of Aberdeen.

www.eddyfamily.com
No. of castles/sites: 1
Rank: 537=/764
Xrefs: Addie; Adie; Eddy

Eason

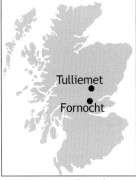

The name may come from 'son of Adam', and the family are believed to be connected to the Toshes of Glentilt, one of the clans that made up Clan Chattan. The Aysons (Easons) held Fornocht from around 1360 or earlier, after they had received a charter from the future Robert II. There appears to have been a castle or small tower at **Fornocht** (or **Fornought**) [NN 947248], which is five or so miles east of Crieff in Perthshire. The Easons held the lands until 1504 when they were sold to the Drummonds.

The Eason family also held **Tulliemet** [NN 996540], one and a half miles east of Ballinluig, further north in Perthshire. There may have been a castle or tower but the present mansion dates from around the turn of the nineteenth century, and is a small classical mansion. By then the property was held by the Dicks.

No. of castles/sites: 2
Rank: 396=/764
Xrefs: Ayson; Esson

Eccles

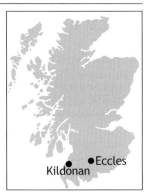

The name is territorial and comes from the lands of Eccles, although there are places with this name in Berwickshire and near Thornhill in Dumfries and Galloway.

Eccles House [NX 848961], two miles west and north of Thornhill, is a mansion of 1830 with later remodelling, but incorporates a tower house dating from the sixteenth century. The lands were held by the Eccles family, one of whom was given remission for a murder in 1526. The property passed to the Maitlands later in the sixteenth century.

Kildonan [NX 227831], half a mile north-west of Barrhill in Ayrshire, was held by the Eccles family from the fifteenth century or earlier, but was a property of the Chalmers family in the seventeenth century. The present building is a large modern mansion, built for the Millers in 1914-23, but it stands on the site of an earlier house.

No. of castles/sites: 2
Rank: 396=/764

Edgar

The name comes from the first name 'Eadgar' or 'Edgar' from Old English, which means 'happy spear'. Edgar, King of Scots in the eleventh century and son of Malcolm Canmore and Margaret, is the first to be recorded in Scotland using the name.

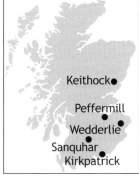

The Edgar family held lands in Nithsdale around the time of the Wars of Independence, as well as in Berwickshire and in Edinburgh. The Adairs (also see that name), who were prominent in the south-west of Scotland, are thought to be descended from the Edgars of Nithsdale.

Sanquhar Castle [NS 786092], south of the village of Sanquhar in Nithsdale in Dumfries and Galloway, is a ruin of a large stronghold, and is associated with the Crichtons. Before it came to them, the castle was held by the Edgars, one of whom was Sheriff of Dumfries in 1329. The ruin is accessible with care.

Kirkpatrick Tower [NY 275701] stood a few miles north-west of Gretna near the English border, but nothing now remains except two date stones. The property was held by the Edgar family, but passed to the Flemings.

Wedderlie House [NT 640515], just north of Westruther in Berwickshire in the Borders, is a mansion of 1680 but incorporates an L-plan tower house dating from the sixteenth century. The lands were held by the

Wedderlie House (M&R)

Polwarths, before passing to the Edgars in 1327, and they were in possession for 400 years. The Stewart Lords Blantyre acquired the property in 1733. The building later became ruinous, but it has been restored and is still occupied. This is one of many castles said to be haunted by a Green Lady.

Keithock [NO 603634] lies a couple of miles north of Brechin in Angus, and was held by the Edgars from the seventeenth century, and perhaps before, until 1790. There is a mansion on the site.

To the south-east of Edinburgh, **Peffermill House** [NT 284717] is an altered seventeenth-century tower house, which rises to three storeys and a garret. The lands were held by the Prestons of Craigmillar, but were sold to the Edgars, and they built the house. It then passed through various families; and Sir Walter Scott

Peffermill House (M&R)

used the house in *The Heart of Midlothian*, calling it Dumbiedykes. The house is still occupied.

www.clanedgar.com
No. of castles/sites: 5
Rank: 240=/764

Edington

The name is territorial and comes from the lands of Edington, which are a mile or so east of Chirnside in Berwickshire in the south-east of the Borders.

Edington Castle [NT 896562] was once a strong castle and was defended by a moat, but it was

abandoned and then demolished in 1777. Only one wall survives. There was also a small tower or bastle house [NT 889552], which was destroyed by the English in the sixteenth century. The lands were held by the Edingtons from the twelfth century, and Walter Edington was taken prisoner at Dunbar in 1296 and was imprisoned in Fotheringhay Castle. David Edington of that Ilk signed a bond of adherence to James VI in 1567, but the property was sold to the Ramsays of Dalhousie in 1594.

No. of castles/sites: 1
Rank: 537=/764

Edmonstone

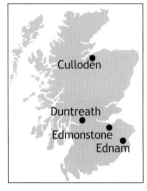

The name comes from the personal name 'Edmund' and 'ton', 'ton' being a settlement or residence. The lands of Edmonstone lie to the south-east of Edinburgh near Dander-hall, and the family may have come to Scotland in the retinue of Queen Mar-garet, wife of Malcolm Canmore, in the eleventh century.

Edmonstone Castle [NT 304704] was held by the family from 1248 or earlier, and Sir William Edmonstone was killed at the Battle of Flodden in 1513. The property passed to the Rait family in the seventeenth century, and then to the Wauchopes of Niddrie. There was a castle but it was replaced by a mansion.

Ednam [NT 737372] was held by the Edmonstones from the fourteenth century, and is located two or so miles north and east of Kelso in the Borders. John Edmonstone married Isabel, widow of James, Earl of Douglas, and Robert II's daughter. The family held the property for 250 years, and have a burial enclosure in the kirkyard [NT 737372] at Ednam. They had a castle or seat at Ednam, but the precise location is not certain.

Culloden House [NH 721465], three and a half miles east of Inverness, is a fine mansion dating from the eighteenth century but incorporating vaulted cellars from an old castle. The property was held by the Mackintoshes but was then a property of the Edmonstones until the property was sold to the Forbeses in 1672. The building is now used as a hotel (01463 790461; www.cullodenhouse.co.uk).

Some miles north of Milngavie near Glasgow in the west of Scotland, **Duntreath Castle** [NS 536811] is a large, altered courtyard castle, which dates from the fifteenth century. The castle had a strong tower, and was a property of the Edmonstones of Culloden from 1445. The castle was abandoned around 1740 for lands at Redhall in Ireland, and became ruinous, but in 1857

Duntreath Castle (M&R)

the building was restored, remodelled and extended. The family had been made Baronets in 1774. By 1958 all but the original keep, and a Victorian range and gatehouse, had been demolished. The house is still apparently occupied by the Edmonstones.

Some of the family went to Shetland in the sixteenth century, and descendants are now the Edmonstons of Buness, which is at Baltasound.

The Edmonstones also held:

Boyne Castle [NJ 612657], near Portsoy, Aberdeenshire; ruined and overgrown castle.
Held by the Edmonstones in the fourteenth century but passed by marriage to the Ogilvies. Still occupied in 1723.

Broich House [NS 641951], near Kippen, Stirlingshire; site of old house or tower house.
Held by the Shaws and then by the Edmonstones in the seventeenth century, but was sold to the Leckies in 1773. Broich was demolished in 1852 and a new mansion, Arngomery House, but built nearby.

Colzium House [NS 729786], near Kilsyth, Glasgow; mansion and site of castle [NS 729788].
The lands were held by the Callanders and by the Livingstones, but the property was held by the Edmonstones of Duntreath in the nineteenth century, who gifted it to the local council. The gardens are open to the public (01236 624031; www.northlan.gov.uk).

Craig of Boyne Castle [NJ 615660], near Portsoy, Aberdeenshire; very ruinous castle.
Held by the Comyns and by the Edmonstones before passing to the Ogilvies of Dunlugas around 1575.

Dunglass Castle [NS 436735], near Dumbarton; some remains of castle.
Held by the Colquhouns, but passed to the Edmonstones in 1738. In 1783 the castle was partly demolished but the property was sold in 1812 to the Buchanans, and they rebuilt the castle. Now derelict or ruinous again and in the grounds of an oil terminal.

Edmonston Castle [NT 070422], near Biggar, Lanarkshire; ruinous castle.
Held by the Edmonstones and named after them, but passed

Edmonston Castle (M&R)

to the Douglases in 1322 and then later went to the Baillies of Walston and then to others.

Mellerstain [NT 648392], near Earlston, Borders; magnificent mansion.
The lands were held by several families and then for two years by the Edmonstones of Ednam (1640-42). The property then passed to the Baillies, then Baillie-Hamiltons, Earls of Haddington, and they built Mellerstain, which is open to the public (01573 410225; www.mellerstain.com).

Newton Castle [NN 731013], near Doune, Stirlingshire; L-plan tower house.
The tower was built by the Edmonstones, hereditary keepers of Doune Castle (which is close by, is in the care of Historic

Newton Castle (M&R)

Scotland, and is open to the public). The family were Jacobites, and in 1708 the Laird of Newton was arrested. The property was sold to John Campbell, a Glasgow merchant, in 1858, and the house is still occupied.

Tulliallan Castle [NS 927888], near Kincardine, Fife; fine ruinous castle.

Held by the Douglas family, then by the Edmonstones from 1410 or earlier, before passing by marriage to the Blackadder family, and then went to the Bruces of Carnock and then to others. The old castle is being restored.

www.edmonstone.com
No. of castles/sites: 14
Rank: 104=/764

Edward

There are two origins from this name, one from the English personal name 'Edward', which means 'happy ward or guardian', and is on record from the middle of the fifteenth century. The other is from 'Udard' or 'Udwart', an Old English personal name. This latter name is on record from the middle of the twelfth century as a surname and, although this spelling was used in the sixteenth century, was then confused with and changed to Edward.

Balruddery [NO 315322], some six miles west of Dundee, was held by the Edward family (from 'Udard', the second origin). There may have been a castle, and there was a mansion dating from 1820 with later extensions, but this was demolished in the 1960s. Campbell of Balruddery is also on record.

Pearsie House [NO 366594], three miles north of Kirriemuir also in Angus, dates from 1820 and may stand on the site of a castle or older house. The lands were held by the Edward family, but passed by marriage to the Wedderburns in 1738.

No. of castles/sites: 2
Rank: 396=/764

Eglinton

The name is territorial and comes from the lands of the same name, which are north of Irvine in Ayrshire. It is derived from 'Eglun', a personal name, and 'ton', 'ton' being a settlement or seat. The name is on record in charters from the beginning of the thirteenth century.

Eglinton Castle [NS 323423] is a huge and once grand castellated mansion, which dates from the eighteenth century, but stands on the site of an old castle. The lands were held by the Eglintons from 1205 or earlier until they passed by marriage to the Montgomerys in the latter half of the fourteenth century. The Montgomerys were made Earls of Eglinton in 1528. The remains of the castle stand in a country park (01294 551776; www.north-ayrshire.gov.uk).

Ardrossan Castle [NS 233424], also in Ayrshire, passed to the Montgomerys at the same time.

No. of castles/sites: 2
Rank: 396=/764

Elder

The name comes from the 'elder' of two members of the same family who have the same name, and is recorded as a surname in Scotland from the fifteenth century.

Knock Castle [NS 194631] is a ruinous tower house, dating from the sixteenth century, and was long held by the Frasers. The old castle was replaced by nearby Knock Castle, a baronial pile built for the Elder family and completed in 1852. The old castle was then turned into a garden folly.

No. of castles/sites: 1
Rank: 537=/764

Ellam

The name comes from the lands and barony of Ellem, which are two or so miles west and south of Abbey St Bathans in Berwickshire in the Borders. The family are mentioned in 1296, and it is possible that there was a castle at, or near, **Ellemford** [NT 730604].

Butterdean or **Kilspindie Castle** [NT 797648] lies four miles south of Cockburnspath, also in Berwickshire. It was held by the Ellem family from the fifteenth century until 1600 or later. Butterdean was later a possession of the Hays of Butterdean, and very little remains of the castle, which formerly had a moat.

No. of castles/sites: 1
Rank: 537=/764
Xrefs: Ellom; Ellem

Elliot

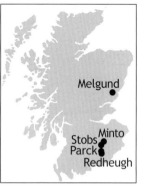

The name probably comes from a personal name from the Old English 'Aelfwuld', and it was spelt 'Elwald' or 'Elwold' in the fifteenth and sixteenth centuries, and then 'Elot'. The family held lands in Liddesdale in the Borders, and like most Border families became notorious for their unruliness and reiving. Many different ways of spelling the name are on record, and different branches of the family adopted specific spellings (which are not replicated here).

Redheugh Castle [NY 498902], two miles north of Newcastleton in the Borders, was the main stronghold of the Elliots, but there are no remains. Robert Elliot, thirteenth chief, was killed at the Battle of Flodden in 1513, and the family were keepers of Hermitage Castle. In 1565 the Elliots feuded with the Scotts, after some of the family had been executed for stealing cattle, but the feud ended in an indecisive battle. James Hepburn, fourth Earl of Bothwell, was wounded in a skirmish with the Elliots, but their lands were devastated in 1569 in retaliation. Redheugh Castle was probably abandoned by the beginning of the seventeenth century. James VI prosecuted a policy of punishments on miscreants in the Borders, and many of the Elliots went to Ireland.

Parck [NY 500910] is half a mile or so north of Redheugh, but again there is nothing left of a tower house. In 1566 John o' the Park, otherwise known as Wee Jock Elliot, stabbed and seriously wounded James Hepburn, fourth Earl of Bothwell, after having been shot himself. Bothwell had been rounding up local members of the Elliot family for reiving. Elliot soon died from his wound, but although Bothwell was injured, he recovered after a visit from Mary, Queen of Scots, at Hermitage Castle. As mentioned above, the Elliots were punished and their lands were ravaged three years later.

Stobs Castle [NT 510084], four miles south of Hawick in the Borders, is a castellated mansion built in the 1790s and designed by Robert Adam. It replaced a castle that was (accidentally) burnt in 1712, when virtually all the

Stobs Castle 1910?

family papers were destroyed. Stobs was held by the Cranstouns, but passed to the Elliots of Stobs, who were made Baronets of Nova Scotia in 1666 and they held the property until the twentieth century. The line continues, but they now apparently live in Australia.

Minto House [NT 573203], five and a half miles north-east of Hawick in the Borders, is a large ruinous Adam mansion, which dates from the 1740s. The mansion replaced an old tower house. The property was held by the Turnbulls, by the Stewarts and by the Scotts, but was sold to the Elliots. Gilbert Elliot was a Lord of Session as Lord Minto in 1705, as was his son, another Gilbert. His daughter was Jane or Jean Elliot and she wrote 'The Flowers of the Forest', lamenting the Battle of Flodden; while his son, another Gilbert, was an author, poet and MP. His son, yet another Gilbert, became Earl of Minto in 1813, as well as Viscount Melgund. Gilbert John Murray Kynmond, fourth Earl, who succeeded in 1891, was Governor General of Canada from 1898-1904, and then Viceroy of India 1905-10. The house has been mostly demolished, having been neglected for years, and set on fire in 1992.

The Elliots also held many other towers and properties:
Arkleton Tower [NY 380914], near Langholm, Dumfries and Galloway; tower replaced by mansion.
  Held by the Maxwells and by the Armstrongs, but from 1671 until the twentieth century was held by the Elliots.
Baholm Tower [NY 515950], near Newcastleton, Borders; site of tower.
  Held by the Elliots.
Borthwickbrae [NT 413135], near Hawick, Borders; mansion on site of castle or older house.
  Held by the Elliots in the eighteenth and nineteenth centuries, now the Eliott Lockharts of Cleghorn.
Breaken (or **Prinkinghaugh**?) **Tower** [NY 544942], near Newcastleton, Borders; site of tower.
  Held by the Elliots. The last vestige was removed in 1792.
Brugh [NT 467058], near Hawick, Borders; site of tower.
  Held by the Scotts of Allanhaugh in 1560, but by 1595 had passed to the Elliots, then by 1632 was held by the Scotts of Buccleuch.
Burnhead Tower [NT 514166], near Hawick, Borders; altered tower house.
  Held by the Scotts or by the Elliots. Hobbie Elliot of Burnhead was accused of engaging in a foray in 1584. The property passed to the Scotts and the tower is still occupied.
Byrsted Tower [NY 568999], near Newcastleton, Borders; site of tower house.
  May have been held by the Elliots or by the Armstrongs.
Clintwood Castle [NY 538910], near Newcastleton, Borders; site of tower.
  Held by the Soulis family, then later probably by the Elliots. There may also have been a tower at **Flight** [NY 534904].
Copshaw Tower [NY 480876], near Newcastleton, Borders; site of tower.
  Held by John Elliot of Copshaw. Ruinous by 1793.
Copshaws Tower [NY 583984], near Newcastleton; site of tower.
  Held by the Elliots of Copshaw.
Dinlabyre [NY 528920], near Newcastleton, Borders; house incorporating tower.
  Held by the Elliots but had passed to the Olivers by the middle of the eighteenth century.
Fatlips Castle [NT 582209], near Jedburgh, Borders; tower house.
  Held by the Turnbulls then by the Stewarts, but was bought by Sir Gilbert Elliot of Minto in 1705. The tower was restored in 1897 but is apparently derelict again.

Foulshiels Tower [NY 492916], near Newcastleton, Borders; site of tower.
  Held by the Elliots.
Gorrenberry Tower [NY 464973], near Newcastleton, Borders; site of tower.
  Held by the Elliots; the tower reputedly had a brownie or a mischievous spirit called a Shellycoat (because his coat was covered in shells so that he rattled when he moved).
Haggishaugh [NY 545944], near Newcastleton, Borders; house on site of tower.
  Held by the Elliots but by the end of the nineteenth century was owned by the Jardines of Dryfeholm. A cannon ball was found here.
Hartsgarth Tower [NY 494926], near Newcastleton, Borders; site of tower.
  Held by the Elliots.
Kellie Castle [NO 608402], near Arbroath, Angus; fine L-plan tower house.
  Perhaps a property of the Elliots from the fourteenth to the seventeenth centuries, but also held by the Ochterlonys, and by several other families.
Larriston Tower [NY 557937], near Newcastleton, Borders; site of tower.
  William Elliot of Larriston was charged with making a raid into Tynedale in 1593.
Melgund Castle [NO 546564], near Brechin, Angus; large and impressive castle.
  Held by the Beatons and by several others but later passed to

Melgund Castle (M&R)

the Elliots, Earls of Minto and Viscounts Melgund from 1813, who held it until 1990. Being restored.
Morton House [NT 254679], Edinburgh; mansion incorporating old work.
  Held by the Sinclairs of Rosslyn, then by the Riggs and by the Trotters of Charterhall, before coming to the Elliotts.
Riccarton Tower [NY 544958], near Newcastleton, Borders; site of tower.
  Held by the Elliots or by the Croziers. Some remains of the tower survive, although these have been built into a sheepfold.
Thorlieshope Tower [NY 571965], near Bonchester Bridge, Borders; site of tower.
  Held by the Elliots.
Wolflee [NT 589093], near Bonchester Bridge, Borders; site of tower.
  Held by the Elliots. A house incorporating a vaulted cellar was rebuilt in 1698 and in the 1820s, but the building was burned down in 1977.

www.elliotclan.com
www.elliotclanusa.com
No. of castles/sites: 27 / Rank: 47=/764
Xref: Ellot; Eliott

Ellis

The name comes from 'Elias', a personal name which was popular in medieval times, and it is recorded as a surname in Scotland from the fifteenth century. The family owned several properties in Edinburgh, in Midlothian and in West Lothian.

Illieston (from **Elliston**) **House** [NT 010700] is some two miles south-east of Broxburn in West Lothian. The house is an altered T-plan tower house, which dates from the seventeenth century. The kings of Scots are

Illieston House (M&R)

said to have had a hunting lodge here, and the lands were held by the Noble family and then by the Grahams, before passing to the Ellis family in the seventeenth century. The property was sold to the Hope Earls of Hopetoun in 1765, and the house is still occupied.

Stenhouse [NT 215717] to the south and west of Edinburgh was held by Patrick Ellis, a wealthy Edinburgh merchant, in 1623; and he extended an L-plan tower house. It had been abandoned by the 1930s, but has since been restored and is now a conservation centre.

Saughton House [NT 205713], to the west of Edinburgh, was a seventeenth-century L-plan tower house, but it was burnt out in the 1950s and was completely demolished. The property belonged to the Watsons, but passed to the Ellis family, who built the tower. It later was used as a private lunatic asylum, and was then bought by the local council. The 1908 the Scottish National Exhibition took place in the grounds, which are now a public park.

Mortonhall [NT 262683] to the south of Edinburgh was long associated with the Sinclairs, but passed to the Ellis family, then to the Trotters. There was a castle which had a moat and drawbridge, but this was removed when a classical mansion was built nearby in 1769. The house has now been divided into three separate dwellings, and there is a caravan and camping site (www.mortonhall.co.uk).

A few miles south-east of Dalkeith in Midlothian is **Southsyde Castle** [NT 369638], a very altered

Southsyde Castle (M&R)

seventeenth-century L-plan tower house. The lands belonged to Newbattle Abbey, but had passed to the Ellis family by 1640.

No. of castles/sites: 5
Rank: 240=/764

Elphinstone

The name is territorial and comes from the lands of Elphinstone, which are two miles south-east of Tranent in East Lothian. The name is on record from the thirteenth century, and the first of the family to hold the lands of Elphinstone appears to have been an Allan de Swinton, and the family name was later changed to that of their lands.

William Elphinstone, who was born illegitimate in Glasgow in 1431, was Chancellor to James III until that king's murder in 1488. He was made Bishop of Aberdeen in 1483 and added a central tower and a choir to St Machar's Cathedral in Aberdeen, although these have now gone. He was also responsible for compiling the Aberdeen Breviary. The remaining part of St Machar's Cathedral is open to the public (01224 485988; www.stmachar.com).

Elphinstone Tower [NT 391698], near Tranent, was a simple (on the outside) keep or tower of three storeys, dating from the fourteenth century. The basement was vaulted and the very thick walls had multitudes of

Elphinstone Tower (M&R)

chambers and stairs contained within them. There was also a laird's lug and peephole, where the laird could listen and watch the hall in secret. The Elphinstones held the lands in the fourteenth and fifteenth centuries. Sir Alexander Elphinstone was killed in 1435 during a raid on Piperden in Northumberland, and the property apparently passed by marriage to the Johnstones soon afterwards. There was an adjoining mansion, but this was demolished in 1865, as was much of the tower, due to subsidence from mine workings. Only a few feet of the base of the keep now survives.

Some six miles north of Falkirk in central Scotland, **Airth** or **Elphinstone Tower** [NS 890889] was held by the Elphinstones from the fourteenth century, and the tower, a plain rectangular building of four storeys, was probably built about 1508 by Sir John Elphinstone. His son, Alexander, was made Lord Elphinstone by James IV but was killed at the Battle of Flodden in 1513; and another of the family, Alexander, was slain at Pinkie in 1547. Yet another Alexander was made a judge of the Supreme Court of Scotland in 1599, and later Lord High Treasurer. The property was sold to the Murray Earls of Dunmore in 1754. The fifth Earl built Dunmore Park, a large Tudor-style mansion, which is itself now a ruin. The basement of Airth Tower was remodelled as the burial vault of the Earls of Dunmore, although it was broken into and ransacked in the 1990s. The line of the Elphinstone Lords Elphinstone continues, and they now apparently live near Tyninghame in East Lothian.

Airth Castle [NS 900869], which is six miles north of Falkirk, consists of a solid keep or tower, dating from the fourteenth century, with later modifications and extensions. Airth was long held by the Bruces until 1642 when it passed to the Elphinstones, and many of the Elphinstone family are buried in the Airth aisle of the nearby ruinous Old Airth Church. The property passed to the Grahams in 1717, and since 1971 Airth has been used as a hotel and country club (01324 831411; www.airthcastlehotel.com).

Craighouse [NT 234709] is a much-altered tower house, dating originally from the sixteenth century, and stands beneath Craiglockhart Hill to the south and west of Edinburgh. It now houses offices for Napier University. Craighouse was held by the Symsons and then by the Dicks, but in 1712 it was a property of Sir Thomas Elphinstone. Elphinstone is said to have stabbed his pretty young wife, Elizabeth Pittendale, to death, wrongly believing she was having an affair with his son. Sir Thomas committed suicide, but a Green Lady began to haunt the building. The hauntings only ceased when Elizabeth's remains were removed from the burial vault of her husband. Or so the story goes. Another ghost said to haunt here is a Jacky Gordon.

The family owned several other properties:
Airdrie House [NS 749654], near Airdrie, Lanarkshire; site of mansion and castle.
  Held by the Clellands and by the Hamiltons, before passing to the Elphinstones, and then to other families until used as a local maternity hospital and then demolished in 1964.
Baberton House [NT 195696], near Edinburgh; mansion incorporating castle.
  Held by the Wardlaws, but passed to the Elphinstones in 1597, and then to the Murrays of Kilbaberton.
Barnton [NT 188758], Edinburgh; site of castle and mansion.
  Held by the Elphinstone Lord Balmerino in 1623, but passed to the Ramsays of Barnton.
Baronial Hall [NS 592641], Gorbals, Glasgow; site of tower house.
  Held by the Elphinstones from 1512. George Elphinstone was knighted by James VI in 1594, and was Provost of Glasgow in 1600, but the property was sold in 1634. It was acquired by the city of Glasgow, and was used as a town hall, school and jail, but had been completely demolished by 1870.

Candacraig [NJ 339111], near Ballater, Aberdeenshire; castle replaced by mansion.

Held by the Elphinstones, but had passed to the Andersons by 1570, and later went to the Forbeses and then to the Wallaces. The house is still occupied and was purchased by Billy Connolly. A cottage on the estate can be rented (www.candacraig.com).

Carberry Tower [NT 364697], near Musselburgh, East Lothian; tower house and mansion.

Held by several families, including by the Riggs and later by the Fullertons, but then passed by marriage to the Elphinstones. A mansion was added to the tower in 1819. The building houses a residential Christian conference centre and accommodation is available (0131 665 3135; www.carberrytower.com).

Croft an Righ House [NT 271742], Edinburgh; altered L-plan tower house.

Probably built by James Stewart, Earl of Moray, but it may have been owned by the Elphinstones at one time.

Cumbernauld Castle [NS 773759], Cumbernauld, Lanarkshire; castle replaced by mansion.

Long held by the Flemings, but passed to Elphinstones in 1747.

Drumkilbo [NO 304449], near Coupar Angus, Perthshire; mansion incorporating some of a castle.

Held by the several families, but passed to Lord Elphinstone in 1953. The building is now a hotel (01828 640445; www.drumkilbo.com).

Glack [NJ 742284], near Inverurie, Aberdeenshire; mansion.

Held by the Elphinstones from 1477 until the eighteenth century. In 1927, this branch eventually succeeded as Elphinstone of Logie, Baronets (which had been dormant since 1743). Glack passed to the Mackenzies, and was then used as part of a psychiatric hospital; the site is to be redeveloped.

Haystoun [NT 259383], near Peebles, Borders; altered L-plan tower house.

Held and built by the Elphinstones, who owned the property

Haystoun (M&R)

from 1500 until 1622, but it later passed to the Hays of Smithfield.

Herbertshire Castle [NS 804830], near Falkirk; site of castle.

Held by the Sinclairs, but passed to the Elphinstone Earl of Linlithgow in 1608, then later passed to the Stirlings and then to others. The castle was demolished in the twentieth century and the grounds are now a public park.

Kildrummy Castle [NJ 454164], Kildrummy, Aberdeenshire; magnificent ruin of a large castle.

Held by several families including by the Cochranes, and then by the Elphinstones from 1507 to 1626, when they were forced to give the property to the Erskine Earls of Mar. In the care of Historic Scotland and open to the public from April to September (01975 571331).

Lochend House [NT 273743], Edinburgh; mansion incorporating part of castle.

Held by the Logans until their forfeiture but passed to Arthur Elphinstone, sixth Lord Balmerino, in 1704, but he was executed in London for his part in the Jacobite Rising after being captured at the Battle of Culloden in 1746. The house is still occupied.

Kildrummy Castle (MC) – see previous column

Logie House (**Logie-Elphinstone**) [NJ 706258], near Inverurie, Aberdeenshire; mansion incorporating tower house.

Held by the Elphinstone family from 1670 until 1903. It was latterly used as a hotel but was damaged by fire in 1974 and only one wing is useable.

Plean Castle [NS 850870], near Stirling; restored castle.

Held by the Airths, by the Somervilles and by the Nicholsons before coming to the Elphinstones. Accommodation is available (01786 480840; www.aboutscotland.co.uk/stirling/plane.html).

Quarrell or **Carron Hall** [NS 891840], near Stenhousemuir, Falkirk; castle or old house replaced by mansion.

Held by several families including by the Bissets, before coming to the Elphinstones, who held it in the seventeenth century. Quarrell later went to the Dundas family.

Renfield [NS 501684], Renfrew; site of castle and of mansion.

Held by several families including by the Elphinstones. The site is now occupied by a golf course.

Skaithmore Tower [NS 888834], near Falkirk; site of tower house.

Held and built by Alexander, fourth Lord Elphinstone, a judge of the Supreme Court of Scotland in 1599, and later Lord Treasurer of Scotland. The tower was modified for use as a coal-pit pumping station, but was then gutted and abandoned to be demolished in the 1960s. The site has been grassed over.

Venlaw or **Smithfield Castle** [NT 253412], Peebles; mansion on site of castle.

Held by the Hays of Smithfield, then by the Dicksons, but was owned by the Elphinstones in the nineteenth century. Smithfield Castle has gone and Venlaw Castle is now a hotel (01721 730384; www.venlaw.co.uk).

Tulliallan Castle [NS 927888], near Kincardine, Fife; fine ruinous hall house.

Held by the Douglas family and then by the Edmonstones from 1410 or earlier until 1468 when it went by marriage to the Blackadders. It later went to the Bruces of Carnock, and then to the Erskines, to the Elphinstones and then to the Osbournes. The castle was replaced by a large mansion, also called Tulliallan Castle, [NS 936881] in 1820 half a mile away, which is now used as the police training college from Scotland. The old castle is being restored.

Westhall [NJ 673266], near Inverurie, Aberdeenshire; L-plan tower house.

Held by the Gordons and then by the Hornes, before passing by marriage to the Elphinstones after 1681. Still occupied.

No. of castles/sites: 26
Rank: 50=/764

Erskine

The name Erskine is territorial in origin and comes from the lands and barony of the same name, which lie just to the north of the present Erskine by the south bank of the River Clyde. The name may mean 'green rising ground', derived from early Brittonic Gaelic. Mary Erskine, the widow of James Hair, was a very wealthy woman and left money for the education of the daughters of Edinburgh burgesses. This foundation, originally the Merchant Maiden Hospital, eventually became Mary Erskine School.

Erskine Castle [NS 462720] was once a strong fortress, but it was replaced by Erskine House in the nineteenth century, and there was no trace of the old castle by 1856. The lands were held by the Erskines from 1226 or earlier, and they supported Robert the Bruce in the Wars of Independence. The Erskines became hereditary keepers of Stirling Castle, and they acquired property around Alloa, and later became Earls of Mar through marriage to the Countess of Mar in her own right. The lands of Erskine were sold to the Hamiltons of Orbiston in 1638, and then to the Stewarts, and the mansion was converted to use as hospital for limbless sailors and soldiers.

Alloa Tower [NS 889925], in Alloa in Clackmannanshire, is a tall and impressive keep or tower, dating from the fifteenth century although there may also be earlier work. There was a courtyard and a later mansion, but these have been demolished after a fire. The property was given to Sir Robert Erskine, Great Chamberlain of Scotland, in 1360, and one of the family was killed at the Battle of Flodden in 1513. Mary, Queen of Scots, was reconciled with Henry Stewart, Lord Darnley, here in 1565, and the queen made the sixth Lord, John Erskine, Earl of Mar; he was later Regent for the young James VI, and James visited the castle. Erskine's sister, Margaret, married Robert Douglas of Lochleven after being a mistress of James V. She had a son by the king, Robert Stewart, who was made Earl of Moray by Mary, Queen of Scots. Mary was imprisoned in Lochleven Castle in 1567, and Margaret Erskine was her jailer, although Mary escaped the following year.

John, sixth Earl of Mar, known as 'Bobbing John', was leader of the Jacobites in the 1715 Jacobite Rising after he felt that he had not received high enough office in the government of King George. The rebellion was poorly led and, after the indecisive battle of Sheriffmuir, Mar was forfeited and had to go into exile. The lands were bought by a relative, but the title was not restored until 1824. John's brother, James, was Lord Justice Clerk as Lord Grange and Lord of Justiciary, and he was married to Rachel Chiesly of Dalry, a great beauty, by whom he had several children. Rachel and he seem to have fallen out and, when she discovered his Jacobite plotting, James had Rachel (Lady Grange) imprisoned, first in central Scotland and then in the Western Isles. Rachel is thought to have died on Skye in 1745 and to be buried at Trumpan.

A large mansion adjoining the castle was destroyed by a fire in 1800, and a portrait of Mary, Queen of Scots, as well as many other treasures, were lost; the smell of smoke is reportedly smelt on the anniversary of the fire. The tower is still owned by the Erskines, but is in the care of The National Trust for Scotland and open to the public (01259 211701; www.nts.org.uk). The family still apparently live near Alloa.

Kildrummy Castle [NJ 454164] is near the village of Kildrummy in Aberdeenshire, and is a fantastic but ruinous castle, and was the main seat of the Earldom of Mar. The fortress and the earldom passed through several hands before coming to the Elphinstones, but was taken

Alloa Tower (M&R)

Kildrummy Castle (M&R)

over by the Erskines in 1626. The castle was captured for Cromwell's forces in 1654, and was damaged in the Jacobite Rising of 1689-90. John Erskine, sixth Earl, (mentioned above) used it as his base in the rebellion of 1715, but six years later it had passed to the Gordons of Wardhouse. The castle was afterwards deliberately dismantled, but the romantic ruin is now in the care of

Historic Scotland and open to the public from April to September (01975 571331).

Braemar Castle [NO 156924], to the north-east of the village of Braemar also in Aberdeenshire, was built by the Erskine Earl of Mar in 1628, and is an altered L-plan tower house with turrets and star-shaped artillery emplacements. The then Earl of Mar supported William and Mary, and the tower was burned by Jacobites led

Braemar Castle 1910?

by John Farquharson of Inverey. The castle was ruinous until 1748, and was held by the Farquharsons and then by the government. It was then restored and reoccupied.

Some four miles north and east of Elie in Fife, **Kellie Castle** [NO 520052] is one of the finest castles in Scotland, and is an E-plan tower house, which dates from the sixteenth century. The building is five storeys in the wings, has a good interior with plaster ceilings, and there is a magnificent walled garden with ancient

Kellie Castle (MC)

roses. The property was held by the Siwards and by the Oliphants, but was sold in 1613 to Sir Thomas Erskine of Gogar, who was a favourite of James VI and was made Earl of Kellie six years later (the earldoms of Mar and Kellie were united in 1835). Erskine had been present at the Gowrie Conspiracy in 1600, and may have been one of those who murdered the Master of Ruthven and the Earl of Gowrie at Gowrie House in Perth. Kellie Castle was abandoned in 1829, but was bought by James Lorimer in 1878 and then restored: his son was Sir Robert Lorimer, the famous architect. There is also a ghost story: Anne Erskine fell to her death from one of the upstairs windows, and unexplained footsteps have been

heard running up a turnpike stair to the chamber. In the care of The National Trust for Scotland and open to the public (01333 720271; www.nts.org.uk).

Standing three mile north-west of Montrose in Angus, **House of Dun** [NO 667599] is a fine classical mansion, built by William Adam for David Erskine, Lord Dun; but it replaced a nearby castle. The Erskines held the lands

House of Dun (MC)

from 1375, and John Erskine of Dun was a scholar and reformer in the time of Mary, Queen of Scots. The castle was the scene of a notorious case of poisoning, reputed witchcraft and murder in 1613, when the young John Erskine, heir to Dun, and his brother, Alexander, were poisoned by Robert Erskine, their uncle, and their three aunts. The older boy died in agony, while Alexander survived after a severe illness, and he eventually succeeded to the lands. Robert Erskine and two of the aunts were executed, while the third had to go into exile. The house is in the care of The National Trust for Scotland and is open to the public (01674 810264; www.nts.org.uk).

The Erskines also owned many other properties:
Airdrie House [NO 567084], near Crail, Fife; altered tower house.
> Held by several families, then by the Erskine Earls of Kellie after 1674.
Alva Castle [NS 901975], near Alva, Clackmannan; site of castle and mansion.
> Held by the Stirlings and by the Menteiths, but passed to the Erskines in 1620. This branch of the family were related to the Earls of Mar, and Sir John Erskine found a rich vein of silver in a nearby glen in 1710: the profits helped to buy him a pardon after being involved in the Jacobite Rising of 1715. The lands were sold to Johnstones of Westerhall in 1775.
Balcomie Castle [NO 626099], near Crail, Fife; L-plan tower house.
> Held by several families, including by the Learmonths, but later passed to the Erskine Earls of Kellie, and now a farmhouse.
Barjarg Tower [NX 876901], near Thornhill, Dumfries and Galloway; tower house and mansion.
> Held by Douglases of Morton, by the Griersons and by the Hunters in 1772, before passing by marriage to the Erskine Lords Tinwald in the nineteenth century.
Board [NS 713750], near Kilsyth, Glasgow; site of castle.
> Held by the Erskines until 1339, when the property was exchanged for Garscadden with the Flemings of Cumbernauld.
Bonnington House [NT 111691], near Ratho, Midlothian; house dating from 1622.
> Held by the Erskines, but by the middle of the seventeenth century had passed to the Foulis Lord Colinton, and then to the Durhams, to the Cunninghams and to the Wilkies of Ormiston.

Brechin Castle [NO 597599], Brechin, Angus; mansion on site of castle.

Held by the Maules, then by the Erskine Earls of Mar, then by the Maules again, and later by the Ramsays of Dalhousie, whose descendants still apparently live here. Brechin Castle Centre is open to the public (01356 626813; www.brechincastle centre.co.uk).

Cambo House [NO 604115], near Kingsbarns, Fife; castle replaced by mansion.

Held by the Cambo family and by the Mortons, and then by the Erskines from the seventeenth century; they were made Baronets in 1821. Two of the family were Lyon King of Arms in the seventeenth century, and the Erskines of Cambo still apparently live near Kingsbarns. The gardens are open to the public (01333 450313; www.camboestate.com).

Cardross House [NS 605976], near Port of Menteith, Stirlingshire; L-plan tower house.

Held by the Erskines from about 1590, and still apparently occupied by the Orr Ewings. Cromwell is said to have garrisoned the castle in the 1650s.

Corgarff Castle [NJ 255086], near Ballater, Aberdeenshire; altered tower house with artillery emplacements.

Held by the Erskine Earls of Mar from 1626, but passed to the Forbeses of Towie. It may have been torched with the death of all the occupants in 1571, when it was occupied by the Forbes family, and the castle was torched again by Jacobites

Corgarff Castle (M&R)

in 1689 and then by government forces in 1716. It was used by the Jacobites in the 1745-46 Rising, and was then restored as a government barracks. It is in the care of Historic Scotland and open to the public (01975 651460).

Culross Palace [NS 986862], Culross, Fife; fine town house.

Built by the Bruces but passed to the Erskines around 1700. The building has been carefully restored by The National Trust for Scotland and is open to the public (01383 880359).

Dirleton Castle [NT 518840], Dirleton, East Lothian; magnificent ruined castle with garden.

Held by the Vauxs, by the Halyburtons and by the Ruthven family, but was owned by the Erskines of Gogar in 1600, then by the Maxwells and by the Nisbets. In the care of Historic Scotland and open to the public all year (01620 850330).

Dryburgh Abbey [NT 591317], near Melrose, Borders; ruined abbey and fortified house.

Held by the Erskine Lords Cardross after the Reformation, and they lived here until 1671. They have a burial vault in the ruin of the church, and a fortified residence was created out of part of the buildings. The property was sold to the Scotts of Ancrum, and the ruins are now in the care of Historic Scotland and are open to the public (01835 822381).

Dunimarle Castle [NS 977859], near Culross, Fife; castle replaced by mansion.

Held by the Blairs, but passed to the Erskines in the nineteenth century.

Fenton Tower [NT 543822], near North Berwick, East Lothian; fine restored tower house.

Held by the Fentons, by the Whitelaws and by the Carmichaels before passing to the Erskines in the seventeenth century. They were made Viscounts Fenton, Lords Dirleton and eventually Earls of Kellie. The tower was ruinous but has been restored and luxury accommodation is available (01620 890089; www.fentontower.co.uk).

Gargunnock House [NS 715944], near Stirling; mansion incorporating old castle.

Held by the Setons, but passed to the Erskine Earls of Mar, then to the Campbells and to the Stirlings. The gardens are open to the public mid April to mid June (01786 860392; www.gardensofscotland.org).

Garscadden Castle [NS 522710], near Bearsden, Dunbartonshire; site of castle and mansion.

Held by the Flemings until 1369, then by the Erskines until 1444, then by the Galbraiths of Gartconnel and by the Colquhouns of Camstradden.

Hallyards [NT 129738], near Kirkliston, West Lothian; ruinous tower house.

Held by the Skenes, but passed to the Erskine Earls of Mar in 1619, then later went to the Marjoribanks family.

Harthill Castle [NJ 687252], near Inverurie, Aberdeenshire; large seventeenth-century castle.

Held by the Leiths, but passed to the Erskines of Pittodrie. Restored in the 1970s and occupied.

Inveramsay [NJ 742240], near Inverurie, Aberdeenshire; site of castle.

Held by the Erskines.

Linlathen House [NO 463329], near Broughty Ferry, Angus; site of castle.

Held by the Grahams of Fintry but then by the Erskines in the nineteenth century.

Mains Castle [NO 410330], near Dundee; courtyard castle.

Held by several families, including by the Erskines and by the Cairds in the nineteenth century who gave the property to the city of Dundee. The castle has been restored and the grounds are a public park.

Mar's Castle [NJ 945078], Aberdeen; site of castle and town house.

Held by the Stewart and then by the Erskine Earls of Mar. The building was dated 1494.

Mar's Wark [NS 794937], Stirling; ruinous but ornate sixteenth-century town house.

Built in 1570 by the first Earl of Mar, Regent of Scotland during the minority of James VI and hereditary keeper of Stirling Castle. The family used the mansion until 1716, and it was then occupied as a barracks and damaged by cannon during the Jacobite Rising of 1745-46. It is in the care of Historic Scotland and is accessible to the public.

Mar's Wark (RWB)

Newhall Tower [NO 598100], near Crail, Fife; site of tower house.

Held by the Meldrums, then by the Erskines of Cambo from the 1680s after the estate had been absorbed into that of Cambo.

Old Sauchie [NS 779883], near Stirling; ruinous L-plan tower house.

Held by the Erskines, but passed to the Ramsays in the eighteenth century and then later to the Gibson-Maitlands.

Pittodrie House [NJ 697241], near Inverurie, Aberdeenshire; mansion incorporating part of a castle.

Held by the Erskines from 1558, and the building was extended several times down the centuries. A chamber which was formerly used as a nursery is said to be haunted, the story going that a servant had died after falling down a stair during a fire. Other ghostly manifestations are reputed to include unexplained footsteps, cries and screams, and the smell of burning: all centred on an old stair. The building has been used as a hotel since 1990 (01467 681444; www.macdonald hotels.co.uk/Pittodrie/).

Ravenscraig Castle [NT 291925], near Kirkcaldy, Fife; fine ruinous castle.

Originally a royal castle, but then pressed upon the Sinclairs, later the Sinclair-Erskines of Rosslyn. The moved to **Dysart House** [NT 302930], a symmetrical Georgian mansion of 1750s with later additions, which apparently became a Carmelite monastery. The property was sold by the family in 1898. Ravenscraig Castle is in the care of Historic Scotland and part is open to the public (01592 412690).

Rosslyn Castle [NT 274628], Roslin Glen, Midlothian; partly ruinous large castle.

Held by the Sinclair Earls of Orkney and Caithness, latterly the Sinclair-Erskine Earls of Rosslyn. Holiday accommodation is available in the castle (01628 825925; www.landmark trust.org.uk).

Scotscraig [NO 445283], near Tayport, Fife; castle replaced by mansion.

Held by several families, including by the Erskines.

Smithfield Castle [NT 253412], near Peebles, Borders; castle replaced by mansion.

Held by the Hays and by the Stevensons before coming to the Erskines and then to other families. The later mansion is now the Castle Venlaw Hotel (01721 730384; www.venlaw.co.uk).

Strathbrock Castle [NT 044717], near Uphall, West Lothian; site of castle.

Held by the Stewarts of Strathbrock and then by the Erskines.

Stravithie Castle [NO 531118], near St Andrews, Fife; site of castle.

Held by Margaret Erskine of Lochleven, jailer of Mary, Queen of Scots; and Lady Margaret gave the estate to James Stewart, Regent Moray.

Tillicoultry Castle [NS 913975], Tillicoultry, Clackmannan; site of castle and mansion.

Held by the Erskines from 1236, but passed to the Colvilles of Culross in 1483, then to the Alexanders and then to others.

Tinwald Place [NY 006800], near Dumfries; castle replaced by mansion.

Held by the Maxwells, and then by the Erskines. Charles Erskine was MP for Dumfriesshire, Dumfries burghs and Wick burghs, and was Lord Advocate in 1737. He was made a Lord of Session as Lord Tinwald in 1744 and four years later was Justice Clerk. The property passed to the Douglas Marquis of Queensberry and then to the Jardines. Tinwald House, which dates from 1740, was designed by William Adam. Tinwald Place was, itself, demolished about 1830.

Tulliallan Castle [NS 927888], near Kincardine, Fife; fine ruinous hall-house castle.

Held by several families, including by the Blackadders and by the Bruces of Carnock, before coming to the Erskines after 1900, although it soon passed to the Elphinstones and then to the Osbournes. The modern **Tulliallan Castle** [NS 936881], built in 1820 and half a mile away, is now a police training college. One story has one part of the later mansion haunted by the sounds of children laughing and playing.

www.erskinclan.com
No. of castles/sites: 42
Rank: 24/764

Eviot

The name is territorial and comes from lands in Angus, and is recorded in charters from the twelfth century, although there are many different spellings of the name.

Balhousie Castle [NO 115244], Perth, is a large castellated mansion, dating from 1860 but including an L-plan tower house of the sixteenth century. The lands were held by the Eviot family until 1478 when they were sold to the Mercers,

Balhousie Castle (M&R)

and then in 1625 passed to the Hay Earls of Kinnoul. The mansion was requisitioned by the army after World War II, and became the regimental headquarters of the Black Watch in 1962. The building also houses a museum about the regiment from its founding in 1739 (0131 310 8530; www.theblack watch.co.uk/museum/ index.html).

No. of castles/sites: 1
Rank: 537=/764

Ewing

The name is an Anglicised form of 'Ewan', and may come from the MacEwans (also see that entry) of Otter in Cowal in Argyll. The family is on record from the twelfth century, and they had lands in Argyll and at Balloch in Dunbartonshire. The family supported the rebellion by the Earl of Argyll in 1685 and suffered for it, and moved to their lands of Balloch, which had been held by the Earls of Lennox. There is a **Balloch Castle** [NS 386826] at the southern end of Loch Lomond, which is a castellated mansion, dating from 1808, and replaced an old castle, little of which survives. Balloch Castle stands in a country park (01389 720620; www.loch lomond-trossachs.org).

Keppoch House [NS 330798] dates from 1820 and is a classical mansion rising to three storeys. It may stand on the site of a castle, and was held by the Stirlings of Glorat before passing to the Ewings in the seventeenth century. From the branch of the family was descended Sir Archibald Orr Ewing, who was an industrialist, landowner and Conservative politician, and he was made a Baronet in 1886.

The family now apparently live at **Cardross House** [NS 605976], which is a couple of miles south of Port of Menteith in Stirlingshire. The house incorporates a small and altered sixteenth-century L-plan tower house to which has been added a long block and other extensions.

Cathkin House [NS 627588], two miles south-east of Rutherglen near Glasgow, is a mansion dating from 1799 but it replaced a castle or older house. The lands were held by several families but passed to the Ewings in 1790, although they took the name MacLea. They built the present mansion, which is now used as a nursing home.

www.clanewing.org
No. of castles/sites: 4
Rank: 278=/764

Fairholme

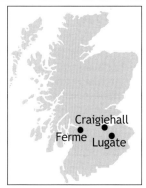

The name comes from the place Fairholm, or Farme, in Ayrshire, and the name is on record in Scotland from the seventeenth century. There was a castle and lands called **Farme** [NS 620624] in Rutherglen near Glasgow, but these apparently have no connection with the family.

Craigiehall House [NT 167754] lies to the west of Edinburgh near Kirkliston, and the present mansion was first built in 1699 by the architect Sir William Bruce. It replaced a castle or older house, and there is a ruinous doocot dated 1672. The lands were held by the Fairholmes from the seventeenth century, and John Fairholme of Craigiehall was treasurer of Edinburgh in 1633-34. The property passed by marriage to William Johnstone, second Earl of Annandale, who built the house, and then Craigiehall later passed to the Hopes of Hopetoun, then to the Hope Weirs, and was later used by the army.

Lugate Castle [NT 444436], which was one mile south-west of Stow in the Borders, stood near the farm but there are little or no remains. The lands passed from the Gardens to the Fairholmes in 1750, and the Fairholmes of Lugate still apparently own the property.

No. of castles/sites: 2
Rank: 396=/764
Xref: Farme

Fairlie

The name is probably territorial and comes from the lands of Fairlie, which are three miles south of Largs in Ayrshire. The family is on record from the fourteenth century, and also held lands near Edinburgh. **Fairlie Castle** [NS 213549], near Largs, is a plain, ruinous but well-preserved keep or tower, dating

Fairlie Castle 1906?

from the fifteenth century and rising to four storeys. The stronghold was built by the Fairlies, but was sold to the Boyles in 1650.

Hermitage of Braid [NT 251703] is in an idyllic spot to the south of Edinburgh, and there is a mansion dating from 1785, as well as a large doocot [NT 248703], which has boxes for nearly 2000 birds. There was a castle or older house, but its location has not been established. The lands were held by the Braid family, but passed by marriage to the Fairlies in the fourteenth or fifteenth century, one of whom much later was to marry the daughter of John Knox. The Fairlies still held the property in the seventeenth century, but later it went to the Gordons. The grounds have been a public park since 1888 and the mansion houses a countryside information centre.

Bavelaw Castle [NT 168628], to the south of Balerno on the outskirts of Edinburgh, is an L-plan tower house, dating from the sixteenth century. It was also owned by the Braids but passed to the Fairlies, then by marriage to the Forresters of Niddrie, then to other families. The castle is still occupied.

The Fairlies also owned:
Ascog House [NS 105633], near Rothesay, Bute; L-plan tower house.
 Held by the Glass family, then by the Fairlies, before passing to the Stewarts in 1587. Can be rented through the Landmark Trust for holidays (01628 825925; www.landmarktrust.org.uk).
Bruntsfield House [NT 252723], Edinburgh; altered Z-plan tower house.
 Held by the Lauders, but owned by the Fairlies from 1603 until 1695 when it passed to the Warrenders. The house is now part of James Gillespie's School.

Bruntsfield House (M&R)

Comiston House [NT 240687], Edinburgh; castle replaced by mansion.
 Held by several families, including by the Fairlies in the sixteenth century. Only a tower survives and the mansion dates from 1820.
Myres Castle [NO 242110], near Auchtermuchty, Fife; Z-plan tower house.
 Held by several families, including by the Scrymgeours, before passing to the Fairlies in 1887, then Myres was used in World War II to house Polish troops. It was sold in 1997 with an asking price of more than £550,000. The gardens are occasionally open to the public and accommodation is available in the castle (01208 821341; www.myres.co.uk/www.gardensof scotland.org).

No. of castles/sites: 7
Rank: 182=/764

Falconer

The name comes from the office of 'falconer', a person who breeds and trains falcons and other birds of prey. The name is recorded on charters in Scotland from the thirteenth century, and may also be a derivation of 'hawker', as in Haulkerton.

Haulkerton Castle [NO 713731], which is one mile north of Laurencekirk in the old county of Kincardineshire, was a property of the Falconers from about 1150, and they were the royal falconers of Kincardine Castle and then Lords Falconer in 1647. Nothing now remains of their castle except two date stones, one with 1556(?) and one 1648. The family moved to nearby Inglismaldie in 1693.

Inglismaldie Castle [NO 644669], some five miles north-east of Brechin further south in Angus, is an altered L-plan tower house, dating from the sixteenth century and rising to three storeys and a garret. It is built from

Inglismaldie Castle (M&R)

a notably red sandstone, and was remodelled as a mansion in 1884. Inglismaldie was held by the Livingstones and then by the Carnegie Earls of Northesk before being sold to the Falconers in 1693. They succeeded to the title Earls of Kintore in 1778, which had been a title of the Keiths. A daughter of the family married Joseph Home of Ninewells, and was the mother of David Hume, the philosopher. Inglismaldie was sold to the Ogilvies in 1960, and the house is still occupied.

The Falconers also held:

Carlowrie Castle [NT 142744], near Kirkliston, West Lothian; site of mansion.
  Held by the Dalziels of Carlowrie in the fifteenth century, but passed to the Marjoribanks and then to the Falconers, then to the Hutchinsons.

Drimmie [NO 285308], near Dundee; site of castle or old house.
  Held by the Ireland family then by the Falconers, but passed to the Kinnairds who built Rossie Priory. This mansion was partly demolished in 1949. The house is available to rent on an exclusive basis (01828 686286/238; www.rossiepriory.com).

Glenfarquhar Castle [NO 718804], near Auchenblae, Kincardineshire; slight remains of a castle.
  Held by the Falconers, but passed to the Gammells, and they built Glenfarquhar Lodge in 1900.

Lauriston Castle [NO 759667], near Laurencekirk, Kincardineshire; mansion incorporating part of a castle.
  Held by the Stirlings then by the Straitons before coming to the Falconers of Phesdo, then went to the Porteous family. The house was ruinous at one time: part was demolished, part was restored.

Monkton House [NT 334703], near Musselburgh, East Lothian; altered L-plan tower house.
  Held by the Hays, then by the Falconers after 1715, then by the Hopes of Pinkie. Still occupied.

Phesdo [NO 676756], near Laurencekirk, Kincardineshire; castle replaced by mansion.
  Held by the Keiths in the seventeenth century then by the Falconers, then by other families. Phesdo House dates from the nineteenth century, at which time the old house or castle was demolished. Phesdo was used to house German prisoners of war in World War II, was for a time a youth hostel, and is now occupied as a residence.

No. of castles/sites: 8
Rank: 160=/764

Farquhar

The name comes from the Gaelic personal name 'Fearchar', which means 'very dear one', and is on record as a surname from the twelfth century.

Some four miles east and south of Mauchline in Ayrshire, **Gilmilnscroft** [NS 556255] is a T-plan house, which dates from the seventeenth century, and it may incorporate a tower house. The lands were held by the Farquhars from the fourteenth to the twentieth century (latterly they were the Farquhar Grays). The building was restored in 1968, and is still occupied.

Mounie Castle [NJ 766287] lies three miles west and north of Oldmeldrum in Aberdeenshire, and is an altered seventeenth-century T-plan house with a round stair-tower. It was held by the Setons, but passed to the Farquhars in 1634, then to the Hays in 1701. The castle is still a private residence.

Tolquhon Castle [NJ 873286], four miles east of Oldmeldrum, is an impressive courtyard castle with ranges of buildings and a neat little drum-towered gatehouse. The original castle was built by the Prestons of Craigmillar, but Tolquhon passed to the Forbes family

Tolquhon Castle (M&R)

in 1420, and they built the present castle. Tolquhon was sold to the Farquhars because of debt in 1716, although the eleventh Forbes laird had to be forcibly ejected from his castle by a detachment of troops in 1718. The property passed to the Gordons Earls of Aberdeen, before being used as a farmhouse and then becoming ruinous. Tolquhon is in the care of Historic Scotland and is open to the public (01651 851286).

No. of castles/sites: 3
Rank: 328=/764

Farquharson

The name comes from the Gaelic personal name, and means 'son of Farquhar' ('son of Fearchar', 'Fearchar' means 'very dear one'). The clan was descended from Farquhar, fourth son of Alexander Shaw of Rothiemurchus, who settled in Mar in 1371.

The Farquharsons were part of Clan Chattan.

Invercauld House [NO 174924], some two miles east and north of Braemar in Aberdeenshire, is a solid castellated mansion with a massive tower, battlements and turrets, and a vaulted cellar from an old tower house is built into the fabric. The lands were held by the Stewarts, but passed by marriage to the Farquharsons, when Donald Farquharson married the heiress of Invercauld. Their son Findlay Mor was Royal Standard Bearer at the Battle of Pinkie in 1547, although he was killed during the fighting. The Farquharsons allied themselves with the Mackintoshes and with Clan Chattan. The clan were Jacobites, and John Farquharson, ninth of Invercauld, fought in the Rising of 1715 although he was imprisoned. It was from here that the Earl of Mar, leader of the Rising, called out the Highlanders for the Old Pretender. Anne Farquharson, daughter of James Farquharson of Invercauld, was married to Mackintosh of Mackintosh. While her husband raised troops for the Hanoverians, she did so for the Jacobites. She led the small contingent that saw off Hanoverian forces, led by Lord Loudoun, at the Rout of Moy, near Inverness, in 1746, although she was briefly imprisoned after the Battle of Culloden. The Farquharsons of Invercauld still flourish, and accommodation is available at Invercauld (01339 741213; www.invercauldcastle.com).

Inverey Castle [NO 086893], four or so miles west of Braemar, was a seventeenth-century tower house, but it was demolished in 1689 following the Battle of Killiecrankie. John Farquharson of Inverey, the 'Black Colonel', murdered John Gordon of Brackley in 1666, as recorded in the old ballad, 'The Baron o' Brackley'. Farquharson fought for the Jacobites in 1689, and defeated a force attacking Braemar Castle, which he then torched. Farquharson summoned servants by firing a pistol, and he is said to haunt Braemar Castle, leaving behind a burning candle. There is a strange tale concerning his own death. The Black Colonel wished to be buried at Inverey, side by side with his mistress, but when he died he was interred at Braemar at the request of his widow and family. His spirit did not apparently rest easy, and three times his coffin mysteriously appeared above ground – and his apparition also terrified his relatives – until they relented and his remains were taken back to Inverey.

Braemar Castle [NO 156924], just to the north-east of Braemar, is an impressive seventeenth-century L-plan

Braemar Castle (M&R)

tower house with turrets crowning the building. It is defended by star-shaped artillery defences, dating from the next century. The castle was built by the Earls of Mar in 1628 and, as they did not support James VII in 1689, the tower was seized and torched by the Black Colonel. John, sixth Earl of Mar, led the 1715 Jacobite Rising, but it fizzled out, and the castle passed to the Farquharsons of Invercauld. It was seized by the government after the 1745-46 rebellion, and then refurbished as a barracks but was later restored as a residence. One story is that Braemar is haunted the ghost of a young blonde-haired woman, who thought that she had been spurned by her new husband and threw herself from the battlements. As mentioned above, the Black Colonel is reputedly another supernatural visitor. The castle was open to the public but this now longer appears to be the case.

Some eight and a half miles east of Braemar is **Monaltrie House** [NO 242952], a long, low whitewashed mansion, which dates from 1704 or earlier. It was burnt in 1746 following the Battle of Culloden. Monaltrie was held by the Farquharsons, who fought for the Marquis of Montrose in the 1640s and then for Charles II at Worcester in 1651. Francis Farquharson of Monaltrie led the Farquharsons at Culloden and, although he survived the battle, he was imprisoned and was lucky to have his execution reduced to exile. He eventually returned and had the village of Ballater built after 1784 when he bought back his estates (he married well). He also improved roads, built inns, and developed the wells at Pannanaich, which became renowned for their restorative properties.

The Farquharsons have a burial aisle at old Crathie Church.

The Farquharsons also held:
Abergairn Castle [NO 358974], near Ballater, Aberdeenshire; ruined tower house.
Held by the Farquharsons.
Allanaquioch [NO 120914], near Braemar, Aberdeenshire; mansion possibly containing old work.
Held by the Farquharsons from the beginning of the seventeenth century.
Allargue House [NJ 259095], near Strathdon, Aberdeenshire; site of old house or castle.
Held by the Farquharsons from the middle of the seventeenth

century. John Farquharson of Allargue was a Jacobite, and was captured at the Battle of Culloden in 1746. He was imprisoned for seven years, and was to be executed, only escaping on the morning of his death, the sentence having been reduced to exile (with Farquharson of Monaltrie).
Baldovie [NO 324541], near Kirriemuir, Angus; site of castle or old house.
Held by the Melvilles and then by the Clayhill family and by the Ogilvies, and then passed to the Farquharsons, who held Baldovie in the nineteenth century.
Balfluig Castle [NJ 586150], near Alford, Aberdeenshire; L-plan tower house.
Held by the Forbeses but sold to the Farquharsons of Haughton in 1753. Latterly used as a farmhouse, then became derelict but now reoccupied. The castle may be visited by written appointment only and accommodation is occasionally available for holidays (020 7624 3200).
Balfour Castle [NO 337546], near Kirriemuir, Angus; part of castle by farmhouse.
Held by the Ogilvies and by the Fotheringhams, but later passed to the Farquharsons. The castle was reduced in size when the farmhouse was added about 1838.
Ballogie [NO 571955], near Aboyne, Aberdeenshire; mansion on older site.
Held by the Forbeses, then by the Inneses, then by the Farquharsons after 1789, and then by the Nichols from 1850. Still occupied.
Balmoral Castle [NO 255952], near Ballater, Aberdeenshire; royal seat on site of castle.
Held by the Drummonds and by the Gordons, but passed to the Farquharsons of Inverey in 1662. James Farquharson of Balmoral was a Jacobite and supported Bonnie Prince Charlie. The Farquharsons got into debt, and had to sell the lands in 1798, probably back to the Gordons, who owned the estate in 1852. That year it was sold to Prince Albert, husband of Queen Victoria, and in 1855 he had the present castle built. It is still often used by the royal family; the gardens, grounds and exhibition are open to the public (01339 742534; www.balmoralcastle.com).
Craibstone House [NJ 873107], near Dyce, Aberdeenshire; site of castle or old house.
Held by the Sandilands but was bought by the Farquharsons of Invercauld.
Finzean House [NO 591934], near Aboyne, Aberdeenshire; site of castle.
Held by the Forbeses, then by the Farquharsons from the middle of the seventeenth century until the twentieth century. Pronounced 'Fingen', Finzean House was burned out in 1934 and a new house was built on the site twenty years later.
Haughton House [NJ 583169], near Alford, Aberdeenshire; castle replaced by mansion.
Held by the Farquharsons from the second half of the seventeenth century.
Kinaldie [NJ 832155], near Kintore, Aberdeenshire; castle replaced by mansion.
Probably held by the Forbeses then by the Patons in 1662, then by the Farquharsons in the eighteenth century.

www.farquharson-clan.co.uk
www.clanfarquharson.org
www.clanfarquharsoncanada.ca
No. of castles/sites: 16
Rank: 86=/764
Xrefs: Chattan

Fawside

The name is territorial and comes from the lands of Fawside or Falside, which are two and a half miles south-west of Tranent in East Lothian. The name is mentioned in records from the middle of the twelfth century.

Falside (or **Fawside**) **Castle** [NT 378710] stands dramatically on a high ridge and is visible for miles around. It is an L-plan tower

Falside Castle (M&R)

house, dating from the fifteenth century, and turrets crown the corners. The lands were held by the Fawside family from the thirteenth or fourteenth century, but they later apparently passed to the Setons. The tower was burned by the English before the Battle of Pinkie in 1547, killing all those within, although the castle was rebuilt. Falside became ruinous around the end of the eighteenth century, but was restored in the 1970s and was reoccupied. The castle is said to be haunted by a Green Lady, the spirit of the lady of the house, dating from the torching of the castle in 1547. Lady Falside is said to have thrown missiles at the English troops and this resulted in the castle being burnt (although Falside is in a strategic position overlooking the battlefield and that might have been enough to seal its fate).

Balmakewan Castle [NO 667663] is some five miles north-east of Brechin in Angus, but little remains and it was replaced by a classical mansion, dating from the 1820s. The lands were held by the Falside family in the fourteenth century, but they passed to the Balmakewans, and then to the Barclays.

No. of castles/sites: 2
Rank: 396=/764
Xrefs: Fawsyde; Falsyde

Fea

The name is found on Orkney, and probably comes from the lands of Fea (pronounced 'Fee-a') on the island of Sanday. Fea is also a common Roma name, and it may be from this.

Carrick House [HY 567384], on the island of Eday in Orkney, is a house of three storeys and has corbiestepped gables. The building dates from the seventeenth century or earlier, and has a courtyard with

Carrick House (M&R)

a wall, which has a date stone with 1633. The house was held by John Stewart, Lord Kinclaven and Earl of Carrick (and the younger brother of the notorious Patrick Stewart, Earl of Orkney) and hence the name Carrick House. On John Stewart's death, the property went to the Buchanans, then to James Fea of Clestrain. It was he who captured John Gow, who had turned to piracy. Gow, born in Stromness in Orkney, was not a very successful buccaneer and managed to run his ship aground on the Calf of Eday, and consequently was caught and executed. The island passed to the Laings, then in 1848 to the Hebden family, who still apparently occupy Carrick House. The house is open to the public: contact 01857 622260 or www.eday.orkney.sch.uk/tourism/carricktour/index.htm to confirm days and times.

No. of castles/sites: 1
Rank: 537=/764

Fenton

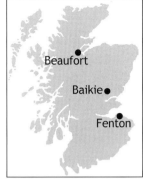

The name is territorial and comes from the lands and barony of Fenton, which are a couple of miles south of North Berwick in East Lothian. The family also held lands in Angus, and John Fenton was sheriff of Forfar in 1261.

Fenton Tower [NT 543822] is a restored sixteenth-century L-plan tower house, although for many years it was ruinous, in a prominent position above the surrounding countryside. The tower rises to four storeys and is dated 1587. The lands were held by the Fentons, but passed by marriage to the Whitelaws, who were forfeited in 1587, then went to the Carmichaels and to the Erskines, who were made Viscounts Fenton. The castle was sacked by Cromwell in 1650, and was restored from ruin in the 1990s. The castle is used in the CBBC series *Balamory* as Archie's Castle. Luxury accommodation available for up to twelve people (01620 890089; www.fentontower.co.uk).

Four or so miles east of Alyth in Angus is the site of **Baikie Castle** [NO 319492], probably originally on an island in a Baikie Loch, which has since been drained. The castle consisted of ranges of buildings around a courtyard with a moat and drawbridge. Baikie was held by the Fentons from the thirteenth century, but passed through heiresses to other families. Baikie went to the Lyons of Glamis in the middle of the fifteenth century.

Beaufort Castle [NH 507430] lies some two miles south and west of Beauly near Inverness, and the present mansion replaced an old castle. The lands were held by

Beaufort Castle 1910?

the Bissets, but passed by marriage to the Fentons, and then went to the Frasers of Lovat, who held the castle until 1990s and still apparently live near here.

No. of castles/sites: 3
Rank: 328=/764

Fergusson

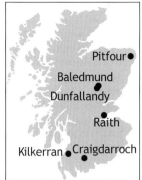

The name comes from 'Fergus's son', and is found in many places of Scotland. Branches of the family claim to be descended from Fergus, Lord of Galloway, in the twelfth century, or even Fergus mac Erc, an early king of Scots. Ferries, Ferres and Faries are contractions of the name.

Robert Fergusson, who was born in Edinburgh in 1750, was a poet and inspiration to Robert Burns, but he committed suicide in a sanatorium when only twenty-four and is buried in the Canongate graveyard. John Duncan Fergusson was one of the Scottish Colourists, along with Peploe, Caddell and Hunter; he died in 1961.

Kilkerran Castle [NS 293005] is seven miles east and north of Girvan in Ayrshire, but very little survives from a strong fifteenth-century castle. Kilkerran was held by the Fergussons, possibly from the twelfth century, but they came into written record in the fifteenth century. The Fergussons supported the Kennedy Earl of Cassillis's feud with the Bargany branch, and were at least present when Gilbert Kennedy of Bargany was slain and perhaps had a hand in his death. Sir John Fergusson of Kilkerran got into debt after joining the Royalist side in the Civil War, but his son was made a Baronet of Nova Scotia in 1703. Two of the family were eminent lawyers.

Two miles to the north and east is the new **Kilkerran** [NS 305030], to where the Fergusson Lord Kilkerran removed about 1730, and which incorporates the old tower of Barclanachan. The lands were held by the Kennedys but were sold in 1683, and the Fergussons built the new house, which has been extended and modified down the years. The Fergussons of Kilkerran still apparently live here.

Dunfallandy [NN 949560], a mile or so south of Pitlochry in Perthshire, is a classical mansion and dates from 1818, but it replaced an old castle. The lands were long held by the Fergussons, who were Jacobites and active in the 1715 and 1745-46 Risings. The laird only escaped execution after the latter rebellion failed because of his young age. A fine Pictish sculpted stone stands nearby [NN 946564], near a monument to General Archibald Fergusson, who died in 1834. The property was sold by the Fergussons in recent times.

At Moulin just to the north of Pitlochry, **Baledmund** [NN 942598] was long held by the family, well before the first charter of 1611. Finlay Ferguson of Baledmund took part in the Jacobite Rising of 1715, although apparently against his will. He was taken prisoner after Preston was captured, and was tried for treason, although he was acquitted. The family flourishes as the Fergusons of Baledmund, and they apparently live at nearby Pitfourie.

Pitfour House [NJ 978491], once called the Blenheim

of Buchan, was a large and grand mansion built in the eighteenth century. It stood by Pitfour Loch, a mile or so west of Mintlaw in Aberdeenshire in the north-east of Scotland; and replaced an old house or castle. The house was built by the Fergussons of Pitfour, one of whom was made a High Court judge, with the title Lord Pitfour, in 1765. Lieutenant Colonel Patrick Fergusson, his son, developed the first breach-loading rifle for the British army. The house was demolished in 1927.

Raith Tower [NT 256917], to the west of Kirkcaldy, was a tower house, but it was remodelled as a folly when Raith House was built in 1694. The lands were held by the Fergussons from the seventeenth century, and they built the new house. The Fergussons of Raith and Novar still apparently live here.

The Fergussons also held:

Caitloch [NX 764918], near Moniaive, Dumfries and Galloway; mansion on site of castle.

Held by the Fergussons of Caitloch. The family were noted Covenanters, and Fergusson of Kaitloch negotiated with the Duke of Monmouth to try to avert fighting at Bothwell Brig in 1679. In the end it was to no avail, and the Covenanters were routed at the battle. The house passed to the MacCalls, and is still occupied.

Carden Tower [NT 226937], near Cardenden, Fife; slight remains of a tower house.

Held by several families before coming to the Fergussons of Raith in 1725. The site has been conserved and is open to the public.

Craigdarroch House [NX 741909], near Moniaive, Galloway; mansion incorporating older house or castle.

Held by the Fergussons of Craigdarroch from the fourteenth century or earlier. Alexander Fergusson of Craigdarroch married Annie Laurie, the subject (and object) of the well-known song. This branch of the Fergussons opposed the Jacobites, and fled from the house in 1745 when Bonnie Prince Charlie arrived here on the long road back from England, looking for lodgings. The house was left in a terrible state. Craigdarroch was sold in 1962, and the house is open in July (01848 200202).

Dalduff Castle [NS 320070], near Maybole, Ayrshire; slight remains of castle.

Held by the Fergussons, then possibly by the Boyles.

Derculich [NN 890524], near Aberfeldy, Perthshire; mansion on site of older house or castle.

Held by the Fergussons in the fourteenth century, but later passed to the Stewarts. The mansion is still occupied.

Farme Castle [NS 620624], Rutherglen, Glasgow; site of castle and mansion.

Owned by several families, including by the Faries in the twentieth century. The building was demolished in the 1960s during the construction of an aluminium works.

Foumerkland Tower [NX 909807], near Dumfries; fine fortified house.

Held by the Maxwells, who built the tower, but was sold to Robert Ferguson in 1720, who also acquired the nearby tower of Isle.

Hallyards [NT 216375], near Peebles, Borders; mansion on site of castle.

Held by the Scotts of Hundleshope in 1647, and then later occupied by the historian Professor Adam Ferguson, and was visited by Sir Walter Scott in 1797.

Inverugie Castle [NK 102484], near Peterhead, Aberdeenshire; ruined castle.

Held by the Cheynes and by the Keiths, before passing to Fergusson of Pitfour in 1764. The tower was blown up in 1899 to try to clear the site.

Isle Tower (M&R)

Isle Tower [NX 935823], near Dumfries; tower house.

Held by the Fergussons from the fourteenth century. Robert Burns farmed Ellisland, an adjoining property.

Loch Beanie [NO 160686], near Spittal of Glenshee, Perthshire; site of castle or seat.

Possibly held by the MacAdies, a branch of the Fergussons.

Moulin [NN 946589], Pitlochry, Perthshire; slight remains of a castle.

The Fergussons held the lands of Moulin (but not the castle), but they were sold to the Murray Earls of Atholl in 1638.

Orroland [NX 773466], near Kirkcudbright, Dumfries and Galloway; mansion incorporating tower house.

Held by the Cutlers but passed by marriage to the Fergussons of Craigdarroch in 1769.

Springkell House [NY 253755], near Ecclefechan, Dumfries and Galloway; castle or old house replaced by mansion.

Held by the Maxwells, but sold to the Fergussons in 1894, and the line (Johnson-Ferguson) continues, although they apparently live in Hampshire.

www.cfsna.org
www.fergus.org
No. of castles/sites: 21
Rank: 63=/764
Xrefs: Ferguson; Ferres; Ferries

Fernie

The name Fernie is territorial and comes from the lands of the same name, which lie some four miles to the west of Cupar in Fife; it is on record from the fourteenth century.

Fernie Castle [NO 316147] is a sixteenth-century L-plan tower house, to which was added a later range with a round tower. The lands appear to have been held by the MacDuffs and by the Balfours, but were a property of the Fernie family in the fifteenth and sixteenth centuries. Fernie then passed to the Lovells and then to others. The building is said to be haunted by a Green Lady, the spirit of a girl who fell to her death from one of the upper chambers. The building is now used as a hotel (01337 810381; www.fernie castle.demon.co.uk).

No. of castles/sites: 1 / Rank: 537=/764

Findlater

The name is territorial and comes from the lands of Findlater, which are a couple of miles east of Cullen in the north-east of Scotland. The family are on record from the fourteenth century when one of them was Sheriff of Buchan, but the property had passed by marriage to the Sinclairs of Rosslyn in 1366. **Findlater Castle** [NJ 542673] dates from the four-

Findlater Castle 1910?

teenth century, and is built on a cliff-top promontory and was defended by two ditches on the landward side. Not much now remains of the castle and the ruins are in a dangerous condition (www.findlater.org.uk/castle.htm).

www.findlater.org.uk
No. of castles/sites: 1 / Rank: 537=/764

Findlay

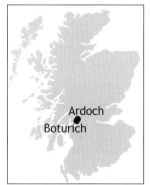

The name comes from the Gaelic personal name 'Fionnlagh', and probably means 'fair hero'. The name is on record as a surname from the middle of the thirteenth century.

   Boturich Castle [NS 387845], a mile or so north of Balloch in Dunbartonshire, is a castellated mansion, dating substantially from 1830, but with older work from a fifteenth-century stronghold. The property was long held by the Haldanes, but passed to the Buchanans of Ardoch, and then in 1850 to the Findlays. The family of the Findlays of Boturich still flourishes, and they apparently live near Alexandria. Holiday accommodation is available at Boturich (www.scottscastles.com). **Ardoch** [NS 412864], also to the north of Balloch, was held by the Bontines and also by the Findlays and by the Buchanans of Ardoch.

No. of castles/sites: 2 / Rank: 396=/764
Xrefs: Finlay; Finlayson

Fisher

The name comes from the occupation of 'fisher' or fisherman, and is recorded from the thirteenth century as a surname. Macinesker is the Gaelic for 'son of the fisherman'.

   Darnick or **Fisher's Tower** [NT 532343], half a mile west of Melrose in the Borders, is a ruinous sixteenth-century tower house, and was built by the Fisher family. It stands near a better-preserved tower house, and these are two of at least five fortified buildings which stood in the village of Darnick.

No. of castles/sites: 1
Rank: 537=/764
Xref: Macinesker

Fithie

The name is territorial and comes from the lands of Fithie or Feithie, which are three and a half miles south-east of Brechin in Angus. There was a castle at **Fithie** [NO 635545], and the lands were a property of the family from the thirteenth century, but passed to the Carnegies in the sixteenth or seventeenth century.

No. of castles/sites: 1
Rank: 537=/764

Fleming

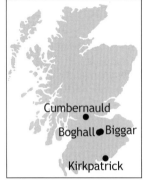

The name comes from French, and simply means that the person was from Flanders, an ancient medieval principality which now occupies parts of Holland, Belgium and France. The Flemings were renowned as merchants, and settled in Scotland from the twelfth century. Sir Alexander Fleming, born in Lochfield in Ayrshire in 1881, discovered penicillin as an antibacterial agent in 1928, although it was not used as such until World War II. He won the Nobel prize in 1945 and died ten years later.

Biggar Castle [NT 043378], on the High Street of the town in Lanarkshire, was once a strong and impressive castle, which dated from the thirteenth century, but nothing survives. It was long held by the Flemings, descended from Baldwin, a Fleming, who was known as 'de Biggar' and was Sheriff of Lanark. The family supported Robert the Bruce, and Sir Malcolm Fleming was with Bruce when John Comyn was killed in Dumfries. The Flemings moved to nearby Boghall in the fourteenth century and the site of castle is occupied by a house.

Boghall Castle [NT 041370], on the south side of Biggar, mostly dates from the sixteenth century, although there was an older stronghold here. Two D-shaped towers survive, but the rest is very ruinous. Edward II stayed at Boghall in 1310. Malcolm Fleming, steward to David II, was made Earl of Wigtown in 1341, although this title went to the Douglases in 1372; Fleming was captured, along with David II, at the Battle of Neville's Cross in 1346.

Sir Malcolm Fleming of Biggar and Cumbernauld was beheaded, along with the Earl of Douglas and his brother, at the Black Dinner of Edinburgh Castle in 1440. In 1458 the family were made Lords Fleming of Cumbernauld, but John Fleming, Chancellor of Scotland, was murdered while out hawking in 1524 by Thomas Tweedie of Oliver and others, which started a feud between the families. Malcolm Fleming, third Lord, was High Chamberlain of Scotland, but he was slain at the Battle of Pinkie in 1547. His daughter was Mary Fleming, one of the 'Four Marys' of Mary Queen of Scots; Mary Fleming was married to William Maitland of Lethington and then to George Meldrum of Fyvie. James, fourth Lord Fleming, was probably poisoned at Dieppe when a commissioner for the wedding of Mary, Queen of Scots, to the Dauphin of France. Mary visited Boghall in 1565, but three years later Boghall was surrendered to the Regent Moray after a siege. In 1605 the Flemings were again made Earls of Wigtown, but a Cromwellian force occupied the castle in 1650. The family supported the Jacobites, but the sixth and last Earl died in 1747 and the castle was soon abandoned.

Biggar Kirk [NT 042378], an impressive cruciform church, on the High Street, was made into a collegiate establishment in 1545 by Malcolm Fleming, third lord, who was slain at Pinkie. The church is open to the public in the summer.

Cumbernauld Castle [NS 773759], in Cumbernauld in central Scotland, was a strong castle, but most of it has gone except for vaulted chambers and other fragments that are built into **Cumbernauld House**. The property was held by the Comyns, but passed to the Flemings in 1306. Mary, Queen of Scots, visited the castle. The National Covenant was signed at Cumbernauld in 1646, and the building was burnt out in 1746 by government dragoons after the Jacobite Rising. The family were subsequently forfeited, and the property went to the Elphinstones in 1747. The castle was replaced by Cumbernauld House, and by the end of nineteenth century the property had passed to Burns of Kilmahew; the house is now used as offices.

The Flemings also held other properties:
Antermony Castle [NS 662765], near Milton of Campsie, Lanarkshire; site of castle and mansion.
  Held by the Flemings from 1424, but passed to the Lennox family and then to the Bells.
Barochan House [NS 415686], near Bridge of Weir, Renfrewshire; mansion incorporating old castle.
  Held by the Flemings from the thirteenth century, and seven of the family were killed at the Battle of Flodden in 1513. The lands passed to the Semples.
Bield Tower [NT 100248], near Tweedsmuir, Borders; house on site of tower house.
  Nether Oliver was held by the Flemings, but passed to the Hays.
Board [NS 713750], near Kilsyth, Lanarkshire; site of castle.
  Held by the Erskines, but passed to the Flemings of Cumbernauld in 1339.
Cardarroch House [NS 638695], near Bishopbriggs, Lanarkshire; site of castle or old house.
  Held by the Peters family, by the Flemings in 1610 and by a William Din in 1627.

Boghall Castle (M&R)

Farme Castle [NS 620624], Rutherglen, Glasgow; site of castle and mansion.

Held by several families before coming to the Flemings after 1645, and then passed to the Duke of Hamilton and then to the Faries, who held it in the twentieth century. The castle was demolished in the 1960s.

Garscadden Castle [NS 522710], near Bearsden, Dunbartonshire; site of castle and mansion.

Held by the Flemings, but in 1369 passed to the Erskines, then to others.

Kilmaronock Castle [NS 456877], near Drymen, Stirlingshire; ruined castle.

Held by the Flemings from 1329, but passed by marriage to the Dennistouns later that century and then to the Cunninghams and to others.

Kirkintilloch Peel [NS 651740], Kirkintilloch, Lanarkshire; site of castle.

Held by the Comyns, but passed to the Flemings, and they moved to Cumbernauld while this property was sold to the Kennedys in 1747. The castle may not have been used after the Wars of Independence, early in the fourteenth century.

Kirkpatrick Tower [NY 275701], near Gretna, Borders; site of tower house.

Held by the Edgars, then by the Flemings. In the ballad Adam Fleming of Kirkpatrick was the suitor of Fair Helen of Kirkconnel Lea, and she was slain taking a shot aimed at Fleming by another suitor, one of the Bells of Blacket. The lovers are said to be buried in Kirkconnel Church. Kirkpatrick may later have been held by the Johnstones or by the Bells.

Oliver Castle [NT 098248], near Broughton, Borders; site of castle.

Over Oliver was a property of the Tweedies, while Nether Oliver passed from the Flemings to the Hays. Lord Fleming was slain by Thomas Tweedie of Oliver in 1524, starting a feud between the two families.

Palacerigg [NS 783733], near Cumbernauld, Lanarkshire; site of castle.

Held by the Flemings of Cumbernauld, but now a country park (01236 720047; www.northlan.gov.uk).

Redhall Castle [NY 290694], near Gretna, Borders; site of castle.

Held by the Flemings in the twelfth century, but passed to the Johnstones.

No. of castles/sites: 16
Rank: 86=/764

Fletcher

The name comes from the Gaelic 'Macanleister', which means 'son of the arrow-maker', and the name was later anglicised to 'Fletcher'. The clan moved to Glenorchy and, despite being allied with the MacGregors, continued to live there after the Mac-

Gregors had lost out to the Campbells of Breadalbane, although the Fletchers, themselves, were to become victims of Campbell machinations. The Fletchers joined the Jacobite Rising of 1715, and many of the clan fought again for the Jacobites in the 1745-46 Rising, although the chief hedged his bets by also sending men to fight for the Hanoverians and so avoided being forfeited. Many of the Fletchers emigrated to the United States and to Canada, and the last chief died in 1911.

Achallader Castle [NN 322442], which is some three or so miles from Bridge of Orchy in Argyll, is a very ruinous sixteenth-century tower house. The lands were held by the Fletchers, but they lost the property to the Campbells, and it was the Campbells who built the existing castle. The story goes that the Campbells tricked the Fletchers into killing an English soldier who was grazing his horses in the chief's cornfield. The Fletchers subsequently fled, and the Campbells then took their lands. The castle was burnt in 1603 by the MacGregors, and in 1689 by Jacobites, and it was not restored. The castle ruin was the scene of a conference in 1691 between John Campbell, first Earl of Breadalbane, and Jacobite Highland chiefs, who agreed to an armistice in exchange for Hanoverian gold.

Saltoun Hall [NT 461685], five or so miles south-west of Haddington in East Lothian, was held by the Morvilles and then by the Abernethys, who were made Lords Saltoun. Saltoun was sold in 1643 to the Fletchers, and the third lord was Sir Andrew Fletcher of Saltoun. He opposed the excesses of the Stewart kings, and had to go into exile, but returned and took part in the unsuccessful Duke of Monmouth's uprising in 1679. He had to escape back to the Continent, and distinguished himself fighting in Hungary against the Ottomans. Fletcher returned to Scotland with William and Mary in 1689, but was then prominent in resisting the Union of Parliaments of Scotland and England in 1707, and was known as 'The Patriot'. His nephew, another Andrew, was the judge at the trial of John Porteous; Porteous was the captain of the guard in Edinburgh and, although found innocent, was taken out by an Edinburgh mob and hanged. The hall was occupied by the Fletchers until the twentieth century, but has been subdivided and is still occupied. The building is reputedly haunted by a Grey Lady. The family still apparently owns the estate, and the line of the Fletchers of Saltoun continues.

The Fletchers also held:

Ballinshoe Tower [NO 417532], near Kirriemuir, Angus; small ruinous tower.
   Held by the Lindsays, but the property passed to the Fletchers in the middle of the seventeenth century.
Caisteal an Duibhe [NN 466423], near Pubil, Perthshire; site of castle.
   Pubil was held by the Fletchers of Glenorchy.
Dunans Castle [NS 041911], near Strachur, Argyll; mansion.
   Held by the Fletchers from the seventeenth century or earlier, and their mausoleum is further downstream on a wooded ridge. The line of the Fletchers of Dunans continues. The castle is said to be haunted by a Grey Lady, but the building was burned out in recent years.
Letham [NO 624457], near Arbroath, Angus; site of castle.
   Held by several families before passing to the Fletchers in the nineteenth century.
Lindertis [NO 337515], near Kirriemuir, Angus; site of castle and mansion.
   Held by the Fletchers before 1780, when it passed to the Wedderburns, then went to the Munros. The castle was replaced by a mansion of 1813 but this building was demolished in 1955.
Rosehaugh [NH 678557], near Fortrose, Ross and Cromarty; site of mansion.
   Held by Sir George Mackenzie of Rosehaugh and then by the Mackenzies of Scatwell in 1688, before being sold to the Fletchers in 1864. They had made a fortune in Liverpool and then in tea and rubber plantations, and built a huge impressive mansion on the site, but this was demolished in 1959.
Woodrae Castle [NO 518566], near Brechin, Angus; site of castle.
   Held by the Valance family and then by Lindsays, but latterly passed to the Fletchers.

www.spaceless.com/fletcher/
No. of castles/sites: 9
Rank: 149=/764
Xref: Macanleister

Folkerton

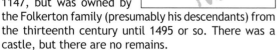

The name is territorial and comes from the lands of Folkerton, which are a couple of miles north of Douglas in the south of Lanarkshire.
   Folkerton Castle [NS 866364], was held by Theobold the Fleming in 1147, but was owned by the Folkerton family (presumably his descendants) from the thirteenth century until 1495 or so. There was a castle, but there are no remains.
   Poneil [NS 840343] lies nearby, and has a similar ownership, although it was also held by the Weirs in 1636. In 1269, however, it is recorded that William, son of Ada de Folkerton, to avoid pain of excommunication, and to deliver the soul of his father from the same, resigned the land called Pollenele [Poneil] in Lesmahagow to the Abbey of Kelso.

No. of castles/sites: 2
Rank: 396=/764

Forbes

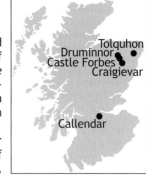

The name is territorial and comes from the lands of Forbes, which lie to the east of Rhynie in Aberdeenshire; the name is on record from the thirteenth century.
   Castlehill at **Druminnor** [NJ 516287], one and a half miles north-east of Rhynie, was the site of the first stronghold on the lands, and was held by the Forbeses from 1271 to 1440, when they moved to Druminnor.
   Druminnor Castle [NJ 513264], one mile south-east of Rhynie, now consists of a much altered keep or tower, first built by the Forbeses in the fifteenth century; the building was modified in the sixteenth century to make it L-plan, and there were later alterations. The family feuded with the Leslies and with the Setons, as well as with the powerful Gordons: twenty Gordons were slaughtered at a banquet held at the castle in 1571. The Battle of Tillyangus was fought soon afterwards, and the Forbeses were routed by the Gordons, and the castle was subsequently sacked. Druminnor was sold in 1770, and the family moved to **Castle Forbes** [NJ 622191], which is a few miles north-east of Alford, also

Castle Forbes 1910?

in Aberdeenshire. There was a tower house, but this was replaced by a large castellated mansion of 1815. A perfumery is located at the castle (01483 730944; www.castleforbes.co.uk).
   One of the enduring achievements of the family is the building of **Craigievar Castle** [NJ 566095], four and a half miles to the south and west of Alford, again in Aberdeenshire. This is a massive L-plan tower house of seven storeys. The lower storeys are very plain, while the upper works are a flourish of corbelling, turrets, gables and chimneys. The building has a magnificent interior and a fine hall with its plaster ceiling and splendid carved fireplace, as well as original panelling on the floors above. The castle was started by the Mortimer family, but they ran out of money and it was purchased and completed by the Forbeses of Menie. William Forbes, a zealous Covenanter, was responsible

Craigievar Castle (RWB)

of Oldmeldrum further north in Aberdeenshire, is an impressive courtyard castle. There is a ruinous keep and later ranges of buildings, along with a neat little gatehouse with drum towers. The original castle was built by the Prestons of Craigmillar, but it passed by marriage to the Forbeses in 1420, who completed the building. Sir Alexander Forbes, sixth laird, died at the Battle of Pinkie in 1547, while William, seventh laird, built the castle as it now is; his finely carved tomb survives at Tarves [NJ 870312], three miles north of Pitmedden, and is open to the public. James VI visited in 1589, during his campaign against the Gordon Earl of Huntly. The tenth laird, another Sir Alexander, saved Charles II's life at the Battle of Worcester in 1651. The Forbeses sold the property to the Farquhars in 1716 because of debts from involvement in the Darien Scheme, although the eleventh Forbes laird had to be forcibly removed from the castle in 1718 by a detachment of soldiers. The building was later used as a farmhouse and then became ruinous. There are tales of a both a White and a Grey Lady haunting the castle, the former a ghost reputed to have been active in recent times. Tolquhon is in the care of Historic Scotland and is open to the public (01651 851286).

Corgarff Castle [NJ 255086], in a remote but picturesque spot some ten miles north-west of Ballater

for the 'putting down' of Gilderoy the freebooter and his band, and having them hanged in Edinburgh. He commanded a troop of horse in the Civil War, and was Sheriff of Aberdeen. Jonathan Forbes of Brux and Paton of Grandhome, who were both Jacobites, hid in the laird's lug to avoid capture. The castle was taken over by The National Trust for Scotland in 1963, and the Forbeses of Craigievar now apparently live near Castle Douglas in Galloway. Craigievar is open to the public, although opening can be restricted (01339 883635; www.nts.org.uk).

Tolquhon Castle [NJ 873286], some four miles east

Corgarff Castle (LF)

in the west of Aberdeenshire, is a tall tower house. It dates from the sixteenth century and rises to four storeys, but was modified in later centuries and has pavilions and star-shaped defences. It was long a property of the Forbeses. The long and bitter feud with the Gordons resulted in one of its most infamous events. Adam Gordon of Auchindoun and a force of his family ravaged through Forbes lands and besieged the castle. Corgarff was held by Margaret Campbell, wife of Forbes of Towie, and twenty-six women, children and servants; the menfolk were away. Margaret, however, would not surrender the castle. Gordon of Auchindoun lost patience after she had shot one of his men in the knee. He had wood and kindling set against the building, and torched the place. The building went up in flames, killing everyone inside. The story is recounted in the ballad 'Edom o' Gordon', although Towie Castle has been suggested as another possible site of the massacre;

Tolquhon Castle (RWB)

nevertheless, ghostly screams have reputedly been heard in the building. The castle saw action in the Jacobite Risings, not least by being torched at least twice more, and was then used as a barracks, first against the Jacobites and then to stop illegal whisky production. The barrack room has been restored and the castle is in the care of Historic Scotland and is open to the public (01975 651460).

Culloden House [NH 721465] is a few miles east of Inverness, and mostly dates from the end of the eighteenth century, but it stands on the site of a formerly strong tower house. It was held by the Mackintoshes and then by the Edmonstones, but was sold to the Forbeses in 1626. Duncan Forbes of Culloden, Provost of Inverness, was a Hanoverian, who fought with Butcher Cumberland at the Battle of Culloden, although he then protested at the terrible treatment that was meted out to Jacobite prisoners following the battle. Many wounded Jacobites were brought to Culloden House after the battle, and then shot: those who were not killed had their skulls bashed in with musket butts. The house is reputedly haunted by the ghost of Bonnie Prince Charlie, although this is disputed. The apparition of a man, dressed in tartan, is supposed to have been witnessed on several occasions in the passages, bedrooms and the lounge. The house is now used as a hotel (01463 790461; www.cullodenhouse.co.uk).

The Forbeses also owned:

Asloun Castle [NJ 543149], near Alford, Aberdeenshire; slight remains of castle.
Held by the Calders, and then by the Forbeses. The Marquis of Montrose spent the night here before defeating the Covenanters, led by General Baillie, at the Battle of Alford in 1645.

Auchernach [NJ 330159], near Strathdon; site of castle and mansion.
Held by the Forbeses. Charles Forbes of Auchernach was master of the barracks of Corgarff Castle towards the end of the eighteenth century, and his son made his fortune in India, becoming a Lieutenant General.

Balfluig Castle [NJ 586150], near Alford, Aberdeenshire; restored L-plan tower house.
Held by the Forbeses, and the castle was torched after the Battle of Alford in 1645. Balfluig was sold to the Farquharsons of Hatton in 1753, used as a farmhouse, then was restored. The castle may be visited by written appointment only and accommodation is occasionally available for holidays (020 7624 3200).

Ballogie [NO 571955], near Aboyne, Aberdeenshire; house on site of mansion and castle.
Held by the Forbeses from 1673 or earlier, but sold to the Innes family in 1789, then went to the Farquharsons and to the Nichols.

Boyndlie House [NJ 915620], near Fraserburgh, Aberdeenshire; mansion with old work.
Held by the Forbeses from the sixteenth century. The line continues although they now apparently live in Australia.

Blackford [NJ 703357], near Rothienorman, Aberdeenshire; castle replaced by mansion.
Held by the Gardens, but passed to the Gellies then to the Forbeses, who held Blackford from about 1702 to 1858.

Breda [NJ 549167], near Alford, Aberdeenshire; castle replaced by mansion.
Held by the Forbeses, but passed to the MacLeans. Breda is reputedly haunted.

Brux Castle [NJ 490169], near Kildrummy, Aberdeenshire; site of tower house.
Held by the Forbeses. Jonathan Forbes of Brux was a Jacobite, and hid in the laird's lug at Craigievar to escape capture.

Bunchrew House [NH 621459], near Inverness; mansion incorporating castle.
Held by the Frasers but was sold to the Forbeses of Culloden in 1622 then returned to the Frasers in 1842. The building is said to be haunted by the wife of one of the owners, and Bunchrew is now a hotel (01463 234917; www.bunchrew-inverness.co.uk).

Byth House [NJ 816565], near Turriff, Aberdeenshire; castle replaced by mansion.
The castle was built by Deacon Forbes of Byth in 1593, but later passed to the Bairds.

Callendar House [NS 898794], Falkirk; magnificent mansion incorporating castle.
Held by the Callendars, by the Livingstones and by others, but latterly passed to William Forbes, a copper merchant, and he and his descendants remodelled and extended the house and held it until the twentieth century. It is now in the care of the local council, although the family of Forbes of Callendar still flourishes (they now apparently live near Castle Douglas in Galloway). Callendar House is open to the public all year (01324 503770; www.falkirk.gov.uk/cultural/).

Candacraig [NJ 339111], near Ballater, Aberdeenshire; castle replaced by mansion.
Held by the Elphinstones and then by the Andersons, but was bought by the Forbeses of Newe in 1867 (see Castle Newe). The present house dates from 1835 although it may incorporate older work. The property had gone to the Wallaces by 1900 and was later purchased by the comedian Billy Connolly. A cottage on the estate can be rented (www.candacraig.com).

Castle Newe [NJ 380124], near Ballater, Aberdeenshire; some remains of castle and mansion.
Held by the Forbes family, who made a fortune in India and were made Baronets in 1823; they still apparently live here.

Castle of King Edward [NJ 722562], near Turriff, Aberdeenshire; little remains of a strong castle.
Held by several families before coming to the Forbeses in 1509.

Colquhonnie Castle [NJ 365126], near Ballater, Aberdeenshire; some remains of tower house.
Held by the Forbeses, but apparently never completed as three of the lairds died during construction. The ruins are said to be haunted by a phantom piper, one of the Forbeses, who fell from the top of the old tower in the 1600s.

Colinton Castle [NT 216694], to south-west of Edinburgh; ruined castle.
Held by the Foulis family, but in 1800 was sold to Sir William Forbes of Pitsligo, a banker, who built nearby Colinton House. Colinton later passed to the Abercrombies, and is now in the grounds of Merchiston Castle School.

Corse Castle [NJ 548074], near Aboyne, Aberdeenshire; ruinous Z-plan tower house.
Held by the Forbeses from 1476. Patrick Forbes of Corse was armour-bearer to James III, and William Forbes built the present castle, after his lands had been raided, stating: 'If God spares my life I shall build a house at which thieves shall knock ere they enter'. One of the family was Patrick Forbes, Bishop of Aberdeen in the seventeenth century; another 'Danzig Willie' who built Craigievar Castle. Corse was raided by Highlanders in 1638, when the laird's cousin was carried off for ransom. The castle was abandoned in the nineteenth century for the nearby mansion, and the Forbeses moved to House of Corse [NJ 547075], which is an attractive Italianate mansion of the 1860s.

Corsindae House [NJ 686088], near Banchory, Aberdeenshire; L-plan tower house.
Held by the Forbeses. In 1605 John Forbes of Corsindae was arrested and taken to Edinburgh for trial, accused of murder. The property had passed to the Duffs of Braco by 1726.

Corse Castle (M&R) – see previous page

Cunningar [NJ 701060], near Banchory, Aberdeenshire; site of castle on motte.

Held by several families including by the Forbeses. It may have been replaced by Midmar Castle, and Cunningar is said to have been abandoned by the end of the sixteenth century because of plague.

Denovan [NS 820834], near Denny, Falkirk; site of castle.

Held by the Forresters and by the Johnstones of Alva, before passing to William Forbes of Callendar in 1830.

Disblair House [NJ 862197], near New Machar, Aberdeenshire; castle replaced by mansion.

Held by the Thompsons and by the Setons, then by the Forbes family: William Forbes of Disblair was a well-known poet. The property passed to the Dyce family about 1750.

Dounreay Castle [NC 983669], near Thurso, Caithness; ruinous castle.

Held by the Sinclairs of Dunbeath, then by the Forbeses, and then by the Mackays of Reay.

Dunipace [NS 837819], near Larbert, Falkirk; site of castle and mansion.

Held by the Livingstones, but passed to the Forbeses of Callendar.

Dunira [NN 738238], near Comrie, Perthshire; reduced mansion on site of tower house.

Held by the Comries, by the Drummonds and by the Dundases, but now apparently occupied by the Forbeses of Rothiemay.

Edingarioch [NJ 621240], near Insch, Aberdeenshire; site of castle or old house.

Held by the Leslies, but passed to the Leiths then to the Forbeses in the seventeenth century, but then back to the Leiths in the following century.

Fettercairn House [NO 656740], near Fettercairn, Aberdeenshire; site of castle and mansion.

Held by the Middletons, but passed to the Belshes, and then from 1797 to the Forbeses of Pitsligo.

Findrack [NJ 609049], near Torphins, Aberdeenshire; castle replaced by mansion.

Held by the Forbeses of Learney, but was sold to the Frasers in 1670. The gardens are occasionally open to the public (www.gardensofscotland.org).

Finzean House [NO 591934], near Aboyne, Aberdeenshire; site of castle and mansion.

Held by the Forbeses, then by the Farquharsons from about 1650. Pronounced 'Fingen'. The building was burned down in 1934 and a new house built on the site twenty years later.

Foveran Castle [NJ 990244], near Ellon, Aberdeenshire; site of castle.

Held by the Turing family, but passed to the Forbeses of Tolquhon about 1750.

Gask House [NJ 730472], near Turriff, Aberdeenshire; site of castle.

Held by the Forbeses but passed to the Duff Earls of Fife in the nineteenth century.

Herbertshire Castle [NS 804830], near Falkirk; site of castle and mansion.

Held by the Sinclairs of Rosslyn and by others before passing to Forbes of Callendar in 1835.

House of Schivas [NJ 898368], near Ellon, Aberdeenshire; fine altered L-plan tower house.

Held by the Schivas family and by others but by 1721 had passed to the Forbeses, then later went to the Gordon Earl of Aberdeen.

Inverernan House [NJ 330110], near Strathdon, Aberdeenshire; castle replaced by mansion.

Held by the Forbeses of Inverernan. 'Black Jock' Forbes of Inverernan took part in the 1715 Jacobite Rising, but was captured and imprisoned in Carlisle Castle, and he died on the night before his execution. The lands passed to the Wallaces and then to the Tennants.

Kinaldie [NJ 832155], near Kintore, Aberdeenshire; castle replaced by mansion.

Probably held by the Forbeses in the fifteenth century, then by the Patons in 1662, then by the Farquharsons.

Learney [NJ 633046], near Torphins, Aberdeenshire; castle or old house replaced by mansion.

Held by the Forbeses in 1670 but passed to the Brebners in the eighteenth century.

Leslie Castle [NJ 599248], near Insch, Aberdeenshire; restored L-plan tower house.

Held by the Leslies, but passed to the Forbeses of Monymusk in the seventeenth century, and they built, or rebuilt, the tower. It was sold to the Leiths in 1771. The tower was ruinous around 1820 but was restored and reoccupied in the 1980s. It was recently put up for sale for offers more than £750,000.

Lickleyhead Castle [NJ 627237], near Insch, Aberdeenshire; fine, altered tower house.

Held by the Leslies and by the Leiths, but passed to the Forbeses in 1625, and they built, or rebuilt, the existing castle. William Forbes, who shot off his own hand while firing a gun, then accepted 5000 merks from the Covenanters to murder Alexander Irvine, a supporter of Montrose, for which Forbes was eventually tried and executed. The property passed to the Hays at the end of the seventeenth century, then went to other families.

Lickleyhead Castle (M&R)

Mains of Balfour [NO 551964], near Aboyne, Aberdeenshire; site of castle or old house.

Held by the Forbeses in the sixteenth and seventeenth centuries.

Medwyn House [NT 143523], near West Linton, Borders; mansion with old work.

Held by the Forbeses in the nineteenth century. The ghostly sounds of horses and a coach are said to have been heard near the house.

Menie House [NJ 978206], near Balmedie, Aberdeenshire; house on site of castle.

Held by the Forbeses and said to be haunted by a Green Lady. Accommodation is available (01358 742885/743092; www.meniehouse.com). A prestigious golf course and holiday complex is to be built on the lands by Donald Trump.

Midmar Castle [NJ 704053], near Banchory, Aberdeenshire; splendid Z-plan tower house.

Held by several families including by the Forbeses.

Monymusk Castle [NJ 688155], near Inverurie, Aberdeenshire; altered tower house.

Held by the Forbeses of Corsindae from the Reformation, and they were made Baronets of Nova Scotia in 1626. The castle is said to have several ghosts, including a Grey Lady and the Party Ghost; and the property was sold in 1712 to the Grants of Cullen. The walled garden is open to the public (01467 651543).

Newhall Castle [NT 175566], near Penicuik, Midlothian; castle replaced by mansion.

Held by the Crichtons, then by the Penicuik family, before passing to Sir David Forbes in 1703. The garden is open by appointment only (01968 660206; www.gardensof scotland.org).

Pitfichie Castle [NJ 677168], near Kemnay, Aberdeenshire; restored tower house.

Held by the Cheynes, then by the Uries, then by the Forbeses of Monymusk in 1657. Ruinous in 1796 but restored in the 1980s and reoccupied.

Pitsligo Castle [NJ 938669], near Fraserburgh, Aberdeenshire; impressive castle with courtyard.

Held by the Frasers but passed to the Forbeses of Druminnor. In 1633 the family were made Lords Pitsligo. Alexander Forbes, fourth Lord Pitsligo, was forfeited for his part in the Jacobite

Pitsligo Castle 1910?

Rising of 1745-46, and the castle was looted by mercenaries. Forbes lived the rest of his life in caves, one of which is still called Lord Pitsligo's Cave, until he died in 1792, aged eighty-four. Sir William Forbes of Pitsligo was a wealthy banker, and was a founder member of the Royal Society of Edinburgh and the Society of Antiquaries of Scotland. He died in 1806. The lands were recovered by the family, but later passed to the Gardens of Troup.

Pittencrieff House [NT 087873], Dunfermline, Fife; T-plan tower house.

Held by several families, including in 1763 by a Colonel Forbes.

The grounds are now a public park (01383 722935/313838; www.fifedirect.org/museums).

Polmood [NT 114270], near Tweedsmuir, Borders; castle replaced by mansion.

Held by the Hunters, but passed to the Forbeses at the end of the eighteenth century.

Rothiemay Castle [NJ 554484], near Huntly, Aberdeenshire; site of castle and mansion.

Held by the Abernethys and by the Gordons, then by the Duffs and by the Forbeses of Rothiemay in 1890. They now apparently live at Dunira, near Comrie in Perthshire. There are ghost stories associated with the castle. One was of the apparition of an old woman, clad in a plaid shawl, which was observed sitting by the fire. Another concerned the phantom of Lieutenant Colonel J. Foster Forbes, seen several times, including by his grandchildren. Other manifestations included the weeping of children, arguing coming from an unoccupied room, and unexplained footsteps in an empty corridor. Rothiemay Castle was completely demolished in 1956.

Skellater House [NJ 315108], near Strathdon, Aberdeenshire; T-plan house.

Held by the Forbeses. George Forbes of Skellater was a Jacobite, and fought at the Battle of Culloden in 1746. John Forbes of Skellater married a Portuguese princess, and became a Field Marshall in the Portuguese army. He died in Brazil in 1809.

Thainstone House [NJ 759186], near Inverurie, Aberdeenshire; mansion on site of castle.

Held by the Forbes family from 1467 to 1717, when it was sold to the Mitchells. The building is said to have a Green Lady, a girl killed in a riding accident or perhaps who died when an earlier house was burned by Jacobites. The house is now a hotel (01467 621643; www.macdonald-hotels.co.uk).

Thornton Castle [NO 688718], near Laurencekirk, Kincardineshire; L-plan tower house.

Held by the Thorntons and by the Strachans before passing to the Forbeses in 1683, then went to the Fullertons and to others. The Strachans of Thornton built an aisle at the Old Kirkyard in Marykirk [NO 686656], which is dated 1615. There is a memorial to Dame Elizabeth Forbes, who died in 1661.

Tillycairn Castle [NJ 664114], near Kemnay, Aberdeenshire; strong and impressive L-plan tower house.

Held by the Gordons but passed to the Forbeses in 1444, and they built the castle. The property went to the Lumsdens, and then to others. The castle was ruinous by 1772 but was restored and reoccupied in the 1980s.

Towie Castle [NJ 440129], near Kildrummy, Aberdeenshire; site of castle.

Held by the Forbeses of Towie. This may have been the place torched by Sir Adam Gordon of Auchindoun – rather than Corgarff Castle – when Margaret Campbell, wife of Forbes of Towie, and twenty-six of her household were burned to death, after she had shot one of Gordon's men in the knee with a pistol. The tale is related in the old ballad 'Edom o' Gordon'. The castle was rebuilt by 1618, remodelled in 1788, but was very ruinous by 1968.

Waterton Castle [NJ 972305], near Ellon, Aberdeenshire; slight remains of tower house.

Held by the Johnstones from 1611, but passed to the Forbeses of Waterton until 1770 or later. John Forbes of Waterton was murdered by the Kennedys of Kermuck in 1652.

www.clanforbes.org
No. of castles/sites: 61
Rank: 14/764

Fordyce

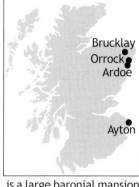

The name comes from the lands of Fordyce, which are near Portsoy in Banff in the far north-east of Scotland. The name is on record from the fifteenth century.

Ayton Castle [NT 929614], a couple of miles south-west of Eyemouth in Berwickshire in the Borders, is a large baronial mansion but occupies the site of an old castle. The lands were held by the Aytons, but passed by marriage to the Homes, and then in 1765 to the Fordyce family, then to the Mitchell-Innes family. The castle is open to the public from May to September (01890 781212/550; www.aytoncastle.co.uk).

Ardoe House [NJ 894017], is four or so miles south-west of Aberdeen, and is a fine castellated mansion of 1839, although it replaced a castle or old house. The property was held by the Meldrums, but was bought by the Fordyce family in 1744, but then was sold to the Ogstouns in 1839. The present mansion is said to be haunted by a White Lady, which is said to be either an apparition of Katherine Ogstoun, or more tragically the ghost of a young girl who was raped and became pregnant, and then killed herself and the child. The building is now a hotel (01224 867355; www.ardoe house.com).

Orrock House [NJ 964196], formerly **Over Blairton** and a mile or so north of Balmedie in Aberdeenshire, is a plain but tall mansion, dating from the end of the eighteenth century, and it replaced a castle or older house. The lands were held by the Mitchells, but passed to the Fordyces in 1770. Alexander Fordyce, a London banker, became bankrupt and had to sell the property to the Orrock family about 1780. John Orrock, a merchant, changed the name to Orrock after lands his family had lost in Fife and he built the house. It is still occupied.

Brucklay Castle [NJ 913502] is a ruinous mansion but incorporates an old tower house. It was held by the Irvines, but was a property of the Fordyce family in the nineteenth century. It stands two or so miles north-east of New Deer, also in Aberdeenshire.

No. of castles/sites: 4
Rank: 278=/764

Forest

The name appears to come from a residence or dwelling in or by a forest, or perhaps may be a shortened version of the post of 'forester' (also see the Forresters). The name is mentioned from the fourteenth century, and Henry Forest was burned for heresy in 1533.

Garrion Tower [NS 797511], which is a couple of miles south of Wishaw in Lanarkshire, is a small tower house, L-plan in design and dating from the sixteenth century, to which has been added a large mansion. The lands belonged to the Bishops of Glasgow, but passed to the Forest family, and then went by marriage to the Hamiltons. The building is occupied as a private residence.

Nemphlar [NS 854447] is another small tower house, dated 1607 and located a couple of miles west and north of Lanark. It was apparently owned by the Forest family, and has the initials DF and DL with the date 1607. The lands had passed to the Carmichaels by 1641.

Gamelshiel Castle [NT 649648], which is a few miles north and west of Cranshaws in East Lothian, was held by the Forest family at the beginning of the sixteenth century. Gamelshiel passed to the Homes in 1679. One story is that a lady of the house was slain by a wolf near Gamelshiel, and her husband buried her savaged body in a corner of the courtyard.

No. of castles/sites: 3
Rank: 328=/764
Xref: Forrest

Forman

Forman or Foreman probably comes from the office of that name, and is mentioned as a surname in Scotland from the thirteenth century.

Hutton Castle [NT 888549], some two miles south and east of Chirnside in Berwickshire in the Borders, is a sixteenth-century tower which has been extended and altered. It was held by the Homes, and is believed to have been sacked by the English in the sixteenth century, but was apparently also a possession of the Formans. Andrew Forman, son of the laird of

Hutton Castle (M&R)

Hutton, negotiated the marriage contract between James IV and Margaret Tudor, and was made Bishop of Moray in 1502 and then Archbishop of St Andrews in 1514 and died eight years later. The building is still occupied as a private residence.

Luthrie [NO 332196], which is some miles north and west of Cupar in Fife, was held by the Crown, and then by the Murrays. Sir Robert Forman of Luthrie is on record in 1555 and was the Lyon King of Arms. There are no remains of a castle or house at the site.

No. of castles/sites: 2
Rank: 396=/764
Xref: Foreman

Forrester

The name comes from the office of 'forester' or 'forest keeper', and the Forresters are mentioned in records in Scotland from the middle of the twelfth century.

Corstorphine Castle [NT 199723], to the west of Edinburgh, was a large and powerful castle with a strong wall, moat and corner towers, but nothing remains except a large doocot. Sir Adam Forrester, who was Keeper of the Great Seal and Deputy Chamberlain of Scotland, held the lands from the 1370s. Sir James Forrester was killed at the Battle of Pinkie in 1547; and the family were made Lords Forrester in 1633. Nearby is Corstorphine Old Parish Church [NT 201728] (which is often open to the public), dating from around 1426, which contains the tombs of Sir Adam Forrester, Lord Provost of Edinburgh (who died in 1405) and his wife, and Sir John Forrester, Lord Chamberlain in the reign of James I, and his wife. The grounds around the castle are still said to be haunted by a White Lady, the ghost of a Christian Nimmo. She stabbed and killed her lover and uncle, John Forrester, second Lord, with his own sword during an argument. They had a daughter, and she said that she only acted in self defence. She was tried and sentenced to death, but although she managed to escape, Christian was recaptured at Fala Moor and executed by beheading in 1679, although she conducted herself with great dignity. Her ghost is said to have been witnessed in recent times.

Tower of Garden [NS 593948], some three and a half miles west of Kippen in Stirlingshire, was held by the Forresters of Garden, who were hereditary keepers of the Torwood for the kings of Scots. They probably built the castle, although it was replaced by Garden, a classical mansion of 1824, and there are no remains of the old tower. The property passed to the Stirlings.

Torwood Castle [NS 836844], four miles north-west of Falkirk, was also held by the Forresters. It is a now ruined sixteenth-century L-plan tower house, which had

Torwood Castle (M&R)

a courtyard. Sir David Forrester was killed at the Battle of Pinkie in 1547, and many of the family were Provosts of Perth. They had a burial aisle at the Church of the Holy Rude in Stirling [NS 793937] (which is open to the public from May to September). The property passed to the Baillies of Castlecary, but then to the Forresters of Corstorphine.

The family also held:

Bantaskine [NS 876800], near Falkirk; site of castle or old house.
> Held by the Forresters from the middle of the fifteenth century, but passed to the Livingstones, then to the Kincaids.

Bavelaw Castle [NT 168628], near Balerno, Edinburgh; restored tower house.
> Held by the Bairds and by the Fairlies, but passed to the Forresters of Niddry, then went to the Mowbrays of Barnbougle in the sixteenth century.

Bedlormie [NS 874675], near Armadale, West Lothian; L-plan tower house.
> Held by the Murrays of Ogilface, then by the Forresters of Corstorphine from 1424 until the sixteenth century, then by the Livingstone Earls of Linlithgow.

Comiston House [NT 240687], Edinburgh; castle replaced by mansion.
> Held by several families including by James Forrester, Lord Provost of Edinburgh.

Denovan [NS 820834], near Denny, Falkirk; site of castle or old house.
> Held by the Forresters, but passed to the Johnstones of Alva, then to others.

Liberton Tower [NT 265697], south-east of Edinburgh; fine restored tower.
> Held by the Dalmahoy family and then by the Forresters before being sold to the Littles in 1587. Available for let through Country Cottages in Scotland (0990 851133; www.cospt. fsnet.co.uk).

Skipness Castle [NR 907577], near Tarbert, Argyll; impressive ruinous castle.
> Held by the MacSweens and by the MacDonalds, but was then

Skipness Castle (M&R)

> given to the Forresters, before going to the Campbells in 1499. In the care of Historic Scotland and open to the public.

Strathendry Castle [NO 226020], near Cardenden, Fife; altered castle.
> Held by the Strathendry family, but passed to the Forresters of Carden and Skipinch in 1496. The castle was visited by Mary, Queen of Scots, then in the 1650s by Cromwell. Strathendry went by marriage to the Douglases of Kirkness around 1700, and is still occupied.

www.forresterfamily.org
No. of castles/sites: 11
Rank: 127=/764

Forret

The name is territorial and comes from the lands of Forret, which are some four and a half miles north of Cupar in Fife. The name was found widely in Fife, and is recorded from the middle of the thirteenth century.

Forret [NO 385208] was held by the Forret family from around the turn of the thirteenth century. One of the family was Thomas Forret, a canon of Inchcolm and vicar of Dollar, who was burnt for heresy at Edinburgh in 1540. In the seventeenth century the lands passed to the Balfours. James Balfour of Forret was knighted in 1674, and was made Lord Forret when he was raised to the Supreme Court.

No. of castles/sites: 1
Rank: 537=/764

Forsyth

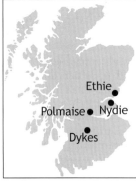

The name has at least two origins, one from a place called Forsyth, the other from 'Fearsithe', meaning 'man of peace'. The family may be descended from 'Forsach', a Norseman who settled in France, his descendants acquiring lands in Northumberland, and then in Scotland. The name is on record in Scotland from the thirteenth century, and the Forsyths held land in Stirlingshire, in Fife, in Lanarkshire and in Aberdeenshire. Alexander Forsyth, who was born in 1768 and was minister of Belhelvie, invented the percussion cap as a more efficient method of firing a bullet than a flintlock.

Polmaise Castle [NS 835924] was an old castle but it was demolished and replaced by a mansion in 1691, itself now gone. The property lies three miles east and south of Stirling, and in the fourteenth century the lands of Polmiase Marischal were given to the Forsyths, one of whom was Constable of Stirling Castle and claviger (or macer) to the king. Polmaise later passed to the Cunninghams, then was held by the Murrays of Touchadam from 1568 until the twentieth century.

Nydie [NO 439174], five or so miles west of St Andrews in Fife, was a castle or old house, but nothing survives except a seventeenth-century doocot. The lands were held by the Forsyths from 1435 until 1608. The fourth laird was Sheriff Depute of Fife, and he was slain at the Battle of Flodden in 1513. James, his grandson, married Elizabeth Leslie, granddaughter of the Earl of Rothes, and the family obtained lands around Falkland.

Dykes Castle [NS 728473] stood two miles west of Stonehouse in Lanarkshire, but there are no remains and the site is apparently occupied by modern housing. The building was ruinous by 1628, but had been held by the Forsyths from 1350, and they built the castle. They story goes that they had defeated an English army and so were given the property. They abandoned Dykes in the first quarter of the seventeenth century.

Some two miles north of Coatbridge in Lanarkshire in central Scotland is the site of **Inchnock Castle** [NS 718694], built in the sixteenth century, but ruinous by the middle of the next century. There are slight remains. It was built by the Forsyths of Dyke, but passed to the Hamiltons of Dalziel and probably then to the Steels.

Ethie Castle [NO 688468], some miles north-east of Arbroath in Angus, is a fine castle with a large altered keep or tower and inner and outer courtyards. Ethie was held by the Beatons, then by the Carnegies, and now apparently by the Forsyths of that Ilk. Accommodation is available in the castle (01241 830434; www.ethiecastle.com).

www.clanforsythsociety.net
www.xmission.com/~forsyth/index.html
No. of castles/sites: 5 / Rank: 240=/764

Fotheringham

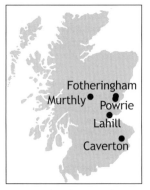

The name is territorial and comes from the lands of Fotheringham, which are four miles south of Forfar in Angus. Fotheringham may originate from 'Fotheringhay' in Northamptonshire (where centuries later Mary, Queen of Scots, was executed), as, although in England, this property was held by David I, King of Scots. The name is on record in Scotland from the thirteenth century, although there is a tradition that the Fotheringham family came to Scotland in the entourage of Queen Margaret, wife of Malcolm Canmore, in the eleventh century.

Fotheringham Castle [NO 459441] was an old stronghold, but was replaced by a large castellated mansion dating from the middle of the nineteenth century. This house has itself been demolished. The lands were held by the family from the fourteenth century until the present day.

Powrie (or **Pourie**) **Castle** [NO 421346] lies a few

Powrie Castle (M&R)

miles north-east of Dundee also in Angus, and was a strong but comfortable castle and residence. It now consists of a ruinous keep or tower, dating from the fifteenth century, with a later, restored wing. The property was held by the Ogilvies, but passed by marriage to the Fotheringhams in 1412, and they built the castle. Powrie was sacked by the Scrymgeours of Dudhope in 1492; and Nicholas Fotheringham of Powrie died at the Battle of Flodden in 1513. The castle was attacked again in 1547 by the English, the same year that one of the family, Thomas Fotheringham, was killed at the Battle of Pinkie. In 1676 the lands were erected into a free barony of Powrie-Fotheringham. Alexander Fotheringham of Powrie fought for the Jacobites at Sheriffmuir during the Rising of 1715 and, although captured, later managed to escape. The family held on to the lands.

Three or so miles south-east of Dunkeld in Perthshire, **Murthly Castle** [NO 070399] is a fine courtyard castle, with a keep and other ranges of buildings. The keep has turrets and rises to four storeys and a garret. It was a property of the Abercrombys and then of the Stewarts of Grandtully in 1615. It passed to the Fortheringhams of Powrie-Fotheringham in the nineteenth century, and is still apparently occupied by them. The castle can be used as a location for weddings and events (01738 494119; www.murthly-estate.com).

Other properties held by the Fortheringhams include:
Baledgarno Castle [NO 276304], near Longforgan, Perthshire; site of castle.
  Held by the Camerons or Cambo family, then by the Grays, before passing to the Fotheringhams in the 1680s.
Balfour Castle [NO 337546], near Kirriemuir, Angus; some remains of a castle.
  Held by the Ogilvies of Balfour, before passing to the Fotheringhams, then went to the Farquharsons.
Ballindean [NO 268299], near Dundee; castle replaced by mansion.
  Held by the Fotheringhams at one time, as well as by the Ruthvens and by the Trotters of Ballindean.
Caverton [NT 752272], near Kelso, Borders; site of tower or old house.
  Held by the Fotheringhams until 1472, then by the Kerrs of Cessford.
Lahill House [NO 445038], near Lower Largo, Fife; castle replaced by mansion.
  Held by the Fotheringhams in the seventeenth century, then by the Halketts.
Murroes Castle [NO 461350], near Broughty Ferry, Angus; restored tower house.
  Held by the Fotheringhams in the fourteenth century. By the nineteenth century the castle was used to house farm labourers

Murroes Castle (M&R)

but it was restored in 1942 and is occupied again. A low roofed chamber is called the 'Goblin Hall' and unexplained sounds of feasting are said to have been heard coming from here; the castle is also said to have a White Lady, known (perhaps unsurprisingly) as the 'Lady in White'.
Tealing House [NO 413380], near Dundee; mansion incorporating castle.
  Held by the Fotheringhams, then by the Giffords of Yester by 1425, then by the Maxwells and by the Scrymgeours.

No. of castles/sites: 10
Rank: 140=/764

Foulis

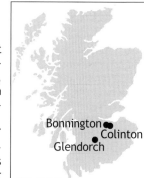

The name is territorial, but could originate from several different locations, and the name is found in records from the thirteenth century.
  Colinton Castle [NT 216694] lies to the southwest of Edinburgh, and is a ruinous L-plan tower house, dating from the sixteenth century but altered in later centuries. The Foulis family acquired Colinton in

Colinton Castle (M&R)

1519, and Henry Foulis of Colinton was Depute Marischal, while his father, James, was an eminent lawyer and was Senator of the College of Justice in 1532. The family were made Baronets of Nova Scotia in 1634, but the castle was torched in 1650, although then restored. In was abandoned in 1800 after being sold to Sir William Forbes of Pitsligo. The painter, Alexander Nasmyth, advised Forbes to unroof and partly demolish the old castle to make it a picturesque ruin as a garden feature for his new house. The ruin is in the grounds of Merchiston Castle School.

The Foulis family also owned:
Bonnington House [NT 111691], near Ratho, Midlothian; seventeenth-century mansion.
  Held by the Erskines, but passed about 1650 to the Foulis Lord Colinton, then to others.
Comiston House [NT 240687], Edinburgh; castle replaced by mansion.
  Held by several families including by Foulis of Colinton in 1531. Only a round tower survives.
Glendorch Castle [NS 871189], near Crawfordjohn, Ayrshire; site of tower house.
  Held by the Foulis family, who were involved in mining gold and lead in the area.
Ravelston House [NT 217741], Edinburgh; slight remains of a castle.
  Held by the Foulis of Ravelston family, but passed to the Keiths in 1726. The castle was replaced by an elegant mansion, which is now home to part of Mary Erskine School.

No. of castles/sites: 5 / Rank: 240=/764
Xref: Fowlis

Francis

The name means a 'Frenchman' or somebody from France, and has the same meaning as the surname 'French'. As a surname Francis is recorded in charters from the twelfth century. William Francis guided Thomas Randolph up the castle rock of Edinburgh in 1313 during the Wars of Independence, and the Scots retook the castle from the English garrison.

Sprouston [NT 755352], one and a half miles northeast of Kelso in the Borders, was held by the Lempitlaw family but they chose the wrong side in the Wars of Independence and were forfeited by Robert the Bruce around 1320. The property was given to the Francis family (perhaps to the William Francis mentioned above). Sprouston was held by the Douglases in the fifteenth century, and then by the Hamiltons in the next century.

Stane Castle [NS 338399] is a small ruinous tower house, one mile east of Irvine in Ayrshire. The lands

Stane Castle (M&R)

were held by the Francis family in 1417, but passed by marriage to the Montgomerys of Greenfield, who built the tower. The castle was later converted to a folly with the insertion of large gothic windows in the 1750s. This became derelict and had to be made safe by the local council.

No. of castles/sites: 2
Rank: 396=/764

Fraser

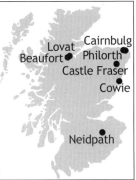

The name comes from a place in France, either from 'Fresel' or 'Freseau'. The Frasers are thought to have come from Anjou, and arrived in Scotland in the twelfth century, as around 1160 the family held lands in East Lothian, and then in the Borders and in Aberdeenshire. Old forms of the names are also recorded as Frissell and Frizelle. One of the family was William Fraser, who was Chancellor of Scotland in 1275 and Bishop of St Andrews from 1279. Fraser was one of the Guardians of the kingdom in 1286 and, fearing civil war among the competing nobles after the death of Alexander III, asked Edward I of England to intercede and help choose the rightful heir. This proved to be less than wise, and hundreds of years of warfare between the two kingdoms followed.

Neidpath Castle [NT 236405], just a mile or so west of Peebles in the Borders, is a plain but impressive keep or tower in a dramatic spot above the River Tweed. The keep dates from the fourteenth century, although it was substantially remodelled down the years. The property was held by the Frasers, and Sir Simon Fraser defeated

Neidpath Castle (LF)

the English at the Battle of Roslin Moor in 1302, but he was later captured and executed, with some barbarity, by the English four years later. The property passed by marriage to the Hays in 1312, then to the Douglases and to the Earls of Wemyss and March. The castle is sometimes open to the public (01721 720333).

Castle Fraser [NJ 724126], which is six and half miles south-west of Inverurie in Aberdeenshire, is a magnificent stately castle, developed out of a Z-plan tower house of 1575 and 1636. There is a courtyard completed by two projecting wings with an arched gateway. The property was held by the Frasers from 1454, and in 1633 the family were made Lords Fraser.

Castle Fraser (RWB)

The Frasers were Covenanters, and their lands were ravaged in 1638 and then again six years later by Montrose. The Frasers were Jacobites, and Charles, fourth Lord, died a fugitive, falling from a cliff, after the 1715 Jacobite Rising. There are stories of blood stains which could not be washed away after the murder of a young woman in the Green Room; as well as the ghostly sound of piano music and the apparition of a woman in a long black gown. In 1976 the property was given to The National Trust for Scotland, and there is a walled garden. The castle is open to the public (01330 833463; www.nts.org.uk)

Cowie Castle [NO 887874] stood one and a half miles north-east of Stonehaven in Kincardineshire, but only traces now survive of the building. It was a property of the Frasers. Alexander Fraser of Cowie was Chamberlain to Robert the Bruce, and in 1316 married Bruce's sister, Mary (who had been hung from a cage outside Roxburgh Castle). Fraser was slain at the Battle of Dupplin Moor in 1332, and his three brothers were killed at Halidon Hill the following year. This branch of the family went on to acquire Philorth, but Cowie passed to the Inneses.

Philorth Castle [NK 003641], two miles south of Fraserburgh in Aberdeenshire, was a large and impressive castle, but little survived a fire of 1915. The

Philorth Castle (M&R)

Frasers of Philorth held the lands from the fourteenth century. In 1669 they gained the title Lords Saltoun, and Alexander, seventeenth laird, built a harbour at Fraserburgh and bankrupted himself in the process, moving here from Carnbulg which had to be sold. The family then moved back to Cairnbulg in 1934 after Philorth was destroyed by fire. There is a rhyming couplet: 'As lang as there's a Cock o' the North, There'll be a Fraser in Philorth'.

Half a mile away is **Cairnbulg Castle** [NK 016640], a large and stately castle consisting of a massive keep or tower of four storeys with other ranges and a strong round tower. The lands were held by the Comyns and

Cairnbulg Castle 1910?

by the Earl of Ross, but passed in 1375 to the Frasers. In 1666 they had to sell Cairnbulg to pay off debts. They moved to Philorth House but, after a fire, they bought back Cairnbulg in 1934.

Kinnaird Head Castle [NJ 999675] in Fraserburgh is a squat but strong keep, which dates from the fifteenth century, and was built by the Frasers of Philorth, and they changed the name of the burgh from Faithlie to Fraserburgh. A lighthouse was constructed into the top of the castle in 1787, and the outbuildings were built around it in 1820 by Robert Stevenson, grandfather of Robert Louis Stevenson. The castle is now part of Scotland's lighthouse museum and is open to the public (01346 511022; www.lighthousemuseum.org.uk). The Wine Tower, which stands nearby, is a small lower tower with three vaulted storeys. The basement has no stair to the floors above, and the upper vault has three finely carved heraldic pendants, with the Fraser arms and those of James V. The story goes that Sir Alexander Fraser of Philorth is said to have had his daughter Isobel's lover chained in the sea cave below the Wine Tower to dissuade them from courting. The plan worked unintentionally rather too well: a storm blew up and the lover was drowned. Isobel cast herself to her death from the Wine Tower, and an apparition is said to been seen here whenever there is a storm.

Just east of Beauly in Inverness-shire is **Lovat Castle** [NH 539461], which was held by another branch of the Frasers, the Frasers of Lovat. The lands were a possession of the Bissets, but passed by marriage to the Frasers in the thirteenth century, and they also settled at Beaufort Castle (see below). Lovat Castle may have been sacked by Cromwell in the 1650s and a new house was built in 1671. The Frasers were Jacobites, and it is said that Lovat was finally destroyed by the Duke of Cumberland after the Battle of Culloden in 1746, and there are no remains.

Beaufort Castle [NH 507430], two and a half miles south and west of Beauly, is a nineteenth-century mansion but replaced an old castle. It too came to the Frasers of Lovat in the thirteenth century, and the castle was besieged by the English in 1303. The Frasers feuded with the MacDonalds of Clan Ranald, which came to battle in 1544 at 'the field of shirts'. The Frasers were

Beaufort Castle 1910?

defeated, and Lord Lovat and his son were both slain. The castle was damaged and captured by Cromwell in 1650. Simon, Lord Lovat, who was active for Bonnie Prince Charlie during the Jacobite Rising of 1745, was condemned to death in 1747: many Frasers had fought and been killed at Culloden the previous year. Just before Lovat was to be executed, seating holding spectators waiting for his hanging collapsed, and killed many of them – which seems to have afforded him some grim amusement. Fraser's son, Simon, Master of Lovat, was also captured but he was pardoned in 1750. The castle was destroyed, and the family forfeited, but Simon recovered the property in 1771, and the titles were all restored by 1857; they built a new house in 1882. The castle had to be sold by the family in the 1990s because of debt, although they apparently still live near Beauly. One of the Brahan Seer's prophesies was that a fox will rear a litter of cubs in the hearth at the castle. Many of the family were buried in Beauly Priory [NH 527465], which is in the care of Historic Scotland and is open to the public.

The Frasers also held:
Aboyne Castle [NO 526995], near Aboyne, Aberdeenshire; tall tower house.
  Held by the Bissets, then by the Frasers, then in 1335 it went to the Keiths and then to the Gordons.
Aldourie Castle [NH 601372], near Inverness; mansion incorporating castle.
  Held by the Frasers, then by the Grants, then by the Mackintoshes in the eighteenth century. The castle is said to be haunted by a Grey Lady.
Ardachy [NH 380075], near Fort Augustus, Inverness-shire; mansion.
  Held by the Frasers of Lovat from the fifteenth century.

Ardendraught [NK 082349], near Cruden Bay, Aberdeenshire; site of castle (location not certain).
  Held by the Frasers in the fifteenth century, but passed by marriage to the Hays.
Belladrum [NH 518417], near Beauly, Inverness-shire; site of castle and mansion.
  Held by the Frasers until the 1820s when it was sold to the Stewarts. Cottage accommodation is available (www.bella drum.co.uk).
Blackcraig Castle [NO 108534], near Blairgowrie, Perthshire; mansion incorporating tower house.
  Held by the Maxwells, but passed to the Allan-Frasers in the nineteenth century. B&B accommodation is available as well as watercolour classes (001250 886251/0131 551 1863).
Braelangwell [NH 696645], near Cromarty; castle replaced by mansion.
  Held by the Urquharts but sold to the Frasers in 1839.
Braikie Castle [NO 628509], near Brechin, Angus; ruinous L-plan tower house.
  Held by the Frasers of Oliver, but passed to the Grays about 1750, then went to the Ogilvies.
Bunchrew House [NH 621459], near Inverness; mansion incorporating castle.
  Held by the Frasers of Lovat but was sold to the Forbeses of Culloden in 1622, but was bought back by the Frasers in 1842. They were later the Fraser-Mackenzies of Allangrange and Bunchrew, and the building is said to be haunted by the ghost of Isobel, wife of Kenneth Mackenzie, twelfth chief. The house is now used as a hotel (01463 234917; www.bunchrew-inverness.co.uk).
Castle Heather [NH 678426], near Inverness; site of castle.
  Held by the Frasers.
Cherry Island [NH 386103], near Fort Augustus, Inverness-shire; site of castle.
  Held by the Frasers and the castle is said to have had a brownie.
Cowie House [NO 880872], near Stonehaven, Kincardineshire; the mansion includes old work.
  Held by the Frasers, then by the Inneses.
Dalcross Castle [NH 779483], near Inverness; restored L-plan tower house.
  Held by the Frasers of Lovat, and they built the castle in 1620, but it passed to the Mackintoshes early in the eighteenth

Dalcross Castle (M&R)

century. Restored from ruin and reoccupied in the twentieth century. Self-catering accommodation is available in the castle and on the estate (0045 3393 4133; www.dalcross.org).
Dores Castle [NO 779968], near Banchory, Aberdeenshire; site of castle.
  Held by the Comyns, then by the Frasers before they moved to Durris House.

Durris House [NO 799968], near Banchory, Aberdeenshire; altered L-plan tower house.

Held by the Frasers from the thirteenth century. The castle was burned by the Marquis of Montrose in 1645 at the same time as Castle Fraser. The Frasers had a burial aisle, built in the sixteenth century, at St Comgall's Parish Church [NO 772965] at Durris, which was rebuilt in 1869. There is a wall tomb. A Green Lady is said to haunt Durris, reputedly the wife of the Fraser lord when Montrose torched the house on 17 March 1645. The property was sold in seventeenth century, and then passed through various hands.

Easter Braikie Castle [NO 637515], near Brechin, Angus; site of tower house.

Held by the Frasers, then the by Striveline (Stirling) family and by others.

Easter Happrew [NT 191395], near Peebles, Borders; site of tower house.

Held by the Frasers in the fourteenth century. It was nearby that William Wallace and Simon Fraser were defeated by the English in 1304.

Elsick House [NO 891947], near Portleithen, Kincardineshire; mansion including older work.

Held by the Frasers, but passed to the Bannermans in 1387, and now apparently occupied by the Carnegie Dukes of Fife.

Erchless Castle [NH 410408], near Beauly, Inverness-shire; altered but fine tower house.

Held by the Frasers, but passed by marriage to the Chisholms in the fifteenth century. Self-catering accommodation available (01463 226990; www.scotland-holiday-homes.co.uk).

Faichfield House [NK 065467], near Peterhead, Aberdeenshire; site of castle or old house.

Held by the Frasers in the seventeenth and eighteenth centuries. Demolished in the 1960s.

Findrack [NJ 609049], near Torphins, Aberdeenshire; castle replaced by mansion.

Held by the Forbeses of Learney, but sold to the Frasers in 1670, and they still held it in the nineteenth century. The gardens are occasionally open to the public (www.gardensof scotland.org).

Ford House [NT 389644], near Pathhead, Midlothian; fine L-plan house of 1680.

Held and built by the Frasers of Lovat. Still occupied.

Fort Augustus [NH 382091], Fort Augustus, Inverness-shire; remains of fort.

Built to defend against the Jacobites, but seized by them in 1746. It was bought by the Fraser Lord Lovat in 1857 and given by him to the Benedictine Order, although the abbey has closed.

Fruid Castle [NT 106180], near Tweedsmuir, Borders; site of castle.

Held by the Frasers, but passed to the Tweedies and to others.

House of Tyrie [NJ 936632], near Fraserburgh, Aberdeenshire; site of castle.

Held by the Frasers, then sold to the Leslies in 1725, before being recovered by the Frasers at the end of the nineteenth century.

Inverallochy Castle [NK 041630], near Fraserburgh, Aberdeenshire; some remains of tower house.

Held by the Comyns, but passed to the Frasers of Lovat.

Invery House [NO 698940], near Banchory, Aberdeenshire; castle replaced by mansion.

Held by the current chiefs, the Fraser Lords Saltoun. The large classical mansion incorporates old work from a castle.

Kinnell Castle [NO 599500], near Friockheim, Angus; site of castle.

Held by the Balnaves family, then by the Frasers in the fourteenth century, then by the Lyons and by others.

Knock Castle [NS 194631], near Largs, Ayrshire; ruinous Z-plan tower house.

Held by the Frasers of Lovat from 1380 to 1645, when it was sold to the Montgomerys of Skelmorlie.

Lonmay Castle [NK 062608], near Fraserburgh, Aberdeenshire; site of castle.

Held by the Frasers.

Moniack Castle [NH 552436], near Beauly, Inverness-shire; altered L-plan tower house.

Held by the Frasers of Lovat. Now houses a wine bar, bistro and tearoom, and Highland Wineries is based at the castle (01463 831283; www.moniackcastle.co.uk).

Muchalls Castle [NO 892908], near Stonehaven, Kincardineshire; well-preserved and impressive castle.

Held by the Frasers, but sold to the Hays in 1415, later passed to the Burnetts, who built the castle.

Oliver Castle [NT 098248], near Broughton, Borders; site of castle.

Held by the Frasers, but passed to the Tweedies.

Overton Tower [NT 685128], near Jedburgh, Borders; ruinous tower house.

Held by the Frasers.

Pitsligo Castle [NJ 938669], near Fraserburgh, Aberdeenshire; large and impressive castle.

Held by the Frasers, but passed to the Forbeses of Druminnor in 1633.

Pittulie Castle [NJ 945671], near Fraserburgh, Aberdeenshire; ruinous tower house.

Held by the Frasers from the fourteenth century until 1630, when it passed by marriage to the Ogilvies.

Powis House [NJ 939081], Aberdeen; castle replaced by mansion.

Held by the Frasers of Powis, then passed to the Leslies and then to the Burnetts.

Red Castle [NH 584495], near Muir of Ord, Ross and Cromarty; altered L-plan tower house.

Held by the Bissets, but passed to the Frasers before going to the Douglases.

Reelig House or **Easter Moniack** [NH 559436], near Beauly, Inverness-shire; mansion.

Held by the Frasers from the seventeenth century, and the Frasers of Reelig still apparently live here.

Savoch Castle [NJ 918389], near Ellon, Aberdeenshire; site of castle, the location uncertain.

Held by the Frasers in the sixteenth century.

Strichen [NJ 944549], Strichen, Aberdeenshire; castle replaced by mansion.

Held by the Frasers. Alexander Fraser of Strichen became a judge of the Court of Session in 1730. Dr Johnston and Boswell visited Strichen, and this branch of the family became Lords Lovat in 1837. The property was sold to the Bairds in 1855, and Strichen House is now roofless.

Touch House [NS 753928], near Stirling; mansion incorporating castle.

Held by the Frasers in 1234 but passed to the Stewarts Earls of Buchan by 1426, then to others.

Urie House [NO 860877], near Stonehaven, Kincardineshire; mansion incorporating castle.

Held by the Frasers, but passed by marriage to the Keith Earls Marischal, then passed to others.

www.fraser-clan.org
www.fraserchief.co.uk
www.thefrasers.com
www.cfsna.com
www.clanfraser.ca
www.fraserclan-cal.net
www.mv.com/ipusers/becky/
No. of castles/sites: 51
Rank: 20/764
Xref: Frissell

French

The name simply means somebody from France (much the same as Francis), and is recorded in Scotland from the middle of the thirteenth century.

Frenchland Tower [NT 102054], just half a mile east of Moffat in Dumfries and Galloway, is an altered sixteenth-century tower house, which is now ruinous. The lands were held by the French family from the thirteenth century. Walter

Frenchland Tower (M&R)

French of Frenchland, although the lover of Lilias Johnstone, is said to have slain the Johnstone laird of nearby Lochhouse, her brother. He fled abroad, and when he returned married another girl. Lillias's ghost is said to haunt Lochhouse.

Thornydykes [NT 613485] was held by the French family in the sixteenth and seventeenth centuries, and they probably had a tower house. The property is six miles east of Lauder, near Westruther in Berwickshire in the Borders. French of Thornydykes also seems to have had a violent dispute with the Graham Earl of Montrose, as James VI called them together to resolve the differences. Adam French of Thornydykes, although only fourteen years of age, was apparently seized from his school in Haddington and was quickly persuaded to wed the daughter of the laird of East Nisbet. The matter came to trial in 1615 on a charge of 'ravishing' among others, but Adam seems to have been quite happy with the arrangement; perhaps his guardian was less so as no dowry appears to have been paid.

No. of castles/sites: 2
Rank: 396=/764

Fullerton

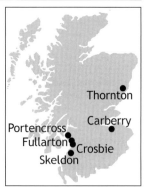

The name is territorial and comes either from the lands of that name to the south of Irvine in Ayrshire or from lands of Fullerton in the sheriffdom of Forfar in Angus. The name is on record from the end of the thirteenth century. The family held lands in both these places, as well as at Kilmichael on Arran. Fullerton may come from the office of 'fowler', a keeper of birds; or could also be derived from 'fuller', meaning a 'bleacher of cloth'; 'ton' means settlement or seat.

Fullarton Castle [NS 319383] to the south of Irvine in Ayrshire, was held by the family in the thirteenth century, but there are no remains of the castle. The Fullertons moved to **Crosbie** or **Corsbie** [NS 344301], a mile or so to the south-east of Troon, also in the thirteenth century. The family built a tower house, but this was replaced by Fullarton House, which dated from 1745 but was completely demolished in 1966. The basement of the old tower survives, as it was later used as an icehouse. The Fullertons held the property until 1805, when it passed to the Bentinck Dukes of Portland.

Reginald Fullerton of that Ilk was taken prisoner at the Battle of Durham in 1346.

The family also held:
Carberry Tower [NT 364697], near Musselburgh, East Lothian; tower house and mansion.
  Held by the Riggs, but passed to several families including to the Fullertons after 1689. Carberry is now a residential Christian conference centre (0131 665 3135; www.carberry tower.com).
Portencross Castle [NS 176488], near West Kilbride, Ayrshire; ruinous but impressive castle.
  Long held by the Boyds, but passed in 1785 to the Fullertons of Overton. The castle featured in the BBC television show *Restoration* (www.portencrosscastle.org.uk).
Skeldon Castle [NS 378138], near Maybole, Ayrshire; some remains of castle.
  Held by the Mures, by the Kennedys and by the Campbells, but much later was a property of the Fullartons, one of whom made a fortune from mining in the early nineteenth century. William Fullarton was born in Patna in India, and hence the name of the mining village 'Patna'. The property was sold to the Duke of Portland in 1867.
Thornton Castle [NO 688718], near Laurencekirk, Kincardineshire; L-plan tower house.
  Long held by the Strachans, but then by other families, including by the Fullertons.

No. of castles/sites: 6
Rank: 212=/764
Xref: Fullarton

Furde

The name comes from a 'ford', a place to cross a river, although there are various spellings, including Foord and Furde. The family is recorded on charters from the beginning of the fifteenth century.

Burncastle [NT 538514], two miles north of Lauder in the Borders, was held by the Furde family in 1493, although soon afterwards passed to the Logans of Restalrig. There was a tower house, but there are no remains.

Also in the Borders, but a couple of miles south-east of Greenlaw, is **Purves Hall** [NT 761447], which was formerly known as Tofts or Nether Tofts. The mansion incorporates a much altered tower house. It was held by the Furdes, then by the Rutherfords, by the Homes, by the Belshes and by the Purvis family in 1670, who changed the name to Purvishall (now Purves Hall). The house is a private residence, and was recently put up for sale for offers of more than £475,000.

No. of castles/sites: 2
Rank: 396=/764
Xrefs: Foord; Ford

Galbraith

The name appears to come from 'one of the Briton' or 'strange or foreign Briton', and the clan may be descended from the Britons of Strathclyde, who had their main fortress at Dumbarton. In Gaelic the clan are known as 'Clan a' Bhreatannaich', and it is possible they came from the royal house of the old kingdom of Strathclyde. The clan held lands in the Lennox from the twelfth century or earlier.

Inchgalbraith Castle [NS 369904], the ruinous remains of which are on an island in Loch Lomond to the south and east of Luss in Dunbartonshire, was a stronghold of the clan, but passed to the Colquhouns of Luss in the sixteenth century. Only a motte remains at **Baldernock** [NS 600751], some miles west and north of Kirkintilloch in central Scotland, but this was the castle of the chiefs of Galbraith in the thirteenth century, although the lands passed to the Hamiltons in the next century. The chiefs of the Galbraiths moved to **Gartconnel Castle** [NS 537732], in Bearsden north of Glasgow, but only a ditch survives of this stronghold. The clan supported Robert the Bruce in the Wars of Independence.

Culcreuch Castle [NS 620876], to the north of Fintry in Stirlingshire, is a fine altered keep or tower, dating from the fifteenth century but extended down the centuries. The Chinese Bird Room, within the old part of the building, has hand-painted Chinese wallpaper dating from 1723, believed to be the only surviving example of this period in Scotland. The castle was held by the chiefs of the Galbraiths, but was sold to the Setons in 1630, and then to the Napiers. The Galbraiths supported the Earls of Lennox, but then had got into serious debt, and line of the chiefs died out in the seventeenth century.

Culcreuch Castle (M&R)

Culcreuch is said to be haunted. The Phantom Harper of Culcreuch relates to events believed to have taken place in 1582. One of the Buchanan family was mortally wounded by Robert Galbraith, son of the sixteenth chief. The dying man was taken to what is now the Chinese Bird Room, accompanied by his mistress. When he died, to comfort herself she began to play a wire-strung harp, known as a clarsach in Gaelic, and it is said that her soft music has often been heard since, particularly in the dead of night. The music has been reported from this and its adjoining room and also in the Laird's Hall. The castle, however, does have a large colony of bats and it has been suggested that they are culprits for these unexplained noises. Another manifestation is that of a cold grey mass, about the height and proportions of a person.

The castle is in a country park and is now a hotel (01360 860228/555; www.culcreuch.com).

The Galbraiths also owned:

Balgair Castle [NS 607884], near Fintry, Stirlingshire; site of tower house.
> Held by the Cunninghams of Glengarnock, but passed to the Galbraiths of Culcreuch in 1563, then went to the Buchanans.

Balvie Castle [NS 535752], near Milngavie, Dunbartonshire; site of castle.
> The lands were held by the Galbraiths of Culcreuch, but passed by marriage to the Logans and then went to others.

Bannachra Castle [NS 343843], near Helensburgh, Dunbartonshire; ruinous tower house.
> Held by the Galbraiths but passed to the Colquhouns, and they built the tower about 1512.

Bardowie Castle [NS 580738], near Milngavie, Dunbartonshire; altered tower house.
> Held by the Galbraiths of Baldernock, but passed by marriage to the Hamiltons of Cadzow in the fourteenth century.

Barskimming [NS 482251], near Mauchline, Ayrshire; castle replaced by mansion.
> Held by the Reids, by the Stewarts and by the Millers before coming to the Galbraiths in the twentieth century, and Barskimming is now apparently home to the Galbraith Barons Strathclyde, who were given the title in 1955.

Craigmaddie Castle [NS 575765], near Milngavie, Dunbartonshire; slight remains of castle.
> Held by the Galbraiths of Baldernock from 1238 or earlier, but passed by marriage to the Hamiltons of Cadzow in the fourteenth century.

Garscadden Castle [NS 522710], near Bearsden, Dunbartonshire; site of castle and mansion.
> Held by the Flemings and by the Erskines, then by the Galbraiths of Gartconnel from 1444 to 1571. Garscadden then went to the Colquhouns.

Kincaid House [NS 650760], Milton of Campsie, Lanarkshire; site of castle.
> Held by the Galbraiths, but the property was sold to the Kincaids in 1280. Their mansion is now the Kincaid House Hotel (0141 776 2226; www.kincaidhouse.com).

Mains Castle [NS 536743], near Milngavie, Dunbartonshire; site of castle and mansion.
> Held by the Galbraiths of Culcreuch, but passed by marriage to the Douglases of Dalkeith in 1373, in whose possession it long remained.

www.clangalbraith.org
No. of castles/sites: 13
Rank: 113=/764

Gardyne

The name is territorial and comes from the lands and barony of Gardyne, which are seven miles north-west of Arbroath in Angus. The name can be spelt either Gardyne or Garden, and is on record at the end of the thirteenth century.

Gardyne Castle [NO 574488] in Angus is an extended tower house, which mostly dates from the fifteenth century but with older work and part of the building has been little altered down the centuries. The lands were held by the

Gardyne Castle (M&R)

Gardynes, who for years feuded with their near neighbours, the Guthries. The trouble is said to have started with a marriage between the families in 1558. Patrick Gardyne was slain in 1578 by William Guthrie, and in 1588 the Gardynes slew a Guthrie chief. Two years later the Guthries fell upon the Gardyne family and murdered their chief and others. Both families were forfeited by James VI, losing their lands, but while the more-powerful Guthries recovered theirs, the Gardyne family never did. The property had passed to the Lyles of Dysart in 1682. The castle is still occupied as a private residence.

The Gardynes also owned the following:

Beannachar or **Banchory** [NJ 915024], near Aberdeen; castle replaced by mansion.
> Held by the Gardynes in the sixteenth century, but passed to the Thomsons. The name Banchory House was from the parish Banchory-Devenick, as opposed to the village of Banchory,

which is in the parish of Banchory-Ternan. Prince Albert stayed here in 1859, and the building is now used to house a Camphill-Rudolph Steiner community school.

Blackford [NJ 703357], near Rothienorman, Aberdeenshire; castle replaced by mansion.

Held by the Gardens in the sixteenth century or earlier, but passed to the Gellies, then went to the Forbeses about 1702.

Castle of Troup [NJ 838663], near Rosehearty, Aberdeenshire; site of castle on cliffs above the sea.

Held by the Comyns or by the Troups and probably by the Keith Earls Marischal but passed to the Gardynes (Gardens) of Troup in 1654. Troup House is a castellated mansion on the site of an older house.

Cononsyth [NO 566464], near Arbroath, Angus; castle replaced by mansion.

Held by the Gardynes until 1578, and then by the Raits.

Delgatie Castle [NJ 755506], near Turriff, Aberdeenshire; impressive tower and mansion.

Long associated with the Hays, but passed to the Gardynes (Gardens) of Troup in 1762, then went to other families before returning to the Hays. The castle is open to the public all year (01888 563479; www.delgatiecastle.com).

Dorlaithers Castle [NJ 703474], near Turriff, Aberdeenshire; site of castle.

Held by the Gardynes in 1618.

Finavon Castle [NO 497566], near Forfar, Angus; ruinous but once strong castle.

Long held by the Lindsays, but then by the Carnegies and by others until it was a possession of the Gardynes in 1815. 'When Finavon Castle runs to sand, The end of the world is near at hand.'

Findon Castle [NJ 795644], near Macduff, Aberdeenshire; earthworks remain from a castle.

Held by the Troup family, then by the Gardynes (Gardens).

Lugate Castle [NT 444436], near Stow, Borders; site of castle.

Held by the Gardyne (Garden) family, but passed to the Fairholmes in 1750, and they apparently still own the property.

Middleton House [NO 583487], near Arbroath, Angus; castle replaced by mansion.

Held by the Gardynes from the beginning of the seventeenth century, and the family, now Bruce-Gardyne of Middleton, still apparently live at Middleton.

Pitsligo Castle [NJ 938669], near Fraserburgh; large and impressive castle.

Held by the Frasers and by the Forbeses, but latterly held by the Gardynes (Gardens) of Troup before passing back to the Forbes family.

No. of castles/sites: 12
Rank: 120=/764
Xref: Garden

Garrioch

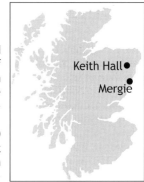

The name is territorial and comes from the lands of Garioch, which are in Aberdeenshire. The name is on record from the thirteenth century.

House of Mergie [NO 796887], four miles west and north of Stonehaven in the old county of Kincardineshire, is a tall tower house, now T-plan, and dates from the seventeenth century, although it has been considerably altered in later years. The lands were a property of the Douglases and later of a Paul Symmer, but were sold to the Garriochs in 1772, one of whom, Alexander Garrioch, was a staunch Jacobite and fought in the 1715 Rising. Mergie later passed to the Duffs.

Keith Hall [NJ 787212], which was known as **Caskieben**, is a Z-plan tower house, dating from the sixteenth century, and lies a mile south of Inverurie in Aberdeenshire. It was held by the Leslies in 1224, but passed to the Garriochs, but then by marriage to the Johnstones in the seventeenth century. Caskieben was sold in 1660 to the Keiths, and they changed the name to Keith Hall. The building has been divided into fourteen separate residences, and is still occupied.

No. of castles/sites: 2
Rank: 396=/764
Xref: Garioch

Gartshore

The name is territorial and comes from the lands of Gartshore, which are a mile or so east of Kirkintilloch in central Scotland.

Gartshore House [NS 692737] was a seventeenth-century mansion, with a double-gabled block, but it was completely demolished in the twentieth century. The lands were held by the Gartshore family from the thirteenth century, but passed to the Murrays of Ochtertyre, and then to others.

No. of castles/sites: 1
Rank: 537=/764

Gavin

The name may be from Gawain, one of the knights of Arthurian legend; and is recorded in Scotland as a surname from the middle of the seventeenth century.

Easter Braikie Castle [NO 637515], six miles south of Brechin in Angus, was a tower house, but it was demolished around 1823 and replaced by a mansion. The lands and old tower were held by several families before being sold to the Gavins in 1752, and from them they passed by marriage to the Bairds.

Langton Castle [NT 756534], two or so miles west of Duns in Berwickshire in the Borders, was once a strong castle but there are no remains, and a later mansion has also been demolished. The lands were long held by the Cockburns, but were sold to the Gavins in 1753; they then passed to the Campbell Marquis of Breadalbane and then to the Baillie-Hamiltons.

No. of castles/sites: 2
Rank: 396=/764

Gayre

The name comes from a family from Cornwall, called 'Kaer' and now 'Gayre', who had held lands in the south-west of England.

Nigg House [NH 804717], five and a half miles east and north of Invergordon in Ross and Cromarty, dates from 1702 but there is older work contained in the outbuildings. There was a bishop's house at Nigg, a large building with a vaulted cellar, but there are no remains above ground. The property was held by the MacCullochs but had passed to the Gayres in the seventeenth century.

Minard Castle [NR 973943], some eight miles or so north-east of Lochgilphead in Argyll, is a modern mansion and has no fortified origins. It dates from the eighteenth century, but was remodelled in later years, and was held by the Campbells when it was known as Knockbuie. It became a hotel, but was sold to the Gayre family in 1974 and accommodation is available (01546 886272; www.minardcastle.com).

No. of castles/sites: 2
Rank: 396=/764

Geddes

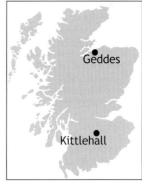

The name is territorial and comes from the lands of the same name, which are a couple of miles south of Nairn to the east of Inverness. It is not clear whether or when the Geddeses were in possession, as the lands had by an early date gone to the Roses, who went on to acquire Kilravock. **Geddes House** [NH 884526] is a fine mansion, dating from 1780 and built after the property had gone to the Mackintoshes. Accommodation is available (01667 452241; www.geddesonline.co.uk).

Kittlehall or **Rachan** [NT 113337], five miles southeast of Biggar in Lanarkshire in central Scotland, was a property of the Geddeses of Rachan from 1406. The Geddeses feuded with the Tweedies of Drumelzier after William Geddes had been cruelly slaughtered by the Tweedies; then in 1592 James Geddes of Glenhigton 'fell victim to the treachery of the Tweedies in Edinburgh'. Rachan was sold to the Tweedies of Quarter in 1752, and later passed to the Marshall family. There was a mansion at Rachan [NT 122345], perhaps on the site of a tower, but this building was demolished in 1956.

There is also the Geddes Barons Geddes, a title created in 1942, and the family apparently now live in Suffolk in England.

Jennie Geddes, a greengrocer on Edinburgh's High Street, is reputed to have thrown her stool at the minister in St Giles on 23 July 1637 as the form of the service was too Catholic for her tastes.

No. of castles/sites: 3
Rank: 328=/764
Xref: Ged

Geils

Geils and Geals are likely to be from the personal name 'Giles', which originally came from the ancient Greek. The name is on record from the beginning of the thirteenth century as a surname. The parish church of Edinburgh was dedicated to St Giles (now St Giles Cathedral).

Geilston House [NS 339783], which is three and a half miles west and north of Dumbarton, is an old house with some early work; there was a tower house. Geilston is from 'Geil's' or 'Gile's' and from 'ton', meaning 'seat' or 'settlement'. It seems likely that the property was held by the Geils family, but by the sixteenth century Geilston had gone to the Woods. The gardens are in the care of The National Trust for Scotland and open to the public from Easter to October (01389 841867).

Ardmore [NS 317785], a couple of miles west of Cardross in Dunbartonshire, is a large mansion with a crenellated central tower. It dates from 1806, but there are three towers from an old castle, dating from the sixteenth or seventeenth centuries, and one has gunloops. The property was held by the Nobles, but passed to the Geils at the end of the eighteenth century, before passing back to the Nobles of Ardmore.

No. of castles/sites: 2
Rank: 396=/764
Xrefs: Geals; Giles

Gellie

The name probably comes from a place in Scotland, and the name is on record from the beginning of the sixteenth century; Gellie was found in Fife, in Angus and in Aberdeenshire.

Blackford [NJ 703357], a mile or so west of Rothienorman in Aberdeenshire, was held by Gardens, but passed to the Gellies, then to the Forbeses around the beginning of the eighteenth century. There was a castle or old house, but this was replaced by a mansion, now reduced in size but still occupied.

No. of castles/sites: 1
Rank: 537=/764

Gemmill

The name means 'the old one', and was a popular first name, although it was spelt in different ways. It is recorded as a surname from the thirteenth century and was found in Ayrshire and in other parts of southern Scotland.

Brockloch Castle [NS 289113], which stood a mile north-west of Maybole in Ayrshire, was a sixteenth-century L-plan tower house, but there are no remains. Brockloch was held by the Gemmills from before 1628. **Templehouse** [NS 405253], which stood three miles east of Prestwick also in Ayrshire, was a castle or old house and may also have been held by the Gemmills.

Countesswells [NJ 871043], four miles west of Aberdeen in the north-east of Scotland, was held by the Sandilands and by the Burnetts, before being sold at the beginning of the nineteenth century to the Gammells, who had made their money in the west of Scotland. They bought several properties in the north-east of Scotland, and the family, 'styled of Forter', have their seats listed in *Burke's* as in Glenisla in Angus and near Kirkliston in West Lothian. **Drumtochty Castle** [NO 699801], some two miles north-west of Auchenblae in north-east Scotland, is a large castellated mansion and dates from 1812. It probably incorporates some of an old castle, and the mansion was built for the Reverend J. S. Gammell of Countesswells. It was later used as a hospital then as a school, and is available to rent (01561 320169; www.drumtochtyunlimited.com).

No. of castles/sites: 4 / Rank: 278=/764
Xref: Gammell

Gibb

The name comes from a diminutive of Gilbert, and is on record from the first quarter of the sixteenth century (also see Gibson).

Carriber or **Easter Carriber Castle** [NS 966751] was a sixteenth century tower house, but it is now ruinous and the remains lie in woodland two or so miles west of Linlithgow in West Lothian. It was built by Rob Gibb, who had been jester to James V, and he married Margaret Shaw, a royal mistress. Robert Gibb of Carriber was principal baillie of the port of Newhaven in 1553. The line continues as the Gibbs of Easter Carriber, although they now apparently live in London.

No. of castles/sites: 1 / Rank: 537=/764

Gibson

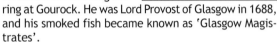

The name comes from 'Gibb's son', 'Gibb' being a diminutive of Gilbert, and the name is on record from the middle of the fourteenth century (also see Gibb).

Walter Gibson, a Glasgow merchant, made a fortune from smoking herring at Gourock. He was Lord Provost of Glasgow in 1688, and his smoked fish became known as 'Glasgow Magistrates'.

Durie House [NO 372025] stands one mile to the north-west of Leven in Fife, and the present three-storey classical mansion dates from 1762. It replaced an older castle or house, and was long held by the Durie family. The property was sold to the Gibsons in 1614, who took the title Lord Durie. Sir Alexander Gibson, an eminent judge, was kidnapped and held prisoner by one of the Armstrongs so that the case he was presiding over would be found in favour of the Earl of Traquair. Durie's son and then his grandson were also well-known lawyers. The family bought the barony of Pentland, south of Edinburgh, and there is a burial vault in Old Pentland Graveyard [NT 262663]. Durie was sold in the eighteenth century to the Christies, and Durie House is still occupied.

The family also held:
Addistoun House [NT 155694], near Ratho, Midlothian; site of castle or old house.
>   Held by the Sutties, and then by the Hoggs and by the Gibsons in the eighteenth century.
Balhouffie [NO 553062], near Anstruther, Fife; site of castle.
>   Held by the Gibsons from 1642 and may have passed to the Pattullos. The house or castle was in ruins by 1802.
Boreland Tower [NT 255480], near Peebles, Borders; site of tower house.
>   Held by the Gibsons and by the Andersons in the seventeenth century, but was then held by the Gibsons in the 1850s.
Clifton Hall [NT 109710], near Broxburn, West Lothian; mansion on site of castle.
>   Held by the Grahams, by the Douglases and by the Wisharts before coming to the Gibsons of Pentland in 1761. The property passed by marriage to the Maitlands, and the building is now used as a school.
Largo Castle [NO 418034], near Lower Largo, Fife; one tower remains from a castle and mansion.
>   Held by the Woods and by the Blacks, before being a possession of the Gibsons of Durie from 1633 to 1663, then went to the Durhams.
Riccarton [NT 183695], near Edinburgh; site of tower house.
>   Held by the Stewarts and by the Craigs, then went by marriage to the Gibsons in 1823. The building was demolished in 1956.

No. of castles/sites: 7
Rank: 182=/764
Xref: Gibsone

Gifford

The name comes from a physical description of the first of the family, who was rather fat and rotund, and is on record from the middle of the twelfth century. The village of Gifford in East Lothian is named after the family; it was originally called Yester.

Yester Castle [NT 556667], some five and a half miles south-east of Haddington also in East Lothian, is a ruinous castle which stands above the meeting place of two rivers. A shattered gatehouse survives as do parts of the curtain wall, but the most memorable part is the

Goblin Hall, Yester Castle (M&R)

vaulted chamber known as the 'Goblin Hall', which is reached down a flight of steps. The lands were held by the Giffords from the twelfth century, and Sir Hugo Gifford, who was reputedly a wizard, built the Goblin (or Hobgoblin of Bo') Hall, although according old tales with the help of magic, spirits or goblins. The Colstoun Pear was a magic pear given by Hugo to his daughter on her marriage to a Brown of Colstoun. So long as her family held and preserved the pear they would prosper; the pear is still preserved, although it was perhaps an inexpensive dowry. Yester Castle was occupied by the

English during the Wars of Independence until recovered by the Scots in 1311. The stronghold later changed hands between the Scots and English in the late 1540s, the last castle in this part of Scotland to be surrendered. Yester passed by marriage to the Hays early in the fifteenth century, and was abandoned by 1800. The Hays were made Lords Yester in 1488 and Earls of Gifford in 1694. **Yester House** [NT 543672], dating from the eighteenth century, replaced the castle, and was designed by William and Robert Adam, although it has since been altered. It is still occupied.

In a peaceful spot twenty or more miles north of Lerwick in Shetland, **Busta** (pronounced 'Boosta') **House** [HU 344670] is a tall white-washed house, which dates from the sixteenth century. Busta was a property of the Giffords of Busta, who had made money as merchants and fish exporters. Thomas Gifford had four sons, but on 14 May 1748 they were all drowned in a boating accident on Busta Voe. Barbara Pitcairn, a maid or guest, was pregnant by the eldest son, and she had papers to prove that they were married. She had a son, Gideon, and he was adopted as Gifford's heir, but Barbara was shunned. She died at just thirty-six in the house of a poor relation in Lerwick. It is said that her sad ghost haunts the building, searching for her son; Gideon, himself, was to have no heirs. Busta is now a hotel (01806 522506; www.bustahouse.com).

The Giffords also owned:
Lennoxlove or **Lethington** [NT 515721], near Haddington, East Lothian; fine impressive castle and mansion.
     Held by the Giffords, but was sold to the Maitlands about 1350, and they built or extended a castle. The property passed through other hands to the Dukes of Hamiltons, and is now their family seat. The castle is open to the public from Easter to October (01620 823720; www.lennoxlove.org).
Morham Castle [NT 557723], near Haddington, East Lothian; site of castle.
     Held by the Morham family, but passed by marriage to the Giffords of Yester in the fourteenth century, but later went to the Hepburn Earls of Bothwell.
Sheriffhall [NT 320680], near Dalkeith, Midlothian; stair-turret survives from a castle.
     Held by the Todd family and by the Scotts of Buccleuch, then by the Giffords in the sixteenth century.
Strachan [NO 657921], near Banchory, Aberdeenshire; motte.
     Held by the Giffords in 1200 but passed to the Durwards.
Tealing House [NO 413380], near Dundee; mansion on site of castle.
     Held by the Fortheringhams, but had come to the Giffords of Yester by 1425 as it then passed by marriage from them to the Maxwells.

No. of castles/sites: 7
Rank: 182=/764

Gilchrist

The name is from Gaelic and means 'servant of Christ'. St Martin's Cross on Iona was carved by one Gilchrist; and Gilchrist was the personal name of one of the Earls of Mar in the twelfth century. There is also a clan called MacGilchrist ('son of Gilchrist').

Ospisdale House [NH 713897], five or so miles west of Dornoch in Sutherland, is an eighteenth-century mansion, but replaced an old castle. The lands were held by the Murrays and by the Grays and by the Gordons, but passed to the Gilchrists, and they held Ospisdale in the seventeenth and eighteenth centuries.

No. of castles/sites: 1
Rank: 537=/764

Gillespie

The name is derived from 'gilleasbuig', the 'ghillie or servant of the bishop'. The name is on record in Scotland from the end of the twelfth century. James Gillespie, a tobacco merchant in Edinburgh, left money for the establishment of a hospital in 1801-02, which later became James Gillespie's School.

Gibliston House [NO 493055], three miles northwest of St Monans in Fife, dates from 1820 but it replaced an older house or castle. The lands were held by the Sibbalds, but passed to the Smiths, and then to the Gillespies. Sir Robert Lorimer, the famous architect, purchased the house in 1916.

Kirkton [NO 447260], three and a half miles north of Leuchars in Fife, is a ruinous mansion with a round corner tower, and incorporates work from the sixteenth century. The lands were held by the Lockharts and by the Balfours, and then by the Youngs. In 1700 Kirkton was occupied by John Gillespie of Newton Rires and, although ruinous at one time, the building has been partly restored.

No. of castles/sites: 2
Rank: 396=/764

Gilmour

The name means 'servant of (St) Mary', and was used as a first name and then as a surname from the thirteenth century; although there are also lands known as Gilmour two miles east of Sanquhar in Dumfries and Galloway. The Gilmour family held several properties around Edinburgh in the seventeenth century. Nothing remains of **Gilmour Castle** [NS 822093], near Sanquhar, although presumably it was owned by the family at some time.

Barbara Gilmour was a Covenanter who fled to Ireland and there learned about a new way of making cheese. Her husband farmed Overhill at Dunlop in Ayrshire, and Barbara is credited with making the first Dunlop cheese. John Boyd Dunlop, who was born in Dreghorn in 1840, developed the first pneumatic tyre in 1888, giving his name to the Dunlop Rubber Company.

Craigmillar Castle [NT 288709], which is to the south-east of Edinburgh and above the new Royal Infirmary at Little France, is a magnificent ruinous castle. There is a large keep or tower, dating from the fourteenth century,

Craigmillar Castle (RWB)

with an inner and an outer courtyard. The lands were held by the Prestons and, after a long and eventful history, passed to the Gilmours in 1660, who remodelled the old stronghold into a more comfortable residence. The castle is now in the care of Historic Scotland and is open to the public (0131 661 4445). The Gilmours of Craigmillar were made Baronets in 1926, and now apparently live in Middlesex in England.

To the south-east of Edinburgh is **Peffermill House** [NT 284717], a tower house of three storeys and a garret with a round stair-tower. The building dates from the seventeenth century, and was held by the Prestons of Craigmillar, then by the Edgars, who built the house. It then passed through other hands until coming to the Gilmours, who held it until 1982. Sir Walter Scott is

believed to have used the house in *The Heart of Midlothian*, calling it Dumbiedykes. The house is in good condition, and still occupied.

Inch House [NT 278709] is also to the south-east of Edinburgh and is not far from Craigmillar. Also known as The Inch, it is a seventeenth-century L-plan tower house, rising to four storeys and incorporating older work. Inch

Inch House (M&R)

was held by the Gilmours from 1600, and Lochend House was burned by William Gilmour of the Inch the following year, after the Logans of Restalrig, who owned Lochend, had been involved in the Gowrie Conspiracy against James VI. Inch appears to have passed to the Winrams, and the house is now a community centre and stands in a public park.

Liberton House [NT 267694], again to the south-east of Edinburgh, is an L-plan house, dating from the seventeenth century, with a main block and a taller wing. The building is harled and orange-washed. The house replaced nearby Liberton Tower, and was built by the Littles in 1605, but later passed to the Gilmours, who held it until 1976. The house has been restored and is occupied, but can be visited strictly by appointment only from March to October (0131 467 7777; www.ngra.co.uk).

Montrave [NO 378067], three or so miles north of Leven in Fife, was a castle or old house but this was replaced by a mansion in 1836, although this has been demolished. The lands were a property of the Andersons, but passed to the Gilmours about 1800, and this branch of the family were made Baronets in 1897. They apparently still live near Montrave.

Lundin Tower [NO 399029], one mile west of Lower Largo in Fife, was incorporated into Lundin House, but this was demolished in 1876 except for a stair-turret. The lands were held by the Lundins and by the Drummonds before passing to the Gilmours in the nineteenth century, who also owned Montrave.

No. of castles/sites: 7 / Rank: 182=/764
Xref: Gilmore

Gladstone

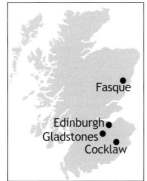

The name is territorial and comes from the lands of Gladstones, which are three and a half miles south-east of Carnwath in Lanarkshire. The name means the 'rocks of the hawk', a 'glede' being a species of hawk. The family are on record from the middle of the thirteenth century.

Gladstone Castle [NT 030428] has gone, but there are two stones with the dates 1619 and 1778 in a barn on the farm which now occupies the site. Gladstones or Easter Gladstones was a property of the Gladstone family from the thirteenth until the end of the seventeenth century. William Gladstone, one of the family, was present at the Battle of Poitiers in 1356. The family later removed to Biggar, and were ancestors of William Ewart Gladstone, who was Prime Minister four times between 1830 and 1851, and had his seat at Fasque (see below) in Kincardine. There are burial markers for the Gladstones in the cemetery of Biggar Kirk [NT 042378], an impressive cruciform church on the High Street of the burgh.

Gladstone's Land [NT 255736] on the Lawnmarket, part of Edinburgh's Royal Mile, is a six-storey tenement with an arcaded front, and was built in 1620. It was the home of well-to-do merchant, Thomas Gladstone. There are unusual tempera paintings, and the rooms and ground-floor shop are furnished and equipped as they would have been in the seventeenth century. The building is in the care of The National Trust for Scotland and is open to the public (0131 226 5856; www.nts.org.uk).

Fasque (formerly **Balmain**) [NO 648755], five miles north-west of Laurencekirk in Kincardineshire, is a fine castellated mansion, built in 1809 for the Ramsays of Balmain. There was a castle here, but there are no traces in the present building. The property passed to William Ewart Gladstone in 1929. He was made Baronet in 1846, and Fasque is still held by the Gladstone family. It is said to be haunted by the ghost of Helen Gladstone, youngest sister of the Prime Minister, as well as the spirit of a butler called MacBean. The house is open to the public but only by appointment for organised groups of twelve or more (01561 340569; www.fasque.com/fasque-estates.co.uk).

The Gladstones also held:
Capenoch House [NX 843938], near Thornhill, Dumfries and Galloway; mansion incorporating older work.
Held by the Griersons, by the Maxwells and by the Kirkpatricks, before coming to the Gladstones in 1850. The house is still apparently occupied by the Gladstones of Capenoch.
Cocklaw Castle [NT 524421], near Hawick, Borders; site of castle.
Held by the Gladstones before 1560, and had been besieged by Henry 'Hotspur' Percy in 1403 after the Battle of Homildon Hill, the events recounted in the *Scotichronicon* by Walter Bower.
Glendye [NO 644864], near Banchory, Aberdeenshire; castle or old house replaced by shooting lodge.
Held by the Carnegies Earls of Southesk, but passed to the Gladstones of Fasque in the nineteenth century.
Phesdo [NO 676756], near Laurencekirk, Kincardineshire; castle replaced by mansion.
Held by the Keiths, by the Falconers of Haulkerton and by the Crombies, before coming to the Gladstones of Fasque in the nineteenth century. Used to house German prisoners of war in World War II, was then a youth hostel, but now occupied again as a residence.

No. of castles/sites: 7
Rank: 182=/764
Xrefs: Gladstains; Gladstones

Glasgow

The name comes from the city of Glasgow in the west of Scotland, and is on record from the middle of the thirteenth century as a surname.

Montgreenan House [NS 343445], three and a half miles north-east of Kilwinning in Ayrshire, was built for the Glasgow family, who made their wealth from a shipping company based in the West Indies, and the building has been used as a hotel since 1982 (01294 850005; www.mont greenanhotel.com). One of the rooms of the house is said to be haunted, although the manifestations are reputed to be mischievous rather than frightening. The mansion replaced **Montgreenan Castle** [NS 342452], which was a property of the Rosses and then of the Cunninghams.

www.geocities.com/glasgowsoc/GlasgowSociety.html
No. of castles/sites: 1
Rank: 537=/764

Glass

The name may simply be from the Gaelic 'glas' meaning 'grey', or may be a shortened form of MacGillieglais 'son of the grey lad'.

Ascog House [NS 105633] stands to the south-east of Rothesay on the Clyde island of Bute. It is an L-plan tower house, and dates from the sixteenth century. It was a property of the Glass family from the fifteenth century, but passed to the Fairlies and then to the Stewarts. It can be rented through the Landmark Trust (01628 825925; www.land marktrust.org.uk).

No. of castles/sites: 1
Rank: 537=/764

Glassford

The name is territorial and comes from the lands of Glassford, which are two miles west of Stonehouse in Lanarkshire. A family of the same name held the lands from the end of the thirteenth century or before until about 1373. There was a castle at **Dykes** [NS 728473], to the north of the present village of Glassford, but nothing survives and this appears to have been built after the Forsyths came into possession. The lands passed to the Semples.

Balvie Castle [NS 535752], one mile west of Milngavie to the north of Glasgow, was replaced by a mansion, which has itself been demolished and Douglas Academy was built on or near the site. The property was held by several families including by the Glassfords, before eventually passing to the Douglases of Mains after 1819.

No. of castles/sites: 2
Rank: 396=/764
Xrefs: Glasford; Glasfurd

Glen

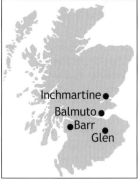

The name is territorial and comes from the lands of Glen, which are four miles south and west of Inner-leithen in the Borders. The family held property in several parts of southern Scotland, and the name is on record from the fourteenth century.

Glen [NT 298330] is a substantial baronial mansion, built in the middle of the nineteenth century for the Tennant family, now Barons Glenconnar, and they still apparently live here. The lands, however, were held by the Glens from the fourteenth century or earlier, and there was apparently a seat or castle, which was mentioned in 1216.

The family also held:
Auchinloss [NS 447401], near Kilmarnock, Ayrshire; site of tower house.
   Held by the Assloss family, then by the Montgomerys, then passed to the Glens then to the Parkers. The lands are now part of Dean Castle Country Park.
Balmuto Tower [NT 221898], near Burntisland, Fife; substantial altered castle.
   Held by the Glens, but had passed to the Boswells by the sixteenth century.
Barr Castle [NS 347582], near Lochwinnoch, Renfrewshire; ruinous but well-preserved tower.
   The castle was built by the Glens, but in the seventeenth

Barr Castle (M&R)

century had passed to the Hamiltons of Ferguslie.
Inchmartine [NO 262281], near Dundee; mansion on site of castle.
   Held by the Glens but passed to the Ogilvies in the middle of the fifteenth century.

No. of castles/sites: 5
Rank: 240=/764

Glendowyn

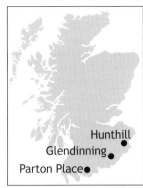

The name is territorial and comes from the lands of the same name, which are eight miles north and west of Langholm in Dumfries and Galloway. **Glendinning Castle** [NY 299965] was once an important place but there are no remains. It was held by the Glendowyns or Glendinnings from the thirteenth century or earlier until the eighteenth century. Sir Adam Glendinning supported Robert the Bruce and accompanied his heart on pilgrimage to Granada in Spain in 1330; Sir Simon Glendinning was slain at Otterburn in 1388; Mathew Glendinning was Bishop of Glasgow and died in 1408. The Glendinnings were one of those mentioned among unruly families in 1587. Glendinning passed to Johnstone of Westerhall in the nineteenth century, and they changed the name to Westerhall and built a mansion on a new site.

Parton Place [NX 710695], a few miles north-west of Castle Douglas also in Dumfries and Galloway, is a modern mansion, but it replaced a castle or older house. Parton was held by the Glendinnings from the fifteenth century until possibly 1850 (or 1720). The family were made Baronets, and John Glendinning, eleventh of Parton, supported Montrose in the 1640s. He was found guilty of treason and was forfeited, and fled to Continent, to return after the Restoration. The property may have passed by marriage to the Murrays in 1720, and Parton Place is apparently now the residence of the Hunter Blairs. **Hunthill** [NT 665191], one mile southeast of Jedburgh in the Borders, was held by the Glendinnings before passing by marriage to the Rutherfords in the fifteenth century. They built a strong tower house, which was later replaced by a mansion.

user.itl.net/~glen/glendinningorigins.html
No. of castles/sites: 3 / Rank: 328=/764
Xref: Glendinning

Gloag

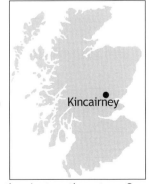

The name is on record from the sixteenth century, and many of the family lived around Dunblane. **Kincairney House** [NO 087441], five miles west of Blairgowrie in Perthshire, is a modern mansion but incorporates earlier work. It was held by the Murrays, but passed to the Gloags in the nineteenth century. One of the family was Lord Kincairney, a judge of the Court of Session.

No. of castles/sites: 1 / Rank: 537=/764

Gordon

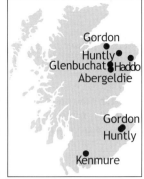

The name is territorial and comes from the lands of Gordon, which are in Berwickshire in the Borders. The family are probably Norman in origin, but are on record in Scotland from the twelfth century. Although the Gordons held lands in the Borders and in Galloway, they became major landowners in Aberdeenshire, so much so that they gave their name to a whole area of the north-east, as well as Earls of Sutherland. Robert Gordon, a successful merchant in Aberdeen who died in 1729, left money for the founding of a charitable establishment for the education of boys. Robert Gordon's College was established in 1750, although it became fee-paying in 1881. Robert Gordon has a memorial in the Kirk of St Nicholas in Aberdeen.

Gordon Castle [NT 646438] stood to the north of the village of Gordon in Berwickshire in the Borders, and there was an old stronghold here, although the exact location is not certain. It was held by the Gordons from the twelfth century, and they supported Robert the Bruce and were given lands in Strathbogie in Aberdeenshire. **Huntly** [NT 618429] is a mile or so away, and there was also a castle here. This property gave its name to the Gordons' more famous stronghold, originally known as Strathbogie, in Aberdeenshire.

Huntly Castle [NJ 532407] is just north of the burgh of Huntly in north-east Scotland, and is an impressive castle and formerly a comfortable residence. The ruins now consist of a large rectangular block with a

Huntly Castle (RWB)

substantial round tower at one end and the remains of a courtyard and other buildings. The upper part of the building has decorative stonework and three oriel windows. The interior has been sumptuous, and there are fine carved fireplaces on the upper floors. The lands were held by the MacDuff Earls of Fife and by the Earls of Atholl, but passed to the Setons and then to the Gordons in the fourteenth century. There was an earlier castle on a nearby motte, and Robert the Bruce stayed here before defeating the Comyn Earl of Buchan in battle in 1307.

This old castle was torched by the Douglas Earl of Moray in 1452, and a new stronghold was built. Perkin Warbreck, a pretender to the English throne, married Catherine Gordon here in 1496, in the presence of James IV. The name of the property was changed from Strathbogie to Huntly in 1506. Alexander Gordon, third Earl (the earldom was originally held by the Setons), led the left flank of the Scottish forces at the Battle of Flodden in 1513, but managed to escape alive. William Gordon, his son, was Bishop of Aberdeen from 1546, although his less than churchman-like behaviour earned him a rebuke from his own chapter; he remained bishop until his death in 1577. George, fourth Earl and the third Earl's grandson, was extremely powerful and he was made Chancellor of Scotland in 1547. He fought at the Battle of Pinkie the same year and, although he was captured by the English, he managed to escape. He rose in rebellion against Mary, Queen of Scots, but his forces were defeated by the forces of Mary's forces at Corrichie in 1562. George died at the battle, reputedly from apoplexy, and his third son, Sir John, was executed. The castle was slighted and pillaged at this time, the treasure from St Machar's Cathedral (presumably purloined by William Gordon – see above) in Aberdeen was seized. George, fifth Earl, was accused of treason and forfeited in 1563, but this was reversed two years later and he was made Chancellor in 1566; he continued to support Mary. The sixth Earl, another George, was probably behind the murder of the Bonnie Earl of Moray in 1592, and two years later he led a Catholic rising against James VI and defeated forces under the Earl of Argyll at the Battle of Glenlivet. Despite this victory, Huntly Castle was attacked by James VI and damaged again, but the castle was restored once again by 1602. The Earl had been pardoned and then was made Marquis of Huntly in 1599. The castle was seized by a Covenanting army in 1640, who destroyed much of the interior. Huntly Castle was then held by the forces of the Marquis of Montrose in 1644, but was captured by General David Leslie three years later after starving out (and subsequently slaughtering) the garrison. George, second Marquis of Huntly, was captured, imprisoned for two years, and then hanged in 1649. George, fourth Marquis, was made Duke of Gordon in 1684, although this title became extinct in 1836.

The castle was garrisoned by Hanoverian soldiers during the Jacobite rising of 1745-46, but by then had been abandoned as a residence. It was then used as a quarry and dump until cleared in 1923. The Gordon Marquises of Huntly and Earls of Aboyne and Enzie still flourish and their seat is listed in *Burke's* as Aboyne Castle.

Some of the materials from Huntly Castle were used to build what is now the Huntly Castle Hotel (www.castlehotel.co.uk), formerly known as Sandiestone and as Huntly Lodge. The building was extended in 1832, and became the seat of the Duke of Gordon's eldest son. It is said to have a Green Lady, the ghost of a girl who found herself with a child but no husband, and who then committed suicide.

An old saying is 'Ne'er misca a Gordon in the raws of Strathbogie', meaning do not insult someone in their own back yard. Huntly Castle is in the care of Historic Scotland and is open to the public (01466 793191).

Gordon Castle or **Bog o' Gight** (pronounced 'Gecht') **Castle** [NJ 350596] is eight and a half miles east of Elgin in Moray, and there was a castle of the Gordons here

Gordon Castle 1910?

from the fifteenth century. It was enlarged and remodelled into a massive mansion from the eighteenth century, and was the seat of the Dukes of Gordon, and then the Dukes of Richmond. It was sold to the government in lieu of death duties in 1936, and deteriorated during World War II. Most of it was demolished when bought back by the Gordon-Lennox family, except for the six-storey block and two separate wings.

Abergeldie Castle [NO 287953] lies five miles west of Ballater in Aberdeenshire, and is an altered tower house of three storeys and an attic, which dates from the sixteenth century. Abergeldie was held by the Gordons from 1482, and James Gordon of Abergeldie was killed at the Battle of Pinkie in 1547. Alexander Gordon of Abergeldie took part in Huntly's rising against Mary, Queen of Scots, in 1562 and was at the Battle of Glenlivet in 1594. During a feud with the Forbeses over land, the seven sons of Gordon of Knock were murdered by Forbes

Abergeldie Castle 1920?

of Strathgirnock, and Forbes was summarily executed by Gordon of Abergeldie. The castle was burnt by the Mackenzies in 1592, Bonnie Dundee used it as a mustering place for Jacobites in 1689, and Abergeldie was captured for William and Mary by General Mackay the same year. The castle was leased to Queen Victoria in the nineteenth century for housing guests, and a mansion was added to the old tower. The later additions have since been demolished, and the castle is still apparently occupied by the Gordons of Abergeldie. The castle is said to be haunted by the spirit of Kitty Rankie, a French maid burnt as a witch. Her ghost has reputedly been seen in the castle, most often in the tall clock tower, and the bell is said to toll when death or misfortune is to strike the family.

Glenbuchat Castle [NJ 397149] is a fine ruinous Z-plan tower house, dating from 1590 and standing four or so miles west of Kildrummy in Aberdeenshire. Glenbuchat was a property of the Gordons, who had an earlier seat **Badenyon** [NJ 340190]. The castle was

Glenbuchat Castle (RWB)

seized by James VI's forces during the Catholic rising of Earl of Huntly in 1594. Brigadier-General John Gordon of Glenbuchat fought for the Jacobites in both the 1715 and 1745-46 Risings, and led the Gordons and Farquharsons at the Battle of Culloden in 1746, when already seventy years of age. He was hunted after the battle, but managed to escape to Norway, disguised as a beggar, and he died in France. The castle was already ruinous by 1738, and was sold to the Duff Earl of Fife and was then replaced by **Glenbuchat House** [NJ 397148]. The old castle is in the care of Historic Scotland and is open to the public (01466 793191).

Rothiemay Castle [NJ 554484] has been demolished, but was an impressive castle and mansion, dating from the fifteenth century but altered and extended down the years. It stood five or so miles north of Huntly, again in Aberdeenshire. Rothiemay was held by the Abernethys, but passed to the Gordons. Mary, Queen of Scots, may have spent a night here in 1562 during Huntly's rebellion, and the castle was attacked by George Gordon of Gight in 1618. William Gordon of Rothiemay, and others, were burnt to death at the castle of Frendraught in suspicious circumstances in 1630. James Crichton of Frendraught and Rothiemay were not

on good terms, although Crichton was later cleared of involvement. In revenge, Lady Rothiemay employed Highlanders to attack Crichton's property, and she was imprisoned in 1635, but later released. Rothiemay was pillaged by the Marquis of Montrose in 1644, and held by Cromwell's forces in the 1650s. The property passed to the Duffs in 1741 and then to the Forbeses, but the building was completely demolished in 1956.

Haddo House [NJ 868347] is a magnificent classical mansion, and lies ten miles north-west of Ellon in Aberdeenshire. It stands on the site of an old stronghold, which was held by the Gordons from 1429, and Patrick Gordon of Haddo was killed at the Battle of Arbroath in 1446. Sir John Gordon of Haddo, who was made a Baronet of Nova Scotia in 1642, was active with the Marquis of Montrose but was captured after being besieged in the castle (or at Kellie) for three days in 1644. He was imprisoned in 'Haddo's Hole' in St Giles Cathedral before being executed by beheading. The castle was destroyed during the siege. Gordon's son Sir George, however, became Lord Chancellor of Scotland and Earl of Aberdeen in 1684, while George, fourth Earl, was Prime Minister but resigned in 1854. John, seventh Earl, was made Marquess of Aberdeen and Temair in 1915 after being Lord Lieutenant of Ireland and Governor General of Canada. The Gordon Marquesses of Aberdeen and Temair and Earls of Haddo, now apparently live in Berkshire in England, while Haddo House is in the care of The National Trust for Scotland and is open to the public (01651 851440; www.nts.org.uk).

Fyvie Castle [NJ 764393], a mile north of Fyvie village, again in Aberdeenshire, is a splendid and massive

Fyvie Castle 1910?

castle with a huge tower house and long wings. The property had several owners during its history, including the Lindsays, the Meldrums, the Seton Earls of Dunfermline, and then the Gordon Earls of Aberdeen from 1733 to 1889, when it went to the Leith family. Fyvie, too, is in the care of The National Trust for Scotland and is open to the public (01651 891266; www.nts.org.uk).

Kenmure Castle [NX 635764] is located a mile south of New Galloway in the south-west of Scotland. It is now ruinous, and consists of a sixteenth-century tower house with later extensions and work. Kenmure was originally held by the Balliols, but passed to the Gordons of Lochinvar about 1297. The castle was torched after the

Kenmure Castle (M&R)

Gordons had welcomed Mary, Queen of Scots, here in 1568. Sir John Gordon was made Viscount Kenmure in 1633, but the castle was burned again by Cromwell in 1650 after the family supported Charles I. William, sixth Viscount, was a Jacobite and was beheaded in the Tower of London after being captured at the Battle of Preston in 1715, and the family were forfeited. The property and title were recovered by 1824 (although the title was dormant in 1847), and the castle had been restored from ruin in the eighteenth century. Kenmure was visited by Robert Burns; but it was stripped for materials after a fire in the 1950s, and remains a ruinous shell.

The Gordons also held:

Abbot House [NT 089875], Dunfermline, Fife; fine town house.
   Held by many families down the centuries, including by the Gordon Earl of Huntly. Now a heritage centre with displays about the house and Dunfermline (01383 733266; www.abbot house.co.uk).

Aboyne Castle [NO 526995], near Aboyne, Aberdeenshire; tall tower house.
   Held by the Bissets, by the Frasers and by the Keiths, but then passed to the Gordons of Huntly by the early fifteenth century. John Gordon, Lord Aboyne, was burned to death with others of his family in an infamous incident at Frendraught Castle in 1630, although the Crichton laird of the stronghold escaped with his folk. The Gordons were made Viscounts Aboyne in 1632 and Earls of Aboyne in 1660. The Campbell Earl of Argyll captured the castle for the Covenanters, and used it as his headquarters in 1640. It has been restored and is still apparently occupied by the Gordons.

Airds [NX 675705], near Castle Douglas, Galloway; site of castle or old house.
   Held by the Gordons in the sixteenth and seventeenth centuries, although there is another site at Airds [NX 729678]. There is a panel in Crossmichael Kirkyard [NX 730670] commemorating William and Robert Gordon of Airds and dated 1629; the Gordons had their burial vault here. The property passed to the Lauries and then to the Moffats in 1877.

Aitkenhead Castle [NS 596603], Glasgow; castle replaced by mansion.
   Held by the Aitkenheads, by the Stewarts, by the Maxwells and by the Hamiltons, before latterly passing to the Gordons.

Aswanley House [NJ 445397], near Huntly, Aberdeenshire; fortified house.
   Held by the Cruickshanks, but passed to the Gordons and then to the Calders in 1440, then to the Duffs of Braco. Holiday accommodation is available and the house can be used as a venue for weddings (01466 700262; www.aswanley.com).

Auchanachie Castle [NJ 498469], near Huntly, Aberdeenshire; altered tower house.
   Held by the Gordons, and was a property of the eldest sons of Avochie.

Auchendolly [NX 768683], near Castle Douglas, Galloway; castle replaced by mansion.
   Held by the Homes and then by the Gordons.

Auchindoun Castle [NJ 348374], near Dufftown, Moray; ruinous L-plan tower house.
   Held by the Ogilvies before coming to the Gordons in 1535.

Auchindoun Castle (M&R)

Adam Gordon of Auchindoun was the leader of a party of Gordons who reputedly torched Corgarff Castle, killing Margaret Campbell, wife of Forbes of Towie, and her family and retainers as told in the old ballad 'Edom o' Gordon'. Auchindoun may have been burnt itself, either in 1544 or 1671 depending on the story, that tale told in the old ballad 'Fair Helen of Auchindoun'. The castle was also sacked in 1592 after the murder of the Bonnie Earl o' Moray at Donibristle by the Marquis of Huntly and Sir Patrick Gordon of Auchindoun. Sir Patrick was killed in 1594 at the Battle of Glenlivet. The castle is in the care of Historic Scotland and can be viewed from close by (01466 793191).

Auchintoul [NJ 615524], near Aberchirder; castle with large round tower.
   Held by the Gordons. Patrick Gordon of Auchintoul was one of the generals of Peter the Great in Russia. Alexander Gordon of Auchintoul, his son, was also a general in the Russian army, but returned to Scotland in 1711 and commanded part of the Jacobite army in 1715. He later wrote a biography of Peter the Great. The property had passed to the Duff Dukes of Fife in the 1890s.

Auchlane Castle [NX 741584], near Castle Douglas, Galloway; site of castle.
   Held by the MacLellans but had passed to the Gordons by 1600, but perhaps then returned to the MacLellans.

Auchmeddan Castle [NJ 850647], near Fraserburgh, Aberdeenshire; site of castle.
   Long held by the Bairds, but then passed to the Gordon Earls of Aberdeen in 1750, then bought back by the Bairds in 1858.

Auchoynanie [NJ 455495], near Keith, Moray; site of castle.
Held by the Gordons.

Avochie Castle [NJ 536466], near Huntly, Aberdeenshire; ruinous tower house.
Held by the Gordons of Avochie, and there is a modern house nearby.

Badenyon Castle [NJ 340190], near Kildrummy, Aberdeenshire; site of castle.
Held by the Gordons of Glenbuchat, and abandoned about 1590 when the family moved to Glenbuchat.

Balbithan House [NJ 812189], near Inverurie, Aberdeenshire; fine L-plan tower house.
Held by the Chalmers family and then by the Hays, but passed to the Gordons early in the eighteenth century, and then went to the Keith Earls of Kintore in 1859. Still occupied.

Balmoral Castle [NO 255952], near Ballater, Aberdeenshire; tower house replaced by mansion.
Held by the Drummonds, then by the Gordon Earls of Huntly, then by the Farquharsons and then by the Gordons again from 1798. They sold it to Prince Albert in 1855, and he later built the present castellated mansion, which is still the residence of the royal family. The gardens, grounds and exhibitions are open to the public from April to July (01339 742534; www.balmoralcastle.com).

Barskeoch [NX 589829], near St John's Town of Dalry, Galloway; site of tower house.
Held by the Gordons in the sixteenth century and may have been at Barskeoch Mains [NX 608833].

Beldorney Castle [NJ 424369], near Keith, Aberdeenshire; large Z-plan tower house.
Held by the Ogilvies but passed to the Gordons about 1500, who built the castle. They got into debt and the property was acquired by the Lyons, although the first Lyon laird was so unpopular that he was murdered by his tenants. The property passed to the Buchans and then to the Grants, and the castle has been restored and is occupied.

Benchar [NN 705989], near Newtonmore, Highland; site of castle or old house.
Held by the Gordons of Huntly and then by the Macphersons.

Birkhall or **Sterin** [NO 348936], near Ballater, Aberdeenshire; castle or old house replaced by mansion.
Held by the Gordons, and the White Lady of Sterin is reputedly a ghost which heralded deaths in the Gordons or the resident family. The property was sold to Prince Albert, and the house was used by Elizabeth Bowes Lyon, the Queen Mother, until her death in 2002, and then by Prince Charles and Camilla for their honeymoon in 2005.

Birse Castle [NO 520905], near Aboyne, Aberdeenshire; mansion incorporating tower house.
Held by the Gordons of Cluny, but was sacked in 1640 by their neighbours who were angry about the Gordons encroaching on their lands. The castle was used by brigands and outlaws in the 1740s, became ruinous, but has been restored and is occupied.

Bishop's Palace [NX 409605], **Penninghame**, near Newton Stewart, Galloway; motte.
Held by the Bishops of Galloway, but passed to the Gordons, who held Penninghame in the sixteenth and seventeenth centuries. Penninghame House [NX 384697] was later used as an open prison.

Blairfindy Castle [NJ 199286], near Tomintoul, Moray; derelict L-plan tower house.
Held by the Grants but passed to the Gordons of Huntly, who built the tower. The Battle of Glenlivet was fought nearby in 1594, when the Gordon Earl of Huntly and Hay Earl of Errol defeated a force led by the Earl of Argyll, with the loss of 700 men.

Blelack [NJ 440036], near Ballater, Aberdeenshire; site of castle or old house.
Held by the Gordons. The house was damaged by fire after the Battle of Culloden in 1746 and it was replaced by a mansion, which has been divided into four dwellings.

Blairfindy Tower (M&R) – see previous column

Bogrie Tower [NX 812849], near Moniaive; house incorporating part of tower.
Held by the Kirks in the 1630s, but passed by marriage to the Gordons of Lochinvar. Now a farmhouse.

Brackley Castle (**House of Glenmuick**) [NO 365945], near Ballater, Aberdeenshire; mansion on site of castle.
Held by the Gordons. John Gordon of Brackley was murdered by John Farquharson of Inverey in 1666, as told in the old ballad 'The Baron of Brackley'. The property was later held by the Mackenzies, who built the present house.

Braid [NT 251703], Edinburgh; castle or old house replaced by mansion.
Held by the Braid family and by the Fairlies, then much later by the Gordons. The Hermitage of Braid became a public park in 1888, and the house is used as a countryside information centre.

Buck o' Bield [NX 581559], near Gatehouse of Fleet, Galloway; site of castle or old house.
Held by the Rutherfords and then by the Gordons by the end of the seventeenth century. William Gordon of Buck o' Bield was shot and killed by Godfrey MacCulloch in 1690. MacCulloch was beheaded in 1697 by the Maiden, an early Scottish guillotine.

Buittle Place [NX 817616], near Dalbeattie, Galloway; altered L-plan tower house.
Held by several families including by the Maxwells and then by the Gordons of Lochinver, who built the tower. It fell ruinous, but was restored and occupied.

Cairnbulg Castle [NK 016640], near Fraserburgh, Aberdeenshire; impressive castle.
Long held by the Frasers, then later by the Gordons, who were in possession in 1899. Restored and then bought back by the Frasers.

Cairston Castle [HY 273096], near Stromness, Orkney; ruinous courtyard castle.
Held by the Gordons in 1587, and Cairston House was later built nearby.

Cardoness Castle [NX 591552], near Gatehouse of Fleet, Galloway; imposing keep or tower and castle.
Long held by the MacCullochs, but passed to the Gordons in 1629 and then went to the Maxwells. Replaced by Cardoness House [NX 566536], and the castle is now in the care of Historic Scotland and is open to the public (01557 814427).

Carnousie Castle [NJ 670504], near Turriff, Aberdeenshire; Z-plan tower house.
Held by the Ogilvies, then bought by the Gordons in 1683, then passed to other families. Restored and occupied.

Carvichen [NJ 540390], near Huntly, Aberdeenshire; site of castle.
Held by the Gordons of Lesmoir, but was sold to the Hays of Mountblairy in 1739, then went to the Dukes of Gordon in 1770.

Castle of Esslemont [NJ 932298], near Ellon, Aberdeenshire; ruinous L-plan tower house.
Held by the Marshalls, by the Cheynes and by the Hays, before being bought by the Gordons in 1728, and they abandoned the castle for a new mansion, Esslemont House, in 1769. The family, now Wolrige Gordon of Hallhead and Esslemont, still apparently lives here.

Clanyard Castle [NX 109374], near Stranraer, Galloway; ruinous L-plan tower house.
Held by the Gordons of Kenmure.

Cluny Castle [NJ 688128], near Inverurie, Aberdeenshire; mansion incorporating tower house.
Held by the Gordons from the fifteenth century.

Colliston Castle [NO 612464], near Arbroath, Angus; Z-plan tower house.
Held by the Reids and by the Guthries, but was bought by the Gordons in 1691, then went to the Chaplin family in 1721. Still occupied.

Craig Castle [NJ 472248], near Rhynie, Aberdeenshire; fine L-plan tower house.
Held by the Comyns and then by the Gordons of Craig, one of whom, Patrick Gordon, died at the Battle of Flodden in 1513. His grandson, another Patrick, was killed at the Battle of Pinkie in 1547, and his son, William, was implicated with his chief,

Craig Castle (M&R)

Huntly, in the murder of the Bonnie Earl of Moray at Donibristle in 1592. They held the property until 1892. Still occupied.

Craighlaw Castle [NX 305611], near Glenluce, Galloway; mansion incorporating tower house.
Held by the Mures but sold to the Gordons of Kenmure in 1513, then passed to the Hamiltons in 1741. Still occupied.

Crogo [NX 759774], near Castle Douglas, Galloway; site of castle or tower house.
Held by the MacNaughts but passed to the Gordons in the fifteenth century.

Culsalmond [NJ 650320], near Huntly, Aberdeenshire; site of castle.
Probably held by the Gordons, although the site may be at Newton House [NJ 661297]. James VI visited during his campaign against the Gordon Earl of Huntly.

Cunningar [NJ 701060], near Banchory, Aberdeenshire; site of castle on motte.
Held by the Browns, then by the Gordons from 1422, then went to the Forbeses, to the Grants and to the Gordons of Cluny.

Cyderhall [NH 758886], near Dornoch, Sutherland; site of castle.
Held by the Gordons.

Davidston House [NJ 419451], near Keith, Aberdeenshire; altered L-plan tower house.
Held by the Gordons.

Dee Castle [NO 438968], near Ballater, Aberdeenshire; site of castle.
Held by the Gordons.

Dinnet [NO 465982], near Ballater, Aberdeenshire; site of castle.
Held by the Gordon Earls of Huntly, but passed to the Wilsons who built Dinnet House [NO 448979], which is a mile to the west.

Dochfour House [NH 604393], near Inverness; castle or old house replaced by mansion.
Held by the Gordon Earls of Huntly but given to the Baillies, who still own it. Available for house parties, conferences, promotions and dinners (01463 861218; www.dochfour.co.uk).

Dornoch Palace [NH 797897], Dornoch, Sutherland; altered castle.
Held by the Gordon Earls of Sutherland after the Reformation. George Sinclair, fourth Earl of Caithness, had the town and cathedral burnt in 1567, and the castle besieged to secure possession of the young Earl of Sutherland (although he is also said to have been abducted from Skibo). The castle held out for a month, but eventually surrendered on fair terms, although hostages given by the garrison were subsequently murdered. The castle was then burnt, and left a ruin until restored in the nineteenth century as a courthouse and a jail. Said to be haunted by the ghost of a man accused of stealing sheep, and the building is now a hotel (01862 810216; www.dornoch castlehotel.com).

Drimnin Castle [NM 547550], near Lochaline, Highland; castle replaced by mansion.
Held by the MacLeans of Coll, but passed to the Gordons who built nearby Drimnin House [NM 554550].

Drumin Castle [NJ 184303], near Tomintoul, Moray; massive ruinous castle.
Held by the Stewarts but later was a possession of the Gordons.

Dunain [NH 626423], near Inverness; castle replaced by mansion.
Held by the Earls of Huntly but given to the Baillies after 1452.

Dundeugh Castle [NX 602880], neat St John's Town of Dalry, Galloway; slight remains of tower house.
Held by the Gordons of Kenmure.

Dunrobin Castle [NC 852008], near Golspie, Sutherland; magnificent castle and mansion.
Long a property of the Sutherlands, but the property and title passed to the Gordons, although the family later took the name of Sutherland. The castle is still held by the Sutherland family, and is open to the public from April to mid October (01408 633177; www.highlandescape.com).

Durris House [NO 799968], near Banchory, Aberdeenshire; altered L-plan tower house.
Held by the Frasers and later by the Innes family, by the Dukes of Gordon and by the MacTires, and then by the Youngs.

Earlstoun Castle [NX 613840], near St John's Town of Dalry, Galloway; altered L-plan tower house.
Held by the Hepburn Earls of Bothwell and by the Sinclairs, but passed by marriage to the Gordons of Airds in 1615. One of the family, William Gordon, was killed at the Battle of Bothwell Brig in 1679, and the castle was occupied by troops fighting against Covenanters. The family became Baronets, and Sir Alexander Gordon, Baronet and son of William, was a Covenanter and was imprisoned and was to be executed, but he was released in 1689. The Gordons have a nineteenth-century mausoleum in the burial ground at Borgue. The castle is still occupied, and the Gordons of Earlston, Baronets, now apparently live in Australia.

Edinglassie Castle [NJ 423388], near Huntly, Aberdeenshire; site of castle.
Held by the Gordons, and torched by government forces during the Jacobite Rising of 1689-90.

Ellon Castle [NJ 960307], Ellon, Aberdeenshire; ruinous castle.

Held by the Comyns and by the Kennedys, but was bought by the Gordons in the seventeenth century. The sons of the then laird were murdered by their tutor, and the property passed to the Gordon Earl of Aberdeen in 1752. The property later went to the Reids.

Fedderate Castle [NJ 897498], near New Deer, Aberdeenshire; ruinous L-plan tower house.

Held by the Crawfords but passed to the Gordons. It was one of the last places to hold out for James VII after the Battle of Cromdale in 1690, but was besieged and captured by William of Orange's forces. It is said to be haunted and its very ruinous state is a result of it being blown up to clear the site.

Ferrar [NO 484989], near Aboyne, Aberdeenshire; castle replaced by house.

Held by the Gordons, then held by the Bruces in the nineteenth century.

Finavon Castle [NO 497566], near Forfar, Angus; ruinous L-plan tower house.

Long held by the Lindsay Earls of Crawford, then much later went to the Carnegies and was then bought by the Gordon Earl of Aboyne in 1775, then went to the Gardynes in 1815. There is a fine doocot, the keys to which are available from the Finavon Hotel.

Findlater Castle [NJ 542673], near Cullen, Aberdeenshire; ruinous castle on cliffs.

Held by the Sinclairs and by the Ogilvies, and then by the Gordons, although it then returned to the Ogilvies, who were made Earls of Findlater in 1633 (www.findlater.org.uk/castle.htm).

Findochty Castle [NJ 455673], near Buckie, Aberdeenshire; ruinous L-plan tower house.

Held by the Gordons, but passed to the Ogilvies and then to the Ords.

Gight Castle [NJ 827392], near Fyvie, Aberdeenshire; ruinous L-plan tower house.

Pronounced 'Gecht'. Held by the Gordons. William Gordon of Gight was killed at the Battle of Flodden in 1513. The sixth laird broke his sword across the head of the Laird of Leask, harassed his second wife's mother to change her will in his favour (at pain of death), and tried to extort money out of his first wife's brother. The seventh laird was a tax collector, but after virtually plundering the town of Banff kept all the money. Catherine Gordon married John Byron, but in 1787 had to sell Gight to pay off his gambling debts. Their son was the poet Lord Byron, and the Gordon Earl of Aberdeen acquired the property. The castle is said to be haunted. A piper was sent to explore a tunnel beneath the building but was never seen again. From time to time it is reputed that his pipes can still be heard.

Glen Tanar [NO 476956], near Aboyne, Aberdeenshire; site of castle.

Held by the Gordon Earls of Huntly, but passed from the family in the nineteenth century.

Glenmuick [NO 372945], near Ballater, Aberdeenshire; site of castle.

Held by the Gordons and then by the Mackenzies.

Golspie Tower [NC 836009], Golspie, Aberdeenshire; site of large tower house.

Held by the Gordon Earls of Sutherland.

Gordonstoun (Plewlands or Ogstoun) [NJ 184690], near Lossiemouth, Moray; mansion incorporating tower.

Held by the Ogstouns and by the Inneses before being bought by the Gordons in 1616, and they renamed the property Gordonstoun. Passed to the Cummings of Altyre in 1795 and is now an exclusive public school. The grounds are occasionally open to the public (01343 837829; www.gordonstoun.org.uk).

Grandhome House [NJ 899117], near Dyce, Aberdeenshire; castle or old house replaced by mansion.

Held by the Keiths, by the Ogilvies, by the Buchanans, by the Gordons, and by the Jaffrays, and then by the Patons.

Greenknowe Tower [NT 639428], near Gordon, Borders; fine ruinous L-plan tower house.

Held by the Gordons, but passed by marriage to the Setons of Touch, who built the tower, and then went to the Pringles of Stichil and then to the Dalrymples. The tower was inhabited until the middle of the nineteenth century, is now in the care of Historic Scotland, and is open to the public.

Greenlaw Tower [NX 741636], near Castle Douglas, Galloway; site of tower house.

Held by the Gordons, and the castle was replaced by a mansion also called Greenlaw [NX 754644]. This is now a ruinous shell after being gutted by fire in the 1970s.

Halleaths [NY 099822], near Lockerbie, Dumfriesshire; site of mansion.

Held by the Gordons and then by the Johnstones.

Hall of Tolophin [NJ 438256], near Rhynie, Aberdeenshire; site of castle.

Held by the Gordons of Craig, and said to have been used as their summer residence.

Hallhead [NJ 525092], near Tarland, Aberdeenshire; altered T-plan tower house.

Held by the Gordons of Hallhead and Esslemont. George Gordon, fourteenth of Hallhead, was a Jacobite in the 1745-46 Rising and was forfeited, but the family regained the property.

Hallhead Castle (M&R)

Later used as a farmhouse.

Halmyre House [NT 174496], near West Linton, Borders; mansion incorporating part of a tower house.

Held by the Tweedies of Drumelzier and by the Murrays of Stanhope, but was bought by the Gordons in 1808.

Helmsdale Castle [ND 027152], Helmsdale, Sutherland; site of castle.

Held by the Earls of Sutherlands, and site of the poisoning of the eleventh Earl of Sutherland, but later passed to the Gordons. Last vestige removed when the A9 was realigned.

House of Schivas [NJ 898368], near Ellon, Aberdeenshire; altered L-plan tower house.

Held by the Schivas family, by the Lipps and by the Maitlands but went to the Gordons in 1467 and then to the Grays in 1509. Later it passed to the Forbeses and then to the Gordon Earl of Aberdeen. Still occupied.

House of Tongue [NC 592588], Tongue, Sutherland; tower house replaced by mansion.

Held by the Mackays, but passed to the Dukes of Sutherland. The gardens are occasionally open to the public (www.gardensofscotland.org).

Huntly House [NT 265739], Canongate, Edinburgh; fine town house.

Held and built by the Gordon Earls and Marquises of Huntly, and now the main museum of local history for Edinburgh (Museum of Edinburgh). It is open all year (0131 529 4143; www.cac.org.uk).

Inverbreakie [NH 715700], near Invergordon, Ross and Cromarty; site of castle.

Held by the Gordons from the beginning of the eighteenth century.

Invergordon Castle [NH 705700], near Invergordon, Ross and Cromarty; site of mansion.

Held by the Gordons from the beginning of the eighteenth century. They changed the name and established the town and port of Invergordon, but the property was held by the MacLeods of Cadboll in the 1870s. The mansion was demolished in 1928.

Inverlochy Castle [NN 120754], near Fort William, Highland; ruinous courtyard castle.

Held by the Comyns but was granted to the Gordon Earls of Huntly in 1505. In the care of Historic Scotland and open to the public (01667 460232).

Invermarkie Castle [NJ 429396], near Keith, Aberdeenshire; site of castle.

Held by the Gordons and then by the Innes family, but was demolished in the seventeenth century. A shooting lodge of the Duffs was built here.

Keithmore [NJ 355391], near Dufftown, Moray; site of castle or old house.

Held by the Ogilvies but passed to the Gordon Earls of Huntly, then to the Duffs, but the lands appear to have returned to the Gordons by 1750.

Kildrummy Castle [NJ 454164], near Kildrummy, Aberdeenshire; magnificent ruinous castle.

After many owners and a long eventful history, Kildrummy passed to the Gordons of Wardhouse in 1731, by when it was already ruinous. It is now in the care of Historic Scotland and is open to the public from April to September (01975 571331).

Killiechassie [NN 864503], near Aberfeldy, Perthshire; site of castle or old house.

Held by the Stewarts but later passed to the Gordons after 1746 and then went to the Douglases in 1863. There is a later mansion.

Kinellar House [NJ 815129], near Kintore, Aberdeenshire; castle replaced by mansion.

Held by the Gordons in 1718.

Kisimul Castle [NL 665979], Castlebay, Barra; fine restored castle on island.

Long a property of the MacNeils, but Barra and the castle were sold to the Gordons of Cluny in 1840 and then went to the Cathcarts. The property was bought back by the MacNeils in 1937 and the castle is now in the care of Historic Scotland and is open to the public from April to October (01871 810313).

Knock Castle [NO 352952], near Ballater, Aberdeenshire; ruinous tower house.

Held by the Bissets but passed to the Gordons of Huntly and this may have been this stronghold which was attacked and destroyed by Clan Chattan in 1590. The Gordons feuded with

Knock Castle (M&R)

the Forbeses and Henry Gordon, second of Knock, was slain in a raid. Later, while the seven sons of the next laird were out cutting peats on Forbes's land, Forbes of Strathgirnock surprised and beheaded all seven sons, and tied their heads to their peat-spades. When the laird of Knock heard of their deaths, he fell down the turnpike stair of his own tower, broke his neck and was also killed. Forbes of Strathgirnock was summarily executed for the deed in his own house by Gordon of Abergeldie. The castle is in the care of Historic Scotland but is not currently open to the public.

Knockbrex [NX 585497], near Gatehouse of Fleet, Galloway; castle or old house replaced by mansion.

Held by the Gordons, who were Covenanters and fought in the Pentland Rising of 1666. John Gordon of Knockbrex, and his brother, Robert, were captured following the Battle of Rullion Green, tried and executed in Edinburgh. Their severed heads decorated the town gate of Kirkcudbright. The property had passed to the Browns by 1895 and they built the present mansion. The mansion can be rented as holiday accommodation (01381 610496; www.lhhscotland.com).

Knockespock House [NJ 544241], near Rhynie, Aberdeenshire; mansion incorporating tower house.

Held by the Gordons. The family, now Fellowes-Gordon, formerly of Knockespoch, apparently now live near Huntly in Aberdeenshire.

Knockgray [NX 578932], near Carsphairn, Galloway; site of castle or old house.

Held by the Gordons in the sixteenth and seventeenth centuries. Gordon of Knockgray was forfeited for treason for his part in the Covenantor Rising which ended in defeat at the Battle of Bothwell Brig in 1679. The property passed to the Kennedys and a later house is now used as a farmhouse.

Leask House [NK 026331], near Ellon, Aberdeenshire; site of castle and ruinous mansion.

Held by the Leasks, who did not get on with the Gordons of Gight. The Gordon sixth laird of Gight broke his sword across the head of Laird of Leask, and some of the Gordons were outlawed for attacking the son of the chief. The Leasks were ruined following the Darien Scheme, and the property went to the Cummings and then to the Gordons of Hilton in the eighteenth century. Leask later passed to the Skenes.

Lesmoir Castle [NJ 470280], near Rhynie, Aberdeenshire; slight remains of castle.

Held by the Gordons. The Covenanter General David Leslie captured the castle in 1647 by draining the moat, and then hanged the garrison in the kind of act of mercy that can be expected from men of God. The property was sold to the Grants of Rothiemurchus in 1759, and they demolished the castle.

Letterfourie [NJ 447625], near Buckie, Aberdeenshire; castle replaced by mansion.

Held by the Leslies and then by the Gordons from the beginning of the sixteenth century for 300 years or so. Sir James of Letterfourie, Admiral of the Fleet, commanded Scottish ships in 1513. James Gordon, third of Letterfourie, was a Royalist and was twice imprisoned, the second time after being captured by General David Leslie. James, fifth lord, was a Jacobite and fought at the Battle of Sheriffmuir in 1715, while Alexander Gordon, seventh of Letterfourie, was in the Life Guards of Bonnie Prince Charlie and was at Culloden in 1746. He then fled abroad to Madeira, but returned in 1760. The Gordons, formerly of Letterfourie, still apparently live in Banffshire.

Lickleyhead Castle [NJ 627237], near Insch, Aberdeenshire; altered L-plan tower house.

Held by several families, including by the Forbeses, but passed to the Gordons, and then to the Leslies at the beginning of the nineteenth century. Still occupied.

Lincluden Collegiate Church [NX 967779], near Dumfries; ruinous collegiate church and later altered dwelling.

Held by the Stewarts, by the Douglases of Drumlanrig and

then by the Gordons of Lochinvar, and then by the Youngs of Lincluden. Now held in the care of Historic Scotland and open to the public.

Little Tarrel [NH 911819], near Tain, Ross and Cromarty; altered L-plan tower house.

Possibly held by the Gordon Earl of Huntly or by the Munros at one time, although also by the Tarrel family and by the MacCullochs. Still occupied.

Loch an Eilean Castle [NH 899079], near Aviemore, Highland; ruinous castle on island.

Held by the Mackintoshes and by the Gordons, then by the Grants.

Lochinvar Castle [NX 656853], near St John's Town of Dalry, Galloway; site of castle on island.

Held by the Balliols but passed to the Gordons in 1297, and they had a stronghold here until 1640 or later, although they moved to Kenmure in the sixteenth century. Gordon of Lochinvar murdered MacLellan of Bombie in Edinburgh's High Street in 1527, but this branch of the family became Viscounts Kenmure in 1633.

Loch Kinord Castle [NO 440996], near Aboyne, Aberdeenshire; site of castle.

Held by the Gordons of Huntly in the sixteenth century. It had been occupied by the Earl of Atholl in 1335 but he was defeated by Andrew Moray and the castle surrendered. It was visited by James IV but was besieged and captured by the Covenanter General David Leslie in 1647. It was razed on order of an act of parliament soon afterwards.

Lynturk Castle [NJ 598122], near Alford, Aberdeenshire; site of castle.

Held by the Strachans, but later passed to the Irvines and then to the Gordons until 1816 when it passed to the MacCombies.

Mains of Mayen [NJ 576477], near Huntly, Aberdeenshire; L-plan tower house.

Held by the Abernethys, and then by the Gordons from 1612. The property passed to the Halketts in 1649 and then to the Abernethys again, then to the Duffs. Restored and occupied.

Mains of Pronie [NJ 446078], near Tarland, Aberdeenshire; site of castle.

Held by the Gordons of Pronie. Tillypronie [NJ 433080] was built by the son of Queen Victoria's physician, Sir James Clark.

Melgund Castle [NO 546564], near Brechin, Angus; restored castle.

Held by the Cramonds, and then by the Beatons, then by the Gordon Marquis of Huntly in the seventeenth century, before passing to the Maules, to the Murrays and then to the Elliot Earls of Minto. Became ruinous but has been restored.

Merton [NX 383640], near Newton Stewart, Galloway; castle replaced by mansion.

Held by the Gordons from the eighteenth century or earlier, but was sold to the Boyds in 1785.

Midmar Castle [NJ 704053], near Banchory, Aberdeenshire; fine Z-plan tower house.

Held by the Browns but passed to the Gordons in 1422 and then to the Forbeses and to the Grants, then to the Gordons of Cluny. Still occupied.

Migvie Castle [NJ 437066], near Ballater, Aberdeenshire; slight remains of castle.

Held by the Rutherfords of Tarland but passed to the Gordon Earl of Huntly.

Muirfad Castle [NX 457631], near Newton Stewart, Galloway; site of castle.

Held by the Gordons of Muirfad, and the last of the family was killed at the Battle of Flodden in 1513.

Old House of Embo [NH 809922], near Dornoch, Sutherland; castle replaced by house.

Held by the Gordons of Embo.

Ospisdale House [NH 713897], near Dornoch, Sutherland; castle replaced by mansion.

Held by the Murrays or by the Grays, then by the Gordons and by the Gilchrists.

Park [NJ 587571], near Aberchirder, Aberdeenshire; fine castle and mansion.

Held by the Gordons, and Sir William Gordon of Park was active for the Jacobites during the 1745-46 Rising. Although he escaped to France, he lost his lands and property, and died in 1751, the estate eventually passing to the Gordon-Duffs. The castle is said to be haunted by a Green Lady, the spirit of a young servant girl who got pregnant and then killed herself. There is also reputedly a spectral monk and the unexplained voices of children and a music box. Open all year to residents by arrangement: painting and writing courses (01466 751667; www.castleofpark.net).

Pitlurg Castle [NJ 436455], near Keith, Aberdeenshire; ruinous Z-plan tower house.

Held by the Gordons, who owned the property until 1724. An effigy of Sir John Gordon of Pitlurg is in the Boray Aisle, the remains of St Martin's Church, at Cairnie.

Place of Tillyfour [NJ 659195], near Inverurie, Aberdeenshire; L-plan tower house.

Held by the Leslies of Wardhouse, but passed to the Gordons after 1640. Restored and occupied.

Poyntzfield or **Ardoch** [NH 711642], near Cromarty; castle replaced by mansion.

Held by the Gordons, but went to the Munros around 1757 and they changed the name to Poyntzfield. Still occupied.

Preston Hall [NT 394658], near Dalkeith, Midlothian; mansion on site of older house or castle.

Held by the Gordons in 1738, but sold to the Callanders in 1789, and their descendants still live here.

Proncy Castle [NH 772926], near Dornoch, Sutherland; slight remains of castle.

Held by the Sutherlands in 1525 but passed to the Gordons of Proncy.

Rathven [NJ 444655], near Buckie, Aberdeenshire; site of castle.

Held by the Chalmers family and then possibly by the Gordons of Letterfourie.

Rothiemurchus [NH 885098], near Aviemore, Highland; castle or old house replaced by mansion.

Held by the Mackintoshes, by the Shaws and by the Dallases of Cantray, then by the Gordons and then by the Grants in the sixteenth century. The estate is open to the public (01479 812345; www.rothiemurchus.net).

Rusko Castle [NX 584605], near Gatehouse of Fleet, Galloway; altered castle.

Held by the Cairns family, but passed by marriage to the Gordons of Lochinvar early in the sixteenth century, and they held it for about 400 years. Restored and occupied.

Ruthven [NJ 510468], near Huntly, Aberdeenshire; site of castle on motte.

Held by the Gordons from the fourteenth century. There is the tomb and stone effigy of Sir Thomas Gordon of Ruthven, Tam o' Ruthven, in the ruins of St Carol's Church at Ruthven. The castle was probably replaced by nearby Auchanachie Castle [NJ 498469].

Ruthven Barracks [NN 764997], near Kingussie, Highland; ruinous barracks.

Held by the Comyns and by the Stewarts, but passed to the Gordon Earls of Huntly in 1451, and was sacked the same year by the MacDonald Earl of Ross. James II visited in 1459, and Mary, Queen of Scots, also visited. The castle was twice damaged by fire, and in 1689 was attacked by Jacobites. The old castle was demolished and a barracks built on the site in 1718. Ruthven was held by government forces in 1746, but was eventually taken and burnt by Jacobite forces after the Battle of Culloden. The ruins of the barracks are in the care of Historic Scotland and are open to the public (01667 460232).

Seggieden [NO 168215], near Perth; site of castle or old house.

Held by the Hay Earls of Kinnoul and then by the Gordons and by the Nairns, before returning to the Hays.

Shirmers Castle [NX 657743], near New Galloway, Galloway; ruinous castle.

Held by the Gordons, and the family supported Mary, Queen of Scots, at the Battle of Langside in 1568. The castle was torched as a result, although it was restored and was still occupied in the eighteenth century.

Skelbo Castle [NH 792952], near Dornoch, Sutherland; ruinous castle.

Held by the Sutherlands of Skelbo, and then by the Gordon Earls of Sutherland.

Stichill House [NT 702392], near Kelso, Borders; site of castle and mansion.

Held by the Gordons of Lochinvar, but passed to the Pringles in 1628 and then to the Bairds and to the Deuchars.

Straloch House [NJ 860210], near New Machar, Aberdeenshire; castle replaced by mansion.

Held by the Cheynes but bought by the Gordons of Pitlurg in 1600. Robert Gordon of Straloch was a mapmaker and historian, and completed the maps of Timothy Pont which were used as the basis of Blaeu's *Atlas Novus* maps of Scotland. Another Robert, his grandson and a successful merchant who traded with the Baltic ports, founded Robert Gordon's College in Aberdeen. The property was sold to the Ramsays in 1758 and then passed to the Irvines of Drum.

Strome Castle [NG 862354], near Lochcarron, Ross and Cromarty; ruinous castle by sea.

Held by the Camerons of Lochiel or by the MacDonald Lord of the Isles, and then by the Gordon Earl of Huntly from 1546. The Gordons had besieged it in 1503, but it passed to the MacDonalds of Glengarry, and was destroyed with gunpowder in 1602 after a long siege. The ruins are accessible (01599 566325).

Terpersie Castle [NJ 547202], near Alford, Aberdeenshire; Z-plan tower house.

Held by the Gordons. It was built by William Gordon, fourth son of Gordon of Lesmoir. He fought at the Battle of Corrichie,

Terpersie Castle (M&R)

when the Gordons were defeated in 1562, but in 1572 was at the Battle of Tillyangus, and killed the champion of the Forbes clan, Black Arthur. He also fought at the Battle of Craibstone and the Battle of Brechin. The castle was burnt in 1645 by Covenanters. George Gordon of Terpersie was involved in the murder of Alexander Clerihew of Dubston in 1707. One of the lairds fought at Culloden in 1746 during the Jacobite Rising and, after the defeat, hid in the castle. His children unwittingly recognised and betrayed him, and he was executed and the family forfeited. The castle was restored in the 1980s and is occupied.

Threave Castle [NX 739623], near Castle Douglas, Galloway; magnificent ruinous castle on island.

Long held by the Douglases and then by the Maxwells, but the property passed to the Gordons in 1873 and they built Threave House [NX 752605], then the property went to The National

Trust for Scotland. The castle is in the care of Historic Scotland and is open to the public from April to September (07711 223101 (mobile)). Threave House and garden can also be visited (01556 502575; www.nts.org.uk).

Tillycairn Castle [NJ 664114], near Kemnay, Aberdeenshire; L-plan tower house.

Held by the Gordons but passed to the Forbeses in 1444 and they built the castle. Then the property went to the Lumsdens, and then to the Gordons again, then to the Lumsdens again.

Tillyhilt Castle [NJ 854318], near Ellon, Aberdeenshire; slight remains of castle.

Held by the Gordons.

Tolquhon Castle [NJ 873286], near Oldmeldrum, Aberdeenshire; fine ruinous castle.

Held by the Prestons and then by the Forbeses, who built much of the present castle, but passed to the Farquhars and then to the Gordon Earls of Aberdeen. In the care of Historic Scotland and open to the public (01651 851286).

Torrish Castle [NC 975185], near Helmsdale; site of castle.

Held by the Gordons in 1621.

Troquhain [NX 681783], near New Galloway, Galloway; site of castle.

Held by the MacLellans but passed to the Gordons, then later went to the Villers-Stuarts.

Urquhart Castle [NH 531286], near Drumnadrochit, Inverness-shire; magnificent ruinous castle by Loch Ness.

Held by several families, including by the Gordon Earl of Huntly from 1476 to 1509, and has a long and violent history. Now in the care of Historic Scotland and open to the public (01456 450551).

Wardhouse [NJ 593289], near Insch, Aberdeenshire; site of castle.

Held by the Leslies in the sixteenth century but passed to the Gordons.

Westhall [NJ 673266], near Inverurie, Aberdeenshire; L-plan tower house.

Held by the Gordons after the Reformation and then by the Hornes in 1681 and then by the Elphinstones. Still occupied.

www.clangordon.org
www.gordon-ca.org
bydand.orcon.net.nz
No. of castles/sites: 149
Rank: 2/764

Gorthy

The name is territorial and comes from the lands of Gorthy, which are five or so miles east of Crieff in Perthshire. There was a castle or tower at **Gorthy** [NN 962237], although the precise location is not certain. The first of the family was Tristram de Gorthy, who was in possession around 1200. The Gorthys held the lands for about 400 years, and successive heads of the family were called Tristram. The property eventually passed by marriage to the Lundies in the sixteenth century.

No. of castles/sites: 1
Rank: 537=/764
Xref: Gorthie

Gourlay

The name probably comes from a place in England, and is on record in Scotland from the end of the twelfth century. The family held lands in Fife and in East Lothian. Norman Gourlay was burned for heresy in Edinburgh in 1534.

Kincraig Castle [NO 466003], one mile west and north of Earlsferry in Fife, was held by the Gourlays of Kincraig in the thirteenth century, but there are no remains. The family held the property for 600 years. **Elie Castle** [NO 488001], also in Fife, was also held by the same family. The castle is an L-plan tower house, dating from the seventeenth century with older work, and rises to three storeys. Some original painting and panelling survives.

Scotstarvit Tower [NO 370113], two miles south of Cupar again in Fife, is a tall and impressive tower house of six storeys and a garret. The tower dates from the

Scotstarvit Tower (M&R)

fifteenth and sixteenth centuries, and was owned by the Inglises and then by the Scotts, before coming to the Gourlays of Craigrothie about 1780. Scotstarvit later passed to others, then to The National Trust for Scotland. The tower is in the grounds of Hill of Tarvit, and can be visited (01334 653127).

Hailes Castle [NT 575758] is a mile or so west and south of East Linton in East Lothian. It is an atmospheric ruin in a (now) peaceful spot above the River Tyne although it had a turbulent history, and dates from the thirteenth century. It was held by the Cospatrick Earls

Hailes Castle (M&R)

of Dunbar and March and by the Gourlay family, before passing to the Hepburns, who held it for hundreds of years. The ruin is in the care of Historic Scotland and open to the public.

No. of castles/sites: 4
Rank: 278=/764

Govan

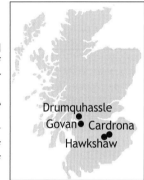

The name is territorial and comes from the lands of Govan, which are near Glasgow. The family held lands from the end of the thirteenth century.

Cardrona Tower [NT 300378] is three and half miles east and south of Peebles in the Borders, and is a small ruinous L-plan tower house, dating from the sixteenth century. Cardrona was held by the Govans from 1386 to 1685, when the property went to the Williamsons. **Hawkshaw Castle** [NT 079225], nine miles south of Broughton also in the Borders, has all but gone, but may have been held by the Govans after 1725: a Govan of Hawkshaw is mentioned in 1819, when he died.

There are also no remains of **Drumquhassle Castle** [NS 483869], a mile or so to the south and east of Drymen in central Scotland. Drumquhassle was held by the Dennistouns, and then by the Buchanans, by the Cunninghams, by the Grahams, and then by the Govans. The castle was replaced by Drumquhassle House, a mansion dating from 1839.

No. of castles/sites: 3
Rank: 328=/764

235

Graham

The name apparently comes from the lands and manor of 'graegham' or 'grey home', which are in England and are recorded in the Domesday Book. The family came to Scotland when David I came to the throne in the twelfth century, and the Grahams were given lands in the Lothians and became major landowners in central Scotland, in Perthshire and in Angus. Patrick Graham was Bishop of Brechin in 1463 and then of St Andrews in 1465. He managed to get the bishopric raised to an archbishopric in 1472, but he seems to have become increasingly insane and he was deprived of the office in 1478 and died soon afterwards. Kenneth Grahame, born in Edinburgh in 1859, moved to London early in his career and in 1908 wrote *The Wind in the Willows*.

Dalkeith House [NT 333679], to the north-west of the town of Dalkeith in Midlothian, is now a U-plan classical mansion, but it stands on the site of an old stronghold going back to the twelfth century. The lands were held by the Grahams from this time, but passed by marriage to the Douglases about 1350. The Douglases lived here for generations, and this branch was made Earls of Morton; but the property eventually passed to the Scott Earls and Dukes of Buccleuch. The house is now used for students from the United States, is said to be haunted, and the grounds are a country park (0131 654 1666/0131 663 5684; www.dalkeithcountrypark.com).

Abercorn Castle [NT 083794] has gone except for a mound, but stood a few miles west and north of South Queensferry in West Lothian. Abercorn was also held by the Grahams but went to the Mures early in the fourteenth century and then to the Douglases. The castle was destroyed by James II's forces in 1455.

Graham's Castle [NS 682858], also known as **Dundaff Castle**, lies four miles east of Fintry in central Scotland. Nothing survives except the impressive moat although this was once a place of some strength. It was the castle of Sir John Graham, who was at Stirling Bridge in 1297, and died fighting alongside William Wallace at Falkirk in 1298. Graham is buried in Falkirk Kirkyard; and Wallace is said to have found refuge at Dundaff. The Grahams were later made Viscounts Dundaff.

Kincardine Castle [NN 948115], just south-east of Auchterarder in Perthshire, was also a substantial castle with a keep or tower and a courtyard, but little now survives. The property came to the Grahams about 1250, and Sir David Graham of Kincardine was taken prisoner after the Battle of Neville's Cross in 1346. The Grahams were made Earls of Kincardine in 1644, but the castle was demolished by the Campbell Earl of Argyll two years later after the campaign led by the Marquis of Montrose. A new symmetrical mansion was built nearby early in

the nineteenth century, and was also called Kincardine Castle [NN 949114].

Old Montrose Castle [NO 675570] has gone completely, but stood three miles west of Montrose in Angus. The lands were exchanged by Robert the Bruce for Cardross with Sir David Graham, a follower of Bruce. The family were made Lords Graham in 1445, and then Earls of Montrose in 1504-05 after William Graham had fought bravely at the Battle of Sauchieburn in 1488. William, first Earl, was killed at the Battle of Flodden in 1513. John, third Earl, was Chancellor of Scotland in 1598-99 and then Viceroy of Scotland. The Grahams of Montrose have a burial vault at St Kattan's Church [NN 973151] in Aberuthven, where there is also the Montrose Mausoleum, constructed for the first Duke of Montrose, who died in 1736. Mugdock had become their favoured residence.

Mugdock Castle [NS 549772] is a mile or so north of Milngavie in Dunbartonshire, and this was formerly a strong courtyard castle, dating from the fourteenth century but it was altered and remodelled down the years. Mugdock was held by the Grahams from the middle of the previous century, and became the residence of the Earls and Marquises of Montrose. One of the family was James Graham, fifth Earl and first Marquis of Montrose, who succeeded his father in 1626 and may have been born here. He joined the Covenanters in 1638, but was opposed to Scottish intervention in the Civil War. Lord Sinclair sacked the castle while Montrose was in prison in 1641. Montrose went on to conduct a brilliant campaign against the Covenanters in 1644-45 winning battles at Tippermuir, Aberdeen, Auldearn, Inverlochy, Alford, and Kilsyth, but was finally surprised and defeated by David Leslie at Philiphaugh in the Borders. Montrose escaped to the continent, where he distinguished himself, but returned to Scotland via Orkney in 1650 to be defeated at Carbisdale the same year, and he was later captured and hanged in Edinburgh. His body was quartered and put on display, but after the Restoration was given a lavish funeral and interred in St Giles Cathedral in Edinburgh. The family was forfeited, and Mugdock was

Mugdock Castle (M&R)

acquired by Montrose's enemy, the Campbell Marquis of Argyll. It was recovered by the Grahams in 1661 when Argyll, himself, was executed. Mugdock was replaced by Buchanan Castle as the main seat of the Grahams, and much of Mugdock was destroyed when a mansion was built here for the Smiths. This house was demolished after World War II, and the ruins of the castle now stand in a public park (0141 956 6100; www.mugdock-country-park.org.uk).

Buchanan Castle [NS 463886] is half a mile west of Drymen in Stirlingshire, and is now a large ruinous mansion which incorporates an L-plan tower house. The lands were held by the Lyles and then by the Buchanans, but when the Buchanans got into financial difficulties it was bought by the Graham Marquis of Montrose in 1682. The Grahams were made Dukes in 1707, and James, first Duke, spent much of his time trying to track down Rob Roy MacGregor. Buchanan Castle was gutted by fire in 1850, and a new house was built four years later, designed by William Burn, while the gardens were modelled by Capability Brown, but have been replaced by a golf course. Rudolf Hess, Hitler's deputy, was imprisoned here after flying to Scotland, but the castle is now ruined although consolidated. Many of the Grahams were buried in the chapter house of Inchmahome Priory [NN 574005], near Aberfoyle in Stirlingshire and on an island in the Lake of Menteith. The ruins of the priory are in the care of Historic Scotland and are open to the public (01877 385294).

Claverhouse Castle [NO 380442] stood seven or so miles north of Dundee but nothing now remains. It consisted of a large keep with a moat and drawbridge. It was held by the Ogilvies, but had passed to the Grahams by the seventeenth century. The Jacobite John Graham of Claverhouse, Bonnie Dundee or Bloody Clavers, took his title from this place and was brought up here. Graham was made Earl of Dundee, and was the victor at the Battle of Killiecrankie in 1689, against the forces of William and Mary, although he was mortally wounded and died during the battle.

The Grahams also held:

Airth Castle [NS 900869], near Falkirk; altered castle and mansion.
  Held by the Airths, by the Bruces and by the Elphinstones, then went to the Grahams from 1717 to 1920. William Graham, seventh Earl of Menteith, was made Earl of Airth (a lesser title) after he had tried to claim the Earldom of Strathearn. The castle is now used as a hotel (01324 831411; www.airthcastlehotel.com).

Ardoch Tower [NS 364768], near Cardross, Dunbartonshire; site of tower house.
  Held by the Bontines, but passed to the Grahams of Gartmore, who built Ardoch House in the 1870s. One of the family was Robert Bontine Cunningham Graham, who became the first president of the Scottish Labour Party in 1888, then the President of the National Party of Scotland in 1928.

Arnfinlay Castle [NS 587955], near Aberfoyle, Stirlingshire; site of castle.
  Held by the Doigs and then by the Grahams at the beginning of the nineteenth century.

Auchindinny House [NT 252613], near Penicuik, Midlothian; mansion with older work.
  Held by the Inglis family, but now apparently occupied by the Maxtone Grahams, formerly of Cultoquhey.

Auchterarder Castle [NN 936133], near Auchterarder, Perthshire; slight remains of castle.
  Held by the Grahams, and Edward I of England stayed at the castle in 1296. The property passed by marriage to the Drummonds.

Balgowan [NN 987237], near Crieff; ruinous building, perhaps on site of castle.
  Held by the Grahams in the sixteenth century or earlier. Thomas Graham of Balgowan was a successful soldier and distinguished himself at Minorca in 1798 and then at Malta two years later. He served in the Peninsular War, and was

Balgowan (STO)

second in command to the Duke of Wellington. Graham was made Lord Lynedoch (also see Lynedoch) of Balgowan in 1814. Balgowan was sold in 1859, and most of the house has been demolished.

Ballanreoch Castle [NS 610794], near Lennoxtown, Dunbartonshire; site of castle.
  Held by the Grahams but passed to the Brisbanes of Bishopton in 1423 and then to the MacFarlanes of Keighton. The castle was rebuilt, used as the Campsie Glen Hotel, was then burned out in the 1980s, but has been restored again.

Ballochtoul Castle [NX 192976], near Girvan, Ayrshire; site of castle.
  Held by the Grahams of Knockdolian but passed to the Boyds of Penkill.

Bogle Walls, Enzieholm [NY 292912], near Langholm, Dumfriesshire; site of castle.
  Held (barony of Westerkirk) by the Avenels but passed by marriage to the Grahams about 1243. Enzieholm was probably later held by the Beatties and by the Scotts.

Boquhan Castle [NS 661935], near Kippen, Stirlingshire; site of castle.
  Held by the Grahams.

Braco Castle [NN 824113], near Dunblane, Perthshire; altered tower house.
  Held by the Graham Earls of Montrose, one of whom was created a Baronet in 1625. The castle was seized by Jacobites in the 1715 Rising, and the Grahams lost the property in the 1790s. It is said to be haunted, and Braco later passed to the Smythes. The grounds are open from February to October by appointment (01786 880437; www.gardensofscotland.org).

Burleigh Castle [NO 130046], near Kinross; remains of castle.
  Held by the Balfours of Burleigh, then by the Irwins and by the Grahams of Kinross.

Carbeth House [NS 524876], near Killearn, Stirlingshire; castle replaced by mansion.
  Held by the Grahams but passed to the Buchanans in 1476, and they built the castle, then went to the Wilsons in the nineteenth century. Still occupied.

Cardross Manor House [NS 385757], near Dumbarton; site of castle or manor.
  Held by the Grahams, but exchanged for the lands of Old Montrose with Robert the Bruce. Bruce built a manor or

fortified house, although the location is not certain, and it is here that he died in 1329. The site is accessible to the public.

Catter Castle [NS 473871], near Drymen, Stirlingshire; site of castle on motte.

Held by the Earls of Lennox and then by the Buchanans, but passed to the Graham Dukes of Montrose, who built a new mansion, Catter House [NS 471871] in 1767.

Claypotts Castle [NO 452319], near Dundee; fine Z-plan tower house.

Held by the Strachans and then by the Grahams of Claverhouse, one of whom was John Graham of Claverhouse, Viscount or 'Bonnie' Dundee. The property went to the Douglas Earls of

Claypotts Castle 1907?

Angus in 1694, and then to the Homes. The castle is in the care of Historic Scotland and is sometimes open to the public (01786 431324).

Clifton Hall [NT 109710], near Broxburn, West Lothian; castle replaced by mansion.

Held by the Grahams of Abercorn in the twelfth century, but passed to the Macalzeans, to the Douglases, to the Wisharts, and then to others, and the mansion is now used to house a school.

Coldoch [NS 699982], near Doune, Stirlingshire; site of castle.

Held by the Spittals, by the Drummonds and by the Stirlings, but passed to the Grahams, who lived at a later mansion.

Craigcrook Castle [NT 211742], Edinburgh; fine Z-plan tower house and mansion.

Held by the Grahams in the fourteenth century, but passed to several different families, including to the Adamsons who built the tower. Still occupied as the offices of Scottish Field (0131 312 4550; www.scottishfield.co.uk).

Craigend Castle [NS 545778], near Milngavie, Dunbartonshire; site of castle and mansion.

Held by the Grahams and part of the Mugdock lands, but was sold to the Smiths in the middle of the seventeenth century, then to the Inglis family, to the Buchanans and to the Wilsons. The building was demolished except for the stables which house a visitor centre for Mugdock Park (0141 956 6100; www.mugdock-country-park.org.uk).

Croft an Righ House [NT 271742], Edinburgh; altered L-plan town or tower house.

Held by James Stewart, Earl of Moray and Regent Moray, but probably later was owned by the Elphinstones and by the Grahams. Taken over by Historic Scotland.

Crookston Castle [NS 524628], near Paisley, Renfrewshire; unusual ruinous castle.

Long held by the Stewarts, but was later owned by several families in succession including the Graham Dukes of Montrose, who sold it to the Maxwells of Pollok in 1757. Held by The National Trust for Scotland, but managed by Historic Scotland and open to the public (0141 883 9606/0131 668 8800).

Cultoquhey [NN 893233], near Crieff, Perthshire; castle replaced by mansion.

Long held by the Maxtones, but they married into the Grahams and changed their name to Maxtone Graham. They sold the

property in 1955, and now live at Auchindinny House, while Cultoquhey is now a hotel (01764 653253).

Darnley Castle [NS 527586], near Barrhead, Glasgow; some remains of tower house.

Held by the Stewarts, later Earls of Lennox, and this is the property from which Mary, Queen of Scots's, second husband, Lord Darnley, took his title. The property was sold to the Graham Marquis of Montrose in 1689, then to the Maxwells of Nether Pollok. It has been renovated and houses a restaurant (0141 876 0458).

Douglaston House [NS 565742], near Milngavie, Dunbartonshire; castle replaced by mansion.

Held by the Grahams, but passed to the Crawfords by 1796, then to the Kerrs by the end of the nineteenth century. Now the clubhouse of a golf course.

Drumquhassle Castle [NS 483869], near Drymen, Stirlingshire; site of castle or old house.

Held by the Dennistouns, by the Buchanans and by the Cunninghams, but was also a property of the Grahams and of the Govans.

Duchray Castle [NS 480998], near Aberfoyle, Stirlingshire; altered tower house.

Held by the Grahams of Downie in 1569, who built the castle.

Duchray Castle (M&R)

It was the mustering point for an army led by the Earl of Glencairn, who defeated a Cromwellian force at Aberfoyle in 1653, but the rising then failed. Two Graham sisters entertained government troops in the 1690s, while the fugitive Rob Roy MacGregor escaped from the back of the building. The castle was torched after the Jacobite Rising of 1745-46, but was restored in 1825 and is still occupied.

Dudhope Castle [NO 394307], Dundee; restored courtyard castle.

Held by the Scrymgeours, but passed to the Grahams in 1688, and this became the chief residence of John Graham of Claverhouse, Viscount or 'Bonnie' Dundee. Used as a woollen mill, barracks and storehouse before being restored for use as offices, and stands in a public park.

Duntrune House [NO 445345], near Dundee; mansion on site of old house or castle.

Held by the Northingtons, by the Ogilvies of Easter Powrie and by the Scrymgeours of Dudhope, but passed to the Grahams of Fintry in the first quarter of the eighteenth century, later the Stirling Grahams. Still occupied.

Finlaystone House [NS 365737], near Port Glasgow, Renfrewshire; mansion incorporating part of castle.

Held by the Dennistouns and then by the Cunninghams, but passed by marriage to the Cunningham Grahams of Gartmore in 1796 but was sold in 1863 because of debt. Now held by the MacMillans, and the grounds are open along with a visitor centre (01475 540505; www.finlaystone.co.uk).

Fintry Castle [NS 641863], near Fintry, Stirlingshire; slight remains of castle.

Held by the Grahams of Fintry and was ruinous by 1724.

Gargunnock House [NS 715944], near Stirling; mansion incorporating old work.

Held by the Grahams but went to the Setons in 1460 and then to others. The gardens are sometimes open to the public (01786 860392; www.gardensofscotland.org).

Gartartan Castle [NS 530978], near Aberfoyle, Stirlingshire; ruinous tower house.

Held by the Lyles and by the MacFarlanes, but passed to the Grahams of Gartmore, and they had moved to Gartmore House by 1780. They owned the property until the twentieth century.

Gillesbie Tower [NY 171919], near Lockerbie, Dumfriesshire; slight remains of tower house.

Held by the Grahams and possibly by the Moffats.

Grahams Walls [NT 162465], near Romanno Bridge, Borders; site of castle.

Held by the Grahams in the fourteenth century, and materials from here were used to build Whiteside Tower and Newlands Church.

Greigston [NO 447111], near St Andrews, Fife; castle or old house replaced by mansion.

Held by the Grahams of Greigston, later Bonar-Grahams, from the sixteenth century or earlier.

Grougar [NS 466388], near Kilmarnock, Ayrshire; possible site of castle.

Held by the Logans, then by the Boyds and then by the Grahams around 1669.

Ha' Tower of Garvock [NO 043145], near Dunning, Perthshire; slight remains of tower.

Held by the Grahams from the fifteenth century. Archibald Graham, third of Garvock, fell at the Battle of Flodden in 1513, and Robert, tenth of Garvock, had to flee abroad after being involved in the Jacobite Rising of 1745-46, but the family kept their lands. The property was sold in 1933, and the house is still occupied. The Graemes formerly of Garvock now apparently live in Hampshire in England.

Hermitage Castle [NY 494960], near Newcastleton, Borders; impressive ruinous castle.

Held by the Dacres and by the Soulis family, then by the Grahams in the fourteenth century but passed by marriage to the Douglases. Later was a possession of the Hepburn Earls of Bothwell and of the Scotts of Buccleuch, but now in the care of Historic Scotland and is open to the public from April to September (01387 376222).

Inchbrackie Castle [NN 903218], near Crieff, Perthshire; site of castle.

Held by the Mercers and then by the Grahams (Graemes), and was destroyed by Cromwell's forces in 1650. Inchbrackie's Ring, a sapphire set in gold, was given to the laird of Inchbrackie by Kate McNiven, a reputed witch, who was burned at Crieff. She spat it into his hand when she was about to be burnt. He had tried to save her, and she promised that if his family kept the ring they would prosper. The Grahams sold the lands in 1882.

Inchmurrin Castle [NS 373863], near Balloch, Dunbartonshire; ruinous castle on island.

Held by the Stewart Earls of Lennox, but passed to the Graham Dukes of Montrose around the beginning of the eighteenth century.

Inchtalla Castle [NN 572004], near Aberfoyle, Stirlingshire; ruinous castle on island.

Held by the Earls of Menteith, a title held by the Comyns, by the Grahams and by the Stewart Dukes of Albany, then by the Graham Earls of Menteith from 1425 with the execution of the second Duke of Albany. William Graham, seventh Earl of Menteith, claimed the Earldom of Strathearn, but this was to the chagrin of James VI and he was demoted and Graham lost the Earldom of Menteith and was made Earl of Airth. The castle was occupied until about 1700, and on other islands are a ruinous priory and the site of dog kennels.

Inchtalla Castle (M&R) – see previous column

Kilbryde Castle [NN 756036], near Dunblane, Stirlingshire; L-plan tower house.

Held by the Graham Earls of Menteith, and they had a stronghold here, but Kilbryde was sold to the Campbells of Aberuchill in 1669, and they rebuilt the castle. The gardens are open to the public by appointment (01786 824505).

Kilbucho Place [NT 095352], near Biggar, Lanarkshire; L-plan house with old work.

Held by the Grahams and then by the Douglases in the fourteenth century, then by the Stewarts of Traquair, and by others. Still occupied.

Kilmardinny [NS 550727], near Bearsden, Dunbartonshire; castle or old house replaced by mansion.

Held by the Colquhouns but passed to the Grahams of Dougalston early in the eighteenth century. It was later held by the Leitch family, and the mansion now houses the Kilmardinny Arts Centre.

Kilpunt, Kilpont or **Kinpont** [NT 098718], near Broxburn, West Lothian; farm on site of castle or old house.

Held by the Kilpont family and then by the Grahams from the fourteenth century. Sir Robert Graham of Kilpont was opposed to James I and was one of his assassins when in 1437 they broke in on the king at Perth and dragged him from the hole where he was hiding and stabbed him to death. Graham was hunted down and then tortured and executed by Joan of Beaufort, James I's queen. John Graham, Lord Kilpont, was one of the captains of the Marquis of Montrose, and was at the Battle of Tippermuir in 1644. Graham argued with James Stewart of Ardvorlich (it has been suggested that they were lovers or that Stewart was angry because his property has been ravaged by Montrose's troops) and Graham was stabbed to death. Kilpont was buried in the chapter house of Inchmahome Priory [NN 574005], which is open to the public. Stewart promptly changed sides and was later pardoned for the killing. The property apparently later went to the Campbells.

Kinross House [NO 126020], near Kinross; mansion near site of castle.

Held by the Douglases, and Kinross House was built by Sir William Bruce, who was Royal Architect to Charles II. The property later went to the Grahams. Gardens open April to September (www.kinrosshouse.com).

Knockdolian Castle [NX 123854], near Ballantrae, Ayrshire; fine tower house.

Held by the Grahams and then by the MacCubbins, and a mansion was built nearby for the MacConnels. A verse associated with the castle is: 'Ye may think on your cradle, I'll think on my stane, And there'll ne'er be an heir, To Knockdolian again.' The story goes that a mermaid used to sing all night from a prominent stone near the castle. This grew so annoying for the lady of the castle that she got her servants to smash the rock. This did indeed get rid of the mermaid, but she returned one last time to sing the above verse. The heir to the lands died in his cradle and the line ended. At least that is the story.

Largie Castle [NO 835760], near Inverbervie, Kincardineshire; site of castle.
Held by the Grahams of Largie.

Linlathen or **Fintry House** [NO 463329], near Broughty Ferry, Angus; site of castle or old house.
Held by the Grahams of Fintry in the first half of the seventeenth century, and they built a mansion, calling it Fintry House. The property was sold in 1803.

Lochleven Castle [NO 138018], near Kinross; ruinous castle on island.
Held by the Douglases of Lochleven, but latter passed to the Bruces of Kinross, and then to the Grahams and to the Montgomerys. The castle is now in the care of Historic Scotland and is open to the public from April to September (07778 040483 (mobile)).

Lynedoch [NO 035289], near Perth; site of castle.
Held by the Grays and then by the Grahams of Balgowan in 1785. Thomas Graham of Balgowan's lovely and talented wife Catherine (her portrait by Thomas Gainsborough is in the National Gallery of Scotland, 'Hon. Mrs Graham') died only six years later. He had the Lynedoch Mausoleum at Methven [NO 026260] built for her. Graham went on to become a distinguished general in the Napoleonic Wars, and was made Baron Lynedoch of Balgowan in 1814. He died in 1843 when ninety-five years old.

Mains or **Fintry Castle** [NO 410330], Dundee; restored courtyard castle.
Held by the Stewarts and by the Douglas Earls of Angus, but passed to the Grahams in 1530, who built the castle. One of

Mains Castle (M&R)

the family, Sir David Graham, nephew of Cardinal Beaton, was executed for plotting to restore Catholicism to Scotland in around 1592. The property was sold to the Erskines in the nineteenth century, and then to the Cairds, and was then given to the people of Dundee. The grounds are now a public park.

Maryton [NO 686563], near Montrose, Angus; site of castle.
Held by the Grahams of Montrose.

Monorgan [NO 321285], near Dundee; site of castle.
Held by the Monorgans, but also by the Grahams and by the Crawfords.

Monzie Castle [NN 873245], near Crieff, Perthshire; small L-plan tower house and mansion.
Held by the Scotts but passed to the Grahams (Graemes) in 1613, but later went to the Campbells and to the Johnstones of Lathrisk. Kate McNiven's Stone [NN 880243] is a five-foot-high standing stone to the south of the drive to the castle. This is said to mark the spot where Kate McNiven, known as 'the Witch of Monzie', was reputedly executed. Kate is said to have cursed the laird of Monzie after being accused of witchcraft (including turning herself into a bee). Kate MacNiven's Craig, on the north side of the Knock of Crieff, is reputed to be where she was put in a barrel and rolled down

Monzie Castle 1910? – see previous column

the slope. The castle is still occupied and is open to the public around mid May to mid June (01764 653110).

Morphie Castle [NO 713642], near Montrose, Angus; site of castle.
Held by the Grahams. At Ecclesgreig [NO 745639] is the Morphie Aisle, which was rebuilt in the nineteenth century.

Mossknowe [NY 281698], near Gretna, Dumfriesshire; castle or old house replaced by mansion.
Held by the Grahams from the sixteenth century or earlier.

Northbar [NS 481693], near Renfrew; castle replaced by mansion.
Held by several families including by the Graham Dukes of Montrose.

Ogilvie Castle [NN 896072], near Auchterarder, Perthshire; slight remains of castle.
Held by the Grahams.

Old Downie [NO 519364], near Monifeith, Angus; site of castle.
Held by the Grahams.

Orchill [NN 866117], near Blackford, Perthshire; site of castle.
Held by the Grahams from the seventeenth century. The architect James Gillespie married the heiress Margaret Graham of Orchill, and then he changed his name to Gillespie Graham. He was born in Dunblane and was a well-known Scottish architect, who designed buildings such as Ayton Castle, Dunninald Castle, Glenbarr Abbey and extended Brodick Castle on Arran; as well as remodelling the mansion, which dates from the eighteenth century, at Orchill. He died in 1855. The property passed to the MacGregors, who built a new mansion nearby [NN 868118] in the 1869, and then to others.

Panholes [NO 888100], near Blackford, Perthshire; site of castle or old house, the location not certain.
Held by the Grahams of Panholes in the sixteenth and seventeenth centuries. The family had a town house on Broad Street in Stirling, which dates from the seventeenth century and has a vaulted basement.

Rednock Castle [NN 600022], near Callander, Stirlingshire; slight remains of tower house.
Held by the Menteiths of Ruskie and then by the Grahams.

Skelmorlie Castle [NS 195658], near Largs, Ayrshire; restored tower house.
Held by the Cunninghams of Kilmaurs and by the Montgomerys, but passed to the Grahams, and they restored and extended the old tower, although these additions have since been demolished after the building was damaged by a fire in 1959. Restored and occupied and self-catering accommodation available (01475 521616; www.aboutscotland.com/ayrshire/skelmorlie.html).

Stapleton Tower [NY 234688], near Annan, Dumfriesshire; ruinous tower house and mansion.
Held by the Irvines but passed to the Grahams, although a Christie Irvine seems to have thought otherwise and attacked the castle in 1626.

Tullybelton [NO 034336], near Bankfoot, Perthshire; castle replaced by mansion.
Held by the Grahams (Graemes) of Inchbrackie, and it was to Tullybelton that the Marquis of Montrose came in disguise in

1644. The property passed to the Robertsons and then to the Richardsons, and the mansion is still occupied.

Wester Kames Castle [NS 062680], near Rothesay, Bute; restored tower house.

Held by the MacKinlays and by the Spences before passing by marriage to the Grahams in 1670, then later it went to the Stuart Marquesses of Bute.

Westhall Tower [NT 048473], near Carnwath, Lanarkshire; slight remains of tower house.

Held by the Grahams from 1477, then by the Hepburns, by the Douglases and by the Lockharts.

www.clan-graham-society.org
www.clan-graham-association.org.uk
No. of castles/sites: 77
Rank: 9/764
Xref: Graeme

Grainger

The name comes from the office of 'granger', originally a person who managed a monastic grange, and the name is recorded in Scotland from the end of the twelfth century. It was Christian Grainger, wife of the minister of Kinneff, who managed to smuggle the Scottish Crown Jewels out of Dunnottar Castle during a siege by Cromwell's forces in 1652. The regalia remained hidden in Kinneff Church until the Restoration of Charles II in 1661.

Warriston [NT 253757] is to the north of Edinburgh, and there was a castle, which was destroyed by the Dalmahoys and by others. The lands were held by the Somervilles and by the Kincaids (and there was a famous murder at Warriston) before passing through the Byres to the Graingers, and then to the Muirs. A cemetery was laid out in part of the grounds

Ayton Castle [NT 929614] is a couple of miles southwest of Eyemouth in Berwickshire in the Borders. This is now a large castellated mansion with turrets, battlements and towers, but stands on the site of an old castle. The property was held by the Aytons, but passed to the Homes, then much later to the Liddell-Grainger family, and they still apparently live here. The castle is open to the public from May to September, Wednesday and Sunday (01890 781212/550; www.aytoncastle.co.uk).

No. of castles/sites: 2
Rank: 396=/764
Xref: Granger

Grant

The Grants probably came to England with William the Conqueror, and the name is most likely from 'le Grande', meaning large or important, although other derivations have been suggested. The family first came to Scotland in the middle of the thirteenth century, and they appear to have been connected with the once powerful family of Bisset. The Grants fought on the Scottish side at the Battle of Dunbar in 1296, where two were taken prisoner although the pair were later released. The Grants held lands in Strathspey, and then the lands of Freuchie.

Castle Grant or **Freuchie Castle** [NJ 041302], one and a half miles north of Grantown-on-Spey in Strathspey, is a large Z-plan tower house, which dates from the fifteenth century. The lands had been held by

Castle Grant (M&R)

the Comyns, but passed to the Grants in the fifteenth century, and this became their main stronghold.

James Grant of Freuchie supported James V and, although the Grants were Protestants, they joined the Marquis of Montrose in the 1640s. The name of the property was changed from Freuchie to Grant in 1694 when the lands were made into the regality of Grant. Ludovick, eighth laird, supported William and Mary and then the Hanoverians against the Stewarts, and fought against the Jacobites in the 1715 and 1745-46 Risings; Castle Grant was occupied by Jacobites. Robert Burns visited in 1787; the castle later became derelict, but is currently being restored. The ghost of Lady Barbara Grant, daughter of a sixteenth-century laird, is said to haunt the castle, although her small apparition is said to be sad rather than terrifying. She was imprisoned in a dark closet for falling in love with the wrong man and died of a broken heart. The family became Earls of

Seafield in 1811, and Barons Strathspey in 1884, and they apparently now live at Lochbuie in Mull.

Urquhart Castle [NH 531286], a mile or so east of Drumnadrochit in Inverness-shire, is a fabulous ruinous castle in a lovely spot by the banks of Loch Ness. This is an ancient site, possibly the fortress of Nechtan, King of Picts, who was converted to Christianity by St

Urquhart Castle (LF)

Columba, after the saint had confronted a fearsome beastie on the loch. The castle saw action in the Wars of Independence, but passed to the Grants of Freuchie in 1509, and they built much of the existing tower house and castle. The MacDonalds seized the castle in 1515, and then again in 1545; and in 1644 the stronghold was sacked by Covenanters. It held out against the Jacobites in 1689, but two years later Urquhart was dismantled to be left a picturesque ruin. The castle is in the care of Historic Scotland and is open to the public (01456 450551).

Ballindalloch Castle [NJ 178365], seven or so miles south-west of Charlestown of Aberlour in Moray, is a splendid stately Z-plan tower house, which was extended and altered in later centuries. The lands were held by the Ballindalloch family, but passed to the Grants in 1499. The castle was sacked by the Gordons during a feud and was burned by the Marquis of Montrose after the Battle of Inverlochy in 1645. Ballindalloch is said to be haunted both by a Green and by a Pink Lady, and another apparition is reputed to be that of General James Grant, who died in 1806. Grant was very proud of the improvements he had made to the estate, and

Ballindalloch Castle (M&R)

his phantom is said to ride around the lands, and to then go to the wine cellar. The house is still occupied by the Macpherson-Grants, and is open to the public from Easter to September (01807 500206; www.ballindallochcastle.co.uk).

Doune of Rothiemurchus [NH 885098], two miles south of Aviemore, is a late-eighteenth-century mansion, and replaced a castle or earlier house. The lands were held by the Mackintoshes, by the Shaws and by the Dallases of Cantray, but passed to the Gordons and then to Grants in 1545. James Grant, seventh of Rothiemurchus, was court-martialled for surrendering a fort to Bonnie Prince Charlie's forces in 1745. Rothiemurchus was home to Elizabeth Grant, author of *Memoirs of a Highland Lady*, and is still held by the Grants of Rothiemurchus. Some stories have the house being haunted by the ghost of a young man who reputedly strangled a servant girl on the stairs, then threw himself to his death. The house reportedly also had a brownie. The estate (and sometimes the house) is open to the public from April to October (01479 812345; www.rothiemurchus.net).

The Grants also held:

Aldourie Castle [NH 601372], near Inverness; mansion incorporating castle.

Held by the Frasers, by the Grants and then by the Mackinstoshes in the eighteenth century, and reputedly haunted by a Grey Lady.

Ballintomb [NJ 213424], near Charlestown of Aberlour, Moray; possible site of castle.

Held by the Grants in the seventeenth century, but passed by marriage to the Duffs.

Balnabreich [NJ 345500], near Keith, Moray; site of castle.

Held by the Grants.

Beldorney Castle [NJ 424369], near Keith, Aberdeenshire; large Z-plan tower house.

Held by several families, including by the Grants. The castle was restored, and is occupied.

Bishop's House [NJ 221631], Elgin, Moray; ruinous fifteenth-century L-plan house.

Held by the Setons after the Reformation, but was a shell by 1851 when the Grant Earl of Seafield decided to demolish it. He was stopped by the protests of locals, and the house was repaired. It is now in the care of Historic Scotland and can be viewed from the road.

Blairfindy Castle [NJ 199286], near Tomintoul, Moray; derelict L-plan tower house.

Held by the Grants, but passed to the Gordons of Huntly, who built the castle.

Castle Hill, Pluscarden [NJ 154571], near Elgin, Moray; site of castle.

Held by several families following the Reformation, including the Grants. The restored Pluscarden Abbey is open to the public (01343 890257; www.pluscardenabbey.org).

Castle Stripe [NJ 185361], near Charlestown of Aberlour, Moray; slight remains of castle.

The predecessor of Ballindalloch Castle. Held by the Ballindalloch family and then by the Grants.

Cunningar [NJ 701060], near Banchory, Aberdeenshire; site of castle on motte.

The predecessor of Midmar Castle; and held by several families, including by the Grants. Cunningar is said to have been abandoned because of plague.

Dalvey or **Grangehill Castle** [NJ 003585], near Forres, Moray; slight remains of castle.

Held by the Dunbars, then by the Grants of Dalvey. They had been made Baronets in 1688, and Sir James Grant was imprisoned for holding Edinburgh for James VII the following year. The Grants built a two-storey classical mansion on the site about 1770. The line of the Grants of Dalvey continues but they apparently now live near Farr in Inverness-shire.

Delnabo [NJ 160170], near Tomintoul, Moray; house on site of castle or older dwelling.

Held by the Grants of Carron in the seventeenth century. Margaret Sinclair, widow of one of the Grants, married Gregor MacGregor, chief of the Glenstrae family, who were proscribed at the time.

Easter Elchies [NJ 279444], near Charlestown of Aberlour, Moray; restored L-plan tower house.

Held by the Grants, and one of the family was Patrick Grant, a well-known judge. The house is now used as offices for the Macallan Distillery; tours available by appointment (01340 871471; www.themacallan.com).

Ecclesgreig or **St Cyrus** [NO 738659], near Montrose, Angus; castle replaced by mansion.

Held by the Burnetts but later passed to the Forsyth Grants, who changed the name to Ecclesgreig to distinguish it from the nearby village of St Cyrus (www.ecclesgreig.com).

Forres Castle [NJ 035588], Forres, Moray; site of castle.

Held by the Murrays and by the Dunbars of Westfield, before passing to the Grants at the beginning of the eighteenth century. The site is now a public park.

Inverallan [NJ 027269], near Grantown-on-Spey, Moray; site of castle.

Held by the Grants from the fifteenth century or earlier.

Invereshie House [NH 841050], near Kingussie, Strathspey; mansion including old work.

Held by the Macphersons, then by the Macpherson-Grants. Accommodation is available (01540 651332; www.kincraig. com/invereshiehouse).

Inverlaidnan [NH 862214], near Carrbridge, Highland; ruins of seventeenth-century house.

Held by the Grants and visited by Bonnie Prince Charlie in 1746. The house was apparently burned, but was rebuilt.

Kilnmaichlie House [NJ 181321], near Tomintoul, Moray; sixteenth-century T-plan house.

Held by the Stewarts of Kilnmaichlie and Drumin, who were Jacobites. After the failure of the Rising of 1745-46, the Grants acquired the property. Now a farmhouse.

Lesmoir Castle [NJ 470280], near Rhynie, Aberdeenshire; slight remains of castle.

Held by the Gordons and sacked by Covenanters in 1647, when the garrison was hanged. Passed to the Grants of Rothiemaise, who dismantled it.

Lethendry Castle [NJ 084274], near Grantown-on-Spey, Speyside; ruinous L-plan tower house.

Held by the Grants and seized by Jacobites in 1690.

Loch an Eilean Castle [NH 899079], near Aviemore, Speyside; ruinous castle on island.

Held by the Stewarts of Badenoch, by the Mackintoshes, then by the Gordons, before coming to the Grants in 1567. It was attacked by Jacobites after their defeat in Cromdale in 1690, but was successfully defended. It was last used in 1715 when Mackintosh of Balnespick was confined here to prevent him opposing the Jacobites.

Mains of Mulben [NJ 353512], near Keith, Moray; house incorporating tower house.

Held by the Grants. John Grant of Mulben fought against the Gordons at the Battle of Glenlivet in 1594. The property later passed to the Macphersons and is now a farmhouse.

Midmar Castle [NJ 704053], near Banchory, Aberdeenshire; magnificent Z-plan tower house.

Held by several families, including by the Grants. Still occupied.

Monymusk Castle [NJ 688155], near Inverurie, Aberdeenshire; tall altered sixteenth-century tower house.

Held by the Forbeses of Corsindae after the Reformation, but was sold in 1712 to the Grants of Cullen, now Monymusk and

Cullen, who apparently still occupy the House of Monymusk. The walled garden is open to the public (01467 651543).

Moy House [NJ 016599], near Forres, Moray; mansion on site of castle.

Held by the Grants in the eighteenth century.

Muckrach Castle [NH 986251], near Grantown-on-Spey, Strathspey; L-plan tower house.

Held by the Grants of Rothiemurchus, and they built the castle about 1598. The castle can be rented as a holiday home (01738 477510; www.muckrachcastle.com).

Pittencrieff House [NT 087873], Dunfermline, Fife; fine T-plan house.

Held by several families after the Reformation, including the Grants, before passing to Andrew Carnegie, who gave the property to the people of Dunfermline. The grounds are now a popular public park (01383 722935/313838; www.fifedirect. org/museums).

Prestongrange House [NT 373737], near Musselburgh, East Lothian; mansion incorporating older work.

Held by the Kerrs and by the Morrisons, then in 1746 was bought by William Grant, Lord Advocate, then passed by marriage to the Grant-Sutties. Now the clubhouse of the Royal Musselburgh Golf Club (01875 810276; www.royalmussel burgh.co.uk).

Rothes Castle [NJ 277490], near Charlestown of Aberlour, Moray; remains of old castle.

Held by several families, including by the Leslies, but sold to the Grants of Elchies in 1700, who held Rothes for eight years, Rothes then passed to the Ogilvies of Findlater, before going to the Grant Earls of Seafield.

Tullochcarron Castle [NJ 180350], near Charlestown of Aberlour, Moray; site of castle.

Held by the Ballindalloch family, but passed to the Grants.

Wester Elchies [NJ 256431], near Charlestown of Aberlour, Moray; site of tower house.

Held by the Grants but demolished in 1970.

www.clangrant.org
www.clangrant-us.org
No. of castles/sites: 35
Rank: 37/764

Midmar Castle (RWB) – see previous column

Gray

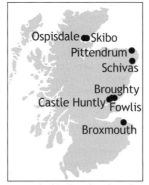

The name comes from the lands of 'Croy' or 'Gray' in Picardy, and was first used as a surname by Fulbert, Great Chamberlain of Robert, Duke of Normandy. The Greys came to England with William the Conqueror, where they held lands at Chillingham in Northumberland. They were recorded in Scotland at the end of the thirteenth century, and supported Robert the Bruce. Sir Andrew Gray was one of those who climbed the castle rock of Edinburgh with Thomas Randolph and seized Edinburgh Castle in 1313. The family were given lands in Perthshire as a reward.

John Gray, a Midlothian farmer who came into Edinburgh for market days with his dog Bobby, died in 1858 and was buried in Greyfriars Kirkyard. His dog kept vigil by his grave side and lived until 1872; some less charitable souls have suggested that Bobby supplemented his diet with gnawing corpses.

Castle Huntly [NO 301292], one mile west and south of Longforgan in Perthshire, is a huge and impressive keep or tower, which rises to four storeys and a garret. The building dates from the fifteenth century, and was built by the Grays. The family were made Lords Gray in 1444, and Andrew, first Lord, was Master of the Household to James II in 1452. He established Fowlis Easter Collegiate Church [NO 322334] in 1453 in the existing parish church; the interior of the building is outstanding as it contains many pre-Reformation features. The Grays went on to use the church as their mausoleum until 1888, and the

building can be visited. Andrew, second Lord, was Justice General of Scotland, and was much involved in the political machinations of the time. Patrick, Andrew's son and his heir, joined with James II in despatching William, sixth Earl of Douglas, at Stirling Castle in 1455, in his case using a battle axe. Patrick, fourth Lord, surrendered Broughty Castle to the English. The line passed to a nephew, Patrick Gray of Buttergask, who was captured after the Battle of Solway Moss in 1542 and had to be ransomed. Patrick, sixth Lord from 1609, supported Elizabeth I of England in the execution of Mary, Queen of Scots, reportedly saying 'the dead don't bite' after her execution. He fell out of favour with James VI and was banished in 1587, although he returned in 1593. Gray died in 1612 and the property was sold to the Lyon Lord Glamis in 1614, then to the Pattersons in 1777, and the building is now used as a Young Offenders' Institution. The castle is said to be haunted by a White Lady. Descendants of the family still flourish as the Campbell-Gray Lords Gray, although they apparently now live in Argyll.

Fowlis or **Foulis Castle** [NO 321334] is a tower house, which dates from the seventeenth century. It stands some five miles north-west of Dundee, and was held by

Fowlis Castle (M&R)

the Maules and by the Mortimers before coming to the Grays in 1337. Sir Alexander Gray of Broxmouth was made Lord Gray of Fowlis, and the family then acquired the lands and built Castle Huntly. Fowlis Castle is currently occupied as a farmhouse.

East of Dundee and by the sea, **Broughty Castle** [NO 465304] is a tall fifteenth-century keep of five storeys. It was given artillery emplacements in the

Castle Huntly (RWB)

Broughty Castle 1907?

nineteenth century, and the wing dates also from this time. The castle was owned and built by the Grays, although during the English attacks on Scotland in 1547-50 Patrick, fourth Lord Gray, handed the castle over to the English. From here, the English harried Dundee and Angus, and the castle was only retrieved with French help in 1550. It was held for Mary, Queen of Scots, in 1571; but was captured by General Monck for Cromwell in 1651. The building now houses a museum (01382 436916; www.dundeecity.gov.uk).

The Grays also owned:

Abbot House [NT 089875], Dunfermline, Fife; fine sixteenth-century house.
> Held by several families, including the Master of Gray, and the house is now a museum with displays on Dunfermline (01383 733266; www.abbothouse.co.uk).

Baledgarno Castle [NO 276304], near Longforgan, Perthshire; site of castle.
> Held by the Grays in the fifteenth century, but passed to the Fotheringhams in the 1680s.

Bandirran [NO 200306], near Coupar Angus, Perthshire; castle replaced by mansion.
> Held by the Grays in the sixteenth century, but passed to the Moncrieffes.

Black Jack's Castle [NO 708535], near Montrose, Angus; site of castle.
> Held by the Grays. The castle may be named after 'Black Jack' or John Gray, son of Patrick, Lord Gray, who owned the castle in the sixteenth century. Gray sacked nearby Red Castle after repeatedly attacking it, but was forfeited in 1581. The old castle had been abandoned by the end of the seventeenth century when a new castle was built nearby [NO 704543], itself replaced in 1824 when Dunninald Castle (see below) was built.

Braikie Castle [NO 628509], near Brechin, Angus; ruinous tower house.
> Held by the Frasers of Oliver, but passed to the Grays about 1750, then went to the Ogilvies.

Broxmouth House [NT 696766], near Dunbar, East Lothian; castle replaced by mansion.
> Held by the Grays before passing to the Homes and then to the Kerrs. Sir Alexander Gray of Broxmouth was made Lord Gray of Fowlis.

Buttergask [NN 877085], near Blackford, Perthshire; site of castle or old house.
> Held by the Grays in the sixteenth century. This branch of the family became Lord Gray, and Patrick Gray of Buttergask, fifth Lord, was captured at the Battle of Solway Moss in 1542.

Carntyne [NS 636651], Glasgow; castle replaced by mansion.
> Held by the Grays of Carntyne after the Reformation.

Carse Gray [NO 464540], near Forfar, Angus; mansion incorporating tower house.
> Held by the Rhynd family, then by the Ruthvens, but in 1741 passed to the Grays. The Gray-Cheapes still apparently own the property.

Crichie [NJ 978453], near Mintlaw, Aberdeenshire; mansion.
> The lands were held by the Leslies and by the Keiths, and possibly by the Grays, but passed to the Stewarts in 1709.

Dalmarnock [NS 615628], Glasgow; castle or old house replaced by mansion.
> Held by the Grays, and then by the Buchanans, who built a mansion in 1800. Parts of the lands were owned by the Woddrops.

Dunninald Castle [NO 704543], near Montrose, Angus; castle replaced by mansion.
> Built to replace Black Jack Castle. The lands were held by the Grays, but passed to the Leightons by 1617 and then to others.

The house is open for some weeks in the summer (01674 674842; www.dunninald.com).

Gilmilnscroft [NS 556255], near Mauchline, Ayrshire; seventeenth-century T-plan house.
> Held by the Farquhars until the twentieth century, latterly the Farquhar Grays.

House of Schivas [NJ 898368], near Ellon, Aberdeenshire; fine altered L-plan tower house.
> Held by the Schivas family and by others before coming to the Grays in 1509, and they probably built the current building. The property had passed to the Forbeses by 1721. It is still occupied.

Invergowrie House [NO 363304], near Dundee; mansion incorporating tower house.
> Held by the Carnegies, then by the Grays, who built or rebuilt the tower in 1568. The lands passed to the Murrays and then to the Clayhills.

Kinfauns Castle [NO 151226], near Perth; mansion on site of castle.
> Long held by the Charteris family, but passed to the Carnegies and to the Blairs and was held by the twelfth Lord Gray in 1741. By 1895 it had gone to the Stewart Earls of Moray. Still occupied.

Kinnell or **Balneave Castle** [NO 599500], near Friockheim, Angus; site of castle.
> Held by the Balnaves family, then by the Frasers and by the Lyons, before coming to the Grays by the end of the sixteenth century.

Lynedoch [NO 035289], near Perth; site of castle.
> Held by the Grays in the sixteenth century. Lynedoch was reputedly the home of Mary Gray who, along with her great friend, Bessie Bell, were struck down by plague sometime in the seventeenth century: their deaths are recounted in an old ballad. The property was later held by the Grahams.

Ospisdale House [NH 713897], near Dornoch, Sutherland; castle replaced by mansion.
> Held by the Murrays or by the Grays, and were a bone of contention which led to much blood-letting, then passed to the Gordons.

Pittendrum [NJ 964670], near Fraserburgh, Aberdeenshire; tall house on site of castle.
> Held by the Cummings and by the Keiths, but by the Grays in the seventeenth century. Sir Walter Gray of Pittendrum built (what was later called) Lady Stair's Close in Edinburgh in 1622, but in 1719 the building was sold to Elizabeth, Dowager Countess of Stair, hence the name.

Red Castle or **Arboll** [NH 892825], near Tain, Ross and Cromarty; site of castle.
> Arboll was held by the Grays.

Skibo Castle [NH 735891], near Dornoch, Sutherland; magnificent mansion on site of castle.
> Held by the Mackays then by the Grays after 1544. The Marquis of Montrose was imprisoned here after being betrayed at Ardvreck Castle. Robert Gray was fined after his wife, Jean Seton, hit one of Montrose's guards with a leg of meat. The old castle was reputedly haunted by the ghost of a young woman murdered here, and the apparition of a dishevelled young woman has reportedly been seen in the castle. A skeleton was later found behind a wall and, when it was buried, the hauntings stopped. The property passed through other hands to Andrew Carnegie in 1895, and he rebuilt the mansion. The castle is now an exclusive country club (www.carnegieclubs.com).

No. of castles/sites: 25
Rank: 52=/764
Xref: Grey

Greenlaw

The name is territorial and comes from the lands of Greenlaw in Berwickshire in the Borders.

There was a castle at **Greenlaw** [NT 719463], but this was abandoned in 1729 and the last remains were cleared away in 1863. The lands were held by the Greenlaw family from the end of the twelfth century or earlier. One of the family was William Greenlaw, Archdeacon of St Andrews in 1361, while another was Gilbert Greenlaw, Bishop of Aberdeen and Chancellor of Scotland, who died in 1422. The property went to the Homes.

No. of castles/sites: 1
Rank: 537=/764

Greenock

The name comes from the burgh of Greenock, which is in Renfrewshire in west-central Scotland. The name comes on record in 1296.

Broadstone Castle [NS 359528] stood one mile south-east of Beith in Ayrshire, but was completely demolished when the present farm was built. The lands were held by the Liddels and by the Montgomerys, but in 1650 were bought by the Greenock family. The castle was occupied until about 1700.

No. of castles/sites: 1
Rank: 537=/764

Gregory

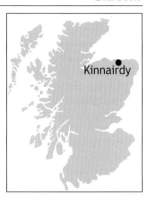

The name comes from the Greek personal name, and means 'vigilant' or more literally 'watchman' (also see Greig, Grierson, and MacGregor). It was used by churchmen in Scotland from the middle of the twelfth century, then as a surname from the fourteenth century.

Kinnairdy or **Kinnairdie Castle** [NJ 609498], a couple of miles south-west of Aberchirder in Aberdeenshire in the north-east of Scotland, is a tall keep or tower of five storeys and a garret, which was altered to L-plan and then extended by a wing. There is fine wood carving in the hall.

The castle was long associated with the Inneses,

Kinnairdy Castle 1910?

but the property was sold to the Crichtons of Frendraught, and then came to the Reverend John Gregory in 1547. It was here that his brother fathered twenty-nine children and built Scotland's first barometer (perhaps his wife needed some time off). The Gregorys went on to have several eminent scientists and doctors among their number, and one of the family, David Gregory, helped to expand the popularity of the work of Sir Isaac Newton and was a professor at Oxford in 1692, while William Gregory was professor of medicine and chemistry at Aberdeen in 1839 and then of chemistry at Edinburgh five years later. The castle eventually returned to the Innes family and the building has been restored and accommodation is available (01463 780833; www.kinnairdy-castle.co.uk).

No. of castles/sites: 1
Rank: 537=/764

Greig

The name comes from 'Giric' or 'Girig', who was one of the early kings of Scots, and is itself derived from Gregory (also see that name, Grierson and MacGregor). It is recorded as a surname from the end of the fifteenth century. Some of the MacGregors change their name to Greig after that clan was proscribed early in the seventeenth century. Samuel Greig, who was born in Inverkeithing in 1735, joined the Russian navy and he was responsible for the destruction of the Turkish fleet at Cheshme during the Russian-Turkish war of 1768-84.

Binsness or **Easterbin** [NJ 030629], three miles north of Forres in Moray, is a mansion, but contains work from the seventeenth century. The lands here became increasingly prone to windswept sand and, despite being a fertile area, were eventually overwhelmed; the area has been planted with trees. The property was held by the Dunbars of Wester Moy in 1620, but is listed as the seat of the Greigs of Binsness in *Burke's*, who apparently live in Hampshire in England.

No. of castles/sites: 1
Rank: 537=/764

Grierson

The name is said to be derived from 'Gregory's son', Gregory meaning 'vigilant' in Greek. Indeed, the family is said to be descended from the MacGregors, from Gilbert MacGregor, second son of the eleventh lord of MacGregor. The name is on record from the end of the fourteenth century.

Lagg Tower [NX 880862] is several miles south-east of Moniaive in Dumfries and Galloway, and was a property of the Griersons from 1408. It was a strong castle with a tower house and courtyard with outbuildings, but it is now quite ruinous. Roger Grierson of Lagg was killed at the Battle of Sauchieburn in 1488, and others of the family were killed at Flodden in 1513. Sir Robert Grierson of Lag was made a Baronet of Nova Scotia in 1685, and was prominent in prosecuting (or persecuting, depending on the viewpoint) Covenanters. In 1685 he surprised an illegal Coventicle and, after killing some of the worshippers (reputedly by rolling them down a hill in a spiked barrel), including James Clement, he denied them a Christian burial, at least according to stories told afterwards. A granite monument marks the spot where the Covenanters died. Grierson went on to become a Jacobite, for which he was fined and imprisoned. He is buried in the cemetery of the old parish church [NX 927832] at Lagg. He died in 1733 in his seventies, and was so fat that one wall of his house in Dumfries had to be demolished to extract him from it. All sorts of stories were told about him. His spit could burn holes where it fell; when he placed his feet in water he made it boil (he had gout); and wine would turn to congealed blood when it was given to him. On the night he died a chariot drawn by horses and surrounded by thunder clouds is said to have taken Grierson off to hell. It seems rather unlikely that Grierson warranted his unholy reputation. Sir Walter Scott used his character in the novel *Red Gauntlet*. The line of the Griersons of Lag, Baronets, continues, and they now apparently live in London.

Rockhall [NY 054754], six miles east of Dumfries, is an altered but slightly severe tower house, dating from the sixteenth century. The lands were held by the Kirkpatricks, but passed by marriage to the Griersons in the fifteenth century. Rockhall was held by Sir Robert Grierson of Lagg. His pet monkey, killed by his servants after his death, is said to haunt the house, blowing a whistle. The property was held by the Griersons until the twentieth century, and is still a private residence.

The Griersons also held:
Barjarg Tower [NX 876901], near Thornhill, Dumfries and Galloway; L-plan tower house.
Held by the Douglas Earls of Morton, but passed in 1587 to the Griersons, and they built the tower. Barjarg went by marriage to the Erskine Lord Tinwald in the nineteenth century, then to the Hunters.

Bardennoch [NX 780914], near Moniaive, Dumfriesshire; site of
   tower house.
   Held by the Rorisons but passed to the Griersons.
Capenoch House [NX 843938], near Thornhill, Dumfries and
   Galloway; mansion incorporating old work.
   Held by the Griersons, but passed in 1606 to the Maxwells,
   and was later held by the Griersons again in 1845 but by 1850
   had gone to the Gladstones. Still occupied.
Dormont [NY 112749], near Lockerbie, Dumfries and Galloway;
   site of castle and mansion.
   Held by the Griersons in 1411, but passed to the Carruthers of
   Howmains around the middle of the sixteenth century.
Garryhorn [NS 296138], near Maybole, Ayrshire; site of castle.
   Held by the Griersons of Lagg from the fifteenth century, and
   said to have been used by Sir Robert Grierson of Lagg when
   pursuing Covenanters.
Old Garroch [NX 589823], near St John's Town of Dalry, Dumfries
   and Galloway; house on site of tower.
   Held by the Asloans, then by the Maxwells and by the Griersons,
   and perhaps also by the Carlyles.

No. of castles/sites: 8
Rank: 160=/764

Gunn

The name is a diminutive
of longer Norse names,
such as Gunnarr, Gun-
nbjorn or Gunnlaug. The
clan are Viking in origin,
and came to Caithness
when they inherited lands
from Harald, Earl of Ork-
ney; the original Gunn or
Gunni was married to Har-
ald's sister. Some of the clan were expelled from Caithness at the end of the sixteenth century and were then
called Gaillie or Gally (meaning 'stranger' in Gaelic).

   Gunn's or **Clyth Castle** [ND 307386] lies eight miles
south and west of Wick in Caithness on a rock above the
sea. This was once a strong and splendid castle, but
virtually nothing remains. The fortress was held by the
Gunns, who had a long and bitter feud with the Keiths
of Ackergill. Dugald Keith attacked the Gunns of
Braemore and carried off Helen Gunn to Ackergill with
ungentlemanly intentions. She threw herself from a
castle tower rather than submit to Keith, and her ghost,
a Green Lady, is said to haunt Ackergill. The Gunns
ravaged the Keiths' lands, but were defeated at battles
at Tannach Moor in 1438 and then again at Dirlot in
1464; the chief of the Gunns and four of his sons were
killed. Another Gunn chief, Justiciar of Caithness, was
'basely' murdered by the Keiths in 1478. James Gunn
slew Keith of Ackergill and his son at Drummoy in
revenge. The fighting weakened the Gunns, and their
power was further diminished by the intervention of
the earls of Caithness and of Sutherland. The Gunns
fought for the Hanoverians during the Jacobite Risings.
The line of the chiefs is now extinct.

   Clan Gunn Heritage Centre and Museum is located
in the old parish church in the village of Latheron (01593
721325; www.caithness.org/community/museums/
clangunn/).

The Gunns also held:
Dirlot Castle [ND 126486], near Watten, Caithness; site of castle.
   Held by the Cheynes but passed to the Gunns in the fifteenth
   century, then later went to the Sutherlands and then to the
   Mackays.
Halberry Castle [ND 302377], near Wick, Caithness; some remains
   of a castle above the sea.
   Held by the Gunns.
Kinbrace [NC 874285], near Kinbrace, Caithness; site of castle
   (location not certain).
   Around 1140 Lady Frakark was burned to death by Svein
   Aliefson here, as told in the sagas. Much later Kinbrace was a
   property of the Gunns.
Latheron Castle [ND 199334], near Dunbeath, Caithness; slight
   remains of a castle.
   Held by the Gunns, but passed to the Sinclairs, who held them
   in the seventeenth century. Latheron House dates from the
   eighteenth century with later additions.

www.clangunnsociety.org
www.clangunn.us / www.gunnclan.net
No. of castles/sites: 5 / Rank: 240=/764
Xref: Gaillie; Gally

Guthrie

The name is territorial and comes from the lands of Guthrie, which are six and a half miles to the southeast of Forfar in Angus; the family are on record from the end of the thirteenth century. James Guthrie, minister of Stirling in 1649 and a leading Protestant reformer, co-operated with the Cromwellian administration and was executed by Charles II in 1661.

Guthrie Castle [NO 563505] in Angus consists of an altered keep of three storeys and a garret to which a modern mansion has been added. The castle stands in acres of mature woodland and there is a walled garden; while inside there are some fine wall paintings. The lands were held by the Guthries, and the present castle was built in 1470. Sir David Guthrie was Armour Bearer to James II and High Treasurer of Scotland, and his son, Sir Alexander Guthrie, was killed at Flodden in 1513. The family had a bitter feud with the Gardynes, which started after a marriage between the two families and the murder of

Guthrie Castle (M&R)

the Guthrie groom. Patrick Gardyne was slain in 1578 by William Guthrie, but ten years later the Gardynes succeeded in murdering a Guthrie laird. Two years after this the Guthries fell upon the Gardyne family and murdered their laird and others. Both families were forfeited by James VI after repeated warnings, losing their lands, but while the Guthries recovered theirs, the Gardynes never did. Guthrie Castle was remodelled by David Bryce in 1848, and was still held by the family in the twentieth century, although the Guthries now apparently live in Australia. The castle is said to have a very kind ghost, the spirit of one of the Guthrie ladies that is believed to be concerned for the welfare of guests. Accommodation is available (01241 828691; www.guthrie castle.com). Sir David Guthrie, Armour Bearer to James II and High Treasurer of Scotland (as mentioned above), founded a collegiate church around 1479 in the existing parish church [NO 567505] at Guthrie. The building has been demolished and replaced by a new church except for what is known as the fifteenth-century Guthrie Aisle; the gateway into the churchyard bears the Guthrie arms and the date 1639. The church can be visited.

The Guthries also owned:

Balgavies Castle [NO 540516], near Letham, Angus; some remains of castle.
   Held by the Ochterlony family, then by the Guthries, but by 1543 had passed to the Prestons, then went to others. Destroyed in 1594.

Colliston Castle [NO 612464], near Arbroath, Angus; fine Z-plan tower house.
   Held by the Reids in 1539, then by the Guthries, who built the castle. Colliston was sold to the Gordons in 1691, then passed through other hands. The building is still occupied.

Craigie [NO 434314], Dundee; mansion possibly on site of older house or castle.
   Held by the Kidds, but passed to the Guthries in 1728. The family still flourishes.

Dysart [NO 695550], near Montrose, Angus; site of castle.
   Held by the Melvilles, then the by Guthries and by the Lyles.

Gagie House [NO 448376], near Dundee; tower house extended into mansion.
   Held by the Olivers, but sold to the Guthries in 1610, and they

Gagie House (M&R)

probably built the old tower. The house is still occupied.

Kair House [NO 769765], near Inverbervie, Kincardineshire; castle replaced by mansion.
   Held by the Sibbalds but passed to the Guthries, then to the Burnetts and to the Kinlochs of Kair.

Kincaldrum [NO 432448], near Forfar, Angus; castle replaced by mansion.
   Held by the Guthries from 1457, and they went on to build Guthrie Castle. The lands passed to the Baxters in the nineteenth century.

Kirkbuddo [NO 502435], near Forfar, Angus; site of castle.
   Held by the Lindsays in the fifteenth century, but later by the Guthries.

Pitforthie [NO 615610], near Brechin, Angus; site of castle or old house.
   Held by the Guthries, one of whom was William Guthrie, born in 1620 at Pitforthie, who was 'one of the holiest and ablest of the experimental divines of Scotland'. Later the property went to the Ochterlonys.

Pitmuies [NO 567497], near Friockheim, Angus; castle or old house replaced by mansion.
   The lands may have been held by the Guthries (this is very close to Guthrie Castle), but passed to the Moodies (Mudies) and then to the Lyells. The house dates from the eighteenth century and there are fine gardens, which are open from April to October (01241 818245; www.pitmuies.com).

Red Castle [NO 687510], near Montrose, Angus; shattered but impressive ruin.
   Held by several families before coming to the Guthries. Can be viewed from a safe distance.

www.clanguthrie.org
No. of castles/sites: 12 / Rank: 120=/764

Haggart

The name is a corruption of MacTaggart, and was found in Perthshire in the sixteenth and seventeenth centuries.

At **Bantaskine** [NS 876800], on the west side of Falkirk, was a castle or old house, but it was demolished in the 1950s and the site is now a public park. The property was held by the Forresters, by the Livingstones and by the Kincaids, before passing to the Haggarts in the nineteenth century.

No. of castles/sites: 1
Rank: 537=/764

Haig

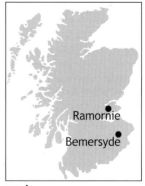

The name comes from 'de Haga' and is Norman in origin, and Haig was originally pronounced 'Hag-e' or 'Hag-he'. The name is recorded in Scotland from the middle of the twelfth century, when Patrus del Hage 'witnessed the sale of two serfs, their sons and daughters and all their progeny'.

Bemersyde House [NT 592334] lies three miles east of Melrose in the Borders, and stands on a rocky knoll beside the River Tweed. The tower house rises to six storeys, and a mansion was added in the eighteenth century. The lands were held by the Haigs from the twelfth century, and the existing castle was built after 1535. Peter Haig, sixth of Bemersyde, fought at the Battle of Bannockburn in 1314; and Gilbert, eleventh lord, was one of the leaders of a Scottish army who defeated the English at the Battle of Sark in 1449, while William, thirteenth lord, died at Flodden in 1513. The tower was burnt by the English in 1545 and had to be restored. William, eighteenth lord, was the King's Solicitor for Scotland in 1626. In 1854 the direct family

Bemersyde House (M&R)

died out, and the house passed to a distant relation. In 1921 Bemersyde was presented to Field-Marshal Douglas Haig for his part in World War I. Haig was born in Edinburgh in 1861 and was made first Earl Haig in 1919. Bemersyde is still apparently held by the Haigs, and the gardens are occasionally open to the public (www.gardensof scotland.org).

The line of the Haigs (formerly) of Bemersyde continues, although they now apparently live in Suffolk in England. It seems then that the old prophecy made by Thomas the Rhymer in the thirteenth century, 'Tide, tide whate'er betide, they'll aye be Haig of Bemersyde' is still sort of true. Another interpretation is that the 'Haig' should be read as 'hag', meaning a 'hag or thicket' clinging to the cliff down to the Tweed, although this does not seem to be much of a prophecy so hardly worth recording.

Ramornie House [NO 318096], half a mile east of Ladybank in Fife, may stand on the site of a castle and was long a property of the Heriots before coming to the Haigs of Ramornie in the nineteenth century. Ramornie is still apparently held by the Haigs.

No. of castles/sites: 2
Rank: 396=/764

Haitlie

The name is on record in Scotland from the first half of the thirteenth century, and the family appear to have been established around the Tweed in the Borders.

Whiteside Peel [NT 644384] is three or so miles south of Gordon, and was probably built by the Haitlies. They held the property from the end of the fifteenth century until 1640, although the lands were earlier a possession of the Homes and of the Haliburtons. The lands passed from the Haitlies to the Edmonstones, then to the Baillies in 1642. They built **Mellerstain** [NT 648392] nearby, which is open to the public (01573 410225; www.meller stain.com).

No. of castles/sites: 1
Rank: 537=/764

Haldane

The name may be territo-rial and come from the lands of Howden, which were given to the family in the twelfth century; or may be from an old per-sonal name 'Healfdene'. The name can also be found spelt as Hadden, Haddon and Howden.

Howden [NT 458269] is a mile or so south and west of Selkirk in the Borders. There is an old motte, with a much reduced ditch and embankment. This may have been the seat of the Haldanes, but they soon moved north.

Gleneagles Castle [NN 929093] lies a couple of miles south and west of Auchterarder in Perthshire, and is now very ruinous. The Haldanes built a new house in 1644 [NN 931088], which was extended and altered in 1750 and again in the middle of the nineteenth century. The lands had passed by marriage to the Haldanes in the twelfth century, and the family fought on the side of Robert the Bruce in the Wars of Independence, and increased their land holdings into the Lennox in Dunbartonshire, were they had a claim to the Earldom of Lennox through an heiress. This was eventually settled, the earldom going to the Stewarts of Darnley, but more lands were given to the Haldanes under the barony of Rusky. Sir John Haldane, fifth of Gleneagles, was killed at the Battle of Flodden in 1513. Another Sir John, eleventh lord, was one of the captains in the Scottish army that was defeated by Cromwell at the Battle of Dunbar in 1650, and he was killed. The Haldanes supported the Hanoverians. The lands were raided and the house was damaged by Jacobites in 1715, and the son of the sixteenth lord, General George Haldane, fought against the Jacobites in the 1745-46 Rising. The house is still apparently occupied by the Haldanes of Gleneagles.

The Haldanes also owned:
Airthrey Castle [NS 813967], near Stirling; mansion.
  Held by the Haldanes, and the mansion was built for them, although they never occupied it. One of the family, Robert Haldane, served in the Royal Navy but then joined his brother James Alexander in missionary and evangelical work. Robert died in 1842. The property had passed to the Abercrombys in 1796, and the house is now part of the University of Stirling.
Boturich Castle [NS 387845], near Balloch, Dunbartonshire; mansion on site of castle.
  Held by the Earls of Lennox, but passed to the Haldanes of Gleneagles in 1425. Boturich was sacked by the MacFarlanes of Arrochar, but passed to the Buchanans of Ardoch in 1792, then to the Findlays. Holiday accommodation is available (www.scottscastles.com).
Lanrick Castle [NN 685031], near Doune, Stirlingshire; site of tower house and mansion.
  Held by the Haldanes of Gleneagles, then later by the MacGregors and then by the tea tycoon William Jardine. The castle was an impressive ruin when it was demolished by its owner in 2002 despite it being listed: a fine of only £1000 was imposed.

Manor Castle [NS 827948], near Stirling; slight remains of a tower house.

Held by the Callendars then by the Dundas family, but was bought by the Haldanes about 1750 before passing to the Abercrombys in 1796.

Rusky Castle [NN 616034], near Callander; site of castle on (now submerged) island in the loch.

The property was held by the Menteiths and by the Napiers of Merchiston before being held by the Haldanes of Gleneagles. The lands were made into the Barony of Haldane, with Rusky as the seat, in about 1509.

No. of castles/sites: 7
Rank: 182=/764
Xrefs: Hadden; Haddon; Howden

Halkett

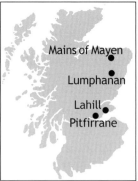

The name appears to be territorial, and may come from the lands of Hawk-head, which are to the east of Paisley in Renfrew-shire, although this was held by the Ross family from an early date. The name is on record from the thirteenth century.

Pitfirrane Castle [NT 060863], which is a couple of miles west of Dunfermline in Fife, has a sixteenth-century tower house at its core, but has been altered

Pitfirrane Castle (M&R)

and extended. Pitfirrane was held by the Halketts from around 1390, one of whom was George Halkett, Provost of Dunfermline, who died by falling from one of the windows of Pitfirrane. The property passed by marriage to the Wedderburns of Gosford, but they assumed the name of Halkett. Sir Peter Halkett of Pitfirrane fought for the Hanoverians against the Jacobites in the Rising of 1745-46, but was taken prisoner at Prestonpans; he died in 1755. The family held the property until 1877 when the castle was sold to the Dalgleishs, and it is now the clubhouse of a golf course.

The family also held:

Lahill House [NO 445038], near Lower Largo, Fife; castle replaced by mansion.

Held by the Fotheringhams in the seventeenth century, but passed to the Halketts by 1845. Now apparently the seat of the Lindesay-Bethune Earls of Lindsay.

Mains of Mayen [NJ 576477], near Huntly, Aberdeenshire; L-plan tower house.

Held by the Abernethys, then by the Gordons, but sold to the Halkett family in 1649, but then passed by marriage back to the Abernethys. Restored in the 1960s.

Peel Ring of Lumphanan [NJ 576037], near Aboyne; motte.

The lands were held by the Durwards, but were a possession of the Halketts in 1370, and then the Irvines in the fifteenth century. The site is in the care of Historic Scotland and is open to the public (01667 460232).

No. of castles/sites: 4 / Rank: 278=/764
Xref: Hacket

Hall

The name is recorded in documents from the thirteenth century, and the name is local in origin.

Fulbar [NS 495678] is one mile west of Renfrew in Renfrewshire, although it is not clear if there was ever a castle here. The lands were held by the Halls from 1370 until the direct line died out about 1550.

Dunglass Castle [NT 766718], one mile north of Cockburnspath in Berwickshire in the Borders, was formerly a place of some strength. It was held by the Homes, but it was destroyed in 1640, and a mansion replaced the castle. The lands passed to the Halls in the seventeenth century, and they were made Baronets of Nova Scotia in 1687. The house was demolished in 1947, and the Halls of Dunglass, Baronets, now apparently live in Derbyshire.

At Dunglass is the substantial ruin of the collegiate church [NT 766718], which has several memorials including to the Halls, and is in the care of Historic Scotland and is open to the public.

A few miles north of west of Coldingham in Berwickshire, **Fast Castle** [NT 862710] is now very ruinous but is in a picturesque spot perched above cliffs. The castle had a long and eventful history, and was owned by several families, including latterly by the Halls. It is possible to visit the ruins, but great care must be taken. **Whitehall** [NT 874551], one mile south of Chirnside also in Berwickshire, is the site of a castle or old house, which was replaced by a mansion, itself much reduced in size. The property was held by the Halls in the eighteenth century, but was sold to the Mitchell-Innes family in 1840.

Killean House [NR 697443], one mile south of Tayinloan in Kintyre in Argyll, is a large baronial mansion, dating from 1875 and replacing and earlier house of 1840. It was built for the wealthy shipowner James Macalister Hall. Accommodation is available at the house and on the estate (01257 266511; www.killean estate.com).

No. of castles/sites: 5
Rank: 240=/764

Halliday

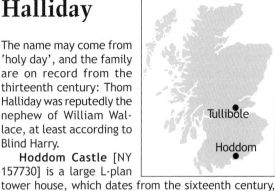

The name may come from 'holy day', and the family are on record from the thirteenth century: Thom Halliday was reputedly the nephew of William Wallace, at least according to Blind Harry.

Hoddom Castle [NY 157730] is a large L-plan tower house, which dates from the sixteenth century, and is located five miles north-west of Annan in Dumfries and Galloway. The property had several owners, including the Maxwells who built the tower, and a Halliday of Hoddom is on record in 1439. The castle now stands in a caravan park (01576 300251; www.hoddom castle.co.uk).

Hoddom Castle (M&R)

Tullibole Castle [NO 053006], just east of Crook of Devon in Perth and Kinross, is an L-plan tower house, dating from the seventeenth century but the building was later extended. There was an earlier stronghold, which was held by the Bishops of St Andrews, but the lands passed to the Herons and then to the Hallidays in 1598. James VI stayed at Tullibole. The property passed to the Moncrieffe family in the eighteenth century and they still apparently occupy it.

website.lineone.net/~c.john.halliday/
No. of castles/sites: 2 / Rank: 396=/764

Tullibole Castle (M&R)

Halyburton

The name is territorial and comes from the lands of that name, which are three miles north-west of Greenlaw in Berwickshire in the Borders. The name may come from the place 'Burton', which then became 'Holy' when a chapel was established.

Halliburton [NT 672484] was held by the family from the twelfth century for at least 200 years, and they may have had a castle. Sir Walter Halyburton was captured after the Battle of Neville's Cross in 1346, and he, or another Sir Walter, was Sheriff of Berwick in the 1370s.

Dirleton Castle [NT 518840], a couple of miles west of North Berwick in East Lothian, is a magnificent ruinous castle, perched on a rock and defended by a deep ditch

Dirleton Castle (M&R)

and formerly by a drawbridge. The building dates from the thirteenth century, and there is a fine round tower with two vaulted chambers, as well as beautiful gardens. The lands were held by the Congiltons and then by the Vauxs, when it saw action in the Wars of Independence, before passing by marriage to the Halyburtons in the fourteenth century. Sir Walter Halyburton was one of the hostages for James I and was made Treasurer in 1438. John Halyburton, his son, was made Lord Halyburton in 1450, and James IV visited in 1505. The family added to the castle, but at the beginning of the sixteenth century Patrick, fifth Lord, only had daughters and Dirleton went by marriage with the heiress, Janet Halyburton, to the Ruthvens, and later went to others. Dirleton is now in the care of Historic Scotland and is open to the public (01620 850330).

Pitcur Castle [NO 252370] stands about three miles south-east of Coupar Angus in Perthshire; and is a massive but now ruinous L-plan tower house, which dates from the sixteenth century. Pitcur was held by the

Chisholms, but passed by marriage to the Halyburtons of Dirleton in 1432. James Halyburton of Pitcur, who was Provost of Dundee from 1550 until 1583, fought against Mary, Queen of Scots, at the Battle of Langside in 1568. The castle was replaced by **Hallyburton House** [NO 248386], dating from 1680, which was remodelled and extended in later centuries. The property was sold to the Menzies family in 1880.

The Halyburtons also owned:

Castle Gogar [NT 164730], near Edinburgh; large L-plan tower house.
    Held by the Setons, but passed to the Halyburtons about 1409, then to the Logans of Restalrig, and then to the Coupers by 1625. Still occupied.

Dryburgh Abbey [NT 591317], near Melrose, Borders; ruinous abbey and fortified residence.
    Held by the Erskines after the Reformation but passed to the Halyburtons and then the Scotts of Ancrum. The abbey ruins are in the care of Historic Scotland and are open to the public (01835 822381)

Eaglescairnie [NT 518696], near Haddington, East Lothian; mansion on site of castle.
    Held by the Halyburtons in the seventeenth century.

Ecclesiamagirdle House [NO 107164], near Perth; T-plan house from 1648 or earlier.
    Held by the Halyburtons of Pitcur after the Reformation, but by 1629 had passed to the Carmichaels of Balmedie.

Hatton Castle [NO 302411], near Coupar Angus, Perthshire; Z-plan tower house.
    Held by the Oliphants, but passed to the Halyburtons of Pitcur in 1627, then to the Mackenzies of Rosehaugh. Restored in the 1980s and still occupied.

Lintrose House or **Fodderance** [NO 225379], near Coupar Angus, Perthshire; mansion incorporating castle.
    Held by the Halyburtons of Pitcur, then by the Murrays.

Mellerstain [NT 648392], near Earlston, Borders; magnificent mansion on site of older house or castle.
    Lands held by the Halyburtons in 1451, but by the end of that century had passed to the Haitlies and was later owned by the Baillies, later Baillie-Hamiltons, for whom the present mansion was built by William and Robert Adam. The mansion is open to the public from Easter, then May to September (01573 410225; www.mellerstain.com)

Mertoun House [NT 618318], near Kelso, Borders; castle replaced by mansion.
    Held by the Halyburtons, but passed to the Scotts of Harden in 1680. The gardens are sometimes open to the public (01835 823236).

Mordington House [NT 951558], near Berwick-upon-Tweed, Borders; site of castle.
    Held by the Mordington family, but passed by marriage to the Halyburtons, then was given to Thomas Randolph by Robert the Bruce, then passed to the Douglases of Dalkeith, and then held to others. An older building was replaced by a mansion in the eighteenth century but this was demolished in 1973.

Whiteside Peel [NT 644384], near Earlston, Borders; remains of tower house.
    Held by the Halyburtons, but passed to the Haitlies, then later to the Baillies (as Mellerstain).

No. of castles/sites: 13
Rank: 113=/764
Xref: Haliburton; Halliburton; Hallyburton

Hamilton

The name comes from Walter fitz Gilbert of Hambledon, who was given the lands of Cadzow (previously held by the Comyns) in Lanarkshire after supporting Robert the Bruce. The name probably comes from lands that fitz Gilbert had held in Northumberland called Homildon (there was later a battle here in 1402, when the Scots were crushed by the English) or perhaps from Hambledon in Yorkshire. Walter fitz Gilbert's original property in Scotland appears to have been in Renfrewshire, but the Hamiltons became one of the most powerful families in Scotland, and gave their name to the burgh of Hamilton in Lanarkshire.

Cadzow Castle [NS 734538] is a mile or so to the south-east of Hamilton, and dates from the twelfth century, although the present ruin is mostly from work

Cadzow Castle 1920?

of about 1540, which included a strong tower with round towers. David Hamilton of Cadzow fought and was captured at the Battle of Neville's Cross in 1346. James, first Lord Hamilton from 1445, married Mary, daughter of James III and widow of Thomas Boyd, Earl of Arran, in 1474, and their son, James, was made Earl of Arran with their castle at Brodick. This gave the family a close connection to the throne, and left them heirs at one time to both James IV and to Mary, Queen of Scots. James, Earl of Arran, played an important part in the minority of James V and allied himself with the English faction. His illegitimate son, John Hamilton, was Archbishop of St Andrews after the murder of Cardinal David Beaton in 1546. He officiated at the baptism of the future James VI, may have been involved in the murders of Lord Darnley and then the Earl of Moray, and he supported Mary, Queen of Scots, after she fled to England in 1568. He was captured when Dumbarton Castle fell and was hanged in 1571. James Hamilton, second Earl of Arran, was Governor of Scotland during the minority of Mary, Queen of Scots. He rebelled against Mary after she married Lord Darnley and remained in exile until 1569 although he then became leader of the Queen's Party until 1573. He was also made Duke of

Chatelherault in France, a title granted by Henri II of France in 1548 to help ensure his support. His son, another James, became third Earl of Arran on his father's death. He was put forward as a candidate for marriage for both Elizabeth of England and for Mary, but he attempted to seize Mary in 1562 and he was then declared insane and incarcerated until his death in 1609. Mary, Queen of Scots, visited Cadzow Castle in 1568 after escaping from Lochleven Castle. The castle was besieged two years later by troops supporting the Earl of Lennox in his fight against the Hamiltons, and the castle surrendered after two days. In 1579 the castle was captured by Regent Morton's forces, and dismantled to be left as a ruin. The castle is in the grounds of Chatelherault, is in the care of Historic Scotland and can be viewed from the exterior (01698 426213).

Brodick Castle [NS 016378], two miles north of the village of Brodick on the island of Arran, is a magnificent castle and mansion, possibly dating from the thirteenth

Brodick Castle (M&R)

century, but modified and extended down the centuries. The property had been held by the Stewarts, then went to the Boyds in 1467, before coming by marriage to the Hamiltons in 1503, and James Hamilton, first Earl of Arran, rebuilt the castle around 1510. It was damaged in a raid of 1528 between feuding Campbells and MacLeans, and again in 1544 by the Earl of Lennox acting for Henry VIII of England. As mentioned above, James Hamilton, third Earl, was declared insane and the Earldom was held by James Stewart of Ochiltree from 1581, who claimed it though his wife, but the Earldom and property were restored to the Hamiltons four years later. John Hamilton, fourth Earl, was Chancellor of Scotland and was made Marquis of Hamilton in 1599. His brother, Claud, became Lord Paisley and Lord Abercorn, and this branch eventually became Dukes of Abercorn, along with many other titles. James Hamilton supported Charles I and was made Duke of Hamilton in 1643. The castle had been seized by the Campbells in 1639, but was retaken by the Hamiltons. The Hamiltons continued to support the Stewarts, and James was one of the commanders at Preston five years later when the king's army was crushed; Hamilton was executed. William, second Duke, was killed at the Battle of Worcester in 1651 when Charles II was defeated, and Brodick was subsequently sacked. The title then passed to Anne, daughter of the first Duke, and there was then a bitter dispute between her and the Dukes of Abercorn about who should succeed, although she also started the building of Hamilton Palace back on the mainland. The Dukedom then went to the Douglases after William Douglas married Anne, Duchess of Hamilton. James Douglas (or Hamilton), fourth Duke, gained a reputation for philandering, and he was a Jacobite although his support was inconstant and he was made Duke of Brandon in 1711; he was killed in a duel the following year.

Extensive additions were made to Brodick Castle in 1844 by James Gillespie Graham for the marriage of Princess Marie of Baden to William, eleventh Duke of Hamilton. In 1958 Brodick was taken over by The National Trust for Scotland, and the castle and grounds are open to the public (01770 302202; www.nts.org.uk).

Hamilton Palace [NS 726504], to the north of the town of Hamilton in central Scotland, was a huge and

Hamilton Palace 1910?

magnificent classical mansion, dating from the beginning of the eighteenth century (and designed by the architect David Hamilton), and was built on the site of a castle known as the Orchard. Mary, Queen of Scots, visited the old castle in the summer of 1563. The building was burned down, probably by the forces of the Regent Morton in 1579, although by 1591 it had been repaired or rebuilt; Hamilton Palace was built on the site. The palace, however, was demolished in 1927 because of mining subsidence. Much of the furniture, paintings and porcelain from here are now on display at Lennoxlove in East Lothian.

Chatelherault Hunting Lodge [NS 737540], two miles to the south-east of Hamilton, is a splendid hunting lodge and kennels, and was built in 1732-44 for James Hamilton, fifth Duke of Hamilton, by the architect William Adam. The building houses a museum and there is a country park with the ruins of Cadzow Castle as well as the Hamilton Mausoleum (01698 426213; www.southlanarkshire.gov.uk). There are memorials to the Dukes of Hamilton in Bothwell Parish Church [NS 705586], which has an interesting burial ground and is open to the public in the summer.

Lennoxlove [NT 515721], which is a mile south of Haddington in East Lothian, had a long association with the Maitlands, and was formerly known as **Lethington**. It was sold to the Stewarts Lords Blantyre, who changed the name to Lennoxlove, then to the Bairds, and Lennoxlove then passed to the Dukes of Hamilton in

Lennoxlove (MC)

1947, and they still own it. Among the treasures it contains are the death mask of Mary, Queen of Scots, and the casket which may have contained the 'Casket Letters'. The castle is has just been refurbished and is open to the public (01620 823720; www.lennoxlove.org).

Kinneil House [NS 983806] lies to the south-west of Bo'ness in Falkirk district, and is a large and impressive

Kinneil House (M&R)

building, dating from the sixteenth century but later altered and extended into a magnificent residence. The lands were held by the Hamiltons from the fourteenth century, and John, fourth Earl of Arran, built a large tower at Kinneil, which was destroyed by the Earl of Morton after the Battle of Langside in 1568. Kinneil was rebuilt and remodelled by the Dukes of Hamilton, although it was occupied by Cromwell's forces in the 1650s. It was abandoned in the 1820s, stands in a public park, and is now in the care of Historic Scotland and can be viewed from the exterior. The area is said to be haunted by the ghost of Ailie or Alice, Lady Lilburne, the young wife of a Cromwellian, or possibly the mistress of the Duke of Hamilton. After having tried to escape, she was imprisoned in one of the upper chambers and then threw herself into the Gil Burn, 200 foot below. Her screams and wails are said still to be heard on dark winter nights, and her spectre is said to haunt the glen.

A few miles to the west and north of Lanark is **Craignethan Castle** [NS 816464], a large and attractive

Craignethan Castle (M&R)

ruin in a picturesque spot. It consists of a massive and squat tower, formerly with a curtain wall and corner towers. There is an outer courtyard with a deep ditch in which there is a caponier. The lands were held by the Douglases, but passed to the Hamiltons. Sir James Hamilton of Finnart, an illegitimate son of James Hamilton, first Earl of Arran, was a talented architect and the King's Superintendent of Palaces, and he built most of the castle. Hamilton became extremely wealthy and was perhaps unscrupulous but he was beheaded for treason in 1540 by James V; the king seized his wealth and property, although Hamilton's son eventually inherited his lands. Mary, Queen of Scots, is said to have spent the night here before the Battle of Langside in 1568. The Hamiltons formed the main part of her army, but were defeated and Mary fled to England. The garrison of Craignethan surrendered, but the castle was retaken by the Hamiltons, was attacked in 1579 and then was given up without a siege. Craignethan was slighted and sacked, and the lands were sold to the Hays in 1655, who built a house in the outer courtyard. Sir Walter Scott featured Craignethan in *Old Mortality*, but called it 'Tillietudlem'. The castle is said to be haunted, especially the newer house in the courtyard, although the apparition of a headless lady has also reportedly been seen, identified by some as Mary, Queen of Scots. Craignethan is in the care of Historic Scotland and is open to the public (01555 860364).

Preston Tower [NT 393742] is a large and foreboding ruinous tower in its own small park in the East Lothian town of Prestonpans. It rises to six storeys, and was held by the Hamiltons from the end of the fourteenth century; they probably built the castle. Preston was torched in 1544 by the Earl of Hertford, and again in 1650 by Cromwell. After being restored, it was accidentally burnt again in 1663, then abandoned for nearby Preston House (which has since been demolished). One of the family was Robert Hamilton, a noted Covenanter and prominent in the victory of Drumclog and the defeat of Bothwell Brig in 1679. He fled to Holland, but he returned in 1688 and died in 1701. The family had been made Baronets of Nova Scotia in 1673, were forfeited in 1684, but then recovered the property in the nineteenth century. The tower was consolidated in 1936, purchased by The National Trust

Preston Tower (M&R)

for Scotland six years later, and is under the guardianship of the local council. The line of the Stirling-Hamiltons of Preston, Baronets, continues, but they now apparently live in King's Lynn in Norfolk in England. Preston Tower is said to be haunted by a Green Lady; and the ruin can be viewed from its attractive gardens (01875 810232).

The Hamiltons also held:
Abercorn Castle [NT 083794], near South Queensferry, West Lothian; site of castle.
  Held by the Douglases, but the castle was destroyed by James II in 1455. The lands passed to the Setons, and then to the Hamiltons. Lord Claud Hamilton, Lord Paisley – fourth son of James, second Earl of Arran and Regent of Scotland during the minority of Mary, Queen of Scots – was made Lord Abercorn in 1568, and his son was made Earl of Abercorn in 1606. The family were made Marquises in 1790 and Dukes of Abercorn in 1868. The family are now the 'senior' branch of the Hamiltons, the Dukes of Hamilton having passed through the female line, and the Dukes of Abercorn apparently live in Northern Ireland.
Airdrie House [NS 749654], Airdrie, Lanarkshire; site of castle and mansion.
  Held by the Clellands, but passed to the Hamiltons in 1490. One of the family was killed at the Battle of Flodden in 1513. The Hamiltons of Airdrie were Covenanters and fought at the Battle of Drumclog in 1679; Airdrie House was captured and garrisoned for James VII. The property passed to the Elphinstones and then to others, and the house was used as a maternity hospital before being demolished when Monklands General Hospital was built.
Aitkenhead Castle [NS 596603], Glasgow; mansion on site of castle.
  Held by several families before coming to the Hamiltons after 1600. John Hamilton of Aitkenhead was Provost of Glasgow in the seventeenth century; the lands later passed to the Gordons.
Ardverikie [NN 508876], Loch Laggan, Highland; mansion.
  Built in 1840 by the Hamilton Marquis of Abercorn; there was a castle [NN 498875] of the Macphersons on an island in Loch Laggan. Ardverikie was visited by Queen Victoria in 1847, passed to the Ramsdens, and was mostly destroyed by fire in 1873. It was rebuilt and the house was used in the BBC series *Monarch of the Glen*. Accommodation is available on the estate and the gardens are occasionally open to the public (01528 544322; www.ardverikie.com).

Auldton [NS 795502], near Wishaw, Lanarkshire; mansion dated 1610.

Held by the Hamiltons of Dalserf. Used as a farmhouse, but has been restored and reoccupied.

Baldernock [NS 600751], near Kirkintilloch, Dunbartonshire; motte.

Held by the Galbraiths, but passed by marriage to the Hamiltons in the second half of the fourteenth century.

Balmacara [NG 800277], near Kyle of Lochalsh, Lochalsh; site of castle or old house.

Held by the Mathesons and by the Mackenzies before going to the Hamiltons, who gave the property to The National Trust for Scotland. The estate is open to the public (01599 566325).

Bardowie Castle [NS 580738], near Milngavie, Dunbartonshire; altered tower house with wing.

Held by the Galbraiths but passed by marriage in the fourteenth century to the Hamiltons of Cadzow, who moved here from

Bardowie Castle 1910?

Craigmaddie. In 1526 John Hamilton of Bardowie was killed by the Logans of Balvie, while his son was slain by the Campbells of Auchenbowie, and in 1591 the family quarrelled with the Grahams of Dougalston, during a series of feuds. In 1707 Mary Hamilton, sister of John Hamilton of Bardowie, married Gregor 'Black Knee' MacGregor, Rob Roy's nephew and chief of the clan. Bardowie passed by marriage to the Buchanans of Leny and Spittal.

Barnbougle Castle [NT 169785], near South Queensferry, Edinburgh; mansion incorporating part of an earlier castle.

Held by the Mowbrays, but sold to the Hamilton Earl of Haddington in 1615, then to the Primroses of Rosebery in 1662 and they rebuilt the castle in 1881. In the grounds of Dalmeny House.

Barncluith or **Baron's Cleugh Castle** [NS 729545], near Hamilton, Lanarkshire; plain tower house.

Built by the Hamiltons in 1583, whose descendants were made Lords Belhaven. Graham of Claverhouse, Bonnie Dundee, spent the night here before the Battle of Bothwell Brig in 1679, when the Covenanters were defeated by the Duke of Monmouth.

Barnhill [NS 679574], near Hamilton, Lanarkshire; site of castle.

Held by the Coats in the seventeenth century, but also a property of the Hamiltons.

Baronial Hall, Gorbals [NS 592641], Glasgow; site of tower house and mansion.

Held by the Elphinstones after the Reformation, but passed to the Hamilton Viscounts Belhaven in 1634. The property went to the City of Glasgow in 1661, and was later used as a town hall, jail and school, before being demolished by 1870.

Barr Castle [NS 347582], near Lochwinnoch, Renfrewshire; well-preserved keep or tower.

Held by the Glens, but passed to the Hamiltons of Ferguslie in the seventeenth century.

Biel [NT 637759], near Dunbar, East Lothian; mansion incorporating castle.

Held by the Hamiltons from the seventeenth century, and they were made Lords Belhaven. The second Lord Belhaven made

a famous speech in the old Scottish parliament in 1706 against the Union of Parliaments. There is a stone plaque on the house bearing the inscription in Latin: 'The first year of the betrayal of Scotland'. The White Lady of Biel is reputedly the ghost of Anne Bruce of Earlshall, and is said to have been seen in the grounds. She was wife of the third Lord Belhaven, who himself died in 1721. The lands were held by the Hamiltons until 1958, and the line continues, although they now apparently live in London. The house can be visited by groups (20-25 people) by appointment only (01620 860355).

Binny [NT 053734], near Broxburn, West Lothian; site of castle or old house.

Held by the Binning family, but the property and the title Lord Binning passed to Thomas Hamilton in 1613. He was made Earl of Melrose in 1619 and then Earl of Haddington in 1627; the family still hold the title Lord Binning.

Blair Castle [NS 968858], near Kincardine, Fife; mansion on site of castle.

The old castle was built by Archbishop John Hamilton of St Andrews in the second half of the sixteenth century. Still occupied.

Boghouse Castle [NS 878236], near Crawfordjohn, Lanarkshire; site of castle.

Built by Sir James Hamilton of Finnart in the sixteenth century. James V entertained his mistress, Catherine Carmichael, here, and the property was exchanged by Hamilton for the barony of Kilmarnock with James V in 1535. Hamilton was executed for treason in 1540, although the property eventually returned to the Hamiltons.

Bonhard House [NT 020799], near Bo'ness, West Lothian; site of tower house.

Held by the Cornwalls, but later passed to the Hamilton Dukes of Hamilton. Bonhard was gutted by fire and demolished in the 1950s.

Boreland Castle [NS 586174], near Cumnock, Ayrshire; site of castle.

May have been held by the Hamiltons.

Broomhill Castle [NS 754508], near Larkhall, Lanarkshire; slight remains of castle and mansion.

Held by the Hamiltons from 1473. Sir John Hamilton of Broomhill died of wounds received at the Battle of Langside in 1568 fighting for Mary, Queen of Scots; and the castle was torched in 1572. It was rebuilt in 1585, and was extended and remodelled in later centuries. Passed to the Birnies, but mostly demolished in 1943. Said to be haunted by a Black Lady.

Carnbroe House [NS 735623], near Coatbridge, Lanarkshire; site of tower house.

Held by the Baillies, but passed to the Hamiltons. Demolished in the middle of the twentieth century.

Carnell [NS 467323], near Kilmarnock, Ayrshire; castle and mansion.

Held by the Wallaces and by the Cathcarts before coming to the Hamiltons in the nineteenth century. The house can be rented as holiday accommodation (01563 884236; www.carnell estates.com).

Carriden House [NT 026808], near Bo'ness, West Lothian; castle and mansion.

Held by several families before coming to the Hamiltons of Letterick in 1601. The family were made Lords Bargany and they built most of the mansion. The property later passed to the Setons and to others. B&B accommodation is available and Carriden is a suitable venue for weddings (01506 829811; www.carridenhouse.co.uk).

Castle Kennedy [NX 111609], near Stranraer, Galloway; large ruinous tower house.

Held by the Kennedys, but passed to the Hamiltons of Bargany, then in 1677 to the Dalrymples of Stair, whose descendants still own it. The gardens are open to the public from April to September (01776 702024; www.castlekennedygardens.co.uk).

Castlemilk or **Carmunnock** [NS 608594], Glasgow; some remains of castle and mansion.

Held by the Comyns and by the Douglases before passing to the Hamiltons in 1455, then it went to the Stewarts of

Castlemilk in Dumfriesshire, and they changed the name from Carmunnock to Castlemilk. Mostly demolished in the 1960s. The area around the castle is said to be haunted.

Cathkin House [NS 627588], near Rutherglen, Glasgow; castle replaced by mansion.

Held by the Douglases and then by the Hamiltons who owned it until the end of the seventeenth century. It passed to the Dunlops and then to others. The building is now used as a nursing home.

Cochno Castle [NS 498745], near Clydebank, Glasgow; tower house replaced by mansion.

Held by the Hamiltons from the Reformation, and two of the family were keepers of Dumbarton Castle. The present Cochno House was built about 1757, and has been owned by the University of Glasgow since 1956.

Coltness Castle [NS 797564], near Wishaw, Lanarkshire; castle replaced by mansion.

Held by several families before coming to the Hamiltons of Udston in the early eighteenth century. It had gone to the Houldsworths by the end of the next century.

Cot or **Cat** or **Coat** or **Kemp** or **Kat** Castle [NS 739457], near Strathaven, Lanarkshire; site of castle.

Held by the Hamiltons from about 1500.

Couston Castle [NS 955712], near Bathgate, West Lothian; slight remains of castle.

Held by the Hamiltons, and then by the Sandilands.

Cowden Hall [NS 466571], near Neilston, Renfrewshire; ruined mansion and site of castle.

Held by several families before coming to the Hamilton Marquis of Clydesdale in 1725, then it went to the Dukes of Hamilton.

Craighlaw Castle [NX 305611], near Glenluce, Galloway; castle and mansion.

Held by the Mures and by the Gordons, before coming to the Hamiltons in 1741. Later additions were demolished in the 1950s and the building is still occupied.

Craigmaddie Castle [NS 575765], near Milngavie, Dunbartonshire; slight remains of castle.

Held by the Galbraiths, but passed by marriage to the Hamiltons of Cadzow, but they had moved to Bardowie before 1566.

Crawfordjohn Castle [NS 879239], near Abington, Lanarkshire; site of castle.

Held by several families, including by the Crawfords and by the Hamiltons. The property was exchanged with Sir James Hamilton of Finnart in 1533, and he probably built Boghouse using materials from here. The property was held by the Crown on Hamilton's execution in 1540, but returned to the Hamiltons in 1553 and they held the lands until 1693.

Dalmeny House [NT 167779], near South Queensferry, Edinburgh; mansion on site of older house.

Held by the Mowbrays of Dalmeny and Barnbougle, but sold to the Hamilton Earl of Haddington in 1615, who sold it to the Primroses of Rosebery in 1662. The Primroses built the fine mansion of Dalmeny House, and it is open to the public in July and August (0131 331 1888; www.dalmeny.co.uk).

Dalserf [NS 801506], near Overton, Lanarkshire; site of castle and later mansion.

Held by the Hamiltons from 1312. Demolished in the twentieth century.

Dalzell House [NS 756550], near Motherwell, Lanarkshire; fine castle and mansion.

Held by the Dalziels but sold to Hamilton of Boggs in 1649. The family became Lords Hamilton of Dalzell, then Barons Hamilton of Dalzell in 1886. The house was remodelled in the 1850s, the north wing was used as a hospital during World War I, and the property was held by the family until 1952. It is said to be haunted by four different ladies (Green, White, Grey and Brown) and has been divided into separate residences. The line of the Hamilton Barons Hamilton of Dalzell continues, and they live in England. The house stands in a public park (0141 304 1907; www.northlan.gov.uk).

Darngaber Castle [NS 729501], near Hamilton, Lanarkshire; motte.

Held by the Hamiltons of Cadzow.

Drumpellier House [NS 716650], near Coatbridge, Lanarkshire; site of castle or old house.

Held by the Hamiltons and then by the Colquhouns, before passing to the Buchanans. The house has been demolished and the grounds are a country park.

Drumry Castle [NS 515710], near Duntocher, Glasgow; site of tower house.

Held by several families and individuals, including Sir James Hamilton of Finnart. Demolished in the 1960s.

Drumsargad or **Cambuslang Castle** [NS 667597], near Hamilton, Lanarkshire; slight traces of castle.

Held by several families before coming to the Hamiltons in 1455 and they held the lands until the 1920s. They lived at Westburn House, but this was demolished in the twentieth century.

Easter Greenock Castle [NS 300755], near Greenock, Renfrewshire; site of large tower house.

Held by several families and individuals including by James Hamilton of Finnart. Demolished to build the railway.

Eddlewood Castle [NS 722518], near Hamilton, Lanarkshire; site of castle.

Held by the Hamiltons of Eddlewood and Neilsland, who owned the property until 1750. The castle may have been destroyed by the Regent Moray after the Battle of Langside in 1568.

Erskine Castle [NS 462720], near Erskine, Lanarkshire; site of castle.

Held by the Erskines but was sold to Sir John Hamilton of Orbiston in 1638, then in 1703 to the Stewart Lords Blantyre, who built a new mansion. In 1916 it was converted into a hospital for limbless sailors and soldiers.

Fairholm [NS 754516], near Larkhall, Lanarkshire; mansion on site of castle.

Held by the Hamiltons from the fifteenth century. Matthew Hamilton of Fairholm was described by John Knox as a 'rank and incorrigible papist', and was captain of Blackness Castle and Linlithgow Palace in 1543. The family, now Stevenson-Hamilton, still apparently live here.

Fala Luggie Tower [NT 425590], near Gorebridge, Midlothian; remains of tower house.

Held by the Douglases and by the Murrays, but by the eighteenth century Fala was owned by the Hamiltons.

Falside Castle [NT 378710], near Tranent, East Lothian; restored L-plan tower house.

Held by the Falside family and by the Setons, but in 1631 was sold to an Edinburgh merchant called Hamilton. Became ruinous but has been restored and reoccupied.

Farme Castle [NS 620624], Rutherglen, Glasgow; site of castle.

Held by several families, including by the Crawfords, before coming to the Hamilton Duke of Hamilton, and then to the Faries. Demolished in the 1960s.

Ferguslie Castle [NS 467637], Paisley, Renfrewshire; site of castle.

Held by the Hamiltons from 1544, and the castle was replaced by Ferguslie House. This building was said to be haunted but has been demolished.

Fingalton [NS 499550], near Barrhead, Renfrewshire; likely site of castle.

Held by the Hamiltons from the fourteenth to sixteenth centuries, and possibly by the Maxwells.

Gallowhill [NS 499650], near Renfrew; castle replaced by mansion.

Held by the Hamiltons, but passed to the Cochrane Earls of Dundonald by the middle of the seventeenth century.

Garrion Tower [NS 797511], near Wishaw, Lanarkshire; tower house and mansion.

Held by the Forest family, then by the Hamiltons. Still occupied.

Gartshore House [NS 692737], near Kirkintilloch, Dunbartonshire; site of castle and mansion.

Held by the Gartshore family, then by the Hamiltons and by the Murrays of Ochtertyre, then by others. Demolished in the twentieth century.

Gilbertfield Castle [NS 653588], near East Kilbride, Ayrshire; ruinous tower house.

Held by the Hamiltons, one of whom was the poet William

Gilbertfield Castle (M&R)

Hamilton of Gilbertfield around the turn of the eighteenth century. Hamilton was responsible for the translation of Blind Harry's epic poem *Sir William Wallace*.

Gilkerscleugh House [NS 900236], near Abingdon, Lanarkshire; site of tower house.

Held by the Hamiltons from 1598 until the nineteenth century; the house was demolished in the twentieth century after a fire.

Grange House [NT 015815], Bo'ness, Falkirk; site of tower house.

Held by the Hamiltons, but sold to the Cadells in 1788. Demolished.

Greenock Castle [NS 280765], Greenock, Renfrewshire; site of castle.

Held by the Cathcarts, but passed to the Hamiltons, then went to the Shaws.

Haggs [NS 722622], near Coatbridge, Lanarkshire; site of castle and later house.

Held by the Hamiltons.

Hallcraig House [NS 829500], near Carluke, Lanarkshire; site of castle and mansion.

Held by the Hamiltons and possibly also by the Stewarts. Demolished in the twentieth century.

Hamilton House [NT 389739], Prestonpans, East Lothian; old mansion.

Held by the Hamiltons, but now in the care of The National Trust for Scotland. House is let and open only by prior arrangement, phone 01721 722502.

Harlawhill [NT 390745], Prestonpans, East Lothian; L-plan house dating from the seventeenth century.

Held by the Hamiltons. Still occupied.

Hills Tower [NT 049481], near Carnwath, Lanarkshire; site of tower house.

Held by the Denholms and by the Baillies of Lamington, then by the Hamiltons and by the Lockharts.

Holm Castle [NS 746474], near Stonehouse, Lanarkshire; site of castle.

Held by the Hamiltons, then by the Rae family, although a Carmichael of Holmhead is mentioned in 1641.

Inchnock Castle [NS 718694], near Coatbridge, Lanarkshire; slight remains of tower house.

Held by the Forsyths of Dykes, but passed to the Hamiltons of Dalyell, then to a John Hay and maybe also to the Steels. Ruinous by the middle of the seventeenth century.

Innerwick Castle [NT 735737], near Dunbar, East Lothian; ruinous castle.

Held by the Stewarts, then by the Hamiltons in 1398. The castle was besieged by the Percys and the fourth Earl of Douglas in 1403. In 1547 the English smoked out the garrison and dismantled the castle, while in 1548 the castle seems again to have been in the hands of the Scots, as the Master of Hamilton and eight other men held Innerwick against the English. Eight of the garrison were picked off with muskets, while the last threw himself to his death from one of the walls. The defences were slighted. The property was sold to the Nisbets in 1663, and was also held by the Maxwells. The castle was complete enough to be used as a base, along with Dirleton and Tantallon, to attack Cromwell's lines of communication in the 1650s.

Karig Lion Castle [NS 987812], Bo'ness, Falkirk; site of castle.

Held by Margaret Lyon, daughter of Lord Glamis and widow of John Hamilton, first Marquis of Hamilton, who himself died in 1604. The castle is marked as being offshore, but the site is now reclaimed land and Kinneil Iron Works was built on it.

Kilbrackmont Place [NO 478057], near Elie, Fife; site of tower house.

Held by the Hamiltons from the end of the sixteenth century or earlier.

Kildonan [NX 227831], near Barrhill, Ayrshire; castle replaced by mansion.

Held by the Eccles family, then by the Chalmerses, but was sold to the Hamiltons around 1830.

Kildonan Castle [NS 037210], Kildonan, Arran; very ruinous castle.

Held by the MacDonald Lords of the Isles, but passed to the Stewarts of Ardgowan, then to the Hamiltons in 1544.

Kingscavil or **Champfleurie** [NT 038766], near Linlithgow, West Lothian; mansion possibly incorporating remains of castle.

Held by the Hamiltons. Patrick Hamilton of Kingscavil was the keeper of Blackness Castle. He took part in jousts at Stirling Castle in 1507, but was slain in 1520 in a fight with the Douglases on Edinburgh's High Street, known as 'Cleanse the Causeway'. Hamilton of Kingscavil's son, Patrick, Abbot of Fearn, became Scotland's first Protestant martyr, and was burned at St Andrews in 1528. Still occupied.

Kinkell [NO 539158], near St Andrews, Fife; site of castle.

Held by the Monypennys of Pitmilly, then by the Hamiltons of Kinkell, and possibly also by the Kinnimonds of Craighall.

Kirkhope Tower or **Daer** [NS 968065], near Elvanfoot, Lanarkshire; site of tower house.

The barony of Daer was created in 1646 for the Douglas Earl of Selkirk, but passed to the Duke of Hamilton in 1885.

Langton Castle [NT 756534], near Duns, Borders; site of castle and mansion.

Held by several families, then latterly by the Baillie-Hamiltons. The building was demolished in the 1950s.

Law Tower [NS 515738], near Bearsden, Dunbartonshire; site of tower house.

Held by the Livingstones, but passed by marriage to Sir James Hamilton of Finnart after 1513, then passed to the Stirlings of Glorat. Demolished in the 1890s.

Lickprivick Castle [NS 616527], near East Kilbride, Lanarkshire; site of castle.

Held by the Lickprivick family and by the Maxwells of Calder before passing to the Hamiltons, who held the property in the sixteenth century. Demolished by 1840 and the site is occupied by a housing estate.

Little Kype [NS 746407], near Strathaven, Lanarkshire; site of castle.

Held by the Bairds and by the Dalziels in 1572, but passed to the Hamiltons. Robert Burns's *Kilmarnock Edition* was dedicated to the fifth son of John Hamilton of Kype.

Lochranza Castle [NR 933507], Lochranza, Arran; fine ruinous castle.

Held by several families, including by the Hamiltons from 1705. The castle is in the care of Historic Scotland and is open to the public.

Mannerston [NT 048790], near Linlithgow, West Lothian; mansion incorporating part of castle.

Held by the Livingstones in 1431, but passed to Sir James Hamilton of Finnart and then to the Bruces of Airth.

Mellerstain [NT 648392], near Earlston, Borders; magnificent mansion on site of older house.

Held by several families before coming to the Baillie-Hamiltons, Earls of Haddington, who built Mellerstain. The house and fine gardens are open to the public from Easter, then from May to September (01573 410225; www.meller stain.com).

Monk Castle [NS 292474], near Kilwinning, Ayrshire; ruinous T-plan tower house.

Held by the Hamiltons.

Monkland House [NS 730633], near Coatbridge, Lanarkshire; site of tower house.

Held by the Kerrs of Ferniehirst, then by the Hamiltons in 1554, then by the Clellands of Monkland, who built the house. The building was demolished after a series of fires in the 1950s, and the site is now occupied by a housing development.

Monkton House [NS 359271], near Prestwick, Ayrshire; site of castle.

Held by the Hamiltons, later Earls of Abercorn, then by the Baillies of Monkton.

Murdostoun Castle [NS 825573], near Newmains, Glasgow; mansion incorporating castle.

Held by the Scotts and by the Inglis family, then passed to the Hamiltons in 1719, then in 1856 went to the Stewarts. The building is now used as a hospital.

Newton Castle [NS 339223], Ayr; site of castle.

Held by the Wallaces of Craigie and by the Hamiltons. The site is now a car park.

Newton House [NS 663613], near Cambuslang, Lanarkshire; site of castle and mansion.

Held by the Douglases, by the Hamiltons of Silvertonhill, and then later by the Montgomerys.

Northfield House [NT 389739], Prestonpans, East Lothian; impressive L-plan house.

Held by the Hamiltons, but had passed to the Marjoribanks family by 1611, then to the Nisbets in 1746, and then to others. The house is in good condition and still occupied.

Ochiltree Castle [NT 032748], near Linlithgow, West Lothian; L-plan tower house.

Held by the Stirlings, then by Sir James Hamilton of Finnart from 1526 to 1540, then went to the Stewarts of Ochiltree. Restored and reoccupied in the 1980s.

Ochiltree Castle [NS 510212], Ochiltree, Ayrshire; site of castle, Held by several families including by Sir James Hamilton of Finnart. Demolished in the middle of the twentieth century.

Old Woodhouselee Castle [NT 258617], near Penicuik, Midlothian; some remains of castle.

Held by the Sinclairs but later by the Hamiltons of Bothwellhaugh. Lady Hamilton and her young child were stripped naked and turned out of their home here by the Regent Moray. The baby died and Lady Hamilton went mad, to die soon afterwards (according to one version), and her ghost is said to haunt the site. Her husband, James Hamilton of Bothwellhaugh, shot and killed Regent Moray at Linlithgow in 1570. The property passed to the Ballantynes and they built a new house, itself gone.

Orbiston House [NS 732580], near Motherwell, Lanarkshire; slight remains of castle.

Held by the Oliphants in the twelfth century, but passed to the Hamiltons, who still held it to 1827.

Pardovan Castle [NT 044773], near Linlithgow, West Lothian; site of castle.

Held by the Hamiltons.

Patrickholm [NS 756500], near Larkhall, Lanarkshire; ruinous mansion on site of castle.

Held by the Hamiltons of Raploch, and is said to have been a meeting place for government forces during Covenanting times.

Penshiel Grange [NT 642632], near Cranshaws, East Lothian; ruinous tower house.

Held by the Hamilton Earl of Melrose in 1621.

Pinmore [NX 206904], near Girvan, Ayrshire; site of castle and mansion.

Held by the Hamiltons. The mansion was burned out and then demolished in 1981.

Pitlessie Castle [NO 336096], near Ladybank, Fife; mansion on site of castle.

Held by the Hamiltons of Binning.

Place of Paisley [NS 485639], Paisley, Renfrewshire; fortified house.

By the abbey and built by the Hamiltons, who had been commendators, and they were made Lords Paisley. This branch went on to be Earls and, much later, Dukes of Abercorn. There is a sad memorial to the children of Claud Hamilton, Lord

Place of Paisley (M&R)

Paisley, in the adjacent Paisley Abbey, which is open to the public (0141 889 7654; www.paisleyabbey.org.uk). The property later passed to the Douglas Earl of Angus then to the Cochranes in 1653. Now the manse for the abbey church.

Plotcock Castle [NS 740501], near Hamilton, Lanarkshire; some remains of tower house.

Held by the Hamiltons. There are tales of the lands around here being haunted by ghosts and witches.

Polmont House [NS 933782], near Falkirk; site of castle and mansion.

Held by the Hamiltons in the seventeenth century, who were made Barons Polmont in 1643. The house was demolished in the twentieth century and the site is occupied by a housing scheme.

Provan Hall [NS 667663], near Coatbridge, Lanarkshire; fine courtyard castle and mansion.

Held by the Baillies, but passed by marriage to the Hamiltons and then to others. Held by The National Trust for Scotland, and open to the public (0141 771 4399).

Prestonfield House [NT 278721], Edinburgh; fine mansion of 1687.

Held by the Hamiltons. Thomas Hamilton of Prestonfield was a Lord of Session in 1607. In 1631 the Prestonfield Aisle was added to Duddingston Kirk [NT 284726] (www.duddingston-kirk.org.uk), and in 1646 Sir James Hamilton of Prestonfield was made hereditary keeper of the nearby Holyrood Park and of Holyroodhouse. The Hamiltons exploited their position by extracting thousands of tons of the stone from the park until 1831 when the House of Lords put a stop to their activity. Prestonfield was burnt out in 1681 by a Protestant mob, and the present house was built for Sir James Dick of Braid six years later. The house has been used as a hotel since 1958 and some of the grounds are used as Prestonfield Golf Course (0131 225 7800; www.prestonfield.com).

Ralston [NS 507642], near Paisley, Renfrewshire; site of castle and mansion.

Held by the Ralstons, then by the Cochrane Earl of Dundonald, then by the Hamiltons and by the Orr family. The house was demolished in 1934.

Ranfurly Castle [NS 384652], near Bridge of Weir, Renfrewshire; small ruinous tower.

Held by the Knox family, then by the Cochrane Earl of Dundonald, then by the Hamiltons of Holmhead, then by the Aitkenheads.

Raploch Castle [NS 763515], near Larkhall, Lanarkshire; site of castle.

Held by the Comyns, then by the Hamiltons from 1312, who built the castle. Gavin Hamilton, son of James Hamilton of Raploch, was commendator of Kilwinning Abbey, a Lord of Session in 1555 and coadjutator of the Archbishopric of St Andrews. He was an opponent of John Knox and was murdered near Restalrig in 1571. Raploch was destroyed after the Battle of Langside in 1568, because of the family's support for Mary, Queen of Scots. The site is occupied by a housing estate.

Redhouse Castle [NT 463770], near Aberlady, East Lothian; large and impressive courtyard castle.

Held by the Douglases, then by the Laings, then passed by marriage to the Hamiltons. George Hamilton, the last of the family, was executed for his part in the 1745-46 Jacobite Rising. The property was forfeited, and the castle was allowed to fall into ruin.

Ridford [NS 455635], near Paisley, Renfrewshire; site of castle.

Held by the Hamiltons.

Ross House [NS 739558], near Hamilton, Lanarkshire; castle replaced by mansion.

Held by the Hamiltons of Rossavon in 1339, but passed to the Aikman family in 1856. Still occupied.

Rough Hill [NS 607553], near East Kilbride, Lanarkshire; site of castle on motte.

Held by the Comyns and by the Douglases before passing to the Hamiltons in 1455.

Rozelle House [NS 338190], Ayr; mansion.

Held by the Hamiltons and they gave the property to the town of Ayr in 1968. The house holds exhibitions and the grounds are open to the public (01292 445447).

Rutherglen Castle [NS 614618], Rutherglen, Glasgow; site of large courtyard castle.

Held by the Hamiltons of Ellistoun. The family supported Mary, Queen of Scots, and the castle was burned by Regent Moray about 1569. The site is occupied by modern buildings.

Saltcoats Castle [NT 486819], near Gullane, East Lothian; ruinous courtyard castle.

Held by the Livingstones, then by the Hamiltons of Pencaitland in the eighteenth century. Occupied until early in the nineteenth century but partly demolished.

Silvertonhill [NS 725547], near Hamilton, Lanarkshire; site of castle and mansion.

Held by the Hamiltons from the beginning of the sixteenth century. The family were made Baronets of Nova Scotia in 1646. The family line continues but they now apparently live in Warwickshire in England. The site of the mansion appears to be occupied by housing.

Skene House [NJ 768097], near Westhill, Aberdeenshire; mansion incorporating castle.

Long held by the Skenes, then by the Duff Earls of Fife, then was sold to the Hamiltons in 1880. Still occupied.

Sorn Castle [NS 548269], near Mauchline, Ayrshire; castle and mansion.

Held by the Keiths of Galston, but passed by marriage to the Hamiltons of Cadzow in 1406, then to the Setons of Winton, then to other families. Guided tours are available in the summer (01290 551555).

Sprouston [NT 755352], near Kelso, Borders; site of tower house.

Held by the Douglases in the fifteenth century, but passed to the Hamiltons of Sprouston in the sixteenth century.

Stoneypath Tower [NT 596713], near East Linton, East Lothian; L-plan tower house.

Held by the Lyles in the fifteenth century, but passed to the Hamiltons of Innerwick, then went to the Douglases of Whittinghame in 1616, then to the Setons. Being restored.

Strathaven Castle [NS 703445], Strathaven, Lanarkshire; ruinous castle.

Held by several families before coming to the Hamiltons in the sixteenth century, and they held the property until 1717, after which it became ruinous. Ruin accessible at all times.

Sundrum Castle [NS 410213], near Ayr; mansion incorporating castle.

Held by the Wallaces of Sundrum from 1373 but passed to the Cathcarts, then to the Hamiltons by 1750. Said to be haunted by a Green Lady, and divided into separate flats. Can be let (01530 244436; www.sundrumcastle.com).

The Peel, Busby [NS 594561], near East Kilbride, Lanarkshire; altered L-plan tower house.

Held by the Douglases, then by the Hamiltons from 1455, then by other families, including by the Semples and by the Houstons of Jordanhill. Still occupied.

Torrance Castle [NS 654526], near East Kilbride, Lanarkshire; mansion incorporating castle.

Held by the Hamiltons, but passed to the Stewarts of Castlemilk in the mid eighteenth century. An outbuilding is now used as a visitor centre and stands in a country park (01355 236644; www.southlanarkshire.gov.uk).

Trabroun [NT 466743], near Haddington, East Lothian; site of castle or old house.

Held by the Heriots, but passed to the Hamiltons in 1605.

Tweedie Castle [NS 727427], near Strathaven, Lanarkshire; site of castle.

Held by the Hamiltons of Silvertonhill, but had passed to the Lockharts of Castlehill by 1900.

Tyninghame House [NT 619798], near Dunbar, East Lothian; mansion incorporating castle.

Held by the Lauders of the Bass, but bought by the Hamilton Earls of Hamilton in 1628. The grounds are accessible and the gardens are occasionally open to the public (www.gardensof scotland.org).

Udston [NS 697558], Hamilton, Lanarkshire; site of castle and later mansion.

Held by the Hamiltons, who were descended from Andrew Hamilton, third son of Sir David Hamilton, second of Cadzow.

West Port House [NT 002770], Linlithgow, West Lothian; L-plan tower house.

Held by the Hamiltons. Mary of Guise, wife of James V, is said to have stayed here. Hamilton of Bothwellhaugh shot and killed the Regent Moray in 1570 from a house nearby after Moray had turned his wife and baby out from their home at Old Woodhouselee.

Winton House [NT 439696], near Tranent, East Lothian; fine mansion incorporating part of a castle.

Long held by the Setons, who were forfeited for their part in the 1715 Jacobite Rising, and the property was sold to the Hamilton Lords Pencaitland in 1779, then to the Nisbets and then to the Ogilvys, who still live here. The house can be visited by guided tours and the gardens are occasionally open to the public (01875 340222; www.wintonhouse.co.uk).

Wishaw House [NS 786565], Wishaw, Lanarkshire; site of castle and mansion.

Held by the Hamilton Lords Belhaven. The mansion was demolished about 1950.

clanhamilton.acomhosting.com
No. of castles/sites: 134
Rank: 5/764

Hannay

The name may comes form the Gaelic 'ap Sheanaigh' or 'O'Hannaidh' for 'son of Senach', and the name is on record from the end of the thirteenth century. James Hannay was Dean of Edinburgh and it was he who was taking the service in 1637 at St Giles Cathedral in Edinburgh when Jennie Geddes is said to have thrown her stool at him and then a riot broke out.

Sorbie Castle [NX 451471] lies two miles west of Garlieston in Galloway, is a substantial and once comfortable L-plan tower house, which dates from the

Sorbie Castle (M&R)

sixteenth century. The Hannays (or Ahannays) held the lands from the fourteenth century, and supported John Balliol in the Wars of Independence. The family got into a long a very bitter feud with the Murrays of Broughton, and John Hannay was slain in 1640. The Hannays of Sorbie were ruined, and the property was sold to the Stewarts of Garlies in the 1670s. The ruin has been consolidated for visitors and is accessible to the public.

Kirkdale Tower [NX 513535], six miles west and south of Gatehouse of Fleet in Galloway, is all but gone and was replaced by nearby **Kirkdale House**, a magnificent classical mansion designed by Robert Adam. The lands may have been held by the Murrays but passed to the Hannays in the sixteenth century. Patrick Hannay of Kirkdale was slain in 1610 by one branch of the Kennedys in a dispute with the Earl of Cassillis. The Hannays of Kirkdale and that Ilk are now chiefs of the family, and they apparently live at Cardoness.

The Hannays also owned:

Balcary Tower [NX 827495], near Dalbeattie, Galloway; mansion on site of castle.
   Held by the Hannays around the turn of the eighteenth century.
Bargaly [NX 462664], near Newton Stewart, Galloway; mansion on site of castle.
   Held by the Herons, then much later by the Hannays, then by the Mackies in the nineteenth century.
Kingsmuir [NO 536084], near Anstruther, Fife; mansion on site of older house?
   Held by the Borthwicks, but passed to the Hannays around 1700, later the Hannay Cunninghams.
Pulcree [NX 593584], near Gatehouse of Fleet, Galloway; earthworks from a castle survive.
   May have been held by the Hannays.

www.clanhannay.com
homepages.rootsweb.com/~lmhannah/Clan_Hanna_Han/
   Page_1x.html
No. of castles/sites: 6
Rank: 212=/764
Xrefs: Ahannay; Hanna

Hare

The name comes from the Irish 'O'hlr', meaning 'descendant or son of Ir'. The name was found in Ayrshire, and is on record in Scotland from the fourteenth century. William Hare was one of the infamous duo of Burke and Hare, who murdered many of their contemporaries and even family members to sell their corpses for dissection in the medical school of Edinburgh University. Hare turned King's Evidence against Burke and he escaped execution and he is said to have died destitute in London sometime in the 1860s.

Blairlogie Castle [NS 827969] is a small L-plan tower house, which dates from the sixteenth century. Blairlogie was held by the Spittal family, then by the Dundases, and then the Hares of Blairlogie in the twentieth century. The family were originally from Ayrshire, and now apparently live in Somerset.

No. of castles/sites: 1
Rank: 537=/764
Xref: Hair

Harvey

The name is from 'Harvey' or 'Hervey', a Breton personal name, and the family came to England along with the Normans. The name is recorded as a surname in Scotland from the fourteenth century.

There was a castle at **Dinnet** [NO 465982], several miles west of Ballater in Deeside in Aberdeenshire, but there are no remains. It was replaced by **Dinnet House** [NO 448979], a tall castellated mansion, dating from 1890, and more than a mile to the west. The lands were held by the Gordon Earls of Huntly, but the house was built for the Wilsons, and is now apparently held by the Humphreys of Dinnet, representatives of the Barclay-Harveys of Dinnet. **Castle Semple** [NS 377602] was a couple of miles east and north of Lochwinnoch in Renfrewshire but was completely demolished when a large classical mansion was built in the eighteenth century, itself demolished in the 1960s. The lands were long a property of the Semples, but passed to the MacDowalls around 1727, then to the Harveys from 1813 or so.

No. of castles/sites: 2 / Rank: 396=/764

Xref: Hervey

Hastings

The name comes from the town in the south of England, near where the Battle of Hastings was fought in 1066. The Hastings family was recorded in Scotland from the twelfth century.

House of Dun [NO 667599] is a few miles north-west of Montrose in Angus, and is a fine classical mansion and replaced an old castle. The lands were held by the Hastings family in the twelfth and thirteenth centuries, and John Hastings was Lord of Dun and sheriff and forester of the Mearns. The property went to the Erskines of Dun, but is now in the care of The National Trust for Scotland and is open to the public (01674 810264; www.nts.org.uk).

Loudoun Castle [NS 506378], one mile north of Galston in Ayrshire, was long the seat of the Campbell Earls of Loudoun but passed, along with the title, by marriage to the Hastings family from England in the nineteenth century; they built much of the existing mansion. The building was burned out and ruined in 1941, and is centre of a theme park (01563 822296; www.loudouncastle.co.uk). The Abney-Hastings are still Earls of Loudoun.

No. of castles/sites: 2 / Rank: 396=/764

Hatton

The name may be territorial and may come from the lands of Hatton, which are a few miles west of Balerno near Edinburgh, or it may be local and come from a family of that name from England.

Hatton House [NT 128687] was an L-plan tower house which had been incorporated into a large old mansion. The tower house dated from the fifteenth century, but the building was gutted by fire and demolished in the 1950s. The lands were a property of the Hatton family from the thirteenth century, but passed to the Lauders in 1377, who built the castle.

No. of castles/sites: 1
Rank: 537=/764

Haulkerston

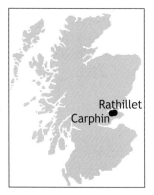

The name probably comes from the lands in the Mearns known as Haulkerton or Hawkerton, which were long held by the Falconers, 'hawker' being another name for the office of 'falconer'. The name was spelt Haulkerston or Halkerstone, and was latterly shortened to Hackston. The name is on record from 1296.

Four miles or so north of Cupar in Fife, **Rathillet House** [NO 359208] is a mansion of 1790 but it replaced a castle, which is on record as being repaired in the thirteenth century. The lands were held by the Lindsays in 1568, but passed to the Hackston family. David Hackston of Rathillet was a noted Covenanter, and was one of those present when Archbishop James Sharp was brutally murdered on Magus Muir in 1679. Hackston fought at the Battle of Bothwell Brig the same year. He was eventually captured and his hands hacked off before he was hanged. The Hackstons held the property until about 1772.

Carphin [NO 319195], several miles to the north-west of Cupar in Fife, was held by the Baillies in the sixteenth century, but later passed to the Hackstons, then went to the Raiths and to the Cooks. There was a castle or old house, but this was replaced by a mansion, which dates from around the turn of the nineteenth century.

No. of castles/sites: 2
Rank: 396=/764

Xrefs: Hackston; Halkerstone

Hay

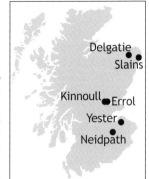

The family are descended from the powerful Norman 'de la Haye' family, who came to England with William the Conqueror. William de la Haye was cupbearer to Malcolm the Maiden, King of Scots, in the twelfth century.

Errol [NO 245228], seven and a half miles east of Perth, was given to William de Haya, by William the Lion, and the Hays had a castle here. Sir Gilbert Hay of Errol was a loyal supporter of Robert the Bruce, and was made hereditary Lord High Constable (an office still held by the Hays), responsible for the monarch's safety, and William, ninth lord, was made Earl of Errol in 1452. Francis Hay, ninth Earl, was summoned for treason in 1594, and went on to fight at the Battle of Glenlivet, where James VI's forces, led by the Earl of Argyll, were defeated. The victory was hollow, however. Hay was forfeited, but returned in 1597 to then be excommunicated in 1608. The Hays left Errol in 1634 to move to Slains, itself now a ruin.

Old Slains Castle [NK 053300] lies four and a half miles to the south-west of Cruden Bay in Aberdeenshire in the far north-east of Scotland. It is now a shattered ruin but was held by the Hays from the fourteenth century, and this was a property of the Earls of Errol. James VI had it destroyed and blown up with gunpowder in 1594 after the Earl had taken part in Huntly's rebellion. The Earls built a new house further down the coast at what is now called Slains.

Slains Castle [NK 102362], formerly known as **Bowness**, is to the east of Cruden Bay, and is in a magnificent location on cliffs above the sea. This has been a grand mansion but is now a stripped shell. Dr Johnson and Boswell visited in 1773, and Bram Stoker had the inspiration for writing *Dracula* here, although Slains was not a ruin at the time. Slains was sold by the Hays in 1916, and unroofed in 1925. There are apparently plans to restore the ruins and turn the castle into a holiday complex. Some accounts also have the castle haunted by the ghost of Victor Hay, twenty-first Earl of Errol. The ruins are accessible with care.

The site of **Kinnoull Castle** [NO 123228] is just to the east of Perth, but there are no remains. The property was held by the Hays from 1360. George Hay of Kinnoull was a gentleman of the bedchamber to James VI, and was one of those who helped James VI during the debacle of the Gowrie Conspiracy in 1600. He was knighted in 1609, and promoted to Chancellor in 1622. After being created Viscount Hay five years later, he was made Earl of Kinnoull in 1633. He is buried in the old church of Kinnoull, where there is an impressive monument to him in the surviving aisle (the rest of the church was demolished in 1836).

Near Turriff in the north-east of Scotland, **Delgatie Castle** [NJ 755506] is an imposing and impressive keep or tower of five storeys, dating from the fifteenth

Delgatie Castle (M&R)

century but with older work. There are later additions, but tempera-painted ceilings survive on the second floor, dating from 1590s. The lands were held by the Comyns but passed to the Hays, and the family were descended from Gilbert Hay, who had fought on the side of Joan of Arc in France. Sir Gilbert Hay of Delgatie, with many others of the family, was killed at the Battle of Flodden in 1513. Mary, Queen of Scots, spent three days at Delgatie after the Battle of Corrichie in 1562, and part of the west wall was battered down by James VI's forces after the Hays had supported Huntly's rebellion of 1594. Sir William Hay of Delgatie was standard bearer to the Marquis of Montrose during the campaign of 1645.

Slains Castle 1903?

265

Although Montrose was defeated at Philiphaugh, Hay managed to return his standard to Buchanan Castle, but he was executed with Montrose at Edinburgh in 1650, and later buried beside him in St Giles Cathedral. The Hays supported the Jacobites during the 1715 and 1745-46 Risings, and Delgatie had passed to the Gardens of Troup by 1762. The building is said to be haunted by the ghost of red-haired young woman known as Rohaise, and she is reputed to haunt a room off the main stair. Delgatie was bought back by the Hays and was made the Clan Hay centre in 1948. It is open all year (01888 563479; www.delgatiecastle.com).

Neidpath Castle [NT 236405] is an impressive keep or tower, and stands in a lovely spot above the Tweed

Neidpath Castle (M&R)

to the west of Peebles in the Borders. Neidpath was originally held by the Frasers but passed by marriage to the Hays in 1312. Mary, Queen of Scots, stayed here in 1563, as did James VI in 1587. The Hays were Royalists, and in 1650 Neidpath held out against Cromwell's forces longer than any other stronghold south of the Forth. Cannon damaged the castle, and the defenders were eventually forced to surrender. The building was partly repaired, and was sold to the Douglases in 1686; it is sometimes open to the public (01721 720333).

Yester Castle [NT 556667] is famous for the Goblin (or Hobgoblin of Bo') Hall, an underground chamber and the most complete part of the shattered ruin. Yester

Yester Castle (M&R)

lies five or so miles to the south-east of Haddington in East Lothian, and was held by the Giffords, but passed by marriage to the Hays early in the fifteenth century. The family were made Lords Yester in 1488, Earls of Tweeddale in 1646, and then Marquises of Tweeddale and Earls of Gifford in 1694. Nearby is the gothic collegiate church (also known as Bothans) [NT 544671], founded by William Hay in 1421, and there is a tablet to Sir William Hay, who died in 1614; access to the church is difficult. **Yester House** [NT 543672], dating from the eighteenth century, replaced the castle, and was designed by William and Robert Adam for the Hays; it is still a private residence, although no longer owned by the family.

The Hays also held:

Ardendraught [NK 082349], near Cruden Bay, Aberdeenshire; site of castle (the location of which is not certain).
Held by the Frasers in the fifteenth century, but passed by marriage to the Hays, who held the property in the sixteenth century. Sir Gilbert Hay of Delgatie and Ardendraught was killed at the Battle of Flodden in 1513. Castle of Esslemont was torched in 1493 during a feud between the Hays of Ardendracht and the Cheynes of Esslemont.

Balbithan House [NJ 812189], near Inverurie, Aberdeenshire; fine L-plan tower house.
Held by the Chalmers, but passed to the Hays in 1690, and then went to the Gordons in the early eighteenth century and then to others. Still occupied.

Balhousie Castle [NO 115244], Perth; mansion incorporating tower house.
Held by the Eviots and by the Mercers, but was sold to the Hays Earls of Kinnoul in 1625. It was used by the army after World War II, and became the regimental headquarters and museum of the Black Watch, which is open to the public (0131 310 8530; www.theblackwatch.co.uk/museum/index.html).

Belton House [NT 644766], near Dunbar, East Lothian; ruinous mansion and castle.
Held by the Cunninghams, but passed by marriage to the Hays of Yester in 1468.

Benholm's Lodging [NJ 936089], Aberdeen; Z-plan tower house.
Held by the Keiths of Benholm, then by Dr Patrick Dun, then went to the Hays of Balbithan, and then to others. It was acquired by the city of Aberdeen in 1918, and moved stone by stone to its present site at Tillydrone to make way for offices.

Bield Tower [NT 100248], Tweedsmuir, Borders; site of tower.
Close to Oliver Castle: Nether Oliver passed from the Flemings to the Hays.

Blackhall Castle [NO 670961], near Banchory, Aberdeenshire; site of castle and mansion.
Held by the Russells, then by the Hays. The building was demolished about 1947 and stone from the castle was used to repair bomb damage to the Houses of Parliament.

Carsegrange [NO 270255], near Dundee; site of castle.
Held by the Hays, but given to Coupar Angus Abbey, then went to the Ogilvies after the Reformation.

Carvichen [NJ 540390], near Huntly, Aberdeenshire; site of castle,
Held by the Gordons of Lesmoir, but passed to the Hays of Mountblairy in 1739, then went to the Duke of Gordon in 1770.

Castle of Esslemont [NJ 932298], near Ellon, Aberdeenshire; ruinous tower house.
Held by the Marshalls and by the Cheynes, but passed to the Hay Earls of Errol in 1626. Twenty years later Covenanters were besieged in the castle, and more than thirty of them were killed. The property was sold to the Gordons in 1728, and they built Esslemont House in 1769, which is apparently still occupied.

Castle of Park [NX 189571], near Glenluce, Galloway; restored L-plan tower house.
Held by the Hays following the Reformation, and Thomas Hay

of Park built the castle in 1590, his father having been commendator of Glenluce Abbey. Park passed to the Cunninghams, but has been restored and can be rented as holiday accommodation (01628 825925; www.landmark trust.org).

Cocklaw Castle [NT 524421], near Hawick, Borders; site of tower house.

Held by the Hays, and besieged by Henry 'Hotspur' Percy in 1403 after the Battle of Homildon Hill, the events recounted in the *Scotichronicon* by Walter Bower. The property had passed to the Gladstones by 1560.

Craigenveoch Castle [NX 237555], near Glenluce, Galloway; site of mansion.

Built for Admiral Sir John Dalrymple-Hay in 1876.

Craignethan Castle [NS 816464], near Lanark; magnificent ruined castle.

Held and built by the Hamiltons, but sold in 1665 to the Hays, who built the house in the outer courtyard. This building has some ghostly tales woven about it. The castle is in the care of

Craignethan Castle 1909?

Historic Scotland and is open to the public (01555 860364).

Cramalt Tower or **Talla** [NT 197227], near Cappercleuch, Borders; site of tower houses (now in Megget reservoir).

Held by the Hays, probably of Tala. The Hays of Tala were religious reformers, and contemporaries of John Knox, in the sixteenth century. One of the family was executed in 1568 for his part in the murder of Lord Darnley.

Crawfordton Tower [NX 796905], near Moniaive, Dumfries and Galloway; tower house replaced by mansion.

Held by the Crichtons in the middle of the seventeenth century, but passed to the Hays and then went to the Walkers in the nineteenth century.

Delvine [NO 123402], near Blairgowrie, Perthshire; site of castle and mansion.

Held by the Hays in the fifteenth century, then by the Ogilvies of Inchmartine, then by the Mackenzies and Muir Mackenzies. Demolished in the 1960s.

Drumcarro [NO 453129], near St Andrews, Fife; site of castle or old house.

Held by the Aytons in 1681 and then by the Hays of Drumcarro in 1709.

Drumelzier Castle [NT 124334], near Broughton, Borders; ruinous tower house.

Held by the Tweedies until 1632 when the property passed to the Hays of Yester, who held it until the middle of the nineteenth century. The castle was replaced by a nearby house, itself now incorporated into farm buildings.

Dunragit House [NX 150582], near Glenluce, Borders; mansion incorporating castle.

Held by the Cunninghams, then by the Baillies, and in the eighteenth century by the Dalrymple-Hays.

Duns Castle [NT 777544], near Duns, Borders; fine mansion incorporating castle.

Held by several families including by the Hays of Drumelzier, whose descendants still own it. The ghost of Alexander Hay, who was killed at the Battle of Waterloo in 1815, is said to haunt the castle. There is a country park and accommodation

is available in the castle (01361 883211; www.duns castle.co.uk).

Dupplin Castle [NO 056195], near Perth; mansion on site of castle. Held by the Oliphants, then by the Douglases of Morton, but passed to the Hay Earl of Kinnoull, one of whom was Lord Chancellor to Charles I. Dupplin passed to the Dewars in 1911. The mansion was burnt out in 1827, was rebuilt but then burned again in 1934.

Faichfield House [NK 065467], near Peterhead, Aberdeenshire; site of castle or old house.

Held by the Frasers and by the Hays. Demolished in the 1960s.

Flemington Tower [NT 166451], near West Linton, Borders; ruinous tower house.

Held by the Hays but passed to the Veitch family. Occupied until the end of the nineteenth century.

Fruid Castle [NT 106180], near Tweedsmuir, Borders; site of castle (part now in reservoir).

Held by the Frasers then by the Tweedies, then later by the Murrays of Stanhope and then the Hay Lord Yester in 1630.

Gourdie [NO 121419], near Blairgowrie, Perthshire; castle replaced by mansion.

Held by the Hays but had passed to the Kinlochs by the beginning of the seventeenth century. The mansion dates from 1714.

Gowrie House [NO 120235], Perth; site of fine fortified town house. Held by the Ruthven Earls of Gowrie and scene of the Gowrie Conspiracy, the result of which was that the Ruthven Earl of Gowrie and his brother were killed and his lands forfeited. The house passed to the Hay Earls of Kinnoull, who entertained Charles II here in 1663. The property passed to the town of Perth, and the building was demolished in 1805.

Haystoun [NT 259383], near Peebles, Borders; altered tower house and courtyard.

Held by the Elphinstones but in 1635 passed to the Hays of Smithfield, who greatly extended the tower house. The family had a burial aisle at the Cross Kirk in Peebles.

Inchnock Castle [NS 718694], near Coatbridge, Lanarkshire; slight remains of castle.

Held by the Forsyths of Dykes, then by the Hamiltons of Dalyell, then went to the Hays. Ruinous by the mid seventeenth century.

Innernytie [NO 129359], near Bankfoot, Perthshire; site of castle or old house.

Held by the Crichtons but passed to the Hays, then went to the Stewarts by the 1670s.

Inshoch Castle [NH 936567], near Nairn, Inverness-shire; ruined Z-plan tower house.

Held by the Hays of Lochloy.

Keillor Castle [NO 268403], near Newtyle, Angus; site of castle. Possibly held by the Hays.

Keillour Castle [NN 979256], near Methven, Perthshire; mansion on site of castle.

Possibly held by the Hays.

Kilspindie or **Butterdean Castle** [NT 797648], near Cockburnspath, Borders; site of castle.

Held by the Ellem family, then went to the Hays of Butterdean.

Kilspindie Castle [NT 462801], near Aberlady, East Lothian; slight remains of castle.

Held by the Douglases, then by the Hays in 1621.

Kininmonth House [NK 033530], near Mintlaw, Aberdeenshire; house on site of castle.

Held by the Hays of Delgatie, but sold to the Cummings around 1682.

Letham [NO 624457], near Arbroath, Angus; site of castle (location not certain).

Held by the Sibbalds and by the Dempsters, and then by the Hays and by the Fletchers in the nineteenth century. Letham Grange [NO 6244568] is a modern mansion dating from 1830.

Leys [NO 262240], near Dundee; site of castle or old house.

Held by the Cairns, then by the Hays of Leys from 1650 to 1850.

Lickleyhead Castle [NJ 627237], near Insch, Aberdeenshire; fine L-plan tower house.

Held by the Leslies, then by the Leiths and by the Forbeses, but passed to the Hays at the end of the seventeenth century, then went to others. Still occupied.

Linplum [NT 553703], near Haddington, East Lothian; site of castle and mansion.

Held by the Hays of Linplum. William Hay of Linplum was an unruly fellow: in 1594 chasing the minister George Chalmers with a pistol, Chalmers only escaping by getting inside the gates of Haddington; then the same year Hay shot another minister, David Ogil, and left him for dead – a crime for which Hay was outlawed. The Hays still held the property in the nineteenth century and the building was used as a farmhouse before being demolished.

Lochloy Castle [NH 926578], near Nairn, Inverness-shire; site of castle.

Held by the Hays. William Hay of Lochloy, who died in 1470, is buried in Elgin Cathedral.

Logie-Almond House [NO 014297], near Perth; tower survives from castle and mansion.

Held by the Hay Earls of Errol, and the lands are said to have been given to them after the defeat of the Vikings at Luncarty

Logie-Almond House (M&R)

in 973. The property passed to the Drummonds in the sixteenth century, then later went to the Murray Earls of Mansfield. The building was already ruinous when it was demolished in the 1960s except for one round tower.

Megginch Castle [NO 242246], near Perth; fine altered Z-plan tower house.

Held by the Hays of Leys at the end of the fifteenth century, but passed to the Drummonds of Lennoch in 1664. The house is still occupied and the extensive gardens are open to the public in July (01821 642222).

Monkton House [NT 334703], near Musselburgh, East Lothian; altered L-plan tower house.

Held by the Hays of Yester following the Reformation, but they were forfeited for their part in the Jacobite Rising of 1715 and the property passed to the Falconers, then to the Hopes of Pinkie. General Monck, Cromwell's commander, is said to have made Monkton his favourite residence in Scotland (perhaps he just found the name easy to remember). Still occupied.

Mordington House [NT 951558], near Berwick-upon-Tweed, Borders; site of castle and mansion.

The lands were held by several families, including by the Hays. An older house or castle was replaced by a mansion in the eighteenth century, but this building was demolished in 1973.

Mounie Castle [NJ 766287], near Oldmeldrum, Aberdeenshire; T-plan tower house.

Held by the Setons and by the Farquhars, but passed to the Hays of Arnbath in 1701, then went back to the Setons. Still occupied.

Mountblairy or **Balravie Castle** [NJ 694546], near Turriff, Aberdeenshire; site of castle and mansion.

Held by the Stewart Earls of Buchan, but passed to the Hays of Mountblairy. One of the family, George Hay, was a lieutenant in Lord Pitsligo's Horse in the Jacobite Rising of 1745-46. Mountblairy was sold around 1800 to the Morrisons, but the mansion has been demolished.

Moyness Castle [NH 951538], near Nairn, Inverness-shire; site of large castle.

Held by the Hays.

Muchalls Castle [NO 892908], near Stonehaven, Kincardineshire; fine courtyard castle.

Held by the Frasers, then sold to the Hays in 1415, but had passed to the Burnetts by 1619 and they built the castle. Said to be haunted by a Green Lady, and is still occupied.

Mugdrum [NO 228184], near Newburgh, Fife; mansion perhaps with older work.

Held by the Coventrys and other families before latterly being held by the Hays. Still occupied.

Muldavit [NJ 504662], near Cullen, Aberdeenshire; site of castle or old house.

Held by the Duffs until 1626, but then passed to the Hays.

Naughton Castle [NO 373246], near Wormit, Fife; very ruinous tower house.

Held by the Hays in the twelfth century, but passed by marriage to the Crichtons in 1494, then back to the Hays about 1625, then went to the Morrisons in 1737 and then passed to the Beatons.

Nunraw Castle [NT 597706], near East Linton, East Lothian; castle and mansion.

Held by the Hepburns of Bothwell after the Reformation, but passed to the Dalrymples then went to the Hays, and a new monastery was founded here in 1946. It is possible to stay in the castle, in the abbey guest house (01620 830228 (guest house); liamdevlin.tripod.com/nunraw/).

Oliver [NT 098248], near Broughton, Borders; site of tower house.

Nether Oliver passed from the Flemings to the Hays.

Pinkie House [NT 353727], Musselburgh, East Lothian; castle and mansion.

Held by the Setons following the Reformation, then by the Hay Marquis of Tweeddale in 1694, then by the Hopes of Craighall in 1778. Now used as part of Loretto School (0131 653 4444; www.lorettoschool.co.uk).

Pitcorthie [NO 570070], near Anstruther, Fife; site of castle or old house.

Held by the Strangs and by the Barclays of Innergellie, before passing by marriage to the Hays of Kinglassie, who held them in the seventeenth century.

Pitfour Castle [NO 199209], near Perth; mansion on site of castle.

Held by the Lindsay Earls of Crawford in the late fifteenth century, then by the Hays and by the Richardsons. The castle has been divided into separate residences.

Place of Snade [NX 847857], near Moniaive, Dumfries and Galloway; site of castle.

Held by the Hays of Yester and by the Cunninghams.

Rannas Castle [NJ 460649], near Buckie, Aberdeenshire; some remains of castle.

Held by the Hays of Rannas. Andrew Hay of Rannas was reputedly seven foot two inches tall and fought for the Jacobites in the 1745-46 Rising. His size made it difficult for him to conceal his identity and, after six years as a fugitive in Scotland, he spent a further eleven years on the continent. He returned in 1763, and in 1789 sold Rannas to clear the debts of his great nephew, who held Leith Hall; his sister had married John Leith.

Renfield [NS 501684], near Renfrew; site of castle and old mansion.
Held by the Stewart Earls of Moray, but passed to the Hays in 1568, then later went to the Campbells of Blythswood and then to the Elphinstones. Demolished in 1935 and the site is occupied by a golf course.

Sandfurd [NO 406242], near Wormit, Fife; site of castle or old house.
The property was also known as Sandfurd Hay (to distinguish it from nearby Sandfurd Nairne), so was held by the Hays.

Seggieden [NO 168215], near Perth; site of castle or old house.
Held by the Hay Earls of Kinnoul, then by the Gordons and by the Nairns, before returning by marriage to the Hays of Seggieden, now Drummond-Hays. They apparently now live in Buckinghamshire in England.

Shieldgreen Tower [NT 274432], near Peebles, Borders; slight remains of tower house.
Held by the Stoddart family in the sixteenth century, but passed to the Hay Earls of Tweeddale in 1656, then went to the burgh of Peebles in 1656.

Smithfield Castle [NT 253412], Peebles, Borders; site of castle.
Held by the Hays of Smithfield in the sixteenth and seventeenth centuries, as well as by the Dicksons. Venlaw Castle, a modern mansion, is built on the site and is now a hotel (01721 730384; www.venlaw.co.uk).

Spott House [NT 679752], near Dunbar, East Lothian; mansion incorporating castle.
Held by the Homes and then by several other families, including by the Hays. Still occupied.

Talla [NT 124214], Tweedsmuir, Borders; site of castle.
Held by the Hays of Tala or Talla, one of whom was executed in 1568 for his part in the murder of Lord Darnley.

Turriff Castle [NJ 722500], Turriff, Aberdeenshire; site of castle.
Held by the Hay Earls of Errol. Robert the Bruce endowed a chapel so that masses would be said for his brother, Nigel, who was executed after being captured at the fall of Kildrummy Castle. A sixteenth-century town house of the Hay Earls of Errol was demolished by road widening.

Urie House [NO 860877], near Stonehaven, Kincardineshire; mansion incorporating part of castle.
Held by the Frasers and by the Keith Earls Marischal, before being sold to the Hays of Errol in 1415, who held it until 1647 when it was sold back to the Keiths, then Urie went to the Barclays and then to the Bairds. The house was abandoned in the 1940s and is now apparently derelict.

Whittinghame Castle [NT 602733], near East Linton, East Lothian; L-plan keep or tower.
Held by several families, including by the Hays, before passing to the Balfours of Balbirnie, whose descendants still apparently live here.

www.clanhay.net
www.clanhay.org
www.clanhay.com
No. of castles/sites: 76
Rank: 10/764

Monkton House (M&R) – see previous page

Hebden

Carrick House

The name probably comes from one of the settlements of that name in Yorkshire in England.

On Eday, an island in Orkney, **Carrick House** [HY 567384] is a building of three storeys with a courtyard, the arched entrance of which is dated 1633. The island was held by the Stewarts, by the Buchanans, by the Feas and by the Laings before passing, along with the rest of the island, to the Hebden family in 1848. The house is open from June to April on Sundays by appointment only (01857 622260; www.eday.orkney.sch.uk/tourism/carricktour/index.htm).

No. of castles/sites: 1
Rank: 537=/764

Heiton

Darnick

The name comes from the place Heiton, which is near Kelso in the Borders, and the name is on record from the turn of the thirteenth century,

Darnick Tower [NT 532343], to the west of Melrose, is a three-storey tower house with a taller stair-tower and a later wing, and the building dates from the fifteenth century. The tower was built by the Heiton family, who held the property from 1425. The building was burnt and 'cast down' by the Earl of Hertford in 1545, although it was soon rebuilt. Sir Walter Scott greatly admired the tower and wished to purchase it, but he was refused.

No. of castles/sites: 1
Rank: 537=/764

Darnick Tower (M&R)

Henderson

The name comes from 'son of Henry', with an intrusive 'd', and is on record in Scotland from the fourteenth century. William Henderson was keeper of Lochmaben Castle in the 1370s. There were also branches of Hendersons in Caithness, which came from the Gunns; and others from Glencoe. Robert Henryson was a renowned poet, who died about 1500, and his work included *The Testament of Cresseid*. Alexander Henderson, who was born in Creich in Fife in 1583, was one of the authors of the National Covenant in 1638. He went on to become one of the negotiators with Charles I but he died in 1646.

Standing a mile or so north of Inverkeithing in Fife, **Fordell Castle** [NT 147854] is a fine Z-plan tower house, with a rectangular main block and two square towers at opposite corners. The building dates from the

Fordell Castle (M&R)

sixteenth century, and there are turrets crowning the corners. The lands were held by the Airths of Plean, but passed by marriage to the Hendersons at the beginning of the sixteenth century. James Henderson of Fordell was Lord Justice Clerk, but was slain, along with his eldest son, at the Battle of Flodden in 1513. Mary, Queen of Scots, stayed at Fordell when one of her ladies, Marion Scott, was married to George Henderson of Fordell, but the castle may have been torched in 1568 because the Hendersons supported Mary. Sir John Henderson, fifth of Fordell, fought in the Civil War, and Fordell was sacked by Cromwell's forces after the Battle of Inverkeithing in 1651. A new mansion was built nearby, although the property passed by marriage to the Duncans of Camperdown, and then to others. The family of the Hendersons of Fordell still flourishes, although they now

apparently live in Australia. The castle is still occupied.

The family had a town house on Church Street in Inverkeithing, known as **Fordell's Lodging** [NT 130830], which dates from the seventeenth century.

Otterston Tower [NT 165852] is close to Fordell, some two miles west of Aberdour. Otterston began as an L-plan tower house, but a mansion was later added and remodelled, although part of this has since been demolished. The property was held by the Hendersons at the beginning of the sixteenth century, but had passed to the Mowbrays of Barnbougle by 1589. They built the tower.

Broomhill House [NT 269674] lay to the south of Edinburgh, but a castle, and then a later mansion, have both been demolished. The property was held by the Hendersons of Fordell from 1508 to 1648. The sister of Sir John Henderson was imprisoned in the Tolbooth of Edinburgh, having been accused of witchcraft. She apparently poisoned herself the night before she was due to be executed. The lands passed to the Bairds of Newbyth and then to the Trotters of Mortonhall.

www.clanhendersonusa.org
www.chebucto.ns.ca/Heritage/Henderson/
home.comcast.net/~buaidh/Henderson.html

No. of castles/sites: 4
Rank: 278=/764
Xref: Henryson

Henry

The name is recorded as a surname from the sixteenth century in Scotland, and was common in parts of Ayrshire and Fife.

Geilston House [NS 339783], a few miles west and north of Dumbarton, is an L-plan house of two storeys, and may date from as early as the fifteenth century, although more probably from 200 years later. It was held by the Geils family and then by the Woods, who had a tower, but was owned by the Donalds and then by Henrys in the nineteenth century. The gardens have been cared for by The National Trust for Scotland since 1983 and are open to the public (01389 841867; www.nts.org.uk).

Hatton Mains [NO 676675] lies five and a half miles north-west of Montrose in the old county of Kincardineshire. The present house dates from the end of the seventeenth century, but may stand on the site of a castle. It was held by the Montgomerys, but was sold to the Henrys in 1920.

No. of castles/sites: 2
Rank: 396=/764
Xref: Hendry

Hepburn

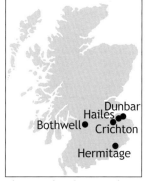

The name comes from the place Hebburn, which is near the grand castle of Chillingham in Northumberland in England, and the family are on record from the end of the thirteenth century.

Hailes Castle [NT 575758] is a ruinous castle, but it is very picturesque and is in a lovely spot above the River Tyne. It dates from the fourteenth century,

Hailes Castle (LF)

and this has formerly been a large and strong fortress. The lands were held by the Earls of Dunbar and March, but were given to the Hepburns in the thirteenth century. Sir Patrick Hepburn played a valiant part in the Battle of Otterburn in 1388 by saving the Douglas banner from falling into the hands of the English. In 1400 the Earl of March and Harry 'Hotspur' Percy, wanting revenge on the Hepburns, attacked the castle without success, and they were themselves routed. Archibald Dunbar captured the castle in 1443, and slew all he found within in the walls. Patrick Hepburn gained the lands of the forfeited Crichtons in 1488 and became Earl of Bothwell and acquired Crichton Castle, as well as becoming Admiral of Scotland (an office the Earls held until 1567), but he was killed at the Battle of Flodden in 1513. His brother, John Hepburn, was prior of St Andrews Cathedral and was responsible for having the massive precinct wall built; he also established St Leonard's College in the burgh. Patrick, his brother, was Bishop of Moray; he was reputedly far from respectable, although he held the office until 1573. Hailes Castle was burnt in 1532, and in 1547 was occupied by Lord Gray of Wilton acting for the English, and then Hugh Douglas of Longniddry held Hailes Castle with fifty men for the English in 1548. James Hepburn, fourth Earl of Bothwell, brought Mary, Queen of Scots, here after abducting her in 1567. The castle was seized and slighted by Cromwell's forces in 1650, but later passed to the Stewarts and

then to the Setons, and was bought by the Dalrymples in 1700, who abandoned it and moved to New Hailes near Musselburgh. There are stories of an underground passage, which appears to have led from Hailes under the river, or even to Traprain Law. And tales that one of the pit prisons is haunted by the spirit of a man imprisoned and starved to death because he had fallen in love with the laird's wife. The castle is now in the care of Historic Scotland and is open to the public.

Hermitage Castle [NY 494960] is a grim and foreboding place, lies in a windswept spot five miles north of Newcastleton in the Borders. The castle is now a ruin but consists of an impressive walled courtyard

Hermitage Castle (M&R)

enclosing ranges of buildings. Hermitage was held by the Dacres, the Soulis family and by the Grahams of Abercorn before passing by marriage to the Douglases (later Earls of Angus) in the fourteenth century, and they exchanged Hermitage for Bothwell Castle in Lanarkshire with the Hepburns in 1492 (at the insistence of James IV, who did not trust the Douglases). Patrick Hepburn had been made the first Earl of Bothwell (from the property in Lanarkshire) by James IV in 1488, and he was High Admiral of Scotland, Keeper of the King's Household and Earl of Orkney. He was killed, along with his son, at the Battle of Flodden in 1513. In 1566 James Hepburn, fourth Earl of Bothwell, was badly wounded in a melee with the Border reiver 'Little Jock' Elliot of Park – the latter was shot and eventually died. Bothwell was paid a visit on his sick bed by Mary, Queen of Scots. Mary and Bothwell were later married (although he divorced his wife to do so), but after the debacle at Carberry the following year he escaped via Spynie Palace and Orkney and Shetland to Norway and then to Denmark. Bothwell was eventually imprisoned on charges by his estranged first wife in the Danish castle of Dragsholm until his death, apparently chained to a pillar for eleven years – his mummified body is said to be preserved there (his ghost is also said to haunt the castle, which is now a hotel). Bothwell was forfeited in 1581, and the titles and property passed to Francis Stewart, fifth Earl of Bothwell, although he was in turn forfeited in 1595, and the castle went to the Scotts of Buccleuch. One of several ghost stories associated with Hermitage is that of an apparition said to be the ghost of Mary, Queen of Scots. The castle is in the care of Historic Scotland and is open to the public (01387 376222).

Bothwell Castle [NS 688594] is near Uddingston and not far from Hamilton in Lanarkshire, and the Earls of Bothwell took their title from the property. It is a fabulous ruin and saw much action in the Wars of Independence. Bothwell was exchanged with the Douglases for Hermitage Castle, and the castle is in the care of Historic Scotland and is open to the public (01698 816894).

The Hepburns also owned:

Alemoor Tower [NT 404157], near Hawick, Borders; site of tower house.
Held by the Hepburn Earls of Bothwell from 1511.

Athelstaneford [NT 533774], near Haddington, East Lothian; site of castle.
Held by the Hepburns, one of whom was Sir John Hepburn of Athelstaneford, who fought in the army of Gustave Adolphus in Sweden and then he entered French service in 1632 and he was made a Marshal of France. The sixteenth-century doocot has been restored to house an unmanned audio-visual display and is open April to September (01620 880378).

Beanston [NT 549763], near Haddington, East Lothian; house dating from 1621.
Held by the Hepburns of Beanston.

Black Castle [NT 738707], near Cockburnspath, Borders; site of castle.
Held by the Hepburns.

Bruce's Castle or Carnock Tower [NS 857878], near Falkirk; ruinous tower house.
Held by the Airths of Plean, but passed to the Hepburns in about 1480, and it was slighted during a family dispute. The property passed to the Bruces of Auchenbowie in the early sixteenth century, then went to the Drummonds.

Colquhalzie [NN 914175], near Crieff, Perthshire; castle replaced by mansion.
Held by the Drummonds, but by 1826 had passed to the Hepburns.

Congalton [NT 544805], near North Berwick, East Lothian; site of castle.
Held by the Congiltons in the thirteenth century and then by Lauders, but much later passed to the Hepburns.

Crichton Castle [NT 380612], near Gorebridge, Midlothian; fantastic ruined castle.
Long held by the Crichtons, but around 1488 passed after the forfeiture of the Crichtons to the Hepburns of Hailes, who were made Earls of Bothwell. The castle was besieged and seized by the Earl of Arran in 1559, and Mary, Queen of Scots, attended a wedding here in 1562. When the Hepburns were

forfeited in 1581, Crichton went to Frances Stewart, fifth Earl of Bothwell, who was himself forfeited in 1595, then passed to other families, including to the Hepburns of Humbie around 1649. Crichton is in the care of Historic Scotland and is open to the public from April to September (01875 320017).

Dolphinton [NT 105465], near West Linton, Lanarkshire; site of castle.
Held by the Hepburns in the fifteenth century.

Dunbar Castle [NT 678794], Dunbar, East Lothian; shattered ruin on rocks by the harbour.
The castle had a long and eventful history, and James Hepburn, fourth Earl of Bothwell, brought Mary, Queen of Scots here after abducting her in 1566. They were later married, but after Carberry he fled to Orkney and the Continent, and she eventually took 'refuge' in England, after which the castle was surrendered and was destroyed. Parts of the ruin are accessible with care.

Dunsyre Castle [NT 073482], near Carnwath, Lanarkshire; site of castle.
Held by the Douglases, among others, as well as by the Hepburns. Until about 1740 the ruins of the castle were still used to hold courts, and the castle 'possessed its instruments of torture'.

Earlstoun Castle [NX 613840], near St John's Town of Dalry, Dumfries and Galloway; altered L-plan tower house.
Held by the Hepburn Earls of Bothwell, but passed to the Sinclairs in the middle of the sixteenth century, and then to the Gordons in 1615.

Elsrickle [NT 062435], near Carnwath, Lanarkshire; site of castle.
Held by the Hepburns in the fifteenth century, but passed to the Woddrops of Dalmarnock by the eighteenth century.

Fairnington House [NT 646280], near Jedburgh, Borders; mansion incorporating castle.
Held by the Burnetts, but had passed to the Hepburns Earls of Bothwell by the late fifteenth century, then went to the Stewarts and then to the Rutherfords.

Gilmerton House [NT 549778], near Haddington, East Lothian; mansion on site of castle or old house.
Held by the Hepburns, but passed to the Kinlochs in the middle of the seventeenth century, and they built the present classical mansion. Still apparently held by them and luxury accommodation is available (01620 880207; www.gilmerton house.com).

Humbie Old Place [NT 467627], near Pathhead, East Lothian; castle replaced by mansion.
Held by the Hepburns, but passed to the Scotts. The gardens are occasionally open to the public (www.gardensof scotland.org).

Crichton Castle (M&R)

Luffness House (M&R) – see next column

Luffness House [NT 476804], near Aberlady, East Lothian; fine castle and mansion.

Held by the Lindsays, then by the Hepburn Earls of Bothwell, then went to the Hope Earl of Hopetoun in 1739.

Markle [NT 579775], near East Linton, East Lothian; some remains of castle.

Held by the Hepburns, but passed to the Stewarts.

Morham Castle [NT 557723], near Haddington, East Lothian; site of castle.

Held by the Hepburn Earls of Bothwell.

Moss Tower [NT 714265], near Kelso, Borders; site of castle.

Probably held by the Hepburn Earls of Bothwell. It stood in a marsh and was sacked in 1524, 1544 and 1570, after which it was left ruinous.

Nunraw Castle [NT 597706], near East Linton, East Lothian; castle and mansion.

Held by the Hepburn Earls of Bothwell after the Reformation, then by the Dalrymples and by the Hays. A new monastery was founded here in 1947, and it is possible to stay in the abbey guest house (01620 830228 (guest house); liamdevlin.tripod.com/nunraw/).

Rickarton [NO 838886], near Stonehaven, Kincardineshire; castle replaced by mansion.

Held by the Rickarton family, but passed by marriage to the Hepburns in the eighteenth century, then went to the Bairds of Urie.

Smeaton Hepburn [NT 593786], near East Linton, East Lothian; castle replaced by mansion.

Held by the Hepburns. Adam Hepburn of Smeaton Hepburn supported Mary, Queen of Scots, and fought for her at the Battle of Langside in 1568. The property passed by marriage to the Buchans, and they took the name Buchan-Hepburn, and they were made Baronets in 1815. The family flourishes, but now apparently lives in St Andrews. The house formerly had many relics of Mary, Queen of Scots.

Walston [NT 060455], near Carnwath, Lanarkshire; site of castle.

Held by the Hepburns in the fifteenth century, but had passed to the Baillies by 1650.

Waughton Castle [NT 567809], near East Linton, East Lothian; ruinous castle and courtyard.

Held by the Hepburns. In 1475 David Hepburn of Waughton was 'interdicted from interfering with the carting of goods dispatched from Haddington', and in 1536 Patrick Hepburn of Waughton had to pay a share of £1000 to build Blackness Castle as a punishment for some misdemeanour. The castle here was sacked by the English in 1547. The dispossessed Robert Hepburn of Waughton raided the castle in 1569.

Westhall Tower [NT 048473], near Carnwath, Lanarkshire; slight remains of a tower.

Held by the Grahams from 1477, then by the Hepburns, by the Douglases and by the Lockharts.

Whitsome [NT 865507], near Chirnside, Borders; possible site of tower house.

Long a property of the Pringles, but had passed to the Hepburns by the sixteenth century.

No. of castles/sites: 30
Rank: 40=/764

Heriot

The name comes from the place and parish of Heriot, which is near the border of Lothian and the Borders. The name is on record from the twelfth century.

Trabroun [NT 466743] lies some three or so miles west and north of Haddington in East Lothian. There may have been a castle and there was a mansion. The lands were held by the Heriot family, and Andrew Heriot of Trabroun fought for Mary, Queen of Scots, at the Battle of Langside in 1568 and was captured, although he was pardoned ten years later. The property passed to the Hamiltons in 1605.

Ramornie House [NO 318096] is located half a mile or so east of Ladybank in Fife, and may stand on the site of a castle or old residence. It was originally held by the Ramornie family but passed to the Heriots and they held the property for some 400 years until the nineteenth century when it went to the Haigs of Ramornie.

Niddrie Marischal [NT 295715], to the east and south of Edinburgh, was a large mansion which incorporated a tower house, but the building has been demolished and the site is now a housing estate. The property was held by the Niddrie family, then possibly by the Heriots, then by the Wauchopes, and then by the Sandilands.

Lennox Castle [NT 174671], near Balerno, was a massive keep, dating from the fifteenth century, but all that remains is part of the vaulted basement. It was held by the Stewart Earls of Lennox (hence the name), but later passed to George Heriot. He is known as 'Jinglin Geordie', and was a goldsmith in the service of Queen Anne and then her husband James VI; after 1603 he spent most of his time in London. Heriot bequeathed his large fortune to found what is now George Heriot's School, and the first building of the school was completed in 1659.

No. of castles/sites: 4
Rank: 278=/764

Heron

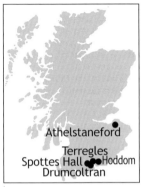

The name comes from the Herons of Chipchase, who were settled in Northumberland in the eleventh century. Heron is probably a nickname for a man with long thin legs, like the bird. Also see the Herring family.

Kirroughtree House [NX 422660] is a mile east of Newton Stewart in Dumfries and Galloway. The present mansion dates from 1719, but replaced an old castle. The lands were held by the Herons from the fourteenth century, after Gilbert Heron had fought on the side of Robert the Bruce. The Herons were one of the Border families who were 'pacified' by James VI. The present house was built by Patrick Heron, who had made his fortune from cattle, and Robert Burns visited several times, and was friends with the then owner. The Herons sold the property in 1873, and the building is now used as a luxury hotel (01671 402141; www.kirrough treehouse.co.uk). Mary Heron, an heiress, married into the Maxwells, and they changed their name to Heron-Maxwell, Baronets, of Springkell. Their line continues, although they now apparently live in Essex.

The Herons also owned:
Bargaly [NX 462664], near Newton Stewart, Dumfries and Galloway; mansion on site of castle.
  Held by the Herons. The present house was built by Andrew Heron, a botanist and agricultural improver. He is buried, along with his wife, in a small tomb near the house. Bargaly later passed to the Hannays, and then to the Mackies.
Drumcoltran Tower [NX 869683], near Dalbeattie, Dumfries and Galloway; L-plan tower house.
  Held by the Herries of Terregles family, but passed by marriage to the Maxwells in 1550, then passed to other families, including to the Herons. In the care of Historic Scotland and open to the public.

No. of castles/sites: 3
Rank: 328=/764

Herries

The name may come from the family of 'Heriz', a Norman family who first settled in Nottinghamshire, but came to Scotland in the eleventh century. Alternatively they may come from the Counts of Vendome in France, who bore three 'herissons' (or 'hedgehogs') on their shield.

Terregles Castle [NX 928775] stood three and a half miles west of Dumfries, but has, along with a classical mansion built to replace it, been completely demolished. The lands were held by the Herries family from the thirteenth century. Andrew, second Lord, was slain at the Battle of Flodden in 1513, and in 1543 the male line died out, and the property passed by marriage in 1547 to the Maxwells, who kept the title Lord Herries. Mary, Queen of Scots, spent some of her last nights here before fleeing to England in 1568, and the castle was probably destroyed soon afterwards.

The Herries family also held:
Athelstaneford [NT 533774], near Haddington, East Lothian; site of castle.
  Held by the Herries family in the fourteenth century, but passed to the Hepburns. There is an unmanned heritage centre in the restored sixteenth-century doocot, which is open April to September (01620 880378).
Blacklaw Tower [NT 052067], near Moffat, Dumfries and Galloway; remains of tower house.
  Held by the Lindsays, but passed to the Herries of Terregles family, then in 1510 went to the Maxwells, then to others.
Drumcoltran Tower [NX 869683], near Dalbeattie, Dumfries and Galloway; L-plan tower house.
  Held by the Herries of Terregles family, but passed by marriage

Drumcoltran Tower (M&R)

to the Maxwells in 1550, then went to others. In the care of Historic Scotland and open to the public.

Hallguards Castle [NY 162728], near Ecclefechan, Dumfries and Galloway; site of castle.

Held by the Bruces, then by the Herries family, then by the Carruthers family. The castle was demolished under the terms of a Border treaty.

Hoddom Castle [NY 157730], near Annan, Dumfries and Galloway; L-plan tower house.

Held by the Carlyles, then by the Herries family in the fourteenth and fifteenth centuries, then by the Carruthers family and then by the Irvines, before passing to the Maxwells, then the property went to others. The castle stands in a caravan and camping site (01576 300251; www.hoddom castle.co.uk).

Mabie [NX 949708], near Dumfries; castle replaced by mansion.

Held by the Kirkconnels, then by the Herries family at the end of the sixteenth century. Now a hotel (01387 263188; www.mabiehouse.co.uk).

Spottes Hall [NX 805662], near Castle Douglas; castle replaced by mansion.

Held by the Maxwells, then by the Young-Herries family in the nineteenth century. In the burial ground of nearby Urr Parish Church are some interesting burial markers, including for the Herries family of Spottes.

Herries of Madinhoip is also on record in 1597, although it is not clear where this property was located.

No. of castles/sites: 8
Rank: 160=/764

Herring

The name perhaps comes from an Old English personal name 'Hering', although it is also recorded as 'Heron' (also see that name). The name is recorded in Scotland from the twelfth century, and the family held lands in Perthshire.

The Herrings held the following properties:

Drumlochy Castle [NO 158469], near Blairgowrie, Perthshire; slight remains of castle.

Held by the Herrings, who feuded with the Blair family, and Drumlochy was destroyed.

Forneth [NO 109447], near Blairgowrie, Perthshire; castle replaced by mansion.

Held by the Herrings but passed to the Speid family.

Glasclune Castle [NO 154470], near Blairgowrie, Perthshire; ruinous Z-plan tower house.

Held by the Herrings in the thirteenth century, but passed to the Blairs of Pittendreich, who had purchased the lands from the Crown. The two families had a long and bitter feud during which Drumlochy Castle (mentioned above) was destroyed.

Gormack [NO 144464], near Blairgowrie, Perthshire; site of castle. Held by the Butters of Gormock, although Wester Gormack was held by the Herrings.

Little Bar [NO 141408], near Blairgowrie, Perthshire; site of tower house.

Held by the Herrings.

Tower of Lethendy [NO 140417], near Blairgowrie, Perthshire; altered tower house.

Held by the Herrings, and they built the original tower. John Graham of Claverhouse was descended from a daughter of the family. The castle may be available to rent (01573 229797; www.ltr.co.uk/properties/scotland/lethendy).

Tullibole Castle [NO 053006], near Crook of Devon, Perthshire; L-plan tower house.

Held by the Herrings from 1513 or before, then sold to the Hallidays in 1598, but passed to the Moncreiffes.

No. of castles/sites: 7
Rank: 182=/764
Xref: Heron

Hogg

The name may come from 'hog', a 'swine' or 'pig', or it may have a quite different origin from Old English 'hoga', meaning 'careful' or 'prudent'. Hogg is used as a surname in Scotland from the eleventh century. James Hogg, the Ettrick Shepherd, was a fine author and poet and was a friend of Sir Walter Scott; his most famous work is probably *The Private Memoirs and Confessions of a Justified Sinner*, published in 1824.

Harcarse [NT 812487] is four miles south and east of Duns in Berwickshire in the Borders. There may have been a castle or old house, but the site is occupied by a farm. Harcarse was held by the Hoggs, possibly from the fourteenth century. Roger Hogg of Harcarse became an advocate in 1661, and was knighted when made a Lord of Session in 1677, taking the title of Lord Harcarse. The family held the property into the eighteenth century or later.

Newliston [NT 110736], to the south-west of Kirkliston in West Lothian, is a tall and impressive classical mansion, built in 1789 and designed by the architect Robert Adam. It replaced an earlier house and the lands were held by the Dalrymples before being sold to the Hoggs in the middle of the eighteenth century. The house and garden are open to the public in the summer (0131 333 3231).

Addistoun House [NT 155694], which is a mile or so south-west of Ratho to the west of Edinburgh, was held by the Sutties, and then by the Hoggs and then by the Gibsons in the eighteenth century.

Raemoir [NO 695995], two miles north of Banchory in Aberdeenshire, is an eighteenth-century mansion, but it includes much older work and there was a castle on the site. It was a property of the Hoggs, but passed to the Innes family, who held it in the nineteenth century, then went to the Cowdrays of Dunecht. The mansion is now a hotel (01330 824844; www.raemoir.com).

No. of castles/sites: 4
Rank: 278=/764

Holbourne

Menstrie Castle [NS 852968], some three miles north-west of Alloa in Clackmannanshire, is a small L-plan tower house, the wing of which has been greatly extended. The lands were held by the Alexanders, but the Holbourne family acquired Menstrie in 1649. One of the family was General James Holbourne, who fought against Cromwell at the Battle of Dunbar in 1650. The property was sold to the Abercrombies in 1719. Menstrie is in the care of The National Trust for Scotland and is open to the public some days (01259 211701; www.nts.org.uk).

Penkaet Castle [NT 427677], one mile south of Pencaitland in East Lothian, is an altered tower house, which dates from the sixteenth century but was altered and extended in later years. The property was held by several families, and has several colourful ghost stories; but was sold to the Holbourn family in 1922. The building is still occupied.

No. of castles/sites: 2
Rank: 396=/764

Home

The name is territorial and comes from the lands and barony of Home (or Hume), which are three miles south of Greenlaw in Berwickshire in the Borders. In medieval and early modern times the name could be spelt either Home or Hume, even within the

Dunglass
Hume ●●
The Hirsel

same family and the same document. The family may be descended from the Cospatrick Earls of Dunbar and March, although it is not clear how much evidence there is for this.

Dunglass Castle [NT 766718] was once a strong castle, and stood a mile north of Cockburnspath, just on the Lothian-Berwickshire border. The lands were held by the Pepdies, but passed by marriage to the Homes of Dunglass. Sir Alexander Home of Dunglass was captured at the Battle of Homildon Hill in 1402, and was killed fighting the English in France in 1424. He had three sons, from whom the main branches of the family were descended. The castle at Dunglass was destroyed in 1640, later passed to the Halls, and a later mansion was demolished in 1947 after a fire. Dunglass Collegiate Church, founded by Sir Alexander Home in 1423, is a fine ruinous building and is open to the public. In the church is the tomb of Sir Thomas Home and his wife, the grandparents of Sir Alexander.

Hume Castle [NT 704414] is some three miles south of Greenlaw, and this was a once important stronghold in the Borders. The lands were held by the Homes from the thirteenth century, and they were made Lords Home in 1473. Alexander, third Lord Home, led the vanguard at the Battle of Flodden in 1513, and escaped the battle. The Regent Albany seized Hume, ravaged the lands, and had Alexander and his brother executed for treason in 1516. George, fourth Lord, was killed before the Battle of Pinkie in 1547 and, after the defeat of the Scots, the English occupied the Homes' lands, although only after overcoming stiff resistance at Hume Castle. Alexander, fifth Lord, took back their properties, slaughtering the English garrison. The castle was visited by Mary, Queen

of Scots; but the Homes fought against her at the Battle of Langside in 1568. In 1569 the stronghold was again besieged by the English with artillery, and within twelve hours had surrendered. In 1573 Alexander, fifth Lord, was arrested and convicted of treason by James VI, and he died after a period of captivity. Alexander, sixth Lord Home, was a favourite of James VI, and in 1605 was made Earl of Home. James, third Earl, was a Royalist, but in 1650 the castle was surrendered to Colonel Fenwick, one of Cromwell's commanders, and was demolished. 'I, Willie Wastle, Stand firm in my castle; And a' the dog o' your toon, Will no pull Willie Wastle doon,' is believed to be from the siege of Hume Castle, and was apparently sent in defiance by the keeper of the castle to Colonel Fenwick.

The old castle was not rebuilt and Home family moved to The Hirsel. This branch of the Homes fought against the Jacobites, and William, eighth Earl, was at the Battle of Prestonpans in 1745. Hume Castle passed to the Home Earls of Marchmont in the eighteenth century, and the castle, which by now was almost 'level with the ground', was rebuilt as a crude folly in 1794. It is open to the public: the key is available from the large house opposite castle.

The Hirsel [NT 829407] is a mansion greatly remodelled the nineteenth century, but it includes much older work from a castle or tower house. It stands near the English border and the River Tweed, to the north of the village of Coldstream. The property is still owned by the Earl of Home, and the garden, museum and craft shop are open to the public (01890 882834; www.hirsel countrypark.co.uk).

The following properties were also held by the Homes:
Auchendolly [NX 768683], near Castle Douglas, Dumfries and Galloway; castle replaced by mansion.
  Held by the Homes and by the Gordons.
Ayton Castle [NT 929614], near Eyemouth, Borders; large mansion on site of castle.
  Held by the Ayton family, but passed by marriage to the Homes. The castle was seized and slighted by the English in 1448, then besieged by the English in 1497-98 when it was believed to be one of the strongest castles between Berwick and Edinburgh. It was held by the English during the invasion of Scotland between 1547-50. The Homes of Ayton were forfeited after their part in the Jacobite rising of 1715, and the property passed eventually to the Liddel-Grainger family and a baronial mansion stands on the site. The castle is open to the public from May to September, Wednesday and Sunday (01890 781212/550; www.aytoncastle.co.uk).
Bassendean House [NT 628458], near Gordon, Borders; mansion incorporating castle.
  Held by the Homes in 1577. George Home of Bassendean had to flee to Holland because of his opposition to James VII. He helped to mastermind the Revolution of 1689, which brought William and Mary to the throne.
Bastleridge [NT 933591], near Eyemouth, Borders; site of tower.
  Long held by the Homes.
Blackadder Castle [NT 856540], near Duns, Borders; site of castle and mansion.
  Held by the Blackadders but passed by marriage to the Homes, perhaps not entirely honestly. The Homes forced Beatrix and Margaret, the young heiresses of the last Blackadder laird, to marry sons of Home of Wedderburn, after besieging them in the castle here. In 1514 Alexander, third Lord Home, sheltered here during his conflict with John, Duke of Albany, and Albany

Hume Castle (M&R)

277

had the castle slighted the following year. Home was executed in 1516. The Homes of Blackadder were made Baronets in 1670-71, but the property later passed to the Houston-Boswells. The Homes, Baronets of Blackadder, still flourish, but now live in Australia. The mansion, which replaced the mansion, was demolished in the 1930s.

Bothwell Castle [NS 688594], near Hamilton, Lanarkshire; fabulous ruinous castle.

Held by the Douglases and others, but by the Homes in the nineteenth century. The castle is in the care of Historic Scotland and open to the public from April to September (01698 816894).

Broxmouth House [NT 696766], near Dunbar, East Lothian; castle replaced by mansion.

Held by the Homes, but later passed to the Kerr Dukes of Roxburgh. Cromwell garrisoned the house and used it as his headquarters in 1650 during the Battle of Dunbar. He is said to have watched the battle from a hillock near the house, now known as Cromwell's Mount.

Bunkle Castle [NT 805596], near Preston, Borders; slight remains of a castle.

Held by the Bonkyls and by the Stewarts, but later passed to the Douglases and then to the Homes.

Claypotts Castle [NO 452319], near Dundee; impressive Z-plan tower house.

Held by the Strachans and by the Grahams, then went to the Douglases and to the Homes. In the care of Historic Scotland and open to the public (01786 431324).

Cockburnspath Castle [NT 785699], Cockburnspath, Borders; ruinous castle.

Held by the Earls of Dunbar, then by the Homes, then by the Sinclairs and by the Douglases in 1546.

Cowdenknowes [NT 5793/1], near Melrose, Borders; strong castle and mansion.

Held by the Homes. An earlier castle was apparently destroyed

Cowdenknowes (M&R)

in 1493. Home of Cowdenknowes was a supporter of the Protestants at the time of the Reformation, and in 1582 was involved in the Raid of Ruthven, when James VI was imprisoned in Ruthven Castle for six months. The house is still occupied, but had passed from the family by the nineteenth century. 'Vengeance! Vengeance! When and where? Upon the house of Cowdenknowes, now and ever mair!' (www.cowden knowes.com)

Deuchar Tower [NT 360280], Yarrow, Borders; some remains of a tower house.

Held by the Homes in 1502, then by the Dalgleishs, then by the Murrays of Deuchar, then by the Dewars.

Douglas Castle [NS 843318], near Douglas, Lanarkshire; site of castle and mansion.

Long held by the Douglases, but latterly passed to the Home Earls of Home. The castle was demolished in 1938 because of subsidence.

Dreghorn Castle [NT 225684], Edinburgh; site of castle.

Held by the Murrays and by the Pitcairns, before coming to the Homes of Kello in 1720, then went to others. The site is occupied by a barracks.

Duns Castle [NT 777544], Duns, Borders; fine castle and mansion.

Held by the Homes of Ayton in 1489, and was damaged by the

Duns Castle 1904?

Earl of Hertford in 1547. It passed to the Cockburns, and then to the Hays of Drumelzier with whose descendants it remains. There is a country park and accommodation is available in the castle (01361 883211; www.dunscastle.co.uk).

Edrington Castle [NT 941534], near Chirnside, Borders; site of tower house.

Held for some time by the Homes of Wedderburn. The castle is said to have been destroyed by the English in 1482 and was also held by the English in the sixteenth century.

Edrom [NT 826559], near Duns, Borders; castle replaced by mansion.

Held by the Homes but passed by marriage through an heiress to the Carmichaels in 1635, apparently not to the liking of the heiress in question, the wedding being forced upon her the Regent Morton

Fast Castle [NT 862710], near Coldingham, Borders; scant ruins perched on cliffs.

Held by the Homes and it was rebuilt in 1521 after being destroyed by the Duke of Albany in 1515. It was seized by the English around 1547, recovered by the Scots before 1566 when Mary, Queen of Scots stayed here, but was recaptured by the English in 1570. Ten years later it passed by marriage to the Logans of Restalrig, and then went to others, including to the Home Earl of Dunbar around 1610. The ruins were reputedly used by smugglers, having a 'secret' cave below the castle. There are tales of treasure buried at Fast, possibly hidden here by Sir Robert Logan of Restalrig. Sir Walter Scott used the old stronghold in his novel *Bride of Lammermoor*, calling it Wolf's Crag. The castle is accessible but great care should be taken – a visit involves a walk and the site is joined to the 'mainland' by a gangway.

Fulton Tower [NT 605158], near Jedburgh, Borders; ruinous tower house.

Held by the Homes of Cowdenknowes, but passed by marriage to the Turnbulls of Bedrule in 1570

Gamelshiel Castle [NT 649648], near Cranshaws, East Lothian; slight remains of castle.

Held by the Forest family, but had passed to the Homes by 1679. One story is that a lady of the house was messily mauled by a wolf near Gamelshiel, and her husband buried her savaged body in a corner of the courtyard.

Greenlaw Castle [NT 719463], Greenlaw, Borders; site of castle.
Held by the Homes, but abandoned in 1729.

Harden [NT 449149], near Hawick, Borders; castle and mansion.
Held by the Homes, but passed to the Scotts in 1501.

Houndwood House [NT 855630], near Granthouse, Borders; mansion incorporating tower.
Held by the Homes following the Reformation, but later passed to the Logans of Restalrig, then to other families. The house was said to be haunted by a ghost called 'Chappie' with manifestations such as unexplained heavy footsteps, knocking and rapping, and deep breathing and moans. The apparition of the lower part of a man, dressed in riding breeches, was also reputedly seen. The story goes that a the fellow was cut in half by troops in the sixteenth century.

Howliston Tower [NT 412489], near Stow, Borders; slight remains of tower.
Held by the Home family in 1626, but had passed to the Mitchells by 1690.

Hutton Castle [NT 888549], near Chirnside, Borders; tower house and mansion.

Hutton Castle (M&R)

Held by the Homes and by the Formans and slighted by the English.

Kilduff House [NT 516774], near Haddington, East Lothian; site of castle or old house.
Held by the Homes in the eighteenth century.

Kimmerghame House [NT 815514], near Duns, Borders; castle replaced by mansion.
Held by the Sinclairs, then by the Homes in the fifteenth and sixteenth centuries. The young Home of Kimmerghame married the equally young heiress of Home of Ayton after she had been kidnapped by other members of her family. Everyone involved was fined, and the couple were imprisoned in Edinburgh Castle for three months. The property passed to the Swintons in the next century.

Lee Tower [NT 328396], near Innerleithen, Borders; ruinous tower house.
Held by the Homes and then by the Kerrs.

Linthill House [NT 937628], near Eyemouth, Borders; altered L-plan tower house.
Held by the Homes. In 1752 the widow of Patrick Home of Linthill was brutally murdered by her servant, Norman Ross. He was executed and is the last man in Scotland to be mutilated and hung in a gibbet afterwards. One story is that Ross's bloody hand prints from the murder can not be washed off. The house is still occupied.

Manderston [NT 810545], near Duns, Borders; fine Edwardian mansion on site of castle.
Held by the Home family in 1628. Sir George Home of Manderston was involved in a witchcraft accusation involving his wife and an Alexander Hamilton. The lady was cleared, but Hamilton implicated many others and himself, and was executed in Edinburgh in 1630. The property passed to the

Millers and the house was virtually rebuilt in the 1900s. Open to the public (01361 883450/882636; www.manderston.co.uk).

Ninewells House [NT 864557], near Chirnside, Borders; mansion on site of earlier house.
Held by the Homes of Ninewells from the fifteenth to the nineteenth century or later. One of the family was David Hume, the famous philosopher and historian, who spent much of his youth here, and visited afterwards. Hume was a religious sceptic and also a Jacobite and this barred him from academic posts, although he was an Under Secretary of State to the Home Department from 1767-69. He died in 1776.

North Berwick Priory [NT 546850], North Berwick, East Lothian; ruinous fortified range.
Held by the Homes after the Reformation.

Old Greenlaw Castle [NT 726448], near Greenlaw, Borders; site of castle.
Held by the Cospatrick Earls of Dunbar, but passed to the Homes.

Paxton House [NT 935530], near Berwick-upon-Tweed, Borders; mansion on possible site of castle.
Built in 1756 for Patrick Home of Billie. The house was for his intended bride, Sophie de Brandt, from the court of King Frederick the Great of Prussia. Paxton is now an outstation of the National Galleries of Scotland, and houses seventy paintings. Open to the public from Easter to October (01289 386291; www.paxtonhouse.com).

Peelwalls [NT 922599], near Eyemouth, Borders; castle replaced by mansion.
Held by the Homes.

Pinkerton [NT 703757], near Dunbar, East Lothian; farm on site of castle or old house.
Held by the Pinkerton family, and by others, before passing to the Homes of Pinkerton, who are on record in 1624.

Polwarth Castle [NT 749500], near Duns, Borders; site of castle.
Held by the Polwarth family, then by the Cospatrick Earl of Dunbar and March and by the Sinclairs of Herdmanston, then by the Homes, who probably built the castle. Sir Patrick Home hid in his own family's burial vault at Polwarth Kirk [NT 750495] after getting into trouble with James VII. Grizel (later the well-known Grizel Baillie of Mellerstain), his twelve-year-old daughter, supplied him with food and drink from Redbraes Castle. Sir Patrick escaped to Holland, and later returned with William of Orange to become Lord Polwarth in 1690 and Earl of Marchmont in 1697; he was made Chancellor in 1696. The property later passed to the Scotts.

Preston Tower [NT 393742], Prestonpans, East Lothian; impressive ruinous tower.
Held by the Homes, but then passed to other families, including to the Hamiltons. The tower stands in a garden from where it can be viewed (01875 810232).

Purves Hall or **Tofts** [NT 761447], near Greenlaw, Borders; mansion incorporating tower house.
Held by the Furde family, then by the Rutherfords, before coming to the Homes. The castle was attacked by the English in about 1544, and it passed to the Belshes by 1610, then to the Purvis family. 'Befa' what e'er befa', there'll aye be a gowk in Purves-ha". Purves Hall was recently put up for sale for offer of more than £450,000.

Quixwood [NT 787632], near Grantshouse, Borders; farm on site of castle or old house.
Held by the Quixwood family but passed to the Homes. Francis Home of Quixwood was an advocate and died in 1721.

Redbraes Castle [NT 746485], near Greenlaw, Borders; site of castle.
Held by the Homes (also see Polwarth). The old castle was remodelled between 1726-35, but was replaced by Marchmont House.

Spott House [NT 679752], near Dunbar, East Lothian; mansion on site of castle.
Held by the Cospatrick Earls of Dunbar, but passed to the Homes. George Home of Spott was made Earl of Dunbar in 1605, although the title became extinct on his death six years

later. There is a magnificent marble and alabaster monument to Home in Dunbar Church [NT 682786], to the south of the burgh. David Leslie, general of the Scottish army, stayed at Spott in 1650 before going on to defeat at the Battle of Dunbar; Cromwell staying here afterwards. The property later passed to other families.

Thornton Tower [NT 739735], near Dunbar, East Lothian; site of tower house.

Held by the Homes, and was held against the English by sixteen men in 1540.

Wedderburn Castle [NT 809529], near Duns, Borders; mansion on site of castle.

Held by the Wedderburns, by the Cospatrick Earls of Dunbar and by the Douglases, before coming to the Homes in the fifteenth century. Mary, Queen of Scots, is believed to have visited. The present house was built for Patrick Home of Billie's new bride, only for Home to catch her in bed with another man on their honeymoon in Venice. The castle can be hired for exclusive use (01361 882190; www.wedderburn-castle.co.uk).

www.clanhome.net
homepages.rootsweb.com/~hume/
No. of castles/sites: 47
Rank: 22=/764
Xref: Hume

Monument to George Home of Spott, Earl of Dunbar (M&R)

Hope

The name is probably local in origin, 'hope' being a common place name element in many parts of lowland Scotland, especially the Borders, and means 'upland valley'. It has also been suggested that Hope is from the family of 'de H'oublons' of Picardy, as 'oublon' means 'hop', which then became 'hope' when translated into English. The name is on record in Scotland from 1296.

Craighall [NO 407107] stood a few miles to the southeast of Cupar in Fife. It was latterly a ruinous but imposing classical mansion and tower house, but the

Craighall 1910?

whole building was demolished in 1955. The property was held by the Kinninmonds, but was sold to the Hopes. Sir Thomas Hope of Craighall, an eminent lawyer, was King's Advocate to Charles I, and was made a Baronet of Nova Scotia in 1628. The property was sold to the Hope Earls of Hopetoun in 1729. The line of the Hopes of Craighall, Baronets, continues, and they now apparently live in London.

Hopetoun House [NT 089790], located by the Firth of Forth a couple of miles to the west of South Queensferry, is a large and grand mansion. It dates from between 1699 and 1707, and was built by William Bruce, but was then remodelled by William Adam from 1721, the work being continued by John and Robert Adam. Hopetoun became the main seat of the Hope family,

Hopetoun House 1920?

who were descended from a younger son of Sir Thomas Hope of Craighall. John Hope of Hopetoun drowned when the frigate *Gloucester* sank, James VII was lucky enough to be rescued. The family became very wealthy in the eighteenth century, and held much land in West Lothian and elsewhere; Charles Hope was made Earl of Hopetoun in 1703. John, fourth Earl, was a soldier and was stationed in the West Indies and in Egypt before assuming command at the Battle of Corunna in 1809 during the Peninsular War when John Moore, his superior, was killed. John, seventh Earl, was the first Governor General of Australia, and was made Marquess of Linlithgow in 1902. The phantom of a man clad in black is said to have been witnessed on a path near the house, a herald of death or misadventure in the Hope family. The castle is owned by a charitable trust, and it is open to the public (0131 331 2451; www.hopetoun house.com). The family have a burial aisle at Abercorn Church [NT 083792], which is a fine old church with an interesting burial ground and which is open to the public.

The Hopes also owned:
Abercorn Castle [NT 083794], near South Queensferry, West Lothian; site of castle.
   Held by several families, including by the Grahams, by the Douglases and by the Hamiltons, before passing to the Hopes in the seventeenth century. The castle was destroyed long before coming to the Hopes.
Balcomie Castle [NO 626099], near Crail, Fife; L-plan tower house.
   Held by the Learmonths, but passed to the Hopes in 1705, then went to the Scotts of Scotstarvit, then to the Erskine Earls of Kellie.
Bridge Castle [NS 944709], near Armadale, West Lothian; castle and mansion.
   Held by the Stewarts and by the Livingstones, then after 1715 went to the Hopes.
Carriden House [NT 026808], near Bo'ness, Falkirk; tower house and mansion.
   Held by several families, including latterly by the Hope Johnstones, two of whom were distinguished admirals. B&B accommodation is available and Carriden is suitable for weddings (01506 829811; www.carridenhouse.co.uk).
Craigiehall House [NT 167754], near Edinburgh; mansion on site of castle.
   Held by the Stewarts, then by the Fairholmes and by the Johnstones, before passing to the Hopes of Hopetoun, then to the Hope Weirs, then to the army.
Granton Castle [NT 225772], Edinburgh; site of castle.
   Held by the Melvilles of Carnbee, then by the Mackenzies of Tarbat, then by the Hopes of Craighall. The property later passed to the Campbell Dukes of Argyll, and the castle was demolished in the 1920s.
Illieston House [NT 010700], near Broxburn, West Lothian; T-plan tower house.
   Held by the Nobles and by the Grahams before passing to the Ellis family, but the property was sold to the Hopes of Hopetoun in 1765.
Kerse House [NS 915817], near Grangemouth, Falkirk; site of castle and mansion.
   Held by the Menteiths, then by the Livingstones and by the Hopes, one of whom was Sir Thomas Hope, Lord Justice General for Scotland; but Kerse later passed to the Dundases (also see Kersie).
Kersie [NS 872912], near Stirling; L-plan tower house.
   Held by the Menteiths, then by the Livingstones and by the Hopes, one of whom was Sir Thomas Hope, Lord Justice General for Scotland; but Kerse later passed to the Dundases (also see Kerse).

Luffness House [NT 476804], near Aberlady, East Lothian; fine castle and mansion.
   Held by the Cospatrick Earls of Dunbar and by the Lindsays, then went to the Hepburns then in 1739 to the Hopes of Hopetoun.
Midhope Castle [NT 073787], near Linlithgow, West Lothian; altered tower house.
   Held by the Drummonds, then by the Livingstone Earls of

Midhope Castle 1910?

Linlithgow, then by the Hopes of Hopetoun. The castle was used to house farm workers after the building of nearby Hopetoun House.
Monkton House [NT 334703], near Musselburgh, East Lothian; L-plan tower house.
   Held by the Hays of Yester, then by the Falconers after 1715, then by the Hopes of Pinkie, who held the property at the end of the nineteenth century.
Niddry or **Niddry-Seton Castle** [NT 097743], near Broxburn, West Lothian; restored L-plan keep or tower.
   Held by the Setons, then by the Hopes in the second half of the seventeenth century.
Ormiston Castle [NT 413677], near Dalkeith, Midlothian; ruinous castle and mansion.
   Held by the Lindsays and by the Cockburns, but was sold to the Hope Earls of Hopetoun in 1748.
Pinkie House [NT 353727], Musselburgh, East Lothian; fine castle and mansion.
   Held by the Setons after the Reformation, but was sold to the Hay Marquis of Tweeddale in 1694, then to the Hopes of Craighall in 1778. The house is part of Loretto, a private school (0131 653 4444; www.lorettoschool.co.uk).
Raehills [NY 064943], near Moffat, Dumfries and Galloway; castle on site of mansion.
   Held by the Johnstones, then by the Hope Earls of Hopetoun.
Rankeilour Castle [NO 330119], near Cupar, Fife; castle replaced by mansion.
   Held by the Rankeillours, then by the Sibbalds of Balgonie, then by the Hopes, later Earls of Hopetoun. This branch of the family were made Baronets in 1932, although they now apparently live at Roy Bridge in Inverness-shire.
Rosyth Castle [NT 115820], near Inverkeithing, Fife; ruinous L-plan tower house.
   Held by the Stewarts of Rosyth, but in the eighteenth century passed to the Primrose Earl of Rosebery, then to the Hope Earl of Hopetoun. The castle stands in the dockyard at Rosyth and is apparently accessible by appointment (0131 668 8800).
Wamphray Tower [NY 128965], near Moffat, Dumfries and Galloway; site of once strong tower.
   Held by the several families, including by the Johnstones, but passed to the Hope Earl of Hopetoun in 1747, and the castle was abandoned at this time.

www.clanhope.org
No. of castles/sites: 21
Rank: 63=/764

Horne

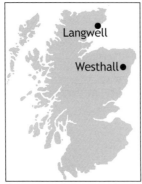

The name comes from the popular Old English or Norse personal name, and is recorded in Scotland from the thirteenth century.

Westhall [NJ 673266] is a small L-plan tower house, dating from the sixteenth century, and stands seven miles north-west of Inverurie in Aberdeenshire. The lands were held by the Gordons

Westhall (M&R)

following the Reformation, but passed to the Hornes in 1681, then by marriage went to the Elphinstones. The house is still occupied.

Langwell Castle [ND 116227], five miles south-west of Dunbeath in Caithness, was replaced by Langwell House, a rambling mansion of the eighteenth century. The property was held by the Sutherlands, but passed to the Sinclairs in 1788, then to the Hornes in 1813 and then to the Dukes of Portland in 1860, who still apparently live here. The garden is open to the public by appointment only (01593 751278; www.gardensof scotland.org).

No. of castles/sites: 2
Rank: 396=/764
Xref: Horn

Horsburgh

The name is territorial and comes from the lands of Horsburgh, which are a couple of miles east and south of Peebles in the Borders. The origin may be from 'Horse' or 'Orse', a personal name, and 'burgh', a settlement or castle. Horsburgh is on record from the middle of the thirteenth century.

Horsburgh Tower [NT 285392] is a very ruinous L-plan tower house, which dates from the sixteenth century. The lands were held by the Horsburghs from the thirteenth century for around the next 700 years.

The Horsburghs also owned:
Hutchinfield Tower [NT 255422], near Peebles, Borders; slight remains of tower house.
　　Held by the Horsburghs, but passed to the Williamsons in 1659.
Manorhead Tower [NT 195276], near Peebles, Borders; slight remains of tower house.
　　Held by the Inglis family, but sold to the Horsburghs around the beginning of the eighteenth century.
Nether Horsburgh Castle [NT 304396], near Peebles, Borders; some remains of tower house.
　　Held by the Horsburghs, but sold to the Shaws of Shillingshaw

Nether Horsburgh Castle (M&R)

in the seventeenth century because of debt.
Pirn [NT 337370], near Innerleithen, Borders; site of tower house and mansion.
　　Held by the Taits, but passed by marriage to the Horsburghs in the eighteenth century. The tower was replaced by Pirn House in about 1700, but this was demolished in 1950 and replaced by a school building.
Purvishill Tower [NT 355375], near Innerleithen, Peebles; slight remains of tower house.
　　Held by the Purvis family, but passed to the Horsburghs.

No. of castles/sites: 6
Rank: 212=/764

Houston

The name is territorial and comes from the barony and lands of Houston, which are a mile to the east and north of Bridge of Weir in Renfrewshire. Also see Johnstone.

Houston House [NS 412672] was a large court-yard castle, dating from the sixteenth century, but only one side remains, dated 1625, which incorporates even older work; a new mansion was built in the eighteenth century. The name comes from 'Hugh's town' from Hugh of Padvinan, whose descendants took the name Houston, and held the lands from the twelfth century. The property passed to the Speirs of Elderslie in 1782.

Houston House [NT 058716], in Uphall in West Lothian, is an altered and extended L-plan tower house of the seventeenth century. The lands were held by the Houstons, one of whom, Sir Peter Houston, was killed at the Battle of Flodden in 1513; and Sir Patrick Houston of Houston was Keeper of the Quarter Seal, but conspired against James V and was slain at the Battle of Linlithgow Bridge in 1526. The property passed to the Sharps in 1569 and they held Houston until 1945, and the building is now used as a hotel (01506 853831; www.macdonald hotels.co.uk/houstounhouse/).

The Houstons also owned:
Cutreoch [NX 467357], near Whithorn, Galloway; site of castle.
  Held by the Houstons in the sixteenth century, but passed to the Agnews in 1732.
Isle of Whithorn Castle [NX 476367], near Whithorn, Galloway; L-plan tower house.
  Held by the Houstons of Drummaston at one time.

Isle of Whithorn Castle (M&R)

Johnstone or **Easter Cochrane Castle** [NS 425623], Johnstone; altered L-plan tower house.
  Held by the Cochranes, but passed to the Houstons in 1733. Frederick Chopin visited the castle in 1848. Most of the mansion was demolished in 1950s: only the oldest part survives in a housing estate.

Jordanhill [NS 538683], Glasgow; site of castle.
  Held by the Crawfords, but later passed to the Houstons and was then sold to the Smiths in 1800.
Mayshiel [NT 622641], near Cranshaws, East Lothian; altered tower house.
  Held by several families before latterly coming to the Houstons of Clerkington. The building is still occupied.
Milliken [NS 418634], near Johnstone, Renfrewshire; site of tower house.
  Held by the Wallaces of Elderslie, but passed to the Houstons, then in 1733 went to the Millikens, and they built a new mansion, which has itself been demolished.
Park [NS 409706], near Bishopton, Renfrewshire; site of castle.
  Held by the Park family, but passed by marriage to the Houstons around the turn of the sixteenth century.
Rossland [NS 442707], near Erskine, Renfrewshire; site of castle.
  Held by the Houston family.
The Peel, Busby [NS 594561], near East Kilbride, Lanarkshire; altered L-plan tower house.
  Held by the Douglases, by the Hamiltons and by the Semples before coming to the Houstons of Jordanhill in 1793. The building is still occupied.

No. of castles/sites: 11
Rank: 127=/764

Howat

The name is from a form of 'Hugh', the diminutive 'How', along with 'at', and is recorded as a surname in Scotland from the fifteenth century.

Mabie [NX 949708], four miles south-east of Dumfries, is the site of a castle, but Mabie House dates from the eighteenth century. The property was held by the Kirkconnels, but passed to the Herries family, and around the end of the nineteenth century was being held by the Howats. The building is now used as a hotel (01387 263188; www.mabiehouse.co.uk).

No. of castles/sites: 1
Rank: 537=/764

Howieson

Craufurdland

The name means 'Howie's son', 'Howie' being derived from 'Hugh', and the name is on record in Scotland from the middle of the fifteenth century. Jock (or Jack) Howieson farmed the lands of Braehead, near Cramond Brig, and he is said to have rescued James V from a band of robbers when the king was disguised at the 'Gudeman of Ballengeich'.

Craufurdland Castle [NS 456408], two or so miles north-east of Kilmarnock in Ayrshire, is a large mansion which incorporates an altered tower house, dating from the sixteenth century. The King's Room has a fine plaster ceiling with the date 1668. The property was held by the Crawfords, but passed to the Howiesons in 1793. The castle was restored in the 1980s, and an underground passage is said to have connected the castle with Dean Castle, to the north of Kilmarnock and some miles away

No. of castles/sites: 1
Rank: 537=/764

Hunt

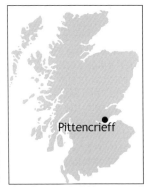

Pittencrieff

The name comes form the Old English 'hunta', meaning 'hunter' or 'huntsman', and is derived from the same root as the surname 'Hunter'.

Pittencrieff House [NT 087873], in Dunfermline, is a fine T-plan mansion, and is surrounded by the grounds of a public park. The lands were held by several families, before coming to the Hunts in 1800, then went to Andrew Carnegie, who gave the property to the people of Dunfermline. The family of Hunt of Pittencrieff and Logie continues, and the family still apparently live in Dunfermline. Pittencrieff House stands in the popular Pittencrieff Park (01383 722935/313838; www.fife direct.org/museums).

No. of castles/sites: 1
Rank: 537=/764

Hunter

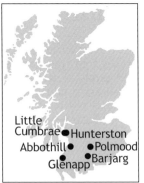

Little Cumbrae ● Hunterston
Abbothill ● ● Polmood
Glenapp ● Barjarg

The name comes form the Old English 'hunta', meaning 'hunter' or 'huntsman', and is derived from the same root as the surname 'Hunt'. The family is said to have come to England in the retinue of Queen Matilda, wife of William the Conqueror, then arrived in Scotland when David I returned to his kingdom in the twelfth century. John and William Hunter were renowned physicians in the nineteenth century and published works on midwifery, gunshot wounds and sexually transmitted disease, and William collected art and other items and his collections were acquired by the University of Glasgow, and both the Hunterian Museum and Art Gallery are open to the public (www.hunterian.gla.ac.uk).

Hunterston Castle [NS 193515], two or so miles north of West Kilbride in Ayrshire, is a strong keep or tower

Hunterston Castle (M&R)

with a crenellated parapet, and dates from the fifteenth century. The Hunters apparently held lands here from the eleventh century, and a grant of 1374 confirmed the property in exchange for a silver penny to be payable to the monarch at Hunterston on the feast of Pentecost. The Hunters were hereditary keepers of the royal forests on Cumbrae and Arran. John Hunter, fourteenth of Hunterston, was killed at the Battle of Flodden in 1513, and his great-grandson, Mungo Hunter, sixteenth of Hunterston, was killed at Pinkie in 1547. The old castle was remodelled as a chauffeur's quarters and a garage after the family moved to the nearby mansion in the eighteenth century. The family still own the property, now represented by the thirtieth laird, and they have apparently moved back to the castle.

Little Cumbrae Castle [NS 153514], on the east side of Little Cumbrae, an island in the Firth of Clyde, is a ruinous keep or tower, dating from the fifteenth century and rising to three storeys and a garret. Little Cumbrae was a property of the Crown, but was administered by the Hunters of Hunterston. There was then a dispute between the Crown and the Hunters over the ownership of falcons, and the property was given to Hew Montgomery, Earl of Eglinton, in 1515. The castle was sacked in the 1650s and was not rebuilt.

Polmood [NT 114270] stood two miles north-east of Tweedsmuir in the Borders, but there are no remains of the castle. The present house forms three sides of a courtyard, and dates from 1638 although it was greatly altered in the nineteenth century. Polmood was a property of the Hunters from the thirteenth century until the end of the eighteenth century when it went to the Forbeses.

Abbothill [NS 370191], a couple of miles south-east of Ayr, is the site of a castle or old house. The lands passed to the Hunters in 1569 and they held them until 1772 when they moved to Barjarg Tower (see below). One of the Hunters of Abbothill became Lord Provost of Edinburgh in the mid eighteenth century. He married Jean Blair, heiress to the lands of Dunskey, and the family became Hunter Blair. They now apparently live at Blairquhan.

Three other buildings owned by the Hunters were **Barjarg Tower** [NX 876901], south of Thornhill in Dumfries and Galloway. This is an L-plan tower house, dating from the sixteenth century but added to and extended, and held by the Hunters in the nineteenth century. **Glenapp Castle** [NX 093808], to the south-east of Ballantrae in Ayrshire, is a grand castellated mansion of 1870, designed by David Bryce and built for the Hunters. The mansion is now is now used as an exclusive luxury hotel and restaurant (01465 831212; www.glenappcastle.com). **Bonnytoun** [NS 454159] lies two or so miles south of Drongan also in Ayrshire, and there was a castle or old house here. The lands were held by the Stewarts of Ochiltree but passed to the Hunters in the middle of the eighteenth century and they held the property until around 1860.

www.clan-hunter-uk.co.uk
www.hunterclanusa.org
www.clanhuntercanada.com
No. of castles/sites: 7
Rank: 182=/764

Partick Castle (M&R) – see next column (Hutchinson)

Hutchinson

The name comes from the French 'Huchon', derived from 'Hugh', and 'son'; and the name is in record from the middle of the fifteenth century. The name could be spelled Hutchinson, Hutcheson, Hutchison or other variations

Partick Castle [NS 559663] stood a couple of miles west of Glasgow Cathedral, and was an L-plan tower house, probably dating from 1611. The castle had gardens and an orchard, and was built by George Hutcheson, probably on the site of a residence of the Bishops of Glasgow. The building was demolished about 1836, and the site is now occupied by a scrap dealers.

Hutchesons' Hall [NS 594652], on Ingram Street in Glasgow, is one of the city's most elegant buildings, and stands on the site of a hospice established by George and Thomas Hutcheson in 1641, who were wealthy lawyers and local philanthropists. There is an audio-visual presentation on Glasgow's Merchant City (0141 552 8391; www.nts.org.uk).

Carlowrie Castle [NT 142744], a mile east of Kirkliston near the border between West Lothian and Edinburgh, has been demolished but the building replaced an earlier house or castle. The lands were held by the Dalziels, by the Marjoribanks and by the Falconers, before passing to the Hutchinsons in the nineteenth century.

No. of castles/sites: 3 / Rank: 328=/764
Xrefs: Hutcheson; Hutchison

Hynd

The name comes from the occupation of peasant from the Old English 'hind', and is on record in Scotland from the middle of the fifteenth century.

Drumcoltran Tower [NX 869683] is an L-plan tower house of three storeys and a garret, and dates from the sixteenth century; it is roofed but does not have internal floors. The property was owned by the Herries of Terregles family then by the Maxwells, by the Irvings, then by the Hynds in 1799, then the property went to the Herons, and then back to the Maxwells in 1875. The tower was occupied until the 1890s, is now in the care of Historic Scotland, and is open to the public.

No. of castles/sites: 1
Rank: 537=/764

Inchmartin

The name is territorial and comes from the lands of Inchmartine, which are nine miles west of Dundee in Perthshire. There was a castle at **Inchmartine** [NO 262281] which was replaced by Inchmartine House, a tall classical mansion dating from the end of the seventeenth century. Some fragments of the castle are apparently built into the bridge at Inchmartine Pow [NO 264278].

The lands were held by the Inchmartin family. Sir Henry de Inch Martine was captured by the English at Dunbar Castle in 1296, another of the family was hanged by the English in 1306, and Gilbert de Inch Martine was killed at the Battle of Durham in 1346. The property passed to the Glens and then by marriage to the Ogilvies in the middle of the fifteenth century.

No. of castles/sites: 1
Rank: 537=/764

Inglis

The name comes from Old English, simply means 'Englishman', and is on record in Scotland from about 1200.

The remains of **Manorhead Tower** [NT 195276] stands about ten miles to the south and west of Peebles in the Borders. The lands were given to the Inglis family in the fourteenth century, reputedly in 1395 after the first Inglis of Manor killed Sir Thomas Struthers, an English champion, in single combat. The property was sold to the Horsburghs at the beginning of the eighteenth century.

Scotstarvit Tower [NO 370113] is two or so miles south of Cupar in Fife, and is a magnificent L-plan tower house of six storeys and a garret. It dates from the fifteenth and sixteenth centuries, and was held by the Inglis family before being sold to the Scotts in 1611. It later passed to other families, and is now in held by The National Trust for Scotland, although administered by Historic Scotland. The key is available at Hill of Tarvit Mansionhouse (01334 653127).

Auchindinny House [NT 252613] is a small mansion with flanking pavilions but incorporates two vaulted chambers from an old castle. The present building was designed by Sir William Bruce and dates from about 1705. Auchindinny was a property of the Inglis family from 1702, but is now apparently held by the Maxtone Grahams.

The Inglis family also held:
Aithernie Castle [NO 379035], near Leven, Fife; some remains of tower house.
> Held by the Lundins, but passed to the Carmichaels and then to the Inglis family. Aithernie then went to the Riggs family, who probably built the castle, then to the Watsons in 1670.

Colluthie House [NO 340193], near Cupar, Fife; mansion incorporating much older work.
> Held by the Ramsays, then by the Carnegies of Colluthie in 1583, then by the Inglis family in 1840, and they renovated the house.

Craigend Castle [NS 545778], near Milngavie, Dunbartonshire; site of castle and mansion.
> Held by the Grahams, but passed to the Smiths and then to the Inglis family, and then to the Buchanans later in the nineteenth century. The site is in Mugdock Country Park (0141 956 6100; www.mugdock-country-park.org.uk).

Cramond Tower [NT 191770], Edinburgh; slim tower house and later mansion.
> Held by the Bishops of Dunkeld, but passed to the Douglases and then in 1622 to the Inglises. They built the fine Cramond House nearby in 1680, and the tower, once part of a much large castle, became ruinous. The Inglis family were made Baronets in 1687 although this became extinct in 1817. Cramond House is home to the Scottish Wildlife Trust, while the tower was restored and reoccupied in 1983.

Eastshield Tower [NS 960500], near Carnwath, Lanarkshire; slight remains of tower house.
> Held by the Inglis family.

Cramond Tower (JM) – see previous page

Murdostoun Castle [NS 825573], near Newmains, Lanarkshire; mansion incorporating castle.

Held by the Scotts but passed to the Inglis family in 1446 and they built the castle. The property passed to the Hamiltons in 1719, and then to the Stewarts. The castle is said to be haunted by a 'Green Lady', seen in the East Dressing Room, although it has not apparently been witnessed for many years. The building is now used as a hospital.

Newmore Castle [NH 680720], near Alness, Ross and Cromarty; slight remains of a castle.

Held by the Munros and by the Mackenzies, but was replaced by Newmore House, a mansion of 1875, a property of the Inglis family and then later of the Oswalds. The building is now used as a nursing home.

Woodhouse Hill or **Woodhouse Manor** [NT 211370], near Peebles, Borders; site of tower house.

Held by the Inglis of Manor family, but passed to the Pringles of Smailholm in 1522, then to Burnetts of Barns and then to the Naesmyths of Posso.

No. of castles/sites: 11
Rank: 127=/764

Innes

The name is territorial and comes from the lands and old barony of Innes, which are four miles east and north of Elgin in Moray. Innes is from 'innis', the Gaelic for 'island', and the name is on record from the eleventh century.

Innes House [NJ 278649] is a fine L-plan tower house, dating from the seventeenth century and designed by William Aytoun, master mason. The building was altered in later years

Innes House (M&R)

with the addition of a steep-pitched roof and has harled walls.

The lands were held by the Innes family from 1160 or earlier, and the family were Flemings (as in from Flanders). John Innes, son of the then laird, was Bishop of Moray and restored Elgin Cathedral after it had been torched by the Wolf of Badenoch in 1390. Sir Robert, eleventh Lord, fought at the Battle of Brechin in 1452 on the side of the Earl of Huntly. James III visited here, and James Innes was his armour bearer; James IV also visited. Alexander, sixteenth Lord Innes, was beheaded by the Regent Morton for murder; while John, seventeenth Lord, resigned the property in favour of Alexander Innes of Crombie, who then became eighteenth Lord, which led to a feud. Alexander, eighteenth Lord, was murdered by Robert Innes of Innermarkie in 1580 in Aberdeen, and Sir Robert, twentieth Lord, was outlawed in 1624, although he was then made a Baronet of Nova Scotia in 1625. The twentieth Lord was a prominent Covenanter, and it was he who built the present house between 1640 and 1653, and he received Charles II at Speymouth in 1650. The family married into the Kerrs in 1666, and eventually succeeded to the Dukedom of Roxburgh in 1805. Innes was sold to James Duff, second Earl of Fife, in 1767, and later passed to the Tennant family. The Duke of Roxburgh would be chief of the Inneses, but he has a double-barrelled surname (Innes-Kerr), which bars him from succeeding.

Balvenie Castle [NJ 326409] is in a pleasant peaceful spot to the north of Dufftown in Moray, and is a fine ruinous courtyard castle, defended by a ditch, with a later L-plan tower and other buildings. It was held by the Comyns, by the Douglases and by the Stewarts before

Balvenie Castle (RWB)

passing to the Inneses of Innermarkie in 1614. The family were made Baronets of Nova Scotia in 1628. The castle was used by the Marquis of Montrose in 1644-45, and the Inneses suffered by supporting the Royalist side in the Civil War, and had to sell the property to the Duffs of Braco in 1687. The Inneses of Balvenie, Baronets, still flourish, but apparently live in Hampshire in England. Balvenie Castle is in the care of Historic Scotland and open to the public from April to September (01340 820121).

The following castles or properties were also held by the family:

Ardtannes [NJ 758201], near Inverurie, Aberdeenshire; site of castle or old house.

Held by the Inneses in the seventeenth century. Walter Innes of Ardtannes is buried in Inverurie churchyard [NJ 780206]. His wife, Marjorie Elphinstone, fell into a coma and was thought to be dead. She was buried, but a sextant attempted to steal her rings, and so unintentionally revived her. She is said to have gone on to marry again.

Asliesk Castle [NJ 108598], near Elgin, Moray; slight remains of tower house.

Held by the Inneses and then by the Brodies.

Ayton Castle [NT 929614], near Eyemouth, Borders; mansion on site of castle.

Long held by the Homes, but in the nineteenth century was held by the Mitchell-Innes family before coming to the Liddell-Graingers. The castellated mansion is open to the public from May to September Wednesday and Sunday (01890 781212/550; www.aytoncastle.co.uk).

Ballogie [NO 571955], near Aboyne, Aberdeenshire; mansion on site of older houses.

Held by the Forbeses, but sold to the Inneses in 1789, then went to the Farquharsons and to the Nichols.

Balnacraig [NJ 604035], near Torphins, Aberdeenshire; castle replaced by mansion.

Held by the Chalmers family, but had passed to the Inneses by 1735. The family were staunch Catholics. James Innes was a Jacobite, and after the Battle of Culloden in 1746 government forces came to capture him and torch the house. Catherine Gordon, his wife, managed to persuade them not to burn them

out as it was her son who owned the property and he was not involved in the Rising. She then got the troops drunk, and they went on their way without either apprehending her husband (who was hiding nearby) or torching the building.

Blackhills [NJ 270587], near Lhanbryde, Moray; castle replaced by mansion.

Held by the Innes family in the seventeenth and eighteenth centuries (see Coxton), and was sold to the Duffs of Fife and then to the Christie family. Cottages can be rented on the estate and the gardens are occasionally open to the public (01343 842223; www.blackhills.co.uk).

Calrossie [NH 804778], near Tain, Ross and Cromarty; site of castle.

Held by the Innes family in the middle of the sixteenth century.

Cowie Castle [NO 887874], near Stonehaven, Kincardineshire; castle replaced by mansion.

Held by the Frasers, then by the Innes family, who lived at Cowie House [NO 880872] until 1975.

Coxton Tower [NJ 262607], near Elgin, Moray; splendid tower house.

Held by the Inneses of Invermarkie from 1523, and they were made Baronets of Nova Scotia in 1685-86. The Inneses of Coxton were Jacobites and fought on the side of Bonnie Dundee and then supported the 1715 and 1745-46 Rising. The property

Coxton Tower (RWB)

was sold to the Duff Earl of Fife and then later to the Christies (www.malcolm.christie.btinternet.co.uk), and the Inneses of Coxton, Baronets, now apparently live in Middlesex.

Crombie Castle [NJ 591522], near Aberchirder, Aberdeenshire; altered L-plan tower house.

Held by the Inneses. James Innes of Crombie, who probably built the house, was killed at the Battle of Pinkie in 1547. A later owner, Alexander Innes, was brutally murdered in Aberdeen by his kinsman, Innes of Innermarkie, in a family dispute. The property passed to the Urquharts in 1631, then to the Meldrums and then to the Duffs.

Dunbeath Castle [ND 158282], near Dunbeath, Caithness; fine E-plan tower house.

Held by the Crichtons, but had passed to the Inneses by 1507, and then went to the Sinclairs of Geanies in 1529.

Durris House [NO 799968], near Banchory, Aberdeenshire; altered L-plan tower house.

Held by the Frasers, then passed to the Innes family in the seventeenth century, one of whom was Cosmo Innes, a distinguished antiquarian. Durris passed to the Duke of Gordon, then to the MacTires and to the Youngs.

Edingight House [NJ 517557], near Cullen, Aberdeenshire; house with old work.

Held and built by the Inneses of Invermarkie, who acquired the property in 1559. Sir Malcolm Rognavald Innes of Edingight was Lord Lyon King of Arms for Scotland from 1981 to 2001.

Elrick House [NJ 883183], near New Machar, Aberdeenshire; castle replaced by mansion.

Held by the Inneses in the sixteenth century, but passed to the Burnetts.

Gordonstoun or **Plewlands** or **Ogstoun** [NJ 184690], near Lossiemouth, Moray; mansion incorporating tower house.

Held by the Ogstouns, but sold to the Inneses in 1473, who sold it to the Gordons in 1616, and they renamed it Gordonstoun. Now home to the well-known public school, and the grounds are occasionally open to the public (01343 837829; www.gordonstoun.org.uk).

Inverbreakie [NH 715700], near Invergordon, Ross and Cromarty; site of castle.

Held by the Inneses, but later passed to the Gordons.

Invermarkie or **Innermarkie Castle** [NJ 429396], near Keith, Moray; site of castle.

Held by the Gordons, but passed to the Inneses. The castle was demolished in the seventeenth century and replaced by a shooting lodge of the Duffs.

Kinnairdy Castle [NJ 609498], near Aberchirder, Aberdeenshire; altered L-plan keep or tower.

Held by the Innes family. Sir Alexander Innes got into trouble with his creditors, and was imprisoned and Kinnairdy was sold to the Crichtons of Frendraught in 1629, then went to others. Accommodation is available (01463 780833; www.kinnairdy-castle.co.uk).

Learney [NJ 633046], near Banchory, Aberdeenshire; castle or old house replaced by mansion.

Held by the Forbeses and by the Brebners before passing by marriage to Innes of Raemoir in the nineteenth century. One of the family was Sir Thomas Innes of Learney, who was Lyon King of Arms; he died in 1971.

Leuchars House [NJ 260649], near Elgin, Moray; castle replaced by mansion.

Held by the Inneses of Leuchars. Still occupied.

Phantassie [NT 598772], near East Linton, East Lothian; site of castle or old house.

Held by the Sharps but passed to the Mitchell-Innes family in the nineteenth century. There is an unusual sixteenth-century doocot, which has 544 nesting boxes, still complete with birds. Open to the public as Preston Mill (and quite smelly, showing why doocots were often built away from residences).

Raemoir [NO 695995], near Banchory, Aberdeenshire; mansion incorporating old work.

Held by the Hoggs, then by the Inneses in the nineteenth century, then went to the Cowdrays of Dunecht. Now a hotel (01330 824844; www.raemoir.com).

Towie Barclay Castle [NJ 744439], near Turriff, Aberdeenshire; altered L-plan tower house.

Long held by the Barclays of Towie, but passed by marriage to the Inneses in the eighteenth century until sold in 1775.

Tulloch Castle [NH 547605], near Dingwall, Ross and Cromarty; mansion incorporating castle.

Held by the Inneses in 1526, then by the Bains from 1542 to 1762, then by the Davidsons. Now a hotel (01349 861325; www.tullochcastle.co.uk).

Whitehall [NT 874551], near Chirnside, Borders; castle replaced by (now reduced) mansion.

Held by the Halls in the eighteenth century, but were sold to the Mitchell-Inneses of Whitehall in 1840, and the family still flourishes.

www.clan-innes.org
No. of castles/sites: 28 / Rank: 44=/764
Xref: Ennis

Ireland

The name is recorded as a surname in Scotland from the thirteenth century. Landowners of that name held property in Perthshire, near Hawick in the Borders, and in Orkney, although the three families do not appear to be related (and the northern Irelands definitely not so). John Ireland, a doctor of the Sorbonne in Paris, returned to Scotland in 1483 and became confessor to James III and was then an ambassador to France the following year.

A few miles to the south-east of Dunkeld in Perthshire, **Murthly Castle** [NO 070399] is a large building and includes an altered keep or tower, dating from the

Murthly Castle (M&R)

fifteenth century. The lands were held by the Ireland family until 1440, and then by the Abercrombys, and then by the Stewarts of Grandtully from 1615. The castle can be used as a location for weddings and events (01738 494119; www.murthly-estate.com).

At **Drimmie** [NO 285308] was a castle or old house, but this was replaced by **Rossie Priory**, a magnificent new mansion. Drimmie had been held by the Ireland family and then by the Falconers, but the Kinnairds moved to Rossie after holding the lands from the end of the fourteenth century. Rossie Priory is available to rent on an exclusive basis and the grounds are open to groups by appointment (01828 686286/238; www.rossie priory.com).

No. of castles/sites: 2
Rank: 396=/764

Irvine

The surname comes from the personal names 'Erewine' and 'Erwinne', and appears on record in the first quarter of the twelfth century. The Irvine (or Irving, Irwin or Irwine) family claim descent from the abbots of Dunkeld in the tenth century. Christopher Irving was a surgeon in the service of Charles II and then to the Cromwellian army of General Monck, and he was also a notable author.

The family settled in lands in Eskdale. The site of **Irvine Tower** [NY 367810] is a couple of miles south of Langholm at **Old Irvine** in Dumfries and Galloway, but the Irvines long held Bonshaw.

Bonshaw Tower [NY 243720], five miles north-east of Annan in Dumfries and Galloway, is a rectangular tower house, which dates from the sixteenth century.

Bonshaw Tower (M&R)

Bonshaw was held by the Irvines from the thirteenth century or earlier, and William de Irwin (or Irvine) was armour bearer to Robert the Bruce. He was given Drum in Aberdeenshire as reward for long service. Bonshaw was sacked in 1544 by the English, but twice successfully withstood sieges by Lord Maxwell in 1585. Francis Irvine of Bonshaw was Provost of Dumfries in the seventeenth century. There is an eighteenth-century house adjacent to the tower. The tower can be visited but by appointment only (01461 500256).

Drum Castle [NJ 796005] is a magnificent castle and mansion, and stands three miles west of Peterculter on Deeside in Aberdeenshire. There is a plain old keep or tower, dating from the thirteenth century, with very thick walls. To this has been added an L-shaped range which, with other buildings, forms the sides of a courtyard. The lands were held by the Irvines from 1323,

Drum Castle (M&R)

and the family became involved in feuds between the Keiths and the Forbeses. Sir Alexander Irvine was killed at the Battle of Harlaw in 1411, slain by and slaying MacLean of Duart 'Hector of the Battles'. The Irvines supported Charles I, and Drum was besieged in 1640, plundered by the Earl of Argyll in 1644, and sacked again in 1645 when the womenfolk were turned out of the castle. Alexander, eleventh laird, caused a scandal when he married Margaret Coutts, a sixteen-year-old local shepherdess (and forty-seven years younger than him), after the death of his first wife. They went on to have three daughters, and the events are featured in the old ballad 'The Laird o' Drum'. The Irvines were Jacobites, and fought in the 1715 and 1745-46 Jacobite Risings. Alexander, fourteenth laird, died from wounds received at the Battle of Sheriffmuir in 1715; and Alexander, seventeenth of Drum, fought at Culloden, although he managed to escape both the aftermath of the battle and forfeiture, after hiding in a secret chamber at Drum and spending several years in exile in France. The property was handed over to The National Trust for Scotland, and the castle and garden in open to the public (01330 811204; www.drum-castle.org.uk). The Irvines of Drum apparently now live near Banchory in Aberdeenshire.

The stone, praying effigies of Sir Alexander Irvine of Drum, who died in 1457, and his wife are in the Kirk of St Nicholas in Aberdeen. The south transept of the church is known as the Drum Aisle, and the church is open to the public (01224 643494; www.kirk-of-st-nicholas.org.uk).

The Irvines also owned:
Auchenrivock Tower [NY 373805], near Langholm, Dumfries and Galloway; slight remains of tower house.
 Held by the Irvines and burned by the English in 1523.
Barra Castle [NJ 792258], near Inverurie, Aberdeenshire; altered L-plan tower house.
 Held by the Kings, by the Setons and by others, before passing to the Irvines in the twentieth century. Still occupied.
Beltie [NJ 629007], near Banchory, Aberdeenshire; site of castle.
 Held by the Irvines from the fifteenth century. Robert Irvine of Beltie was killed at the Battle of Brechin in 1452.

Brucklay Castle [NJ 913502], near New Deer, Aberdeenshire; extended but ruinous tower house.

Probably held by the Irvines, but passed to the Fordyce family in the nineteenth century.

Burleigh Castle [NO 130046], near Kinross, Perthshire; partly ruinous courtyard castle.

Long held by the Balfours, but latterly passed to the Irwins, then to the Grahams of Kinross.

Drumcoltran Tower [NX 869683], near Dalbeattie, Dumfries and Galloway; L-plan tower house.

Held by the Herries family and by the Maxwells before being bought by the Irvines in 1669, and they held it until 1799. It then passed to the Hynds, to the Herons, and then to the Maxwells. The tower is in the care of Historic Scotland and open to the public.

Easter Clune Castle [NO 612914], near Banchory, Aberdeenshire; castle replaced by mansion.

Held by the Irvines and there is a stone with the initials of Alexander Irvine and his wife and the date 1719.

Gribton [NX 921800], near Dumfries; castle replaced by mansion.
Held by the Maxwells and then by the Irvines from 1682. William Irvine of Gribton, seventeenth chief, was active for the Jacobites. The property was sold in 1814, and at the end of the nineteenth century was owned by the Lamonts. The Irvings of Gribton now apparently live in Australia.

Hoddom Castle [NY 157730], near Annan, Dumfries and Galloway; L-plan tower house.

Held by several families, including by the Herries family then by the Maxwells and by the Carruthers family. Passed to the Irvines in 1549 and they fought for Mary, Queen of Scots, at Langside in 1568. The castle was seized the same year by Douglas of Drumlanrig, and the following year was recaptured by forces loyal to Mary. It was then blown up by the English in 1570. The castle was rebuilt but had passed to the Murrays of Cockpool around 1627, and then passed through several families. The castle stands in a caravan and camping park (01576 300251; www.hoddomcastle.co.uk).

Kellie Castle [NO 608402], near Arbroath, Angus; fine L-plan tower house and courtyard.

Held by several families, including by the Ochterlonys and by the Elliots before being purchased by the Irvines in 1614, who remodelled the building. It later went to the Maule Earl of Panmure.

Kingcausie [NJ 863001], near Peterculter, Aberdeenshire; mansion on site of castle.

Held by the Irvines of Kingcausie from around 1535, and they were descended from the Irvines of Drum. Alexander Irvine, sixth of Kingcausie, was an active Royalist and had a price of 5,000 merks on his head. He was murdered in 1644 by a William Forbes. The house or castle was burnt in 1680. John Irvine, eighth of Kingcausie, was a Jacobite and joined the Jacobite Rising of 1715, and he restored Kingcausie. The property is apparently still owned by the same family, now the Irvine-Fortescues of Kingcausie. The house is said to be haunted by the ghost of a two-year-old child. James Turner Christie, the infant, fell down the stairs, after slipping through his nanny's arms, and was killed.

Kirkconnel Tower [NY 192752], near Ecclefechan, Dumfries and Galloway; slight remains of a tower house.

Held by the Irvines, who moved here from Kirkconnel, near Springkell, in 1609. Kirkconnel Hall is a modern mansion, and is now used as a hotel (01576 300277; www.kirkconnel hall.co.uk).

Kirkconnel Tower [NY 253752], near Ecclefechan, Dumfries and Galloway; site of tower house.

Held by the Bells in 1426, but they were forfeited in 1455 and the property went to the Irvines, who moved to the Kirkconnel, mentioned above, in 1609. This was probably the home of Helen Irvine (or Maxwell) of Kirkconnel, heroine of one of the Border Ballads. She was slain by a rejected suitor, one of the Bells of Blacket House. Helen got in the way of a bullet meant

for her lover, Adam Fleming; the lovers are said to be buried in Kirkconnel Church. The property passed to the Maxwells.

Lynturk Castle [NJ 598122], near Alford, Aberdeenshire; site of castle.

Held by the Strachans until 1550, then passed to the Irvines, then went to the Gordons and to the MacCombies.

Monboddo House [NO 744783], near Laurencekirk, Kincardineshire; castle and mansion.

Held by the Barclays then by the Strachans and by the Irvines, who held Monboddo in 1635, then passed to the Burnetts. The house was abandoned but reoccupied in the 1970s with the demolishing of the modern mansion. The building stands in a housing estate of aspiring but feeble castlettes.

Peel Ring of Lumphanan [NJ 576037], near Aboyne, Aberdeenshire; motte.

Held by the Durwards, then by the Halketts in 1370, then by the Irvines in the fifteenth century. The site is in the care of Historic Scotland and is open to the public (01667 460232).

Pitmurchie [NJ 602023], near Aboyne, Aberdeenshire; site of castle.

Held by the Irvines in the fifteenth century.

Robgill Tower [NY 248716], near Annan, Dumfries and Galloway; mansion incorporating mansion.

Held by the Irvines until the nineteenth century, and was burned by the English in 1544. The tower was complete until demolished to the basement about 1850 and the remains built into a new mansion.

Stapleton Tower [NY 234688], near Annan, Dumfries and Galloway; ruinous tower house.

Held by the Irvines, but passed to the Grahams. There was some dispute over ownership, however, and in 1626 a Christie Irvine captured the castle in a surprise attack.

Straloch House [NJ 860210], near New Machar, Aberdeenshire; castle replaced by mansion.

Held by the Cheynes and by the Gordons, then by the Ramsays, then passed by marriage to the Irvines of Drum.

Whitehill [NY 149748], near Ecclefechan, Dumfries and Galloway; castle replaced by mansion.

Held by the Irvines from 1549. John Irvine of Whitehill, called Jock o' Milk, was killed in a Border raid in the sixteenth century. The family married into the Bells, and became Bell-Irving of Whitehill, and the family still apparently lives at Whitehill.

Woodhouse Tower [NY 251715], near Annan, Dumfries and Galloway; ruinous tower house.

Held by the Irvines.

www.clanirwin.org
No. of castles/sites: 25
Rank: 52=/764
Xrefs: Irving; Irwin

Jackson

The name comes from 'Jack's son', Jack being a pet-name of both James and of John. The name is on record in Scotland from the beginning of the fifteenth century.

There may have been a castle at **Westquarter** [NS 913787], two miles east of Falkirk in central Scotland, but both it and a later mansion, which dated from the seventeenth century, have gone. The lands were held by the Livingstones, but were a possession of the Jacksons of Halhill about 1890. The mansion was demolished in 1934, but there is a fine old doocot, which is dated 1647. The doocot is in the care of Historic Scotland and is accessible to the public.

Udston [NS 697558], in Hamilton in Lanarkshire, was long held by the Hamiltons but in the nineteenth century was held by the Jacksons. There was a castle but this was replaced by a mansion although this has also been demolished.

No. of castles/sites: 2
Rank: 396=/764

Jamieson

The name means 'son of James' (or 'Jamie', a pet-name for James), and is on record in Scotland from the beginning of the fourteenth century.

Nothing survives of **Kilmory Castle** [NS 051611] except one small turret. It is a few miles south-west of Rothesay on Bute, and was held by the Jamiesons of Kilmorie, hereditary coroners of Bute; the lands passed to the Stewarts in 1780.

Kilallan House [NS 383689], a mile or so west of Kilmacolm in Renfrewshire, is a strongly built house of the seventeenth century, rising to two storeys and a garret. In 1659 Reverend Alexander Jamieson was ordered to remain in the house by the Privy Council. It was believed that Jamieson had been attacked by the 'Witches of Pollok', and the Council may have feared he was bewitched or possessed.

No. of castles/sites: 2
Rank: 396=/764
Xrefs: James; Jameson

Jardine

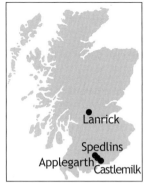

The name is derived from 'jardin', which means 'garden or orchard' in French, although this means that their seat was originally near a garden, rather than that they were, themselves, gardeners. The family came to England with William the Conqueror, and are recorded in Scotland from the middle of the twelfth century.

Applegirth or **Applegarth** [NY 105840] is two miles north-west of Lockerbie in Dumfries and Galloway, and there was a tower house but there are no remains. The lands were held by the Dunwoodies in the thirteenth century, but passed to the Jardines in the next century, and they still held the lands at the end of the sixteenth century.

Spedlins Tower [NY 098877] is close by, a few miles north and east of Lochmaben. It is a fine large tower house, dating from the fifteenth century, but remodelled about 1602, and then again in later centuries. The lands

Spedlins Tower (M&R)

were held by the Jardines from the fourteenth century or perhaps from 200 years earlier, and this appears to have been their principal seat. Sir Alexander Jardine of Applegirth, along with Lord Maxwell, defeated English raiders in 1402, taking 300 prisoners. The Jardine's lands were ravaged in 1547, but the Jardines retaliated with French help the same year, raiding into England. The family were made Baronets of Nova Scotia in 1675, and the chiefs are still styled 'of Applegirth', but they apparently live in Cumbria in England. The tower was abandoned for nearby **Jardine Hall** [NY 100876], a splendid nineteenth-century classical mansion, and became ruinous but the tower was restored in the 1970s and is still occupied. Jardine Hall, however, was completely demolished in 1964.

Spedlins was said to have been haunted by the ghost of a miller, called Dunty Porteous, who had the misfortune to be imprisoned here after trying to burn down his own mill. The laird took the key to the dungeon with him to Edinburgh; and Porteous gnawed at his own feet and hands before eventually dying of hunger. His ghost is then said to have manifested itself with all sorts of activity, until contained in the dungeon by a bible. Once when the bible was removed for repair, the ghost is said to have followed the family to nearby Jardine Hall. His presence has not been reported since the tower was restored.

The Jardines also owned:
Bower of Wandel [NS 952228], near Abingdon, Lanarkshire; very ruinous castle.
  Held by the Jardines from the twelfth century for about 500 years. James V is said to have used the castle when hunting.
Castlemilk [NY 150775], near Annan, Dumfries and Galloway; mansion in site of castle.
  Held by the Bruces and then by the Stewarts and by the Maxwells. The castle was replaced by a splendid new mansion,

Castlemilk 1901?

which dates from 1866, and has a sumptuous interior. Sir Robert Jardine, for whom the house was built, was a successful merchant and MP for Dumfriesshire, and made his fortune from tea and opium trafficking. The family were made Baronets in 1885, and still apparently live here.
Haggishaugh [NY 545944], near Newcastleton, Borders; site of tower house.
  Held by the Elliots and then by the end of the nineteenth century by the Jardines of Dryfeholm
Lanrick Castle [NN 685031], near Doune, Stirlingshire; site of castle and mansion.
  Held by the Haldanes of Gleneagles, then by the MacGregors and then in 1840 by William Jardine, the tea tycoon, who built the mansion. Although an impressive ruin, it was completely demolished in 2002 by its owner, although a listed building. The owner was only fined £1,000.
Tinwald Place [NY 006800], near Dumfries; castle replaced by mansion.
  Held by the Maxwells, but passed to the Erskines, then to the Douglas Marquis of Queensberry, before being bought by the Jardines in 1884. Tinwald House, which dates from 1740, was designed by William Adam.

www.nexicom.net/~drjardine_825/
No. of castles/sites: 7
Rank: 182=/764

Jeffrey

Jeffrey or Jaffrey comes from the personal name 'Godfrith' in Old English. The surname was found in Aberdeenshire, and is recorded from the end of the thirteenth century.

Kingswells House [NJ 862064], a couple of miles west of Aberdeen and east of Westhill, dates from the seventeenth century, and was restored in 1854. It was held by the Jaffreys from 1587. Alexander Jaffrey of Kingswells was Provost of Aberdeen in 1636, and he, or another of the name, fought against Cromwell at the Battle of Dunbar in 1650, where he was badly wounded. He became a Quaker round about the same time, died in 1673 and is buried with his wife and others of his faith at a nearby burial ground [NJ 857066]. Andrew Jaffrey, fourth Laird, was also buried here. Kingswells passed to the Edmonds and then to the Calderwoods.

Grandhome House or **Dilspro** [NJ 899117], which is to the south-east of Dyce to the north of Aberdeen, incorporates work from the seventeenth century or earlier. It was held by several families, including by the Jaffrays, before coming to the Patons of Farrochie, who changed the name to Grandhome.

To the west of Edinburgh is **Craigcrook Castle** [NT 211742], fine altered Z-plan tower house. It was held by several families, including by the Adamsons who built the castle. Lord Francis Jeffrey, the well-known judge and editor of the 'Edinburgh Review', had William Playfair remodel the building. Lord Jeffrey's ghost is said to haunt the building. Many disturbances have been reported, including unexplained footsteps and noises, things being moved around and thrown, and the doorbell ringing when nobody is apparently present. The castle now houses the offices of the magazine Scottish Field (0131 312 4550; www.scottishfield.co.uk).

No. of castles/sites: 3
Rank: 328=/764
Xref: Jaffrey

Craigcrook Castle (M&R)

293

Johnstone

The name means 'John's ton' (John's 'seat or settlement'), and there are various places of that name in Scotland. The main branch of the family had lands in Annandale in what is now Dumfries and Galloway, and elsewhere, but the name may also be from lands of that name near Dalkeith in Midlothian and from St John's Town of Perth, and from elsewhere. James Johnstone, born in Edinburgh in 1719, was an aide-de-camp of Bonnie Prince Charlie in the Jacobite Rising of 1745-46, and was known as the 'Chevalier de Johnstone'. He wrote an account of the rebellion after escaping abroad following the Battle of Culloden, and he joined the French army and fought at Louisbourg and Quebec. He died in 1800. Also see Houston.

Lochwood Tower [NY 085968] is a ruinous L-plan tower house, and dates from the fifteenth or sixteenth century. It stands five miles south of Moffat in Dumfries and Galloway, and was the main stronghold of the Johnstones of that Ilk, who held by the lands from the fourteenth century. The family were Wardens of the West March. Adam Johnstone, one of the lairds, fought against the English at the Battle of the Sark in 1448; he also took part in the actions against the Douglases, and gained more lands in 1455. A later laird, John Johnstone, fought at the Battle of Pinkie in 1547, and Lochwood Tower was held by the English from then for three years, but was later burnt by the Maxwells and by the Armstrongs in 1585. The Johnstones feuded with the Maxwells and, along with other Border families, defeated the Maxwells at the Battle of Dryfe Sands in 1593, killing Lord Maxwell, and the wounds given by the Johnstones became known as a 'Lockerbie Lick'. The feud continued, however, and Sir James Johnstone was slain in 1608 by the ninth Lord Maxwell. Another Sir James Johnstone was made Earl of Hartfell in 1643, and supported the Marquis of Montrose, and was at the Battles of Kilsyth and Philiphaugh, both in 1645. He was captured after the latter battle, and narrowly escaped execution; but in 1661, following the Restoration, he was made Earl of Annandale. Lochwood was abandoned around 1724, and the Johnstones married into the Hopes. The family is now Hope Johnstone Earls of Annandale and Hartfell, and they apparently live at nearby Raehills [NY 064943]. This is a large mansion, dating from 1728 but later modified and extended. It probably stands on the site of castle as there is a dated stone with 163?.

Lochhouse Tower [NT 082034] is a mile south of Moffat, and is a strong tower house, rising to three storeys and an attic, and dating from the sixteenth century. Lochhouse was held by the Johnstones of Corehead in the sixteenth and seventeenth centuries, and was restored in the 1980s. The tower is said to be haunted by the ghost of Lillias Johnstone, the then laird's

Lochhouse Tower (M&R)

sister. She fell in love with Walter French of Frenchland. Her brother and French had a furious argument during which Johnstone was slain. French fled abroad and when he returned he married another girl. Lillias wished for no other lover, and after her death her ghost reputedly returned to haunt the tower.

The Johnstones also owned:

Alva Castle [NS 901975], near Alva, Clackmannan; site of castle and mansion.
Held by several families, including by the Erskines, before being sold to the Johnstones of Westerhall in 1775, with whose descendants it remained until 1929. The lands were sold because of debt, and the house was demolished after being used by the army for target practice in World War II.

Auldton [NT 094058], near Moffat, Dumfries and Galloway; site of castle or tower house.
Held by the Moffats but passed to the Johnstones in 1608. The Johnstones had a long-running, bitter feud with the Moffats: Robert Moffat of Auldton was slain in 1557 and a house the Moffats were in was burned and they were slain as they tried to escape.

Blacklaw Tower [NT 052067], near Moffat, Dumfries and Galloway; slight remains of tower house.
Held by several families, including by the Johnstones in 1592.

Breconside Tower [NT 109022], near Moffat, Dumfries and Galloway; small altered tower house.
Held by the Johnstones and now a farmhouse.

Bridgemuir [NY 093845], near Lochmaben, Dumfries and Galloway; site of tower house.
Held by the Johnstones in the sixteenth century, but passed to the Charteris family, who were in possession at the end of the seventeenth century.

Buittle Place [NX 817616], near Dalbeattie, Dumfries and Galloway; L-plan tower house.
Held by the Balliols and by the Douglases, before passing to the Johnstones in 1455, then later went to the Maxwells in the sixteenth century and later to the Gordons.

Carnsalloch [NX 971803], near Dumfries; castle replaced by mansion.
Held by the Maxwells, then by the Johnstones, who were in possession in the nineteenth century, although the family, the Campbell Johnstons, now apparently live in Wiltshire in England.

Carriden House [NT 026808], near Bo'ness, West Lothian; altered tower house.

Held by several families, including latterly by the Hope Johnstones, two of whom were distinguished admirals. B&B accommodation is available and the house is suitable for weddings (01506 829811; www.carridenhouse.co.uk).

Cochrane Castle [NS 418616], near Johnstone, Renfrewshire; site of castle.

Held by the Cochranes, but bought by the Johnstones of Cochrane in about 1760.

Corehead [NT 072124], near Moffat, Dumfries and Galloway; site of tower house.

Held by the Johnstones.

Cornal Tower [NT 112044], near Moffat, Dumfries and Galloway; slight remains of tower.

Held by Carruthers of Mouswald, but passed to the Johnstones of Corehead, then to the Douglas Dukes of Queensberry after 1633.

Corrie [NY 197843], near Lockerbie, Dumfries and Galloway; site of tower house.

Held by the Corrie family, but had passed to the Johnstones of Corrie by the sixteenth century.

Craigieburn [NT 117053], near Moffat, Dumfries and Galloway; castle replaced by mansion.

Held by the Johnstones, but passed to the Lorimers. Craigieburn House dates from the eighteenth century, and the gardens are open to the public from Easter to October (01683 221250).

Craigiehall House [NT 167754], near Kirkliston, West Lothian; mansion on site of castle.

Held by the Stewarts and then by the Fairholmes, before passing by marriage to William Johnstone, second Earl of Annandale and first Marquis of Annandale, who built the house in 1699. The property passed to the Hopes of Hopetoun, then was later used by the army.

Curriehill Castle [NT 165678], near Balerno, Edinburgh; site of castle.

Held by the Skenes, then later by the Johnstones. Sir Archibald Johnston, Lord Warriston, served Oliver Cromwell as Lord Clerk Register and sat for a time in the House of Lords. At the Restoration he was forfeited and he fled abroad, but he was captured in France and was brought to Edinburgh and executed at the Market Cross in 1663.

Denovan [NS 820834], near Denny, Falkirk; site of castle or old house.

Held by the Forresters, then by the Johnstones of Alva, and then passed to the Forbeses of Callander in 1830.

Elphinstone Tower [NT 391698], near Tranent, East Lothian; much reduced keep or tower.

Held by the Elphinstones, but passed to the Johnstones in the fifteenth century. In 1545 George Wishart was brought from nearby Ormiston, and at Elphinstone was handed over to Cardinal Beaton, who took Wishart back to St Andrews for trial for heresy and execution by burning in 1546. The tower had to be demolished because of subsidence caused by old mine workings.

Elshieshields Tower [NY 069850], near Lochmaben, Dumfries and Galloway; L-plan tower house.

Held by the Johnstones, and burnt by Maxwell of Kirkhouse in 1602. The tower was restored and is still occupied.

Fairholm [NY 125812], near Lockerbie, Dumfries and Galloway; site of castle or old house.

Held by the Johnstones.

Glendinning Castle [NY 299965], near Langholm, Dumfries and Galloway; site of castle.

Long held by the Glendinning family, but passed to the Johnstones of Westerhall in the nineteenth century.

Halleaths [NY 099822], near Lockerbie, Dumfries and Galloway; site of mansion.

Held by the Gordons and then by the Johnstones.

Elshieshields Tower (M&R) – see previous column

Hilton [NT 881507], near Chirnside, Borders; site of castle or old house.

Held by the Johnstones from 1633. Archibald Johnstone, second of Hilton, was murdered in his bed by William Home, Sheriff of Berwickshire, in 1671. The two had argued after a dispute during a game of cards. Home took the argument to Johnstone's bedroom and stabbed him nine times. Johnstone had also been one of those involved in the abduction of the young heiress of Ayton and her subsequent marriage to the equally young Home of Kimmerghame, a matter that got them all, including the young couple, fined and imprisoned. The Johnstones held the lands until about 1800.

Holehouse [NS 897718], near Armadale, Dumfries and Galloway; altered tower house.

Held by the Johnstones in the sixteenth century.

Johnstounburn House [NT 460616], near Dalkeith, Midlothian; mansion on site of castle.

Probably held by the Johnstones in about 1250, but had passed to the Borthwicks by the seventeenth century, then went to the Browns and then to others. There is reputedly a tunnel from the building to Soutra Hill, which is about two miles away.

Keith Hall or **Caskieben** [NJ 787212], near Inverurie, Aberdeenshire; Z-plan tower house.

Held by the Garriochs, but passed by marriage to the Johnstones of Caskieben in the seventeenth century. They were made Baronets of Nova Scotia in 1626, but the property was sold to the Keiths in 1660 and they changed the name to Keith Hall. Arthur Johnstone, son of the then laird, studied medicine in Padua in 1624, and was a Latin poet and scholar; he became rector of King's College in Aberdeen in 1637. The line of the Johnstones of Caskieben, Baronets, continues.

Kimmerghame House [NT 815514], near Duns, Borders; castle replaced by mansion.

Held by the Sinclairs and then by the Homes in the sixteenth and seventeenth centuries, but later passed to the Johnstones then to the Swintons in the second half on the eighteenth century.

Kinnelhead Tower [NT 028017], near Moffat, Dumfries and Galloway; some remains of tower house.

Held by the Johnstones, apparently until 1965.

Kirkpatrick Tower [NY 275701], near Gretna, Dumfries and Galloway; site of tower house.

Held by the Edgars and by the Flemings, and probably by the Johnstones and by the Bells.

Kirkton Tower [NY 132838], near Lockerbie, Dumfries and Galloway; site of strong tower house.

Held by the Johnstones of Kirkton in the sixteenth century; many members of the family were buried at Kirkpatrick-Juxta.

Knock [NY 299908], near Langholm, Dumfries and Galloway; site of tower house.

Probably held by the Moffats, but was bought by the Johnstones in 1609 (although see Auldton above).

Knockhill or **Duke of Hoddom**s [NY 166740], near Lockerbie, Dumfries and Galloway; castle replaced by mansion.

Held by the Johnstones. Andrew Johnstone of Knockhill was transported to the West Indies for his part in the Jacobite Rising of 1745-46. He returned in 1777.

Lathrisk House [NO 273085], near Glenrothes, Fife; mansion on site of castle.

Held by the Setons of Parbroath, but passed to the Johnstones, who held the property from 1783 until the twentieth century.

Lockerbie Tower [NY 136815], Lockerbie; site of towers.

Held by the Johnstones. Two towers in the burgh were besieged and captured by the Earl of Morton in 1585. One tower withstood another attack in 1593 when Lord Maxwell attempted to capture and destroy it. The Johnstones surprised Lord Maxwell at the siege, and the Maxwells were defeated and Lord Maxwell slain at the Battle of Dryfe Sands, the wounds given by the Johnstones being known as a 'Lockerbie Lick'. The tower was later used as the town jail, and survived into the twentieth century. The new police station is built on the site.

Lunelly Tower [NY 197824], near Lockerbie, Dumfries and Galloway; slight remains of tower house.

Held by the Corries, but passed to the Johnstones in 1516 and they built the tower.

Marjoribanks [NY 077998], near Moffat, Dumfries and Galloway; site of castle or old house.

Held by the Marjoribanks family until 1630 when the property was bought by the Johnstones.

Mellingshaw Tower [NT 037088], near Moffat, Dumfries and Galloway; slight remains of tower house.

Held by the Johnstones.

Monzie Castle [NN 873245], near Crieff, Perthshire; altered L-plan tower house.

Held by the Scotts, by the Grahams and by the Campbells, before being bought by the Johnstones of Lathrisk in 1869. Open mid May until mid June (01764 653110).

Muirhead [NY 129818], near Lockerbie, Dumfries and Galloway; site of tower house.

Held by the Johnstones.

Netherplace [NY 137811], near Lockerbie, Dumfries and Galloway; site of strong tower.

Probably held by the Johnstones.

Newbie Castle [NY 174647], near Annan, Dumfries and Galloway; site of castle.

Held by the Corries, but sold to and passed to the Johnstones, although only after a prolonged dispute with the Corries.

Old Graitney [NY 312663], near Gretna, Dumfries and Galloway; site of castle.

Held by the Johnstones of Graitney, and was burnt by the Maxwells in 1585.

Pitkierie [NO 559060], near Anstruther, Fife; site of mansion.

Held by the Pitkerrie family but a Johnstone of Pitkierie is on record in 1767.

Poldean [NT 104001], near Moffat, Dumfries and Galloway; site of tower house.

Held by the Bells and by the Johnstones.

Raecleugh Tower [NT 038118], near Moffat, Dumfries and Galloway; slight remains of tower house.

Held by the Johnstones of Raecleugh.

Redhall Castle [NY 290694], near Gretna, Dumfries and Galloway; site of castle.

Held by the Flemings, then by the Johnstones.

Runstonfoote [NT 140085], near Moffat, Dumfries and Galloway; site of castle.

Held by the Johnstones.

Sarkbridge [NY 326669], near Gretna, Dumfries and Galloway; site of castle.

Held by the Johnstones.

Stonehouse Tower [NY 296682], near Gretna, Dumfries and Galloway; site of tower house.

Probably held by the Johnstones.

Tundergarth Castle [NY 176807], near Lockerbie, Dumfries and Galloway; site of castle.

Held by the Johnstones.

Wamphray Tower or **Leithenhall** [NY 128965], near Moffat, Dumfries and Galloway; site of tower house.

Held by the Corries, but passed to the Kirkpatricks then to the Johnstones in 1476. It was occupied by William Johnstone, the 'Galliard'. His horse-stealing raid and death, and Willie o' Kirkhill's subsequent revenge, are recorded in the old ballad 'The Lads of Wamphray'. John Johnstone of Wamphray was imprisoned in his own home for his part in the Jacobite Rising of 1745-46, and only escaped execution by changing places with a kinsman. The property was sold to the Hope Earl of Hopetoun in 1747, and the castle was abandoned at this time and became ruinous. The story goes that for some 300 years the building had a brownie. A new laird took over Wamphray, but managed to anger the brownie by giving it new clothes, and it departed, saying: 'Ca', cuttee, ca'! A' the luck o' Leithenha', Gangs wi' me to Bodsbeck Ha'!'

Warriston [NT 253757], Edinburgh; site of castle or old house.

Held by the Somervilles and by the Kincaids, but passed to the Johnstones. Sir Archibald Johnstone (as mentioned above), Lord Warriston, held the property, and was one of those who composed the National Covenant in 1638 and was a Lord of Session in 1641. He was involved in the Cromwellian government in the 1650s. After the Restoration in 1661, he was captured in France, imprisoned in the Tower of London and found guilty of treason, then taken to Edinburgh, where he was hanged in 1663. He lands and property were also forfeited in 1660, and the property passed to other families.

Waterton Castle [NJ 972305], near Ellon, Aberdeenshire; site of tower house.

Held by the Bannermans, but was bought by the Johnstones in 1611, then passed to the Forbeses.

Westerhall Tower or **Glendinning** [NY 320893], near Langholm, Dumfries and Galloway; altered tower house.

Held by the Johnstones of Westerhall, who owned the lands for more than 400 years. They were made Baronets of Nova Scotia in 1700. The Johnstones of Westerhall, Baronets, now apparently live in Leicestershire in England. In the old burial ground at Westerkirk is the Johnstone Mausoleum [NY 313904], which was built in 1790 and was designed by Robert Adam.

Westraw or **Westerhall** [NS 947429], near Lanark; old house.

Held by the Carmichaels, then by the Johnstones in the fifteenth and sixteenth centuries. The lands were sold in 1605, and the family moved to Glendinning in Dumfriesshire, which they renamed Westerhall.

www.johnstoneclan.org.uk
www.clanjohnston.org
www.johnston.asn.au
No. of castles/sites: 57
Rank: 18/764
Xref: Johnston

Kay

The name may be come from either a contraction of Mackay, or from an English family called 'Kay' or 'Kaye', which was recorded in England in the thirteenth century. This derivation for the English name may be from 'Kei', an early personal name from Welsh, and an alternative spelling is 'Keay'. The name is recorded in Scotland from the fourteenth century, and was not uncommon in Perthshire.

Snaigow House [NO 084430], four miles east of Dunkeld in Perthshire, may stand on the site of an earlier house or castle. There was a mansion dating from the 1820s, but this was demolished in the 1960s because of dry rot and replaced with the present classical mansion. The property was held by the Keays, but passed to the Coxes of Snaigow.

The site of **Edinbellie Castle** [NS 577890] is two miles east of Balfron in central Scotland, and Edinbellie was held by the Napiers of Merchiston. In 1750 the sons of Rob Roy MacGregor forcibly abducted Jean Kay from here. She was a young widow and heiress to Edinbellie, and was (probably) forced to marry Robin Oig MacGregor, or she may have done so of her own accord. When she died, her family protested to the authorities as the lands then passed to the MacGregors, and Robin Oig was hanged three years later.

No. of castles/sites: 2
Rank: 396=/764
Xref: Keay

Keith

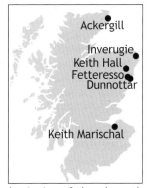

The name is territorial and comes from the lands of Keith, which are a few miles south of Pencaitland in East Lothian. There are legends concerning the origins of the family. One is that they are descended from the Catti who came from Germany and then arrived in Scotland at the beginning of the eleventh century. One of the Catti then slew a Danish leader at the Battle of Barrie in 1010. A few years later Malcolm II took Lothian after the Battle of Carham in 1018, and the Catti were rewarded with the lands of Keith in East Lothian. Alternatively, the Keiths comes from a Norman called Hervey, who married an heiress and held the lands from the middle of the twelfth century. The Keiths became very powerful and held lands from East Lothian in the south to Caithness in the north.

Keith Marischal [NT 449643] is three miles south of Pencaitland in East Lothian, is a very altered and extended L-plan tower house, dating from the sixteenth

Keith Marischal (M&R)

century. An older castle was built by the Keiths, who had been made Marischals from the fourteenth century or earlier. This important office involved ensuring the monarch's safety within parliament and looking after the royal regalia. Sir Robert Keith was a friend and supporter of Robert the Bruce, and he was given Hallforest in Aberdeenshire. He commanded the Scottish horse at Bannockburn but was killed at the Battle of Neville's Cross in 1346. The Keiths were made Earls Marischal in 1458 and became extremely powerful and owned extensive estates after marrying heiresses. George Keith, fourth Earl Marischal, negotiated James VI's marriage to Anne of Denmark, and in gratitude to the King of Denmark sent him a ship-load of timber to be used in the building of Keith Marischal. Agnes Simpson lived at Keith Marischal. She was accused of witchcraft by James VI, who charged her with raising a storm to drown him and his new bride on their way home from Denmark, as well as being responsible for the death of Archibald Douglas, eighth Earl of Angus. After torture the unfortunate woman confessed, and she was strangled, then burnt. Keith Marischal is still occupied.

Dunnottar Castle [NO 882839] is one of the most fabulous castles in Scotland, and stands on a cliff-girt promontory above the sea, a couple of miles south of Stonehaven in Kincardineshire. There was a stronghold in the twelfth century, and the present ruinous buildings include a tower, courtyard, chapel and the entrance into the castle up a steep ascent and then through a tunnel. The property was held by the Keiths from 1382 after they exchanged their property of Struthers with the Lindsays for Dunnottar. Dunnottar already had a long history. Donald, King of Scots, was slain here by Vikings in 900, and William Wallace captured the castle from the English in 1296, reputedly slaughtering 4000 men. William Keith, fifth Earl Marischal, was a noted scholar, and founded Marischal College in Aberdeen, now part of the University of Aberdeen. By the beginning of the sixteenth century, Dunnottar was one of the strongest fortresses in Scotland. Mary, Queen of Scots, stayed here in 1562, and the Marquis of Montrose unsuccessfully besieged Dunnottar in 1645. William, ninth Earl, entertained King Charles II here in 1650, and in 1651 the Scottish regalia was brought here for safekeeping when Cromwell invaded. General Lambert and Cromwell's forces besieged the castle in 1652, but the castle was only reduced after eight months by starvation and mutiny. The regalia and state papers were smuggled out to be hidden in nearby Kinneff Church until recovered at the Restoration. The garrison of the castle had been commanded by Sir Robert Keith, fourth son of the sixth Earl Marischal, and he was made Earl of Kintore in 1677. William, seventh Earl Marischal, was captured and imprisoned in the Tower of London until released at the Restoration. In 1685 Covenanters, numbering some 167 women and men, were forced into one of the cellars and nine died while twenty-five escaped; there is a memorial in Dunnottar Parish Church to those who perished. The castle was held for William and Mary in 1689 and many Jacobites were imprisoned here. George,

tenth Earl Marischal, joined the Jacobite Rising of 1715, and was subsequently forfeited. The Duke of Argyll partly destroyed Dunnottar in 1716, and it was more fully slighted two years later. The Earl Marischal became the Prussian ambassador to the Court of France and Governor of Neufchatel, and his brother, James Keith, rose to the rank of Major-General in the Russian army and Field Marshall in the service of Frederick of Prussia in 1747. He was killed at Hochkirch in 1758.

Dunnottar Parish Church [NO 863852] was begun by the Keiths, but the present building dates from 1782. The Marischal Aisle, built by the fifth Earl in 1582, was restored by Marischal College in Aberdeen in 1913 (also see above), and many of the Keiths were buried here. There is also the poignantly sad carved memorial of 1622 to Mary Keith, the young daughter of William, fifth Earl Marischal, in St Marnoch's Church at Benholm [NO 804692]. Death, in the form of skeleton, has been carved stabbing the Earl and his wife through the chest with spears.

Sightings of several ghosts have been reported at Dunnottar, including the apparition of a teenage girl in a dull plaid dress; a young deer hound; a tall Scandinavian-looking man; and noises of a meeting coming from Benholm's Lodging when the building was empty. The castle is open to the public all year (01569 762173; www.dunechtestates.co.uk).

Keith Hall [NJ 787212], once known as **Caskieben**, is a mile to the south-east of Inverurie in Aberdeenshire, and is a Z-plan tower house, dating from the sixteenth century but extended by a large mansion in 1662. The property was held by the Leslies, by the Garriochs and by the Johnstones, before being sold to the Keiths about 1660. This branch of the family were made Earls of Kintore in 1671 after they had ensured that the Scottish regalia had not fallen into the hands of Cromwell's forces at Dunnottar. William Keith, second Earl of Kintore, was a Jacobite and fought at the Battle of Sheriffmuir in 1715. The family are still Earls of Kintore and apparently still live at Keith Hall, although the castle has been divided into separate flats and residences.

Ackergill Tower [ND 352547], which stands a couple of miles north of Wick in Caithness, is a very impressive tower and mansion, dating from the fifteenth century and rising to five storeys. The property was held by the Cheynes, but passed to the Keith Earls Marischal about

Dunnottar Castle (M&R)   *Ackergill Tower 1910?*

1350. The Keiths had a long and very bitter feud with the Gunns. This reputedly started when Dugald Keith desired Helen Gunn of Braemore, and seized her from her father's house, killing many of her folk and carrying her off to Ackergill. Helen was a great beauty, but she wanted nothing to do with Keith. When her position became hopeless, she threw herself from the top of the tower and was killed. Her ghost, a 'Green Lady', is said to have began to haunt the castle from that day. Whatever the truth of its origins, the feud was very bloody. The Gunns ravaged the Keiths' lands, but were defeated at battles at Tannach Moor in 1438, and again at Dirlot in 1464. The chief of the Gunns and four of his sons were killed. Another Gunn chief, Justiciar of Caithness, was 'basely' murdered by the Keiths in 1478. James Gunn slew Keith of Ackergill and his son, at Drummoy, in revenge in 1518. The Keiths also had trouble with the great family of Sinclair. Alexander Keith of Ackergill was kidnapped by the Sinclair Earl of Caithness, and in 1556 the castle was besieged by the Sinclairs, before being sold to them in 1612; Sir Robert Keith of Benholm had also attacked the castle in a family dispute. Ackergill later passed to the Oliphants and then to the Dunbars of Hempriggs. The castle can be hired for totally exclusive use (01955 603556; www.ackergill-tower.co.uk).

The Keiths also owned:

Aboyne Castle [NO 526995], near Aboyne, Aberdeenshire; tall tower house.
Held by the Bissets, by the Frasers and then by the Keiths from 1335, but by the early fifteenth century had passed to the Gordons. The castle is still occupied.

Aden House [NJ 981479], near Peterhead, Aberdeenshire; ruined mansion on site of castle.
Held by the Keiths, but passed to the Russells of Montcoffer in 1758. The lands are now a country park (01771 622807; www.aberdeenshire.gov.uk/heritage).

Badenheath Castle [NS 713724], near Cumbernauld, Lanarkshire; site of castle.
Held by the Boyds, then by the Keiths from 1708.

Balbithan House [NJ 812189], near Inverurie, Aberdeenshire; fine L-plan tower house.
Held by the Chalmers family and by others, before passing to the Keith Earls of Kintore in 1859. Still occupied.

Barmagachan [NX 613494], near Kirkcudbright, Dumfries and Galloway; old house.
Held by the Keiths, but passed by marriage to the Muirs in 1459, then went to the MacLellans.

Benholm Castle [NO 804705], near Inverbervie, Aberdeenshire; ruinous keep or tower.
Held by the Lundies, by the Ogilvies, and then by the Keith Earls Marischal. It was from Benholm that the fifth Earl's widow stole money and jewels 'to a great amount' in 1623. The property was sold to the Scotts in 1623. Has been, or is about to be, restored, and said to be haunted.

Benholm's Lodging [NJ 936089], Aberdeen; altered Z-plan tower house.
Held by the Keiths of Benholm, and built by Sir Robert Keith of Benholm, brother to William, fifth Earl Marischal. There was a dispute in the family over property, and Sir Robert seized and garrisoned Deer Abbey, and besieged his brother's castle of Ackergill in Caithness.

Boddam Castle [NK 133419], near Peterhead, Aberdeenshire; ruinous courtyard castle.
Held by the Keiths of Ludquharn, who were later made Baronets of Nova Scotia. In the eighteenth century Sir William

Keith of Ludquharn was Surveyor General for the Southern District of the Americas and also became Lieutenant Governor of Pennsylvania, although he was later to die in poverty. Others of his family were Jacobites, who fought in the Rising of 1715.

Castle of Troup [NJ 838663], near Rosehearty, Aberdeenshire; site of castle within Iron Age fort.
Held by the Troups but may have passed by marriage to the Keiths before being sold to the Gardynes in 1654. The castle was replaced by Troup House.

Clackriach Castle [NJ 933471], near Ellon, Aberdeenshire; slight remains of castle.
Held by the Keiths.

Covington Castle [NS 975399], near Lanark; ruinous castle.
Held by the Keith Earls Marischal from the beginning of the fourteenth century until 1368 when Covington went to the Lindsays and then to others.

Crichie [NJ 978453], near Mintlaw, Aberdeenshire; site of castle or old house.
Held by the Leslies, by the Keiths and by the Grays before passing to the Stewarts in 1709.

Fetteresso Castle [NO 843855], near Stonehaven, Kincardineshire; mansion on site of castle.
Held by the Strachans, but passed by marriage to the Keith Earls Marischal in the fourteenth century, and they built the

Fetteresso Castle 1910?

castle. Fetteresso was torched by the Marquis of Montrose in 1645. James VIII, the old Pretender, stayed here over Christmas 1715 during the Jacobite Rising; the Keiths were forfeited for being Jacobites. The castle had been completely rebuilt in 1671, later passed to the Duffs, and has since been divided into separate flats. The castle is said to be haunted by a Green Lady, and manifestations include an apparition with a baby in her arms and the sounds of unexplained footsteps. There are also stories of a tunnel linking Fetteresso to a house in Stonehaven and to Dunnottar Castle.

Forse Castle [ND 224338], near Dunbeath, Caithness; remains of castle.
Held by the Cheynes, but passed to the Keiths, then to the Sutherlands.

Grandhome House or **Dilspro** [NJ 899117], near Dyce, Aberdeenshire; mansion incorporating old work.
Held by the Keiths, then by the Ogilvies and by others.

Hallforest Castle [NJ 777154], near Inverurie, Aberdeenshire; ruinous castle.
Held by the Keith Earls Marischal from 1309. The castle was visited by Mary, Queen of Scots, in 1562. Hallforest was used until about 1639, and is said to have often been attacked in the fighting before and during the Civil War in the seventeenth century.

House of Auchiries [NJ 977606], near Fraserburgh, Aberdeenshire; old house.
Held by the Keith Earls Marischal in the seventeenth century, but sold to the Ogilvies in 1703, then later went to the Forbeses. Part is used as a farm while other parts are ruinous.

Inverugie Castle [NK 102484], near Peterhead, Aberdeenshire; ruinous castle.

Held by the Cheynes, but passed by marriage to the Keith Earls Marischal. The Keiths were Jacobites, and were forfeited and forced into exile after the Jacobite Rising of 1715. As mentioned above, James Keith, born at Inverugie in 1696,

Inverugie Castle 1910?

rose to the rank of Major-General in the Russian army and Field Marshall in the service of Frederick of Prussia in 1747.

Keith Inch Tower [NK 138458], near Peterhead, Aberdeenshire; site of L-plan tower house.

Held by the Keith Earls Marischal, but passed to the Arbuthnotts after the 1715 Jacobite Rising.

Kintore Castle [NJ 794163], near Inverurie, Aberdeenshire; site of castle.

Held by the Keiths from 1309. The family were made Earls of Kintore in 1677 after Sir Robert Keith, fourth son of the sixth Earl Marischal, had led the garrison at the siege of Dunnottar Castle.

Kirktonhill [NO 692659], near Montrose, Angus; site of castle and mansion.

Held by the Keiths, but owned by the Taylors from the eighteenth century.

Ludquharn [NK 035455], near Peterhead, Aberdeenshire; site of castle.

Held by the Keiths, who built Boddam Castle.

Old Maud [NJ 917469], near Maud, Aberdeenshire; site of castle.

Held by the Keith Earls Marischal. The site of castle was destroyed when the railway was built, although the railway is now dismantled.

Phesdo [NO 676756], near Laurencekirk, Kincardineshire; castle replaced by mansion.

Held by the Keiths of Phesdo in the seventeenth century, but passed to the Falconers of Haulkerton, then to the Crombies and to the Gladstones of Fasque. Phesdo House is a large two-storey house, which dates from the beginning of the nineteenth century.

Pitmedden House [NJ 885281], near Ellon, Aberdeenshire; mansion on site of castle.

Held by several families including by the Keiths, and there is a five-acre walled garden, which is open to the public from May to September (01651 842352; www.nts.org.uk).

Pittendrum [NJ 964670], near Fraserburgh, Aberdeenshire; castle replaced by mansion.

Held by the Comyns, then by the Keiths of Pittendrum in the sixteenth century, then by the Grays in the next century.

Ravelston House [NT 217741], Edinburgh; slight remains of castle.

Held by the Foulis family but passed to the Keiths in 1726. The newer house is now part of Mary Erskine's School.

Ravenscraig Castle [NK 095488], near Peterhead, Aberdeenshire; ruinous L-plan tower house.

Held by the Cheynes, but passed by marriage to the Keiths of Inverugie in the fourteenth century, and they built the castle. James VI visited in 1589.

Rickarton [NO 838886], near Stonehaven, Kincardineshire; castle replaced by mansion.

Held by the Rickarton family, then by the Hepburns and by the Bairds of Urie (then Keiths from the 1930s) Viscounts Stonehaven from 1870.

Sorn Castle [NS 548269], near Mauchline, Ayrshire; altered castle.

Held by the Keiths of Galston. Sir William Keith of Galston was one of the knights who returned from Spain with the heart of Robert the Bruce and took it to Melrose Abbey where it is still buried. Sorn passed to the Hamiltons of Cadzow in 1406, and then went to others. The castle is open some days in the summer (01290 551555).

Struthers Castle [NO 377097], near Cupar, Fife; ruinous L-plan tower house.

Held by the Keiths, but was exchanged for Dunnottar with the Lindsays of The Byres. On the face of it does not seem a very even swop...

Tannadyce House [NO 484577], near Forfar, Angus; castle or old house replaced by mansion.

Held by the Keiths but passed to the Lyons in the fourteenth century.

Urie House [NO 860877], near Stonehaven, Kincardineshire; mansion incorporating castle.

Held by the Frasers, but passed by marriage to the Keiths, then was sold to the Hays of Errol in 1415. In 1647 it was bought back by the Keiths, then went to the Barclays of Mathers, then to the Bairds.

Usan House [NO 723553], near Montrose, Angus; mansion on site of castle.

Held by the Leightons, but passed to the Scotts and then to the Keiths, and then to others.

www.thekeithclan.com / www.clankeith.org
www.keithclan.com / www.clankeithusa.org
No. of castles/sites: 38 / Rank: 29=/764

Kelloe

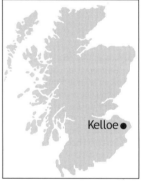

The name is territorial and comes from the lands of Kelloe, which are a couple of miles east of Duns in Berwickshire in the Borders. John Kello was the minister of Spott in East Lothian when he strangled his wife and then impaled her on a meat hook. He then went on to take services and preach sermons before confessing; he was hanged in 1570. Kelloe Bastle [NT 828543] was a small tower hour or bastle, and the site is in a field. The property was held by the Kelloe or Kelly family, but had passed to the Buchans by the eighteenth century. Kelloe, a mansion, was held by the Fordyce-Buchans in the nineteenth century.

No. of castles/sites: 1 / Rank: 537=/764
Xrefs: Kello; Kellow

Kelly

The name is territorial and comes from the lands of Kelly, which are a couple of miles west of Arbroath in Angus, although there are also lands of the same name in Fife and in Renfrew. It may also possibly be from Kelloe (see that name). Kelly is also a very popular surname in Ireland, and comes from 'O'Caellaigh', meaning 'son of Ceallach', a personal name which may mean 'strife'. **Kellie Castle** [NO 608402] is a fine keep or tower, dating from the fifteenth century, extended to L-plan and forming one corner of a courtyard. The lands were held by the Mowbrays but probably also by the Kelly family, before passing to the Stewarts, then in 1402 to the Ochterlony family and then to others. The castle is still occupied.

www.kellycln.com
No. of castles/sites: 1
Rank: 537=/764
Xref: Kellie

Kelso

The name comes from the burgh of Kelso, which is in the Borders, and the name is mentioned from about 1200.

Kelsoland or **Brisbane** [NS 209622] is a couple of miles north of Largs in Ayrshire and was a four-storey mansion, dating from the seventeenth century, but built on the site of an old stronghold. The lands belonged to the Kelso family from the thirteenth century, but were sold to the Shaws of Greenock in 1624, and they built the house ten years later. The property was bought back by the Kelso family in 1650, but in 1671 was sold to the Brisbanes of Bishopton, and they changed the name to Brisbane House. The Brisbanes held the property until the twentieth century, but the house was unroofed in the 1930s and has been mostly demolished.

No. of castles/sites: 1
Rank: 537=/764

Kemp

The name is believed to come from Norse 'kempa' or Old English 'cempa' and means 'warrior champion'. The name is on record in Scotland from the beginning of the fifteenth century. George Meikle Kemp was the architect of the Scott Monument in Edinburgh; he died in 1844.

Durie House [NO 372025], one mile north of Leven in Fife, is a three-storey classical mansion dating from 1762 and is built on the site of castle. The lands were long held by the Duries, but were for a time a property of Sir Alexander Kemp, a favourite of James V, who then apparently took the surname Durie. The Duries were later forfeited and the property was sold to the Gibsons in 1614 and then in the eighteenth century to the Christies. The house is still occupied.

No. of castles/sites: 1 / Rank: 537=/764

Kene

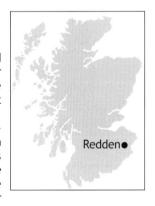

A family of this name held the lands of Redden (or Reveden), which are three and a half miles north-east of Kelso in the Borders, perhaps being in possession from the thirteenth century, although there is said to have been a grange of Kelso Abbey here. There was probably a tower house somewhere near the present farm of **Redden** [NT 786375]. John Kene of Redden was a writer to the signet in 1609, but the property had passed to the Kerrs by the middle of the seventeenth century.

No. of castles/sites: 1 / Rank: 537=/764

Brisbane (Kelsoland) (M&R) – see previous column (Kelso)

301

Kennedy

The name comes from the Gaelic for 'ugly headed', and the family claim descent from the Earls of Carrick, of whom sprang Robert the Bruce; the title Earl of Carrick is now one of those held by Prince Charles. The Kennedys had considerable possessions in the south part of Ayrshire, and were known as the 'Kings of Carrick', as well as holding lands in Galloway. They were also prominent in Ireland.

Dunure Castle [NS 253158] stands on a rocky promontory above the sea, five or so miles north west of Maybole in Ayrshire, and is now a shattered ruin. It was held by the Kennedys from 1360 or so, and James

Dunure Castle (M&R)

Kennedy married Mary, daughter of Robert III; their son, another James, was Bishop of St Andrews and founded St Salvator's College. John Kennedy of Dunure founded Maybole Collegiate Church [NS 301098] in 1384 in the existing parish church, and the remains of the building were used as a burial aisle by the Kennedys. David, third Lord Kennedy, was made Earl of Cassillis in 1509, but was killed at the Battle of Flodden in 1513 (the family's main stronghold was by now Cassillis: see below). In 1570 Allan Stewart, Commendator of Crossraguel Abbey, was roasted in sop at Dunure by the Kennedys until he signed the lands of the abbey over to them (the Kennedys had in fact donated most of the property to the abbey in the first place). Gilbert Kennedy of Bargany, an enemy of Cassillis, stormed the castle and rescued the Commendator, apparently doing some damage to the buildings. This led to a feud with the Kennedys of Bargany. Dunure may have been blown up sometime around the middle of the seventeenth century, and it appears to have been systematically dismantled. Ghostly cries have reputedly been heard coming from the chamber in which Allan Stewart was roasted. The ruins are accessible.

Cassillis House [NS 341128], three miles north-east of Maybole, is a strong keep or tower to which extensions were made in the seventeenth century and again in 1830. The lands were held by the Montgomerys, but passed to the Kennedys in 1373. Gilbert, second Earl of Cassillis, was assassinated in 1527 by Sir Hugh Campbell of Loudoun, Sheriff of Ayr. Gilbert, third Earl, was captured

Cassillis House (M&R)

at the Battle of Solway Moss by the English in 1542. He was Treasurer from 1554 until his death, probably by being poisoned, at Dieppe when a commissioner for the marriage of Mary, Queen of Scots, to the Dauphin of France. Another son of the second Earl was Quentin Kennedy, commendator of Crossraguel Abbey, condemned abuses within the church but he argued with John Knox and other Protestant reformers. The fourth Earl, another Gilbert, fought for Mary at the Battle of Langside in 1568. In 1570 the Earl went on to boil the Commendator of Crossraguel Abbey, Allan Stewart, in sop to persuade him to sign over the lands of the abbey. In 1601 John, fifth Earl, with 200 men, ambushed and murdered Gilbert Kennedy of Bargany in a snow-storm, during a dispute over land, but deviously escaped punishment. Bargany's son-in-law, John Mure of Auchendrane, took his revenge by slaying Sir Thomas Kennedy of Culzean, younger son of the Earl of Cassillis. Mure and his son were less lucky than the Earl, and were caught, tried and executed in 1611. This inspired Sir Walter Scott's play *Auchendrane*, or *The Ayrshire Tragedy*. John, sixth Earl, was Justice General 1649, and supported the Presbyterian cause during the Restoration. Archibald, twelfth Earl, was created first Marquis of Ailsa in 1831. Cassillis was the main seat of the Kennedys until the 1770s when they moved to their splendid new mansion of Culzean.

One story is that Cassillis House is haunted by the ghost of Lady Jean Hamilton, wife of John, sixth Earl. It is said that her apparition has been seen at a window. The tale behind the haunting (which does not appear to have any historical basis) is that Lady Jean was in love with Johnie Faa, the gypsy laddie of the old ballad. They ran off together, but the Earl was having none of it, pursued and caught them, and hanged Johnie from a tree and made his wife watch.

The family returned to Cassillis in the 1940s, and the house is still occupied by the Kennedy Marquis of Ailsa and Earl of Cassillis.

Culzean Castle [NS 233103], four and a half miles west of Maybole, is a magnificent mansion, which was built by the architect Robert Adam and dates from the end of the eighteenth century. The building incorporates parts of a sixteenth-century L-plan tower house. The elegant interior includes the spectacular Oval Staircase and the Circular Saloon. The Kennedys owned the lands from the twelfth century. Thomas Kennedy of Culzean was murdered by John Mure of Auchendrane in the course of a feud after the slaying of Gilbert Kennedy of Bargany. The castle was completely rebuilt for the Earls of Cassillis, and apartments within the building were reserved for use by President Dwight Eisenhower for his services to Britain during World War II. The castle has several ghost stories, including the apparition of a young woman and tales of a ghostly piper who plays on stormy nights and to herald events in the family. Culzean passed to The National Trust for Scotland in 1945, and stands in a country park (01655 884455; www.culzean castle.net).

The Kennedys also owned:

Ailsa Craig Castle [NX 023995], island in the Firth of Clyde; ruinous tower house.
Held by the Kennedys from after the Reformation, and they built the castle. It is from the island that the Marquises of Ailsa take their title. In 1597 Ailsa Craig was captured by Hugh Barclay of Ladyland and held for the Spanish. The island can be visited (01465 713219; www.ailsacraig.org.uk).

Ardmillan Castle [NX 169945], near Girvan, Ayrshire; ruinous tower house.
Held by the Kennedys of Bargany from 1476 or earlier, and was visited by Mary, Queen of Scots, in 1563. It passed to the Crawfords of Baidland in 1658, but the castle was burned out in the twentieth century.

Ardstinchar Castle [NX 086824], near Ballantrae, Ayrshire; some remains of castle.
Held by the Kennedys and built about 1450. Hugh Kennedy of Ardstinchar fought for Joan of Arc at the siege of Orleans in France. Ardstinchar was visited by Mary, Queen of Scots, in 1563. In 1601 Gilbert Kennedy, sixteenth laird of Bargany and Ardstinchar, was slain by the Earl of Cassillis over a dispute about lands. Much of the castle was demolished about 1770.

Auchtyfardle Castle [NS 826409], near Lesmahagow, Lanarkshire; site of castle.
Held by the Dowane family and by the Weirs before passing to the Kennedys.

Balneil [NX 179639], near Glenluce, Galloway; site of castle.
Held by the Kennedy Earls of Cassillis, before passing to the Vauxs of Barnbarroch, then to others.

Balsarroch House [NW 994691], near Leswalt, Galloway; ruinous house with old work.
Held by the Kennedys in the seventeenth century, but passed to the Rosses.

Baltersan Castle [NS 282087], near Maybole, Ayrshire; L-plan tower house.
Held by the Kennedys of Pennyglen; the lands had passed from

Baltersan Castle (M&R)

Crossraguel Abbey after the commendator had been tortured. The castle is to be restored (www.baltersan.com).

Barbieston [NS 368142], near Maybole, Ayrshire; site of castle and mansion.
Held by the Dalrymples, but passed to the Kennedys, later Earls of Cassillis, in the later part of the fourteenth century.

Barclanachan or **Kilkerran** [NS 305030], near Maybole, Ayrshire; castle replaced by mansion.
Held by the Kennedys until 1686 when sold to the Fergussons. Still occupied.

Bargany Castle [NS 244003], near Girvan, Ayrshire; castle replaced by mansion.
Held by the Kennedys. Gilbert Kennedy of Bargany was murdered by the Kennedy fourth Earl of Cassillis in 1601 during a dispute over land. The gardens of the mansion are open from March to October (01465 871249).

Blairquhan [NS 367055], near Maybole, Ayrshire; fine mansion incorporating castle.
Held by the MacWhurters, then by the Kennedys in the fifteenth century, then by the Whitefoords in 1623. It is now owned by the Hunter Blairs and is open to the public (01655 770239; www.blairquhan.co.uk).

Brockloch Castle [NS 289113], near Maybole, Ayrshire; site of L-plan tower house.
Held by the Kennedys. It was nearby that the Earl of Cassillis ambushed and mortally wounded Gilbert Kennedy of Bargany.

Brunston Castle [NS 261012], near Girvan, Ayrshire; slight remains of tower house.
Held by the Kennedys. 'Black Bessie' Kennedy lived here after the death of her third husband, William Baillie of Carrick. Her relatives, the Bargany branch and the Earls of Cassillis, had a long and bitter quarrel over the possession of Bessie and her lands, which ended with the murder of Gilbert Kennedy of Bargany in 1601.

Carlock [NX 095770], near Ballantrae, Ayrshire; site of castle.
Held by the Kennedys in 1696.

Castle Kennedy [NX 111609], near Stranraer, Galloway; fine ruinous tower house.
Held by the Kennedys from 1482, and the castle was built by the fifth Earl of Cassillis. It passed to the Hamiltons, then to the Dalrymples of Stair. It was gutted by fire in 1716, and the Dalrymples built the nearby fabulous Lochinch Castle. Castle Kennedy remains a ruin and stands in fine gardens, which are open from April to September (01776 702024; www.castle kennedygardens.co.uk).

Castle Kennedy (LF) – see previous page

Dalquharran Castle (M&R) – see previous column

Craigneil Castle [NX 147853], near Ballantrae, Ayrshire; ruinous castle.

Held by the Kennedys. Robert Bruce is said to have sheltered here during the Wars of Independence. It was used by the Kennedys when travelling between Cassillis and Castle Kennedy, but is said to have then been a prison and a place of execution. The property had passed to the MacConnels of Knockdolian by the end of the nineteenth century.

Craigoch [NX 305467], near Glenluce, Galloway; site of castle.

May have been held by the Kennedys.

Craigoch Castle [NX 013668], near Leswalt, Galloway; site of tower.

May have been held by the Kennedys.

Craigskean [NS 299149], near Maybole, Ayrshire; site of castle.

Held by the Kennedys.

Crossraguel Abbey [NS 275084], near Maybole, Ayrshire; ruinous abbey with tower house.

Held by the Kennedys after the Reformation following the roasting of the commendator Allan Stewart by the Earls of Cassillis. In the care of Historic Scotland and open to the public from April to September (01655 883113).

Cruggleton Castle [NX 484428], near Garlieston, Galloway; slight remains of a courtyard castle.

Held by several families, including by James Kennedy, who was denounced as an outlaw after he seized Alexander Myrton and imprisoned him in the castle dungeon.

Cumstoun Castle [NX 683533], near Kirkcudbright, Galloway; some remains of tower house.

Held by the Kennedys, then the by MacLellans and by others.

Daljarroch or **Daljarrock** [NX 196882], near Girvan, Ayrshire; mansion on site of castle.

Held by the Kennedys in the seventeenth and eighteenth centuries. Alexander Kennedy of Daljarrock, along with his sons and wife, was in 1609 charged with waylaying Andro McChrutter with a view to killing him.

Dalquharran Castle [NS 273019], near Girvan, Ayrshire; ruinous castle and mansion.

Held by the Kennedys of Culzean.

Drummellan Castle [NS 298032], near Maybole, Ayrshire; site of castle.

Held by the Kennedys from the fourteenth century.

Ellon Castle [NJ 960307], Ellon, Aberdeenshire; ruinous castle.

Held by the Comyns, but passed to the Kennedys of Kermuck (or Kinmuck). They were outlawed for the murder of John Forbes of Waterton in 1652, and the property was sold to the Gordons.

Fergus Loch [NS 395183], near Ayr; site of castle.

Held by the Kennedy Earls of Cassillis.

Glenays Castle [NS 285180], near Ayr; site of castle.

Held by the Montgomerys of Bridgend and by the Kennedys.

Greenan Castle [NS 312193], near Ayr, Ayrshire; ruinous tower house by the sea.

Held by the Davidsons but was sold to the Kennedys in 1588. Sir Thomas of Kennedy of Culzean, younger son of the Earl of Cassillis, spent his last night at Greenan in 1602 before being murdered by John Mure of Auchendrane; Mure was executed in 1611 for the deed. Greenan has been suggested as the site of King Arthur's Camelot.

Inch Crindil [NX 104608], near Stranraer, Galloway; site of castle.

Held by the Kennedys from 1482, and used by them until they moved to Castle Kennedy in 1607.

Kilhenzie Castle [NS 308082], near Maybole, Ayrshire; altered tower house.

Held by the Bairds but passed to the Kennedys in the seventeenth century.

Kinmuck or **Kermuck Castle** [NJ 988353], near Ellon, Aberdeenshire; site of castle.

Held by the Kennedys of Kermuck from 1413, and materials from the stronghold were used to build Ellon Castle.

Kirkhill Castle [NX 146859], near Ballantrae, Ayrshire; ruinous L-plan tower house.

Held by the Kennedys of Bargany. One of the family was Sir Thomas Kennedy of Kirkhill, Lord Provost of Edinburgh in 1680. Kirkhill was sold to the Bartons in 1843.

Kirkintilloch Peel [NS 651740], Kirkintilloch, Dunbartonshire

Held by the Comyns and by the Flemings, but was bought by the Kennedys in 1747.

Kirkmichael House [NS 342085], near Maybole, Ayrshire; mansion incorporating part of castle.

Held by the Kilpatricks, but had passed to the Shaw-Kennedys by the end of the nineteenth century. Now used as a school.

Knockdaw Castle [NX 151896], near Ballantrae, Ayrshire; site of tower house.

Held by the Kennedys.

Knockdon Castle [NS 305132], near Maybole, Ayrshire; site of castle.

Held by the Kennedys.

Knockgray [NX 578932], near Carsphairn, Galloway; house on site of castle.

Held by the Gordons, but passed to the Kennedys after 1679, and they still apparently live here.

Knocknalling [NX 597848], near St John's Town of Dalry, Galloway; site of castle or old house.

Held by the Kennedys in 1450.

Lochmodie Castle [NS 263024], near Maybole, Ayrshire; castle site.

Probably held by the Kennedys.

Maybole Castle [NS 301100], Maybole, Ayrshire; altered L-plan tower house.

Held and built by the Kennedys. This is another location given for the hanging of Johnie Faa, the gypsy laddie (Cassillis being the other). The building is used as the factor house for the estates of the Kennedy Marquises of Ailsa. Maybole formerly had several fine town houses, including those of Kennedy of Knockdaw, Kennedy of Culzean, and Kennedy of Ballimore. John Kennedy of Dunure founded Maybole Collegiate Church [NS 301098] in 1384 in the existing parish church, and the remains of the building were used as a burial aisle by the Kennedys Earls of Cassillis and the family.

Maybole Castle (RWB) – see previous page

Newark Castle [NS 324173], Ayr; altered tower house.
    Held by the Kennedys of Bargany. Mary, Queen of Scots, may have stayed here after the Battle of Langside in 1568. The property passed to the Crawfords of Camlarg, but was bought by the Kennedy Earls of Cassillis in 1763.
Old Halls of Craig [NX 172598], near Glenluce, Galloway; site of castle.
    Held by the Kennedys until sold in 1615.
Pinwherry Castle [NX 198867], near Ballantrae, Ayrshire; ruinous L-plan tower house.
    Held by the Kennedys until sold to the Pollocks in 1644.
Ravenstone Castle [NX 409441], near Whithorn, Galloway; altered tower house.
    Held by the MacDowalls, but passed to the MacLellans and then to the Kennedys, then to the Stewarts and to others.
Romanno Tower [NT 167483], near West Linton, Borders; castle replaced by mansion.
    Held by the Romanes family and by the Murrays, then by the Penicuiks of Newhall, before being bought by the Kennedys in 1720 and they still held it in the nineteenth century.
Sinniness Castle [NX 215532], near Glenluce, Galloway; slight remains of tower house.
    Held by the Kennedys, but passed to the Dalrymples of Stair.
Skeldon Castle [NS 378138], near Maybole, Ayrshire; remains of castle built into cottage.
    Held by the Mures, then by the Kennedys and by the Campbells, then later by the Fullartons. A mansion was built nearby.
Stair [NS 442239], near Tarbolton, Ayrshire; fine L-plan tower house.
    Held by the Montgomerys, then by the Kennedys of Dunure in the fourteenth century, then passed to the Dalrymples of Stair in 1421.
Stranraer Castle or **Castle of St John** [NX 061608], Stranraer, Galloway; restored L-plan tower house.
    Held by the Adairs, then by the Kennedys in 1596 and by the Dalrymples of Stair in 1680. The building houses a museum about the castle and is open from Easter to mid September (01776 705544; www.dumgal.gov.uk).
Underwood Castle [NS 390292], near Prestwick, Ayrshire; mansion on site of castle.
    Held by the Kennedys from the eighteenth to the twentieth century.

www.kennedysociety.net / www.clankennedy.org
www.kennedysociety.org
No. of castles/sites: 54
Rank: 19/764

Kerr

The name derives from 'kjrr', which means 'marsh dweller' in Norse, and can be spelt Kerr, Ker, Carr or Carre. The family became very powerful on the Border, and the name is first mentioned in records in Scotland at the end of the twelfth century. The name can also be found on Arran, but here has a different origin, coming from 'ciar', which means 'dusky' in Gaelic. The Border Kerrs claim descent from two Norman (as in from Normandy) brothers, who moved to Roxburghshire from Lancashire in England. The two main branches of the family descended from these brothers: the Kerrs of Ferniehirst from Ralph; and the Kers of Cessford from John. Despite being so closely connected and related, the two branches of the Kerrs often fought among themselves.

Ferniehirst Castle [NT 653179], a mile or so south of Jedburgh in the Borders, is an altered and extended tower house, which incorporates work from the sixteenth century. The original entrance leads to a stair known as the 'Left-Handed Staircase', the story being that when Sir Andrew Kerr, who was himself left-handed, returned from the Battle of Flodden in 1513 he had his followers trained to use their weapons with their left hands. This is said to be the origin of 'Corrie-fisted' or 'Kerr-handed'. The castle was first built in 1470 and this branch was made Wardens of the Middle Marches in 1502, but Ferniehirst was sacked by the English in 1523. The castle was recaptured with French help in 1549, and the leader of the English garrison was beheaded. Sir Thomas Kerr, protector of Mary, Queen of Scots,

Ferniehirst Castle (M&R)

invaded England in 1570, hoping to have her released, but all that resulted was a raid on Scotland, during which Ferniehirst was damaged. James VI attacked the castle in 1593, because of help given by the family to Francis Stewart, fifth Earl of Bothwell, whom the king accused of witchcraft and treason (among other things). The castle was rebuilt about 1598. Between 1934 and 1984 it was leased by the Scottish Youth Hostel Association, except for during World War II when it served as an army billet. The castle is said to be haunted by a Green Lady, although the story is refuted. The Kerr Marquises of Lothian and Earls of Ancram, still own the castle but apparently live in London. The castle is open to the public in July (01835 862201).

Many of the family were buried in the north transept of Jedburgh Abbey [NT 650204], a mile or so north of Ferniehirst, which has been restored. The ruins of the abbey are in the care of Historic Scotland and are open to the public (01835 863925).

The site of **Ancrum** or **Ancram House** [NT 625245] is a few miles north-west of Jedburgh. Robert Kerr of Ferniehirst built a castle in 1558, but it was destroyed by fire in 1873 and, although rebuilt, was demolished in 1970. This branch of the family were made Earls of Ancram in 1633, and married into the Kerr Earls of Lothian.

Newbattle Abbey [NT 333660] lies a mile south-west of Dalkeith in Midlothian, and the abbey was founded by David I in 1140. After the Reformation, the property of the wealthy establishment was given to the Kerrs of Ferniehirst. They were made Lords Newbattle in 1591, and then Earls of Lothian in 1606. In 1631 William Kerr

Newbattle Abbey (M&R)

of Ferniehirst married Ann Ker of Cessford, helping to heal the feud between the two branches, and the family were made Marquises of Lothian in 1701. Most of the abbey buildings were demolished, but the fine vaulted undercroft of the dormitory and reredorter, and other buildings, were incorporated into a fortified dwelling for the family; and good plasterwork and wood carving survives. Newbattle was remodelled and extended down the centuries into a large mansion. The eleventh Marquis of Lothian gave the building to the nation, and it is now an adult education college. The old part of the building has a reputation for being haunted. There are also tales

of a Grey Lady, said by some to be the spirit of a girl who was killed when she fell in love with one of the monks, as well as stories of spectral monks haunting the grounds. The building is a venue for conferences, events and weddings (0131 663 1921; www.newbattle abbeycollege.ac.uk).

Cessford Castle [NT 738238] is a massive brooding ruin, and lies some miles south of Kelso in the Borders. It is a squat L-plan castle, rising to three storeys in the main block, and dating from the fifteenth century or earlier. It was surrounded by a curtain wall, and then apparently another wall and ditch beyond this. The lands were held

Cessford Castle (MC)

by the Sinclairs, but passed to the Kerrs, and they soon became rivals of the Ferniehirst branch. Sir Andrew Kerr of Cessford fought and survived the Battle of Flodden in 1513, and became a Warden of the Marches, although Cessford was damaged by the English in 1519. The castle was besieged four years later, when the English reckoned it the third strongest fortress in Scotland. Cessford was torched in 1543 and then was sacked a year later, again by the English. Sir Walter Kerr, also a Warden, was banished to France for his part in the murder of Walter Scott of Buccleuch in 1552, and was active against Mary, Queen of Scots: this branch of the Kerrs fought against her at the Battle of Langside in 1568. The Kerrs were made Earls in 1616, and then Dukes of Roxburghe in 1704. The castle was abandoned around 1650, and materials from here were used to build Floors Castle.

Floors Castle [NT 711346] is a massive castellated mansion, and dates from 1721 and was designed by the architect William Adam, although the building was remodelled by William Playfair in the nineteenth

Floors Castle 1910?

century. Floors stands a mile to the north-west of Kelso, and is on the site of a castle or older house. Floors was built for John Ker, the first Duke of Roxburghe. The family, now Innes-Ker and holding the titles of Dukes of Roxburghe, Marquis of Bowmont and Cessford, Earl of Roxburghe, Earl of Kelso, Viscount Broxmouth, and others, still own Floors (they would also be chiefs of the Innes family, but clan chiefs are not allowed to have double-barrelled names). The ghost of a gardener is said to haunt the outside of the main entrance; and the apparition of a horseman has been seen in the grounds. This may be linked to the death of James II, who was killed besieging Roxburgh Castle, which is on the estate. Floors Castles and the grounds are open the public from April to mid October (01573 223333; www.floors castle.com).

The Dukes used Kelso Abbey (once the richest abbey in Scotland but now very ruinous) as a burial place, and part of the transept is walled off; the ruin is open to the public. The Dukes also have a burial vault at Bowden Kirk [NT 554303], two or so miles south of Melrose, which is a long building dating partly from the fifteenth century. There is also a carved seventeenth-century laird's loft for the Kers. The church is open the public.

The Kerrs also owned:

Abbotsgrange [NS 931811], Grangemouth, Falkirk; site of castle and mansion.
Held by the Livingstones, then by Elizabeth Kerr, wife of James Bellenden of Auchinoul in 1611 and then by the Dukes of Roxburgh, before passing to the Drummonds.

Broxmouth House [NT 696766], near Dunbar, East Lothian; castle replaced by mansion.
Held by the Grays and by the Homes, but passed to the Ker Dukes of Roxburghe, who hold the title Viscount Broxmouth.

Castle of Faldonside [NT 502328], near Melrose, Borders; site of castle.
Held by the Kerrs.

Castle of Holydean [NT 537303], near Melrose, Borders; slight remains of castle.
Held by the Kerrs of Cessford, and probably built about 1570.

Cavers Carre [NT 551268], near Melrose, Borders; mansion on site of castle.
Held by the Kerrs.

Caverton [NT 752272], near Kelso, Borders; site of castle or old house.
Held by the Fortheringhams, but passed to the Kerrs of Cessford in the sixteenth century, being held by the 'younger of Cessford'.

Chatto [NT 770176], near Morebattle, Borders; site of castle or old house.
Held by the Rutherfords in the fourteenth century, but passed to the Kerrs of Chatto, and they held it into the nineteenth century and possibly later.

Colquhar Tower [NT 332416], near Innerleithen, Borders; some remains of tower house.
Held by the Kerrs, and later by the Morrisons.

Cherrytrees [NT 810293], near Town Yetholm, Borders; castle or old house replaced by mansion.
Held by the Rutherfords and by the Taits but passed to the Kerrs in the seventeenth century.

Corbet Tower [NT 776239], near Morebattle, Borders; restored tower house.
Held by the Kerrs. Burned by the English in 1522 and 1544, although rebuilt, then restored in the nineteenth century.

Crag Tower [NT 690190], near Jedburgh, Borders; site of tower house.
Held by the Colvilles, then by the Kerrs in 1502.

Dolphinston Tower [NT 683150], near Jedburgh, Borders; site of tower house.
Held by the Ainslies but passed by marriage to the Kerrs in the sixteenth century. The tower had a brownie, which was angered by an inappropriate present and left, saying: 'Since ye've gien me a harden ramp, Nae mair o' your corn I will tramp.' A farm stands on the site of the castle.

Douglaston House [NS 565742], near Milngavie, Dunbartonshire; castle replaced by mansion.
Held by the Grahams, but passed to the Crawfords, then to the Kerrs by the end of the nineteenth century. The mansion is now a golf clubhouse.

Fairnilee [NT 458327], near Galashiels, Borders; altered tower house.
Held by the Kerrs of Linton at the end of the sixteenth century, but passed to the Rutherfords.

Graden Tower [NT 799300], near Kelso, Borders; site of tower house.
Held by the Kerrs of Graden.

Greenhead Tower [NT 492295], near Selkirk, Borders; site of tower house.
Held by the Browns in the fourteenth century, but passed to the Kerrs, who held the property in the sixteenth and seventeenth centuries.

Harviestoun Castle [NS 937978], near Tillicoultry, Clackmannan; site of castle and mansion.
Held by the Taits and by the Orrs, then latterly by the Kerrs of Harviestoun, who presented Castle Campbell to The National Trust for Scotland.

Hirendean Castle [NT 298512], near Penicuik, Midlothian; slight remains of tower house.
Held by the Kerrs after the Reformation, but possibly passed to the Scotts.

Hoselaw Tower [NT 802318], near Town Yetholm, Borders; site of tower house.
Held by the Somervilles, then by the Kerrs and by the Reids.

Kersland [NS 306508], near Dalry, Ayrshire; site of castle.
Held by the Kerrs in 1604.

Killumpha Tower [NX 113407], near Stranraer, Galloway; tower house.
Held by the Kerrs in the nineteenth century.

Kippilaw House [NT 548286], near Melrose, Borders; mansion incorporating part of castle.
Held by the Kerrs from the sixteenth century to 1822.

Lee Tower [NT 328396], near Innerleithen, Borders; ruinous tower house.
Held by the Homes and then by the Kerrs.

Littledean Tower [NT 633314], near Kelso, Borders; ruinous castle.
Held by the Kerrs, and burnt by the English in 1544. The grounds around the castle are said to be haunted by a ghostly horseman.

Littledean Tower (TP)

The story goes that this is the apparition of one of the lairds who dallied with a witch and was then strangled by her severed arm. The Kerrs of Littledean are buried at Maxton Church.

Lochtower [NT 805282], near Kelso, Borders; site of tower house formerly in loch.

Held by the Kerrs and torched by the English in 1523. Sir Walter Scott used the then ruin and surrounding area as 'Avenel Castle' in the *Monastery*.

Lurdenlaw Tower [NT 769321], near Kelso, Borders; site of tower house.

Held by the Scotts, then by the Kerrs in the fifteenth century.

Malleny House [NT 166667], near Balerno, Edinburgh; mansion incorporating work from a castle.

Held by the Hamiltons, then by the Kerrs and by the Murrays of Kilbaberton, then by others. The gardens are in the care of The National Trust for Scotland and are open to the public (0131 449 2283; www.nts.org.uk).

Masterton House [NT 345636], near Newtongrange, Midlothian; site of castle and mansion.

May have been held by the Kerrs.

Maxton [NT 613302], near St Boswells, Borders; possible site of castle.

Held by the Maxtones and by the Barclays, but had passed to the Kerrs by the sixteenth century.

Mersington Tower [NT 775443], near Greenlaw, Borders; site of castle.

Held by the Kerrs, then by the Swintons, and was torched by the English in 1545.

Monkland House [NS 730633], near Coatbridge, Ayrshire; site of castle.

Held by the Kerrs, but passed to the Hamiltons, who held the property in 1554. The site is occupied by a housing development.

Morriston Tower [NT 595423], near Earlston, Borders; site of tower house.

Held by the Kerrs of Morriston, some of whom are buried at Ledgerwood Church.

Mowhaugh Tower [NT 816204], near Morebattle, Borders; site of tower house.

Held by the Stewarts and by the Mow family, as well as by Kelso Abbey and by the Kerrs. The castle was besieged by the English in 1546, who managed to undermine the tower and make it collapse, killing those inside.

Nisbet House [NT 795512], near Duns, Borders; altered tower house.

Held by the Nisbets, then by the Kerrs in the seventeenth century, then later by the Sinclairs.

Old Jeddart [NT 670144], near Jedburgh, Borders; site of tower house.

Probably held by the Kerrs.

Prestongrange House [NT 373737], near Musselburgh, East Lothian; mansion incorporating old work.

Held by the Kerr Earls of Lothian, but passed to the Morrisons in 1609, then to the Grants and to the Sutties. The building is now a golf clubhouse (01875 810276; www.royalmussel burgh.co.uk).

Redden or **Reveden** [NT 786375], near Kelso, Borders; site of tower or old house.

Held by the Kene family but had passed to the Kerrs by the middle of the seventeenth century.

Smailholm Tower [NT 637346], near Kelso, Borders; fine plain tower house.

Held by the Kerrs in the fifteenth century, but passed to the Pringles and then to the Scotts of Harden. In the care of Historic Scotland and open to the public (01573 460365).

Stone Hill [NT 654208], near Jedburgh, Borders; site of castle.

Held by the Kerrs of Ferniehirst.

Sunlaws House or **Roxburghe House** [NT 705295], near Kelso, Borders; mansion incorporating old work.

Held by the Kerrs of Chatto and now the Dukes of Roxburghe. Bonnie Prince Charlie was entertained here in November 1745. The building is said to be haunted by a Green Lady, reputed to be searching for her baby, as well as by other ghosts. The present mansion is now used as a hotel (01573 450331; www.roxburghe.net).

Wallace's Tower [NT 700304], near Kelso, Borders; ruinous L-plan tower house.

Held by the Kerrs of Cessford.

Windydoors Tower [NT 432398], near Galashiels, Borders; slight remains of tower house.

Held by the Kerrs.

Yair House [NT 452328], near Selkirk, Borders; mansion on site of castle.

Held by the Pringles of Whytbank but passed to the Kerrs of Yair by 1588. The lands were bought back by the Pringles in the seventeenth century and they held them until World War I.

www.kerrfamilyassociation.com
No. of castles/sites: 48
Rank: 21/764
Xrefs: Ker; Carr

Kidd

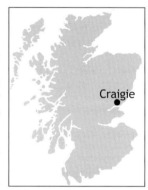

Craigie

The name may be derived from a diminutive of Chris topher or from the Old English 'Cydd(a)' or 'Cyddi'. The name was found in Dundee and in Arbroath, and is on record from the middle of the fourteenth century. Cap tain William Kidd, who was born in Greenock in 1650, was captain of a merchant ship and he settled in New York. He became a privateer and then a notorious pirate; he was hanged at Wapping in 1701.

Craigie [NO 434314], two or so miles to the east and north of Dundee, was held by the Kidds (Kyds) in the sixteenth century, and they had a burial vault at Kilcraig [NO 418309]. There may have been a castle or residence at Craigie. The property passed to the Guthries of Craigie in 1723, and they built Craigie House.

No. of castles/sites: 1
Rank: 537=/764
Xref: Kyd

Kilconquhar

The name comes from the 'church of (St) Conquhar', and the lands are two miles north of Elie in Fife. The name is on record from the first quarter of the thirteenth century.

Kilconquhar Castle [NO 494027] is a large mansion dating from the nineteenth century, but the building incorporates a sixteenth-century tower house of five storeys with turrets. The property belonged to the Kilconquhar family, and Adam Kilconquhar, who became Earl of Carrick through his wife, Margaret, was slain in 1270 in the 'Holy War' in Acre; Margaret went on to marry Robert Bruce and was the mother of Robert I, King of Scots. The property later went to the Earls of Dunbar and March, then later to the Bellendens (or Bannatynes), and then to the Carstairs. The building is now part of a time-share development (01333 340501; www.kilconquhar castle.co.uk).

No. of castles/sites: 1
Rank: 537=/764

Kilconquhar Castle (M&R)

Kilmaron

The name is territorial and comes from the lands of Kilmaron, which are one mile to the north-west of Cupar in Fife. **Kilmaron Castle** [NO 357162] was a modern building, dating from 1820, but was demolished in the twentieth century. The lands were probably held by the Kilmaron family in the thirteenth and fourteenth centuries. The later castle was built for the Baxters of Kilmaron, and the property had also been held by the Maitlands and by the Lows.

No. of castles/sites: 1 / Rank: 537=/764

Kincaid

The name is territorial and comes from the lands of Kincaid, which are to the south of Milton of Campsie in central Scotland. The family claim descent from Earls of Lennox, and the name is descriptive and may mean a 'pass' or 'steep place' from Gaelic, or 'of the head of the rock'. John Kincaid, from Tranent in East Lothian, was a witch-pricker in the middle of the seventeenth century, a profession that paid well, although he was eventually himself discredited and outlawed.

Kincaid House [NS 650760], a mansion which was extended in 1712 and 1812, is most likely built on the site of a castle. The lands were held by the Earls of Lennox and by the Galbraiths, before passing to the Kincaid family in 1280 (the family took their surname from their lands). One of the family helped recapture Edinburgh Castle in 1296, and he was later made Constable of that castle. Malcolm Kincaid lost his left arm in a melee and the Kincaids then feuded with the Lennox family of Woodhead. Malcolm Kincaid was to have worse luck; he was then slain by one of the Stirlings of Glorat in 1581. The family also held lands in Edinburgh and near Falkirk, and members of the family supported the Jacobites. Kincaid House is now used as a hotel (0141 776 2226; www.kincaidhouse.com). It has been suggested that **Broken Tower** [NS 613741], three miles west of Kirkintilloch was the original seat of the Kincaid family. There were some remains in 1860 but nothing now remains.

Warriston [NT 253757] to the north of Edinburgh was held by the Kincaids from 1581. A castle had been besieged by the Dalmahoys and other families a couple of years before. John Kincaid of Warriston married the lovely Jean Livingstone of Dunipace. The couple did not get on, and Kincaid may have mistreated his wife. Robert Weir, a servant, beat John Kincaid to death. The murder was ill conceived, and those involved were soon identified and condemned to death. Robert Weir was broken on the wheel, the nurse was burnt to death, and in 1600 Jean Livingstone was executed by beheading. The property passed to the Johnstones.

Craiglockhart Castle [NT 226703], to the south-west of Edinburgh, is a small ruinous keep or tower, possibly dating from as early as the thirteenth century. The Kincaids held the lands from the sixteenth century, but the property passed to the Lockharts of The Lee. The ruin is in the grounds of Napier University.

To the west of Falkirk, **Bantaskine** [NS 876800] was a castle or old house, but it was demolished in the 1950s and the site is now a public park. The lands were held by the Forresters, but passed to the Livingstones and then to the Kincaids. Alexander Kincaid of Bantaskine was Lord Provost of Edinburgh in 1776.

Auchenreoch Castle [NS 678767], some three miles to the west and south of Kilsyth in central Scotland, was a tower house of the Kincaid family, although it later passed to the Buchanans.

www.kincaid.kinkead.net
No. of castles/sites: 6
Rank: 212=/764

King

The name is found in several parts of Scotland, including in Berwickshire, in Fife and in Aberdeenshire, although it is the latter where the family held lands. The name is on record in Scotland from the middle of the thirteenth century. A later family of Kings were made Baronets of Campsie in 1888, although they now live in the USA.

Barra Castle [NJ 792258] is an altered L-plan tower house, dating from the seventeenth century but including even older work. Barra lies three miles northeast of Inverurie in Aberdeenshire, and was held by the King family from the middle of the thirteenth century. The family feuded with the Setons of Meldrum, one of the Kings having slain a Seton in 1530. The property was, however, sold to the Setons, who in turn sold it to the Reids in 1658. Barra later passed to the Ramsays and then to the Irvines, and is still occupied.

Dudwick Castle [NJ 975370] was four miles northeast of Ellon also in Aberdeenshire, but the building was demolished in about 1860. The mansion had incorporated an old castle, and it was held by the Mitchells before passing to the Kings. One of the family was General James King, who fought in the Swedish army of Gustave Adolphus, and King was made Lord Ythan in 1642. King later returned to Sweden, where he died in 1652.

Tertowie House [NJ 822102], a couple of miles north of Westhill again in Aberdeenshire, is a baronial mansion of 1867 and 1905, but replaced an old house or castle. Tertowie was held by the Kings from the sixteenth century or earlier, but much later was used as student accommodation. It was recently put up for sale, and has its own gymnasium and nuclear bunker.

No. of castles/sites: 3
Rank: 328=/764

Barra Castle (M&R)

Kinloch

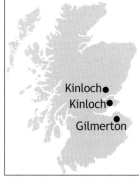

The name is territorial and comes from the lands of Kinloch, which are a couple of miles north-west of Ladybank in the parish of Collessie in Fife. The name is from the Gaelic 'ceann loch' meaning 'head of the loch', and there was apparently a loch here although it has since been drained. The family also held property at Kinloch three miles south-east of Alyth in Angus, and could have got their name from here.

Kinloch House [NO 280123] in Fife dates from about 1700 but stands on the site of a castle or old house. The property was held by the Kinlochs, but passed to the Balfours of Kinloch, and then to the Kinnears in the nineteenth century.

Kinloch House [NO 268444] in Angus replaced an old castle or house, which dated from the seventeenth century, but the building was ruinous by 1791 and had been demolished by 1900. It was a property of the Kinlochs until the twentieth century. Their mausoleum, standing on the south side of the A94, has a small tower and dates from 1861. The Kinlochs of Kinloch were made Baronets in 1873 and now live in London.

Gilmerton House [NT 549778] is three miles east and north of Haddington in East Lothian, and is a classical mansion dating from the middle of the eighteenth century which was extended in 1828. The lands were held by the Hepburns, but were bought by the Kinlochs, successful Edinburgh merchants, in 1655. The family were made Baronets of Nova Scotia in 1686. Francis Kinloch, sixth Baronet, was tragically murdered by Archibald, his brother, in 1795, just a few days after his father had died. Archibald was tried for the murder, but was given over to the care of his own family because of his insanity at the time of the crime. The Kinlochs still apparently live at the house, and luxury accommodation is available (01620 880207; www.gilmertonhouse.com).

The Kinlochs also owned:
Alderstone House [NT 044662], near Livingston, West Lothian; altered tower house.
   Held by the Kinlochs in the middle of the sixteenth century, and they built the tower. Alderstone passed to the Sandilands Lord Torphichen in 1656, then went to the Mitchells of Todhaugh in 1692, then to others. The building is used as company offices.
Aldie Castle or **House of Aldie** [NT 052977], near Crook of Devon, Perthshire; extended tower house.
   Held by the Mercers of Aldie, then by the Murray Lord Nairne, and then by the Kinlochs.
Altries [NO 840987], near Peterculter, Aberdeenshire; mansion incorporating old work.
   Held by the Kinlochs in the nineteenth century.

Athelstaneford [NT 533774], near Haddington, East Lothian; site of castle.
   Held by the Herries family and by the Hepburns, but the lands passed to the Kinlochs in the seventeenth century. There is a heritage centre in the restored sixteenth-century doocot, open from April to September (01620 880378).
Cruivie Castle [NO 419229], near Balmullo, Fife; large ruinous castle
   Held by the Kinlochs, but passed by marriage to the Sandilands of Calder about 1490, then went to the Ramsays and then to the Carnegies, later Earls of South Esk.
Gourdie [NO 121419], near Blairgowrie, Perthshire; castle replaced by mansion.
   Held by the Hays, but passed to the Kinlochs by the beginning of the seventeenth century, and they held Gourdie for more than 300 years.
Kair House [NO 769765], near Arbuthnott, Kincardineshire; castle replaced by mansion.
   Held by the Sibbalds, by the Guthries, and by the Burnetts before coming to the Kinlochs of Kair.
Logie House [NO 394521], near Kirriemuir, Angus; plain extended tower house.
   Held by the Wisharts, then by the Kinlochs of Kilrie, who held the property in the twentieth century.
Markle [NT 579775], near East Linton, East Lothian; some remains of castle.
   Held by the Hepburns, but later passed to the Stewarts and then to the Kinlochs.
Marlee House [NO 149445], near Blairgowrie, Perthshire; tower house replaced by mansion,
   Probably held by the Kinloch family in the fifteenth century, but later passed to the Browns.
Meigle House [NO 285447], Meigle, Perthshire; mansion on site of castle.
   Held by the Lyon Earls of Strathmore, then by the Murrays before being sold to the Kinlochs in 1871.
Nevay [NO 330445], near Newtyle, Fife; site of castle or old house.
   Held by the Nevay family, but passed by marriage to the Kinlochs around 1700, although they were forfeited for their part in the Jacobite Rising of 1745-46.
Newark Castle [NO 518012], near Elie, Fife; ruinous castle.
   Held by the Kinlochs, but passed to the Sandilands of Cruivie, then to the Leslies, to the Anstruthers and then to the Bairds of Elie (www.inverie.com).
Pitlochie Castle [NO 175095], near Auchtermuchty, Fife; site of castle.
   Held by the Kinlochs, but passed to the Lundies of Balgonie by 1452, then to the Sandilands.

No. of castles/sites: 17
Rank: 83=/764

Kinnaird

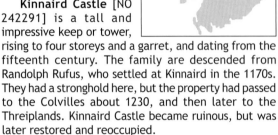

The name is territorial and comes from the lands and barony of the same name, some nine miles east and north of Perth; the name is on record from the twelfth century.

Kinnaird Castle [NO 242291] is a tall and impressive keep or tower, rising to four storeys and a garret, and dating from the fifteenth century. The family are descended from Randolph Rufus, who settled at Kinnaird in the 1170s. They had a stronghold here, but the property had passed to the Colvilles about 1230, and then later to the Threiplands. Kinnaird Castle became ruinous, but was later restored and reoccupied.

Inchture [NO 280285], eight miles west of Dundee, was originally held by the Kirkcaldy family, but passed by marriage to the Kinnairds in 1396, and they held the lands until the twentieth century. There was a tower house, which was probably replaced by Moncur Castle and then by Rossie Priory. John Kinnaird of Inchture was probably killed at the Battle of Flodden in 1513; and Sir George Kinnaird of Inchture, who supported the Royalists throughout the civil war, was knighted by Charles II in 1661, and was made Lord Kinnaird of Inchture in 1682. Patrick, third Lord, opposed the Union of the Parliaments of 1707.

Moncur Castle [NO 284295], which is nearby, is a ruinous Z-plan tower house, and was held by the Moncurs in the fifteenth century, but was later occupied by the Kinnairds. It was gutted by fire in the eighteenth century.

Rossie Priory or **Drimmie** [NO 285308] is also close by. Drimmie House was replaced by Rossie Priory, which was a magnificent castellated mansion, but this was mostly demolished in 1949 and the remains remodelled by Sir Basil Spence. The lands were held by the Ireland family and by the Falconers before coming to the Kinnairds. Rossie Priory is available to rent on an exclusive basis and grounds are open to groups by appointment (01828 686286/238; www.rossie priory.com).

Culbin [NH 995615] is a few miles north-west of Forres in Moray. The lands were held by the Murrays, but passed by marriage to the Kinnairds in the fifteenth century. They had a castle, but this was overwhelmed by sand along with the lands in the seventeenth century. Walter Kinnaird and his wife, Elizabeth Innes, have a fine tombstone, dated 1613, in Dyke kirkyard. The area around Culbin is now planted with trees, and is accessible to the public.

www.kinnaird.net
ClanKinnaird.tripod.com/kinnairdhomeindex.html
No. of castles/sites: 5
Rank: 240=/764

Kinnear

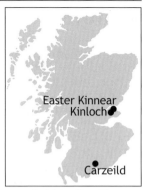

The name is territorial and comes from the lands of Kinnear, which are in the north part of Fife, two or so miles south of Wormit. The family is on record from the middle of the twelfth century.

There are only slight remains of **Easter Kinnear Castle** [NO 404232], which was held by the Kinnears from the thirteenth century for 400 years or more. Wester Kinnear was owned by Balmerino Abbey, and Henry Kinnear was made commendator of the abbey.

Kinloch House [NO 280123], a couple of miles north-west of Ladybank also in Fife, was held by the Kinlochs and then by the Balfours, but was owned by the Kinnears in the nineteenth century. There was a castle or old house, but the present building dates from about 1700, although it was remodelled in 1859 and then again in the 1920s.

Carzeild [NX 969818] is three miles north of Dumfries, and appears to be the seat of the Balfour-Kinnears. There was a tower house but this has gone, and there is a later mansion.

No. of castles/sites: 3
Rank: 328=/764

Kinninmont

The name is territorial, and probably comes from the lands of Kinninmonth, which are three and a half miles south-east of Cupar in Fife, although there are other places in Scotland with the same name. The spelling of the name has many variations from Kinninmont to Kynynmound.

The family may have had a castle or house at **Kinninmonth** [NO 424125], but their main seat was nearby at **Craighall** [NO 407107]. There was a tower house, which dated from the sixteenth century, added to which was a classical

Craighall (M&R)

mansion. The tower was built by the Kinninmonts, who held the lands from the twelfth century. Craighall passed to the Hopes, but the building was abandoned and was an impressive ruin when it was demolished in 1955.

Kinkell [NO 539158], a couple of miles to the east of St Andrews also in Fife, was held by the Monypennys of Pitmillie and by the Hamiltons of Kinkell, but possibly also by the Kinninmonts of Craighall.

Melgund Castle [NO 546564], four and a half miles south-west of Brechin in Angus, is an impressive and imposing building, and has been undergoing restoration. It was a property of the Beatons, then of the Gordons, of the Maules and of the Murrays. The direct line of the Kinninmont family died out in the eighteenth century when a heiress married into the Murrays of Melgund, although they later became Elliot Murray Kynynmound Earls of Minto and Viscounts Melgund. **Minto House** [NT 573203], five and a half miles north-east of Kelso in the Borders, is a ruinous mansion and tower house, and the property, long held by the Elliots, gives its name to the Earldom of Minto.

No. of castles/sites: 5
Rank: 240=/764
Xrefs: Kinninmond; Kynymound

Kirk

The name is local in origin, and means a seat or settlement near a church or kirk, and is on record from the middle of the fifteenth century. Robert Kirk, the minister of Aberfoyle, is said to have been taken off to faeryland, and he wrote *The Secret*

Commonwelth of Elves, Faunes and Fairies as well as a translation of psalms into Gaelic. Legends surround his death in 1692, not the least that he was imprisoned by the fairies in Doon Hill and still languishes there.

Bogrie Tower [NX 812849] is now used as a farmhouse, and is a reduced tower house, which was partly demolished in 1680. It was held by the Kirk or Kirko family in 1630, but passed by marriage to the Gordons of Lochinvar. Bogrie is four miles south of Moniaive in Dumfries and Galloway.

Also near Moniaive is **Sundaywell Tower** [NX 811845], which was also held by the Kirk or Kirko family in the sixteenth and seventeenth centuries. Both towers were used as places of refuge by Covenanters in the seventeenth century. The remains of this tower house are built into the farmhouse.

No. of castles/sites: 2
Rank: 396=/764
Xrefs: Kirko; Kirkhoe

Kirkcaldy

The name comes from the lands of Kirkcaldy in Fife, now the site of a large burgh, and Kirkcaldy is on record as a surname from the end of the thirteenth century. The name itself may come from 'Kil (or Kirk) Culdee', the 'church or chapel of the Culdees', an early Christian order of monks.

Grange [NT 270886] is a mile north of Kinghorn in Fife, and the mansion incorporates some of a tower house, which dates from the sixteenth century and has a round tower. The lands were held by the Kirkcaldys from 1540 or earlier. James Kirkcaldy of Grange was Lord High Treasurer to James V and to Mary, Queen of Scots. He was forfeited, and the property passed to the Hamiltons, but it was then recovered by Sir William Kirkcaldy, his son, in 1564. He had been involved in the murder of Cardinal David Beaton, and was captured and sent to France, where he distinguished himself as a soldier. He returned and joined the rebellion against Mary and the fourth Earl of Bothwell in 1567, pursuing Bothwell all the way to Shetland. However, after her flight to England, Kirkcaldy held Edinburgh Castle for Mary from 1571-73. Although he surrendered on the condition he would not be harmed, he was hanged after the fall of the castle. The family was forfeited, and the property passed to the Douglases, then to the Stewarts, but Grange returned to the Kirkcaldy family. The last of the line died in 1739, and the property then went to the Melvilles.

Inchture [NO 280285], some eight miles west of Dundee, was a property of the Kirkcaldy family, but passed by marriage to the Kinnairds in 1396. There was a castle, but all traces have gone. The Kinnairds held the lands until the twentieth century.

Three or so miles to the east of Cowdenbeath in Fife are the remains of Hallyards Castle [NT 212914]. This was a substantial courtyard castle, dating from the sixteenth century, but little survives. Hallyards was held by the Skenes, but passed to Sir James Kirkcaldy of Grange, mentioned above, but then appears to have returned to the Skenes.

No. of castles/sites: 3
Rank: 328=/764

Kirkconnel

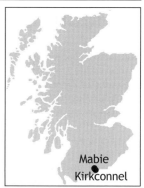

The name is territorial and comes from the lands of Kirkconnel, which are a few miles south of Dumfries, and the name is on record from the fourteenth century.

Kirkconnel House [NX 979679] is a large mansion and incorporates an altered tower house at one end. The old part dates from the sixteenth century, and was extended into an L-plan. The property was held by the Kirkconnels from

Kirkconnel House (LF)

1320 or earlier, but passed by marriage to the Maxwells in 1410, and they built the tower. The house is still occupied, and is available to rent as holiday accommodation (01381 610496; www.lhhscotland.com).

Mabie [NX 949708] is nearby and was also held by the Kirkconnels. The present house is a mansion of three storeys and dates from the seventeenth century, but there was a castle or older house here. The property had passed to the Herries family by the end of the sixteenth century, and it was later owned by the Howats. The building is now used as a hotel (01387 263188; www.mabiehouse.co.uk).

No. of castles/sites: 2
Rank: 396=/764

Kirkpatrick

The name comes from Kirkpatrick, a kirk or church dedicated to St Patrick, and the name is on record from the middle of the twelfth century.

Closeburn Castle [NX 907921], which is a few miles south-east of Thornhill in Dumfries and Galloway, has a massive keep or tower, dating from the fourteenth century, to which has been added a modern mansion. The lands were held by the Kirkpatricks from the twelfth century, although some stories have the family settled in this area for 300 years before this. Roger Kirkpatrick, along with John Lindsay of Dunrod, joined Robert the Bruce in stabbing John Comyn to death in a church in Dumfries in 1306, both of them helping 'mak siccar'. Sir Roger Kirkpatrick of Closeburn captured the castles of Dalswinton and Caerlaverock from the English in 1355, but he was murdered by Sir James Lindsay in 1357 during a quarrel at Caerlaverock. Sir Thomas Kirkpatrick was taken prisoner after the Battle of Solway Moss in 1542, and the Kirkpatricks were made Baronets of Nova Scotia in 1685. The Empress Eugenie, wife of Napoleon III, was descended from the family, and many of the Kirkpatricks are buried at Garvald. A red-breasted swan was said to appear here as a portent of a death in the Kirkpatrick family after one had been shot by a son of the house. Closeburn was damaged by fire in 1748, and sold in 1783. It is still occupied and, although the line of the Kirkpatricks, Baronets, continues, they now apparently live in Australia.

The Kirkpatricks also owned:

Auldgirth [NX 915868], near Thornhill, Dumfries and Galloway; site of castle.
> Held by the Kirkpatricks in the middle of the seventeenth century.

Capenoch House [NX 843938], near Thornhill, Dumfries and Galloway; mansion with old work.
> Held by the Griersons and by the Maxwells, but passed to the Kirkpatricks in 1780, before returning to the Griersons in 1845. It is now apparently held by the Gladstones of Capenoch and is still occupied.

Conheith or **Conheath** [NY 005701], near Dumfries; site of tower house.
> Long held by the Maxwells, but appears also to have been a property of the Kirkpatricks.

Friars Carse [NX 925850], near Dumfries; mansion on site of castle.
> Held by the Kirkpatricks after the Reformation, but passed to the Maxwells, then to other families. The building is now used as a hotel (01387 740388; www.classic-hotels.net).

Kirkmichael House [NS 342085], near Maybole, Ayrshire; mansion incorporating part of a castle.
> Probably held by the Kirkpatricks, but had passed to the Shaw-Kennedys by the end of the nineteenth century. Now used as a school.

Rockhall [NY 054754], near Dumfries; altered L-plan tower house.
> Held by the Kirkpatricks, but passed by marriage to the Griersons of Lagg in the fifteenth century, and remained with them for about 500 years. Still occupied.

Ross Castle [NY 067887], near Lochmaben; site of castle.
> Held by the Kirkpatricks from the fifteenth century or earlier.

Torthorwald Castle [NY 033783], near Dumfries; ruinous tower on motte.
> Held by the Torthorwald family, but passed by marriage to the Kirkpatricks in the thirteenth century, then went to the Carlyles in 1418. The property passed to the Douglases, and the castle was occupied until about 1715.

Tynron Doon [NX 819939], near Moniaive, Dumfries and Galloway; site of castle within Iron Age fort.
> Held by the Kirkpatricks, and Robert the Bruce is believed to have sheltered here after murdering John Comyn in Dumfries.

Wamphray Tower [NY 128965], near Moffat, Dumfries and Galloway; slight remains of tower house.
> Held by the Corries and by the Kirkpatricks, but passed to the Johnstones in 1476.

www.geocities.com/Heartland/6540/
members.tripod.com/~PPPat/
No. of castles/sites: 11
Rank: 127=/764

Kirkwood

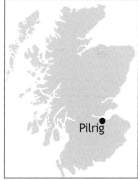

The name is local, and there are several place from where it could have originated, including in Ayrshire, in Lanarkshire and in Dumfriesshire. The name is on record from the middle of the fifteenth century. The Kirkwood Barons Kirkwood, a title created in 1951, apparently live in Sheffield in Yorkshire.

Pilrig House [NT 265757] is to the north and east of Edinburgh and now stands by a public park. It is an altered L-plan tower house, dating from the seventeenth century, and was held by the Monypennys from the sixteenth century. Pilrig passed to Gilbert Kirkwood, a goldsmith, in 1623, and he may have built the tower; and then went to the Balfours in 1716. The house was given to the city of Edinburgh and, after a long period of neglect, was restored into individual dwellings. It stands by a public park.

No. of castles/sites: 1
Rank: 537=/764

Pilrig House (M&R)

Knight

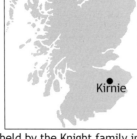

The name comes from the military position of knight, and is on record as a surname in Scotland from the fourteenth century.

Kirnie Tower [NT 349373] stood a mile north-east of Innerleithen in the Borders, but the last vestige was cleared away in 1840. It may have been held by the Knight family in the seventeenth century.

No. of castles/sites: 1
Rank: 537=/764

Knox

The name is territorial and comes from the lands of Knock, one mile south of Renfrew. These were given to an Adam son of Uchtred, who then became 'of Knock', which over time became 'Knox'. Robert Knox, born in Edinburgh in 1791, was keeper of the Anatomy Museum in Edinburgh and he was responsible for purchasing corpses for dissection. He had dealings with Burke and Hare, but he was cleared at the subsequent trial, but then had to go to London to find work.

There was a manor house at **Knock** [NS 491662], a mile to the south of Renfrew, but it is not clear if this is the correct place; the site is now in a housing estate. Also in Renfrewshire is **Ranfurly Castle** [NS 384652], just to the south-west of Bridge of Weir, a small and ruinous keep or tower with a courtyard. The buildings date from the fifteenth century, and Ranfurly was a property of the Knox family, one of whom was the famous Protestant reformer John Knox. Knox had been a follower of George Wishart and joined the murderers of Archbishop David Beaton in St Andrews Castle in 1546. He was captured when the castle fell and was a galley slave of the French. He was freed and preached in England and then in Geneva, but returned to Scotland and took part in anti-French, anti-Catholic and anti-Mary activities. He wrote the *History of the Reformation*. **John Knox House** [NT 262738], on the Royal Mile of Edinburgh and one of the oldest houses in the capital, is said to be where Knox died in 1572. The house is open to the public (0131 556 9579). Another of the family was Andrew Knox, the Protestant Bishop of the Isles, who was important in trying to pacify the clans and to implement the Bond and Statutes of Iona. He died in 1633. Ranfurly was sold to the Cochrane Earls of Dundonald in 1665, then passed to others. **Craigends House** [NS 419662], a couple of miles to the north-east of Kilbarchan again in Renfrewshire, was a castellated mansion dating from 1857 but it was demolished 100 years later. It incorporated old work, and the lands may have been held by the Knoxs of Ranfurly before going to the Cunninghams in the middle of the fifteenth century. **Markhouse** [NO 517582], some miles west of Brechin in Angus, is the site of a castle. John Knox of Markhouse is mentioned in 1723.

In the far south of East Lothian is **Mayshiel** [NT 622641], which stands four and a half miles north-west of Cranshaws. It is a plain L-plan tower house, dating from the seventeenth century, and has been much altered. The lands were held by several families, but passed to the Knoxs in the eighteenth century, then went to the Cunninghams, and then to others. The house is still occupied.

No. of castles/sites: 6
Rank: 212=/764

Laidlaw

The name come from the place Laidlawsteil, which is four and a half miles west of Galashiels in the Borders, although there may have also been a place of this name near West Linton. Alternatively, the name may come England where there are families with similar spellings. The name in on record in Scotland from the end of the thirteenth century, and is mainly found in the Borders; the family had links to the Scotts.

Mossfennan or **Mosfennan** [NT 117317] is five miles south-east of Biggar and two miles south-west of Drumelzier in Tweeddale in the Borders. There was tower house but it was replaced by Mossfennan House in the eighteenth century. The Laidlaws apparently held the lands during part of the seventeenth and eighteenth centuries, although the property was sold to the Welsh family in 1753.

No. of castles/sites: 1
Rank: 537=/764

Laing

The name is descriptive and is the Scots (or Old English) for 'long' or 'tall', and is on record from the end of the thirteenth century. Eppie Laing, who lived in Anstruther, was accused of witchcraft and was burned after the boat carrying the builder of the lighthouse on the Isle of May was caught in a storm and the builder drowned.

Overtoun Castle or **House** [NS 424761] is a large baronial mansion, dating from the middle of the nineteenth century, and stands a mile or so north-east of Dumbarton. It is probably built on the site of an old castle, and in the fourteenth century the lands were held by the Colquhouns, but they passed to the Laings, who owned them in the seventeenth century. Overtoun was sold to James White in 1859, a successful chemical manufacturer, and the house and some of the estate were given over to the people of Dumbarton. The mansion is now used as a Christian Centre for Hope and Healing, and the estate around the house is open to the public with formal gardens and a nature trail (www.overtounhouse.com).

Redhouse Castle [NT 463770] is a mile south of Aberlady in East Lothian, and is a large and impressive ruinous courtyard castle, which dates from the sixteenth century. Redhouse was owned by the Douglases, but passed to the Laings, one of whom was John Laing, Keeper of the Royal Signet. The property then went by marriage to the Hamiltons, the last of whom was executed after the Jacobite Rising of 1745-46. The property was forfeited and the castle became ruinous.

Carrick House [HY 567384] is a fine courtyard house of the seventeenth century, and stands on the Orkney island of Eday. The property belonged to several families, including to the Laings and to the Hebdens from 1848, who still apparently live here. The house is open for some days during the summer (01857 622260; www.eday.orkney.sch.uk/tourism/carricktour/index.htm).

No. of castles/sites: 3 / Rank: 328=/764
Xref: Lang

Redhouse (M&R)

Lamb

The name comes from a Norse personal name, and the family are on record from the end of the thirteenth century. Also see Lammie, and the family had links to the Lamonts.

The Lambs were prominent burgesses in Leith, and they built **Lamb's House** [NT 269764] in Leith, a fine example of a sixteenth-century town house with a flourish of corbelling and gables. Mary, Queen of Scots, rested here after arriving at Leith from France in 1561. The Lamb family emigrated to America around the beginning of the nineteenth century, and the house was restored in the 1960s and is now an old people's day centre.

No. of castles/sites: 1
Rank: 537=/764

Lamberton

The name is territorial and comes from the barony and lands of Lamberton, which are just inside the Scottish border, a few miles north-east of Berwick-upon-Tweed in Berwickshire. The name is on record from the twelfth century.

There was a tower house at **Lamberton** [NT 965573], which was burned and destroyed, along with the village, by the Earl of Hertford in 1545. This tower was probably held by the Rentons, but there may have been an older stronghold which was a property of the Lamberton family, who held the lands in the middle of the twelfth century. William Lamberton, Bishop of St Andrews, was a supporter of Robert the Bruce and was instrumental in freeing Scotland from the English during the Wars of Independence. The property passed by marriage to the Leslies around the turn of the fifteenth century.

No. of castles/sites: 1
Rank: 537=/764

Lambie

The name is a pet-name for 'Lamb', an old Norse personal name, and spelt both 'Lambie' and 'Lammie', as well as 'L'Amy', supposedly from a French origin. The surname is recorded in Scotland from the end of the thirteenth century. Andrew Lammie was one of those accused of the murder of David Rizzio at Holyroodhouse in 1565. The name also has links to the Lamonts and also see the Lambs.

Barns [NO 597068] stood a mile to the west and south of Crail in Fife, but the castle or old house which was there has been demolished. The property was held by several families, including by the Lambies in the fourteenth century, and later by the Cunninghams and by the Anstruthers.

Dunkenny [NO 355477] is some four and a half miles south of Kirriemuir in Angus and just to the north of Eassie. There was a castle, although this appears to have been replaced by a mansion. The lands were held by the Lambies (or L'Amys) from 1542 or earlier until the twentieth century. Dunkenny was also apparently held by the Lindsays as David Lindsay of Dunkenny was Bishop of Edinburgh.

No. of castles/sites: 2
Rank: 396=/764
Xrefs: Lammie; L'Amy

Lamont

The name is Norse in origin and means 'lawman' or 'law giver', which in Gaelic became 'Ladhman'. The family claim descent from the son of one of the O'Neill princes of Tyrone, and the name is on record in Scotland from the middle of the thirteenth century. The Lamonts settled in Argyll, and were very powerful in Cowal until the Campbells took a (bloody) hand.

The ruins of **Toward Castle** [NS 119678] lie seven miles south of Dunoon in Cowal. This was once a strong fortress, consisting of a keep and a walled courtyard with an arched gateway. The lands were held by the Lamonts from 1200 or earlier, and Mary, Queen of Scots, visited in 1563. The Lamonts were Royalists and in the

Toward Castle (M&R)

1640s they raided the Campbell lands of Kilmun. The Campbells retaliated by moving a large army into Cowal, and besieged Toward Castle and Ascog Castle. Sir James Lamont, the chief, agreed to surrender the castles on condition that his people should be allowed to go free. The Campbells agreed, but then went back on their word. They massacred and mistreated any Lamonts they found, including old folk, women and children. They took many of the captives back to Dunoon where they hanged thirty-six gentlemen from one tree, while others were buried alive in pits. Many Lamonts changed their name to Black after the slaughter. Archibald, eighth Earl of Argyll and first Marquis, chief of the Campbells, was tried in 1661 for this, treason (he had also co-operated with the Cromwellian administration) and other crimes and he was executed, although the Lamonts never got any other compensation. Toward Castle was destroyed and not reused, the chiefs moving to Ardlamont, although a new mansion was built near Toward in the 1820s. This new mansion is now a school, and the ruins of the old castle are in the grounds.

Asgog Castle [NR 946705] is a couple of miles south-west of Tighnabruaich on Cowal, and is a very ruinous keep and courtyard. Ascog dates from the fifteenth century, and suffered the same fate as Toward Castle.

Ardlamont House [NR 981659] is further south again, and is a modern mansion, although it may incorporate some of an old castle. This became the chief's main castle, although the Lamonts never recovered their power and continued to lose out to the Campbells. The last chief sold the property in 1893. The Lamonts had a burial vault at Kilfinan Parish Church [NR 934789], dating from 1633, although the church itself is much older.

The Lamonts also held:

Carrick Castle [NS 194944], near Lochgoilhead, Argyll; restored keep or tower.
> Held by the Lamonts, but passed to the Campbell Earls of Argyll in 1368.

Gribton [NX 921800], near Dumfries; castle replaced by mansion.
> Held by the Maxwells and by the Irvines, but had passed to the Lamonts by the end of the nineteenth century.

Kilmory Castle [NR 870868], near Lochgilphead, Argyll; mansion on site of castle.
> Briefly held by the Lamonts before passing to the Campbells in 1575, who owned the property until 1828. The building is now council offices and the gardens are open to the public (01546 604360; www.argyll-bute.gov.uk/content/leisure/heritage/kilmory).

Knockamillie Castle [NS 152711], near Dunoon, Argyll; slight remains of castle.
> Held by the Lamonts, but was another stronghold which was destroyed by the Campbells in 1646.

www.clanlamont.ca
home.pcmagic.net/ogdenj/lamont/
No. of castles/sites: 7
Rank: 182=/764
Xrefs: Lamond; Macerchar

Landale

The name is territorial and comes from the lands of Landale, a property in the Borders, possibly near Kelso. The family are on record from the end of the twelfth century.

Dalswinton Castle [NX 945841], some six miles north of Dumfries, is a shattered ruin, and was replaced by an elegant mansion, dating from 1785, and called **Dalswinton House** [NX 943841]. The property was built for the Millers, but was sold to the Landales of Dalswinton, who still apparently live here and come from Fife. The gardens are occasionally open to the public (www.gardens ofscotland.org).

No. of castles/sites: 1
Rank: 537=/764
Xrefs: Landel; Landells

Lathrisk

The name is territorial and comes from the barony and lands, which are four or so miles north of Glen-rothes in Fife. **Lathrisk House** [NO 273085] is a mansion mostly dating from the eighteenth century, but it incorporates vaulted cellars from a cas-tle. The lands were held by the Lathrisk family from before 1296, but passed by marriage to the Setons of Parbroath. Lathrisk was later held by the Johnstones, and the mansion is still occupied.

No. of castles/sites: 1
Rank: 537=/764

Lauder

The name is territorial and comes from the lands and place of Lauder in the Borders. The name is on record from the end of the thirteenth century, and the family held lands in Lothian, in Edinburgh and in the Borders. Thomas Lauder was Bishop of Dunkeld in 1452 and he completed much work on the cathedral there, as well as building a bridge at Dunkeld. The cathedral, now the parish church, is open to the public (01350 727688; www.dunkeldcathedral.org.uk).

Lauder Tower [NT 530475] stood near Lauder Church, and there was a castle here, formerly with gardens and orchards, although all traces have gone. The tower was built on lands held by the Lauders, and the castle (or perhaps another tower) was incorporated into Lauder Fort; the fort was occupied and strengthened by the English in 1548, although it was retaken only two years later by the Scots with French help. The last remains of the fort were demolished at the end of the seventeenth century.

Tyninghame House [NT 619798], three miles west and north of Dunbar in East Lothian, is a large mansion built around a courtyard, and incorporates work from the sixteenth century or earlier. It was remodelled down the centuries, and was held by the Lauders of the Bass, although the lands were a property of the Archbishops of St Andrews. The Lauders spent the winters at Tyninghame, and the summer on the Bass Rock in the Firth of Forth. The Hamiltons purchased the lands in 1628, and the house is still occupied. The grounds are open to the public and the gardens are occasionally open (www.gardensofscotland.org).

Bass Rock [NT 602873] is a massive volcanic plug and it rises out of the sea about three miles north-east of North Berwick, also in East Lothian. Both the Bass and Tyninghame are associated with St Baldred. The Bass was held by the Lauders from 1318, and they had a castle, which was developed into an artillery fortification. The Lauders supported Mary, Queen of Scots, but the rock was sold to the Crown in 1671, who used the Bass as a prison for Covenanters and later for Jacobites. The castle was dismantled in 1701, and a lighthouse was built on the islands. The Bass can be visited by boat from North Berwick (01620 892838 (boat trips) or 01620 892197 (tourist information office)).

The Lauders also owned:
Blyth [NT 132458], near West Linton, Borders; site of castle or old house.
   Held by the Douglas Earls of Morton, but passed to the Lauders in the fifteenth century. Alexander Lauder of Blyth was slain at the Battle of Flodden in 1513. The property passed to the Veitchs of Dawyck, then went to others.

Bruntsfield House [NT 252723], Edinburgh; altered Z-plan tower house.

Held by the Lauders from 1381 until the beginning of the seventeenth century. Sir Alexander Lauder was Provost of Edinburgh, as was his son, another Alexander, but he was killed at the Battle of Flodden in 1513. The property was sold to the

Bruntsfield House (M&R)

Hatton House (M&R)

Fairlies of Braid in 1603, then to the Warrenders, and is now part of James Gillespie's School. The house, especially the upper storeys, are said to be haunted by a Green Lady. The tale goes that the remains of a murdered woman (and some times her child) were found in a secret room which had been sealed up, discovered when the number of windows on the outside of the building did not match that on the inside. The details are similar to that of Wrightshouses, and may have come along with the school to Bruntsfield House, although many castles have Green Ladies.

Congalton [NT 544805], near North Berwick, East Lothian; site of castle or hall-house.

Held by the Congalton family, although a Lauder of Congalton is also on record, and much later the property passed to the Hepburns.

Edrington Castle [NT 941534], near Chirnside, Borders; site of tower house.

The castle was probably held by the Lauders, but passed to the Homes of Wedderburn. Edrington is said to have been destroyed by the Duke of Gloucester in 1482, and was returned to the Scots in 1534 after being held by the English for some years. A fragment is built into a farm.

Glenbranter [NS 112978], near Strachur, Argyll; site of mansion.

Held by the MacBraynes by others, but sold to Sir Harry Lauder in 1916, although he only lived here for a few years. Lauder was born in Portobello in 1870, and he became a famous entertainer, both in Britain and abroad; he was knighted in 1919 and died in 1950. Lauder only lived at Glenbranter for a few years, and his son died in 1916 during the war. The lands were sold to the Forestry Commission and the mansion was demolished in the 1950s. The site is occupied by a car park.

Grange House [NT 258718], Edinburgh; site of L-plan tower house.

Held by several families including by the Wardlaws, by the Cants, by the Dicks and by the Lauders. Bonnie Prince Charlie stayed here in 1745. One of the family was Sir Thomas Dick Lauder, who was an author and encouraged the establishment of art and technical colleges. The house reputedly had many ghosts, one of whom was reputedly a miser, who is said to have rolled a ghostly barrel of gold through the house. The house was demolished in 1936.

Hatton House [NT 128687], near Balerno, Edinburgh; site of tower house and mansion.

Held by the Hattons, but passed to the Lauders in 1377, and they built a castle. One of the family was killed fighting for

the Black Douglases in the 1450s, and their property was forfeited, although the castle had to be besieged in 1453 to wrest it from them. It was recovered by the Lauders, and strengthened by them in 1515. James Hepburn, fourth Earl of Bothwell, stayed at Hatton the night before he abducted Mary, Queen of Scots, in 1567. In the 1580s Sir William Lauder argued with his son and wife, and had them imprisoned here. The property passed to the Maitlands in 1652.

Johnscleugh [NT 631665], near Cranshaws, East Lothian; plain tower house.

Long held by the Lauder family and now a farmhouse.

Penkaet or **Fountainhall Castle** [NT 427677], near Pencaitland, East Lothian; altered tower house.

Held by several families before coming to the Lauders in 1685, who changed the name to Fountainhall. One of the family was Sir John Lauder, Lord Fountainhall, who was a lawyer and collected historical and legal documents. The Lauders were made Baronets in 1690 and held the property until 1922 when it was sold to the Holbourn family. In recent years the name has been changed to Penkaet Castle, and the castle is still occupied. The Dick-Lauders, Baronets, now apparently live in Australia. The castle has many stories of ghosts, and was investigated in the 1920s. Many unexplained noises and events were recorded, although the investigation was not perhaps as convincing as it could have been.

Quarrelwood Castle [NJ 181642], near Elgin, Moray; site of castle.

Held by the Lauders about 1350, but passed to the Sutherlands in the early sixteenth century.

Whitslaid Tower [NT 557446], near Lauder, Borders; ruinous tower house.

Held by the Lauders or by the Maitlands, but passed to the Montgomerys of Macbiehill in the mid seventeenth century.

Woodhall [NT 433680], near Pencaitland, East Lothian; mansion incorporating tower house.

Held by the Setons and by the Sinclairs of Herdmanston, but passed to the Lauders in the nineteenth century. Woodhall had become ruinous, but was restored and reoccupied.

No. of castles/sites: 15
Rank: 94=/764

Laurie

The name is probably from a diminutive of Laurence, although it has also been suggested it is from the Scots word 'lowrie', meaning 'foxy'. The name is on record on Scotland as a surname from the seventeenth century.

Maxwelton House or **Glencairn Castle** [NX 822898], a couple of miles east of Moniaive in Dumfries and Galloway, is a fine courtyard castle and mansion, which dates from the seventeenth century. The property was owned by the Dennistouns, but passed to the Cunninghams of Kilmaurs, before being purchased by the Laurie family in 1611. The Lauries changed the name to Maxwelton, and this was the home of the heroine of the song 'Annie Laurie'; Annie married Alexander Fergusson of Craigdarroch in the 1720s. The Lauries sold the property in 1966, and Maxwelton is still occupied.

Airds [NX 675705] is six miles north of Castle Douglas in Dumfries and Galloway, and there was a castle or old house known as Airds, although there are two possible locations. The lands were held by the Gordons, but passed to the Lauries and then to the Moffats in 1877.

Polmont House [NS 933782], three miles east of Falkirk in central Scotland, dated from the eighteenth century but probably stood on the site of a castle. The property had been held by the Hamiltons, but the house was built after it had passed to Gilbert Laurie, who had been Lord Provost of Edinburgh. The house was demolished in the twentieth century and the site is occupied by a housing scheme.

A few miles north-west of Lesmahagow in Lanarkshire, **Blackwood House** [NS 773433] stands on the site of an old stronghold or house. The lands were held by the Weirs, but passed to the Lauries, but then went to the Hope Veres by the end of the nineteenth century. The mansion was itself demolished and replaced by a 'timbercabin-style' house.

No. of castles/sites: 4
Rank: 278=/764
Xref: Lawrie; Lowrie

Law

The name is local and means 'hill', and there are many places in Scotland from where the surname could have originated. Alternatively it may come from 'Law', a diminutive for Lawrence, and is also found spelt 'Low' (also see that name). It is on record from the fifteenth century, and was common in Glasgow in the following century. James Law was Bishop of Orkney in 1605 and he did much to integrate the islands into Scotland; he was made Archbishop of Glasgow in 1615 and died in 1632.

Lauriston Castle [NT 204762], which is to the north and west of Edinburgh at Davidson's Mains, is a fine castle and mansion, which was extended by William

Lauriston Castle (M&R)

Burns in the 1820s. The lands were held by several families, including by the Napiers, but passed to the Laws in 1683. One of the family was John Law of Lauriston, an economist and writer, who was made Comptroller of France in 1720. Lauriston later went to the Reids, who gave it to the city of Edinburgh. The castle is open to the public by guided tour and stands in fine grounds (0131 336 2060; www.cac.org.uk).

Clatto Castle [NO 358073] is some miles south of Cupar in Fife, and the present mansion, which was remodelled in the nineteenth century, replaced an old stronghold built some 300 years previously. Clatto was held by the Ramsays, and then by the Learmonths, but was held by the Law family in the nineteenth century.

No. of castles/sites: 2
Rank: 396=/764

Lawson

The name comes from 'Law's son', 'Law' being a diminutive for 'Lawrence'. The name is on record in Scotland from the end of the thirteenth century, and is also found spelt 'Lowson'.

Baddingsgill House [NT 131549], which is a couple of miles north-west of West Linton in the Borders, incorporates vaults from a tower house into the later mansion. The tower house was held by the Lawsons, although the property was later owned by the Marshalls of Rachan.

Balthayock Castle [NO 174230], some three or so miles east of Perth, is a strong and substantial keep or tower, dating from the fourteenth century, although later altered. There is a mansion nearby but this is now ruinous. The lands were held by the Blairs, but in the nineteenth century went to the Lawsons, although they sold it the same century. The castle is still occupied.

No. of castles/sites: 2
Rank: 396=/764
Xref: Lowson

Lawtie

The name is apparently territorial, and comes from the lands of Lawtie (or 'Laithis') in Ayrshire. The lands had passed to the Fullartons around 1350, although their location has not been established.

Inaltrie Castle [NJ 518631] stood three miles south of Cullen in Moray, but little remains now except for one wall. The castle dated from the thirteenth century, and the lands were a property of the Lawties of Inaltrie before being sold to the Ogilvie Earl of Findlater around 1721.

No. of castles/sites: 1
Rank: 537=/764

Learmonth

The name comes from the lands of Learmonth, which are in Berwickshire in the Borders, although the location has not been established. The name was not uncommon in this part of Scotland, and is on record from the thirteenth century.

Rhymer's Tower [NT 572383] at **Earlston** (or **Ercildoune**), three miles north-east of Melrose in the Borders, is a small ruinous keep or tower, probably dating from the fifteenth century. The tower is associated with Thomas Learmonth, known as True Thomas or Thomas the Rhymer, a thirteenth-century poet and seer. In his youth, Thomas is said to have spent seven years in faeryland, after falling asleep under the Eildon Tree, where he met and kissed the Queen of the Faeries. Returning considerably older, wiser and more farsighted, he became famed for his predictions. After a further seven years he reputedly returned to faeryland. Many of his predictions are said to have come true down the years, although written sources only exist from the seventeenth century. Earlston was a property of the Purvis family in the fourteenth century.

Dairsie Castle [NO 414160] is some three miles east and north of Cupar in Fife, and the castle is a much restored Z-plan tower house, which dates from the sixteenth century but was virtually rebuilt in the 1990s. The lands were a property of the bishops and archbishops of St Andrews, and David II is said to have spent much of his boyhood at Dairsie. The property was held by the Dairsie family, before passing by marriage to the Learmonths in the sixteenth century, and they built the old castle. Sir James Learmonth of Dairsie was Master of the Household for James V, and was Provost of St Andrews in 1546. One of the family besieged Blebo Hole, seat of the Trails, in 1599. The property passed to the Spottiswoode family in 1616, and then to the Morrisons.

Balcomie Castle [NO 626099], one and a half miles north and east of Crail also in Fife, is a fine L-plan tower house, which rises to five storeys and a garret, and dates from the sixteenth century. The lands originally belonged to the Balcomie family, but passed to the Learmonths of Clatto in 1526. Mary of Guise stayed at Balcomie after landing at Fifeness on her way to marry James V. Sir James Learmonth of Balcomie was one of the Fife Adventurers who in 1598 tried to take land on Lewis and was slain for his pains. The property passed to the Hopes, and then to others. The building is said to be haunted by the whistling spirit of a young man, imprisoned and starved to death because he would not stop whistling.

The Learmonths also owned:

Clatto Castle [NO 358073], near Cupar, Fife; castle replaced by mansion.

 Held by the Ramsays, but passed to the Learmonths, who built the old castle. Much later Clatto passed to the Law family.

Dean House [NT 235740], Edinburgh; site of tower house.

 Held by the Nisbets of Dean, and then later by John Learmonth, who had Telford Bridge built. The building was demolished in 1845 when the cemetery was laid out.

Isle of May [NT 655995], Firth of Forth; ruins of priory, later fortified.

 The island was held by the Learmonths after the Reformation, but then passed to the Balfours of Montquhandie, later to Cunningham of Barnes, and then to others. The island can be visited with trips leaving from Anstruther from May to September (01333 310103/01333 451152).

No. of castles/sites: 6
Rank: 212=/764

Leask

The name is territorial and comes from the lands of Leask, which are a few miles north-east of Ellon in Aberdeenshire in north-east of Scotland. The name is on record from the fourteenth century.

 Leask House or **Pitlurg** [NK 026331] is now a ruinous shell of a mansion, after being burnt out in 1927, but it replaced a castle. The lands were held by the Leask family from the thirteenth century or earlier. The family was allied with the Hays, but the Gordons seem to have borne them a serious grudge, harrying the Leasks repeatedly in 1615. George Gordon, sixth of Gight, or Adam, his brother, broke his sword across the head of Alexander Leask at his own gates, and some of the Gordons were outlawed for attacking Alexander's son; George Gordon of Gight was eventually outlawed. The Leask family held the property until the end of the seventeenth century, but they invested heavily in the Darien scheme and were then ruined. The property was sold to the Cummings, then passed to the Gordons, who changed the name to Pitlurg; although it was changed back when it later was acquired by the Skenes.

mysite.wanadoo-members.co.uk/clanleask1/index.jhtml
No. of castles/sites: 1
Rank: 537=/764

Leckie

The name is territorial, and comes from the lands and barony of Leckie, which are west of Gargunnock and six or so miles west of Stirling. The name also has links to the Mac-Gregors.

 Leckie, now **Old Leckie House** [NS 690946], is a T-plan tower house with a centrally placed stair-turret, and dates from the sixteenth century. The lands were held by the Leckie family from the fourteenth

Old Leckie House (M&R)

century or earlier, and they built the original castle. The family are believed to be descended from a son of one of the Earls of Lennox, but the property was sold to the Moirs in 1659, who held it into the twentieth century.

 Broich House [NS 641951], to the north-west of Kippen in Stirlingshire, has been demolished but appears to have occupied the site of an old stronghold which was defended by a ditch and rampart. Broich was replaced by Arngomery House, a mansion of the nineteenth century. The lands were held by the Shaws and by the Edmonstones, before being sold to the Leckies in 1773.

No. of castles/sites: 2
Rank: 396=/764
Xref: Lecky

Leighton

The name comes from the barony of the same name in Bedfordshire in England, and is first on record in Scotland at the end of the twelfth century. Many of the family were eminent churchmen, and Henry Leighton was Bishop of Moray, and then of Aberdeen, and he was responsible for much of the work of St Machar's Cathedral in Aberdeen in 1422-40. His carved tomb is located in the south transept; the church and ruins are open to the public (01224 485988; www.stmachar.com). Robert Leighton was principal of the University of Edinburgh and then the Protestant Bishop of Dunblane. Leighton donated some 1500 books to establish the Leighton Library in Dunblane, which is open to the public (01786 822296; www.dunblane cathedral.org.uk). He was made Archbishop of Glasgow but he resigned his office in 1674 and went to England.

Usan House [NO 723553] stands a couple of miles south of Montrose in Angus, and the mansion probably incorporates part of an old stronghold. The lands were held by the Leightons from the thirteenth century, and they had a castle, which was rebuilt in 1608. Alexander Leighton, who came from the family, was a Puritan author who wrote *Zion's Plea Against Prelacy* in 1630. His work did not go down with the Episcopalian authorities of the day, and the poor man had his ear cut off. The property later passed to the Scotts, then to the Keiths and finally to the Alstons.

No. of castles/sites: 1 / Rank: 537=/764

Leitch

The name comes from the Old English for 'doctor' ('leech'), and the name is on record in Scotland from the first quarter of the fourteenth century. A family of this name held the lands of Kildavanan on the west side of Bute in the fifteenth century, but the lands passed to the Stewarts.

Kilmardinny House [NS 550727], in Bearsden to the north of Glasgow, stands on the site of a castle or old house. The building was remodelled and given a new front in the nineteenth century. Kilmardinny was held by the Colquhouns and by the Grahams of Dougalston before passing to the Leitch family. The mansion now houses the Kilmardinny Arts Centre.

No. of castles/sites: 1 / Rank: 537=/764
Xref: Leach

Leith

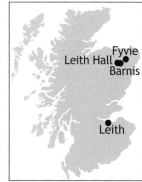

The name probably comes from the port and burgh of Leith, which is now part of Edinburgh. The name is on record from the fourteenth century, and the family became landowners in Aberdeenshire, although their origins are not clear.

Barnis or **Netherhall** [NJ 640257], a mile or so south and east of Insch in Aberdeenshire, was held by the Leiths from the fourteenth century. William Leith of Barnis was Provost of Aberdeen in 1350, as was his son, Laurence, at the beginning of the fifteenth century. There was probably a castle at or near Netherhall. Nearby **Edingarioch** [NJ 621240], further south of Insch, was owned by the Leslies, but passed to the Leiths in 1499, who sold it to the Forbeses in the seventeenth century, before it passed back to the Leiths.

Leith Hall [NJ 541298] is a few miles north-east of Rhynie also in Aberdeenshire, and is a fine altered tower house, dating from the seventeenth century. Turrets crown the corners, and ranges were built in following

Leith Hall (MC)

years to encircle a courtyard. Small drum towers were added in the nineteenth century. The lands were a property of the Leiths until 1945, and the family were made Baronets in 1923, although by then they were Forbes-Leith. The hall has reports of ghosts, including the sighting of a bearded and bandaged man. The bogle is thought to be John Leith, who was killed in a brawl and shot in the head in 1763, or perhaps Colonel Alexander Leith, who died in 1900 and had fought at the Battle of Balaclava. Apparitions of a woman in Victorian dress have also reputedly been seen, as well as a young child and governess. The property is now in the care of The National Trust for Scotland, and the house and extensive grounds are open to the public (01464 831216; www.nts.org.uk). The Leith family now apparently live at Dunachton, near Kingussie in Strathspey.

Fyvie Castle [NJ 764393], eight miles south of Turriff and a mile north of Fyvie village again in Aberdeenshire,

Fyvie Castle (MC)

is one of the most magnificent castles in Scotland. The massive building was added to down the centuries, each family who owned it adding a new tower. It has a fine interior and the main turnpike stair is decorated with twenty-two coats of arms. Many of the chambers are panelled in wood, and have plaster ceilings and tempera painting. The castle had many legends and a famous ghost story, and was owned in turn by the Lindsays, by the Prestons, by the Meldrums, by the Setons, by the Gordons and then finally by the Leiths, then Forbes-Leiths, from 1889. The castle is now in the care of The National Trust for Scotland and the castle, gardens and grounds are open to the public (01651 891266; www.nts.org.uk).

The Leiths also held:

Aquhorthies or **House of Aquhorthies** [NJ 729200], near Inverurie, Aberdeenshire; castle replaced by mansion.
 Held by the Leiths in the seventeenth century. The house was used as a Roman Catholic seminary from 1799-1829, but was then remodelled as a house and occupied by the Blairs.

Dunachton Castle [NH 820047], near Kingussie, Strathspey; castle replaced by mansion.
 Held by the MacNivens and then by the Mackintoshes, but much later the property passed to the Forbes-Leiths of Fyvie, Baronets, and they apparently still live at Dunachton.

New Leslie or **Castle Croft** [NJ 588253], near Insch, Aberdeenshire; site of castle.
 Held by the Leslies, then by the Leiths from 1600 to 1650. The castle was ruinous by 1724.

Freefield House [NJ 676314], near Inverurie, Aberdeenshire; castle replaced by mansion.
 Held by the Leiths. George Leith of Freefield was killed by Leslie of Pitcaple, starting a feud between the families.

Glenkindie House [NJ 437140], near Kildrummy, Aberdeenshire; castle replaced by mansion.
 Held by the Strachans, but later passed to the Leiths. Still occupied.

Harthill Castle [NJ 687252], near Inverurie, Aberdeenshire; Z-plan tower house.
 Held by and built by the Leith family, who were in possession of the lands from 1531. One of the family, Patrick Leith, was noted for his boldness and leadership in the army of the Marquis of Montrose. He was captured by General Middleton in 1647, and beheaded at the age of twenty-five years. The last Leith of Harthill apparently deliberately torched the castle, and the property passed to the Erskines of Pittodrie. The building was restored in the 1970s and is occupied.

Leslie Castle [NJ 599248], near Insch, Aberdeenshire; restored tower house.
 Held by the Leslies, but passed to the Forbeses then to the Leiths of Leith Hall in 1671. The castle was ruinous in 1820

but was restored in the 1980s, and was then recently put up for sale for offers of more than £750,000.

Lickleyhead Castle [NJ 627237], near Insch, Aberdeenshire; fine altered L-plan tower house.
 Held by the Leslies, then by the Leiths, before being sold to the Forbeses in 1625, then went to other families. The building is still occupied.

No. of castles/sites: 12
Rank: 120=/764

Harthill Castle (M&R) – see previous column

Lempitlaw

The name is territorial and comes from the lands of Lempitlaw, which are three or so miles east of Kelso in the Borders. The name is on record from the end of the twelfth century, and in 1580 a family of that name held lands in Lanark.

 There was a tower house at **Lempitlaw** [NT 787327] but this was destroyed by the English in 1547. The family, however, appear to have been forfeited by Robert the Bruce in the first quarter of the fourteenth century (well before the tower was built) and Lempitlaw was later held by the Dalgleish family.

 Nearby **Sprouston** [NT 755352] also had a tower house and the lands may have been held by the Lempitlaw family before going to the Francis family in the fourteenth century.

No. of castles/sites: 2
Rank: 396=/764

Lennox

The name comes from the old Earldom of Lennox, which covered not only Dunbartonshire, but also parts of Renfrew, of Stirling and of Perthshire. Lennox is believed to come from 'smooth stream' in Gaelic, and the Earls were settled in their lands by the end of the twelfth century.

They were one of the most powerful families in Scotland, and supported Robert the Bruce in the Wars of Independence. The family married into, and were allied with, the Stewart Dukes of Albany, who virtually ruled Scotland during the reign of Robert III and then the captivity of James I. James was eventually released from England, and had Murdoch, second Duke of Albany, beheaded, along with the Earl of Lennox, in 1425. The lands of the earldom were then divided between the Menteiths of Ruskie and the Stewarts of Darnley. Although the former got much of the land, the latter got the title, and Henry Stewart, Lord Darnley and Mary Queen of Scots's husband, was the son of the Earl of Lennox. The title stayed with the Stewarts, and in 1579 the holder was made Duke of Lennox. The family went on to become the Gordon-Lennox Dukes of Richmond, Gordon and Lennox, along with other titles; and they now apparently live in Sussex in England.

The Lennox family itself also held castles and land in Scotland, and one branch became established in Kirkcudbright in Galloway.

Antermony Castle [NS 662765], near Milton of Campsie, Dunbartonshire; site of castle and mansion.
  Held by the Flemings, but passed to the Lennox family.

Balcastle [NS 702782], near Kilsyth, Dunbartonshire; site of castle on motte.
  Held by the Earls of Lennox, but passed to the Callanders, then by marriage to the Livingstones.

Balcorrach Castle [NS 614789], near Milngavie, Dunbartonshire; site of castle.
  Held by the Lennox family. This branch of the family was descended from Donald, son of Duncan, eighth Earl of Lennox. They lived at Balcorrach from 1421 until they moved to Woodhead around 1570.

Ballagan or **Campsie Castle** [NS 572796], near Milngavie, Dunbartonshire; site of castle.
  Held by the Earls of Lennox, and then by the Stirlings from 1522 to 1756.

Balloch Castle [NS 386826], Balloch, Dunbartonshire; earthworks from a castle.
  Held by the Earls of Lennox until 1425, when it passed to the Stewarts of Darnley, who were made Earls of Lennox. It then passed through several families. Balloch Castle, a large mansion, was first built about 1808 and now houses a visitor centre (01389 720620; www.lochlomond-trossachs.org).

Bencloich Castle [NS 635785], near Kirkintilloch, Dunbartonshire; site of castle.
  Held by the Lennox family from 1421, but later passed to the Livingstones of Kilsyth.

Boturich Castle [NS 387845], near Balloch, Dunbartonshire; mansion on site of castle.
  Held by the Earls of Lennox, but passed to the Haldanes of Gleneagles in 1425. Holiday accommodation is available (www.scottscastles.com).

Cally Castle [NX 598554], near Gatehouse of Fleet, Galloway; ruinous tower house.
  Held by the Stewarts, then by the Murrays and by the Lennoxes. William Lennox, younger of Cally, was accused of 'forethought felony and oppression in Kirkcudbright' in 1508, but the Lennox family still held by the property in 1637. Cally passed to the Murray-Stewarts of Broughton and they built Cally House [NX 600549], which is now a hotel (01557 814341; www.cally palace.co.uk).

Cameron House [NS 376831], near Alexandria, Dunbartonshire; castle replaced by mansion.
  Held by the Lennox family, then by others, but was sold to the Smolletts in 1763. The house is now a luxury hotel and leisure centre (01389 755565; www.cameronhouse.co.uk).

Catter Castle [NS 473871], near Drymen, Stirlingshire; site of castle on impressive motte.
  Held by the Earls of Lennox, who abandoned it for Inchmurrin, but later passed to the Buchanans.

Colzium Castle [NS 729788], near Kilsyth, Dunbartonshire; castle replaced by mansion.
  Held by several families until latterly by the Lennox family, who gifted the property to the local council in 1937. The grounds are open to the public and the house is available to hire for conference or functions (01236 624031; www.northlan.gov.uk).

Duntreath Castle [NS 536811], near Milngavie, Dunbartonshire; large altered courtyard castle.
  Held by the Earls of Lennox, but on their forfeiture passed to the Edmonstones of Culloden.

Faslane Castle [NS 249903], Faslane, Dunbartonshire; motte.
  Held by the Earls of Lennox, although the castle was abandoned by the end of the fourteenth century. The property passed to MacAulays of Ardencaple, then to the Colquhouns of Luss.

Gordon Castle [NJ 350596], near Elgin, Moray; reduced mansion and castle.
  Held by the Gordons, latterly Gordon-Lennox Dukes of Richmond, Gordon and Lennox. The property was sold in 1936 in lieu of death duties, but was bought back by the family, although the castle was partly demolished and now looks a bit odd. There is a burial aisle of the family at Dipple [NJ 328579].

Inchmurrin Castle [NS 373863], island in Loch Lomond, Dunbartonshire; ruinous castle.
  Home of the widow of Murdoch Stewart, second Duke of Albany, after he been executed along with his sons by James I in 1425. She had been imprisoned in Tantallon Castle for two years, and died at Inchmurrin in 1460. This part of the Earldom, along with the title, went to the Stewarts of Darnley. In 1506 James IV stayed at the castle, as did James VI in 1585 and in 1617. The island passed to the Graham Dukes of Montrose around the beginning of the eighteenth century, and the castle was ruinous by 1724.

Kilmaronock Castle [NS 456877], near Drymen, Stirlingshire; ruinous castle.
  Held by the Earls of Lennox, but passed to the Flemings in 1329, then went to others.

Maiden Castle [NS 643785], near Kirkintilloch, Dunbartonshire; motte.
  Held by the Earls of Lennox.

Old Dalquhurn House [NS 390780], near Dumbarton; site of castle or old house.
  Held by the Earls of Lennox and then by the Spreulls from the fourteenth century, but was bought by the Dennistouns in 1620. The property passed to the Smolletts in 1692. The house has been demolished and a church occupies the site.

327

Place of Bonhill [NS 390793], near Alexandria, Dunbartonshire; site of castle and mansion.

Held by the Lennox family, but passed to the Lindsays in the fifteenth century and then went to the Smolletts.

Plunton Castle [NX 605507], near Gatehouse of Fleet, Galloway; L-plan tower house.

Held by the MacGies, but passed to the Lennox family, who built the tower, then passed by marriage to the Murrays of Broughton.

Rosneath Castle [NS 272823], Rosneath, Dunbartonshire; site of castle and mansion.

Held by the Earls of Lennox, but passed to the Campbells of Argyll. The site is now a caravan park.

Shandon [NS 257878], near Faslane, Dunbartonshire; motte.

Held by the Earls of Lennox.

Woodhead Castle [NS 606783], near Milngavie, Dunbartonshire; ruinous L-plan tower house.

Held by the Lennoxes of Balcorrach in 1572. The Lennoxes of Woodhead feuded with the Kincaids until the families were united by marriage. The castle was left a picturesque ruin when nearby Lennox Castle was built about 1840. This mansion was sold to the city of Glasgow in 1927, and the family moved to England.

No. of castles/sites: 21
Rank: 63=/764

Leny

The name is territorial and comes from the lands of Leny, which are a mile or so west and north of Callander in Stirlingshire. The name comes on record from the thirteenth century. The surname was also found on Orkney from the place called Linay.

Leny House [NN 613089] is a sixteenth-century L-plan tower house, which has been extended by a large mansion, encasing the old castle on three sides. The property was held by the Leny family, but passed by marriage to the Buchanans, who held it until the twentieth century. The building is now used as a hotel (01877 331078; www.lenyestate.com).

No. of castles/sites: 1
Rank: 537=/764
Xrefs: Lennie; Lenny

Leslie

The name is territorial and comes from the lands and barony of Leslie, which are three miles south-west of Insch in Aberdeenshire. The family claim descent from Bartholomew (or Bartolf), who came to Scotland in the entourage of Queen Margaret, wife of Malcolm Canmore, in the 1060s. Malcolm made Bartholomew keeper of Edinburgh Castle, and the family became established in Aberdeenshire, and then in Fife and elsewhere.

Leslie Castle [NJ 599248] is an L-plan tower house, dating from the seventeenth century but standing on the site of an older stronghold. There was a courtyard

Leslie Castle (M&R)

and moat, but these have gone. The lands were held by the Leslies from the eleventh or twelfth century. Malcolm, Bartolf's son, was made Constable of the royal castle at Inverurie (Bass of Inverurie). Through marriage the Leslies gained other properties, but the lands of Leslie were sold to the Forbes of Monymusk in the seventeenth century, and they probably built, or rebuilt, the present castle. The castle became ruinous but was restored in the 1980s and then later was put up for sale for offers of more than £750,000.

Leslie House [NO 259019], to the north of Glenrothes in Fife, was previously known as **Fettykil** of **Fythkill**, but the name was changed when it came into the possession of the Leslie family in the thirteenth century. There was a castle, but it was replaced by the present courtyard mansion, which was rebuilt as a classical mansion of three storeys after a fire in 1763. The mansion is currently used as a Church of Scotland eventide home, but this may be about to close.

Ballinbreich Castle [NO 271204] is a couple of miles north-east of Newburgh by the Tay in Fife. The building is now the impressive ruin of a large courtyard castle. The Leslies acquired the lands in 1312, and the family were made Earls of Rothes (a property in Moray) in 1457.

Ballinbreich Castle (M&R)

William Leslie, third Earl, was killed at the Battle of Flodden in 1513. George, fourth Earl, was one of the commissioners for the marriage of Mary to the Dauphin of France. He died in mysterious circumstances, along with the Earl of Cassillis and others, after becoming ill at Dieppe in France: it is thought that they were poisoned. Norman, Master of Rothes, was one of those responsible for the murder of Cardinal Beaton, but went on to fight in France and was killed after the Battle of Renti in 1554. The castle was visited by Mary, Queen of Scots, in 1565. John, sixth Earl and grandson of Alexander, fifth Earl, led the Covenanters in 1638, and John, seventh Earl, was captured at the Battle of Worcester in 1651 and remained in prison until 1658. He was made Treasurer of Scotland in 1663 after the Restoration and then Chancellor four years later, and then Duke of Rothes in 1680; this title was extinct on his death, although the earldom continued through his daughter. Ballinbreich was sold to the Dundases of Kerse in the nineteenth century. The Leslie Earls of Rothes now apparently live in Salisbury in Wiltshire in England.

Three or so miles east of Glenrothes, also in Fife, is **Balgonie Castle** [NO 313007] which consists of a fine keep or tower, dating from the fourteenth century and of five storeys, with a walled courtyard. The lands were held by the Sibbalds and then by the Lundies, but in 1635 were bought by Alexander Leslie. He fought for Gustavus Adolphus of Sweden during the Thirty Years War and was made a Field Marshall. Leslie was captured at Alyth in Angus after the Battle of Dunbar in 1650 while on the losing side against Cromwell, and was imprisoned in the Tower of London, only the intervention of the Queen of Sweden saving his life. He died at Balgonie in 1661. Balgonie was captured and plundered by Rob Roy MacGregor in 1716, and was sold in 1824 to the Balfours of Whittinghame. The castle has many ghost stories, including of a Green Lady and of an apparition which might have been Leslie himself; a skeleton was also found buried beneath the floor in 1912. The castle is open to the public (01592 750119; www.balgonie-castle.com).

The Leslies also held:

Aikenway Castle [NJ 291509], near Charlestown of Aberlour, Moray; slight remains of castle.
Held by the Leslies around 1450.

Balquhain Castle [NJ 732236], near Inverurie, Aberdeenshire; ruinous castle.
Held by the Leslies from 1340, and the castle was sacked in

Balquhain Castle (M&R)

1526 during a feud with the Forbes family. Mary, Queen of Scots, spent the night here before the Battle of Corrichie in 1562, when her forces defeated the Gordons of Huntly. In 1746 Balquhain was burnt by the forces of the Duke of Cumberland, and was probably never restored.

Birkhill House [NO 336234], near Wormit, Fife; castle or old house replaced by mansion.
Held by the Leslies in the seventeenth century, but later passed to the Scrymgeour Earls of Dundee, and they apparently still live here. The gardens are occasionally open to the public (www.gardensofscotland.org).

Cairnie [NO 635420], Arbroath, Angus; site of castle or old house.
Probably held by the Abernethys, then by the Leslies in the thirteenth century, but long a property of the Aikmans.

Castle Croft or **New Leslie** [NJ 588253], near Insch, Aberdeenshire; site of castle.
Held by the Leslies from about 1470, but passed to the Leiths around 1600, and the castle was ruinous by 1724.

Chanonry [NH 727567], Fortrose, Ross and Cromarty; part of the cathedral buildings was a fortified tower.
The lands of the abbey were fought over by the Leslies of Balquhain and the Mackenzies of Kintail. The Mackenzies won out, and were made Earls of Seaforth in 1623.

Crichie [NJ 978453], near Mintlaw, Aberdeenshire; castle replaced by mansion.
Held by the Leslies, but passed to the Keiths and then to others.

Cushnie Castle [NJ 525111], near Alford, Aberdeenshire; some remains of castle.
Held by the Cushnies, but passed to the Leslies in the early fourteenth century, then to the Lumsdens in 1509.

Drumdollo Castle [NJ 606387], near Huntly, Aberdeenshire; site of castle.
Held by the Leslies in the sixteenth century.

Drummuir [NJ 407448], near Keith, Aberdeenshire; altered L-plan tower house.
Held by the Leslies, but the tower was built by the Abercrombys, and the property later passed to the Duffs. The modern Drummuir Castle has guided tours some days and there are holiday cottages on the estate (01542 810225; www.drummuirestate.co.uk).

Eden Castle [NJ 698588], near Banff, Aberdeenshire; some remains of castle.

Held by the Meldrums, but had passed to the Leslies by 1613. Alexander Leslie of Eden wrote the ballad 'The Banks o' Deveron Water' for Helen Christie. The castle was sold to the Duff Earl of Fife in 1712.

Edingarioch [NJ 621240], near Insch, Aberdeenshire; site of castle or old house.

Held by the Leslies, but passed to the Leiths in 1499, then to the Forbeses.

Fetternear House [NJ 723171], near Inverurie, Aberdeenshire; slight remains of castle.

Held by the Leslies after the Reformation, who built a tower house in the 1560s. The property passed to the Abercrombies of Birkenbog in 1627, but later returned to the Leslies. The Fetternear Banner, a pre-Reformation banner of the fraternity of the Holy Blood, was kept here by the Leslies. Patrick Leslie of Fetternear was a count of the Holy Roman Empire. The present house was burnt out in 1919 and is a large ruin.

Findrassie Castle [NJ 195651], near Elgin, Moray; site of castle.

Held by the Leslies of Findrassie from the sixteenth century until 1825. The present house, dating from 1780, has vaulted outbuildings.

Folla [NJ 705344], near Rothienorman, Aberdeenshire; possible site of castle or old house.

Held by the Leslies from the seventeenth to the nineteenth century.

House of Tyrie [NJ 936632], near Fraserburgh, Aberdeenshire; site of old house or castle.

Long held by the Frasers, but was sold to the Leslies in 1725, although the property was recovered by the Frasers at the end of the nineteenth century.

Keir House [NS 770989], near Stirling; mansion incorporating part of castle.

Held by the Leslies, but passed to the Stirlings in 1448.

Keith Hall or **Caskieben Castle** [NJ 787212], near Inverurie, Aberdeenshire; altered Z-plan tower house.

Held by the Leslies in 1224, but passed to the Garriochs and then to the Johnstones, then later to the Keiths, who changed the name from Caskieben to Keith Hall. The house has been divided into flats.

Kininvie House [NJ 319441], near Dufftown, Moray; altered L-plan tower house.

Held by the Leslies from 1521. The stone effigy and tomb of Alexander Leslie of Kininvie, who died about 1549, are located in Mortlach Parish Church [NJ 323392]. James V is reputed to have hidden in the kitchen of Kininvie while travelling as the 'Gudeman of Ballengeich'. The house was extended in 1840, and the Leslies still apparently own the property. It is occupied, although the family now apparently live in Midlothian.

Lamberton [NT 965573], near Berwick upon Tweed, Borders; site of tower house.

Held by the Lambertons, but passed by marriage to the Leslies around 1400. There was a later tower house, probably built by the Rentons, but this was destroyed by the English in 1545.

Letterfourie [NJ 447625], near Buckie, Aberdeenshire; castle replaced by mansion.

Held by the Leslies, but passed to the Gordons in the sixteenth century.

Lickleyhead Castle [NJ 627237], near Insch, Aberdeenshire; fine L-plan tower house.

Held by the Leslies, but passed to the Leiths, who built most of the existing castle, but then passed to the Hays, to the Duffs and to others.

Lour [NO 478462], near Forfar, Angus; site of castle.

Held by the Abernethys, but then passed to several families, including to the Leslies, and then to the Carnegies.

Mugdrum [NO 228184], near Newburgh, Fife; mansion incorporating older work.

Held by the Arnotts and then by the Leslies in the seventeenth century, then by the Cheapes in 1678 and then by others.

Newark Castle [NO 518012], near Elie, Fife; ruinous castle.

Held by the Kinlochs and by the Sandilands, then was bought by the Covenanter General Sir David Leslie in 1649. Leslie served under Gustavus Adolphus of Sweden, and joined the Covenanters in 1643. He fought at Marston Moor the following year, defeated the Marquis of Montrose at Philiphaugh a year later, and then led a campaign up the west coast of Scotland in 1647. He was one of the leaders of the Scottish army that was defeated by Cromwell at Dunbar 1650. He escaped but was captured after defeat at the Battle of Worcester the following year, after which he spent nine years in the Tower of London. He was made Lord Newark and died in 1682. Newark is said to be haunted by a Green Lady, the ghost of Jean Leslie, daughter of Sir David Leslie. The property passed to the Anstruthers, and then to the Bairds of Elie (www.inverie.com).

Newton House [NJ 662297], near Inverurie, Aberdeenshire; castle replaced by mansion.

Held by the Leslies at one time.

Pitcairlie House [NO 236148], near Auchtermuchty, Fife; mansion incorporating castle.

Held by the Abernethys, but passed by marriage to the Leslies in 1312, one of whom was David Leslie of Newark. The family

Pitcairlie House (M&R)

became bankrupt and the lands were sold to the Cathcarts of Carbiston in the eighteenth century. The house is still occupied, and holiday self-catering accommodation is available (01337 827418; www.pitcairlie-leisure.co.uk).

Pitcaple Castle [NJ 726261], near Inverurie, Aberdeenshire; Z-plan tower house.

Held by the Leslies from 1457. The fourth laird slew George Leith of Freefield, starting a feud between the families. James IV visited Pitcaple, as did Mary, Queen of Scots, in 1562. In 1650 the Marquis of Montrose was imprisoned here on his way

Pitcaple Castle (M&R)

to Edinburgh to be executed, and Charles II visited the same year. The laird was killed at the Battle of Worcester in 1651 fighting for Charles. The castle passed by marriage to the Lumsdens in 1757. When a robin is found in the castle it is reputedly the harbinger of bad news and the herald of death. A robin was discovered when the laird was killed at the Battle of Worcester in 1651, although later appearances of the birds are sketchy. The castle is still occupied.

Place of Tillyfour [NJ 659195], near Inverurie, Aberdeenshire; L-plan tower house.

Held by the Leslies of Wardhouse from 1508, who built a castle, but the property passed to the Gordons after 1640. The building was restored about 1884 and is still occupied.

Powis House [NJ 939081], Aberdeen; castle replaced by mansion.

Held by the Frasers, but passed to the Leslies and then to the Burnetts. The house is now a community centre, while the grounds were used to build a housing estate.

Rothes Castle [NJ 277490], near Charlestown of Aberlour, Moray; remains of castle.

Held by the Leslies, who were made Earls of Rothes in 1457. The castle was burnt by the Innes family, and may have been damaged by Montrose. It was slighted around 1660 to prevent it being used by brigands, who were raiding the area. The Leslies lived in Fife, but were created Dukes of Rothes in 1680, although they reverted to Earls when the first Duke died without sons; the Earldom of Rothes continued through his daughter. Rothes was sold to Grant of Elchies in 1700.

Tullos House [NJ 703218], near Inverurie, Aberdeenshire; ruinous L-plan castle or house.

Held by the Leslies of Balquhain, and used until the end of the eighteenth century.

Wardhouse [NJ 593289], near Insch, Aberdeenshire; site of castle.

Held by the Leslies in the sixteenth century but passed to the Gordons.

Warthill House [NJ 710315], near Rothienorman, Aberdeenshire; castle replaced by mansion.

Held by the Cruickshanks, but passed by marriage to the Leslies about 1518, and it is still apparently occupied by their descendants.

www.clanlesliesociety.org
No. of castles/sites: 38
Rank: 29=/764
Xref: Lesley

Lestalric

The name is territorial and comes from the lands, now an area of Edinburgh, of Restalrig, which were originally known as Lestalric, and formerly pronounced 'Lestarick'. The name is on record from the end of the twelfth century.

Lochend House or **Restalrig Castle** [NT 273743] is to the east of Edinburgh, and the present mansion incorporates part of an altered castle, which dated from the sixteenth century or before. The lands were held by the Lestalric family in the thirteenth century, but passed by marriage to the Logans in the following century. The Logans held them until 1601, when they passed to the Elphinstone Lords Balmerino. The house is still occupied.

No. of castles/sites: 1
Rank: 537=/764
Xref: Restalrig

Lickprivick

The name is territorial and comes from the lands of the same name, which are a mile or so south-west of East Kilbride in Lanarkshire. The name was spelt in various ways down the centuries. Robert Lekprevivk was a printer in Edinburgh and he was made King's Printer in 1568.

Lickprivick Castle [NS 616527] incorporated an old keep or tower, and the castle had towers and battlements. It dated from the fourteenth century, and was long a property of the Lickprivick family, but the lands may have eventually passed to the Maxwells of Calderwood. The castle has been completely demolished, and the site is occupied by a housing estate.

No. of castles/sites: 1
Rank: 537=/764
Xrefs: Lapraik; Lekprevick

Liddel

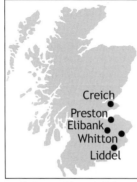

The name is local in origin, probably from Liddel and Liddesdale in the Borders, although there is also a barony of the same name in Cumbria in England. The family are on record from the fourteenth century. There is a **Liddel Castle** [NY 510900], a couple miles north and east of Newcastleton, although it is not clear if it was ever held by a family of that name, being a possession of the Soulis family. The castle was visited by Edward I, and was probably destroyed early in the fourteenth century and not reused.

Elibank Castle [NT 397363] is four miles east of Innerleithen in the Borders, and is a ruinous L-plan tower house of the sixteenth century. The lands were held by the Liddels, but passed to the Murrays in about 1594. The castle was a ruin by 1722. **Whitton Tower** [NT 759222], two miles south of Morebattle also in the Borders, was held by the Liddel family in the middle of the twelfth century, but had passed to the Bennets by 1523. Their tower house, now ruinous, was sacked by the English that year, and then again in 1545.

The site of **Broadstone Castle** [NS 359528] is a mile south-east of Beith in Ayrshire, and the last remains were removed when the farm of Broadstonehall was built. The lands were held by the Liddels in 1452, but probably were later a possession of the Montgomerys and then of the Greenock family.

Creich Castle [NO 329212] is a ruinous L-plan tower house, dating from the sixteenth century, and five miles north-west of Cupar in Fife. It was held by the Liddels, but they were forfeited for treason and the property was sold to the Beatons in 1502.

Preston Tower [NT 393742] is located to the south-east of Prestonpans in East Lothian, and is an impressive and stark L-plan tower of six storeys. It stands in its own garden. The property was held by the Homes and by the Setons, before passing to the Liddels, and then the property went by marriage to the Hamiltons. The tower was torched in 1544 and then again in 1650, and is now a ruin. It can be viewed from the exterior and the attractive gardens are open from dawn to dusk (01875 810232).

No. of castles/sites: 5
Rank: 240=/764
Xrefs: Liddal; Liddle

Lindsay

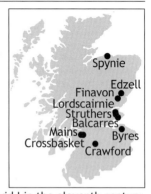

The name is probably territorial and Norman in origin, coming from 'de Limesay', north of Rouen in France, or perhaps from territory in Lincolnshire in England. The family had wide possessions on both sides of the border, after Sir Walter de Lindissie came to Scotland with David I in the eleventh century.

Crawford Castle [NS 954213], to the north of the village of Crawford in Lanarkshire, was also known as **Lindsay Tower**, but there are now only slight remains of the old stronghold. The family long held the lands,

Crawford Castle (M&R)

and it was from Crawford that the Earldom was created in 1398.

The Lindsays added their seal to the Declaration of Arbroath in 1320. Sir David Lindsay took part in the famous tournament at London Bridge in 1390, and he defeated his English opponent. Lindsay was made Earl of Crawford in 1398, and was also High Lord Admiral of Scotland. The lands and castle of Crawford passed to the Douglases in 1488, but the Lindsays kept the title.

Finavon Castle [NO 497566] was once a strong and important fortress, but it is now very ruinous. It stands four or so miles north-east of Forfar in Angus, and passed to the Lindsay of Crawford in 1375. David, third Earl, and his brother-in-law, Ogilvie of Inverquharity, were both badly wounded at Battle of Arbroath in 1446, and were brought to Finavon. The Earl soon died, and his wife suffocated Ogilvie, her own brother, with a pillow to ensure the succession of her own son. The fourth Earl, known as 'The Tiger' or 'Earl Beardie', was a ruthless fellow. Earl Beardie hanged a minstrel from hooks who had (correctly) predicted the defeat of the Lindsays at the Battle of Brechin in 1452. Crawford fled after the battle, but James II pardoned him as the king was more interested in destroying Lindsay's allies, the Black Douglases. On the Covin Tree, reputedly grown from a chestnut dropped by a Roman soldier, the fourth Earl hanged Jock Barefoot for cutting a walking stick from the tree. Jock's ghost is said to haunt the castle.

David, fifth Earl, became Lord High Admiral, Lord Chamberlain and High Justiciary; while John, sixth Earl, was slain at the Battle of Flodden in 1513. In 1530, David, eighth Earl, was murdered by a Dundee cobbler in a brawl; and David, tenth Earl, married Margaret, daughter of Cardinal Beaton, at Finavon in 1546. The property was sold in 1629 to Lord Spynie, after Edzell became the Earls of Crawford main seat. The title of the Earl of Crawford was eventually united with that of the Earls of Balcarres. Finavon fell into the ruin, although a fine doocot survives and is in the care of The National Trust for Scotland.

Edzell Castle [NO 585693] lies some six miles north of Brechin in the north of Angus. It is a grand ruinous tower and castle with a magnificent walled garden. It was held by the Stirlings of Glenesk, but passed to the Lindsay Earls of Crawford in 1357. Mary, Queen of Scots, held a Privy Council at Edzell in 1562, and stayed in the castle; Cromwell garrisoned Edzell in 1651. During the Royalist uprising of 1653, John Lindsay was kidnapped

Edzell Castle (M&R)

from Edzell, but he was rescued by Cromwell's forces.

One story associated with the castle is that the one of the Lindsays lairds was cursed by a gypsy woman after he had hanged her sons for poaching. The tale goes that his pregnant wife died that day, while Lindsay was himself devoured by wolves. This goes rather against Edzell being known as the 'Kitchen of Angus', apparently due to the generous hospitality of the Lindsays.

The castle is said to be haunted by a White Lady, reputedly the spirit of Catherine Campbell, second wife of David Lindsay, ninth Earl of Crawford. She was thought to have died suddenly in 1578, but is said to have been interred alive in the Lindsay Burial Aisle [NO 582688] at Edzell Old Church. She eventually regained consciousness when a sextant tried to steal her rings, and one version has her dying of exposure at the castle gates, although others that she lived on for many years.

The Lindsays got into serious debt, and had to sell Edzell to the Maule Earls of Panmure. The castle was garrisoned by Hanoverian troops, who did much damage, and the building was abandoned soon afterwards. Edzell is now in the care of Historic Scotland, and the ruined castle, splendid walled garden and the Lindsay Burial Aisle are all open to the public (01356 648631).

Balcarres House [NO 476044] is a few miles north of Elie in Fife. The large mansion incorporates a Z-plan tower house of the sixteenth century. Good oak panelling, carving and plasterwork survive in the house. There is an extensive garden, and a ruined chapel from 1635 serves as the family burial ground. The lands were held by the Lindsays of Menmuir from 1587, and the family became Lord Balcarres in 1633, and then Earls of Balcarres in 1651. Charles II visited the same year. Colin, third Earl, fought for James VII, and had to flee to Holland between 1693 and 1700. He returned and joined the Jacobites in 1715, but was then confined to Balcarres for the rest of his life. Alexander Lindsay, sixth Earl of Balcarres, also became the Earl of Crawford in 1808, and the Lindsays still apparently occupy Balcarres. The gardens are occasionally open to the public (www.gardensofscotland.org).

Byres [NT 495770] is a couple of miles north of Haddington in East Lothian but little remains except for the ruin of a small tower or keep. The property was originally held by the Byres family, but passed to the Lindsays of the Byres. Patrick, sixth Lord Lindsay of Byres, supported the Reformation and was involved in the plot to murder Rizzio. He took a leading part in compelling Mary, Queen of Scots, to abdicate, and was a party in the Ruthven Raid when James VI was confined in Huntingtower Castle. John, tenth Lord Lindsay of Byres, was created Earl of Lindsay in 1633. He joined the Covenanters and fought at Marston Moor in 1644 against Charles I.

Struthers Castle [NO 377097], four miles south of Cupar in Fife, is a ruinous L-plan tower house, rising to four storeys and dating from the sixteenth century. It was held by the Keiths, but was exchanged for Dunnottar with the Lindsays of The Byres in 1392. Struthers became the main stronghold of this branch of the family, who later succeeded to the Earldom of Crawford. Mary, Queen of Scots, visited Struthers in 1565, Charles II stayed at the castle in 1651, and it was occupied by Cromwell's forces two years later.

The Lindsays also owned:
Alyth Castle [NO 247485], near Blairgowrie, Perthshire; slight remains of castle.
Held by the Lindsay Earls of Crawford from 1303 to 1620.
Auchenskeoch Castle [NX 917588], near Dalbeattie, Galloway; ruinous Z-plan tower house.
Held by the Lindsays, then by the Crichtons and by the Mackenzies.
Auchmull Castle [NO 585748], near Edzell, Angus; site of castle.
Held by the Lindsays. Perhaps built by Sir David Lindsay, Lord Edzell, as a refuge for his son who was implicated in the murder of his uncle, Lord Spynie.
Balgavies Castle [NO 540516], near Letham, Angus; slight remains of castle.
Held by several families, including by the Lindsays, but the castle was destroyed in 1594 by James VI.
Balmungo [NO 523148], near St Andrews, Fife; site of castle or old house.
Held by the Pringles, and then by the Lindsays in the eighteenth century, and then by the Maitlands and by the Bayne-Meldrums.

Ballinshoe Tower [NO 417532], near Kirriemuir, Angus; ruinous tower house.
Held by the Lindsays, but passed to the Fletchers in the middle of the seventeenth century.

Barntalloch Tower [NY 353878], near Langholm, Dumfries and Galloway; slight remains of tower house on motte.
Held by the Coningsburgh family, but passed to the Lindsays in 1285.

Barnyards [NO 479576], near Forfar, Angus; site of castle.
Held by the Lindsays.

Belstane Castle [NS 850515], near Carluke, Lanarkshire; site of tower house.
Held by the Livingstones, then by the Lindsays, by the Maxwells and by the Douglases.

Blacklaw Tower [NT 052067], near Moffat, Dumfries and Galloway; slight remains of tower house.
Held by the Lindsays from around 1315, but passed to the Herrieses of Terregles, then to the Maxwells, to the Johnstones and to the Douglases.

Brandy Den [NO 478610], near Brechin, Angus; site of castle.
Held by the Mowats of Fern, but passed to the Lindsay Earls of Crawford after 1450, then went to the Carnegies. The castle was abandoned for Vayne.

Careston Castle [NO 530599], near Brechin, Angus; fine Z-plan tower house.
Held by the Dempsters, then by the Lindsays, who extended the castle, then by the Carnegies and by the Adamsons. The castle is said to be haunted by a White Lady, which is reported to wander from chamber to chamber. The spirit of Jock Barefoot, slain for not delivering a message, is also said to haunt the building (as well as Finavon). Careston is still occupied.

Carsluith Castle [NX 495542], near Creetown, Galloway; L-plan tower house.
Held by the Cairns family, then by the Lindsays from 1460. James Lindsay, Chamberlain of Galloway, probably built the tower, but his son was killed at the Battle of Flodden in 1513 and the property passed by marriage to the Browns. In the care of Historic Scotland and open to the public.

Castlehill of Barcloy [NX 854524], near Dalbeattie, Galloway; site of castle.
Held by the Lindsays at the end of the sixteenth century, but later passed to the Stewarts and then to the MacLellans.

Cockburn House [NT 147651], near Balerno, Edinburgh; seventeenth-century house.
Held by the Lindsays from 1468 until 1670 when the property went to the Chieslys, who then built the present house. Still occupied.

Comyn's Castle [NS 628563], near East Kilbride, Lanarkshire; motte.
Held by the Comyns, but passed to the Lindsays of Dunrod. The Lindsays moved to the nearby castle of Mains [NS 627560] in the fifteenth century.

Corb Castle [NO 164568], near Blairgowrie, Perthshire; site of castle.
Held by the Lindsay Earls of Crawford, then by the Rattray family in the seventeenth century.

Covington Castle [NS 975399], near Lanark; ruinous castle.
Held by the Keith Earls Marischal, but passed to the Lindsays in 1368, who built the castle, then Covington was sold to the Lockharts in 1679.

Craigie Castle [NS 408317], near Kilmarnock, Ayrshire; ruins of hall house and castle.
Held by the Lindsays in the thirteenth century, but passed to the Craigies, then to the Wallaces of Riccarton in 1371.

Crossbasket Castle [NS 665563], near East Kilbride, Lanarkshire; altered tower house.
Held by the Lindsays of Dunrod, whose main seat was Mains, and used as a dower house. It now houses a nursery and stores donations for the American-based 'Missionaries of the Latter Day Rain'.

Crossbasket Castle (M&R) – see previous column

Daviot Castle [NH 730405], near Inverness; slight remains of castle.
Held by the Lindsay Earls of Crawford, but passed to the Mackintoshes.

Dowhill Castle [NT 118973], near Kinross, Perth and Kinross; ruinous tower house.
Held by the Lindsays of Dowhill from the end of the fourteenth century. James Lindsay of Dowhill was one of those who helped Mary, Queen of Scots, escape from Lochleven Castle in 1568 but the family got into financial difficulty and the lands were sold. The property had passed to Robert Adam, the famous architect, by 1740, although Martin Lindsay of Dowhill, the last laird, took part in the Jacobite Rising of 1745-46. Although tried for treason, he was acquitted. The descendants of the Lindsays of Dowhill were made Baronets in 1962 and apparently live in London.

Duddingston [NT 102776], near South Queensferry, West Lothian; castle replaced by mansion.
Held by the Lindsays but passed by marriage to the Dundases in the sixteenth century.

Dunkenny [NO 355477], near Kirriemuir, Angus; site of castle.
Held by the Lambies, but may have also been held by the Lindsays as David Lindsay of Dunkenny was Bishop of Edinburgh.

Dunnottar Castle [NO 882839], near Stonehaven, Kincardineshire; wonderful ruinous castle on cliffs.
Held by the Lindsays of the Byres but swopped for Struthers in Fife with the Keith Earls Marischal in 1382. The castle is open all year (01569 762173; www.dunechtestates.co.uk).

Dunrod Castle [NS 224732], near Greenock, Renfrewshire; site of castle.
Held by the Comyns, but passed to the Lindsays. John Lindsay of Dunrod 'made sure' that the Red John Comyn was dead after Robert the Bruce had stabbed him in a church in Dumfries. The property was sold to the Stewarts of Blackhall in 1619, and the last Lindsay laird made a living selling charms to sailors and eventually died in a barn. 'In Innerkip the witches ride thick, And in Dunrod they dwell; But the greatest loon among them a', Is auld Dunrod himsel.'

Evelick Castle [NO 205260], near Perth; large ruinous L-plan tower house.
Held by the Lindsays of Evelick from 1497. One of the family, Thomas Lindsay, was brutally murdered here by his step-brother, James Douglas, in 1682. Douglas stabbed Lindsay five times, held him under the water in a burn, and finally dashed his brains out with a rock. Douglas was tried and executed for the crime. Allan Ramsay, the famous portrait painter, ran off with Margaret Lindsay, daughter of Sir Alexander Lindsay of

Evelick Castle (M&R)

Evelick, and made her his second wife. The family disapproved of Ramsay, but his painting of his wife hangs in the National Gallery of Scotland. The last Lindsay of Evelick was drowned in 1799. There are stories of a White Lady of Evelick, although it is not clear if the apparition of a woman in a white dress is directly connected with the castle. The ghost has reputedly been seen at Lady's Brig, which is on the road between Evelick and Kilspindie, near Balmyre, and on the road itself.

Fairgirth House [NX 879565], near Dalbeattie, Galloway; castle replaced by mansion.

Held by the Lindsays in the sixteenth century.

Farnell Castle [NO 624555], near Brechin, Angus; altered tower house.

Held by the Campbells after the Reformation, but passed to the Lindsays in 1568 then went by marriage to the Carnegies of Kinnaird. The castle housed farm labourers at one time, but has been restored and reoccupied.

Feddinch House [NO 485135], near St Andrews, Fife; castle or old house replaced by mansion.

Held by the Symsons and by the Aytons, and then by the Lindsays in the eighteenth and nineteenth centuries, and then by the Wedderburns. Accommodation is available (01334 470888; www.feddinch-house.com).

Fyvie Castle [NJ 764393], near Fyvie, Aberdeenshire; splendid massive castle.

Originally held by the Lindsays. William the Lyon held court here in 1214, as did Alexander II in 1222. Edward I of England stayed in 1296, during the Wars of Independence, and then Robert the Bruce in 1308. Margaret Keith, wife to the Earl of Crawford, was besieged here by her nephew, and the property passed to the Prestons in 1402; then to the Meldrums, to the Setons, to the Gordons and to the Leiths. Thomas the Rhymer is recorded as having made a prophecy concerning Fyvie; this was probably before the Lindsays were in possession. When the castle was first being built, stones were removed from church lands by demolishing a nearby chapel, but fell into a nearby river. The then laird refused Thomas shelter in the castle, and the Rhymer is said to have prophesied that unless the three stones were recovered the castle and estate would never descend in direct line for more than two generations. Only two of the stones were found, and the prophecy is said to have come true. One of the stones is in the charter room, while another is reported to be built into the foundations – and were said to 'weep', oozing with water, when tragedy is going to strike the owners. The castle is now in the care of The National Trust for Scotland and is open to the public (01651 891266; www.nts.org.uk).

Garleton Castle [NT 509767], near Haddington, East Lothian; mostly ruinous castle.

Held by the Lindsays. Sir David Lindsay of the Mount, the famous sixteenth-century author who wrote *The Satire of the*

Three Estates, is thought to have been born here. Garleton passed to the Towers of Inverleith, who sold it to the Setons. The building is said to be haunted.

Herbertshiel [NO 862753], near Inverbervie, Kincardineshire; site of castle, the location not certain.

Held by the Lindsays.

Invermark Castle [NO 443804], near Edzell, Angus; ruinous castle.

Held by the Lindsays of Crawford. David, ninth Earl of Crawford, died here in 1558. David, son of Lord Edzell, hid here in 1607 after being involved in the murder of his uncle, Lord Spynie, in Edinburgh.

Inverquiech Castle [NO 277497], near Alyth, Angus; slight remains of castle.

The Lindsays were keepers of the castle in 1394, but the property later passed to the Rollo family.

Kilbirnie House [NS 304541], near Kilbirnie, Ayrshire; ruinous castle.

Held by the Barclays and by the Crawfords, before being bought by the Lindsay Earl of Crawford in 1661. Kilbirnie passed to the Boyle Earls of Glasgow in 1833. The house was gutted by fire in the eighteenth century and was never rebuilt.

Kilspindie Castle [NO 219258], near Perth; site of castle.

Held by the Lindsays. William Wallace and his mother are supposed to have taken refuge here, according to a poem by Blind Harry; and there are stories of a White Lady.

Kinblethmont [NO 638470], near Arbroath, Angus; slight remains of castle.

Held by the Lindsay Earls of Crawford, but passed to the Carnegies.

Kingask [NO 541145], near St Andrews, Fife; site of castle.

Held by the Lindsay Earls of Crawford in 1669.

Kirkbuddo [NO 502435], near Forfar, Angus; site of castle.

Held by the Lindsays in the late fifteenth century, but later owned by the Guthries.

Kirkforthar House [NO 297049], near Glenrothes, Fife; ruinous castle.

Held by the Lindsays from 1488 or earlier until the nineteenth century.

Lordscairnie Castle [NO 348178], near Cupar, Fife; large ruinous castle, formerly on an island.

Held by the Lindsay Earls of Crawford from around 1350. Alexander Lindsay, the fourth Earl, 'Earl Beardie' or the 'Tiger

Lordscairnie Castle (M&R)

Earl', probably built the castle. It was abandoned in the eighteenth century, and the loch was drained in about 1803. There is reputedly treasure buried at Lordscairnie, and the castle is said to be haunted by a spectre of the fourth Earl, which can be seen playing cards with the de'il at midnight on Hogmanay.

Lour [NO 478462], near Forfar, Angus; site of castle.

Held by the Abernethys, but passed by marriage to the Lindsays, then to other families, including to the Carnegies.

Luffness House [NT 476804], near Aberlady, East Lothian; fine castle and mansion.

Held by the Earls of Dunbar, but passed by marriage to the Lindsays in the twelfth century, and they built a strong castle. The property (or at least part of it) was given to the Church in memory of Sir David Lindsay, a crusader. He died in the 1160s while on crusade, and on his deathbed promised land for a religious house provided his body was returned to Scotland. A Carmelite friary was built nearby in 1293, some of which survives, including the stone burial slab of a crusader. There was a French fort at Luffness in 1549, and the property passed to the Hepburns. The Hopes acquired the castle and still apparently live here.

Mains Castle [NS 627560], near East Kilbride, Lanarkshire; plain keep or tower.

Held by the Comyns, but had passed to the Lindsays of Dunrod by 1382. One of the Lindsay lairds, while curling on the ice of a nearby loch, was angered by a servant, and had a hole cut

Mains Castle 1910?

in the ice and drowned the man by forcing him under the ice. Mains was sold because of debt in 1695 and soon became ruinous. The castle is reputedly haunted by the ghost of a young woman strangled by her jealous husband after he found her with another man. Her (gallant?) lover escaped out of a window on knotted sheets, but she was too slow and was throttled. The castle has been restored.

Menmuir [NO 534643], near Brechin, Angus; site of castle.
Held by the Lindsays and by the Rollo family.

Monikie Castle [NO 517390], near Monifieth, Angus; site of castle.
Held by the Lindsays.

The Mount [NO 339162], near Cupar, Fife; site of castle or old house.

Held by the Lindsays. Sir David Lindsay of the Mount, the famous sixteenth-century playwright and author who wrote *The Satire of the Three Estates*, among other works. He was knighted in 1542 and died in 1555. A farm may occupy the site.

Ormiston Castle [NT 413677], near Dalkeith, Midlothian; ruinous castle and mansion.

Held by the Lindsays, but passed to the Cockburns in the fourteenth century.

Pitairlie Castle [NO 502367], near Monifieth, Angus; site of castle.
Held by the Lindsays from the fifteenth century for about 200 years before passing to the Maules.

Pitcruvie Castle [NO 413046], near Lower Largo, Fife; ruined castle.

Held by the Lindsays, but sold to the Watsons in the seventeenth century.

Pitfour Castle [NO 199209], near Perth; castle replaced by mansion.
Held by the Lindsay Earls of Crawford in the late fifteenth century, but passed to the Hays and then to the Richardsons. The castle has been divided but is still occupied.

Pitroddie [NO 214252], near St Madoes, Perthshire; site of castle.
Held by the Lindsays of Evelick in 1665.

Pitscottie [NO 418131], near Cupar, Fife; site of castle or old house?
Held by the Lindsays, and Robert Lindsay of Pitscottie was the author of *History and Chronicles of Scotland*, which covers the period from 1436 to 1575, and is an important contemporary account of the period of the Reformation.

Pittormie [NO 417185], near Cupar, Fife; site of castle or old house.
Held by the Lindsays in the sixteenth century. One of the family was David Lindsay, minister of Leith and Moderator of the General Assembly of the Church of Scotland. He is believed to have been one of the few of the clergy who prayed for Mary, Queen of Scots, before her execution, and officiated at the wedding of James VI to Anne of Denmark. He was made Bishop of Ross, and died in 1613. The property passed to the Meldrums in the eighteenth century.

Place of Bonhill [NS 390793], near Alexandria, Dunbartonshire; site of castle and mansion.
Held by the Lennox family, then by the Lindsays in the fifteenth century, before passing to the Smolletts. The site appears to be occupied by a school.

Quiech Castle [NO 426580], near Kirriemuir, Angus; site of castle.
Held by the Comyns, but had passed to the Lindsays by the seventeenth century.

Rathillet House [NO 359208], near Cupar, Fife; castle replaced by mansion.
Held by the Lindsays in 1568, but passed to the Hackstons or Halkerstons.

Ruthven Castle [NO 302479], near Alyth, Angus; remains of castle.
Held by the Lindsay Earls of Crawford, but had passed to the Crichtons by 1510, and then went to the Ogilvies of Coul, who built a new mansion.

Spynie Palace [NJ 231658], near Elgin, Moray; fine ruinous castle with massive tower.
Held by the Bishops of Moray, but sold to the Lindsays after

Spynie Palace (M&R)

the Reformation. Alexander Lindsay, fourth son of the tenth Earl of Crawford, was made Lord Spynie in 1590, but he was killed by his nephew in 1607. The second Lord, another Alexander, joined the forces of Gustave Adolphus in Sweden and then commanded the armies of Charles I in Scotland. George, third Lord, died without issue. In the care of Historic Scotland and open to the public (01343 546358).

The Binns [NT 051785], near Linlithgow, West Lothian; fine seventeenth-century mansion.
Held by the Meldrums, then by the Lindsays in the sixteenth century who in 1559 sold the property to the Livingstones, and then to the Dalziels in 1612. The house is in the care of

The National Trust for Scotland and is open to the public in the summer (01506 834255).

Vayne Castle [NO 493599], near Brechin, Angus; ruinous Z-plan tower house.

Held by the Mowats, but passed to the Lindsay Earls of Crawford in 1450, then went to the Carnegie Earls of Southesk in 1594. An elegant new mansion was built at Noranside [NO 472609], which is apparently now a prison. The ruins of Vayne Castle are said to be haunted.

Wauchope Castle [NY 354840], near Langholm, Dumfries and Galloway; site of castle.

Held by the Lindsays from 1285, but may have been a possession of the Moffats at one time.

Wemyss Castle [NO 497524], near Forfar, Angus; site of castle.

Held by the Lindsays. The castle may have been at West Mains of Turin [NO 518532].

West Barcloy [NX 855532], near Dalbeattie, Galloway; site of tower house.

Held by the Lindsays at the end of the sixteenth century, then by the Stewarts and by the MacLellans.

Woodrae Castle [NO 518566], near Brechin, Angus; site of castle.

Held by the Valance family, but passed to the Lindsays. In the late seventeenth century Sir James Lindsay of Woodrae killed an Ogilvie of Ballinshoe. The castle later passed to the Fletchers.

Wormiston House [NO 612095], near Crail, Fife; L-plan tower house.

Held by the Spences and by the Balfours before passing to the Lindsays in 1621. The gardens are occasionally open to the public (www.gardensofscotland.org).

www.clanlindsay.com
www.clanlindsayusa.org
No. of castles/sites: 73
Rank: 11/764

Lipp

The name is an old Aberdeenshire surname, and is recorded in Scotland from the middle of the thirteenth century.

House of Schivas [NJ 898368], five and a half miles north-west of Ellon in Aberdeenshire in the north-east of Scotland, is a fine but altered L-plan tower house, which dates from the sixteenth century. The lands were held by the Schivas family, but passed by marriage to the Lipps, before going to the Maitlands in the fifteenth century, and then Schivas passed to other families. It was used as a farmhouse, but was damaged by fire in 1900 and was later restored and reoccupied as a residence.

No. of castles/sites: 1
Rank: 537=/764

Lithgow

The name comes from a contraction of Linlithgow, a royal burgh with a palace and old church in West Lothian. The surname is recorded from the beginning of the fourteenth century. William Lithgow, who was born in Lanark around 1582, was known as 'Lugless Will' as he had had his ears cut off. He travelled widely in Europe and the near East and the accounts of is travels were published in 1614.

Ormsary House [NR 740720], eight miles west and north of Tarbert in Knapdale in Argyll, is a baronial mansion, which may date from the end of the eighteenth century, but there was an older house or castle. The lands were held by the Campbells from the 1650s or earlier, but passed to the Lithgow family, who were shipbuilders from Port Glasgow, around 1900. They were made Baronets in 1925, and still apparently live here.

No. of castles/sites: 1
Rank: 537=/764

Little

The name means as it sounds, 'little' or 'small', but may also be derived from 'Liddel', the name of a river and dale in the Borders, and so would be from the same origin as the Liddel family. The Littles settled in Ewesdale and in Eskdale in what is now Dumfries and Galloway.

Meikledale [NY 375930] is located some five miles or so north of Langholm, and there may have been a tower house, although now there is only a farm. The lands were held by the Littles from the thirteenth century or earlier. Edward Little of Meikledale supported William Wallace, and the lands were confirmed to the family in the fifteenth century. The Littles were recorded as one of the unruly families in the Borders in 1587, and were scattered during the pacification of the Borders by James VI. Many of them went to Ireland, then to North America and to Australia and New Zealand. Kirkton Tower [NY 368907] and Sorbie [NY 365901], both of which are also by the Ewes Water north of Langholm, were also held by the family.

Foulitch Tower [NT 256436] was a couple of miles north of Peebles, but there are no remains. It was held by the Caverhills in the sixteenth century, then by the Williamsons, before passing to the Littles of Winkston. Winkston Tower [NT 245430] is nearby, and is an altered tower house, which has been reduced in height. Winkston was a property of the Dicksons, but was also held by the Littles.

Liberton Tower [NT 265697] is a plain old keep or tower, and stands to the south-east of Edinburgh. It was long held by the Dalmahoys, but was bought by William Little, Provost of Edinburgh, in 1587. He built nearby Liberton House, and abandoned the castle. The old tower is available for let, including through Country Cottages in Scotland (0990 851133; www.cospt.fsnet.co.uk).

Liberton House [NT 267694] is an L-plan tower house of the seventeenth century, and was built by William Little (as mentioned above). The property soon passed to the Gilmours and was held by them until 1976. The house has been restored in recent years, and can be visited by prior appointment only from March to October (0131 467 7777; www.ngra.co.uk). There are stories that the house is haunted.

www.nwrain.net/~little/
www.clanlittlesna.com
No. of castles/sites: 7
Rank: 182=/764

Livingstone

The name may be territorial and come from the lands of Livingston, which are in West Lothian and where there is now a town of that name. Alternatively, the lands were called after their owner, one 'Leving', who came to Scotland in the twelfth century. His settlement or seat was then called 'Leving's ton'. David Livingstone, who was born in Blantyre in 1813, was a missionary and explorer and he searched for the sources of the Nile. He met Stanley in 1871 and returned to Scotland, but he went back to Africa where he died two years later. The David Livingstone Centre, in Blantyre, is a museum in the tenement where he was born and is open to the public (01698 823140). The MacLea clan also took the name Livingstone and also see MacLea.

Livingston Peel [NT 040676] was once a strong castle with a wet moat, high ramparts and a tower. The lands were held by the Livingstones, and the castle was occupied by the English in 1302 and 1313, although it was presumably recovered after the Battle of Bannockburn the next year. The family became Earls of Callendar and of Linlithgow, but the lands passed to the Murrays, and then to the Cunninghams, and then to the Primrose Earl of Rosebery in 1812. The castle was then demolished.

Callander Castle [NN 629076] is to the south of the Stirlingshire holiday town, but only earthworks and one fragment of masonry survive. Callander was held by the Livingstones from the fifteenth century.

Callendar House [NS 898794] in Falkirk, on the other hand, is a magnificent and massive ornate mansion, with turrets and towers. There was a strong castle on the site, with a deep ditch and courtyard, part of the buildings of which is incorporated into the present building. The lands were held by the Callendar family, but the family were forfeited in 1345 after supporting Edward Balliol, and their property went to the Livingstones. Sir Alexander Livingstone of Callendar was one of the Guardians of James II, and the young king was brought here after being removed from

Callendar House 1910?

Edinburgh Castle. The Livingstones were party to the Black Dinner at Edinburgh in 1440, when William, the young sixth Earl of Douglas, and his brother David was summarily executed, and in retaliation the Douglases imprisoned Livingstone and slew his son. The Livingstones became Lords Livingstone in 1458, and Mary, Queen of Scots, stayed at Callendar several times in the 1560s; one of her 'Four Marys', Mary Livingstone, was the daughter of Alexander, fifth Lord. William, sixth lord, fought for Mary at the Battle of Langside in 1568. The family were made Earls of Linlithgow in 1599, and then of Callendar in 1641. The Livingstones supported the Stewarts, and the castle was stormed and captured by Cromwell in 1651. The Livingstones were forfeited for their part in the 1715 Jacobite Rising, and the house was leased to the Boyd Earl of Kilmarnock, although in their turn the Boyds were forfeited after the Rising of 1745-46, and William Boyd, fourth Earl of Kilmarnock, was beheaded. The property passed to William Forbes of Callendar, a copper merchant, and it is now in the care of the local council and stands in a public park. The house is open to the public all year (01324 503770; www.falkirk.gov.uk/cultural/).

Bachuil House [NM 863438] is an eighteenth-century building, and stands in a pretty spot on the Argyll island of Lismore. The property was held by the Livingstones from 1641 or long before, although they lost many of their lands to Campbell of Airds. The Livingstones changed their name from MacLea or Macleay, and are hereditary keepers of the staff of St Moluag, a sixth-century saint. The staff is still kept at Bachuil, and can be viewed by appointment (01631 760256). The much-reduced but attractive Cathedral of St Moluag [NM 860434] lies to the south-east, and is open to the public. The Livingstones, chiefs of the MacLea clan, still live at Bachuil.

The Livingstones also owned:

Abbotsgrange [NS 931811], Grangemouth, Falkirk; site of castle and mansion.
   Held by the Livingstones in 1543, but passed to the Kerrs in 1611 and later to the Drummonds.

Almond or Haining Castle [NS 956773], near Linlithgow, West Lothian; ruinous keep and courtyard.
   Held by the Crawfords, but passed to the Livingstones in 1540, and they changed the name from Haining to Almond in 1633. James, third son of the Earl of Linlithgow, was created Baron Livingstone of Almond. The family were forfeited after the Jacobite Rising of 1715. The building is now by an industrial plant.

Balcastle [NS 702782], near Kilsyth, Dunbartonshire; site of castle of motte.
   Held by the Earls of Lennox and by the Callendar family, before passing by marriage to the Livingstones.

Bantaskine [NS 876800], Falkirk; site of castle or old house.
   Held by the Forresters, but passed to the Livingstones, one of whom, Alexander Livingstone, was killed fighting for the Covenanters. The property passed to the Kincaids and then to the Haggarts. The laird had a substantial lodging in the High Street of Falkirk; and the site at Bantaskine is now a public park.

Bedlormie [NS 874675], near Armadale, West Lothian; L-plan tower house.
   Held by the Murrays of Ogilface, then by the Forresters of Corstorphine and by the Walkers, before passing by marriage

to the Livingstone Earls of Linlithgow, who held Bedlormie until 1853.

Belstane Castle [NS 850515], near Carluke, Lanarkshire; site of tower house.
   Held by the Livingstones, but passed to the Lindsays, then to the Maxwells and to the Douglases.

Bencloich Castle [NS 635785], near Kirkintilloch, Dunbartonshire; site of castle.
   Held by the Lennox family, but passed to the Livingstones of Kilsyth. The castle was almost entire in 1804, but has been completely demolished.

Biggar Castle [NT 043378], Biggar, Lanarkshire; site of castle.
   Held by the Flemings, but the site passed to a Reverend Livingston in 1659, and the site was occupied in turn by an inn, slaughter house, school, and now a house.

Bridge Castle [NS 944709], near Armadale, West Lothian; altered L-plan tower house.
   Held by the Stewarts but sold to William, Lord Livingstone, in the 1580s and he altered the building. The Livingstones became Earls of Linlithgow in 1599, but were forfeited for their part in the Jacobite Rising of 1715. The property passed to the Hopes, and the castle is still occupied.

Castle Cary [NS 786775], near Cumbernauld, Lanarkshire; fine castle.
   Held by the Livingstones, but passed to the Baillies in the seventeenth century, then to the Dunbars of Fingask. The castle is still occupied (www.castle-cary.org).

Castle Hill, Slamannan [NS 856732], near Falkirk; site of castle.
   Held by the Livingstones from 1470 until 1716.

Colzium Castle [NS 729788], near Kilsyth, Dunbartonshire; slight remains of tower house.
   Held by the Callendar family, but passed by marriage to the Livingstones. The castle was demolished to build the nearby house [NS 729786], and the property passed to the Edmonstones of Duntreath. Later the property was gifted to the local council, and the grounds are open to the public (01236 624031; www.northlan.gov.uk).

Drumry Castle [NS 515710], near Duntocher, Glasgow; site of castle.
   Held by the Callendar family, but passed to the Livingstones in 1346. Sir Robert Livingstone of Drumry was Lord Treasurer of Scotland, but he was executed in 1447. The last Livingstone laird was slain at the Battle of Flodden in 1513, and the property passed by marriage to Sir James Hamilton of Finnart, then went to the Crawfords and to the Semples. It latterly housed farm labourers, but was demolished in the 1960s.

Dunipace [NS 837819], near Larbert, Falkirk; site of castle.
   Held by the Livingstones in the fifteenth century. Jean Livingstone, a daughter of the house, was executed in 1600 for her part in the death of her husband, John Kincaid, at Warriston in Edinburgh. David Livingstone of Dunipace was made a Baronet of Nova Scotia in the seventeenth century, but Dunipace was later held by Forbes of Callendar.

Dunlappie or Poolbrigs [NO 587679], near Brechin, Angus; possible site of castle.
   Held by the Abernethys, and then much later by the Livingstones.

Edingham Castle [NX 839626], near Dalbeattie, Galloway; slight remains of tower house.
   Held by the Livingstones of Little Airds.

Glentirran [NS 668944], near Kippen, Stirlingshire; site of castle or old house.
   Held by the Livingstones from the sixteenth century or earlier. Sir Alexander Livingstone of Glentirran was made a Baronet of Nova Scotia in 1685. The property passed to the Campbells in the eighteenth century.

Inglismaldie Castle [NO 644669], near Brechin, Angus; altered L-plan tower house.
   Held by the Livingstones in 1588, but passed to the Carnegie Earls of Northesk in 1635, then later went to the Falconers of Halkerton and then to the Ogilvies.

Jerviswood House [NS 884455], near Lanark; altered L-plan tower house.

Held by the Livingstones, who built the original tower, but sold to the Baillies of Lamington in 1636. The house was restored and reoccupied.

Kerse House [NS 915817], Grangemouth, Falkirk; site of castle and mansion.

Held by the Menteiths of West Kerse, then by the Livingstones and by the Hopes, but later went to the Dundas Marquis of Zetland.

Kersie [NS 872912], near Stirling; L-plan tower house.

Held by the Menteiths of West Kerse, then by the Livingstones and by the Hopes, but later went to the Dundas Marquis of Zetland.

Kilsyth Castle [NS 717786], Kilsyth, Dunbartonshire; site of castle.

Held by the Livingstones, who were Royalists. The castle was garrisoned in 1650, but Kilsyth was soon captured by Cromwell's forces and the tower was blown up, while the rest of the buildings were burned. The Livingstones were made Viscounts Kilsyth in 1661, but were forfeited after the Jacobite Rising of 1715.

Law Tower [NS 515738], near Bearsden, Dunbartonshire; site of tower house.

Held by the Livingstones but passed by marriage to Sir James Hamilton of Finnart, then went to the Stirlings of Glorat and to the Crawfords of Kilbirnie.

MacDuff's Castle [NT 344972], East Wemyss, Fife; ruinous castle.

Held by the MacDuffs and by the Wemyss family, before passing by marriage to the Livingstones. The property later passed to the Hamiltons, to the Colvilles and then to the Wemyss family again.

Mannerston [NT 048790], near Linlithgow, West Lothian; mansion incorporating castle.

Held by the Livingstones of Mannerston in 1431, but later passed to Sir James Hamilton of Finnart, then to the Bruces of Airth.

Midhope Castle [NT 073787], near Linlithgow, West Lothian; altered tower house.

Held by the Drummonds, then by the Livingstone Earls of Linlithgow, then by the Hopes. Apparently being restored.

Ogilface Castle [NS 927690], near Bathgate, West Lothian; site of castle.

Held by the Murrays but passed to the Livingstone Earls of Linlithgow. Ogilface is said to have been used by Covenanters as a place of refuge.

Old Place [NS 690780], near Kilsyth, Dunbartonshire; site of castle.

Held by the Livingstones of Kilsyth.

Quarter House [NT 100334], near Broughton, Borders; site of tower house.

Held by the Livingstones, but passed to the Murrays and then to the Tweedies in 1741.

Saltcoats Castle [NT 486819], near Gullane, East Lothian; unusual ruinous castle.

Held by the Livingstones, but passed to the Hamiltons of Pencaitland in the eighteenth century.

The Binns [NT 051785], near Linlithgow, West Lothian; fine early mansion.

Held by the Livingstones of Kilsyth, but was sold to the Dalziels in 1612, the most famous of whom was General Tam. The house is in the care of The National Trust for Scotland and is open to the public (01506 834255; www.nts.org.uk).

Westquarter [NS 913787], near Falkirk; site of castle and mansion.

Held by the Livingstones in the seventeenth century, but then by the Jacksons of Halhill in about 1890. There is a fine doocot, which is in the care of Historic Scotland and is accessible to the public.

www.clanlivingstone.com
www.clanmclea.co.uk
No. of castles/sites: 37
Rank: 32=/764
Xref: MacLea

Lochore

The name is territorial and comes from the lands of the same name, which are a few miles north of Cowdenbeath in Fife.

Lochore Castle [NT 175959] is quite ruinous and stands on a motte on what was originally an island in a loch. The courtyard enclosed ranges of buildings and had round corner towers. The island was known as Inchgall, 'island of strangers', and the castle was built by Duncan of Lochore, and was then held by his descendants in the fourteenth century. It apparently passed to the Valances, and in 1547 was thought to be one of the four strongest castles in Fife. Lochore went to the Wardlaws of Torrie and then to the Malcolms of Balbedie. The area was devastated by mining, but has since been restored and landscaped and is now a public park (01592 414300).

No. of castles/sites: 1
Rank: 537=/764

Saltcoats Castle (M&R) – see next column

Lockhart

The name comes from the Old French personal name 'Locard', and was spelt in many different ways. The family were given lands in Lanarkshire and in Ayrshire after to coming to Scotland following the Norman invasion of England.

The Lee [NS 854465], a couple of miles north-west of Lanark, was held by the Lockhart family from the twelfth century. The Lockharts supported Robert the Bruce, and Sir Simon Lockhart was one of those who went on crusade to Spain with Bruce's heart. He is said to have been instrumental in its safe return to Scotland and to have been the keepers of the key to the casket, and changed the spelling of their name to 'Lock Heart', later 'Lockhart'. Their coat of arms was also altered (although the variation of the spelling of the name does not seem to have been much affected). While on crusade, Lockhart also reputedly acquired what is now known as the Lee Penny, a healing amulet consisting of a dark-red gem set in a silver coin. This stone was said to cure bleeding, fever, illnesses of animals and even the bites of mad dogs, when dipped in water. The authorities investigated its use in the seventeenth century, suspecting witchcraft, but decided its use was merely superstitious so did not warrant a righteous burning. Alan Lockhart of The Lee was killed at the Battle of Pinkie in 1547, and Sir James Lockhart of The Lee was appointed to the Supreme Court Bench as Lord Lee, and was imprisoned in the Tower of London for being a Royalist. Sir William, his son, fought at the battles of Preston and then at that of Worcester in 1651. He married Oliver Cromwell's niece, and was then ambassador to France and commanded English soldiers at the siege of Dunkirk. The Lee was held by the Lockharts until the twentieth century.

The Lockharts also held:

Barr Castle [NS 502365], Galston, Ayrshire; massive keep or tower.
Held by the Lockharts. William Wallace is said to have taken refuge here during the Wars of Independence. John Lockhart of Barr was an ardent Protestant and had George Wishart preach here in 1545, and John Knox do the same some years later. Barr was sold to the Campbells of Cessnock in 1670, and is now a masonic hall.

Carnwath House [NS 975465], Carnwath, Lanarkshire; site of castle and mansion.
Held by the Somervilles, but passed to Lockhart of The Lee in the seventeenth century, then to the Dalziels around 1639. Before 1674 the property returned to the Lockharts of The Lee and Carnwath, and they were made Baronets in 1806. Sir George Lockhart of Carnwath, Lord President of the Court of Session, defended Archibald Campbell, ninth Earl of Argyll, after Argyll had rebelled against James VII but Argyll was executed. Lockhart found against John Chiesly of Dalry in a divorce settlement, and in 1689 Chiesly shot and killed Lockhart. Chiesly was caught, had his arm hacked off and he was then executed. Lockhart's son, another George, was a Jacobite and was arrested in 1715. He fled abroad but was

killed in a duel in 1731. Carnwath House was demolished when a new clubhouse for the golf course was built. Members of the family were buried in the north transept of the collegiate church [NY 393760] at Carnwath; the rest of the building has been demolished.

Carstairs Castle [NS 939461], Carstairs, Lanarkshire; site of castle.
Held by the Hamiltons and by the Stewarts before passing to the Lockharts. Materials from the castle were used to build the parish church.

Castlehill [NS 788534], Cambusnethan, near Wishaw, Lanarkshire; slight remains of a castle.
Held by the Bairds, by the Stewarts and by the Somervilles, before passing to the Lockharts of Castlehill, later Sinclair-Lockharts, who still held the property in the twentieth century. The site is said to be haunted by a headless horsemen.

Cleghorn House [NS 898461], near Lanark; site of castle and mansion.
Held by the Lockharts from the end of the fifteenth century. The family were cautioned in 1579 after supporting the 'rebel' Hamiltons. The family, now Eliott Lockhart of Cleghorn, still apparently live at Cleghorn.

Covington Castle [NS 975399], near Lanark; ruinous castle.
Held by the Keith Earls Marischal and by the Lindsays, but passed to the Lockharts in 1679. One of the family was Sir George Lockhart, President of the Court of Session. He was

Covington Castle (M&R)

shot and killed by John Chiesly of Dalry in 1689 (see Carnwath House).

Craiglockhart Castle [NS 875450], near Lanark; site of castle.
Held by the Lockharts of The Lee. William Wallace is said to have used the castle before an attack on Lanark, and to have sheltered in nearby caves after murdering Hazelrig, the English sheriff.

Craiglockhart Castle [NT 226703], Edinburgh; small ruinous keep or tower.
Held by the Kincaids, but later passed to the Lockharts of The Lee. Now located in the grounds of Napier University.

Dean Castle [NS 437394], near Kilmarnock, Ayrshire; fine restored castle.
Held by the Lockharts and by the Soulis family, then by the Balliols, before being given to the Boyds by Robert the Bruce. Much later the castle was given to the people of Kilmarnock, and it stands in a public park and is open to the public (01563 522702; www.deancastle.com).

Dunsyre Castle [NT 073482], near Carnwath, Lanarkshire; site of castle.
Held by the Newbigging family and by the Douglases and by the Hepburns, before later passing to the Lockharts of The Lee.

Hallbar Tower or **Braidwood Castle** [NS 839471], near Carluke, Lanarkshire; restored tower house.
Held by the Douglas Earls of Angus, but then passed through others until going to the Lockharts of the Lee in about 1662.

Holiday accommodation is available (0845 090 0194; www.vivat.org.uk).

Hills Tower [NT 049481], near Carnwath, Lanarkshire; site of tower house.

Held by the Denholms, by the Baillies of Lamington, by the Hamiltons and then by the Lockharts.

Kerelaw Castle [NS 269428], near Kilwinning, Ayrshire; altered ruinous castle.

Held by the Lockharts in 1191, but passed to the Cunningham Earls of Glencairn. The castle was replaced by a mansion, but this has been demolished.

Kirkton [NO 447260], near Leuchars, Fife; ruinous mansion with old work.

Held by the Lockharts, but passed to the Balfours and then to the Gillespies.

Kirkton of Carluke [NS 844502], near Carluke, Lanarkshire; site of castle and mansion.

Held by the Weirs of Stonebyres, but passed to the Lockharts of The Lee in 1662. Demolished in about 1950.

Ogs Castle [NT 030446], near Carnwath, Lanarkshire; site of castle.

Held by the Lockharts, but passed to the Patersons in the eighteenth century.

Torbrex Castle [NT 027552], near Carnwath, Lanarkshire; site of castle.

Held by the Somervilles but had passed to the Lockharts of Cleghorn by 1649.

Tweedie Castle [NS 727427], near Strathaven, Lanarkshire; site of castle.

Held by the Hamiltons of Silvertonhill, but had passed to the Lockharts of Castlehill by 1900. The site is occupied by a farm.

Waygateshaw House [NS 825484], near Lanark; courtyard castle with tower.

Held by the Murrays of Touchadam, but passed by marriage to the Lockharts of The Lee in 1539. One of the family, Stephen Lockhart, was included in the indictment in 1572 for the murder of Lord Darnley. The family were forfeited for their share in the Pentland Rising of 1666, but later recovered the property. Waygateshaw was sold to the Weirs in 1720. The house has been restored and is occupied.

Westhall Tower [NT 048473], near Carnwath, Lanarkshire; some remains of tower house.

Held by the Grahams, by the Hepburns, by the Douglases and by the Lockharts. The site was excavated and cleared in the 1980s.

Westshield [NS 946494], near Lanark; site of castle and mansion.

Held by the Denholm family, but passed to the Lockharts of The Lee in the seventeenth century. Demolished in the 1980s after a fire.

www.clanlockhart.org
www.clanlockhartsociety.com
www.clanlockhart-us.org
No. of castles/sites: 22
Rank: 58=/764

Logan

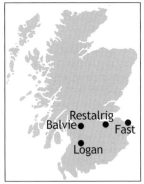

The place name Logan is not uncommon in Scotland, and the surname is territorial and probably comes from the lands of Logan, which are just east of Cumnock in Ayrshire. The name is on record from the beginning of the thirteenth century. Sir Robert Logan and Sir Walter Logan were two of the Scottish knights who accompanied Robert the Bruce's heart on crusade against the Moors in Granada.

Logan [NS 589207] was held by the Logans from 1230 or earlier, and they were in possession until 1802 when the property went to the Cunninghams. There was a mansion, Logan House, but this appears to have been at least partly demolished; there may also have been a castle.

Restalrig Castle, now **Lochend House**, [NT 273743] is to the east of Edinburgh, and the house incorporates part of an altered castle, dating from the sixteenth

Lochend House (M&R)

century. The lands were held by the Lestalric or Restalrig family, but passed by marriage to the Logans of Grougar (also in Ayrshire) about 1400. Sir Robert Logan of Grougar married the heiress of Restalrig, and was made Lord High Admiral by Robert III and that same year defeated English ships in the Firth of Forth. The Logans were forfeited in 1601 for their alleged part in the Gowrie Conspiracy, and the castle was torched by William Gilmour of the Inch. Sir Robert Logan, the last laird, is said to have buried treasure at Fast Castle. Restalrig passed to the Elphinstones, and the house is still occupied.

The Logans also held:

Balvie Castle [NS 535752], near Milngavie, Dunbartonshire; site of castle.

Held by the Galbraiths but passed by marriage to the Logans and they built the castle. John Logan of Balvie and his two sons slew John Hamilton of Bardowie at nearby Blairskaith. The property was sold to the Colquhouns of Luss around 1600, and there was a mansion but this was demolished when Douglas Academy was built.

Burncastle [NT 538514], near Lauder, Borders; site of castle.

Held by the Foord family, but had passed to the Logans of Restalrig by the first part of the sixteenth century.

Caroline Park House [NT 227773], Granton, Edinburgh; mansion incorporating tower house.

Caroline Park House (M&R)

The original tower house was built by Andrew Logan in 1585, but the property passed to the Mackenzies of Tarbat in 1683, then to the Campbell Dukes of Argyll, then to the Scott Dukes of Buccleuch. The house is still occupied.

Castle Gogar [NT 164730], Edinburgh; large L-plan tower house.

Held by the Setons and by the Halyburtons, before coming to the Logans of Restalrig, but then passed to the Coupers, who built the castle. The building is still occupied.

Coltness Castle [NS 797564], near Wishaw, Lanarkshire; castle replaced by mansion.

Held by the Somervilles, but passed to the Logans of Restalrig in 1553, then was sold to the Stewarts of Allanton in 1653. The mansion dates from about 1800, and had a picture gallery some 200-foot long.

Couston Castle [NT 168851], near Aberdour, Fife; L-plan tower house.

Held by the Logans of Couston, then by the Murrays. Restored in 1985.

Edrom [NT 826559], near Duns, Borders; castle replaced by mansion.

Held by the Homes and by the Carmichaels, before passing to the Logans in the nineteenth century. The mansion dates from the eighteenth century and is still occupied.

Fast Castle [NT 862710], near Coldingham, Borders; ruinous castle on cliffs.

Held by the Homes, but passed by marriage to the Logans in 1580. The castle was abandoned about twenty years later on the Logan's forfeiture for their alleged part in the Gowrie Conspiracy. The castle was reputedly used by smugglers, having a 'secret' cave below the castle. There are tales of treasure buried here, possibly hidden by Sir Robert Logan of Restalrig, who died in 1606. The castle passed to the Douglases, back to the Homes and then to the Arnotts. The ruins can be visited although great care must be taken: a visit involves a walk and the castle is joined to the 'mainland' by a gangway.

Gartconnel Castle [NS 537732], Bearsden, Dunbartonshire; site of castle.

Held by the Galbraiths of Culcreuch, but passed by marriage to the Logans of Restalrig around 1400.

Grougar [NS 466388], near Kilmarnock, Ayrshire; possible site of castle.

Held by the Logans from the thirteenth to the fifteenth century. Sir Robert Logan of Grugar married the heiress of Restalrig around 1400. Grougar passed to the Boyds and then to the Grahams.

Houndwood House [NT 855630], near Granthouse, Borders; mansion incorporating tower house.

Held by the Homes after the Reformation, but passed to the Logans of Restalrig. Mary, Queen of Scots, is said to have visited in 1565. The property passed to the Turnbulls in the eighteenth century, then to other families. The house is to be haunted by a ghost called 'Chappie' with unexplained heavy footsteps, knocking and moans. The apparition of the lower part of a man, dressed in riding breeches, is said to have been witnessed, and the story is that the poor fellow was slain and had his torso cut in two, sometime in the sixteenth century.

Knockshinnoch Tower [NS 609126], near New Cumnock, Ayrshire; site of strong castle.

Held by the Dunbars, but passed to the Logans in the middle of the eighteenth century.

Logan's Rais [NS 505605], near Barrhead, Renfrewshire; site of tower house.

Presumably a property of the Logans.

Pittarthie Castle [NO 522091], near Elie, Fife; L-plan tower house.

Held by the Monypennys of Pitmilly and by the Murrays before passing to the Logans in 1598. Pittarthie soon went to the Borthwicks and then to others, including to the Cunninghams. Being restored.

Preston [NT 795573], near Duns, Borders; site of tower houses.

Held by the Logans of Restalrig: one tower house was at West Preston, another one at East Preston.

Renton Peel [NT 824654], near Coldingham, Borders; site of tower house.

Held by the Logans of Restalrig, and torched by the English in 1545.

Reston [NT 883621], near Coldingham, Borders; site of tower house.

Held by the Logans of Restalrig.

Whitehouse [NT 187766], Cramond, Edinburgh; altered L-plan tower house.

Held by the Logans, but passed to the Primroses, then to other families. Still occupied.

www.clanlogansociety.com
No. of castles/sites: 20
Rank: 70=/764

Logie

The name is territorial, although there are many places in Scotland from where it could come.

Logie House [NO 408206] stands three miles west of Leuchars in Fife, and the mansion incorporates part of an L-plan tower house, which dates from the sixteenth century. The lands were held by the Logies in the thirteenth century. Two of the family may have been taken prison after the Battle of Dunbar in 1296, and Sir John Logie of Logie was one of those accused of conspiring against Robert the Bruce in 1320. The property passed to the Wemyss family, and they held Logie until the end of the sixteenth century or later.

No. of castles/sites: 1
Rank: 537=/764

Lorane

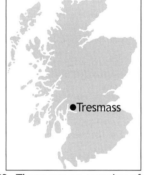

The name comes from Lorraine, the province of France, and is recorded in Scotland from the thirteenth century.

Tresmass [NS 428753], which was a castle two miles east of Dumbarton, was held by the Colquhouns, then later by the Lorraine or Lorane family after 1543. There are no remains of the building which stood here.

No. of castles/sites: 1
Rank: 537=/764
Xrefs: Lorraine; Lorrain

Lorimer

The name comes from the profession of making items, such as bits, stirrups and spurs, for riding horses. The name is on record in Scotland from the twelfth century, and as a surname was found in Angus, in Stirlingshire, in the Lothians and in Dumfries and Galloway.

Craigieburn [NT 117053], two miles or so east of Moffat in Dumfries and Galloway, is an eighteenth-century mansion, but replaced a tower house which was held by the Johnstones and dated from the sixteenth century. This was the birthplace of Jean Lorimer, called 'Chloris' by Robert Burns, and Burns visited the house and woods. The gardens are open to the public from Easter to October (01683 221250).

Kellie Castle [NO 520052] stands two or so miles north of St Monans in Fife, and is a fine E-plan tower house, dating from the sixteenth century, and with lovely

Kellie Castle (MC)

gardens. The lands belonged to the Erskine Earls of Kellie, but the castle was abandoned in 1829 and became derelict. James Lorimer, Professor of Public Law at Edinburgh University, leased Kellie in 1878 and proceeded to restore it. Sir Robert Lorimer, his son, spent most of his childhood at Kellie, and was later a famous architect after working with Sir Robert Rowand Anderson. Lorimer restored many buildings, such as the church of Paisley Abbey and St John's Church in Perth, as well as designing and rebuilding many houses and the Scottish National War Memorial at Edinburgh Castle. Kellie Castle is now in the care of The National Trust for Scotland and is open to the public. (01333 720271).

Gibliston House [NO 493055] dates from 1820, but replaced a castle or older house. The building stands three miles north-west of St Monans, also in Fife. The lands were held by the Sibbalds, then by the Smiths and by the Gillespies, before being bought by Sir Robert Lorimer in 1916.

No. of castles/sites: 3
Rank: 328=/764

Loudon

The name is territorial and comes from the lands of Loudoun, which are a mile north-east of Galston in Ayrshire, and the name is on record from the end of the twelfth century.

Loudoun [NS 516377] was held by the Loudons in the twelfth century, but passed by marriage to the Crawfords, and later went to the Campbells. The Loudons had a castle on a motte, but this was later destroyed by the Kennedy Earl of Cassillis in the fifteenth century. The Campbells moved to the new Loudoun Castle [NS 506378], which is now a large but ruinous castellated mansion.

Terringzean Castle [NS 556205], a mile or so west of Cumnock also in Ayrshire, was also held by the Loudon family, but passed by marriage to the Crawfords. Not much remains of the castle, which had a keep and a courtyard with a ditch, except an octagonal tower.

No. of castles/sites: 2
Rank: 396=/764
Xref: Loudoun

Lovell

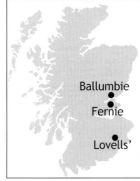

The name means 'little wolf', and is not uncommon in France. The family appear to have come to Scotland from Somerset in England, and held lands in the Ewesdale and in Eskdale, before moving north to Angus and Fife.

Lovells' Castle [NT 499140] is the to the south-west of Hawick in the Borders, but nothing remains except a motte. The family held the property from the thirteenth century or earlier. The Lovells supported the English against Robert the Bruce, and they were forfeited and their lands were given to the Douglases.

Ballumbie Castle [NO 445344] is a ruinous courtyard castle, dating from the fourteenth century, and lying four or so miles to the north-east of Dundee. The lands were held by the Lovells from around 1350 until the seventeenth century. Henry Lovell of Ballumbie was a very unruly fellow in the 1560s, and James Durham of Pitkerro fled his house in terror of Lovell, and the minister of Monifieth had his manse torched by Lovell.

Fernie Castle [NO 316147] is four miles west of Cupar in Fife, and is an altered and extended L-plan tower house, which dates from the sixteenth century. The property was held by the MacDuffs and by the Balfours, then by the Fernies in the fifteenth century. Fernie passed by marriage to the Lovells, but they sold it to the Arnots in 1586, after which it then passed by marriage back to the Balfours. The building is said to be haunted by a Green Lady, the ghost of a girl who fell to her death from one of the upstairs windows. The castle is now a hotel (01337 810381; www.ferniecastle. demon.co.uk).

No. of castles/sites: 3
Rank: 328=/764

Low

The name is local in origin, perhaps from 'law' meaning 'hill', and is on record in Scotland from the fourteenth century (but also see Law).

Blebo, which is three miles east of Cupar in Fife, was a property of the Trails from the fourteenth century, but came to the Beatons, who held it until 1900. There was a castle at **Blebo Hole** [NO 423134] but a new mansion was built at **Blebo House** [NO 423145], which was completely refurbished when bought by the Lows. One of the family was the founder of the William Low supermarket chain. Blebo passed from the family in 1951, but the house is still occupied. **Kilmaron Castle** [NO 357162] was also latterly held by the Lows, and Sir James Low was made a Baronet in 1908. The mansion, a mile to the north-west of Cupar, was built in 1820 for the Baxters of Kilmaron, and has no older origins. The building was demolished in the twentieth century and only the stables survives.

No. of castles/sites: 2 / Rank: 396–/764

Lowis

The name comes from the lands of that name near Loch of Lowes south of Peebles in the Borders. The name is on record from the beginning of the fourteenth century.

Castlehill Tower or **Castlehill of Manor** [NT 214354] is a few miles south and west of Peebles, and dates from the fifteenth century, although it is now quite ruinous. The lands were held by the Lowis of Manor family from early in the fifteenth century, and they built the tower. The property was sold to the Veitchs in 1637, then passed to the Baillies of Jerviswood, and then to other families. The building was abandoned about 1840. **Plora Tower** [NT 359360], two miles east of Innerleithen also in the Borders, was also held by the Lowis family, but little remains although it may still have been roofed in 1838.

Merchiston Castle [NT 243717] is a fine L-plan tower house, which dates from the fifteenth century, but has been incorporated into Napier University. The property was held by the Napiers, but Merchiston was sold to the Lowis family in 1668, although they got into debt and had to sell it themselves in 1728. The castle was later used as a school (Merchiston Castle School, now at Colinton), but is now part of Napier University.

No. of castles/sites: 3 / Rank: 328=/764

Lumsden

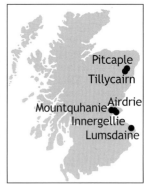

The name is territorial and comes from the lands of Lumsden, or Lumsdaine, which are a couple of miles to the north-west of Coldingham in Berwickshire in the Borders, and the name is on record from the middle of the twelfth century.

Lumsdaine [NT 873690] was held by the family from the twelfth century, and they went on to acquire lands in Fife and in Aberdeenshire in the first half of the fourteenth century. **Blanerne Castle** [NT 832564], three miles to the east and north of Duns in the Borders, was held by the Lumsdens from 1329, after it had passed to them by marriage from the Blanerne family. The present remains are of an L-plan block, which dates from the sixteenth century, but there was also an older stronghold at Blanerne.

Tillycairn Castle [NJ 664114], five and a half miles south-west of Kemnay in Aberdeenshire, is a strong and impressive L-plan tower house, which is four storeys in height and dates from the sixteenth century. The lands were held by the Gordons, but passed to the Forbeses, and then to the Lumsdens in 1580. Later Tillycairn went to the Burnetts, and then to the Gordons. The castle became ruinous, but was bought back and restored in 1980 by the Lumsdens.

Pitcaple Castle [NJ 726261], four miles north-west of Inverurie also in Aberdeenshire, is a fine Z-plan tower house with two round towers and a turret which have conical roofs. The castle was derelict by the end of the eighteenth century, but was restored and then extended in the succeeding years. The lands were long held by the Leslies, but passed by marriage to the Lumsdens in 1757. Pitcaple is still apparently occupied by the Burges-Lumsdens of Pitcaple.

The Lumsdens also owned the following properties:

Airdrie House [NO 567084], near Crail, Fife; altered tower house.
  Held by the Dundemore family, but passed to the Lumsdens in the fifteenth century, one of whom was Sir John Lumsden, President of the Court of Session. The Lumsdens were buried in the cemetery at Crail Parish Church, where there is a fine memorial to the family. The lands went to the Turnbulls of Pittencrieff in 1602, and then to others. The house is still occupied.

Auchry Castle [NJ 788507], near Turriff, Aberdeenshire; site of castle.
  Held by the Cummings, but had passed to the Lumsdens by the nineteenth century.

Buchromb [NJ 313439], near Dufftown, Moray; site of castle and mansion.
  Held by the Lumsdens.

Clova House [NJ 456224], near Rhynie, Aberdeenshire; castle replaced by mansion.
  Held by the Lumsdens until the nineteenth century or later. Harry Leith Lumsden of Clova and Auchindoir established the nearby village of Lumsden in 1825.

Cushnie Castle [NJ 525111], near Alford, Aberdeenshire; castle replaced by mansion.

Held by the Cushnie family, but passed to the Leslies, and then to the Lumsdens in 1509. One of the family was Andrew Lumsden, Secretary to Bonnie Prince Charlie during the Jacobite Rising of 1745-46. Lumsden fled to Rome after the rebellion failed and joined James, the Old Pretender, until James's death in 1766. A couple of years later he returned to Scotland, and he was pardoned in 1778.

Innergellie House [NO 575052], near Kilrenny, Fife; castle replaced by mansion.

Held by the Drummonds, by the Beatons and by the Barclays of Kippo, before passing to the Lumsdens of Airdrie in 1642. Sir James Lumsden fought for Gustave Adolphus of Sweden, and then at Marston Moor in 1644 and at the Battle of Dunbar in 1650. He was captured after the battle but was later released. Innergellie remained with the Sandys-Lumisdaines until the 1960s.

Lathallan Castle [NO 460063], near Ellie, Fife; site of castle.

Held by the Spences, but passed to the Lumsdens.

Mountquhanie Castle [NO 347212], near Cupar, Fife; ruinous tower house.

Held by the Balfours, then went to the Lumsdens of Innergellie about 1600. Major-General Robert Lumsden, a veteran of the

Mountquhanie Castle (M&R)

Gustave Adolphus wars, fought against Cromwell at the Battle of Dunbar in 1650, and was Governor of Dundee in 1651. He surrendered to a Roundhead army led by General Monk, but was murdered by English troops and the town was sacked and looted, and many of the inhabitants slaughtered. Mountquhanie was sold to the Crawfords in 1676.

Pittillock House or **Conland** [NO 278052], near Glenrothes, Fife; mansion incorporating castle.

Held by the MacDuffs and by the Bruces, but passed to the Lumsdens, who held the property until 1651. Pittillock passed to the Baillies of Falkland and then to the Balfours of Balbirnie. Still occupied.

Rennyhill [NO 573049], near Anstruther, Fife; castle replaced by mansion.

Held by the Lumsdens.

Stravithie Castle [NO 531118], near St Andrews, Fife; site of castle.

Held by the Lumsdens, but was later a property of the Erskines and of the Douglases. The castle was entire in 1710, apparently with a ditch and drawbridge and surrounded by trees and ornamental walks, but there is now no trace.

www.geocities.com/BourbonStreet/4826/lumsden.html
www.alumsden.freeserve.co.uk
No. of castles/sites: 15
Rank: 94=/764
Xref: Lumsdaine

Lundie

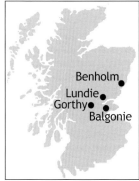

The name is probably territorial in origin, coming from the lands of Lundie near Coupar Angus in Perthshire or from a place of the same name near Doune in Stirlingshire. Lundie is very close in spelling to Lundin, and the two may have been confused as both families held property in Fife. **Lundie Castle** [NO 309361] in Angus has now gone, as has a mansion built to replace it; while a later building, also known as Lundie Castle, has a date stone from the old stronghold with 1683. The lands may have been held by the Lundie family, but were long held by the Duncans. One of the family, Adam Duncan, was a famous admiral, and defeated a Dutch fleet at Camperdown in 1797. The modern Lundie Castle now stands in a public park.

Balgonie Castle [NO 313007], three or so miles east of Glenrothes in Fife, is a fine restored keep or tower, which is five storeys in height, in a courtyard with ruinous

Balgonie Castle (M&R)

ranges of building. The property was held by the Sibbalds, but was a property of the Lundies. Sir Robert Lundie, later Lord High Treasurer, extended the castle about 1496. James IV visited the same year, as did Mary, Queen of Scots, in 1565. The property was sold to the Leslies in 1635. The castle is said to be haunted by a Green Lady, Green Jeanie, believed to be the spirit of one of the Lundies. The bogle has reputedly been seen in recent times, and was recorded in 1842 as being a well-known ghost. The castle has been restored and is open to the public (01592 750119; www.balgonie-castle.com).

Pitlochie Castle [NO 175095] stood a few miles west and south of Auchtermuchty in Fife, but there are no remains. Pitlochie was held by the Kinloch family, but had passed to the Lundies of Balgonie by 1452. The property was apparently held by them in 1557 when the tower and fortalice are mentioned, but the Sandilands are also recorded as holding the lands. **Lathallan Castle** [NO 460063] has also gone but stood five miles north and east of Elie, again in Fife. The property was held by the Spences, but passed to the Lumsdens and may have been held by the Lundies in 1596.

Benholm Castle [NO 804705] stands a couple of miles

south-west of Inverbervie in Kincardineshire, and is a ruinous fifteenth-century castle. It was a property of the Benham family but passed to the Lundie family by marriage to an heiress around the end of the fourteenth century, and they built the castle. Benholm later passed to the Ogilvies and then to the Keith Earls Marischal. The building is being restored, but is said to be haunted.

Gorthy [NN 962237], some five or so miles east of Crieff in Perthshire, was long a property of the Gorthy family but passed by marriage to the Lundies in the sixteenth century. The property appears to have then gone to the Murrays by the first quarter of the seventeenth century. There was a small castle or tower house, but there are no remains.

www.lundie.org
No. of castles/sites: 6
Rank: 212=/764

Lundin

As noted earlier, the names Lundin and Lundie are very similar, given the different spellings used, but the Lundins appear to have been descended from a Robert de London. He was given lands in Fife, which were then presumably called after the family.

Lundin Tower [NO 399029] stood a mile west of Lower Largo in Fife, and the tower house had been incorporated into a later mansion. The whole building, except for a stair-turret, was demolished in 1876. The original stronghold belonged to the Lundin family, who held the property from the twelfth century. The family were hereditary 'doorwards' to the kings of Scots. Some of them moved north, where they were given lands in Aberdeenshire, and they changed their name to Durward (see that family). Mary, Queen of Scots, is said to have stayed at Lundin Tower in 1565. The property passed by marriage to the Maitlands, but the surname was kept as Lundin. Robert Lundin fought at the Battle of Worcester for the Royalists in 1651, but he was captured, imprisoned and then heavily fined. Lundin passed, again by marriage, to the Drummonds in 1670, and they were made Earls of Melfort in 1685. The family were forfeited after the 1745-46 Jacobite Rising. Lundin was later held by the Gilmours.

Aithernie Castle [NO 379035] is a very ruinous tower house, which dated from the seventeenth century; and it stands a mile or so north of Leven, also in Fife. The lands belonged to the Lundins in the thirteenth century, but passed to the Carmichaels, and then to the Inglis family, and then to others.

www.lundie.org
No. of castles/sites: 2
Rank: 396=/764

Luss

The name comes from the parish and lands of Luss, which are on the west side of Loch Lomond in Dunbartonshire. The lands were held by the Luss family, and are on record from the thirteenth century; there may have been a castle or seat at Luss [NS 360930]. The property passed by marriage to the Colquhouns, when the 'Fair Maid of Luss', heiress of Godfrey the sixth of Luss, married Sir Robert Colquhoun.

No. of castles/sites: 1
Rank: 537=/764

Lundin Tower 1903? – see previous column (Lundin)

Lyle

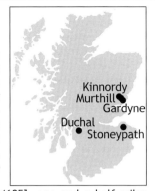

The name comes from 'd'Isle', which is from the French and means 'of the isle or island'. The family were settled in Northumberland in England, but are first on record in Scotland from the twelfth century, and the name was also spelled Lyell.

Duchal Castle [NS 334685], one and a half miles west and south of Kilmacolm in Renfrewshire, is now a shattered ruin, but this was once a strong keep and courtyard, and was built in the thirteenth century. Duchal was a property of the Lyles, who were made Lords Lyle in 1440 and then Lord High Justiciars of Scotland. Robert Lyle, second Lord Lyle, fought against James III at Sauchieburn in 1488, but the family then took part in the Lennox rebellion against James IV the following year. The king besieged Duchal, bringing with him the cannon Mons Meg. Lyle was forfeited, although the family regained the lands and held them until the middle of the sixteenth century when the male line failed. The property passed to the Montgomerys of Lainshaw, and then to the Porterfields. The castle was said to have been haunted by the spirit of an excommunicated monk in the thirteenth century, a violent and aggressive bogle. The son of the laird eventually confronted it one night. In the ensuing battle he was slain, but the ghost also left. **Duchal House** [NS 353680], was built about 1768, although part may date from 1710, and the gardens are occasionally open to the public (www.gardens ofscotland.org).

Murthill [NO 463574] is some four or so miles north of Forfar in Angus by the River South Esk. The lands were held by the Lyles from 1375 and there may have been a castle. One of the family was Hercules Lyle, who was killed at the Battle of Falkirk in 1746. This branch acquired Gardyne, and later Kinnordy, which is still apparently held by the Lyell Barons Lyell.

The Lyles also held:

Buchanan Castle [NS 463886], near Drymen, Stirlingshire; ruined mansion and castle.
    Held by the Lyles in the fourteenth century, but passed to the Buchanans and then to the Grahams.
Dysart [NO 695550], near Montrose, Angus; possible site of castle.
    Held by the Melvilles, by the Guthries, and then by the Lyles.
Gardyne Castle [NO 574488], near Arbroath, Angus; fine altered tower house.
    Held by the Gardynes of Leys, but passed to James Lyle of Dysart, and the family remained in possession until the twentieth century. The castle is still occupied.
Gartartan Castle [NS 530978], near Aberfoyle, Stirlingshire; ruinous Z-plan tower house.
    Held by the Lyles, but passed to the MacFarlanes in 1531, who built the castle, then later went to the Grahams of Gartmore.
Kilmacolm Castle [NS 361693], Kilmacolm, Renfrewshire; site of castle.
    Held by the Lyles and by the Porterfields.

Kinnordy [NO 366553], near Kirriemuir, Angus; castle replaced by mansion.
    Held by the Ogilvies of Inverquharity, but bought by the Lyles of Gardyne in 1770, who still apparently hold it. The family were made Baronets in 1894 as the Lyell Barons Lyell.
Pitmuies [NO 567497], near Friockheim, Angus; castle or old house replaced by mansion.
    Held by the Guthries and by the Mudies before in 1846 going to the Lyell Baronets of Kinnordy. The property passed from the Lyells but the fine gardens are open to the public from April to October (01241 818245; www.pitmuies.com).
Shielhill [NO 428574], near Forfar, Angus; mansion on site of castle.
    Held by the Ogilvies, but passed to the Lyles.
Stoneypath Tower [NT 596713], near East Linton, East Lothian; L-plan tower house.
    Held by the Lyles from the middle of the fifteenth century, but passed to the Hamiltons of Innerwick, then to others. Undergoing restoration.

No. of castles/sites: 11
Rank: 127=/764
Xref: Lyell

Lynn

The name comes from a waterfall ('Linn' from Gaelic) on the Caaf Water, which is to the west of Dalry in Ayrshire.

Lynn House [NS 284489] stands near the waterfall, and there was apparently an old stronghold which was held by the Lynn family from 1296 (or earlier) until the end of the fifteenth century (or later).

Larg Castle [NX 167644], which stood four miles north and west of Glenluce in Galloway, was held by the Lynns in the seventeenth century, but there are no remains. The lands had been held by Soulseat Abbey and then by the Vauxs of Longcastle and Barnbarroch, before passing to the Lynns.

No. of castles/sites: 2
Rank: 396=/764
Xref: Lyne

Lyon

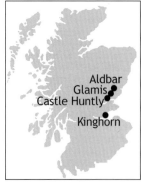

The family claim descent from a French family called 'de Leon', who is believed to have come to Scotland with Edgar, one of St Margaret's sons, when Edgar fought against the rival Donaldbane (or Donald III). Edgar had the victory in 1097, and Donald was imprisoned. The 'de Leons' or 'Lyons' were then given lands in Perthshire, including at Forteviot.

Glamis Castle [NO 387481] is a splendid stately castle of massive size, which was extended out of a keep or tower first built in the fourteenth century. The castle was added to down the centuries with lower wings and round towers, and the battlements were replaced by turrets and dormer windows. The predecessor of the present Glamis was reputedly intended to be built on the **Hill of Denoon** [NO 348438]. The story goes that the area was the realm of supernatural beings, and the Queen of the Faeries did not want humans in her realm. The foundations of the castle were repeatedly cast down, and it was decided to build Glamis at its present site. Malcolm II is said to have been slain at Glamis in 1034, although if he was it was in an earlier building. Glamis is traditionally associated with Macbeth, and in the old keep is 'Duncan's Hall', but any connection is probably only based on Shakespeare's play.

Sir John Lyon was Chancellor of Scotland and married Joanna or Jean, daughter of Robert II; and the family were made Lords Glamis in 1445. Janet Douglas was the beautiful widow of John Lyon, sixth Lord Glamis, and, unfortunately for her, sister of the Earl of Angus, for whom James V had an abiding hatred. Janet remarried, wedding Alexander Campbell of Skipness, but she was accused of trying to poison the king and also of witchcraft, which were most likely baseless accusations. Although she acquitted herself well, it made no difference and the poor woman was burned to death

on Castle Hill in Edinburgh in 1537, half blind from her long imprisonment. Her husband had died trying to escape from the castle, and her infant son was only imprisoned because he was too young to be executed. Janet's ghost, a Grey Lady, is said to haunt the castle, and has sometimes reputedly been witnessed in the chapel. The castle and lands were plundered, but were restored to her son John Lyon after the death of James V in 1542. Mary, Queen of Scots, stayed at Glamis in 1562. In 1578 John, eight Lord, who was Chancellor of Scotland and Keeper of the Great Seal, was killed in a brawl with the Lindsays in Stirling, and his brother, Thomas, was one of those involved in the kidnapping of the young James VI in the 'Raid of Ruthven' in 1582. Patrick, ninth Lord, was made Earl of Kinghorne in 1606, and the family were made Earls of Strathmore in 1677. John, fifth Earl, was slain fighting for the Jacobites at Sheriffmuir in 1715, and James VII was entertained at Glamis the following year. The Lyons did not come out for the Jacobites in the 1745-46 rebellion, and the Duke of Cumberland stayed here, although it is said that the bed he used was subsequently destroyed. The castle has gained a reputation for being haunted, and among the stories is the famous walled-up chamber where the ghost of Alexander Lindsay, fourth Earl of Crawford, 'Earl Beardie', is said to have to play cards until the 'day of doom'. The ninth Earl married the heiress of George Bowes of Streatlam and the family are now the Bowes-Lyon Earls of Strathmore and Kinghorne. Elizabeth, the Queen Mother, who died in 2002, was the daughter of the fourteenth Earl. The castle is open to the public from April to October (01307 840393; www.glamis-castle.co.uk).

The Lyon family also owned:

Aldbar Castle [NO 572577], near Brechin, Angus; site of altered castle.

Held by the Cramond family, but sold to the Lyons in 1577. One of the family was Thomas Lyon and he was among those who kidnapped the young James VI and held him in Ruthven Castle (Huntingtower) in what became known as the Ruthven Raid. It was he who told his king: 'Better bairnis grete than grown men', when James was feeling upset. Aldbar was later sold to the Sinclairs, then went to the Youngs and to the Chalmers of Balnacraig, who held the property into the twentieth century; the castle was completely demolished in 1965.

Baikie Castle [NO 319492], near Alyth, Angus; site of castle.

Held by the Fentons in the thirteenth century, but passed to the Lyons of Glamis about 1450.

Balintore Castle [NO 290590], near Kirriemuir, Angus; mansion.

Held by the Lyons in 1865 but passed to the Chirnside family. Abandoned in the 1960s.

Beldorney Castle [NJ 424369], near Keith, Moray; Z-plan tower house.

Held by the Ogilvies and by the Gordons, but then passed to John Lyon because of debt. Lyon was very unpopular and was murdered by his own tenants. Beldorney passed to the Buchans and then to the Grants, and the castle is occupied after being restored.

Castle Huntly [NO 301292], near Longforgan, Perthshire; impressive castle.

Held by the Grays but was bought by the Lyons of Glamis in 1614, who sold it to the Pattersons in 1777. There was said to

Glamis Castle (RWB)

Castle Huntly (M&R)

Tannadyce House [NO 484577], near Forfar, Angus; castle replaced by mansion.

Held by the Keiths, but passed by marriage to the Lyons of Glamis, then later went to the Ogilvies and then to the Neishes.

Thornton Castle [NO 397465], near Forfar, Angus; site of castle or old house.

Probably held by the Lyons.

www.clanlyon.org
No. of castles/sites: 15
Rank: 94=/764

Kinghorn Castle (M&R) – see previous column

be a tunnel from here to Glamis Castle. Castle Huntly is reputedly haunted by a White Lady, the ghost of one of the Lyons. The story goes that the poor girl was with child but without a husband, and was imprisoned in an upstairs chamber. She tried to escape but fell to her death. At one time her apparition was reportedly often seen, both in the building and especially around the Bogle Bridge. The castle is now a Young Offenders' Institution.

Cossans Castle [NO 393498], near Kirriemuir, Angus; site of castle.
Held by the Lyons in the fifteenth century.

Denoon Castle [NO 348438], near Kirriemuir, Angus; site of castle.
Believed to be where the predecessor to Glamis stood.

Fletcherfield Castle [NO 403522], near Kirriemuir, Angus; site of tower house.
Held by the Lyons.

Forteviot [NO 055176], near Perth; site of palace.
Traditionally the palace of the kings of Scots, and where Kenneth MacAlpin murdered his rivals in the ninth century. It may have been used by William the Lion, and the lands were a property of the Lyons in the fourteenth century.

Karig Lion Castle [NS 987812], Bo'ness, Falkirk; site of castle.
Held by Margaret Lyon, daughter of Lord Glamis and widow of John Hamilton, Marquis of Hamilton, who himself died in 1604.

Kinghorn Castle or Glammis Tower [NT 269871], Kinghorn, Fife; site of castle.
Originally a royal castle. Alexander III fell from cliffs nearby in 1286 on his way to the castle to meet his young wife Yolande de Dreux. The property passed to Sir John Lyon of Glamis, Chancellor of Scotland, in the fourteenth century, a descendant of whom was made Earl of Kinghorne in 1606. Kinghorn was burnt by the English in 1547 after the Battle of Pinkie. There are tales of a Grey Lady, the phantom of Yolande, which has reputedly been seen searching for her husband in the area in and around the Kingswood.

Meigle House [NO 285447], Meigle, Perthshire; castle replaced by mansion.
Held by the Lyons of Glamis, but passed to the Murrays.

MacAdam

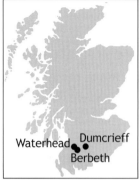

The name means 'son of Adam', and is recorded in Scotland from the twelfth century. The clan owned lands in the south of Ayrshire and in Dumfries and Galloway in the south-west of Scotland. The MacAdams of Berbeth (or Craigengillan) are said to have been descended from the MacGregors.

Banck Castle [NX 558939], near Carsphairn, Galloway; site of castle.
  Held by the MacAdams of Waterhead, and believed to have been destroyed by fire.
Berbeth or **Craigengillan** [NS 473028], near Dalmellington, Ayrshire; site of castle or old house replaced by mansion.
  Held by the MacAdams and their descendants from 1580 until 1999. Many of the family were buried at Dalmellington [NS 480060] where they had a mausoleum. Craigengillan is a fine mansion, dating from the eighteenth century but remodelled down the years. A holiday cottage is available on the estate, and there is a riding school and other activities (01292 551818; www.craigengillan.com).
Blackcraig Castle [NS 634082], near New Cumnock, Ayrshire; site of castle.
  Held by the Crawfords, but sold to the MacAdams after 1550. This has been identified as the site of a house (or even the birthplace) of Sir William Wallace, used by him after the murder of the Sheriff of Ayr in 1297 and then before his capture at Robroyston in 1305.
Chapelhouse [NS 634279], near Muirkirk, Ayrshire; slight remains of a tower house.
  Held by the MacAdams.
Dumcrieff [NT 102036], near Moffat, Dumfries and Galloway; castle replaced by mansion.
  Held by the Murrays and by the Clerks of Penicuik, but was the home of John Loudoun Macadam, of road-making fame, in 1758 when he was a child. MacAdam emigrated to America in 1783, but he returned and when sixty years of age he was made Surveyor General of the Bristol Turnpike Trust. He pioneered the surfacing of roads using tar and small stones. Dumcrieff passed to other families.
Holm of Dalquhairn [NX 655990], near Carsphairn, Dumfries and Galloway; site of castle or old house.
  Held by the MacAdams in 1568, when visited by the Regent Moray: the MacAdams did not support Mary, Queen of Scots. The property had passed to the MacMillans by the middle of the seventeenth century.
Meikle Auchrae [NX 645945], near Carsphairn, Dumfries and Galloway; site of castle or old house.
  Held by the MacAdams in the middle of the sixteenth century.
Sauchrie Castle [NS 303147], near Maybole, Ayrshire; castle replaced by mansion.
  Held by the Chalmers family in the eighteenth century, but passed to the MacAdams.
Waterhead Castle [NS 543115], near Dalmellington, Ayrshire; site of castle.
  Held by the MacAdams of Waterhead. The noted Covenanter Gilbert MacAdam of Waterhead was shot by John Reid of Ballochmyle at Kirkmichael in 1685.

No. of castles/sites: 9
Rank: 149=/764

MacAdie

The name comes from the 'son of Adie', and was used for the Fergussons of Balmacruichie. They probably had a seat or stronghold on a crannog in **Loch Beanie** [NO 160686], which is three or so miles east of Spittal of Glenshee in Perthshire, as they were lairds of Glenshee and Strathardle.

No. of castles/sites: 1
Rank: 537=/764

MacAlexander

The name means 'son of Alexander', and is on record in Scotland from the end of the fourteenth century. The clan held lands in Ayrshire, and MacAlister is the Gaelic form of the name, and also see Alexander.

Drummochreen [NS 280026] is four or so miles south of Maybole, and the property was held by the MacAlexanders from the fifteenth century for 300 years or so. They claimed descent from the Lords of the Isles, and were ardent Covenanters in the seventeenth century. They had a castle, but little survives except one upstand of masonry and some remains of a ditched courtyard.

No. of castles/sites: 1
Rank: 537=/764

Tarbert Castle (M&R) – see next column (MacAlister)

MacAlister

The name means 'son of Alasdair' or 'son of Alexander', and is recorded in Scotland from the middle of the fifteenth century. Allison is another variation. The clan claimed descent from Alastair Mor, son of Donald of the Isles, who flourished in the middle of the thirteenth century. The clan were granted lands in the north of Kintyre, and also see the section on the Alexanders.

Loup or **Luib** [NR 763580] is some ten miles southwest of Tarbert in Kintyre in Argyll, and there was a castle or old house, probably dating from the seventeenth century or earlier, which was replaced by a newer dwelling. The lands were held by the MacAlisters of Loup, chiefs of the clan and constables of **Tarbert Castle** [NR 867687], which is to the east of the village of Tarbert in the Knapdale area of Argyll. The MacAlisters raided Arran and then Bute, and Archibald MacAlister, heir to Tarbert, was executed in Edinburgh. The MacLeans took over as constables of the castle in the first half of the sixteenth century. The MacAlisters also held lands at **Ardpatrick** [NR 753593], nine and a half miles south-west of Tarbert. There was a castle but it was replaced by Ardpatrick House in the second half of the eighteenth century. By then the property had passed to the Campbells of Skipness.

Some of the family moved to central Scotland, and held the lands of Menstrie, changing their name to Alexander (also see the Alexanders) or possibly to Allison or Alison. The family supported the Jacobites and fought at the Battle of Killiecrankie in 1689, although they do not appear to have taken part in the later rebellions, having been forced into the Hanoverian forces of the Campbells. The MacAlisters held Loup into the eighteenth century but the lands were eventually sold.

Glenbarr Abbey [NR 669365], which is some twelve miles north of Campbeltown in Kintyre, is a gothic mansion, dating from the eighteenth century. The house is held by the MacAlisters and houses the Clan MacAlister Centre; it is open to the public from Easter to October (01583 421247; www.kintyre-scotland.org.uk/glenbarr; www.clanmcalister.org/glenbarr.html).

Killean House [NR 697443], one mile south of Tayinloan in Kintyre in Argyll, is a large baronial mansion, dating from 1875 and replaced an earlier house of 1840. The mansion was built for the wealthy shipowner James Macalister Hall. Accommodation is available at the house and on the estate (01257 266511; www.killean estate.com).

www.clanmcalister.org
members.aol.com/macaliste2/
No. of castles/sites: 5
Rank: 240=/764
Xrefs: MacAlaster; MacAlexander

MacArthur

The name means 'son of Arthur' and this is believed to be one of the most ancient of clans. The name is derived from the old Irish for 'bear'; the legends associated with King Arthur and the Round Table are still popular. The MacArthurs supported Robert the Bruce, and benefited at the expense of the MacDougalls when Bruce became undisputed king. The clan was made keepers of Dunstaffnage Castle, near Oban in Argyll, but John MacArthur, chief of the MacArthurs, was beheaded by James I; the Campbells became keepers of the castle. One branch of the family were hereditary pipers to the MacDonalds of Sleat, another armourers to the MacDonalds of Islay, and there are also the MacArthur Campbells, who were established in Strachur. MacArthurs fought on both sides in the Jacobite Risings, and many of the clan emigrated in the eighteenth century to the West Indies, to North America and to Australia. There is currently no clan chief.

Ardbrecknish House [NN 069212] is some seven or so miles north of Inveraray on the east shore of Loch Awe. The mansion incorporates an old tower or keep in the West Tower, perhaps dating from the fifteenth century. The lands were held by the MacDougalls, but passed to the MacArthurs in the fourteenth century after they had supported Bruce. The MacArthurs became relatively powerful and held considerable lands around Lochawe, but then came into conflict with the Campbells of Inverawe. Some of the MacArthurs were drowned in a skirmish with the Campbells, but the MacArthurs held the lands until 1751. The property passed to the Thorpes and the house is now a hotel (01866 833223; www.loch-awe.co.uk).

Nearby **Inistrynich** [NN 106235] or **Tirevadich** was also held by the MacArthurs, and there was a castle or hall-house on the peninsula in Loch Awe. In 1567 Duncan MacArthur of Tireivadich, his son and several of his clan were drowned in a melee with the Campbells. The lands were held by the MacArthurs until the middle of the eighteenth century.

www.clanarthur.com
www.clannarthur.com
No. of castles/sites: 2
Rank: 396=/764
Xref: Arthur

MacAskill

The name means 'son of Askell', 'Askell' being a Norse personal name. The family were established on the island of Skye on the west coast of Scotland.

Dun Sgathaich [NG 595121] is some eight miles north and west of Armadale, and is in a lovely spot on the north coast of Sleat on Skye. The ruins are perched on a rock, and the entrance was reached up a flight of stairs defended by a tower, drawbridge and door. There was probably a stronghold on the rock from early times, and the present remains date from the fourteenth century or earlier. The property was held by the MacAskills, and there are many legends associated with the place. The fortress was associated with the hero Diarmid, a companion of Finn MacCool, and this is where he came to be instructed by the warrior-queen Sgathaich. Another tale has the castle being built by a witch in a single night. The MacLeods were in possession of Dun Sgathaich by the fourteenth century, and this part of Skye eventually passed to the MacDonalds. William MacAskill, probably of Eabost a few miles to the south of Dunvegan, led the MacLeods in a battle against the MacDonalds at Eynot in the sixteenth century. There is a museum at Dunvegan about Angus MacAskill, who was seven foot nine inches tall.

Calgary Castle or **House** [NM 377513] is some ten miles west of Tobermory on Mull, and is a petite baronial mansion, and has no defensive past although there was an older building on the site. The castle dates from about 1823, and was built for the MacAskills. Calgary on the west coast of Canada gets its name from here. Colonel James MacLeod stayed at Calgary House and fell in love with a daughter of the owner, and in 1876 called the place in Canada Calgary in commemoration of meeting her. Self-catering accommodation is available at the castle (01449 741066; www.calgary-castle.com).

No. of castles/sites: 2
Rank: 396=/764
Xrefs: MacAsgill; MacAskell

MacAughtrie

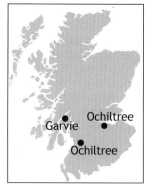

The name is found in Galloway, and is recorded in Scotland from the fifteenth century. The MacAughtries held land in Galloway and in Argyll; the name apparently became Anglicised to Ochiltree.

There were two Ochiltree castles in Scotland: **Ochiltree Castle** [NT 032748], three and a half miles east and south of Linlithgow in West Lothian, is an altered sixteenth-century tower house, while the **Ochiltree Castle** [NS 510212], in Ayrshire, was demolished about 1950. Neither of these building, however, appears to have been held by the Ochiltree or MacAughtrie family.

The site of **Garvie Castle** [NS 035903] is some ten miles south-west of Strachur on Cowal. The lands were a property of the Campbells of Argyll, but were also held by the MacAughtries.

No. of castles/sites: 1
Rank: 537=/764
Xref: Ochiltree

MacAulay

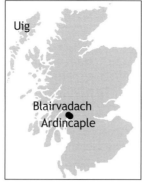

The name comes from two sources. One is 'son of Amalghaidh', an Irish personal name, and the clan became established in Dunbartonshire. They claimed descent from a son of the Earl of Lennox, and may have been linked to the MacGregors with whom they had a long association. A separate origin for the name is found on Lewis and in the Western isles, from 'son of Amlaib', which is a Gaelic rendition of the Norse name 'Olaf'.

The MacAulays of Uig on Lewis were an old clan, and were enemies of the Morrisons of Ness. This led to bloodshed and battles, in which the MacLeods of Lewis and the Mackenzies of Seaforth got involved. The Morrisons were using Dun Carloway when there were suffocated in their sleep by the MacAulays.

The name is on record from the end of the thirteenth century. Zachary MacAulay was the manager of a plantation in Jamaica and became prominent in the anti-slavery movement, and his son, Thomas Babington MacAulay, was MP for Edinburgh and Secretary for War from 1839-41. He wrote *History of England*, and was made a baron in 1857.

Ardincaple Castle [NS 282830], to the West of Helensburgh in Dunbartonshire, was an old stronghold, dating from the twelfth century, but was remodelled down the centuries into a large castellated mansion. The old castle had a moat, as well as a brownie. The lands were held by the MacAulays, but by the eighteenth century the castle was in ruins and the chiefs in debt, and the property was sold to the Campbells in 1767. The mansion was rebuilt, but was mostly demolished in 1957.

Blairvadach Castle [NS 263853], a mile north and west of Rhu in Dunbartonshire, was also held by the MacAulays of Ardincaple. There was a tower house, dating from the sixteenth century, but this was replaced by a mansion after the property was sold to Andrew Buchanan, a Glasgow merchant.

Only a motte survives of nearby **Faslane Castle** [NS 249903], a stronghold of the Earls of Lennox on the eastern side of the Gare Loch, which is believed to have been abandoned by the end of the fourteenth century. The lands were then held by the MacAulays of Ardincaple, and then later by the Colquhouns of Luss.

www.macaulay.org
No. of castles/sites: 3
Rank: 328=/764
Xref: MacAuley

MacBain

The name MacBain or MacBean probably comes from Gaelic 'bheathain', meaning 'lively one'. The name is on record from the fourteenth century, and the clan supported Robert the Bruce. They fought for the MacDonalds at the Battle of Harlaw in 1411, where many of the MacBains were killed. The MacBains were part of Clan Chattan (also see Mackintosh).

Kinchyle [NH 622380], six miles south-west of Inverness, was held by the MacBains, although it is not clear whether they had a seat or a castle. They took part in the Jacobite Risings of 1715, after which many were transported; and in the rebellion 1745-46. Major Gillies MacBean fought bravely at the Battle of Culloden in 1746, resisting an onslaught of government dragoons, but was slain, along he killed thirteen dragoons. It was also a MacBain who helped Cameron of Locheil, who had been wounded, from the battlefield and so saved his life, although Locheil died aboard a French ship fleeing Scotland. The lands of the MacBains were sold in the 1760s.

www.clanmacbean.net
No. of castles/sites: 1
Rank: 537=/764
Xref: MacBean; Chattan

MacBrayne

The name means 'son of the judge', 'Brayne' coming from 'brieve' or 'brehon', a man who was trained in and dispensed law as laid out through oral tradition. The office became hereditary, although doubt has been cast on how fair such a system could be when the office passed from father to son. Caledonian MacBrayne is now the main ferry company for the Western Isles, and was run by David MacBrayne in 1879.

Glenbranter [NS 112978], which is three miles south-east of Strachur in Cowal in Argyll, was held by the MacBraynes from the end of the eighteenth century. There was a mansion, but this was demolished in the 1950s after the lands were sold to the Forestry Commission by Sir Harry Lauder, who had purchased the estate in 1916.

No. of castles/sites: 1
Rank: 537=/764

MacCall

The name comes from 'son of Cathal', 'Cathal' being a personal name. The clan is believed to be descended from the MacAulays, members of whom came to the lowlands in the sixteenth century to escape trouble in Argyll.

Guffockland [NS 730124], which is four miles west and north of Sanquhar in Nithsdale in Dumfries and Galloway, was held by the MacCalls until the seventeenth century. They may have had a castle or seat at Guffockland, but they also had a tower house at Tower [NS 756119], two miles to the east.

Caitloch [NX 764918], which is a mile north-west of Moniaive also in Dumfries and Galloway, is a small mansion, but replaced or stood on the site of a castle. The lands were held by the Fergussons, but later passed to the MacCalls, and the mansion is still occupied.

To the north and a few miles east of Glasgow near Broomhouse was **Daldowie House** [NS 674619]. It was a substantial symmetrical mansion, dating from 1745 with later additions, and replaced an earlier house. The mansion was demolished and all that remains is an old doocot. The lands were held by the Stewarts, then by the Bogle family in 1724 and then by the MacCalls, who were descended from the family of Guffockland. The family of Pollock-McCall of Daldowie still flourishes.

www.theclanmccall.org
No. of castles/sites: 4
Rank: 278=/764

MacCombie

The name is from the Gaelic 'MacComaidh', which is a contraction of 'MacThomaidh', meaning 'son of Tommie or Tommy', from a diminutive of the personal name 'Thomas'. In English the name is Thomson, and many of the clan ended up with this form, particularly in Perthshire. The 'b' of MacCombie was introduced towards the end of the eighteenth century. The MacCombies held lands in Glenshee, although the use of either MacCombie or MacThomas were interchangeable, while another variation is Combie. The MacCombies were part of Clan Chattan (see Mackintosh).

Finegand [NO 141662], three and a half miles south and east of Spittal of Glenshee in Perthshire, was held by the clan from 1571 or earlier, and there is a charter from this date. There was a castle or old house, but nothing survives except a stone with the date 1658. The Cockstane [NO 141643] (Clach na Coileach in Gaelic) was a gathering point for the clan in times of trouble.

Some twelve or so miles to the north of Alyth in Glen Isla and also in Perthshire, **Forter Castle** [NO 183646] is a restored sixteenth-century tower house, L-plan and rising to four storeys. The castle had been plundered and burned in 1640, and when the property was sold by the Ogilvies to the MacCombies they built a new castle at **Crandart** [NO 188675], further up the glen. It dated from 1660, but the clan were not to enjoy their new possession for long. The chief got into a bitter and costly feud with the Ogilvies, and he had to sell his lands in 1676. **Dod** [NO 492499], which was a couple of miles east of Forfar in Angus, was a small castle of the MacCombies but it went to the Ogilvies. The line of the MacThomases of Finegand continues, although they apparently now live in Parsons Green in London in England. Self-catering accommodation is available at Forter Castle (www.hoseasons.co.uk).

Lynturk Castle [NJ 598122] is all but gone except for earthworks, and it was replaced with a house in the nineteenth century. It is located three miles south-east of Alford in Aberdeenshire, and was a property of the Strachans, of the Irvines and of the Gordons, before passing to the MacCombies in 1816.

www.clanmacthomas.org
www.macthomasnorthamerica.com
No. of castles/sites: 5
Rank: 240=/764
Xrefs: Chattan; Combie; MacComie; MacThomas; Thomson

MacConnel

The name probably comes from variation in the spelling of MacDonnell, or from 'son of Conall', 'Conall' being an old personal name meaning 'high powerful'. The name is on record from the seventeenth century, and was found in Argyll.

Knockdolian Castle [NX 123854] is three or so miles north-east of Ballantrae in Ayrshire, and is a sixteenth-century tower house, a property of the Grahams and of the MacCubbins. It was replaced by Knockdolian House, which dates from 1842 and was built for the MacConnels.

Craigneil Castle [NX 147853] is also in Ayrshire, but five miles north-east of Ballantrae. It is now ruinous, but is said to have been used as a prison and place of execution. Craigneil was built by the Kennedys, although by the end of the nineteenth century the lands were held by the MacConnels of Knockdolian.

No. of castles/sites: 2
Rank: 396=/764

MacCorquodale

The name means 'son of Thorketill', from the Norse personal name, which means 'Thor's kettle', and the name is on record from the fifteenth century.

The clan held a stronghold on **Eilean Tighe Bhainn** [NN 044249], an island in **Loch Tromlee** (although the property was also known as **Phantilands**), which is a mile or so north of Kilchrenan and Loch Awe in Argyll; the name means 'isle of the white house' in Gaelic. It was a property of the MacCorquodales of Phantilands, and consisted of a sixteenth-century tower and courtyard. They claimed descent from Thorkil or Thorketill, who is said to have retrieved the severed head of Alpin, Kenneth's father and king of the Dalriadan Scots, from the Picts. The MacCorquodales were described in 1612 as 'notorious thieves and supporters of Clan Gregour [the MacGregors]'. The castle was sacked by Alasdair Colkitto MacDonald in 1646, and is now very ruinous.

No. of castles/sites: 1
Rank: 537=/764
Xref: MacCorckindale

MacCrindle

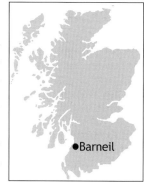

The name is a form of MacRanald (more usually known as Clanranald), a branch of the MacDonalds, and was found in Ayrshire and in Galloway.

Barneil [NS 366085], which is five miles east of Maybole in Ayrshire, was held by the MacCrindles in the sixteenth century, but passed to the Boyds of Trochrague. There may have been a castle or an old house, although the site is now a farm.

No. of castles/sites: 1 / Rank: 537=/764

MacCubbin

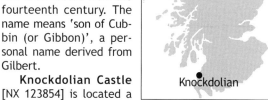

The name was found in Dumfries and Galloway, and is on record from the fourteenth century. The name means 'son of Cubbin (or Gibbon)', a personal name derived from Gilbert.

Knockdolian Castle [NX 123854] is located a few miles north of Ballantrae in Ayrshire, and stands near the sea. There is a tower house, which dates from the sixteenth century, although this was later replaced by a mansion. Knockdolian was held by the Grahams, but passed to the MacCubbins, who made extensive repairs to the tower house in the seventeenth century. The property later passed to the MacConnels. 'Ye may think on your cradle, I'll think on my stane, and there'll ne'er be an heir to Knockdolian again.' A story goes that a mermaid used to sing all night from a stone on the seashore near the castle. This so angered the lady of the house that she had the rock broken up. The mermaid returned only once more to sing the above verse; the heir to the lands died in his cradle and the line died out.

No. of castles/sites: 1
Rank: 537=/764
Xref: MacGibbon

Knockdolian Castle (M&R)

357

MacCulloch

The origin of the name is not certain, but it may be from 'son of (the) boar', which is from the Gaelic 'MacC(h)ullach'. The name is on record in Scotland from the end of the thirteenth century, and the clan became important in Galloway, although

there were also MacCullochs in Ross-shire in the north.

Cardoness Castle [NX 591552] is a tall and impressive tower house, and stands to the south-west of Gatehouse of Fleet in Galloway. The tower rises to four storeys

Cardoness Castle (MC)

and formerly a garret, and dates from the end of the fifteenth century. There was a courtyard, but this is mostly very ruinous. The lands passed by marriage to the MacCullochs from around 1450, and they built the castle. They were an unruly and violent lot: James MacCulloch, second laird, was outlawed in 1471 and again in 1480. His successor, Ninian, robbed his father's widow of all her goods. Thomas MacCulloch, his son, besieged the Adairs of Dunskey in 1489, and soon after plundered the castle of his kinsman, MacCulloch of Adair. Thomas died at the Battle of Flodden in 1513. The property went to Alexander MacCulloch in 1516, and he raided the Isle of Man in the 1530s, commemorated by the Isle of Man verse: 'God keep the good corn, the sheep, and the bullock, From Satan, from sin, and from Cutlar M'Culloch'. The last of the family was Sir Godfrey MacCulloch, who shot William Gordon of Buck (or Bush) o' Bield in 1690, fled abroad, returned and was spotted in a church in Edinburgh. He was beheaded in 1697 by the Maiden, an early Scottish guillotine preserved in the Museum of Scotland in Edinburgh. The property had passed to the Gordons and then to the Maxwells and the castle was replaced by **Cardoness House** [NX

566536]. There are stories of a curse which afflicted the owners of Cardoness Castle, leading each family to eventual ruin. Cardoness Castle is in the care of Historic Scotland and is open to the public (01557 814427).

Ardwall [NX 581547] is nearby, a little further south of Cardoness, and is a mansion dating from 1767, which was extended in the nineteenth century. The lands were held by the MacCullochs (although also apparently by the Turners for several generations). David MacCulloch, fifth of Ardwall, was a Covenanter, and fought at the Battle of Bothwell Brig in 1679. He then fled abroad, but returned in 1689. The property may still be held by the MacCullochs of Ardwall, although their residence is given as in Edinburgh by *Burke's*.

The MacCullochs also held:

Ardwell House [NX 103455], near Stranraer, Galloway; castle replaced by mansion.
  Held by the MacCullochs, and then later by the MacTaggart Stewarts. The mansion dates from the eighteenth century, with later remodelling, and the garden and grounds are open to the public from April to October (01776 860227).

Auchneight [NX 110334], near Stranraer, Galloway; site of castle or hunting lodge.
  Held by the MacCullochs.

Barholm Castle [NX 521529], near Gatehouse of Fleet, Galloway; fine L-plan tower house.
  Held by the MacCullochs. John Knox used Barholm as a place of refuge before fleeing to the continent. In 1579 John Brown

Barholm Castle (M&R)

of Carsluith was called to account for the murder of MacCulloch of Barholm. Major John MacCulloch of Barholm was executed for his part in the Pentland Rising, and subsequent Battle of Rullion Green, in 1666. The castle has been restored and is still occupied (www.barholm.net).

Druchtag Motte [NX 349467], near Port William, Galloway; fine motte.
  The lands were held by the MacCullochs and then by the Maxwells.

Hills Tower [NX 912726], near Dumfries; restored castle.
  Held by the Maxwells, but passed to the MacCullochs of Ardwall in the middle of the seventeenth century.

Killaser Castle [NX 096451], near Stranraer, Galloway; slight remains of castle.
  Held by the MacCullochs of Ardwell.

McCulloch's Castle [NX 997577], near New Abbey, Dumfriesshire; site of castle.
  Held by the MacCullochs, but the seat was moved to a new site after the property had passed to the Murrays. Later owners

were the Carnegie Earls of South Esk, the Craiks (who built Arbigland House), and the Blacketts.

Myrton Castle [NX 360432], near Whithorn, Galloway; ruinous L-plan tower house.

Held by the MacCullochs. Sir Alexander MacCulloch of Myrton burnt Dunskey Castle in 1503, and was the King's Master Falconer. James IV visited Myrton in 1504 (and 1511) during a

Myrton Castle (M&R)

pilgrimage to the shrine of St Ninian at Whithorn and to visit mistresses. The tower was ruined by the late seventeenth century, and a new house was built nearby. Myrton was sold to the Maxwells of Monreith in 1685. Legend has it that when this parish was united with Glasserton, the pulpit and bell were removed from Kirkmaiden church and were to be transported by sea across Luce Bay to a church of the same name near the Mull of Galloway. A strange storm blew up and the boat foundered, sinking with the pulpit and bell. The wraith-bell is said to ring from the depths of Luce Bay whenever one of the MacCullochs is near death.

Nigg House [NH 804717], near Invergordon, Ross and Cromarty; site of castle or old house.

Held by the MacCullochs but passed to the Gayres in the seventeenth century. The MacCullochs of Tarrel, Plaids, Kindeace, and Glastulich are recorded as being followers of the Earl of Ross.

Tarrel [NH 911819], near Tain; site of tower houses.

Held by the Tarrel family but passed to the MacCullochs, and then perhaps to the Munros. There were castles at both **Little Tarrel** [NH 911819], a restored tower house, and **Meikle Tarrel** [NH 900810], all traces of which have gone, but it is not clear who built them and whether they were later held by the Munros.

Torhouse Castle [NX 396554], near Wigtown, Galloway; ruinous tower house.

Held by the MacCullochs.

No. of castles/sites: 15
Rank: 94=/764

MacDonald

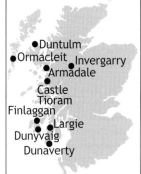

The name comes from 'son of Donald', and the original Donald was the son of Reginald and grandson of Somerled; the English equivalent of the name is Donaldson. There are numerous spellings of the name, such as MacDonnell, MacConnel and MacConnochie, and there were several related branches of the clan, including the Lords of the Isles, of Clanranald, the MacDonnells of Glengarry, the MacDonalds of Sleat, the MacDonalds of Largie, the Maclans (or MacDonalds) of Glencoe and the Maclans of Ardnamurchan.

James Donaldson was a successful bookseller and publisher, and when he died he left money to build and run Donaldson's Hospital. The building, a magnificent pile, was designed by William Playfair and was completed in 1851. It housed Donaldson's School for the Deaf, although the building is to be sold and houses built in the grounds.

James Ramsay MacDonald, who was born in Lossiemouth in 1866, was an MP for Labour from 1906, and was then Prime Minister in 1924 and 1925-35.

Finlaggan [NR 388681], which lies three miles west of Port Askaig on the Isle of Islay, is the site of the centre of power of the MacDonald Lords of the Isles. All that

Finlaggan (M&R)

remains are foundations of buildings on two islands in Loch Finlaggan. The larger island, Eilean Mor, has the ruins of a chapel and other buildings, as well as several carved graveslabs, while the smaller island, Eilean na Comhairle or 'island of council', has what are probably the remains of a tower or castle. There was a kingdom of the Isles (or Sudreys), which was subject to Norway, from about 900, and this included all the islands off western Scotland as well as Kintyre and the Isle of Man. Somerled, who was of mixed Norse and Scottish descent, was instrumental in pushing out the Norsemen and establishing himself in their territories. He probably founded Saddell Abbey [NR 785321] in Kintyre about 1160, but he got into conflict with Malcolm IV, King of Scots. This came to arms in 1164 and Somerled raised an army, but he was reputedly assassinated near

Renfrew. He was succeeded by his sons Reginald in Kintyre and Islay, Dugald in Lorn, Mull and Jura, and Angus in Bute, Arran and North Argyll. Reginald refounded Iona Abbey around 1208 and founded Iona Nunnery around the same time. Reginald's son, Donald, was the progenitor of the MacDonalds.

The Western Isles became part of the kingdom of Scots three years after the Battle of Largs in 1263. Angus Og MacDonald, grandson of Donald (mentioned above), was a friend and supporter of Robert the Bruce, and Angus fought at the Battle of Bannockburn in 1314. Angus died at Finlaggan in 1328, and his son, John of Islay, was the first to use the title 'Lord of the Isles'. John was married to Amy MacRuari, the heiress of the MacRuari lands of Garmoran, a huge property including much of the Outer Hebrides and other lands, and they appear to have had a son called Ranald, who is believed to have been the progenitor of Clanranald. John, Lord of the Isles, married her and they appear to have had a son Ranald. John went on to divorce Amy, and married Margaret, a daughter of Robert II, although Ranald was given considerable lands, including Moidart and the Uists. John founded or refounded Oronsay Priory [NR 349889] around 1340. It was from Angus Og's other son, Iain, that the MacIains (or MacDonalds) of Glencoe were descended. The independence of the Lords, however, and their power and influence, especially after they had acquired the Earldom of Ross, caused constant trouble for the kings of Scots. A campaign in pursuit of the Earldom by Donald, second Lord, led to the bloody Battle of Harlaw in 1411, and Alexander, third Lord, was twice imprisoned by James I. The power of the Lords reached its zenith with the fourth Lord, John, who had secured the Earldom of Ross. John entered into the Treaty of Westminster/Ardtornish in 1461, an agreement whereby Scotland would be divided up between the Earl of Douglas, the Lord of the Isles and the English king Edward IV. James III was in no position to resist John at that time, but James IV was much stronger and eventually destroyed the power of John in a campaign in 1493. John was stripped of all his titles, his properties were forfeited, and he was imprisoned in Paisley Abbey until his death in 1503. Attempts were made to restore the Lordship, but these were ultimately unsuccessful, although other branches of the MacDonalds survived and prospered. Finlaggan itself was held by the MacGillespie family after the Lordship collapsed, and they may have had a house on the island; Islay was eventually to become a property of the Campbells. There is a visitor centre at Finlaggan, and the islands can be reached via a boardwalk (01496 810629; www.fin laggan.com).

The Lords of the Isles were buried at Iona Abbey [NM 287245] on the Isle of Iona by the Street of the Dead, and the restored St Oran's Chapel, which dates from the eleventh century, is associated with the Lords.

Dunyvaig Castle [NR 406455], three miles east of Port Ellen on the south of the Isle of Islay, is a shattered ruin of what was once a strong castle. A small tower or keep stood on a steep rock on the shore, and there was an inner and an outer courtyard. The stronghold was held by the Lords of the Isles, but passed to the MacIains

Dunyvaig Castle (MC)

of Ardnamurchan after the MacDonald keeper rebelled against the Crown. The property was leased back to the MacDonalds in 1519, but was then given to the Campbells in 1543, who leased it back after much dispute to a branch of the MacDonalds. The Rhinns of Islay, however, and the north part of Jura were given to the MacLeans of Duart, to the chagrin of the MacDonalds. In 1598 the last MacDonald of Dunyvaig defeated the MacLeans at the Battle at Gruinart, and killed Lachlan MacLean of Duart. MacDonald was, however, then ordered to surrender the castle, and was forfeited in 1608; Dunyvaig was put into the stewardship of the Bishops of the Isles for the King. In 1612 the castle was taken by Alasdair 'Old' Colkitto MacDonald, but it was retaken by the Campbells of Cawdor in 1615 after the Campbells had bought the island, and although Colkitto escaped, the rest of his men were slain or later hanged. Fighting continued under Sir John MacDonald and the castle changed hands again. It was besieged and taken by 'Old' Colkitto in 1647. After a siege by a Covenanter army under David Leslie the same year it was forced to surrender when the water supply failed, and Colkitto was finally hanged from the walls. The Campbells of Cawdor occupied the castle until about 1677, but demolished the building soon afterwards, and moved to **Islay House** [NR 334628] and the island remained with branches of the Campbells. The ruin of Dunyvaig has mostly crumbled away but it has been consolidated and can be visited.

Castle Tioram [NM 663725] stands on a tidal island in a beautiful spot three miles north of Acharacle in Moidart in the western Highlands. Although ruinous, the building consists of a massive curtain wall into which a tower house and ranges of buildings were added in the sixteenth century. As mentioned above, Amy MacRuari was the heiress of the MacRuari lands of Garmoran, a huge property which included Moidart and the Uists in the Outer Hebrides. John, Lord of the Isles, married her and they appear to have had a son Ranald, but John took the opportunity to marry Margaret, a daughter of Robert II, and divorced Amy. Ranald, her son, was given many of the possessions of the MacRuaris, including Moidart and the Uists. Castle Tioram was modified (or built) by Amy MacRuari, and became the seat of the MacDonalds of Clan Ranald. Ranald, first Chief, died here in 1386, and Alan, second Chief, fought at the bloody Battle of Harlaw in 1411 on the side of the Lord

Castle Tioram (M&R)

of the Isles. Allan MacDonald, fourth Chief, was executed by James IV in 1505 after taking part in pillaging Atholl. The sixth Chief was assassinated, while Ian Moidartch, eighth Chief, was kidnapped and held in Edinburgh Castle in 1544; he escaped and recovered his lands after Castle Tioram had been seized. In 1554 the stronghold was attacked by a force under the Earls of Huntly and of Argyll, and Cromwell's forces occupied the castle in 1651 after a siege. John, twelfth Chief, had fought on the side of the Marquis of Montrose, as did his son, Donald. During the Jacobite Rising of 1715, the castle was torched so that Hanoverian forces could not use it, and Allan, fourteenth Chief, led the left wing of the Jacobite forces and was killed at the battle of Sheriffmuir that year. The castle was never reoccupied, but Rachel Chiesly, Lady Grange, was imprisoned here for a few weeks in 1732 before being taken to the outer isles. Ranald, son of Ranald, the then Chief, and known as Young Clanranald, led the clan contingent during the Jacobite Rising of 1745-46. Ranald fled to France after the Battle of Culloden, but he was allowed to return nine years later. The chiefs sold the property to the Gordons in 1849, and many people were subsequently cleared from their lands. The line of the chiefs and captains of Clanranald continues, and the present chief now apparently lives near Killin in central Scotland. Clan Ranald had a set of reputedly magic bagpipes which, when played, are said to have ensured victory in battle.

Ormacleit Castle [NF 740319], nine and a half miles north of Lochboisdale on South Uist in the Outer Hebrides, is a T-plan tower house, and is one of the last castles to be built in Scotland: it was started in 1701 and completed seven years later. It was built for Allan, chief of Clanranald, but it was destroyed by fire in 1715; said to have been set alight during a riotous party. It happened, though, that this was also on the eve of the Battle of Sheriffmuir, at which Alan was killed. The building was never restored, and the family moved to Nunton House [NF 764535] on Benbecula. The property was sold to the Gordons in 1838.

Flora MacDonald, daughter of Ranald MacDonald of Milton, was born in 1722 on South Uist. After the Battle of Culloden in 1746, Bonnie Prince Charlie was a fugitive in the Hebrides and Flora helped the prince travel from the Uists to Skye, disguised as Betty Burke, an Irishwoman. The couple parted on Skye, and she was later taken and imprisoned including in the Tower of London, but she was eventually released without punishment. Flora married Allan MacDonald of Kingsburgh in 1750, and they had several children before emigrating to America in 1774 (when she was fifty-two years old). Their timing was unfortunate as Flora and her husband supported the British in the American War of Independence, and Flora had to return in 1779, and she came back to live on Skye. She died in 1790, apparently wrapped in the sheets in which Bonnie Prince Charlie had slept, and is buried at Kilmuir to the north of the island.

Invergarry (or Glengarry) Castle [NH 315006], seven miles south-west of Fort Augustus in Lochaber in the Highlands, is a magnificent ruined tower house, the present building dating from the seventeenth century. Glengarry was long a property of the MacDonnells of Glengarry, a branch of Clanranald, and descended from a younger brother of Ranald, son of Amy MacRuari (as mentioned above). The fortress stands on the 'Rock of

Invergarry Castle 1910?

the Raven', and this is the slogan of the family. The MacDonnells supported Charles I, and the castle was burnt in 1654 by forces of General Monck during Cromwell's occupation of Scotland. The clan was forfeited but recovered the lands after the Restoration. In 1688 Alastair MacDonald of Glengarry fortified the castle for James VII, but eventually submitted to the government of William and Mary in 1692. Invergarry was seized by Alasdair Dubh of Glengarry in 1715 and he fought at Sheriffmuir the same year, but the stronghold was recaptured by Hanoverian forces in 1716. The castle was back in the hands of the MacDonnells by 1731, and during the Jacobite Rising of 1745-46 was twice visited by Bonnie Prince Charlie. John MacDonnell of Glengarry and his son, Alistair Ruadh, were imprisoned after the Rising, although Alistair became a spy for the Hanoverian government, and then chief of the clan from 1754. Invergarry had been burnt by the 'Butcher' Duke of Cumberland. A new mansion was built nearby, on the site of which is the Glengarry Castle Hotel. The lands were sold in the nineteenth century to the Earl of Dudley, and the MacDonnell chiefs of Glengarry now apparently live in London in England. The castle stands in the grounds of the Glengarry Castle Hotel (01809 501254; www.glengarry.net).

Caisteal Camus (or Chamius) [NG 671087], also known as Knock Castle, three and a half miles north of Armadale on the Isle of Skye, stands on a steep headland with a ditch defending the landward side, but the buildings are very ruinous. Dun Sgathaich [NG 595121], is eight miles north and west of Armadale. The shattered ruin crowns a rock by the shore, and it was formerly protected by a drawbridge. Meaning 'dun of shadows', Dun Sgathaich is associated with Diarmid, a companion of Finn MacCool. The warrior queen Sgathaich trained men in the art of fighting, and Diarmid came here to be instructed by her. Another tradition is that the castle was built in a single night a witch. Both the castles are situated in the fertile south of the island, which is called Sleat, which was held by the MacAskills and by the MacLeods of Dunvegan. The MacDonalds, however, acquired the lands early in the fifteenth century after a period of strife when both castles were besieged. This branch of the MacDonalds was descended from Hugh, a younger son of Alexander, Lord of the Isles. Both castles were captured by the forces of James I in 1431. The property was forfeited to the Crown around 1493 with the destruction of the Lord of the Isles by James IV, but the castles were besieged by the MacLeods in support of the MacDonalds in 1515, although to no avail. The lands were eventually granted to the MacDonalds of Sleat, but by 1689 they had abandoned both the castles and were based at Duntulm, further north on Skye.

Duntulm Castle [NG 410743], six and a half miles north of Uig in Trotternish, is again a shattered ruin but it is located in a picturesque spot above cliffs, looking out to the Outer Hebrides. This part of Skye was originally held by the MacLeods, but was acquired by the MacDonalds of Sleat in the seventeenth century. The MacDonalds of Sleat were made Baronets of Nova Scotia in 1625, and Sir James, second Baronet, supported the Marquis of Montrose and led men into England in

Duntulm Castle 1925?

1651; while Sir Donald, fourth Baronet, fought for the Jacobites at the Battle of Killiecrankie in 1689, and also joined the rising of 1715. Duntulm was abandoned for Monkstadt House [NG 380676], which is two miles north of Uig. The house was first built as a dower house but it was rebuilt in 1732. The chief of the MacDonalds of Sleat did not openly support the Jacobite Rising of 1745-46, although Bonnie Prince Charlie was sheltered and helped by the clan, including by Flora MacDonald (see above). The MacDonalds left in 1798 for Armadale in

Sleat, and Monkstadt was used by tacksmen who held the nearby lands. The house was ruinous by the middle of the twentieth century.

Armadale Castle [NG 640047] is at the village of Armadale on the southern side of the island, back in the lands of Sleat. There was an older house nearer the shore, but the present building was begun in 1815 for Lord MacDonald of Sleat. Flora MacDonald's mother was married to Hugh MacDonald of Sleat. Flora came to Armadale after helping the Bonnie Prince and was arrested near here; she was later married at Armadale to Allan MacDonald of Kingsburgh in 1750. Dr Samuel Johnson visited in 1773. The present mansion was burned out and is now ruinous, and in 1925 the MacDonalds of Sleat, Baronets, moved to Ostaig. Some of the outbuildings of the castle now house the Museum of the Isles and Clan Donald Centre. There are woodland gardens and nature trails, as well as a walled garden and accommodation is available (01471 844305/227; www.clandonald.com).

The MacDonalds also held:

Achamore House [NR 644477], near Ardminish, Island of Gigha; mansion on site of older residence.
    The island was held by the MacDonald Lords of the Isles, but after their forfeiture passed to the MacNeills of Taynish. Gigha much later passed to other hands, and was bought by its residents in 2002. The gardens of Achamore House are open to the public and there is B&B at the house (01583 505385; www.AchamoreHouse.com/www.gigha.org.uk).

Airds Castle [NR 820383], Carradale, Kintyre, Argyll; some remains of castle.
    Held by the MacDonald Lords of the Isles, but passed to the Reids of Barskimming in 1498. Carradale House is a large nineteenth-century mansion (www.carradale.org.uk).

Ardtornish Castle [NM 692426], near Lochaline, Lochaber; ruinous hall house on rocky crag.
    Held by the MacInnes clan but then by the MacDonald Lords of the Isles. It was here that John MacDonald, Lord of the Isles and Earl of Ross, signed the treaty of Westminster-Ardtornish in 1461 – by which he, the Earl of Douglas, and Edward IV of England agreed to divide Scotland between them. The property went to the MacLeans after the forfeiture of the Lords of the Isles. Ardtornish House [NM 703475] is a mansion of 1856-66 and the gardens are open in the summer and there is self-catering accommodation on the estate (01967 421288; www.ardtornish.co.uk).

Aros Castle [NM 563450], near Salen, Isle of Mull; ruinous castle in fine location.
    Held by the MacDougalls but passed to the MacDonalds, later Lords of the Isles, by the beginning of the fourteenth century. Aros went to the MacLeans of Duart on the Lords' forfeiture, and then later to the Campbells.

A' Chrannog [NR 294674], near Bridgend, Isle of Islay, Argyll; fortification.
    Built by Sir James MacDonald in 1615 when his family were trying to recover their lands on Islay.

Balconie Castle [NH 625652], near Alness, Ross and Cromarty; site of castle and mansion.
    Held by the Murrays, but the MacDonalds of Balconie are on record in the seventeenth century. The later mansion was demolished in the 1960s or 70s.

Balloan Castle [NH 160830], near Ullapool, Ross and Cromarty; mansion on site of castle.
    Held by the Earls of Ross, and then later by the MacDonnels or MacDonalds and by the Mackenzies. Inverbroom House [NH 182837], formerly known as Balloan House, stands nearby.

Borve Castle [NF 774506], near Balivanich, Isle of Benbecula; ruinous castle.

Held by the MacDonalds and Borve was occupied until 1625 or so, and was then burned down in the eighteenth century. This branch of the clan were Clanranald.

Breachacha Castle [NM 159539], near Arinagour, Isle of Coll; restored castle and later mansion.

The island was held by the MacDonalds, later Lords of the Isles, from early in the fourteenth century, but then changed hands between the MacDonalds, the MacNeils and the MacLeans of Coll and of Duart. A new mansion was built nearby [NM 159540], and the old castle became ruinous, although it was restored in the 1960s.

Cairnburgh Castle [NM 308450] and [NM 305447], Treshnish Isles, near Isle of Mull; ruinous castle on two islands.

Held by the MacDougalls of Lorn but was given to the MacDonalds, later Lords of the Isles, in 1309, before passing to the MacLeans of Duart. Last garrisoned in the 1745-46 Jacobite Rising.

Caisteal Bheagram [NF 761371], near Lochboisdale, Isle of South Uist; small ruinous castle on lochan in island.

Held by the Clanranald branch of the MacDonalds.

Caisteal Mhic Cneacail [NH 124943], near Ullapool, Ross and Cromarty; site of castle.

Probably held by the MacDonnels or MacDonalds, although the name means 'Nicholson's Castle'.

Caisteal Uisdean [NG 381583], near Uig, Isle of Skye; ruinous but solid castle.

The lands were held by the MacDonalds of Sleat, and the name means 'Hugh's Castle'. Hugh MacDonald, the builder, was outlawed for piracy, his exploits extending even to the fishermen of Fife, although he was later pardoned and made steward of Trotternish. However, he plotted to overthrow his MacDonald kin by slaughtering them at Castle Uisdean. The plot was discovered when letters were mixed up; Hugh was eventually caught about 1602 at Dun an Sticar on North Uist and he was then imprisoned in Duntulm Castle. He was given salted beef and no water, and when the pit where he had been buried was finally opened his skeleton was found with a broken pewter jug, which he had destroyed with his teeth. His skull and thigh bones were kept in a window of the parish church until buried in 1827. His ghost is said to be one of those that haunt Duntulm Castle.

Cara House [NR 641443], Isle of Cara, near Tayinloan, Kintyre, Argyll; ruinous old house.

Held by the MacDonalds of Largie. The house and island are said to have had a brownie, although the origins suggest more of a ghost as he was said to be the spirit of a MacDonald murdered by the Campbells. The ghost was said to be bearded and dressed in green.

Castle Loch Heylipol [NL 986435], near Scarinish, Isle of Tiree; mansion on site of castle in loch.

Held by the MacDonalds, later Lords of the Isles, but passed to the MacLeans and then later to the Campbells of Argyll. The mansion is said to be haunted by a Green Lady and by the bogle of a factor called MacLaren.

Castle of King Edward [NJ 722562], near Turriff, Aberdeenshire; fragments remain of a strong castle.

Held by the Comyns, by the Ross family and by the Stewarts, before passing to the MacDonald Lords of the Isles and Earls of Ross. They were forfeited in 1455 and the property had passed to the Forbeses by 1509.

Claig Castle [NR 472627], Am Fraoch Eilean, near Isle of Jura; some remains of castle.

Held by the MacDonalds, later Lords of the Isles, and is said to have been used as a prison as well as a stronghold and to extort money from vessels using the sound. The slogan of the MacDonalds was 'Fraoch Eilean', the name of the island on which the castle stands.

Coroghon Castle [NG 288055], Isle of Canna; slight remains of castle on a steep rock.

Held by Clanranald branch of the MacDonalds, and the name

Coroghon means 'fetters'. The site is said to be haunted by the ghost of a woman imprisoned here by one of the MacDonald Lords of the Isles, possibly his beautiful wife, who had fallen in love with one of the MacLeans.

Delny Castle [NH 735724], near Invergordon, Ross and Cromarty; site of substantial castle.

Held by the Earls of Ross and by the MacDonald Lords of the Isles when they held that title. Later went to the Munros and the site is occupied by a farm.

Dun Aonais [NF 889737], near Lochmaddy, Isle of North Uist; remains of dun on island in lochan.

Held by the MacDonalds. The dun was occupied until 1516 or later, and takes its name from a MacDonald Aonghais Fionn, 'Angus the Fair', its last occupier.

Dun Athad [NR 284406], near Port Ellen, Isle of Islay; remains of dun.

The dun was reused by Sir James MacDonald in 1615 when he was trying to reclaim the island for his family.

Dun Bhoraraic [NR 417658], near Port Askaig, Isle of Islay; remains of broch.

Used by the MacDonalds in medieval times.

Dun Chonnuill [NM 680125], Garvellach Islands, Firth of Lorn; ruinous castle.

Held by the MacDougalls, and then later by the MacDonalds and then by the MacLeans, descendants of whom are still hereditary keepers and captains of the castle.

Dun an Sticar [NF 898778], near Lochmaddy, Isle of North Uist; impressive ruinous dun on island in loch reached by two causeways.

The dun was still in use by Hugh MacDonald, one of the MacDonalds of Sleat, until 1602. He sheltered here after plotting to slaughter his kin, but was eventually captured to be starved to death in Duntulm Castle, on Trotternish, in Skye.

Dunaverty Castle [NR 688074], near Campbeltown, Kintyre, Argyll; slight traces of a once important castle.

On an ancient site, the stronghold was held by the MacQuillans and then later by the MacDonalds, later Lords of the Isles; Robert the Bruce is said to have been sheltered here. In 1493 James IV seized the castle from the MacDonalds, but it was almost immediately retaken and the king's governor was hanged from the walls, within sight of the king's departing ship. Archibald MacDonald's 300-strong garrison was massacred to a man after surrendering to the Covenanter forces of General David Leslie in 1647: among the slain was Archibald Mor MacDonald, the chief of the MacDonalds of Sanda. The castle was finally dismantled during Argyll's rebellion of 1685, and little remains.

Dundonald Castle [NR 700445], near Killean, Kintyre, Argyll; slight remains of castle.

Held by the MacDonald Lords of the Isles but later went to the Campbells. Killean House is a large impressive pile, built for the wealthy shipowner James Macalister Hall. Accommodation is available on the estate (01257 266511; www.killean estate.com).

Gorm Castle [NR 235655], near Bowmore, Island of Islay; slight remains of castle.

Held by the MacDonald Lords of the Isles and once a place of some strength. This part of Islay went to the MacLeans and the castle was besieged by the MacDonalds in 1578. Gorm was used by the MacLeans before they were defeated at the Battle of Traigh Gruinart in 1598. The property went to the Campbells, but the castle was used by Sir James MacDonald in 1615, and then was garrisoned by the Campbells in the 1640s.

Inverie [NM 776995], near Mallaig, Lochaber, Highland; site of castle.

Held by the MacDonnels or MacDonalds of Glengarry, and is believed to have been destroyed following the 1745-46 Jacobite Rising.

Island Muller Castle [NR 756224], near Campbeltown, Kintyre, Argyll; ruinous castle.

Held by the MacDonalds.

Keppoch Castle [NN 270807], near Spean Bridge, Lochaber, Highland; site of castle.

Held by the MacDonnels or MacDonalds of Keppoch, but passed to the Mackintoshes in 1690. The lands were disputed with the Mackintoshes, and the last clan battle was fought here. The castle was demolished in 1663 after the Keppoch Murder.

Kildonan Castle [NS 037210], near Brodick, Isle of Arran; ruins of small castle.

Held by the MacDonalds but went to the Stewarts of Ardgowan in 1406, and then later to the Hamiltons.

Kilkerran Castle [NR 729194], Campbeltown, Kintyre, Argyll; site of castle.

Held by the MacDonald Lords of the Isles, but it may have been rebuilt by James IV during his campaign against the Lords, and then used by James V in 1536. The lands were given to the Campbells and there was much bloodshed and then the planting of lowlanders. The Campbells changed the name of the place from Kilkerran to Campbeltown.

Kingsburgh House [NG 393554], near Uig, Isle of Skye; old house.

Held by the MacDonalds and mentioned in 1557. Bonnie Prince Charlie was brought here in 1746 while a fugitive from Hanoverian forces. Allan MacDonald of Kingsburgh married Flora MacDonald. The house is a private residence.

Loch Kinellan [NH 472576], near Strathpeffer, Inverness-shire; site of castle on island in loch.

Held by the Earls of Ross and then by the MacDonald Lords of the Isles when they held that title, but the property went to the Mackenzies. One story associated with Kinellan is that the then Earl of Ross sent his wife, Margaret, back to John MacDonald, Lord of the Isles, her brother. Margaret happened to have one eye, and the Earl had her accompanied by a one-eyed horse, a one-eyed servant, and one-eyed dog. Angering the Lord of the Isles in this way would not seem very sensible, although there is a very similar tale from Duntulm on Skye, where the lady was a MacLeod and her husband a MacDonald of Sleat.

Largie Castle [NR 708483], near Tayinloan, Kintyre, Argyll; some remains of castle.

Held by the MacDonalds of Largie (or Clan Ranaldbane, the Ranald Bane in question had distinguished himself in battle at Inverlochy in 1431), descendants of the Lord of the Isles, from the middle of the fifteenth century until the twentieth century. The clan had connections with the Bisset Earls of Antrim in Ireland, and also held the nearby island of Cara, which is just to the south of Gigha. Largie Castle is said to have been razed by the Covenanter general David Leslie in 1647 after the MacDonalds had been defeated at a battle at Ronachan. The clan were forfeited but recovered the property in 1661. John, fourteenth of Largie, tried to join the Jacobite Rising of 1745-46, but had to abandon his venture when a kettle of boiling water was poured over his foot. Flora MacDonald was related to the family and visited Largie several times. The family moved to 'new' Largie Castle, half a mile to the north-east of Tayinloan. The old castle is said to have had a brownie, which also frequented their house on the island of Cara. The clan became Moreton-MacDonald of Largie, and then Maxwell MacDonald, and apparently still live near Tayinloan. The MacDonalds of Largie had a burial vault at the Old Parish Church at Killean [NR 695446], where there are several carved burial slabs and the remains of a cross.

Loch an Sgoltaire Castle [NR 386972], near Scalasaig, Isle of Colonsay; ruinous castle.

The island was held by the MacDuffies, and then to the MacDonalds in the seventeenth century, and then to the Campbells of Argyll and then to the MacNeills. **Colonsay House** [NR 395968] dates from 1722 and has fine gardens which are open to the public some days (01951 200211; www.colonsay.org.uk).

Lochranza Castle [NR 933507], near Brodick, Isle of Arran; fine ruinous castle in picturesque location.

Held by the MacDonalds and by the Stewarts of Menteith, by the Campbells and by the Montgomerys, later Earls of Eglinton. The ruin is in the care of Historic Scotland and is open to the public (key available locally).

Moil Castle [NR 725210], Campbeltown, Kintyre, Argyll; site of castle.

Held by the MacDonald Lords of the Isles (and see Kilkerran Castle).

Moy Castle [NM 616247], Lochbuie, near Craignure, Isle of Mull; fine ruinous castle in lovely spot.

The lands were held by the MacDonalds, but passed to the MacLaines in 1360 and they built the castle.

Muiravonside [NS 965753], near Linlithgow, West Lothian; site of castle and mansion.

Held by the Tinsdales, by the Rosses, by the MacLeods and then by the MacDonalds of Largie after 1742, before passing to the Stirlings. The house was demolished in the twentieth century and the grounds are a public park.

Rammerscales House [NY 081777], near Lockerbie, Dumfries and Galloway; fine mansion.

Held by the Bells, who may have had a castle, but passed to the Mounsey family and then to the Bell MacDonalds. The house and gardens are open to the public for a month in the summer (01387 810229; www.rammerscales.co.uk).

Rineten [NJ 276003], near Ballater, Aberdeenshire; site of castle.

Held by the MacDonalds of Rineten, and Rineten House, which dates from the eighteenth century or earlier, may stand on the site of the castle.

Saddell Castle [NR 789316], near Campbeltown, Kintyre, Argyll; fine restored castle.

The lands were held by the MacDonalds, and Robert the Bruce is said to have been sheltered here. The property passed to the Bishops of Argyll, and then to the Campbells and to the Ralstons who remodelled the building. The castle was restored in the 1970s and can be rented as holiday accommodation through the Landmark Trust (01628 825925; www.landmark trust.org.uk).

Scorrybreac [NG 487439], near Portree, Isle of Skye; site of old house.

Long held by the Nicholsons but was sold to the MacDonalds at the beginning of the nineteenth century.

Skipness Castle [NR 907577], near Tarbert, Argyll; fine ruinous castle.

Held by the MacSweens but passed to the MacDonalds, later Lords of the Isles, who held the property until their forfeiture in 1493. The castle went to the Forresters and then to the Campbells. Near the castle is **Skipness House** [NR 907578], built for the Graham family at the end of the nineteenth century. The castle or house is said to have a Green Lady, and the castle is in the care of Historic Scotland and is open to the public.

Strome Castle [NG 862354], near Lochcarron, Ross and Cromarty; very ruinous castle.

Held by the Camerons of Locheil or by the MacDonald Lords of the Isles, but passed to the Gordon Earl of Huntly in 1546 and then to the MacDonnels or MacDonalds of Glengarry. The castle was blown up in 1602 by the Mackenzies of Kintail and the ruins are accessible (01599 566325).

Taynish [NR 725831], near Tayvallich, Argyll; castle or old house replaced by mansion.

Held by the MacDonald Lords of the Isles, but went to the MacNeills in 1440. Taynish House is a small mansion dating from the seventeenth century and it was restored as holiday accommodation after being gutted by fire (01764 681606; www.aboutscotland.co.uk).

www.clandonald.org.uk
www.highlandconnection.org/clandonaldmain.html
www.clan-donald-usa.org
No. of castles/sites: 59
Rank: 15/764
Xrefs: Clanranald; Donaldson; MacConnell; MacDonnell

MacDougall

The name means 'son of Dougall', 'Dougall' being a personal name, and the clan claim descent from Dugall, son of the great Somerled, who fought for and acquired much of the western seaboard of Scotland. The MacDougalls held Lorn, Mull and Jura, and the name was assumed by the clan in the middle of the thirteenth century. Duncan MacDougall founded Ardchattan Priory, near Connel in Argyll, in the 1230s, and there are tombs dating from about 1500 for two of the priors, brothers, who were MacDougalls; the ruins are open to the public. The MacDougalls supported John Balliol and the Comyns in the Wars of Independence, which put them on the wrong side when Robert the Bruce secured the throne. The clan were forfeited, although they recovered some of their property and influence in the 1340s.

Dunollie Castle [NM 852314] stands in a prominent position on a headland, a mile to the north of Oban in Argyll. There is a strong but ruinous tower, much

Dunollie Castle (M&R)

overgrown, along with the remains of other buildings. This has been a fortified site since the days of the kings of Dalriada in the sixth and seventh centuries, and probably long before that. In 698 the stronghold was taken and destroyed, and the present castle was built by the MacDougalls of Lorn. A MacDougall force defeated Bruce at Dalry, nearly killing him and wrenching a brooch from his cloak. This brooch become known as the Brooch of Lorn and was kept at the castle, then at Gylen Castle on Kerrera. Bruce returned and ravaged the MacDougall lands in 1309 after defeating them at the Pass of Brander. In 1644 Dunollie was attacked by Argyll, and in 1647 the castle was besieged by General David Leslie and an army of Covenanters and was sacked and burnt. It was attacked again in 1715 when the MacDougalls were fighting for the Stewarts during the Jacobite Rising. John MacDougall of Dunollie was captured and was to be transported, but he was later pardoned. The lands were

forfeited, but were restored by 1745. The MacDougalls built nearby Dunollie House [NM 853315] in 1746 or earlier, although there was already a house here dating from about 1600, and the old stronghold was abandoned. The castle is still owned by the MacDougalls but is in a dangerous condition. There are stories of a phantom piper or Highlander haunting the ruins.

Gylen Castle [NM 805265] is on the south coast of Kerrera (three miles from where the ferry lands), and is a fine and elegant small tower house, standing in a

Gylen Castle (M&R)

prominent and picturesque spot. Gylen was (and is) a property of the MacDougalls. An earlier castle here was where Alexander II may have died during an expedition to recover the Western Isles in the mid thirteenth century, although Dalrigh, near Horse Shoe Bay, is given as an alternative site. The existing castle, built by Duncan MacDougall, was completed in 1582, but was captured and torched (along with Dunollie) by a Covenanter army, led by General David Leslie, in 1647. The Brooch of Lorn was stolen, and not returned by the Campbells of Inverawe until the nineteenth century. The castle was never restored, although it has been consolidated and is open to the public at all reasonable times (www.gylencastle.co.uk).

Dunstaffnage Castle [NM 882344], three and a half miles north-east of Oban, is an impressive courtyard castle with a high curtain wall and later gatehouse range. A stronghold here was held by the kings of Dalriada in

Dunstaffnage Castle (and chapel) (TP)

the seventh century, and is believed to have been one of the places where the Stone of Destiny was kept. The present castle was built by the MacDougalls. Dunstaffnage was besieged and captured by Robert the Bruce in 1309 after the MacDougalls had been defeated at the Pass of Brander. Bruce made the castle a royal property with the Campbells as keepers. There is a fine ruined chapel [NM 881344] nearby in an atmospheric setting, dating from the thirteenth century, which incorporates the Campbell burial aisle, dated 1740. The castle is said to be haunted by a Green Lady or gruagach, also known as the Ell-maid of Dunstaffnage. The castle is in the care of Historic Scotland and is open to the public (01631 562465).

The MacDougalls also held:

Ardbrecknish House [NN 069212], near Inveraray, Argyll; mansion incorporating tower house.
> Held by the MacDougalls, but passed to the MacArthurs in the fourteenth century. There is a ghost story, which has two phantom bloodhounds, 'MacDougall's Hounds', appearing from the hearth, stretching and then leaving through a closed window. Another tale has the spectre of an old housekeeper with a candle being seen in the dead of night. The activity is said to be friendly rather than frightening. The building is now a hotel (01866 833223; www.loch-awe.co.uk).

Ardfad Castle [NM 769194], near Clachan, Isle of Seil, Argyll; some remains of castle and courtyard.
> Held by the MacDougalls of Ardencaple, and replaced by Ardencaple House [NM 764193] but later passed to the Campbells of Breadalbane.

Ardlarach [NM 736090], near Toberonochy, Isle of Luing, Argyll; farm house.
> Held by the MacDougalls from the beginning of the seventeenth century. The building is said to be haunted by the ghost of the wife of one of the MacDougall owners. Her son was slain at the Battle of Talaveera in 1809 during the Peninsular War, and unexplained noises were reported on the night he died, although it is her ghost which is now said to haunt the house.

Ardmaddy Castle [NM 788164], near Kilninver, Argyll; mansion incorporating castle.
> Held by the MacDougalls, who built the old castle, but passed to the Campbells. The fine gardens are open to the public and holiday accommodation is available on the estate (01852 300353; www.gardens-of-argyll.co.uk).

Aros Castle [NM 563450], near Tobermory, Isle of Mull, Argyll; ruinous castle.
> Held and built by the MacDougalls, but passed to the MacDonalds at the beginning of the fourteenth century, then later went to the MacLeans of Duart and then to the Campbells.

Cairnburgh Castle [NM 308450] & [NM 305447], Treshnish Isles, off Isle of Mull, Argyll; ruinous castle.
> Held by the MacDougalls, but passed to the Crown, with the MacDonalds as keepers, in 1309.

Caisteal nan Con [NM 765136], Isle of Torsa, Argyll; ruinous keep or tower.
> Held by the Campbells, by the MacDougalls of Rarey, and by the MacLeans.

Castle Coeffin [NM 853437], Isle of Lismore, Argyll; ruinous castle.
> Held and built by the MacDougalls, but the lands passed to the Stewarts and then to the Campbells. The castle is said to be named after Caifen, the son of a Norse king, who lived here. His sister, Beothail, died of a broken heart after her betrothed was slain. Her spirit was said to haunt the castle, and did not find peace until she was buried beside her love in Norway.

Dun Chonnuill [NM 680125], Garvellach Isles, Argyll; ruinous castle.
> Held by the MacDougalls, then later by the MacDonalds and by the MacLeans. One story is that a MacLauchlan from Ireland took and fortified the island in the fourteenth century.

Fincharn Castle [NM 898044], near Kilmartin, Argyll; ruinous tower house.
> Held by the MacDougalls against Robert the Bruce in 1308, but passed to the Scrymgeours in the fourteenth century, then later returned to the MacDougalls. One tale is that one of the chiefs, Mac Mhic Iain, wronged the wife of one of his men, who took his revenge by burning the castle and slaying the chief.

Gallanach Castle [NM 827260], near Oban, Argyll; castle replaced by mansion.
> Held by the MacDougalls of Gallanach, and the lands were still owned by them in the twentieth century (Patten-MacDougall). At Kilbride [NM 857257] is a burial aisle, now roofless, for the MacDougalls; the church, dedicated to St Bride, is ruinous but there are interesting memorials

Inistrynich [NN 106235], near Inveraray, Argyll; site of castle.
> Held by the MacDougalls, but passed to the MacArthurs.

Lunga House [NM 795064], near Arduaine, Argyll; mansion incorporating work from a castle.
> Held by the Campbells of Craignish, but passed to the MacDougalls of Lunga in the 1780s. Self-catering and B&B accommodation available (01852 500237; www.lunga.com).

Makerstoun House [NT 672315], near Kelso, Borders; mansion incorporating castle.
> Held by the Corbetts, then by the MacDougalls from 1373 to 1890, when it went to the Scotts of Gala. It was sacked by the Earl of Hertford in 1545. The house is now apparently the residence of the Biddulphs of Ledbury.

Rarey [NM 832206], near Kilninver, Argyll; castle replaced by mansion.
> Held by the MacDougalls, but given to the Campbells in 1311, although it was later recovered by the MacDougalls.

www.macdougall.org
No. of castles/sites: 19
Rank: 72=/764

Castle Coeffin (M&R) – see previous column

MacDowall

The name may come from 'dark stranger', in Gaelic 'dubh gall'; or it may be a variation on MacDougall, with a soft 'g'. The clan claimed descent from the powerful Lords of Galloway, whose line came to an end when Devorgilla, heiress of the lordship, married John Balliol. Her son was John I, King of Scots, but he was deposed by Edward I and so began the Wars of Independence. Not surprisingly, the MacDowalls supported John Balliol, so making them enemies of Robert the Bruce.

Garthland Castle [NX 077554] stood a few miles south of Stranraer in Galloway, and consisted of a square tower, which rose to forty-five foot, and other buildings. It was completely demolished in the nineteenth century to build a farm. Garthland was a property of the MacDowalls of Garthland from the thirteenth century. Dougal MacDowall (or MacDougall) captured Thomas and Alexander Bruce, brothers of Robert the Bruce, and in 1307 handed them over to Edward I of England for execution. Edward Bruce, their brother, attacked Galloway, and Dougal was slain in battle the following year. Uchtred MacDowall of Garthland was killed at the Battle of Flodden in 1513, along with his son and heir, and John MacDowall of Garthland was slain at the Battle of Pinkie in 1547. The castle was replaced by Garthland House, but the property was sold in the nineteenth century. The line of the MacDowalls of Garthland continues, but they now apparently live in Canada.

The MacDowalls also owned:
Auchness Castle [NX 106447], near Stranraer, Galloway; altered tower house.
  Held the MacDowalls and now used as a farmhouse.
Balgreggan [NX 089500], near Stranraer, Galloway; site of castle and mansion.
  Held by the MacDowalls, but passed to the Maitlands
Barr Castle [NS 347582], near Lochwinnoch, Renfrewshire; keep or tower and courtyard.
  Held by the Glens then by the Hamiltons of Ferguslie, then much later by the MacDowalls of Garthland.
Castle Semple [NS 377602], near Lochwinnoch, Renfrewshire; site of castle and mansion.
  Long held by the Semples, but the property had passed to the MacDowalls by 1727, and they built a new mansion, although this was demolished in the 1960s. Castle Semple Country Park is open to the public (01505 842882).
Corsewall Castle [NW 991715], near Stranraer, Galloway; some remains of castle.
  Held by the Stewarts of Dreghorn and by the Campbells of Loudoun, before passing by marriage to the MacDowalls in 1547. John MacDowall of Garthland and Corsewall was killed the same year at the Battle of Pinkie. The castle was replaced by nearby Corsewall House, which dates from the eighteenth century, and the lands are now apparently held by the Carrick-Buchanans of Drumpellier and Corsewall.

Drumgin Castle [NX 402444], near Whithorn, Galloway; site of tower house.
  Held by the MacDowalls.
Freugh Tower [NX 111562], near Stranraer, Galloway; site of tower house.
  Held by the MacDowalls from the fifteenth century or earlier. In 1654 the tower was burnt and the family moved to Balgreggan; the MacDowalls of Freugh were made Earls of Dumfries in 1768.
Heston Island [NX 839503], near Dalbeattie, Galloway; site of castle.
  Held by the MacDowalls, but burned by Edward Bruce, brother of Robert the Bruce, in 1308. The island was used in the 1330s and 40s by Edward Balliol, and the lands were long held by Dundrennan Abbey.
Logan House [NX 097426], near Stranraer, Galloway; slight remains of castle.
  Held by the MacDowalls until the twentieth century, and the old stronghold was replaced by Logan House in 1702. Andrew MacDowall of Logan was a Lord of Session in 1755, and wrote *Institutional Laws of Scotland*. There is a botanic garden, a specialist garden of the Royal Botanic Garden in Edinburgh, which is open to the public from March to October (01776 860231; www.rbge.org.uk).
Longcastle [NX 394469], near Whithorn, Galloway; slight remains of castle.
  Held by the MacDowalls from 1330 or earlier but passed to the Vaux family around the Reformation.
Machermore Castle [NX 416644], near Newton Stewart, Galloway; mansion incorporating castle.
  Held by the MacDowalls, although by 1866 had passed to the Dunbars. The building is now a nursing home.
Old Place of Mochrum [NX 308541], near Glenluce, Galloway; fine castle and courtyard.
  Held by the Dunbars, but passed to the MacDowalls in 1694,

Old Place of Mochrum (M&R)

who were made Earls of Dumfries in 1768, then in 1876 Mochrum went to the Stuart Marquess of Bute.
Ravenstone Castle [NX 409441], near Whithorn, Galloway; altered ruinous tower house.
  Held by the MacDowalls, but had passed to the MacLellans by 1560, then went to the Kennedys and to the Stewarts.

No. of castles/sites: 14
Rank: 104=/764
Xref: MacDouall

MacDuff

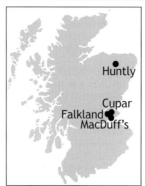

The name means 'son of Duff', and 'Duff' comes from 'dubh', pronounced 'doo' or 'doov', the Gaelic for 'black', probably referring to the colouring of complexion or of hair. It was used as a first name for centuries, and Dubh or Duff was a king of Scots in the tenth century. The MacDuffs are mentioned in Shakespeare's play of *Macbeth*, when Lady MacDuff and her babes are slaughtered on the orders of Macbeth. There is no evidence that this ever happened, but the MacDuffs became Thanes and then Earls of Fife, and are on record from the twelfth century. Malcolm, Earl of Fife, founded Culross Abbey in 1217; the ruins and the church are open to the public.

The MacDuffs had the honour of crowning the kings of Scots. Isobel MacDuff, Countess of Buchan but wife of a Comyn and sister of the then Earl of Fife (who was the hands of Edward I), crowned Robert the Bruce, but was then imprisoned in a cage hanging from the walls of Berwick Castle. The MacDuffs later supported the English, and the Earl was imprisoned in Kildrummy Castle, where he died in 1336. The title passed to Robert Stewart, later Duke of Albany, in 1372. The MacDuff line ended, although the Duffs (see that family), who were probably related, rose to prominence in the seventeenth century. They were from the north-east of Scotland, and were made Earls and then Dukes of Fife, although the title is now held by the Carnegie Earls of Southesk.

The MacDuffs held the following properties:
Airdit House [NO 412200], near Leuchars, Fife; site of castle and mansion.
    Held by the MacDuffs, but passed to the Stewarts, who held Airdit in 1425 when Murdoch, the then Duke and Earl of Fife (and second Duke of Albany), was forfeited and executed. The property passed to the Douglases and then to the Ainslies.
Barnslee [NO 304015], near Markinch, Fife; site of castle.
    Held by the MacDuffs. One story is that an underground passage goes from here to Maiden Castle, about three miles away.
Cairneyflappet or **Strathmiglo Castle** [NO 220102], near Auchtermuchty, Fife; site of castle.
    Held by the Earls of Fife in the twelfth century, but passed to the Scotts of Balwearie who built the castle, and then to others. It was demolished in 1734.
Castle Hill [NT 563850], North Berwick, East Lothian; large motte.
    Probably held by the MacDuff Earls of Fife. The Earls had a ferry from North Berwick to Earlsferry in Fife.
Cupar Castle [NO 376146], Cupar, Fife; site of castle.
    Held by the MacDuffs and located on School Hill. It was captured by Edward I of England in 1296, and visited by the future Edward II in 1303. One tale makes the castle the place where MacDuff's wife and babes were murdered on the orders of Macbeth, but Dunimarle is a more likely location - if such an event ever took place.
Falkland Palace [NO 254075], Falkland, Fife; fine palace.
    Held by the MacDuff Earls of Fife, who had a castle here although it was destroyed by the English in 1337. The castle

was rebuilt, and in 1371 passed to Robert Stewart, Duke of Albany and Earl of Fife. The existing building is a magnificent palace, which was used by the monarchs of Scotland until Charles II, and then by George IV. The building was restored, although part is ruinous after a fire, and is now in the care of The National Trust for Scotland (01337 857397; www.nts.org.uk).
Fernie Castle [NO 316147], near Cupar, Fife; altered tower house.
    Held by the MacDuff Earls of Fife, but passed to the Balfours and then to the Fernies, then to others. Fernie is now a hotel (01337 810381; www.ferniecastle.demon.co.uk).
Huntly or **Strathbogie Castle** [NJ 532407], near Huntly, Aberdeenshire; motte and magnificent ruinous castle.
    Held by the MacDuff Earls of Fife, and they built a castle on the nearby motte. The property passed to the Gordons and they moved their stronghold to the present site, which was developed down the years. In the care of Historic Scotland and open to the public (01466 793191).
Lindores Castle [NO 265168], near Newburgh, Fife; site of castle.
    Held by the MacDuff Earls of Fife but destroyed by Edward I in 1300. Nearby William Wallace defeated an English force, led by the Earl of Pembroke, in 1298.
MacDuff's Castle [NT 344972], East Wemyss, Fife; ruinous castle.
    Held by the MacDuff Earls of Fife, but destroyed by Edward I. The property passed to the Wemyss family and they built the present castle, but the property later went by marriage to the Livingstones and then to others.
Maiden Castle [NO 349015], near Methil, Fife; motte and bailey castle.
    Held by the MacDuff Earls of Fife. One story is that a tunnel from here goes to Barnslee, about three miles away.
Pittencrieff [NO 373159], near Cupar, Fife; site of castle or old house.
    Held by the Balfours, but passed to the MacDuffs.
Pittillock House [NO 278052], near Glenrothes, Fife; mansion incorporating tower house.
    Held by the MacDuff Earls of Fife, but passed to the Bruces and to the Lumsdens, then to others.

www.clanmacduff.org
groups.msn.com/ClanMacduffAssociationofNorthAmerica
No. of castles/sites: 13
Rank: 113=/764

MacDuffie

The name comes from 'MacDubhshithe', meaning 'son of Dubhshithe', a personal name which means 'son of the black man of peace' or the 'son of the dark fairy'; MacPhee or MacFie also comes from this name. The MacDuffies held the Hebridean island of Colonsay, and some were supposed to be blessed with mystical powers, the tradition being that they were descended from a seal-woman. An alternative is also Duffie.

Loch an Sgoltaire Castle [NR 386972] is two miles to the north of Scalasaig on Colonsay, and was held by the MacDuffies from early times. One of the chiefs is said to have defeated the English knight, Sir Gile de Argentine, at the Battle of Bannockburn in 1314. The MacDuffies supported the MacDonalds and fought along with them in 1615 when the MacDonalds attempted to retrieve the Isle of Islay. One of the MacDuffie chiefs signed the Statutes of Iona, and was later murdered in 1623. Some of clan went to Lochaber and are said to have fought at the Battle of Culloden in 1746. The island passed in the seventeenth century to the MacDonalds, and then to the Campbells and then to the MacNeills. On the neighbouring tidal isle of Oronsay is the Oronsay Cross, located at the old priory [NR 349889]. This is a fine medieval carved cross, decorated with a figure of Christ being crucified and with foliage, and has the inscription 'this is the cross of Colinus, son of Cristinus MacDuffie'. Many of the MacDuffies were buried at the priory, and there is also the stone effigy of Sir Donald MacDuffie, who was one of the priors.

Dun Eibhinn [NR 382944], north-west of Scalasaig, was also used by the MacDuffies in medieval times, and means 'fort of Eyvind', from a Norse name. The ruin is of a well-preserved Iron Age fort, and there is a plaque by a lay-by on the road.

Airds [NM 909450], which is a few miles north of Benderloch in Argyll, is a mansion dating from the eighteenth century, but it replaced an older house or castle. The lands were held by the Campbells, but by the end of the nineteenth century Airds was owned by the MacPhees.

www.macfiesocietyofamerica.com
www.geocities.com/Heartland/Meadows/4399/
    macfie.html
No. of castles/sites: 3
Rank: 328=/764
Xrefs: Duffie; MacFie; MacPhee

MacEarchan

The name is from 'son of Earchan', possibly from 'son of the horse lord', and the family are on record from the sixteenth century. It is possible the clan are a branch of the Mac-Donalds, or possibly they are descended from the people who lived here from the times of the Romans, known as the 'horse folk' or 'Epidii'.

Tangy Loch [NR 695279] is four or so miles north-west of Campbeltown on Kintyre in Argyll. There was a castle or fortified house on an island in the loch, which was reached by a causeway. The lands were held by the Bishops of the Isles, but were given to the Campbells in 1576. The MacEarchans of Tangy are believed to have lived here in the seventeenth century, and they held the lands until 1709 when they went to the Semples. In Campbeltown is the Campbeltown Cross [NR 720204], a fine fifteenth-century carved cross, decorated on both sides. The cross was brought from Kilkivan in the seventeenth century, and is dedicated to the MacEarchans, possibly to Colin MacEarchan, who was chief in 1499. There is another cross shaft in Kilkerran burial ground.

Killellan [NR 680159], four miles south-west of Campbeltown, was also held by the MacEarchans from 1499 or earlier, although they lost the property following the campaign by the Marquis of Montrose. They recovered their lands in 1659, and held them until the 1740s. There was probably a house or castle at Killellan, and there are the ruins of an old building.

No. of castles/sites: 2
Rank: 396=/764
Xrefs: MacAchin; MacEachen

MacEwan

The name means 'son of Ewen', and the MacEwens claimed descent from the kings of Ireland, along with the MacNeils and with the MacLachlans. MacEwan is on record from the thirteenth century, and the clan held lands at Otter on Cowal in Argyll. Some of the MacEwens appear to have been bards or poets to the Campbells. Elspeth MacEwan was executed in 1698 in Kirkcudbright after being found guilty of witchcraft.

Castle Ewen [NR 916796] is a mile or so west and north of Kilfinan in Cowal in Argyll, and was a stronghold of the MacEwans of Otter. The old stronghold reused an Iron Age dun, and is marked by a cairn. The clan lost their power and lands to the Campbells in the fifteenth century, and became a broken clan. The castle was also known as MacEwen's Castle and Caisteal Mhic Eoghainn, and was excavated in the 1960s.

Ballimore [NR 922833] is three miles to the north of Kilfinan and was also held by the MacEwans of Otter, and lost at the same time. At Ballimore is a steep-sided motte, and on the summit are two burial enclosures of the Campbells of Otter, dating from the nineteenth century. **Ballimore House** [NR 924833] is a fine castellated mansion.

Bardrochat [NX 153853] is eight miles south of Girvan in Ayrshire, and dates from the nineteenth century. It was built for Robert McEwen, and the McEwens, Baronets since 1953, apparently still own Bardrochat although the live in Edinburgh, according to *Burke's*. The MacEwans owned the lands from the eighteenth century or earlier.

Marchmont [NT 746485], three miles north-east of Greenlaw in the Borders, was held by the same family, and is a mansion dating from the eighteenth century. The mansion replaced Redbraes Castle, a property of the Homes, which was then demolished.

No. of castles/sites: 4
Rank: 278=/764
Xref: MacEwen

MacFarlane

The name comes from 'son of Parlan', an Old Irish personal name, and is on record from the twelfth century. The clan held lands around Loch Lomond and around Loch Long, as well as property in the north-east of Scotland. The clan claimed descent from the Earls of Lennox.

Arrochar House [NN 297039] was a seat or castle of the MacFarlanes, who held the lands from the twelfth century. They supported Robert the Bruce, sheltering him when needed, and then fighting at the Battle of Bannockburn in 1314. The eleventh chief was slain at Flodden in 1513, and Duncan, thirteenth chief, at Pinkie in 1547. The clan sacked Boturich Castle in the early sixteenth century. They were allied with the Earls of Lennox, and when Lord Darnley, husband of Mary, Queen of Scots, and son of the Earl, was murdered, they opposed their queen, and fought against Mary at the Battle of Langside in 1568. They were on the side of the Marquis of Montrose at the Battle of Inverlochy in 1645, but their lands were ravaged by Cromwell's forces in the 1650s. The clan did not come out for the Jacobites, and the lands were sold in 1767, passing to the Colquhouns of Luss, the clan's former enemies: Sir Humphrey Colquhoun had been murdered at Bannachra Castle by the MacFarlanes or MacGregors in 1592. MacFarlane's Lantern was a full moon, a night good for reiving and thieving cattle. The building was said to be haunted by a Green Lady, the ghost either of a murdered wife or a daughter who was imprisoned because she had fallen in love with the wrong man. The site of Arrochar House is occupied by the Claymore Hotel (01301 702238).

The MacFarlanes also held:
Ballanreoch Castle [NS 610794], near Lennoxtown, Dunbartonshire; site of castle.
    Held by the Grahams and by Brisbanes of Bishopton, before coming to the MacFarlanes of Keighton in 1652, and they built a later mansion. They sold the property in 1921.
Ballingrew [NS 692990], near Doune, Stirlingshire; site of castle or old house.
    Held by the Doigs, but passed by marriage to the MacFarlanes.
Eilean Vhow Castle [NN 332128], near Tarbet, Dunbartonshire; ruinous tower house.
    Held by the MacFarlanes, and may have been their main seat after the destruction of Inveruglas Castle in the 1650s. James VI had visited the castle, and the clan moved to Arrochar in 1697.
Gartartan Castle [NS 530978], near Aberfoyle, Stirlingshire; ruinous Z-plan tower house.
    Held by the Lyles, but passed to the MacFarlanes in 1531, and they built the castle. It went to the Grahams of Gartmore, who abandoned the old castle and built a new mansion.

Inveruglas Castle [NN 323096], near Tarbet, Dunbartonshire; ruinous Z-plan tower house on island.

    Held by the MacFarlanes. The castle was sacked and torched by Cromwell's forces in the 1650s, and the clan moved to Eilean Vhow Castle and then to Arrochar.

Tarbet or **Claddach Castle** [NN 320047], Tarbet, Dunbartonshire; site of castle.

    Held by the MacFarlanes, and possibly built by Robert the Bruce.

Tighvechtichan [NN 312045], near Tarbet, Dunbartonshire; site of tower or old house.

    Held by the MacFarlanes, and used to get 'tolls' from those using the drove road.

www.macfarlane.org
No. of castles/sites: 8
Rank: 160=/764
Xref: MacPharlane

MacGie

The name is from 'son of Aodh' ('son of Hugh'), and has the same derivation as MacKay. It was spelt both MacGie and MacKie, and the clan is on record from the end of the thirteenth century and held lands in Galloway. The MacGies may originally have come from Moray.

    Balmaghie [NX 718633], some three miles west of Castle Douglas in Galloway, was held by the family from the fifteenth century or earlier and they had a castle here.

    A mile or so east and north of Newton Stewart also on Galloway are the ruins of **Larg Tower** [NX 432663], and the MacGies held the lands from around 1320. Sir Patrick MacGie of Larg was one of the original lairds who was 'planted' in Ulster at the beginning of the seventeenth century.

    The clan also held **Livingstone** [NX 715677], near Castle Douglas and site of a tower house or castle in a park; and **Plunton Castle** [NX 605507], a few miles south of Gatehouse of Fleet, again in Galloway. This is an L-plan tower house of the sixteenth century, and was held by the MacGies in the early sixteenth century, before passing to the Lennox family and then to the Murrays of Broughton.

    Bargaly House [NX 462664], three or so miles east of Newton Stewart, dates from 1691 and may be built on the site of an older dwelling or castle. The property was owned by the Herons and then by the Hannays, before coming to the MacGies in the nineteenth century.

No. of castles/sites: 5
Rank: 240=/764
Xrefs: MacGhie; MacKie

MacGilchrist

The name is from the Gaelic, and means 'son of the servant of Christ' (also see Gilchrist), and the family were given lands by Alexander II in the middle of the thirteenth century.

    Fincharn Castle [NM 898044], five and a half miles north of Kilmartin in Argyll, may have been held by the MacGilchrists before it passed to the MacDougalls, who held it for the English in 1308. The castle is a strong but ruinous tower house and courtyard, which dates from the sixteenth century but may incorporate much earlier work. It had passed to the Scrymgeours in 1370, and they held the property until 1688.

    Northbar [NS 481693] is two or so miles north-west of Renfrew and was held by the MacGilchrists in 1672 and probably much earlier. There was a castle, but it was replaced by Northbar House; and the property passed to the Semples in 1741, then to the Buchanans and then to the Stewart Lords Blantyre.

No. of castles/sites: 2
Rank: 396=/764

MacGillespie

The name is from Gaelic and means 'son of the bishop', and is mentioned from the middle of the thirteenth century. The name was found in Islay, in Ayrshire, in Bute and in other parts of Scotland. Also see Gillespie.

    Finlaggan [NR 388681] was a seat and castle of the MacDonald Lords of the Isles, and is located some three miles west of Port Askaig on Islay. The remains are located on two islands in a loch. The MacDonalds were attacked by James IV and their power broken, the last Lord of the Isles dying in Paisley Abbey. The MacGillespie family probably occupied the island after the fall of the lords, although Islay was to become a property of the Campbells. The islands and visitor centre at Finlaggan are open to the public (01496 810629; www.finlaggan.com).

No. of castles/sites: 1
Rank: 537=/764

MacGillivray

The name comes from 'Mac Gille-bhrath', meaning 'son of the servant of judgement'. The clan probably came from Argyll, and some of them stayed in Morvern and on Mull, while others settled on lands south of Loch Ness in Inverness-shire and became allied with Clan Chattan (see Mackintosh). They are on record from the sixteenth century. William MacGillivray, a professor of natural history, wrote *A History of British Birds* and is regarded as the father of British Ornithology; there is a small museum about his work at Northton [NA 992898] on the Isle of Harris. James Pittendreigh MacGillivray was made King's sculptor in Scotland in 1921.

Dunmaglas [NH 593223], six or so miles east of Inverfarigaig on the south bank of Loch Ness in Inverness-shire, was held by the MacGillivrays from the middle of the sixteenth century or earlier. The clan fought in both the 1715 and 1745-46 Jacobite Risings for the Jacobites. Many of the clan were at the Battle of Preston in 1715, but were captured after they surrendered. Alexander MacGillivray of Dunmaglas led the Clan Chattan contingent in the Jacobite army. The Jacobites were victorious at Falkirk in 1746, but were slaughtered at Culloden the same year, and the MacGillivray slain are buried near the Well of the Dead on the battlefield. The last lands were sold in 1890. Nearby **Dalcrombie** [NH 612295] was also held by the clan.

www.mcgillivray.us / www.clan-macgillivray.zoomshare.com
No. of castles/sites: 2 / Rank: 396=/764
Xrefs: Chattan

MacGowan

The name is from Gaelic, and means 'son of the smith'. The name is on record from the beginning of the sixteenth century, and the clan was settled in Dumfries and Galloway and elsewhere.

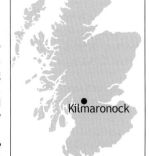

Kilmaronock Castle [NS 456877] is a ruinous keep or tower, formerly of four storeys, and is located a mile south-west of Drymen in Stirlingshire in central Scotland. The lands were held by several families, including by the Cochrane Earls of Dundonald, before coming to John McGoune in the eighteenth century. There is a modern mansion nearby.

No. of castles/sites: 1 / Rank: 537=/764
Xrefs: MacGoune

MacGregor

The name means 'son of Gregory (or Gregor)', and the clan claim descent from the ancient royal family of Scotland through the hereditary bishops of Glendochart. The clan are on record from the end of the fourteenth century, and they held lands in Glenstrae, in Glenorchy and in Glenlochy. Although the MacGregors are believed to have fought for Robert the Bruce, that king gave the barony of Loch Awe to the Campbells of Argyll, which was probably not the best way to reward the MacGregors for their support. The most famous of all the clan was Rob Roy MacGregor, who fought in the Jacobite Risings. After the clan were proscribed (meaning that they were outlawed and anyone with the name MacGregor could not hold lands or property and they could be killed without punishment for the killer) in the seventeenth century, many of the clan changed their names, and variations used were Gregorson, Gregory, Greig, Grier as well as names such as Black, Campbell, Comrie and Drummond. James MacGregor, who was the Dean of Lismore in 1514, compiled an important collection of material dating from as early as the fourteenth century, his work being known as *The Book of the Dean of Lismore*. Sir James MacGrigor, trained in Edinburgh and in Aberdeen as a surgeon, and then joined the army and served in Flanders, in the West Indies and in India. He was chief of medical staff to the Duke of Wellington in the Peninsular War.

Glenstrae Castle [NN 138296] was a couple of miles north-west of Dalmally in Argyll, but nothing of the castle survives. It was held by the MacGregors of Glenstrae and Stronmilchan from the fourteenth century. Alasdair MacGregor of Glenstrae, eighth Chief, fought at the Battle of Pinkie in 1547. Gregor MacGregor of Glenstrae fought against the Campbells of Glenorchy, who acquired the barony, and was captured and beheaded at Balloch in 1570. It was he who had earlier made the renowned MacGregor's Leap, across the River Lyon, while trying to evade capture. In 1602 some of the clan raided the lands of Colquhouns of Luss, and the following year this came to battle at Glenfruin. The MacGregors were victorious, but the clan was then proscribed by James VI, while Alasdair MacGregor, the chief, was executed. Many of the MacGregors were buried at Dysart, near Dalmally. Glenstrae passed to the Campbells, and the castle was burnt in 1611 by Sir Duncan Campbell. Members of the clan fought for the Jacobites in the 1715 and the 1745-46 Jacobite risings.

Sir John Murray MacGregor of MacGregor was a lieutenant colonel in the army of the British government and was made a Baronet in 1795. The MacGregors of MacGregor, Baronets, now apparently live at **Bannatyne** [NO 294410] in Angus.

The MacGregors also owned:

Aberuchill Castle [NN 745212], near Comrie, Perthshire; L-plan
tower house.

Held by the MacGregors, but passed to the Campbells in 1596,
and they built the tower. The MacGregors, however, continued
to extort money from the Campbells. The castle was damaged
by the Jacobites in 1689, but after the 1715 Jacobite Rising
the Campbell laird decided to stop paying blackmail. However,
when Rob Roy MacGregor, with a band of clansman, appeared
during a dinner party the Campbells quickly found the money.
The house was occupied until gutted by a recent fire.

Balhaldie [NN 812050], near Dunblane, Stirlingshire; site of castle
or old house.

Held by the MacGregors (Drummonds) until the nineteenth
century. This branch of the MacGregors claimed to be chiefs
of the clan in 1714, but it went to others. They were Jacobites.

Edinample Castle [NN 601226], near Lochearnhead, Stirlingshire;
restored Z-plan tower house.

Held by the MacGregors, but passed to the Campbells after

Kilchurn Castle 1910? – see previous column

Jardine. It was an impressive ruin, but was completely
demolished in 2002 and its owner was found guilty of
contravening building regulations but was only fined £1000.

Orchill [NN 866117], near Blackford, Perthshire; mansion on site
of castle.

Long held by the Grahams but passed to the MacGregors in
the 1860s. They built a new mansion [NN 868118], an
impressive baronial pile, but did not hold the property for
long.

Stronmilchan [NN 153278], near Dalmally, Argyll; site of castle.

Held by the MacGregors of Glenstrae, and it had a moat and
drawbridge.

www.clangregor.org
No. of castles/sites: 12
Rank: 120=/764
Xrefs: Gregorson; Greig

Edinample Castle 1906?

the MacGregors were proscribed. The castle is believed to
have been built by Sir Duncan Campbell of Glenorchy.

Eilean Molach [NN 488083], near Aberfoyle, Stirlingshire; castle
on island.

Held by the MacGregors.

Glengyle Castle [NN 385135], near Aberfoyle, Stirlingshire; site
of castle.

Held by the MacGregors, and Rob Roy's father was styled 'of
Glengyle'.

Inversnaid [NN 348097], near Loch Lomond, Stirlingshire; slight
remains of barracks.

The lands were held by the MacGregors, and the barracks
were built following the 1715 Rising, although Rob Roy attacked
the garrison during construction. Rob Roy held property in
the area, and probably inherited the lands from his father
Donald MacGregor of Glengyle. Rob Roy was forfeited for his
part in the 1715 Rising, but was pardoned in 1725. He had
been responsible for much blackmail – the term being credited
as an invention of the clan – and thievery, including the taking
of £1000 from rents of the Marquis of Montrose, although it is
likely he had nothing to do with this particular piece of robbery.
MacGregor died at Balquhidder in 1734. His son and cousin
seized the barracks in 1745.

Kilchurn Castle [NN 133276], near Dalmally, Argyll; photogenic
ruinous castle.

Held by the MacGregors, but passed to the Campbells of
Glenorchy, who built (or rebuilt) the castle. Kilchurn was
apparently damaged by the MacGregors, but was soon
strengthened. The castle was garrisoned during the Jacobite
Risings, but was unroofed by 1775. It is in the care of Historic
Scotland and is open to the public by boat from nearby Loch
Awe pier (01866 833333).

Lanrick Castle [NN 685031], near Doune, Stirlingshire; site of castle
and mansion.

Held by the Haldanes of Gleneagles, but passed to the
MacGregors of MacGregor, then in 1840 went to William

MacGruder

The name is from Gaelic
and means 'son of (the)
brewer', is on record from
the fifteenth century, and
the name was not uncom-
mon in Perthshire. There
was also a more northerly
branch who were dis-
persed among the Frasers
and other clans.

Craigneach Castle [NJ
238425], three or so miles west of Charlestown of
Aberlour in Moray, was probably held by the MacGruder
family. It was an L-plan tower house, but little survives
except foundations. The castle was attacked and looted
by Covenanters in 1645.

No. of castles/sites: 1
Rank: 537=/764
Xref: MacGruar

MacIan

The name is from the Gaelic 'Maclain', and simply means 'son of John', 'Iain' apparently being the most popular name in Gaelic-speaking areas at one time. The MacIans of Ardnamurchan claim descent from Iain, son of Angus Og, from whom the Lords of the Isles were descended; the MacIains or MacDonalds of Glencoe were also descended from Iain. The name is recorded in Scotland from 1296.

Mingary Castle [NM 502631] is to the east of Kilchoan on the Ardnamurchan peninsula and looks across to Tobermory on the Isle of Mull. Mingary is a strong but ruinous courtyard castle, dating from the thirteenth century and with later ranges constructed within the walls. Mingary was built by the MacIans of

Mingary Castle (M&R)

Ardnamurchan, but was occupied by James IV in 1493 and 1495 during his campaigns against the MacDonalds; and was sacked or slighted in 1517. The MacIans supported the MacDonalds in the 1550s, and MacLean of Duart captured the chief of MacIan, and then unsuccessfully besieged the castle with Spanish soldiers from an Armada galleon in Tobermory Bay. The Campbells, however, took Mingary from the MacIans. The castle can be reached from along the shore from Kilchoan pier, and there is a ferry service from Tobermory.

On the south coast of the Isle of Islay in a lovely spot, **Dunyvaig Castle** [NR 406455] is near Lagavulin Distillery, three miles east of Port Ellen. Dunyvaig was long held by the MacDonalds, but was given to the MacIans of Ardnamurchan at the end of the fifteenth century. The property was leased back to the MacDonalds and then passed to the Campbells. The castle had a long and bloody history, but is now very ruinous, although the site, in a picturesque spot, can be visited.

No. of castles/sites: 2
Rank: 396=/764
Xref: Maclain

MacIlvaine

The name is Gaelic and comes from 'Mac Gille Bheathain', which means 'son of the servant of St Bean'. The family held lands in Galloway and in Carrick in south Ayrshire, and are on record from the fourteenth century.

Grimmet Castle [NS 446064] stood a couple of miles west of Dalmellington in Ayrshire, although the exact location has not been determined. The lands were long a property of the MacIlvaines, and were still held by them in the seventeenth century or later. Gilbert MacIlvaine, heir of Grimmet, was killed at the Battle of Fawsyde, near Pinkie, in 1547.

Standing three or so miles west of Maybole in Ayrshire, **Thomaston Castle** [NS 240096] is a ruinous courtyard castle, which dates from the thirteenth century, but with a much later L-plan tower house. The property was held by Thomas Bruce, nephew of the warrior king, but passed to the Corries of Kelwood, then by marriage to the MacIlvaines of Grimmet in 1632. They occupied it until around 1800.

No. of castles/sites: 2
Rank: 396=/764
Xref: MacGilvane

MacInnes

The name is Gaelic, and comes from 'son of Angus'. The clan held lands on Loch Aline across the narrow sound from the Isle of Mull.

Kinlochaline Castle [NM 697476], which is two miles north of Lochaline, was held by the Mac-Inneses, hereditary bowmen to the MacKinnons. The old stronghold, which is in a striking location, is a rectangular tower or keep of four storeys. Following the murder of the laird and his sons by the MacKinnons at nearby Ardtornish in 1319, the lands were given to the Ma-

Kinlochaline Castle (M&R)

cLeans of Duart and then to the Campbells, although the MacInneses appear to have been keepers of the castle. The castle was damaged by the Marquis of Montrose's lieutenant Alasdair Colkitto MacDonald in 1644, then later by Cromwell's forces in the 1650s, and then by the Campbell Earl of Argyll in 1679 during a feud. Kinlochaline was ruinous after 1690, but was then restored. Most of the MacInnes clan followed the Campbells in their opposition to the Jacobite rebellion of 1745-46, but some of MacInneses fought for the Jacobites at the Battle of Culloden. Many of them then emigrated to Canada and to New Zealand.

www.macinnes.org
No. of castles/sites: 1
Rank: 537=/764

MacIntyre

The name is from Gaelic and means 'son of the carpenter or wright'. Stories have the clan descended from a nephew of the great Somerled, although the tale of how he helped Somerled secure his bride seems a little unlikely. MacTire is a

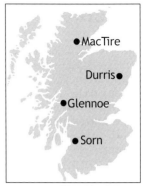

shortened form of the same name. The MacIntyres settled on the south side of Glen Etive, and a legend has them finding the glen by following a white cow in their herd.

Glennoe [NN 055343] is about four miles north-east of Taynuilt in Argyll, and was held by the MacIntyres from the thirteenth century. They had a castle or house, and Duncan MacIntyre, who died in 1695, is buried in a fine tomb at Ardchattan Priory [NM 971349], on the other side of Loch Etive. The chiefs, perhaps sensibly, supported the Campbells, although members of the clan fought for both the Marquis of Montrose at the Battle of Inverlochy in 1645 and then later for the Jacobites. Duncan Ban MacIntyre, also known in Gaelic as Donnachaidh Ban nan Oran, was born in Glenorchy in 1724, and he was in the Hanoverian forces defeated by the Jacobites at Falkirk in 1746, and was later part of the Edinburgh Guard. He was also a renowned poet and bard, although he could not write and his verse had to be dictated. There is a monument of 1859 dedicated to him in a prominent position a mile or so south-west of Dalmally [NN 144259]. The chief of the MacKinnons left for America at the end of the eighteenth century, and the lands had passed into other hands by 1810.

MacTire Castle [NH 652883] stood three miles east and south of Bonar Bridge in Sutherland, but only traces remain within the ramparts of an Iron Age fort. The castle was built by the MacIntyres or MacTires, and was ruinous by the end of the sixteenth century.

Sorn Castle [NS 548269] is an altered and extended keep or tower, which dates from the fourteenth century and stands three or so miles east of Mauchline in Ayrshire. The property belonged to the Keiths of Galston, but passed through other families before coming to the McIntyres around 1900. The family still apparently live at Sorn, and the castle is open to the public for some weeks in the summer (01290 551555).

Durris House [NO 799968] is a few miles east of Banchory on Deeside, and is an altered and extended L-plan tower house with later work. The lands were held by the Frasers, then passed to others, before later coming to the MacTires, who had made a fortune in India. Durris was then bought by James 'Paraffin Young' in 1871, but has since been divided.

www.macintyreclan.org
No. of castles/sites: 4
Rank: 278=/764
Xrefs: MacTire

MacIver

The name is from Gaelic and means 'son of Iver or Ivar', from the Norse personal name, and it is on record from the beginning of the thirteenth century. 'Iver' was a common personal name in medieval times, and it is not possible to identify from which Iver the clan takes their name.

Glendarroch [NR 849866], two or so miles south and west of Lochgilphead in Argyll, is also known as **Robber's Den** and **Kilduskland**. The site is defended by gorges on two sides and by a rock-cut ditch, and there are some remains of two buildings. As the name suggests, this was reputedly the refuge of brigands, and is said to have been used by the MacIvers in the seventeenth century.

No. of castles/sites: 1
Rank: 537=/764

MacKay

The name is from the Gaelic 'MacAodh' or 'son of Hugh'. The clan may be descended from 'Aodh' or 'Aedh', who was Abbot of Dunkeld and Earl of Fife, and whose son was the Earl of Ross in the twelfth century. The MacKays became established in Sutherland in the thirteenth century, although another clan with that name were also settled for many centuries in Kintyre. The MacKays of the north became powerful enough to raise 4000 men, but also came into conflict with the Earls of Sutherland. Donald and his son, Iye, were murdered by the Sutherlands of Duffus in Dingwall Castle in 1370. The MacKays fought for Charles I in the Civil War, and Sir Donald MacKay was made a Baronet of Nova Scotia in 1627 and was then created Lord Reay the following year (he would have been made Earl of Strathnaver but the Civil War put a halt to the creation of that title); he had to go into exile in Denmark in 1649. The chiefs settled in Holland, where they prospered. The MacKays became Protestant and Hugh MacKay of Scourie led the government forces who were defeated at the Battle of Killiecrankie in 1689; he then went to Holland where he was killed at Steinkirk in 1692. The clan fought against the Jacobites in the Risings of 1715 and 1745-46. The MacKay Lords Reay (see House of Tongue below) still flourish, and they apparently have residences at Kasteel Ophemert in the Netherlands and in London in England.

The MacKays held the following in the far north of Scotland:
Balnakeil House [NC 391687], near Durness, Sutherland; altered and extended house.
> Held by the MacKays from 1611; it later passed to Lord Reay.
Bighouse [NC 892648], near Thurso, Sutherland; mansion.
> Held by the MacKays of Bighouse, who held the lands from 1597. They had an early residence at **Kirkton** [NC 890614], and Bighouse is said to be haunted by a Green Lady. The house is now an exclusive hotel and restaurant (01641 531207; www.bighouseestate.com).
Borve or **Farr Castle** [NC 725642], near Bettyhill, Sutherland; ruined tower house and courtyard.
> Held by the MacKays. Said to have been captured and destroyed by the Earl of Sutherland in the middle of the sixteenth century, and then besieged with cannon in 1655. The original stronghold is thought to have been built by a Norseman called Torquil.
Caisteal Bharraich [NC 581567], near Tongue, Sutherland; ruinous tower house.
> Held by the Bishops of Caithness and then by the MacKays.
Dirlot Castle [ND 126486], near Watten, Caithness; site of castle.
> Held by the Cheynes and by the Gunns, then by the Sutherlands, and then by the MacKays from 1499.
Dounreay Castle [NC 983669], near Thurso, Caithness; ruinous castle.
> Held by the Sinclairs of Dunbeath, but passed to the Forbeses, then to the MacKay Lords Reay. It was still occupied in 1863 and is now in the grounds of the Dounreay Nuclear Plant.
House of Tongue [NC 592588], near Tongue, Sutherland; tower house replaced by mansion.
> Held by the MacKays, and was the main seat of Lord Reay. Sir

Donald MacKay recruited men to fight in Denmark and then with Gustave Adolphus of Sweden. He was knighted in 1616, and was made Lord Reay in 1628. He was a Royalist and held Newcastle, but when it fell he was captured, although he was released in 1645. He returned to Denmark in 1649 and died the same year. John, second Lord, was also a Royalist, while Donald James, eleventh Lord, was born in the Hague (where the MacKays had settled), and went on to be Governor of Bombay in 1885-90. The property was acquired by the Dukes of Sutherland, and is still apparently held by them, although the MacKay Lords Reay still flourish. The gardens of House of Tongue are occasionally open to the public (www.gardensof scotland.org).

Loch Stack Castle [NC 275434], near Scourie, Sutherland; site of castle.

Held by the MacKays of Reay.

Melness [NC 581608], near Tongue, Sutherland; older house replaced by mansion.

Held by the MacKays from the fourteenth century. It was nearby that a French ship carrying Jacobite gold ran aground. The crew made it to the shore with the treasure, but after a brief battle they surrendered to a force made up mostly of MacKays.

Sandside House [NC 952652], near Reay, Sutherland; site of castle or old house.

Held by the MacKays, and the first Lord Reay built a house here in 1628, although there was already a building on the site. The lands passed to the Bentinck Duke of Portland, and the present large mansion dates from the middle of the eighteenth century. The gardens are occasionally open to the public (www.gardensofscotland.org).

Scourie [NC 156450], Scourie, Sutherland; site of castle or old house.

Held by the MacKays. As mentioned above, Hugh MacKay of Scourie led the government forces who were defeated at the Battle of Killiecrankie in 1689; he then went to Holland where he was killed at Steinkirk in 1692. The lands went to the Earls and Dukes of Sutherland, and Scourie House dates from 1846.

Skibo Castle [NH 735891], near Dornoch, Sutherland; mansion on site of castle.

The castle was captured by the MacKays in 1544, but it passed to the Grays and then to others, including to Andrew Carnegie who built a magnificent new mansion. The mansion is now home to an exclusive country club (www.carnegieclubs.com).

Shiels [NJ 656094], near Alford, Aberdeenshire; site of castle or old house.

Held by the MacKays of Shiels. Charles MacKay of Shiels, who died in 1794, was a captain of a merchant ship which traded with the West Indies. There is a later house of 1742.

Ugadale [NR 784285], near Campbeltown, Kintyre, Argyll; ruins of house and dun.

Held by the MacKays, possibly from the fourteenth century. They were in possession for about 300 years, when Ugadale then passed by marriage to the MacNeils.

www.clan-mackay.co.uk
www.clanmackaysociety.org
www.mackaycountry.com
No. of castles/sites: 14
Rank: 104=/764
Xrefs: Mackay; Morgan

House of Tongue (M&R) – see previous page

Mackenzie

The name means 'son of Kenneth', from the Gaelic 'MacCionneach', 'Coinneach' being a personal name derived from 'fair or bright'. The family are on record from the middle of the thirteenth century, and settled in and around Lochaber.

Roderick Mackenzie, an officer in Lord Elcho's troop of horse, is said to have closely resembled Bonnie Prince Charlie. Roderick is said to have given his life to save the Prince, and Hanoverian troops, thinking that they had killed Charlie, hacked off Roderick's head; there is a monument to him in Glenmoriston. Sir Alexander Mackenzie, who was born in Stornoway around 1763, emigrated to Canada and travelled across the Rockies to the Pacific. He wrote an account of his adventures in 1801, was knighted the following year, and returned to Scotland. Sir Compton Mackenzie, who was born in England in 1883, wrote many novels including most notably *Whisky Galore*, which was turned into an Ealing comedy.

Eilean Donan Castle [NG 881259] is one of the most picturesque castles in Scotland, and it stands on a small island in Loch Duich on the road to Skye. The castle consists of a strong tower and walled courtyard, and

Eilean Donan Castle (M&R)

was long held by the Mackenzies of Kintail; it may have been given to them after they helped defeat the Norseman at the Battle of Largs in 1263. Robert the Bruce sheltered at Eilean Donan in 1306, and twenty-five years later Thomas Randolph executed fifty wrongdoers and spiked their heads from the castle walls. Alasdair Mackenzie of Kintail supported James III in his fight with the Earls of Ross and was rewarded with more lands. Duncan Mackenzie, Alasdair's son, has a fine tomb at Beauly Priory [NH 527465], in the attractive village of Beauly near Inverness, and the north transept was restored in 1901 as the Kintail burial aisle; there is also the tomb of Prior Mackenzie, who died in 1479. The remains of the priory church are open to the public. Eilean Donan was captured by the Earl of Huntly in 1504, and five years later the MacRaes became constables of the castle. In 1539 Eilean Donan was besieged by Donald Gorm MacDonald, a claimant to the Lordship of the Isles, but he was killed by an arrow shot from the castle. By the seventeenth century, the Mackenzies were very powerful and had lands from the island of Lewis in the far west to the Black Isle in the east; in 1623 they were made Earls of Seaforth after acquiring the lands of Fortrose Cathedral. The Mackenzies fought against the Marquis of Montrose, but changed side when Charles I was executed. The clan supported the Jacobites, and William Mackenzie, fifth Earl of Seaforth, had the castle garrisoned with Spanish troops during the Jacobite rising of 1719, but three frigates battered the castle into submission with cannon, and it was blown up from within with barrels of gunpowder. The Spaniards, supported by Scottish Jacobites, were defeated at the Battle of Glenshiel. The ghost of one of the Spanish soldiers, slain at the castle or battle, is said to haunt Eilean Donan with his head under his arm. The Earl of Seaforth was forfeited and lost the lands and titles. The clan later regained the title, but it became extinct in 1815. Eilean Donan had been left very ruinous until being completely rebuilt in the twentieth century. It is a fine building and is open to the public from April to October (01599 555202; www.eileandonancastle.com).

Brahan Castle [NH 513549] stood three or so miles south-west of Dingwall, but it has been completely demolished except for one wall. It was held by the Mackenzies of Brahan, and were the patrons of the Brahan Seer, Kenneth Mackenzie or Coinneach Odhar, who was born at Uig on Lewis. The Earls of Seaforth eventually lost everything as the Brahan Seer foretold in around 1670. Isabella, third Countess of Seaforth, asked the Brahan Seer why her husband had not returned from Paris, and was furious to be told that her husband had been straying with a French lady. She ordered that the Brahan Seer was to be burnt in a barrel of tar on Chanonry Point on the Black Isle. The Brahan Seer then predicted that the last clan chief would follow his sons to the grave, deaf and dumb, and that one of his daughters would kill the other. This did not save him, of course, but his prophecy is said to have come true. The last chief became deaf through illness and finally too weak to speak after seeing his four sons predecease him. His eldest daughter succeeded him, but a carriage she was driving, near Brahan, overturned and killed her sister.

Lying a few miles west of Dingwall in Ross and Cromarty, **Castle Leod** [NH 485593] is a fine L-plan tower house, dating from the seventeenth century but with later additions. The lands were held by the Mackenzies, and Castle Leod was built by Sir Roderick Mackenzie of Coigach about 1610. His grandson, Sir George Mackenzie of Tarbat, was made Viscount Tarbat in 1685, then Earl of Cromartie in 1703, but George, third Earl, was forfeited for his part in the Jacobite Rising of 1745-46. The Mackenzies had fought at the Battle of Falkirk in 1746, but the Earl and his son were surprised and captured at Dunrobin Castle the same year. The Earl was imprisoned in the Tower of London and was sentenced to death, but he got a remission in 1749. The

Castle Leod (M&R)

property and titles were eventually recovered, and a wing was added to the castle in 1854. The castle is still apparently occupied by the Mackenzie Earls of Cromartie and Viscounts Tarbat. The Mackenzies also held Lewis for many years, which had been a property of the MacLeods of Lewis, and the name of the castle commemorates the association of the two clans.

The Mackenzies also held:

Ardvreck Castle [NC 240236], near Inchnadamph, Sutherland; ruinous castle in fine spot.
Held by the MacLeods of Assynt, who built the castle. The property later passed to the Mackenzies, who had sacked the castle in 1672, but they were forfeited following the Jacobite Risings. The lands passed to the Earls of Sutherland in 1758.

Auchenskeoch Castle [NX 917588], near Dalbeattie, Galloway; some remains of castle.
Held by the Lindsays and by the Crichtons, but later passed to the Mackenzies.

Balloan Castle [NH 160830], near Ullapool, Ross and Cromarty; site of castle.
Held by the Earls of Ross, and possibly later passed to the MacDonnels or to the MacDonalds or to the Mackenzies.

Ballone Castle or **Castlehaven** [NH 929838], near Tain, Ross and Cromarty; large Z-plan tower house.
Held by the Earls of Ross then by the Dunbars of Tarbat, but passed to the Mackenzies in 1623. The family were made Earls of Cromartie in 1703 and changed the name of the property to Castlehaven. The old stronghold was abandoned for Tarbat House, a three-storey classical mansion, in the late seventeenth century, and was ruined by 1680. It is being restored.

Balmacara [NG 800277], near Kyle of Lochalsh, Lochalsh, Highland; site of castle or old house.
Held by the Mathesons, but later passed to the Mackenzies and then to the Hamiltons. The estate is in the care of The National Trust for Scotland and is open to the public (01599 566325)

Belmont Castle [NO 286439], near Blairgowrie, Perthshire; mansion incorporating tower house.
Held by the Nairnes of Dunsinane, but passed in the seventeenth century to Sir George Mackenzie of Rosehaugh, called by some 'Bluidy Mackenzie' for his apparently ruthless persecution of Covenanters. The property later passed to other families, and is now a nursing home.

Bunchrew House [NH 621459], near Inverness; mansion with older work.

Held by the Frasers but was sold to the Forbeses of Culloden in 1622, but was then bought back by the Frasers in 1842. The building is said to be haunted by the ghost of Isobel, wife of Kenneth Mackenzie, twelfth Chief of the Mackenzies, although the ghost is reputed to be a gentle spirit. A portrait of her hangs in the hotel. The family became Fraser-Mackenzie of Allangrange and Bunchrew, and they still apparently live at Bunchrew, although not at the house, which is now a hotel (01463 234917; www.bunchrew-inverness.co.uk).

Calda House [NC 244234], near Inchnadamph, Sutherland; ruinous house.

Held by the Mackenzies, who built the house in 1660 as a replacement for Ardvreck Castle. The family were said to have held riotous parties, and soon became short of money. The house was plundered and torched in 1737. The Mackenzies were forfeited after the Jacobite Rising, and the house was sold to the Earl of Sutherland in 1758, then was burned by the MacRaes in 1760 and was never restored.

Caroline Park House or **House of Royston** [NT 227773], Edinburgh; mansion incorporating tower house.

Held by the Logans but was acquired by Sir George Mackenzie

Caroline Park House (M&R)

of Tarbat in 1683, who built much of the present mansion. The house is reputedly haunted by a Green Lady, the apparition of Lady Royston, wife of Sir James Mackenzie, younger son of Lord Tarbat. On certain nights the ghost is said to rise from an old well and then appears in the courtyard and rings a bell. The property passed to the Campbell Duke of Argyll who changed the name from Royston to Caroline Park.

Castle Hill [NJ 154571], Pluscarden, Moray; site of castle.

Held by several families after the Reformation, including by the Mackenzies of Tarbat. The abbey here was ruinous but has been restored as a Benedictine monastery and is open to the public (01343 890257; www.pluscardenabbey.org).

Chanonry [NH 727567], Fortrose, Ross and Cromarty; ruinous cathedral and site of fortified tower.

After the Reformation the lands of the cathedral were fought over by the Mackenzies of Kintail and by the Leslies of Balquhain. The Mackenzies won out, and were made Earls of Seaforth in 1623. They were forfeited in 1716 for their part in the Jacobite Rising, although they later recovered their lands. The Brahan Seer was burnt in a barrel of tar at nearby Chanonry Point.

Coul House [NH 463563], near Strathpeffer, Ross and Cromarty; castle replaced by mansion.

Held by the Mackenzies of Coul, who owned the property until the nineteenth century. The family were made Baronets in 1673, and now apparently live in London in England. Sir George Stewart Mackenzie of Coul, who died in 1848, discovered the composition of diamonds as carbon crystals. The building is now used as a hotel (01997 421487; www.coulhousehotel.com).

Delvine [NO 123402], near Blairgowrie, Perthshire; site of castle or old house.

Held by the Hays and by the Ogilvies of Inchmartine, before passing to the Mackenzies, latterly Muir Mackenzies, from the seventeenth century for about 200 years. The family were made Baronets in 1805, and now apparently live in Dorset in England.

Dochmaluag Castle [NH 521601], near Dingwall, Ross and Cromarty; ruinous tower house.

Held by the Mackenzies from the fifteenth century.

Earlshall [NO 465211], near Leuchars, Fife; fine courtyard castle.

Long a property of the Bruces of Earlshall, but passed to the Mackenzies at the end of the nineteenth century, then to others. The gardens are occasionally open to the public (www.gardensofscotland.org).

Fairburn Tower [NH 469523], near Muir of Ord, Ross and Cromarty; altered tower house.

Held by the Mackenzies. It featured in one of the Brahan Seer's prophecies, when a cow managed to climb all way to the watch-chamber at the top of the tower. It could not be brought down again until it had calved – an event, according to the Seer, heralding the end of the Mackenzies of Kintail and Seaforth.

Flowerdale [NG 814754], near Gairloch, Ross and Cromarty; castle replaced by mansion.

Held by the Mackenzies after Red Hector, son of Mackenzie of Kintail, was granted Gairloch in 1494.

Glack [NJ 742284], near Inverurie, Aberdeenshire; castle and old house replaced by mansion.

Held by the Elphinstones, and then by the Mackenzies. The old house and mansion were both used as a psychiatric hospital but the site is to be redeveloped.

Glenmuick [NO 372945], near Ballater, Aberdeenshire; site of castle and mansion.

Held by the Gordons, but had passed to the Mackenzies in the nineteenth century, who had made their fortune in silk from India and built the mansion. They were made Baronets in 1890 and now apparently live in Cornwall in England.

Granton Castle [NT 225772], Edinburgh; site of large castle.

Held by the Melvilles of Carnbee, then bought by Sir George Mackenzie of Tarbat, then went to the Hopes of Craighall and to the Campbell Duke of Argyll. It was demolished in the 1920s.

Hatton Castle [NO 302411], near Coupar Angus, Angus; Z-plan tower house.

Held by the Oliphants and by the Halyburtons of Pitcur, then by the son of Mackenzie of Rosehaugh, before returning to the Oliphants.

Kilcoy Castle [NH 576512], near Muir of Ord, Ross and Cromarty; Z-plan tower house.

Held by Alexander Mackenzie, son of the eleventh baron of Kintail, chief of the clan, from 1618 and he built the castle. It

Kilcoy Castle (M&R)

was ruinous at one time but has been restored and is still occupied.

Kinkell Castle [NH 554543], near Dingwall, Ross and Cromarty; tower house.

Held by the Mackenzies of Gairloch, then later was used as a farmhouse, before being restored and reoccupied.

Lews Castle [NB 419335], Stornoway, Lewis, Outer Hebrides; mansion on site of castle or old house.

Held by the MacLeods, but passed to the Mackenzies at the end of the sixteenth century, who had a house known as **Seaforth Lodge**. They sold the island to the Mathesons in 1844 and they built Lews Castle. The building stands in a public park and the grounds are open to the public (www.lews-castle.com).

Loch Kinellan [NH 472576], near Strathpeffer, Ross and Cromarty; site of castle on crannog.

Held by the Mackenzies of Seaforth. Robert the Bruce is said to have visited William, fourth Earl of Ross, at Loch Kinellan, although his wife and womenfolk had been delivered up to the English by the Earl. The widow of Kenneth Mackenzie was kidnapped from the island in 1494 by a band of Munros; they were pursued and slaughtered near Castle Leod.

Loch Slin Castle [NH 849806], near Tain, Ross and Cromarty; ruinous castle on island.

Held by the Munros in the seventeenth century and then by the Mackenzies.

Logie [NH 750761], near Milton, Ross and Cromarty; site of castle.
Held by the Mackenzies in the seventeenth century.

Milliken [NS 418634], near Johnstone, Renfrewshire; probable site of tower house.

Held by the Wallaces of Elderslie, by the Houstons and by the Millikens, before passing to the Mackenzies.

Newmore Castle [NH 680720], near Alness, Ross and Cromarty; slight remains of castle.

Held by the Munros and then by the Mackenzies, and was replaced by Newmore House, dating from 1875, which was built by the Inglis family.

Ord House [NH 514505], near Muir of Ord, Ross and Cromarty; mansion on site of castle or older house.

Held by the Mackenzies. The building is said to be haunted by the ghost of a lady, witnessed in both corridors and one of the bedrooms. The ghost has also been held responsible for removing pictures, presumably because of a dislike for them, and propping them neatly and unbroken against walls. Ord House is now a hotel (01463 870492; www.ord-house.co.uk).

Red Castle [NH 584495], near Muir of Ord, Ross and Cromarty; altered and ruined L-plan tower house.

Held by several families before coming to the Mackenzies from 1570 to 1790. The house was burned in 1649, and the property later passed to Baillies of Dochfour. The castle is now a shell.

Red Castle (M&R)

Rosehaugh [NH 678557], near Fortrose, Ross and Cromarty; site of mansion.

The property was bought by Sir George Mackenzie of Rosehaugh, nephew of the Earl of Seaforth, and he apparently built the first house here. Mackenzie is a controversial figure and is widely accused of persecuting Covenanters, earning him the name 'Bluidy Mackenzie,' and he was at the trial of Archibald Campbell, ninth Earl of Argyll, who was subsequently executed for treason. Mackenzie was also a respected author

Rosehaugh House 1906?

and established the Advocates' Library in Edinburgh. He was buried in an elaborate tomb in Greyfriars Kirkyard (which is open to the public) in Edinburgh; his ghost is said to haunt several pubs and the burial ground in a series of unpleasant (but unlikely) manifestations, such as scratching unwary visitors. His spectral presence was not enough, it seems, to stop his tomb being despoiled and a skull being removed. Rosehaugh was sold to the Mackenzies of Scatwell in 1688 and then to the Fletchers in 1864 and they built a huge impressive mansion on the site; this was demolished in 1959.

Scatwell House [NH 399559], near Strathpeffer, Ross and Cromarty; mansion incorporating castle or old house.

Held by the Mackenzies of Scatwell. The family were made Baronets of Nova Scotia in 1702-03, and now live in Canada. The property passed to the Bells in 1885.

Scotsburn [NH 720761], near Invergordon, Ross and Cromarty; site of castle.

Held by the Mackenzies in the seventeenth and eighteenth centuries.

Shank House [NT 334611], near Gorebridge, Midlothian; ruinous seventeenth-century mansion.

Held by the Shank family but apparently occupied by Sir George Mackenzie of Rosehaugh. Sold to the Dundases of Arniston in 1753.

Tarbat House [NH 772737], near Alness, Ross and Cromarty; site of castle and house and ruinous mansion.

Held by the Munros but sacked by Jacobites in 1745 as the clan did not support Bonnie Prince Charlie. It passed to the Mackenzies. Sir George Mackenzie of Tarbat opposed the Cromwellian administration and was made a Lord of Session in 1661. In 1685 he was made Viscount Tarbat, in 1702 he was made Secretary of State for William and Mary, and he was made Earl of Cromartie the following year. The house was occupied until the 1960s but is now a shell.

Tarradale Castle [NH 553488], near Beauly, Ross and Cromarty; site of castle.

Held by the Comyns, but the lands passed to the Mackenzies of Fairburn, and then to the Bains. The present Tarradale House is a field studies centre for Aberdeen University.

www.clan-mackenzie.org.uk
www.clanmackenzie.com
No. of castles/sites: 40
Rank: 26/764
Xrefs: Kennethson; MacKenzie

MacKerrell

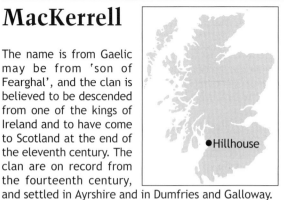

The name is from Gaelic may be from 'son of Fearghal', and the clan is believed to be descended from one of the kings of Ireland and to have come to Scotland at the end of the eleventh century. The clan are on record from the fourteenth century, and settled in Ayrshire and in Dumfries and Galloway.

Hillhouse [NS 343338] is two or so miles north and east of Troon in Ayrshire, and was held by the MacKerrells from the sixteenth century or earlier. The family are believed to be descended from Sir John MacKerrell, who played a valiant part in the Battle of Otterburn in 1388 by capturing Raoul de Percy, brother of Henry Hotspur. John, eighth laird, born in 1762 was a silk merchant in Paisley. Prince Louis Napoleon, later Emperor of France, stayed at Hillhouse in 1839 while attending the Eglinton Tournament. The property was sold in 1895 to the Bentinck Duke of Portland. The McKerrells of Hillhouse now apparently live at Lochmaben in Dumfries and Galloway.

http://clanmckerrell.50free.net
No. of castles/sites: 1
Rank: 537=/764

MacKinlay

The name is Gaelic and means 'son of Finlay', or 'Finlayson' in English.

Wester Kames Castle [NS 062680] is a small restored tower house, dating from the sixteenth century, with a courtyard. It stands a few miles northwest of Rothesay on the island of Bute in the Firth of Clyde, and the lands were originally held by the MacKinlays. An argument about an archery contest led to the Crown granting the property to the royal butler, a fellow called MacDonald, but who then took the name Spence, from 'Dis-spenser'. The property later passed to the Grahams and then to the Stuart Marquess of Bute.

homepages.rootsweb.com/~mckinlay/
members.tripod.com/~McKinley783/
No. of castles/sites: 1
Rank: 537=/764
Xref: Finlayson

MacKinnon

The name means 'son of Fingon', and 'Fingon' was a personal name from Gaelic and means 'fair born'. The clan claim descent from Kenneth MacAlpin, the 'first' king of a united Scotland in the ninth century. The clan held lands on the islands of Mull and of Skye, and one story is that they were given these lands as a reward for sheltering Robert the Bruce on Arran.

Caisteal Maol [NG 758264], which is also known as Dunakin or Dun Haakon, is a shattered ruinous keep or tower, which dates from the fifteenth century. It stands overlooking the narrows between the Isle of Skye and the mainland, not far from the modern bridge, at Kyleakin. The castle was held by the MacKinnons and

Caisteal Maol 1910?

the story goes that the MacKinnon chief was married to a Norse princess, who became known as Saucy Mary. Much of their income came from her enterprising habit of drawing a heavy chain across the narrow sound and extracting tolls from ships wanting to use the waters. It is said that she was buried beneath a large cairn on the top of Beinn na Caillaich. King Haakon of Norway is said to have marshalled his forces beneath the castle before going on to defeat at the Battle of Largs in 1263, and so the castle was named Dun Haakon or Dunakin. After James IV's death at Flodden in 1513, a conclave of chiefs was held at Caisteal Maol and agreed to restore the Lordship of the Isles, but the attempt failed. The castle was probably abandoned sometime around the middle of the seventeenth century. The site is accessible, and a hoard of coins was found in one of the walls in 1951. There is a branch of clan called the MacKinnons of Dunakin, and they apparently live in Tanzania.

Dun Ringill [NG 562171] is at Kilmarie on the Isle of Skye, eleven miles south of Broadford on the road to Elgol, reached along the foreshore. It was first built in the Iron Age as a dun with mural passageways. The entrance has lintels in place but is choked with rubble, and there are two small rectangular buildings within the wall. The place was used by the MacKinnons, although castle is too grand a word for the existing structure. The MacKinnons fought for the Marquis of Montrose at the battles of Auldearn and at Inverlochy in 1645, and a MacKinnon regiment fought for Charles II at Worcester six years later. The clan were Jacobites, fighting at the battles of Sheriffmuir in 1715, Glenshiel in 1719 and Culloden in 1746. Iain Og, chief of the clan, helped Bonnie Prince Charlie following Culloden in 1746 and rowed him over to the mainland from Skye; the prince had been sheltered in a cliff near Elgol. Iain Og was given the recipe for Drambuie, a whisky liqueur, although the original ingredients included brandy instead of whisky. Whether this was sufficient recompense for the next four years spent by MacKinnon in captivity in a prison ship at Tilbury is debateable. By then the MacKinnons had moved to what is now **Strathaird House** [NG 551180]. The last chief died in 1808, although the line was eventually established through a younger son, and the present chief of the MacKinnons apparently lives in Somerset in England.

Dun Ara [NM 427577] is in a quiet spot five miles west of Tobermory on the island of Mull. The stronghold stands on a rock, and probably occupies the site of an ancient fort. A wall runs around the summit and there are ruins of buildings. This part of Mull was held by the MacKinnons from 1354 or earlier, and Dun Ara appears to have still been in use in the seventeenth century.

www.cmksna.org
No. of castles/sites: 3
Rank: 328=/764

Mackintosh

The name is from old Gaelic, and means 'son of the leader or chief'. There were two main branches of the family, one that settled in Perthshire at Dalmunzie and were descended from Ewan, the son of John of Islay; and other Mackintoshes settled around Inverness, Strathspey and Nairn. The clan were an integral part of Clan Chattan, a grouping of smaller and less-powerful clans, which joined into a confederation for their own protection and advancement. The Mackintoshes and Clan Chattan had a long feud with the Camerons after the latter clan had seized Tor Castle and the surrounding lands. The Mackintoshes fought for the Marquis of Montrose in 1645, and then supported the Jacobites, and many of the Mackintoshes and of Clan Chattan were captured after the Battle of Preston in 1715. William Mackintosh of Borlum was one of the leaders of the Rising, although he managed to escape from captivity. Many Mackintoshes (and members of Clan Chattan) also died at the Battle of Culloden in 1746. Mackintosh of Clan Chattan, the chief of the associated clans, now apparently lives in Zimbabwe.

Charles Mackintosh, born in Glasgow in 1766, developed a water-proof material by combining rubber with a constituent of tar, and the process went on to bear his name. He patented the process in 1823. Charles Rennie Mackintosh, born in Glasgow in 1868, studied at Glasgow Art School and is renowned as a designer and artist. He won the competition to design Glasgow School of Art in 1894, and other notable buildings are Cranston's Tea Rooms, the Hill House and the Scotland Street School, which is now a museum.

The clan held several properties:
Aldourie Castle [NH 601372], near Inverness; mansion incorporating castle.
Held by the Frasers and by the Grants before passing to the Mackintoshes in the eighteenth century. The building is said to be haunted by a Grey Lady.
Benchar [NN 705989], near Newtonmore, Highland; possible site of castle or old house.
Held by the Mackintoshes, and then by the Macphersons.
Blervie Castle [NJ 071573], near Forres, Moray; ruinous Z-plan tower house.
Held by the Comyns and by the Dunbars, but was bought by the Mackintoshes in the eighteenth century. Blervie was then sold to the Duffs of Braco.
Borlum [NH 652414], near Inverness; castle replaced by mansion.
Held by the Mackintoshes. One of the family was William Mackintosh of Borlum, who led part of the Jacobite forces in the Rising of 1715. He marched his troops south to Preston in the north of England, along with Viscount Kenmure, but there they were attacked and had to surrender. Mackintosh was captured but escaped in 1716, although he was seized again three years later. He was luckier than Viscount Kenmure, who was executed; Mackinstosh died in 1743. **Ness Castle**, a modern mansion, is built on the site.

Castle Stuart [NH 742498], near Inverness; impressive tower house.
Held by the Mackintoshes, but granted to James Stewart, Earl of Moray. The castle was seized by the Mackintoshes in a

Castle Stuart (RWB)

dispute over ownership and compensation, and an agreement was reached. Accommodation is available (01463 790745; www.castlestuart.com (also www.brigadoon.co.uk)).

Culloden House [NH 721465], near Inverness; mansion incorporating part of castle.
Held by the Mackintoshes and by the Edmonstones, but was sold to the Forbes family in 1626. Said to be haunted by the ghost of Bonnie Prince Charlie, and now a hotel (01463 790461; www.cullodenhouse.co.uk).

Dalcross Castle [NH 779483], near Inverness; L-plan tower house.
Held by the Frasers of Lovat, but passed to the Mackintoshes in the eighteenth century. Hanoverian troops were marshalled here prior to the Battle of Culloden in 1746. The castle became ruinous but has been restored and reoccupied. Self-catering accommodation is available in the castle and on the estate (0045 3393 4133; www.dalcross.org).

Dalmunzie [NO 092710], near Spittal of Glenshee, Perthshire; castle replaced by mansion.
Held by the Mackintoshes (or MacRitchies) of Dalmunzie until the twentieth century, and the later house is now a hotel (01250 885224; www.dalmunzie.com).

Daviot Castle [NH 730405], near Inverness; some remains of castle.
Held by the Lindsay Earls of Crawford, but later passed to the Mackintoshes, and they built a later house. The family of Mackintosh of Daviot-Kinrara flourishes, and they apparently live in London in England.

Dunachton Castle [NH 820047], near Kingussie, Highland; slight remains of castle.
Held by the MacNivens then by the Mackinstoshes of Torcastle about 1500. The castle was burned down in 1689 by the MacDonalds of Keppoch, and not rebuilt. The lands are now held by the Forbes-Leiths of Fyvie, Baronets, and they apparently live at Dunachton.

Geddes [NH 884526], near Nairn, Inverness-shire; castle or old house replaced by mansion.
Held by the Geddeses, but passed to the Roses and then to the Mackintoshes, who built the mansion. The house can be rented (01667 452241; www.geddesonline.co.uk).

Halhill Castle [NH 759519], near Inverness; site of castle.
Held by the Mackintoshes, but passed to the Dunbars, although the castle was plundered in 1513 by a party of Mackintoshes and of Roses.

Keppoch Castle [NN 270807], near Spean Bridge, Lochaber, Highland; site of castle near motte.
Held by the MacDonalds of Keppoch, but passed to the Mackintoshes in 1690. The ownership of the lands was disputed with the Mackintoshes, and the last clan battle was fought

here. The castle was demolished in 1663 after the Keppoch Murder.

Loch an Eilean Castle [NH 899079], near Aviemore, Strathspey, Highland; ruinous castle.
Held by the Mackintoshes, then by the Gordons and by the Grants.

Moy Castle [NH 775343], near Inverness; slight remains of castle.
Held by the Mackintoshes. It was nearby, at Moy Hall, that in 1746 forces under the Montgomery Earl of Loudoun tried to capture Bonnie Prince Charlie, but were themselves surprised and routed by only a few Jacobites.

Rait Castle [NH 894525], near Nairn, Inverness-shire; fine ruinous castle.
Held by the Cummings whose wedding feast for the Mackintoshes ended with many of the Cummings being slain. The laird blamed his love-struck daughter for the violence, and pursued her round the castle. She climbed out a window, but he chopped off her hands and she fell to her death. Her ghost, in a blood-soaked wedding dress, is said to haunt the ruins. The property passed to the Mackintoshes, then to the Campbells of Cawdor. The Duke of Cumberland is said to have stayed here before victory at Culloden in 1746. Moves are afoot to get the castle consolidated (www.saveraitcastle.org).

Rothiemurchus [NH 885098], near Aviemore, Strathspey, Highland; castle replaced by mansion.
Held by the Mackintoshes and by the Dallases of Cantray before passing to the Grants. Open to the public (01479 812345; www.rothiemurchus.net).

Tor Castle [NN 133786], near Fort William, Lochaber, Highland; massive ruinous castle.
Held by the Mackintoshes, but seized by the Camerons in the fourteenth century, who rebuilt it to defend themselves against the MacDonalds of Keppoch.

www.cmna.org
No. of castles/sites: 18
Rank: 76=/764
Xrefs: MacRitchie; Chattan

Loch an Eilean Castle 1910?

MacLachlan

The name means 'son of Lachlann or Lochlainn', and the clan claimed descent from the kings of Ulster, and came to Scotland when they were defeated by Brian O'Neill. Their chief Donall MacLochlainn was slain in battle in 1241 along with many of his clan, but by the end of the thirteenth century the survivors were settled by Loch Fyne.

Castle Lachlan [NS 005953] is a substantial and impressive castle, with ranges of buildings enclosing a small courtyard. It stands seven miles south-west of Strachur in Argyll on the north side of Lachlan Bay. There was an older castle of the clan, referred to in a charter of 1314, and it may have been on an island in Loch Fyne. The family supported Robert the Bruce in the Wars of Independence, and also sensibly treated well with the Campbells. The clan were Jacobites and fought at Killiecrankie with Bonnie Dundee in 1689. They were also out in the 1715 and 1745-46 Jacobite Risings, and Lachlan MacLachlan, chief of the clan, was killed at the Battle of Culloden in 1746. The castle was attacked by a Hanoverian warship, although it did little damage. The MacLachlans kept their lands as the property had already been given to the eldest son who had taken no part in the Rising. The castle was not rebuilt and a new house, (now) a large castellated mansion also called Castle Lachlan [NS 013956] with a dominating battlemented tower, was built nearby. The property is still apparently held by the chiefs, and the old castle was said to have had a brownie. Holiday accommodation is available in the new castle (01369 860669; www.castlelachlan.com).

The clan have a burial aisle at the St Bride's Old Parish Church at Kilmorie [NS 011952], dating from the fifteenth century, although now without a roof.

www.maclachlans.org / www.clanmaclachlan.org.uk
www.clanlachlan.ca
No. of castles/sites: 2 / Rank: 396=/764
Xref: Lachlan

Castle Lachlan (M&R)

MacLaine

The name is from the Gaelic 'Mac Gille Eathain', and means 'son of the servant of (St) John'. The MacLaines and the MacLeans are descended from Gillean of the Bloodaxe, a strong warrior in the thirteenth century, and the clan fought on the side of Robert the Bruce at Bannockburn in 1314. The clan was granted land on Mull and the MacLaines of Lochbuie came from Hector the Stern, while Lachlan Lubanach was the progenitor of the MacLeans of Duart. The different spellings for branches of the same clan were only adopted in the sixteenth century.

Moy Castle [NM 616247] is a plain but striking tower house in a beautiful location on the beach at Lochbuie, some ten miles south-west of Craignure on the island of Mull. It dates from the fifteenth century. The MacLaines

Moy Castle (M&R)

held the property, after acquiring the lands from the MacDonald Lords of the Isles around 1360. Iain the Toothless, the chief, and his son and heir, Ewen of the Little Head, fought in 1538 over the latter's marriage settlement: apparently Ewen's wife was not satisfied with their house on a fortified island in Loch Squabain [NM 631307], and desired something more luxurious. Ewen was slain in the subsequent battle, his head being hewn off and his horse riding away for two miles with the decapitated body. A cairn [NM 649326?] was said to mark the spot where Ewen finally fell from his horse, but has been destroyed. His ghost, the headless horseman, is said to been seen riding in Glen Mor on a dun-coloured horse, sometimes with a green cloak, when one of the MacLaines is about to die, or the hooves of his horse have been heard. There are also tales of a ghostly black dog. Ewen was buried on Iona where his grave can apparently still be seen.

The MacLeans and the MacLaines were not always on the best terms. One story is that MacLean of Duart, desiring Lochbuie, imprisoned one of the MacLaine chiefs on the Treshnish Isle of Cairnburg to prevent him producing an heir. His only female companion was an old and less than beautiful woman who, however, he contrived to make pregnant. MacLaine, himself, was murdered, but the woman managed to escape, and produced a son, Murdoch, who eventually regained the property. Murdoch MacLaine of Lochbuie supported the Marquis of Montrose and fought at the Battle of Kilsyth in 1645 and then raided Campbell lands. His possessions were forfeited, but were regained after the Restoration in 1661. The MacLaines and the MacLeans rode with 300 men to join Bonnie Dundee in 1689 and fought at Killiecrankie. The castle was abandoned in 1752, and when Boswell and Johnson visited Lochbuie in 1773 they stayed in a small house nearby, which was in turn replaced by **Lochbuie House** [NM 616249], a large Georgian mansion with lower wings. The MacLaines sold the property in the twentieth century, although apparently kept possession of the castle. There is a burial vault with an armorial panel, dating from 1864, at the old chapel [NM 626236], as well as a number of eighteenth-century memorials. The chief of the MacLaines of Lochbuie apparently lives in South Africa.

www.maclaineoflochbuie.com
members.tripod.com/maclainelochbuie/
No. of castles/sites: 2
Rank: 396=/764

MacLaren

The name means 'son of Laurence' from Gaelic, and is on record from the thirteenth century. There are several different spellings including MacLaren and Maclaurin. The clan held lands in Tiree and in and around Balquhidder in Stirlingshire. The clan claim descent from Lorn, the son of Fergus MacErc, who was king of Dalriada in the sixth century. MacLaren's Loup is another name for the Devil's Beeftub, which is near Moffat. A Jacobite named MacLaren had been captured in 1746 but managed to escape by wrapping his plaid about him and rolling down the steep slope into a mist.

Auchleskine [NN 543209] is a couple of miles north and west of Strathyre in Stirlingshire. It was held by the MacLarens, who had had lands around Balquhidder, but were later tenants from 1370 when the Earldom of Strathearn was kept by the Crown. The clan may have been at Bannockburn in 1314, but fought at Sauchieburn for James III in 1488, and then at the Battle of Flodden in 1513 and the Battle of Pinkie in 1547. The MacLarens were not on best terms with their neighbours the MacGregors, and many MacLarens were slain and their lands taken by the MacGregors in 1558. The MacLarens were Jacobites and took part in the battles of Killiecrankie in 1689, then Sheriffmuir in 1715 and then the disaster of Culloden, during which thirteen were killed and fourteen wounded as part of the Stewart of Appin regiment. Donald MacLaren was captured after the battle and was to be imprisoned in Carlisle but he managed to escape and lived as a fugitive until 1757 when there was a general amnesty. The chief of the MacLarens was styled as 'of Achleskine'.

Ardveich or **Dalveich Castle** [NN 615244] was two miles east of Lochearnhead also in Stirlingshire, and was believed to be a Z-plan tower house, but little or nothing survives. It was held by the MacLarens of Ardveich from the thirteenth century, but later passed to the Stewarts.

Dreghorn Castle [NT 225684] stood to the south of Edinburgh, and dated from the seventeenth century, but all remains have gone, as has the mansion built to replace it. The lands were held by the Murrays, then passed through several families to John Maclaurin, Lord Dreghorn, after his elevation to the bench. Dreghorn then passed to the Trotters on his death in 1796, and they built a mansion, which was destroyed by the army in 1955; the site is now a barracks.

www.clanmaclarenna.org
www.clanmaclarensociety.com
No. of castles/sites: 3
Rank: 328=/764
Xref: Maclaurin

MacLea

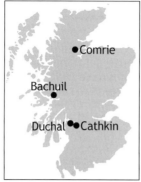

The name is often thought to mean 'son of (the) physician', but the origin is likely to be from 'son of Dunsleve'. 'Dunsleve' was a personal name, and then over the years this got reduced to MacLea. The name also became anglicised to Livingstone, and also see that name. **Comrie** [NH 414560], some four and a half miles west and south of Strathpeffer in Ross and Cromarty, is believed to have been the seat of the clan in the sixteenth century, but the MacLeas had an ancient association with the Isle of Lismore in the Firth of Lorn in Argyll.

Bachuil House [NM 863438] is a couple of miles north of Achnacroish on the island of Lismore, and is an eighteenth-century house. The property was held by the Livingstones from 1641 or much earlier, although they lost many of their lands to Campbell of Airds. The Livingstones changed their name from MacLea or Macleay, and are hereditary keepers of the staff of St Moluag, who was a sixth-century saint. The staff is still kept at Bachuil, and can be viewed by appointment (01631 760256). The much-reduced but attractive Cathedral of St Moluag [NM 860434] lies to the southeast. The Livingstones, chiefs of the MacLea clan, still live at the house.

Donald MacLea or Livingstone was one of the guard of Stewart of Ardshiel at the Battle of Culloden in 1746. MacLea prevented the White Banner of the Stewarts from falling into the hands of the Hanoverian forces and managed to return it to Appin.

Duchal Castle [NS 334685], which is a mile or so south of Kilmacolm in Renfrewshire, is now very ruinous and was replaced by **Duchal House** [NS 353680], which dates from the eighteenth century. The property was held by the Lyles and others before coming to the Maclay Barons Maclay, the title being created in 1922. The family were shipowners during World War I and one of the family was Minister of Shipping and in the War Cabinet. The gardens of Duchal House are occasionally open to the public (www.gardensofscotland.org).

Cathkin House [NS 627588], which is two miles south-east of Rutherglen near Glasgow, dates from 1799 but replaced an older house or castle. It was held by the Douglases, by the Hamiltons and by the Dunlops before coming to the MacLeas. The building is now used as a nursing home.

www.clanmclea.co.uk
No. of castles/sites: 4
Rank: 278=/764
Xrefs: Livingstone; Maclay; MacLae

MacLean

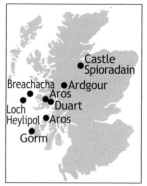

The name is from the Gaelic 'Mac Gille Eathain', and means 'son of the servant of (St) John'. The MacLeans are descended from Gillean of the Bloodaxe, a strong warrior in the thirteenth century, and the clan fought on the side of Robert the Bruce at Bannockburn in 1314. The clan was granted land on the Isle of Mull and the MacLeans of Duart claim descent from Lachlan Lubanach, while the MacLaines of Lochbuie came from Hector the Stern. The different spellings for branches of the same clan were only adopted in the sixteenth century. The MacLeans held lands on the Island of Mull, on Islay, on Jura, on Tiree, on Coll, in Knapdale and in Morvern. On the Isle of Iona, between the abbey and the nunnery, is MacLean's Cross [NM 285242], a fine fifteenth-century carved stone cross, and the stone effigy of Anna MacLean, prioress of the nunnery of Iona who died in 1543, is in the Abbey Museum.

John MacLean, who was born in 1879 and was a Glasgow teacher, was an antiwar Communist and revolutionary. He was imprisoned in 1915 and lost his job but he was made Soviet Council to Scotland in 1918. He was imprisoned again but continued to campaign for the Scottish Workers Republican Party.

Duart Castle [NM 749354] is a magnificent and daunting stronghold, perched on a rock and guarding the Sound of Mull, a few miles south of Craignure on the island of Mull. It dates from the thirteenth century, and consists of a strong curtain wall and a substantial keep or tower, which was added in about 1390. Later ranges were built with the courtyard. Lachlan Lubanach married Elizabeth, daughter of the Lord of the Isles, granddaughter of Robert II, King of Scots, and was granted the first known charter for Duart dated 1390 as her dowry. While fighting with the MacDonalds, the sixth Chief, Red Hector, was killed at the Battle of Harlaw in 1411, slaying and being slain by Sir Alexander Irvine of

Duart Castle (LF)

Drum. During a battle between the clan in 1538, Ewen MacLaine of Lochbuie was slain and beheaded in battle – and his ghost, the headless horseman, rides in Glen Mor. Sir Lachlan MacLean, despite being one of the most powerful chiefs on the western seaboard at the time, was killed on the Isle of Islay, along with many of his clan, by the MacDonalds at the Battle of Traigh Gruinart in 1598. Lachlan Cattanach, eleventh Chief, became so unhappy with his Campbell wife that he had the poor woman chained to a rock in the Firth of Lorn to be drowned at high tide. She was rescued, however, and was taken to her father, the Campbell Earl of Argyll. As a result, MacLean was murdered in his bed in Edinburgh by Sir John Campbell of Cawdor. In 1608 MacLean of Duart, along with many other chieftains, was kidnapped and imprisoned while being entertained aboard ship off Aros Castle on Mull. Sir Lachlan MacLean was made a Baronet of Nova Scotia in 1631, and his son, Sir Hector, was killed at the Battle of Inverkeithing in 1651. In 1674 the castle was acquired by the Campbell Earl of Argyll, who also gained most of the MacLeans' lands, although not without much bloodshed in the following years. The MacLeans remained staunch supporters of the Stewarts throughout the Jacobite Risings, and fought at Killiecrankie in 1689 and in the later rebellions. Although garrisoned, Duart was not used as a residence, and was abandoned after the Jacobite Rising of 1745-46 to become derelict and roofless. It was acquired in 1911 by Fitzroy MacLean, who restored Duart, and the castle is still owned by the MacLeans of Duart and Morvern, although they now live in Perthshire. The castle is open to the public in the summer (01680 812309; www.duart castle.com).

The MacLeans also held:

Ardgour House [NM 995638], near Corran, Ross and Cromarty; castle replaced by mansion.

Held by the MacDonalds, but passed to the MacLeans of Ardgour in the fifteenth century, and this branch of the clan were also known as Clan Tearlach. Ewen, second of Ardgour, was slain at the Battle of Bloody Bay on Mull around 1482. The clan followed the Marquis of Montrose, but Allan, seventh lord, was later pardoned. The chiefs did not take part in the Jacobite Risings, and the MacLeans of Ardgour now apparently live at Salachan at Ardgour. Ardgour can be rented as self-catering accommodation (0141 337 6669; www.iolair.co.uk).

Ardtornish Castle [NM 692426], near Lochaline, Ardnamurchan, Highland; ruinous castle.

Held by the MacDonald Lords of the Isles, but passed to the MacLeans at the end of the fifteenth century, and was abandoned around 200 years later. Accommodation is available on the estate (01967 421288; www.ardtornish.co.uk).

Aros Castle [NM 563450], Aros, Isle of Mull, Argyll; ruinous castle by the sea.

Once an important place. Built by the MacDougalls and then held by the MacDonald Lords of the Isles, Aros passed to the MacLeans after 1493. On the orders of James VI in 1608, Lord Ochiltree lured many independently minded island chiefs onto his ship, where they were imprisoned and sent to Edinburgh for punishment. They were forced to sign the Bond and Statutes of Iona, which greatly curtailed their power. In 1674 the Campbell Earl of Argyll occupied Aros (and Duart) with 2000 men to punish the MacLeans of Duart, and there was much bloodshed. The lands passed to the Campbells, and Aros lost importance to Tobermory (which has a better harbour).

Aros Castle [NR 645968], Glengarrisdale, Isle of Jura, Argyll; site of castle.

Held by the MacLeans, who came into possession of the north part of Jura; the southern part was held by the MacDonalds, but by 1620 the lands had passed to the Campbells who complained they were being harassed by the MacLeans. This came to battle in 1647, and a force of Campbells surprised the MacLeans at Glen Garrisdale, slaying many of them. There is a tradition that the severed head of one of the MacLeans, along with two limb bones, adorned a cairn near MacLean's Skull Cave [NR 647970]. The castle was still in use in 1690 when the Campbell constable took action against the MacLeans who had not taken the Oath of Allegiance to William and Mary.

Breachacha Castle [NM 159539], Isle of Coll, Argyll; substantial restored castle.

Held by the MacDonalds, by the MacNeils and by the MacLeans. It was seized by the MacLeans of Coll in 1431, but they feuded

Breachacha Castle (AC)

with the MacLeans of Duart, who captured the castle in 1578. Donald MacLean of Coll garrisoned it against the Campbell Earl of Argyll in 1679. **New Breacachadh Castle** [NM 159540] was built nearby in 1750, and the old castle became ruinous; Dr Johnston and Boswell visited in 1773. The property passed to the Stewarts of Glenbuchie in 1856, but the old castle was bought and restored by a descendant of the MacLeans in 1965. The castle has been reoccupied, and is now used for the Project Trust, a scheme to involve young people in development work around the world. Nearby is the MacLean burial ground, above Crosapol bay.

Breda [NJ 549167], near Alford, Aberdeenshire; castle replaced by mansion.

Held by the Forbeses, but later passed to the MacLeans and they built the mansion. Breda is reputedly haunted.

Cairnburgh Castle [NM 308450] & [NM 305447], Treshnish Isles, Argyll; remains of castle on two islands.

Held by the MacDougalls of Lorn, then by the MacDonald Lords of the Isles, and then by the MacLeans of Duart. One story is that MacLean of Duart had the chief of the MacLaines of Lochbuie imprisoned here to prevent him producing an heir. MacLaines's only female companion was an old, not overly pleasing woman, whom he made pregnant. MacLaine himself was murdered, but the woman managed to escape and produced a son, who eventually recovered Lochbuie. James IV had the castle besieged in 1504 when held by the rebellious Lachlan MacLean. The castles were surrendered to the Covenanter General David Leslie in 1647, and many of the books and records which had been rescued from Iona were destroyed during a siege by Cromwell's forces in the 1650s. Although the castles held out against attacks by the Campbells in 1679, they were again surrendered in 1692. The castles were garrisoned during both the 1715 and 1745-46 Jacobite Risings.

Caisteal nan Con [NM 584487], near Lochaline, Highland; simple ruinous castle.

Held by the MacLeans of Duart, and said to have been used as a hunting lodge by those occupying Aros Castle. The name means 'castle of dogs'.

Caisteal nan Con [NM 765136], Isle of Torsa, Argyll; simple ruinous castle.

Held by the Campbells and by the MacDougalls of Rarey, before passing to the MacLeans. Presumably also used as a hunting lodge, although Torsa is not a large island.

Castle Loch Heylipol [NL 986435], Isle of Tiree, Argyll; castle replaced by house on former island.

Held by the MacDonalds, then by the MacLeans and by the Campbell Earls and Dukes of Argyll. The castle was besieged by the Campbells in 1678-79, became ruinous, and was replaced by the factor's house. The building is said to be haunted by a Green Lady, as well as the spirit of the factor, who died on the threshold of his new house before he could enter it.

Castle Spioradain [NH 603375], Bona Ferry, near Inverness; site of castle, formerly on an island.

Held by the MacLeans of Dochgarroch around 1420, and the site gained a reputation for being haunted: the name means 'castle of spirits'. The story goes that there was a long-running feud between the MacLeans and the Camerons of Lochiel. This resulted in several Camerons being executed and their corpses were hung from the walls, but the MacLeans retaliated in kind with much slaughter. The ghosts of the dead are said to have become united in death and terrorised the castle and the area. The site, however, was destroyed when the Caledonian Canal was built, and it is said that human bones were found.

Dochgarroch [NH 617409], near Inverness; site of castle or old house.

Held by the MacLeans, also known as Clan Tearlach, from the sixteenth century, and the clan were allied to Clan Chattan. The clan were Jacobites and fought at Killiecrankie in 1689 and Sheriffmuir in 1715. The line continues as the MacLeans of Dochgarroch, who apparently have residences in Glen Urquhart, in Edinburgh and in Morvern.

Drimnin Castle [NM 547550], near Lochaline, Highland; site of castle.

Held by the MacLeans of Coll in the sixteenth century, and demolished in the 1830s. MacLean of Drimnin led the clan during the Jacobite Rising of 1745-46 and was killed at the Battle of Culloden. The castle was replaced by nearby **Drimnin House** [NM 554550], although by that time the property had passed to the Gordons.

Dun Chonnuill [NM 680125], one of the Garvellach Isles, Argyll; ruinous castle.

Held by the MacDougalls, and then later by the MacDonalds and by the MacLeans. The MacLeans of Dunconnel apparently live at Strachur House in Argyll, and are hereditary keepers and captains of Dunconnel.

Eilean Amalaig Castle [NM 708298], Loch Spelve, Isle of Mull, Argyll; site of castle on island.

Held by the MacLeans of Duart. The clan marshalled their birlinns or galleys here. Sir Lachlan MacLean of Duart was warned not to sail his galleys anticlockwise around the island or trouble would befall. He ignored this warning, and soon afterwards was killed on Islay, along with many of his clan, by the MacDonalds at the Battle of Traigh Gruinart in 1598.

Glensanda Castle [NM 824469], near Lochaline, Kingairloch, Highland; ruinous castle.

Held by the MacMasters but passed to the MacLeans in the fifteenth century. The castle was built by Ewen MacLean of Kingairloch in about 1450, and restoration is proposed or undergoing.

Gorm Castle [NR 235655], Loch Gorm, Isle of Islay, Argyll; slight traces of castle in island.

Held by the MacDonalds, but passed to the MacLeans who had come to hold this part of Islay (the Rhinns). This was contested by the MacDonalds, and they came to battle at Traigh Gruinart in 1598. The MacLeans were slaughtered, and Lachlan MacLean

of Duart was killed. A party of MacLeans sheltered in Kilnave Chapel [NR 285715], on the western shore of Loch Gruinart, which was then burned down and all of them perished, except one man. The castle and the island passed to the Campbells. Gorm Castle was still in use in 1745 but is now very ruinous.

Kingairloch [NM 836531], Kingairloch, Highland; castle or old house replaced by mansion.

Held by the MacLeans of Kingairloch from 1509, and they were a branch of Clan Tearlach. Hector MacLean of Kingairloch fought at the Battle of Kilsyth in 1645. While many of the chief's kin and clan fought for the Jacobites, and several were killed at the Battle of Culloden in 1746, Lachlan MacLean of Kingairloch took no part in the rebellion and retained the lands. The MacLeans of Kingairloch now apparently live in North America. The house can be rented as holiday accommodation (01967 411242; www.kingairloch-holidays.co.uk).

Kinlochaline Castle [NM 697476], near Lochaline, Highland; altered castle.

Held by the MacInneses, but passed to the MacLeans of Duart after the chief of MacInnes had been murdered along with his sons by the MacKinnons. The castle was damaged by Alasdair Colkitto MacDonald in 1644, and later by Cromwell's forces in the 1650s. The castle was attacked by the Campbell Earl of Argyll in 1679 during a feud. It was abandoned about 1690, but is about to be or has been restored as a house.

Strachur [NN 091016], Strachur, Argyll; castle replaced by mansion.

Strachur House is apparently occupied by the MacLeans of Dunconnel, hereditary keepers and captains of Dun Chonnuill castle on the Garvellachs, who were made Baronets in 1957. The gardens of Strachur are occasionally open to the public (www.gardensofscotland.org).

Tarbert Castle [NR 867687], Tarbert, Knapdale, Argyll; ruinous castle.

Although a royal castle, the lands were held by the MacAlisters and then by the MacLeans and by the Campbells.

Torloisk House [NM 410458], near Dervaig, Mull, Argyll; castle or old house replaced by mansion.

Held by the MacLeans of Torloisk from the sixteenth century. Hector MacLean of Torloisk supported the Marquis of Montrose, and Donald MacLean of Torloisk fought at Sheriffmuir in 1715. The line became Clephane Compton MacLean, and now apparently live at Ripon in Yorkshire. The house can be rented as holiday accommodation (01381 610496; www.lhh scotland.com).

Westfield House [NJ 163654], near Elgin, Moray; castle replaced by mansion.

Held by the MacLeans of Westfield from the nineteenth century.

www.maclean.org
www.clan-maclean.org
www.clanmacleanatlantic.org
No. of castles/sites: 25
Rank: 52=/764
Xrefs: Maclean

Tarbert Castle (M&R)

MacLellan

The name is from Gaelic and comes from 'son of the servant of (St) Fillan': there may be two saints called Fillan in Scotland, both from the early times of the church, one from the sixth century and one from the eighth. The name is on record from the middle of the thirteenth century, and the clan were numerous and held lands in Galloway.

Bombie Castle [NX 708501] is a mile or so east of Kirkcudbright in Galloway, but all that remains of what was a large and strong castle is the enclosing ditch. The lands were held by the MacLellans, and MacLellan of Bombie supported William Wallace. The MacLellans feuded with the Douglases, and Sir Patrick MacLellan was murdered in 1452 at Threave Castle by the Earl of Douglas. The MacLellans had their revenge by helping to besiege, capture and sack Threave after the fall of the Black Douglases in 1455. William MacLellan of Bombie was killed at the Battle of Flodden in 1513, while MacLellan of Bombie was murdered in Edinburgh's High Street in 1527 by a Gordon of Lochinvar. Sir Thomas MacLellan of Bombie, Provost of Kirkcudbright, acquired the lands and buildings of the Franciscan Greyfriars Monastery in Kirkcudbright in 1569, and later those of the old royal castle. In 1582 he completed a new tower house in the burgh, MacLellan's Castle, abandoning Bombie. He is commemorated by a large monument of 1597 in Greyfriars [NX 683511] in the burgh, which is near MacLellan's Castle (see below). The monument has the stone effigy of a knight in armour. The church is open to the public.

MacLellan's Castle [NX 683511] in Kirkcudbright is a fine large L-plan tower house, dating from the sixteenth century and now ruinous, although complete to the wallhead. The MacLellans were made Lords

Kirkcudbright in 1633, and one of the family fought at the Battle of Philiphaugh in 1645. They abandoned the castle around 1752 because of financial troubles, and it was sold to the Maxwells of Orchardton, and then to the Douglas Earl of Selkirk in 1782. It was soon ruinous and is now in the care of Historic Scotland and is open to the public from April to September (01557 331856).

The MacLellans also held:

Auchlane Castle [NX 741584], near Castle Douglas, Galloway; slight remains of castle.

Held by the MacLellans from the fourteenth century, but had passed to the Gordons by 1600, although it may have later returned to the MacLellans.

Balmangan Tower [NX 651456], near Kirkcudbright, Galloway; slight remains of tower house.

Held by the MacLellans until 1605 or later, but had passed to the Maxwells by the eighteenth century.

Barmagachan [NX 613494], near Kirkcudbright, Galloway; small tower house.

Held by the Keiths and by the Muirs, but bought by the MacLellans in 1511. Robert MacLellan of Barmagachan, a Covenanter, was forfeited for his part in the Pentland Rising of 1666. He escaped, however, with banishment to America; others were less lucky. The property was sold by the family in 1737.

Barscobe Castle [NX 660806], near New Galloway, Galloway; L-plan tower house.

Held by the MacLellans, who built the castle. They were Covenanters and Barscobe was occupied by the family until

Barscobe Castle (M&R)

1779. It was used as a farmhouse, but has been restored and reoccupied as a residence.

Bombie [NY 319886], near Langholm, Dumfriesshire; site of tower house.

May have been held by the MacLellans.

Castlehill of Barcloy or **West Barcloy** [NX 854524], near Dalbeattie, Galloway; site of castle in the remains of an Iron Age fort.

Held by the Lindsays and by the Stewarts, but had passed to the MacLellans by 1715.

Cumstoun Castle [NX 683533], near Kirkcudbright, Galloway; some remains of tower house.

Held by the Kennedys, by the MacLellans, by the Dunbars and by the Montgomerys, then later by the Maitlands. The castle was replaced by Compstone, a mansion built in the nineteenth century.

MacLellan's Castle (M&R)

Lochfergus [NX 699511], near Kirkcudbright, Galloway; site of castle on former island.

Held by Fergus, Lord of Galloway, then later by the MacLellans, whose castle was torched in 1499.

Raeberry Castle [NX 699437], near Kirkcudbright, Galloway; slight remains of castle on cliff tops.

Held by the MacLellans. It was from Raeberry that Patrick MacLellan of Bombie was seized and taken to Threave Castle in 1452, and was then murdered by the Earls of Douglas. Raeberry had been demolished by the middle of the sixteenth century.

Ravenstone Castle or **Castle Stewart** [NX 409441], near Whithorn, Galloway; altered tower house.

Held by the MacDowalls, but had passed to the MacLellans by 1560. It may have also come to the Kennedys, but the name was changed to Castle Stewart when it went to that family.

Troquhain [NX 681783], near New Galloway, Galloway; site of castle.

Held by the MacLellans but passed to the Gordons.

West Barcloy [NX 855532], near Dalbeattie, Galloway; site of tower house.

Held by the Lindsays and by the Stewarts but was a possession of the MacLellans by 1715.

www.clanmaclellan.net
No. of castles/sites: 14
Rank: 104=/764

MacLeod

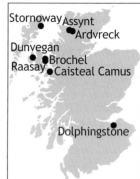

The names means 'son of Leod', 'Leod' being a Norse personal name, and the Leod on question is believed to have been the son of King Olaf the Black, the Viking ruler of the kingdom of Man (Man actually covered much of the western seaboard of Scotland). When his father died, Leod got Lewis and Harris and part of Skye, and the clan became established at Dunvegan to the north of Skye. There were two main branches of the MacLeods descended from Leod's sons: those of Lewis, then of Raasay and Assynt, of Cadboll, and of Geanies, descended from Thorkil or Torquil; and those of Dunvegan and Harris, descended from Tormod.

Dunvegan Castle [NG 247491], a mile north of the village of Dunvegan on the north of Skye, dates from the fourteenth century and formerly stood on an island. There is a massive keep or tower, the famous Fairy Tower, and a hall block, as well as many later extensions. The castle was restored in the nineteenth century and given turrets and battlements. Dunvegan has been held by MacLeods since 1270. They supported Robert the Bruce during the Wars of Independence, and the clan fought at the bloody Battle of Harlaw in 1411. Dunvegan was visited by James V in 1540, and the king was reputedly entertained on the top of MacLeod's Tables – flat-topped hills. The MacLeods fought at the Battle of Worcester for Charles II in 1651 but lost 500 men, which made them reluctant to take part in the Jacobite Risings. In fact MacLeod of Dunvegan refused to join Bonnie Prince Charlie unless he had significant French help, which was perhaps wise. The castle is still owned by the chiefs of the MacLeod, although the twenty-ninth Chief died recently. There are many fascinating items at Dunvegan, including Rory Mor's Horn, which holds more than a pint of claret, which the heir of the MacLeods had to empty in one go; and the Dunvegan Cup, gifted to the clan by the O'Neils of Ulster in 1596 after Sir Roderick MacLeod, or Rory Mor, had led 500 men to their aid. There are also mementoes of Bonnie Prince Charlie and Flora MacDonald, and information about St Kilda, which was

Dunvegan Castle 1910?

formerly a property of the family. And, of course, there is the famous Fairy Flag, 'Am Bratach Sith' in Gaelic. It is made from silk, comes from the Middle East, and dates from around 400-700 AD, predating Dunvegan Castle. The flag is believed to give victory to the clan whenever unfurled, and reputedly did so at the battles of Glendale in 1490 and Trumpan in 1580. The flag could also charm the fish out of Dunvegan Loch, and make the marital bed of the chiefs especially fruitful. There are different stories as to its origin, not least that it was given to one of the chiefs by his faerie wife at their parting. This is said to have taken place at the Fairy Bridge, three miles to the north east, at a meeting of rivers and roads. The castle is open to the public all year (01470 521206; www.dunvegan castle.com). There was a college of piping of the MacCrimmons, renowned pipers to the MacLeod chiefs, at Borreraig. Many of the MacLeods were buried at St Mary's Chapel [NG 256478] at the village of Dunvegan, where they had a burial enclosure.

St Clement's Church [NG 047833] at Rodel on Harris is an impressive and substantial church, dating from the sixteenth century. Housed in the building is the splendid carved tomb of Alasdair Crotach MacLeod, built in 1528, although he did not die for another twenty years. The carvings include the stone effigy of a man in full armour, surrounded by panels of saints and other decorations – particularly a galley, castle and hunting scene: the inscription reads: 'this tomb was prepared by Lord Alexander, son of Willielmus MacLeod, Lord of Dunvegan, in the year of Our Lord 1528'. There is another tomb nearby, which also has the effigy of an armoured man and dates from 1539.

Mary MacLeod (or Mairi Nighinn Alasdair Ruaidh), born at Rodel around 1615, was a Gaelic bard or poetess, and she wrote laments for the MacLeod chiefs and their family members. She is believed to have been about ninety when she died.

Brochel Castle [NG 585463] is a small and very ruinous stronghold, perched on a rock, and located seven miles north of Clachan on Raasay. It was held by the MacLeods of Raasay, and the last chief resident at Brochel was probably Iain Garbh around 1648, after which the clan seat was moved to Kilmaluag near Clachan.

Raasay House [NG 546366] dates from 1747 and was built to replace the old tower house nearby at Kilmaluag. It stands at Clachan and the chiefs moved here in the seventeenth century. The MacLeods of Raasay supported the Jacobites and sent 100 men to join the Rising of 1745-46. After the defeat at Culloden, Bonnie Prince Charlie was briefly sheltered on Raasay. The island was raided in retaliation for the MacLeods' support of the Jacobites, and Brochel and Kilmaluag were both torched, along with every other dwelling on Raasay: the islanders' boats were holed and 280 cows and 700 sheep were slaughtered. The chiefs then built Raasay House, and it was here that Dr Johnson and Boswell were lavishly entertained in 1773. It was on the summit of Dun Caan, the highest hill of the island, that James Boswell, fortified with mutton, bread, cheese, punch and brandy, danced a Highland jig. The MacLeods of Raasay were buried at Kilmaluag.

The chiefs got into debt and sold Raasay in 1846, and the island then had several owners who did little for the people of the island. Raasay House had become derelict but has been restored as the Raasay Outdoor Centre, and there are a variety of activities (01478 660266; www.raasay-house.co.uk).

Assynt Castle or **Eilean Assynt** [NC 189251], four miles north-west of Inchnadamph in the north-west of the mainland, was built on an island in Loch Assynt although little remains. It was held by the MacLeods of Assynt, and the island was besieged in 1585 by the MacKays of Strathnaver, then again in 1646 by the Mackenzies. Eilean Assynt may have been used as a prison after the clan chief moved to Ardvreck.

Ardvreck Castle [NC 240236], one and a half miles north-west of Inchnadamph, is an impressive ruinous castle standing on a peninsula in the loch, and was built by the MacLeods of Assynt. It was at Ardvreck that James Graham, Marquis of Montrose, took refuge in 1650 after losing the Battle of Carbisdale. Montrose was turned over to the Covenanters, and subsequently executed in Edinburgh, his body dismembered and displayed in public. The castle was sacked in 1672 by the Mackenzies and was replaced by **Calda House** [NC 244234], itself

Brochel Castle (GC)

Ardvreck Castle (M&R)

torched in 1760 and not restored. Ardvreck is said to be haunted by the despairing ghost of the daughter of the MacLeod chief who built the castle. The story goes that the devil offered to build him the stronghold if his daughter was wed to him. The chief agreed, but the girl threw herself out of one of the windows when she found out what he had done. There is also said to be the ghost of a tall man, dressed in grey, who only converses in Gaelic. The castle is accessible but is dangerously ruinous.

Angus MacLeod, chief of the clan, founded the church at Assynt [NC 249220] in the fifteenth century and there are the remains of the MacLeod Mausoleum in the burial ground.

The MacLeods also held:

Bearasay [NB 121425], Isle of Bearasay, near Isle of Great Bernera, Lewis, Outer Hebrides; ruins remain on an island.
  Held by Neil MacLeod about 1610, but he was captured when his wife and children were left on a skerry to drown, and he was executed in 1613.

Cadboll Castle [NH 879776], near Tain, Ross and Cromarty; substantial ruinous L-plan tower house.
  Held by the Clyne family, then by the MacLeods of Cadboll, but later passed to the Sinclairs. The building was apparently badly damaged by Alexander Ross of Balnagown as he was ordered to repair it in 1572-74. Cadboll was abandoned for the nearby house in the early eighteenth century, and part of the old castle is used as a farm store.

Caisteal Camus [NG 671087], near Armadale, Isle of Skye, Highland; ruinous castle.
  Also known as **Knock Castle** and **Caisteal Chamius**. Held by the MacLeods in the fifteenth century, but later passed to the MacDonalds. In an attempt to resurrect the Lordship of the Isles in 1515, the castle was besieged unsuccessfully by Alastair Crotach MacLeod. The castle is said to be haunted by a Green Lady, and was recently put up for sale.

Caisteal Mhicleod [NG 816202], near Shiel Bridge, Lochaber, Highland; ruinous dun and castle.
  Held by Alastair Crotach MacLeod, and still in use in the sixteenth century. It is said that a nursemaid dropped a baby from a window to its death here.

Dolphingstone Castle [NT 384729], near Tranent, East Lothian; site of castle.
  Held by the Ainslies, but also by the MacLeods at one time.

Dun Sgathaich [NG 595121], near Armadale, Sleat, Isle of Skye, Highland; ruinous castle on rock by sea.
  Held by the MacAskills but passed to the MacLeods in the fourteenth century. They managed to defend themselves against the MacDonald Lord of the Isles in 1395 and 1401, but early in the fifteenth century the property passed to the MacDonalds. The castle is now very ruinous but is in a lovely spot.

Duntulm Castle [NG 410743], near Uig, Isle of Skye, Highland; some remains of castle on cliffs.
  Held by the MacLeods and built on the site of an Iron Age stronghold reused by the Norsemen. James V visited in 1540, but the property passed to the MacDonalds in the seventeenth century. The castle is said to have had several ghosts. One was said to be the spirit of Margaret, a sister of MacLeod of Dunvegan, who was married to one of the MacDonalds. She had lost an eye in an accident, but her husband cast her out, sending her packing back to Dunvegan on a one-eyed horse with a one-eyed servant and one-eyed dog. Her weeping ghost is said to haunt the castle. The MacDonalds later moved to Monkstadt and then to Armadale in Sleat.

Eilean Ghruididh [NG 951693], Loch Maree, near Kinlochewe, Ross and Cromarty; site of castle on island.
  Held by the MacBeaths in the thirteenth century, and then by the MacLeods from about 1430 to 1513.

Geanies Castle [NH 894798], near Tain, Ross and Cromarty; site of castle.
  Held by the MacLeods of Geanies, but had passed to the Sinclairs by 1624, then went to the Murrays. There is a later house.

Gunnery of MacLeod [NF 933815], near Borve, Isle of Berneray, near North Uist, Outer Hebrides; site of castle.
  Held by the MacLeods of Berneray. Norman MacLeod of Berneray was born here in 1614. He was laird of the island, a famous scholar, and fought at the Battle of Worcester in 1651.

Invergordon Castle [NH 705700], near Invergordon, Ross and Cromarty; site of castle and mansion.
  Held by the Gordons, then by the MacLeods of Cadboll in the 1870s.

MacLeod's Castle [NB 442305], near Stornoway, Isle of Lewis, Outer Hebrides; site of castle.
  Held by the MacLeods of Lewis, but was demolished by Cromwell's forces in 1653. The island passed to the Mackenzies and they built a house on the site of which is **Lews Castle** [NB 419335], itself built in the nineteenth century, after the island had passed to the Mathesons. The grounds around Lews Castle are open to the public (www.lews-castle.com). The chiefs of the clan were buried at St Columba's Church at Aignis [NB 484322], where there is a ruinous church and burial ground. There are two carved stones within the church: one of the effigy of a warrior and is believed to be Roderick, seventh Chief, while the other is for Margaret, daughter of Roderick MacLeod of Lewis, who died in 1503.

Muiravonside [NS 965753], near Linlithgow, West Lothian; site of castle and mansion.
  Held by the Tinsdales and by the Roses, before passing to the MacLeods in 1742, then to the Stirlings. The grounds are a public park.

Stornoway Castle [NB 423327], Stornoway, Lewis, Outer Hebrides; site of castle.
  Held by the MacLeods of Lewis, and an older stronghold may have dated from the eleventh century when it was owned by the MacNicols. The MacLeods either drove the MacNicols from Lewis or forcibly married a MacNicol heiress, or both. The castle was captured by the Gordon Earl of Huntly in 1506, but held out against the Campbell Earl of Argyll in 1554, before being demolished by Cromwell's forces in 1653. His own garrison were reputedly subsequently massacred by the islanders. The last remains of the old castle were removed in the nineteenth century, and the site is thought to be under the old pier.

www.clan-macleod-scotland.org.uk
www.clanmacleodusa.org
www.clanmacleod.org
No. of castles/sites: 21
Rank: 63=/764
Xref: Macleod

Duntulm Castle (M&R) – see prev. column

MacMaster

The name means 'son of the master (a cleric)', and the name was found in Dumfries and Galloway, but there were also MacMasters who held land in the north-west of Scotland.

On the north side of Loch Linnhe, **Glensanda Castle** [NM 824469] is a small square tower, dating from the fifteenth century, and located some ten miles east of Lochaline in Kingairloch in a very remote spot (by road although now close to the huge quarry). The lands were held by the MacMasters, but passed to the MacLeans of Kingairloch in the fifteenth century, possibly with a little skulduggery. The MacLeans built the castle.

Ardgour House [NM 995638], one mile west of Corran also on the north side of Loch Linnhe in Ross and Cromarty, is a mansion of 1765 with later additions but stands on the site of a castle or old house. The lands were also a possession of the MacMasters but, like Glensanda, passed to the MacLeans. The house can be rented as holiday accommodation (0141 337 6669; www.iolair.co.uk).

No. of castles/sites: 2
Rank: 396=/764

Glensanda Castle (M&R)

MacMillan

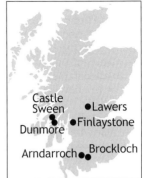

The name means 'son of (the) bald or tonsured (person)' from Gaelic, and is a reference to being the descendant of a priest or a monk. In the early days of the church in Scotland churchmen were allowed to marry and there were hereditary bishops. The clan held lands at Loch Tay and in Knapdale, and another branch had property in Dumfries and Galloway. Kirkpatrick MacMillan, who was a blacksmith at Keir, is credited with making the first bicycle in 1840. Alexander and Daniel MacMillan, grandsons of an Arran farmer, founded the publishing house of MacMillan and Company in London in 1843.

Lawers [NN 684395] is eight miles east of Killin, and stands under Ben Lawers on the north side of Loch Tay in Perthshire. This may have been the seat of the chief of the MacMillans, who is believed to have sheltered Robert the Bruce. The clan went on to fight at Bannockburn in 1314, but Lawers had passed from the clan by 1370, and was long held by the Campbells. The MacMillans were given lands in Knapdale by the Lords of the Isles.

Castle Sween [NR 712789] is in a magnificent spot by the sea on the banks of Loch Sween, and is an early ruinous courtyard castle with ranges of buildings and

Castle Sween (M&R)

towers. The MacMillans were given lands at Knap (the chiefs were styled 'of Knap'), and held the castle, which was built by the MacSweens, from 1362. The MacMillan Tower of the stronghold is named after them, and to the south is Kilmory Knap Chapel [NR 703752] which houses the finely carved MacMillan's Cross, decorated with a figure of Christ on the cross. The castle passed to the Campbells, and it is now in the care of Historic Scotland; both the old castle and Kilmory Knap are open to the public.

Dunmore House [NR 793619] is on the north side of West Loch Tarbert, six or so miles south-west of Tarbert in Knapdale in Argyll. The present ruin appears to be the shell of a tower house, but the building apparently

393

only dates from the nineteenth century and was only gutted by fire in 1985. The lands were a property of the MacMillans, and they became chiefs in 1742. They sold Dunmore to the Fraser Campbells at the beginning of the nineteenth century.

Brockloch [NX 802844] stood four miles south and east of Moniaive in Dumfries and Galloway, but little survives of a tower house. Brockloch was a property of the MacMillans, who are believed to have been descended from Gilbert MacMillan, Baron of Ken, who was a companion of Robert the Bruce. The MacMillans also owned **Arndarroch** [NX 616894], where there was a castle, and **Holm of Dalquhairn** [NX 655990], the site of an old house or stronghold, both near Carsphairn, in the seventeenth century.

Three miles east of Port Glasgow in Renfrewshire is **Finlaystone House** [NS 365737], a grand mansion, dating from 1760 and later, but incorporating some of an old castle. The property was held by the Cunninghams for hundreds of years, but is now owned by the MacMillans. The grounds and gardens are open to the public and the visitor centre has Clan MacMillan exhibits (01475 540505; www.finlaystone.co.uk).

www.clanmacmillan.org
www.macmillanclan.org
www.clanmacmillanaus.freeservers.com
No. of castles/sites: 7
Rank: 182=/764
Xrefs: Milligan

MacNab

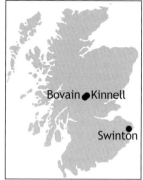

The name is from the Gaelic 'Mac an Aba', which means 'son of the abbot', and the English equivalent being Abbotson. The abbots of the early church in Scotland could be married, and bishoprics and other offices were hereditary. The clan claim descent from the abbot of Glendochart and Strathearn from the royal line of the kings of Dalriada. The name is on record from the beginning of the twelfth century, but the MacNabs fought against Robert the Bruce and were forfeited. They went on to hold lands in Glendochart, around Loch Tay and Killin in Perthshire.

John MacNab, who came from Clackmannanshire and was a herd boy, made a fortune as a captain and shipowner. He died in 1802 and left money for the founding of Dollar Academy.

Bovain [NN 541306] is some three miles south-west of Killin, but there are no remains; the lands were held by the MacNabs from the fourteenth century. The MacNabs and the MacNeishes fought at the Battle of Glenboltachan in 1522, and the MacNeishes were defeated and sorely pressed. The MacNeishes began to raid neighbouring clans lands from their island fortress of Ellanrayne Castle. In 1612 the MacNabs crossed the mountains with a boat to get them out to the island and slew the chief of the MacNeishes and most of his folk. The MacNabs then used (a representation of) MacNeish's head as their heraldic crest. The MacNabs sent 300 men to the defeat of the Battle of Worcester in 1651. The chiefs of the MacNabs did not support the Jacobite Risings, and John MacNab fought for the Hanoverians and was captured at the Battle of Prestonpans in 1745 and was imprisoned in Doune Castle. The clan lost many of their lands to the Campbells in the nineteenth century. Members of the family are buried in the MacNab burial ground on Inchbuie, a small island in the Falls of Dochart in Killin. The burial ground can be visited by getting the key from the Breadalbane Folklore Centre (01567 820254), which also has information about the clan. The MacNabs of MacNab now apparently live at Leuchars in Fife.

The clan also held:
Acharn [NN 756438], near Kenmore, Perthshire; site of castle.
    Held by the MacNabs from the fifteenth century or earlier.
Eilean Ran Castle [NN 577334], near Killin, Stirlingshire; site of castle on an island.
    Held by the MacNabs in 1525 and burnt out in the middle of the seventeenth century. The lands passed to the Campbells.
Kinnell House [NN 578329], near Killin, Stirlingshire; mansion incorporating castle.
    Held by the MacNabs from 1580 to the twentieth century, but passed to the Campbells. The chiefs lived here, and Francis MacNab, then chief, lived in some style and eccentricity, although he did not apparently have the funds to finance his

lifestyle. MacNab is probably best remembered for Sir Henry Raeburn's impressive portrait of him in full Highland dress. MacNab was succeeded by his nephew Archibald as chief, but Archibald escaped his creditors by fleeing to Canada.

Swinton [NT 819471], near Coldstream, Borders; castle replaced by mansion.
  Held by the Swinton family, but had passed to the MacNabs by the nineteenth century.

www.macnab.org
www.mcnabb.us
No. of castles/sites: 5
Rank: 240=/764
Xref: Abbotson

MacNaught

The MacNaughts are a branch of the Mac-Naughtons, and the name means 'son of Nechtan', which was the name of Pictish kings. The name was shortened when this branch of the family came to Galloway, and they are first on record in 1296.

Crogo [NX 759774] is ten or so miles north of Castle Douglas in Dumfries and Galloway, and there was a tower house which stood in its own park. There are no remains, but the lands were held by the MacNaughts before passing to the Gordons in the fifteenth century.

Kilquhanity [NX 766705] is also north of Castle Douglas, and there was a castle or old house, again with its own park. The lands were held by the MacNaught family from 1360 to about 1680. The present mansion was built in 1820 and is now used as a school.

No. of castles/sites: 2
Rank: 396=/764
Xrefs: MacNutt

MacNaughton

The name means 'son of Nechtan', and the clan claimed descent from the mormaers or rulers of Moray; there were several Pictish kings called Nechtan. The MacNaughtons were given lands at Loch Fyne, which put them into contact with their powerful neighbours, the Campbells.

Dubh Loch Castle [NN 114107] stood by the side of Loch Dubh, a couple of miles north-east of Inveraray in Argyll, but nothing is left except a mound. It was held by the MacNaughtons, and the clan supported the MacDougalls against Robert the Bruce, although they changed sides and fought with the Bruce at the Battle of Bannockburn in 1314. The clan made Dunderave their main seat in the fifteenth century, and Dubh Loch Castle is said to have been abandoned because of an outbreak of plague.

Dunderave Castle [NN 143096] is not far from Dubh Loch, and is three miles east of Inveraray on the north bank of Loch Fyne. It is a restored L-plan tower house with a large round tower at one corner, and is dated 1596. The MacNaughtons were Royalists and fought in the ill-prepared and unsuccessful rising of 1653 against the Cromwellian occupation. Iain, the last MacNaughton holder, intended to wed the younger daughter of Sir James Campbell of Ardkinglas, but after some trickery found himself married to the wrong woman. After fleeing

Dunderave Castle (M&R)

to Ireland with his love the younger daughter, Dunderave passed to the Campbells, probably around 1689. Iain had been a Jacobite and had fought at Killiecrankie, which may have been reason enough not to stay. The castle became ruinous but was restored in 1911-12 for the Noble family, and it is still occupied. The MacNaghtens of MacNaghten flourished and the line continues, although they apparently live at Dunderarve in Antrim in Northern Ireland.

Fraoch Eilean Castle [NN 108251], two mile northeast of Inveraray, was a strong castle with a hall house and courtyard, but it is now ruinous and overgrown. It dates from the twelfth or thirteenth century and was occupied for about 400 years. It was held by the MacNaughtons from 1267 but later passed to the Campbells of Inverawe. A tale about the island is that the hero Fraoch journeyed to the island to fetch apples for the fair Mego but was slain by a serpent guarding the fruit. Fraoch, however, means heather in Gaelic, and the name probably just means 'heathery island'.

www.clanmacnaughton.org
No. of castles/sites: 3
Rank: 328=/764
Xrefs: MacNaghten

MacNeil

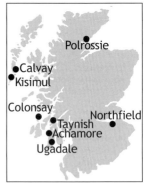

The name means 'son of Neil', and the clan claim descent from Neil of the Nine Hostages, High King of Ireland at the end of the fourth century. The clan held the island of Barra and part of Uist in the Hebrides, and went on to hold property in Kintyre and in Knapdale as well as on the islands of Colonsay and of Gigha.

Kisimul Castle [NL 665979] stands on a small island in Castle Bay to the south of the island of Barra in the Outer Hebrides. A curtain wall runs around the island and there is a keep or tower, a hall and a chapel. Neil of the Castle built a stronghold here in 1030, or so it is claimed, and the MacNeils are believed to have fought at Bannockburn in 1314 and were given lands in Kintyre

Kisimul Castle (1920?)

as reward. One of Kisimul's most unpleasant reputed occupants was Marion of the Heads, second wife of MacNeill of Barra, who ensured her own son's succession by beheading her stepsons. The castle was besieged several times during the clan wars and kinstrife. Some of the clan fought at the Battle of Worcester in 1651, then at the Battle of Killiecankie in 1689, and then in the 1715 Jacobite Rising. The clan nominally supported Bonnie Prince Charlie in the Jacobite Risings and the chief was imprisoned, but they did no actual fighting. In 1750 an agent reported to the exiled Bonnie Prince Charlie that MacNeil of Barra would bring 150 men to a new rising in Scotland. Roderick, twenty-first of Barra, went bankrupt and was forced to sell Barra and all his lands in 1840. The castle and estate were bought back by the MacNeils of Barra in 1937, and the old stronghold was restored in the 1950s and 60s. Kisimul is now in the care of Historic Scotland and is open to the public (01871 810313).

Many of the MacNeils and their kin were buried at Cille Bharra [NF 704077], six miles north of Castlebay on Barra. There are several carved grave slabs, as well as three chapels, one of which has been reroofed. The burial ground is open to the public.

The following properties were also held by the clan:

Achamore House [NR 644477], Isle of Gigha, Argyll; mansion on site of castle or old house.

The island was held by the MacDonalds but on their forfeiture in 1493 went to the MacNeills of Taynish, and they apparently had a residence or castle here in 1590. There was fighting with the MacDonalds and MacLeans over possession, and Gigha was ravaged by pirates in 1530 when the laird was slain, and was raided again in 1555. In 1790 Gigha was sold to another branch of the MacNeills, the MacNeills of Colonsay, who held it until the middle of the nineteenth century. Many of the MacNeills were buried at Kilchattan [NR 644482], where there is the ruin of a chapel in a picturesque spot and several carved burial slabs, including one thought to be for Malcolm MacNeill of Gigha, who died in 1493. Gigha then went through a succession of owners, including the Scarletts and James Horlick until the island was bought by its residents in 2002. B&B accommodation is available at Achamore House and the fabulous Achamore Gardens are open to the public all year (01583 505385; www.AchamoreHouse.com/www.gigha.org.uk).

Breachacha Castle [NM 159539], Isle of Coll; tower and courtyard.

Held by the MacDonalds, but then passed between the MacDonalds, the MacLeans and the MacNeils, and then went to the MacLeans.

Caisteal Calvay [NF 817182], near Lochboisdale, Isle of South Uist, Outer Hebrides; ruinous castle on island.

Held by the MacNeils until about 1600. Bonnie Prince Charlie sheltered here after defeat at Culloden in 1746.

Castle Sinclair or **Dun Mhic Leod** or **Iain Garbh's Castle** [NL 648997], near Castlebay, Isle of Barra, Outer Hebrides; ruinous tower house.

Held by the MacNeils.

Castle Sween [NR 712789], near Tayvallich, Argyll; fine ruinous castle by the sea.

Held by the MacSweens and by others until it passed to the MacNeils who held it for the MacDonald Lords of the Isles. It later passed to the Campbells, and is now in the care of Historic Scotland and is open to the public.

Colonsay House [NR 395968], Isle of Colonsay; eighteenth-century mansion.

The island was held by the MacDuffies but in the seventeenth century passed to the MacDonalds and then to the Campbell Dukes of Argyll. In 1701 the MacNeills acquired the island by exchanging Crerar with the Campbells for Colonsay, and many of them were buried at Oronsay Priory [NR 351889] on the nearby island. Duncan MacNeill was Solicitor General in 1834-35, and was then Lord Advocate and Justice General. He was made Baron Colonsay and Oronsay, and died in 1874. Colonsay is now a possession of Lord Strathcona, and there are fine gardens at Colonsay House which are open to the public from April to September and accommodation is also available (01951 200211; www.colonsay.org.uk). The 'big house' on Colonsay is said to have had a brownie (fairy or gruagach), which also acted as a herdsman.

Loch an Sgoltaire Castle [NR 386972], Isle of Colonsay; castle replaced by mansion.

The island was held by the MacDuffies, then by the MacDonalds and by the Campbells, before coming to the MacNeils in 1701.

Lossit House [NR 633202], near Campbeltown, Kintyre, Argyll; site of castle or old house,

Held by the MacNeils in the seventeenth and eighteenth centuries.

Northfield House [NT 389739], Prestonpans, East Lothian; altered impressive L-plan tower house.

Held by the Hamiltons but passed to the MacNeils in 1890. It is still occupied.

Polrossie [NH 724884], near Dornoch, Sutherland; site of castle or old house.

Held by the MacNeils. Thomas MacNeil of Creich, who was the then laird, had an argument with Mowat of Freswick in 1427, pursued him to St Duthac's Chapel [NH 786823] at Tain, and then burned down the building with its thatched roof and slaughtered Mowat and his men. MacNeil was captured and executed, and the lands passed to the Murrays,

Taynish [NR 725831], near Tayvallich, Argyll; castle replaced by mansion.

Held by the MacNeils from 1440 along with the island of Gigha from 1493. Torquil MacNeil was also made constable of Castle Sween, which is on the other side of the loch, but this passed by marriage, along with some of the lands, to the MacMillans. The lands were held by the MacNeils well into the eighteenth century, but later passed to the Campbells of Inverneill. The house was gutted by fire, but then restored and has been converted into holiday accommodation (01764 681606; www.aboutscotland.co.uk).

Tirfergus [NR 664184], near Campbeltown, Kintyre, Argyll; site of castle or old house.

Held by the MacNeils of Tirfergus and Lossit.

Ugadale [NR 784285], near Campbeltown, Kintyre, Argyll; ruin of dun and later building.

Held by the Mackays, possibly from the fourteenth century, but passed to the MacNeils about 300 years later, who held Ugadale into the nineteenth century. The Ugadale Brooch is said to have been given to Gilchrist MacKay by Robert the Bruce and then was held by the MacNeils of Ugadale, latterly at Lossit.

www.the-macneils.org.uk
www.clanmacneilusa.net
www.clanmacneilincanada.ca
No. of castles/sites: 14
Rank: 104=/764
Xrefs: MacNeill; Neill; Neilson

MacNeish

Loch Earn

The name comes from 'son of Angus or Naos', and so has the same origin as MacInnes and MacAngus. The clan held lands in Strathearn, and are on record from the fifteenth century.

Loch Earn Castle or **Ellanrayne Castle** [NN 690243] was once a strong place but is now quite ruinous. It stands on an island in Loch Earn near St Fillans, and was a property of the MacNeishes. The MacNabs and the MacNeishes fought at the Battle of Glenboltachan in 1522, and the MacNeishes were defeated and sorely pressed. The MacNeishes survived by raiding neighbouring clans. In 1612 the MacNabs climbed the mountains with a boat, rowed out to the island, and slew the chief of the MacNeishes and many of his people. The MacNeishes never recovered from the slaughter.

No. of castles/sites: 1
Rank: 537=/764
Xref: Neish

MacNicol

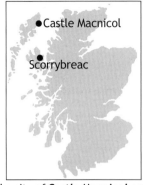

The name comes from 'son of Nicol', a Norse personal name, and the clan held lands on both Lewis and on Skye, as well as in other parts of Scotland. Many of the MacNicols changed their name to Nicolson (also see Nicolson), and this surname is still common in the north of Skye. The site of **Castle Macnicol** or **Stornoway Castle** [NB 423327] is under the pier in Stornoway harbour on Lewis and this was the original stronghold of the MacNicols, who held the island of Lewis from an early date. The island passed to the MacLeods in the fourteenth century by forcible marriage to a MacNicol heiress, but some stories have Leod, a Viking, seizing the castle from the MacNicols; both are possible, of course. The castle had an eventful history before being destroyed in the middle of the seventeenth century by Cromwell's forces. **Scorrybreac** [NG 487439] lies to the east of Portree on the island of Skye, and was for centuries the seat of the MacNicols. The clan may have been given Scorrybreac after fighting at the Battle of Largs in 1263; James V is believed to have spent a night at Scorrybreac in 1540. The MacNicols did not come out for the Jacobites, although some of the clan fought at the Battle of Culloden in 1746. The last chief sold to the lands to the MacDonalds at the beginning of the nineteenth century. The chiefs were buried at Skeabost [NG 418485] on an island (with a bridge) in the River Snizort, and there is a footpath along the coast from Scorrybreac.

www.clanmacnicol.org
www.clanmacnicolcanada.com / www.clanmacnicol.com
No. of castles/sites: 2 / Rank: 396=/764
Xrefs: MacNeacail; Nicolson

MacNiven

The name is from Gaelic and means 'son of the holy one', from 'Mac Naoimh'. The MacNivens were associated with the MacNaughtons, and later were dependent on the Campbells. MacNiven (or NicNiven) appears to have been a traditional name for witches and Kate MacNiven was the Witch of Monzie. **Dunachton Castle** [NH 820047] stood some five miles east and north of Kingussie in the Highlands, but nothing is left except a cellar built into the present mansion. The lands were held by the MacNivens, but passed to the Mackintoshes of Torcastle about 1500. The castle was burned out in 1689.

No. of castles/sites: 1 / Rank: 537=/764

Macpherson

The name comes from 'son of the parson', and it is thought that the clan are descended from Murdo Cattanach, a priest from near present-day Kingussie. Ferson is a contraction of Macpherson, and the Macphersons were part of Clan Chattan, and held lands in and around Badenoch and Strathspey. These are said to have been given to them by Robert the Bruce on the condition that the clan did their bit to destroy the Comyns. Three of the branches of the clan were from brothers: Kenneth of Cluny; Iain of Pitmain; and Gillies of Invereshie. Clan Chattan and the Camerons had a bitter feud, and this ended up in a rather gladiatorial contest, fought on the North Inch of Perth in the presence of Robert III in 1396. Up to thirty of each clan were chosen to fight to the death to resolve their differences. Clan Chattan 'won', when the last Cameron left alive fled and swam the Tay to escape.

Cluny Castle or **Cluny Macpherson** [NN 645942] lies some five miles or south south-west of Newtonmore in Strathspey, and there was a stronghold here of the Macphersons, which dated from the fourteenth century. Euan Macpherson of Cluny was one of the leaders of the Jacobite Rising of 1745-46. When the Jacobites were withdrawing from Derby and returning north, he defeated a large force of Hanoverian troops at Clifton Moor in Cumbria. After the Jacobites were defeated, Macpherson hid in a cave known as 'Cluny's Cage' (two miles north-east of the castle), constructed from trees and brushwood. Macpherson eventually managed to escape from Scotland in 1755, but died soon afterwards in France. The castle had been sacked and razed by the army of the Duke of Cumberland, and the present clan chief apparently lives at Newton Castle near Blairgowrie in Perthshire. The fate of the family is said to have rested with a black pipe chanter, believed, by some, to have fallen from heaven. The Clan Macpherson Museum, on the High Street of Newtonmore, is open from April to October (01540 673332); the clan gathering is held in Newtonmore each August. The present Cluny Castle is a nineteenth-century mansion and stands on the site of the old stronghold.

The Macphersons also held:
Balavil House [NH 791027], near Kingussie, Strathspey, Highland; castle replaced by mansion.
> Held by the Macphersons, and home of James Macpherson, who became famous (and infamous) for the translation (or creation) of the poems of Ossian from Gaelic into English in the 1760s, although he had used much old material. Balavil is now apparently held by the Macpherson-Fletchers and serviced accommodation is available (01828 633383; www.scottscastles.com).
Ballindalloch Castle [NJ 178365], near Charlestown of Aberlour, Moray; fine Z-plan tower house.
> Held by the Ballindallochs, but was built by the Grants, then later passed to the Macphersons, now the Macpherson-Grants.

The castle is open to the public from Easter to September (01807 500206; www.ballindallochcastle.co.uk).

Benchar [NN 705989], near Newtonmore, Strathspey, Highland; site of castle or old house.

Held by the Gordons of Huntly, then by the Mackintoshes and by the Macphersons, who have a burial enclosure in the cemetery.

Gartincaber House [NN 698001], near Doune, Stirlingshire; mansion incorporating old work.

Held by the Buchanans, but passed to the Macphersons in the eighteenth century, then went to others.

Invereshie House [NH 841050], near Kingussie, Strathspey, Highland; mansion incorporating old work.

Held by the Macphersons from the fourteenth century. William Macpherson of Invereshie captured Blair Castle for the Marquis of Montrose in 1644. The property later passed to the Macpherson-Grants, and accommodation is available (01540 651332; www.kincraig.com/invereshiehouse).

Loch Laggan Castle [NN 498875], Loch Laggan, Highland; site of castle.

Held by the Macphersons and used as a hunting lodge. The mansion house of **Ardverikie** [NN 508876], built in 1840 by the Hamilton Marquis of Abercorn, was visited by Queen Victoria in 1847. It was used in the BBC series *Monarch of the Glen*. Accommodation is available and the gardens are occasionally open to the public (01528 544322; www.ardverikie.com).

Loch a' Phearsain [NM 855135], near Kilmelford, Argyll; fortified island.

Said to have been occupied by an outlaw called Macpherson in the seventeenth century.

Mains of Mulben [NJ 353512], near Keith, Moray; mansion incorporating tower house.

Held by the Grants but later passed to the Macphersons. The house is still occupied and is used as a farm.

Newton Castle [NO 172453], Blairgowrie, Perthshire; fine Z-plan tower house.

Long held by the Drummonds, but passed to the Macphersons of Cluny Macpherson, who still apparently live here.

Pitmain House [NH 760006], Kingussie, Strathspey, Highland; site of castle or old house.

Held by the Macphersons from the fourteenth century. The present building houses part of the Highland Folk Museum, and the Macphersons of Pitmain now apparently live in Duror of Appin in Argyll.

www.clan-macpherson.org
www.clan-macpherson.ca
No. of castles/sites: 11
Rank: 127=/764
Xrefs: Cattanach; Chattan; Ferson

Newton Castle (M&R)

MacQuarrie

The name comes from Gaelic, and means 'son of Guaire', an old personal name which meant 'noble or proud', and the clan are said to have a similar origin to the MacKinnons. The MacQuarries were long associated with the island of Ulva, which nestles off the west coast of the Isle of Mull in the Western Isles.

Dun Ban or **Glackingdaline Castle** [NM 384416] lies in the narrow channel between the isles of Ulva and Gometra, and stands on an islet with steep slopes. There is the ruin of a small rectangular building on the summit. The island was held by the MacQuarries from 1473, and probably from much earlier. The clan fought at the Battle of Bannockburn in 1314, and the MacQuarries supported the attempts of the MacDonalds to re-establish the Lords of the Isles in 1545. The chief was one of those seized on ship off Aros Castle on Mull and then imprisoned, before signing the Bond and Statutes of Iona in 1608. The clan fought at the Battle of Inverkeithing in 1651, when the chief and many of his folk were slain; and the Battle of Culloden in 1746, when many of the clan were also killed: a stone at the battlefield marks their burial place. The chiefs of the MacQuarries had a house [NM 442389] near the present **Ulva House**, although the site is now occupied by a farm steading, but the chiefs got into debt and had to sell the lands in the eighteenth century. The island can be visited (www.ulva.mull.com).

One of the family became Governor of New South Wales from 1809-1821, and he returned to Mull and purchased the Gruline estate, and built the Macquarie Mausoleum [NM 549399], three miles south of Salen on Mull. The mausoleum is in the care of the National Trust of Australia.

www.albanach.org/macquarrie/
members.tripod.com/~clanmacquarrie/
No. of castles/sites: 1
Rank: 537=/764
Xref: MacCreary

MacQuillan

The name means 'son of Colin' from Gaelic, and the clan are said to have been brought to Scotland by the O'Donnells of Tirconnel in the fifteenth century as good warriors. They are, however, mentioned earlier.

Dunaverty Castle [NR 688074] was located eight miles south of Campbeltown at the far south of the Mull of Kintyre in Argyll. This was once a strong and important castle on a promontory above the sea, but virtually nothing survives. An ancient stronghold of Dalriada, Dunaverty was captured and burnt on more than one occasion. It was garrisoned against the Vikings before the Battle of Largs in 1263, when it was held by the MacQuillans. It passed to the MacDonald Lords of the Isles, and was besieged several times until it was dismantled in the seventeenth century after the garrison had been slaughtered by a Covenanter army in 1647.

No. of castles/sites: 1
Rank: 537=/764

Macrae

The name comes from Gaelic, and probably means 'son of grace or prosperity'. The clan may first have been established at Clunes near Beauly in Inverness-shire, but then became settled in Kintail in Wester Ross in the fourteenth century. They were keepers of the Mackenzie castle of Eilean Donan and Chamberlains of Kintail.

Inverinate [NG 910225] is a couple of miles north of Shiel Bridge in Kintail, and was held by the Macraes, who were keepers of **Eilean Donan Castle** [NG 881259] for the Mackenzies from 1509. Eilean Donan was besieged by Donald Gorm MacDonald in 1539, a claimant to the Lordship of the Isles, but he was killed by an arrow shot from the castle by Duncan Macrae of Kintail. Eilean Donan was destroyed by gunpowder in the 1719 Rising, but was rebuilt and restored in the twentieth century. It is in a very picturesque place and is an interesting building; Eilean Donan is open in the summer (01599 555202; www.eileandonancastle.com).

Conchra [NG 885278] is three and a half miles east of Auchtertyre near Dornie in Lochalsh, and the present mansion dates from about 1760. The property was also held by the Macraes. Iain Mor Macrae of Conchra, chief of the clan, was slain along with many of his folk at the Battle of Sheriffmuir in 1715. The next rising was four years later, but Eilean Donan Castle was destroyed and the Jacobites were defeated at Glenshiel. The Macraes did not come out for Bonnie Prince Charlie in 1745, although members of the clan fought for the Jacobites at Culloden the following year. Conchra House was the seat of the MacRaes, and is now a hotel (01599 555233; www.conchrahouse.co.uk).

Clunes or **Muir of Clunes** [NH 554414], three and a half miles south-east of Beauly in Inverness-shire, was long held by the Macraes, and there was probably a castle.

There was a castle and then a mansion at **Ochiltree** [NS 510212] in Ayrshire, but these have both gone. The lands were held by several families before coming to the Macraes in 1737; James MacRae, who had been born at Ochiltree, had been Governor of Madras in 1725. He left the property to a family he adopted called the MacGuires, although the house was demolished in the middle of the twentieth century.

Houston House [NS 412672], one mile east and north of Bridge of Weir in Renfrewshire, dates from the eighteenth century but replaced an old castle. The property was held by the Stewarts of Lennox but was also bought by James Macrae and then later went to the Speirs of Elderslie in 1782.

Pitcon Castle [NS 299506] is also in Ayrshire, a mile north and east of Dalry, and was replaced by a mansion in the eighteenth century. Pitcon was owned by the Boyds but was sold to the Macraes in the 1770s.

www.clanmacrae.org
www.macrae.org
www.clanmacrae.ca
www.clanmacrae.org.au
No. of castles/sites: 7
Rank: 182=/764
Xref: MacRae

Macredie

The Macredies came from Ireland, and Andrew Macredie was Provost of Stranraer at the beginning of the eighteenth century.

Perceton or **Pierston House** [NS 354406] is two or so miles east and north of Irvine in Ayrshire. The present mansion dates from the eighteenth century, but there was a castle here and nearby there is also a moated site, dating from the twelfth century. The lands were long held by the Barclays, but the property was bought by the Macredies in 1720, but then later passed to the Mures. There are the remains of an old church [NS 351406], which was used as a burial place for the Macredies and Mures of Perceton. The present mansion is the headquarters of North Ayrshire Council.

No. of castles/sites: 1
Rank: 537=/764
Xref: Macreadie

Skipness Castle (M&R) – see next column (MacSween)

MacSween

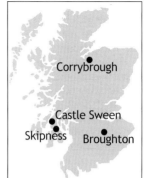

The name comes from 'son of Sueno or Sween', 'Sween' being an old Norse personal name, although it may be derived from 'son of Suibne', a Gaelic name which means 'well-going' or 'good-going'. The name can be spelt either Mac-Queen (the 'q' can be a 'w' sound) or MacSween. The clan claim descent from the Irish High Kings, and they held lands in Argyll and then in Strathearn near Tomatin. They were part of Clan Chattan, and are said to have settled at Corrybrough after escorting a the daughter of Clan Ranald when she was to be married to one of the Mackintoshes.

Castle Sween [NR 712789] is ten or so miles north-west of Tarbert (although much further by road), and stands on the shore of Loch Sween. The castle dates from the twelfth century, when this part of Scotland

Castle Sween (M&R)

was still under Norse rule, and is named after Sueno or Sween, who was Lord of Knapdale. The castle was held by the MacSweens until the middle of the thirteenth century, and then passed to other clans and families. Castle Sween is a fine ruin with an impressive walled courtyard with ruinous ranges of building, and is in the care of Historic Scotland and is open to the public.

Skipness Castle [NR 907577] is seven miles to the south of Tarbert, and is located on the east side of Kintyre overlooking the Isle of Arran. It is an impressive and well-preserved stronghold with a strong wall and tower house. The first stronghold here was built by the MacSweens around 1247, but Skipness passed to the MacDonald Lords of the Isles and then to the Campbells. The castle is also in the care of Historic Scotland and is open to the public.

Corrybrough [NH 818295] is a mile east of Tomatin by the River Findhorn near Inverness, and was held by the MacQueens from the sixteenth century or earlier. They joined Clan Chattan and were known as Clan Revan. The chiefs eventually emigrated to New Zealand, and the lands were sold by the nineteenth century. Corrybrough is now a sporting estate and accommodation is available (01738 451600; www.sport.ckdfh.co.uk/corrybrough.htm).

Broughton Place [NT 117372], five miles east of Biggar in the Borders, appears to be a tower house, but was actually built in 1938 and designed by the famous architect Basil Spence. There was, however, a tower house, some of which may be incorporated into the present building. It was held by the Murrays of Broughton, but passed to Robert Macqueen, Lord Braxfield, around 1755. He was a famous judge and was employed by the Crown after the forfeiture of many Jacobite supporters following the 1745-46 Rising. He also gained a fearsome reputation for his heavy sentencing of criminals, and he presided at the trial of Thomas Muir and other radicals in 1793. The house has a gallery (01899 830234; www.broughtongallery.co.uk).

No. of castles/sites: 4
Rank: 278=/764
Xrefs: MacQueen

MacWhirter

The name comes from Gaelic, and means the 'son of (the) harper'. The name is on record from the middle of the fourteenth century, when David II granted some land to Patrick, the son of Michael, harper of Carrick. This property soon passed to the Kennedys.

●Blairquhan

Blairquhan [NS 367055] is seven miles south-east of Maybole in the south part of Ayrshire, and is now a large castellated mansion, dating from the 1820s. This new house replaced an old stronghold, one part of which was called McWhurter's Tower, which dated from the fourteenth century, but this was demolished along with a range of 1573. The property passed to the Kennedys in the fifteenth century, then to the Whitefoords and then to the Hunter Blairs, who still apparently own it. The castle is open to the public in the summer (01655 770239; www.blairquhan.co.uk).

www.macwhirter.com
www.mcwherter.com
No. of castles/sites: 1
Rank: 537=/764
Xrefs: MacWhurter; MacChruiter

Main

The name could have several origins, including from the area of France called 'Maine', from the personal name 'Mayne', or in the northern parts of Scotland from a diminutive for 'Magnus'. The name is on record from the fifteenth century.

Lochwood

Bishop's House, Lochwood [NS 692666] was a few miles north-west of Coatbridge in central Scotland, but there are no remains. As the name suggests, it was owned by the Bishops and Archbishops of Glasgow and was used as a hunting lodge. They are said to have linked the Molendinar burn, Hogganfield, Frankfield and Bishops lochs with a canal system so that they could sail here by barge from Glasgow Castle near the cathedral. The lands passed to the Main family after the Reformation.

No. of castles/sites: 1
Rank: 537=/764
Xrefs: Mayne; Mann

Mair

The name comes from the office of crier or herald for the king, or king's sergeant. The surname is on record from the thirteenth century.

Wyseby

Wyseby [NY 241724] is four miles north-east of Annan in Dumfries and Galloway, and the present house dates from the end of the eighteenth century, but stands on the site of a castle or old house. The lands were held by the Mair family, and the house is still occupied.

No. of castles/sites: 1
Rank: 537=/764

Maitland

The name has been interpreted as a nickname meaning 'bad wit' or poor wit', although some have seen this as unlikely. The family are probably descended from one of the companions of William the Conqueror, and the name is found in England in the twelfth and thirteenth centuries. The Maitlands are recorded in Scotland from 1227.

Old Thirlestane Castle [NT 564474] was the original stronghold of the family and dates from the middle of the thirteenth century, or perhaps earlier. It stands two miles to the east of Lauder in the Borders, but little remains. The Maitlands moved to the present Thirlestane Castle (see below) in around 1595, but they also owned Lethington, which is now known as Lennoxlove.

Lennoxlove or **Lethington Castle** [NT 515721] is a fine L-plan castle, dating from the fourteenth century, but with later extensions and remodelling. It stands just to the south of Haddington in East Lothian, and was

Lennoxlove (M&R)

known as Lethington for most of its history. It was originally a property of the Giffords but was sold to the Maitlands around 1350. William Maitland of Lethington and Thirlestane was slain at the Battle of Flodden in 1513, and the castle was burnt by the English in 1549. Sir Richard Maitland of Lethington was a Lord of Session and Keeper of the Privy Seal, and his son, William, secretary to Mary, Queen of Scots, lived here. He was involved in the plot to murder Lord Darnley and fought against Mary at the Battle of Langside in 1568, but then secretly supported her after she had fled to England. He was taken prisoner after Edinburgh Castle was captured in 1573 and died, possibly having been

poisoned, soon afterwards. Sir John, William's brother, was Keeper of the Privy Seal in 1567, and was made a Lord of Session in 1581 and then Chancellor in 1587; he was created Lord Thirlestane three years later. The property was sold to the Stewart Lord Blantyre in the eighteenth century, during whose ownership the name was changed, then it went to the Bairds and then to the Dukes of Hamilton in 1947, who still own it. Among the treasures it contains are the death mask of Mary, Queen of Scots, and the casket which may have contained the 'Casket Letters'. The castle has just been renovated and is open to the public (01620 823720; www.lennox love.org).

Thirlestane Castle [NT 540473], which is close to Lauder in the Borders, is a magnificent castle and mansion, and is a very imposing edifice. It dates from the sixteenth century, but was extended in 1670 by the well-known architect Sir William Bruce, and there are fine plaster ceilings. The present castle was built by Sir John Maitland, James VI's chancellor, but it was John Maitland, Duke of Lauderdale, a very powerful man in Scotland, who had the house remodelled. Lauderdale was Secretary of State for Scotland from 1661-80, but he was eventually replaced after the Covenanter uprising which ended with their defeat at the Battle of Bothwell Brig. His ghost is said to haunt Thirlestane, as well as St Mary's Church in Haddington where he was buried in 1682; his ghost is described as an important looking man with long curly hair. His intestines and brain were kept in a separate lead urn near his coffin, and on several occasions his coffin was found to have moved around in the burial vault. It was thought that this was because of some supernatural manifestation until it was realised that when the River Tyne was high it flooded the vault.

Bonnie Prince Charlie stayed at Thirlestane Castle in 1745 on his way south. The Maitland Earls of Lauderdale and Viscounts Maitland still flourish and apparently have residences in Edinburgh and in London. Thirlestane Castle is open to the public from April to October (01578 722430; www.thirlestanecastle.co.uk). St Mary's Kirk in Haddington is a large cruciform church with a central tower. The church has a marble monument to John Maitland, Lord Thirlestane and Chancellor of

Thirlestane Castle (M&R)

Scotland, who died in 1595, below which is the Lauderdale family vault, and the church is open to the public at Easter and then from May to September (01620 823109; www.stmaryskirk.com).

The Maitlands also held:

Auchen Castle [NT 063035], near Moffat, Dumfries and Galloway; castle replaced by mansion.

Held by the Kirkpatrick family and others before passing to the Maitlands in the fifteenth century, and then much later went to the Johnstones. They built a new mansion, also called **Auchen Castle** [NT 063047], half a mile to the north, which is now a hotel (01683 300407; www.auchencastle.com).

Auchengassel Castle [NX 826994], near Thornhill, Dumfries and Galloway; site of castle.

Held by the Maitlands in 1582.

Balgreggan [NX 089500], near Stranraer, Dumfries and Galloway; site of castle and mansion.

Held by the MacDowalls, but Balgreggan House, which has also been demolished, was a property of the Maitlands in the nineteenth century.

Balmungo [NO 523148], near St Andrews, Fife; site of castle or old house.

Held by the Pringles and then by other families including by the Maitlands.

Brunstane Castle [NT 201582], near Penicuik, Midlothian; ruinous L-plan tower house.

Held by the Crichtons, and then by the Maitlands from 1632, and they extended the castle.

Brunstane House [NT 316725], Edinburgh; altered L-plan tower house.

Held by the Crichtons, and then by John Maitland, later Duke

Brunstane House (M&R)

of Lauderdale, from 1632 to 1733 when it was sold. The house has been divided but is still occupied.

Clifton Hall [NT 109710], near Broxburn, West Lothian; castle replaced by mansion.

Held by several families before coming to the Gibsons of Pentland in 1761, and they were later the Gibson-Maitland family. The mansion is used as a school.

Cumstoun Castle [NX 683533], near Kirkcudbright, Dumfries and Galloway; castle replaced by mansion.

Held by several families before coming to the Maitlands in the eighteenth century, and the castle was replaced by a nineteenth-century mansion. The Maitlands of Cumstoun and Dundrennan still apparently live here.

Eccles House [NX 848961], near Thornhill, Dumfries and Galloway; mansion incorporating tower house.

Held by the Eccles family, but passed to the Maitlands in the sixteenth century.

Hallbar Tower [NS 839471], near Carluke, Lanarkshire; restored tower house.

Held by the Douglas Earls of Douglas then by the Stewarts of

Gogar before passing to the Maitlands of Thirlestane in the sixteenth century, then soon went to the Douglases and then to the Lockharts of The Lee around 1662. Holiday accommodation is available (0845 090 0194; www.vivat. org.uk).

Hatton House [NT 128687], near Balerno, Edinburgh; site of castle and mansion.

Held by the Hattons and by the Lauders, then by the Maitlands in 1652, who built much of the mansion that was then demolished in the 1950s. The property was sold to the Davidsons of Muirhouse in 1792, then was sold again in 1870.

House of Schivas [NJ 898368], near Ellon, Aberdeenshire; fine altered L-plan tower house.

Held by the Schivas family and then by the Lipps, but passed to the Maitlands in the fifteenth century then to the Gordons in 1467, then to others. The house is still occupied.

Inveresk Lodge [NT 348716], near Musselburgh, East Lothian; L-plan tower house.

Held by the Maitlands of Thirlestane after the Reformation, but was sold to the Scotts of Buccleuch in 1709 and then went to others. The gardens are open to the public (01721 722502; www.nts.org.uk).

Kilmaron Castle [NO 357162], near Cupar, Fife; site of mansion. Held latterly by the Maitlands. Demolished in the twentieth century.

Lundin Tower [NO 399029], near Lower Largo, Fife; tower remains from mansion and castle.

Held by the Lundins, then passed by marriage to the Maitlands, but they changed their name to Lundin. It later passed by marriage to the Drummonds and then the Gilmours. The castle was replaced by Lundin House but this was demolished except for a stair-turret in 1876.

Old Sauchie [NS 779883], near Stirling; ruinous L-plan tower house. Held by the Erskines and by the Ramsays, then from 1865 by Sir Alexander Gibson-Maitland.

Scotscraig [NO 445283], near Tayport, Fife; castle replaced by mansion.

Held by the several families, but latterly passed to the Maitlands.

Tibbers Castle [NX 863982], near Thornhill, Dumfries and Galloway; slight remains of castle.

Held by the Siwards, but passed to the Dunbar Earls of March, then to the Maitlands of Auchen in 1489, and then to the Douglases of Drumlanrig in 1592. Stands in the grounds of Drumlanrig Castle.

Whitslaid Tower [NT 557446], near Lauder, Borders; ruinous tower house.

Held by the Maitlands, but by the mid seventeenth century passed to the Montgomerys of Macbiehill.

www.clanmaitland.org.uk
www.lauderdale.u-net.com
No. of castles/sites: 22
Rank: 58=/764

Hallbar Tower (M&R) – see prev. column

Makgill

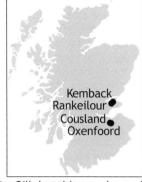

The name comes from 'Mac an Gall', meaning 'son of the stranger', and is recorded in Scotland from the thirteenth century. The family originally held lands in Galloway, but they moved north and acquired property in Fife and in Midlothian. The name was originally spelt MacGill, but this was changed to Makgill at an early date.

Three miles to the west of Cupar in Fife was **Rankeilour Castle** [NO 330119], although there are no remains of the stronghold mentioned in 1540; a mansion was built on the site in the nineteenth century. The property was owned by the Rankeillours, then by the Sibbalds of Balgonie and then by the Makgills. Sir James Makgill was a Lord of Session and took the title Lord Rankeillour. He was one of the Privy Councillors to Mary, Queen of Scots, but was involved in the murder of Rizzio and fell out of favour. After she was imprisoned in England, he was one of those that brought accusations against Mary and was then ambassador to England. The property passed to the Hopes. Rankeilour House, a mansion dating from the beginning of the nineteenth century, was built by the fourth Earl of Hopetoun.

Oxenfoord Castle or **Nether Cranston Riddel** [NT 388656], some three or so miles east and south of Dalkeith in Midlothian, is an impressive Adam mansion, built in the 1780s and later enlarged, but incorporating

Oxenfoord Castle (1925?)

an L-plan tower house from the sixteenth century. The lands were held by the Riddels, but passed to the Makgills in the twelfth century. David Makgill of Oxenfoord was King's Advocate in 1582; and the family were made Viscounts Oxfuird in 1661. The lands and titles passed to the Dalrymples of Stair in 1760, and from 1931 the mansion was used as a school, although this closed in 1984. The gardens are occasionally open to the public (www.gardensofscotland.org).

Cousland Tower [NT 377683], also near Dalkeith, is a very ruinous tower house, dating from the sixteenth century. The tower was burnt after the Battle of Pinkie in 1547, and passed from the Sinclairs of Rosslyn to the Makgills in the seventeenth century; Cousland then went to the Dalrymples of Stair. This branch of the family succeeded to the properties of the Makgills of Oxenfoord, becoming Hamilton-Dalrymple-MacGill.

Kemback House [NO 418155] is three and a half miles east of Cupar in Fife, and is an eighteenth-century mansion, although it replaced an older house or castle. Kemback was held by the Schivas family, but passed to the Makgills in the late seventeenth century, and they held it until 1906.

Old Lindores Castle [NO 264168] was located two miles south-east of Newburgh also in Fife, but again there are no remains; the property was also owned by the Makgills.

Rumgally House [NO 407149], also to the east of Cupar, incorporates an L-plan tower house, and has a round tower. The lands were held by the Scotts of Balwearie, then by the Wemyss family, but belonged to James Makgill, minister of Largo, in 1658. Accommodation is available (01334 653388; www.sol.co.uk/r/rumgally/).

No. of castles/sites: 6
Rank: 212=/764
Xrefs: Macgill; MacGill

Malcolm

The name comes from MacCallum or 'Mac Gille Chaluim', which means 'son of the servant or disciple of Columba'. Alternatively, Malcolm could be translated as 'Maol Chaluim', where 'maol' means bald or shaven, in this case as a tonsure. So the name would be from the 'monk or tonsured one of Columba'. It could also be that Malcolm was a personal name which was then used as a surname: four kings of Scots were called Malcolm. The spelling Malcolm, however, was not apparently used by the family until the eighteenth century. Ronald MacCallum was made constable of Craignish Castle in 1414, and the clan held lands in Argyll and then in Fife.

Poltalloch [NR 814965] is two or so miles south and west of Kilmartin in mid Argyll, and the lands were held by the Campbells but were granted to the Malcolms in 1562. The clan seems to have done little of note, at least as far as getting involved in battles and feuds. There was a castle or older house, but the present Poltalloch House dates from 1830, although it has been stripped and is now a shell. Members of the family are buried at Kilmartin [NR 834988], where there is a good number of carved slabs and an old stone cross in the church.

Duntrune Castle [NR 794956] is not far from Poltalloch and is in a lovely spot on the north side of Loch Crinan. The castle was built in the thirteenth century, and a wall encloses a courtyard with a later L-plan tower house. The buildings were remodelled in the eighteenth century and again in the 1830. The property was long held by the Campbells, but was sold to the Malcolms of Poltalloch in 1792 and they still apparently own the castle. Duntrune is said to have a

phantom piper, and holiday cottages are available on the estate (01546 510283; www.duntrune.com).

Balbedie [NT 198995] lies in Fife, some four miles north of Lochgelly, but little remains of a castle or old house, which was built in the seventeenth century or earlier. Previously held by the Colvilles, the lands had passed to the Malcolms by 1612. John Malcolm of Balbedie was Chamberlain of Fife in the seventeenth century, and his son, Sir John, was made a Baronet of Nova Scotia in 1665. The Malcolms of Balbedie, Baronets, now apparently live in Surrey in England.

Lochore Castle [NT 175959] is a ruinous fourteenth-century keep and courtyard, and formerly stood on an island in a loch. Lochore was held by the Wardlaws of Torrie before the lands came to the Malcolms of Balbedie. The area was destroyed by mining but was restored and landscaped, and the lands are now a public park (01592 414300).

www.Clan-MacCallum-Malcolm.3acres.org
No. of castles/sites: 4
Rank: 278=/764
Xref: MacCallum

Duntrune Castle (M&R)

Marjoribanks

The name is pronounced 'Marchbanks', and may come from lands in Annandale or elsewhere, or possibly from lands given as dowry on the marriage of Marjorie, daughter of Robert the Bruce, which the became known as Marjoriebanks. This latter explanation seem less likely than a simple mis-spelling. The lands in Annandale,

three miles south of Moffat, which were held by the Marjoribanks family are now known as Marchbank.

Marjoribanks (now **Marchbank**) [NY 077998] was held by Thomas Marjoribank of that Ilk. He was made Lord Provost of Edinburgh in 1540, and in 1549 became a judge, with the title Lord Ratho, from other lands he held.

Balbardie House [NS 975695] was a fine classical mansion, dating from 1793 and designed by Robert Adam, but it was demolished in 1955 due to subsidence. The mansion stood to the north of Bathgate in West Lothian, and the lands were bought by the Marjoribanks in 1624. Christian Marjoribanks married George Heriot 'Jingling Geordie', who founded the famous school in Edinburgh. Andrew Marjoribanks of Balbardie was an eminent lawyer and Writer to the King in 1716. The property was sold in 1869.

The following properties were also held by the family:
Bathgate Castle [NS 981680], Bathgate, West Lothian; earthworks survive from castle.
   The property was held by the Marjoribanks family in the eighteenth century.
Carlowrie Castle [NT 142744], near Kirkliston, West Lothian; site of mansion and older house.
   Held by the Dalziels of Carlowrie, but passed to the Marjoribanks family in the eighteenth century, then to the Falconers and then to the Hutchinsons.

Craigcrook Castle (M&R)

Craigcrook Castle [NT 211742], Edinburgh; extended tower house.
   Held by the Grahams, then later by the Marjoribanks family in the sixteenth century, then by the Adamsons and by others. The building is now used as offices for *Scottish Field* (0131 312 4550; www.scottishfield.co.uk).
Hallyards [NT 129738], near Kirkliston, West Lothian; ruinous tower house.
   Held by the Skenes and by the Erskines before being bought by the Marjoribanks family in 1696.
Leuchie House [NT 572833], near North Berwick, East Lothian; mansion on site of older house.
   Held by the Marjoribanks family in the early part of the seventeenth century, or perhaps before that, but was sold to the Dalrymples in 1701 (www.leuchie.com).
Northfield House [NT 389739], Prestonpans, East Lothian; fine L-plan tower house.
   Held by the Hamiltons, but passed to Joseph Marjoribanks, an

Northfield House (M&R)

Edinburgh merchant, in 1611; Northfield was sold to the Nisbets in 1746.

www3.sympatico.ca/mjbnks/
No. of castles/sites: 8
Rank: 160=/764
Xref: Marchbanks

Marshall

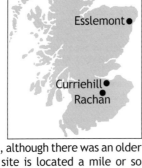

The name means 'horse servant', and comes from French. It was an important office at one time, but it also came to mean a simple groom. The name is on record in Scotland from the twelfth century.

Castle of Esslemont [NJ 932298] is a very ruinous L-plan tower house, although there was an older stronghold here, and the site is located a mile or so west and south of Ellon in Aberdeenshire in the northeast of Scotland. Esslemont was owned by the Marshalls in the twelfth century, but passed by marriage to the Cheynes.

Curriehill Castle [NT 165678], a mile north of Balerno, has gone, but was held by several families, including John Marshall, Lord Curriehill.

Rachan [NT 122345], five miles east of Biggar in the Borders, was held by the Geddes family and by the Tweedies before coming to the Marshall family in 1897. There was an older house which was replaced in the middle of the nineteenth century by a new mansion, but this was demolished in the 1950s. **Kittlehall** [NT 113337], close by and five miles south-east of Biggar in the Borders, is the site of the tower house. Kittlehall was also a property of the Geddeses of Rachan and then of the Tweedies before passing to the Marshall family in 1897. The Marshalls of Rachan now apparently own **Baddingsgill** [NT 131549], which is a couple of miles north-west of West Linton, also in the Borders.

No. of castles/sites: 5
Rank: 240=/764

Martin

The name may have come from one of three origins. One is simply from the personal name 'Martin'; another a contraction of the name 'St Martin', a family which apparently once held lands in East Lothian; and the third is from a contraction of 'MacMartin'. The name is on record in Scotland from the end of the twelfth century. Martin Martin, the factor to the MacLeods, wrote *Voyage to St Kilda* in 1698 and *Description of the Western Isles* five years later.

Carden Tower [NT 226937], one mile south and east of Cardenden in Fife, was once a place of some strength and importance, but very little is left of an L-plan tower house, which dated from the sixteenth century. The lands were held by the Martin family from 1482 or earlier, and they built the tower. Carden passed to the Wemyss family in 1623, and then to others. The site had been cleared and conserved, and is accessible.

No. of castles/sites: 1
Rank: 537=/764
Xref: MacMartin

Mathers

The name apparently comes from the place Mathers, which is six miles north and east of Montrose in the old county of Kincardineshire. The name is on record from the middle of the fifteenth century.

Kaim of Mathers or **Mathers Castle** [NO 763649] sat on cliffs but little is left of the fifteenth-century stronghold. It is not clear if it was ever owned by the Mathers family; the property was held by the Barclays from 1351.

Provan Hall [NS 667663], three and a half miles west and north of Coatbridge in central Scotland, is a fine courtyard house with a sixteenth-century tower house forming one side, completed by other buildings and a wall with an arched gateway. The lands passed to the Baillies after the Reformation, then passed through several hands until Provan Hall came to Reston Mathers; his ghost is said to haunt the building. The building is managed by the local council and is open to the public (0141 771 4399).

No. of castles/sites: 1
Rank: 537=/764
Xrefs: Matters; Mather

Matheson

The name comes from Gaelic, and means 'son of (the) bear', in Highland and Gaelic-speaking areas, or more prosaically from the 'son of Matthew' in lowland Scotland. The clan is mentioned from the middle of the thirteenth century, and held lands in Lochalsh and in Kintail, before branches moved to Shiness in Sutherland and Bennetsfield on the Black Isle. The Mathesons supported the MacDonald Lords of the Isles and fought for them at the bloody Battle of Harlaw in 1411. The chiefs became associated with the Mackenzies, and Iain Dubh Matheson was slain at the siege of Eilean Donan Castle in 1539. Dugall Matheson of Balmacara was chamberlain of Lochalsh in 1631. Their power diminished after conflict with the MacLeods and then a feud with the MacDonalds of Glengarry, and their lands passed to the Mackenzies. The line of the chiefs went through the Mathesons of Bennetsfield.

Later Mathesons prospered, however, and in 1844 Sir James Matheson purchased Lewis and Great Bernera in the Outer Hebrides. Matheson, son of Donald Matheson of Shiness, had helped found Jardine, Matheson and Company, a business established in Canton and Hong Kong for trading in tea. The islands were sold to Lord Leverhulme in 1918. The Mathesons of Matheson, Baronets of Lochalsh since 1851 and the chiefs of the clan, apparently now live in Norfolk in England.

The Mathesons held the following properties:

Ardross Castle [NH 611741], near Alness, Ross and Cromarty; mansion incorporating older work.
   Held by the Munros, but passed to the Mathesons, then in 1880 went to the Perrins family, one of the owners of the Lea and Perrins company.

Attadale [NG 925391], near Strathcarron, Ross and Cromarty; old house replaced by mansion.
   Held by the Mathesons from 1730 to the 1880s, and they did much to improve the estate and were influential in getting the railway from Inverness built. Subsequent owners developed the gardens, which are open to the public (01520 722603; www.attadale.com).

Balmacara [NG 800277], near Kyle of Lochalsh, Highland; old house replaced by mansion.
   Held by the Mathesons, possibly from the ninth century. The lands later passed to the Mackenzies, and then to the Hamiltons. The gardens here are in the care of The National Trust for Scotland and the estate is open to the public (01599 566325).

Bennetsfield [NH 678536], near Munlochy, Ross and Cromarty; site of castle or old house.
   Held by the Mathesons from the end of the seventeenth century, and they became chiefs. John Matheson, second of Bennetsfield, fought for the Jacobites at the Battle of Culloden in 1746, although most of his clan were Hanoverians, but he managed to escape punishment. Members of the family are buried in the old graveyard [NH 664546] near Easter Suddie.

Brahan Castle [NH 513549], near Dingwall, Ross and Cromarty; site of castle and mansion.
   Long held by the Mackenzies, but the Mathesons of Brahan apparently live at Brahan.

Lews Castle [NB 419335], Stornoway, Lewis, Outer Hebrides; mansion on site of old house.
   The island was held by the MacLeods then by the Mackenzies, but was sold to Sir James Matheson in 1844 and the family built Lews Castle on the site of **Seaforth Lodge**. The property was sold to Lord Leverhulme in 1918 and the grounds of Lews Castle are now a public park (www.lews-castle.com).

Shiness [NC 539143], near Lairg, Sutherland; site of castle or old house.
   Held by the Mathesons from the fifteenth century, and they were baillies to the Earls of Sutherland. Donald Matheson of Shiness fought against the Jacobites in the Rising of 1715. The chiefs got into debt, and the property passed to the Dukes of Sutherland in 1809. As mentioned above, Sir James Matheson, son of Donald Matheson of Shiness, founded Jardine, Matheson and Company, which traded tea from China, and Matheson made a fortune. Matheson bought Lewis and Great Bernera in 1844, although these were sold to Lord Leverhulme in 1918.

www.clanmatheson.org
No. of castles/sites: 7
Rank: 182=/764
Xref: MacMathan

Maule

Edzell
Brechin
Panmure

The name comes from the place Maule in France, and the family were Norman in origin, having come to England with William the Conqueror and secured lands in Yorkshire. They arrived in Scotland in the reign of David I in the twelfth century. The Maules first held lands in Midlothian, but came to prominence in Angus.

Panmure Castle [NO 546376] was once a strong courtyard castle, rhomboid in plan, with corner towers, as well as having a hall and a chapel. It stood two or so miles north of Carnoustie in Angus, and was still in use in the middle of the seventeenth century. The stronghold was replaced by **Panmure House** [NO 537386], which was rebuilt in the middle of the nineteenth century, but this building has been demolished except for the stables.

The lands passed by marriage to the Maules about 1224. The castle was held by the English in the Wars of Independence, but was recaptured by the Scots in 1306. It may have been abandoned for many years, but had been rebuilt before 1487. Sir Thomas Maule of Panmure was killed at the Battle of Harlaw in 1411, while his grandson, another Sir Thomas, was slain at the Battle of Flodden in 1513. Patrick Maule was made Earl of Panmure in 1633, and George Maule, his son, fought for the Royalists at the battles of Dunbar in 1650 and then at Inverkeithing the following year, where he was wounded. James, fourth Earl, proclaimed James VII king, and fought for the Jacobites at the Sheriffmuir in 1715, and was wounded and captured. Harry Maule, one of the most successful Jacobite leaders, rescued James and they fled to the Continent. The Maules were forfeited but later recovered their titles. The Maules had a burial vault at Panbride Parish Church, which was built by George, third Earl of Panmure, in 1681.

Brechin Castle [NO 597599] is to the west of Brechin also in Angus, and the mansion incorporates some of an L-plan tower house, dating from the sixteenth century,

Brechin Castle 1905?

although there was a stronghold from early times. John Balliol, 'Toom Tabard', was forced to abdicate as King of Scots here by Edward I of England in 1296. Sir Thomas Maule defended the castle for three weeks against the English in 1303, but was slain by a missile from a catapult. The castle was held by the Maules, but passed to the Erskine Earl of Mar, until sold back to the Maule Earl of Panmure in 1646; they built the existing mansion in 1711. The family was forfeited for its part in the 1715 Jacobite Rising, but the property was bought back by a relation and the title restored. The property later passed through marriage to the Ramsays of Dalhousie, and Brechin Castle is still apparently occupied by the Earl of Dalhousie; the Ramsays also hold the title Earl of Panmure. Brechin Castle Centre is open to the public and features Pictavia with information and displays on the Picts (01356 626813; www.brechincastle centre.co.uk).

The following castles were also held by the Maules:

Ardestie Castle [NO 505342], near Monifieth, Angus; site of castle.
Held by the Maule Earls of Panmure.

Auchterhouse [NO 332373], near Dundee; mansion incorporating part of castle.
Held by the Ramsays, then by the Stewart Earls of Buchan and Moray, before passing to the Maule Earls of Panmure in 1660, then went to the Ogilvie Earls of Airlie.

Balmossie [NO 476326], near Broughty Ferry, Angus; site of castle.
Held by the Maule Earls of Panmure.

Carmyllie Castle [NO 546432], near Letham, Angus; site of castle.
Held by the Strachans, and then by the Maules of Panmure from 1640.

Edzell Castle [NO 585693], near Brechin, Angus; fine ruinous castle with walled garden.
Long held by the Lindsays, but bought by the Maule Earls of Panmure in 1715, although forfeited by them after the Jacobite Rising of 1745-46. The Maules recovered the property in 1764

Edzell Castle 1910?

but the castle was soon abandoned. In the care of Historic Scotland and open to the public (01356 648631).

Fowlis Castle [NO 321334], near Dundee; altered tower house.
Held by the Maules from 1330, but passed to the Mortimers, and then to the Grays in 1377.

Kellie Castle [NO 608402], near Arbroath, Angus; fine castle.
Held by several families, then from 1679 by the Maule Earls of Panmure. It was lost after the Jacobite Rising of 1715, but was recovered by the Maules, and Kellie is still occupied.

Melgund Castle [NO 546564], near Brechin, Angus; impressive castle.
   Held by the Beatons and by the Gordons in the seventeenth century, before coming to the Maules and then went to the Murrays and then to others.
Pitairlie Castle [NO 502367], near Monifieth, Angus; site of castle.
   Held by the Lindsays, but passed to the Maules in the seventeenth century or later.

No. of castles/sites: 11
Rank: 127=/764

Mawer

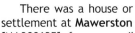

Mawerston

The name comes from the Gaelic 'maor', a steward or lesser officer, and the name is on record from the end of the fifteenth century and was common in Speyside. The family had links to the Gordons.
   There was a house or settlement at **Mawerston** [NJ 300635], four or so miles east of Elgin in Moray, and this property was owned by the family in 1608.

www.maverfamily.com
No. of castles/sites: 1
Rank: 537=/764
Xrefs: Maver; Mavor

Maxtone

Cultoquhey

Auchindinny
Maxton

The name is territorial and comes from the lands and barony of Maxton, which are a mile or so south-east of St Boswells in the Borders. John Maxton, born in Pollokshaws in 1885, was a school teacher who joined the Independent Labour Party. He was imprisoned in 1916 for trying to organise a general strike, and was then an MP from 1922-46.
   The family held lands at **Maxton** [NT 613302] in the twelfth century, but these had passed to the Barclays before the century was out. The Maxtones moved to Perthshire.
   Cultoquhey [NN 893233] is two miles north-east of Crieff in Perthshire, and there was a tower house, which had its own park, in the sixteenth century; the name is pronounced 'Cultoowhey'. The Maxtones held the lands from 1410 or earlier, and Robert Maxtone of Cultoquhey was killed at the Battle of Flodden in 1513. Kate McNiven, who was burnt after being accused of witchcraft, reportedly made a prophecy about the Maxtones: when a 'gleg-eyed' laird was born, a treasure should be found at Cultoquhey.
   The Maxtones have also been credited with the following verse:
   From the greed of the Campbells;
   From the ire of the Drummonds;
   From the pride of the Grahams;
   From the wind of the Murrays;
   Good Lord deliver us.
   The family, later Maxtone Graham, held the property until 1955 when Cultoquhey was sold. The building is now used as a hotel (01764 653253), and the family now apparently live at **Auchindinny House** [NT 252613], one mile north-east of Penicuik in Midlothian. This building is a small mansion with flanking pavilions, designed by Sir William Bruce and dating from about 1705, and it incorporates two vaulted chambers from an earlier castle or house.

No. of castles/sites: 3
Rank: 328=/764
Xref: Maxton

Maxwell

The name is believed to come from 'Maccus Well', a fishing pool on the Tweed near Kelso in the Borders. The 'Maccus' in question seems to have come from England and was granted lands in the twelfth century: the family of Maxton may have sprung from the same source. Sir John Maxwell was Chamberlain of Scotland, and the family were to become major landowners in Dumfries and Galloway, and then in Renfrewshire and in Lanarkshire. John Maxwell, Bishop of Ross and a Privy Councillor, was in 1637 one of those who helped to compile the controversial Prayer Book. He was deprived of office the following year, but went to Ireland where he was made Archbishop of Tuam in 1643.

James Clerk-Maxwell, who was born in Edinburgh in 1831, was a professor of natural law at Aberdeen before moving to King's College in London and then to Cambridge in 1871. He has been described as one of the greatest geniuses of the nineteenth century, and he made many discoveries, including in the fields of physics, electricity and magnetism.

Caerlaverock Castle [NY 026656] is a magnificent ruinous fortress with a water-filled moat. The castle is triangular in shape with a towered gatehouse and fine ranges of buildings around a central courtyard. There are round towers at the two other corners, one of which is known as Murdoch's Tower, called so because Murdoch, second Duke of Albany, was imprisoned in it before being executed in 1425. The lands were held by the Maxwells, and the castle was built by them in the thirteenth century. Caerlaverock was captured by the English in 1300, after a siege by Edward I of England, the event being commemorated in a poem in medieval French 'Le Siege de Kalavreock'. The castle was held by the English until 1312, when the keeper Sir Eustace Maxwell

Caerlaverock Castle (RWB)

joined the Scots. He successfully resisted an English attack, but afterwards slighted the castle. The castle was repaired in the 1330s. Herbert Maxwell submitted to Edward III of England in 1347, and ten years later Roger Kirkpatrick captured the castle for the Scots, although Kirkpatrick was later murdered here. Herbert Maxwell of Caerlaverock was made Lord Maxwell in 1445, and there was further rebuilding of the castle in 1452-88 by Robert, second Lord Maxwell. He added the machicolated parapets to the towers, and remodelled the gatehouse. James V visited the castle before defeat at Solway Moss in 1542; John, fifth Lord Maxwell, was captured by the English at the battle. Caerlaverock was handed over to the English three years later, but was then recaptured by the Scots, only to be taken and slighted by the English in 1570. Sir John Maxwell of Terregles, son of Robert, fifth Lord, commanded the Queen's cavalry at the Battle of Langside in 1568 (see below). The Maxwells had a bitter feud with the Johnstones, and this came to battle in 1593 near Lockerbie and the Maxwells were routed and John Maxwell, eighth Lord and Warden of the West Marches, was slain; the family also feuded with the Douglases over the Earldom of Morton. The eighth Lord, another John, was imprisoned in Edinburgh Castle but managed to escape in 1607. The feud with the Johnstones continued, however, and he was executed in 1612 for murdering the chief of the Johnstones. The castle was remodelled again in 1634, then six years later the Earl eventually had to surrender the castle to Covenanters after a siege of thirteen weeks. Caerlaverock was then reduced by demolishing part of the curtain wall and one corner tower, and unroofing the rest. The Maxwells moved to Terregles, and then to Traquair House (see Stewart). Caerlaverock Castle is now in the care of Historic Scotland and is open to the public (01387 770244).

Terregles Castle [NX 928775] was a few miles west of Dumfries, but both it and the classical mansion built to replace in 1789 have been demolished. The lands were held by the Herries family, but passed by marriage, along with the title Lord Herries, to Sir John Maxwell of Terregles (later fifth Lord Maxwell) in 1547. Mary, Queen of Scots, stayed here for a few days in 1568 before travelling on to Dundrennan Abbey and England after being defeated at Langside: Sir John had commanded her cavalry at the battle. The castle may have been destroyed soon afterwards. William Maxwell, fifth Lord Herries, was Warden of the West Marches (although the feud with the Johnstones continued even after the dispute was sent to arbitration in 1597). Robert, tenth Lord Maxwell, was made Earl of Nithsdale in 1620, but the Maxwells were forfeited in 1716 for their part in the Jacobite Rising. William, fifth Earl, was captured after the Battle of Preston and only managed to avoid execution when his wife, Winifred, had a Mrs Mills swap places with him, allowing him to flee from the Tower of London, dressed as a woman. The couple fled to the Continent and then to Rome, where the Countess became governess to Henry Benedict, younger brother of Bonnie Prince Charlie. The mansion at Terregles was demolished in 1964, and the Maxwells did not recover the earldom.

Monreith or **Myrton** [NX 360432] is a few miles west and north of Whithorn in Galloway. Myrton is a ruinous L-plan tower house, built on a motte and dating from the sixteenth century, and was replaced by **Monreith House** [NX 356429], a large country house, close by, in 1791. The lands were held by the MacCullochs, but were purchased by the Maxwells of Monreith in 1685, who removed to Myrton from nearby Dowies, and they built Monreith House. The Maxwells of Monreith have a mausoleum in Kirkmaiden churchyard at the village of Monreith, but they now apparently live in England; Monreith House is still occupied.

Orchardton Tower [NX 817551] is unique and is the only round tower house in Scotland. The building dates from the fifteenth and sixteenth centuries, and lies four miles south of Dalbeattie in Dumfries and Galloway. The lands were held by the Cairns, and they built the tower, but it passed by marriage to the Maxwells about 1550. Sir Robert Maxwell was wounded and then captured at Culloden in 1746 after fighting for the Jacobites. He was taken to Carlisle for trial and probable execution, and tried to destroy his personal papers. Luckily for him, he was prevented, and his commission as an officer in the French army was discovered. He was then treated as a prisoner of war, and was exiled to France rather

Newark Castle (M&R)

three sides of a courtyard, the last side formerly completed by a wall. The lands were held by the Dennistouns, but passed by marriage to the Maxwells of Calderwood in 1402. James IV visited Newark several times. One of the family, Patrick Maxwell, was involved in the murders of Patrick Maxwell of Stanely in 1584 and then the Montgomery Earl of Eglinton in 1596, during feuds with those families. The castle was eventually abandoned by the family as a residence, but was then used to house workers. The castle is now in the care of Historic Scotland and is open to the public from April to September (01475 741858).

Pollok House [NS 549619] in the Pollokshaws area of Glasgow, is a fine mansion, dating from 1750 but remodelled in the 1890s. The mansion replaced an old castle, and the property was held by the Maxwells from the middle of the thirteenth century. The property was given to the city of Glasgow in 1966, and the Burrell Collection is located in the grounds. The house is open to the public and features include the Stirling Maxwell collection of Spanish and European paintings, furniture, ceramics and silver, which was collected by Sir William Stirling-Maxwell, who was MP for Perthshire. Pollok House is in the care of The National Trust for Scotland (0141 616 6410; www.nts.org.uk).

Orchardton Tower (MC)

than being executed. Maxwell later returned to Orchardton, and Sir Walter Scott made use of this story in his novel *Guy Mannering*. The tower was replaced by **Ordchardton House** [NX 811532], a large baronial mansion, and the property passed to the Douglases in 1785. Orchardton Tower is in the care of Historic Scotland and is open to the public.

Newark Castle [NS 331745] stands on a low promontory in the sea at Port Glasgow in Renfrewshire. Newark is an impressive castle, developed out from a simple tower of the fifteenth century, but now with ranges forming

The Maxwells also owned:

Aitkenhead Castle [NS 596603], Glasgow; castle replaced by mansion.
Held by the Stewarts and then by the Maxwells in the fourteenth century, and then by the Hamiltons after 1600.

Annan Castle [NY 192668], Annan, Dumfries and Galloway; site of castle and tower house.
Held by the Bruces, but the Maxwell Lord Herries built a new tower house in the burgh in the 1560s, although this has been demolished.

Ardwall [NX 581547], near Gatehouse of Fleet, Dumfries and Galloway; mansion on site of castle.
Held by the MacCullochs, although the property may have passed to the Maxwells at one time.

Arkland Tower [NX 803980], near Moniaive, Dumfries and Galloway; site of tower house.
Held by the Maxwells. Robert Maxwell of Arkland was a notable agricultural improver in the middle of the eighteenth century, and a new mansion was built near by.

Arkleton Tower [NY 380914], near Langholm, Dumfries and Galloway; site of tower house.
Held by the Maxwells, but passed to the Armstrongs in 1537, then later went to the Elliots.

Auldhouse [NS 557605], near Barrhead, Lanarkshire; altered L-plan tower house.
Held by the Maxwells from about 1450 until early in the seventeenth century. George Maxwell was involved in a witch trail at Gourock in 1676, and later he fell ill with a 'hot and fiery distemper'. Dolls of him, which were stuck with pins, were found in the house of a widow, and the poor woman and her family were accused of witchcraft and burned at Paisley. The house is still occupied.

Balmangan Tower [NX 651456], near Kirkcudbright, Dumfries and Galloway; slight remains of tower house.
Held by the MacLellans until 1605 or later, but had passed to the Maxwells by the eighteenth century.

Barclosh Castle [NX 855624], near Dalbeattie, Dumfries and Galloway; slight remains of tower house.
Held by the Maxwell Lord Herries.

Belstane Castle [NS 850515], near Carluke, Lanarkshire; site of tower house.
Held by the Livingstones and by the Lindsays, before passing to the Maxwells and then to the Douglases.

Bishopton House [NS 422717], near Bridge of Weir, Renfrewshire; L-plan tower house.
Held by the Brisbanes, but passed to other families, then went to the Maxwells of Pollok, then later to the Stewart Lord Blantyre. Now used as a convent.

Blackcraig Castle [NO 108534], near Blairgowrie, Perthshire; tower house and mansion.
Held by the Maxwells from 1550 or earlier, but was owned by the Allan-Frasers in the nineteenth century. B&B accommodation is available as well as watercolour classes (01250 886251/0131 551 1863).

Blacklaw Tower [NT 052067], near Moffat, Dumfries and Galloway; slight remains of tower house.
Held by the Lindsays then passed to Herries of Terregles, then to the Maxwells in 1510, then to the Johnstones by 1592 and then to the Douglases of Fingland.

Blawarthill [NS 520687], near Clydebank, Glasgow; site of castle.
Held by the Maxwells in the seventeenth century.

Breckonside Tower [NX 840889], near Moniaive, Dumfries and Galloway; slight remains of tower house.
Held by the Maxwells of Breckonside.

Broomholm Tower [NY 372817], near Langholm, Dumfries and Galloway; site of tower house.
Held by the Maxwells.

Buittle Place [NX 817616], near Dalbeattie, Dumfries and Galloway; restored L-plan tower house.
Held by the Douglases and by the Johnstones, but was a property of the Maxwells in the sixteenth century, then went to the Gordons of Lochinvar, who built the tower.

Calderwood Castle [NS 658560], near East Kilbride, Lanarkshire; castle replaced by mansion.
Held by the Calderwoods, then by the Maxwells, a branch of the Maxwells of Pollok, from 1363, who owned it for about 500 years.

Capenoch House [NX 843938], near Thornhill, Dumfries and Galloway; mansion incorporating older work.
Held by the Griersons, but passed to the Maxwells in 1606 but returned to the Griersons and then went to others. Still occupied.

Cardoness Castle [NX 591552], near Gatehouse of Fleet, Dumfries and Galloway; impressive castle.
Long held by the MacCullochs, but passed to the Gordons in 1629, then to the Maxwells. **Cardoness House** [NX 566536] is a large mansion. The castle is in the care of Historic Scotland and is open to the public (01557 814427).

Carmunnock or **Castlemilk** [NS 608594], near Glasgow; slight remains of castle and mansion.
Held by several families before being exchanged by the

Maxwells for the lands of Castlemilk near Annan, which were held by the Stewarts. The Stewarts changed the name from Carmunnock to Castlemilk, and had a large castle and mansion, although this has been demolished.

Carnsalloch [NX 971803], near Dumfries, Dumfries and Galloway; castle replaced by mansion.
Held by the Maxwells and then by the Johnstones.

Castlemilk [NY 150775], near Annan, Dumfries and Galloway; castle replaced by mansion.
Held by the Stewarts of Castlemilk until exchanged for lands near Glasgow (Carmunnock, now Castlemilk) with the Maxwells. A large mansion was built nearby, and was a property of the Jardines at the turn of the nineteenth century.

Cavens Castle [NX 958572], near New Abbey, Dumfries and Galloway; site of castle.
Held by the Douglas Earls of Morton, but passed to the Maxwells in 1581 along with the Earldom, then went to the Murrays. Maxwell of Cavens murdered Sir Robert Maxwell of Dinwiddie in around 1605. At **Cavens** [NX 977584] there is a mansion, dating from the eighteenth century and now used as a country house hotel (01387 880234; www.cavens.com).

Chapelton [NX 798667], near Castle Douglas, Dumfries and Galloway; site of castle or old house.
Held by the Maxwells, but passed to the Biggars and then to the Wilsons. A farmhouse probably stands on the site.

Conheith [NY 005701], near Dumfries, Dumfries and Galloway; site of tower house.
Held by the Maxwells from 1400 to 1783, then passed to the Kirkpatricks and then to the Rannie family.

Corra Castle [NX 867662], near Dalbeattie, Dumfries and Galloway; slight remains of tower house.
Held by the Maxwells. Mary, Queen of Scots, was brought here in 1568 following defeat at Langside on her way to Terregles Castle and eventual imprisonment in England.

Cowhill Tower [NX 952824], near Dumfries; ruinous L-plan tower house.
Held by the Maxwells, but was burnt in 1560 and again in 1745 by Jacobites. The family were involved in a feud with their kin the Maxwells of Kirkhouse in 1583, and Archibald Maxwell of Cowhill and William, his son, were later tried for murder. The castle was replaced by **Cowhill House** [NX 950827], which was built by George Johnston, a merchant from Liverpool.

Crookston Castle [NS 524628], near Paisley, Renfrewshire; fine ruinous castle.
Held by the Stewarts, then by others, including by the Maxwells of Pollok. Now in the care of Historic Scotland and open to the public (0141 883 9606).

Dalswinton Castle [NX 945841], near Dumfries; slight remains of castle.
Held by the Comyns and then by the Stewarts and then by the Maxwells. The castle was replaced by **Dalswinton House** [NX 943841], which was built by the Millers, and the gardens of the house are occasionally open to the public (www.gardens ofscotland.org).

Dargavel House [NS 433693], near Bishopton, Renfrewshire; altered L-plan tower house.
Held by the Maxwells from the middle of the sixteenth century. Patrick, third of Dargavel, was slain in fighting with the Johnstones in 1593. The Maxwells of Dargavel now apparently live in north Wales.

Darnley Castle [NS 527586], near Barrhead, Lanarkshire; some remains of castle.
Held by the Stewarts, later Earls of Lennox. One of the family was Henry Stewart, Lord Darnley, second husband of Mary Queen of Scots. The property passed to the Graham Dukes of Montrose then to the Maxwells of Nether Pollok, who owned it in the nineteenth century. The remaining part has been renovated and is now a restaurant (0141 876 0458).

Dewar [NT 349489], near Peebles, Borders; site of castle or old house.
Held by the Dewars, but was bought by the Maxwells in the seventeenth century, and passed to the Cranstouns.

Dinwoodie [NY 108907], near Lochmaben, Dumfries and Galloway; site of castle.

Held by the Dunwoodies, but later passed to the Maxwells. Sir Robert Maxwell of Dinwiddie was murdered by Maxwell of Cavens around 1605.

Dirleton Castle [NT 518840], near North Berwick, East Lothian; magnificent ruinous castle.

Held by several families including by the Vauxs, by the Halyburtons and by the Ruthvens, before passing to the Maxwells. Sir James Maxwell was made Earl of Dirleton in 1646, but the title became extinct on his death seven years later. In 1649 several women and men, who had confessed to witchcraft after the witch-finder, John Kincaid, had found 'devil's marks' on them, were imprisoned in the castle, later to be strangled and burned at the stake. In 1650 the castle was besieged by General Monck, during Cromwell's invasion of Scotland. A party of mosstroopers had been attacking Cromwell's lines of communication, with some success, but they were quickly forced to surrender; three of the leaders were subsequently shot. The property was sold to Sir John Nisbet in 1661, who built **Archerfield** [NT 505841] to replace the castle, and the ruins of Dirleton are in the care of Historic Scotland and are open to the public (01620 850330).

Dowies [NX 381430], near Whithorn, Dumfries and Galloway; altered tower house.

Held by the Maxwells from 1481 to 1683 when they moved to Myrton castle. The building was used as a farmhouse, then became derelict, but has been restored and reoccupied as a residence.

Druchtag Motte [NX 349467], near Port William, Dumfries and Galloway; impressive motte.

Held by the MacCullochs and by the Maxwells, and there may have been a later castle.

Drumcoltran Tower [NX 869683], near Dalbeattie, Dumfries and Galloway; L-plan tower house.

Held by the Herries of Terregles family, but passed by marriage to the Maxwells in 1550. It was sold to the Irvings in 1669, then to the Hynds and then to the Herons, before returning to the Maxwells in 1875. The tower is in the care of Historic Scotland and is open to the public.

Dubs [NS 516591], near Barrhead, Lanarkshire; altered tower house.

Held by the Maxwells from 1271 to the 1830s. Maxwell of Dubs fought for the Hanoverians during the Jacobite Rising of 1745. It is said that he hid his money, not trusting family or bankers, in Darnley Glen, but he never returned to retrieve it.

Dumfries Castle [NX 975754], Dumfries; site of castle.

Held by the Maxwells. The burgh was burned several times by the English. Lord Maxwell, after sacking the English town of Penrith in revenge, built a tower house in **Dumfries** [NX 971762] in 1545 as a fortress and refuge (in Castle Street). This building is said to have had four storeys with a vaulted basement, a turnpike stair and turret. The tower was taken and the burgh sacked by the English in 1547, and again in 1570. It was garrisoned in 1675 when in need of repair, but by 1724 had been demolished and the site is occupied by a church.

Duncow [NX 970833], near Dumfries; site of castle or old house.

Held by the Comyns and by the Boyds, but passed to the Maxwells, who sold the lands in 1782.

Ethie Castle [NO 688468], near Arbroath, Angus; fine altered castle.

The lands were held by the Maxwells but passed to Arbroath Abbey and then to the Beatons and then to the Carnegies. Accommodation is available (01241 830434; www.ethie castle.com).

Fenton Tower [NT 543822], near North Berwick, East Lothian; restored L-plan tower house.

Held by the Fentons, by the Whitelaws, by the Carmichaels and by the Erskines before passing to the Maxwells of Innerwick in 1631. The castle was sacked by Cromwell's forces in 1650 and was long ruinous but has since been restored. Luxury accommodation is available in the building (01620 890089; www.fentontower.co.uk).

Fingalton [NS 499550], near Barrhead, Lanarkshire; possible site of castle.

Held by the Hamiltons, but also by the Maxwells at one time.

Flask Tower [NY 373884], near Langholm, Dumfries and Galloway; site of tower house.

Held by the Maxwells.

Foumerkland Tower [NX 909807], near Dumfries; restored fortified house.

Held by the Maxwells after the Reformation, but was sold to

Foumerkland Tower (M&R)

the Fergusons in 1720. Still occupied.

Friars Carse [NX 925850], near Dumfries; mansion on site of castle.

Held by the Kirkpatricks, but passed to the Maxwells of Tinwald in 1634, then to the Riddels of Glenriddell, and then to the Crichtons. The building is now a hotel (01387 740388; www.classic-hotels.net).

Glenlee [NX 607807], near New Galloway, Dumfries and Galloway; castle replaced by mansion.

Held by the Millers, then by the Maxwells but by the end of the nineteenth century had passed to the Smiths. Glenlee is reputedly haunted by a Grey Lady, one story being that she was involved in the death of her husband as he was riddled with lice.

Glenshinnoch [NX 811532], near Dalbeattie, Dumfries and Galloway; castle replaced by mansion.

Held by the Cairns family, but passed by marriage to the Maxwells in the sixteenth century, and then went to the Douglases in 1785.

Gribton [NX 921800], near Dumfries; castle replaced by mansion.

Held by the Maxwells and then by the Irvines, then later by the Lamonts.

Guffockland [NS 730124], near Sanquhar, Dumfries and Galloway; site of castle or old house.

Held by the MacCalls, but may have passed to the Maxwells sometime in or after the seventeenth century.

Haggs Castle [NS 560626], Glasgow; altered L-plan tower house.

Held by the Maxwells and built by John Maxwell of Pollok in 1585. It was used by Covenanters, and the Maxwells were heavily fined in 1684, although they were saved from paying by the Revolution five years later. Haggs was abandoned around 1753 for Pollok House, but Haggs was restored and extended around 1890. It was Glasgow's Museum of Childhood, but was then sold and converted into flats.

Hills Tower [NX 912726], near Dumfries; castle and courtyard.
   Held by the Maxwells, and the family eventually succeeded

Hills Tower (M&R)

to the Earldom of Nithsdale, but the property passed by
marriage to the MacCullochs of Ardwall about 1650.

Hoddom Castle [NY 157730], near Annan, Dumfries and Galloway;
massive L-plan tower house.
   Held by the Carlyles and by others, but the castle was built
after it had passed to the Maxwell Lord Herries. It was seized
by Douglas of Drumlanrig in 1568, recaptured by supporters
of Mary, Queen of Scots the next year, but was then taken and
sacked by the English in the next again year. It was rebuilt but
had been acquired by the Murrays of Cockpool about 1627.
Now stands in a caravan park (01576 300251;
www.hoddomcastle.co.uk).

Innerwick Castle [NT 735737], near Dunbar, East Lothian; ruinous
castle.
   Held by the Stewarts, then by the Hamiltons, then by the
Maxwells. The castle was sufficiently complete to be used as a
base, along with Dirleton and Tantallon, to attack Cromwell's
lines of communication in the 1650s. The property later went
to the Nisbets.

Isle Tower [NY 028689], near Dumfries; slight remains of tower.
   Held by the Maxwells.

Kenmure Castle [NX 635764], near New Galloway, Dumfries and
Galloway; ruinous tower house.
   Held by the Balliols, then possibly by the Maxwells, before
being a property of the Gordons for hundreds of years.

Kirkconnel House [NX 979679], Dumfries; castle and mansion.
   Held by the Kirkconnel family, but passed by marriage to the
Maxwells in 1410, and they built the old castle. The house is
still occupied and is available to rent as holiday accommodation
(01381 610496; www.lhhscotland.com).

Kirkconnel Tower [NY 253752], near Ecclefechan, Dumfries and
Galloway; site of tower house.
   Held by the Bells, then by the Irvines, before passing to the
Maxwells in 1648, who were made Baronets of Nova Scotia in
1682 and they built **Springkell House** [NY 255752]. Helen of
Kirkconnel Lea, who was shot by a spurned admirer as
recounted in the old ballad, may have been a Maxwell rather
than an Irvine. The lovers are said to be buried in Kirkconnel
Church

Kirkhouse [NX 981592], near New Abbey, Dumfries and Galloway;
site of castle or old house.
   Held by the Douglases and then by the Maxwells from 1581
until about 1750. One of the family, Sir James Maxwell, was
made the Earl of Dirleton in 1646, although the title became
extinct on his death, seven years later.

Kirkconnel House (M&R) – see previous column

Langholm Tower [NY 361849], Langholm, Dumfries and Galloway;
slight remains of tower house.
   Held by the Armstrongs but passed to the Maxwells. It was
held by the English in 1544, but was recaptured by the Scots
three years later. The property was sold to Douglas of
Drumlanrig and the tower was abandoned by 1725.

Langholm Tower [NY 365855], Langholm, Dumfries and Galloway;
remains of tower house.
   Held by the Armstrongs but passed to the Maxwells then to
the Douglases of Drumlanrig. The basement of the tower is
built into the former Buccleuch Arms Hotel.

Langrig [NS 536550], near Barrhead, Lanarkshire; site of tower
house.
   Held by the Maxwells, who moved to the Mearns in 1449.

Lee Castle [NS 580590], near East Kilbride, Lanarkshire; site of
castle.
   Held by Cochrane of The Lee, but passed to the Pollocks of
Balgray and then to the Maxwells.

Lickprivick Castle [NS 616527], near East Kilbride, Lanarkshire;
site of castle.
   Held by the Lickprivick family, but passed to the Maxwells of
Calderwood. The site is occupied by a housing estate.

Lochmaben Castle [NY 088812], Lochmaben, Dumfriesshire;
ruinous castle.
   Held by the Bruces and then by the Crown with the Maxwells
as hereditary keepers. James VI besieged the castle and took
it from the Maxwells, and gave the property to John Murray,
who was Groom to the king, and Murray was made Earl of
Annandale in 1625.

MacLellan's Castle [NX 683511], Kirkcudbright, Dumfries and
Galloway; large ruinous tower house.
   Held and built by the MacLellans, but was bought by the
Maxwells of Orchardton in 1752 then was sold to the Douglas
Earl of Selkirk thirty years later. It is in the care of Historic
Scotland and open to the public from April to May (01557
331856).

Mayshiel [NT 622641], near Cranshaws, East Lothian; altered tower
house.
   Held by the Stewarts and by the Cockburns before passing to
the Maxwells of Fenton. Alexander Maxwell fought at the Battle
of Worcester in 1651 for Charles II, but was taken prisoner
and imprisoned in the Tower of London. The lands passed to
the Knoxs, who held them in the eighteenth century, then
went to others. The house is still occupied.

Mearns Castle [NS 553553], Barrhead, Lanarkshire; altered keep
or tower.
   Held by the Pollocks, but passed by marriage to the Maxwells
of Caerlaverock in 1300, and they had a stronghold. The
present building dates from 1449. One of the family was killed

at the Battle of Flodden in 1513, while another, an ambassador to France, was imprisoned in the Tower of London in 1542 until ransomed. The castle passed to the Stewarts of Blackhall.

Moure Castle [NX 382433], near Whithorn, Dumfries and Galloway; site of castle.

Held by the Mundeville family, but passed by marriage to the Maxwells in 1451, who moved to Dowies.

Munches [NX 831589], near Dalbeattie, Dumfries and Galloway; castle replaced by mansion.

Held by the Maxwells from the sixteenth century for about 400 years.

Newton Mearns [NS 535560], near Barrhead, Lanarkshire; site of castle.

Held by the Maxwells and the site is occupied by housing.

Old Garroch [NX 589823], near St John's Town of Dalry, Dumfries and Galloway; old house.

Held by the Asloane family, but later passed to the Maxwells, then to the Griersons and possibly to the Carlyles.

Penkaet Castle [NT 427677], near Pencaitland, East Lothian; altered tower house.

Held by the Maxwells, but passed to the Cockburns and then to the Pringles in 1636, then to others. Still occupied.

Portrack Castle [NX 935832], near Dumfries; slight remains of castle.

Held by the Maxwells and replaced by the elegant Portrack House [NX 939830].

Repentance Tower [NY 155723], near Annan, Dumfries and Galloway; tower house.

Built by John Maxwell, Lord Herries, who had demolished a chapel to build Hoddom Castle, and then built this tower as recompense, probably at the insistence of the Archbishop of

Repentance Tower (M&R)

Glasgow, whose chapel it was. It survived a siege by the English in 1570 and is surrounded by a graveyard.

Spottes Hall [NX 805662], near Castle Douglas, Dumfries and Galloway; site of castle or old house.

Held by the Maxwells in the sixteenth and seventeenth centuries, but passed to the Young-Herries family in the nineteenth century. The house is still occupied.

Springkell House [NY 253755], near Ecclefechan, Dumfries and Galloway; castle replaced by mansion.

Held by the Maxwells from 1609 or earlier. They were made Baronets of Nova Scotia in 1682, and became Heron-Maxwells in the nineteenth century. Springkell was sold to the Fergusons in 1894, and the Heron-Maxwells, Baronets, now apparently live in Essex in England.

Stanely Castle [NS 464616], near Paisley, Renfrewshire; ruinous altered keep or tower.

Held by the Dennistouns, but passed by marriage to the Maxwells of Newark, who built the castle. Sold to the Rosses of Hawkhead in 1629, then passed to the Boyle Earls of Glasgow, the castle now stands in Paisley Waterworks and the basement is flooded.

Tealing House [NO 413380], near Dundee; mansion incorporating castle.

Held by the Fotheringhams, but passed to the Giffords of Yester and then by marriage to the Maxwells, then to the Scrymgeours in 1710.

Threave Castle [NX 739623], near Castle Douglas, Dumfries and Galloway; magnificent ruined castle on island.

Held by the Douglases, but they were forfeited in 1455 and the Maxwells became keepers. The Maxwell keeper was captured by the English at Solway Moss in 1542 and he turned the castle over to the English. It was recaptured by the Earl of Arran in 1545. Threave was besieged by an army of Covenanters for thirteen weeks in 1640, until the Maxwells were forced to surrender it. The castle was slighted and partly dismantled and was used to hold French prisoners in the Napoleonic wars. It is now in the care of Historic Scotland and is open to the public from April to September (07711 223101 (mobile)).

Tinwald Place [NY 006800], near Dumfries; castle replaced by mansion.

Held by the Maxwells, but passed to the Erskines then to the Douglas Marquis of Queensberry, then to the Jardines.

Wreaths Tower [NX 953565], near New Abbey, Dumfries and Galloway; slight remains of tower house.

Held by the Douglases but passed to the Maxwells, then possibly back to the Douglases.

www.maxwellsociety.com
www.clanmaxwellusa.com
www.clanmaxwell.com
No. of castles/sites: 87
Rank: 8/764

Meiklejohn

Edradynate

The name, which means 'muckle John' or 'big John' is descriptive of the first person to be given it, and the name is on record in Scotland from the sixteenth century.

Edradynate House [NN 885521], two and half miles north-east of Aberfeldy in Perthshire, is a modern mansion, but there are what may be the remains of a castle close by at **Edradynate** [NN 881521]. The property was held by the Robertsons, but later passed by marriage to the Stewart Meiklejohns of Edradynate, who held it until the twentieth century. They now apparently live in Edinburgh, and Edradynate House can be rented as holiday accommodation (01738 451600; www.scotland-holiday-homes.co.uk/perthshire/edradynate.html).

No. of castles/sites: 1
Rank: 537=/764

Meldrum

The name is territorial and comes from the lands and barony of Meldrum, which are one mile to the north of Oldmeldrum in Aberdeenshire in the north-east of Scotland. The family came to own several castles and properties in this part of the country as well as in Fife and in other parts of Scotland.

Meldrum House [NJ 812291] is a large mansion, which was extended down the centuries, but it incorporates the vaulted basement of an old castle. The lands were held by the Meldrums from 1236 until the middle of the fifteenth century. The male line died out and the property passed by marriage to William Seton, although he was slain at the Battle of Brechin in 1452. The house is reputedly haunted by a Green (or a White) Lady, and is now used as a hotel (01651 872294; www.meldrumhouse.co.uk).

Fyvie Castle [NJ 764393], just north of Fyvie village in Aberdeenshire, is a magnificent and impressive building, which incorporates a massive tower house and very long wings; the interior is as splendid as the exterior.

Fyvie Castle (RWB)

The property was owned by several families in turn including by the Prestons, and then by the Meldrums in 1433 before passing to the Seton Earls of Dunfermline in 1596. The castle is in the care of The National Trust for Scotland and is open to the public (01651 891266; www.nts.org.uk).

The Meldrums also owned:

Ardoe House [NJ 894017], near Aberdeen; castle replaced by mansion.
Held by the Meldrums, but was bought by the Fordyce family in 1744, and was then sold to the Ogstouns in 1839. The present mansion dates from 1879, is said to be haunted by a White Lady, and is now a hotel (01224 867355; www.ardoe house.com).

Balmungo [NO 523148], near St Andrews, Fife; site of castle or old house.
Held by the Pringles and then by the Lindsays and by the Maitlands, and then by the Bayne-Meldrums in the twentieth century.

Cleish Castle [NT 083978], near Kinross, Perth and Kinross; L-plan tower house.
Held by the Meldrums, and this was the home of William Meldrum, the *Squire Meldrum* of Sir David Lindsay of The Mount. Meldrum courted Marjorie Lawson, widow of Sir John

Cleish Castle (M&R)

Haldane of Gleneagles, but he was set upon and left for dead in 1517; it is thought that Haldane's brothers disapproved of his attention and attacked him. Meldrum survived the mauling and went on to be Sheriff Depute of Fife in 1522. The Colvilles owned the castle from 1530; much later it became ruinous but it was restored and is occupied. The gardens are occasionally open to the public (www.gardensofscotland.org).

Craigfoodie [NO 407180], near Cupar, Fife; castle or old house replaced by mansion.
Held by the Beatons in 1711 and then by the Meldrums in the eighteenth and nineteenth centuries.

Crombie Castle [NJ 591522], near Aberchirder, Aberdeenshire; altered L-plan tower house.
Held by the Innes family, then later by the Urquharts, by the Meldrums and by the Duffs.

Dumbreck Castle [NJ 898289], near Ellon, Aberdeenshire; site of castle.
Held by the Dumbreck family, but passed to the Meldrums, who built the castle.

Eden Castle [NJ 698588], near Banff, Aberdeenshire; slight remains of Z-plan tower house.
Held and built by the Meldrums, but passed to the Leslies by 1613, then later went to the Duff Earls of Fife.

Hatton Manor [NJ 709420], near Turriff, Aberdeenshire; castle replaced by mansion.
Held by the Allardyces, but passed to the Meldrums who exchanged the property with the Allardyce family for Pitcarry. It was also a property of the Dempsters at one time, before it passed to the Duffs in 1709.

Kincaple [NO 465182], near St Andrews, Fife; castle or old house replaced by mansion.
Held by the Duddingstons and by the Melvilles, but passed to the Meldrums who held the lands in the eighteenth and nineteenth centuries and they built the present house.

Newhall Tower [NO 598100], near Crail, Fife; site of castle.
Held by the Meldrums in 1578.

Pitcarry [NO 830740], near Inverbervie, Kincardineshire; site of castle.

Held by the Allardice family, but was exchanged with the Meldrums for the lands of Auchterless in 1547.

Pittormie [NO 417185], near Cupar, Fife; site of castle or old house.

Held by the Lindsays, but was held by the Meldrums in the eighteenth century.

The Binns [NT 051785], near Linlithgow, West Lothian; fine early mansion on site of castle.

Held by the Meldrums from before 1478. William Meldrum of Cleish and the Binns was the 'Squire Meldrum' of Sir David Lindsay (see Cleish above). The property was sold to the Lindsays in 1559, and it then went to the Livingstones and then to the Dalziels who were long in possession. The castle is now in the care of The National Trust of Scotland and is open to the public in the summer (01506 834255; www.nts.org.uk).

Tullibody [NS 865945], near Alloa, Clackmannan; site of castle and mansion.

Held by the Meldrums, but passed to the Abercrombies about 1655. Demolished in the 1960s.

No. of castles/sites: 16
Rank: 86=/764

Eden Castle (M&R) – see previous page

Melrose

The name comes from the burgh of Melrose, which is in the Borders and has a picturesque ruinous abbey [NT 550344], which is in the care of Historic Scotland and is open to the public (01896 822562).

In **West Linton** [NT 149519], which is in the north-west part of the Borders, is a small L-plan tower house, dating from the sixteenth century but later altered. The tower was held by the Melrose family.

No. of castles/sites: 1
Rank: 537=/764

Melville

The name comes from the barony of 'Maleville' in Normandy in France, and the family came to England with William the Conqueror during the Norman invasion of England. The Melvilles settled in Scotland in the reign of David I in the twelfth century, and were given lands in Midlothian. There are many different spellings of the name down the centuries.

Melville Castle [NT 310669], one and a half miles west of Dalkeith in Midlothian, is a symmetrical castellated mansion, designed by James Playfair and dating from the end of the eighteenth century, but it stands on the site of an old stronghold. The lands were held by the Melvilles from the twelfth century, but the property passed by marriage to the Rosses of Hawkhead some 200 years or so later. Much later Melville was sold to the Rennies, and then later passed by marriage to Henry Dundas, who was made Viscount Melville. The house has recently been restored and is now a hotel (0131 654 0088; www.melvillecastle.com).

Raith Tower [NT 256917] is a mile or so to the west of Kirkcaldy in Fife, but little remains of a tower house. The Melvilles held the lands from the thirteenth century or earlier. James Melville of Raith was a favourite of James V, and was captain of Dunbar Castle and Master General of the Ordnance. He was one of those accused of the murder of Archbishop David Beaton at St Andrews Castle in 1546, and he was executed four years later. Raith was sold to the Fergusons in the seventeenth century, and they abandoned the old tower for Raith House. The current Raith Tower, west of Raith House, is a derelict nineteenth-century Gothic folly.

Melville House [NO 298138], four and a half miles west of Cupar in Fife, is a tall classical mansion, and dates from 1692 when it was built to replace the bishop's palace at **Monimail** [NO 299141] (see below). It appears to stand on the site of a fortified building, and there are cellars from a building of the sixteenth century. Melville was held by the Balfours of Pittendreich after the Reformation, but passed to the Melvilles in 1592. The family were made Lords Melville of Monimail in 1616, and then George Melville was made Earl of Melville in 1690 after playing an active part in the Revolution of 1689. The Melvilles married into the Leslie family, and David, George's son, became Earl of Leven in 1681. He fought at the Battle of Killiecrankie on the government side, and then in Ireland and in Flanders. He was made commander-in-chief in Scotland in 1706 but he lost the post six years later. The family still hold the titles Earl of Melville, Earl of Leven, Viscount Kirkcaldy – and others. The family lived at Melville House until 1950, but now apparently reside near Grantown-on-Spey in Moray.

The family also held:

Baldovie [NO 324541], near Kirriemuir, Angus; site of castle or old house.
Held by the Melvilles. Andrew Melville, one of nine sons of the laird, was born at Baldovie in 1545. Melville was a supporter of the Presbyterian system of church government, and did much to increase its adoption. This was not much to the liking of James VI, and Melville was exiled from Scotland. The property passed to the Clayhills in 1615, then later to the Ogilvies and then to the Farquharsons.

Balwearie Castle [NT 251903], near Kirkcaldy, Fife; ruinous castle.
Held by the Scotts, but passed to the Melville Earls of Melville at the end of the seventeenth century.

Carden Tower [NT 226937], near Cardenden, Fife; slight remains of tower house.
Held by the Martin family, then by the Betsons and by the Melville Earls of Melville, then by the Fergusons of Raith in 1725. The site is accessible to the public.

Carnbee Place [NO 530067], near Pittenweem, Fife; site of castle.
Held by the Melvilles, one of whom was killed at Flodden in 1513, but was sold to the Moncreiffes in 1598.

Cassingray [NO 490070], near St Andrews, Fife; possible site of castle or old house.
Held by the Carstairs family, but passed to the Melvilles. James Melville of Cassingray was the main collector of Hearth Tax, having been appointed to the post by Parliament.

Dysart [NO 695550], near Montrose, Angus; possible site of castle.
Held by the Melvilles, then by the Guthries and by the Lyles.

Glenbervie House [NO 769805], near Stonehaven, Kincardineshire; mansion incorporating castle.
Held by the Melville family from the twelfth century, and Edward I of England stayed here. John Melville, Sheriff of Kincardine, was murdered and boiled in a cauldron on Hill of Gravock by four local lairds, who drank some of the broth, and were afterwards outlawed. The property passed to the Auchinlecks in 1468, and then to others. The house is still occupied.

Grange [NT 270886], near Kinghorn, Fife; mansion incorporating part of tower house.
Held by the Kirkcaldy family, but passed to the Melvilles after the Kirkcaldy line died out in 1739. The gardens are occasionally open to the public (www.gardensofscotland.org).

Granton or **Royston Castle** [NT 225772], Edinburgh; site of castle.
Held by the Melvilles of Carnbee from the twelfth century until sold to the Mackenzies of Tarbat, then passed to the

Kinblethmont [NO 638470], near Arbroath, Angus; some remains of castle.
Held by the Melvilles in the twelfth century, but had passed to the Lindsays by the end of the sixteenth century, and then to the Carnegies, who built or rebuilt the castle.

Kincaple [NO 465182], near St Andrews, Fife; castle or old house replaced by mansion.
Held by James Melville, Constable of St Andrews Castle in 1587, but the property went to the Meldrums, who held Kincaple in the eighteenth and nineteenth centuries, and they built the present house.

Monimail Tower [NO 299141], near Cupar, Fife; tower house.
Held by the Balfours after the Reformation, but was bought by the Melvilles in 1592. The family were made Lords Melville of Monimail in 1616, and Earls of Melville in 1690. Nearby **Melville House** [NO 298138] (see above) was built in 1692 to replace Monimail. The tower can be visited (01337 810420).

Murdocairnie [NO 354195], near Cupar, Fife; site of castle or old house.
Held by the Melvilles of Raith in the sixteenth century. Sir Robert Melville was ambassador to England and tried to save Mary, Queen of Scots, from being executed, although so vigorously that he was nearly imprisoned himself. He took the title Lord Murdocairney when he was elevated to the bench.

Old Manse [NO 567036], Anstruther Easter, Fife; L-plan tower house.
Held by the Reverend James Melville around 1571.

Rossend Castle [NT 225859], Burntisland, Fife; altered tower house.
Long held by the Duries but passed to the Melvilles of Murdocairnie. The castle was briefly held against Cromwell, but was soon captured by his forces, and he stayed at Rossend in 1651. The property passed to the Wemyss family, later became derelict, but was restored and is now an office.

Seafield Tower [NT 280885], near Kinghorn, Fife; ruinous castle above sea.
Held by the Moultray family until about 1715, and the lands then passed to the Melville Earls of Melville.

Tayport or **Ferryport-on-Craig Castle** [NO 457291], Tayport, Fife; site of castle.
Held by the Melvilles, but by the seventeenth century had passed to the Duries, and later held by the Douglases of Glenbervie.

No. of castles/sites: 21
Rank: 63=/764

Granton Castle (M&R)

Hopes of Craighall and then to the Campbell Dukes of Argyll. The castle was demolished in the 1920s.

Halhill Tower [NO 292132], near Cupar, Fife; site of tower house.
Held by the Cummings of Inverallochy and by the Balnaves family, but later went to the Melvilles. One of the family was Sir James Melville, courtier and diplomat, who died in 1607. The castle was demolished by Lord Melville when he added the lands to Melville Park.

Menteith

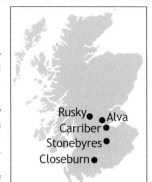

The name comes from the part of Scotland and old earldom called Menteith, which is in central Scotland west of Stirling. The name comes on record in the first half of the thirteenth century, and another spelling is Monteith. There was an Earldom of Menteith, which is on record from 1164, but it was held by the Comyns and then by the Crown before going to Robert Stewart, Duke of Albany, but then, on the forfeiture and execution of his son in 1425, to the Graham family.

The Menteiths held the following castles and properties:

Alva Castle [NS 901975], near Alva, Clackmannan; site of tower house and mansion.

Held by the Stirlings, then by the Menteiths, but passed to the Erskines in 1620. The tower was incorporated into a mansion, but this building has been completely demolished.

Carriber Castle [NS 966751], near Linlithgow, West Lothian; slight remains of tower house.

Held by the Gibbs, but the property passed to the Menteiths in 1640.

Carse Castle [NS 924823], near Falkirk; possible site of castle.

Held by the Menteiths of Kerse.

Carstairs Castle [NS 939461], Carstairs, Lanarkshire; site of castle.

Held by several families before coming to Henry Monteith in 1819, and he built a mansion which is now St Charles Hospital; he also replanned Carstairs.

Closeburn Castle [NX 907921], near Thornhill, Dumfries and Galloway; impressive castle.

Long held by the Kirkpatricks, but was sold to the Stewart-Menteiths in 1783, who were made Baronets in 1838. A few years later the property passed to the Bairds. The Stuart-Menteiths, Baronets, now apparently live near Castle Douglas in Dumfries and Galloway; Closeburn is still occupied.

Hill House [NT 092860], Dunfermline, Fife; mansion incorporating castle.

Held by the Menteiths of Randieford from 1621, when William Menteith of Randieford acquired the lands. The walls are adorned with religious sayings.

Kerse House [NS 915817], near Grangemouth, Falkirk; site of castle and mansion.

Held by the Menteiths, then by the Livingstones, by the Hopes and by the Dundas family, later Marquises of Zetland.

Kersie [NS 872912], near Stirling; L-plan tower house.

Held by the Menteiths, then by the Livingstones, by the Hopes and by the Dundas family, later Marquises of Zetland. Now used as a farmhouse.

Rednock Castle [NN 600022], near Callander, Stirlingshire; slight remains of castle.

Held by the Menteiths of Ruskie, but a later castle was built by the Grahams.

Rusky or **Ruskie Castle** [NN 616034], near Callander, Stirlingshire; site of castle on former island.

Believed to have been held by Sir John Menteith, who imprisoned William Wallace in Dumbarton Castle before having him taken to London for execution. Menteith had been captured by the English in 1296, but he was released the following year and was made Sheriff of Dumbarton. Robert the Bruce made Menteith Earl of Lennox in 1307, and he was one of the magnates to add his seal to the Declaration of Arbroath. The property was held by the Menteiths of Rusky until the 1470s, when the main line ended. Rusky appears to have passed to the Napiers of Merchiston, but was later held by the Haldanes of Gleneagles. The lands were made into the Barony of Haldane, with Rusky as the seat in 1508-09. There were no remains by the end of the nineteenth century, and the level of the loch has been raised, drowning the island.

Stonebyres House [NS 838433], near Lanark; site of castle and mansion.

Long held by the Weirs, but was bought by the Menteiths in 1845 who remodelled the building; the house was, however, demolished in 1934.

No. of castles/sites: 11
Rank: 127=/764
Xref: Monteith

Menzies

The name, which is pronounced 'Mingiz', is Norman in origin, and it comes from 'Mesniere' in France. The family came to England following the invasion by the William the Conqueror, where they became known as Manners and whose descendants became the Dukes of Rutland. The name is recorded in Scotland from 1224 and Robert Menzies was Great Chamberlain of Scotland. He was granted lands in Glen Lyon and others parts of Perthshire. Sir Robert Menzies fought on the side of Robert the Bruce and was given more property, and added his seal to the Declaration of Arbroath in 1320.

Comrie Castle [NN 787486] is now a ruinous L-plan tower house, which stands four and half miles west of Aberfeldy in Perthshire. The castle was built and held by the Menzies family, but was burned out in 1487, and the clan moved to Weem and what is now known as Castle Menzies. Comrie was repaired and used by branches of the family until around 1715.

Castle Menzies [NN 837496], which was originally known as **Place of Weem**, is closer to Aberfeldy and is a magnificent extended tower house, Z-plan but now with a later wing. The original Place of Weem was built after 1487 but was sacked fifteen years later by Neil Stewart of Garth. Sir Robert Menzies was incarcerated at Garth and was forced to sign away some of his lands by Stewart, who claimed them as part of a dowry settlement. The case was found against Stewart and he was forced to make restitution. The Menzies clan fought against the Marquis of Montrose, and the then chief was killed in a skirmish, and his son was then slain at the Battle of Inverlochy in 1645. The castle was occupied by Cromwell's forces, under General Monck, in the 1650s, but the family were made Baronets of Nova Scotia in 1665. The chiefs did not support the Jacobite Risings, and the castle was captured and occupied by Jacobites in 1715. Bonnie Prince Charlie stayed here for two nights

in 1746, but four days later the castle was occupied by Hanoverian forces, led by the Duke of Cumberland. The chiefs again did not support the Rising, but many of the clan, including their leader Menzies of Shian, were killed at the Battle of Culloden in 1746. The last of the Menzies line died in 1918, and the castle was used as a Polish Army medical supplies depot during World War II. The castle became derelict, but is being restored by a trust established by the Clan Menzies Society, who acquired the building in 1957. Castle Menzies is open to the public (01887 820982; www.menzies.org).

Meggernie Castle [NN 554460] is a very attractive, gleaming and turreted tower house of five storeys, to which has been added a mansion. It stands some eight miles north of Killin in Perthshire, and was held by the

Meggernie Castle 1910?

Campbells, before passing to the Menzies family of Culdares. James Menzies of Culdares, 'Old Culdares', was a Jacobite who took part in the Rising of 1715, and was then exiled. He was allowed to return and later sheltered Jacobite fugitives while entertaining government troops during the 1745-46 Rising. Meggernie is reputedly haunted by the ghost of the wife of one of the Menzies lairds. The story goes that the laird slew his wife in a jealous rage and cut her body in half to hide it. He managed to bury her lower half, but not her other remains which were concealed in an upper chamber. The upper floors of the castle are said to be haunted by the apparition of her upper body, while her lower half haunts the lower floors and the burial ground. The property later passed to the Stewarts of Cardney, and the castle is a private residence.

Pitfodels Castle [NJ 918032] was to the south-west of Aberdeen but little remains of the castle, and the old stronghold was replaced by Norwood Hall. The property was held by the Reids, but passed by marriage to the Menzies family in the sixteenth century, and they also had a house, **Pitfodel's Lodging** [NJ 945063] in Aberdeen, although this has been demolished. Pitfodels Castle was apparently abandoned about 1622. Sir Gilbert Menzies of Pitfodels supported the Marquis of Montrose, and was at Inverlochy in 1645; and the family were also Jacobites. The family founded the Catholic College of Blairs, although this is now closed. Norwood Hall, built

Castle Menzies (M&R)

for the Ogstoun family, stands nearby the site of Pitfodels and is now a hotel (01224 868951; www.norwood-hall.co.uk).

The Menzies clan also held:

Arnprior Castle [NS 613949], Arnprior, Stirlingshire; site of castle.

Held by the Menzies family at the end of the sixteenth century, but passed to the Buchanans.

Blairs [NJ 883008], near Cults, Kincardineshire; castle replaced by mansion and seminary.

Held by the Menzies family from the sixteenth century. John Menzies of Pitfodels gave the property to the Catholic Church in 1829 as a college for boys hoping to become priests, and also helped found St Margaret's Convent in Edinburgh. The college closed in 1986, although the chapel and a museum are open to the public.

Bolfracks [NN 822481], near Aberfeldy, Perthshire; castle replaced by mansion.

Held by the Stewarts, but passed to the Menzies family in the eighteenth century, and then went to the Campbells of Breadalbane in the nineteenth century. The fine gardens are open to the public from April to October (01887 820344; www.rannoch.net/Bolfracks-Garden/).

Cammo House [NT 174747], near Edinburgh; site of castle or old house and mansion.

Held by the Niddrie family and then by the Menzies family, who were in possession at the end of the seventeenth century. Cammo later went to the Clerks and then to others, and the mansion was demolished after 1975. The grounds are now a country park and there is a visitor centre.

Culdares [NN 728469], near Fortingall, Perthshire; possible site of castle or old house.

Held by the Moncreiffes, but passed to the Menzies family. Colonel James Menzies of Culdares was a Royalist officer during the Civil War in the seventeenth century and was wounded nine times in various fights. Menzies of Culdares fought for the Jacobites in the 1715 Rising, but was captured after the rebellion and was exiled to North America. He was an agricultural improver, and introduced the larch to Scotland. He was too old to take part in the 1745-46 Rising, but sent Bonnie Prince Charlie a fine horse. Many Jacobites were sheltered in Glen Lyon following the failure of the rising.

Durisdeer Castle [NS 891042], near Carronbridge, Dumfriesshire; site of castle.

Held by the Menzies family, and occupied by the English during the Wars of Independence. Probably demolished by the end of the fourteenth century.

Enoch Castle [NS 879009], near Thornhill, Dumfriesshire; site of castle.

Held by the Menzies family, and said to have been captured by William Wallace in 1296. It was sold to the Douglas Duke of Queensberry in 1703, then to the Scott Dukes of Buccleuch.

Finlarig Castle [NN 575338], near Killin, Stirlingshire; ruinous castle.

Held by the Menzies family, but passed to the Campbells, who built or rebuilt the castle in the 1620s. There is a ruinous mausoleum close by, and the site is accessible with care.

Fordyce Castle [NJ 556638], near Portsoy, Aberdeenshire; restored L-plan tower house.

Held by the Dunbars and by the Ogilvie Earls of Findlater, but the castle was built by Thomas Menzies of Durn, Provost of Aberdeen. Part of the castle can be rented as holiday accommodation (01261 843722; www.fordycecastle.co.uk).

Maryculter House [NO 845999], near Aberdeen; mansion incorporating part of castle.

Held by the Menzies family, who built a house in the seventeenth century on the site of a house of the Knights Templar. The stone effigies of Gilbert Menzies (who died in 1452) and Marjorie his wife were taken from the ruinous church at Maryculter to the Kirk of St Nicholas in Aberdeen, which is

Finlarig Castle (M&R) – see previous column

open to the public (01224 643494; www.kirk-of-st-nicholas.org.uk). Maryculter House is now used as a hotel (01224 732124; www.maryculterhousehotel.com).

Pitcur Castle [NO 252370], near Coupar Angus, Angus; massive ruinous tower house.

Held by the Chisholms and by the Halyburtons of Dirleton, but the property was sold to the Menzies family in 1880. The castle was replaced by **Hallyburton House** [NO 248386], dating from 1680.

Shian or **Wester Shian** [NN 842400], near Aberfeldy, Perthshire; site of castle.

Held by the Menzies family. Menzies of Shian led the 300-strong force from the clan in the 1745-46 Jacobite Rising, held the rank of colonel, and was killed during the fighting.

Whitehouse [NT 187766], Cramond, Edinburgh; altered L-plan tower house.

Held by several families, including by the Menzies family after 1676.

www.menzies.org

No. of castles/sites: 18
Rank: 76=/764
Xref: Manners

Fordyce Castle (M&R) – see previous column

Mercer

The name is believed from come from the profession of 'mercier' from French, meaning a 'draper' or a 'merchant'. The family are on record in Scotland from the thirteenth century.

Meikleour House [NO 153387] is a few miles south and west of Blairgowrie in Perthshire, and is a substantial mansion, which stands on the site of several earlier houses. Meikleour was held by the Mercers from 1162, and Henry Mercer of Meikleour was killed at the Battle of Flodden in 1513. The Mercers gave lands to St John's Church [NO 121233] in Perth so that they could be buried there (the church is open to the public; www.st-johns-kirk.co.uk). Meikleour passed by marriage to the Murray Lords Nairne in the eighteenth century, and later to the Marquises of Landsdowne, although they kept the name Mercer. Charles Mercer of Meikleour, Lord Nairne, was killed in action in 1914. The house is still occupied by the family, and the Meikleour Hedge, a famous beech hedge which lines the A93 along the edge of the estate, is 100-foot high. The gardens are occasionally open to the public (www.gardensofscotland.org).

The Mercers also held:

Aldie Castle [NT 052977], near Crook of Devon, Perthshire; tower house.
  Held by the Mercers of Aldie, but later passed to the Murray

Aldie Castle (M&R)

Lords Nairne and then to the Kinlochs. The house was restored and is occupied.

Balhousie Castle [NO 115244], Perth; mansion incorporating tower house.
  Held by the Eviots, but bought by the Mercers in 1478, and several of the family were Provosts of Perth, and then passed to the Hay Earls of Kinnoul in 1625. Balhousie is the regimental headquarters and museum of the Black Watch, and is open to the public (0131 310 8530; www.theblackwatch.co.uk/museum/index.html).

Balhousie Castle (M&R) – see previous column

Dunbarney House [NO 111196], near Perth; castle replaced by mansion.
  Held by the Mercers in 1455, but passed to the Oliphants and then to the Craigies.

Huntingtower Castle [NO 083252], near Perth; magnificent castle.
  Held by the Ruthvens and by the Murrays, but was bought by the Mercers in 1805, and the building was used to house labourers in the calico printing industry. The Mercers, formerly of Huntingtower, now apparently live in London in England. The castle is in the care of Historic Scotland and is open to the public (01738 627231).

Inchbrackie Castle [NN 903218], near Crieff, Perthshire; site of castle.
  Held by the Mercers, but had passed to the Grahams (Graemes) by 1513.

No. of castles/sites: 6
Rank: 212=/764

Huntingtower Castle 1910?

Merry

The name is on record in Scotland from the beginning of the seventeenth century, and one William Merry was executed for murder in the Grassmarket of Edinburgh in 1682.

Belladrum [NH 518417], three and a half miles south of Beauly near Inverness, is a modern mansion but stands on or near the site of a castle. The lands were held by the Frasers, but were sold to the Stewarts and then to the Merry family in 1857. The estate was sold 120 years later, and cottage accommodation is available (www.belladrum.co.uk).

No. of castles/sites: 1
Rank: 537=/764

Middlemast

The name comes from the lands of Middlemast, probably near Kelso in the Borders, which the family held in the sixteenth century. The surname Middlemast is on record in Scotland from 1406, and variations in spelling include Middlemas and Middlemiss.

Grieston Tower [NT 314358] was a mile or so south-west of Innerleithen, but although there were some ruins in 1857, nothing now survives. The lands were held by the Middlemast family in the sixteenth and seventeenth centuries.

No. of castles/sites: 1
Rank: 537=/764
Xref: Middlemas; Middlemiss

Middleton

The name is territorial in origin and, although there are other lands with the same name, are believed to have come from Middleton of Conventh (Conventh was the old name for Laurencekirk) in the old county of Kincardineshire.

Fettercairn House [NO 656740] was previously known as **Middleton**, and is half a mile north-east of Fettercairn village. There was a castle, but it was replaced by Fettercairn House, which was begun in 1666 and was extended down the centuries into a large mansion with a Jacobean front. The lands were held by the Middletons from the twelfth century, and a Robert Middleton was captured by the English at Dunbar Castle in 1296. John Middleton of Coldham was a famous soldier in the seventeenth century. He was part of the forces that defeated the Marquis of Montrose at Philiphaugh in 1645, but was on the Royalist side at the defeat of Preston in 1648, and he was then wounded and captured at Worcester in 1651. He escaped to France but returned two years later and led an unsuccessful Royalist rising in Scotland in 1653. He was made Earl of Middleton at the Restoration after 1661, but the family were forfeited following the Jacobite Rising of 1715. Fettercairn had passed to the Belshes, then went to the Forbeses of Pitsligo and then to Lord Clinton. The house is still occupied.

Just to the south-west of Fettercairn is **Balbegno Castle** [NO 639730], an altered L-plan tower house, dating from the sixteenth century but extended by a mansion two centuries later. The property was long held by the Woods, but was sold to the Middletons in 1687, and later passed to the Ogilvies and then to the Ramsays.

Pitgarvie [NO 669695] is three or so miles south and west of Laurencekirk, and was held by the Middleton family at the end of the seventeenth century. There was a castle or old house, and the site is probably occupied by a farm.

No. of castles/sites: 3
Rank: 328=/764

Millar

The name comes from the profession of 'miller', an important but not always popular occupation in medieval times. The name is widespread throughout the English-speaking parts of Scotland and is more commonly spelt 'Millar' in Scotland. The name is on

record from the twelfth century, but was an indication of a person's profession rather than a surname. Hugh Miller, who was born in Cromarty in 1802, was a stone mason by trade but educated himself and then became a banker, writer and geologist; he shot himself in 1856. Hugh Miller's Cottage in Cromarty is in the care of The National Trust for Scotland and is open to the public (01381 600245).

The Millars or Millers owned the following properties:

Balmanno Castle [NO 144156], near Bridge of Earn, Perthshire; restored L-plan tower house.

Held by the Balmanno family and others before being used as a farmhouse. It was purchased by the Millers, who were Glasgow shipowners, and was restored by the architect Sir Robert Lorimer for them from 1916.

Barskimming [NS 482251], near Mauchline, Ayrshire; castle replaced by mansion.

Held by the Reids, then by the Stewarts, but passed to the Millers in 1691. They were made Baronets in 1778, and Sir William Miller was Lord President of the Court of Session. Barskimming was sold to the Galbraiths in the twentieth century.

Blair Castle [NS 968858], near Kincardine, Fife; mansion in site of castle or old house.

Held by the Hamiltons, then latterly by the Millers, who were timber merchants and were made Barons of Inchyra in 1962. They now apparently live in Hampshire in England.

Craigentinny House [NT 290747], Edinburgh; altered L-plan tower house.

Held by the Nisbets, but passed to the Millers, who were wealthy Edinburgh merchants, and they remodelled the old tower. They built the extraordinary Christie Miller Mausoleum, a fantastic carved marble monument to themselves, which can be seen in Craigentinny Crescent. Craigentinny House is now used as council offices, after a wing was destroyed in an air raid in World War II.

Dalswinton Castle [NX 945841], near Dumfries; castle replaced by mansion.

Held by the Maxwells but passed to the Millers, who built the elegant **Dalswinton House** [NX 943841] from 1785. Patrick Miller of Dalswinton was a merchant, then a deputy Governor of the Bank of Scotland. The gardens of the house are occasionally open to the public (www.gardensofscotland.org).

Glenlee [NX 607807], near New Galloway, Dumfries and Galloway; castle replaced by mansion.

Held by the Millers in the eighteenth century, two of whom, Sir Thomas Miller and his son Sir William, were eminent judges. They were made Baronets in 1788, and the family now apparently live in Devon in England. The property passed to the Maxwells and then to the Smiths, and is said to be haunted by a Grey Lady.

Manderston [NT 810545], near Duns, Borders; castle replaced by mansion.

Held by the Homes but the present house was rebuilt for Sir

Manderston 1904?

James Miller, a millionaire racehorse owner, whose family had acquired the property in 1890. Some stories have the house haunted by the apparition of a woman on the main stairs, the ghost identified in one account as Lady Eveline, Sir James's wife. The house is open to the public from mid May to mid September (01361 883450/882636; www.manderston.co.uk).

Rossie Castle [NO 702561], near Montrose, Angus; site of castle and mansion.

Held by the Rossie family, then by several other families, but had passed to the Millars by 1880.

No. of castles/sites: 8
Rank: 160=/764
Xref: Miller

Milligan

The name is from Gaelic and means 'small bald or shaven one', probably a reference to the tonsure from the early church in Scotland. The name has several spellings, including Milligan and Milliken; and the family held lands in Dumfries and Galloway, and then later in Renfrewshire.

Blackmyre [NX 863973] is a couple of miles north of Thornhill in Dumfries and Galloway, and there was a castle or tower house here, although the exact location is not now known. The lands were held by the Milligans in the sixteenth and seventeenth centuries.

Milliken [NS 418634] is a mile or so west of Johnstone in Renfrewshire, and the lands were held by the Wallaces of Elderslie and then by the Houstons, before being acquired by James Milliken, a wealthy sugar merchant, in 1733. He demolished a previous building, probably a tower house, although his new house was itself damaged by a fire and replaced by new Grecian-style mansion, which was then itself replaced by a new house in the 1920s. The property had passed to the Napiers by 1829 and then went to the Mackenzies, and then to others.

No. of castles/sites: 2
Rank: 396=/764
Xrefs: Milliken; Mullikin

Milne

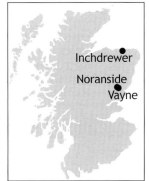

The name comes from a person living or occupying a mill ('Millar' or 'Miller'), or it may come from the Gaelic word 'maol', and describes a bald fellow or priest with a tonsure. The name is on record from the fourteenth century.

Alexander Mylne was Abbot of Cambuskenneth and the first Lord President of the College of Justice in 1532; Walter Mill or Mylne, parish priest of Lunan, was burnt for heresy in 1558 when already more than eighty years old. The Milnes or Mylnes were masons to the kings of Scots for several generations and then architects and civil engineers. They supervised projects such as the remodelling of Holyrood Palace, the building of part of what is now George Heriot's School, the design of the Tron Kirk in Edinburgh, and the design of the North Bridge in Edinburgh. Alexander Milne, who was born at Fochabers in 1742, emigrated to America and made a fortune. He left $100,000 to establish a free school in Fochabers, which was opened in 1846.

Vayne Castle [NO 493599] is a very ruinous Z-plan tower house, dating from the sixteenth century, and materials from here were used to build the nearby farmhouse. Vayne stands seven miles west of Brechin in Angus, and the property was held by the Mowats, by the Lindsay Earls of Crawfords and by the Carnegie Earls of Southesk, before being bought by the Mill family in 1766. They built an elegant new house at **Noranside** [NO 472609], which is apparently now a prison.

Inchdrewer Castle [NJ 656607], three miles south-west of Banff in the north-east of Scotland, is an altered L-plan tower house, dating from the sixteenth century but was extended in later years. Inchdrewer was owned by the Curror family, but was sold to the Ogilvies of Dunlugas, who were made Lords Banff in 1692. The house was torched and Lord Banff slain, the story going that he was murdered by his own servants who were robbing Lord Banff when he unexpectedly returned home. An alternative explanation is that he was killed by John Milne of Boyndie Milne after Lord Banff had insulted Milne's young wife, although Milne was cleared of murder that same year. The castle is now owned and was restored by the Grinnell-Milnes, descendants of John Milne.

No. of castles/sites: 2
Rank: 396=/764
Xrefs: Mill; Mylne

Mitchell

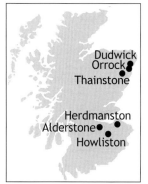

The name comes from the name Michael, the sound being changed when pronounced 'Michel' in French. The name is on record in Scotland from the fifteenth century. James Mitchell was a prominent Covenanter, but fled to Holland after the failure of the Pentland Rising in 1666. He tried to shoot and kill Archbishop James Sharp, but was later arrested and then executed himself in 1678.

James Leslie Mitchell, born in 1901, was a journalist, soldier and traveller, and wrote under the name Lewis Grassic Gibbon. He wrote *The Scots Quair*, the first volume of which, *Sunset Song*, was recently voted the most popular Scottish book in a survey.

The following properties were held by the Mitchells:
Alderstone House [NT 044662], near Livingstone, West Lothian; altered tower house.
Held by the Kinlochs and by the Sandilands Lord Torphichen, but it was bought by John Mitchell of Todhaugh in 1692. Much later it passed to the Bruces and then to the Whitelaws. Currently used as company offices.
Dudwick Castle [NJ 975370], near Ellon, Aberdeenshire; site of castle and mansion.
Held by the Mitchells but had passed to the Kings by 1725. The castle was later used as a farmhouse but was completely demolished about 1860.
Herdmanston [NT 474700], near Haddington, East Lothian; site of tower house.
Held by the Sinclairs, although a Mitchell of Herdmanston is on record in 1438.
Howliston Tower [NT 412489], near Stow, Borders; slight remains of tower.
Held by the Homes, but was owned by the Mitchells in 1690. Built into the farm.
Orrock House or **Over Blairton** [NJ 964196], near Balmedie, Aberdeenshire; castle replaced by mansion.
Held by the Mitchells from 1708, but passed to the Fordyce family in 1770, then later went to the Orrocks, who changed the name from Over Blairton.
Thainstone House [NJ 759186], near Inverurie, Aberdeenshire; castle or old house replaced by mansion.
Held by the Forbeses, but was bought by the Mitchells in 1717. An older house here was sacked by Jacobites in 1745, and Sir Andrew Mitchell was Under Secretary for Scotland in the 1740s and then ambassador to the Court of Prussia in the time of Frederick the Great. The building is said to be haunted by a Green Lady, the ghost of a daughter of a laird who died in a riding accident. Thainstone is now a hotel (01467 621643; www.macdonald-hotels.co.uk).

No. of castles/sites: 6
Rank: 212=/764

Moffat

The name probably comes from the Moffat Water and the burgh of Moffat in Dumfries and Galloway. The family are mentioned from the thirteenth century, and they held lands in Annandale. Dr Robert Moffat, born in Ormiston in 1795, was a missionary and explorer in Africa; his son-in-law was David Livingstone.

Auldton [NT 094058], to the north and east of Moffat, and Granton, which was further north, were held by the Moffats, perhaps from the eleventh century, and they had a castle or seat. The Moffats supported Robert the Bruce, fought at the Battle of Bannockburn in 1314 and were prominent in the fourteenth century. They had a long-standing and bitter feud with the Johnstones, and the head of the family, Robert Moffat of Auldton, was slain in 1557. The house in which the Moffats were sheltering was burned and they were slaughtered as they tried to escape. The family had lost their lands by 1608; they passed to their enemies, the Johnstones.

The Moffats also held lands further north at Granton or Grantoun, as mentioned above, on the east side of the River Annan, and may have had a tower house. Granton House [NT 074099] is an attractive classical mansion of three storeys, dating from 1830.

The Moffats also held:
Airds [NX 675705], near Castle Douglas, Dumfries and Galloway; site of castle.
   Held by the Gordons, but passed to the Lauries and then to the Moffats in 1877.
Boadsbeck Castle [NT 148093], near Moffat, Dumfries and Galloway; site of tower house.
   Held by the Moffats, who (as mentioned above) had a long feud with the Johnstones. Boadsbeck is said to have had a brownie, which came here after deserting the Johnstones of Wamphray. Some versions have the brownie going in the other direction, leaving after being given inappropriate food, crying: 'Ca', brownie, ca'! A' the luck o' Bodbeck's Awa' to Leithenha'!' This may be a reference to the feud, but the lands were bought back by the Moffats in the twentieth century.
Gillesbie Tower [NY 171919], near Lockerbie, Dumfries and Galloway; slight remains of tower house.
   Held by the Grahams, but also possibly by the Moffats at one time.
Knock [NY 299908], near Langholm, Dumfries and Galloway; site of tower house.
   Held by the Moffats. Adam Moffat of Knock fought at the Battle of Bannockburn in 1314, but Knock was sold to the Johnstones in 1609.
Wauchope Castle [NY 354840], near Langholm, Dumfries and Galloway; site of castle.
   Held by the Lindsays, but may have been a property of the Moffats at one time.

www.clanmoffat.org
No. of castles/sites: 6
Rank: 212=/764

Moir

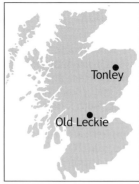

The name comes from the Gaelic 'mor', meaning 'big' and is descriptive. The name was not uncommon in Aberdeenshire, and is on record from the beginning of the fourteenth century.

Old Leckie House [NS 690946], which is six or so miles west of Stirling, is a T-plan house, which dates from the sixteenth century. It was held by the Leckie family in the fourteenth century, but was bought by the Moirs in 1659, and they were in possession until the twentieth century. Bonnie Prince Charlie was entertained at the house by the wife of the then laird in 1745, while her husband was imprisoned in Stirling Castle.

Tonley House [NJ 611135] is some three miles east and south of Alford in Aberdeenshire, and is now an impressive ruin. It stands on or near the site of a castle, and was greatly altered and extended in the nineteenth century. Tonley was a property of the Byres family, but passed by marriage to the Moir family after 1790, although they took the name Moir Byres. The lands were sold in 1947.

No. of castles/sites: 2
Rank: 396=/764

Moncreiffe

The name comes from the barony and lands of Moncreiffe, which are three miles south-east of Perth. There have been many different ways to spell the name, not least those still represented: Moncreiffe of that Ilk, Moncrieff of Kinmonth, the Moncreiff Barons Moncreiff, and Scott Moncrieff, formerly of Fossoway. The origin is from the Gaelic 'monadh croibhe', which means 'hill of the sacred bough', and the name is on record from the thirteenth century. The present **Moncreiffe House** [NO 138193] stands on the site of a mansion, which dated from 1679 and was designed by Sir William Bruce, and probably also on the site of castle. The mansion suffered a catastrophic fire in 1957, killing the twenty-third laird, although a new house was built on the site.

The lands were a property of the Moncreiffes from 1248. The family are said to have sheltered William Wallace. Sir John Moncreiffe of that Ilk and John of Easter Moncreiffe were both killed at the Battle of Flodden in 1513, and William Moncreiffe was captured following the Battle of Solway Moss in 1542 and was imprisoned in the Tower of London. Sir John Moncreiffe was made a Baronet of Nova Scotia in 1628, but signed the National Covenant ten years later. The Moncreiffes of that Ilk still apparently own the property.

The Moncreiffes also held:

Balcaskie House [NO 526035], near Pittenweem, Fife; mansion incorporating castle.
  Held by the Strangs, but passed to the Moncreiffes after 1615, who extended the house and new wings were added in 1665 by Sir William Bruce. Much of Bruce's original interior remains, including painted ceilings by De Witt and plaster by Dunsterfield. The property passed to the Stewarts of Grandtully, then to the Nicholsons, and then to the Anstruthers, who apparently still own it.

Bandirran [NO 200306], near Coupar Angus, Perthshire; castle replaced by mansion.
  Held by the Grays in the sixteenth century, but passed to the Moncreiffes, who were in possession until 1928.

Carnbee Place [NO 530067], near Pittenweem, Fife; castle replaced by mansion.
  Held by the Melvilles but bought by the Moncreiffes in 1598.

Culdares [NN 728469], near Kenmore, Perthshire; site of castle or old house.
  Held by the Moncreiffes but passed to the Menzies family at the end of the sixteenth century.

Hallyards Castle [NT 212914] or **Camilla**, near Cowdenbeath, Fife; slight remains of castle.
  Held by the Skenes and by the Kirkcaldys of Grange, but passed to the Moncreiffes of Reedie in 1788, and they changed the name of the property to Camilla.

Moredun Hall or **Easter Moncreiffe** [NO 145193], near Perth; slight remains of castle.
  Held by the Moncreiffes from the thirteenth century. John Moncreiffe of Easter Moncreiffe was slain at Flodden in 1513.

Myres Castle [NO 242110], near Auchtermuchty, Fife; Z-plan tower house.
  Held by several families before coming to the Moncreiffes of

Reedie about 1750, but later passed to the Bruces. Still occupied and the gardens are occasionally open to the public while accommodation is available in the castle (01208 821341; www.myres.co.uk/www.gardensofscotland.org).

Randerston [NO 608108], near Crail, Fife; L-plan tower house.
  Held by the Balcomie family and then by the Mortons, but was bought by the Moncreiffes of Balcaskie in 1629, who sold it to the Balfours of Denmylne in 1663. Randerston is now a farmhouse.

Reedie [NO 234107], near Auchtermuchty, Fife; site of castle or old mansion.
  Held by the Moncreiffes of Reedie, who moved to Myres Castle about 1750.

Tullibole Castle [NO 053006], near Crook of Devon, Perthshire; L-plan tower house.
  Held by the Herring family, but passed to the Hallidays, and then by marriage to the Moncreiffes in the eighteenth century. Henry James Moncreiffe, second of Tullibole, was a Lord of Session in 1888. The house is still apparently occupied by the Moncreif Barons Moncreif.

www.moncreiffe.org
No. of castles/sites: 11 / Rank: 127=/764
Xref: Moncrieff

Moncur

The name may come from the French 'mon', meaning 'my', and 'coeur', meaning 'heart', so 'my heart', and the name is on record from the thirteenth century. **Moncur Castle** [NO 284295] is some nine miles east and north of Perth, and is a ruinous Z-plan tower house, rising to three storeys with round towers at both ends. It was a property of the Moncurs, and Robert Moncur was one of those taken prisoner at Dunbar Castle in 1296. The property later passed to the Kinnairds, and the castle was gutted by fire in the eighteenth century; it was not restored.

No. of castles/sites: 1 / Rank: 537=/764

Monorgan

The name is territorial and comes from the lands of Monorgan, which are six miles west of Dundee in Perthshire. The lands were held by the Monorgan family, who are on record from the fourteenth century, and there was a castle at **Monorgan** [NO 321285]. It is not clear when the Monorgans lost the property, but it is on record as being held by the Grahams and also by the Crawfords.

No. of castles/sites: 1 / Rank: 537=/764
Xref: Monorgund

429

Montgomery

The name comes from a Norman family, who held the Castle of Sainte Foy de Montgomery. The Montgomerys came to England in the forces of William the Conqueror, and acquired much property and gave their name to the county in Wales. The family were established in Scotland from the middle of the twelfth century, and held lands principally in Renfrew and in Ayrshire but also in other parts of Scotland.

Eaglesham Castle [NS 571520], at or near the village of Eaglesham in Renfrewshire to the south of Glasgow, was held by the Montgomerys from 1165 after Robert Montgomery had married a daughter of Walter the High Steward. Sir John Montgomery, ninth of Eaglesham, captured Harry 'Hotspur' Percy at the Battle of Otterburn in 1388, and built a new castle at Polnoon with the proceeds of the ransom. The present Eaglesham Castle or House is a grand modern mansion, and the motte site was used for meetings and festivals. **Polnoon Castle** [NS 586513] became the main seat of the Montgomerys, but little now remains. Polnoon is three miles south-west of East Kilbride and not far from Eaglesham, but was ruinous by the end of the seventeenth century.

Eglinton Castle [NS 323423] is a mile or so north of Irvine in Ayrshire, and is a huge but very ruinous castellated mansion, dating from the eighteenth century but built on the site of an old stronghold. The property passed to marriage from the Eglinton family to the Montgomerys in the fourteenth century. Hugh Montgomery fought for James IV at the Battle of Sauchieburn in 1488, and was made Earl of Eglinton in 1508. The Montgomerys had a bitter and bloody feud with the Cunningham Earl of Glencairn, and they sacked Kerelaw Castle, and in retaliation the Cunninghams attacked and torched Eglinton. Hugh, third Earl, fought for Mary, Queen of Scots, at Langside in 1568 (Jean, Countess of Eglinton, who died in 1562, is buried in Holyrood Abbey), and the fourth Earl, another Hugh, was murdered in 1586 near the bridge of Annick by the

Eglinton Castle 1930?

John Cunningham of Clonbeith and Cunningham of Robertland, and others of that family. The Montgomerys slew every Cunningham they could find in revenge, and slaughtered Cunningham of Clonbeith. The title and lands passed by marriage to the Setons, and the seventh Earl, another Hugh, fought for the Royalists at Marston Moor. The castle was replaced by a large mansion in 1802, and it was at the new castle that the Eglinton Tournament was held in 1839, a splendid but expensive medieval tournament, attracting thousands of visitors. The house was abandoned when the family ran out of money, not least by building a harbour at Ardrossan. Eglinton was unroofed in 1925, was blown up in the 1950s, and the shell of the house partly demolished in 1973. The family are now represented by the Montgomerie Earls of Eglinton and Winton, and they now apparently live near Cargill in Perthshire. The ruin stands in a public park (01294 551776; www.north-ayrshire.gov.uk).

The Montgomerys also held:

Ardrossan Castle [NS 233424], Ardrossan, Ayrshire; ruinous castle.
  Held by the Ardrossan or Eglinton family, but passed by marriage to the Montgomerys. Sir John Montgomery, who fought at the battles of Otterburn in 1388, capturing Harry 'Hotspur' Percy, and then at Homildon Hill in 1402, remodelled the castle. The family sheltered at Ardrossan in 1528 when their castle at Eglinton was sacked and burnt by the Cunninghams. Ardrossan was dismantled in the 1650s to build the Cromwellian Citadel at Ayr.

Auchans [NS 355346], near Troon, Ayrshire; ruinous altered L-plan house.
  Held by the Wallaces, then by the Cochranes of Coldoun, then by the Montgomery Earls of Eglinton. Auchans was the home of the beautiful Susanna Kennedy of Culzean, widow of the

Auchans (M&R)

ninth Earl. She remained a staunch Jacobite until her death in 1780 at the age of ninety-one years old. The poet Allan Ramsay dedicated his work *The Gentle Shepherd* to her, and one story is that in her old age she trained rats to eat with her at meal times.

Auchinloss [NS 447401], near Kilmarnock, Ayrshire; site of tower house.
  Held by the Assloss family, but passed to the Montgomerys in 1616, but then went to the Glens and to the Parkers. The lands are now part of Dean Castle Country Park.

Ballikillet Castle [NS 172560], near Millport, Isle of Cumbrae, Ayrshire; site of castle or old mansion.
  Held by the Montgomerys, who owned much of the island until the eighteenth century.

Brigend Castle [NS 334177], near Ayr; remains of castle.
  Held by the Montgomerys of Bridgend.

Broadstone Castle [NS 359528], near Beith, Ayrshire; site of castle.
  Held by the Liddels in 1452, but apparently passed to the Montgomerys before being sold to the Greenock family in 1650.

Cassillis House [NS 341128], Maybole, Ayrshire; altered castle and mansion.
  Held by the Montgomerys, but passed by marriage to the Kennedys in 1373, who still own it, now Marquises of Ailsa and Earls of Cassillis.

Cloak Castle [NS 344605], near Lochwinnoch, Renfrewshire; site of castle.
  Held by the Montgomerys.

Clonbeith Castle [NS 338455], near Kilwinning, Renfrewshire; slight remains of castle.
  Held by the Cunninghams. John Cunningham of Clonbeith murdered Hugh Montgomery, fourth Earl of Eglinton, in 1586 during a feud. He was pursued by the Montgomerys and cut to pieces. The property was sold to the Montgomery Earl of Eglinton in 1717.

Coilsfield Castle [NS 444265], near Mauchline, Ayrshire; site of castle and mansion.
  Held by the Cunninghams of Caprington, but bought by the Montgomerys in 1661 and they held the property until the twentieth century. The castle was replaced by Montgomerie House in 1798, but the house was burnt out in 1969 and then demolished.

Corslie Castle [NS 545593], near Barrhead, Lanarkshire; site of tower house.
  Held by the Montgomery Earls of Eglinton.

Cumstoun Castle [NX 683533], near Kirkcudbright, Galloway; slight remains of tower house.
  Held by several families, including by the Montgomerys in 1595, but had passed to the Maitlands by the eighteenth century.

Duchal Castle [NS 334685], near Kilmacolm, Renfrewshire; slight remains of castle.
  Held by the Lyles, but passed to the Montgomerys of Lainshaw in 1544, and then was sold to the Porterfields and then to others. The gardens of nearby **Duchal House** [NS 334685] are occasionally open to the public (www.gardensofscotland.org).

Dunskey Castle [NW 994534], near Portpatrick, Galloway; fine ruinous castle in cliffs.
  Held by the Adairs of Kilhilt, but was bought by the Montgomerys in 1620, then was sold to John Blair in 1660. The castle is accessible by foot from Portpatrick, but may be going to be restored.

Giffen Castle [NS 377507], near Beith, Ayrshire; slight remains of castle.
  Held by the Montgomerys of Eglinton but demolished in 1920.

Glenays Castle [NS 285180], near Ayr; site of castle.
  Held by the Montgomerys of Bridgend and then by the Kennedys.

Hatton Mains [NO 676675], near Montrose, Angus; castle replaced by mansion.
  Held by the Montgomerys, but was sold to the Henry family in 1920.

Hessilhead Castle [NS 379533], near Beith, Ayrshire; site of castle.
  Held by the Montgomerys of Eglinton, one of whom, Alexander Montgomery, was a well-known poet.

Knock Castle [NS 194631], near Largs, Ayrshire; ruinous Z-plan tower house.
  Held by the Frasers of Lovat, but was sold to the Montgomerys of Skelmorlie in the seventeenth century, and then passed through several families.

Ladyland Castle [NS 324579], near Kilbirnie, Ayrshire; castle replaced by mansion.
  Held by the Barclays and by the Montgomerys before being bought by the Cochranes in 1717. The present house dates from 1817-21.

Lainshaw Castle [NS 410453], near Stewarton, Ayrshire; site of castle.
  Held by the Stewarts but passed to the Montgomerys in 1570,

then was sold to the Cunninghams in 1779. The present Lainshaw House is a classical mansion with later additions. The building is said to have a Green Lady, reputed to be the apparition of Elizabeth Cunningham, wife of Montgomery of Lainshaw. She may have been involved in the plot which resulted in the murder of the Hugh Montgomery, fourth Earl of Eglinton, in 1586. The ghost is said to have been witnessed wearing a green dress and carrying a candle; the rustle of her dress is also reportedly been heard.

Little Cumbrae Castle [NS 153514], Isle of Little Cumbrae, Ayrshire; ruinous castle.
  Held by the Hunters of Hunterston, but passed to the Montgomery Earls of Eglinton in 1515. Sir Alexander (Seton), sixth Earl, imprisoned Archibald Hamilton, a supporter of Cromwell, in the castle before sending him to Stirling to be hanged. Cromwell had the castle sacked, and it was not reoccupied.

Lochleven Castle [NO 138018], near Kinross, Perthshire; ruinous castle on island in loch.
  Held by the Douglases, by the Bruces and by the Grahams before passing to the Montgomerys. The castle is in the care of Historic Scotland and is open to the public from April to October (07778 040483 (mobile)).

Lochranza Castle [NR 933507], Lochranza, Isle of Arran, Ayrshire; fine ruinous castle.
  Held by the MacDonalds, by the Stewarts of Menteith and by the Campbells, before passing to the Montgomerys, later Earls of Eglinton. James IV used the castle as a base from which to

Lochranza Castle (M&R)

harry the MacDonald Lords of the Isles in the 1490s, and it was occupied by the forces of James VI in 1614 and by Cromwell in the 1650s. It was sold to the Hamiltons in 1705, but is now in the care of Historic Scotland and is open to the public (key available locally).

Macbiehill [NT 185514], near West Linton, Borders; site of castle and mansion.
  Held by the Montgomerys in the middle of the seventeenth century, and they were made Baronets in 1801, and they now apparently live in Kinross. The property passed to the Beresfords before the end of the eighteenth century.

Montfode Castle [NS 226441], near Ardrossan, Ayrshire; some remains of Z-plan tower house.
  Held by the Montgomerys.

Newton House [NS 663613], near Cambuslang, Lanarkshire; site of castle and mansion.
  Held by the Douglases and by the Hamiltons of Silvertonhill but later went to the Montgomerys.

Saltcoats [NS 243411], Saltcoats, Ayrshire; site of castle.
  The burgh was held by the Montgomery Earl of Eglinton in 1529.

Seagate Castle [NS 320392], Irvine, Ayrshire; ruinous tower and town house.
  Held by and built by the Montgomerys, later Earls of Eglinton, who owned the property from 1361. Mary, Queen of Scots,

431

visited the castle in 1563, and it was occupied until about 1746, when the tenth Earl had the roof removed.

Skelmorlie Castle [NS 195658], near Largs, Ayrshire; restored tower house.

Held by the Cunninghams of Kilmaurs, but passed to the Montgomerys in 1461. Sir James Montgomery, tenth of Skelmorlie, was imprisoned in 1684 for sheltering Covenanters, was an MP for Ayrshire, but then became a Jacobite and died

Skelmorlie Castle 1920?

in Paris in 1694. The next laird, Sir Robert, fought in the War of the Spanish Succession and was granted lands in South Carolina. The property then went to the Graham family in 1852 who extended the castle, and it is still occupied. The Montgomerys of Skelmorlie had a burial aisle and loft in Largs Old Kirk [NS 200594] from 1646, called the Skelmorlie Aisle. There are a number of burial monuments, as well as a painted ceiling, and the key can be acquired from nearby Largs Museum. Self-catering accommodation is available in Skelmorlie Castle (01475 521616; www.aboutscotland.com/ ayrshire/skelmorlie.html).

Southannan Castle [NS 209538], near Largs, Ayrshire; ruinous castle.

Held by the Semples, but had passed to the Montgomerys of Eglinton by the nineteenth century.

Stair [NS 442239], near Tarbolton, Ayrshire; fine altered L-plan tower house.

Held by the Montgomerys, but passed by marriage to the Kennedys of Dunure in the fourteenth century, then later went to the Dalrymples of Stair.

Stane Castle [NS 338399], near Irvine, Ayrshire; ruinous tower house.

Held by the Francis family, but passed by marriage to the Montgomerys of Greenfield and they built the castle. The castle was turned into a folly in the 1750s.

Stanhope Tower [NT 123297], near Drumelzier, Borders; site of tower house.

Held by the Murrays, but sold to the Montgomerys in 1767. They were made Baronets in 1801, Sir James Montgomery having been Lord Advocate for Scotland in 1766, and they now apparently live in Kinross.

Stobo Castle [NT 173367], near Drumelzier, Borders; castle replaced by mansion.

Held by the Murrays, but bought by the Montgomerys in 1767. The building is now used as a health spa (01721 725300; www.stobocastle.co.uk).

Whitslaid Tower [NT 557446], near Lauder, Borders; slight remains of tower house.

Held by the Lauders or by the Maitlands, but had passed to the Montgomerys of Macbiehill in the mid seventeenth century.

www.clanmontgomery.org
No. of castles/sites: 39
Rank: 27=/764
Xref: Montgomerie

Monypenny

The name probably comes from a family from Normandy, and they came to England, where they were called 'Mannipenni' and 'Manipenyn'. They were given lands in Fife, where they became a prominent family.

Pitmilly House [NO 579134], half a mile east of Boarhills in Fife, is a modern mansion but it stands at or near the site of a castle. The lands were held by the Monypennys from the twelfth century. John Monypenny of Pitmully was a Scottish ambassador to Edward III of England in the fourteenth century, and the family were made Lords Monypenny around 1464. Isobel Monypenny, daughter of the then laird, was mother of Cardinal David Beaton; nevertheless David Monypenny of Pitmilly, an ardent Reformer, was captured at St Andrews Castle after the murder of Beaton in 1546. Monypenny was imprisoned in France, was later pardoned, but he was then seized by the French again. The family held the property until 1974, and now apparently live in West Sussex in England.

The Monypennys also held:

Kinaldy Castle [NO 513104], near St Andrews, Fife; site of castle.
Held by the Aytons until the eighteenth century, then by the Monypennys.

Kinkell [NO 539158], near St Andrews, Fife; site of castle.
Held by the Monypennys of Pitmilly, then by the Hamiltons of Kinkell, and possibly by the Kinnimonds of Craighall.

Pilrig House [NT 265757], Edinburgh; restored L-plan tower house.
Held by the Monypennys from the sixteenth century, but passed to the Kirkwoods in 1623, then to the Balfours. It was restored and divided into flats in 1985.

Pittarthie Castle [NO 522091], near Elie, Fife; L-plan tower house.
Held by the Monypennys of Pitmilly, but passed to the Murrays in 1590, then to the Logans and then to others. The castle is being restored.

No. of castles/sites: 5
Rank: 240=/764
Xref: Moneypenny

Pittarthie Castle (M&R)

Moodie

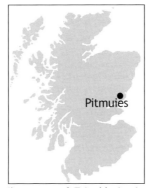

The name may come from 'modig', the Old English for 'courageous', and it is on record in Scotland from the middle of the thirteenth century. The name was not uncommon in Angus, and the family held **Pitmuies** or **House of Pitmuies** [NO 567497], which is one and a half miles west of Friockheim in Angus, although in 1876 Pitmuies went to the Lyell Baronets of Kinnordy. There are fine gardens, which are open to the public (01241 818245; www.pitmuies.com).

No. of castles/sites: 1
Rank: 537=/764
Xref: Mudie

Mordington

The name is territorial and comes from the lands of Mordington, which are a few miles west of Berwick-upon-Tweed near the English border. The name means the seat or 'ton' of the Saxon 'Mordyn', 'Morthing' or 'Mording', hence 'Mordington'.

Mordington [NT 951558] was held by the family from after 1200, and one of the family, William Mordington, was Chancellor of Scotland in the reign of Alexander II in the thirteenth century. The lands appear to have passed by marriage to the Halyburtons, but the property was given to Thomas Randolph by Robert the Bruce. Mordington later passed to the Douglases of Dalkeith and then to others. There was a castle but there are no remains.

No. of castles/sites: 1
Rank: 537=/764

Morham

The name is territorial and comes from the lands of Morham, which are a few miles to the south-east of Haddington in East Lothian; the name is on record from the twelfth century.

Morham Castle [NT 557723] has gone but the lands were held by the family of that name from around the middle of the twelfth century. Herbert Morham was imprisoned by the English in Rockville Castle in 1296. The property passed by marriage to the Giffords of Yester in the fourteenth century, and then later went to the Hepburn Earls of Bothwell.

Kimmerghame House [NT 815514], a couple of miles to the south and east of Duns in the Borders, is a grand mansion but there was a castle or old house here before the mansion was built. The lands were held by the Morhams from around 1320, but had passed to the Sinclairs by the fifteenth century, and then went to the Homes and to others.

To the east of Carnoustie in Angus is **Panbride** [NO 572358], and there was probably a castle here, although there is no trace; Panbride House is a modern mansion. The property was held by the Morhams from the twelfth century, but had passed to the Ramsays by 1519 and then went to the Carnegies.

Rankine Castle or **Castle Rankine** [NS 787819] was two miles west of Denny in central Scotland, but there is nothing left. The stronghold had a tower and a barbican and was still occupied in the sixteenth century. The lands were a property of the Morhams in about 1300, and they probably built the castle.

No. of castles/sites: 4
Rank: 278=/764

Morrison

The name has two origins, one from the Gaelic-speaking Hebrides, the other from lowland parts of Scotland. The Gaelic origin means 'son of (the) servant of the Virgin (St Mary)', or may come from an Irish family, the 'O'Muirgheasains', who were bards and keepers of the relics of St Columcille. The Morrisons settled on Lewis, and were judges and held lands. The clan got into a bitter feud with the MacAulays of Uig which led to raiding and murder, and the Morrisons got the worst of it when the MacLeods of Lewis supported the MacAulays. The Morrisons, however, then supported the Mackenzies of Kintail against the MacLeods of Lewis, although more of them were killed. The Mackenzies eventually won out, although this does not seem to have benefited the Morrisons much. They were long in possession of Ness, to the north of the Isle of Lewis in the Outer Hebrides.

Dun Eistean [NB 536650] is on a small island above the sea to the east of Five Penny Ness at the far northern tip of Lewis. There are traces of a building and a wall and this was the stronghold of the Morrisons of Ness, and dates from the sixteenth century or earlier. A bridge gives access to the site.

Dun Carloway [NB 190412], further south on Lewis to the south-west of Carloway, was originally an Iron Age broch, but it was used by the Morrisons of Ness in

Dun Carloway (JM)

the seventeenth century. One of the MacAulays of Uig managed to climb the tower and then suffocated the sleeping Morrisons by dropping smouldering heather into the broch. The broch is open to the public.

The English derivation of the name is from 'Maurice's son', and is mentioned in Scotland from the middle of the fifteenth century. Robert Morison, who was born in Aberdeen in 1620, studied science and medicine and was physician to Gaston, Duke of Orleans, and he was then physician and botanist to Charles II before becoming

a Professor at Oxford. Thomas Morrison, who made a fortune as a builder in Edinburgh, left money to found Morrison's Academy in Crieff.

The following properties were held by the Morrisons:
Colquhar Tower [NT 332416], near Innerleithen, Borders; slight remains of tower house.
   Held by the Kerrs and then by the Morrisons.
Conzie Castle [NJ 595450], near Huntly, Aberdeenshire; ruinous tower house.
   Held by the Morrisons and by the Dunbars.
Dairsie Castle [NO 414160], near Cupar, Fife; restored Z-plan tower house.
   Held by the Learmonths and by the Spottiswoodes, but passed to the Morrisons after 1650 and later went to the Scotts of Scotstarvit. The castle was very ruinous but was rebuilt in the 1990s.
Frendraught Castle [NJ 620418], near Huntly, Aberdeenshire; restored house on site of castle.
   Long held by the Crichtons, but passed to the Morrisons in about 1690. The house is still occupied.
Mountblairy or **Balravie** [NJ 694546], near Turriff, Aberdeenshire; castle replaced by mansion.
   Held by the Stewart Earls of Buchan and by the Hays, before being bought by the Morrisons around 1800. The castle was replaced by **Mountblairy** [NJ 692545], which was a magnificent classical mansion dating from 1791 and extended in 1825, but this building been demolished.
Naughton Castle [NO 373246], near Wormit, Fife; ruinous tower house and courtyard.
   Held by the Hays and by the Crichtons before going to the Morrisons in 1737, then passed to the Beatons in the nineteenth century.
Prestongrange House [NT 373737], near Musselburgh, East Lothian; mansion incorporating old work.
   Held by the Kerr Earls of Lothian but passed to the Morrisons in 1609 before being sold to the Grants in 1746. The building is now the clubhouse of the Royal Musselburgh Golf Club (01875 810276; www.royalmusselburgh.co.uk).

www.clanmorrison.net
www.clanmorrison.org

No. of castles/sites: 9
Rank: 149=/764
Xref: Morison

Mortimer

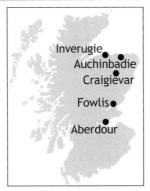

The name comes from the barony of 'Mortemer' in Normandy, and the name is derived from 'dead sea'. The name is on record in Scotland from the twelfth century, and William Mortimer was captured with William the Lion at Alnwick in 1174, although he was soon released.

Aberdour Castle [NT 193854] is a partly ruinous but fine castle, dating from the fourteenth century but extended down the centuries. There is an original

Aberdour Castle (M&R)

painted ceiling, and a splendid walled garden. The property was held by the Mortimers, one of whom gave his name to 'Mortimer's Deep', the stretch of water between Inchcolm and the mainland. This Mortimer gave land to the abbey so that he might be buried on the holy island of Inchcolm, but his coffin ended up in the sea. The story goes that he was a wicked fellow and the abbot did not want his remains on Inchcolm, and one version has a storm blowing up, while another has the monks casting his remains overboard; it may, of course, be a pun on the name Mortimer. The castle passed to Thomas Randolph and then to the Douglases, who were long in possession. Aberdour Castle is now in the care of Historic Scotland and is open to the public (01383 860519).

Craigievar Castle [NJ 566095], four and a half miles south and west of Alford in Aberdeenshire, is one of the best castles in Scotland, and is a fantastic L-plan tower house of seven storeys and the walls are pink-washed. The lower floors are very plain, while the upper works abound with gables, turrets, chimney stacks and corbelling. There are some good interiors, including the hall and panelled rooms on the floors above. The lands were held by the Mortimers from 1457 or earlier, and they started to built the castle, but ran out of money and the property was sold to the Forbeses in 1610. The Forbeses finished the castle and their descendants held it until 1963 when it went to The National Trust for Scotland. Craigievar is open to the public (01339 883635).

The Mortimers also owned:

Auchinbadie [NJ 688585], near Banff, Aberdeenshire; motte.
> Held by the Mortimers until 1716 when the line ended with two heiresses.

Fowlis Castle [NO 321334], near Dundee; tower house.
> Held by the Maules, but passed to the Mortimers and then went by marriage to the Grays of Broxmouth in 1377, and they later built the tower. Now used as a farmhouse.

Inverugie Castle [NJ 152687], near Elgin, Moray; site of castle.
> Held by the Youngs, but the present house was built in 1864 after the property had passed to the Mortimers.

No. of castles/sites: 5
Rank: 240=/764

Craigievar Castle (M&R) – see previous coumn

Morton

One derivation of the name is territorial and comes from the lands of Myreton or Morton, about four miles east of Cupar in Fife, from which the family got their name. Another is local from the place and lands of Morton in Annandale in Dumfries

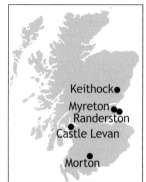

and Galloway. There is a castle at Morton [NX 891992], but it never seems to have been owned by the Morton family, although they do have associations with the Douglases (who were Earls of Morton). The castle is in the care of Historic Scotland and can be visited.

   Randerston [NO 608108] is three or so miles north of Crail in Fife, and is an altered L-plan tower house, which dates from the sixteenth century, and has two turrets. The lands were held by the Balcomie family, but passed to the Myrtouns or Mortons, and they probably built the tower. Randerston was sold to the Moncreiffes of Balcaskie in 1629, and then to the Balfours of Denmylne; it is now a farmhouse. Crail Collegiate Church [NO 614080] was founded in the existing church by William Myrton in 1517, and it is a fine building which is open to the public

   Cambo House [NO 604115], a mile south of Kingsbarns also in Fife, is a classical mansion, rebuilt after a fire in 1878, but it stands on or near the site of a castle. Cambo was a possession of the family of the same name, but passed to the Mortons in 1364 and they held it until the seventeenth century. Cambo went to the Erskines, and the gardens are open to the public all year (01333 450313; www.camboestate.com).

   A mile or so west of Gourock in Renfrewshire is **Castle Levan** [NS 216764], a strong tower or keep of the fourteenth century, to which has been added a later wing. The castle was built by the Mortons, but was sold to the Semples in 1547, and then later passed to the Stewarts of Inverkip. Castle Levan has been restored and is occupied, but is said to be haunted by a White Lady, and B&B accommodation is available (01475 659154; www.castle-levan.com).

Keithock [NO 603634], a couple or so miles north of Brechin in Angus, was held by several families including by the Bowies, but was owned by the Mortons at the end of the nineteenth century. The present mansion replaced an old house or castle.

No. of castles/sites: 4
Rank: 278=/764
Xref: Myrtoun

Morville

The Morvilles or de Morvilles were a Norman family who came to Scotland in the twelfth century. They were Constables of Scotland in the twelfth and thirteenth centuries until they were forfeited by Robert the Bruce after supporting John Balliol. Hugh Morville founded Kilwinning Abbey [NS 303433], in Kilwinning, in 1262, although little of the buildings of the abbey now remains.

They held the following properties:
Borgue [NX 633483], near Kirkcudbright, Galloway; ruinous mansion.
   Held by the Morvilles, who had a castle. It is likely that it was destroyed by the men of Galloway in the 1170s during a rising against the king of Scots. The property later passed to the Blairs.
Glengarnock Castle [NS 311574], near Kilbirnie, Ayrshire; slight remains of castle.
   Held by the Morvilles, but passed to the Riddels and then to the Cunninghams.
Newton Don [NT 709372], near Kelso, Borders; castle replaced by mansion.
   Held by the Morvilles, but passed to the Douglases in the fourteenth century. The later mansion is still occupied.
Saltoun Hall [NT 461685], near Haddington, East Lothian; fine mansion incorporating castle.
   Held by the Morvilles, but passed to the Abernethys before 1300. The mansion has been divided but is still occupied.

No. of castles/sites: 4
Rank: 278=/764

Castle Levan (M&R)

Mossman

The name is on record in Scotland from the fifteenth century. William Mossman was executed by beheading after being found guilty of the slaying of Ralph Weir in 1532.

John Knox House [NT 262738], which is on the High Street of Edinburgh, is believed to date from the fifteenth century and may be the oldest house in the capital. It was home to James Mossman, keeper of the Royal Mint to Mary, Queen of Scots. He supported Mary and was captured after the fall of Edinburgh Castle and was then executed in 1573.

John Knox House (M&R)

The house gets its name from the tradition that this was where the Protestant reformer John Knox died in 1572. The original floor in the Oak Room survives, and there is a magnificent painted ceiling. An exhibition covers the life of Knox, and there is also information about Mossman (0131 556 9579).

No. of castles/sites: 1 / Rank: 537=/764

Moultray

The name is on record in Scotland from the end of the thirteenth century, and the family held lands in Edinburgh: General Register House is built on what was the estate. **Seafield Tower** [NT 280885] is a mile or so north of Kinghorn in Fife, and is a ruinous tower house, dating from the sixteenth century; a round corner turret is known as the Devil's Tower. The lands were held by the Moultrays until they were forfeited following the Jacobite Rising of 1715 and they then went to the Melvilles.

No. of castles/sites: 1 / Rank: 537=/764
Xrefs: Moutray; Moultrie

Mounsey

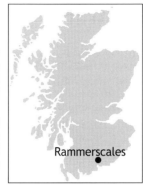

The name comes from French and means 'of the Mount', and is on record in Scotland from the end of the thirteenth century. Aman Mounceaux was the warden of Lochmaben Castle in Dumfries and Galloway at the end of the fourteenth century.

Rammerscales House [NY 081777], three miles south of Lockerbie in Dumfriesshire, is a fine classical mansion, dating from the eighteenth century and rising to four storeys, and there was a probably a castle here. Rammerscales was owned by the Bells, but passed to the Mounsey family in the eighteenth century. The house is said to be haunted by the ghost of Dr James Mounsey, who had the house built and died in 1773. He was physician to Tsar Peter of Russia, but Mounsey lived in fear of his life after returning to Scotland following the assassination of the tsar. Supernatural activity is reported to be mostly witnessed in the library, and evacuees from Glasgow, who were billeted here during World War II, were so apprehensive that they slept in the stables rather than in the house. Rammerscales is now a property of the Bell MacDonald family, has fine grounds, and is open to the public in the summer (01387 810229; www.rammerscales.co.uk).

No. of castles/sites: 1
Rank: 537=/764
Xrefs: Mounsie; Mouncey

Mow

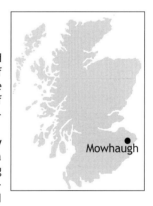

The name is territorial and comes from the lands of Mow or Molle, which are some three and a half miles south-east of Morebattle in the Borders.

Mowhaugh or **Mow Tower** [NT 816204] was a strong tower house, dating from the sixteenth century. The lands were held by the Mows from the twelfth or thirteenth century, and they were in possession of the property for some 500 years. The tower was besieged by the English in 1546 and destroyed by undermining the wall, killing those inside. The laird of Mow was slain at Raid of Redeswire in 1575, although the Scots had the victory.

No. of castles/sites: 1
Rank: 537=/764
Xref: Molle

Mowat

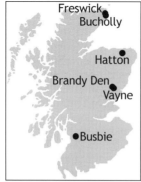

The name comes from the French 'monthault' or Latin 'monte alto', which is translated as 'of the high mountain'. The family was from France but went to Wales before coming to Scotland in the twelfth century. Many of the Mowats achieved high office, and they held lands in Angus and elsewhere; William Mowat was one of those to add his seal to the Declaration of Arbroath in 1320. Another of the family, Bernard, was from the Borders and was sentenced to be drawn and hanged for opposing the English at Methven and other 'crimes'.

The name became widespread in many places in Scotland, and the Mowats held the following properties:

Brandy Den or **Fern** [NO 478610], near Brechin, Angus; site of castle.

Held by the Mowats of Fern from about 1300 to 1450, when the property passed to the Lindsay Earls of Crawford and then to the Carnegies. The castle was abandoned for **Vayne Castle** [NO 493599].

Bucholly or **Freswick Castle** [ND 382658], near Wick, Caithness; ruinous castle and courtyard on promontory above the sea.

Held by the Mowats of Bucholly in the thirteenth century, and

Bucholly Castle (M&R)

they built the castle. In 1427 Mowat of Freswick, and his followers, were burned to death in the chapel of St Duthac at Tain by MacNeil of Creich. The property was sold to the Sinclairs of Rattar in 1661 and by then the castle had already been abandoned for **Freswick House** [ND 378671]. Bucholly was said to be 'strongly expressive of the jealous and wretched condition of the tyrant owners'.

Busbie or **Cunninghamhead Tower** [NS 392409], near Kilmarnock, Ayrshire; site of castle.

Held by the Mowats until the beginning of the seventeenth century. The castle was demolished in the 1950s when it was already ruinous.

Freswick House [ND 378671], near Wick, Caithness; seventeenth-century house.

Built by the Mowats (see Bucholly above) but was sold to the Sinclairs of Rattar in 1661. The house was badly damaged during a thunderstorm in the 1770s but was remodelled, restored and is still occupied.

Hatton Castle [NJ 758469], near Turriff, Aberdeenshire; mansion incorporating castle.

Held by the Mowats from the thirteenth century, but was sold to the Duffs in 1723 and they built the mansion. The walled garden is open to the public by appointment (01888 562279; www.gardensofscotland.org).

Vayne Castle [NO 493599], near Brechin, Angus; ruinous Z-plan tower house.

Held by the Mowats from around the end of the twelfth century until 1450 when the property went to the Lindsay Earls of Crawford and then to the Carnegies, and the castle dates from the sixteenth century.

www.gatheringoftheclans.com
No. of castles/sites: 6
Rank: 212=/764
Xref: Mouat

Busbie Tower (M&R) – see previous column

Mowbray

The name probably comes from the barony of 'Mombray' in the Calvados region of France, and the family came to England during the Norman invasion, and then to Scotland at the beginning of the thirteenth century.

Standing in the policies of Dalmeny House, **Barnbougle Castle** [NT 169785] lies some two or so miles east of South Queensferry to the west of Edinburgh. The present building dates mostly

Barnbougle Castle (M&R)

from the nineteenth century, but it incorporates cellars from an old castle. The lands were held by the Mowbrays of Barnbougle and Dalmeny, and they also had a residence called **Dalmeny House** [NT 159776] on the estate. The property was sold in 1615 to the Hamilton Earls of Haddington, who in turn sold it to the Primrose Earls of Rosebery, and they built the fine mansion of **Dalmeny House** [NT 167779], demolishing the old Dalmeny House. A ghostly dog is said to haunt the grounds of Barnbougle, and is heard howling or seen when the laird of Barnbougle is about to die. The legend dates from when Sir Roger Mowbray went off on Crusade, and this is reputedly the origin of the name 'Hound Point', just to the north-west of Barnbougle, and now the haunt of oil tankers. Dalmeny House is open to the public in July and August and there are fine walks (0131 331 1888; www.dalmeny. co.uk).

Inverkeithing Friary [NT 129827] was a Franciscan establishment founded around 1268 by Philip Mowbray. The site is now a public garden, although the former guest house survives; a museum is located on the upper floor of the building, which is open to the public (01383 313595/838).

The Mowbrays also owned:
Bavelaw Castle [NT 168628], near Balerno, Edinburgh; restored L-plan tower house.
  Held by the Bairds, by the Fairlies and by the Forresters before passing to the Mowbrays of Barnbougle and then went to the

Bavelaw Castle (M&R)

Dundases in the sixteenth century, and then to the Scotts. Restored in about 1900 and still occupied.
Kellie Castle [NO 608402], near Arbroath, Angus; fine and restored fortified house.
  Held by the Mowbrays, but probably passed to the Kellys then to the Stewarts then to the Ochterlony family from 1402, then to others. The castle is still occupied.
Methven Castle [NO 042260], near Perth; large castle with round towers.
  Held by the Mowbrays in the eleventh century, but passed to the Stewart Earls of Atholl, and then to the Crown from 1427. It later passed to the Stewart Dukes of Lennox and to the Smythes of Braco, before being restored as company offices.
Otterston Tower [NT 165852], near Aberdour, Fife; mansion incorporating tower house.
  Held by the Hendersons, but had passed to the Mowbrays of

Otterston Tower (M&R)

Barnbougle by 1589, and they built the tower and held it into the nineteenth century. The tower is still occupied.

No. of castles/sites: 7
Rank: 182=/764
Xref: Moubray

Muirhead

The name comes from one of the many places in Scotland called 'Muirhead' or 'Morehead', and the name is on record from the end of the fourteenth century. The name probably comes from 'muir', which means 'heath or grassy moor', so the name means 'head of the heath'.

The family owned the following properties:

Billies [NX 724573], near Kirkcudbright, Galloway; site of castle or old house.

Held by the Muirheads in the sixteenth and seventeenth centuries.

Herbertshire Castle [NS 804830], near Falkirk; site of large tower house.

Held by the Sinclairs of Rosslyn, by the Elphinstone Earls of Linlithgow and by the Stirlings, before being purchased by

Herbertshire Castle (M&R)

William Morehead in 1768. Herbertshire went to the Forbeses of Callander in 1835 but was demolished in the twentieth century and the grounds are now a public park.

Lauchope House [NS 781617], near Motherwell, Lanarkshire; site of strong tower house.

Held by the Muirheads. Hamilton of Bothwellhaugh (the Muirhead laird was Hamilton's brother-in-law) was sheltered here after he had shot the Regent Moray at Stirling in 1570. The tower was torched as a result, although it was rebuilt. Demolished in 1956.

Linnhouse [NT 062630], near West Calder, West Lothian; altered L-plan tower house.

Held by the Tennants, but passed to the Muirheads about 1631, and they were in possession until they sold it in 1767. The house is still occupied.

www.clanmuirhead.com
No. of castles/sites: 4
Rank: 278=/764
Xref: Morehead

Mundeville

The name comes from French, and means 'of the great town', and comes from 'Mandeville', a place in Normandy. The family were Earls of Essex in England, but are on record in Scotland from the second half of the thirteenth century. Roger Mandeville was one of the competitors for the Scottish throne at the end of the thirteenth century; the name Mundeville or Mundell is still found in Dumfries and Galloway.

Moure Castle [NX 382433] was four or so miles northwest of Whithorn in Galloway, but little now survives of the old stronghold. Moure was a property of the Mundeville family, but passed by marriage to the Maxwells in 1451.

No. of castles/sites: 1
Rank: 537=/764
Xref: Mundell

Munro

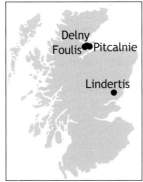

The name may come from 'man of Roe', and the clan perhaps originated from Ireland. They settled in Ross and Cromarty in the north of Scotland as early as the eleventh century, after Donald, progenitor of the Munros, had helped Malcolm II against Viking invaders. They had been given the lands on the condition that they should find a snowball in midsummer, if required to do so. Donald Monro, who was Archdeacon of the Isles in the sixteenth century, wrote *Description of the Western Isles*, an important early account of the area; he was a minister after the Reformation. Alexander Monro was a Professor of Anatomy at the University of Edinburgh and founded Edinburgh School of Medicine. His son and grandson, both also Alexander, were also physicians and anatomists, and they wrote several books on the subject. Neil Munro, born in 1864 and from Inveraray, wrote *Pari Handy* series and other stories.

Foulis Castle [NH 589642] stands five miles south-west of Alness in Ross and Cromarty, and is a two-storey whitewashed mansion, which incorporates part of an old tower house with gunloops. Foulis was held by the Munros from the twelfth century or earlier, and they had a stronghold here. The clan is believed to have fought at the Battle of Bannockburn in 1314 and then at the Battle of Halidon Hill in 1333, when the Scots were defeated. One of the chiefs, Robert Munro, was killed at the Battle of Pinkie in 1547; while another Robert, known as the 'Black Baron', joined the army of Gustave Adolphus in the Thirty Years War and was killed at Ulm in 1633. The family were made Baronets of Nova Scotia the following year. The clan opposed the Jacobites and Sir Robert Munro, sixth Baronet and a distinguished soldier, was killed at Falkirk during the Rising in 1745-46. The castle was sacked and burnt by Jacobites the same year. The house was rebuilt as a large classical mansion in 1754-92, and the Munros held the property into the twentieth century. The house is still apparently occupied, although the Munros of Foulis-Obsdale, Baronets, now apparently live in London in England.

The Munros also owned:

Allan [NH 815771], near Tain, Ross and Cromarty; site of castle.
Held by the Munros.

Ardross Castle [NH 611741], near Alness, Ross and Cromarty; mansion incorporating old work.
Held by the Munros, but passed to the Mathesons and then to the Perrins, of Worcestershire sauce fame.

Auchenbowie House [NS 798874], near Stirling; mansion incorporating tower house.
Held by the Cunninghams of Polmaise and by the Bruces, before passing by marriage to the Munros in 1708. The house is still occupied.

Contullich Castle [NH 637705], near Alness, Ross and Cromarty; site of castle.
Held by the Munros, and thought to have first been built in the eleventh century.

Delny Castle [NH 735724], near Invergordon; site of castle.
Held by the Earls of Ross but passed to the Munros. Delny was held by Black Andrew Munro in 1512, reputedly an unpleasant character, who was hanged at Balnagown by the Rosses some ten years later. Among much other mayhem, Munro made his female servants thresh corn naked, which would have been unbearably painful. Another version is that he was murdered by his own household in 1522. His ghost is said to haunt Balnagown Castle, and reputedly to be witnessed by women.

Docharty [NH 534603], near Dingwall, Ross and Cromarty; site of tower house.
Held by the Munros, one of whom was Black Andrew as mentioned above. Mary, the daughter of the house, along with three other Marys from neighbouring properties, entertained James IV with harp-playing at Dingwall Castle in 1503. The property passed to the Bains of Tulloch in 1533.

Fyrish House [NH 614690], near Alness, Ross and Cromarty; mansion on site of castle.
Held by the Munros, and was home to Sir Hector Munro, a general who served in India and put down a rising at Patna.

Lindertis [NO 337515], near Kirriemuir, Angus; site of castle and mansion.
Held by the Fletchers and then by the Wedderburns in 1780, before coming to the Munros. Sir Hugh Munro of Lindertis devised the Munro classification of mountains of more than 3000 feet in 1891. The family had been made Baronets in 1825, and now apparently live in Vermont in the USA.

Little Tarrel [NH 911819], near Tain, Ross and Cromarty; altered and restored L-plan tower house.
Held by the Gordon Earls of Huntly and by the Tarrels and by the MacCullochs, and then by the Munros.

Loch Slin Castle [NH 849806], near Tain, Ross and Cromarty; ruinous castle.
Held by the Munros in the seventeenth century, and then by the Mackenzies.

Meikle Daan [NH 688847], near Edderton, Ross and Cromarty; old house.
Held by the Munros.

Meikle Tarrel [NH 900810], near Tain, Ross and Cromarty; site of castle.
Held by Tarrel family, by the MacCullochs and by the Munros.

Milnton or **Tarbat House** [NH 772737], near Alness, Ross and Cromarty; slight remains of tower house.
Held by the Munros, who built the castle about 1500. It was sacked by Jacobites in the 1745-46 rebellion. The property passed to the Mackenzie Viscounts Tarbat and Earls of Cromartie, and they built **Tarbat House** [NH 770736], a classical mansion of 1787. The old castle was remodelled as part of the garden. Tarbat House was burned out in the twentieth century and is now a shell.

Newmore Castle [NH 680720], near Alness, Ross and Cromarty; slight remains of castle.
Held by the Munros and then by the Mackenzies. Replaced by Newmore House, which was built in 1875 by the Inglis family.

Novar House [NH 612680], near Alness, Ross and Cromarty; mansion on site of castle.
Held by the Munros. One of the family was General Sir Hector Munro, who served in India in the second half of the eighteenth century. The gardens are occasionally open to the public (www.gardensofscotland.org).

Pitcalnie or **Culnaha** [NH 810730], near Cromarty; site of castle.
Held by the Munros at the beginning of the sixteenth century.

Poyntzfield or **Ardoch** [NH 711642], near Cromarty; mansion on site of old house or castle.
Held by the Gordons but passed to the Munros about 1757 and they changed the name from Ardoch to Poyntzfield, called after the laird's wife (whose name was Poyntz). Still occupied.

www.clanmunro.org.uk / www.clanmunrousa.org
www.clanmunroassociation.ca / www.clanmunroaustralia.org
No. of castles/sites: 18 / Rank: 76=/764
Xrefs: Munroe; Monroe

Murdoch

The name comes from Gaelic, and is derived from two personal names 'Mui-reach' and 'Murchadh'. The former means 'belonging to the sea', and the latter 'sea warrior', an apt name for a Viking. As a personal name, 'Murdoch' is on record from the twelfth century, but it was not used as a surname until later. Murdoch, son of Robert Stewart, Duke of Albany, was beheaded by James I in 1425.

Cumloden or **Old Risk** [NX 443695] lies three miles north-east of Newton Stewart in Galloway, but little remains except the foundations of the castle. The lands were held by the Murdochs of Cumloden from the fourteenth century. They had supported Robert the Bruce and were given the property in return. Cumloden passed to the Stewart Earls of Galloway in the eighteenth century, and they built **Cumloden House** [NX 4176770], a low rambling mansion, in the nineteenth century.

Gartincaber House [NN 698001], two miles south-west of Doune in Stirling, is an altered mansion, which dates from the seventeenth century and incorporates work from a castle. The property belonged to the Buchanans and possibly to the Doigs, but later passed to the Murdochs, then Burn-Murdochs. They no longer hold Gartincaber and now apparently live in London in England.

No. of castles/sites: 2
Rank: 396=/764
Xref: Murdock

Mure

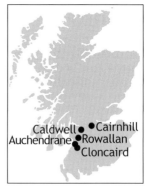

The name appears to have two derivations, one from Gaelic and the other from English. In Gaelic 'mor' or 'more' means 'big' or 'large', and is descriptive; while 'muir' means 'heath or grassy moor', from Middle English. Thomas Muir, born in Glasgow in 1765, qualified as an advocate before becoming a radical and supporting the French Revolution. He was outlawed for sedition and was caught and then sentenced to be transported to Australia for fourteen years. He was rescued by an American ship and went to France where he died in 1798. John Muir, who was born in Dunbar in 1838, emigrated to America where he campaigned for the conservation of forests and wild places, and he helped found the first National Park. His birthplace in Dunbar is open to the public (01368 865899; www.jmbt.org.uk).

Rowallan Castle [NS 435424] is three miles north of Kilmarnock in Ayrshire, and is a magnificent courtyard castle with a drum-towered gatehouse. The building dates from the sixteenth century, but the lands were held by the Mures of Rowallan after passing by marriage from the Comyns. Elizabeth Mure, daughter of Adam Mure of Rowallan, was married to Robert II, and their

Rowallan Castle (M&R)

son became Robert III. Members of the family were slain at Flodden in 1513, and Mungo Mure of Rowallan was killed at the Battle of Pinkie in 1547. The family opposed Mary, Queen of Scots, and became Covenanters in the seventeenth century. William Mure of Rowallan allowed coventicles, which were illegal meeting of Covenanters, to be held in his castle, and he was imprisoned. The property passed to the Boyle Earls of Glasgow, then to the Campbell Earls of Loudoun, and then to the Corbetts. Rowallan is apparently now in the care of Historic Scotland but is not currently open to the public.

Four miles west of Neilston in Renfrewshire is **Caldwell Tower** [NS 422551], a small tower house, rising to three storeys and dating from the sixteenth century. The property was held by the Caldwell family, but was long a possession of the Mures of Caldwell. Sir John Mure of Caldwell was slain in 1550 by the Cunninghams and by the Aikets, and a later Robert was killed in battle about 1640. William Mure was involved with the Covenanters in the Pentland Rising, which ended in defeat in 1666 at Rullion Green. He fled abroad and his lands were forfeited to be given to William Dalziel of The Binns; Mure's wife and daughters were imprisoned in Blackness Castle. The castle fell into disrepair and, although the Mure family recovered the property in 1690, the castle never seems to have been reoccupied. The family moved to Hall of Caldwell in the eighteenth century, and then to Caldwell House, designed by Robert Adam, in 1773. The Mures held the property into the twentieth century, but now apparently live in Tasmania in Australia.

The Mures also owned:

Abercorn Castle [NT 083794], near South Queensferry, West Lothian; site of castle.
Held by the Avenels and by the Grahams before passing by marriage to the Mures in the early fourteenth century. Abercorn then passed to the Douglases, but was destroyed by the forces of James II in 1455, and later went to the Setons and to others.

Annieston Castle [NS 997366], near Biggar, Lanarkshire; slight remains of tower house.
Held by the Mures (or Muirs) in the seventeenth and eighteenth centuries.

Auchendrane Castle [NS 335152], near Ayr; site of castle.
Held by the Mures. John Mure of Auchendrane murdered Sir Thomas Kennedy of Culzean, younger son of Gilbert, third Earl of Cassillis, in revenge for the murder of Muir's son-in-law, Gilbert Kennedy of Bargany, in a feud with the Earl of Cassillis. The Earl had managed to escape punishment for this earlier killing, but Mure and his son were caught, tried and executed in 1611. The property passed by marriage to the Cathcarts in 1793, and was sold to the Coats family of Paisley in 1868. The castle was replaced by Blairstone House.

Barmagachan [NX 613494], near Kirkcudbright, Galloway; small tower house.
Held by the Keiths but passed by marriage to the Muirs in 1459, and then was sold to the MacLellans in 1511.

Cairnhill House [NS 756641], near Airdrie, Lanarkshire; site of castle and mansion.
Held by the Wallaces but bought by the Mure (or More) family in 1641, then went by marriage to the Nisbets. The family is now styled More Nisbett of The Drum and Cairnhill, and they apparently live at The Drum.

Cassencarie House [NX 476577], near Wigtown, Galloway; ruinous tower house and mansion.
Held by the Mures. Alexander Muir Mackenzie, who came from the family, was made a Baronet in 1805.

Cloncaird Castle [NS 359075], near Maybole, Ayrshire; castle and mansion.
Held by the Mures from 1494 or earlier. Patrick Mure of Cloncaird was killed at the Battle of Flodden in 1513. The property passed from the family but the castle is still occupied. The apparition of a man is said to have been seen often on the stairs, even in recent times.

Cowden Hall [NS 466571], near Neilston, Renfrewshire; ruinous mansion incorporating old work.
Held by the Spreull family, by the Blairs and by the Hamilton Marquis of Clydesdale, before passing to the Mures of Craigends in 1766.

Craighlaw Castle [NX 305611], near Glenluce, Galloway; mansion incorporating tower house.
Held by the Mures but was sold to the Gordons of Kenmure in 1513 then later went to the Hamiltons. Extended in 1870 but partly demolished in the 1950s and still occupied.

Glanderston Castle [NS 499563], near Barrhead, Renfrewshire; castle replaced by mansion.
Held by the Stewart Earls of Lennox in 1507, but passed by marriage to the Mures of Caldwell. The Mures had a long and bitter feud with the Maxwells of Nether Pollok.

Little Caldwell [NS 414550], near Uplawmoor, Renfrewshire; site of tower house.
Held by the Mures of Caldwell.

Nether Auchendrane or **Blairstone** [NS 338167], near Ayr; mansion incorporating old work.
Held by the Mures, but now a nursing home.

Perceton House [NS 354406], near Irvine, Ayrshire; castle replaced by mansion.
Held by the Morvilles, then by others, before latterly passing to the Mures of Perceton. The house is now the headquarters of North Ayrshire Council.

Pokelly [NS 442458], near Stewarton, Ayrshire; site of castle.
Held by the Mures (or Muirs) from the thirteenth century for around 400 years or more.

Skeldon Castle [NS 378138], near Maybole, Ayrshire; remains of castle built into castle.
Held by the Mures, then by the Kennedys and by the Campbells. The castle was replaced by Skeldon House, a small classical mansion.

Warriston [NT 253757], Edinburgh; site of castle or old house.
Held by the Somervilles, by the Kincaids and by the Johnstones, then by others, before coming to the Mures (or Muirs). A cemetery was laid out on part of the lands.

www.theclanmuir.org
No. of castles/sites: 18
Rank: 76=/764
Xrefs: Muir; More

Murray

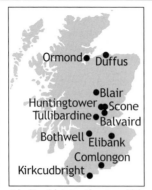

The name is territorial in origin and comes from the province of Moray, which covered a large area in the north of Scotland, larger than the present district of Moray. The family were probably Flemish, and they were in England after the Norman conquest, but they arrived to Scotland with David I in the twelfth century. They were given lands in Moray, hence their name, but also in Sutherland, in Clydesdale and elsewhere.

Bothwell Castle [NS 688594], stands by the Clyde, a few miles north and west of Hamilton near Uddingston in Lanarkshire. It is one of the best early castles in Scotland and is a very impressive ruin. The magnificent round keep was partly demolished, but enough survives to show what a fabulous building this was. There is also a large walled courtyard with round towers and ranges of buildings within the walls.

This was a property of the Murrays (or Morays) from the middle of the twelfth century, having passed from the Oliphants, and it was the Murrays who built the castle. Bothwell was in a strategic position during the Wars of Independence and changed hands several times between the Scots and the English. The castle was the headquarters of the English Aymer de Valence, Earl of Pembroke, Edward I's Warden of Scotland. Bothwell was surrendered to the Scots in 1314, and the keep was partly demolished at this time and, although it was later made defensible, it was never restored to its former glory. The castle was rebuilt by Edward Balliol, but then was taken by the Scots and slighted again by Sir Andrew Murray, around 1337. The last Murray laird died from the plague about 1360, and the property went to the Douglases and then to others, including to the Hepburns Earls of Bothwell and then back to the Douglases, later Earls of Forfar. Bothwell is now in the care of Historic Scotland and is open to the public (01698 816894).

Bothwell Castle (M&R)

Duffus Castle [NJ 189672], three miles north-west of Elgin in Moray, is an impressive motte and bailey castle, and dates from the twelfth century, having been built by Freskin, Lord of Strathbrock, from whom both the Murrays (Morays) and the Sutherlands were descended. A large tower was built on the motte, but this was eventually too much for the mound and half of it collapsed. David I visited Duffus, but the castle was slighted by the Scots in 1297, and passed to the Cheynes, who rebuilt it in stone. The property then passed to the Sutherland Lord Duffus, who held the property until 1843; the castle is now in the care of Historic Scotland and open to the public (01667 460232).

Ormond or **Avoch Castle** [NH 696536], three miles south-west of Fortrose on the Black Isle in Ross and Cromarty, was once a strong castle but little remains. This part of the Black Isle was formerly in Moray, and was a property of the Murrays. One of the family was Sir Andrew Moray who, along with William Wallace, defeated an English army at the Battle of Stirling Bridge in 1297. He died soon afterwards, and Wallace went on to defeat at Falkirk the following year. Moray's son, another Andrew, was made Guardian of Scotland in 1332, and did much to free Scotland from Edward Balliol and the English. He was responsible for the capture of Kildrummy Castle in 1335, and Bothwell Castle in 1336 (as mentioned above). Murray died here two years later, and the lands went to the Douglases, although that family was forfeited in 1455, and Hugh Douglas, Earl of Ormond, got his head lopped off. The castle was probably destroyed in about 1650, and the sacrament house, a mural cupboard in which the consecrated elements of bread and wine were retained for the use of the sick and the dying, now at the parish church Avoch, may have come from the Chapel of Our Lady at the castle.

Tullibardine Castle [NN 910139] was completely demolished in 1833, but was two or so miles north of Auchterarder in Perthshire, and appears to have been a large and very impressive building. The nearby chapel [NN 909134], which is in the care of Historic Scotland and is open to the public, was founded by Sir David Murray of Tullibardine in 1446, and has been used as a burial place by the Murrays since the Reformation. The building is one of the most complete examples of a small collegiate church in Scotland.

Tullibardine was a property of the Murrays from 1284, and Andrew Murray of Tullibardine supported Edward Balliol, playing an important part in ensuring victory at Dupplin Moor, and he was executed for treason in 1332. Sir William, son of the then laird (another Sir William), was slain at Flodden in 1513; another Sir William was Comptroller from 1565-82 and, although initially supporting Mary, Queen of Scots, turned against her after she married the Earl of Bothwell. Sir John Murray was also Comptroller to the royal household in the reign of James VI and was made Earl of Tullibardine in 1606, while his son, another William, had been one of those who were present at the Gowrie Conspiracy at Perth in 1600 and saved the James VI's life. The Murrays were made Marquises in 1676, while another branch became Earls and then Dukes of Atholl in 1703. William Murray, Marquis of Tullibardine, fought in the 1715 and in the 1719 Jacobite Risings, and then was also out for Bonnie Prince Charlie. He was captured following the Battle of Culloden in 1746 and died in captivity in the Tower of London. The title is now held by the Dukes of Atholl.

Blair Castle [NN 867662] is a rambling white-washed mansion, which incorporates part of an old castle dating from the thirteenth century. The building was remodelled in the eighteenth century, turning it into a plain mansion, but it was rebuilt and restored in 1872. The Comyns had a stronghold here, and the property

Blair Castle 1920?

was held by the Earls of Atholl, before the castle, lands and title passed to the Murrays by marriage in 1629. The Marquis of Montrose used Blair as a mustering point before the Battle of Tippermuir, and in 1653 the castle was besieged, captured and partly destroyed with gunpowder by Cromwell's forces. Blair was complete enough for the young Earl of Atholl to try to recapture it the following year. The castle was garrisoned by Bonnie Dundee, John Graham of Claverhouse, in 1689, and it was here that his body was brought after he was killed at the Battle of Killiecrankie. The Earls of Atholl were made Marquises, and then Dukes of Atholl in 1703, and gained the sovereignty of the Isle of Man in 1736, which they held until 1765 when it was given to the Crown. Bonnie Prince Charlie stayed at Blair in 1745, during the Rising. The following year the castle was held by Hanoverian forces, and attacked and damaged by Lord George Murray, Bonnie Prince Charlie's general and the Duke of Atholl's brother: it is the last castle in Britain to have been besieged. Robert Burns visited Blair in 1787. The castle is the home of the Atholl Highlanders, Britain's only remaining private regiment. The Dukes of Atholl and Marquises of Tullibardine now apparently live in South Africa, and the castle is open to the public (01796 481207; www.blair-castle.co.uk).

Huntingtower Castle [NO 083252] is a couple of miles north-west of Perth, and is a fine well-preserved castle. The castle consists of two towers, one from the fifteenth century, and one from the next century, which were built close together but formerly had no direct connection. A joining block was later built, and there are some original painted walls and ceilings, dating from the sixteenth century.

The lands were originally held by the Ruthvens, and

Huntingtower Castle (M&R)

the stronghold was known as Ruthven Castle, but the property was forfeit and the name proscribed following the Gowrie Conspiracy in 1600. The property went to William Murray, Earl of Dysart, then to the Murrays of Tullibardine, and then to the Marquises and Dukes of Atholl. Huntingtower was the birthplace of Lord George Murray, the Jacobite general (and brother of the Duke of Atholl, who supported the Hanoverians). Murray was involved in both the 1715 and the 1719 Rising, but then had to go into exile. Having been pardoned, he returned to Scotland and then reluctantly took part in the 1745-46 rebellion. Lord George is credited with the early successes of the Jacobite campaign, although there was friction between him and the Bonnie Prince. The rising reached its bloody conclusion at Culloden in 1746, a battle Murray probably would have not chosen to fight at that time or that place. He escaped abroad and died in Holland in 1760. Huntingtower was sold to the Mercers in 1805, and is now in the care of Historic Scotland and is open to the public (01738 627231).

Balvaird Castle [NO 169118], four miles south of Bridge of Earn in Perth and Kinross, is a fine well-preserved L-plan tower house, which dates from the fifteenth century. Balvaird was a property of the Barclays, but passed to the Murrays of Tullibardine in 1500 and they

Balvaird Castle (M&R)

built the castle. Balvaird can be visited, although check opening (01786 431324).

This branch of the family were later made Viscounts Stormont and Earls of Mansfield. **Stormont** [NO 190421] is two miles south of Blairgowrie, also in Perthshire, and there was a castle here. Stormont was a property of the Murrays of Gospertie, one of whom, Sir David, had saved James VI's life at Perth in the Gowrie Conspiracy in 1600. Murray was made Viscount Stormont in 1621, although their main seat was at Scone.

Scone Palace [NO 114267] is two or so miles north of Perth, and is a massive castellated mansion, dating from 1802, but incorporating old work, possibly from 1580 or even from the abbot's lodging of the former abbey. The abbey here was an important place, and the kings of Scots were inaugurated at the moot hill. Scone went to the Ruthvens after the Reformation but, as

Scone Palace (MC)

mentioned above, Sir David Murray of Gospertie had been one of those to save the king's life in the Gowrie Conspiracy at Perth in 1600, and the family were granted the Ruthvens' possession at Scone. The Murrays were made Viscounts Stormont in 1602, and Earls of Mansfield in 1776. James VIII and III held 'court' here in 1716 during the Jacobite Risings, and James Murray, second son of the fifth Viscount, supported the Jacobites and escaped to France. He helped negotiate the marriage of James 'the Old Pretender', and he was made Earl of Dunbar in the Jacobite peerage. Bonnie Prince Charlie visited on his way south in 1745. On the Moot Hill is Scone Palace Chapel, used as a mausoleum and containing the exuberant alabaster monument to commemorate the first Viscount Stormont. The Murray Earls of Mansfield and Viscounts Stormont still flourish, and the palace is open to the public (01738 552300; www.scone-palace.co.uk).

Elibank Castle [NT 397363] lies four miles east of Innerleithen in the Borders, and is a ruinous L-plan tower house of four storeys and a garret, which dates from the sixteenth century. Sir Gideon Murray was chamberlain to Walter Scott of Buccleuch, and received the lands in 1594. He captured Walter Scott of Harden, a Border reiver, in 1611 but offered him his life if Scott would marry Murray's daughter Agnes, 'Muckle Mou'd Meg', rather than be hanged. Harden sensibly married the girl. Murray's son, Patrick, was made a Baronet of

Nova Scotia in 1628 and then became Lord Elibank in 1643. Patrick, second Lord, was fined for supporting the Marquis of Montrose, and the castle was a ruin by 1722. Alexander Murray, son of the fourth Lord Elibank, was a Jacobite, and the family were made Viscounts Elibank in 1911. They now apparently live in London in England.

Comlongon Castle [NY 079690] is a substantial keep or tower, rising to five storeys, and standing alongside a castellated mansion. Comlongon is located eight or so miles south-east of Dumfries, and was held by the Murrays of Cockpool from 1331. The family became Earls

Comlongon Castle (LF)

of Annandale in 1624 (although the title was not to remain with the Murrays for long), and later Earls of Mansfield. The castle is said to be haunted by sad spirit of Marion Carruthers, heiress of Mouswald. She was betrothed to one of the Douglases of Drumlanrig, but did not want to marry and was sheltered in the castle. Either through despair or the helping hands of the Douglases she fell from the top of the tower and was killed. The Douglases gained the lands of Mouswald, but Marion's ghost is said to haunt the building. Comlongon was sold by the eighth Earl of Mansfield in 1984, and the mansion was restored and is now a hotel (01387 870283; www.comlongoncastle.co.uk).

The Murrays also held:
Abercairny [NN 913226], near Crieff, Perthshire; house on site of castle and mansion.
 Held by the Murrays of Abercairny from around 1299 after one of the family married Mary, heiress of Malise, Earl of Strathearn. The were still in possession in the twentieth century.
Aberscross [NC 705050], near Dornoch, Sutherland; site of castle (location not certain).
 Held by the de Moravia (Murray) family when they moved to Sutherland at the end of the twelfth century.
Aberuchill Castle [NN 745212], near Comrie, Perthshire; fine L-plan tower house.
 On lands held by the MacGregors and then by the Murrays of Abercairny, but went to the Campbells in 1594 and they built the present castle.

Airth or **Dunmore Tower** [NS 890889], near Falkirk; simple keep or tower.

Held by the Elphinstones, but was bought by the Murrays in 1754 after they had been made Earls of Dunmore in 1686. George, fifth Earl, had Dunmore Park built, a large Tudor-style mansion, which is itself now a ruin. The basement of Airth Tower has been the burial vault of the Earls of Dunmore since 1820, but was broken into and despoiled in the early 1990s. The Murray Earls of Dunmore now apparently live in Australia.

Aldie Castle [NT 052977], near Crook of Devon, Perthshire; altered tower house.

Held by the Mercers of Aldie, but passed to the Murray Lord Nairne and then to the Kinlochs. Still occupied.

Amhuinnsuidhe Castle [NB 049078], near Tarbert, Isle of Harris, Outer Hebrides; mansion.

Held by and built for the Murray Earls of Dunmore, but later passed to Lord Leverhulme. Accommodation is available at the castle (01859 560200; www.amhuinnsuidhe-castle.co.uk).

Arbigland House [NX 989574], near Kirkbean, Dumfriesshire; castle replaced by mansion.

Held by the MacCullochs, then by the Murrays, by the Carnegie Earls of South Esk, by the Craiks, who built the present mansion, and then by Blacketts, who still apparently own it.

Ardoch [NN 842097], near Braco, Perthshire; castle or old house replaced by mansion.

Held by the Stirlings but in the nineteenth century was a property of the Drummond-Morays.

Auchencruive Castle [NS 387235], near Ayr; mansion on site of castle.

Held by the Wallaces and by the Cathcarts, but passed to the Murrays in 1758, then to the Oswalds from 1764 to 1925. The grounds are open to the public,

Baberton House [NT 195696], Edinburgh; mansion incorporating tower house.

Held by the Elphinstones but passed to the Murrays and the present house was built by Sir James Murray of Kilbaberton, Master of Works to the Crown. The house is still occupied.

Ballencrieff House [NT 487783], near Haddington, East Lothian; restored castle.

Held by the Murrays from the fourteenth century, and the present castle was built by John Murray, first Lord Elibank,

Ballencrieff House (M&R)

around 1586, after an older stronghold had been destroyed by the English in the 1540s. Sir Gideon Murray held the castle in 1615 and was Depute Treasurer for Scotland. General James Murray, born here in 1721, was Governor of Canada in 1763. Dr Samuel Johnson and James Boswell visited Ballencrieff in 1773. The castle was burnt out in 1868, but was restored in the 1990s and is occupied. It was recently put up for sale (01875 870784; www.ballencrieff-castle.com).

Balmanno Castle [NO 144156], near Bridge of Earn, Perthshire; L-plan tower house.

Held by the Balmanno family and by the Auchinlecks, who built the castle, but had passed to the Murrays of Glendoick by the later seventeenth century. Balmanno went to the Belshes of Invermay in 1752, then to others, and is still occupied.

Bedlormie [NS 874675], near Armadale, West Lothian; L-plan tower house.

Held by the Murrays of Ogilface, then by the Forresters of Corstorphine from 1424, and then by others.

Black Barony or **Darnhall Castle** [NT 236472], near Peebles, Borders; altered L-plan tower house.

Held by the Murrays from 1412, and they built the castle. Sir John Murray of Darnhall was knighted by James VI, and enclosed his lands, earning the nickname 'The Dyker'. His son, Sir Archibald, was made a Baronet of Nova Scotia in 1628. The Murrays of Blackbarony, Baronets, now apparently live in Argentina, and Barony Castle is a centre for events and courses and can be rented for exclusive use (01721 730395; www.initialstyle.co.uk).

Black Castle of Moulin [NN 946589], near Pitlochry, Perthshire; site of castle on former island.

Held by the Campbells and by the Fergusons, but the property was purchased by the Murray Earls of Atholl in 1638.

Broughton House [NX 682511], Kirkcudbright, Galloway; old house.

Held by the Murrays of Broughton, and they had a town house here, which dated from the seventeenth century or earlier, but was later the home and studio of E. A. Hornel, one of the Glasgow Boys. The house is in the care of The National Trust for Scotland and is open to the public after recent refurbishment (01557 330437; www.nts.org.uk).

Broughton Place [NT 117372], near Biggar, Borders; mansion on the site of tower house.

Held by the Murrays, and John Murray of Broughton was Secretary to Bonnie Prince Charlie. After the failure of the Jacobite Rising of 1745-46, he remained in Scotland to guard the Loch Arkaig treasure: 40,000 Louis d'Ors, which has never been found. He was captured but escaped punishment by denouncing the Fraser Lord Lovat, who was less lucky and was executed. The property was sold to Robert MacQueen, Lord Braxfield, and is still occupied (01899 830234; www.broughtongallery.co.uk).

Callands House [NT 155459], near Romannobridge, Borders; house on site of tower house.

Held by the Aitkens, but was bought by the Murrays in 1840.

Cally Castle [NX 598554], near Gatehouse of Fleet, Galloway; ruinous tower house.

Held by the Stewarts in the thirteenth century, but later passed to the Murrays and then to the Lennoxes by the beginning of the sixteenth century. The castle was replaced by **Cally House** [NX 600549] in the eighteenth century. This building was extended in 1835 and later, and was held by the Murray-Stewarts of Broughton. The building is said to have a Green Lady, the phantom of a servant or nanny who was murdered by being thrown from one of the windows, and the house is now a hotel (01557 814341; www.callypalace.co.uk).

Carrick Castle [NS 194944], near Lochgoilhead, Argyll; restored castle.

Held by the Lamonts and by the Campbell Earls of Argyll, but later passed to the Murray Earls of Dunmore.

Cavens Castle [NX 958572], near New Abbey, Dumfries and Galloway; site of castle.

Held by the Douglas Earls of Morton and by the Maxwells, but later passed to the Murrays and then to the Oswalds, who built nearby Cavens House. The house is now used as a hotel (01387 880234; www.cavens.com).

Cluggy Castle [NN 840234], near Crieff, Perthshire; ruinous tower.

Held by the Comyns, then by the Oliphants and by the Murrays of Tullibardine from the end of the fifteenth century, and one of the family fell at Flodden in 1513. Still occupied in 1650 but abandoned for Ochtertyre.

Cobairdy [NJ 575438], near Huntly, Aberdeenshire; mansion on site of castle.

Held by the Murrays and then by the Burnetts.

Cockpool Castle [NY 070677], near Annan, Dumfriesshire; site of castle.

Held by the Cockpool family, but passed to the Murrays of Cockpool, who held the property from 1350 to 1450 when they built nearby Comlongon Castle. Cockpool was occupied by the English from 1547 to 1550.

Cringletie House [NT 234445], near Peebles, Borders; mansion on site of tower house.

Held by the Murrays. Alexander Murray of Cringletie fought in the forces of General Wolfe at Quebec, and was recognised for his gallantry. The mansion is now a hotel (01721 725750; www.cringletie.com).

Cromarty Castle [NH 794670], Cromarty; castle replaced by mansion.

Held by the Urquharts, but the property was bought by the Murray Lord Elibank in 1763 but then went to the Rosses eight years later and they built the mansion. They still apparently live here.

Culbin [NH 995615], near Forres, Moray; site of castle or old house.

Held by the Murrays from the thirteenth century but passed to the Kinnairds two centuries later. Sand overwhelmed what was very fertile land, although this has been stabilised in recent times by growing trees. The forest is accessible to the public.

Darnaway Castle [NH 994550], near Forres, Moray; mansion incorporating part of castle.

Held by Sir Thomas Randolph and by the Douglas Earls of Moray, then went in 1455 to the Murrays before passing to James Stewart, Earl of Moray, in the sixteenth century. Their descendants still apparently own the castle.

Denork [NO 454138], near St Andrews, Fife; site of castle or old house.

Held by the Murrays of Denork and Claremont in the sixteenth and seventeenth centuries. **Claremont** [NO 459146] is to the north-east.

Deuchar Tower [NT 360280], Yarrow, Borders; slight remains of tower house.

Held by the Homes and by the Dalgleishs, but had passed to the Murrays of Deuchar by 1643, then later went to the Dewars.

Dollerie [NN 904208], near Crieff, Perthshire; castle replaced by mansion.

Held by the Murrays from the fifteenth century, and one of the family was Alexander Murray, who was a well-known explorer and geologist, and was the first director of the Geological Survey of Newfoundland; he died in 1884. The house may still be occupied by the Murrays.

Dreghorn Castle [NT 225684], Edinburgh; castle and mansion replaced by mansion.

Held by the Murrays in the seventeenth century, one of whom was Sir William Murray, Master of Works to Charles II. Dreghorn passed to other families but was demolished in the 1950s and the site is now occupied by a barracks.

Drumsargad Castle [NS 667597], near Hamilton, Lanarkshire; slight remains of castle.

Held by the Oliphants but passed to the Murrays in the thirteenth century and they held Drumsargad until 1370 when the property went to the Douglases, then later to the Hamiltons.

Drumstinchall [NX 884580], near Dalbeattie, Galloway; mansion on site of castle.

Held by the Murrays from 1527 to about 1750, and then later passed to the Cochranes and to others.

Dumcrieff [NT 102036], near Moffat, Dumfriesshire; mansion on site of tower house.

Held by the Murrays but passed to the Clerks of Penicuik, then to John Loudoun Macadam in 1785, and then to others.

Dunkeld House [NO 024427], Dunkeld; site of castle and mansion.

Held by the Murrays, later Dukes of Atholl, and it was stormed and blown up by Cromwell's forces in 1653. Rebuilt in 1679, it was demolished at the beginning of the nineteenth century. A new mansion was built for the Duke of Atholl in 1900 and this is now the Dunkeld House Hotel (01350 727771; www.hilton.co.uk/dunkeld).

Fala Luggie Tower [NT 425590], near Gorebridge, Midlothian; slight remains of tower house.

Held by the Douglases but passed to the Murrays in the fourteenth century and they held it for more than 200 years. John Murray of Falahill was known as 'the Outlaw' and is associated with Hangingshaw. Fala was owned by the Hamiltons in the eighteenth century.

Forres Castle [NJ 035588], Forres, Moray; site of castle.

Held by the Murrays in the fifteenth century, although also said to have been a property of the Dunbars of Westfield from the fourteenth century for some 300 years, then of the Grants. The site is now a public park.

Fowlis Castle [NO 321334], near Dundee; altered tower house.

Held by the Maules, by the Mortimers and by the Grays, then bought by the Murrays of Ochtertyre in 1669. Used as a farmhouse.

Fruid Castle [NT 106180], near Tweedsmuir, Borders; site of castle, now in reservoir.

Held by the Tweedies, but later passed to the Murrays of Stanhope and then to the Hay Lord Yester from the 1630s.

Gauldwell Castle [NJ 311452], near Dufftown, Moray; slight remains of castle.

Held by the Murrays, and Mary, Queen of Scots, stayed here in 1562.

Geanies Castle [NH 894798], near Tain, Ross and Cromarty; site of castle.

Held by the MacLeods of Geanies and by the Sinclairs, but was bought by Kenneth Murray, a merchant from Tain, in 1828. The castle was replaced by the eighteenth-century Geanies House.

Glendoick House [NO 208237], near Perth; mansion incorporating part of a tower house.

Held by the Murrays, one of whom, Sir Thomas Murray, was made a Lord of Session (Glendoick) in 1674, but the property passed to the Craigies in 1726 and then to the Coxes. Still occupied and the gardens are open mid April to mid June; there is a garden centre and restaurant (01738 860205; www.glendoick.com).

Glenrath Tower [NT 218324], near Peebles, Borders; site of tower house.

Held by the Veitchs then by the Murrays in the seventeenth century.

Gorthy [NN 962237], near Crieff, Perthshire; site of castle, location uncertain.

Held by the Gorthy family and by the Lundies, then by the Murrays; David Murray of Gorthy was a poet and courtier, and died in 1629.

Halmyre House [NT 174496], near West Linton, Borders; mansion including part of a tower house.

Held by the Tweedies of Drumelzier, but passed to the Murrays of Stanhope, who were in possession in the eighteenth century, and then was sold to the Gordons in 1808.

Hangingshaw [NT 397303], near Selkirk, Borders; site of castle.

Held by the Murrays of Philphaugh. One laird was the 'outlaw' John Murray of Falahill who – according to the ballad – came before James IV on charges of treasonably occupying the Ettrick Forest, although he claimed that he had recovered the territory from the English. An agreement was reached whereby Murray acknowledged James as his king, and the king made Murray Sheriff of Ettrick Forest. The old house was burnt out at the end of the eighteenth century and replaced by the present mansion of 1846.

Hoddom Castle [NY 157730], near Annan, Dumfriesshire; L-plan tower house.

Held by several families, including by the Maxwells, before coming to the Murrays of Cockpool in 1627, and then went to the Carnegies in 1653, and then to others. Now in a caravan park (01576 300251; www.hoddomcastle.co.uk).

Hopeton Tower [NT 249467], near Peebles, Borders; site of tower house.

Held by the Murrays of Black Barony in the seventeenth century.

Hundleshope [NT 230364], near Peebles, Borders; site of castle or old house.

Held by the Turnbulls, by the Murrays, by the Scotts and by the Campbells.

Inchbervie Castle [NO 123329], near Perth; slight remains of castle.

Held by the Nairn family and then by the Murray Lords Nairne. The third Lord Nairne, a Jacobite, had to flee from the dining room of the castle after the Rising of 1745-46 to avoid capture.

Invergowrie House [NO 363304], near Dundee; mansion incorporating tower house.

Held by the Carnegies and by the Grays, but went to Sir David Murray, one of those who had killed the Earl of Gowrie and his brother in the Gowrie Conspiracy in 1600. The property passed to the Clayhills in 1615, and the house is now divided into flats.

Invershin Castle [NH 573964], near Bonar Bridge, Sutherland; slight remains of castle.

Held by the Murrays, from whom the Sutherlands are descended.

Kildrummy Castle [NJ 454164], Kildrummy, Aberdeenshire; fabulous ruinous castle.

Held by several families down the centuries, including by the Murrays. The castle was besieged by the Earl of Atholl acting for the English in 1335, but was successfully defended by Robert the Bruce's sister, Christian. Her husband, Sir Andrew Moray, the Regent, relieved the castle and killed the Earl of Atholl at or after the Battle of Culbean. Kildrummy is in the care of Historic Scotland and open to the public (01975 571331).

Kincairney House [NO 087441], near Blairgowrie, Perthshire; mansion on site of castle.

Held by the Murrays of Glendoick in the seventeenth century, but then passed to others. Still occupied.

Langshaw Tower [NT 516397], near Galashiels, Borders; slight remains of tower house.

Held by the Borthwicks and then by the Murrays.

Lintrose or **Fodderance House** [NO 225379], near Coupar Angus, Angus; mansion incorporating part of castle.

Held by the Halyburtons but later passed to the Murrays.

Livingston Peel [NT 040676], Livingston, West Lothian; slight remains of castle.

Held by the Livingstones, then later by the Murrays, and one of the owners, Sir Patrick Murray of Livingstone, collected plants and formed the basis of the Old Physic Garden, the first botanic garden in Edinburgh. The property was later owned by the Cunninghams and by the Primrose Earl of Rosebery.

Lhanbryde [NJ 275613], near Elgin, Moray; site of castle or old house.

Held by the Murrays in the thirteenth century. Sir Malcolm Murray of Lhanbryde was Sheriff of Perth.

Lochmaben Castle [NY 088812], Lochmaben, Dumfriesshire; ruinous castle.

Held by the Bruces and then by the Crown with the Maxwells as hereditary keepers. James VI besieged the castle and took it from the Maxwells, and gave the property to John Murray, who was Groom to the king; Murray was made Earl of Annandale in 1625.

Logie-Almond House [NO 014297], near Perth; site of castle and mansion.

Held by the Hay Earls of Errol but passed to the Drummonds and then to the Murray Earls of Mansfield. One round tower survives.

Logierait Castle [NN 975513], near Dunkeld, Perthshire; slight remains of castle.

Held by the Stewarts and there is a Celtic cross memorial to the Murray sixth Duke of Atholl on the site.

Luthrie [NO 332196], near Cupar, Fife; site of castle or old house.

Held by John Murray, barber-surgeon to James V, but was also a property of the Formans and of the Stewarts.

Malleny House [NT 166667], near Balerno, Edinburgh; altered mansion with old work.

Held by the Hamiltons and by the Kerrs, then by the Murrays of Kilbaberton, who built the present house, then by the Scotts of Murdostoun and by the Primrose Lord Rosebery. Now in the care of The National Trust for Scotland and the gardens are open to the public (0131 449 2283; www.nts.org.uk).

McCulloch's Castle [NX 997577], near New Abbey, Dumfriesshire; site of castle.

Held by the Murrays and they moved to a new site at Arbigland. The property passed to the Carnegie Earls of Southesk, to the Craiks in 1679 and then to the Blacketts.

Meigle House [NO 285447], near Coupar Angus, Perthshire; castle or old house replaced by mansion.

Held by the Meigle family and then by the Murrays in around 1785, then was sold to the Kinlochs in 1871. Patrick Murray was a friend of Sir Walter Scott in 1785, and Scott is reputed to have written parts of his novels here.

Meikleour House [NO 153387], near Blairgowrie, Perthshire; mansion on site of castle and old houses.

Held by the Mercers, but passed by marriage to the Murray Lords Nairne in the eighteenth century, and later the Marquises of Landsdowne. The house is apparently occupied by their descendants, and the Meikleour Hedge is a 100-foot-high beech hedge which lines the A93 along the edge of the estate. The gardens are occasionally open to the public (www.gardensof scotland.org).

Melgund Castle [NO 546564], near Brechin, Angus; impressive castle.

Held by the Cramonds and by the Beatons, then by others including by the Murray Kynynmounds, and it has undergone restoration.

Minto House [NT 573203], near Hawick, Borders; site of castle and mansion.

Held by the Turnbulls, and then by the Elliots and by the Murray Kynynmounds, Earls of Minto. John Murray Kynynmound, fourth Earl and who succeeded in 1891, was Governor General of Canada 1898-1904, and Viceroy of India 1905-10. The house has been mostly demolished.

Mount Lothian [NT 271693], near Penicuik, Midlothian; farm on site of castle or old house.

May have been held by the Abernethys and some have suggested that there was a priory or house here of the Knights Templars. Mount Lothian was held by the Murrays in the eighteenth century.

Mugdrum [NO 228184], near Newburgh, Fife; mansion including old work.

Held by the Coventrys, by the Ormes, by the Arnotts and by the Leslies, then by the Cheapes. It was occupied by Lord George Murray, the Jacobite general, before the Rising of 1745, and then went to the Hays.

Mukkersy [NO 117340], near Bankfoot, Perthshire; site of castle.

Held by the Nairnes of Mukkersy but probably passed to the Murray Dukes of Atholl along with Strathurd after the Jacobite Rising of 1745-46.

Murraythwaite [NY 128727], near Annan, Dumfriesshire; castle replaced by mansion.

Held by the Murrays from the fifteenth to the twentieth century. The house dates from the eighteenth century.

Newton [NT 332699], near Musselburgh, Midlothian; mansion incorporating castle.

Held by the Newtons and then later by the Murrays of Newton and then by the Wauchope Lord Edmonstone. Still occupied.

Ochtertyre [NN 839236], near Crieff, Perthshire; castle replaced by mansion.

Held by the Comyns and by the Oliphants before passing to the Murrays of Ochtertyre, who held the property from the fifteenth century for some 400 years or so. Patrick Murray of Ochtertyre was killed at the Battle of Flodden in 1513, and the family were made Baronets of Nova Scotia in 1673. The early nineteenth-century family mausoleum was built on the site of Monzievaird Parish Church, but is now a roofless ruin.

The (Keith) Murrays of Ochtertyre, Baronets, apparently now have residences in Powys in Wales and at Greenwich in England according to *Burke's*.

Ogilface Castle [NS 927690], near Bathgate, West Lothian; site of castle.

Held by the de Bosco (Wood) family, but passed to the Murrays and then to the Livingstone Earls of Linlithgow. Used by Covenanters as a place of refuge in the seventeenth century.

Old Place of Broughton [NX 456452], near Garlieston, Galloway; site of castle.

Held by the Murrays of Broughton.

Ospisdale House [NH 713897], near Dornoch, Sutherland; castle replaced by mansion.

Held by the Murrays or by the Grays, and the lands were a bone of contention which led to much blood-letting. Later held by the Gordons and by the Gilchrists.

Outerston [NT 330570], near Gorebridge, Midlothian; site of castle or old house replaced by farm.

Held by the Murrays in the seventeenth century.

Parton Place [NX 710695], near Castle Douglas, Galloway; castle replaced by mansion.

Held by the Glendinnings, but passed by marriage to the Murrays in 1720 and is now apparently held by the Hunter Blairs.

Philiphaugh [NT 459283], near Selkirk, Borders; site of castle and mansion.

Held by the Murrays from 1461, but passed to the Strang Steels in the nineteenth century. There is a modern house on the site.

Pittarthie Castle [NO 522091], near Elie, Fife; L-plan tower house.

Held by the Monypennys of Pitmilly, then by the Murrays from 1590 to 1598, then by the Logans and by others. The castle is being restored.

Pittheavlis Castle [NO 097222], near Perth; altered L-plan tower house.

Held by the Rosses of Craigie, and by others, then by the Murrays, after which it was used as a farmhouse. Had been divided and is occupied.

Polmaise Castle [NS 835924], near Stirling; site of castle and mansion.

Held by the Forsyths and by the Cunninghams, but passed by marriage to the Murrays of Touchadam, who were in possession from 1568 into the twentieth century. The site is now apparently occupied by a sewerage works.

Polrossie [NH 724884], near Dornoch, Sutherland; site of castle or old house.

Held by the MacNeils, but passed to the Murrays in the fifteenth century.

Quarter House [NT 100334], near Broughton, Borders; tower house replaced by mansion.

Held by the Livingstones, by the Murrays, and then by the Tweedies from 1741.

Romanno Tower [NT 167483], near West Linton, Borders; tower house replaced by mansion.

Held by the Romanes family and then by the Murrays of Romanno from 1513 to 1676, and was apparently held against James VI in 1591. Romanno passed by marriage to the Penicuiks of Newhall and then to the Kennedys.

Spott House [NT 679752], near Dunbar, East Lothian; mansion incorporating old work.

Held by several families including by the Homes, then later went to the Murrays and then to others.

Stanhope Tower [NT 123297], near Drumelzier, Borders; site of castle.

Long held by the Murrays but was sold to the Montgomerys in 1767 (www.murrayofstanhope.com).

Steuarthall or **Wester Polmaise** [NS 826927], near Stirling; site of tower house.

Held by the Murrays of Touchadam, but was sold to the Cowans early in the seventeenth century and then went to the Stirlings of Garden. The site has been cleared.

Stobo Castle [NT 173367], near Drumelzier, Borders; tower house replaced by mansion.

Held by the Murrays but was sold to the Montgomerys in 1767.

Stobo Castle 1905?

Now used as a luxurious health spa (01721 725300; www.stobocastle.co.uk).

Strathbrock Castle [NT 044717], near Uphall, West Lothian; site of castle.

Held by a Fleming called Freskin in the twelfth century, and he went on to build Duffus Castle in Moray. Freskin was the ancestor of both the Murrays and of the Sutherlands, but the property passed to the Erskines. Middleton Hall may be on the site and is now a residential home for the elderly.

Strathurd Castle or **House of Nairne** [NO 074328], near Bankfoot, Perthshire; site of castle and mansion.

Held by the Nairnes who built the imposing House of Nairne, but this was demolished following the Jacobite Rising (the Nairnes were forfeited) after the property had passed to the Murray Duke of Atholl.

Waygateshaw House [NS 825484], near Lanark; courtyard castle.

Held by the Murrays of Touchadam, but passed by marriage to the Lockharts in 1539, then later went to the Weirs and then to the Steels. Still occupied.

Whitslade Tower [NT 112350], near Broughton, Borders; slight remains of tower house.

Held by the Porteous family, then by the Murrays of Stanhope and by the Dicksons.

Woodend [NN 938221], near Crieff, Perthshire; castle replaced by mansion.

Held by the Oliphants, but passed to the Murrays of Woodend, who held Woodend in the latter part of the sixteenth century and then into the seventeenth century. It was sold to the Watts about 1750 and is still occupied.

www.clanmurray.org
www.freepages.genealogy.rootsweb.com/~murrayclan/
index.html
No. of castles/sites: 107
Rank: 6/764
Xref: Moray

Muschett

The name comes from 'Montfiguet' or 'Mont-fiquet', which is a place in Normandy in France, and the name is on record in Scotland from the middle of the twelfth century. William de Monte Fuchet held the town of Dundee for the English in 1312, but it may have been the same William who added his seal to the Declaration of Arbroath in 1320. The family held lands in Perthshire and in Menteith, although most of their possessions passed by marriage to the Drummonds. Nichol Muchett of Boghall was hanged for the murder of his wife in Holyrood Park in 1720.

The Muschetts held:

Burnbank [NS 710988], near Doune, Stirlingshire; site of castle.
Held by the Muschetts.

Cargill [NO 157374], near Blairgowrie, Perthshire; site of castle on motte.
Held by the Muschetts, but passed by marriage to the Drummonds in the fourteenth century.

Kincardine Castle [NS 721986], near Doune, Stirlingshire; site of castle.
Held by the Muschetts but passed by marriage to the Drummonds in the fourteenth century.

Stobhall [NO 132344], near Perth, Perthshire; fine courtyard castle.
Held by the Muschetts but passed to the Drummonds in 1360, and Stobhall became the Drummonds' main seat until 1487. Now home to the Drummond Earls of Perth, and the gardens and chapel are open to the public (01821 640332; www.stobhall.com).

No. of castles/sites: 4
Rank: 278=/764
Xrefs: Muchet; Montfiquet

Naesmith

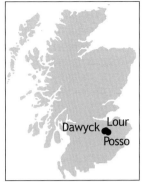

The name comes from the profession of 'knife smith', although there is also a story that one of the family had to repair the armour of Alexander III in the thirteenth century. He did the job badly but then went on to fight well, the king remarking that he was 'nae smith'. The family are on record from the fifteenth century. Alexander Naesmyth, who was born in Edinburgh in 1758, was a pupil of Allan Ramsay and became a well-known portrait painter, one of his most famous pictures being that of Robert Burns.

The Naesmiths held the following lands:

Dawyck House [NT 168352], near Peebles, Borders; castle or old house replaced by mansion.
Held by the Veitch family but passed to the Naesmiths towards the end of the seventeenth century. Sir James Naesmith, who died in 1706, was known as the 'Deil o' Dawick' from his perhaps less than honest dealings as a lawyer and property owner. He was made a Baronet of Nova Scotia in 1706, and his son, another Sir James, was a keen botanist. The property passed to the Balfours in the nineteenth century, and Dawyck Botanical Garden is nearby.

Lour Tower [NT 179356], near Peebles, Borders; slight remains of tower house within Iron Age fort.
Held by the Veitch family, but passed to the Naesmiths towards the end of the eighteenth century. It was still in use in 1715.

Posso Tower [NT 200332], near Peebles, Borders; some remains of tower house.
Held by the Bairds of Posso, but passed by marriage to the Naesmiths. Michael Naesmith of Posso fought for Mary, Queen of Scots, at Langside in 1568, after which he was exiled. Several of the family were slain in 1588 by the Scotts of Tushielaw. James Naesmith of Posso was Royal Falconer to James VI, and his son held the same office for Charles I. The tower was ruined by 1775 and was replaced by a new house nearby. The family now apparently live in Wiltshire in England.

Woodhouse Hill [NT 211370], near Peebles, Borders; site of tower house.
Held by the Inglises of Manor, then by the Pringles of Smailholm and by the Burnetts of Barns, and then part was owned by the Naesmiths of Posso in the seventeenth and eighteenth centuries.

No. of castles/sites: 4
Rank: 278=/764
Xrefs: Naysmith; Naesmyth

Nairne

The name is of local origin and comes from the burgh of Nairn, which is in the north of Scotland some miles east of Inverness. The name is on record from the middle of the fourteenth century.

Sandfurd (now **St Fort**) [NO 417258], but also on record as **Sandford Nairne**, is a mile or so south of Newport-on-Tay in Fife. The lands were long a property of the Nairnes of Sandfurd, and they built a castle at the beginning of the fifteenth century. Alexander Nairne of Sandfurd was the King's Shield Bearer to James II, and was slain in a trial by combat at the North Inch in Perth in 1453 after being accused of treason. A later Alexander was a Gentleman of the Bedchamber to James VI; and Alexander's son, Sir Thomas, was fined at the Restoration for complicity in the overthrow of Charles I. The family were accused of attending coventicles in 1671 and the fines imposed bankrupted the estate so that it had to be sold in 1720. Sandfurd was held by the Stewarts in 1795, and they built the new mansion, but this building was demolished in the 1960s.

Mukkersy [NO 117340] is three and a half miles east of Bankfoot in Perthshire, and there was a castle or old house although there are apparently no remains. The lands were held by the Nairnes of Mukkersy from the middle of the sixteenth century. Strathurd was also acquired by the family.

Strathurd Castle [NO 074328] was close by, some two miles south of Bankfoot. Strathurd was a property of the Crichtons, but passed to the Nairnes of Mukkersy in the middle of the seventeenth century. Sir Robert Nairne of Strathurd was made Lord Nairne in 1681. The family built the magnificent **House of Nairne** in 1710, and it was once known as 'The Glory of Strathord'. The mansion was designed by Lady Margaret Nairne, and was a massive symmetrical building of five storeys. The family supported the Jacobites in the 1715 and 1745-46 Risings and Bonnie Prince Charlie was entertained here. The Nairnes were forfeited after the Rising failed and the title was lost. The lands (and those of Mukkersy) were sold to the Murray Dukes of Atholl, and they demolished the House of Nairne. The title was restored to the Nairnes in 1824.

The Nairnes also held:

Belmont Castle [NO 286439], near Blairgowrie, Perthshire; mansion incorporating tower house.
    Held by the Nairnes of Dunsinnan, but went to the advocate Sir George Mackenzie of Rosehaugh - who earned the name 'Bluidy Mackenzie' in the seventeenth century. The building is now a nursing home.

Drumkilbo [NO 304449], near Coupar Angus, Perthshire; mansion incorporating castle.
    Held by the Tyries, but Drumkilbo was bought by the Nairnes in 1650 and they held it for about 200 years. The house is available to rent on an exclusive basis (01828 640445; www.drumkilbo.com).
Dunsinnan House [NO 167329], near Perth; castle replaced by mansion.
    Held by the Collace family, but then by the Nairnes from the fifteenth century for four hundred years. The family have a burial vault at the Old Parish Church at Collace [NO 197320].
Inchbervie Castle [NO 123329], near Perth; slight remains of castle.
    Held by the Nairne family, but passed to the Murrays, who succeeded to the title Lord Nairne in 1683.
Seggieden [NO 168215], near Perth; site of castle or old house.
    Held by the Hay Earls of Kinnoul and by the Gordons, before coming to the Nairnes, and then passed to the Hays again.

No. of castles/sites: 8
Rank: 160=/764
Xref: Nairn

Napier

The family claim descent from the Earls of Lennox, and it has been suggested that the name might be from 'naperer', an officer in charge of linen and tableware to a king. A more fanciful origin may from the days of William the Lyon in the twelfth century when a young knight fought so bravely that the king remarked he had 'nae peer'. The family held land in Menteith in central Scotland as well as in Edinburgh and elsewhere.

Merchiston Castle [NT 243717], which stands in the Merchiston area to the south of Edinburgh, is a strong tower, altered with the addition of a wing to L-plan, and dating from the fifteenth century. There were later extensions but these have been demolished, and the castle is now incorporated into Napier University. The alternative might well have been its demolition, but slapping a corridor through the wing in the midst of rigid concrete building is not the best.

The lands were held by the Craigies, but passed to the Napiers in the middle of the fifteenth century, and they built the tower; three of the family were Lord Provosts of Edinburgh and Sir Alexander Napier was Comptroller for various periods between 1449 and 1461 and was an ambassador to England. Sir Alexander Napier was slain at the Battle of Flodden in 1513, while Alexander Napier of Merchiston was killed at Pinkie in 1547. Mary, Queen of Scots, visited the castle, but it was attacked by the Regent Morton in 1572, who bombarded it from Edinburgh Castle, although with questionable success. Sir Archibald Napier later refused to surrender Merchiston to the Regent Mar, and it resisted another siege. Sir Archibald was made Master of the Mint in 1576 and he built Lauriston Castle. John Napier, the inventor of logarithms, was born at Merchiston in 1550. Sir Archibald Napier was made a Baronet in 1627 and the family were also made Lords Napier of Merchistoun that year. The two titles parted company

as the Lordship could pass through the female line, but the Baronetcy of Nova Scotia could not; the latter passed by marriage to the Scotts, but they took the name Napier. Admiral Sir Charles Napier, grandson of the fifth Lord Napier, commanded the Portuguese navy and was made Count St Vincent, and his brother, Sir William, served in the Peninsular War. Merchiston was sold to the Lowis family in 1668, but they had to sell it in 1728 when they became bankrupt. The buildings housed a school in the nineteenth century, but Merchiston Castle School found a new site at Colinton in 1924. The Napiers of Merchistoun and Ettrick lived at Thirlestane until the 1960s when their house was demolished because of dry rot and they now apparently reside in England; the Napiers of Merchistoun, Baronets, apparently live in South Africa.

The Napiers also owned:

Ardmore [NS 317785], near Cardross, Dunbartonshire; castle replaced by mansion.
   Long held by the Nobles, but a Napier of Ardmore is on record in the seventeenth century.

Balgair Castle [NS 607884], near Fintry, Stirlingshire; site of tower house.
   Held by the Cunninghams of Glengarnock then by the Galbraiths of Culcreuch and by the Buchanans, but may also have been owned by the Napiers of Gartness.

Culcreuch Castle [NS 620876], near Fintry, Stirlingshire; fine castle and mansion.
   Long a property of the Galbraiths of Culcreuch, but passed to the Setons, then to the Napiers in 1632 and they held it until 1796. Culcreuch was then acquired by the Speirs family, then by others, and is now a hotel and stands in a country park (01360 860228/555; www.culcreuch.com).

Edinbellie Castle [NS 577890], near Balfron, Stirlingshire; site of tower house.
   Held by the Napiers of Merchiston from 1509, and has been suggested as the birthplace of John Napier in 1550, who invented logarithms, rather than Merchiston.

Gartness Castle [NS 502865], near Drymen, Stirlingshire; site of castle.
   Held by the Napiers from 1495.

Kilmahew Castle [NS 352787], near Cardross, Dunbartonshire; ruinous castle.
   Held by the Napiers from the later thirteenth century for more than 500 years.

Lauriston Castle [NT 204762], Edinburgh; castle and mansion.
   Held by the Forresters, but the tower house was built by the Napiers of Merchiston in the sixteenth century. The property

Merchiston Castle (M&R)

Lauriston Castle (MC)

453

was sold to the Dalgleishs in 1656, and then passed to other families before being given to the city of Edinburgh. The castle is open to the public and stands in a public park (0131 336 2060; www.cac.org.uk).

Milliken [NS 418634], near Johnstone, Renfrewshire; castle replaced by later houses.

The property was held by several families, including by the Napiers around 1829, before it passed to the Mackenzies. The Napiers built a Grecian-style mansion but this has been demolished.

Old Ballikinrain [NS 561880], near Balfron, Stirlingshire; mansion incorporating castle.

Held by the Napiers from the seventeenth century until 1862. Burnt out by suffragettes, and was later used as a residential school.

Rusky Castle [NN 616034], near Callander, Stirlingshire; site of castle on island.

Held by the Menteiths of Rusky until the 1470s, then by the Napiers of Merchiston, who had a claim to the Earldom of Lennox but did not pursue it, and then by the Haldanes of Gleneagles.

Thirlestane Tower [NT 281154], near Ettrick, Borders; ruinous L-plan tower house.

Held by the Scotts, but passed by marriage to the Napiers of Merchiston in 1699, and they built a new mansion and lived here until 1965 when the house had to be demolished because of dry rot. The family now apparently live in England.

Wrychtishousis [NT 247724], Edinburgh; site of castle and mansion.

Held by the Napiers but passed to the Clerks in 1664. The site later housed James Gillespie's School and then the Blind Asylum but has been completely demolished.

www.napier.ac.uk/depts/clan_napier/
No. of castles/sites: 13
Rank: 113=/764

Neilson

The name means 'Neil's son', and there are at least two origins. The Neilsons of Craigcaffie claimed descent from Neil, Earl of Carrick, who died in 1256 (or possibly from Neil, an illegitimate son of Robert the Bruce, although this seems more unlikely), and they long held property in Galloway. There were also a family of the name who held land in Inverness-shire.

Craigcaffie Tower [NX 089641] is three miles northeast of Stranraer in Galloway, and is a sixteenth-century tower house, which has been restored. Craigcaffie was held by the Neilsons from the fourteenth century until 1791, when it passed to the Dalrymples of Stair. The tower was later used by farm labourers, but is now a residence again.

Nothing survives of **Corsock Castle** [NX 758748], which was seven miles north of Castle Douglas, also in Dumfries and Galloway, and was replaced by **Corsock House** [NX 760755], a castellated mansion of the nineteenth century. The old castle was held by the Neilsons, one of whom was Robert Nelson of Corsock, a noted Covenanter; there is a memorial to him in the kirkyard of Kilpatrick Durham Church. A panel from the castle is built into Corsock House, and the gardens of the house are open to the public by appointment only (01644 440250; www.gardensofscotland.org).

No. of castles/sites: 2
Rank: 396=/764
Xrefs: Nelson; Nielson

Neish

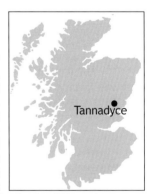

The name is a rendition of Angus (also see MacNeish), and is recorded in Scotland from the fifteenth century.

Tannadyce House [NO 484577] is a nineteenth-century mansion, and stands some five or so miles north of Forfar in Angus, on the north bank of the River South Esk. The lands of Tannadyce were held by the Leiths, by the Lyons and by the Ogilvies, before being sold to the Neishes in 1870.

No. of castles/sites: 1
Rank: 537=/764

Craigcaffie Tower (M&R) – see next column (Nielson)

Nevay

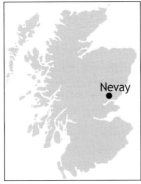

The name is territorial and comes from the lands and parish of Nevay, a couple of miles north-east of Newtyle in Angus; the name is on record from 1219.

Nevay [NO 330445] was held by the family of the same name from the thirteenth century or earlier. David Nevay of Nevay was raised to the Supreme Court Bench. The family ended in an heiress, and the property passed by marriage to the Kinlochs around 1700.

No. of castles/sites: 1
Rank: 537=/764
Xref: Nevoy

Newbigging

The name is territorial, but there are several possible places of origin, including near Carnwath, near Musselburgh in East Lothian, and two Newbiggings in Angus.

Newbigging [NT 015460], some two miles east of Carnwath in South Lanarkshire, was held by the family from the thirteenth century or earlier, and Thomas Newbigging provided a market cross for the village. The property passed by marriage to the Carmichaels in the middle of that century.

Dunsyre Castle [NT 073482] is several miles to east of Carnwath, and the property was probably held by the same family of Newbiggings. Dunsyre passed to the Douglases in 1368 and later went to the Lockharts of The Lee.

No. of castles/sites: 2
Rank: 396=/764

Newton

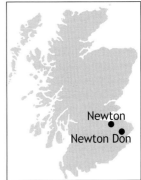

The name is local in origin and there are numerous places called this, and the name is on record from the thirteenth century.

Newton [NT 332699] is two miles south of Musselburgh in Midlothian, and the nineteenth-century mansion incorporates vaulted cellars from an old castle. A round tower has gunloops and has a doocot on its top storey. The property was held by the Newtons from the thirteenth century for about 400 years, and two of the family probably gave homage to Edward I of England in 1296. The lands passed to the Murrays of Newton in the seventeenth century, and then to the Wauchope Lord Edmonstone. The building is still occupied.

Standing in wooded parkland, **Newton Don** [NT 709372], which is in the Borders two miles north of Kelso, is an eighteenth-century mansion with later additions, but it replaced a castle or older house. The lands were held by the Morvilles, by the Balliols and by the Douglases, before being owned by the Newton family. The property passed to the Don family, and they changed the name to Newton Don. Newton Don later passed to the Balfours of Whittinghame and they still apparently live here.

No. of castles/sites: 2
Rank: 396=/764

Nichol

The name comes from the diminutive of Nicholas, which means 'victorious people' from ancient Greek. The name is on record from the middle of the sixteenth century, and may be a contraction of either MacNicol or Nicholson.

Ballogie or **Tillysnaught** [NO 571955] is a modern mansion but it stands on the site of earlier houses. The property is located four miles south-east of Aboyne in Aberdeenshire, and was held by the Forbeses, by the Inneses in 1789 and by the Farquharsons before being owned by the Nicol family, who were in possession in 1850. The Nicols of Ballogie still apparently live here.

No. of castles/sites: 1
Rank: 537=/764
Xrefs: Nicol; Nichols

Nicholson

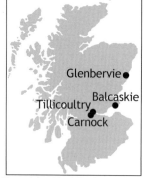

The name is from 'Nicol's son', from a diminutive of Nicolas or Nicholas, which means 'victorious people' from ancient Greek, and is on record from the end of the thirteenth century. The name is MacNicol in Gaelic, but some of the clan changed their name to Nicolson, especially on Skye (see MacNicol). Nichol and Nicol may be a contraction of the name.

Carnock House [NS 865882] was a two or so miles west of Airth in Stirlingshire, but the building was demolished in 1941. It was a long three-storey house with corbiestepped gables and dormer windows. Carnock was held by the Somervilles, by the Bruces and by the Drummonds of Carnock, before passing to the Nicolsons in 1634. The family were made Baronets of Nova Scotia in 1637 (as were the Nicholsons of Lasswade some years before). The property passed to the Shaws of Greenock in the eighteenth century, and they held it for the next 200 years. The Nicolsons, Barons Carnock, are descended from the family and apparently have houses in London and in Devon in England according to *Burke's*.

Balcaskie House [NO 526035] is a mile or so north-west of Pittenweem in Fife, and is a symmetrical mansion, dating from the seventeenth century and incorporating an earlier tower house. The house has been owned by several families, including by the Nicolsons of Kennay before 1698, when it passed to the Anstruthers, who still apparently occupy it.

Glenbervie House [NO 769805], several miles south-west of Stonehaven in Aberdeenshire, was held by the Melvilles, then by the Auchinlecks, by the Douglases and by the Burnetts of Leys before passing to the Nicholsons in 1721. The house is still occupied and the gardens are occasionally open to the public (www.gardensofscotland.org).

Tillicoultry Castle [NS 913975], which stood just north-west of Tillicoultry in Stirlingshire, is the site of a castle and mansion. The property was held by the Erskines, by the Colvilles of Culross and by the Alexanders of Menstrie, but had passed to the Nicholsons in 1693 before later going to the Wardlaw-Ramsays of Whitehill. The mansion replaced the castle in 1806 but this was demolished around 1938.

No. of castles/sites: 4
Rank: 278=/764
Xrefs: Nicolson; MacNichol

Niddrie

The name is territorial and comes from the lands of Niddrie, which are to the south and east of Edinburgh, and the name is on record from the thirteenth century.

Niddrie Marischal [NT 295715] was a fine large mansion and tower house, but it has been demolished and housing estates were built in the grounds. The lands were held by the Niddrie family in the thirteenth and fourteenth centuries, but the property passed to the Heriots and then to the Wauchopes. The mansion was occupied until the 1930s.

To the west of Edinburgh is **Cramond Tower** [NT 191770], which is a tall and narrow tower house, formerly part of a larger building. The property was owned by the Niddries, but was exchanged for the lands of Cammo with the Bishops of Dunkeld. Much later this part of Cramond passed to the Douglases and then to the Inglises, and they built nearby Cramond House.

Cammo House [NT 174747] was a mile or two to the south, and was held by the Niddries. The property later passed to the Menzies family and they built a mansion, which may have been on the site of a castle. The property passed to the Clerks and then to the Watsons of Saughton and was occupied until 1975. Cammo was given to The National Trust for Scotland and but the house was then vandalised and set on fire. The building was then demolished, and the grounds are now a country park.

No. of castles/sites: 3
Rank: 328=/764
Xref: Niddry

Nisbet

The name is territorial and comes from the lands of Nisbet, which are a couple of miles south of Duns in Berwickshire in the Borders, and the family are on record from the twelfth century.

Nisbet House [NT 795512] is an altered tower house, dating from the seventeenth century with a main block and two round towers. There is a later

Nisbet House (M&R)

wing and the walls are pierced by many gunloops. The family owned the property from the twelfth century, and Philip Nesbit was one of those who swore fealty to Edward I in 1296. Alexander Nisbet supported the Royalists, and his son Sir Philip Nisbet fought with the Marquis of Montrose, but he was captured after the defeat of Philiphaugh in 1645. He was taken to Glasgow and there executed; two of his brothers were also slain in the fighting: Major Alexander Nisbet was killed at York in 1644 and Colonel Robert Nisbet was executed with Montrose at Edinburgh in 1650. Adam Nisbet was the youngest son and went on to become a famous writer on heraldry and history. The property passed to the Kerrs, and then to the Sinclairs in the nineteenth century. The house is still occupied.

A mile to the south of Airdrie in central Scotland, **Cairnhill House** [NS 756641] was an attractive mansion, remodelled in 1841, but incorporating a classical mansion from the previous century. Cairnhill was held by the Wallaces and by the Mores (Mures) from 1641, but passed by marriage to the Nisbets in the 1750s. Cairnhill House was demolished in 1991, except for the

doocot and the stables, although the family still apparently own the property.

The Drum or **Drum House** [NT 301688] is to the south and east of Edinburgh and is an Adam mansion, dating from the 1720s and 30s. The Drum was held by the Somervilles, but passed to the More Nisbetts in the eighteenth century. The family is now styled More Nisbett of The Drum and Cairnhill, and they apparently live at The Drum, although they also have a residence in London according to *Burke's*.

The Nisbets also owned:

Carfin [NS 769575], near Carfin, Lanarkshire; site of tower house.
  Held by the Baillies but had passed to the Nisbets by 1710.

Craigentinny House [NT 290747], Edinburgh; altered L-plan tower house.
  Held by the Nisbets of Dean, who built the tower, in the

Craigentinny House (M&R)

sixteenth and seventeenth centuries. The property passed to the Millers, was damaged by an air raid in World War II, and is now used as council offices.

Dean House [NT 235740], Edinburgh; site of tower house.
  Held by the Nisbets of Dean. William Nisbet of Dean was Provost of Edinburgh when James VI visited Edinburgh in 1617, and Nisbet was knighted. The property passed to the Learmonths, but the building was demolished in 1845 when the cemetery was laid out. Wooden panels from the great hall are in the Museum of Scotland in Edinburgh.

Dirleton Castle [NT 518840], near North Berwick, East Lothian; magnificent ruinous castle.
  Held by several families, but latterly by the Nisbets from 1663, and they built **Archerfield** [NT 505841]. Archerfield was altered down the centuries, including by Robert Adam, then was used by the army in World War II, but was stripped in the 1960s, when it was being used as a farm store. It has recently been restored and there is a golf course in the grounds (www.archerfieldgolfclub.com). Dirleton Castle is in the care of Historic Scotland and is open to the public (01620 850330), and there are fine gardens.

Innerwick [NT 735737], near Dunbar, East Lothian; ruinous castle.
  Held by the Stewarts, by the Hamiltons and by the Maxwells before being sold to the Nisbets in 1663.

Marlfield House [NT 735255], near Kelso, Borders; mansion incorporating tower house.
  Held by the Bennets in the seventeenth century, but passed

457

to the Nisbets. Said to be haunted by a ghost that pushes past people in corridors.

Northfield House [NT 389739], Prestonpans, East Lothian; fine L-plan tower house.

Held by the Hamiltons and by the Marjoribanks family, but was bought by the Nisbets in 1746, and then later passed to the Symes. Still occupied.

Sornhill [NS 509342], near Galston, Ayrshire; L-plan tower house.
Held by the Nisbets, but was sold to the Campbells in 1553. Used as a farmhouse, but apparently now derelict.

Winton House [NT 439696], near Tranent, East Lothian; fine mansion of 1620 with older work.

Held by the Quincys and by the Setons, then later by the Nisbet Hamiltons, then by the Ogilvys from 1920. The house is still occupied and can be visited (01875 340222; www.wintonhouse.co.uk).

www.nesbittnisbet.org.uk
www.nisbetts.co.uk
www.ibydeit.com
No. of castles/sites: 11
Rank: 127=/764
Xref: Nesbitt

Niven

The name was originally a personal name, and it means 'little saint': it was found in Ayrshire and Galloway. Niven is on record as a surname from the end of the thirteenth century (also see MacNiven).

Monkredding House [NS 325454], two miles north-east of Kilwinning in Ayrshire, is a small tower house, altered in later years and extended by a mansion. The buildings now form three side of a courtyard. The lands were held by the Nevans or Nivens from the sixteenth century or earlier, but the property had passed to the Cunninghams of Clonbeith by 1698. The house is still occupied.

No. of castles/sites: 1
Rank: 537=/764
Xrefs: Nevan; Nevin

Noble

The Nobles came from England and settled on lands in East Lothian at the end of the twelfth century, and then held other properties, including property in Dunbartonshire.

Illieston House [NT 010700] is an altered T-plan tower house, which dates from the seventeenth century. It is located a couple of miles south-east of Broxburn in West Lothian, and was held by the Noble family in the middle of the sixteenth century or earlier before passing to the Grahams and then to the Ellis family. The house is still occupied.

Ardmore [NS 317785], two miles west of Cardross in Dunbartonshire, stands on Ardmore Point in the Firth of Clyde. There was a castle, of which three towers remain, one with gunloops. The property was held by the Nobles of Ardmore from the sixteenth century, and the family apparently now live in Kent in England. The grounds are managed by the Scottish Wildlife Trust.

Ardardan or **Ferme Castle** [NS 331785], which is also near Cardross, also belonged to the Nobles from the middle of the sixteenth century and they may have held the property for some three centuries. There was a tower house, but there are no remains.

A few miles east of Inveraray in Argyll is **Ardkinglas House** [NN 175104], a mansion dating from 1906 and designed by Sir Robert Lorimer for the Nobles. There

Ardkinglas House 1910?

was a castle at Ardkinglas, which was held by the Campbells, and it apparently had three towers and a courtyard. According to *Burke's*, the Nobles of Ardkinglas apparently have residences in Edinburgh and on Skye. The woodland garden at Ardkinglas, which has a fine collection of rhododendrons and conifers, is open to the public (01499 600261/263; www.ardkinglas.com).

Dunderave Castle [NN 143096] is also near Inveraray, and is on the north bank of Loch Fyne. The castle is a sixteenth-century L-plan tower house of four storeys, and it was long a property of the MacNaughtons before passing to the Campbells. The castle was roofless when it was restored and extended for the Nobles by Sir Robert Lorimer in 1911-12. Dunderave is still occupied.

No. of castles/sites: 5 / Rank: 240=/764

Northington

The name is local in origin and appears to come from 'Northincheton', or possibly from 'Nothingham', in Caithness, and is on record from the fourteenth century.

Duntrune House [NO 445345], a few miles east and north of Dundee in Angus, is a house of 1825 in a fine location, and it replaced an older house or castle dating from the sixteenth century. The lands were given to a Walter Northington by Robert the Bruce in the fourteenth century, but passed to the Ogilvies of Easter Powrie and then to the Scrymgeours of Dudhope in the fifteenth century, and then to others. The house is still occupied.

No. of castles/sites: 1
Rank: 537=/764

Norval

The name comes from a shortened form of 'Normanville', and the name may come from either of two places in France. The name is on record in Scotland from the end of the twelfth century.

Cardonald Castle [NS 526645] stood in the Cardonald area of Glasgow but there are no remains. The property was held by the Norval family until 1296 or later, but passed to the Stewarts of Darnley, who held it in the fifteenth century.

Descendants of the Norvals went on to hold the lands of **Gargunnock** [NS 715944], which are five miles west of Stirling. There was a castle at Gargunnock, some of which is incorporated into Gargunnock House. The gardens of the house are open for some weeks in the spring and summer (01786 860392; www.gardensof scotland.org). The Stewarts built a large castle at Cardonald, which went to the Stewarts of Blantyre, but the building was demolished in 1848 and replaced by a farmhouse.

No. of castles/sites: 1
Rank: 537=/764
Xref: Norvel

Ochterlony

The name is territorial and comes from the lands of Ochterlony or Auchterlony, which appear to have been a mile or so north-east of Letham in Angus. This property was also apparently known as **Balmadies** and as **Auchtermeggities**, however, and there was a castle at **Ochterlony** [NO 553497], which was replaced by Balmadies House. This property had passed to the Piersons of Balmadies by 1600 and they held it into the nineteenth century; the Ochterlonys held the lands from the thirteenth century or earlier. They also appear to have been in possession of **Balgavies Castle** [NO 540516], some remains of which survive. This stood two miles to the north and east of Letham, but passed to the Guthries, then to the Prestons and then to others.

The family also owned several other properties in Angus and in Kincardineshire:

Flemington Tower [NO 527556], near Forfar, Angus; ruinous L-plan tower house.
    Held by the Dishington family, but passed to the Ochterlonys. The Ochterlony family supported the Jacobites in the Rising of 1745-46, and fugitives hiding in the castle only narrowly escaped discovery. The castle was abandoned in 1830, and was then used to house farm workers.

Guynd [NO 564418], near Arbroath, Angus; castle replaced by mansion.
    Held by the Beatons in the sixteenth century, then by the Ochterlony family in the next two centuries. Ochterlony of Guynd probably fought at the Battle of Culloden in 1746 for the Jacobites. He and two other fugitives hid in the hills, then sailed from Montrose in an open boat; they were picked up by a Swedish ship and taken to Gothenberg.

Kellie Castle [NO 608402], near Arbroath, Angus; fine fortified house.
    Held by the Mowbrays, by the Kellys and by the Stewarts before passing to the Ochterlony family in 1402. William Ochterlony of Kellie was sheriff of Forfar in 1514. Kellie was sold to the Irvines in 1614 and later passed to the Maule Earls of Panmure.

Kellie Castle (M&R)

Kintrockat [NO 568592], near Brechin, Angus; site of castle or old house.

Held by the Cramonds but passed to the Ochterlonys. One of the family was Major General Ochterlony, after they had settled in Russia in 1794. Ochterlony was in the service of the Czar, and was slain at the Battle of Inkerman in 1854 during the Crimean War.

Pitforthie [NO 615610], near Brechin, Angus; site of castle or old house.

Held by the Guthries, but passed to the Ochterlonys. One of the descendants of the family was Sir David Ochterlony, an eminent soldier, who fought in the Indian subcontinent and was made a Baronet.

Tillyfruskie [NO 622929], near Banchory, Aberdeenshire; castle replaced by mansion.

Held by the Ochterlony family.

No. of castles/sites: 8
Rank: 160=/764
Xref: Auchterlony

Airlie Castle (M&R) – see next column (Ogilvie)

Ogilvie

The name is territorial and comes from the lands and barony of Ogilvie, which was in the parish of Glamis in Angus. The name is on record from the end of the twelfth century. John Ogilvie, who was born in Aberdeenshire in 1579, was a Jesuit and was hanged in 1615. He is recognised as a Catholic martyr and was beatified in 1929 and canonised in 1976, making him a saint.

Claverhouse Castle [NO 380442] stood several miles north of Dundee and a couple of miles south of Glamis in Angus. The places was also known as Hatton of Ogilvie and Tower of Glenogilvie, and there was a castle with a keep and a moat and drawbridge, but there are no remains. The lands were held by the Ogilvies from the twelfth century or earlier, and Sir Patrick Ogilvie of Claverhouse led the Scottish forces fighting the English on the side of Joan of Arc in France. The property passed to the Grahams, and John Graham of Claverhouse, Bonnie Dundee or Bloody Clavers, took his title from this place.

Airlie or **Errolly Castle** [NO 293522], four or so miles north-east of Alyth in Angus, is a mansion which incorporates some of an old castle, and a deep ditch defended the landward side of an angle of land between two rivers. The castle was built in 1432 by the Ogilvies, and James Ogilvie was made Lord Ogilvie in 1491. His daughter, Marion, was the mistress (and probably wife) of Cardinal David Beaton, Archbishop of St Andrews, and they had several children; her ghost is said to haunt Claypotts Castle. One of the family was slain at the Battle of Pinkie in 1547, and Mary, Queen of Scots, visited the castle. Although it had previously withstood sieges, in 1640 it was captured and sacked by the Earl of Argyll with 4000 troops; James Ogilvie, first Earl of Airlie from 1639, had fled Scotland rather than sign the National Covenant. The ballad 'The Bonnie House o' Airlie' tells how the pregnant wife of Ogilvie was turned out of doors - probably at Forter Castle rather than Airlie - by Argyll after the castle had been taken, pillaged and partly demolished. Argyll himself is supposed to have taken a hand in the destruction with a hammer; the Ogilvies later torched Castle Campbell near Dollar in Clackmannanshire in revenge. Ogilvie joined the Marquis of Montrose, and fought bravely at Kilsyth. Ogilvie's son, another James, was captured at the defeat of Philiphaugh in 1645, although he later managed to escape from St Andrews Castle on the night before his execution by swopping clothes with his sister. He was forfeited, but recovered the property at the Restoration. David Ogilvie, son of (what would have been) the fourth Earl fought in the Jacobite Rising of 1745-46, but had to flee Scotland to France. He was pardoned in 1778, but the title was not recovered until 1826. The castle was not rebuilt and it was replaced by a mansion in 1793. A ram, the 'Doom of Airlie Castle', is said to circle the castle when one of the family is near death or bad fortune is about to strike. The Earls of Airlie still apparently own the property.

Cortachy Castle [NO 398597] is a fine altered courtyard castle, which dates from the fifteenth century and stands three or so miles north of Kirriemuir in Angus.

Cortachy Castle 1920?

The property passed to the Ogilvies in 1473, and then to the Earls of Airlie; when Airlie was destroyed, the Earls moved to Cortachy. Charles II spent a night at Cortachy in 1650 in the 'King's Room', and the following year the castle was sacked by Cromwell. The castle is still apparently owned by the Ogilvies, and Cortachy has an interesting ghost story. The building is said to be haunted by the spirit of a drummer, whose drums are heard before one of the family is going to die. This reportedly happened on several occasions in the nineteenth century, although the evidence for ghostly activity is not perhaps as strong as it might be. The gardens of the castle are occasionally open to the public (www.airlieestates.com/www.gardensofscotland.org).

Inverquharity Castle [NO 411579] is also north of Kirriemuir, and is an altered keep or tower, which rises to four storeys and an attic, with later extensions. It was held by the Ogilvies of Inverquharity from 1420. One of the family, Alexander, was (reputedly) smothered

Inverquharity Castle (M&R)

at Finavon Castle by his sister in 1446; and Sir John Ogilvie of Inverquharity was slain by the Lindsays in 1581. The family were made Baronets of Nova Scotia in 1625. Alexander Ogilvie of Inverquharity was captured after the Battle of Philiphaugh in 1645, while fighting for the Marquis of Montrose, and beheaded in Glasgow; members of the family also fought at Culloden for the Jacobites in 1746. Inverquharity is said to have been haunted by a Sir John Ogilvie. Desiring the beautiful daughter of the local miller, John White, Ogilvie had her father hanged when she refused him, then raped her and her mother. Ogilvie was then struck down dead, although his ghost is said to have so plagued the castle that it had to be abandoned at one time. The property was sold in the late eighteenth century, and the Ogilvys of Inverquharity, Baronets, became ensconced at Winton House in East Lothian.

Winton House [NT 439696] is three miles to the south-east of Tranent in East Lothian, and is a fine

Winton House (M&R)

Renaissance mansion, which incorporates an old castle, and has some magnificent chimneys. Winton was long held by the Setons, but they were forfeited following the Jacobite Rising of 1745-46 and the property eventually came to the Ogilvys in 1920. The house is occupied and open to the public (01875 340222; www.wintonhouse.co.uk).

Findlater Castle [NJ 542673] is located on high cliffs a couple of miles east of Cullen in Aberdeenshire, but only ruins remain of the old stronghold. Owned by the Sinclairs, the property passed to the Ogilvies, although in 1560 the laird of the time disinherited his son and signed the property over to the Gordons. The Ogilvies got the property back, but the castle was abandoned after 1600 when the Ogilvies moved to Cullen; they were made Earls of Findlater in 1633. The castle is accessible but great care should be taken (www.findlater.org.uk/castle.htm).

Cullen House [NJ 507663] is to the south-west of the village on the north coast of Aberdeenshire, and

Findlater Castle 1904? – see previous page

was built above a deep ravine. The core of the house is an L-plan tower house but it was extended down the centuries until it had 386 rooms. The Ogilvies built the castle, and (as mentioned above) became Earls of Findlater in 1633, although the building was plundered by Royalists in 1645. James Ogilvie, fourth Earl of Findlater, was one of those responsible for securing the union of the Scottish and English parliaments in 1707, and he had been made Earl of Seafield in 1701 as well as Lord High Commissioner. The castle was sacked again in 1745-46 during the Jacobite Rising. It is reputed that the ghost of James Ogilvie, third Earl of Seafield, haunts the castle. Although in good health most of the time, Ogilvie suffered from episodes of uncontrollable rage, and during one of these in 1770 he murdered his factor, and then killed himself in remorse at what he had done. The property was sold by the family in 1981, and was converted into flats in 1984-85. The Ogilvy-Grant Earls of Seafield now apparently live at Old Cullen.

Cullen Collegiate Church [NJ 507663], to the south-west of the centre of Cullen, was established in 1543 by Alexander Ogilvie (presumably of Findlater), whose canopied tomb and stone effigy survives in the building, and there are burial monuments to the Earls of Seafield.

The Ogilvies also owned:

Alyth Castle [NO 247485], near Alyth, Perthshire; slight remains of castle.
　　Held by the Lindsays Earls of Crawford, although the village was made a burgh of barony for the Ogilvie Earl of Airlie in 1488.

Auchindoun Castle [NJ 348374], near Dufftown, Moray; ruinous L-plan tower house.
　　Held by the Ogilvies after 1482 and before passing to the Gordons by 1535. In the care of Historic Scotland and open to the public (view from exterior) (01667 460232).

Auchterhouse [NO 332373], near Dundee, Angus; mansion incorporating castle.
　　Held by the Ramsays, by the Stewarts and by the Maules before passing to the Ogilvie Earls of Airlie.

Balbegno Castle [NO 639730], near Fettercairn, Kincardineshire; altered L-plan tower house.
　　Held by the Woods, and then by the Middletons in 1687 and then by the Ogilvies, then by the Ramsays in the nineteenth century. The building is apparently not currently occupied.

Baldovie [NO 324541], near Kirriemuir, Angus; site of castle or old house.
　　Held by the Melvilles, but passed to the Clayhills and then to the Ogilvies in the seventeenth century, then to the Farquharsons in the nineteenth century.

Balfour Castle [NO 337546], near Kirriemuir, Angus; slight remains of castle.
　　Held by the Ogilvies, and may have been built for Marion Ogilvie, mistress (or wife) of Cardinal David Beaton, and their many children. Balfour later passed to the Fotheringhams and then to the Farquharsons.

Balnagarrow [NO 378573], near Kirriemuir, Angus; site of tower house.
　　Held by the Ogilvies.

Barras Castle [NO 856804], near Stonehaven, Kincardineshire; slight remains of castle or old house.
　　Held by the Ogilvies of Barras, and demolished in 1862. Sir George Ogilvie of Barras was one of the commanders of the garrison of Dunnottar Castle when it was besieged by Cromwell's forces and he helped to save the Scottish Crown Jewels from falling into the hands of the English. He was made a Baronet of Nova Scotia in 1660.

Beldorney Castle [NJ 424369], near Keith, Aberdeenshire; altered Z-plan tower house.
　　Held by the Ogilvies, but passed to the Gordons about 1500 and they built the castle. Beldorney went to the Lyons, to the Buchans and then to the Grants and is still occupied.

Benholm Castle [NO 804705], near Inverbervie, Kincardineshire; ruinous castle and mansion.
　　Held by the Lundies, but passed to the Ogilvies, then to the Keith Earls Marischal and to the Scotts. Said to be haunted.

Bolshan Castle [NO 617521], near Friockheim, Angus; site of castle.
　　Held by the Ogilvies of Lintrathen in the fifteenth century, and they probably built the castle. Bolshan was sold to the Carnegie Earl of Southesk in 1634, then went to others.

Boyne Castle [NJ 612657], near Portsoy, Aberdeenshire; ruinous castle.
　　Held by the Edmonstones but passed by marriage to the Ogilvies, who built the castle after 1575. Occupied in 1723.

Braikie Castle [NO 628509], near Brechin, Angus; derelict L-plan tower house.
　　Held by the Frasers of Oliver, but passed to the Grays around 1750 and then to the Ogilvies.

Buchragie House [NJ 659644], near Banff, Aberdeenshire; slight remains of castle or old house.
　　Held by the Ogilvies.

Carnousie Castle [NJ 670504], near Turriff, Aberdeenshire; Z-plan tower house.
　　Held by the Ogilvies, but the lands were raided in the 1640s and the family had to sell the property to the Gordons in 1683. Later used as a piggery, but restored and reoccupied.

Carsegrange [NO 270255], near Dundee, Perthshire; site of castle or old house.
　　Held by the Ogilvies of Carsegrange.

Clova Castle [NO 322734], near Kirriemuir, Angus; slight remains of tower house.
　　Held by the Ogilvies. They also had another castle or old house at **Clova** [NO 327732]

Clunie Castle [NO 114440], near Blairgowrie, Perthshire; ruinous L-plan tower house.
　　Held by the Crichtons, but later passed to the Ogilvies and then to the Coxs of Lochlee in 1892.

Coull [NO 444590], near Forfar, Angus; site of castle.
　　Held by the Ogilvies of Coull, who moved to Ruthven around 1744.

Craig Castle [NO 254527], near Alyth, Angus; site of castle.
　　Held by the Ogilvies, and reputed to have been destroyed by James VI's forces in 1595, and was then sacked again by the Earl of Argyll in the 1640s. The lands passed to the Carnegies of Kinnaird in the seventeenth century.

Craig of Boyne Castle [NJ 615660], near Portsoy, Aberdeenshire; ruinous castle.
　　Held by the Edmonstones or by the Comyns but passed to the Ogilvies of Dunlugas about 1571, and they built Boyne Castle, further up stream.

Delvine [NO 123402], near Blairgowrie, Perthshire; site of castle and mansion.

Held by the Hays and then by the Ogilvies of Inchmartine until the seventeenth century, and then by the Mackenzies.

Deskford Castle [NJ 509617], near Cullen, Aberdeenshire; slight remains of castle.

Held by the Sinclairs and then by the Ogilvies, who moved to Cullen.

Dod or **Burnside** [NO 492499], near Forfar, Angus; site of small castle.

Held by the MacCombies, but passed to the Ogilvies. The name of the property is said to have been changed from Dod to Burnside because the then laird did not like being called 'Doddie'.

Duntrune House [NO 445345], near Dundee; mansion on site of castle.

Held by the Northingtons but passed to the Ogilvies of Easter Powrie, and then to the Scrymgeours of Dudhope in the fifteenth century. Duntrune then passed to the Grahams of Fintry and others, and is still occupied.

Easter Braikie Castle [NO 637515], near Brechin, Angus; site of tower house.

Held by the Frasers and by the Stirlings, but passed to the Ogilvies, and then to others, including to the Gavins from 1752.

Findochty Castle [NJ 455673], near Buckie, Aberdeenshire; ruinous L-plan tower house.

Held by the Gordons but passed to the Ogilvies and then to the Ord family in 1568.

Fordyce Castle [NJ 556638], near Portsoy, Aberdeenshire; L-plan tower house.

Held by the Dunbars in 1499, but passed to the Ogilvie Earls of Findlater, and then the Menzies family of Durn, who built the school. Restored and accommodation is available (01261 843722; www.fordycecastle.co.uk).

Forglen House [NJ 696517], near Turriff, Aberdeenshire; mansion incorporating part of castle.

Held by the Ogilvies of Dunlugas, but passed by marriage to the Abercrombies, who built the present house. Still occupied.

Forter Castle [NO 183646], near Alyth, Angus; L-plan tower house.

Held by Ogilvies and the castle was pillaged and burned by the Earl of Argyll in 1640, as was Airlie. The property went to

Forter Castle (M&R)

the MacThomas or MacCombie clan, who feuded with the Ogilvies, although it was the MacThomases who were ruined. The castle was restored and is occupied, and self-catering accommodation is available (www.hoseasons.co.uk).

Gella [NO 375655], near Kirriemuir, Angus; site of small tower house.

May have been held by the Ogilvies.

Grandhome or **Dilspro House** [NJ 899117], near Dyce, Aberdeenshire; castle replaced by mansion.

Held by the Keiths, and then by the Ogilvies, by the Buchanans

and by others, before going to the Patons of Farrochie, who changed the name from Dilspro to Grandhome.

Halhill Castle [NH 759519], near Inverness; site of castle.

Held by the Mackintoshes and by the Dunbars of Cumnock and Durris in 1502, then passed to the Ogilvies. Halhill was then sacked by the Mackintoshs and the Roses in 1513.

House of Auchiries [NJ 977606], near Fraserburgh, Aberdeenshire; castle or old house.

Held by the Keith Earls Marischal but was bought by the Ogilvies in 1703, who held it for about 100 years. Now a farm while part is ruinous.

House of Skeith [NJ 504603], near Cullen, Aberdeenshire; site of castle or old house.

Held by the Ogilvies.

Inaltrie Castle [NJ 518631], near Cullen, Aberdeenshire; slight remains of castle.

Held by the Lawties of Inaltrie, but was bought by the Ogilvie Earl of Findlater around 1721.

Inchdrewer Castle [NJ 656607], near Banff, Aberdeenshire; altered L-plan tower house.

Held by the Currors, but bought by the Ogilvies of Dunlugas in the sixteenth century and they built the castle. The family were made Lords Banff in 1692. The house was torched and

Inchdrewer Castle (M&R)

Lord Banff slain in 1712, the story going that he was murdered by his own servants who were robbing him when he unexpectedly returned home, and they then burned the building to hide the evidence. An alternative explanation is that he was killed by John Milne of Boyndie Milne after Lord Banff had insulted Milne's young wife, although Milne was cleared of murder that same year. Inchdrewer later passed to the Abercrombies of Birkenbog and has been restored.

Inchmartine [NO 262281], near Dundee, Perthshire; site of castle on former island.

Held by the Glens, but passed to the Ogilvies in the middle of the fifteenth century and they held Inchmartine for about 300 years. Fragments of this building may be built into the bridge at Inchmartine Pow [NO 264278], where there is a stone with the date 1643 and the initials S/PO for Patrick Ogilvie. The castle was replaced by Inchmartine House in the seventeenth century.

Inglismaldie Castle [NO 644669], near Brechin, Angus; altered L-plan tower house.

Held by the Livingstones and by others, but was sold to the Ogilvies in 1960 and the castle is still occupied.

Inshewan [NO 447569], near Forfar, Angus; mansion on site of castle.

Held by the Ogilvies from 1474 to the twentieth century, and the Ogilvys of Inshewan still flourish.

Keithmore [NJ 355391], near Dufftown, Moray; castle or old house replaced by mansion.

Held by the Ogilvies of Deskford in 1490 but later passed to the Gordons of Huntly and then to the Duffs, but had returned to the Gordons by 1750.

Keltie Castle [NO 008133], near Dunning, Perthshire; L-plan tower house.

Held by the Bonnars and by the Drummonds, but passed to the Ogilvie Earl of Airlie in 1812 then to Lord Rollo in 1833, then to others. Still occupied.

Kinnell or **Balneave Castle** [NO 599500], near Friockheim, Angus; site of castle.

Held by the Balnaves family, and then by others, including by the Ogilvies at one time.

Kinnordy [NO 366553], near Kirriemuir, Angus; mansion on site of castle.

Held by the Ogilvies of Inverquharity but sold to the Lyles of Gardyne in 1770, and they apparently still own it.

Kinrive [NO 388629], near Kirriemuir, Angus; site of tower house.

May have been held by the Ogilvies.

Lochindorb Castle [NH 974364], near Grantown-on-Spey, Highland; ruinous castle on island.

Held by the Stewarts, by the Douglases and by the Campbells of Cawdor before coming to the Ogilvie Earls of Seafield in 1750.

Lumgair [NO 851807], near Stonehaven, Kincardineshire; site of castle or old house.

Held by the Ogilvies of Lumgair; Lumgair is, however, very close to another Ogilvie property at East Mains of Barras (Barras Castle). The family also owned a town house in **Stonehaven** [NO 875858] at 51 High Street, which dates from the seventeenth century and is said to be haunted by a Green Lady. There is also said to be a tunnel linking the house to Dunnottar Castle and to Fetteresso Castle.

Milton Keith Tower [NJ 429512], Keith, Moray; slight remains of tower house.

Held by the Ogilvies after the Reformation, but passed to the Oliphants in the late seventeenth century.

Newton Castle [NO 230602], near Kirriemuir, Angus; site of castle.

Held by the Ogilvies, and destroyed by the Earl of Argyll in 1640.

Lintrathen or **Peel of Lintrathen** [NO 263540], near Alyth, Angus; site of castle.

Held by the Ogilvies, and Sir Walter Ogilvie of Lintrathen was High Treasurer of Scotland to James I in the fifteenth century. This branch of the family acquired Airlie.

Pittensear (now **Pittensair**) [NJ 282607], near Lhanbryde, Moray; site of old house.

Held by the Chalmers family but passed to the Ogilvies. One of the family was William Ogilvie who was a Professor of Philosophy at King's College in Aberdeen in 1762.

Pittulie Castle [NJ 945671], near Fraserburgh, Aberdeenshire; ruinous tower house.

Held by the Frasers, but passed by marriage to the Ogilvies in 1630.

Portsoy Castle [NJ 585660], Portsoy, Aberdeenshire; site of castle.

Held by the Ogilvies of Boyne in 1550.

Powrie or **Wester Powrie Castle** [NO 421346], near Dundee; partly ruinous castle.

Held by the Ogilvies from about 1170, but passed to the Fotheringhams in 1412, and they built the castle.

Rochelhill [NO 375451], near Glamis, Angus; site of castle.

Held by the Ogilvies and a doocot survives.

Rothes Castle [NJ 277490], near Charlestown of Aberlour, Moray; ruinous castle.

Held by several families including by the Leslies, and then latterly by the Ogilvie Earl of Findlater in 1708, and then by the Grants.

Ruthven Castle [NO 302479], near Alyth, Angus; slight remains of castle.

Held by the Lindsay Earls of Crawford and by the Crichtons, but bought by the Ogilvies of Coull in 1744, who built a new house; this was held by the Ogilvies into the twentieth century.

Shielhill [NO 428574], near Forfar, Angus; mansion on site of castle.

Held by the Ogilvies, but passed to the Lyles.

Stonehaven [NO 876855], Kincardineshire; old house.

51 High Street is a seventeenth-century town house of three storeys, which was held by the Ogilvies of Lumgair. The house is said to be haunted by a Green Lady. There are also stories of a tunnel linking this house to Fetteresso and to Dunnottar Castle.

Tannadyce House [NO 484577], near Forfar, Angus; mansion on site of castle.

Held by the Keiths and by the Lyons, but had passed to the Ogilvies in the nineteenth century, and they sold it to the Neishes in 1870.

Wedderburn Castle or **Easter Powrie** [NO 435352], near Dundee, Angus; site of castle.

Held by the Douglas Earls of Angus, but passed to the Ogilvies and then to the Wedderburns who changed the name to Wedderburn Castle.

No. of castles/sites: 68
Rank: 12/764
Xref: Ogilvy

Tilquhillie Castle (M&R) – see next page (Ogstoun)

Ogstoun

The name is territorial, and comes from the lands of Ogstoun, which are now known as Gordonstoun, three or so miles south-west of Lossiemouth in Moray. The family are on record from the beginning of the thirteenth century.

Ogstoun (or **Plewlands**) or (now) **Gordonstoun** [NJ 184690], a mansion, incorporates a sixteenth-century tower house, which has been extended and much altered with a classical front. The property was held by the Ogstouns, and Alexander Hogeston did homage for his lands in 1296. The family sold the lands to the Inneses in 1473, who sold them in turn to the Gordons in 1616, and the Gordons renamed the property. The building now houses Gordonstoun School, and was attended by many of the privileged including Prince Charles and the Duke of Edinburgh. The gardens are occasionally open to the public (01343 837829; www.gordonstoun.org.uk).

Tilquhillie Castle [NO 722941] is a mile or so southeast of Banchory in Aberdeenshire, and is a tall Z-plan tower house, which dates from the sixteenth century and rises to three storeys and an attic. Tilquhillie was held by the Ogstouns following the Reformation, but passed by marriage to the Douglases of Lochleven, and they built the castle. The castle is still occupied.

Ardoe House [NJ 894017] is a fine castellated mansion, dating from 1879, and it replaced a castle or older house. Ardoe lies four and a half miles to the south-west of Aberdeen to the south of the River Dee; and the lands were held by the Meldrums and by the Fordyces before coming to the Ogstouns in 1839; the Ogstouns had made their money from the manufacture of soap. The building is said to be haunted by a White Lady, and she may be the apparition of Katherine, wife of Alexander Milne Ogstoun. An alternative identity has been given as the daughter of a former owner who was raped and then made pregnant, and killed herself and her baby. The house is now used as a hotel (01224 867355; www.ardoe house.com).

Norwood Hall [NJ 918032], two miles south-west of Aberdeen, stands near the site of the old castle of Pitfodels, but the hall was rebuilt for the Ogstoun family in 1881. The property had been held by the Reids and by the Menzies family of Pitfodels. The hall is said to have two ghosts. One is reputedly the apparition of the mistress of Colonel James Ogstoun as Ogstoun would not leave his wife for her; while the other is said to the ghost of Ogstoun himself, seen in the dining room. The building is now used as a hotel (01224 868951; www.norwood-hall.co.uk).

No. of castles/sites: 4
Rank: 278=/764
Xref: Ogston

Oliphant

The Oliphants or Olifards were a Norman family, and held lands in Northamptonshire in England before moving to Scotland in the twelfth century. They became major landowners in Perthshire, as well as in Caithness, in Lanarkshire and in other parts of the country.

Aberdalgie Castle [NO 081202] was about three or so miles south-west of Perth, but the old stronghold has been demolished and a classical mansion built on the site. The lands were a property of the Oliphants of Aberdalgie. Sir William Oliphant of Aberdalgie defended Stirling Castle from the English for three months, but was imprisoned in London after the castle fell. He was released, was given lands by Robert the Bruce, and added his seal to the Declaration of Arbroath in 1320. His gravestone, now much weathered, survives in a wall of the newer church, near the site of the Old Parish Church [NO 080203] in the Aberdalgie village. Sir Laurence Oliphant of Aberdalgie was made Lord Oliphant around 1458, and he founded Greyfriars, a friary, in Perth two years later, the burial ground [NO 120223] of which is the only part to survive. The Oliphants held Aberdalgie until the sixteenth century. Colin, Master of Oliphant and Sir Laurence's son, was killed at the Battle of Flodden in 1513, and Laurence, third Lord Oliphant, was captured at Solway Moss in 1542, and was only released after a large ransom was paid. The fourth Lord, another Laurence, supported Mary Queen of Scots and fought for her at Langside in 1568; he is buried in the old kirk at Wick. The Oliphants had got into a feud with the Sutherlands, in which the Sinclair Earls of Caithness also got involved. The fourth Lord's son was exiled and drowned at sea after being accused of involvement in the Raid of Ruthven in 1582; the lands had to be sold after his brother inherited. Aberdalgie is apparently now a property of the Dewars, Barons Forteviot.

About four miles east of Auchterarder is **Gask** or **Gascon Hall** [NN 986175]. This property was held by the Colvilles but was purchased by the Oliphants of Aberdalgie, and there was a stronghold here from the thirteenth century. **Old House of Gask** dates from the seventeenth century and is a large courtyard house, which was remodelled in the 1930s. The Oliphants of Gask were Jacobites, and fought in the Risings of 1689, 1715 and 1745-46. Bonnie Prince Charlie is said to have visited here, and the house was burnt by Hanoverian troops in 1746. Laurence Oliphant was an aide-de-camp to Bonnie Prince Charlie and had to flee abroad after the defeat at Culloden, but he was allowed to return in 1763. Carolina Oliphant, Lady Nairne, the well-known Jacobite songwriter, was born here. She used the penname Mrs Bogan of Bogan, and wrote 'Charlie is My Darling' and 'Will You No Come Back Again?'. The nearby house of **Gask** [NN 995189] was built in 1801 and is an elegant classical mansion with later alterations. The Oliphants sold Gask in 1902, and moved to Ardblair.

Ardblair Castle [NO 164445] is to the west of Blairgowrie in Perthshire, and is a fine L-plan tower house with a courtyard, and dates from the sixteenth

Ardblair Castle 1910?

century. The lands were held by the Blairs of Balthayock, but passed by marriage to the Oliphants of Gask in 1792, and there are many Jacobite mementoes at Ardblair. The castle is still apparently occupied by the Kington Blair Oliphants of Ardblair and Gask. This is another castle said to be haunted by a Green Lady, dressed in green silk, who searches through the chambers of the castle. She is reputed to be the ghost of Lady Jean Drummond of nearby Newton, who had fallen in love with one of the Blairs of Ardblair. The families feuded, and Lady Jean seems to have died of a broken heart, drowned in a local marsh, although there are several versions of the story and she is also said to haunt Newton Castle. Accommodation is available at Ardblair although it must be pre-booked (01250 873155).

The Oliphants also held:
Ackergill Tower [ND 352547], near Wick, Caithness; fine altered tower and mansion.
    Held by the Cheynes, then by the Keiths and by the Sinclairs, before passing to the Oliphants, then to the Dunbars of Hempriggs, who held Ackergill until the 1980s. The castle can be rented for totally exclusive use (01955 603556; www.ackergill-tower.co.uk).
Balcraig Castle [NO 312400], near Alyth, Angus; site of castle.
    Held by the Oliphants.
Berriedale Castle [ND 121224], near Dunbeath, Caithness; slight remains of castle.
    Held by the Cheynes and by the Sutherlands, but had passed to the Oliphants by 1526. It was sold to the Sinclair Earls of Caithness in 1606.
Castle of Old Wick [ND 369488], near Wick, Caithness; ruinous castle on cliffs.
    Held by the Cheynes and by the Sutherlands, but then by the Oliphants. It was sold to the Sinclairs, after they had besieged and seized it, in 1606; then it later went to the Campbells of Glenorchy and to the Dunbars of Hempriggs. Now in the care of Historic Scotland and open to the public although great care should be taken if visiting (01667 460232).
Cluggy Castle [NN 840234], near Crieff, Perthshire; ruinous castle.
    Held by the Comyns, but granted to the Oliphants, then to the Murrays of Tullibardine at the end of the fifteenth century.
Condie [NO 075117], near Forgandenny, Perthshire; site of castle.
    Held by the Condie family and located some miles south of

Newton of Condie (see below). The property passed to the Oliphants.
Condie or **Newton of Condie** [NO 076182], near Forgandenny, Perthshire; site of castle and mansion.
    Held by the Colvilles of Cleish but bought by the Oliphants in 1601, who still held the lands 300 years later. The family are still styled as the Oliphants of Condie, although they now apparently live on Skye.
Drumsargad Castle [NS 667597], near Hamilton, Lanarkshire; slight traces of castle.
    Held by the Oliphants, but passed to the Murrays, and then to the Douglases and to the Hamiltons.
Dunbarney House [NO 111196], near Perth; castle replaced by house.
    Held by the Mercers in 1455, but passed to the Oliphants, who were in possession in the sixteenth century. Later went to the Craigies.
Dupplin Castle [NO 056195], near Perth; mansion on site of castle.
    Held by the Oliphants, and probably built or rebuilt by Sir William Oliphant, the hero of Stirling Castle. The Battle of Dupplin was fought nearby in 1332, and Edward Balliol and the English were victorious, although the success was short lived. The burgesses of Perth destroyed the castle in 1461 because of a dispute with Lord Oliphant. The castle was rebuilt, but the property was sold to the Douglas Earls of Morton, and then to the Hay Earls of Kinnoul, and they built the mansion. It is now apparently held by the Dewars.
Hatton Castle [NO 302411], near Coupar Angus, Angus; Z-plan tower house.
    Held by the Oliphants but passed to the Halyburtons of Pitcur

Hatton Castle (M&R)

in 1627, then to others, before being bought back by the Oliphants and restored in the 1980s. The castle had to be sold, however, because of financial difficulties.
Hazelside Castle [NS 815289], near Douglas, Lanarkshire; site of castle.
    Held by the Dicksons, but later passed to the Oliphants.
Kellie Castle [NO 520052], near Elie, Fife; magnificent castle with fine gardens.
    Held by the Siwards but the present castle was started after it had passed to the Oliphants, who held the lands from 1360 to 1613. The property was then sold to the Erskines of Gogar, who were made Earls of Kellie. The castle is now in the care of The National Trust for Scotland and is open to the public (01333 720271; www.nts.org.uk).
Mains of Catterline [NO 865786], near Stonehaven, Kincardineshire; possible site of castle.
    Held by the Oliphants, but passed to the Arbuthnotts in the seventeenth century.
Milton Keith Tower [NJ 429512], Keith, Moray; slight remains of tower house.
    Held by the Ogilvies, but passed to the Oliphants in the late

seventeenth century. It had already been abandoned when it was destroyed in 1829.

Ochtertyre [NN 839236], near Crieff, Perthshire; castle replaced by mansion.

Held by the Comyns, but passed to the Oliphants in the thirteenth century, then went to the Murrays.

Orbiston House [NS 732580], near Motherwell, Lanarkshire; site of castle.

Held by the Oliphants in the twelfth century, but passed to the Hamiltons, who held the property until 1827.

Pittheavlis Castle [NO 097222], near Perth; altered L-plan tower house.

Held by the Rosses of Craigie and by the Stewarts, who probably built the tower. Then was owned by the Oliphants of Bachiltron by 1636, then later by the Murrays. The castle has been divided and is still occupied.

Rossie House [NO 084183], near Perth; mansion incorporating older work.

Held by the Oliphants. The gardens are open by appointment only (01738 812265; www.gardensofscotland.org).

Rossie Ochil [NO 087130], near Perth; mansion incorporating castle or older house.

Held by the Blairs, but passed to the Oliphants of Condie in 1583.

Struie Castle [NO 079114], near Forgandenny, Perthshire; some remains of castle.

Held by the Stirlings but passed to the Oliphants.

Struiehill [NO 064105], near Forgandenny, Perthshire; probable site of castle.

Held by the Stirlings but passed to the Oliphants.

Turin House [NO 545527], near Forfar, Angus; mansion on site of castle.

Held by the Oliphants in the sixteenth century, but passed to the Carnegies of Lour and Turin.

Williamston [NN 972220], near Perth; altered tower house.

Held by the Blairs of Kinfauns, but was bought by the Oliphants. The house was built for Oliphant of Gask after he was disinherited. Instead of marrying the forty-five-year-old sister of the Marquis of Douglas – as his family wished – he married a daughter of the Minister of Gask.

Woodend [NN 938221], near Crieff, Perthshire; castle replaced by mansion.

Held by the Oliphants, but passed to the Murrays, who held it in the seventeenth century. It is still occupied.

No. of castles/sites: 28
Rank: 44=/764
Xrefs: Oliphaunt; Olifard

Oliver

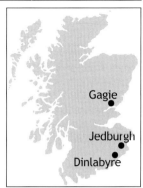

The name is on record in Scotland as a surname from the end of the twelfth century, and the family may be descended from Olyver, son of Kyluert, who was a follower of the Earl of March in the same century. The family held lands around Jedburgh in the Borders, as well as elsewhere.

The Olivers held:

Dinlabyre [NY 528920], near Newcastleton, Borders; house incorporating tower house.

Held by the Elliots, but had passed to the Olivers by the middle of the eighteenth century.

Dykeraw Tower [NT 629085], near Jedburgh, Borders; site of castle.

Held by the Olivers, and burnt by the English in 1513.

Gagie House [NO 448376], near Dundee; mansion and tower house.

Held by the Olivers (Oliphants?), but passed to the Guthries in 1610, who probably built the original tower house. It is still occupied.

Hindhaughead [NT 643103], near Jedburgh, Borders; site of castle.

Held by the Olivers, and the castle and village were destroyed by the English in 1513.

Mervinslaw Pele [NT 672117], near Jedburgh, Borders; ruined tower house.

Held by the Olivers.

Northbank Peel [NT 661095], near Jedburgh, Borders; slight remains of tower.

Held by the Olivers.

Slacks Peel (or **Lustruther?**) [NT 628091], near Jedburgh, Borders; small ruinous tower house.

Held by the Olivers.

No. of castles/sites: 7
Rank: 182=/764

Kellie Castle (M&R) – see previous page

Orde

The name is territorial and comes from at least two possible sources: the lands of Orde, now Kirkurd, a few miles south-west of Romanno Bridge in the Borders; and there were also lands of this name in Aberdeenshire in the far north-east of Scotland,

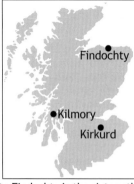

although this branch moved to Findochty in the sixteenth century. There are also lands called Ord, near Muir of Ord in Ross and Cromarty, but these do not appear to have been held by the Orde family (being a property of the Mackenzies). The name is on record from the end of the thirteenth century.

Kirkurd [NT 139446], near Romanno Bridge, was held by the Ordes, but had passed to the Scotts by the middle of the fifteenth century. There was a tower house, but there are no remains.

Findochty Castle [NJ 455673] is a couple of miles east and north of Buckie in Aberdeenshire in the far north-east of Scotland. The castle is a ruinous sixteenth-century L-plan tower house, and the property was held by the Gordons and by the Ogilvies before coming to the Orde family in 1568. Findochty was exchanged for their original lands of Ord; and the family were responsible for developing the village as a fishing port.

Kilmory Castle [NR 870868], one mile south of Lochgilphead in Argyll, is said to date from the fourteenth century but the present building is a large castellated mansion. The lands were held by the Lamonts and by the Campbells before passing by marriage to the Orde family in 1828, and they held them for more than 100 years. The Ordes had been made Baronets in 1790, and the Campbell-Ordes, Baronets, now apparently live in Tennessee in the United States. The house is now used by the local council but the fine gardens and grounds are open to the public (01546 604360; www.argyll-bute.gov.uk/content/leisure/heritage/kilmory).

No. of castles/sites: 3
Rank: 328=/764
Xref: Ord

Orme

The name comes from Old Norse 'Ormr', and means 'serpent', and it was used as a personal name and then a surname. Orme is on record in Scotland from the middle of the twelfth century, and the family were established around Newburgh in Fife, while

Henry Orme was abbot of nearby Lindores in 1502.

Mugdrum [NO 228184] is just to the east of Newburgh in Fife, and the present mansion dates from the eighteenth century, although there was an older house or castle. The lands were held by the Coventrys, but passed to the Ormes, and Mugdrum was then held by the Arnotts and by others. It was used by Lord George Murray, the Jacobite general, before the Rising of 1745-46, and the lands were later held by the Hays. The house is still occupied.

No. of castles/sites: 1
Rank: 537=/764
Xref: Orm

Ormiston

The name is territorial but comes from two places: the lands of Ormiston, four miles east of Dalkeith in Midlothian; and the lands of the same name three or so miles south and west of Kelso in the Borders. The name is on record in Scotland from the middle of the twelfth century.

Ormiston Castle [NT 413677], four miles east of Dalkeith, is mostly gone, although part was built into Ormiston Hill House. This became ruinous, although it appears to have been restored. The lands were held by the Ormistons in the thirteenth century, but passed to the Lindsays and then to the Cockburns in the next century. The castle was torched in 1547 by the Scots as Cockburn had sided with the English, and the property passed to the Hope Earl of Hopetoun in 1746.

Nothing remains of **Ormiston Tower** [NT 700279], three and a half miles south and west of Kelso, except a mound. The property was also held by the Ormistons in the thirteenth century, and they built a castle. James Ormiston of that Ilk was paid for his part in the taking and destruction of Jedburgh Castle 1409, and the Ormistons were later accused of being involved in the murder of Lord Darnley. The Ormistons of that Ilk had a 'deadly' feud with the Kerrs of Cessford, and several Ormistons were forfeited for treason in 1592. The tower had been torched by the English in 1523 and the barmkin was burnt in 1544, again by the English. The property passed to the Dicksons in the seventeenth century, and the Ormiston family still flourishes, although they now apparently live in Devon in England.

Westhouses [NT 527354] is a mile to the north-west of Melrose in the Borders. There was a strong tower house here, dating from the fifteenth century and furnished with gunloops, but this was completely demolished at the beginning of the nineteenth century. The property was held by the Ormistons, and there was also a village near the castle, although all traces of it have gone.

No. of castles/sites: 3
Rank: 328=/764

Orr

The name may be descriptive and come from the Gaelic 'odhar', meaning 'sallow'; although it was a common surname in the west of Scotland from the thirteenth century, possibly from lands of that name. The family held lands in Renfrewshire but were also found in Kintyre from the middle of the seventeenth century.

The Orrs held several properties:

Castle Campbell [NS 962994], near Dollar, Clackmannan; fantastic ruinous castle in fine location.
Long held by the Campbells, but latterly held by the Taits and by the Orrs before passing to The National Trust for Scotland in the middle of the twentieth century, although it is managed by Historic Scotland. The castle is open to the public all year (01259 742408).

Harviestoun Castle [NS 937978], near Tillicoultry, Clackmannan; site of mansion.
Held by the Taits and then by the Orrs in the nineteenth century.

Kinnaird House [NS 885849], near Stenhousemuir, Falkirk; mansion on site of castle.
Held by the Colvilles and by the Bruces, before coming to the Orrs, and they built the new mansion.

Larabank or **Lorabank Castle** [NS 328586], near Kilbirnie, Ayrshire; site of castle.
Held by the Orrs for many years.

Ralston [NS 507642], near Paisley, Renfrewshire; site of castle and mansion.
Held by the Ralston family, then by the Cochrane Earls of Dundonald and by the Hamiltons, but passed to the Orrs in 1800, and they built the mansion (which has since been demolished).

Stobcross [NS 570655], Glasgow; site of castle or old house.
Held by the Andersons, but bought by the Orrs in the eighteenth century. The mansion was demolished about 1850.

www.orrnamestudy.com
No. of castles/sites: 6
Rank: 212=/764

Castle Campbell (M&R)

Orrock

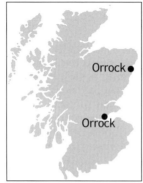

The name is territorial and comes from the lands of Orrock, which are a mile or so north-west of Burntisland in Fife, and the family is on record from the thirteenth century. Alexander Orrock of Sillebawbe was mint-master in 1538, and 'bawbee', originally a coin worth three Scots pence, may have taken its name from the lands which he held.

Orrock [NT 220881] was held by the family from the middle of the thirteenth century for some 400 years. They had a castle or mansion, from which a date stone of 1704 survives, but the lands were sold in the 1750s to the Beatons and the Orrock family moved to Aberdeenshire.

Orrock House [NJ 964196], one and a half miles north of Balmedie to the north of Aberdeen in Aberdeenshire in the north-east of Scotland, was purchased by the family about 1780. There is a tall and plain mansion, which replaced an earlier house or castle. The lands had been held by the Mitchells and by the Fordyce family, but were bought by the Orrock family in about 1780. The Orrocks renamed their new property Orrock House: it had been called **Over Blairton**. The house is still occupied.

No. of castles/sites: 2
Rank: 396=/764

Osborn

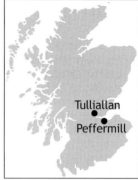

The name comes from the Old Norse personal name 'Asbjorn', which means 'divine bear'. Osborn is on record as a personal name from the eleventh century in Scotland, but it was not used as a surname until much later.

Peffermill House [NT 284717] is to the south-east of Edinburgh, and the building is an altered tower house of three storeys, which dates from the seventeenth century. The lands belonged to the Prestons of Craigmillar, and then to the Edgars, who built the house. Peffermill then passed to the Osborns, and then to the Alexanders and to the Gilmours. The house is still occupied.

Tulliallan Castle [NS 927888] is a fine ruinous hall house, dating from the fourteenth century and located just north of Kincardine in Fife. The castle was replaced by a new mansion, also called **Tulliallan Castle** [NS 936881], about half a mile away, in 1820. The lands were held by several families including by the Blackadders, but latterly passed to the Osborns. The new mansion is now a police training college, and one story has one part of the house haunted by the sounds of children laughing and playing.

No. of castles/sites: 2
Rank: 396=/764
Xref: Osborne

Oswald

The name comes from the Old English personal name 'Oswald', which means 'divine power'. The name is on record as a surname from the middle of the seventeenth century.

Skirling Castle [NT 072398] is a couple of miles north-east of Biggar in Lanarkshire, but virtually nothing survives of the old stronghold except the moat. Skirling was held by the Cockburns, but was blown up on the orders of Regent Moray in 1568. The property passed to the Carmichaels and was held by the Oswalds in 1683.

Auchencruive Castle [NS 387235] stood three miles east of Ayr, but was demolished when **Oswald Hall**, formerly Auchencruive House, an Adam mansion of 1767, was built on the site. The hall was built for the Oswald family, who held the property from 1764 until 1925; Auchencruive had previously belonged to the Wallaces, to the Cathcarts and to the Murrays. The building has been owned by the Scottish Agricultural College since 1927 and the grounds are accessible to the public.

Cavens Castle [NX 958572] stood six miles south of New Abbey in Dumfries and Galloway but all traces of the old stronghold have gone. The castle was replaced by **Cavens House** [NX 977584], which was built by the Oswalds; the lands had been owned by the Douglas Earls of Morton, by the Maxwells and by the Murrays. Cavens House dates from the eighteenth century and is now a hotel (01387 880234; www.cavens.com).

Newmore Castle [NH 680720] is two or so miles north-east of Alness in Ross and Cromarty, but little remains except the vaulted basement and a stair-turret. Newmore was a property of the Munros and then of the Mackenzies, but Newmore House was built after it had passed to the Inglis family. This was later the seat of the Oswalds of Newmore and Auchincruive, but the house is now a residential home.

No. of castles/sites: 4
Rank: 278=/764

Otterburn

The name comes from the place of the same name which is near Morebattle in the Borders; the name is on record from the first half of the fifteenth century.

Redhall Castle [NT 190718] is to the west of Edinburgh, and is a ruinous and overgrown castle, which dates from the sixteenth century. Redhall was held by Sir Adam Otterburn, King's Advocate in 1524, Provost of Edinburgh five years later, and Scottish ambassador to prevent Border skirmishes with the English. The castle was besieged by Cromwell's forces in 1650, and fell after a two-day attack. The castle was demolished for materials to build Redhall House, but there is a doocot nearby with a sixteenth-century panel bearing the Otterburn arms.

Auldhame [NT 602847] is a ruinous and picturesque L-plan tower house, which stands above the sands at Seacliff, three or so miles east of North Berwick in East Lothian; the beach side is complete to the wall head. The property was acquired by Sir Adam Otterburn, and he probably built the castle, although it later passed to the Colt family. There was a village and church but these have gone, and the remains of the castle are crumbling.

No. of castles/sites: 2
Rank: 396=/764

Auldhame (M&R)

Paisley

The name is local in origin and comes from the burgh of Paisley, near Glasgow in the west of Scotland, and the name is on record from the end of the twelfth century. The Paisleys, or Pasleys, of Craig in the Borders probably have a different origin for their name, and it may come from the lands of (How)pasley. **Old Howpasley** [NT 349067] is eleven miles south-west of Hawick, and there was a tower house, although it was held by the Scotts of Howpasley when it was torched by the English in the 1540s. There are no remains.

Craig [NY 341884] was a few miles north-west of Langholm in Dumfries and Galloway, but nothing survives of a tower house. The lands were held by the Pasley family, one of whom was Admiral Thomas Paisley, who defeated a French fleet in 1794.

No. of castles/sites: 2
Rank: 396=/764

Palmer

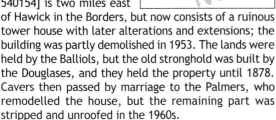

The name comes from someone who had visited the Holy Land on Crusade, and then carried a palm branch as a token. The name is on record in Scotland from the beginning of the thirteenth century.

Cavers House [NT 540154] is two miles east of Hawick in the Borders, but now consists of a ruinous tower house with later alterations and extensions; the building was partly demolished in 1953. The lands were held by the Balliols, but the old stronghold was built by the Douglases, and they held the property until 1878. Cavers then passed by marriage to the Palmers, who remodelled the house, but the remaining part was stripped and unroofed in the 1960s.

No. of castles/sites: 1
Rank: 537=/764

Panton

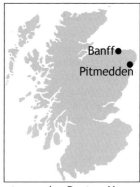

The origin of the name in Scotland is not clear, but there is a parish and an old family of Panton in Lincolnshire in England. Alisaunder Paunton of Lanarkshire is one of those recorded on the Ragman Roll, and the family also held lands in the north-east of Scotland. **Castle Panton** and a **Panton House** are mentioned in the north-eastern burgh of Banff.

Pitmedden House [NJ 885281] dates from the seventeenth century, with later remodelling, but stands on the site of a castle. Pitmedden is located four miles west and south of Ellon in Aberdeenshire. The property was held by the Pantons in 1436, but passed to the Setons, and then to the Bannermans in the seventeenth century, and then to the Keiths. There is a magnificent five-acre walled garden with formal planting, which is in the care of The National Trust for Scotland and is open to the public (01651 842352; www.nts.org.uk).

No. of castles/sites: 1
Rank: 537=/764

Park

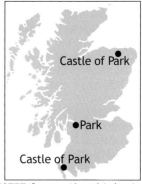

The name is territorial and comes from the lands of Park, which are a mile or so west of Bishopton in Renfrewshire, although there are several other properties with this name in Scotland. There are also two Castles of Park, one [NX 189571] near Glenluce in Galloway and one [NJ 587571] near Aberchirder in Aberdeenshire, although neither was apparently owned by a family of that name. The Park family is on record from the beginning of the thirteenth century. Mungo Park, born at Foulshiels in the Borders in 1771, was a doctor and explorer who travelled widely in Africa. He was drowned in 1806 after being attacked by natives.

Park [NS 409706], near Bishopton, was held by a family of that name, and they built a castle in the thirteenth century. The property passed to the Houstons, probably by marriage as the Park line ended with three daughters, around the turn of the sixteenth century. There are no traces of the old stronghold.

No. of castles/sites: 1
Rank: 537=/764

Parker

The name comes from the office of park-keeper of 'parker', which was a more important occupation that it may seem today (much as with 'forester'): hunting in parks was extremely important. The name Parker is on record in Scotland from 1296, although its use as a surname, as opposed to an occupation, is later.

Auchinloss or **Assloss** [NS 447401] is two miles northeast of Kilmarnock in Ayrshire, and there was a tower house here, which dated from the sixteenth century. Auchinloss (or Assloss) belonged to the family of the same name until it passed to the Montgomerys in 1616, and then to the Glens and to the Parkers. One of the family, Colonel William Parker, was a friend of Robert Burns in the eighteenth century. The lands are now part of the Dean Castle Country Park.

No. of castles/sites: 1
Rank: 537=/764

Paterson

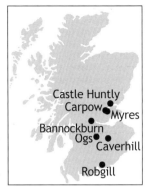

The name comes from the Scottish form of 'Patrick's son', and is a common surname north of the Border; it is MacPhaidraig or MacPatrick in Gaelic. There may be a separate origin for the name in Argyll, which is from the 'son of (the) servant of St Patrick'. The Patersons held lands around Loch Fyne in the thirteenth century, but also held properties in many other parts of the country. Perhaps the most famous holder of the name from Scottish history was William Paterson, who was born in Tinwald in Dumfriesshire in 1658. He is credited with being instrumental in establishing the Bank of England and with the rather less successful Darien Scheme; he died bankrupt and in poverty. John Paterson was Bishop of Galloway and then of Edinburgh before being made Protestant Archbishop of Glasgow in 1687.

The Patersons held the following properties:
Bannockburn House [NS 809889], near Stirling; mansion with older work.
  Held by the Rollos, but passed to the Patersons. The family were Jacobites, and were forfeited following the rising of 1715. They recovered the property, but then had Bonnie Prince Charlie stay at the house during the 1745-46 Rising. It was during this time that Charlie met Clementina Walkinshaw, who very quickly became his mistress. She followed him into exile after he had fled Scotland following Culloden, and they had a daughter, Charlotte, in 1753. Charlotte was made Duchess of Albany, although this was a Jacobite title. Bannockburn House is still occupied.
Castle Huntly [NO 301292], near Longforgan, Perthshire; impressive altered castle.
  Long held by the Grays and then by the Lyon Lord Glamis, before being bought by the Patersons in 1777. They owned the castle well into the twentieth century, although it is now a Young Offenders' Institution.

Castle Huntly (STO)

473

Caverhill Tower [NT 216383], near Peebles, Borders; site of tower house.

Held by the Caverhills but passed to the Patersons of Caverhill in the sixteenth century, and they probably built the tower.

Dundemore [NO 303189], near Cupar, Fife; some remains of castle or old house.

Held by the Dunmores, but Dundemore passed to the Patersons in the fifteenth century.

Myres Castle [NO 242110], near Auchtermuchty, Fife; Z-plan tower house.

Held by the Coxwells then by the Scrymgeours, before passing to the Patersons in 1611, and they held it until about 1750 when it went to the Moncreiffes of Reedie; then Myres went to others. The property was put up for sale in 1997 for offers over £550,000. Accommodation is available in the castle and the gardens are occasionally open to the public (01208 821341; www.myres.co.uk/www.gardensofscotland.org).

Ogs Castle [NT 030446], near Carnwath, Lanarkshire; site of castle.
Held by the Lockharts, but passed to the Patersons in the eighteenth century, then went to others.

Old House of Carpow [NO 204174], near Newburgh, Fife; ruinous house including old work.
Held by the Patersons from the sixteenth to the eighteenth century.

Robgill Tower [NY 248716], near Annan, Dumfriesshire; mansion incorporating part of tower house.
Held by the Irvines but had passed to the Pattersons by about 1890.

www.pattersonheritage.co.uk
No. of castles/sites: 8
Rank: 160=/764
Xrefs: Patterson; MacPatrick; MacPhaidraig

Paton

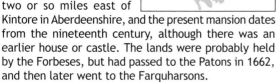

The name comes from a diminutive of Patrick, and the name was recorded in Scotland from the fifteenth century. The family held property in Aberdeenshire, and possibly in Midlothian.

Kinaldie [NJ 832155] is two or so miles east of Kintore in Aberdeenshire, and the present mansion dates from the nineteenth century, although there was an earlier house or castle. The lands were probably held by the Forbeses, but had passed to the Patons in 1662, and then later went to the Farquharsons.

Grandhome House or Dilspro [NJ 899117] is a few miles away, south-east of Dyce also in Aberdeenshire, and the present mansion has work from the seventeenth century or earlier. The property was held by the several families, including by the Gordons and by the Jaffrays, before passing to the Patons of Farrochie around the end of the seventeenth century. They changed the name from Dilspro to Grandhome. Paton of Grandhome was a Jacobite, and hid in the laird's lug at Craigievar to avoid capture.

No. of castles/sites: 2
Rank: 396=/764

Patrick

The name comes from the popular personal name 'Patrick', which comes from Latin and means 'a patrician', although its popularity most probably came from St Patrick. The surname comes on record in the fifteenth century, and it was common in Ayrshire. Woodside House [NS 352553] stands one miles north-east of Beith in Ayrshire, and the castellated mansion incorporates a tower house of the sixteenth century. The property was held by the Ralstons, but in 1834 was sold to the Patricks. Ladyland Castle [NS 324579], two and a half miles north of Kilbirnie also in Ayrshire, has been reduced to a fragment and was replaced by the picturesque house of Ladyland [NS 322578], which dates from 1817-21. The lands were owned by the Barclays, then by the Cochranes, then went by marriage to the Patricks of Woodside in the nineteenth century. The house is now apparently occupied by the Kennedy-Cochran-Patricks.

No. of castles/sites: 2 / Rank: 396=/764

Pattullo

The name is territorial or local in origin and comes from 'Pittillock', which became 'Pattullo', although there are places of that name near Freuchie in Fife and in Glenfarg in Perthshire. The name is spelt in many different ways down the years.

Pittillock House [NO 278052], two miles north of Glenrothes in Fife, is a symmetrical mansion, dating from about 1850, but it incorporates a sixteenth-century L-plan tower house. The lands were held by the MacDuffs, but were a property of the Pattullos in 1305. They then went to the Bruces, followed by the Lumsdens, the Baillies and the Balfours.

Gibliston House [NO 493055] dates from 1820 and replaced a castle or older house; it lies three miles north-west of St Monans also in Fife. The lands were held by the Pattullos in the fourteenth century, but later passed to the Sibbalds, who held them in the seventeenth century, and then Gibliston went to other families. Sir Robert Lorimer, the well-known architect, purchased the house in 1916. Balhouffie [NO 553062] is a few miles away and is two or so miles north of Anstruther again in Fife, and there was a castle or old house here, although there are no remains. The lands were held by the Gibsons, and then probably by the Pattullos in 1779. A mansion here, however, was in ruins by 1802.

No. of castles/sites: 3 / Rank: 328=/764
Xrefs: Pattillo; Patullo; Pittillock

Paxton

The name comes from the lands of the same name, which are a few miles west of Berwick-upon-Tweed by the English border in Berwickshire, and is on record from the thirteenth century. The name comes from the personal name 'Pac', and from 'ton', meaning 'settlement' or 'seat', so 'Pac's ton'.

Paxton House [NT 935530], four or so mile west of Berwick-upon-Tweed in Berwickshire in the Borders, is a fine Adam classical mansion, with a colonnaded main block and flanking wings, and dates from the middle of the eighteenth century, and there may have been a castle or tower house at Paxton or near the house. The lands were held by the Paxtons from the thirteenth century or earlier, but later passed to the Homes, and they built the house. The mansion is now an outstation of the National Galleries of Scotland and on display are seventy works or art; the house is open to the public (01289 386291; www.paxtonhouse.com).

No. of castles/sites: 1
Rank: 537=/764

Penicuik

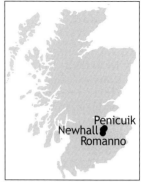

The name is territorial and comes from the lands and barony of Penicuik, which is now a burgh, in Midlothian, and the name is on record from the middle of the thirteenth century.

Penicuik or Terregles Tower [NT 220596] was half a mile to the southwest of the town of Penicuik, but this was demolished around 1700, and a folly was built on the site some fifty years later. The lands of Penicuik had been held by the Penicuik family from the twelfth century until they sold them in 1604. The property was acquired by the Clerks of Penicuik, who built the impressive Penicuik House [NT 217592], which is now a shell, although the grounds are occasionally open to the public (www.gardens ofscotland.org).

Newhall Castle [NT 175566] was half a mile or so to the south-west of Penicuik, but any remains of the old castle may have been built into a new house of 1703. This present building was remodelled in 1785 and 1852. The lands were held by the Crichtons, before being sold to the Penicuik family in 1646, and they held Newhall until 1703 when it was sold to the Forbeses. The gardens of the house are open to the public by appointment only (01968 660206; www.gardensofscotland.org).

Romanno Tower [NT 167483], two or miles south of West Linton in the Borders, was a sixteenth-century tower house. The old tower was replaced by Romanno House in the eighteenth century. The property was held by the Romanes family and by the Murrays of Romanno, but passed to the Penicuiks of Newhall after 1676, and was then sold to the Kennedys in 1720, who still held it at the end of the nineteenth century. Romanno Bridge was apparently the scene of a battle between two Romany families, the Faws and Shaws, in 1683.

No. of castles/sites: 3
Rank: 328=/764
Xref: Pennycook

Pepdie

The Pepdies were an old Border family.

Dunglass Castle [NT 766718] was a strong castle, dating from the fourteenth century, and stood a mile north of Cockburnspath in Berwickshire in the Borders. Dunglass was held by the Pepdies of Dunglass, but passed by marriage to the Homes, and then to the Douglases in 1516. The castle was replaced by a mansion after being blown up in 1640, but the mansion was demolished in 1947. There is a fine collegiate church near the site of the castle, founded by the Homes in 1423. The church is in the care of Historic Scotland and open to the public.

No. of castles/sites: 1 / Rank: 537=/764

Peters

The name comes from a shortened version of Peterson, 'Peter' being a personal name from the Latin 'Petrus', which means a 'rock'. The name is on record in Scotland from the beginning of the fourteenth century.

Cardarroch House [NS 638695] has gone, but it stood one mile east of Bishopbriggs in Lanarkshire. Cardarroch was a T-plan house, rising to two storeys, and dated from 1625 or earlier. The property was owned by the Peters family at one time, but was held by the Flemings in 1610.

No. of castles/sites: 1 / Rank: 537=/764
Xref: Peterson

Cardarroch House (M&R)

476

Phin

The name comes from the old personal name of 'Finn', which is found in Old English, in Norse and in Gaelic. Phin is recorded as a surname from the end of the thirteenth century.

Pittencrieff House [NT 087873] is a fine T-plan house, which rises to three storeys and an attic, and it stands in the public park in Dunfermline in Fife. It was built using materials from the nearby royal palace and abbey buildings, and was owned by the Setons after the Reformation. Pittencrieff then passed through several families before coming to the Phins after 1763, but by the turn of the nineteenth century had gone to the Hunts. Pittencrieff was bought by Sir Andrew Carnegie in 1908, who gave the property to the people of Dunfermline, and the house sits in a popular public park (01383 722935/313838; www.fifedirect.org/museums).

No. of castles/sites: 1
Rank: 537=/764
Xrefs: Fin; Finn

Pierson

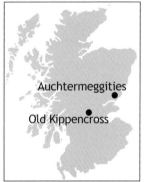

The name can be derived from two origins: one from 'son of Pierre', the French for 'Peter', and the other from a contraction of MacPherson, often spelt 'Pearson'. The name is on record from the end of the thirteenth century.

Auchtermeggities or **Balmadies House** (or **Ochterlony**) [NO 553497] was one or so miles north-east of Letham in Angus, but nothing remains of the castle and Balmadies House, a later mansion, is probably built on the site. The property may have been known as Ochterlony and owned by a family of that name, but the Piersons held the lands of Balmadies from 1600 or earlier until the nineteenth century.

Old Kippencross [NS 785999] is a mile south of Dunblane in Stirlingshire, and the eighteenth-century classical mansion includes the lower storey of an L-plan tower house. The property was held by the Pearsons in 1624, but passed to the Stirlings of Kippendavie after 1768.

No. of castles/sites: 2
Rank: 396=/764
Xref: Pearson

Pinkerton

The name comes from the barony and lands of Pinkerton, which are three or so miles east of Dunbar in East Lothian. The name is on record in Scotland from the end of the thirteenth century. Allan Pinkerton, born in Glasgow in 1819, emigrated to America and founded the famous detective agency in Chicago in 1850.

There appears to have been a castle or old house at **Meikle Pinkerton** [NT 703757], but all that remains is a seventeenth-century beehive doocot with nest boxes for 750 birds. The barony was later held by the Stewart Duke of Albany and then by the Campbell Earl of Argyll in 1483, and then by the Homes of Pinkerton.

No. of castles/sites: 1 / Rank: 537=/764

Pirie

The name is most likely to come from the diminutive of 'Pierre', from the French for 'Peter'. The name was common in Aberdeenshire and there was a family of Piries in Paisley from the end of the fifteenth century.

The Piries held the lands of **Iriewells** [NJ 905286], a mile north-east of Pitmedden to the north of Aberdeen. There is, however, no record of a castle.

No. of castles/sites: 1 / Rank: 537=/764
Xref: Pirrie

Pitblado

The name is territorial and comes from the lands of Pitbladdo, which are two miles north of Cupar in Fife.

Pitbladdo [NO 363172] was held by the family of the same name, who are on record in the fifteenth and sixteenth centuries. There was a castle or old house, but the property probably passed to the Stewarts and then to the Russells.

members.shaw.ca/pitblado.genealogy
No. of castles/sites: 1 / Rank: 537=/764
Xref: Pitbladdo

Pitcairn

The name is territorial and comes from the lands of Pitcairn, which are to the north of Glenrothes in Fife. The name is on record from the middle of the thirteenth century. Pitcairn Island is named after Robert Pitcairn, a midshipman in the Royal Navy who was born in Fife; he was the first to see the island in 1767.

Pitcairn House [NO 270026] is now quite ruinous, but enough survives to show that it rose to two storeys and probably had a vaulted basement. The building dates from the seventeenth century, and was excavated in the 1980s. The lands were a property of the Pitcairn family, one of whom appears on the Ragman Roll of 1296. Andrew Pitcairn and his seven sons were all slain at the Battle of Flodden in 1513. Robert Pitcairn, Commendator of Dunfermline Abbey, was one of those who went to England with the Regent Moray to make sure Mary, Queen of Scots, was executed. The Pitcairns supported the Jacobites in the 1715 and 1745-46 Jacobite Risings.

Abbot House [NT 089875], on Maygate in Dunfermline, is a fine sixteenth-century (or earlier) house, which was built or used by the commendator of nearby Dunfermline Abbey. The lands of the abbey were acquired by Robert Pitcairn (see above), who died in 1584; he is buried in the nave of the abbey church where there is a monument to him. The property soon passed to other families, including to the Seton Earls of Dunfermline. The house is now a heritage centre, and has displays about the house and Dunfermline (01383 733266; www.abbothouse.co.uk).

Dreghorn Castle [NT 225684] stood to the south of Edinburgh, and dated from the seventeenth century or earlier, but it has been demolished and the site is occupied by Dreghorn Barracks. Dreghorn was held by the Murrays in 1671, but then passed to the Pitcairns, then to the Homes of Kello in 1720, and then to others. The last vestige of the castle, and the mansion that replaced it, had been cleared by the 1960s.

No. of castles/sites: 3 / Rank: 328=/764
Xref: Pitcairns

Abbot House (M&R)

477

Pitcon

The name is territorial and come from the lands of the same name, one mile north and east of Dalry in Ayrshire, and the name is on record from the thirteenth century.

Pitcon Castle [NS 299506] was an old castle but it was replaced by **Pitcon**, a mansion dating from the second half of the eighteenth century. The lands were held by the Pitcon family from the thirteenth century or earlier before coming to the Boyds, who sold the property to the Macraes in the 1770s.

No. of castles/sites: 1
Rank. 537–/764
Xref: Petcon

Pitkerrie

The name is territorial and comes from the lands of Pitkerrie (now Pitkierie), one and a half miles north of Anstruther in Fife. The lands were held by the Pitkerrie family from the end of the thirteenth century or earlier, and a William Pitkerrie rendered homage in 1296. The property may have gone to the Johnstones, as Johnstone of Pitkeirie is on record in 1767.

There was a mansion at **Pitkierie** [NO 559060], which may have replaced a castle, but there are no remains except a doocot; the site is probably occupied by the present farm.

No. of castles/sites: 1
Rank: 537=/764

Pollock

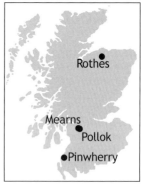

The name is territorial and comes from the lands of Pollok or Pollock, which are to the north-west of Newton Mearns in Renfrewshire. The name may mean 'little pool' from Gaelic, and the family are descended from Fulbert, who was given the lands at the end of the twelfth century. The name was pronounced 'Pook'.

Pollok Castle [NS 522570] incorporated part of an old castle, although it was rebuilt towards the end of the seventeenth century, and then again after a fire in

Pollok Castle (M&R)

1882. The property was held by the Polloks, who also held lands in Moray. John Pollok of Pollok supported Mary, Queen of Scots, and fought for her at the Battle of Langside in 1568. John Pollok, his son, was killed in 1593 at Lockerbie, while supporting the Maxwells in a feud against the Johnstones. The Polloks were a turbulent lot and were involved in feuding with local families, but were made Baronets in Nova Scotia in 1703 and they held the property until the twentieth century. The house was demolished in 1947 and only foundations survive. Near the site of the house is a motte, which was probably the original stronghold of Fulbert de Pollok.

The Pollocks also owned:
Arthurlie House [NS 504588], near Barrhead, Renfrewshire; mansion on site of older houses.
  Held by the Polloks from 1372 to 1479. The house was reused as part of St Mary's Convent.
Lee Castle [NS 580590], near East Kilbride, Renfrewshire; site of castle.
  Held by the Cochranes of Lee, but passed to the Pollocks of Balgray in the sixteenth century, and then to the Maxwells. The foundations were removed in the 1840s when human bones were discovered in 'subterranean houses', the bones said to be of 'almost superhuman magnitude'.

Mearns Castle [NS 553553], near Barrhead, Renfrewshire; altered castle.
> Held by the Polloks but passed by marriage to the Maxwells in 1300. The building was restored from ruin to link two Church of Scotland buildings in 1971.

Netherplace [NS 520556], near Barrhead, Renfrewshire; castle replaced by mansion.
> Held by the Polloks.

Pinwherry Castle [NX 198867], near Ballantrae, Ayrshire; ruinous tower house.
> Held by the Kennedys but was bought by the Polloks in 1644. Abandoned by the end of the eighteenth century.

Rothes Castle [NJ 277490], near Charlestown of Aberlour, Moray; ruinous castle.
> Held by the Polloks, and Edward I visited in 1296. The property passed by marriage to the Watsons then to the Leslies (whose title Earl of Rothes is from here), and much later to the Grants and to the Ogilvies.

www.clanpollock.com
No. of castles/sites: 7
Rank: 182=/764
Xref: Pollok

Pinwherry Castle (M&R)

Polwarth

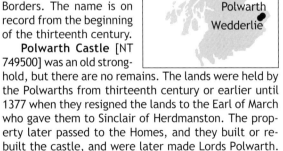

The name is territorial and comes from the lands of Polwarth, which are two or so miles south-west of Duns in Berwickshire in the Borders. The name is on record from the beginning of the thirteenth century.

Polwarth Castle [NT 749500] was an old stronghold, but there are no remains. The lands were held by the Polwarths from thirteenth century or earlier until 1377 when they resigned the lands to the Earl of March who gave them to Sinclair of Herdmanston. The property later passed to the Homes, and they built or rebuilt the castle, and were later made Lords Polwarth. The lands later went to the Scotts.

Wedderlie House [NT 640515] is a mile north of Westruther also in Berwickshire, and is a mansion of 1680, although it includes an L-plan tower house from the previous century. It was held by the Polwarths, again from an early date, but passed to the Edgars, who themselves held Wedderlie for some 400 years. The house is said to be haunted by a Green Lady.

No. of castles/sites: 2 / Rank: 396=/764

Pont

The name is probably territorial and comes from the lands of Kilpont (now Kilpunt), which are to the south and east of Broxburn in West Lothian. The name is on record from the thirteenth century, and there are variations in spelling, such as Kilpont, Kilpunt, Kinpont, Kinpunt, Kilpuc and Pont. Robert Pont (or Kynpont) was provost of Trinity College in Edinburgh and was made a Lord of Session in 1573. His son, Timothy Pont, compiled a series of maps covering Scotland in the 1580s and 1590s. His work was used as the basis of *Blaeu's Atlas Novus* maps of Scotland, although many of Pont's original maps have been lost. The surviving maps are held in the National Library of Scotland and are available online (www.nls.uk).

Kilpunt or **Kilpont** [NT 098718], near Broxburn, was held by John Kilpuc in 1296, but the property passed to the Grahams in the fourteenth century. There was a castle or house, but this was replaced by a farm in about 1750, and nothing apparently remains except an old doocot.

No. of castles/sites: 1
Rank: 537=/764
Xrefs: Kilpont; Kilpunt; Kilpuc; Kinpont

Porteous

The family held lands by the Tweed, south of Broughton in the Borders, but the origin of the name is not clear; the name is on record from the fifteenth century. Perhaps the best known Porteous from Scottish history was John Porteous, who was in charge of the city guard of Edinburgh in 1736. His men opened fire on a crowd at the hanging of Andrew Wilson, and killed and wounded many. He was sentenced to death, but then reprieved, so the Edinburgh mob broke into the Tolbooth and hanged him anyway. Dunty Porteous, a miller, was long said to haunt the dungeon of Spedlins Tower after being starved to death there.

Hawkshaw Castle [NT 079225] is nine miles south of Broughton in the Borders, and there was a castle, dating from the fourteenth century, but little now remains. The lands were held by the Porteous family until 1725, but then probably passed to the Govans.

Whitslade Tower [NT 112350] is further north, just two miles south of Broughton, but again little survives except the vaulted basement of a sixteenth century tower house. Whitslade was owned by the Porteous family, but later passed to the Murrays of Stanhope and then to the Dicksons. There was another property near here called **Glenkirk**, which also belonged to the Porteous family.

Lauriston Castle [NO 759667], some four miles south-east of Laurencekirk in Kincardineshire, is much reduced and has been remodelled, but once consisted of a keep or tower and a courtyard, which dated the thirteenth century. The lands were held by the Stirlings and by others until coming to the Falconers of Phesdo in 1695, then later Lauriston was a property of the Porteous family. The house became ruinous, part was demolished, while part has been rebuilt and reoccupied.

No. of castles/sites: 3
Rank: 328=/764

Porterfield

The name comes from the important office of door-keeper or 'porter', and the lands which the family owned as the hereditary porters of Paisley Abbey, were called Porterfield. The name is on record from the middle of the fifteenth century. **Porterfield** [NS 495670] is to the west of Renfrew and east of the White Cart River, and was held by the family of the same name. There was probably a castle or old house, but the site is now in an industrial works. The family also appear to have had a house on the High Street of Glasgow known as **Porterfield Mansion** [NS 597651].

Duchal Castle [NS 334685] is a mile or so south of Kilmacolm, also in Renfrewshire, but little now remains of the castle. The old stronghold was abandoned for nearby **Duchal House** [NS 353680], which was built about 1768, although part may date from 1710. The lands were long held by the Lyles, but passed to the Montgomerys of Lainshaw in 1544, and then were bought by the Porterfields. They held them until the middle of the nineteenth century, and Duchal then passed to the Shaw-Stewarts of Ardgowan. The gardens of the house are occasionally open to the public (www.gardensof scotland.org). **Kilmacolm Castle** [NS 361693] itself was to the south of the old part of the town, and was held by the Lyles and then by the Porterfields.

Comiston House [NT 240687], to the south of Edinburgh, dates from 1815 but there was a castle, of which only a round tower with gunloops and a doocot survives. The property was held by many families, including by the Cants and then by the Porterfields and by the Forresters.

No. of castles/sites: 4 / Rank: 278=/764

Prendergast

The name comes from the place in Wales of the same name, and the family came to Scotland in the middle of the twelfth century and gave their lands their name.

Prendergast (now **Prenderguest**) [NT 919595] is about three miles south-west of Eyemouth in Berwickshire in the Borders. There may have been a tower house, and Prenderguest was burnt by Sir George Douglas in 1528. The property was held by the Robertsons in the nineteenth century.

No. of castles/sites: 1 / Rank: 537=/764

Preston

The name is territorial and comes from the lands and barony of **Preston**, later called **Gourtoun** and now known as Craigmillar. Preston is from 'priest's town', and the name is on record from the first quarter of the thirteenth century.

Craigmillar Castle [NT 288709] is a magnificent ruinous castle in a prominent location to the south-east of Edinburgh. A large L-plan keep stands within two walled courtyards, and is further

Craigmillar Castle (M&R; reconstruction)

defended by a ditch. The inner courtyard enclosed ranges of buildings, including a kitchen and a long gallery. The property was held by the Prestons from 1374, and they built a new castle on the site of an old stronghold. In 1477 James III imprisoned his brother John, Earl of Mar, in one of its cellars, where John died. The Earl of Hertford burnt the castle in 1544, after valuables placed here by the citizens of Edinburgh had been seized. James V visited the castle to escape 'the pest' in Edinburgh. Mary, Queen of Scots, used Craigmillar often, and fled here in 1566 after the murder of Rizzio by, among others, her second husband Lord Darnley. It was also here that James Stewart, Earl of Moray, James Hepburn, Earl of Borthwick, and William Maitland of Lethington reputedly plotted Darnley's murder. Sir Simon Preston of Craigmillar was Lord Provost of Edinburgh three times from 1538 until 1560; Mary, Queen of Scots, lodged in his house in Edinburgh after surrendering at Carberry in 1567. James VI also stayed at Craigmillar, but the property was sold to the Gilmours in 1660. A walled-up skeleton was found in one of the vaults in 1813. The ruins are in the care of Historic Scotland and are open to the public (0131 661 4445]).

Fyvie Castle [NJ 764393], a mile north of the village of Fyvie in Aberdeenshire, is a huge and grand castle and mansion, formerly built around a courtyard. The building has a profusion of turrets, dormer windows and carved finials. The property was owned by many families in its history, starting with the Lindsays, then by the

Prestons from 1402 to about 1433, then by the Setons, by the Gordons and by the Leith family before passing to The National Trust for Scotland. The castle is open to the public (01651 891266; www.nts.org.uk).

Tolquhon Castle [NJ 873286], four miles east of Old Meldrum also in Aberdeenshire, is a fine courtyard castle, with an old keep, later ranges of buildings and a

Tolquhon Castle (M&R)

small drum-towered gatehouse. The old keep was built by the Prestons of Craigmillar, but Tolquhon passed by marriage to the Forbeses in 1420, and they built most of the existing building. The castle is in the care of Historic Scotland, and is open to the public (01651 851286).

Valleyfield [NT 005872] is a mile south east of Culross, and there was a large and attractive mansion, but this has been demolished and all that remains is the fine parkland. The lands were held by the Prestons from the middle of the sixteenth century, and Sir George Preston was made a Baronet in 1637. Coal was mined on the estate, and Preston Island in the Firth of Forth is named after them. One of family, George Preston, was in command of Edinburgh Castle during the Jacobite Rising of 1745-46, and held out against Bonnie Prince Charlie's forces. The old salt pans near Valleyfield and Culross are being filled in with ash from the Longannet Power Station to reclaim the lands. The Preston family held the property well into the nineteenth century.

The Prestons also owned:

Airdrie House [NO 567084], near Crail, Fife; altered tower house.
  Held by the Dundemore family, then passed through several hands before coming to the Prestons at the turn of the seventeenth century, then went to the Anstruthers and then to the Erskine Earls of Kellie. Still occupied.

Balgavies Castle [NO 540516], near Letham, Angus; slight remains of castle.
  Held by the Ochterlonys and by the Guthries, but passed to the Prestons in 1543, then went to the Lindsays. Balgavies was destroyed by James VI in 1594.

Peffermill House [NT 284717], Edinburgh; altered tower house.
  Held by the Prestons of Craigmillar, but sold to the Edgars, who built the house, then later went to other families. Still occupied.

Uttershill Castle [NT 235594], near Penicuik, Midlothian; very ruinous castle.
  Held by the Prestons of Craigmillar, but sold to the Clerks of Penicuik. Later used as a gunpowder store.

No. of castles/sites: 8
Rank: 160=/764

Primrose

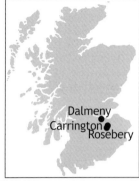

The name is local and taken from the place of the same name a couple of miles south of Dunfermline in Fife. The name may be mean 'tree of the moor' from Old British. The Primroses apparently held lands in Fife, but they came to prominence when they owned properties in Midlothian, and the name is on record from the middle of the twelfth century.

Carrington [NT 318605] is two miles south-west of Gorebridge in Midlothian, although it is not certain if there was a castle or old house here. The lands were held by the Primrose family from the middle of the seventeenth century. Sir Archibald Primrose of Carrington was a Royalist and was captured after the Battle of Philiphaugh in 1645, but he was saved from execution. When he was freed he was made a Baronet of Nova Scotia in 1651, and he fought at the Battle of Worcester for Charles II the same year. Primrose was forfeited, but recovered the estates after the Restoration. He was made Lord Justice General from 1676-78, and acquired the lands of Barnbougle and Dalmeny.

Rosebery or **Clerkington House** [NT 305574] is a few miles away, some four miles south-west of Gorebridge. Clerkington, a large and ancient mansion house, was demolished in 1805-12 and replaced by Rosebery House. The property was bought by the Primroses in 1695, and the family was made Viscounts Rosebery in 1700, and then Earls of Rosebery three years later. The property was sold in 1712, but bought back by the fourth Earl in 1821.

Lying in the grounds of Dalmeny House to the east of South Queensferry, **Barnbougle Castle** [NT 169785] stands on the site of an ancient castle, but the present building was rebuilt at the end of the nineteenth century. The lands were owned by the Mowbrays, and then by the Hamilton Earls of Haddington before being bought by the Primroses in 1662. The ruins of Barnbougle were rebuilt around 1880 by Archibald Philip Primrose, fifth Earl of Rosebery, who was Foreign Secretary in 1886 and 1892-94, and Prime Minister from 1894-95. He supported Scottish Home Rule, and wrote many historical works. The family had built nearby Dalmeny House.

Dalmeny House [NT 167779] is a Tudor Gothic mansion, and was built in 1814-17, and there are vaulted corridors and a splendid hammer-beam hall, although the main rooms are in classical style. The present building replaced an old house or castle also called Dalmeny House, and the new house was built by the Primroses. The family still apparently live here and they have many titles including Earl of Rosebery, Viscount Inverkeithing, Baron Primrose and Inverkeithing, as well as Viscount of Rosebery, Lord Primrose and Dalmeny, Earl of Midlothian, and several others. Dalmeny House

is open to the public in July and August (0131 331 1888; www.dalmeny.co.uk).

The Primroses also owned:

Dunipace [NS 837819], near Larbert, Falkirk; site of castle and mansion.

Held by the Livingstones, but later passed to the Primroses. Sir Archibald Primrose of Dunipace fought for the Jacobites and was executed at Carlisle in 1746. The property later passed to the Forbeses of Callendar.

Inverkeithing [NT 131829], Fife; altered town house.

Rosebery House is a much altered sixteenth-century townhouse in Inverkeithing and is named after the Primrose Earl of Rosebery who bought it in 1711.

Livingston Peel [NT 040676], Livingston, West Lothian; site of castle.

Held by the Livingstones, then by the Murrays and by the Cunninghams before passing to the Primrose Earl of Rosebery in 1812.

Malleny House [NT 166667], near Balerno, Edinburgh; mansion with old work.

Held by several families before coming to the Primrose Earl of Rosebery in 1882. Malleny is now in the care of The National Trust for Scotland and the gardens are open to the public (0131 449 2283; www.nts.org.uk)

Pitreavie Castle [NT 117847], near Dunfermline, Fife; altered castle and mansion.

Held by the Wardlaws, but was owned briefly by the Primroses from 1703-11 when it went to the Blackwood family, then others, before being used by the armed forces for many years. Pitreavie was recently put up for sale.

Rosyth Castle [NT 115820], near Inverkeithing, Fife; impressive ruinous castle.

Held by the Stewarts of Rosyth, but passed to the Primrose Earl of Rosebery in the eighteenth century, and then went to the Hope Earls of Hopetoun. The castle is within the grounds of the dockyard, in the care of Historic Scotland, and can be visited by appointment only (0131 668 8800).

Whitehouse [NT 187766], Cramond, Edinburgh; altered L-plan tower house.

Held by the Logans, but passed to Gilbert Primrose, surgeon to James VI, who died in 1616. Whitehouse was sold to the Corse family, then went to others, and is still occupied.

No. of castles/sites: 11
Rank: 127=/764

Smailholm Tower (LF) – see next column (Pringle)

Pringle

The name appears to be territorial, and comes from the lands of Hoppringle, which are four miles north of Stow in the Borders. The origin of the name may be from 'son of the pilgrim', 'ap' meaning 'son of' and 'pringle' coming from pilgrim. The Pringles certainly went to Rome with the Douglases, but the origin is speculative. The family held much land in the Borders and was long associated with the Black Douglases, being their squires, but this ended with the downfall of this branch of the Douglases in 1455. The Pringles, however, prospered around Galashiels and elsewhere.

Hoppringle Castle [NT 434511] stood north of Stow in Lauderdale in the Borders and was once a place of some strength and importance, but nothing remains and the site of the castle is probably occupied by a farm. This was the original stronghold of the family.

Smailholm Tower [NT 637346] is a few miles west of Kelso also in the Borders, and is a plain and somewhat stark tower house, perched on a rock in a windswept location. The small courtyard is ruinous, but the tower is in good condition. The lands were held by the Pringles from the middle of the fifteenth century. The Pringles had been squires of the Black Douglas family before the Douglases were overthrown by James II in 1455. David Pringle of Smailholm was killed, together with his four sons, at the Battle of Flodden in 1513. The tower was attacked by the English in 1543, and again in 1546, when the garrison of Wark made off with sixty cattle and four prisoners. The property was sold to the Scotts of Harden in 1645, and the tower is now in the care of Historic Scotland and is open to the public (01573 460365).

Buckholm Tower [NT 482379] is an impressive but ruinous L-plan tower house, dating from the sixteenth century, and located a mile north and west of Galashiels on the side of Buckholm Hill. The lands were held by the Pringles, although they were convicted of treason in 1547. One of the lairds, in the seventeenth century, is said to have been a cruel man who enjoyed tormenting Covenanters in his basement. He was cursed by the wife of one of his victims and afterwards lived in great terror. Pringle's ghost can reputedly be seen running from a pack of ravening dogs on the anniversary of his death, and screams and cries reportedly heard from the basement of the tower.

The Pringles also owned:
Balmungo [NO 523148], near St Andrews, Fife; site of castle or old house.
  Held by the Pringles one of whom, George Pringle of Balmungo, was a major in the army of Gustave Adolphus of Sweden. The property later went to the Lindsays, then to the Maitlands and the Bayne-Meldrums.

Blackhouse Tower [NT 281273], near Cappercleuch, Borders; ruinous tower house.
  Held by the Douglases, but had passed to the Pringles by 1509, then Blackhouse went to the Stewarts of Traquair by the end of that century.
Blindlee Tower [NT 471373], near Galashiels, Borders; site of tower house.
  Held by the Pringles, and John Pringle of Blindlee was killed at the Battle of Flodden in 1513.
Chapelhill [NT 245422], near Peebles, Borders; altered tower house.
  Held by the Pringles from the middle of the sixteenth century, and they built the tower. Chapelhill was sold in 1657, and later passed to the Williamsons.
Colmslie Tower [NT 513396], near Galashiels, Borders; ruinous tower house.
  Held by the Borthwicks and by the Cairncross family, but was a possession of the Pringles in the seventeenth century.
Craigcrook Castle [NT 211742], Edinburgh; fine Z-plan house.
  Held by several families, including by the Pringles. Still occupied as the offices of *Scottish Field* (0131 312 4550; www.scottishfield.co.uk).
Greenknowe Tower [NT 639428], near Gordon, Borders; fine ruinous L-plan tower.
  Held by the Gordons and by the Setons of Touch, who built the tower, but passed to the Pringles of Stichill in the

Greenknowe Tower (M&R)

seventeenth century, one of whom Walter Pringle was a noted writer and Covenanter. Greenknowe later passed to the Dalrymples and was occupied until the middle of the nineteenth century. In the care of Historic Scotland and open to the public.
Haining or **The Haining** [NT 469280], near Selkirk, Borders; castle or old house replaced by mansion.
  Held by the Riddels but passed to the Pringles in the seventeenth century. John Pringle was an advocate, who was made a Lord of Session with the title Lord Haining. The family built a classical mansion and the house is still occupied.
Muirhouse Tower [NT 473452], near Stow, Borders; site of tower house.
  Held by the Pringles.
Newhall or **Craiglatch (Craigleith)** [NT 423386], near Galashiels, Borders; possible site of castle.
  Held by the Pringles from the fifteenth century, and a fortalice is mentioned at Craigleith.
Old Gala House [NT 492357], Galashiels, Borders; mansion incorporating tower house.
  Held by the Douglases, but passed to the Pringles of Gala, and

then went by marriage to the Scotts in 1632. The building now houses a museum (01896 752611; www.scotborders. gov.uk/outabout/museums).

Penkaet Castle or Fountainhall [NT 427677], near Pencaitland, East Lothian; altered tower house.

Held by the Maxwells and by the Cockburns, then by the Pringles from 1636 to 1685, when the property was sold to the Lauders. The castle is said to be haunted and is still occupied.

Stichill House [NT 702392], near Kelso, Borders; site of mansion and castle or old house.

Held by the Gordons of Lochinver, but was sold to the Pringles in 1628. The family were made Baronets of Nova Scotia in 1682-83, and one of the family was Sir John Pringle, an eminent physician. In the kirkyard of the old church [NT 711383] at Stichill is a burial enclosure for the Pringles of Stichill. The property passed to the Bairds in the middle of the nineteenth century, and they built a massive castellated mansion, but this was demolished in 1938. The Pringles of Stichell, Baronets, still flourish.

Torsance Castle [NT 456424], near Stow, Borders; house on site of castle.

Held by the Pringles.

Torwoodlee Tower [NT 467378], near Galashiels, Borders; large ruinous tower house.

Held by the Pringles from 1509 or earlier, and was sacked by the Elliots in 1568. The tower was rebuilt, and the Pringles sheltered Covenanters at Torwoodlee, but it was abandoned in 1783 for nearby Torwoodlee House, a symmetrical mansion with flanking pavilions and screen walls.

Whitsome [NT 865507], near Chirnside, Borders; site of castle.

Held by the Pringles from the thirteenth century. They supported Robert the Bruce and they were forfeited, but recovered the property when Bruce became king. Robert Pringle of Whitsome was squire to James, Earl of Douglas, at the Battle of Otterburn in 1388, and was present at James's death although the Douglases won the battle. The Pringles were given Smailholm in 1402. The village of Whitsome was burned by the English in 1482, and the property later passed to the Hepburns.

Whytbank Tower [NT 442377], near Galashiels, Borders; ruinous tower house.

Held by the Pringles. James Pringle of Whytbank fought at the Battle of Solway Moss in 1542. Alexander, fourth of Whytbank, supported the Cromwellian administration and was fined after the Restoration. The tower was occupied until 1790, fell ruinous, but has been restored. The line of the Pringles of Whytbank continues, and members of the family were buried in Melrose Abbey [NT 543341], which is in the care of Historic Scotland and is open to the public (01896 822562).

Woodhouse Hill or Manor [NT 211370], near Peebles, Borders; site of tower house.

Held by the Ingles of Manor, but passed to the Pringles of Smailholm in 1502, and then went to the Burnetts of Barns in the late sixteenth century.

Yair House [NT 452328], near Selkirk, Borders; castle replaced by mansion.

Held by the Pringles of Whytbank, and then by the Kerrs of Yair. The lands were bought back by the Pringles in the seventeenth century and they held them until World War I. Members of the family were buried at Melrose Abbey [NT 543341], which is in the care of Historic Scotland and is open to the public (01896 822562).

www.jamespringle.co.uk
No. of castles/sites: 22
Rank: 58=/764
Xref: Hoppringle

Purves

The name may come from 'parveys' or 'parvis', the porch or enclosed area by a church, where lawyers and others used to meet to discuss business. The family are on record from the beginning of the thirteenth century.

Purvishill Tower [NT 355375] stands a mile or so east of Innerleithen in the Borders, but little survives of the sixteenth-century tower house except a stony mound. The property was owned by the Purves family, possibly from as early as the eleventh century, but it later went to the Horsburghs.

Rhymer's Tower [NT 572383] is a small ruinous castle in the village of **Ercildoune** or Earlston, near Melrose, also in the Borders. The tower is associated with Thomas the Rhymer, the thirteenth-century poet and seer, but in the fourteenth century was a property of the Purves family. Saunders Purves of Earlston became an assured Scot in 1547 and supported the English.

Mossfennan [NT 117317] lies some two miles south-west of Drumelzier in Tweeddale in the Borders, and there was a tower house but this was replaced by a mansion. The lands were a property of the Purves family, but passed to the Laidlaws, who held Mossfennan in the sixteenth century, and then went to the Welsh family.

A couple of miles north of Penicuik in Midlothian is the site of **Fulford Tower** [NT 238645], which was also known as **Woodhouselee**. There was a castle, but it was incorporated into a later mansion, although this was completely demolished in 1965. The lands were held by the Purves family in the seventeenth century, and one story is that the building was haunted by the ghost of Lady Hamilton, more usually linked to Old Woodhouselee.

Purves Hall [NT 761447], a few miles south-east of Greenlaw in Berwickshire in the Borders, was formerly known as **Tofts** or **Nether Tofts**. The mansion incorporates a much altered tower house, and was held by several families including by the Belshes, before passing to the Purveses about 1670. They changed the name to Purves Hall, and presumably have the following verse aimed at them: befa' what e'er befa', there'll aye be a gowk in Purves-ha'. The building was used as a hotel, but is now a residence again, and was recently put up for sale for offers of more than £475,000.

No. of castles/sites: 5
Rank: 240=/764
Xref: Purvis

Quarrel

Carron Hall

The name is territorial and comes from the lands of Quarrell, which are to the east of Stenhousemuir near Falkirk in Central Scotland. The name means 'quarry', and the family are on record from the end of the thirteenth century.

There was a castle or old house at **Quarrell** [NS 891840], the lands later known as **Carron Hall**, but this building was replaced by a mansion in the eighteenth century or earlier. The Quarrel family left Scotland in about 1420 and went to Northamptonshire, and Quarrell was then held by the Redheughs, by the Bissets, by the Elphinstones and by the Dundas family.

No. of castles/sites: 1
Rank: 537=/764

Quincy

Leuchars
Lathrisk
Winton

The name comes from a family who were land-owners in Northampton-shire, originally from Quinci or Quincay in France; the name is on record in Scotland from the middle of the eleventh century. The family were made Earls of Winchester in 1207, and they became powerful landowners in Scotland, after Roger Quincy married Helen, the daughter of Alan Lord of Galloway, and he was Constable of Scotland. On Roger's death the Earldom of Winchester lapsed. The family were opposed to, and then forfeited by, Robert the Bruce.

Lathrisk House [NO 273085], near Glenrothes, Fife; mansion on site of castle.
  Held by the Quincys, although the mansion and castle date from long after their ownership. Later a property of the Lathrisk family, then of the Setons and of the Johnstones.
Leuchars Castle [NO 454219], Leuchars, Fife; site of castle.
  Held by the Quincys, who had a stronghold on Castle Knowe, but they were forfeited and the lands went to the Wemyss family. Leuchars was demolished by Robert the Bruce, but was rebuilt in support of Edward Balliol in 1336. The castle was retaken by the Scots, then appears to have been destroyed. There was a later tower house but this has also been demolished. The parish church of St Athernase [NO 455215], a fine old building on a mound in a prominent position in the village, dates from 1183 and it was first built by the Quincy family; it can be visited.
Winton House [NT 439696], near Tranent, East Lothian; fine mansion.
  Held by the Quincys but passed to the Setons, and then later went to the Hamiltons, then Nisbet Hamiltons, and then to the Ogilvys, who still own Winton. Guided tours of the house are available some days and the gardens are occasionally open to the public (01875 340222; www.wintonhouse.co.uk).

No. of castles/sites: 3 / Rank: 328=/764

Quixwood

Quixwood

The name is territorial and comes from the lands of Quixwood, which are two or so miles south-west of Grantshouse in Berwick-shire in the Borders. There may have been a castle or old house at **Quixwood** [NT 787632] but the site is now a farm. Arnold Quix-wood was a large landowner in the early part of the thirteenth century, and made several gifts of land to Coldingham Priory; Robert Quixwood was prior of Coldingham from 1315 to 1322. The property later passed to the Homes, who held Quixwood in 1721.

No. of castles/sites: 1 / Rank: 537=/764

Rae

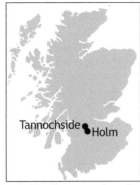

The name may be of local origin, and the family were numerous in parts of Dumfriesshire. The name is on record from the thirteenth century.

Tannochside House [NS 716620] was demolished in the 1950s, but it stood two miles south of Coatbridge in central Scotland. The house replaced a castle or older residence, and was held by the Raes in 1698 before passing to the Whitelaws in the next century and then to the Hosiers and to others. The site is occupied by housing.

Holm Castle [NS 746474] has also gone but lay half a mile north-west of Stonehouse, again in Lanarkshire. It was a property of the Hamiltons and probably of the Carmichaels, but passed to the Rae family in the nineteenth century, by which time the castle was already ruinous.

No. of castles/sites: 2
Rank: 396=/764

Raffles

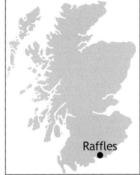

The name comes from the lands of the same name, which are some miles west and north of Annan, in the parish of Mouswald in Dumfries and Galloway, and the name is on record from the beginning of the thirteenth century.

Raffles Tower [NY 086721] is now very ruinous, although it dated from the sixteenth century, after the lands had passed to the Carruthers family. The Raffles family held the property from the thirteenth century until after 1361, and they may have had a stronghold here.

No. of castles/sites: 1
Rank: 537=/764

Rait

The name may be territorial in origin, and comes from the lands of that name which are a couple of miles south of Nairn near Inverness, or perhaps from Raith: there are places of that name in Fife and in Ayrshire. The name may be Germanic in origin and come from 'Rhet', and the family gave their name to the lands. The family later held property in Kincardineshire and in Angus, and are on record from the end of the thirteenth century.

Rait Castle [NH 894525] is a fine but ruinous hall-house, first built in the thirteenth century, but altered in later years. It was a property of the Raits, but Sir

Rait Castle (M&R)

Alexander Rait killed the third Thane of Cawdor around 1395, and fled south, where his son married the heiress of Hallgreen. Rait passed to the Cummings and then to the Mackintoshes, and then went to the Campbells of Cawdor. The Duke of Cumberland is said to have stayed here before Culloden in 1746, and the castle is reputed to be haunted by the apparition of a handless girl in a blood-soaked dress. There are moves afoot to have the castle ruin consolidated (www.saveraitcastle.org).

Hallgreen Castle [NO 832721] is to the east of Inverbervie in Kincardineshire, and is an altered L-plan tower house, which rises to three storeys and an attic. There are turrets at the corners, and it may incorporate much earlier work. Hallgreen was owned by the Dunnets, who had a stronghold here, but passed by marriage to the Raits in the fifteenth century, one of whom was captain of the guard to James IV. Hallgreen became derelict but has been restored (perhaps rather unsuccessfully, at least in appearance), and is said to be haunted by several ghosts.

The Raits also held:
Anniston [NO 674486], near Arbroath, Angus; site of castle or old house and later mansion.
Held by the Raits in the eighteenth and nineteenth centuries.

James Rait of Anniston commanded a regiment of lancers in Spain in the 1830s and was decorated for bravery.

Cononsyth [NO 566464], near Arbroath, Angus; site of castle or old house.

Held by the Gardynes, but was a property of the Raits in the seventeenth century.

Pitforthie [NO 615610], near Brechin, Angus; site of castle or old house.

Held by the Guthries and by the Ochterlonys, but also by the Raits at one time.

Red Castle [NO 687510], near Montrose, Angus; shattered but impressive ruinous castle.

Held by the Barclays and then by others before coming to James Rait, an Episcopal minister, then passed to the Guthries.

Snadon [NO 731655], near St Cyrus, Kincardineshire; site of castle or old house.

Held by the Raits in the 1670s.

No. of castles/sites: 7
Rank: 182=/764

Raith

The name is probably local in origin, possibly from Raith near Monkton in central Scotland and was also found in Ayrshire; it may be a variation in spelling of 'Rait' (also see that name). There was a Raith Tower, to the west of Kirkcaldy in Fife, but this was a property of the Melvilles and was not apparently held by the Raith family. The surname is on record from the fifteenth century.

Carphin [NO 319195] is six miles north-west of Cupar in Fife, and the present mansion, dating from around the turn of the nineteenth century, replaced a castle or old house. Carphin was held by the Baillies, but passed to the Halkerstons and then to the Raiths and then to the Cooks.

No. of castles/sites: 1
Rank: 537=/764

Ralston

The name means the 'Ralph's seat or town', 'Ralph' being a diminutive of Randolph, which comes from the Old English for 'cunning wolf'. The name is on record from the end of the thirteenth century.

Ralston [NS 507642] is two miles north of Paisley in Renfrewshire, and was held by the family from the thirteenth century, and the Ralstons are said to be descended from a son of the Earl of Fife. Hugh Ralston of Ralston was killed at the Battle of Pinkie in 1547. The family held the lands until 1704, when the property was sold to the Cochrane Earls of Dundonald, and then later Ralston passed to the Hamiltons and then to the Orrs. There was a castle, which was replaced by Ralston House in 1810, although this building was itself demolished in 1934.

Woodside House [NS 352553], a mile north-east of Beith in Ayrshire, incorporates an old tower house of 1551 into the mansion, which was then altered and extended down the centuries. Woodside was held by the Ralstons from 1551 to 1772, but was later a property of the Patrick family.

Saddell Castle [NR 789316] is a fine altered keep or tower, dating from the fifteenth century and rising to four storeys. The castle is located eight miles north of Campbeltown in Kintyre, and was built by the Bishop of Argyll in 1507. The Campbells of Argyll took it over, but the Ralstons were tenants and they remodelled the building in the 1650s. The castle was superseded by **Saddell House** [NR 791318], a three-storey symmetrical mansion, built at the end of the eighteenth century. The castle has been restored and can be rented as holiday accommodation from the Landmark Trust (01628 825925; www.landmarktrust.org.uk).

No. of castles/sites: 3
Rank: 328=/764

Saddell Castle (M&R)

487

Ramornie

The name is territorial and comes from the lands and barony of Ramornie, half a mile or so east of Lady-bank in Fife. The lands were a property of the Ramornie family from the fourteenth century or ear-lier, and Sir John Ramornie was one of those who seized David, Duke of Rothesay, son of Robert III, and imprisoned him in Falkland Palace in 1402; David was starved to death. There was a castle or old house at **Ramornie** [NO 318096], and Ramornie House stands on the site.

The property passed to the Heriots in the fifteenth century and they held the property for some 400 years when it went to the Haigs of Ramornie, who are apparently still in possession.

No. of castles/sites: 1
Rank: 537=/764

Ramsay

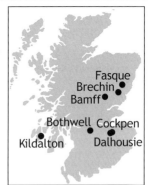

The name is apparently local from Ramsey in Huntingdonshire, and the family came to Scotland with David I in the twelfth century, and he gave them lands in Midlothian. Allan Ramsay, who was born in Edinburgh in 1713, was a famous artist and portrait painter and he went to London where he was much in demand.

Dalhousie Castle [NT 320636], which stands a mile or so south-east of Bonnyrigg in Midlothian, is a grand and imposing stronghold and mansion. It dates from the thirteenth century with later additions and extensions, including a tower house in the sixteenth century, and there is a large round tower at one corner. The lands were held by the Ramsays from the thirteenth century,

Dalhousie Castle (M&R)

and William Ramsay of Dalhousie added his seal to both the Ragman Roll of 1296 and the Declaration of Arbroath in 1320. Sir Alexander Ramsay was active for the Scots against the English during the Wars of Independence. He was, however, starved to death by William Douglas, the Knight of Liddesdale, in Hermitage Castle in 1342 after he was made Sheriff of Teviotdale, an office the Douglases coveted; Ramsay's ghost is said to haunt Hermitage. William Ramsay, Sir Alexander's brother, was captured at the Battle of Neville's Cross in 1346. In 1400 the castle was held successfully against Henry IV of England, but Sir Alexander Ramsay of Dalhousie was killed at the Battle of Homildon Hill in 1402, as was another Alexander at the Battle of Flodden in 1513. The family supported Mary, Queen of Scots, and fought for her at Langside in 1568. In 1633 William Ramsay was created the first Earl of Dalhousie, and he had the castle much extended and remodelled. He fought at Marston Moor against the king in 1644, and then was in the force that defeated Montrose the following year at Philiphaugh. Cromwell besieged and captured the castle in the 1650s. Many of the later Earls were soldiers and fought in foreign wars and in different parts of the British Empire. The Ramsays lived at the castle until about 1900, and many of them were buried in the family vault at Cockpen. **Dalhousie Grange** [NT 318640] was used as a dower house. The Ramsays then moved to Brechin Castle, and Dalhousie was used as a school from 1925-50. The castle has several ghost stories, including that of a Grey Lady, the spirit of a Lady Catherine, mistress to one of the Ramsays who was starved to death by his vengeful wife, as well as the spirit of a dog and a lad who fell from the battlements. The building is now used as a hotel (01875 820153; www.dalhousiecastle.co.uk).

Brechin Castle [NO 597599] is an impressive castle and mansion to the west of the 'city' of Brechin in Angus. It was at the castle that it is believed that John Balliol, 'Toom Tabard', was forced to abdicate by Edward I of England in 1296. The property was long held by the Maules, later the Earls of Panmure, but it is now apparently the seat of the Ramsays of Dalhousie, who also have a residence in London according to *Burke's*. The Brechin Castle Centre is open to the public, and there is also Pictavia, with information and displays on the Pict's carved stones and artefacts (01356 626813; www.brechincastlecentre.co.uk).

Balmain or **Fasque** [NO 648755] is five miles northwest of Laurencekirk in Kincardineshire, and the present castellated mansion (called Fasque) of 1809 stands on or near the site of an old stronghold. The lands were held by the Ramsays of Balmain, and they supported James III at Sauchieburn in 1488 and their lands and titles were forfeited. They recovered Balmain, and were made Baronets of Nova Scotia in 1625. The mansion was built for Sir Alexander Ramsay, but the property passed to the Gladstones in 1829, and the Ramsays of Balmain, Baronets, still flourish but now apparently live in Australia. Fasque is open to the public by appointment for organised groups of twelve or more (01561 340569; www.fasque.com/fasque-estates.co.uk).

The Ramsays also owned:

Auchterhouse [NO 332373], near Dundee; mansion incorporating part of castle.
   Held by the Ramsays in the thirteenth century, and William Wallace is said to have visited the castle. Auchterhouse passed to the Stewart Earls of Buchan, and then to others.
Balbegno Castle [NO 639730], near Fettercairn, Kincardineshire; altered L-plan tower house.
   Held by the Woods, by the Middletons and by the Ogilvies before passing to the Ramsays in the nineteenth century.
Bamff House [NO 222515], near Alyth, Perthshire; castle and mansion.
   Held by the Ramsays from 1322, and Neis Ramsay was physician to Alexander II. Alexander Ramsay served as physician to James VI and Charles I, and in 1666 Charles II created Gilbert Ramsay a Baronet after bravery at the Battle of Rullion Green in 1666. The house is still occupied and self-catering accommodation is available adjoining the castle (01828 633739; www.scottscastles.com).
Barnton Tower [NT 188758], Edinburgh; site of castle.
   Held by the Crichtons and by the Elphinstone Lords Balmerino, but was a property of the Ramsays of Balmain until 1885.
Barra Castle [NJ 792258], near Inverurie, Aberdeenshire; altered L-plan tower house.
   Held by the Kings and by the Reids before coming to the

Ramsays in 1750. Barra was later held by the Irvines and is still occupied.
Bothwell Castle [NS 688594], near Uddingston, Lanarkshire; fine massive ruinous castle.
   Held by the Douglases and then by the Crichtons, but passed to John Ramsay of Balmain who was a favourite of James III and was made Lord Bothwell. He lost the title and property after following James III at Sauchieburn in 1488 and fled to England; the property was given to Patrick Hepburn, Lord Hailes. The castle passed back to the Douglases after being exchanged for Hermitage and is now in the care of Historic Scotland and is open to the public (01698 816894).
Carrington [NT 318605], near Gorebridge, Midlothian; possible site of castle or old house.
   Held by the Ramsays, who had a house at Whitehill, but passed to the Primroses.
Clatto Castle [NO 358073], near Cupar, Fife; mansion on or near site of castle.
   Held by the Ramsays from the thirteenth century for about 300 years, when Clatto passed to the Learmonths, and then to the Law family. The castle apparently had an underground passageway which led to a cave at Clatto.
Cockpen [NT 325637], near Bonnyrigg, Midlothian; site of castle or old house.
   Held by the Ramsays. Sir Andrew Ramsay of Cockpen was Provost of Edinburgh during the reign of Charles II. The property passed to the Cockburns, but was bought by the Ramsay Earl of Dalhousie in 1785, and the house was demolished soon afterwards. 'The Laird o' Cockpen', written by Carolina Oliphant, Lady Nairne, concerns one of the lairds in the seventeenth century: 'The Laird o' Cockpen, he's proud and he's great, His mind is ta'en up wi' the things o' the state; He wanted a wife his braw house to keep, But favour wi' wooin' was fashious to seek.' The lady he was courting was not impressed, and refused his proposal of marriage. A waistcoat, believed to have belonged to the laird, is kept in the vestibule of the Cockpen and Carrington Parish Church.
Colluthie House [NO 340193], near Cupar, Fife; mansion incorporating castle.
   Held by the Ramsays in the fourteenth century, but passed to the Carnegies of Colluthie, and then to the Inglises.
Colstoun House [NT 514712], near Haddington, East Lothian; mansion incorporating tower house.
   Long held by the Browns, but passed to the Ramsay Earls of Dalhousie in 1805.
Corston Tower [NO 208098], near Auchtermuchty, Fife; ruinous castle.
   Held by the Ramsays of Carnock in the fifteenth century. Sir John Ramsay of Corston (or Balmain) was made Lord Bothwell in 1483, although he did not hold the lands for long as he refused to swear allegiance to James IV in 1488 and Bothwell was given to the Hepburns. Corston passed to the Colquhouns in 1669.
Cruivie Castle [NO 419229], near Balmullo, Fife; large ruinous castle.
   Held by the Kinlochs and by the Sandilands of Calder, but passed to the Ramsays in 1540 and then to the Carnegies around 1583.
Easter Deans [NT 226532], near Penicuik, Midlothian; farmhouse incorporating tower house.
   Held by the Ramsays.
Edington Castle [NT 896562], near Chirnside, Borders; site of castle.
   Held by the Edington family, but was a property of the Ramsays of Dalhousie in 1594.
Foulden Bastle [NT 920555], near Chirnside, Borders; site of tower house.
   Held by the Ramsays. In the graveyard of Foulden Church is a stone for Ramsay of Dalhousie with the inscription: 'Hier lyeth ane honorabil man Georg Ramsay in Fulden Bastle who departit 4 Jan 1592 and of his age 74'. Ramsay was apparently a notorious Border reiver.

Fuirdstone Castle [NO 542589], near Brechin, Angus; site of castle.
   Held by the Ramsays in the 1570s, but passed to the Carnegies.
Inverleith House [NT 245753], Edinburgh; possible site of castle.
   Held by the Ramsays but passed to the Tower family. Inverleith House dates from 1774 and is now in the Royal Botanic Gardens.
Kellie Castle [NO 608402], near Arbroath, Angus; fine fifteenth-century castle.
   Held by several families, including by the Ochterlonys and by the Maules before coming to the Ramsay Earls of Dalhousie.
Kildalton Castle [NR 437475], near Port Ellen, Isle of Islay, Argyll; large mansion.
   Held by the Ramsays, and is now apparently derelict. The Ramsays are said to have been cursed by an old woman after the family had the inhabitants of the area forcibly emigrated to the Americas. John Ramsay and his wife are said to have died soon afterwards and the estate was soon bankrupted.
Old Sauchie [NS 779883], near Stirling; ruinous L-plan tower house.
   Held by the Erskines but passed to the Ramsay family in the eighteenth century, and then to the Gibson-Maitlands in 1865.
Panbride House [NO 572358], near Carnoustie, Angus; castle replaced by mansion.
   Held by the Morhams but had passed to the Ramsays by 1519, and then went to the Carnegies.
Scotscraig [NO 445283], near Tayport, Fife; castle replaced by mansion.
   Held by the Scotts of Balwearie in the thirteenth century then by the Duries and by the Ramsays, before passing to the Buchanans and then to others.
Straloch House [NJ 860210], near New Machar, Aberdeenshire; castle replaced by mansion.
   Held by the Cheynes and by the Gordons, but bought by the Ramsays in 1758, then passed by marriage to the Irvines of Drum.
Tillicoultry Castle [NS 913975], near Tillicoultry, Clackmannan; site of castle and mansion.
   Held by the Erskines, then by others, before coming to the Wardlaw-Ramsays of Whitehill at the end of the nineteenth century.
Whitehill House [NT 296620], near Bonnyrigg, Midlothian; mansion on site of castle or old house.
   Held by the Ramsays of Whitehill from the middle of the seventeenth century or earlier for about 200 years. The family have a burial vault at the Old Parish Church [NT 322611] near Carrington village. The house was later used as St Joseph's Hospital by the Sisters of Charity of St Vincent de Paul, who cared for disabled children, but this was closed in the 1990s.
Whitehouse [NT 187766], Cramond, Edinburgh; tower house and mansion.
   Held by the Logans and by others until bought by the Ramsays in 1788 and they held Whitehouse until the second half of the nineteenth century. Still occupied.

www.clanramsay.org
No. of castles/sites: 30
Rank: 40=/764
Xref: Ramsey

Corston Tower (M&R) – see previous page

490

Randolph

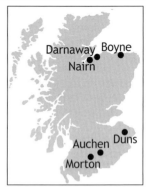

The name comes from Sir Thomas Randolph, Earl of Moray, and the nephew of Robert the Bruce. He supported the English after being freed by them but was then captured by James Douglas and changed sides and supported Bruce. Randolph was one of those who captured Edinburgh Castle in 1314, and he commanded one wing of the Scottish army at Bannockburn the same year. He was made Guardian of the Realm in 1329 after the death of Bruce, as well as Regent for the young David II, but he died at Musselburgh, followed a few weeks later by his son and heir; they may have been poisoned. They were succeeded by John, Randolph's younger son, and he defeated Edward Balliol at the Battle of Annan in 1332. He was made a joint Guardian of Scotland, but he was captured in 1341 and spent the next years in captivity. He was released but was slain at the Battle of Neville's Cross in 1346 without issue; on his death the Randolph's possessions went to other families.

The following castles were owned or built by the Randolphs:
Auchen Castle [NT 063035], near Moffat, Dumfries and Galloway; ruinous castle.
   Held by the Kirkpatricks, but may have been built or rebuilt by Thomas Randolph, and it was later owned by the Douglases and by the Maitlands.
Boyne Castle [NJ 612657], near Portsoy, Aberdeenshire; ruinous castle.
   Held by Thomas Randolph in 1320, but passed to the Edmonstones and then to the Ogilvies.
Darnaway Castle [NH 994550], near Forres, Moray; mansion incorporating some of a castle.
   The original castle was built by Thomas Randolph when he

Darnaway Castle – hall (M&R)

was made Earl of Moray, but the property passed to the Dunbars and then to the Douglases and then to the Stewart Earls of Moray. Darnaway incorporates a fourteenth-century hall-block from an old castle in the mansion. The oak roof of the hall is particularly fine, rivalling that of Parliament Hall.

Duns Castle [NT 777544], Duns, Borders; fine altered castle and mansion.

The original castle may have been built by Thomas Randolph, but the property passed to the Homes of Ayton, and then to the Cockburns and to the Hays. The castle stands in a country park and accommodation is available (01361 883211; www.dunscastle.co.uk).

Morton Castle [NX 891992], near Thornhill, Dumfries and Galloway; ruinous castle.

Held by the Adairs, but passed to Thomas Randolph, and then later to the Douglases, later still Earls of Morton. Morton is in the care of Historic Scotland and is open to the public.

Nairn Castle [NH 885566], Nairn, Inverness-shire; site of castle.

The lands were held by Thomas Randolph, although the castle had the Calders as keepers.

No. of castles/sites: 6
Rank: 212=/764
Xref: Randolf

Rankeilour

The name is territorial and comes from the lands of Rankeilour, which are three miles west and south of Cupar in Fife. The family is on record from the end of the thirteenth century.

Rankeilour Castle [NO 330119] is now just a site, and a new mansion, Rankeilour House, was built at the beginning of the nineteenth century. The lands were held by the family of Rankeilour, but passed to the Sibbalds of Balgonie and then to the Makgills. Sir James Makgill was a Lord of Session and took the title Lord Rankeillour. The property later passed to the Hope Earls of Hopetoun.

No. of castles/sites: 1
Rank: 537=/764

Rattray

The name is territorial and comes from the lands and barony of Rattray, which are a mile or so east of Blairgowrie/Rattray in Perthshire; the name is on record from the middle of the thirteenth century.

Rattray Castle [NO 210454] stood on an S-shaped motte, but little else remains except the mound. The family held the property from the eleventh century. Eustace Rattray was captured by the English after the Battle of Dunbar in 1296, and another Eustace, sixth laird, was accused and then cleared of being involved in a plot to replace Robert the Bruce with William Soulis. Rattray was the main seat of the Rattrays until 1516 when the Earl of Atholl had the Rattray family driven from the castle after they had succeeded to lands around Fortingall. The family moved to Craighall-Rattray, although they still own the site of their old stronghold.

Craighall-Rattray [NO 175480], a couple of miles north of Rattray, is a baronial mansion, dating from the nineteenth century, but the building incorporates part of a tower house. Craighall-Rattray stands on a hill above a river, and the castle was defended by a ditch and towers on the landward side. It was originally a property of the Scotts of Balwearie, but passed to the Rattrays at the beginning of the sixteenth century, or from much earlier. Patrick Rattray of Craighall was driven from Rattray Castle in 1516 by the Earl of Atholl, who also kidnapped his nieces and then had Rattray murdered in his own chapel in 1533; Thomas Rattray of Craighall was Bishop of Dunkeld in 1627. The family supported Charles I, and as a result the castle was besieged by Cromwell's forces around 1650, and John Rattray was captured after the Battle of Worcester in 1651 and imprisoned in the Tower of London. A Jacobite fugitive was sheltered at Craighall during the 1745 Rising, although the laird of the time did not come out for the Jacobites. John Rattray, youngest son of the laird, was physician to Bonnie Prince Charlie, and only escaped execution when Duncan Forbes of Culloden intervened on his behalf. Sir Walter Scott visited the castle in 1793, and used it in *Waverley*, calling it Tullyveolain Castle. The castle is reputedly haunted by a Grey Lady, and there are stories of a poor serving girl being flung from one of the windows when she would not reveal the whereabouts of the family after the castle had been seized by Cromwell's forces. Accommodation is available (01250 874749; www.craighall.co.uk).

Corb Castle [NO 164568] is seven miles north of Rattray, but little remains except a mound. The property was held by the Lindsays of Crawford, but was owned by the Rattrays in the seventeenth and eighteenth centuries.

www.clanrattray.org
No. of castles/sites: 3 / Rank: 328=/764

Redheugh

The name is territorial and comes from the lands of Reidhaugh, which are near Comrie in Perthshire, although the name also occurs in other places in Scotland including in the Borders. **Redheugh Castle** [NY 498902] stood a couple of miles north of Newcastleton in the Borders, although nothing remains; Redheugh was, however, the main stronghold of the Elliots.

The Redheughs did hold the lands of **Cultybraggan** [NN 769197], which lie two miles south of Comrie in Perthshire, and there was probably a castle or tower house here, although the location is far from certain. The lands were held by the Redheugh family in 1590 but later passed to the Drummonds. Cultybraggan is the site of a former German prisoner of war camp, and was also used to house the national civil and military command and control centre should there be a nuclear strike.

Quarrell or **Carron Hall** [NS 891840] is to the east of Stenhousemuir near Falkirk in central Scotland, and there may have been a castle or old house here although this was replaced by a mansion. The lands were held by the Quarrell family until 1420 but then passed to the Redheughs and then to the Bissets, who were in possession in the sixteenth century.

No. of castles/sites: 2
Rank: 396=/764
Xrefs: Reidheugh; Reddoch

Reid

The name is descriptive and means 'red haired' or with a ruddy complexion, and the name is on record from the end of the thirteenth century.

The Reids owned the following properties:
Affleck Castle [NO 493389], near Monifeith, Angus; tall L-plan tower house.
Held by the Auchinlecks, but passed to Reid family in the middle of the seventeenth century. The family was forfeited in 1746 for their part in the Jacobite Rising. On seeing government troops coming to take the castle, the lady of the house and her maid fled to Dundee with many of the castle's valuables, and they eventually joined her husband in France.
Airds Castle [NR 820383], near Carradale, Kintyre; very ruinous castle.
Held by the MacDonald Lord of the Isles, but was given to Sir Adam Reid of Barskimming in 1498, although it was later recovered by the MacDonalds, later to return to the Reids. **Carradale House** [NR 807378] is a castellated mansion, dating from the middle of the nineteenth century.
Ballochmyle House [NS 521264], near Mauchline, Ayrshire; castle replaced by mansion.
Held by the Reids in the seventeenth century, and John Reid of Ballochmyle shot the noted Covenanter, Gilbert MacAdam of Waterhead, at Kirkmichael in 1685. Ballochmyle passed to the Whitefoords and then to the Alexanders, and the building was used as a hospital until 2000. The site is to be redeveloped, restoring the house, and luxury homes are to be built in the grounds.
Barra Castle [NJ 792258], near Inverurie, Aberdeenshire; L-plan tower house.
Held by the Kings then by the Setons, but passed to the Reids in 1658 and then went to the Ramsays in 1750. Still occupied.
Barskimming [NS 482251], near Mauchline, Ayrshire; castle replaced by mansion.
Held by the Reids from 1375 to 1615 when the property was sold to the Stewarts, then passed to the Millers and later to the Galbraiths.
Colliston Castle [NO 612464], near Arbroath, Angus; Z-plan tower house.
Held by the Reids from 1539 but passed to the Guthries, who built the castle, and Colliston later passed to the Gordons.

Colliston Castle (M&R)

Daldilling [NS 576263], near Mauchline, Ayrshire; site of castle.

Held by the Reids, one of whom is said to have been a persecutor of Covenanters and to have hanged his victims here (perhaps John Reid of Ballochmyle mentioned above).

Ellon Castle [NJ 960307], Ellon, Aberdeenshire; ruinous castle and site of mansion.

Held by the Comyns, by the Kennedys and by the Gordons, before coming to the Reids after Sir James Reid was physician to Queen Victoria and was made a Baronet in 1897. The Reids now apparently live at Lanton Tower near Jedburgh.

Hoselaw Tower [NT 802318], near Town Yetholm, Borders; site of tower house.

Held by the Somervilles, then by the Kerrs and by the Reids.

Isle of Whithorn Castle [NX 476367], Whithorn, Galloway; L-plan tower house.

Held by the Houstons, but was owned by John Reid, Superintendent of Customs, in 1830. Still occupied.

Lanton Tower [NT 618215], near Jedburgh, Borders; altered tower house and mansion.

Held by the Cranstons and by the Douglases of Cavers, but it is now apparently occupied by the Reids of Ellon, Baronets.

Lauriston Castle [NT 204762], Edinburgh; fine tower house and mansion.

Held by several families, then latterly by the Reids, who gave

Lauriston Castle (MC)

it to the people of Edinburgh. The castle stands in a public park and is open to the public by guided tour (0131 336 2060; www.cac.org.uk).

Robertland Castle [NS 441470], near Stewarton, Ayrshire; mansion on site of castle.

Held by the Cunninghams, latterly Fairlie-Cunninghames of Robertland, but the barony is now owned by the Reids of Robertland, and they apparently live here.

No. of castles/sites: 13
Rank: 113=/764
Xrefs: Read; Reed

Rennie

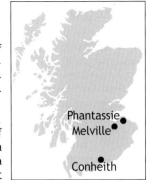

The name is a variant of Rainy, often Rannie or Rennie, and was found in Angus in the fifteenth century.

Conheith [NY 005701], a few miles south of Dumfries, is the site of a tower house, although a later mansion was built nearer the River Nith at **Conheath** [NX 995697]. The lands were held by the Maxwells until 1783, but were owned by the Rannie family in 1876.

Melville Castle [NT 310669] is a fine mansion, a mile or so to the west of Dalkeith in Midlothian, and stands on the site of a castle. The present building is a symmetrical castellated edifice of three storeys, and was built at the end of the eighteenth century. The property was held by the Melvilles, but was bought by David Rennie in 1705. Melville passed by marriage through Elizabeth Rennie to Henry Dundas, Viscount Melville, a very powerful fellow in the Scotland of his day. The building is said to be haunted by the ghost of Elizabeth Rennie, and during recent renovations an apparition of a woman was seen to walk through a wall, later found to be a blocked-up door. An alternative identification of the apparition has been made as Mary, Queen of Scots. The castle is now a hotel (0131 654 0088; www.melvillecastle.com).

Phantassie [NT 598772], to the north of East Linton, was held by the Rennies in the nineteenth century. There was an old house or castle, and there is a fine, unusual doocot, which dates from the sixteenth century, and has some 544 nesting boxes. The property was held by the Sharps and then by the Mitchell-Innes family before coming to the Rennies, one of whom was George Rennie, a successful agricultural improver. Rennie's brother was a colleague of James Watt, and was later a civil engineer and designer of bridges, and his sons continued the family business.

No. of castles/sites: 3
Rank: 328=/764
Xrefs: Rannie; Rainy

Renton

The name comes from the lands and parish of that name, which are four miles west of Coldingham in Berwickshire in the Borders. The name itself is believed from 'Rein' or 'Raegen' (which comes from Old English and is derived from the personal name 'Raegenweald') and 'ton' (meaning 'settlement' or 'seat') so 'Rein's ton' or 'Renton'.

Renton Peel [NT 824654] has gone, and all that remains is a mound near a farm house. The lands were held by the Rentons from the twelfth century, and they were hereditary foresters of Coldingham. Renton passed to the Logans of Restalrig, and the tower was torched by the English in 1545. The remains were demolished in the eighteenth century.

Lamberton [NT 965573] is near the English Border, some four miles north-east of Berwick-upon-Tweed. There was a tower house, and the lands were held by the Lambertons before passing to the Leslies and then to the Rentons, who probably held the tower. The tower was torched and destroyed, along with the village, by the English in 1545. The only trace of the settlement is the slight remains of the church, where James IV and Margaret Tudor are said to have been married.

Mordington House [NT 951558] is close by, and is more than three miles west and north of Berwick-upon-Tweed. There was a castle, which was replaced by a Georgian mansion, which was itself demolished in 1973. The property was owned by the Mordingtons, and then passed through several families before coming to the Rentons of Lamberton. Cromwell used a castle or house here as his headquarters in July 1650.

Three miles north and west of Chirnside, **Billie Castle** [NT 851596] is a very ruinous old stronghold which had a keep or strong tower and a courtyard. Held by the Dunbars and then by the Douglases, the property passed to the Rentons on the forfeiture of the Earls of Angus in 1540. Only four years later it was one of the many places in southern Scotland that was destroyed by the English during the Rough Wooing.

No. of castles/sites: 4
Rank: 278=/764

Richardson

The name means 'Richard's son', 'Richard' itself being from the Old English for 'powerfully rich'. The name is on record from the first quarter of the fourteenth century.

Smeaton Castle [NT 347699] is two miles north of Dalkeith in Midlothian, and is an altered courtyard castle with part of a curtain wall and two surviving round corner towers. The lands passed to the Richardsons before or at the Reformation, and they held the property until they sold it in 1780. Smeaton is now a farm.

Formerly known as **Gedeleth** and **Werty Gellet**, **Broomhall** [NT 077837] is a few miles south-west of Dunfermline in Fife. The present house is a long classical mansion, dating from the end of the seventeenth century and rising to three storeys, but it stands on the site of a tower house or castle. The lands were bought by the Richardsons after the Reformation, but they were sold to the Bruces at the beginning of the seventeenth century, and they then changed the name to Broomhall. The building is now used as a hotel and restaurant (01259 763360; www.broomhallcastle.co.uk).

Some five or so miles east of Perth, **Pitfour Castle** [NO 199209] is a mansion of 1784 and 1829, but it may include work from an older stronghold which stood on the site. Pitfour was owned by the Lindsay Earls of Crawford and by the Hays, but passed to the Richardsons, Baronets since 1630, who still held it into the twentieth century but now apparently live in Surrey in England. The castle has been divided but is still occupied.

Tullybelton [NO 034336] is two and a half miles west and south of Bankfoot in Perthshire, and a castle or tower house here was replaced by a mansion built in the nineteenth century. The lands were held by the Grahams (Graemes) of Inchbrackie, then by the Robertsons and by the Richardsons in the eighteenth and nineteenth centuries. Tullybelton then passed to the Barries, shipowners and merchants in Dundee.

Ballathie House [NO 146367], seven miles south of Blairgowrie also in Perthshire, dates from the middle of the nineteenth century and again replaced an old house or castle. Owned by the Drummonds, later Earls of Perth, the property passed to the Blairs and then to the Richardsons of Tullybelton, and then to the Coats family of Paisley in 1910. The building is now used as a hotel (01250 883268; www.ballathiehousehotel.com).

No. of castles/sites: 5
Rank: 240=/764

Richmond

The name probably comes from the castle, town and parish of Richmond in Yorkshire, and the name is on record in Scotland from the sixteenth century.

Kincairney House [NO 087441], five miles west of Blairgowrie in Perthshire, dates from the nineteenth century but incorporates older work. Kincairney was held by the Murrays in the seventeenth century, then by the Gloags but was then a property of the Richmonds of Kincairney from 1850. The Richmonds are descended from a family who owned lands and farmed around Kilmarnock in the sixteenth century, and now apparently live in Australia.

No. of castles/sites: 1
Rank: 537=/764

Rickarton

The name is territorial or local, and comes from 'Richard's ton'. There are places of this name in several parts of Scotland, including in Ayrshire, in the Borders, in Clackmannan, in Lanarkshire, in Midlothian and in West Lothian. It does not appear that a family of that name held these lands, except for Rickarton in Kincardineshire.

Rickarton [NO 838886] is two or so miles south-west of Stonehaven in Kincardineshire, and there was a castle or old house which was replaced by a small mansion of 1830. The lands were held by the Rickarton family, who were in possession until the eighteenth century when the property passed to the Hepburns. Rickarton later went to the Bairds of Urie, and the house is still occupied.

No. of castles/sites: 1
Rank: 537=/764
Xref: Riccarton

Riddell

The name may have two origins, one from Ryedale in Yorkshire, the other from a family from Gascony. The former settled in the Borders, while the family from France held the lands of Cranstoun Riddel.

Riddell Tower [NT 516245] was incorporated into Riddell House, but this building is now ruinous. The remains lie four miles southeast of Selkirk in the Borders, and the lands were held by the Riddells from the middle of the twelfth century. Nearby in woodland are the remains of a motte and bailey castle [NT 520249], which was built by the Riddells in around 1150, and on the site of which is the General's Tower, a folly of 1885. The family were made Baronets of Nova Scotia, but are probably most distinguished for doing little of note. The Riddells held the property until 1823, and the Riddells of Riddell, Baronets, apparently now live at Morpeth in Northumberland in northern England. Riddell had passed to the Sprots by the end of the nineteenth century, but the house was burnt out in 1943 and remains a shell. The Riddells have a burial vault at Bowden Kirk [NT 554303], two or so miles south of Melrose; the church dates partly from the fifteenth century and is open the public.

Nearby was **Lilliesleaf Tower** [NT 537253], also a property of the Riddells, again from the middle of the twelfth century until 1823. They had a tower house or castle, but there are no remains.

The Haining [NT 469280] is also to the south of Selkirk, and there is a classical mansion with an arcaded portico, which dates from 1794. There was an old castle or house here, and the lands were owned by the Riddells before passing to the Pringles in the seventeenth century. The house is still occupied.

Two or so miles south of Morebattle, also in the Borders, is **Whitton Tower** [NT 759222], a ruinous sixteenth-century tower house. Whitton was held by the Liddel family and by the Bennets, and was sacked twice by the English. The property passed to the Riddells by 1602, and they rebuilt the tower.

Oxenfoord Castle or **Cranstoun Riddel** [NT 388656] is a magnificent Adam mansion of 1780-85, which encases an L-plan tower of the sixteenth century. It lies three or so miles east and south of Dalkeith in Midlothian, and was held by the Riddells before passing to the Makgills, who held it for centuries. Oxenfoord Castle was used as a school from 1931 to 1984, and the gardens are occasionally open the public (www.gardensof scotland.org).

Friars Carse [NX 925850] is six miles north of Dumfries and is a modern mansion although it stands on the site of a castle and may incorporate older work. Friars Carse was owned by the Kirkpatricks, then by the Maxwells of Tinwald, before passing to the Riddells of

Glenriddell. Robert Burns was a frequent visitor when he farmed nearby Ellisland at the end of the eighteenth century, being close friends with the then laird, Robert Riddell, and Burns wrote some of his poems at Friars Carse. The property later passed to the Crichtons, one of whom Dr Crichton founded the Crichton Royal Institute, a hospital, in the nineteenth century. Friars Carse is now used as a hotel (01387 740388; www.classic-hotels.net).

Glengarnock Castle [NS 311574], a couple of miles north of Kilbirnie in Ayrshire, is now very ruinous. Owned by the Morvilles, it passed to the Riddells, and Mary,

Glengarnock Castle (M&R)

Queen of Scots, visited in 1563. Glengarnock went to the Cunninghams in 1614, but was abandoned and stripped in the eighteenth century.

No. of castles/sites: 7
Rank: 182=/764
Xref: Riddle

Rigg

The name is local in origin, and there are many place names in which Rigg is an element; the name is on record from the middle of the sixteenth century.

Carberry Tower [NT 364697] is two miles north-east of Dalkeith in Midlothian and it was near here that Mary, Queen of Scots, surrendered in 1567. The tower was built by Hugh Rigg around 1543, and his building may have been rather too ornate for some

Carberry Tower (M&R)

tastes: 'Auld Hugh Rigg was very very big, But a bigger man than he, When his cherubs chirped, Upon his new house of Carberee!' The property passed to the Blairs of Lochwood in 1659, and then to others. The building now houses a residential Christian conference centre and accommodation is available (0131 665 3135; www.carberrytower.com).

Aithernie Castle [NO 379035] is now very ruinous, and lies a mile or so north of Leven in Fife. The tower house dated from the seventeenth century, when the property was held by the Riggs; Aithernie had been owned by the Lundins, by the Carmichaels and by the Inglises. The property was sold to the Watsons in 1670.

Morton House [NT 254679], to the south of Edinburgh, is a tall plain house, which dates from 1702, but it includes old work from a castle or previous house. Owned by the Sinclairs of Rosslyn, it passed to the Riggs in 1800, one of whom, Thomas Rigg, was High Sheriff of Edinburgh. The property was later held by the Trotters of Charterhall and then by the Elliotts, and Morton House is still occupied.

No. of castles/sites: 3
Rank: 328=/764

Roberton

The name is territorial and comes from the manor and then parish of Roberton, which is to the north of Abington in South Lanarkshire. In the twelfth century the property was held by one 'Robert', and being his settlement or 'ton', the lands were called 'Roberton' (the Robertsons are not linked to the Robertsons, although no doubt the two have sometimes been confused). Robert's motte and bailey castle was a mile or so south of present village of **Roberton** [NS 941272]. The family did not support Robert the Bruce and were subsequently forfeited. The motte was possibly last used by Mary of Stirling and she resigned her lands in 1346 hoping for a pardon from David II, son of Robert the Bruce.

The family did, however, acquire the lands of Earnock, which are a mile west of Hamilton also in Lanarkshire. There was a castle or old house at **Earnock** [NS 699545], which was incorporated into **Earnock House**, a mansion, but this has been demolished and the site is occupied by a housing estate. The property was held by the Robertons from 1380 or earlier. James Roberton of Earnock fought on the side of Gustave Adolphus of Sweden in 1631, and the family were Covenanters. By 1889 the property had passed to the Watsons.

Lauchope House [NS 781617], some three and a half miles east of Motherwell also in Lanarkshire central Scotland, was an attractive mansion which incorporated a strong old tower. This was demolished in 1956. Lauchope was long held by the Muirheads, but by the twentieth century had passed to the Robertons.

No. of castles/sites: 3
Rank: 328=/764

Robertson

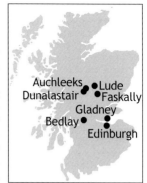

The Robertsons or Clan Donnachaidh ('Duncan son'), pronounced 'Donnachie', claim descent from Crinan, Abbot of Dunkeld and are named after Fat Duncan, one of his descendants, who fought for Robert the Bruce. Duncan is said to have made Duncan's Leap, on the River Ericht in Rannoch, when scouting out a camp of the MacDougalls. The name Robertson is said to come from his and his clan's decisive participation in the Battle of Bannockburn. Bruce is said to have remarked: 'Hitherto, you have been called the son of Duncan, but henceforth you shall be called my children', and so Robertson. The clan held much land in Perthshire. Dob, Dobbie, Hob, Hobbie, Robin and Rob are diminutives for Robert, and from this comes Dobson, Hobson, Robinson and Robson as well as Roberts.

Dunalastair [NN 710589], a few miles east of Kinloch Rannoch, were held by the Robertsons of Struan, and this was the seat of their chiefs. There was a castle, which was replaced by **Dall House** [NN 594565], now part of Rannoch School. Robert Reoch Robertson captured the murderers of James I in 1437, and gave them into the hands of the queen, who put them to death. The Robertsons supported the Marquis of Montrose and fought at Inverlochy in 1645. Alexander, known as the Poet Chief, fought for the Jacobites at Killiecrankie in 1689 and was forfeited. He was allowed to return but was captured after Sheriffmuir in 1715, although he managed to escape. He was allowed to return again, but then took part in the 1745-46 Rising at the age of 75 and fought at Prestonpans; he escaped to France and died there. There is an old graveyard [NN 708587], where members of the clan are buried. The lands were sold to the MacDonalds of Dalchosnie around 1855, and they built a substantial new mansion at **Dunalastair** [NN 710580], but this is now ruinous. The chief of the Robertsons now apparently lives in Kent.

Lude [NN 886656] is half a mile or so north-east of Blair Atholl, and there was a castle or old house. This was replaced by Lude House, which was designed by William Burn and dates from 1831. The lands were a property of the Robertsons. Alexander Robertson of Lude fought on the side of the Marquis of Montrose at the Battle of Tippermuir in 1644, and Lude was later torched by Cromwell's forces in the 1650s. Lady Lude was an enthusiastic Jacobite, and raised her men to join Bonnie Prince Charlie in 1745. Her tenants seem to have been less keen and, by the time the Jacobites arrived in Edinburgh, only Robertson of the Mains of Lude and her nephew had not deserted. Lady Lude threatened to hang the 'deserters' from her gatepost. The Robertsons of Lude held the property until 1874.

The Clan Donnachaidh (Robertson) Museum is in Bruar in Perthshire.

The following properties were also held by the Robertsons:

Auchleeks [NN 741646], near Kinloch Rannoch, Perthshire; castle replaced by mansion.

Held by the Robertsons from the 1530s, and the second laird, Charles Robertson, was known as 'Charles of the Strings' because of his skill with the harp. Duncan Robertson of Auchleeks was wounded at the Battle of Culloden in 1746. The property was sold by the family in 1962, and the garden is occasionally to the public (www.gardensofscotland.org).

Bedlay Castle [NS 692701], near Kirkintilloch, Dunbartonshire; L-plan tower house.

Held by the Boyds of Kilmarnock, but was bought by the Robertson Lord Bedlay in 1642, who extended the castle. The property was sold in 1786, and later passed to the Campbells of Petershill and then to the Christies. The building is said to be haunted by the bearded apparition of Bishop Cameron or one of the Campbell lairds.

Edradynate Castle [NN 881521], near Aberfeldy, Perthshire; site of fortified residence.

The lands were held by the Robertsons and later by the Stewart Meiklejohns.

Eilean nam Faoileag [NN 530577], near Kinloch Rannoch, Perthshire; site of castle on island.

Held by the Robertsons of Struan, and said to have been used as a refuge and as a prison.

Faskally House [NN 917601], near Pitlochry, Perthshire; castle or old house replaced by mansion.

Held by the Robertsons, but passed to the Butter family, who built a new mansion. Faskally House is now owned by the Scottish Executive and is an outdoor centre. Nearby is Old Faskally House, the former dower house, and this was the site of the original residence.

Fearnan [NN 725446], near Kenmore, Perthshire; site of castle or old house.

Held by the Robertsons of Struan and then by the Campbells.

Fordie or **Lawers** [NN 799230], near Crieff, Perthshire; tower house replaced by mansion.

Held by the Campbells, but much later passed to the Robertsons, and the building is now used as a college of agriculture.

Gladney House [NT 280908], Kirkcaldy, Fife; site of mansion.

Held by the Clerks but passed to the Robertsons. Mary Robertson of Gladney married the famous architect William Adam; their sons Robert and James were born here. By the 1870s the building was used as a boarding house and it was demolished with other slums in the 1930s; there are no remains.

Pitcastle [NN 973554], near Pitlochry, Perthshire; ruinous house or tower.

Held by the Robertsons, and the studded door from the castle and other items are kept at Blair Castle.

Prenderguest [NT 919595], near Eyemouth, Borders; site of castle and/or mansion.

Held by the Prendergast family but a property of the Robertsons in the nineteenth century.

Tullybelton [NO 034336], near Bankfoot, Perthshire; castle replaced by mansion.

Held by the Grahams (Graemes) of Inchbrackie, then by the Robertsons and by the Richardsons, then went to the Barries.

Wrychtishousis [NT 247724], Edinburgh; site of castle and mansion.

Held by the Napiers and by the Clerks, then by the Robertsons of Lawers. Robertson's servant witnessed the apparition of a headless woman with a baby in her arms rising from the hearth stone of his room. When the building was demolished a few years later, the decapitated body of a woman and child were found beneath the hearth – or so the story goes.

www.robertson.org
www.donnachaidh.com
No. of castles/sites: 14 / Rank: 104=/764
Xrefs: Duncanson; Donnachaidh; Dobson; Robinson

Rollo

The name is Norse in origin, and Sigurd Rollo was Earl of Orkney, but his descendants became established in Normandy. The Rollos accompanied their kinsmen William the Conqueror to England, and then came to Scotland in the reign of David I in the twelfth century. The family was given lands in Perthshire, and the name was also spelt Rollock. Peter Rollock was Bishop of Dunkeld in 1585 and then a Lord of Session. Robert Rollock was the first Principal of the University of Edinburgh, and died in 1599.

Duncrub [NO 007157] is four or so miles north-east of Auchterarder, but both a castle, and the large mansion which replaced it, have been demolished. The lands were held by the Rollo family from 1380. William and Robert Rollo of Duncrub both died at the Battle of Flodden in 1513; while Sir William Rollo, son of the then laird, was executed by beheading in 1645 after being captured at the Battle of Philiphaugh fighting for Montrose. The family were made Lords Rollo in 1651. Robert, fourth Lord, fought for the Jacobites in the 1715 Rising, but gave himself up and was later pardoned and died at Duncrub in 1758. Many of the family were distinguished soldiers, and the Rollos held the property at the end of the nineteenth century. They now apparently live near Dunning, and hold the titles Lords Rollo and Barons Dunning.

The family also held:

Balloch Castle [NO 263495], near Alyth, Perthshire; farm on site of castle.

Held by the Rollos.

Bannockburn House [NS 809889], near Stirling; mansion with old work.

Held and originally built by the Rollo family, but passed to the Patersons, who were Jacobites. The house is still occupied.

Dumcrieff [NT 102036], near Moffat, Dumfriesshire; castle replaced by mansion.

Held by the Murrays, then by other families, before coming to the Rollo Lord Rollo in the nineteenth century.

Inverquiech Castle [NO 277497], near Alyth, Perthshire; slight remains of castle.

Held by the Lindsays but passed to the Rollos.

Keltie Castle [NO 008133], near Dunning, Perthshire; plain L-plan tower house.

Held by the Bonnars, by the Drummonds and by the Ogilvie Earl of Airlie before passing to the Rollo Lord Rollo in 1833, and then went to others. Still occupied.

Menmuir or **Manmure** [NO 534643], near Brechin, Angus; site of castle.

Held by the Rollos from the sixteenth century but later passed to the Lindsays.

members.aol.com/rolloclan/
No. of castles/sites: 7
Rank: 182=/764
Xref: Rollock

Romanes

The name is territorial and comes from the manor of **Rothmaneic** (now **Romanno**), which is a couple of miles south of West Linton in Tweeddale in the Borders. The family are on record from the middle of the thirteenth century until 1513 when an heiress married into the Murrays of Falahill and Philiphaugh. There was a tower house at **Romanno** [NT 167483] but this was replaced by Romanno House in the eighteenth century.

No. of castles/sites: 1
Rank: 537=/764
Xrefs: Romanis; Romans

Rome

The name comes from Dumfriesshire, and the family were long under the protection of the Johnstones of Gretna. In the seventeenth century the Romes flourished for a while and held the lands of Dalswinton, which are six miles north of Dumfries in the south of Scotland. **Dalswinton Castle** [NX 945841] was a strong castle and was seized by the English in 1309 and again in 1355. It had been a property of the Comyns, of the Stewarts and of the Maxwells, but for some years in the seventeenth century was held by the Rome family. Little of the castle now survives and it was replaced by **Dalswinton House** [NX 943841], an elegant mansion which dates from 1785. The gardens of the house are occasionally open to the public (www.gardensofscotland.org).

No. of castles/sites: 1
Rank: 537=/764
Xref: Roome

Rorison

Rorison is the Anglicization of the Gaelic 'MacRuari' (also see that name). The family had been Lords of Bute but they left the island after the Stewarts assumed the lordship in the reign of Robert II, and the Rorisons then held the lands of Bardannoch (now Bardennoch) during the sixteenth century, which are just to the north of Moniaive in Dumfries and Galloway. There was a small tower house at **Bardennoch** [NX 780914], but the site appears to be occupied by a farm. Bardannoch later passed to the Griersons.

No. of castles/sites: 1
Rank: 537=/764
Xrefs: MacRuari; Rorieson

499

Rose

The name comes from Ros, near Caen in Normandy in France, and the family came to England with William the Conqueror. The family were granted lands in the north of Scotland and are on record from the twelfth century.

Geddes [NH 884526] is two or so miles south of Nairn in Inverness-shire, and there was an old house or possibly a castle, but this was replaced by Geddes House, a fine mansion dating from 1780. The Roses held the property from the twelfth century, and the family married into the Bissets of Kilravock in 1293, and that property passed to them. The Roses of Kilravock and Geddes had a burial vault [NH 888529] near Rait Castle. Geddes later passed to the Mackintoshes, who built the present house. The house can be rented (01667 452241; www.geddesonline.co.uk).

Kilravock Castle [NH 814493], which is six miles south-west of Nairn, is a plain, massive and imposing keep or tower of five storeys, and the building was altered and extended in the following centuries. The property had passed to the Roses in 1293, and they built the castle. Mary, Queen of Scots, visited Kilravock in 1562, and Hugh, the future seventeenth laird, entertained Bonnie Prince Charlie two days before the Battle of Culloden in 1746. The next day the Duke of Cumberland visited on his way to the battlefield, and his host was Hugh, the sixteenth laird. Robert Burns stayed in 1787. The property is still owned by the Roses, and the castle is now a guest house, youth hostel and sports centre, and the garden is open to the public (01667 493258; www.kilravockcastle.com).

Holme Rose [NH 806486] is a short distance to the west, and there is a mansion, probably on the site of an older house or castle. The lands were held by the Roses from the sixteenth century to 1939, when the property was sold. The line continues but they now apparently live in England.

Just to the south-west of Nairn is Balblair [NH 873553], a mansion which includes work from the seventeenth century. Balblair was held by the Rose family, although a party of Cummings are said to have been murdered here by the Mackintoshes. The building housed some of the troops of the Duke of Cumberland's army before Culloden in 1746. The building is now a residential home for old people.

www.clanrose.org
No. of castles/sites: 4
Rank: 278=/764

Kilravock Castle (RWB)

Ross

The name appears to have at least two origins, one from the south and one from the north. The family of Ros or Ross held lands in Ayrshire and in Renfrewshire, and come on record in the twelfth century. This branch came from Yorkshire in England. In the

north the name originated from the area of northern Scotland known as Ross, possibly meaning 'promontory' from Gaelic. The Earls of Ross were recognised as such from the middle of the thirteenth century. They fought for the Scots at Largs in 1263, but William, Earl of Ross, was responsible for placing Robert the Bruce's wife and womenfolk into the hands of the English even though they were in a place of sanctuary in St Duthac's Chapel at Tain. Bruce forgave the Earl, and William fought at Bannockburn in 1314 and added his seal to the Declaration of Arbroath six years later. Euphemia Ross, who was the widow of John Randolph, third Earl of Moray, married Robert II in 1372 and her sons became the Earl of Strathearn and the Earl of Atholl. The male line of the Earls of Ross died out in 1372 when the last Earl, William, died. His daughter Euphemia, Countess of Ross, was married to Walter Leslie, but after his death without issue she married Alexander Stewart, the Wolf of Badenoch. Stewart seems to have been more interested in acquiring the Earldom than he was in his wife, and it was not a happy union; he abandoned her and he was excommunicated by the Bishop of Moray. The Earldom later went to the MacDonald Lords of the Isles before coming into the hands of the Crown after a period of unrest and bloodshed. The Rosses of Balnagown were descended from the Earls of Ross.

Balnagown Castle [NH 763752], eight miles northeast of Alness, is an altered tower house, which dates from the fourteenth century, but it was extended in later years. The castle was first built by the Ross family in 1375. Alexander, eighth laird, terrorised his neighbours, and was imprisoned in Tantallon Castle. He died in 1592, but his son, George, was also a turbulent

Balnagown Castle 1910?

fellow, and held John Ross in Balnagown Castle after seizing him in Edinburgh. George was also accused of much murder, and with aiding the fugitive Earl of Bothwell. Katherine, his sister and wife of Robert Munro of Foulis, was charged with witchcraft, incantation, sorcery and poisoning, but although some of her acquaintances were burned, she managed to escape prosecution by getting her own people onto the jury at her retrial – a sensible precaution as the charges were then found not proven. David Ross of Balnagown led his clan against Cromwell at the Battle of Worcester in 1651, but he was captured after the battle and imprisoned in the Tower of London. The clan lost the property because of debt in the eighteenth century, and Balnagowan was bought by the Rosses of Hawkhead, of the southerly branch. The castle has stories of two ghosts. Black Andrew Munro was a man believed guilty of many dastardly deeds, and he was hanged from one of the windows of Balnagown in 1522. His ghost is said to haunt the castle, and to manifest itself to women. The other is a Grey Lady, the ghost of a young woman, clad in a grey dress with auburn hair and green eyes. The tale goes that her skeleton is walled up somewhere in the building. The property remained with the Ross family until 1978. Cottages are available to rent on the estate (01862 843601; www.balnagown-estates.co.uk).

Tain Through Time, in Tain in Ross and Cromarty, has information about the Ross clan, as well as displays on the burgh as a pilgrimage site and much else (01862 894089; www.tainmuseum.org.uk).

Hawkhead Castle [NS 501626] lay a mile east of Paisley in Renfrewshire, and there was a strong keep or tower, which was incorporated into a mansion, itself remodelled down the centuries. Hawkhead was a property of the Rosses from the middle of the fifteenth century, and they built the castle. The Rosses of Hawkhead were hereditary keepers of Renfrew Castle, and they were made Lords Ross in 1490. John, second Lord, was killed at the Battle of Flodden in 1513. The family became very wealthy and bought much other property, including Balnagown Castle from the northern branch of the family. The Lordship had become extinct in 1754, but a new lordship, Ross of Hawkhead, was created in 1815. Hawkhead passed from the Rosses to the Boyle Earls of Glasgow, the lands were divided, and a psychiatric hospital was built on part of the estate. The site of the castle is now occupied by Hawkhead Hospital.

The Rosses also held:

Achnacloich Castle [NH 670734], near Alness, Ross and Cromarty; site of castle.

 Held by the Rosses in the fifteenth and sixteenth centuries. The Rosses of Achnacloich apparently got into a legal dispute, lasting over four generations and into the eighteenth century, with the Mackenzies of Dundonnel, which apparently bankrupted the Rosses and they lost Achnacloich.

Arnage Castle [NJ 936370], near Ellon, Aberdeenshire; Z-plan tower house.

 Held by the Cheynes and by the Sibbalds, but sold to John Ross, who was later Provost of Aberdeen, in 1702. Restored and occupied.

Arthurlie House [NS 504588], near Barrhead, Renfrewshire; mansion on site of castle.

Held by the Polloks, but part of the estate later passed to the Rosses of Hawkhead.

Auchlossan House [NJ 571021], near Aboyne, Aberdeenshire; altered fortified house.

Held by the Rosses from 1363 to 1709. Captain Francis Ross of Auchlossan was killed at the Battle of Malplaquet, and he was the last of the line. Still occupied.

Balgone House [NT 567825], near North Berwick, East Lothian; L-plan tower house and mansion.

Held by the Rosses of Hawkhead, but passed to the Semples and then to the Sutties of Addiston in 1680.

Balloan Castle [NH 160830], near Ullapool, Ross and Cromarty; site of castle.

Held by the Earls of Ross, but passed to the MacDonnels or MacDonalds, or to the Mackenzies.

Balconie Castle [NH 625652], near Alness, Ross and Cromarty; site of castle.

Held by the Earls of Ross.

Balneil [NX 179639], near Glenluce, Galloway; site of castle.

Held by the Kennedy Earls of Cassillis and by the Vauxs of Barnbarroch, then went to the Rosses in the seventeenth century, then passed by marriage to the Dalrymples of Stair in 1634. They moved to Carscreugh.

Balsarroch House [NW 994691], near Leswalt, Galloway; old ruinous house.

Held by the Kennedys in the seventeenth century, but passed to the Rosses.

Caisteal nan Corr or **Invercassley** [NC 466012], near Lairg, Sutherland; slight remains of tower house.

Held by the Rosses at one time.

Carscreugh Castle [NX 223599], near Glenluce, Galloway; ruinous mansion and tower house.

Held by the Vauxs, then by the Rosses of Balneil then passed by marriage the Dalrymples of Stair. Said to be haunted by a White Lady.

Castle of King Edward [NJ 722562], near Turriff, Aberdeenshire; ruins of strong castle.

Held by the Comyn Earls of Buchan, but passed to the Earls of Ross, to the Stewarts and to the MacDonald Earls of Ross, then went to the Forbeses in 1509.

Cromarty Castle [NH 794670], near Cromarty; castle replaced by mansion.

Held by the Urquharts then by the Murray Lords Elibank, but passed to the Rosses in 1771. The old castle was reputed to be haunted, and the Rosses of Cromarty still apparently live near here.

Inch Castle [NS 515675], near Renfrew; site of castle.

Held by the Stewarts, but passed to the Ross family towards the end of the fifteenth century and they held it until 1732. The property was sold to the Speirs of Elderslie in 1760 and they built Elderslie House. Demolished in 1924, the site of the house is partly occupied by the Braehead shopping centre.

Melville Castle [NT 310669], near Dalkeith, Midlothian; mansion on site of castle.

Held by the Melvilles, but passed to the Rosses of Hawkhead in the late fourteenth century, but was sold to the Rennies in 1705 and then passed by marriage to the Dundases. Now a hotel (0131 654 0088; www.melvillecastle.com).

Montgreenan Castle [NS 342452], near Kilwinning, Ayrshire; mansion by slight remains of castle.

Held by the Rosses and then later by the Cunninghams. The mansion was built for the Glasgow family and is now a hotel (01294 850005; www.montgreenanhotel.com).

Muiravonside [NS 965753], near Linlithgow, West Lothian; site of castle and mansion.

Held by the Tinsdales but passed to the Rosses from 1421 to 1742, when the property went to the MacLeods and then later to the Stirlings. The house was demolished and the grounds are now a country park.

Pitcalnie [NH 810730], near Cromarty; site of castle.

Held by the Munros but passed to the Rosses in the eighteenth century, and they became chiefs of the Ross clan. There may be a farm on the site.

Pittheavlis Castle [NO 097222], near Perth; L-plan tower house and mansion.

Held by the Rosses of Craigie, but sold to the Stewarts in 1586, then passed to the Oliphants and to the Murrays. Divided and still occupied.

Portencross or **Ardneil Castle** [NS 176488], near West Kilbride; site of castle and ruinous castle.

Held by the Rosses but passed to the Boyds after the Wars of Independence, who held Portencross until 1785. The castle can be viewed from the exterior and there are plans to restore it (www.portencrosscastle.org.uk).

Provost Ross's House [NJ 935060], Aberdeen; fine town house.

Held by Provost John Ross of Arnage in 1702, and he was involved in trading with Holland and died in Amsterdam in 1714. Now houses part of Aberdeen's Maritime Museum (01224 337700; www.aberdeencity.gov.uk).

Rossie Castle [NO 702561], near Montrose, Angus; site of castle and later mansion.

Held by the Rossie family, by the Carnegies and by the Scotts of Logie before passing to Hercules Ross, who made a fortune in Jamaica, in 1783. He built a new mansion which was a castellated building with turrets and battlements. The property had passed to the Millars by 1880, and the mansion was demolished in 1957.

Sanquhar Castle [NS 786092], near Sanquhar, Dumfries and Galloway; ruinous castle.

Held by the Edgars and by the Ross family, but passed by marriage to the Crichtons in the fourteenth century. Much later went to the Douglases of Drumlanrig, and the ruins can be viewed from nearby.

Shandwick Castle [NH 858745], near Balintore, Ross and Cromarty; ruined house and site of castle.

Held by the Rosses and Sir Ronald Ross of Shandwick was an eminent physician and discovered the cause of malaria.

Stanely Castle [NS 464616], near Paisley, Renfrewshire; ruinous castle.

Held by the Dennistouns, but passed to the Maxwells of Newark and then went to the Rosses of Hawkhead in 1629. Stanely passed to the Boyle Earl of Glasgow around 1750, and is now in Paisley Waterworks, the basement being flooded.

Tarbet Castle [NS 215470], near West Kilbride, Ayrshire; site of castle.

Held by the Rosses of Tarbet, and demolished in 1790.

Tartraven Castle [NT 005726], near Linlithgow, West Lothian; site of castle.

Held by the Rosses in the sixteenth and seventeenth centuries.

www.clanrossassociation.org

No. of castles/sites: 29
Rank: 42=/764

Stanely Castle (M&R)

Rossie

The name is territorial in origin, and comes from the lands of Rossie, which are two miles east of Auchtermuchty in Fife.

Rossie House or **Hall of Rossie** [NO 265120] incorporated an older house or tower house, but this part was demolished when a wing was built on the site. The lands were held by the Rossies, but passed to the Scotts, and then to the Cheapes, who held them until 1839.

Rossie Castle [NO 702561] was a mile or so to the south-west of Montrose in Angus, but there are no remains. The lands were also held by the Rossies but also passed to the Scotts. There was a modern mansion, also known as Rossie Castle and built in 1800, but this has apparently been demolished. The property was held by the Millars in 1880.

Craig House or **Castle** [NO 704563], one mile south of Montrose in Angus, is a fine courtyard castle, dating from the fifteenth century. The lands were held by the Rossies, but passed to the Woods, who built the original castle, and later went to the Carnegies. Maryton [NO 686563], three miles west and south of Montrose, was probably also held by the Rossie family but passed to the Grahams of Montrose. There was a castle here.

No. of castles/sites: 4
Rank: 278=/764

Royal Castles

Holyroodhouse [NT 269739] is at the foot of the Royal Mile beside the Scottish Parliament building. The palace has ranges of buildings around a courtyard, the oldest of which dates from the sixteenth century and housed the private chambers for James V. The present building was designed by Sir William Bruce for Charles II in 1671-78. The palace was built on the site of the Holyrood Abbey, which was founded in 1128 and named after the Black Rood of St

Holyroodhouse (M&R)

Margaret. The abbey was pillaged in 1322 and in 1385 by the English, but the guest range was found to be a comfortable alternative to Edinburgh Castle. James IV and James V both added to the building, although the English burnt the abbey in 1544 and again three years later. David Rizzio, Mary Queen of Scots's secretary, was murdered here in her presence in 1566, and Bonnie Prince Charlie stayed here for six weeks during the Jacobite Rising of 1745-46. The Duke of Cumberland also made it his residence. The palace is said to be haunted by a Grey Lady, and Holyroodhouse is the official residence of the monarch in Scotland. It is open to the public (0131 556 5100; www.royalcollection.org.uk).

Balmoral Castle [NO 255952] is a large baronial mansion with a tall turreted and battlemented tower, but stands on the site of an old castle. It lies seven miles west of Ballater in Aberdeenshire. The lands were held by the Drummonds, by the Farquharsons, and by the Gordons, but were sold to Prince Albert, husband of Queen Victoria, in 1852. They built a new mansion, which is still the holiday home of the royal family. The gardens, grounds and exhibitions are open to the public (01339 742534; www.balmoralcastle.com).

503

Balmoral Castle 1930? – previous page

Also not far from Ballater is **Birkhall** (or **Sterin**) [NO 348936] and the present house dates from around 1715, although it replaced an older house or castle. The property was held by the Gordons, but was also sold to Prince Albert. Birkhall was used by Elizabeth Bowes Lyon, the Queen Mother, until her death in 2002; and was also where Prince Charles and the Duchess of Cornwall went for their honeymoon in 2005.

Castle of Mey [ND 290739], seven miles north-east of Castletown in Caithness, is an altered Z-plan tower house, rising to three storeys and an attic, and dating

Castle of Mey 1920?

from the sixteenth century. There are later alterations and additions. Castle of Mey was owned by the Sinclair Earls of Caithness, but was sold to Elizabeth Bowes Lyon, the Queen Mother, who had it restored. This was one of her favourite residences, although it is said to be haunted by a Green Lady, the ghost of one of the earl's daughters who fell to her death. The Queen Mother died in 2002, and the castle is open to the public in the summer (01847 851473; www.castleofmey.org.uk). The Queen Mother came from the Bowes Lyon family, who own **Glamis Castle** [NO 387481] near Forfar in Angus. Glamis is a magnificent building and is open to the public from April to October (01307 840393; www.glamis-castle.co.uk).

Edinburgh Castle [NT 252735] is in a wonderful location on a rock in the middle of Scotland's capital and was one of the two most important castles in Scotland. There are many buildings and points of interest, including St Margaret's Chapel, which dates from the twelfth century; the huge cannon, Mons Meg; the Scottish War Memorial; the Great Hall; also the Scottish Crown Jewels and the famous Stone of Destiny. There has been a

Edinburgh Castle (AC)

fortress here from earliest times, and this is where St Margaret, wife of Malcolm Canmore, died in 1093. The castle saw action in the Wars of Independence, and it was captured from the English in 1313 when the Scots, led by Thomas Randolph, scaled the rock; and then again in 1341 when the Scots disguised themselves as merchants bringing food. William, the young sixth Earl of Douglas, and his brother, David, were murdered at the 'Black Dinner' in Edinburgh Castle in 1440, along with Sir Malcolm Fleming of Cumbernauld. The Douglases besieged the castle in retaliation. It was at the castle that Mary, Queen of Scots, gave birth to the future James VI; and it was later besieged successfully by Covenanters in 1640 and then by Cromwell in 1650, and then unsuccessfully by Jacobites in 1715 and in 1745. The castle is in the care of Historic Scotland and is open to the public (0131 225 9846).

Stirling Castle [NS 790940] dominates the burgh of Stirling in central Scotland, and also stands on a rock, controlling an important crossing of the Forth. Buildings are ranged around courtyards, and among many points of interest are the King's Old Building, Great Hall with is hammerbeam roof, the Chapel Royal and the massive kitchen. There was a fortress here from the twelfth century or earlier, and both Alexander I and William the Lion died at the castle. It was seized by Edward I in 1304, but was restored to the Scots after Bannockburn in 1314. Murdoch, Duke of Albany, and his sons were executed in the castle in 1425, and James II and James III were both born here. William, eighth Earl of Douglas,

Stirling Castle (M&R)

was summarily murdered by James II and his corpse was thrown out of one of the windows in 1452. Mary, Queen of Scots, was crowned in the old chapel in 1543, and James VI was baptised in 1566. Charles I and Charles II both visited, and Stirling was besieged by Cromwell's forces but soon surrendered. The castle was garrisoned in the Jacobite risings of 1715 and 1745-46, and was besieged rather ineffectually by the Jacobites. It was used by the army until 1964, and is said to be haunted by several ghosts, including a Green Lady, a Pink Lady, and the apparition of a kilted man. The castle is also in the care of Historic Scotland and is open to the public (01786 450000).

Dumbarton Castle [NS 400745] is in a commanding position overlooking the burgh and the Firth of Clyde on a hill by the sea. The name means 'fortress of the Britons', and this was the seat of the kings of the ancient

Dumbarton Castle (JS)

kingdom of Strathclyde. It was a very strong place, and has a long and eventful history. William Wallace was held in the castle in 1305 before being taken to England and execution. James IV besieged the castle to eject the Earl of Lennox, and it was from here that he conducted his campaign against the MacDonald Lord of the Isles in the 1490s. The castle changed hands several times, and the young Mary, Queen of Scots, sheltered at Dumbarton before being taken to France for marriage to the Dauphin. The castle was then involved in the fighting in the seventeenth century, but was completely remodelled in the following years, so that little of the medieval castle is now left except for the portcullis arch. The castle is also in the care of Historic Scotland and open to the public (01389 732167).

Inverness Castle [NH 667451] was in a strategic position in the north of Scotland. Macbeth is said to have had a stronghold at Inverness, which was destroyed by the forces of Malcolm Canmore. Inverness Castle was held by the English during the Wars of Independence, but was taken by Robert the Bruce in 1310. James I had many Highland chiefs seized at Inverness in 1427 and they were not released until they gave pledges of good behaviour. The MacDonald Lords of the Isles showed what he thought of this by returning two years later and destroying Inverness, although the castle held out. James I, James III and James IV stayed at the castle; and Mary Queen of Scots's forces took the castle from the Gordons in 1562. The Marquis of Montrose failed to capture it in 1644, but the castle was seized by Royalists

in 1649. The castle was captured by Jacobites in 1715 and then blown up by Jacobites in 1746 after the Battle of Culloden. A mock castle stands on the site.

Linlithgow Palace [NT 003774] is a fine ruinous palace, with ranges around an internal courtyard with a splendid carved fountain, which has been recently restored.

Linlithgow Palace (M&R)

There was a castle here from the twelfth century, and it stands in the West Lothian burgh of Linlithgow. It was held by the English, but was retaken by the Scots by driving a cart underneath the portcullis. The castle was left ruinous, but was rebuilt by the kings of Scots and this became one of their favourite residences. James III and James IV had work done, and Mary, Queen of Scots, was born here in 1542. The palace was occupied by Charles I and James VII when Duke of York, as well as being visited by Bonnie Prince Charlie and the Duke of Cumberland; but the building was gutted by fire after Hanoverian forces sheltered here following defeat at the Battle of Falkirk in 1746. The palace is in the care of Historic Scotland and is open to the public (01506 842896).

Falkland Palace [NO 254075] had ranges of buildings around a courtyard, but only one of these is now complete, while another is ruinous and the third is mostly gone. The palace lies in the village of Falkland in Fife, and the gatehouse range is complete and has a twin-towered gateway. There was a castle from the thirteenth

Falkland Palace (RWB)

century, which was destroyed by the English in 1337. David, Duke of Rothesay and eldest son of Robert III, died at Falkland in 1402, probably starved to death by his uncle, the Duke of Albany. Falkland was another preferred residence of the Scottish monarchs, and was remodelled by James III, James IV and James V, who died here in 1542. Other royal visitors include Mary, Queen of Scots, James VI, Charles I and Charles II, as well as George IV in 1822. The gatehouse block was restored after 1887, and the palace is now in the care of The National Trust for Scotland and is open to the public (01337 857397; www.nts.org.uk).

Dunfermline Palace [NT 089872] is in the middle of Dunfermline town in Fife, and adjacent to the abbey church. The palace is ruinous but is an impressive building. The abbey was founded by St Margaret and Malcolm Canmore, and the remains of Robert the Bruce (although not his heart) are buried in the church. Other kings buried at Dunfermline include Edgar, Alexander I, David I, Malcolm IV and Alexander III. There was a royal palace here from the fourteenth century, although the place was pillaged and torched by Edward I in

Dunfermline Palace (M&R)

1303-04. David II was born at the palace in 1323, the building was probably burned in 1385 by the English, and James I was born here in 1394. James IV, James V and Mary, Queen of Scots, all stayed at the palace. The building was remodelled by Queen Anne, wife of James VI, and Charles I was another royal birth in 1600. The palace was unroofed by 1708, and the ruins of the palace and domestic buildings of the abbey, and part of the abbey church, are in the care of Historic Scotland and are open to the public (01383 739026).

The following are a selection of royal castles, residencies and palaces:

Aberdeen [NJ 942060], Aberdeen; site of royal palace.
    Said to have been used by Malcolm Canmore in the eleventh century.

Aberdeen Castle [NJ 944063], Aberdeen; site of castle.
    Held by the English, and visited by Edward I, although William Wallace is said to have burned 100 English ships in the harbour. The castle was destroyed in 1308 and probably not reused.

Auldearn Castle [NH 917557], near Nairn, Inverness-shire; motte.
    Built by William the Lion, but passed to the Dunbars of Cumnock in 1511.

Ayr Castle [NS 335222], Ayr; site of castle.
    Built by William the Lion, and torched by Robert the Bruce in 1298, but was occupied by the English in 1306 and then retaken by the Scots in 1314. The castle was garrisoned by the French in 1542, but the remains were demolished by Cromwell and used to built a citadel at Ayr.

Berwick Castle [NT 999590], Berwick-upon-Tweed, England; slight remains of castle.
    The castle was captured by Edward I in 1296, although the burgh was devastated and reputedly 16,000 people were slain. It was here that the Ragman Roll were compiled, the lists of seals of the many Scots who did homage to Edward I. The burgh and castle were recovered by the Scots in 1318, but then changed hands many times until 1482 when burgh finally fell to the English for the last time. It was at the castle that Isabella Duff, Countess of Buchan, had been imprisoned for four years in a cage hung from the walls as punishment for crowning Robert the Bruce. Most of the castle was destroyed when the railway station and line were built, but there are some remains at and near the station.

Blervie Castle [NJ 071573], near Forres, Moray; ruinous Z-plan tower house.
    Probably originally a royal castle in the thirteenth century, but passed to the Dunbars who built the tower.

Clackmannan Tower [NS 905920], Clackmannan; tower house.
    Site of royal castle, possibly from as early as the twelfth century, but the lands passed to the Bruces and they built the present tower.

Clunie Castle [NO 111440], near Blairgowrie, Perthshire; slight remains of castle.
    There may have been a palace of Malcolm Canmore here, and then later there was a royal castle. Edward I stayed in 1296. The building had been completely demolished by the beginning of the sixteenth century and the remains used to build the nearby tower house.

Cromarty Castle [NH 794670], Cromarty; mansion on site of castle.
    There was a royal castle here from the twelfth century, but the property passed to the Urquharts, who had defended the castle against the English in about 1300.

Cullen Castle [NJ 509670], Cullen, Aberdeenshire; site of castle.
    Royal castle, and it was here that Elizabeth de Burgh, second wife of Robert the Bruce, died. Bruce founded a chapel nearby, at which prayers were to be said for her 'in perpetuity'.

Cupar Castle [NO 376146], Cupar, Fife; site of castle.
    Site of royal castle, which dated from the twelfth or thirteenth century. It was seized by Edward I in 1296 and was visited by the future Edward II in 1303. This is one of the places where it is said that Lady MacDuff and her babes were murdered on the orders of Macbeth.

Dingwall Castle [NH 553589], Dingwall, Ross and Cromarty; slight remains of castle.
    William the Lion built a royal castle at Dingwall in the twelfth century, and it later passed to the Earls of Ross. Macbeth's father is said to have had a stronghold at Dingwall, and Macbeth to have been brought up here. Thorfinn the Mighty, the Norse Earl of Orkney, who was probably related to Macbeth, also had a residence at Dingwall

Doune Castle [NN 728011], near Doune, Stirlingshire; fine partly ruinous castle in a picturesque spot.
    Built by the Stewart Dukes of Albany but retained by the Crown on their forfeiture in 1425, and used by the widows of James III, James IV and James V. Visited by Mary, Queen of Scots, and another castle she is said to haunt. The property went to the Stewart Earls of Moray and the castle is now in the care of Historic Scotland and is open to the public (01786 841742).

Dumfries Castle [NX 975754], Dumfries; earthworks.
    Site of royal castle built by William the Lion in 1214. It was held by the English in 1298, then briefly by Robert the Bruce in 1306 after he stabbed Comyn, then by the English until 1314. Destroyed in 1357.

Doune Castle (M&R) – see previous column

Dundee Castle [NO 404302], Dundee; site of castle.

Held by the English, damaged by William Wallace, repaired by Edward I, but then destroyed by Robert the Bruce in 1312 and not rebuilt.

Dundonald Castle [NS 364345], near Troon, Ayrshire; fine ruinous castle in a prominent location.

Held by the Stewarts and used and remodelled by Robert II, who died here in 1390, and Robert II, who may have also died here in 1406. The property went to the Cochranes and the ruins are open to the public (01563 851489; www.dundonald castle.org.uk).

Edderton Castle [NH 716838], near Tain, Ross and Cromarty; site of castle.

Built by William the Lion in the twelfth century.

Elgin Castle [NJ 212628], Elgin, Moray; site of castle.

Royal castle, which was visited by Edward I in 1296 and again in 1303, but it was taken by the Scots five years later and not rebuilt. King Duncan is said to have died here in the eleventh century from wounds inflicted by Macbeth at a battle near Spynie.

Forfar Castle [NO 456507], Forfar, Angus; site of castle.

Used by Alexander II and William the Lion, and also associated with Malcolm Canmore and St Margaret. Held by the English and visited by Edward I in 1296, but was taken by the Scots, who slaughtered the garrison on Christmas Day 1298 and slighted the castle. It was rebuilt but seized again by the Scots in 1313. Abandoned by the 1330s.

Forres Castle [NJ 035588], Forres, Moray; site of castle.

Royal castle, dating from the twelfth or thirteenth centuries, but later passed to the Murrays or to the Dunbars of Westfield. This is believed to be where Dubh, King of Scots, was murdered in 966 by the keeper of the castle. His corpse was hidden in a deep pool, but the story goes that the sun would not shine on the spot until Dubh's body was found and given a decent burial.

Glasgow Castle [NS 602655], Glasgow; site of castle.

This was a royal castle in 1258, and was taken by William Wallace in 1296, although it was garrisoned by the English two years later. It passed to the Bishops of Glasgow.

Haddington Castle [NT 513738], Haddington, East Lothian; site of castle.

Built in the twelfth or thirteenth century, and the site is probably occupied by the County Buildings. It was visited by William the Lion and was the birthplace of Alexander II in 1268. The sixth Earl of Atholl was apparently murdered here in 1242.

Hunter's Hall [NT 494357], Galashiels, Borders; site of castle.

Used as a hunting lodge by the kings of Scots, and the site is occupied by housing.

Jedburgh Castle [NT 647202], Jedburgh, Borders; site of castle.

Dated from the twelfth century; Malcolm IV died here in 1165. Alexander II was married to Yolande de Dreux at the castle in

1285, although a ghostly apparition foretold of his impending death, which came true when he fell off cliffs at Kinghorn. The castle was held by the English from 1346 to 1409, when it was recaptured by the Scots and razed. A jail was built on the site of the castle, and is open to the public (01835 864750; www.scotborders.gov.uk/outabout/museums).

Kincardine Castle [NO 671751], near Fettercairn, Kincardineshire; slight remains of castle.

This was a strong royal castle, dating from the twelfth century and visited by William the Lion and Alexander II. John Balliol may have been forced to abdicate here by Edward I and he visited in 1296. Robert II stayed here in 1383, and then Mary, Queen of Scots, in 1562. The building was demolished in 1646.

Kinclaven Castle [NO 158377], near Blairgowrie, Perthshire; slight remains of castle.

Built by Alexander II in the 1230s on the site of an older stronghold said to have been used by Malcolm Canmore. Edward I stayed in 1296 although it was seized by William Wallace in the following year. It was captured by Edward III in 1335, then slighted again, and was still apparently in use in 1455.

Kindrochit Castle [NO 152913], near Braemar, Aberdeenshire; slight remains of castle.

Used by Robert II, who issued charters from here at the end of the fourteenth century. It was later held by the Drummonds and then by the Stewarts. The castle is said to have been destroyed by cannon when the inhabitants caught plague.

Kinghorn Castle [NT 269871], Kinghorn, Fife; site of castle.

Royal castle, which dated from the twelfth century. It was from near here that Alexander III fell from cliffs on his way to the castle to meet his young wife Yolande de Dreux in 1286. The property passed to the Lyons, who take the title Earl of Kinghorne from here.

Kingsbarns Castle [NO 599126], near Crail, Fife; site of castle.

Royal castle which had barns to store grain for Falkland Palace.

King's Haugh [NJ 363303], near Dufftown, Moray; site of castle.

Said to have been a residence of Malcolm Canmore.

Kirkcudbright Castle [NX 677508], Kirkcudbright, Galloway; site of castle.

May have been built by Malcolm IV after a rising in Galloway, although it is first mentioned in 1288. Edward I stayed here for ten days in 1300. The property passed to the Douglases.

Lanark Castle [NS 875435], Lanark; site of castle.

Used by the kings of Scots in the twelfth century, but occupied by the English during the Wars of Independence until taken by Robert the Bruce in 1310. It is believed that William Wallace massacred the garrison here, and slew Hazelrig, the English governor, after his wife, Marion Braidfute, had been killed by Hazelrig.

Lochleven Castle [NO 138018], Kinross; ruinous castle on island.

Royal castle from 1257 and stormed by William Wallace after being taken by the English, and it was besieged by the English in 1301. It was visited by Robert the Bruce, and then held against Edward Balliol in 1335. Lochleven passed to the Douglases and was later used as the prison for Mary, Queen of Scots, although she escaped in 1568. The castle can be visited in the summer from Kinross (07778 040483 (mobile)).

Lochmaben Castle [NY 088812], Lochmaben, Dumfriesshire; ruinous castle.

The castle was built by Edward I in 1298, but was besieged by the Scots in 1299 and 1301. It was seized by Robert the Bruce in 1306, went back to the English, but then was surrendered to the Scots in 1314. It was held by the English from 1333 to 1384 when it was captured by the Douglases. It was at Lochmaben that the army assembled which went on to defeat at Solway Moss in 1542, and Mary, Queen of Scots, attended a feast here in 1565. James VI captured the castle from the Maxwells in 1588. The castle is now very ruinous, but is in the care of Historic Scotland and the site can be visited.

Malcolm's Tower [NT 087873], Dunfermline, Fife; slight remains of castle.

This is believed to be the site of a castle of Malcolm Canmore, and where St Margaret, his wife, founded Dunfermline Abbey. It was at the tower that Maud, later wife of Henry I of England, was born.

Menmuir or **Manmure** [NO 534643], near Brechin, Angus; site of castle.
This was a royal palace or castle, and dated from the thirteenth century. It later passed to the Rollo family and then to the Lindsays.

Montrose Castle [NO 710568], Montrose, Angus; site of castle.
Royal castle, dating from the twelfth century. It was used by William the Lion and was visited by Edward I in 1296. It may have been where John Balliol abdicated the same year, was captured by William Wallace, and probably destroyed by Robert the Bruce around 1308. It was rebuilt, held by the English, recaptured by the Scots, and had been abandoned by the 1330s. Sir James Douglas may have set out for Granada from Montrose, to take the heart of Robert the Bruce on a crusade.

Palace an Righ [NN 717593], near Tummel Bridge, Perthshire; site of castle.
Site of a royal palace.

Peebles Castle [NT 249403], Peebles, Borders; site of castle.
Royal castle. This may be where Henry, Earl of Huntingdon, son of David I and father of kings Malcolm IV and William I the Lyon, died in 1152. William, Alexander II and Alexander III all stayed here. The castle was garrisoned by the English between 1301-02, and Edward I visited.

Perth Castle [NO 119238], Perth; site of castle.
Royal castle, which was washed away in 1210 along with the bridge. It was rebuilt then taken by Edward I in 1298. It was seized by Robert the Bruce in 1311 and the walls were demolished and the moat filled in. It was taken by Edward III and rebuilt, but was recaptured for the Scots in 1339, and was probably abandoned soon afterwards.

Rosneath Castle [NS 272823], near Rosneath, Dunbartonshire; site of castle.
Royal castle, dating from the twelfth century, but replaced by a later tower house and then mansion. The old castle is said to have been destroyed by William Wallace, and the lands passed to the Earls of Lennox.

Rotmell [NO 004470], near Dunkeld, Perthshire; site of castle.
Royal castle, finally demolished in 1810.

Roxburgh Castle [NT 713337], near Kelso, Borders; site of castle.
Formerly a strong courtyard fortress, and a royal castle, and was used by many of the monarchs. It was occupied by the

Roxburgh Castle 1918?

English, and Mary, sister of Robert the Bruce, was hung from a cage suspended from the walls in 1306. The castle was retaken by James Douglas in 1314, but was held by the English from the 1330s for many years. It was besieged several times by the Scots, including in 1417 and then in 1460 when James II was killed when the cannon he was standing beside exploded. The castle was stormed and demolished and little now remains. There was an important royal burgh near the castle, with a substantial church and many tenements, but these have gone. The ruins are in the grounds of Floors Castle.

Scrabster Castle [ND 107692], near Thurso, Caithness; slight remains of castle.
Held by the Bishops of Caithness, but then a royal castle, before passing to the Sinclairs. Harald Maddadson, Earl of Orkney, seized and destroyed a stronghold here in 1201, capturing the bishop and other lords. William the Lion brought the area under the control of the kings of Scots, and had Maddadson blinded and castrated.

Selkirk Castle [NT 470281], Selkirk, Borders; motte and bailey.
Royal castle in the twelfth and thirteenth centuries, and was used by William the Lion, Alexander II and Alexander III. Held by the English in 1302, taken by the Scots but then seized again by the English in 1311. It was then stormed by the Scots, demolished and not reused.

Tarbert Castle [NR 867687], Tarbert, Argyll; ruinous castle.
Royal castle, dating from the thirteenth century, but rebuilt down the centuries. Magnus Barelegs, King of Norway, had his longship taken across the isthmus here in 1098 to emphasise his possession of the Isles and of the peninsula of Kintyre. The

Tarbert Castle 1920?

castle was strengthened by Robert the Bruce, and it was used by James IV. It was later held by the Campbells, and it had been abandoned by the middle of the eighteenth century.

Thunderton House [NJ 215615], Elgin, Moray; altered tower house.
May incorporate part of a royal castle, dating from the fourteenth century, but was later held by the Sutherland Lord Duffus and by the Dunbars of Thunderton. Visited by Bonnie Prince Charlie and now a public house (01343 554921; www.thundertonhouse.co.uk).

Wigtown Castle [NX 437550], Wigtown, Galloway; site of castle.
Royal castle, dating from the thirteenth century, and probably built by Alexander III. Held by the English, but stormed by William Wallace in 1297, was then retaken by the English, and then finally demolished by the Bruces about 1310.

No. of castles/sites: 58
Rank: 16=/764

Ashiesteel House 1905? – see next column (Russell)

Russell

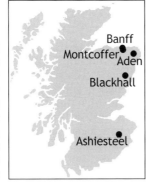

The name may be derived from 'rous', which means 'red', and refers to hair colour or to a ruddy complexion: 'rufus' means the same. The name is on record in Scotland from the twelfth century. The family held lands in the north-east of Scotland as well as in the Borders.

Ashiesteel House [NT 432351] is three miles west of Galashiels in the Borders, and the mansion incorporates a tower house dating from the seventeenth century. Ashiesteel was owned by the Russells, but was later home to Sir Walter Scott, who rented the property from William Scott, his uncle, and Scott wrote several of his works here.

Banff Castle [NJ 689642] is to the east side of Banff in Aberdeenshire, but little now remains of the castle except ditches and ramparts with a section of what has been a strong curtain wall. An Adam mansion was built within the walls in the eighteenth century. Owned by the Comyns and then by the Sharps, the property later passed to the Russells, who acquired Montcoffer.

Montcoffer House [NJ 685613] is two miles to the south of Banff, and is a mansion dating from 1670 but the building was remodelled in 1825 with the addition of two-storeyed bow-windows. The lands were a property of the Campbells, but passed by marriage to the Russells around the turn of the eighteenth century. They then acquired Aden, and Montcoffer was sold to the Duff Dukes of Fife in 1750. Montcoffer is still occupied.

Ten or so miles east of Peterhead, **Aden House** [NJ 981479] is now a ruinous shell, but it replaced an old castle. The present building dates from 1832, and was built by the Russells of Montcoffer after they had acquired the property from the Keiths. They sold Aden in 1937, and the mansion was said to be haunted by the ghost of one of the daughters of the owners. She is said to have run off with a servant lad, but then haunted one of the bedchambers, although what circumstances would have caused this are not known. It is said that the 'haunted' portion of the chamber was walled off. The grounds of the house are now a country park and are open to the public (01771 622807; www.aberdeen shire.gov.uk/heritage).

Blackhall Castle [NO 670961] was two miles west of Banchory also in Aberdeenshire, but there is nothing left of what was a strong castle and then a later mansion. The property was latterly held by the Russells and then by the Hays.

No. of castles/sites: 5
Rank: 240=/764
Xref: Russel

Rutherford

The name is territorial, and comes from the lands of Rutherford, which are three miles east of St Boswells in the Borders. There are two rather fanciful stories about how the family got its name: one has the progenitor of the family finding a little known ford at which one of the kings of Scots could cross the Tweed and was rewarded with the property; another have the English being massacred at the crossing and the calling it 'rue the ford'.

Rutherford [NT 643303] was held by the family of that name from the middle of the twelfth century or earlier. Sir Richard Rutherford was a favourite of Robert II and was ambassador to England in 1398. There may have been a castle or old house at Rutherford, although if there was its location has not been established. The lands had passed to the Stewarts of Traquair by the early sixteenth century, and then went to others.

Hunthill [NT 665191] is a mile to the south-east of Jedburgh also in the Borders, and there was a strong tower house, on the site of which is a nineteenth-century house. Owned by the Glendinnings, the property passed by marriage to the Rutherfords in the fifteenth century, and they built the tower. The family were made Lords Rutherford in 1661, and General Andrew Rutherford, the first Lord, was governor of Tangier in Morocco, although he was slain in 1664. The title is now extinct.

Eggerston Castle [NT 691115] was also near Jedburgh, although six miles to the south and east. It is just a site now, but it was held by the Rutherfords. Eggerston was seized by 'assured' Scots for the English in 1544, but the Rutherfords were one of the families who routed the English at Ancrum Moor the following year. Thomas Rutherford, the Black Laird of Eggerston, was one of those influential in defeating at the English at Carter's Bar in 1575 after a dispute had arisen between the Wardens of the Marches. The family were Royalists, and one of the lairds was badly wounded fighting against Cromwell at the Battle of Dunbar in 1650.

The family also owned:
Ashintully Castle [NO 101613], near Kirkmichael, Perthshire; L-plan tower house.
  Held by the Spaldings, before passing to the Rutherfords in 1750. It is said to be haunted by a Green Lady, and is still occupied. Holiday accommodation is available (01250 881237; www.ashintully.com).
Buck o' Bield [NX 581559], near Gatehouse of Fleet, Galloway; site of castle or house.
  Held by the Rutherfords from 1630 or before, and occupied by Samuel Rutherford, the Covenanting minister of Anwoth. The property passed to the Gordons.
Chatto [NT 770176], near Morebattle, Borders; site of castle or old house.
  Held by the Rutherfords from the fourteenth or early fifteenth century. Robert Rutherford of Chatto is said to have played a decisive part in winning the Battle of Otterburn for the Scots

in 1388. The property had passed to the Kerrs by the seventeenth century.

Cherrytrees [NT 810293], near Town Yetholm, Borders; castle or old house replaced by mansion.

Held by the Rutherfords in 1523 but had passed to the Taits by 1605, and then went to the Kerrs the same century.

Fairnilee [NT 458327], near Galashiels, Borders; altered tower house.

Held by the Kerrs of Linton, but passed to the Rutherfords. Alison Rutherford, later married to Patrick Cockburn, wrote 'The Flowers of the Forest' here, which commemorates the

Fairnilee (M&R)

disastrous Battle of Flodden in 1513. There was a large mansion but this has been demolished.

Fairnington House [NT 646280], near Jedburgh, Borders; mansion incorporating tower house.

Held by the Burnets, by the Hepburn Earls of Bothwell and by the Stewarts, but passed to the Rutherfords in 1647. Still occupied.

Glendevon Castle [NN 976055], near Dollar, Clackmannan; altered Z-plan tower house.

Held by the Douglas Earls of Douglas and by the Crawfords before passing to the Rutherfords in the eighteenth century. It was used as a farmhouse.

Hundalee Tower [NT 646187], near Jedburgh, Borders; site of tower house.

Held by the Rutherfords.

Lauriston Castle [NT 204762], Edinburgh; fine castle and mansion.

Held by the Napiers and by several other families including by the Rutherfords. The castle is now owned by the city of Edinburgh and stands in a public park and is open to the public (0131 336 2060; www.cac.org.uk).

Migvie Castle [NJ 437066], near Ballater, Aberdeenshire; slight remains of castle.

Held by the Rutherfords of Tarland, and then by the Gordon Earl of Huntly.

Purves Hall or **(Nether) Tofts** [NT 761447], near Greenlaw, Borders; mansion incorporating tower house.

Held by the Furdes, then by the Rutherfords, then by the Homes and then by the Belshes in 1610, then by the Purves family, who changed the name from Tofts to Purves Hall. Said to be haunted by a Green Lady and still occupied; recently put up for sale.

No. of castles/sites: 15
Rank: 94=/764

Ruthven

The name is territorial and comes from the lands of Ruthven (pronounced 'Rooven'), which are a couple of miles to the north-west of Perth, and are now known as Huntingtower. The family were descended from Thor son of Swein, who held lands in Tranent, and then his son Swan acquired further property in Perthshire around the end of the twelfth century.

Huntingtower or **Ruthven Castle** [NO 083252] is a fine old castle, the earliest part of which is a keep or tower of the fifteenth century. A new tower house was built nearby in the next century, and then a joining block was added. There was a courtyard and other buildings, although these have gone; but some chambers have painted walls and ceilings. The Ruthvens fought against the English during the Wars of Independence, and they were made Sheriffs of Perth in 1313, and then Lords Ruthven in 1488. William, Master of Ruthven, was killed at Flodden in 1513. Mary, Queen of Scots, visited the castle in 1565 while on honeymoon with Darnley, although Patrick, third Lord, took part in the murder of Rizzio, Mary's secretary. William, fourth Lord, was made Earl of Gowrie in 1581, and the following year kidnapped the young James VI in the 'Raid of Ruthven', and held him in Huntingtower for a year. James VI escaped during a hunting trip and the Earl was beheaded in 1585.

The space between the battlements of the two towers of Huntingtower is known as 'The Maiden's Leap'. Dorothy, daughter of the first Earl of Gowrie, is said to have jumped from one tower to the next. While visiting her lover, John Wemyss of Pittencrieff, in his chamber, and about to be discovered by her mother, she leapt to the other tower and returned to her own bed before being discovered. She eloped with her lover the following night.

Huntingtower Castle (RWB)

John Ruthven, third Earl of Gowrie and his brother, Alexander, Master of Ruthven, were murdered at Gowrie House in Perth in 1600 by James VI and his followers. These events became known as the 'Gowrie Conspiracy', and it may have been a plot to murder or kidnap James VI. The Ruthvens were forfeited, their lands seized, and their name was proscribed. The castle was renamed Huntingtower, and was given to the Murrays who sold it to the Mercers in 1805. It was used to house workers in the calico printing industry. A new earldom of Gowrie was created in 1945, and the second Earl apparently lives in London in England. The castle is said to be haunted by a Green Lady, sometimes known as My Lady Greensleeves. Her appearance is said to foretell death, but she has also apparently been helpful to a child near death and a man being robbed. Huntingtower is in the care of Historic Scotland and is open to the public (01738 627231).

Dirleton Castle [NT 518840] is a magnificent ruinous castle perched on a rock two or so miles west of North Berwick in East Lothian. The oldest part is a drum tower with two vaulted polygonal chambers from the thirteenth century, and other towers and ranges were

Dirleton Castle (RWB)

added in the following years. The property was held by the Congiltons and then by the Vaux family, who built the first castle. It sustained a hard siege in 1298, and passed to the Halyburtons and then to the Ruthvens by marriage to the heiress Janet Halyburton in the sixteenth century. The Ruthvens remodelled the buildings, but the property was forfeited after the Gowrie Conspiracy in 1600 and was given to the Erskines of Gogar and then passed to others. The castle was seized by Cromwell's forces in 1650, but is now in the care of Historic Scotland and there are fine gardens (01620 850330).

The Ruthvens also owned:
Ballindean [NO 268299], near Dundee; castle replaced by mansion. Held by the Fotheringhams, but had passed to the Ruthvens by the middle of the sixteenth century. The name was proscribed after the Gowrie Conspiracy, but an Act of Parliament in 1641 allowed this branch of the family to use their family name again as they had not been involved in the plot. The property passed to the Trotters.
Carse Gray [NO 464540], near Forfar, Angus; mansion incorporating tower house. Held by the Rynd family, but was bought by the Ruthvens in

1641. Carse was acquired by the Grays in 1741 and they added the 'Gray' to the name. It is apparently held by the Gray-Cheapes.
Gowrie House [NO 120235], Perth; site of fine fortified town house. Held by the Countess of Huntly, but was sold to the Ruthven Earls of Gowrie, and this was the scene of the Gowrie Conspiracy in 1600. The property passed to the Hay Earls of Kinnoul and was later used as a barracks before being demolished in 1805. The site is occupied by the County Buildings.
Rohallion Castle [NO 039401], near Dunkeld, Perthshire; Z-plan tower house.
    Held by the Ruthvens, and William, first Earl of Gowrie, sheltered here after involvement in the Raid of Ruthven in 1582. He did not escape for long and had his head snuck off three years later.
Scone Palace [NO 114267], near Perth; large mansion on site of abbey and palace.
    Held by the Ruthvens from 1580, but they were forfeited in 1600 and the property went to the Murrays, whose descendants the Earls of Mansfield and Viscounts Stormont built the palace and still own the property. The palace is open to the public from April to October (01738 552300; www.scone-palace.co.uk).
Trochrie Castle [NN 978402], Dunkeld, Perthshire; slight remains of Z-plan tower house.
    Held by the Ruthvens, and the tower was torched in 1545.

No. of castles/sites: 8
Rank: 160=/764

Rynd

The name comes from the parish of the same name, which is in Perthshire. The family is on record in Scotland from the fourteenth century.

Carse [NO 464540], later **Carse Gray**, is two or so miles north of Forfar in Angus, and the present house incorporates an altered T-plan tower house, which dates from the seventeenth century. The family were involved in feuding between the Ogilvies, the Guthries and others of their neighbours. The property was sold to the Ruthvens in 1641 then later went to the Grays, whose descendants, now the Gray-Cheapes, still apparently own Carse Grey.

Broxmouth House [NT 696766] is a mile or so southeast of Dunbar in East Lothian, but the present mansion dates from the end of the eighteenth century; there was an earlier house or castle on the site. The lands appear to have been held by the Grays and then by the Rynds in 1470, but Broxmouth went to the Homes and then to the Kerr Dukes of Roxburgh, one of whose titles is Viscount Broxmouth. The house is still occupied.

No. of castles/sites: 2
Rank: 396=/764
Xrefs: Rhind; Rind

Sanderson

The name comes from the diminutive for Alexander, 'Sandy', hence 'Sandy's son' or Sanderson, Sandison or Sandeson. The surname is on record from the first half of the fifteenth century.

The lands of **Balvie** [NS 535752] lie one mile west and north of Milngavie to the north of Glasgow, and there was a castle here. This was replaced by a mansion, which was itself demolished in the twentieth century so that Douglas Academy could be built. The lands were held by several families, being sold to the Colquhouns of Luss around 1600 and then passing to the Sandersons. From them, the property went to the Campbells and then to others.

No. of castles/sites: 1
Rank: 537=/764
Xrefs: Sandison; Sandeson

Sandilands

The name is territorial and comes from the lands of Sandilands, which are three or so miles south of Lanark by the Douglas Water, and the family are on record from the fourteenth century.

Sandilands [NS 892385] was held by the Douglases, but was given to the Sandilands in the 1330s after they had distinguished themselves in the Wars of Independence. The family acquired Calder by marriage, but it is not clear if they had a castle or seat at Sandilands itself.

Calder House [NT 073673] is a couple of miles east of Livingston in West Lothian. Calder was also a property of the Douglas family, but passed by marriage to the Sandilands in the fourteenth century. John Sandilands of Calder and his uncle were assassinated by the Douglases because the Sandilands had supported James II in the 1450s. Sir James Sandilands was Preceptor of the powerful religious-military Order of the Knights of St John, whose headquarters were at the Preceptory of Torphichen, and after the Reformation Sandilands was made Lord Torphichen, acquiring much of their lands. John Knox held a service at Calder in 1556 as Sir James was one of his friends. James, seventh Lord, fought against the Jacobites at the Battle of Sheriffmuir in 1715. The family have a burial vault at Mid Calder Parish Church [NT 074673], and the Sandilands Lords Torphichen still apparently own the property.

Torphichen Preceptory [NS 972727], four miles south and west of Linlithgow also in West Lothian, was the main seat of the Knights Hospitallers from the twelfth century. William Wallace held a convention of barons here in 1298, as did Edward I after winning the Battle of Falkirk against Wallace the same year. The last Preceptor of the Order in Scotland was Sir James Sandilands, and the property was made into a temporal

Torphichen Preceptory (M&R)

lordship for him in 1564. The Sandilands family moved to Calder House, and the Preceptory was probably abandoned as a residence. The crossing and the transepts of the church survive, and are open to the public some days (01506 653475/0131 668 8800).

The Sandilands also owned:
Alderstone House [NT 044662], near Livingstone, West Lothian; altered tower house.
    Held by the Kinlochs, but went to the Sandilands Lord Torphichen in 1656, who sold it to John Mitchell of Todhaugh in 1692. Alderstone passed to the Bruces and then to the Whitelaws and is used as company offices.
Bold [NT 374374], near Innerleithen, Borders; site of tower house.
    Held by the Sandilands from the twelfth century, but passed to the Stewarts of Traquair and then to the Cranstouns.
Countesswells [NJ 871043], near Aberdeen; castle replaced by mansion.
    Held by the Sandilands, and John Sandilands of Countesswells was Provost of Aberdeen in the seventeenth century. Countesswells passed to the Burnetts, and then to the Gamills.
Couston Castle [NS 955712], near Bathgate, West Lothian; slight remains of castle.
    Held by the Hamiltons and then by the Sandilands.
Craibstone House [NJ 873107], near Dyce, Aberdeenshire; mansion on site of older house or castle.
    Held by the Sandilands from 1606 until sold to the Farquharsons of Invercauld. The Sandilands of Lagganmore are descended from this family, and apparently now live near Kilninver in Argyll.
Cruivie Castle [NO 419229], near Balmullo, Fife; large ruinous castle.
    Held by the Kinlochs, but passed by marriage to the Sandilands of Calder around 1490, before going to the Ramsays and then to the Carnegies of Colluthie.
Murieston Castle [NT 050636], near West Calder, West Lothian; ruinous tower house.
    Held by the Sandilands, then by the Cochranes and possibly by the Williamsons, and then by the Steels.
Newark Castle [NO 518012], near Elie, Fife; ruinous castle.
    Held by the Kinloch family, but passed to Sandilands of Cruivie. The Sandilands family became bankrupt and sold the castle to the Covenanter General Sir David Leslie in 1649. Newark later passed to the Anstruthers and then to the Bairds of Elie, and is said to be haunted by a Green Lady. The castle can be viewed from the exterior (www.inverie.com).
Niddrie Marischal [NT 295715], Edinburgh; site of castle and mansion.
    Held by the Niddries, by the Heriots and by the Wauchopes, but passed to the Sandilands and then returned by marriage to Wauchopes in 1608. The mansion was occupied to the 1930s, but was then demolished and a housing estate built.
Northbar or **Oldbar** [NS 481693], near Renfrew; castle replaced by mansion.
    The lands were held by the Knights Templars and by the Knights of St John, but came into the possession of the Sandilands, before going to the Stewart Earls of Lennox and then to others. Nothing remains of the castle and it was replaced by Northbar House in about 1742.
Pitlochie Castle [NO 175095], near Auchtermuchty, Fife; site of castle.
    Held by the Kinlochs and by the Lundies, but was also owned by the Sandilands.
Pitteadie Castle [NT 257891], near Burntisland, Fife; ruinous castle.
    Held by the Valance family, but passed to the Sinclairs and then to the Sandilands family, and then to the Boswells of Balmuto and then to the Calderwoods in 1671.

No. of castles/sites: 15
Rank: 94=/764

Schivas

The name is territorial and comes from the lands of Schivas, which are five or so miles north-west of Ellon in Aberdeenshire. The name is on record from the end of the fourteenth century.
    House of Schivas [NJ 898368] is a fine altered L-plan tower house with a large round tower, and dates from the sixteenth century. The property was held by the Schivas family, but passed to the Lipps and then to the Maitlands in the fifteenth century, then to the Gordons, to the Grays and to the Gordon Earls of Aberdeen. House of Schivas was used as a farmhouse, was restored after a fire in 1900 and is still occupied.
    Kemback House [NO 418155] is three or so miles east of Cupar in Fife, and the present building dates from the eighteenth century, but replaced an earlier house or castle. Kemback was held by the Schivas family in the sixteenth and seventeenth centuries, but then passed to the Makgills, who held Kemback until 1906. Kemback House, Dura Den and Dairsie Bridge are said to be haunted by a White Lady. She is reputed to be the wife of one of the lairds, who was a Covenanter, and when she would not reveal his whereabouts the poor woman was hanged from Dairsie Bridge. A chamber in Kemback House is apparently known as the White Lady's Room.

No. of castles/sites: 2
Rank: 396=/764
Xrefs: Shivas; Chivas

Newark Castle (M&R) – see previous column (Sandilands)

Scott

Scott comes from the name given to the Irish who attacked the shores of Scotland and England, and the name is said to mean 'pirate'. The name first comes on record in the first quarter of the twelfth century, and the Scotts went on to be one of the most powerful clans on the Border, as well as holding property in Fife and elsewhere.

Buccleuch or **Rankilburn Castle** [NT 328143] stood a few miles east of Ettrick in the Borders, and dated from the sixteenth century. The castle was built on the site of an older stronghold but there are no remains of the castle or its predecessor. The Scotts held the property from the thirteenth century, and supported Robert the Bruce during the Wars of Independence. Sir Michael Scott of Buccleuch fought at the Battle of Halidon Hill in 1333, and was killed at the Battle of Durham thirteen years later. Walter Scott of Buccleuch fought at Flodden in 1513, Ancrum Moor in 1545 and Pinkie in 1547, and in 1526 he had tried to rescue the young James V from the Earl of Angus. The castle was burnt in 1544 by the English, and the Scotts had a bitter feud with the Kerrs of Cessford after slaying several of them in 1526; Scott was murdered by the Kerrs in the High Street of Edinburgh in 1552. A later Walter Scott of Buccleuch rescued 'Kinmont' Willie Armstrong from Carlisle Castle in 1596, the events told in the old ballad 'Kinmont Willie'. Scott went to the continent and fought the Spanish and Dutch in the service of the Prince of Orange. The Lordship of Buccleuch was created for him in 1606, and Walter, second Lord, was made Earl in 1612. A Dukedom was created for James, Duke of Monmouth, on his marriage to Anna, Countess of Buccleuch, in 1663. Monmouth was executed for leading a rebellion against James VII in 1685; Anna was Duchess in her own right and died in 1732.

Branxholme Castle [NT 464116], three miles south-west of Hawick also in the Borders, is an altered tower house, rising to five storeys and dating from the sixteenth century. The old tower was incorporated into a mansion built in 1790 with later work. The lands came to the Scotts in 1420, and the castle was burned by the English in 1532 and then held against them fifteen years later. It was slighted by the Scotts, but this was done more thoroughly by the English in 1570 by blowing up the castle with gunpowder. As mentioned above, the Scotts were eventually made Dukes of Buccleuch, but they also became Dukes of Queensberry, which they obtained from the Douglases, along with Drumlanrig Castle. Branxholme Castle was remodelled by William Burn for Walter, fifth Duke, in 1837. *The Lay of Last Minstrel*, written by Sir Walter Scott, takes place at Branxholme, and the Dukes of Buccleuch still apparently own the property.

Branxholme Castle (M&R)

Kirkhope Tower [NT 379250] is a mile north-west of Ettrick Bridge in the Borders, and is a restored sixteenth-century tower house, which rises to four

Kirkhope Tower (M&R)

storeys and an attic. It was long held by the Scotts, although it was torched by the Armstrongs in 1543. This was the childhood home of the famous Border reiver 'Auld Wat', Walter Scott of Harden. He was one of those, along with Walter Scott of Buccleuch, who rescued Kinmont Willie from Carlisle Castle in 1596. Some twenty years before, he married Mary or Marion Scott of Dryhope, known as the 'Flower of Yarrow'. She is the heroine of another of the Border Ballads 'The Dowie Dens of Yarrow', which tells of the slaughter of her lover and seven of her brothers.

Bowhill [NT 426278] is a large and rambling mansion, a few miles west of Selkirk again in the Borders, and dates from the eighteenth century although it may stand on the site of a castle or old house. Bowhill is held by the Dukes of Buccleuch, and has fine collections of paintings and furniture, including the Duke of

Bowhill 1905?

Monmouth's saddle and his execution shirt. Newark Castle is in the grounds, and the house is open to the public (01750 22204; www.boughtonhouse.org.uk).

Three miles north and west of Thornhill in Dumfriesshire is **Drumlanrig Castle** [NX 851992], a magnificent courtyard mansion, dating from the

Drumlanrig Castle (M&R)

seventeenth century although with older work. There are higher rectangular towers at the corners, which have pepper-pot turrets. The lands were a property of the Douglases for generations, but passed to the Scotts of Buccleuch in 1810, and the family are also now Dukes of Queensberry. There is a fine collection of pictures, and a Leonardo de Vinci which was stolen from here was found in 2007. The castle is said to be haunted by at least three ghosts: Lady Anne Douglas, dressed in white, with a fan in one hands and her head under her arm; the ghost of a monkey or a similar creature; and the apparition of a girl in a flowing dress. The property is still owned by the Montagu-Douglas-Scott Dukes of Buccleuch and Queensberry, and other titles they hold are Marquess of Dumfriesshire, and Earls of Drumlanrig, Buccleuch, Sanquhar and Dalkeith, and Viscounts Nith, Torthorwald and Ross, and more. The castle is open to the public (01848 331555; www.drumlanrig.com).

Dalkeith House [NT 333679], to the north west of the burgh of Dalkeith in Midlothian, is a U-plan classical mansion which incorporates work from an old castle. The property was also long a property of the Douglases,

and had a long and eventful history, before coming to the Scotts of Buccleuch in 1642. Anna, Duchess of Buccleuch, stayed here and had the house remodelled. Bonnie Prince Charlie stayed here for two nights in 1745, and the house became one of the main seats of the Dukes of Buccleuch and Queensberry until 1885. The family had a burial vault, the Buccleuch Aisle, in St Nicholas Buccleuch Parish Church [NT 330670] in Dalkeith; the church is open to the public (www.stnicholasbuccleuch.org.uk). Dalkeith Palace is now used for students from colleges of Wisconsin in the USA, and is said to be haunted by a Green Lady. The grounds are a country park and are open to the public (0131 654 1666; www.dalkeith countrypark.com).

Balwearie Castle [NT 251903] is now ruinous and it is located two or so miles south and west of Kirkcaldy in Fife. Balwearie passed by marriage to the Scotts in the thirteenth century, although the present ruins date from 200 years later. Balwearie may have been the home of Sir Michael Scott, thought to have been born at Aikwood in the Borders, who was a scholar and studied at Oxford, Toledo and Padua, and is sometimes known as 'the Wizard' because of his reputed supernatural powers. He is said to have died about 1250, and is also associated with Glenluce Abbey. A later Michael, or perhaps the same, was a member of the party that went to Norway to bring Princess Margaret, the Maid of Norway, home after the death of Alexander III in 1286. Sir Andrew Scott of Balwearie was killed when the Scots stormed and seized Berwick in 1355, and Sir William, a later lord, was captured after the Battle of Flodden in 1513; while another Sir William was wounded fighting for Mary, Queen of Scots, at Langside in 1568. Thomas Scott of Balwearie, Justice Clerk, died in 1539, and his apparition, with a company of devils, is said to have appeared to James V at Linlithgow on the night of his death; Scott told the king that he was damned for serving him. The Scotts held the property until the end of the seventeenth century, when it passed to the Melville Earls of Melville. Balwearie has been suggested as the site of the bloody events described in the old ballad 'Lamkin'. The mason who built the castle was not paid the agreed fee and took his revenge by murdering the son and wife of the house. The mason and the nurse, his accomplice, were subsequently executed.

Scotstarvit Tower [NO 370113] is a fine and well preserved L-plan tower house, which rises to six storeys and a garret, and stands in the policies of Hill of Tarvit, two miles south of Cupar in Fife. Scotstarvit was held by the Inglis family, but passed to the Scotts in 1611. Sir John Scott of Scotstarvit was an eminent historian and was a Lord of Session as Lord Scotstarvit in 1632. He helped with Blaeu's *Atlas Novus* maps of Scotland and wrote *The Staggering State of Scots Statesmen*, as well as other works. The property later went to the Gourlays of Craigrothie and to others, before going to The National Trust for Scotland. The tower is in the care of Historic Scotland and the key is available from Hill of Tarvit (01334 653127).

Abbotsford [NT 508343] is a fine castellated mansion, dating from the beginning of the nineteenth century and was home to the famous writer, statesman, antiquarian and historian Sir Walter Scott, author of *Ivanhoe*, the *Waverley* novels, and a collector of ballads. The mansion lies two miles west of Melrose in the Borders, and was built by Scott to house his impressive collections of armour and weapons, as well as Rob Roy MacGregor's gun, a crucifix of Mary, Queen of Scots, Claverhouse's pistol and the Marquis of Montrose's sword. Sir Walter got into debt and worked increasingly hard to try to pay this off, and his health suffered and he died in 1832. His ghost is said to haunt the building, especially the dining room. Abbotsford is open to the public (01896 752043; www.scotts abbotsford.co.uk). Scott is buried in Dryburgh Abbey, his tomb marked by a pink granite monument; the ruins of the abbey are in the care of Historic Scotland and are open to the public (01835 822381).

The Scotts also held:

Aikwood Tower [NT 420260], near Selkirk, Borders; restored tower house.

Held by the Scotts of Harden in the seventeenth century, but said to have been the residence of Master Michael Scott in the

Aikwood Tower (M&R)

thirteenth century. The tower became ruinous, but has been restored.

Allanmouth or **Allanhaugh Tower** [NT 455102], near Hawick, Borders; slight remains of tower house.

Held by the Scotts and in ruins by 1663.

Ancrum or **Ancram House** [NT 625245], near Jedburgh, Borders; mansion on site of castle.

Held by the Kerrs, who were made Earls of Ancram in 1633, but passed to the Scotts. The Battle of Ancrum Moor was fought nearby in 1545. The mansion was demolished in 1970.

Ardross Castle [NO 509006], near Elie, Fife; slight remains of castle.

Held by the Dishington family, but sold to the Scotts of Elie in 1607, and then to the Anstruthers towards the end of that century.

Ashiesteel House [NT 432351], near Galashiels, Borders; mansion incorporating tower house.

Held by the Russells, but was the home of Sir Walter Scott from 1804-12. It was here that he wrote *The Lay of the Last Minstrel*, *The Lady of the Lake*, *Marmion*, and part of the *Waverley* novels.

Balcomie Castle [NO 626099], near Crail, Fife; L-plan tower house.

Held by several families including by the Scotts of Scotstarvit, and now used as a farmhouse.

Bavelaw Castle [NT 168628], near Balerno, Edinburgh; L-plan tower house.

Held by the Braids and by others, but passed to the Scotts of Harperigg in 1628, and then became ruinous. Restored and reoccupied.

Benholm Castle [NO 804705], near Inverbervie, Kincardineshire; ruinous castle.

Held by the Lundies, by the Ogilvies and by the Keith Earls Marischal, but bought by the Scotts in 1659, who added the mansion. The castle was used as a hospital by Polish troops during World War II and became ruinous. Said to be haunted.

Bogle Walls, Enzieholm [NY 292912], near Langholm, Borders; site of castle.

Held by the Grahams, by the Beatties, then by the Scotts in the eighteenth century.

Broadhaugh [NT 449093], near Hawick, Borders; site of tower house.

Held by the Scotts of Allanhaugh.

Brotherton Castle [NO 803676], near Laurencekirk, Kincardineshire; mansion on site of castle.

Held by the Brotherton family, but passed to the Scotts of Logie in the seventeenth century, who still held it into the twentieth century. Brotherton was abandoned as a residence in 1949, and now houses Lathallan School.

Brugh [NT 467058], near Hawick, Borders; site of tower house.

Held by the Scotts of Allanhaugh in 1560, but had passed to the Elliots by 1595, and then became part of the Buccleuch lands in 1632.

Burnhead Tower [NT 514166], near Hawick, Borders; tower house.

Held by the Scotts who were in possession of the lands from the fifteenth century. The tower and house are occupied, and the Scotts of Burnhead now apparently live in London in England.

Cairneyflappet or **Strathmiglo Castle** [NO 220102], near Auchtermuchty, Fife; site of castle.

Held by the Scotts of Balwearie in the sixteenth century, and the laird built or rebuilt the castle so he could entertain James V. It is said to have been rather quickly and poorly built, and 'Cairneyflappet' was a nickname given to it by James V. The town hall steeple was built from the remains, and the lands passed to the Balfours of Burleigh about 1600 and then to the Skenes of Hallyards. The castle is said to have had a brownie, which is reputed to have stolen food from the stores. Strathmiglo Collegiate Church [NO 216103] was founded by Sir William Scott in 1528 in an existing church. The old church has gone and the present building dates from 1785 and later.

Caroline Park House or **Royston House** [NT 227773], Granton, Edinburgh; mansion incorporating tower house.

Held by the Logans, by the Mackenzies of Tarbat and then by the Campbell Dukes of Argyll before coming to the Scott Dukes of Buccleuch. The house is said to be haunted by a Green Lady, and a ghostly cannon ball is also said to have been witnessed several times smashing through the window of the Aurora Room. Still occupied.

Cash Tower [NO 222099], near Auchtermuchty, Fife; site of tower.

Held by the Scotts in 1548.

Cessnock Castle [NS 511355], near Galston, Ayrshire; castle and mansion.

Held by the Campbells, then passed to the Dicks, to the Wallaces, to the Scotts and then to the De Fresnes in 1946. Still occupied.

Craighall [NO 175480], near Blairgowrie, Perthshire; mansion incorporating tower house.

Held by the Scotts of Balwearie, but passed to the Rattrays at the beginning of the sixteenth century, and they still apparently own it. Sir Walter Scott visited the castle in 1793, and used it in *Waverley*, calling it Tullyveolain Castle. Accommodation is available (01250 874749; www.craighall.co.uk).

Crumhaugh Tower [NT 485138], near Hawick, Borders; very ruinous tower house.

Held by the Scotts of Goldielands and Crumhaugh in the seventeenth and eighteenth centuries.

Curriehill Castle [NT 165678], near Balerno, Edinburgh; site of castle.

Held by the Skenes, by the Johnstones and by the Andersons, before coming to the Scotts of Malleny and then went to the Marshall Lord Curriehill.

Dairsie Castle [NO 414160], near Cupar, Fife; restored Z-plan tower house.

Held by the Learmonths and by the Spottiswoodes, but later passed to the Morrisons and then to the Scotts of Scotstarvit. The castle was very ruinous but has been rebuilt and restored.

Dalgleish Tower [NT 260083], near Eskdalemuir, Borders; site of tower house.

Held by the Dalgleish family until 1630 when Dalgleish passed to the Scotts of Buccleuch. The tower had been destroyed by the English in 1547.

Dean Castle [NS 437394], near Kilmarnock, Ayrshire; fine restored castle.

Long held by the Boyds, but sold in the eighteenth century to the Cunningham Earls of Glencairn and then to the Scotts of Balcomie and then to the Howards. Later given to the people of Kilmarnock, and stands in a public park and is open to the public (01563 522702; www.deancastle.com).

Drumlanrig's Tower [NT 502144], Hawick, Borders; L-plan tower house.

Held by the Douglases of Drumlanrig, and was the only building left unburnt after the English torched the burgh in 1570. It was later occupied by Anna, Duchess of Buccleuch, wife of the executed Duke of Monmouth; and was then used as a prison and then a hotel. It now houses a museum (01450 373457; www.scotborders.gov.uk/outabout/museums).

Dryburgh Abbey [NT 591317], near Melrose, Borders; ruinous remains of abbey and later residence.

Held by the Erskines after the Reformation, but passed to the Scotts of Ancrum. Sir Walter Scott is buried in the abbey, and the ruins are in the care of Historic Scotland and are open to the public (01835 822381).

Dryhope Tower [NT 267247], near Cappercleuch, Borders; ruinous tower house.

Held by the Scotts, and Dryhope was the home of Mary (or

Dryhope Tower (M&R)

Marion) Scott, the 'Flower of Yarrow'. The ballad the 'Dowie Dens of Yarrow' records the bloody events associated with her suitors; she married Walter 'Auld Wat' Scott of Harden in 1576. The tower was slighted in 1592, but was rebuilt by 1613.

Dunninald Castle [NO 704543], near Montrose, Angus; mansion on site of older house.

Held by the Grays and by the Scotts in the eighteenth century, but later passed to the Arklays. The castle is open to the public (01674 674842; www.dunninald.com).

Eckford Tower [NT 709261], near Kelso, Borders; site of tower house.

Held by the Burrells but passed to the Scotts in the fifteenth century, and was torched by the English in 1554 and in 1570.

Eldinhope Tower [NT 305238], near Cappercleuch, Borders; slight remains of tower house.

Held by the Scotts of Howpaslie, and then by the Scotts of Branxholme, later Earls of Buccleuch.

Elie House [NO 496008], Elie, Fife; mansion incorporating old work.

Held by the Anstruthers but had passed to the Scotts by the seventeenth century, then later went to the Bairds. Used as a convent.

Enoch Castle [NS 879009], near Thornhill, Dumfriesshire; site of castle.

Held by the Menzies family, then by the Douglas Dukes of Queensberry, then in 1803 by the Scott Dukes of Buccleuch.

Ettrick House [NT 259144], near Selkirk, Borders; site of castle.

Held by the Scotts.

Gamescleuch Tower [NT 284147], near Selkirk, Borders; slight remains of tower house.

Held by the Scotts of Tushielaw until 1530, then Gamescleuch passed to the Scotts of Thirlestane. The tower was built for Simon Scott at the end of the sixteenth century, but is said to have never been occupied as his step-mother poisoned him on the eve of his marriage.

Goldielands Tower [NT 478128], near Hawick, Borders; ruinous tower house.

Held by the Scotts in 1446, and Scott of Goldielands was ordered to demolish Dryhope Tower in 1592. Walter Scott of Goldielands was one of the leaders of the party that helped to rescue Kinmont Willie from Carlisle Castle in 1596, as recounted in the old ballad, and his burial marker is now in the Hawick Museum. The last laird of Goldielands was hanged from his own gates for treason.

Grangemuir [NO 539040], near Pittenweem, Fife; mansion on site of castle.

Held by the Scotts in the sixteenth century, then by the Bruces and by the Wallaces. The older building was said to be haunted by the ghost of a pretty young woman who was murdered by one of her admirers.

Hallyards [NT 216375], near Peebles, Borders; mansion incorporating work from a tower house.

Held by the Scotts of Hundleshope in 1647, and then by the historian Professor Adam Ferguson, and was visited by Sir Walter Scott in 1797.

Harden [NT 449149], near Hawick, Borders; mansion incorporating tower house.

Held by the Homes but passed to the Scotts in 1501. One of the family was Auld Wat of Harden, a Border reiver, who married Marion or Mary Scott, the 'Flower of Yarrow'. The family moved to Mertoun in the eighteenth century, but the house was later restored and reoccupied by the Home Lord Polwarth.

Hassendean Castle [NT 547203], near Hawick, Borders; site of tower house.

Held by the Scotts. Sir Alexander Scott of Hassendean was killed at the Battle of Flodden in 1513.

Hermitage Castle [NY 494960], near Newcastleton, Borders; impressive ruinous castle.

Held by several families, including by the Douglases and by the Hepburn Earls of Bothwell, then by the Scotts of Buccleuch. The castle is now in the care of Historic Scotland and is open to the public from April to September (01387 376222).

Hirendean Castle [NT 298512], near Penicuik, Midlothian; slight remains of tower house.

Held by the Kerrs after the Reformation, and then possibly by the Scotts.

Horsleyhill [NT 532193], near Hawick, Borders; site of tower house.

Probably held by the Scotts.

Humbie Old Place [NT 467627], near Pathhead, East Lothian; mansion on site of castle or old house.

Held by the Hepburns but passed by marriage to the Scotts,

who were Lords Polwarth from 1835. The gardens are occasionally open to the public (www.gardensofscotland.org).

Hundleshope [NT 230364], near Peebles, Borders; site of castle or old house.

Held by the Turnbulls as well as by the Murrays, by the Scotts and by the Campbells.

Inveresk Lodge [NT 348716], near Musselburgh, East Lothian; L-plan house.

Held by the Maitlands of Thirlestane after the Reformation and then bought by the Scotts of Buccleuch in 1709, then went to others. The gardens are in the care of The National Trust for Scotland and are open to the public (01721 722502; www.nts.org.uk).

Isle of May [NT 655995], near Anstruther, Firth of Forth; ruinous priory and later dwelling.

Held by several families after the Reformation, including by the Scotts of Balcomie and by the Scotts of Scotstarvit. The island can be visited (01333 310103/01333 451152).

Killernie Castle [NT 032924], near Cowdenbeath, Fife; slight remains of tower house.

Held by the Colvilles of Easter Wemyss, by the Duries and then by the Scotts of Balwearie.

Kirkurd [NT 139446], near Romannobridge, Borders; site of tower house.

Held by the Orde family, and then by the Scotts from the middle of the fifteenth century. Walter Scott of Kirkurd was rewarded by James II with large grants of land for his loyalty at the Battle of Arkinholm in 1455. This branch of the family eventually became Dukes of Buccleuch.

Lessudden House [NT 595306], near Melrose, Borders; altered tower house.

Held by the Scotts of Lessudden. The family were persecuted for being Quakers, and were fined and their children taken from them. Sir Walter Scott was descended from the family, and the house is still occupied.

Lugton [NT 327677], near Dalkeith, Midlothian; site of castle.

Held by the Douglases and then by the Scotts of Buccleuch from 1693.

Makerstoun House [NT 672315], near Kelso, Borders; mansion incorporating castle.

Held by the Corbetts and then by the MacDougalls, but passed to the Scotts of Gala in 1890 and then to the Biddulphs of Ledbury. Still occupied.

Malleny House [NT 166667], Balerno, Edinburgh; old mansion with round tower.

Held by the Hamiltons, by the Kerrs and by the Murrays of Kilbaberton before coming to the Scotts of Murdieston, then was sold to the Primrose Lord Rosebery in 1882. The gardens are in the care of The National Trust for Scotland and are open to the public (0131 449 2283; www.nts.org.uk).

Mangerton Tower [NY 479853], near Newcastleton, Borders; slight remains of tower.

Held by the Armstrongs, but passed to the Scotts in 1629.

Mertoun House [NT 618318], near Kelso, Borders; castle replaced by mansion.

Held by the Halyburtons and then by the Scotts of Harden, later Lords Polwarth from 1680 to 1912, and then by the Dukes of Sutherland. The gardens and grounds are open to the public (01835 823236).

Minto House [NT 573203], near Hawick, Borders; ruinous castle and mansion.

Held by the Turnbulls and by the Scotts, but passed to the Elliots, who became Earls of Minto. The house was burnt in 1992.

Monzie Castle [NN 873245], near Crieff, Perthshire; altered L-plan tower house.

Held by the Scotts in the fifteenth century, but passed by marriage to the Grahams in 1613, then later went to the Campbells, to the Johnstones of Lathrisk and to the Crichtons. Still occupied and open to the public (01764 653110).

Moss Tower [NT 714265], near Kelso, Borders; site of castle.

Held by the Earls of Bothwell and by the Scotts of Buccleuch. It was burnt by the English in 1523, in 1544 and in 1570, when it was left as a ruin.

Murdostoun Castle [NS 825573], near Newmains, Lanarkshire; mansion incorporating castle.

Held by the Scotts; Sir Michael Scott, heir of Murdostoun, fought at the Halidon Hill in 1333, and was slain at the Battle of Durham in 1346. Murdostoun went to the Inglis family in 1446, and they built the castle, then Murdostoun later passed to the Hamiltons and to the Stewarts. Said to be haunted by a Green Lady.

Newark Castle [NT 421294], near Selkirk, Borders; impressive ruinous castle.

Held by the Douglases and was altered for Anna, Duchess of Monmouth and Buccleuch, about 1700. Wordsworth visited the castle in 1831 with Sir Walter Scott. The ruin has been consolidated and is in the grounds of Bowhill (01750 22204; www.boughtonhouse.org.uk).

Old Gala House [NT 492357], Gala, Borders; mansion incorporating tower house.

Held by the Douglases and by the Pringles of Gala, before passing by marriage to the Scotts of Gala. The Scotts of Gala still flourish, and apparently have residences near Gala and in London according to *Burke's*. Old Gala House is now used as a community and art centre, and there is a museum (01896 752611).

Old Howpasley [NT 349067], near Hawick, Borders; site of tower house.

Held by the Scotts of Howpasley, and the tower was torched by the English in 1543 or 1547 or both.

Pitlour [NO 209113], near Auchtermuchty, Fife; castle replaced by mansion.

Held by the Scotts in the fifteenth and sixteenth centuries, but was sold to the Skenes in 1683. The present Pitlour, a fine classical mansion, was built in 1783-4.

Polwarth Castle [NT 749500], near Duns, Borders; site of castle.

Held by the Homes but much later by the Scotts, who also got the title Lord Polwarth in the nineteenth century. The Hepburne-Scott Lords Polwarth now apparently live in Devon in England.

Queen Mary's House [NT 651206], Jedburgh, Borders; T-plan tower house.

Held by the Scotts of Ancrum. Mary, Queen of Scots, stayed in a chamber on the second floor. She was very ill and lay for many days near to death after her visit to James Hepburn, fourth Earl of Bothwell, at Hermitage Castle in 1566. Above Mary's chamber is another similar room where the Queen's 'Four Marys' are supposed to have stayed. The building is open to the public, and houses a museum displaying exhibits relating to the visit by Mary to Jedburgh (01835 863331).

Rossie Castle [NO 702561], near Montrose, Angus; site of castle.

Held by the Rossies, but had passed to the Scotts of Logie by 1650, then went to the Millars by 1880.

Rossie House [NO 265120], near Auchtermuchty, Fife; house on site of castle.

Held by the Rossies but passed to the Scotts in 1630, then to the Cheapes.

Rumgally House [NO 407149], near Cupar, Fife; house incorporating work from a tower house.

Held by the Scotts of Balwearie from 1528, and then possibly by the Wemyss family and by the Makgills. B&B accommodation is available (01334 653388; www.sol.co.uk/r/rumgally/).

Salenside Castle [NT 464207], near Selkirk; site of tower house.

Andrew of Salenside is one of those listed as riding to the help of Kinmont Willie, according to the old ballad of the same name.

Scotscraig [NO 445283], near Tayport, Fife; castle replaced by mansion.

Held by the several families including by the Scotts of Balwearie in the thirteenth century, then by the Duries and by others.

Sheriffhall [NT 320680], near Dalkeith, Midlothian; slight remains of castle.
Held by the Scotts of Buccleuch after the Reformation, and then by the Giffords in the sixteenth century.

Smailholm Tower [NT 637346], near Kelso, Borders; impressive tower house.
Held by the Kerrs, then by the Pringles, and then by the Scotts of Harden in 1645. Sir Walter Scott came here as a boy as his grandfather held nearby Sandyknowe. The tower is in the care of Historic Scotland and is open to the public (01573 460365).

Spottiswoode House [NT 603499], near Lauder, Borders; site of tower house and mansion.
Held by the Spottiswoodes, then by the Bells and in 1836 the property passed by marriage to Lord John Douglas-Montagu-Scott (of the Dukes of Buccleuch).

Stirches [NT 498162], near Hawick, Borders; altered tower house.
Held by the Scotts from 1501 or earlier, but passed to the Chisholms in 1650. It has been used as a Roman Catholic Home for Ladies, called St Andrew's Convent, since 1926.

Sunderland Hall [NT 479319], near Selkirk, Borders; mansion on the site of castle.
Held by the Scotts, then later Scott Plummers, from the middle of the nineteenth century. The family apparently now live at Dryburgh Abbey House near St Boswells.

Synton [NT 487223], near Selkirk, Borders; site of tower house and mansion.
Held by the Scotts and this branch of the family died out in 1720.

Thirdpart House [NO 589067], near Crail, Fife; site of castle or old house.
Held by the Scotts of Scotstarvit.

Thirlestane Tower [NT 281154], near Ettrick, Borders; ruinous L-plan tower house.
Held by the Scotts of Thirlestane, and the family were made Baronets of Nova Scotia in 1666. Thirlestane passed by marriage to the Napiers of Merchiston in 1699. The third son of Robert Scott of Thirlestane is said to have been treacherously slain by his brother-in-law, John Scott of Tushielaw, the story told in the old ballad 'The Dowie Dens of Yarrow'.

Thirlestane Tower [NT 803287], near Kelso, Borders; site of tower house.
Held by the Scotts. The tower was said to have had a 'warlock's room', probably the laboratory of Dr Scott, a well-known alchemist and physician to Charles II.

Todrig Tower [NT 430197], near Hawick, Borders; house incorporating tower house.
Held by the Scotts of Todrig.

Tushielaw Tower [NT 300172], near Ettrick, Borders; some remains of tower house.
Held by the Scotts. Adam Scott, known as 'The King of the Borders' and 'The King of Thieves'. He was executed by beheading in Edinburgh by James V in 1530. John Scott of Tushielaw is said to have been responsible for the treacherous murder of Walter Scott, third son of Robert Scott of Thirlestane – the story being related in one version of the old ballad, 'The Dowie Dens of Yarrow'. The castle would appear to have been ruined by 1630.

Usan House [NO 723553], near Montrose, Angus; mansion incorporating old work.
Held by the Leightons, by the Scotts, by the Keiths and by the Alstons. The Scotts of Logie-Montrose and Usan still flourish and apparently have residences near Montrose, in Inverness-shire and in Essex in England according to *Burke's*.

Westhouses or Allanhaugh [NT 527354], near Melrose, Borders; site of tower house.
Held by the Ormistons, but apparently passed to the Scotts of Buccleuch, although this may be a confusion with Allanmouth Tower, south of Hawick.

Whitchesters [NT 469110], near Hawick, Borders; probable site of tower.
Held by the Scotts.

Whitslade Tower [NT 429180], near Hawick, Borders; site of tower.
Held by the Scotts of Whitslaid, and burnt in 1502.

www.clanscott.org.uk
www.clanscott.org
www.homepages.rootsweb.com/~clnscott/main.htm
No. of castles/sites: 92
Rank: 7/764

Scougal

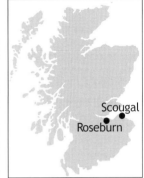

The name is territorial and comes from the lands of Scougal, now Seacliff, which are three or so miles east and south of North Berwick in East Lothian.

Seacliff or **Scougal Tower** [NT 613844] is a small and ruinous tower house, which dates from the sixteenth century. The lands were held by the Scougal family from the thirteenth century or earlier. Murdoch Stewart, Duke of Albany, was charged with (among other things) the cruel slaughter of John of Scougal in 1379 and Albany was executed. Another of the family, Patrick Scougal, was the Protestant Bishop of Aberdeen from 1664-82 and his son, Henry, was Professor of Divinity at King's College in Aberdeen in the 1670s. Near the site of the tower is the ruin of Seacliff House, built in 1750 and remodelled in the nineteenth century, but burnt out in 1907; it remains an impressive ruin.

Roseburn House [NT 226731] lies to the west of Edinburgh, and is an altered and extended L-plan tower house. The walls are whitewashed and there is a

Roseburn House (M&R)

courtyard. The property was owned by the Scougals, and Oliver Cromwell spent a night here in 1650. One of the family was Sir James Scougal, who was Senator of the College of Justice in 1697.

No. of castles/sites: 2
Rank: 396=/764

Scrymgeour

The name comes from 'skirmisher' and means 'swordsman', and originates from Middle English. The name is on record from the end of the thirteenth century, and the Scrymgeours may have been settled in Fife before they came to prominence in Dundee and in Angus.

Dudhope Castle [NO 394307] is to the south of Dundee Law to the north and west of the city. It is a courtyard castle with two long ranges with round corner towers and a towered gatehouse; there was also a tower house but this has been demolished. The lands were held by the Scrymgeours after they had rendered valuable service at the Battle of Stirling Bridge in 1298 as hereditary standard bearers of the Scottish army. Sir Alexander Scrymgeour had fought alongside William Wallace, and then supported Robert the Bruce, although

Dudhope Castle (M&R)

he was captured after the Battle of Methven in 1306 and then hanged by the English. His son, Nicholas, carried the Standard at Bannockburn eight years later, and his son, Sir John, was slain at Dupplin Moor in 1332. Sir James Scrymgeour of Dudhope fought and was killed at the Battle of Harlaw in 1411, and Sir James Scrymgeour of Dudhope was banished for his part in the Ruthven Raid, but returned and was Provost of Dundee in 1588. James VI visited Dudhope in 1617. The family were made Viscounts Scrymgeour in 1641, and John, second Viscount, was killed at the Battle of Marston Moor three years later. John, third Viscount, was made Earl of Dundee in 1660, after he fought on the side of the Marquis of Montrose and carried the Standard on the march to Worcester in 1651. The Royalists were defeated and, although he escaped from the battle, he was taken prisoner three years later and the property was forfeited. John recovered the property, but when he died Dudhope was seized by the acquisitive Duke of Lauderdale. Dudhope was sold to the Grahams of Claverhouse, and the castle was later used as a woollen mill and as a barracks. The family apparently now live

at Birkhill near Cupar in Fife, and their titles include Earl of Dundee, Viscount Dudhope, Hereditary Royal Standard Bearer of Scotland and Constable for Dundee. Dudhope Castle has been restored and is used as offices, while the grounds are a public park.

The family also held:

Birkhill House [NO 336234], near Wormit, Fife; castle replaced by mansion.

> Held by the Leslies but passed to the Scrymgeours, who held the lands from the eighteenth century. Birkhill is now apparently the seat of the Earls of Dundee. The gardens are occasionally open to the public (www.gardensofscotland.org).

Duntrune House [NO 445345], near Dundee; castle replaced by mansion.

> Held by the Northingtons and by the Ogilvies of Easter Powrie, and then by the Scrymgeours of Dudhope in the fifteenth century. The property had passed to the Grahams of Fintry by the first quarter of the eighteenth century, then went to others. Still occupied.

Fincharn or **Glassery Castle** [NM 898044], near Kilmartin, Argyll; ruinous tower house.

> Held by the MacDougalls and by the MacGilchrists, but was owned by the Scrymgeours from 1370 to 1688. One of the family, John Scrymgeour of Glassery, was Standard Bearer and died from wounds received at the Battle of Flodden in 1513. The castle later returned to the MacDougalls. One tale is that one of the chiefs, Mac Mhic Iain (the Gaelic title for the Scrymgeours), insulted and tried to steal the wife of one of his men, who took his revenge by burning the castle and slaying the chief.

Myres Castle [NO 242110], near Auchtermuchty, Fife; Z-plan tower house.

> Held by the Coxwells but passed by marriage to the Scrymgeours, and they built the castle in 1530. John Scrymgeour was Master of Works to James V; Mary, Queen of Scots, visited Myres on hunting trips. The property passed to the Patersons and then to the Moncreiffes of Reidie in 1750. It then passed through several families, and was put up for sale in 1997 with an asking price of more than £550,00. Accommodation is now available in the castle and the gardens are occasionally open to the public (01208 821341; www.myres.co.uk/www.gardensofscotland.org).

Tealing House [NO 413380], near Dundee; mansion incorporating part of an old tower.

> Held by the Fotheringhams, by the Giffords of Yester and by the Maxwells, before being bought by the Scrymgeours in 1710.

Wedderburn Castle [NO 435352], near Dundee; site of castle.

> Held by the Douglas Earls of Angus, then by the Ogilvies and by the Wedderburns, but then passed by marriage to the Scrymgeours at the end of the eighteenth century. The family owned Wedderburn into the twentieth century, and their seat is apparently now Birkhill.

www.scrimgeourclan.org.uk
No. of castles/sites: 7
Rank: 182=/764
Xref: Scrimgeour

Sempill

The origin of the name is not known, although the family were established in Renfrewshire from the twelfth century, and they were hereditary sheriffs of Renfrew.

Elliston or **Elliotston Castle** [NS 392598] is a few miles west and south of Johnstone in Renfrewshire, and is a large and ruinous castle and courtyard, which dated from the fifteenth century. The lands were held by the Sempill family from before 1344, and they were made Lords Sempill in 1488. Sir John, first Lord Sempill, was killed at the Battle of Flodden in 1513. The castle was abandoned about 1550 for Castle Semple.

Castle Semple [NS 377602], two miles east and north of Lochwinnoch, was been completely demolished. The old castle had been replaced by a large classical mansion, but this was itself demolished in the 1960s, although one wing and the stable block survives. The old castle was built by the Sempills, and Robert Sempill, later third Lord, was captured after the Battle of Pinkie in 1547. Although originally supporting Mary, Queen of Scots, he turned against her at Carberry in 1567, supported her abdication and imprisonment, and led the vanguard of the forces against her at the Battle of Langside the following year. His son, John, was accused of being one of those in the plot to assassinate Regent Morton, and he was sentenced to death although this was commuted to imprisonment, and he was eventually released. The family were Hanoverians, and fought against the Jacobites in 1715, and in 1746 at the Battle of Culloden. Hugh, twelfth Lord Sempill, was a Brigadier General and commanded the left wing of the Hanoverian army. The castle, however, had passed to the MacDowalls by 1727, and they demolished they old stronghold and built the mansion; the Sempill, Lords Sempill, now apparently live in Edinburgh. Near the site of the old castle is Castle Semple Collegiate Church [NS 377601], roofless but standing to the wallhead, which contains the elaborate tomb of its founder, John, first Lord Sempill, who fell at Flodden. Castle Semple country park is open all year (01505 842882).

The Sempills also owned:

Balgone House [NT 567825], near North Berwick, East Lothian; L-plan tower house.
　Held by the Rosses of Hawkhead, but passed to the Sempills, then by marriage to the Sutties of Addiston in 1680. Still occupied.

Barochan House [NS 415686], near Bridge of Weir, Renfrewshire; mansion including work from a tower house.
　Held by the Flemings, but passed to the Sempills in the sixteenth century, and they held Barochan until 1863. The existing building is almost all modern, the old part of the house having being demolished in 1947 because of dry rot.

Belltrees Peel [NS 363587], near Lochwinnoch, Renfrewshire; ruinous tower house.
　Held by the Stewarts, but passed to the Sempills. Sir James Sempill of Belltrees was educated with James VI and became ambassador to France in 1601.

Bishopton House [NS 422717], near Bridge of Weir, Renfrewshire; L-plan tower house.
　Held by the Brisbanes, then by others including by the Sempills, before going to the Maxwells of Pollok and to the Stewart Lords Blantyre. Now part of the Convent of the Good Shepherd.

Castle Hill, Busby [NS 589562], near East Kilbride, Lanarkshire; slight remains of castle.
　Held by the Sempills, but passed to the Stewarts of Minto in 1490.

Castle Levan [NS 216764], near Gourock, Renfrewshire; restored L-plan tower house.
　Held by the Mortons, but was bought by the Sempills before 1547, and then passed to the Stewarts of Inverkip in 1649. B&B accommodation is available (01475 659154; www.castle-levan.com).

Cathcart Castle [NS 586599], near Rutherglen, Glasgow; slight remains of castle.
　Held by the Cathcarts, but passed to the Sempills in 1546. Although the family fought against her at Langside, Mary, Queen of Scots, is said to have stayed here the night before the battle in 1568. The castle was abandoned for Cathcart House, although both these buildings have now been demolished. The site is in Linn Park (0141 637 1147; www.glasgow.gov.uk).

Dykes Castle [NS 728473], near Stonehouse; site of castle.
　The property was long held by the Forsyths but it passed to the Sempills in the seventeenth century and was then sold to the Stewarts of Castlemilk in 1710.

Drumry Castle [NS 515710], near Duntocher, Glasgow; site of castle.
　Held by the Callendars, by the Livingstones and by others, but passed to the Sempills in 1545. Demolished in the 1960s.

Northbar or **Oldbar** or **Semple House** [NS 481693], near Renfrew; castle replaced by mansion.
　Held by the MacGilchrists, but passed to the Sempills in 1741, and Northbar was sold to the Buchanans in 1798, then to the Stewart Lords Blantyre in 1812.

Place of Paisley [NS 485639], Paisley; old fortified house by abbey.
　Held by the Hamiltons after the Reformation, then by the Sempills, before being recovered by the Hamiltons. It later passed to the Douglas Earls of Angus and to the Cochranes, and is now used as the manse for the abbey church.

Southannan Castle [NS 209538], near Largs, Ayrshire; slight remains of castle.
　Long held by the Sempills, and Mary, Queen of Scots, visited in 1563, but then Southannan later passed to the Montgomerys of Eglinton.

Tangy Loch [NR 695279], near Campbeltown, Kintyre, Argyll; site of castle.
　Held by the Campbells and by the MacEarchans, but passed to the Sempills in 1709.

The Peel, Busby [NS 594561], East Kilbride, Lanarkshire; altered L-plan tower house.
　Held by the Douglases and by the Hamiltons, then by others including by the Sempills and by the Houstons of Jordanhill in 1793. Still occupied.

No. of castles/sites: 16
Rank: 86=/764
Xref: Semple; Sempie

Seton

The name is believed to have come from Sai, a village near Exmes in Normandy in France. Seiher de Say was given lands in East Lothian by David I in the twelfth century, and called his new property Sayton or Seton. There is apparently no direct evidence for this, and the lands were often spelt Seaton.

Seton House [NT 418751] is a classical mansion, designed by Robert Adam and dating from the end of the eighteenth century. The lands lie a mile or so northeast of Tranent in East Lothian, and there was a castle here and then a splendid palace, but this was demolished when the new house was built. Christopher Seton was Robert the Bruce's brother-in-law and supporter. He is believed to have saved Bruce's life at the Battle of Methven in 1306, but was captured after the battle and then brutally executed by the English. Sir Alexander Seton, perhaps his brother, was one of the Scottish nobles to add their seals to the Declaration of Arbroath in 1320. Sir Alexander was Governor of Berwick when the burgh surrendered in 1333 and his son was hanged by the English. The family were made Lords Seton in 1448. The Setons married into the Gordons and their descendants were the powerful Earls of Huntly. George, third Lord Seton, was killed at the Battle of Flodden in 1513. The old castle was destroyed by the English in 1544, and a new house known as the Palace was built on the site. George, fifth Lord Seton, was a friend and supporter of Mary, Queen of Scots, and she fled to Seton Palace after the murder of David Rizzio in 1566. She also visited with the Earl of Bothwell after the assassination of Lord Darnley, her second husband. The following year her army camped at the castle the night before 'defeat' at Carberry Hill. The Setons helped to rescue Mary from imprisonment in Lochleven Castle, after which she stayed at another of their properties, Niddry Castle. They fought for her at Langside in 1568 but were defeated and the fifth Lord escaped to Flanders, although he later returned and was one of

the judges at the trial of the Earl of Morton for the murder of Darnley: Morton was beheaded. Mary Seton, daughter of George, fifth Lord Seton, was one of the 'Four Marys' of Mary, Queen of Scots; she never married and stayed with her Queen until her execution in 1587; Mary Seton then went into a nunnery in France. The Setons were made Earls of Winton in 1600, and then also Earls of Dunfermline six years later, the first of whom was Sir Alexander Seton, Chancellor of Scotland. Seton Palace was damaged during the 1715 Jacobite Rising, having been held for three days by Highlanders against Hanoverian forces, after which the Setons were forfeited for supporting the Jacobites. The house was left a ruin and was then demolished in 1790. A fine collegiate church [NT 418751] stands near the house. It was founded in 1492 by George, fourth Lord Seton, although it was looted and burned by the English in 1544. There are the stone effigies of one of the Setons and his wife, but it is not known who they were in life. The church is in the care of Historic Scotland and open to the public in the summer (01875 813334).

Fyvie Castle [NJ 764393] is a magnificent castle and mansion, and stands to the north of Fyvie village in Aberdeenshire. There is a massive tower house with very long wings, and the building has a flourish of turrets, dormer windows, statues and carved finials. There are fine interiors, including the main turnpike stair which has twenty-two coats of arms for local families. The property was owned by several families down the years: by the Lindsays, by the Prestons and by the Meldrums before passing to the Seton Earls of Dunfermline in 1596, the first of whom, Sir Alexander, was Chancellor of Scotland. The Marquis of Montrose occupied the castle in 1644, and it was held by Cromwell's men in the 1650s. The Setons were Jacobites and were forfeited following the Jacobite Rising of 1689-90. The property passed to the Gordon Earls of Aberdeen in 1733, and then to the Leith family. The castle is said to be haunted. The most

Seton Palace (M&R)

Fyvie Castle (M&R)

famous story is that of Lillias Drummond, wife of Sir Alexander Seton, first Earl of Dunfermline. She died in 1601, most likely of natural causes, having given birth five times, but she may have been starved to death by her husband, who remarried quickly after her death. Lillias and Seton had had several daughters, but no sons and it may be that he wanted a male heir. Her ghost is said to have carved her name on the window sill of the newlyweds' bedroom, what is now the Drummond Room, the night of their wedding – and the writing can still be seen: D[ame] LILLIES DRUMMOND, on the outside of the window sill. Her ghost, a Green Lady, is said to have been witnessed many times down the years, sometimes as a portent of death. The castle is also said to have a Grey Lady, the spirit of a woman starved to death in the castle (Lillias died at Dalgety in Fife and is probably buried in St Bridget's Kirk there); and the spirit of a trumpeter or drummer, another herald of death. The castle stands in fine ground, is in the care of The National Trust of Scotland, and is open to the public (01651 891266).

Winton House [NT 439696], three miles south-east of Tranent, is a magnificent Renaissance mansion, which dates from 1620 and later, and is built on the site of an old stronghold. There are fine stone twisted chimneys and some splendid plaster ceilings. The lands were held by the Quincys, but were given to the Setons after that family was forfeited. Lord Seton built a castle here about 1480, which was later sacked by the English. The Setons

Winton House (RWB)

were made Earls of Winton in 1600, and much of the present house dates from 1620. Charles I visited in 1633. George, fifth Earl, was forfeited for his part in the Jacobite Rising of 1715. He was imprisoned in the Tower of London after being captured at the Battle of Preston, although he managed to escape and went to Rome. The property passed to the Hamilton Lords Pencaitland in 1779, and then to the Ogilvys in 1920 and they still apparently live here. The house is open to the public by guided tours and the gardens are occasionally open to the public (01875 340222; www.wintonhouse.co.uk).

The Setons also owned:

Abbot House [NT 089875], Dunfermline, Fife; fine restored town house.

Held by the Setons after the Reformation, and they were made Earls of Dunfermline, although the house passed to the Stewarts, to the Master of Gray, to the Gordon Earl of Huntly and to others. There are stories that the building is haunted by a ghostly monk. The house is used as a heritage centre and has displays about the house and Dunfermline (01383 733266; www.abbothouse.co.uk).

Abercorn Castle [NT 083794], near South Queensferry, West Lothian; site of castle.

Held by the Douglases and by the Hamiltons, but passed to the Setons, and they were made Baronets of Nova Scotia in 1663. The Setons of Abercorn, Baronets, now apparently live in Australia.

Barnes Castle [NT 529766], near Haddington, East Lothian; ruinous castle.

Held by the Setons from the thirteenth century, and Sir John Seton of Barnes started to build the castle. He spent much of his life as a diplomat at the court of Philip II of Spain. James VI recalled him, and made him Treasurer of the Household, but Seton died in 1594 before the castle was completed.

Barra Castle [NJ 792258], near Inverurie, Aberdeenshire; L-plan tower house.

Held by the Kings, and the they feuded with the Setons of Meldrum, one of the Kings having slain a Seton in 1530. Barra was bought by the Setons, who sold it to the Reids in 1658. The property was later held by the Ramsays and by the Irvines, and the castle is still occupied.

Bishop's House [NJ 221631], Elgin, Moray; ruinous town house.

Held by the Setons after the Reformation, but later went to the Grant Earls of Seafield, who began to demolish it before protests stopped the destruction. The building is in the care of Historic Scotland and can be viewed from the road.

Carriden House [NT 026808], near Bo'ness, West Lothian; altered tower house.

Held by several families before being bought by the Setons, then later passed to the Cornwalls of Bonhard and then to the Hope Johnstones. Still occupied, B&B accommodation is available, and the house is suitable for weddings (01506 829811; www.carridenhouse.co.uk).

Castle Gogar [NT 164730], near Edinburgh; large L-plan tower house.

Held by the Setons in the fourteenth century, but passed to the Halyburtons about 1409, then went to the Logans of Restalrig and then to the Coupers who built the castle. Still occupied.

Castle Hill [NJ 154571], Pluscarden, Moray; site of castle near abbey.

Held by the Setons, later Lords Urquhart, after the Reformation, but was sold to the Mackenzies of Kintail in 1595. It then passed through several families. The abbey was refounded in 1948 and can be visited (01343 890257; www.pluscardenabbey.org).

Culcreuch Castle [NS 620876], near Fintry, Stirlingshire; fine castle and mansion.

Held by the Galbraiths, but was bought by the Setons in 1630 before being sold to the Napiers two years later. Later held by the Speirs family, and the castle has one of the largest colonies of bats in Britain. There are also some fine interiors, including the Chinese Bird Room. The castle stands in a country park and is a hotel (01360 860228/555; www.culcreuch.com).

Dalgety [NT 169838], near Aberdour, Fife; site of castle or old house.

Held by the Setons and this was the favourite residence of Sir Alexander Seton, Earl of Dunfermline and Chancellor of Scotland, who died at Pinkie House in 1622. Lillias Drummond, his first wife, died at Dalgety in 1601; her ghost is said to haunt Fyvie Castle. Seton (and presumably Lillias as well) is buried in the now ruinous shell of nearby St Bridget's Kirk where there is a burial vault. The church is in the care of Historic Scotland and is open to the public. The fourth Earl was forfeited for supporting the Jacobites in 1689-90.

Disblair House [NJ 862197], near New Machar, Aberdeenshire; site of castle or old house.

Held by the Thompsons and by the Setons in the sixteenth century, but passed to the Forbeses and then to the Dyce family.

Elphinstone Tower [NT 391698], near Tranent, East Lothian; very ruinous castle.

Held by the Setons, but passed to the Elphinstones in the thirteenth century. Demolished due to subsistence.

Falside or **Fawside Castle** [NT 378710], near Tranent, East Lothian; restored L-plan tower house.

Held by the Falside family and by the Setons. The tower was burnt by the English before the Battle of Pinkie in 1547, suffocating those inside. Became ruinous but was restored in the 1970s. The building is said to have a Green Lady.

Gargunnock House [NS 715944], near Stirling; mansion incorporating tower house.

Held by the Setons in 1460, but later passed to the Erskine Earls of Mar, and then to the Campbells and to the Stirlings. Still occupied and the gardens are open to the public (01786 860392; www.gardensofscotland.org).

Garleton Castle [NT 509767], near Haddington, East Lothian; partly ruinous castle.

Held by the Lindsays then later by the Towers of Inverleith before being bought by the Setons. Said to be haunted.

Gordon Castle [NT 646438], Gordon, Borders; site of castle.

Held by the Gordons, but passed to the Setons in 1580.

Greenknowe Tower [NT 639428], near Gordon; fine ruinous L-plan tower house.

Held by the Gordons but passed by marriage to the Setons of Touch, who built the castle. Greenknowe went to the Pringles

Greenknowe Tower (LF)

of Stichil in the seventeenth century. Now in the care of Historic Scotland and open to the public.

Hailes Castle [NT 575758], near East Linton, East Lothian; fine ruinous castle in scenic location.

Long held by the Hepburns, but passed to the Stewarts and then to the Setons, who sold to the property to the Dalrymples in 1700. The Dalrymples moved to what is now Newhailes, near Musselburgh, and the castle became ruinous. Hailes is in the care of Historic Scotland and is open to the public.

Lathrisk House [NO 273085], near Glenrothes, Fife; mansion on site of castle.

Held by the Quincys and by the Lathrisk family, before being owned by the Setons of Parbroath and then by the Johnstones.

Meldrum House [NJ 812291], near Oldmeldrum, Aberdeenshire; mansion incorporating part of castle.

Held by the Meldrums, but passed to the Setons in the middle of the fifteenth century. William Seton, first of Meldrum, was killed fighting for the Gordons at the Battle of Brechin in 1452; and Alexander Seton of Meldrum was murdered in 1526 by the Master of Forbes and John Strachan of Lynturk. The property went to the Urquharts in 1670, is said to be haunted by a ghostly lady, and is now a hotel (01651 872294; www.meldrumhouse.co.uk).

Mounie Castle [NJ 766287], near Oldmeldrum, Aberdeenshire; T-plan tower house.

Held by the Setons, but passed to the Farquhars in 1634, and then went to the Hays, before being recovered by the Setons, who sold it in 1970. Still occupied.

Niddry or **Niddry-Seton Castle** [NT 097743], near Broxburn, West Lothian; restored L-plan tower.

Held by the Setons. One of the family, George Seton, was killed at the Battle of Flodden in 1513. Mary, Queen of Scots, came here after she had escaped from Lochleven Castle in 1568. The property passed to the Hopes later in the seventeenth century. Restored and still occupied.

Parbroath Castle [NO 322176], near Cupar, Fife; slight remains of castle.

Held by the Setons, one of whom supported Mary, Queen of Scots, and captured and held Broughty Castle against the Lords of the Congregation in 1571.

Pinkie House [NT 353727], Musselburgh, East Lothian; fine tower house and mansion.

Held by the Setons, one of whom, Sir Alexander, was Earl of Dunfermline, Lord Fyvie and Chancellor to James VI. He altered the house in 1613, and died here in 1622. The Setons were forfeited in 1690 because of their support for James VII. The

Pinkie House (RWB)

property was sold to the Hay Marquis of Tweeddale in 1694, then to the Hopes of Craighall, and the house is now part of Loretto School (0131 653 4444; www.lorettoschool.co.uk). Pinkie House is said to be haunted by a Green Lady, which has also been identified as Lillias Drummond, Sir Alexander Seton's first wife, although she apparently died at Dalgety. Her ghost, or another, is said to be sometimes accompanied by a child, and she is also believed to haunt Fyvie Castle.

Pitmedden House [NJ 885281], near Ellon, Aberdeenshire; mansion on site of castle.

Held by the Pantons, but passed to the Setons. Alexander Seton of Pitmedden was a Royalist and was slain when he was shot through the heart at Dee Bridge while carrying the king's standard in 1639. Sir Alexander Seton of Pitmedden was an eminent lawyer and was made a Baronet of Nova Scotia in 1683-84. Pitmedden passed to the Bannermans, then to the Keiths. The fine walled garden is open to the public (01651 842352; www.nts.org.uk).

Pittencrieff House [NT 087873], Dunfermline, Fife; T-plan house.

Held by the Setons and then by the Wemyss family after the Reformation, then by others. The house stands in a popular public park (01383 722935/313838; www.fifedirect.org/museums).

Preston Tower [NT 393742], Prestonpans, East Lothian; impressive ruinous tower.

Held by the Setons in the thirteenth century, but passed to the Liddels and then to the Hamiltons at the end of the fourteenth century. Stands in a public garden and can be viewed from the exterior (01875 810232).

Shethin [NJ 886326], near Ellon, Aberdeenshire; site of castle.

Held by the Setons, but demolished by Covenanters in 1644.

Sorn Castle [NS 548269], near Mauchline, Ayrshire; altered and extended castle.

Held by the Keiths of Galston and then by the Hamiltons of Cadzow, but passed to the Setons of Winton. James VI visited, and it was held against the Covenanters. Sorn was sold to the Campbell Earl of Loudoun about 1680, then went to the Somervilles and to the MacIntyres. Still occupied and open to the public (01290 551555).

Stoneypath Tower [NT 596713], near East Linton, East Lothian; L-plan tower house.

Held by the Lyles, by the Hamiltons of Innerwick and by the Douglases of Whittinghame, but passed to the Setons. The tower is being restored.

Touch House [NS 753928], near Stirling; altered tower house and mansion.

Held by the Frasers and by the Stewart Earls of Buchan before passing to the Setons around the end of the fifteenth century. Sir Alexander Seton of Touch was Armour Bearer to James IV, and the next lord, Sir Alexander, fell at the Battle of Flodden in 1513. The Laird of Touch was one of five lords involved in an unsuccessful attempt to put James VII on the throne in 1708, an exploit in which Rob Roy MacGregor was implicated. Touch passed by marriage to the Seton-Stewarts of Allanton and Touch, who held it until 1930. Still occupied.

Tranent Tower [NT 404729], Tranent, East Lothian; ruinous L-plan tower house.

Held by the Setons but passed to the Valance family in the seventeenth century.

Whittinghame Castle [NT 602733], near East Linton, East Lothian; altered keep or tower.

Held by the Earls of Dunbar and by the Douglases, but passed to the Setons in 1650, then to the Hays and then to the Balfours, who still apparently own it.

Woodhall [NT 433680], near Pencaitland, East Lothian; mansion incorporating tower house.

Held by the Setons, but passed to the Sinclairs of Herdmanston in 1488 and then later to the Lauders. Still occupied.

No. of castles/sites: 37
Rank: 32=/764

Shand

The name is on record in Scotland from the sixteenth century, and the name appears to have been found most often in the north-east part of Scotland.

Arnhall House [NO 613691], six and a half miles north of Brechin in Angus, is an attractive mansion, dating from about 1750, and it replaced an old castle. The property was held by the Carnegies and then by the Brodies, but the property passed to the Shands in 1814.

No. of castles/sites: 1
Rank: 537=/764

Shank

The name is territorial and comes from the lands of Shank, which are half a mile west of Gorebridge in Midlothian, and the name is on record from the thirteenth century.

Shank House [NT 334611], near Gorebridge, is a ruinous mansion, dating from the seventeenth century or earlier, and it may stand on the site of a castle. The lands were long held by the Shank family, and Murdoch Shank, son of the laird of Shank, is said to have discovered and taken charge of the body of Alexander III of Scotland, after he had fallen from cliffs at Kinghorn in 1286. He was given lands at Kinghorn in Fife by Robert the Bruce. Shank stayed with the family into the sixteenth century or later, but was apparently held by George Mackenzie of Rosehaugh and then was later sold to the Dundases of Arniston in 1753. The lands were absorbed into the Arniston estate and the house became ruinous. John Reid wrote *The Scots Gard'ner* at Shank in 1683.

No. of castles/sites: 1
Rank: 537=/764
Xref: Shanks

Sharp

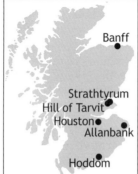

The name is on record in Scotland from the end of the fourteenth century, and the family owned lands in Fife and in Aberdeenshire in the sixteenth and seventeenth centuries. The name is also often spelt Shairp. The most famous member of the family was probably James Sharp, who was the Protestant Archbishop of St Andrews in the 1660s and 70s; he was born at Banff Castle. He was accused of being involved in the persecution of Covenanters and pursuing his own interests, making him extremely unpopular. He was shot in 1668 but survived the attack, and was then brutally murdered in front of his daughter at Magus Muir near St Andrews in 1679.

The Sharps owned the following properties:

Allanbank House [NT 864546], near Duns, Borders; site of castle and mansion.

Held by the Stewarts, but later passed to the Kirkpatrick Sharpes. The house was said to be haunted by the ghost of 'Pearlin Jean', the spirit of girl dressed in lace, who reputedly caused all number of disturbances. The mansion was demolished in 1969.

Banff Castle [NJ 689642], Banff, Aberdeenshire; mansion within ramparts of castle.

Held by the Comyns but passed to the Sharps. This was the birthplace of Archbishop James Sharp in 1618, but the property passed to the Russells. An Adam mansion was built about 1750.

Hill of Tarvit Mansion House [NO 380119], Cupar, Fife; fine mansion.

Rebuilt for Mr F. B. Sharp, a Dundee industrialist, by Sir Robert Lorimer so that Sharp could display his fine collections of paintings, tapestries and furniture. There are formal gardens and the house is open to the public (01334 653127; nts.org.uk). Scotstarvit Castle [NO 370113] is nearby; key from the house.

Hoddom Castle [NY 157730], near Annan, Dumfries and Galloway; L-plan tower house.

Held by several families before coming to the Maxwells, who built the tower. Hoddom later passed to the Murrays of Cockpool and to the Carnegie Earls of Southesk, before being bought by the Sharp family in 1690. They extended the castle, but this new work has been demolished. Hoddom was sold in 1878 and the tower now stands in a caravan park (01576 300251; www.hoddomcastle.co.uk).

Houston House [NT 058716], near Uphall, West Lothian; extended L-plan tower house.

Held by the Houstons, but passed to the Sharps in 1569 or so. Sir John Sharp, an advocate for the queen, received a pair of hawking gloves from Mary, Queen of Scots, which were long kept at the house. One of the family was Archbishop Sharp, who was murdered at Magus Muir in 1679 (as mentioned above). Sharp of Houston voted against the Act of Union of 1707 during the last Scottish Parliament. The property was sold by the family in 1945 and the house is now a hotel (01506 853831; www.macdonaldhotels.co.uk/houstounhouse/).

Phantassie [NT 598772], near East Linton, East Lothian; site of castle or old house.

Held by the Sharps but passed by marriage to the Mitchell-Innes family in the nineteenth century. There is a fine doocot, which is in the care of The National Trust for Scotland and is open to the public as Preston Mill.

Scotscraig [NO 445283], near Tayport, Fife; castle replaced by mansion.

Held by the Scots of Balwearie, then by others, before being a possession of the Sharps in the seventeenth century. Sold to the Colvilles, then went to the Dalgleishs and then to the Maitlands.

Staneyhill Tower [NT 092784], near South Queensferry, West Lothian; ruinous L-plan tower house.

Held by the Sharps of Staneyhill.

Strathtyrum House [NO 491172], near St Andrews, Fife; castle or old house replaced by mansion.

The property was bought by James Sharp, Archbishop of St Andrews. The property later went to the Cheapes who still apparently own it. Strathtyrum House, which dates from the eighteenth century, can be used for weddings and luxury accommodation is available on an exclusive basis (01334 473600; www.strathtyrumhouse.com).

No. of castles/sites: 10
Rank: 140=/764
Xref: Shairp

Hoddom Castle 1911?

Shaw

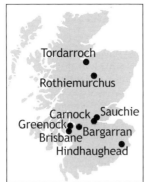

There are two branches of the family with different origins: one from the north and one from the south.

The northern branch, also known as Clan Aedh or Ay, is said to be descended from the MacDuff Earls of Fife, when one of them was made keeper of Inverness Castle. The clan acquired lands at Rothiemurchus, and they were part of the confederation of small clans known as Clan Chattan (see Mackintosh). The clan were on bad terms with the Comyns, which meant they supported Robert the Bruce and fought at the Battle of Bannockburn in 1314. The clan were led by Shaw 'Bucktooth' at the trial by battle at the North Inch of Perth in 1396. Clan Chattan had a bitter feud with the Camerons, and was settled in front of Robert III when thirty of each side fought it out: Clan Chattan won when the last Cameron left alive swam for the shore.

Doune of Rothiemurchus [NH 885098], two miles south of Aviemore in Strathspey, is an eighteenth-century mansion, which replaced a castle or earlier house. The lands were held by the Dallases of Cantray, and by the Mackintoshes and by the Shaws. James Shaw of Rothiemurchus was killed at the Battle of Harlaw in 1411. Rothiemurchus passed to the Gordons and then to the Grants, with whose descendants it remains. The estate is open to the public from April to October and there is a visitor centre (01479 812345; www.rothie murchus.net).

Tordarroch Castle [NH 677335], some seven miles south of Inverness, was once a strong tower but little or nothing survives. Tordarroch was held by the Shaws from 1468 and they fought for the Jacobites in the 1715 Rising. The two sons of the then laird fought at Preston, but were captured after the battle and one died after becoming ill in captivity while the other, Angus, was transported. He returned in 1722 but was then reluctant to get involved in the 1745-46 Rising, although many Shaws fought at Culloden. The castle was replaced by Tordarroch House, but the Shaws of Tordarroch now apparently live near Conon Bridge in Ross and Cromarty.

The lowland name is perhaps territorial in origin, and the Shaws or Schaws are on record from the end of the thirteenth century.

Sauchie Tower [NS 896957], which stands two miles north of Alloa in Clackmannan, is a square keep or tower of four storeys. It dates from the fifteenth century and there was a courtyard with later ranges but these have been demolished. The lands were held by the Annan family but passed to the Shaws in 1420, and they built the castle. The family plotted against James III, and Sir James Shaw, Governor of Stirling Castle, refused the king access to his son, later James IV. James III was

Sauchie Tower (M&R)

murdered soon afterwards in 1488 after the Battle of Sauchieburn. The family were Masters of the King's Wine Cellar in 1529, and the family built a mansion in the courtyard of the castle, and then moved to **Schawpark** [NS 905947], near Fishcross, but both these buildings have been demolished. The property went to the Cathcarts in 1752, and Sauchie Tower became ruinous but is being restored.

Bargarran [NS 463709] was to the north of Erskine in Renfrewshire, near the Clyde. It appears to have been held by the Stewarts of Barscube, but passed to the Shaws. There was an old mansion with an enclosing wall, and this was the home of Christian, daughter of John Shaw of Bargarran. She was at the centre of a notorious witch trial, when she claimed that she had been tormented by witches after she had been cursed in 1696 and 1697. Several people were tried and executed at Paisley, but this case has been likened to the Salem witch hunt in America. Some have suggested that Christian was at best hysterical, others that she maliciously concocted the evidence. Whatever the truth of it, she was later influential in making thread from yarn, which became a very important industry in Paisley.

The Shaws also owned:

Brisbane House or **Kelsoland** [NS 209622], near Largs, Ayrshire; site of castle and mansion.
  Held by the Kelso family, but was bought by the Shaws of Greenock in 1624, and they built the house. It was sold back to the Kelso family in 1650, but the name was changed after it went to the Brisbanes of Bishopton in 1671 and they held it until the twentieth century. The mansion was unroofed in 1938, and then was demolished.

Broich House [NS 641951], near Kippen, Stirlingshire; castle replaced by mansion.
  Held by the Shaws in the sixteenth century, then by the Edmonstones in the next century, then by the Leckies in 1773. Arngomery House is a nineteenth century mansion.

Carnock House [NS 865882], near Airth, Stirlingshire; site of tower house.
  Held by the Somervilles, by the Bruces and by others before passing to the Shaws of Greenock in the eighteenth century and they were still in possession into the twentieth century. Demolished in 1941.

Dalquhairn [NS 905725], near Falkirk; site of castle or old house.
  Held by the Shaws in the eighteenth century, and they were forfeited for their part in the Jacobite Rising of 1715.

Easter Greenock Castle [NS 300755], Greenock, Renfrewshire; site of castle.
  Held by the Stewarts of Castlemilk and then by the Hamiltons,

but passed to the Shaws of Sauchie in 1540, then later went to the Cathcarts and then to the Stewarts again. Demolished to build a railway.

Greenock Castle [NS 280765], Greenock, Renfrewshire; site of castle.

Held by the Cathcarts and by the Hamiltons and then by the Shaws. The castle was replaced by a mansion.

Hindhaughead [NT 643103], near Jedburgh, Borders; slight remains of castle.

Held by a Lady Shaw in the seventeenth century. The castle had been sacked, along with the village, by the English in 1513.

Keirs Castle [NS 430081], near Dalmellington, Ayrshire; slight remains of castle.

Held by the Crawfords, but Keirs was a property of the Shaws in 1696. One story is that William Wallace besieged Keirs Castle, but was driven from the walls.

Nether Horsburgh Castle [NT 304396], near Peebles, Borders; slight remains of tower house.

Held by the Horsburghs, but was bought by the Shaws of Shillingshaw when the Horsburghs got into debt.

Polkemmet House [NS 925650], near Whitburn, West Lothian; site of castle and mansion.

Held by the Cairns and then the Shaws, but was sold to the Baillies in 1820. The house was demolished in the twentieth century and the grounds are now Polkemmet Country Park (01501 743905).

www.clanshaw.net / www.cplx.net/SHAW/
No. of castles/sites: 14 / Rank: 104=/764
Xrefs: Chattan; Shaw; Aedh

Easter Greenock Castle (M&R) – see previous page

Sheriff

The name comes from the office of 'sheriff', which comes from Old English 'shire-reeve'. The name is on record in Scotland from 1400.

Stenhouse [NS 879829] was a seventeenth-century L-plan tower house, and stood two miles north of Falkirk

in central Scotland. The lands were held by the Watsons but passed to the Bruces of Stenhouse in 1611 and they built the tower. The property passed to the Sheriffs of Carronvale in the nineteenth century, but Stenhouse was demolished in the 1960s and the site is occupied by a housing estate.

No. of castles/sites: 1 / Rank: 537=/764

Sibbald

The name comes from the personal name 'Sigebeald', meaning 'victoriously bold', or from 'Saebeald', meaning 'sea-bold', from Old English. The name is on record as a surname in Scotland from the thirteenth century.

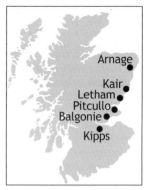

The Sibbalds held the following properties:

Arnage Castle [NJ 936370], near Ellon, Aberdeenshire; restored Z-plan tower house.

Held by the Cheynes, but Arnage was bought by the Sibbalds in 1643 and they sold Arnage to John Ross, who was later Provost of Aberdeen, in 1702. Still occupied.

Balgonie Castle [NO 313007], near Glenrothes, Fife; fine castle and courtyard.

Held by the Sibbalds from before 1246, but passed by marriage to the Lundies around 1496. Later went to the Leslies and

Balgonie Castle (LF)

then to the Balfours of Whittinghame, and the castle is said to have several ghosts, including a Green Lady. Balgonie is open to the public (01592 750119; www.balgonie-castle.com).

Gibliston House [NO 493055], near St Monans, Fife; castle replaced by mansion.

Held by the Pattullos, but passed to the Sibbalds, who held the lands in the seventeenth century. Gibliston later went to the Smiths, then to Sir Robert Lorimer in 1916.

Kair House [NO 769765], near Arbuthnott, Aberdeenshire; castle replaced by mansion.

Held by the Sibbalds, and John Sibbald of Kair was minister of St Ternan's Church at Arbuthnott (which is open to the public) in the middle of the seventeenth century. There is a plaque to him in the church, but the property passed to the Guthries, then to the Burnetts and then to the Kinlochs.

Kipps Castle [NS 989739], near Linlithgow, West Lothian; ruinous tower house.

Held by the Boyds, but passed to the Sibbalds. One of the family was Sir Robert Sibbald, seventeenth-century naturalist (he established a Physic Garden in Edinburgh in 1667) and antiquary, a founder member of the Royal College of Physicians of Edinburgh in 1681, and first professor of medicine at Edinburgh four years later. He was the king's physician (and geographer) in Scotland.

Letham [NO 624457], near Arbroath, Angus; site of castle.
Held by the Sibbalds from the fifteenth century for 300 or so years. Passed then to the Dempsters at the end of the eighteenth century, then to the Hays and to the Fletchers, and there is a modern mansion at Letham Grange, which is apparently now a hotel (01241 890373).

Pitcullo Castle [NO 413196], near Leuchars, Fife; restored L-plan tower house.
Held by the Sibbalds, but passed to the Balfours in the sixteenth

Pitcullo Castle (M&R)

century, then went to the Trents. Restored in the 1960s and 1970s and reoccupied.

Rankeilour Castle [NO 330119], near Cupar, Fife; castle replaced by mansion.
Held by the Rankeillour family, but passed to the Sibbalds of Balgonie and then to the Makgills and to the Hopes. The Hopes built Rankeillour House in the nineteenth century.

No. of castles/sites: 8
Rank: 160=/764

Sinclair

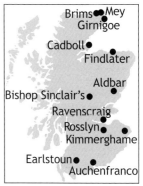

The name comes from 'St Clare', which is located in Pont d'Eveque in Normandy in France, and the St Clares followed William the Conqueror when he invaded England in 1066. The family came to Scotland in the twelfth century and held lands in the Borders and in Midlothian and other parts of southern Scotland before acquiring the Earldom of Orkney and the Lordship of Shetland. The family came to own much property in Caithness as well as in the south and east of Scotland. John Sinclair, Bishop of Ross, officiated at the wedding of Mary, Queen of Scots, to Henry Stewart, Lord Darnley, in 1565.

Rosslyn Castle [NT 274628] is a couple of miles south of Loanhead in Midlothian, and the romantic ruins are enough to indicate that this was once a large, strong and princely stronghold. The keep or main tower is ruinous but a range from the sixteenth century is almost complete. The Sinclairs held the lands from twelfth or thirteenth century, and during the Wars of Independence an English army was heavily defeated by the Scots in 1303 near the castle. The Sinclairs fought for Robert the Bruce at Bannockburn in 1314, and Sir Henry Sinclair was one of the nobles to add his seal to the Declaration of Arbroath. Sir William, who probably built the keep, set out on crusade with Robert the Bruce's heart, and was killed fighting the Moors in Granada in 1330. Henry Sinclair was made Earl of Orkney in 1379 by the King of Norway, and he conquered the Faroes, and discovered Greenland and probably the northern part of North America. The second Earl, another Henry, was captured by the English at the Battle of Homildon Hill in 1402, and was Admiral of Scotland. Rosslyn Castle was accidentally burnt in 1452. The Sinclairs were forced to resign the Earldom of Orkney and were given Ravenscraig in Fife in compensation as well as the Earldom of Caithness from 1455 (Orkney was a much wealthier earldom). Rosslyn Castle was sacked and torched by the Earl of Hertford in 1544, and was attacked again in 1650 by Monck during Cromwell's invasion; a Covenanting mob also damaged it in 1688. The property

Rosslyn Castle (and chapel) 1907?

passed by marriage to the Sinclair (St Clair)-Erskines, who were made Earls of Rosslyn in 1802, and they still own the castle. A spectre of a dog, killed with its English master after the battle in 1302, reputedly haunts the castle, and its howling has been reported. There are also stories of a spectre of a black knight on a black horse being seen in the glen. A great treasure is said to be buried within the old castle, and there is reputed to be a White Lady who guards it. She can only be woken and the treasure found by blowing a trumpet when standing on the correct step of one of the staircases. Part of the castle is habitable, and can be rented through the Landmark Trust (01628 825925; www.land marktrust.org.uk). Rosslyn Chapel was founded by William Sinclair, Earl of Caithness and Orkney, in 1446, and the building is open to the public (0131 440 2159; www.rosslyn-chapel.com). The chapel is richly carved and there is the famous Apprentice Pillar. Beneath the crypt is the burial vault for the Sinclairs, where ten of the Earls and their kin lie, formerly in full armour without coffins; there are also memorials to the Sinclairs in the chapel. Ghostly flames were said to be flare from the chapel when one of the Sinclairs was about to die.

Girnigoe Castle [ND 379549], also known as **Castle Sinclair**, is some three miles north of Wick in Caithness on cliffs above the sea; this used to be thought of as two castles but current thinking is that it was one large fortress. Not much remains of what is known as Castle

Girnigoe Castle (M&R)

Sinclair, while Girnigoe is a substantial ruin above cliffs, the main part of which is a U-plan block which rises to five storeys on the cliff side.

The Sinclairs were forced to resign the Earldom of Orkney, which was much wealthier, and had to content themselves with Caithness and with Ravenscraig in Fife. William Sinclair, second Earl of Caithness, built a castle here but he was slain at the Battle of Flodden in 1513; and the next Earl, John, was slain in battle in 1529 on Orkney. In 1571 George, fourth Earl, had John, Master of Caithness, his son and heir, imprisoned in the dungeons for seven years after having apparently tried to make peace with their enemies, the Earls of Sutherland, without first consulting his father. The story goes that

the Master was fed on salted beef, and denied water so that he died mad with thirst. The fifth Earl, another George, built Castle Sinclair, but feuded with the Earl of Sutherland, and then put down a rebellion in Orkney in 1615 by the Stewart Earls of Orkney. Cromwell had the castle garrisoned in the 1650s. George, sixth Earl, had huge debts which were acquired by the Campbells of Glenorchy, and they claimed the Earldom of Caithness. This was contested by Sinclair of Keiss, and came to battle at Altimarlech in 1679, where the Sinclairs were slaughtered in such numbers that the Campbells reportedly could cross the river without getting their feet wet. The Sinclairs recovered the earldom in 1681, but the castle was damaged during the attack, and was not reused. The property passed to the Dunbars of Hempriggs, but was sold back to the Sinclairs about 1950, and the castle is now held in trust. The current Earl of Caithness apparently lives in Oxfordshire in England. The ruins are accessible with great care but should viewed from a safe distance (www.castle-sg.org/ www.clansinclair.org).

Ravenscraig Castle [NT 291925] is an impressive ruinous castle and courtyard, and it dates from the fifteenth century and is one of the first strongholds in

Ravenscraig Castle (M&R)

Britain to be built for artillery, both defensive and offensive. It had been a royal stronghold and Mary of Gueldres died here in 1463. Ravenscraig was forced upon the Sinclairs when they resigned the Earldom of Orkney, and they completed the castle and it was occupied until about 1650. The property passed by marriage to the Sinclair (St Clair)-Erskines, Earls of Rosslyn, who moved to **Dysart House** [NT 302930], a symmetrical mansion of 1755 with later additions (and now a Carmelite monastery). Ravenscraig was sold by the family in 1898, and the castle is now in the care of Historic Scotland and part of the building is open to the public.

Castle of Mey [ND 290739], which is seven miles north-east of Castletown in Caithness, is an altered Z-plan tower house, which rises to three storeys and an attic, and dates from the sixteenth century. Mey was a property of the Sinclair Earls of Caithness from 1566 and they built the castle. William Sinclair, eldest son of George Sinclair of Mey, while a student at Edinburgh High School, shot and killed Bailie MacMorran in 1595; he was later Sir William Sinclair of Cadboll. MacLeod of Assynt, who betrayed the Marquis of Montrose, was

Castle of Mey 1910?

imprisoned in the Castle of Mey. The property was sold to the late Queen Mother in 1952, who had it restored. The building is said to be haunted by a Green Lady, the ghost of a daughter of George, the fifth Earl. She fell in love with a ploughman, and her father had her imprisoned in one of the attic rooms. She threw herself from one of the windows, and her sad spectre reportedly haunts the castle. The castle is open to the public (01847 851473; www.castleofmey.org.uk).

The Sinclairs were not noted for avoiding a fight with their neighbours:

'Sinclair, Sutherland, Keith and Clan Gunn,
    There was never peace when they four were in.'

The Sinclairs also held:

Ackergill Tower [ND 352547], near Wick, Caithness; fine castle and mansion.
  Held by the Cheynes and by the Keiths before passing to the Sinclairs, then went to the Oliphants and to the Dunbars of Hempriggs. The castle can be rented for totally exclusive use (01955 603556; www.ackergill-tower.co.uk).

Aldbar Castle [NO 572577], near Brechin, Perthshire; site of castle.
  Held by the Cramonds and then by the Lyon Lord Glamis, but was later bought by the Sinclairs, then passed to the Youngs and to the Chalmers of Balnacraig who held it into the twentieth century. The castle was demolished in 1965.

Auchenfranco Castle [NX 893724], near Dumfries; site of strong castle.
  Held by the Douglases but passed to the Sinclairs. William Sinclair of Auchenfranco was murdered by one of the MacNaughts in 1542. The property passed to the Corries in the eighteenth century.

Berriedale Castle [ND 121224], near Dunbeath, Caithness; slight remains of castle.
  Held by the Cheynes, by the Sutherlands and by the Oliphants before being bought by the Sinclair Earls of Caithness in 1606.

Bishop Sinclair's Tower [NO 077457], Dunkeld, Perthshire; site of castle.
  Probably built by William Sinclair, who was Bishop of Dunkeld from 1309. He was active on behalf of Robert the Bruce, and is known as the 'fighting bishop' because in 1317 he rallied the Scots against an English attack on Dunfermline. He crowned Edward Balliol in 1333, and died in 1337.

Bower Tower [ND 230619], near Castleton, Caithness; site of tower house.
  Held by the Sinclairs.

Braal Castle [ND 139601], near Thurso, Caithness; ruinous castle.
  Held by the Stewarts and by the Crichtons, but had passed to the Sinclair Earls of Caithness by 1547, then went to the Sinclairs of Ulbster. They built the nearby castellated mansion, which has been divided into separate flats.

Brabster Castle [ND 316695], near Castletown, Caithness; slight remains of castle.
  Held by the Sinclairs, and the castle was replaced by Brabstermire House, a two-storey eighteenth-century house.

Brims Castle [ND 043710], near Thurso, Caithness; ruinous L-plan tower house.
  Held by the Sinclairs of Dunbeath and occupied into the twentieth century (www.brims.co.uk). The castle is said to have a White Lady, the ghost of the daughter of James Sinclair of Uttersquoy. The attractive young woman was lover to Patrick Sinclair of Brims, but the story goes that he tired of her, murdered her and then hid her body in the castle before later having her secretly buried.

Bucholly Castle [ND 382658], near Wick, Caithness; ruinous castle on cliffs.
  Held by the Mowats but was bought by the Sinclairs of Rattar in 1616. It was replaced by Freswick House, and Bucholly was said to be 'strongly expressive of the jealous and wretched condition of the tyrant owners'.

Cadboll Castle [NH 879776], near Tain, Ross and Cromarty; ruinous L-plan tower house.
  Held by the Clyne family and by the MacLeods of Cadboll but passed to the Sinclairs. Sir William Sinclair of Cadboll, when a student at Edinburgh High School, shot and killed Baillie MacMorran in 1595. The building was apparently damaged by Alexander Ross of Balnagown as he was ordered to repair the damage in 1572-74. The castle was abandoned for the nearby house, and part is used as a farm store.

Carfrae Peel [NT 502551], near Lauder, Borders; ruinous tower house.
  Held by the Sinclairs.

Castle Hill [NJ 154571], Pluscarden, Moray; site of castle by abbey.
  Held by several families following the reformation including by the Sinclair Earls of Caithness in 1649, then by the Brodies of Lethen and by others. The abbey is restored and can be visited (01343 890257; www.pluscardenabbey.org).

Castle Mestag [ND 340764], Isle of Stroma, Caithness; slight remains of castle on rock.
  Held by the Sinclairs but passed to the Kennedys, and they built a later mansion.

Castle of Old Wick [ND 369488], near Wick, Caithness; old ruinous castle.
  Held by the Cheynes, by the Sutherland Lord Duffus and then by the Oliphants. During a feud between the Oliphants, Sutherlands and Sinclairs, the castle was starved into submission and captured in 1569 by John, Master of Caithness. It was bought by the Sinclairs in 1606 (or 1644), but passed to the Campbells of Glenorchy, then to the Dunbars of Hemprigg until 1910. It is now in the care of Historic Scotland and can be visited although great care should be taken (01667 460232).

Catcune Tower [NT 351605], near Gorebridge, Midlothian; site of L-plan tower house.
  Held by the Borthwicks but passed to the Sinclairs, who probably built the tower.

Cessford Castle [NT 738238], near Kelso, Borders; impressive ruinous castle.
  Held by the Sinclairs in the fourteenth century, but passed to the Kerrs, who were long in possession and in residence, and the Kerrs built the castle.

Cockburnspath Castle [NT 785699], near Cockburnspath, Borders; ruinous castle.
  Held by the Cospatrick Earls of Dunbar and by the Homes before passing to the Sinclairs, who sold it to the Douglases in 1546. The old castle was replaced by Cockburnspath House.

Cot Castle [NS 739457], near Strathaven, Lanarkshire; site of castle.
  Held by the Hamiltons for many years but then passed to Lord Lee and then went by marriage to the Sinclairs.

Cousland Tower [NT 377683], near Dalkeith, Midlothian; slight remains of tower house.
  Held by the Sinclairs of Rosslyn, but passed to the Makgills of Cranstoun in the seventeenth century and then to the Dalrymples of Stair.

Cullen House [NJ 507663], near Cullen, Aberdeenshire; altered and extended castle.

Held by the Sinclairs but passed by marriage to the Ogilvies of Auchleven and they built the castle. The Ogilvies became Earls of Findlater and long held the property. Developed into a large mansion, and divided but occupied.

Deskford Castle [NJ 509617], near Cullen, Aberdeenshire; slight remains of tower house.

Held by the Sinclairs and then by the Ogilvies who abandoned it for what is now Cullen House.

Dounreay Castle [NC 983669], near Thurso, Caithness; ruinous castle.

Held by the Sinclairs of Dunbeath from 1564. This was disputed by the Sinclair Earl of Caithness, and the castle was besieged

Dounreay Castle (M&R)

in 1614. The building was occupied by Cromwell's forces in the 1650s, but later passed to the Forbeses after 1726, then to the Mackays of Reay, and later of Tongue. It is in the grounds of the nuclear plant.

Dunbeath Castle [ND 158282], near Dunbeath, Caithness; fine E-plan tower house on cliffs.

Held by the Crichtons and by the Innes family before it passed to the Sinclairs of Geanies in 1529. They built much of the present castle, and Dunbeath was seized by the Marquis of Montrose in 1650, although it was quickly retaken after he was defeated at Carbisdale. The Sinclairs were made Baronets in 1704, and now apparently live in London in England; the castle is still occupied.

Earlstoun Castle [NX 613840], near St John's Town of Dalry, Galloway; altered L-plan tower house.

Held by the Hepburn Earls of Bothwell, but passed to the Sinclairs in the middle of the sixteenth century, then went by marriage to the Gordons of Airds in 1615. Still occupied.

Evelaw Tower [NT 661526], near Westruther, Borders; ruinous L-plan tower house.

Held by the Douglases but passed by marriage to the Sinclairs of Longformacus, who sold it to the Smiths in 1731.

Findlater Castle [NJ 542673], near Cullen, Aberdeenshire; ruinous castle on cliffs.

Held by the Sinclairs in the twelfth century, but passed to the Ogilvies and then to the Gordons, then to the Ogilvies again, who abandoned Findlater for Cullen. The castle can be viewed from a safe distance (www.findlater.org.uk/castle.htm).

Freswick House [ND 378671], near Wick, Caithness; tall and old house.

Held by the Mowats but was sold to the Sinclairs of Rattar in 1661. Still occupied.

Geanies Castle [NH 894798], near Tain, Ross and Cromarty; site of castle.

Held by the MacLeods, but had passed to the Sinclairs by 1624,

who sold it to the Murrays in 1838. Replaced by Geanies House.

Haimer Castle [ND 143673], near Thurso, Caithness; site of castle.

Held by the Sinclairs.

Hempriggs House [ND 359473], near Wick, Caithness; castle replaced by mansion.

Held by the Sinclairs but passed to the Dunbars of Hempriggs. Now a residential home.

Herbertshire Castle [NS 804830], near Falkirk; site of large castle.

Held by the Sinclairs of Rosslyn, but passed to the Elphinstone Earls of Linlithgow in 1608, then to the Stirlings and to others. This is said to have been the birthplace of the Black Douglas, the Good Sir James, who was a friend and captain of Robert the Bruce.

Herdmanston [NT 474700], near Haddington, East Lothian; site of strong L-plan tower house.

Held by the Sinclairs from 1160, and this branch of the family gained the title Lord Sinclair from another line. The tower was seized by Lord Gray of Wilton, acting for the English, in 1548. The Sinclair Lords Sinclair now apparently live near St John's Town of Perth in Galloway.

Keiss Castle [ND 357616], near Wick, Caithness; impressive ruinous castle on cliffs.

Held by the Sinclairs, and the castle was abandoned for nearby new **Keiss Castle** [ND 35561/], which was built in 1755 but

Keiss Castle (M&R)

was altered in later years. The old castle is dangerously ruined.

Kimmerghame House [NT 815514], near Duns, Borders; castle replaced by mansion.

Held by the Morhams and then by the Sinclairs in the sixteenth century, then by the Homes in the next century. Burnt out and only partly rebuilt.

Kirkwall Castle [HY 448109], Kirkwall, Orkney; site of castle.

Held by the Sinclair Earls of Orkney, but eventually passed to the Stewarts. The last remains were used to build the tolbooth and town hall, and nothing remains.

Knockhall Castle [NJ 992265], near Newburgh, Fife; ruinous L-plan tower house.

Held and built by the Sinclairs of Newburgh in 1565, but sold to the Udnys in 1633. Burned accidentally in 1734 and never restored.

Knockinnan Castle [ND 181312], near Dunbeath, Caithness; slight remains of castle.

Held by the Sinclairs, and may never have been completed.

Knocknalling [NX 597848], near St John's Town of Dalry, Galloway; castle replaced by mansion.

Held by the Kennedys but later passed to the Sinclair Lords Sinclair.

Langwell Castle [ND 116227], near Dunbeath, Caithness; slight remains of castle.

Held by the Sutherlands and replaced by Langwell House, a rambling mansion, but was bought by the Sinclairs in 1788, then went to the Hornes in 1813 and then to the Dukes of Portland, who still apparently own it. The garden is open by appointment only (01593 751278; www.gardensof scotland.org).

Latheron Castle [ND 199334], near Dunbeath, Caithness; slight remains of castle.

Held by the Gunns, but passed to the Sinclairs, who held the lands in the seventeenth century.

Logan House [NT 204630], near Penicuik, Midlothian; slight remains of castle.

Held by the Sinclairs of Rosslyn. One story is that Sir William Sinclair, third Earl of Orkney, wagered his life that he could help the king kill a famous white stag before it escaped across the Glencorse Burn. This he did and was granted the lands in reward, although he was later slain fighting the Moors. The property was held by Cowans in the nineteenth century.

Longformacus [NT 685573], near Duns, Borders; castle replaced by mansion.

Held by the Earl of Moray and by the Earls of Dunbar before passing to the Sinclairs, who held Longformacus for many generations.

Morton House [NT 254679], Edinburgh; mansion with old work.

Held by the Sinclairs of Rosslyn from the fourteenth century, but had passed to the Riggs by 1800, then to the Trotters of Charterhall and to the Elliotts. The house is still occupied.

Mortonhall [NT 262683], Edinburgh; castle replaced by mansion.

Held by the Sinclairs of Rosslyn, but passed to the Ellis family and then to the Trotters, who built a classical mansion in 1769. There is a caravan and camping site and house can be rented on the estate (www.mortonhall.co.uk).

Nisbet House [NT 795512], near Duns, Borders; altered tower house.

Held by the Nisbets, but passed to the Kerrs and was held by the Sinclairs in the nineteenth century.

Old Woodhouselee Castle [NT 258617], near Penicuik, Midlothian; slight remains of tower house.

Held by the Sinclairs in the sixteenth century, but passed to the Hamiltons of Bothwellhaugh. Said to be haunted by the despairing ghost of Lady Hamilton.

Peelhill [NT 683572], near Longformacus, Borders; site of tower house.

Held by the Earls of Moray then by the Earls of Dunbar, but passed to the Sinclairs of Rosslyn, who probably built the tower.

Pitteadie Castle [NT 257891], near Burntisland, Fife; strong but ruinous castle.

Held by the Valance family, but passed to the Sinclairs and then to the Sandilands, to the Boswells of Balmuto and then to the Calderwoods.

Polwarth Castle [NT 749500], near Duns, Borders; site of castle.

Held by the Polwarth family, then by the Cospatrick Earls of March, then by the Sinclairs of Herdmanston, and then by the Homes, who probably built the castle. It later passed to the Scotts.

Ravensneuk Castle [NT 224590], near Penicuik, Midlothian; slight remains of castle.

Held by Oliver Sinclair of Pitcairn, favourite of James V and leader of the Scottish forces at the disastrous Battle of Solway Moss in 1542. Passed to the Clerks of Penicuik, who demolished much of it.

Scrabster Castle [ND 107692], near Thurso, Caithness; slight remains of castle.

Held by the Sinclairs but the Earls of Sutherland were made keepers of the castle in 1544. Scrabster House may be on the site.

Stevenson [NT 170430], near Peebles, Borders; site of tower house.

Held by the Swintons but passed by marriage to the Sinclairs in the seventeenth century who held it into the nineteenth century or later.

Stevenson House [NT 544748], near Haddington, East Lothian; mansion incorporating part of castle.

Held by the Sinclairs from the sixteenth century or earlier. The Sinclairs of Stevenson were patrons of the Holy Blood altar in St Mary's Kirk in Haddington (which is open to the public). The family were made Baronets of Nova Scotia in 1636, and became Sinclair-Lockharts. The property passed to the Dunbars in the twentieth century and the Sinclair-Lockharts, Baronets, apparently now live in New Zealand.

Strathaven Castle [NS 703445], Strathaven, Lanarkshire; ruinous castle.

Held by the Bairds and then by the Sinclairs, before passing to the Douglases and then to the Stewarts and then to the Hamiltons. The building has been clumsily consolidated but the site is accessible.

Strom Castle [HU 395475], near Lerwick, Shetland; slight remains of castle.

Held by the Sinclairs.

Thurso Castle [ND 125689], Thurso, Caithness; ruinous mansion on site of castle.

Held by the Sinclairs of Greenland and Rattar in 1612. Thurso Castle was the home of Sir John Sinclair of Ulbster, who

Thurso Castle (M&R)

compiled the *Statistical Account of Scotland* and died in 1835. The family have a burial vault nearby [ND 336418]. The Sinclairs were made Baronets in 1786 and then Viscounts in 1952. The Sinclair Viscounts Thurso still apparently live in Caithness.

Whitekirk [NT 595816], near North Berwick, East Lothian; altered tower house.

Held by Oliver Sinclair of Pitcairn, favourite of James V and general at the disastrous battle of Solway Moss in 1542. The tower was burnt in the following years by the English. Restored and occupied; can be viewed from the burial ground of the church.

Woodhall [NT 433680], near Pencaitland, East Lothian; mansion incorporating tower house.

Held by the Setons, but passed to the Sinclairs of Herdmanston in 1488 and they held it to the eighteenth century. Woodhall passed to the Lauders, was restored in 1884, and is occupied.

www.clansinclair.org
www.clansinclairusa.org
www.clansinclaircanada.ca
home.vicnet.net.au/~clansinc/
sinclair.quarterman.org
No. of castles/sites: 63
Rank: 13/764
Xref: St Clair

Siward

The name comes from the Old English personal name 'Sigeweard', which means 'victorious guard'. Siward was Earl of Northumberland, and he is thought to have defeated Macbeth at Dunsinane in 1054, although he apparently lost his son in the battle. Macbeth escaped and was not hunted down for another three years. The Siwards are on record in Scotland from the twelfth century, but supported the English in the Wars of Independence to their ruin when Robert the Bruce was victorious.

Tibbers Castle [NX 863982] is a couple of miles north and west of Thornhill in Dumfries and Galloway. This was once a strong castle, with a rampart and ditch which enclosed a hall and other buildings. The courtyard had round towers at the corners and there was a barbican. The lands were held by the Siwards, who were sheriffs of Dumfries. One story is that the Romans previously used the site and it is named after Tiberius Caesar. The Siward family sided with Edward I of England, who visited here in 1298, although the castle is said to have been captured by William Wallace. Tibbers was seized by the Scots in 1306, but was swiftly retaken by the English, who hanged the garrison. Tibbers was once again retaken by the Scots by 1314, and may have then been dismantled. The lands passed to the Earls of March and then to the Maitlands of Auchen and to the Douglases of Drumlanrig. The castle now stands in the park surrounding Drumlanrig Castle.

Kellie Castle [NO 520052] is a magnificent E-plan castle, dating from the sixteenth century and with a fine walled garden. An older stronghold was held by the Siwards, but the present building was begun after it had passed to the Oliphants in the fourteenth century. Kellie went to the Erskines, later Earls of Kellie, and is now in the care of The National Trust for Scotland and is open to the public (01333 720271).

No. of castles/sites: 2
Rank: 396=/764
Xref: Seward

Skene

The name is probably territorial and comes from the lands of Skene, which are four miles north-west of Westhill to the west of Aberdeen. A story about the origin is that one of the Robertsons of Struan managed to save the life of the king, and he fought off the attack with a dirk or 'sgian', pronounced 'sgee-in', hence 'Skene'. The lands were given to the rescuer, and he called them after the weapon which made his fortune. Gilbert Skene, who died in 1599, was physician to James VI.

Skene House [NJ 768097] is a large castellated mansion, remodelled and extended in the middle of the nineteenth century, but the building incorporates a large and strong keep or tower, which had three vaulted storeys and dates from the fourteenth century. The property was owned by the Skenes from 1318 or earlier after they had supported Robert the Bruce. Adam Skene was killed at the Battle of Harlaw in 1411, Alexander Skene died at Flodden in 1513, and another laird, also Alexander, died at Pinkie in 1547. Alexander Skene of Skene, who died in 1727, was said to be a wizard who had acquired his power studying on the contintent. He would procure the unbaptised corpses of babies on which his familiars would feast. The story goes that a spectral carriage, in which he and the devil are riding, reputedly crosses the Loch of Skene at midnight on New Year's Eve only to sink before it reaches the bank. The Skenes owned the property until it passed to the Duff Earls of Fife in 1827, and then later it went to the Hamiltons.

The Skenes also held:
Cairneyflappet or **Strathmiglo Castle** [NO 220102], near Auchtermuchty, Fife; site of castle.
Held by the Scotts of Balwearie, and believed to have been rather shoddily built and hence the name. The lands passed to the Balfours of Burleigh and then to the Skenes of Hallyards in the eighteenth century. The castle is said to have had a brownie, which is reputed to have stolen food from the stores. The building was demolished in 1734, and the steeple of the town hall was built from the remains.
Curriehill Castle [NT 165678], near Balerno, Edinburgh; site of castle.
Held by the Skenes, and the castle was defended against Mary, Queen of Scots, by the family. Sir John Skene of Curriehill was an eminent sixteenth-century lawyer, and was raised to the Supreme Court Bench in 1594. He was knighted and made a Baronet of Nova Scotia in 1626. The property passed to the Johnstones and then to others.
Hallyards [NT 129738], near Kirkliston, Edinburgh; ruinous tower house.
Possibly held by the Skenes, by the Erskine Earls of Mar and by the Marjoribanks family.
Hallyards Castle [NT 212914], near Cowdenbeath, Fife; slight remains of castle.
Held by the Skenes. James V stayed here on his way to Falkland Palace, after the rout at Solway Moss in 1542, and died soon afterwards at the Palace. The castle is said to have been the

mustering point for Fife Jacobites in the 1715 Rising. Hallyards passed by marriage to Moncrieffes of Reidie in 1788, and Skene of Skene, fourteenth of Hallyards, now apparently lives in Edinburgh.

Leask House [NK 026331], near Ellon, Aberdeenshire; site of castle and ruinous mansion.

Held by the Leask family, and later by the Cummings, by the Gordons and then by the Skenes. The mansion was burnt out in 1927.

Lethenty Castle [NJ 764254], near Inverurie, Aberdeenshire; site of castle.

Held by the Skenes, and the castle was sacked by Covenanters in 1640 and again five years later.

Mains of Dyce [NJ 889138], near Dyce, Aberdeenshire; possible site of castle.

Held by the Skenes of Dyce and there is a nineteenth-century mansion.

Parkhill House [NJ 898140], near Dyce, Aberdeenshire; site of castle.

Held by the Skenes of Dyce. Parkhill House, which dated from the eighteenth century, was demolished around 1960, and a new house built.

Pitlour [NO 209113], near Auchtermuchty, Fife; castle replaced by mansion.

Held by the Scotts and then by the Skenes.

Provost Skene's House [NJ 943064], Aberdeen; fine town house.

Held by George Skene of Rubislaw, a wealthy merchant and Provost of the city, from 1669. The Duke of Cumberland stayed here for six weeks in 1746 on his way to Culloden and the defeat of the Jacobites at Culloden. There are fine plaster ceilings and wood panelling, and the painted gallery has a unique cycle of tempera wall and ceiling painting depicting Christ's life. The house is a museum and open to the public (01224 641086; www.aagm.co.uk).

Rubislaw [NJ 919056], Aberdeen; site of castle or old house.

Held by the Skenes from around the middle of the sixteenth century. Sir George Skene of Rubislaw was Lord Provost of Aberdeen, and bought the house now known as Provost Skene's House (see above). James Skene of Rubislaw was a friend of Sir Walter Scott and drew sketches to illustrate some of the *Waverley* novels, and William Forbes Skene, descended from the Skenes of Rubislaw, was made Historiographer Royal for Scotland in 1881.

www.clanskene.org
No. of castles/sites: 12
Rank: 120=/764

Smith

The name comes from the occupation of smith, a metal worker and armourer and an important profession. The name is in record in Scotland from the end of the twelfth century, and it can be spelt Smith, Smyth or Smythe. Adam Smith, who was born in Kirkcaldy in 1723, was a Professor at the University of Glasgow and wrote the hugely influential *An Inquiry into the Nature and Causes of the Wealth of Nations* in 1776. James Smith was the overseer of King's Works for James VII, and was the architect for buildings including Dalkeith Palace, Melville Castle and the Canongate Parish Church in Edinburgh.

The Smiths or Smyths owned the following properties:

Balhary [NO 264466], near Blairgowrie, Perthshire; castle replaced by mansion.

Held by the Smyths from around 1588 to 1876.

Bardmony House [NO 250452], near Blairgowrie, Perthshire; house incorporating old work.

Held by the Smyths following the Reformation.

Braco Castle [NN 824113], near Dunblane, Perthshire; altered tower house.

Held by the Graham Earls of Montrose, but the property passed to the Smythes in 1790. Said to be haunted, and the grounds are open by appointment from February to October (01786 880437; www.gardensofscotland.org).

Colonsay House [NR 395968], near Scalasaig, Isle of Colonsay; mansion.

The island was held by the MacDuffies and by the MacNeills before passing to Lord Strathcona, the first of whom was Sir Donald Alexander Smith, who was Governor of the Hudson Bay Company and then High Commissioner for Canada in London in 1896. The mansion dates from 1722 and the fine gardens are open to the public some days (01951 200211; www.colonsay.org.uk).

Craigend Castle [NS 545778], near Milngavie, Dunbartonshire; site of castle and mansion.

Held by the Grahams but passed to the Smiths, one of whom started the Glasgow booksellers John Smith and Son in 1751. The property passed to the Inglises and then to the Wilsons. Demolished in the twentieth century, and the stables now house a visitor centre for Mugdock Park (0141 956 6100; www.mugdock-country-park.org.uk).

Evelaw Tower [NT 661526], near Westruther, Borders; ruinous L-plan tower house.

Held by the Douglases then by the Sinclairs of Longformacus, but was bought by the Smiths in 1731.

Gibliston House [NO 493055], near St Monans, Fife; castle replaced by mansion.

Held by the Pattullos and by the Sibbalds before coming to the Smiths, then went to the Gillespies and then to Sir Robert Lorimer in 1916.

Glassingall [NN 798045], near Dunblane, Stirlingshire; mansion on site of castle or old house.

Held by the Chisholms but passed to the Smiths in the nineteenth century, and then to the Wallaces.

Glenlee [NX 607807], near New Galloway, Galloway; castle replaced by mansion.

    Held by the Millers and by the Maxwells but was owned by the Smiths at the end of the nineteenth century.

Jordanhill [NS 538683], Glasgow; site of castle.

    Held by the Crawfords, but passed to the Houstons and then to the Smiths; Archibald Smith of Jordanhill was a prosperous Glasgow merchant. The Smiths of Jordanhill now apparently live in Australia.

Methven Castle [NO 042260], near Perth; restored castle.

    Held by several families including by the Stewarts, but passed

Methven Castle (M&R)

    to the Smythes of Braco in 1664 and they held Methven until 1923, when it was sold. Now used as company offices.

Mugdock Castle [NS 549772], near Milngavie, Dunbartonshire; ruinous castle.

    Long held by the Grahams but was a property of J. Guthrie Smith when a large mansion was built in the ruins. The house was used by the government during World War II but was demolished soon afterwards. In Mugdock Country Park (0141 956 6100; www.mugdock-country-park.org.uk).

Peelwalls [NT 922599], near Eyemouth, Borders; castle replaced by mansion.

    Held by the Homes, but owned by the Smiths of Peelwalls in the eighteenth century. The family are now apparently the Smiths of Cumledge, a property near Duns in the Borders.

Pitgair Castle [NJ 774606], near Macduff, Aberdeenshire; site of castle.

    Held by the Smiths in the eighteenth century.

www.clansmithsociety.org

No. of castles/sites: 14
Rank: 104=/764
Xrefs: Smythe; Smyth

Smollett

The origin of the name is not clear, but it is on record in Scotland from the beginning of the sixteenth century and the family held lands in Dunbartonshire.

    Place of Bonhill [NS 390793] was to the south of Alexandria, and there was a mansion which included work from an older house or castle. The property was held by the Lennox family and by the Lindsays, but was bought by the Smolletts in 1648. The Smolletts married into the Telfers, and became Telfer Smolletts. The house was demolished around 1950 and a school occupies the site, and the family, the Telfer Smolletts of Bonhill, now apparently live near Alexandria and also in Devon in England according to *Burke's*. It is said that a subterranean passageway led down from a hidden entrance behind the drawing room fireplace of Place of Bonhill to the banks of the River Leven. A piper was sent to explore the passage, but then vanished without trace. Afterwards it was said that faint pipe music could often be heard within the walls.

    Cameron House [NS 376831], two miles north of Alexandria, is a magnificent mansion and dates from 1830, but it may stand on the site of or incorporate an old castle of the fourteenth century. The lands were held by the Lennox family, then by the Charterises, by the Dennistouns and by the Colquhouns, before being bought by the Smolletts in 1763. Dr Johnson and Boswell visited in 1772, and Tobias Smollett, the well-known author, came from the family. One of the rooms of Cameron House is said to be haunted, and the freezing over of Loch Lomond was said to herald a death in the resident family, but over the years this was in fact shown not to be the case. The Smolletts sold the property in 1986, and the house is now a luxury hotel and leisure centre (01389 755565; www.cameronhouse.co.uk).

    Old Dalquhurn House [NS 390780] stood a couple of miles north of Dumbarton in the village of Renton. The house was a plain old building, rising to three storeys, but was demolished and the site is occupied by a church. The lands were held by the Earls of Lennox, by the Spreulls and by the Dennistouns, but were acquired by the Smolletts in 1692. This was the birthplace of well-known author Tobias Smollett, and there is a monument [NS 388782], a sixty-foot column, to the writer near the site of the house. Smollett studied medicine at the University of Glasgow and was the author of several successful books, including *Humphrey Clinker* in 1771.

    Renton is named after Celia Renton, who was a daughter-in-law of the Smolletts.

No. of castles/sites: 3
Rank: 328=/764

Somerville

The name originates from Somerville, an estate and now town, which is near Caen in Normandy in France. The family came to England in 1066 with William the Conqueror during the Norman invasion, and then settled in Scotland in the reign of David I in the twelfth century. They held lands in central Scotland and in the Borders.

Carnwath House [NS 975465] stood at the village of the same name in Lanarkshire, and there was a castle, which was incorporated into the house, a plain mansion of two storeys. This house was demolished in 1970 when a new clubhouse was built for Carnwath Golf Club. An earlier castle is located at the west end of the village [NS 975467] on an impressive motte, and was constructed by Sir John Somerville of Carnwath and Linton. The motte is particularly steep, and access to a blockhouse was by a tunnel, through the base, then a stairwell to the centre. Carnwath was a property of the Somervilles from 1140, and Sir William Somerville, fifth laird, fought for the Scots against the Norsemen at the Battle of Largs in 1263. The family joined William Wallace and fought at Biggar where the English were defeated, and then supported Robert the Bruce. The family were made Lords Somerville around 1430. John, third Lord, was wounded at the Battle of the Sark in 1448, and Hugh Somerville was captured at Solway Moss in 1542. The family supported Mary, Queen of Scots, and Hugh, the then laird, was badly injured fighting for her at Langside in 1568. James Somerville, tenth Lord, fought at the Battle of Dunbar in 1650. The family got into debt and sold the property to Lockhart of The Lee in the seventeenth century, and Carnwath later passed to the Dalziels and then back to the Lockharts.

Sir Thomas Somerville founded a collegiate establishment in the existing parish church [NY 393760] at Carnwath in 1424, but only a fragment survives. There is a tomb with two damaged stone effigies, thought to be memorials for the family.

Couthalley Castle [NS 972482] lies a mile or so northwest of Carnwath, and was an L-plan tower house with a courtyard and further towers and a gatehouse, but little remains. Couthalley was the chief stronghold of this branch of the Somervilles from the mid twelfth century, and was burnt by the English in 1320, although soon rebuilt. The family became Barons Somerville in 1430, before they removed to Drum in Midlothian in 1583. The castle had been besieged in 1557, but was rebuilt and then remodelled in 1586. James V visited, as did Mary, Queen of Scots, in 1563, and James VI. James Somerville, thirteenth Lord, was a Hanoverian and an aide-de-camp to Cope at Prestonpans and Hawley at Falkirk during the 1745-46 Jacobite Rising. This branch of the family died out in 1870.

Linton Tower [NT 774262] stood some six and a half miles to the south-east of Kelso in the Borders, but there are no remains. The property belonged to the Somervilles from the twelfth century. The Linton worm or dragon, which plagued the area, is said to have been defeated by Sir John Somerville, who was given the lands and knighted because of this feat of beast slaying. The property may have passed to the Dalgleishs, and Linton Tower was torched in 1523 and then destroyed by the English in 1547.

The Somervilles also owned:

Carnock House [NS 865882], near Airth, Stirlingshire; site of tower house.
    Held by the Somervilles, but was then owned by the Bruces of Auchenbowie in the sixteenth century. Carnock then passed to others but was demolished in 1941.

Castlehill [NS 788534], Cambusnethan , near Wishaw, Lanarkshire; castle replaced by mansion.
    Held by the Bairds but passed to the Stewarts and then to the Somervilles, then to the Lockharts. **Cambusnethan House** [NS 781530] replaced the castle, and Castlehill was said to be haunted by a headless horseman.

Coltness Castle [NS 797564], near Wishaw, Lanarkshire; site of castle.
    Held by the Somervilles but passed to the Logans of Restalrig in 1553, then to the Stewarts of Allanton and then to others.

Corehouse Castle [NS 882414], near Lanark; slight remains of tower house.
    Held by the Bannatynes, then by the Somervilles of Cambusnethan in 1695, then by the Cranstouns by the nineteenth century. **Corehouse** [NS 882416], a mansion of the 1820s, was built nearby, and it is open for about one month in the spring and summer (01555 663126).

Cormiston Towers [NT 001372], near Biggar, Lanarkshire; site of castle.
    Held by the Somervilles at one time.

Drum House or **The Drum** [NT 301688], near Edinburgh; mansion on site of castle.
    Held by the Somervilles and they occupied the castle and then built the mansion. James Somerville of Drum was killed after a duel with Thomas Learmonth in 1682. Drum is now

Drum House (M&R)

apparently owned by the More Nisbetts of The Drum and Cairnhill.

Hoselaw Tower [NT 802318], near Town Yetholm, Borders; site of tower house.
    May have been held by the Somervilles, but passed to the Kerrs and then to the Reids.

Plean Castle [NS 850870], near Stirling; restored castle.
  Held by the Airths of Plean, but passed by marriage to the
  Somervilles in 1449, and was sold to the Nicholsons in 1643,
  then went to the Elphinstones. Accommodation is available
  (01786 480840; www.aboutscotland.co.uk/stirling/
  plane.html).

Peel [NS 594561], near East Kilbride, Lanarkshire; altered L-plan
  tower house.
  Held by several families, including by the Douglases, by the
  Hamiltons, by the Sempills, by the Houstons, as well as by the
  Somervilles.

Sorn Castle [NS 548269], near Mauchline, Ayrshire; altered and
  extended castle.
  Held by the Keiths of Galston then others before coming to
  the Somervilles at the end of the eighteenth century. It later
  passed to the MacIntyres, who still apparently own it, and it
  is open to the public for some weeks in the summer (01290
  551555).

Torbrex Castle [NT 027552], near Carnwath, Lanarkshire; site of
  castle.
  Held by the Somervilles but had passed to the Lockharts of
  Cleghorn by 1649.

Warriston [NT 253757], Edinburgh; site of castle or old house.
  Held by the Somervilles, and their castle or house was besieged
  by the Dalmahoys and others in 1579. The property passed to
  the Kincaids, and was associated with both the kidnap of Lady
  Warriston and the murder of John Kincaid. Warriston later
  went to the Johnstones and then to others, and a cemetery
  was laid out in the grounds. There is a sundial of 1624 from
  Warriston at Fettes College.

No. of castles/sites: 15
Rank: 94=/764

Soulis

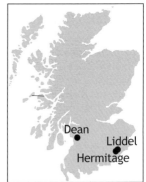

The family came from France, and went to England with William the Conqueror following the Norman invasion. They came to Scotland with David I in the twelfth century, and held lands in the Borders and in Ayrshire. The family were related to the kings of Scots and Nicholas Soulis was a Competitor for the throne after the death of Alexander III, springing as he did from an illegitimate daughter of Alexander II.

Hermitage Castle [NY 494960] is an impressive and brooding ruinous fortress in a somewhat bleak location some five miles north of Newcastleton in the Borders. The castle dates from the thirteenth century, and a strong wall encloses ranges of buildings and a small internal courtyard. The lands were held by the Dacres, but passed to the Soulis family, who strengthened an

Hermitage Castle (MC)

existing castle. William Soulis plotted against Robert the Bruce, apparently trying to place himself on the throne (see above), and he was imprisoned in Dumbarton Castle in 1320 for the rest of his life and his property was seized. The castle passed to the Grahams, and then to the Douglases and to the Hepburns, and then to the Scotts. The castle is an oppressive place, and has several ghost stories. One is that Hermitage is haunted by the ghost of Mary, Queen of Scots, clad in a white frock; another that the spirit of Alexander Ramsay, who was starved to death here, also has been witnessed in the ruins. Another story is that one of the Soulis family, perhaps Nicholas or William, was a wicked fellow and said to be a warlock. Many local children were apparently seized by Soulis and never seen again. The local people, according to one story, eventually rebelled and Soulis was wrapped in lead and boiled in a cauldron at the nearby stone circle of Nine Stane Rig until both him and the metal were dissolved; Hermitage is said to be troubled by his restless bogle. The castle is now in the care of Historic Scotland and is open to the public from April to September (01387 376222).

The family also owned:
Clintwood Castle [NY 538910], near Newcastleton, Borders; site of castle.
> Held by the Soulis family before they moved to Liddel Castle. A later tower house was built here, a property of the Elliots.

Dean Castle [NS 437394], near Kilmarnock, Ayrshire; fine restored castle.
> Held by the Lockharts and by the Soulis family, who had a castle nearby, and then by the Balliols and then by the Boyds, who long were associated with Dean. The castle is in a country park and is open to the public (01563 522702; www.dean castle.com).

Liddel Castle [NY 510900], near Newcastleton, Borders; earthworks survive from a castle.
> Held by the Soulis family, and Edward I of England visited in 1296 and then again two years later. The castle was probably destroyed early in the fourteenth century and never reused.

No. of castles/sites: 4
Rank: 278=/764

Spalding

The name comes from the place of Spalding in Lincolnshire in England, and the name is on record from the first quarter of the thirteenth century. The family held lands in Angus and in Perthshire.

Ashintully Castle [NO 101613], which is two miles north-east of Kirkmichael in Perthshire, is a fine L-plan tower house, which rises to four storeys and dates from the sixteenth century. The building was altered in later centuries, and was long a property of the Spald-

Ashintully Castle (M&R)

ings. Andro Spalding was besieged in the castle in 1587, and was then badly treated by a band of Stewarts and of Blairs. The castle is said to be haunted a Green Lady or Green Jean. The young woman held the castle in her own right but she was brutally murdered by her uncle, who slit her throat and murdered her servant (who was concealed by pushing her corpse up the chimney) so that the property would be his. He dragged his poor niece's body off to the nearby burial ground and there disposed of her. The Green Lady is reputedly seen at the family burial ground and in the castle. Two other ghosts are said to haunt the grounds: a messenger, slain when the laird believed he had not delivered a message; the other 'Crooked Davie', a pedlar hanged for trespass. The castle passed to the Rutherfords in 1750 and is still occupied. Holiday accommodation is available (01250 881237; www.ashintully.com).

Ballzordie [NO 562652] is four or so miles north-west of Brechin in Angus, and there was a castle or old house here. The lands were held by the Spaldings in the fourteenth century after one of them had helped the Scots recapture Berwick-upon-Tweed from the English. The lands passed to the Symmers, and they held them for several generations until about 1750. Also to the north of Brechin is the nearby property of **Kilgarie** [NO 565660], and the Spaldings had a castle here.

Whitefield Castle [NO 089617] is one mile northwest of Kirkmichael in Perthshire, and is a ruinous L-

Whitefield Castle (M&R)

plan tower house of the sixteenth century. Whitefield was owned by the Spaldings, but the upper works were taken down to build the nearby farm.

No. of castles/sites: 4
Rank: 278=/764

Speid

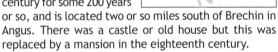

The name is on record in Scotland from the beginning of the fifteenth century, and the family held properties in the east of Scotland.

Ardovie [NO 593565] was held by the Speids from the seventeenth century for some 200 years or so, and is located two or so miles south of Brechin in Angus. There was a castle or old house but this was replaced by a mansion in the eighteenth century.

Forneth [NO 109447], around four miles west of Blairgowrie in Perthshire, was held by the Herrings or Herons, but passed to the Speids, who held Forneth in the nineteenth and twentieth centuries. There was a castle or old house here in the sixteenth century, but this was replaced by Forneth House, a whitewashed mansion in a pleasant spot.

No. of castles/sites: 2
Rank: 396=/764
Xref: Speed

Speirs

The name is from 'Speir's son', and the 'Speir' may be from the Old French for 'watchman'. The name is on record in Scotland from the sixteenth century.

Just to the east of Renfrew by the Clyde, **Inch Castle** or **Elderslie House** [NS 515675] is the site of a strong castle on an island but the old stronghold has gone. The property was owned by the Stewarts and by the Rosses, but the property passed to the Speirs family in 1760 after the old castle had become ruinous. Alexander Speirs of Elderslie was a Glasgow Tobacco Lord, and has been described as a 'mercantile god of Glasgow'. He bought several other estates, and died in 1782. Elderslie House was built close by and was called after the Elderslie, near Paisley. The mansion dated from the 1770s, but was enlarged and remodelled in later years, and was then demolished in 1924 and there is no trace. The site is no longer an island and is partly occupied by the Braehead Shopping Centre.

Houston House [NS 412672] lies one mile east of Bridge of Weir in Renfrewshire, but little survives of a courtyard castle, except one altered range of 1625 but with earlier work. A mansion replaced the rest of the castle, and this was extended in the nineteenth century. Houston was held by the Stewart Earls of Lennox but went to Alexander Speirs of Elderslie in 1782.

Culcreuch Castle [NS 620876] is just north of Fintry in Stirlingshire, and is an altered castle and mansion, dating from the fifteenth century. Culcreuch was owned by the Galbraiths of Culcreuch and then by the Setons and by the Napiers, but passed to Alexander Speirs of Elderslie in 1796. He built a large and profitable cotton mill on his estate, but the property passed from the family in 1875. The castle sits in a country park and the building is now used as a hotel (01360 860228; www.culcreuch.com).

No. of castles/sites: 3
Rank: 328=/764

Spence

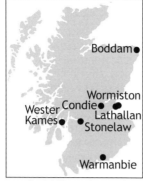

The name comes from the office of custodian of the larder or provision room, and is derived from 'despense' in Old French. The name is on record in Scotland from the thirteenth century, and the family held lands in Fife and in Perthshire. Thomas Spence was Bishop of Galloway in 1448, and was then Keeper of the Privy Seal, and then Bishop of Aberdeen from 1459.

Lathallan Castle [NO 460063] lay five miles north and east of Elie in Fife, and the old stronghold was held by the Spences. John Spence of Lathallan was in parliament in 1434, and another of the family features in the old ballad 'Sir Patrick Spens' when the ship he was captaining was lost with all hands. One of the family, Patrick Spence, was an Officer in the Company of the Scots Guard to the French king and he settled in Gascony. The Spences were Jacobites and got into debt and had to sell the property in the eighteenth century; Lathallan passed to the Lumsdens. The Spences of Lathallan now apparently live in Australia.

The Spences also owned:

Boddam Castle [NK 133419], near Peterhead, Aberdeenshire; ruinous castle on cliffs.
   Held by the Spences at one time, but passed to the Keiths of Ludquharn.

Condie or **Newtown of Condie** [NO 076182], near Bridge of Earn, Perthshire; site of castle and mansion.
   Held by the Colvilles of Cleish and by the Spences. John Spence of Condie was Lord Advocate, and prosecuted John Knox for treason, although Knox was acquitted: Spence was, himself, a Reformer and may have had no enthusiasm for the task. Condie went to the Oliphants in 1601. There original **Condie Castle** [NO 075117] was some miles to the south, but there are no remains.

Crail Castle [NO 613074], Crail, Fife; site of castle.
   The Spences were constables of the castle, and the lands were given to the Spences of Wormiston, who may have rebuilt it.

Kilspindie Castle [NT 462801], near Aberlady, East Lothian; slight remains of castle.
   Held by the Spences, but passed to the Douglases, who built the tower, and then went to the Hays.

Stonelaw Tower [NS 619609], near Rutherglen, Glasgow; slight remains of castle.
   Held by the Spences, several of whom were Provosts of Rutherglen. Demolished in 1965.

Warmanbie [NY 196689], near Annan, Dumfries and Galloway; castle replaced by mansion.
   Held by the Carruthers family from the end of the sixteenth century, but had passed to the Spencers by 1943 and then went to others. The mansion is said to be haunted.

Wester Kames Castle [NS 062680], near Rothesay, Bute; small tower house.
   Held by the MacKinlays and then by the MacDonalds, who were royal butlers and took the name Spence. Wester Kames passed by marriage to the Grahams in 1670, fell ruinous, and was later restored.

Wormiston House [NO 612095], near Crail, Fife; L-plan tower house.
   Held by the Spences of Wormiston, Constables of Crail, from the end of the fourteenth century. They supported Mary, Queen of Scots, during the 1570s, and then went to Sweden where they were made counts. Wormiston passed to the Balfours and then to the Lindsays. The house was rebuilt in the 1980s and is occupied. There is a seventeenth-century walled garden and a woodland garden, which are occasionally open to the public (www.gardensofscotland.org).

No. of castles/sites: 10
Rank: 140=/764
Xrefs: Spens; Spencer

Spittal

The name comes from 'hospital', which in medieval times were hostelries or hotels rather than places of healing (which were called infirmaries). The name is on record in Scotland from the thirteenth century, and Spittal is a common place name element.

Blairlogie Castle [NS 827969] is a small L-plan tower house, which dates around 1513, with a later wing; and it lies three miles north-east of Stirling. Blairlogie was

Blairlogie Castle (M&R)

owned by the Spittal family from late in the fifteenth century to 1767, when the property went by marriage to the Dundases of Blair, and then passed to others. The building was used as a farmhouse and is occupied.

Coldoch [NS 699982] is to the south-west of Doune also in Stirlingshire. Robert Spittal of Stirling, tailor to James IV, probably built a stronghold here about 1513, although there are no remains. The property was also held by the Drummonds, by the Stirlings and by the Grahams.

No. of castles/sites: 2
Rank: 396=/764
Xref: Spittel

Spottiswoode

The name is territorial and comes from the lands of that name, which are five and a half miles east of Lauder in Berwickshire in the Borders. The name is on record from the end of the thirteenth century and, although the family were never extensive landowners, they were influential in sixteenth- and seventeenth-century Scotland.

Spottiswoode House [NT 603499] was an imposing mansion, which was designed by William Burn and dated from the 1830s, and included much of an old tower house. The property was held by the Spottiswoode family from the thirteenth century, and Robert Spotteswode's seal appears on the Ragman Roll of 1296. William Spottiswoode of Spottiswoode was killed at the Battle of Flodden in 1513. The Reverend John Spottiswoode of that Ilk was opposed to Mary, Queen of Scots, describing her as 'that wicked woman, whose iniquity, knowen and lawfully convict, deserveth more than ten deaths'. One of the family was John Spottiswoode, Protestant Archbishop of St Andrews and Lord Chancellor of Scotland, who crowned Charles I. Spottiswoode was in St Giles Cathedral when Jenny Geddes is said to have thrown her stool at the officiating minister as she did not approve of the style of service; a riot followed. Another of the family was Sir Robert Spottiswoode, Lord President of the Court of Session. He supported the Marquis of Montrose and was captured following the Battle of Philiphaugh in 1645. Spottiswoode was executed by beheading with the Maiden, an early type of guillotine, the following year. The property was sold to the Bells in 1620 but was bought back by the Spottiswoodes in 1700. Spottiswoode passed by marriage to Lord John Douglas-Montagu-Scott, but the house was demolished in 1928.

Dairsie Castle [NO 414160], three miles east and north of Cupar in Fife, is a heavily rebuilt and restored Z-plan tower house, which dates from the sixteenth century, although there was an older stronghold on the site. David II spent much of his childhood at Dairsie, and it was associated with the Learmont family. The property passed to the Spottiswoodes in 1616, and in 1621 the nearby church was built by John Spottiswoode, Archbishop of St Andrews. He is said to have written much of the *History of the Church and State of Scotland* at Dairsie. The property went to George Morrison, father-in-law of Sir Robert Spottiswoode, and then later to the Scotts of Scotstarvit. The castle became quite ruinous, but was restored in the 1990s and is occupied.

No. of castles/sites: 2
Rank: 396=/764
Xref: Spottiswood

542

Spreull

The family were settled in Dunbartonshire and held lands there from the thirteenth century or earlier.

Cowden Hall [NS 466571], to the west of Neilston in Renfrewshire, is now very ruinous but the mansion included work from a fourteenth-century stronghold. The lands were held by the Spreull family from 1306 to 1662, when they were sold to the Blairs. Cowden Hall passed through other hands and was a property of the Mures of Craigends in 1766.

Dalmuir Castle [NS 481713] has gone, but it stood on Castle Street in Clydebank, near Glasgow. Dalmuir was a property of the Spreulls from late in the thirteenth century. One of the family was John Spreull, a Covenanter, who was imprisoned on the Bass Rock. The property passed to the Collins family, who held it in the nineteenth century. They built a mansion called **Dalmuir House** [NS 484716], although this was demolished in 1905.

Old Dalquhurn House [NS 390780] was a couple of miles north of Dumbarton in the village of Renton, in a prominent position by the River Leven. It was a plain building of three storeys with a lower wing, but the building has been demolished and the site is occupied by a church. The lands were held by the Earls of Lennox but were held by the Spreulls from the fourteenth century until they were sold to the Dennistouns in 1620. Dalquhurn later passed to the Smolletts, and the famous writer Tobias Smollett was born at Old Dalquhurn in 1721.

No. of castles/sites: 3
Rank: 328=/764

Sproat

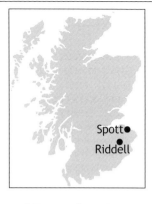

The name may come from either an Old English or Norse personal name, and the family probably came to Scotland following the Norman invasion of England in 1066. The name is first recorded in Scotland in 1262, and was spelt several ways including Sproat, Sprott and Sprot.

George Sprott, a notary of Eyemouth in the Borders, was found guilty of concocting letters between Robert Logan of Restalrig and the third Earl of Gowrie, and of being involved in the Gowrie Conspiracy of 1600; Sprott was executed in 1608.

Riddell Tower [NT 516245], four miles south-east of Selkirk in the Borders, is incorporated into the later Riddell House, but both mansion and castle are now ruinous. The lands were held by the Riddell family from 1150 to 1823, but were held by the Sprots at the end of the nineteenth century. The house was gutted by fire in 1943.

Spott House [NT 679752] lies a couple of miles south of Dunbar in East Lothian, and the mansion of 1830, designed by William Burn, includes work from an old castle. Spott was held by several families over the years, including by the Homes, but later passed to the Sprot family and then to the Watts. It is still occupied.

No. of castles/sites: 2
Rank: 396=/764
Xrefs: Sprot; Sprott

Stark

The name is on record in Scotland from the fourteenth century.

Auchinvole House [NS 714769] was to the south of Kilsyth in central Scotland, and was a plain but altered L-plan tower house with a turret at one corner. The property was owned by the Starks, and held by them in 1629, but may later have gone to the Wallaces. The building was said to be haunted by the apparition of a woman, seen looking out from one of the windows. She had been betrothed, but her lover was murdered and then buried near the house. Both in life and death she is reputed to have gazed forlornly from the window. The house has been demolished and all that survives is the doocot and some walling.

Gartshore House [NS 692737], which stood a mile or so east of Kirkintilloch in Lanarkshire, has also been demolished. It was a mansion of two storeys with a

Gartshore House (M&R)

double gable, and dated from the seventeenth century. Held by the Gartshore family, it later passed to the Hamiltons and then to the Murrays of Ochtertyre, then in the eighteenth century to the Starks of Auchinvole. It was later occupied by the Whitelaws of Gartsherrie.

Ballindean [NO 268299], eight or so miles west of Dundee in Perth and Kinross, was held by the Starks at one time, the first of whom is said to have been a Robertson of Struan who fled here after being involved in a feud. Ballindean had passed to the Ruthven by the middle of the sixteenth century, and then to others. There was a castle but this was replaced by a new house and then by Ballindean House, which dates from 1832.

No. of castles/sites: 3
Rank: 328=/764

Steel

The name is local in origin, and there are places with this name in several parts of Scotland, including in Ayrshire, in Berwickshire and in Dumfriesshire. The name is on record from the middle of the thirteenth century.

The Steels owned:

Inchnock Castle [NS 718694], near Coatbridge, Lanarkshire; slight remains of tower.

Held by the Hamiltons of Dalziel and then by Hays, but also appears to have been held by the Steels as there was a tomb [NS 719692] for the family.

Murieston Castle [NT 050636], near West Calder, West Lothian; ruinous tower house.

Held by the Sandilands, by the Cochranes and by the Williamsons, but was owned by the Steels in 1903.

Philiphaugh [NT 459283], near Selkirk, Borders; mansion near site of tower or old house.

Held by the Murrays but passed to the Strang Steels in the nineteenth century. **Philiphaugh House** [NT 437279] replaced the earlier house, and was a picturesque mansion, but this was demolished in the 1960s and a new house was built.

Waygateshaw House [NS 825484], near Lanark; courtyard castle.

Held by the Murrays of Touchadam, by the Lockharts and by the Weirs, but latterly passed to the Steels. Restored and occupied.

No. of castles/sites: 5
Rank: 240=/764

Stewart

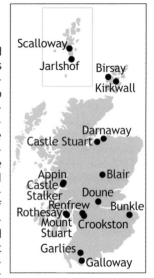

The name comes from Old English and originally was 'stiward', meaning 'sty-warden', and a person who cared for beasts and animals. By the eleventh century, however, the name had come to mean a person who looked after the household of another, and in Scotland the High Steward was both the chief of the royal household, collected taxes, administered justice and was also next in power to the king during time of war. The Fitz Allans appear to have come from Breton to England and then to Scotland in the reign of David I in the twelfth century. Walter Fitz Allan, first mentioned in 1142, was made High Steward of Scotland, and over the years his heirs took the name Steward, which then became Stewart ('t' and 'd' sound very alike in Scots). The spellings Stuart and Steuart are misspellings of Stewart, usually believed to have been introduced by the French while Mary, Queen of Scots, was in that country.

Walter, mentioned above, led the forces that defeated the great Somerled (although tradition has it that Somerled was assassinated in his camp before the battle), and he was given extensive lands in Renfrewshire. James, fifth High Steward, swore allegiance to Edward I of England during the Wars of Independence, but he went on to support both William Wallace and Robert the Bruce. Walter, James's son, married Marjorie Bruce, the daughter of Robert the Bruce. When Robert's son David died without heirs, the throne went to Robert Stewart, Marjorie's son and Bruce's grandson, and the Stewart dynasty was born (also see the section on royal castles and residences).

The Stewarts were to have many branches, many descended from children, both legitimate and illegitimate, of the Stewart monarchs, and at different times held many titles, supplying Dukes of Albany and of Rothesay, and the Earls of Menteith, of Lennox, of Strathearn, of Ross, of Atholl, of Moray, of Mar, of Buchan, of Arran, of Angus, of Fife, of Orkney, of Bothwell, and of Galloway; as well as many other lords, bishops and archbishops, abbots and commendators.

Renfrew Castle [NS 509680] stood in Renfrew, and the castle dated from the twelfth century or earlier. Some remains survived in 1775, but there is now no trace. A soap works was built on the site and then a mansion, but this has been demolished. The castle was built by Walter Fitzalan, the High Steward of Scotland. Renfrew was attacked by Somerled, Lord or King of the Isles, in 1164 but Somerled was assassinated before the castle could be taken. Paisley Abbey [NS 486640], which is also in Renfrewshire, was founded in 1163 by Walter as a Cluniac Priory and was dedicated to St Mirren. The priory was raised to an abbey in 1219, and it is here that it is believed that Marjorie, daughter of Robert the Bruce, was buried, her tomb marked by a stone effigy. Marjorie was married to Walter, the then High Steward, and their son was Robert II, the first of the Stewart monarchs. The abbey church was restored in the nineteenth century and it is open to the public (0141 889 7654; www.paisleyabbey.org.uk).

Bunkle Castle [NT 805596], two miles north and east of Preston in Berwickshire in the Borders, was a large, strong castle but nothing survives except some upstands of masonry. The property passed by marriage to the John Stewart in 1288; he was the son of Alexander, the High Steward. John was killed at the Battle of Falkirk in 1298, but his sons went on to inherit many lands and titles. Alexander was Earl of Angus, Alan Earl of Lennox, Walter the progenitor of the Earls of Galloway, and James the progenitor of the Earls of Atholl, Buchan and Traquair, as well as the Lords of Lorn and Innermeath.

One of the many branches of the Stewarts were those of Appin, who were descended from Alexander, fourth High Steward of Scotland. The Stewarts had been made Lords of Lorn, but this title passed by marriage to the Campbells in 1483.

Castle Stalker [NM 921473], about eight miles north of Connel in Appin in Argyll, is a fine and impressive tower house on a small island at the mouth of Loch Laich. The building dates from the sixteenth century, although it was restored from ruin in the 1960s. Castle Stalker was built by Duncan Stewart of Appin, who was made Chamberlain of the Isles for his part in helping James IV destroy the MacDonald Lord of the Isles; James IV visited. Allan Stewart of Appin, along with five of his sons, were slain at the Battle of Flodden in 1513. The assassination of John Campbell of Cawdor in 1592 started a feud between the family and the Campbells. The Stewarts of Appin fought at the Battle of Inverlochy, under the Marquis of Montrose, in 1645 against the Campbells. In 1620 the castle had been sold to the Campbells, but the Stewarts retrieved it after a long siege in 1685; a Stewart garrison surrendered to William and Mary's forces five years later. In 1715 the clan fought for the Jacobites at Sheriffmuir during the Jacobite Rising. Dugald, ninth Chief, did not support the 1745-46 Rising, but the clan were led by Stewart of Ardshiel; eighty of the clan were slain at the Battle of Culloden in 1746. The chief sold the lands in 1765, and the castle was abandoned about 1780, although by then the Stewarts had built **Appin House** [NM 933494], which stands seven and a half miles north of Benderloch in Argyll. There was an older castle or house, but the present classical mansion dates from early in the eighteenth century. The chief of the Stewarts of Appin still lives in Argyll and Castle Stalker can be visited (01883 622768; www.castlestalker.com).

Ballachulish House [NN 048593], further north in Lochaber, also dates from the eighteenth century. This was a property of the Stewarts of Appin, and it was from an earlier house that in 1692 Campbell of Glenorchy ordered the start of the Massacre of Glencoe. The house is said to be haunted by several ghosts, one of which is reputedly the bogle of one of the Stewarts of Appin, who rides up to the door and there vanishes. The building is now used as a fine hotel (01855 811266; www.balla chulishhouse.com).

Rothesay Castle [NS 086646], in the village of Rothesay on the Island of Bute, is an unusual round walled castle with a large gatehouse, and is defended by a wet moat. There was a castle here in the thirteenth century which was attacked by Norsemen in the 1230s, who cut a hole in the wall with their axes. Rothesay was captured in 1263 by King Haakon of Norway, although he was defeated at the Battle of Largs and had to retreat. The Stewarts were keepers of the castle, and the stronghold saw action in the Wars of Independence. The castle was a favourite residence of Robert II and Robert III, who may have died here in 1406. In 1401 Robert III had made his son, David, Duke of Rothesay, a title since taken by the eldest son of the kings of Scots and currently held by Prince Charles. David, himself, did not fare so well and was starved to death by his uncle Robert Stewart, Duke of Albany, at Falkland the following year. The castle was besieged by the Earl of Ross in 1462, by the Master

Castle Stalker (LF)

Rothesay Castle (M&R)

of Ruthven in 1527, and in 1544 Rothesay was captured by the Earl of Lennox on behalf of the English. It had been visited by James V, who completed the gatehouse block. In the 1650s the castle was held for Charles I, but it was later taken by Cromwell, whose men damaged the buildings. Argyll's forces torched the castle in 1685. James Stewart was made Earl of Bute in 1703, and the family were made Marquesses in 1796, and also became Earls of Dumfries in 1803. The castle was very ruinous until 1816 when it was repaired, and it was partly rebuilt for the second Marquess of Bute between 1872 and 1879. Rothesay is now in the care of Historic Scotland and the building is open to the public (01700 502691). The Crichton-Stuart Marquesses of Bute moved to Mount Stuart, further south on the island.

Mount Stuart [NS 105595], which lies five miles south of Rothesay on Bute, is a grand gothic building, built for the third Marquess of Bute after a fire of 1877 had devastated an earlier house. There are many acres of fine grounds and the house is open to the public (01700 503877; www.mountstuart.com).

Doune Castle [NN 728011] is a magnificent pile in a picturesque spot near the village of Doune to the north and west of Stirling. The castle was built by Robert Stewart, who was Duke of Albany from 1398. Albany was the third son of Robert II, and was also the Earl of Menteith and of Fife; he virtually ruled Scotland during the latter part of the reign of Robert II and then his brother Robert III. Albany's dominance was rivalled by David, son of Robert III and Duke of Rothesay, but David died in 1402 in mysterious circumstances at Falkland and he is believed to have been murdered by his uncle. The Duke of Albany's position was further strengthened when James, the second son of James III, was captured by the English; it is possible that Albany also had a hand in this. When Albany died in 1420, his son, Murdoch, succeeded him as Regent and as Duke, but when James I

Doune Castle (LF)

was freed in 1424 he had Murdoch executed the following year. Doune was kept as a royal hunting lodge, prison, and dower house for the widows of James III, James IV and James V. It was occasionally used by Mary, Queen of Scots, and was held by forces loyal to her until 1570. The castle was partly restored and rebuilt in the nineteenth century, and the building is in the care of

Historic Scotland and is open to the public (01786 841742).

Duke Murdoch's Castle [NN 473014], three and a half miles west of Aberfoyle in Stirlingshire, was built as a hunting lodge by Murdoch Stewart, second Duke of Albany, although he was executed in 1425.

Ruthven [NN 764997], one mile south of Kingussie in Strathspey in the Highlands, is the site of a strong castle but this building was replaced by a barracks in 1718, although impressive earthworks remains. The barracks are ruinous after being torched in 1746 during the Jacobite Rising. The old castle dated from the thirteenth

Ruthven Barracks (M&R)

or fourteenth century, and the property was held by the Comyns. Ruthven was later held by Alexander Stewart, fourth son of Robert II, and better known as the 'Wolf of Badenoch'. Alexander was the Lord of Badenoch and Earl of Buchan, although he abandoned his wife and his actions got him excommunicated by the Bishop of Moray. Stewart retaliated by burning the burgh and cathedral of Elgin, seat of the Bishop, and Forres as well. Alexander died in 1406 and was buried in Dunkeld Cathedral, where a stone effigy marks his tomb; the cathedral is open to the public (01350 727688; www.dunkeldcathedral.org.uk). The story also goes, however, that Alexander dabbled in the black arts, and that a dark visitor to Ruthven challenged him to a chess match. In the morning there was nobody left alive, and the ghosts of Alexander and his men are said to haunt the castle. The ruinous of the barracks are in the care of Historic Scotland and are open to the public (01667 460232). One of his sons, another Alexander, led the royal forces at Harlaw in 1411 (see Kindrochit).

Balloch Castle [NS 386826], in Balloch at the south end of Loch Lomond in Dunbartonshire, dates from the thirteenth century although little remains of the castle except earthworks. The castle was a property of the Earls of Lennox, but Malcolm, Earl of Lennox, supported the Dukes of Albany and was father-in-law of Murdoch, second Duke. Malcolm was forfeited and executed in 1425, and much of the property as well as the earldom passed to the Stewarts of Darnley, and Sir John Stewart was made Earl of Lennox in 1473. The present Balloch Castle, a castellated mansion, dates from 1808 and now houses a visitor centre (01389 720620; www.lochlomond-trossachs.org).

Darnley Castle [NS 527586] stood one and a half miles east of Barrhead in Lanarkshire, but little remains now except a round stair-turret built into a later building. Darnley was a property of the Stewarts, and (as mentioned above) Sir John Stewart of Darnley was made Earl of Lennox in 1473. In 1513 Matthew, the second Earl, led the right flank of James IV's army at the Battle of Flodden and was slain; John, third Earl, died in 1526 attempting to rescue the young James V from the clutches of the Earl of Angus. Matthew, fourth Earl, supported the English during the reign of Mary, Queen of Scots, and he was married to Margaret, the daughter of Margaret Tudor and the Earl of Angus, and so also had a claim to the English throne. Henry Stewart, Lord Darnley, their son, was married to Mary, Queen of Scots, in 1565; Mary and Darnley's son was James VI. Darnley, however, was party to the murder of David Rizzio, and Darnley was himself murdered at Kirk o' Field in 1567, having been strangled after his lodging was blown up with gunpowder. Matthew, the fourth Earl, became the Regent for the infant James VI in 1571 after Mary fled to England. Matthew was, however, shot and killed the same year in Stirling.

Matthew was succeeded by Esme Stewart, who was made Duke of Lennox in 1581. Esme had spent many years in France and he was suspected of being a Catholic agent and he eventually returned to France. The title eventually went to an illegitimate son of Charles II in 1675, uniting the title with the Duke of Richmond; in 1876 the sixth Duke was also made Duke of Gordon.

Crookston Castle [NS 524628], three miles to the east of Paisley in Renfrewshire, is an unusual X-plan castle, although it is now ruinous. Crookston was held by the Stewarts from the thirteenth century, and they became Earls of Lennox. During the rebellion of the Earl of Lennox in the fifteenth century, James IV bombarded the castle with the large cannon, Mons Meg (now to be seen on the battlements of Edinburgh Castle), leading to a quick surrender. The damage included the virtual destruction of two of the corner towers. The castle was seized in 1544 by the Regent Arran and Cardinal Beaton while the Earl of Lennox was besieged in Glasgow Castle. Mary and Lord Darnley may have been betrothed here, and they stayed at the castle after their

Crookston Castle (LF)

marriage. The property passed to the Graham Dukes of Montrose and then to others; Crookston is now in the care of Historic Scotland and is open to the public (0141 883 9606).

Darnaway Castle [NH 994550], which stands four miles south-west of Forres in Aberdeenshire, is a large classical mansion, dating from 1810, but incorporating a hall block from a much older castle. This block has an exceptional oak roof. The castle was held by the Earls of Moray, having been built by Thomas Randolph. The property and title passed to the Dunbars, to the Douglases and then to the Murrays, but in 1563 was then given by Mary, Queen of Scots, to James Stewart, an illegitimate son

Darnaway Castle 1910?

of James V, and her half-brother. James was prominent in her administration but he turned against her after she married Darnley and he went to England. He returned to Scotland and was apparently involved in the murders of both David Rizzio and then Darnley; he then fought against Mary at Langside in 1568. He was made Regent for the young James VI but he was assassinated at Linlithgow by the Hamiltons in 1570. James's daughter married into another branch of the Stewarts (who had acquired the property of Inchcolm Abbey), and her son, another James, became Earl of Moray. This James got into a feud with the Gordons of Huntly. Huntly had been given a commission to capture Moray as he was suspected of being involved in a plot against James VI. The Gordons besieged Donibristle Castle in 1592 and set it alight, and Moray escaped to the beach where he was cornered and then stabbed. Moray reportedly said, as he was dying after Gordon of Gight had slashed him across the face with his sword: 'You have spoilt a better face than your own.' Moray's mother had a painting made of his hewn body, which is now kept at Darnaway Castle; the story is told in the old ballad 'The Bonnie Earl o' Moray'. Some tales have an apparition of Moray being seen on the beach, its hair blazing, near where he was slain. Charles, sixth Earl, was made a Baronet in 1681, and Darnaway Castle is still apparently the seat of the Stuart Earls of Moray.

Castle Stuart [NH 742498], six miles north-east of Inverness, is a magnificent tower house, mostly dating from the early seventeenth century but probably incorporating older work. The property was held by the Mackintoshes but went to James Stewart, Earl of Moray, in 1563. The castle was completed by James Stewart,

Castle Stuart (M&R)

Earl's Palace, Kirkwall (AC)

third Earl, about 1625, although it was seized by the Mackintoshes in a dispute about ownership and compensation. The Mackintoshes were bought off, and castle was restored to the Stewarts. Castle Stuart was abandoned and unroofed about 1835, but it has been restored and accommodation is available (01463 790745; www.castlestuart.com (also www.brigadoon.co.uk)). One of the turret chambers is said to be haunted by a fearsome bogle.

Blair Castle [NN 867662], seven or so miles north of Pitlochry in Perthshire, is a magnificent whitewashed mansion which incorporates some of an ancient castle. The castle was built by the Comyns in 1263, but the property was owned by the Earls of Atholl, and this title came to Walter Stewart, youngest son of Robert II, in 1404. He was made Earl of Strathearn in 1427 and, as he had a good claim to the throne, his grandson (although there were other reasons as well), Sir Robert Stewart, and others murdered James I at Perth in 1437. Walter, however, was executed along with the assassins. The title later went to John Stewart, son of Joan (wife of James I) by her second husband, in 1455. John Stewart, Earl of Atholl, supported Mary, Queen of Scots, and fought for her at Corrichie in 1562. He did, however, turn against her and he was made Chancellor in 1578 after she had fled to England; he died the following year. The property and title passed to John Murray, Master of Tullibardine, in 1629 after he married an heiress. The castle saw action during the Cromwellian occupation and the Jacobite Risings, and Blair Castle is home to the Atholl Highlanders, Britain's only remaining private regiment. The castle and grounds are open to the public (01796 481207; www.blair-castle.co.uk).

Earl's Palace, Kirkwall [HY 449107] is a fantastic palace, dating from early in the seventeenth century, and with unusually large oriel windows. The palace was built by Patrick Stewart, the illegitimate half-brother of Mary, Queen of Scots; his father, Robert, had been made Earl of Orkney in 1581 and he was also made Earl. He (and then his son Patrick) oppressed the Orcadians and Shetlanders after acquiring the property of the Bishopric of Orkney. Robert died in 1593 and Patrick was

imprisoned in 1609. Patrick's son, another Robert, led a rebellion in the islands in 1614, capturing the palace and **Kirkwall Castle** [HY 448109] (no remains of which survive), as well as Earl's Palace at Birsay. The rising was put down by the Earl of Caithness, and Patrick and Robert Stewart were both executed in Edinburgh in 1615. The Bishops of Orkney occupied the palace until 1688 after which it fell ruinous. The adjacent **Bishop's Palace** [HY 449108] may date from as early as the twelfth century, and this is where King Haakon of Norway died in 1263 after defeat at the Battle of Largs. The building was remodelled as part of the Earl's Palace, and both buildings are in the care of Historic Scotland and are open to the public (01856 871918). **Earl's Palace, Birsay** [HY 248279] stands twelve miles north of Stromness on the Orkney mainland, and is a ruinous courtyard castle, dating from the sixteenth century. The palace was started by Robert Stewart, Earl of Orkney, about 1574 and completed by his son, Patrick. The building was badly damaged in a gale of 1868, and is in the care of Historic Scotland and is open to the public (01856 721205/841815). **Carrick House** [HY 567384], on the Orkney island of Eday, was held by and named after John Stewart, Lord Kinclaven and Earl of Carrick, and the younger brother of the notorious Patrick, Earl of Orkney. The house dates from the seventeenth century with older work, and rises to three storeys with a courtyard. The house is open occasionally by appointment in the summer (01857 622260; www.eday.orkney.sch.uk/tourism/carricktour/index.htm).

On Shetland, Robert and Patrick Stewart used a house at **Jarlshof** [HU 398095], twenty miles south of Lerwick. There are the remains of a sixteenth-century building, but there are also remains from the Bronze Age, Iron Age and Pictish and Viking periods, making this one of the most remarkable archaeological sites in Europe. The site is in the care of Historic Scotland and is open to the public (01950 460112). **Scalloway Castle** [HU 404392], in the village of Scalloway to the west of Lerwick, is a fine L-plan tower house, dating from 1600 and rising to four storeys. The castle was built by Patrick Stewart, Earl of Orkney, but had been abandoned by the end of the seventeenth century. Scalloway is also in the care of Historic Scotland and may be visited (01856 841815).

Scalloway Castle (M&R) – see previous page   *Traquair House (M&R)*

Garlies Castle [NX 422692], some two and a half miles north-east of Newton Stewart in Galloway, is a ruinous and overgrown courtyard castle with the remains of a keep. Garlies was held by the Stewarts from 1263, and they were descended from Alexander, High Steward of Scotland in 1263. Sir Alexander Stewart of Garlies fought for James III at the Battle of Sauchieburn in 1488, and his son, Alexander, was a favourite of James IV and died with his king at Flodden in 1513. His son, another Alexander, was captured after the Battle of Solway Moss in 1542. Sir Alexander Stewart of Garlies was made Earl of Galloway in 1623.

Galloway House [NX 478453], fifteen or so miles south of Newton Stewart and one mile south of Garlieston, is a large plain mansion which dates from 1740. The Earls held the property until the turn of the twentieth century but it was then sold. The house was used as a residential school for some years, but is now a private residence again; the Stewart Earls of Galloway now apparently live in Castle Douglas. The gardens, created in 1740 by Lord Garlies, are currently under restoration but are open to the public (01988 600680; www.gallowayhousegardens.co.uk).

Traquair House [NT 330354], which stands one mile south of Innerleithen in the Borders, is a large, impressive and extended tower house. Traquair may be the oldest continuously inhabited house in Scotland as it is said to incorporate work from the twelfth century. In the thirteenth century the lands were held by the Douglases but the property went through several families until it was sold the Stewart Earls of Buchan in 1478. James Stewart, son of the Earl of Buchan, became the first laird; he was killed at the Battle of Flodden in 1513. Mary, Queen of Scots, visited with Lord Darnley in 1566, and John Stewart, fourth laird, helped her escape from Lochleven Castle in 1568. The bed where she slept some of her last nights in Scotland was rescued from Terregles and is preserved at Traquair. John Stewart of Traquair was made Earl of Traquair in 1633. The Marquis of Montrose fled here after the Battle of Philiphaugh in 1645, but was refused entry. Charles, fourth Earl,

married Mary Maxwell, daughter of the Earl of Nithsdale, and she gave birth to seventeen children in sixteen years. The Earl was a Jacobite and was imprisoned in the Tower of London after the 1715 Jacobite Rising, although he managed to escape with the help of his sister-in-law. Bonnie Prince Charlie visited the house on his way south in 1745 to invade England. He entered Traquair through the famous Bear Gates. One story is that Charles, fifth Earl, closed and locked the gates after Charlie's departure, swearing they would not be unlocked until a Stewart once more sat on the throne of the country; they are still locked. The Earldom became extinct on the death of the eighth Earl but the house is still owned by the Maxwell Stuarts, and is open to the public (01896 830323; www.traquair.co.uk).

The Stewarts also held:
Abbot House [NT 089875], Dunfermline, Fife; fine town house in good location by abbey church.
    Originally held by Dunfermline Abbey and used by the commendators. After the Reformation the abbey lands were acquired by the Pitcairns and went to the Seton Earls of Dunfermline and then to John Stewart, Earl of Arran, and then passed to others. The house is said to have a ghostly monk and is now a heritage centre and is open to the public (01383 733266; www.abbothouse.co.uk).
Airdit House [NO 412200], near Leuchars, Fife; site of castle and mansion.
    Held by the MacDuffs but passed to the Stewart Dukes of Albany until 1425 when Murdoch, second Duke, had his head snuck off. Airdit went to the Douglases and then to the Ainslie family.
Aitkenhead Castle [NS 596603], Glasgow; castle replaced by mansion.
    Held by the Aikenhead family, but went to the Stewarts and then to the Maxwells in the fourteenth century and then to the Hamiltons. The mansion dates from 1806.
Allanbank House [NT 864546], near Duns, Borders; site of castle and mansion.
    Long held by the Stewarts. Robert Stewart of Allanbank was made a Baronet of Nova Scotia in 1687, and the story goes that he met a fetching and innocent your girl called Jean in Paris and they became lovers. Stewart, however, planned to return to Allanbank without her but the girl tried to stop him leaving and was trampled to death under the horse's hooves of his carriage. The ghost, 'Pearlin Jean', is said then to have gone to Allanbank and began to haunt the grounds and house;

the room in which the ghost was most commonly seen was abandoned. The property passed to the Kirkpatrick Sharpe family but the mansion was completely demolished in 1969.

Allanton House [NS 850580], near Newmains, Lanarkshire; site of castle and mansion.

Held by the Stewarts, who were descended from Alexander Stewart, fourth High Steward of Scotland. Allanton was visited by Cromwell in 1650, and was later held by the Seton-Stewarts of Allanton and Touch, possibly until 1930. The mansion was demolished in the twentieth century.

Ardpatrick Castle [NR 753593], near Tarbert, Knapdale, Argyll; castle replaced by mansion.

Held by the Stewarts and by the MacAlisters before passing to the Campbells of Skipness, who held Ardpatrick in the eighteenth century. The mansion dates from the same century.

Ardveich or **Dalveich Castle** [NN 615244], near Lochearnhead, Stirlingshire; site of castle.

Held by the MacLeans but passed to the Stewarts who held Ardveich in the eighteenth century.

Ardvorlich [NN 633229], near St Fillans, Perthshire; castle replaced by mansion.

Held by the Stewarts from 1580. Margaret Drummond, wife of the first laird, was driven insane when her brother was murdered by the MacGregors in 1589 – she found his head with some bread and cheese in its mouth. During a quarrel the second laird slew John Stewart of Kilpont in 1644, but was pardoned and he distinguished himself in the Covenanter army of David Leslie. Clach Dearg ('red stone'), held for many years by the family, is a crystal mounted in silver, which was famed for curing sick people or cattle when they drank water in which it had been dipped. The stone is now kept by the Museum of Scotland. The MacDonald Stone [NN 633232], near the Ardvorlich Burn, has the legend: 'Near this spot were interred the bodies of seven MacDonalds of Glencoe killed when attempting to harry Ardvorlich', with the date 1620. The Stewarts still apparently hold Ardvorlich.

Arthurlie House [NS 504588], near Barrhead, Renfrewshire; mansion on site of older houses.

Held by the Polloks, and then by the Rosses and the Stewarts of Castlemilk, who were in possession in the eighteenth century. Now part of St Mary's Convent.

Ascog House [NS 105633], near Rothesay, Isle of Bute; L-plan tower-house.

Held by the Glass family and by the Fairlies, but the property was held by the Stewarts from 1587 until the middle of the eighteenth century. The house can be rented as holiday accommodation (01628 825925; www.landmarktrust.org.uk).

Auchindarroch [NN 003554], near Ballachulish, Argyll; house.

Held by the Stewarts of Appin, and said to be haunted by a ghost known as the Maid of Glen Duror.

Auchterhouse [NO 332373], near Dundee; mansion incorporating reduced castle.

Held by the Ramsays then by the Stewart Earls of Buchan from 1497 or earlier, and they built the castle, and then went to the Stewart Earls of Moray. Auchterhouse passed to the Maules in 1660 and then to the Ogilvies of Airlie. The house was used as a hotel but this appears to have closed.

Auldhouse [NS 557605], near Barrhead, Renfrewshire; altered tower house.

Held by the Stewarts and then by the Maxwells from around 1450, and they built the tower house. The building has been divided but is occupied.

Balcaskie House [NO 526035], near Pittenweem, Fife; mansion incorporating tower house.

Held by several families, including by Sir William Bruce in 1665, but the property then went to the Stewarts of Grandtully and then to the Nicholsons and then to the Anstruthers in 1698. Still occupied.

Balnakeilly House [NN 946598], near Pitlochry, Perthshire; mansion on site of castle.

Held by the Stewarts from the sixteenth century, and their descendants apparently still live here. The grounds are occasionally open to the public (www.gardensofscotland.org).

Balvenie or **Mortlach Castle** [NJ 326409], near Dufftown, Moray; fine ruinous castle.

Held by the Comyns and by the Douglases, before being given to the Stewart Earls of Atholl in 1455. Mary, Queen of Scots, probably visited in 1562, but the property was sold to Innes of Invermarkie in 1614, and it then went to others. Balvenie is now in the care of Historic Scotland and is open to the public from April to September (01340 820121).

Bar (or **Bargarran?**) **Castle** [NS 463709], near Erskine, Renfrewshire; site of castle.

Held by the Stewarts of Barscube from 1490 until 1673, and then by the Shaws.

Barskimming [NS 482251], near Mauchline, Ayrshire; site of castle.

Held by the Whites and then by the Reids until 1615 when the property was sold to the Stewarts. They held Barskimming until 1691 when it went to the Millers. The present house is a plain classical mansion which was built when the old house was burnt down.

Bathgate Castle [NS 981680], Bathgate, West Lothian; earthworks of castle.

The property was given to Marjorie, daughter of Robert the Bruce, and she married Walter the High Steward, and from her the Stewarts went on to inherit the throne. Walter died here in 1328. The castle was dismantled in the fourteenth century, and the property was later held by the Marjoribanks.

Belladrum [NH 518417], near Beauly, Inverness-shire; site of castle.

Held by the Frasers but sold to the Stewarts in the 1820s who sold it to the Merry family in 1857. Cottage accommodation is available (www.belladrum.co.uk).

Belltrees Peel [NS 363587], near Lochwinnoch, Renfrewshire; tower house on former island.

Held by the Stewarts in the fifteenth century but passed to the Semples.

Binny [NT 053734], near Broxburn, West Lothian; site of castle or old house.

Held by the Binning family and by the Hamiltons, but Binny House, dating from 1840s, was owned by the Stewarts of Binny. The building is now used for young people with eating disorders.

Bishopton House [NS 422717], near Bridge of Weir, Renfrewshire; L-plan tower house.

Held by the Brisbanes, and then by several families, including by the Stewart Lords Blantyre in the nineteenth century. Now part of the Convent of the Good Shepherd.

Blackhall Manor [NS 490630], Paisley, Renfrewshire; old house.

Held by the Stewarts from 1396 or earlier, and the house was built by Stewart of Ardgowan and Blackhall in the sixteenth century. Sir Archibald Stewart of Blackhall was made a Baronet of Nova Scotia in 1667. The building was being used as a farmhouse after 1710 but was later ruinous before being restored and reoccupied in the 1980s. The family became Shaw-Stewart, Baronets, and they apparently live near Inverkip in Renfrewshire.

Blackhall Manor (M&R)

Blackhouse Tower [NT 281273], near Cappercleuch, Borders; ruinous tower house.

Held by the Douglases and by the Pringles, and then by the Stewarts of Traquair, who were in possession at the end of the sixteenth century.

Blantyre Priory [NS 686594], near Hamilton, Lanarkshire; slight remains of priory.

Held by the Stewarts of Minto after the Reformation, and the family were made Lords Blantyre in 1606. That year Lady Blantyre left with her daughters for Cardonald, leaving Lord Blantyre in the building. The reason given was the ghostly activities and unexplained noises that plagued the household at night. One of the family was Frances Stewart, Duchess of Richmond and Lennox, who was the model for Britannia on British coins. She was responsible for having the name of Lethington Castle changed to Lennoxlove.

Blyth [NT 132458], near West Linton, Borders; site of old house.

Held by several families, including by the Veitchs of Dawyck, and then by the Stewarts of Traquair from 1635 until 1739 when Blyth went to the Geddes family and then to others.

Bold [NT 374374], near Innerleithen, Borders; site of tower house.

Held by the Sandilands family but passed to the Stewarts of Traquair in the seventeenth century, and then Bold went to the Cranstons.

Bonnytoun [NS 454159], near Drongan, Ayrshire; site of castle or old house.

Held by the Stewarts of Ochiltree in the sixteenth century but passed to the Hunters about 1750.

Bonskeid [NN 885611], near Pitlochry, Perthshire; site of castle or old house.

Held by the Stewarts from the end of the fifteenth century and then by the Barbours, who were related, in the nineteenth century. Bonskeid House was remodelled as a baronial mansion, and the property was bought by the YMCA in 1951.

Bothan an Lochain [NN 982781], near Blair Atholl, Perthshire; site of palace or castle.

Held by the Stewart Earls of Atholl. James V was entertained here but the building burned down afterwards. The area around Glen Tilt was used for hunting by Scottish monarchs, including by Mary, Queen of Scots.

Braal Castle [ND 139601], near Thurso, Caithness; ruinous castle.

Held by the Stewarts by 1375 but passed to the Crichtons around 1450, and then to the Sinclairs. They built a mansion which has been divided into flats.

Breachacha Castle [NM 159539], near Arinagour, Isle of Coll; castle and mansion.

The island was a property of the MacLeans of Coll and others, but passed to the Stewarts of Glenbuchie in 1856 although the property was bought back by a descendant of the MacLeans in 1965.

Bridge Castle [NS 944709], near Armadale, West Lothian; large altered and extended castle.

Held by the Stewarts but sold to the Livingstones in 1580. Still occupied.

Brodick Castle [NS 016378], near Brodick, Isle of Arran; fine large castle and mansion.

Held by the Stewarts of Menteith, who built the original castle. The castle was held by the English during the Wars of Independence until 1307 when it was recaptured by the Scots, perhaps led by Robert the Bruce. The castle was damaged by English ships in 1406, and by the MacDonald Lord of the Isles about 1455. The property passed to the Boyds in 1467 and then to the Hamiltons. James Hamilton, third Earl, was declared insane and the Earldom was held by James Stewart of Ochiltree from 1581, who claimed it though his wife, although he only held the title and property for four years before it went back to the Hamiltons. The building is now in the care of The National Trust for Scotland and is open to the public (01770 302202; www.nts.org.uk).

Caberston Tower [NT 369376], near Innerleithen, Borders; site of tower.

Held by the Stewarts of Caberston in 1563.

Cally Castle [NX 598554], near Gatehouse of Fleet, Galloway; slight remains of tower house.

Held by the Stewarts in the thirteenth century, but passed to the Murrays and then to the Lennox family. **Cally House** [NX 600549], replaced the castle in 1763, and was held by the Murray-Stewarts of Broughton. The building is said to have a Green Lady, the phantom of a servant or a nanny who was murdered by being thrown from one of the windows. The building is now the Cally Palace Hotel (01557 814341; www.callypalace.co.uk).

Cardney House [NO 050453], near Dunkeld, Perthshire; castle or old house replaced by later mansion.

Held by the Stewarts, and Marion Stewart of Cardney was a mistress of Robert II, and it was from her that the Stewarts of Airntully, of Dalguise and of Murthly were descended. Marion was sister to Robert, Bishop of Dunkeld, who was later one of the hostages exchanged for the return of James I.

Cardonald Castle [NS 526645], Glasgow; site of castle.

Held by the Norvals and then by the Stewarts of Darnley from early in the fifteenth century, and they built a large castle here in 1565. The castle was built by James Stewart, who died in 1584, and is buried in Paisley Abbey. His epitaph records that he was once Captain of the Scots Guard to the French Royal house. The property passed to the Stewarts of Blantyre in 1584, but the castle was demolished in 1848, and replaced by a farm house; the family moved to Erskine House. This house is now a private residence.

Careston Castle [NO 530599], near Brechin, Perthshire; extended and altered tower house.

Held by the Dempsters, and then by others, before being bought by the Stewarts of Grandtully in 1707, and they remodelled the building seven years later. Careston went to the Adamsons in the nineteenth century, is said to have a White Lady, and is still occupied.

Carstairs Castle [NS 939461], Carstairs, Lanarkshire; site of castle.

Held by several families before coming from the Hamiltons to the Stewarts after 1535 and then to the Lockharts.

Castle Campbell (or **Gloom**) [NS 962994], near Dollar, Clackmannan; fine partly ruinous castle in picturesque spot.

Held by the Stewarts, but the property passed by marriage to Colin Campbell, first Earl of Argyll and Chancellor of Scotland, and he had the name changed to Castle Campbell by an Act of Parliament in 1489. The property was held by the Campbells until early in the nineteenth century but is now in the care of Historic Scotland and is open to the public (01259 742408).

Castle Hill [NS 589562], Busby, near East Kilbride, Lanarkshire; slight remains of castle on hillock.

Held by the Semples but passed to the Stewarts of Minto in 1490.

Castlehill of Barcloy [NX 854524], near Dalbeattie, Galloway; site of castle in the remains of fort above sea.

Held by the Lindsays at the end of the sixteenth century as well as by the Stewarts and then by the MacLellans. Probably replaced by a tower near West Barcloy [NX 855532]

Castlehill [NS 788534], Cambusnethan, near Wishaw, Lanarkshire; slight remains of castle.

Held by the Bairds and then by the Stewarts, by the Somervilles and by the Lockharts. The site is said to be haunted by a headless horsemen.

Castle Levan [NS 216764], near Gourock, Renfrewshire; restored L-plan tower house.

Held by the Mortons and by the Semples but passed to the Stewarts of Inverkip in 1649. Said to be haunted by a White Lady, and the building is still occupied. B&B accommodation is available (01475 659154; www.castle-levan.com).

Castlemilk [NY 150775], near Annan, Dumfries and Galloway; site of castle.

Held by the Bruces and then by the Stewarts of Castlemilk but they exchanged this property for Carmunnock (see below) near Rutherglen with the Maxwells. The castle was destroyed by Cromwell's forces in the 1650s. The mansion, dating from 1866, was built by the Jardines and is still occupied.

Castlemilk or Carmunnock [NS 608594], near Rutherglen, Glasgow; some remains of castle and mansion.

Held by several families before being exchanged for Castlemilk near Annan with the Maxwells and the Stewarts renamed the property Castlemilk. Mary, Queen of Scots, may have stayed here rather than at Craignethan the night before the Battle of Langside in 1568. Through marriage and inheritance the family name eventually became Crawfurd Stirling Stuart. Bought by Glasgow Corporation in 1938, Castlemilk was occupied as a children's home until the early 1960s. It was then mostly demolished, despite protests, in 1969. The building is said to have been haunted by a Green Lady, and also by the 'Mad Major', an apparition who was said to gallop up to the house by moonlight. This was believed to be the return of Captain William Stirling Stuart from Waterloo.

Castle Shuna [NM 915482], Isle of Shuna, near Connel, Argyll; ruinous tower house.

Held by the Stewarts of Appin and said to have never been completed.

Castle Stewart (or Calcruchie) [NX 379691], near Newton Stewart, Galloway; ruinous castle.

Held by the Stewarts, and named after Colonel William Stewart, who made his fortune fighting for Gustave Adolphus of Sweden in the 30 Years War during the seventeenth century.

Castle Sween [NR 712789], near Crinan, Argyll; impressive ruinous castle.

Held by the MacSweens but then by the Stewarts of Menteith from 1262 until 1362 when the castle went to the MacNeills and then to the MacMillans, and then to the Campbells. The ruins are in the care of Historic Scotland and are open to the public.

Castle of King Edward or Kinedder [NJ 722562], near Turriff, Aberdeenshire; some remains of castle.

Held by the Comyns and then by the Ross family and by Alexander Stewart, the Wolf of Badenoch, then by the MacDonald Earl of Ross, and then by the Forbeses.

Castlewigg [NX 428432], near Whithorn, Galloway; site of castle and mansion.

Held by the Vaux family but was bought by the Stewarts of Bardye and Tonderghie in 1584. The building was derelict by the 1950s and has been demolished.

Clachary [NX 424603], near Newton Stewart, Galloway; site of castle.

Held by the Stewarts, later Earls of Galloway, and Mary, Queen of Scots, stayed here with the Master of Garlies in 1563.

Clochfoldich [NN 895531], near Aberfeldy, Perthshire; site of castle or old house.

Held by the Stewarts of Clochfoldich from the beginning of the seventeenth century or earlier. The present mansion dates from 1828.

Coltness Castle [NS 797564], near Wishaw, Lanarkshire; site of castle and mansion.

Held by the Somervilles and by the Logans, but was bought by the Stewarts of Allanton in 1653, but by the early eighteenth century had gone to the Hamiltons and then to the Houldsworths. They built a new mansion incorporating the castle, but this building was demolished in the 1980s.

Corsewall Castle [NW 991715], near Stranraer, Galloway; some remains of castle.

Held by the Stewarts of Dreghorn, but passed to the Campbells of Loudoun in 1333 and then went to the MacDowalls.

Cortachy Castle [NO 398597], near Kirriemuir, Angus; fine altered and extended castle.

Held by the Stewart Earls of Strathearn, who had a castle here, but the property had passed to the Ogilvies in 1473 and they still hold it. The gardens of the castle are occasionally open to the public (www.airlieestates.com/www.gardens ofscotland.org).

Craigiehall House [NT 167754], Edinburgh; castle or old house replaced by mansion.

May have been held by the Stewarts in the fifteenth century,

but was a property of the Fairholmes in the seventeenth, and later of the Johnstones and of the Hopes. The mansion dates from 1699.

Craigton [NN 680054], near Callander, Stirlingshire; possible site of castle.

Held by the Stewarts in the seventeenth century.

Crichie [NJ 978453], near Mintlaw, Aberdeenshire; castle or old house replaced by mansion.

Held by several families before coming to the Stewarts in 1709 and the family, now the Burnett-Stuarts of Crichie, apparently still live here.

Crichton Castle [NT 380612], near Gorebridge, Midlothian; magnificent ruinous castle.

Held by the Crichtons and then by the Hepburns, later Earls of Bothwell, but the property passed on the forfeiture of James Hepburn, fourth Earl, to Francis Stewart, fifth Earl. Stewart's

Crichton Castle (M&R)

mother was Hepburn's sister, and he added the Renaissance range in the 1580s and remodelled much of the rest of the castle. Francis Stewart was, himself, such a wild and unruly fellow that in 1593 he was also forfeited after being accused of witchcraft and much else. The property then went to other families, and is now in the care of Historic Scotland and is open to the public from April to September (01875 320017).

Croft an Righ House [NT 271742], Edinburgh; altered L-plan tower house.

Probably first built by James Stewart, Earl of Moray and Regent of Scotland; he was shot and killed in Linlithgow in 1570. The property may have also been held by the Elphinstones and by the Grahams, and now houses offices of Historic Scotland.

Cruggleton Castle [NX 484428], near Garlieston, Galloway; some remains of castle.

Held by several families, including by Robert Stewart, commendator of Whithorn Priory, who was besieged here by John Fleming, fifth Lord Fleming, who was trying to seize the priory's lands. Later Stewart of Garlies captured Cruggleton in a surprise night attack. The property went to others and the castle was ruinous by the 1680s.

Culgruff [NX 738667], near Castle Douglas, Galloway; castle or old house replaced by mansion.

Held by the Stewarts from 1595 or earlier until the twentieth century, and apparently now a hotel.

Daldowie [NS 674619], Glasgow; site of castle and mansion.

Held by the Stewarts in the fourteenth century and Sir Robert Stewart of Daldowie fought at Bannockburn in 1314, but later was a property of the Bogle family and then of others. The building was demolished and the site appears to be occupied by a crematorium.

Dalguise [NN 991478], near Dunkeld, Perthshire; castle or old house replaced by mansion.

Held by the Stewarts from the middle of the fifteenth century. Beatrix Potter holidayed here from 1871 for about ten years, and the Stewarts held Dalguise until 1896.

Dalswinton Castle [NX 945841], near Dumfries; slight remains of castle.

Held by the Comyns, and the castle saw action in the Wars of Independence. Robert the Bruce gave the lands to his son-in-law, Walter Stewart, who was married to Bruce's daughter Marjorie. The castle was rebuilt, captured from the English in 1355, and destroyed again along with the castle at Dumfries two years later as part of the terms of the release of David II from captivity in England. Sir John Stewart of Dalswinton was captured by the English at the Battle of Homildon Hill in 1402; the lands later passed to the Maxwells. The elegant **Dalswinton House** [NX 943841], which dates from 1785, is still occupied, and the gardens are occasionally open to the public (www.gardensofscotland.org).

Derculich [NN 890524], near Aberfeldy, Perthshire; castle or old house replaced by mansion.

Held by the Fergussons but had passed to the Stewarts by the eighteenth century. The mansion was extended in the nineteenth century and again in the 1930s, and is still occupied.

Deskie Castle [NJ 198302], near Tomnavoulin, Moray; slight remains of castle.

Held by the Stewarts.

Donibristle Castle [NT 157827], near Inverkeithing, Fife; site of castle and mansion.

Held by the Stewarts, who became Earls of Moray by marriage. The castle was besieged by the Gordons in 1592 during a feud, and James Stewart, Earl of Moray, was hunted down and slain. The tale is related in the ballad the 'Bonnie Earl o' Moray'. The castle was torched but it was rebuilt, and the building was burned down again in 1858; two service wings survive.

Drumin Castle [NJ 184303], near Tomintoul, Moray; massive ruinous castle.

May have been built by Alexander Stewart, the Wolf of Badenoch, or by his son. It was later sold to the Gordons, but may have returned to the Stewarts. The family were Jacobites, and were forfeited after the Rising of 1745-46.

Duchal Castle [NS 334685], near Kilmacolm, Renfrewshire; slight remains of castle.

Long held by the Lyles, but passed to other families, and then to the Shaw-Stewarts of Ardgowan by the end of the nineteenth century, then to others. The castle had been replaced by **Duchal House** [NS 353680], which was built about 1768; the gardens are occasionally open to the public (www.gardens ofscotland.org).

Dunbar Castle [NT 678794], Dunbar, East Lothian; shattered ruinous castle.

Held by the Earls of Dunbar, but was remodelled for artillery by Robert Stewart, Duke of Albany, around 1515. Robert's father was Alexander, the son of James III, and Robert spent much of his life in France. He was made Governor of Scotland from 1515 until 1524 but he returned to France, where he died in 1536 without an heir. The Hepburns were later keepers of the castle.

Dundas Castle [NT 116767], near South Queensferry, West Lothian; massive castle.

Long held by the Dundas family until 1875 when the property went to the Stewarts, now Stewart-Clarks. The castle is available for exclusive hire for weddings or corporate hospitality (0131 319 2039; www.dundascastle.co.uk).

Dundonald Castle [NS 364345], near Troon, Ayrshire; imposing ruinous castle.

Held and built by the Stewarts in the thirteenth century, and the castle was slighted during the Wars of Independence. Dundonald was extended and remodelled around 1350 by Robert II, who died at Dundonald in 1390. Robert III also used the castle, and he may have died here in 1406. The property

was sold to the Cochranes in 1636. The castle is open to the public from April to October (01563 851489; www.dundonald castle.org.uk).

Dunduff Castle [NS 272164], near Maybole, Ayrshire; L-plan tower house.

Held by the Stewarts but passed to the Whitefoords in the seventeenth century. Still occupied.

Dunoon Castle [NS 175764], Dunoon, Cowal, Argyll; some remains of castle.

Held by the Stewarts, but was captured by Edward Balliol and the English in 1334, although recovered by the Scots soon afterwards. The town was burnt by the Earl of Lennox for the English in 1544, although the castle remained in Scottish hands. Mary, Queen of Scots, visited in 1563. In 1646 the Campbells massacred the Lamonts at Dunoon after a raid on Lamont territories. The castle was abandoned in the 1650s and the site is now a public park.

Dunrod Castle [NS 224732], near Greenock, Renfrewshire; site of castle.

Held by the Comyns and then long a property of the Lindsays but was bought by the Stewarts of Blackhall in 1619 after the Lindsays had got into financial trouble.

Dykes Castle [NS 728473], near Stonehouse, Lanarkshire; site of castle.

Held by the Forsyth family but passed to the Semples and the sold to the Stewarts of Castlemilk in 1710. The site appears to be occupied by a housing scheme.

Easter Greenock Castle [NS 300755], Greenock, Renfrewshire; site of castle.

Held by the Stewarts of Castlemilk, but passed to the Hamiltons and then to the Shaws, to the Cathcarts and then back to the Stewarts. The family moved to Ardgowan and the castle was sublet while the cellar was used as a prison. The building was demolished in 1886 to built the railway.

Eilean Dearg Castle [NS 008771], island in Loch Riddon or Ruel, Cowal, Argyll; ruinous castle.

Held by the Stewarts at the end of the thirteenth century but was a possession of the Campbells from 1440 or earlier. Blown up in 1685 and not rebuilt.

Eliock House [NS 796074], near Sanquhar, Dumfriesshire; partly ruinous mansion incorporating castle.

Held by the Dalziels and then by the Crichtons, but Eliock was sold to the Stewarts of Balquhane in 1593, but then returned to the Dalziels in the seventeenth century and then went to the Veitchs.

Erskine [NS 462720], Erskine, near Glasgow; castle replaced by mansion.

Held by the Erskine family but went to the Hamiltons and then to the Stewart Lords Blantyre in 1703. The castle was abandoned for **Erskine House** [NS 454724], a large mansion dating from 1828. Since 1916 the mansion has been used as a hospital for wounded and maimed servicemen and women.

Fairnington House [NT 646280], near Jedburgh, Borders; mansion incorporating tower house.

Held by the Hepburn Earls of Bothwell but when they were forfeited went, along with Crichton, to Francis Stewart, fifth Earl of Bothwell. Fairnington had gone to the Rutherfords by 1647 and is still occupied.

Falkland Palace [NO 254075], Falkland, Fife; magnificent partly ruinous royal palace.

Held by the MacDuff Earls of Fife and then by Robert Stewart, Duke of Albany and Earl of Fife. Stewart had David, Duke of Rothesay, his nephew and the heir of Robert III, imprisoned here and starved to death, or murdered, in 1402. The second Duke was forfeited in 1425 and the Crown kept the palace and it was used by many of the monarchs of Scotland; James V died here in 1542. The palace was little used after the Union of the Crowns in 1603 and deteriorated until 1887 when part was restored by the third Marquess of Bute. The building is now in the care of The National Trust for Scotland and is open to the public (01337 857397).

Farme Castle [NS 620624], Rutherglen, Glasgow; site of castle and mansion.

Held by the Stewarts from the fourteenth century, but then by the Douglases and by the Crawfords, and then went to the Stewarts of Minto, who were in possession in 1645. Farme later went to the Flemings, to the Dukes of Hamilton and to the Faries, but the building was demolished in the 1960s.

Fatlips Castle [NT 582209], near Jedburgh, Borders; tower house.

Long held by the Turnbulls, but passed to the Stewarts who sold the property to the Elliots of Minto in 1705.

Feddal [NN 824089], near Braco, Perthshire; ruinous house.

Held by the Stewarts. The stable and staff quarters have been renovated and can be rented as holiday accommodation (01764 663071; www.duchally.com).

Fincastle House [NN 870622], near Killiecrankie, Perthshire; mansion with old work.

Held by the Stewarts but Fincastle had gone to the Colquhouns by the nineteenth century.

Garth Castle or **Caisteal a Cuilean Curta** [NN 764504], near Aberfeldy, Perthshire; restored and plain keep or tower.

Held and built by Alexander Stewart, Wolf of Badenoch, Lord of Badenoch and Earl of Buchan, fourth son of Robert II. In 1502 Nigel Stewart of Garth burned nearby Weem Castle over a dispute about property and he was nearly executed. Stewart was suspected of murdering his wife and was imprisoned here until his death in 1554; the castle is said to be haunted by her ghost. The castle was restored in the 1980s.

Gauldwell Castle [NJ 311452], near Dufftown, Moray; some remains of castle.

Held by the Murrays, and then by the Earls of Moray, who were Stewarts from the fifteenth century, but later passed to the Erskines; Mary, Queen of Scots, stayed here in 1562.

Glanderston Castle [NS 499563], near Barrhead, Renfrewshire; site of castle and mansion.

Held by the Stewart Earls of Lennox but passed by marriage to the Mures of Caldwell.

Glasserton House [NX 419377], near Whithorn, Galloway; mansion on site of castle.

Held by the Stewart Earls of Galloway.

Gourock Castle [NS 244771], Gourock, Renfrewshire; site of castle.

Held by the Douglases until 1455 when the property went to the Stewarts of Castlemilk. The castle was demolished in 1747.

Grandtully Castle [NN 891513], near Aberfeldy, Perthshire; fine tower house and mansion.

Held by the Stewarts from the fourteenth century, and restored

Grandtully Castle (M&R)

and reoccupied by the Stewarts in the 1920s.

Grange [NT 270886], near Kinghorn, Fife; mansion incorporating tower house.

Held by the Kirkcaldy family, but the family were forfeited after 1573 and the property went to the Douglases and then

to the Stewarts, before returning to the Kirkcaldy family and then later to the Melvilles.

Greenock Castle [NS 280765], Greenock, Renfrewshire; site of castle.

Held by the Cathcarts and by the Hamiltons and by the Shaws of Greenock, later Shaw-Stewarts. They built a new mansion.

Hailes Castle [NT 575758], near East Linton, East Lothian; large ruinous castle in lovely location.

Long held by the Hepburns, but after the forfeiture of the fourth Earl of Bothwell Hailes went to Francis Stewart, fifth Earl of Bothwell, and then to the Setons and then to the Dalrymples of Hailes. They moved to Newhailes, near Musselburgh, and Hailes Castle is now in the care of Historic Scotland and is open to the public.

Hallbar Tower [NS 839471], near Carluke, Lanarkshire; restored tower house.

Held by the Douglases but was acquired by the Stewarts of Gogar in 1581, and in the same century went to the Maitlands and then to others. Holiday accommodation is available (0845 090 0194; www.vivat.org.uk).

Hallcraig House [NS 829500], near Carluke, Lanarkshire; site of castle and mansion.

Held by the Hamiltons and possibly by the Stewarts, but the building was demolished in the twentieth century.

Hartshaw Tower [NS 958915], near Clackmannan; site of castle.

Held by the Stewarts of Rosyth; Hartshaw Mill and Farm were built from the remains.

Hermitage Castle [NY 494960], near Newcastleton, Borders; oppressive and impressive ruinous castle.

Held by several families before coming to the Earls of Bothwell, but on the forfeiture of James Hepburn, fourth Earl, the property went to Francis Stewart, fifth Earl, although he was himself forfeited by James VI in 1593. Hermitage went to the Scotts of Buccleuch but is now in the care of Historic Scotland and is open to the public from April to September (01387 376222).

Hillside [NT 191856], near Burntisland, Fife; site of castle and mansion.

Held by the Stewarts of Dunearn in the nineteenth century and visited by James Hogg among others.

House of Urrard [NN 908634], near Pitlochry, Perthshire; mansion on site of castle or old house.

Held by the Stewarts from the sixteenth century, and it was from, or near, the house that the shot that slew John Graham of Claverhouse, Bonnie Dundee, was fired during the Battle of Killiecrankie in 1689. James Stewart of Urrard fought, and was wounded, at the Battle of Ticonderoga in Canada in 1758.

Houston House [NS 412672], near Bridge of Weir, Renfrewshire; some remains of castle.

Held by the Stewart Earls of Lennox, but passed to the MacRaes, and most of the castle was demolished in 1780 except for one block when a new house was built. The property passed to the Speirs family and the building was extended in 1872 and 1893.

Inchmurrin Castle [NS 373863], near Balloch, Dunbartonshire; ruinous castle on island in Loch Lomond.

Held by the Earls of Lennox, and was the residence of the widow of Murdoch Stewart, Duke of Albany, who had been executed along with his sons by James I. She was imprisoned in Tantallon Castle for two years, and died at Inchmurrin in 1460. This part of the Earldom, along with the title, went to the Stewarts of Darnley. In 1506 James IV stayed at the castle, as did James VI in 1585 and 1617. The property went to the Grahams of Montrose at the beginning of the eighteenth century and the building was ruinous by 1724.

Inchtalla Castle [NN 572004], near Aberfoyle, Stirlingshire; ruinous castle on island in the Lake of Menteith.

Part of the Earldom of Menteith and held by the Comyns and then by the Grahams but in 1361 passed by marriage to Robert Stewart, first Duke of Albany. The second Duke was executed in 1425 and the property went back to the Grahams. Walter Stewart, Earl of Menteith and who died in 1295, and his

Countess were buried on the nearby island of Inchmahome, and in the chapter house of the priory are their stone effigies, formerly part of a table tomb. The castle on Inchtalla was occupied until about 1700 and had been built (or rebuilt) with materials from the priory on another of the islands in the loch. The priory is in the care of Historic Scotland and is open to the public in the summer (01877 385294).

Innernytie [NO 129359], near Bankfoot, Perthshire; site of castle or old house.

Held by the Crichtons and by the Hays, but was a possession of the Stewarts in the 1670s.

Innerwick Castle [NT 735737], near Dunbar, East Lothian; ruinous castle in fine location.

Held by the Stewarts but passed to the Hamiltons in 1398, and then later went to others.

Inverkip Castle [NS 205728], near Greenock, Renfrewshire; ruinous castle on cliffs.

The castle saw action in the Wars of Independence, and the property was acquired by the Stewarts in 1390 and they built the present castle, probably incorporating some of the original

Inverkip Castle (M&R)

building. The castle was abandoned with the building of Ardgowan, a classical mansion, early in the nineteenth century.

Invermay Tower [NO 061163], near Perth; tower house.

Held by the Bonnar family and then by the Stewarts, but passed to the Belshes family, who built a new house near the tower.

Inch Castle [NS 515675], near Renfrew; site of castle on former island.

Held by the Stewarts but by the end of the fifteenth century the property went to the Ross family and later to the Speirs family. The castle had been rebuilt as a large tower house but was ruinous by the eighteenth century. It was replaced by Elderslie House but this was demolished in 1924 and the site of the castle is partly occupied by the Braehead Shopping Centre.

Inchcolm Abbey [NT 191827], island in the Firth of Forth, near Aberdour, Fife; ruinous abbey.

Held by the Stewarts after the Reformation, and this branch became Earls of Moray after marrying the heiress of the Regent Moray (see Donibristle). The ruins of the abbey are in the care of Historic Scotland and are open to the public (01383 823332; 0131 331 4857; www.maidoftheforth.co.uk)

Inchinnan Castle [NS 482697], near Erskine, Renfrewshire; site of castle.

Held by the Stewarts from 1151, and then by the Stewart Earls of Lennox; the castle was rebuilt and enlarged about 1506 by Matthew Stewart, second Earl of Lennox. Although the property went to the Crown in 1571, Inchinnan returned to the Stewarts, eventually to the Earls of Lennox and Richmond, but they sold the lands to the Campbells. There

were substantial remains of the building in 1710 but nothing now remains.

Kames Castle [NS 064676], near Rothesay, Isle of Bute; impressive castle.

Long held by the Bannatyne family but later passed to the Stewarts of Bute.

Kellie Castle [NO 608402], near Arbroath, Angus; fine and impressive tower house.

Held by the Mowbrays and by the Kellys, but was then a property of the Stewarts until 1402 when the property went to the Ochterlony family and then to others. Still occupied

Kelspoke Castle [NS 106541], near Rothesay, Isle of Bute; slight remains of castle.

Held by the Stewarts in the sixteenth and seventeenth centuries.

Kilbucho Place [NT 095352], near Biggar, Lanarkshire; old house.

Held by the Grahams and by the Douglases before passing to the Stewarts of Traquair in 1631. Kilbucho then passed to the Dicksons around 1650, and then to others, and the building is still occupied.

Kildonan Castle [NS 037210], near Brodick, Isle of Arran; some remains of castle.

Held by the MacDonalds and then by the Stewarts, but passed to the Hamiltons.

Kildrummy Castle [NJ 454164], Kildrummy, Aberdeenshire; shattered but impressive ruin.

Held by several families as the main stronghold of the Earldom of Mar, including by Alexander Stewart, son of the Wolf of Badenoch. Alexander made himself Earl by forcible marriage to Isabella Douglas, Countess of Mar in her own right, in 1404. Alexander led the king's forces at the Battle of Harlaw in 1411 against the army of the MacDonald Lord of the Isles and Earl of Ross; there were heavy casualties on both side. The property went to the Crown in 1435, and then to the Cochranes, to the Elphinstones and to the Erskines. The castle was deliberately dismantled and used as a quarry in the eighteenth century, but the fine ruin is now in the care of Historic Scotland and is open to the public (01975 571331).

Killiechassie [NN 864503], near Aberfeldy, Perthshire; castle or old house replaced by mansion.

Held by the Stewarts from the seventeenth century or earlier. The Stewarts of Killiechassie fought on the right flank for the Jacobites at the Battle of Culloden in 1746, and took heavy casualties. The property later passed to the Gordons and then to the Douglases.

Kilmory Castle [NS 051611], near Rothesay, Isle of Bute; slight remains of castle.

Held by the Jamiesons of Kilmorie, but had passed to the Stewarts in 1780.

Kilnmaichlie House [NJ 181321], near Tomintoul, Moray; old house.

Held by Alexander Stewart, the Wolf of Badenoch, and was then a property of the Stewarts of Kilnmaichlie and Drumin. The family were Jacobites, and after the failure of the Jacobite Rising of 1745-46, the Grants acquired the property. Now a farmhouse.

Kindrochit Castle [NO 152913], Braemar, Aberdeenshire; some remains of castle.

Kindrochit was a Royal castle, but in 1390 it was granted to Sir Malcolm Drummond. While supervising work on it, he was kidnapped and died in captivity about 1402, possibly at the hands of Alexander Stewart, son of the Wolf of Badenoch. Isabella, Countess of Mar, was forced to marry Stewart at Kildrummy Castle in 1404. Stewart then acquired both the Earldom of Mar and the Lordship of Garioch from her. The castle was ruinous by 1618 and was excavated in the 1920s.

Kinfauns Castle [NO 151226], near Perth; mansion on site of castle.

Long held by the Charteris family, but passed through several families, including to the Stewart Earls of Moray in 1895, and then went to others. The building is still occupied.

Kirkhill House [NT 074723], near Broxburn, West Lothian; altered tower house.

Held by the Stewart Earls of Buchan in 1770; the house and

associated buildings were converted into flats and houses in the 1970s.

Kyle Castle [NS 647192], near Cumnock, Ayrshire; some remains of castle.

Held by the Cunninghams but later passed to the Stewarts of Bute.

Lainshaw Castle [NS 410453], near Stewarton, Ayrshire; castle replaced by mansion.

Held by the Stewarts but passed to the Montgomerys in 1570 and then to the Cunninghams in 1570. The mansion, Lainshaw House, dates from 1800 and was used latterly as an old people's home although the building is apparently to be converted into flats. It is said to be haunted be a Green Lady.

Lennox Castle [NT 174671], near Balerno, Edinburgh; ruinous keep.

Held by the Stewart Earls of Lennox, and the castle was visited for hunting by Mary, Queen of Scots, the Regent Morton, and James VI. There was reputedly a tunnel from the castle to another building on the opposite bank of the river. The property passed to the Heriots.

Lennoxlove or **Lethington** [NT 515721], near Haddington, East Lothian; fine castle and mansion.

Long a property of the Maitlands, the property was bought by the Stewart Lord Blantyre. Instrumental in having the name changed to Lennoxlove was Frances Stewart, Duchess of Richmond and Lennox, a great beauty, who is said to have been the model for Britannia and to have helped raise the finance for the transaction. The property passed to the Bairds and then to the Dukes of Hamilton, and Lennoxlove is open to the public (01620 823720; www.lennoxlove.org).

Lincluden Collegiate Church [NX 967779], near Dumfries; ruinous collegiate church.

The property of the church passed to Provost Stewart after the Reformation, and he altered some of the buildings into a residence. Lincluden later went to the Douglases, then to the Gordons and to the Youngs. The ruins of the church are in the care of Historic Scotland and are open to the public.

Loch an Eilean Castle [NH 899079], near Aviemore, Strathspey, Highland; ruinous castle on island.

Held and probably built by Alexander Stewart, the Wolf of Badenoch, but passed to the Mackintoshs and then the Gordons and the Grants.

Lochindorb Castle [NH 974364], near Grantown-on-Spey, Highland; ruinous castle on island.

Held by the Comyns, and then later by Alexander Stewart,

Lochindorb Castle (M&R)

the Wolf of Badenoch, and then by the Douglas Earls of Moray. The castle was not used after 1455 although the lands were held by the Stewart Earls of Morays and then by the Campbells of Cawdor.

Lochranza Castle [NR 933507], near Brodick, Isle of Arran; fine ruinous castle in scenic location.

The castle may have been built by the Stewarts of Menteith, or by the MacDonalds or by the Campbells. Lochranza passed to the Montgomerys, later Earls of Eglinton, and then to the Hamiltons. The ruin is in the care of Historic Scotland and is open to the public (key available locally).

Logierait Castle [NN 975513], near Dunkeld, Perthshire; some remains of castle.

Held by the Stewarts. Rob Roy MacGregor escaped from here

in 1717, and the Jacobites used the castle to confine prisoners captured after the Battle of Prestonpans in 1745.

Lour [NO 478462], near Forfar, Angus; site of castle.

Held by the Abernethys in 1264 and then by the Lindsays, but passed to the Stewarts before going to the Leslies and then to the Carnegies in the seventeenth century. There is a later house.

Luthrie [NO 332196], near Cupar, Fife; site of castle or old house.

Held by the Murrays and by the Formans but Sir William Stewart of Luthrie, Lyon King of Arms, is on record in 1567.

Mains Castle [NO 410330], Dundee; courtyard castle.

Held by the Stewarts, but passed to the Douglas Earl of Angus and then the Grahams, who built the present castle, and then to others. The castle has been restored and the grounds are Caird Park.

Markle [NT 579775], near East Linton, East Lothian; ruins of castle.

Held by the Hepburns and then by the Stewarts and by the Kinlochs.

Mar's Castle, Aberdeen [NJ 945078]; site of castle and town house.

Held by the Stewart Earls of Mar, although the Earldom changed hands and was later held by the Erskines.

Mayshiel [NT 622641], near Cranshaws, East Lothian; altered tower house.

Held by the Stewarts from 1586 but passed to the Cockburns in the seventeenth century and then went to others. Still occupied.

Mearns Castle [NS 553553], near Barrhead, Renfrewshire; altered castle.

Held by the Pollocks and then to the Maxwells, but was a property of the Stewarts of Blackhall after 1648. The castle was ruinous at one time but was restored in 1971 to link two Church of Scotland buildings.

Meggernie Castle [NN 554460], near Killin, Perthshire; magnificent tower house and mansion.

Held by the Campbells and by the Menzies family before passing to the Stewarts of Cardney after 1745 and they held Meggernie until 1895. The castle is said to be haunted and is still occupied.

Methven Castle [NO 042260], near Perth; altered and extended castle.

Held by the Mowbrays and then by the Stewart Earls of Atholl, but they were forfeited in 1427 and Methven was retained by the Crown. The property was given to Esme Stewart by James VI in 1584, and was then held by the Dukes of Lennox until in 1664 it was sold to the Smythes of Braco. The building was derelict when restored in the 1980s as company offices.

Minto House [NT 573203], near Hawick, Borders; ruinous mansion incorporating castle.

Held by the Turnbulls and then by the Stewarts, by the Scotts and by the Elliots. The castle was damaged by fire in 1992 and is very ruinous.

Mountblairy or **Balravie** [NJ 694546], near Turriff, Aberdeenshire; site of castle and mansion.

Held by the Stewart Earls of Buchan, but passed to the Hays and then around 1800 to the Morrisons. The nearby mansion, which dated from 1791, has been demolished.

Murdostoun Castle [NS 825573], near Newmains, Lanarkshire; mansion incorporating a castle.

Held by the Scotts, by the Inglis family and by the Hamiltons before it was bought by Robert Stewart, Provost of Glasgow, in 1856. Stewart was responsible for getting Glasgow's water supply from Loch Katrine, and this was the first building to have electric light in Scotland. The building is said to have been haunted by a Green Lady, and is now used as a hospital.

Murthly Castle [NO 070399], near Dunkeld, Perthshire; altered and extended castle.

Held by the Ireland family and then by the Abercrombies before passing to the Stewarts of Grandtully in 1615. A new mansion was built nearby in 1829 but this was demolished in 1949, and Murthly had by then passed to the Fotheringhams. The building is still occupied and can be used as a location for weddings and events (01738 494119; www.murthly-estate.com).

Northbar or **Oldbar** [NS 481693], near Renfrew; castle replaced by mansion.

Held by the Sandilands and then by the Stewart Earls of Lennox and then by the Graham Dukes of Montrose and by the MacGilchrists. The property later went to the Semples and then to the Stewart Lords Blantyre in 1812. The mansion dates from around 1742.

Ochiltree Castle [NT 032748], near Linlithgow, West Lothian; altered tower house on a ridge.

Held by the Stirlings and by the Hamiltons before coming to the Stewarts around 1540. It was later used as a farmhouse but was restored and reoccupied in the 1980s.

Ochiltree Castle [NS 510212], Ochiltree, Ayrshire; site of castle and mansion.

Held by the Colvilles and by the Hamiltons but the property was acquired by the Stewarts of Avondale in 1534. One of the family, James Stewart of Ochiltree, was made Earl of Arran in 1581 (as the third Hamilton holder was declared insane and Stewart's wife was descended from the first Hamilton Earl), and Chancellor of Scotland from 1584-85. He was overthrown in that year, losing the Earldom which returned to the Hamiltons; Stewart was then murdered in 1596. In 1609 Lord Stewart of Ochiltree was involved in the murder of James, Lord Torthorwald. Ochiltree went to the Cochranes and then to others, but the building was demolished around 1950 and a modern house is built on the site.

Old House, New Abbey [NX 962662], New Abbey, Dumfriesshire; old house.

Held by the Browns but by 1622 was the property of the Stewarts of Shambellie. The ruins of Sweetheart Abbey are nearby and are open to the public.

Old Place [NS 680568], Blantyre, near Hamilton; site of castle or old house.

Held by the Stewarts of Minto after the Reformation, although they appear to have used Blantyre Priory and then Cardonald as their residence. Old Place was demolished about 1800 and a farm was built on the site.

Old Place of Mochrum [NX 308541], near Glenluce, Galloway; fine courtyard castle with two towers.

Held by the Dunbars and by the MacDowalls before coming to the Stuart Marquesses of Bute in 1876. The castle was ruinous at one time but has been restored and is occupied.

Old Risk or **Cumloden** [NX 443695], near Newton Stewart, Galloway; some remains of castle.

Long held by the Murdochs but the property passed to the Stewart Earls of Galloway in the eighteenth century. They built **Cumloden House** [NX 4176770], a low rambling mansion.

Ormiston Tower [NT 315378], near Innerleithen, Borders; site of castle and mansion.

Held by the Stewarts of Traquair from 1583 until 1789 when it was sold to William Chambers, and later it was owned by the Thorburns. The tower was demolished in 1805 when Glenormiston House was built, itself demolished in the 1950s.

Perceton or **Pierston House** [NS 354406], near Irvine, Ayrshire; castle or old house replaced by mansion.

Held by the Morville family but Robert the Bruce gave the property to the Stewarts. Sir James Stewart of Pierston was killed at the Battle of Halidon Hill in 1333. Perceton later went to the Douglases and then to the Barclays and to the Mures. The present Perceton, dating from the eighteenth century, is the headquarters of the North Ayrshire Council.

Physgill House [NX 428366], near Whithorn, Galloway; castle replaced by mansion.

Held by the Stewarts from the seventeenth century or earlier. Captain John Stewart of Physgill was killed at the Battle of Prestonpans in 1745 during the Jacobite Rising, and is buried in the cemetery of the old parish church at Prestonpans. The present mansion dates from 1780.

Pinkerton [NT 703757], near Dunbar, East Lothian; site of castle or old house.

Held by the Pinkerton family, but passed to the Stewart Dukes

of Albany and then to the Campbells of Argyll in 1483 and then to the Homes. There is a large beehive doocot.

Pittenweem Priory [NO 549027], Pittenweem, Fife; remodelled priory.

Held by the Stewarts of Darnley in 1606 and the buildings were given to the burgh.

Pittheavlis Castle [NO 097222], Perth; L-plan tower house.

Held by the Rosses but was bought by the Stewarts in 1586 and they probably built the tower. The property had passed

Pittheavlis Castle (M&R)

to the Oliphants by 1636, and then to others. Pittheavlis was used as a farmhouse but it was later divided into separate dwellings.

Ravenstone Castle or **Castle Stewart** [NX 409441], near Whithorn, Galloway; altered ruinous tower house.

Held by the MacDowalls, by the MacLellans and by the Kennedys, but was a property of the Stewarts in the mid seventeenth century when it was known as Castle Stewart. It later passed to the Borthwicks and was unroofed in 1948.

Red Castle [NO 687510], near Montrose, Angus; impressive but crumbling ruin.

Held by the Barclays and by the Earls of Ross, but passed to the Stewarts of Innermeath in 1328 and then later to others, including the Guthries. The ruins are accessible but are in a dangerous condition.

Renfield [NS 501684], Renfrew; site of castle or old house.

Held by the Stewart Earls of Moray, but passed to the Hays in 1568 and then went to the Campbells. The castle was replaced by Blythswood House, but this was itself demolished in 1935; the site of both the castle and mansion are now occupied by a golf course.

Riccarton [NT 183695], Edinburgh; site of castle and mansion.

Held by the Stewarts, having been given to Walter Stewart, the High Steward, by Bruce on his marriage to Marjorie, daughter of Robert the Bruce, but later passed to the Craigs and then to the Gibsons. The building was demolished in 1956.

Rosyth Castle [NT 115820], near Inverkeithing, Fife; fine ruinous castle.

Held by the Stewarts of Rosyth from 1428 until around 1700. In the 1440s, Walter Bower, Abbot of Inchcolm, compiled a history of Scotland, known as the *Scotichronicon*, for the family. Robert Stewart of Rosyth was a supporter of Mary, Queen of Scots, and a later lord, James Stewart, was imprisoned in 1647 for being a Royalist. Rosyth was sacked by Cromwell's forces in 1650. The property went to the Primrose Earl of Rosebery, then to the Hope Earl of Hopetoun. The castle stands in a dockyard surrounded by reclaimed land, is in the care of Historic Scotland and can be visited (0131 668 8800).

Rosyth Castle (M&R) – see previous page

Rothiemay Castle [NJ 554484], near Huntly, Aberdeenshire; site of castle and mansion.

Held by the Abernethys but was bought by the Stewart Lord Ochiltree in 1612 and it was then sold to the Gordons in 1617. Later it went to the Duffs and then to the Forbes family. There were several ghost stories associated with the building but it was demolished in 1956.

Rutherford [NT 643303], near St Boswells, Borders; site of castle or old house.

Held by the Rutherfords but had passed to the Stewarts of Traquair by early in the sixteenth century. Rutherford later went to the Dons and then to the Antrobus family.

Sandfurd [NO 417258], near Newport-on-Tay, Fife; site of castle and mansion.

Long held by the Nairnes but the property was owned by the Stewarts in 1795. They demolished the old castle and built a new mansion, but this was itself demolished in the 1960s.

Shambellie House [NX 960665], near Dumfries; mansion.

Held by the Stewarts of Shambellie from the seventeenth century or earlier. The mansion dates from the nineteenth century and is now home to the National Museum of Costume, which is open to the public (01387 850375; www.nms.ac.uk/costume).

Shillinglaw Castle [NT 326335], near Innerleithen, Borders; site of castle or old house.

Held by the Stewarts of Shillinglaw in the seventeenth century.

Sorbie Castle [NX 451471], near Garlieston, Galloway; ruinous castle.

Long held by the Hannays but was purchased by the Stewarts of Garlies, Earls of Galloway, in the 1670s. The castle was used until 1748 but is now a consolidated ruin and is accessible to the public.

Stewart Tower or **Airntully Castle** [NO 091362], near Murthly, Perthshire; site of castle.

Held by the Stewarts, descended from an illegitimate son of Robert II. Regent Moray ordered Stewart of Airntully to destroy any idolatrous images in Dunkeld Cathedral in 1560.

Strathaven Castle [NS 703445], Strathaven, Lanarkshire; ruinous castle.

Held by the Bairds, by the Sinclairs and by the Douglases before coming in 1457 to Andrew Stewart, Lord Avondale, an illegitimate grandson of the Duke of Albany, who built, or rebuilt, the castle. The property passed to the Hamiltons and it was occupied until 1717. It became ruinous and a skeleton, sealed up in one of the walls, is said to have been found when part of the castle was demolished. The ruin is accessible to the public.

Strathbrock Castle [NT 044717], near Uphall, West Lothian; castle replaced by mansion.

Held by the Stewarts and then by the Erskines. **Middleton Hall**, which dates from around 1700, may stand on the site and is now a residential home for the elderly.

Stravithie Castle [NO 531118], near St Andrews, Fife; site of castle.

Held by the Lumsdens and then by Lady Margaret Erskine of Lochleven, jailer of Mary, Queen of Scots. Lady Margaret gave the estate to James Stewart, Earl of (and Regent) Moray, her illegitimate son by James V. Moray was shot and killed at Linlithgow in 1570. The castle was entire in 1710 but there are now no remains.

Tonderghie [NX 443357], near Whithorn, Galloway; site of castle or old house.

Held by the Stewarts from the seventeenth century; the present mansion dates from the end of the nineteenth century.

Torrance Castle [NS 654526], near East Kilbride, Lanarkshire; rambling mansion incorporating castle.

Held by the Torrance family and by the Hamiltons before being sold to the Stewarts of Castlemilk in 1652. The Stewarts held it until 1947. The castle is a private residence but one of the outbuildings is a visitor centre for Calderglen Country Park (01355 236644; www.southlanarkshire.gov.uk).

Touch House [NS 753928], near Stirling; castle and mansion.

Held by the Frasers but went to the Stewart Earls of Buchan and then to the Setons around the end of the fifteenth century. Touch passed by marriage to the Seton-Stewarts of Allanton and Touch around 1750, and they held the property until 1930. The building was used as a hospital but it is now a private residence again.

Tower Rais or **Stewart's Rais** [NS 511594], near Barrhead, Renfrewshire; site of castle.

Held by the Stewarts of Darnley from 1449 or earlier. The building was ruinous by late in the eighteenth century and was demolished in 1932.

Troquhain [NX 681783], near New Galloway, Galloway; site of castle.

Held by the MacLellans and by the Gordons before going to the Villers-Stuarts.

Ward of Lochnorris [NS 539205], near Cumnock, Ayrshire; castle replaced by mansion.

Held by the Crawfords and the Dalrymple Earls of Dumfries; they built **Dumfries House** [NS 541204] in 1757. Dumfries House passed to the Crichton-Stuart Marquesses of Bute and was recently put up for sale.

Wedderlie House [NT 640515], near Westruther, Borders; mansion incorporating castle.

Held by the Polwarths and then long by the Edgars, but went to the Stewart Lords Blantyre in 1733. Although ruinous at one time, it has been restored and the building is said to be haunted by a Green Lady.

Wester Kames Castle [NS 062680], near Rothesay, Isle of Bute; tower house.

Held by the MacKinlays and by the Spences and by the Grahams. The tower became ruinous but was restored by the Stuart Marquess of Bute.

www.stewartsociety.org
www.clansstewart.org
No. of castles/sites: 212
Rank: 1/764
Xrefs: Stuart; Steuart

Stirling

The name comes from the castle and town of Stirling, which lies at a strategic place in central Scotland on a crossing of the Forth. Stirling itself means 'place of strife', and there have been many battles near here, not least Stirling Bridge in 1297. The family of that name are on record from the middle of the twelfth century, and they held lands in Stirlingshire and in the north part of Lanarkshire, as well as elsewhere.

Cadder Castle [NS 605728] stood three or so miles west and south of Kirkintilloch in central Scotland. The castle has gone and the site is occupied by Cadder House, now the clubhouse for a golf course but dating in part from 1624. The lands were a property of the Stirlings of Cadder or Calder, who held the property from the twelfth century. Sir John Stirling, sixth of Cadder, was killed at the Battle of Halidon Hill in 1333. Janet Stirling was forcibly married to Sir James Stirling of Keir, who acquired the property in the 1530s. John Knox is said to have preached at Cadder, and the line of the Stirlings of Cadder continues, although they apparently now live in London in England.

The Stirlings also held:

Alva Castle [NS 901975], Alva, Clackmannan; site of castle and mansion.
Held by the Stirlings, but passed to the Menteiths and then to the Erskines and then to the Johnstones of Westerhall.

Arnhall Castle [NS 764986], near Stirling; ruinous L-plan tower house.
Held by the Dow family but passed by marriage to the Stirlings of Keir. A scene from *Monty Python and the Holy Grail* was filmed here.

Ardoch [NN 842097], near Braco, Perthshire; castle or old house replaced by now ruinous mansion.
Held by the Stirlings from the sixteenth century or earlier. One of the family, Sir Thomas Stirling, served in the Scots Brigade in Holland in the 1740s and 50s, and then fought in Canada and commanded the Black Watch in the American War. The mansion dates from the eighteenth century but is now ruinous.

Balglass Castle [NS 585876], near Killearn, Stirlingshire; site of castle.
Held by the Stirlings of Craigbarnet from 1468, and William Wallace is said to have sheltered here during the Wars of Independence. Balglass passed to the Bontines in the seventeenth century.

Ballagan or **Campsie Castle** [NS 572796], near Milngavie, Dunbartonshire; site of castle.
Held by the Earls of Lennox, then by the Stirlings of Ballagan from 1522 to 1756. Replaced by Ballagan House.

Coldoch [NS 699982], near Doune, Stirlingshire; castle replaced by mansion.
Held by the Spittals and by the Drummonds, then later by the Stirlings and then by the Grahams.

Craigbarnet Castle [NS 594790], near Lennoxtown, Dunbartonshire; site of castle and mansion.
Held by the Stirlings. John Stirling, third of Craigbarnet, was armour bearer to James I and comptroller of the royal household. James IV visited Craigbarnet in 1507; this branch of the family were keepers of Dumbarton Castle. The castle was abandoned in 1660 for a new mansion, but the site was cleared for planting trees in the twentieth century.

Drumpellier House [NS 716650], near Coatbridge, Lanarkshire; site of castle and mansion.
Held by the Hamiltons, by the Colquhouns and by the Buchanans, before coming to the Stirlings. Rear Admiral Sir James Stirling of Drumpellier who was later made Governor of Western Australia. Drumpellier was bought back by the Buchanans. The house was later demolished and the site is occupied by housing and the grounds are Drumpellier Country Park (www.northlan.gov.uk).

Easter Braikie Castle [NO 637515], near Brechin, Angus; site of castle.
Held by the Frasers and then by the Stirlings, but latter passed to the Ogilvies, then to others. Demolished in 1823 and replaced by mansion.

Edzell Castle [NO 585693], near Brechin, Angus; fine ruinous castle.
Held by the Stirlings of Glenesk, but passed by marriage to the Lindsays, who long held it. Edzell later went to the Maules but is now in the care of Historic Scotland and is open to the public (01356 648631).

Fairburn Tower [NH 469523], near Muir of Ord, Ross and Cromarty; castle replaced by mansion.
Long held by the Mackenzies, but passed to the Stirlings in the nineteenth century, and they apparently now live near Muir of Ord in Ross and Cromarty. The house is now a nursing home.

Faskine [NS 760631], near Airdrie, Lanarkshire; site of castle or old house.
Held by the Clellands, but passed to the Stirlings of Cadder. John Stirling of Faskine was Lord Provost of Glasgow; and Sir Walter Stirling of Faskine was prominent in the Royal Navy and was made commander-in-chief of the fleet in the eighteenth century. His son was made a Baronet in 1800, and others of the family distinguished themselves in the Navy. This title is now extinct. Faskine is said to be the site of the execution of those accused of witchcraft.

Gargunnock House [NS 715944], near Stirling; mansion incorporating castle.
Held by the Setons, by the Erskines and by the Campbells, but was sold to the Stirlings in the nineteenth century. They still apparently own it; the gardens are open for some weeks in the summer (01786 860392; www.gardensofscotland.org).

Glorat House [NS 641779], near Milton of Campsie, Lanarkshire; mansion incorporating part of castle.
Held by the Stirlings from 1430, one of whom Sir John Stirling was armour bearer to James I. George Stirling of Glorat was keeper of Dumbarton Castle and died of wounds received at Pinkie in 1547. Another Stirling of Glorat killed Malcolm Kincaid in 1581; and George Stirling of Glorat was made a Baronet of Nova Scotia in 1666. The house is still occupied by the Stirlings, or was until recently.

Herbertshire Castle [NS 804830], near Falkirk; site of castle and mansion.
Held by the Sinclairs of Rosslyn and by the Elphinstones, but passed to the Stirlings who sold it to the Muirheads in 1768.

Keir House [NS 770989], near Stirling; mansion incorporating part of castle.
Held by the Leslies, but passed to the Stirlings in 1448. The house was burned at the Battle of Sauchieburn in 1488. The Stirlings of Keir fought for the Jacobites in both the 1715 and 1745-46 Risings, and the family were forfeited, although they later recovered their lands after buying them back. James, tenth of Keir, had been imprisoned during the 1745-46 Rising. Sir William Stirling-Maxwell, son of Archibald Stirling of Keir, was MP for Perthshire and married the daughter of John Maxwell of Pollok. He collected many works of art and artefacts, which are on display at Pollok House in Glasgow (0141 616 6410). Keir House is still occupied.

Keir House (STO) – see previous page

Keppoch House [NS 330798], near Helensburgh, Dunbartonshire; castle replaced by mansion.
  Held by the Stirlings of Glorat in 1545, but passed to the Ewings. Still occupied.

Lauriston Castle [NO 759667], near Laurencekirk, Kincardineshire; castle and mansion.
  Held by the Stirlings, but passed to the Straitons, and then to others. Part has been demolished, part is occupied.

Law Tower [NS 515738], near Bearsden, Dunbartonshire; site of castle.
  Held by the Livingstones then by the Hamiltons, but was bought by the Stirlings of Glorat.

Moat [NS 941272], near Abington, Lanarkshire; motte.
  Held by the Robertons and then by Mary of Stirling, who did not support Robert the Bruce and tried to get herself a pardon from David I by resigning her lands.

Muiravonside [NS 965753], near Linlithgow, West Lothian; site of castle and mansion.
  Held by the Tinsdales, by the Rosses and by the MacLeods, before coming to the Stirlings after 1742, and they held the property into the twentieth century. The mansion was demolished in the 1970s and the grounds are a country park.

Ochiltree Castle [NT 032748], near Linlithgow, West Lothian; altered L-plan tower house.
  Held by the Stirlings, and one of the family was made Bishop of Dunblane in the fifteenth century, then passed to the Hamiltons and to the Stewarts. Restored and is occupied.

Old Kippencross [NS 785999], near Dunblane, Stirlingshire; mansion incorporating tower house.
  Held by the Pearsons, but passed to the Stirlings of Kippendavie after 1768.

Steuarthall [NS 826927], near Stirling; site of castle.
  Held by the Murrays of Touchadam and by the Cowans before passing by marriage to the Stirlings of Garden. Rachel Chiesly, Lady Grange, wife of James Erskine, was probably imprisoned here after discovering that her husband was involved in Jacobite plotting. She was taken out to the Hebrides in 1732 and she is believed to have died on Skye. The site was cleared in the 1980s.

Struie Castle [NO 079114], near Forgandenny, Perthshire; some remains of castle.
  Held by the Stirlings but passed to the Oliphants.

Struiehill [NO 064105], near Forgandenny, Perthshire; probable site of castle.
  Held by the Stirlings but passed to the Oliphants.

Tower of Garden [NS 593948], near Kippen, Stirlingshire; tower house replaced by mansion.
  Held by the Forresters, but was bought by the Stirlings early in the seventeenth century. Sir Archibald Stirling of Garden was Senator of the College of Justice as Lord Garden, and he was a prominent Royalist. Archibald, the next laird, was imprisoned after trying to restore James VII in the Jacobite

rebellionette in 1708. The Stirlings of Garden apparently still own the property.

Woodside or **Glenbervie** [NS 851845], near Larbert, Falkirk; mansion on site of castle.
  Held by the Bruces but passed to the Stirlings, who renamed it. Still occupied.

www.clanstirling.org
No. of castles/sites: 29
Rank: 42=/764
Xref: Striveline

Stoddart

The name comes from the occupation of 'stot-hird', a person who looked after bullocks (or 'stots'). The name is on record from the last quarter of the fourteenth century.
  Shieldgreen Tower [NT 274432] is two or so miles north-east of Peebles in the Borders, but very little now remains of the tower house except a mound. Shieldgreen was held by the Stoddarts in the sixteenth century, but passed to the Hay Earl of Tweeddale in 1656, and then went to the burgh of Peebles.

No. of castles/sites: 1
Rank: 537=/764

Stormonth

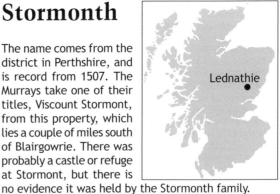

The name comes from the district in Perthshire, and is record from 1507. The Murrays take one of their titles, Viscount Stormont, from this property, which lies a couple of miles south of Blairgowrie. There was probably a castle or refuge at Stormont, but there is no evidence it was held by the Stormonth family.
  The Stormonth (now Stormonth Darling) family did (and apparently do) hold **Lednathie** [NO 340630], which stands in a tranquil spot in Glen Prosen, some miles north of Kirriemuir in Angus. The family held the lands from 1683, and James Stormonth of Lednathie served as an officer in the Jacobite army during the Rising of 1745-46.

No. of castles/sites: 1
Rank: 537=/764
Xref: Stormont

Strachan

The name is territorial and comes from the lands of Strachan (pronounced 'Strawn'), which are three or so miles south-west of Banchory in Kincardineshire. The name was spelt in many different ways down the years, and is on record from about 1200.

Thornton Castle [NO 688718], one and a half miles north-west of Laurencekirk in Kincardineshire, is an altered L-plan tower house, part of which may date from the fourteenth century. The property was held by the Thorntons, but passed by marriage to the Strachans in 1309. The Strachans were appointed to act against Jesuits and seminary priests in 1590, but Strachan of Thornton had to pay 10,000 merks to keep the peace with Sir Robert Arbuthnott during a feud in 1616. Sir Alexander Strachan of Thornton was made a Baronet of Nova Scotia in 1625. The Strachans of Thornton built an aisle at the Old Kirkyard in Marykirk [NO 686656], which is dated 1615. There is a memorial to Dame Elizabeth Forbes, who died in 1661. The property passed to the Forbeses of Newton in 1683, then to others. The castle is still occupied.

The Strachans owned:

Carmyllie Castle [NO 546432], near Letham, Angus; site of castle.
Held by the Strachans, but had passed to the Maules of Panmure by 1640. There is a story about a buried castle here and a pile of gold; the gold can be seen in the distance when the sun shines on it, but the way to the treasure can never be discovered.

Claypotts Castle [NO 452319], near Dundee; fine Z-plan tower house.
Held by the Strachans from about 1560 and they built the castle, but the property passed to the Grahams, one of whom was John Graham of Claverhouse, and then later to the Douglas

Craigcrook Castle [NT 211742], Edinburgh; fine altered tower house, now Z-plan.
Held by several families down the years, including by the Adamsons who built it, but later passed to the Strachans. Still occupied as the offices of *Scottish Field* (0131 312 4550; www.scottishfield.co.uk).

Fetteresso Castle [NO 843855], near Stonehaven, Kincardineshire; mansion incorporating part of castle.
Held by the Strachans, but passed by marriage to the Keith Earls of Marischal in the fourteenth century and they built the castle. The property later went to the Duffs, became ruinous and then was divided and occupied.

Glenkindie House [NJ 437140], near Kildrummy, Aberdeenshire; mansion with old work.
Held by the Strachans, and was pillaged by Donald Farquharson of Monaltrie in 1639, then torched in 1644 by Argyll. The property passed to the Leiths.

Lynturk Castle [NJ 598122], near Alford, Aberdeenshire; site of castle.
Held by the Strachans. John Strachan of Lynturk was involved in the murder of Alexander Seton of Meldrum in 1526. Strachan besieged Kildrummy Castle in 1531, and managed to get the Master of Forbes executed by implicating him in a plot to assassinate James V; Strachan went into exile in 1550. The property passed to the Irvines, to the Gordons and then to the MacCombies. Ruinous by 1782.

Monboddo House [NO 744783], near Laurencekirk, Kincardineshire; tower house and site of mansion.
Held by the Barclays but had passed to the Strachans by 1593, and then went to the Irvines and to the Burnetts. The older part is still occupied but the mansion has been demolished, although 'executive' homes have been built in the grounds.

Strachan [NO 657921], near Banchory, Kincardineshire; motte.
Held by the Strachans, by the Giffords and by the Durwards, then later went to the Reids.

Tarrie [NO 643449], near Arbroath, Angus; site of castle.
Held by the Strachans of Tarrie in the seventeenth and eighteenth centuries, but later passed to the Carnegies.

Whitehouse [NT 187766], Cramond, Edinburgh; altered L-plan tower house.
Held by several families, including by the Strachans in the middle of the eighteenth century, but was sold to the Ramsays in 1788. Still occupied.

No. of castles/sites: 11
Rank: 127=/764

Claypotts Castle (M&R)

Earls of Angus and then to the Homes. Claypotts is said to be haunted by a White Lady, and also to have had a brownie. The castle is in the care of Historic Scotland and is sometimes open to the public (01786 431324).

Strang

The name could either come from the Old French 'estrange', meaning 'stranger or foreign'; or from the Scots 'strang' meaning 'strong'. The name is on record in Scotland from the middle of the thirteenth century. The Strangs held lands in Fife, and some of them also went to Orkney. One member of this branch, Sir Robert Strange, fought with the Jacobites at Culloden, but went on to become a distinguished engraver, specialising in historical prints, and he settled in London.

Balcaskie House [NO 526035] is a mile or so north of Pittenweem in Fife, and is now a U-plan symmetrical mansion, but the building includes old work from an L-plan tower house. John Strang of Balcaskie died at the Battle of Pinkie in 1547, and the property was sold in 1615, passing to the Moncreiffes and then to Sir William Bruce in 1665. Much of his original interior survives, but Balcaskie passed to others before going to the Anstruthers in 1698, and they still apparently live here.

Pitcorthie [NO 570070] is close by and is three miles north of Anstruther, although there are no remains of a castle or old house. The lands of **West Pitcorthie** were owned by the Strangs from the fourteenth century, but passed to the Barclays of Innergellie and then to the Hays of Kinglassie, who held them in the seventeenth century.

No. of castles/sites: 2 / Rank: 396=/764
Xref: Strange

Strathendry

The name is territorial and comes from the lands of Strathendry, which are four miles north of Cardenden in Fife; the name comes on record from the thirteenth century.

Strathendry Castle [NO 226020] consists of a keep or tower of three storeys and an attic with a round stair tower. There is a courtyard enclosing ranges of building dating from the nineteenth century. The lands were held by the Strathendry family from 1226 until the property passed by marriage to the Forresters of Carden and Skipinch in 1496. Strathendry then went to the Douglases of Kirkness and then to the Clephanes of Carslogie, and is still occupied.

No. of castles/sites: 1 / Rank: 537=/764

Stratton

The name is territorial and comes from the lands and barony of that name, which are near Liberton to the south of Edinburgh. There were, however, also baronies of that name in Ayrshire and in Fife, and the Strattons held lands in Midlothian, in Angus, in Kincardineshire and in West Lothian.

Straiton [NT 273667], four and a half miles south of Edinburgh Castle, was held by the family from the thirteenth century or earlier, and Alexander Stratton was one of those who added his seal to the Declaration of Arbroath in 1320. There was a hall house, although there are no remains, and the Strattons were still in possession in the middle of the fifteenth century.

Lauriston Castle [NO 759667] is four miles to the south of Laurencekirk in Kincardineshire, and a castle was extended by a mansion in the eighteenth century. Owned by the Stirlings, the property was then held to the Strattons from the thirteenth century until 1695. The castle was captured by the English under Edward III in 1336. One of the family, Alexander Stratton, was slain at the Battle of Harlaw in 1411; and another, David Stratton, an early Protestant martyr, was executed for heresy in 1534 at Greenside in Edinburgh. Lauriston passed to the Falconers of Phesdo and then later to the Porteous family. The mansion and castle have been partly demolished, but the remaining part is occupied.

Kirkside [NO 738637] lies three miles north and east of Montrose in Angus, and is substantially an eighteenth-century mansion, although it incorporates older work. Kirkside was held by the Strattons from 1582 to 1872, and the building is still occupied.

Seabegs [NS 824798], to the south-east of Bonnybridge in West Lothian, was held by the Strattons in the twelfth century. There are the remains of a motte, and the property may have later passed to the Cunninghams.

No. of castles/sites: 4
Rank: 278=/764
Xrefs: Straiton; Straton

Sutherland

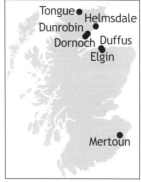

The name is territorial in origin, and comes from a large area of north and north-east Scotland, which was the 'southern land' to the Norsemen who held Orkney and Caithness. The Sutherland family are believed to be descended from a Fleming called Freskin, from whom the Murrays also come. Freskin established a castle at Duffus, but it is the great fortress and mansion of Dunrobin which became the seat of the family.

Dunrobin Castle [NC 852008] is a mile to the north-east of Golspie in Sutherland, and is now a splendid fairy-tale castle, developed out of an old stronghold but remodelled in modern times by Sir Robert Lorimer. The Sutherland family were made Earls of Sutherland in 1235, and Kenneth, fourth Earl and Regent of Scotland, was slain at the Battle of Halidon Hill in England in 1333. William, the next Earl, was murdered in a feud with the Mackays in 1370, and the sixth Earl, Robert or Robin, is believed to have built the first castle (or perhaps rebuilt an older stronghold), which is named after him; he died in 1446. John, eighth Earl, was declared unfit, and the Earldom passed to the Gordons, who were related to the Sutherlands. In 1567 Isobel Sinclair poisoned John, eleventh Earl, and his wife at Helmsdale Castle, hoping to secure the succession of her son, but the future twelfth Earl escaped and she managed to poison her own son; she committed suicide before she could be executed. The young Earl of Sutherland escaped to Dornoch Palace or Skibo Castle, where he was eventually captured by the Earl of Caithness and forced to marry Lady Barbara Sinclair, who was twice his age. When he came of age he divorced her, and assumed the title. John, sixteenth Earl, took the name Sutherland, and supported the Hanoverians in the Jacobite Rising of 1715. The Jacobites seized Dunrobin, but they soon surrendered and the Mackenzie Earl of Cromartie was captured. The male line of the Sutherlands failed, and the property went through an heiress to the Marquess of Stafford, and they were made Dukes of Sutherland in 1833. Done for whatever motives, the family are remembered for their brutal treatment, when many of their own tenants were cleared from lands they had held for generations. The third Duke contributed much of his money to the building of the railway to the north. The male line failed again, and the Earldom and Dukedom have parted company: the Earldom went to the present Countess of Sutherland, while the Dukedom went to the next male heir, the Earl of Ellesmere. During World War I the castle was used as a naval hospital, and then as a boys' public school between 1963 and 1972. The castle is said to be haunted by the ghost of a girl, although there are different versions of the tale behind her appearance. One that she tried to elope with her lover but fell to her death from an upstairs window; another that she had been seized by one of the earls who desired her, but she refused him and also fell to her death. Dunrobin is still apparently held by the Countess of Sutherland, who has residence at House of Tongue and in London according to *Burke's*, and the castle is open to the public from April to mid October (01408 633177; www.highlandescape.com).

House of Tongue [NC 592588] is a mile or so north of Tongue in the very far north of Scotland. There was a tower house of the Mackays, but the present mansion dates from 1678. House of Tongue was held by the Mackay Lords Reay, but is apparently now a property of the Countess of Sutherland. The gardens are occasionally open to the public (www.gardensofscotland.org).

The Sutherlands also owned:
Ardvreck Castle [NC 240236], near Inchnadamph, Sutherland; ruinous castle.
　Held by the MacLeods of Assynt and then by the Mackenzies, but was sold to the Earl of Sutherland in 1758.
Berriedale Castle [ND 121224], near Dunbeath, Caithness; slight remains of castle.
　Held by the Cheynes in the fourteenth century, but passed by marriage to the Sutherlands, then to the Oliphants by 1526, and then to the Sinclair Earls of Caithness in 1606.
Castle of Old Wick [ND 369488], near Wick, Caithness; ruinous castle on cliffs.
　Held by the Cheynes and then by the Sutherland Lords Duffus, then by the Oliphants, by the Sinclairs, by the Campbells of Glenorchy and by the Dunbars of Hempriggs. Now in the care of Historic Scotland and open to the public (01667 460232).
Clyne [NC 895060], near Brora, Sutherland; site of castle or old house.
　Held by the Clyne family, but passed by marriage to the Sutherlands around 1550 and they still held the property in the middle of the eighteenth century.

Dunrobin Castle (M&R)

Cnoc Chaisteal [NH 777900], near Dornoch, Sutherland; site of castle.

Believed to have been built by the Sutherlands of Evelix about 1570.

Dirlot Castle [ND 126486], near Watten, Caithness; site of castle.

Held by the Cheynes and by the Gunns, then by the Sutherlands, and then by the Mackays in 1499.

Dornoch Palace [NH 797897], Dornoch, Sutherland; altered castle.

Held by the Bishops of Caithness, but passed to the Earls of Sutherland after the Reformation. George Sinclair, fourth Earl of Caithness, had the town and cathedral burnt and the castle besieged in 1567 to secure possession of the young Earl of Sutherland, although he is also said to have been abducted from Skibo. The castle held out for a month, but eventually surrendered on fair terms, although hostages given by the garrison were subsequently murdered. The castle was then burnt, and left a ruin until restored in the nineteenth century as a courthouse and jail. The palace is said to be haunted by the ghost of a man accused of stealing sheep, and there are stories of an underground passageway linking the palace to the nearby cathedral, into which all the bishop's wealth was placed following the Reformation. Should the treasure ever be found, the story goes that this will herald the end of the Earls and Dukes of Sutherland. Dornoch Castle is now a hotel (01862 810216; www.dornochcastlehotel.com) and Dornoch Cathedral is also open to the public.

Duffus Castle [NJ 189672], near Elgin, Moray; fine motte and bailey castle.

Held and built by Freskin, Lord of Strathbrock, whose descendants were both the Sutherlands and the Murrays. Duffus later passed to the Cheynes, but then went by marriage to the Sutherlands in 1350 and they held the lands until 1843. The castle was sacked by the Douglas Earl of Moray in 1452, and again by Royalists in 1645. John Graham of Claverhouse, Bonnie Dundee, stayed here in 1689. The castle was abandoned for nearby **Duffus House** [NJ 176685], which rises to three storeys, at the end of the seventeenth century, although the building was altered in 1840, and it is now part of Gordonstoun school. The Sutherlands of Duffus have a burial aisle at St Peter's Church [NJ 175688] at (Old) Duffus, which is open to the public.

Forse Castle [ND 224338], near Dunbeath, Caithness; ruinous castle on promontory.

Held by the Cheynes and by the Keiths, then by the Sutherlands and the castle was abandoned in the eighteenth century. Forse House was built some two miles to the north, and is a symmetrical mansion of three storeys of 1753. It is still occupied.

Golspie Tower [NC 836009], Golspie, Sutherland; site of large tower house.

Held by the Earls of Sutherland.

Helmsdale Castle [ND 027152], Helmsdale, Sutherland; site of castle.

Held by the Earls of Sutherland. It was here that in 1567 Isobel Sinclair, the Earl's aunt, poisoned John, eleventh Earl of Sutherland, and his wife in order make her own son Earl. She also tried to poison the Earl's heir, but the cup of poison was drunk by her own son, who died two days later. She killed herself before being executed in Edinburgh. The whole affair was apparently a plot hatched by George Sinclair, fourth Earl of Caithness.

Kinsteary [NH 927543], near Nairn, Inverness-shire; castle replaced by mansion.

Held by the Sutherlands of Kinsteary from the sixteenth century, but perhaps also a possession of the Campbells of Cawdor.

Langwell Castle [ND 116227], near Dunbeath, Caithness; slight remains of castle.

Held by the Sutherlands, and the castle was replaced by Langwell House, a mansion dating from the eighteenth century. The property was sold to the Sinclairs in 1788, then passed to

the Hornes and then to the Dukes of Portland, who still apparently occupy it. The garden is open by appointment only (01593 751278; www.gardensofscotland.org).

Loch Brora [NC 856060], near Brora, Sutherland; site of castle.

Held by the Earls of Sutherland.

Proncy Castle [NH 772926], near Dornoch, Sutherland; slight remains of castle.

Held by the Sutherlands in 1525, but passed to the Gordons of Proncy.

Mertoun House [NT 618318], near Kelso, Borders; castle replaced by tower house.

Held by the Halyburtons, but passed to the Scotts of Harden, then to the Dukes of Sutherland in 1912. Mertoun Gardens are open to the public (01835 823236).

Quarrelwood Castle [NJ 181642], near Elgin, Moray; site of castle.

Held by the Lauders, but passed to the Sutherlands in the early sixteenth century, who held the property until about 1750.

Scourie [NC 156450], Scourie, Sutherland; site of castle or old house.

Long held by the Mackays but passed to the Earls and (later) Dukes of Sutherland after 1692.

Shiness [NC 539143], near Lairg, Sutherland; site of castle.

Held by the Mathesons but passed to the Earls of Sutherland in 1809.

Skelbo Castle [NH 792952], near Dornoch, Sutherland; ruinous castle.

Held by the Sutherlands of Skelbo, and a castle here was captured by Robert the Bruce in 1308. This branch of the Sutherlands acquired the Lordship of Duffus in the fourteenth century. William Sutherland, Lord Duffus, was slain by the Gunns at Thurso in 1530. Alexander, his son, sacked and burnt the cathedral and town of Dornoch in 1567, and again in 1570. The family was forfeited for their part in the Jacobite Rising of 1715. The property was acquired by the Earls of Sutherland.

Skibo Castle [NH 735891], near Dornoch, Sutherland; mansion on site of castle.

Held by the Mackays, by the Grays, by the Dowalls and by the Dempsters of Dunnichen, and the building was remodelled for the Sutherlands in 1872 but was then purchased by Andrew Carnegie in 1895. It is now an exclusive country club (www.carnegieclubs.com).

Swiney Castle [ND 232345], near Dunbeath, Caithness; site of castle.

Held by the Sutherlands of Forse, and was replaced by Swiney House about 1730.

Thunderton House [NJ 215615], Elgin, Moray; altered castle.

Held by the Sutherland Lord Duffus, but passed to the Dunbars of Thunderton and is now a public house (01343 554921; www.thundertonhouse.co.uk).

www.clansutherland.org.uk
www.clansutherland.org
No. of castles/sites: 25
Rank: 52=/764

Duffus Castle (M&R) – see previous column

Suttie

The name is probably local in origin, and is on record from the beginning of the seventeenth century.

Addistoun House [NT 155694] is a mile or so south-west of Ratho to the west of Edinburgh, and there appears to have been a castle or old house, which had its own park. The house was rebuilt in the eighteenth century and later. The lands were probably held by the Sutties in the seventeenth century, but passed to the Hoggs and then to the Gibsons. The family married into the Sempills of Balgone.

Lying a couple of miles south and east of North Berwick in East Lothian, **Balgone House** [NT 567825] is an L-plan tower house, dating from the seventeenth century, to which has been added a later mansion. Balgone was held by the Rosses of Hawkhead and then by the Sempills, but passed by marriage to the Sutties of Addiston in 1680. The family were made Baronets of Nova Scotia in 1702, now Grant-Suttie as the name of Grant was added when they married the heiress of the Grants of Prestongrange.

Prestongrange House [NT 373737] is two miles east of Musselburgh, also in East Lothian; and the large mansion includes work from the sixteenth century although it was extensively remodelled and extended in later years. Owned by the Kerr Earls and Marquises of Lothian, it was sold to the Grants in 1746 and then passed by marriage to the Sutties of Balgone. The building is now the clubhouse of the Royal Musselburgh Golf Club (01875 810276; www.royalmusselburgh.co.uk).

No. of castles/sites: 3
Rank: 328=/764

Cranshaws Castle (M&R) – see next column

Swinton

The name is territorial and comes from the lands of Swinton, which are four and half miles north of Coldstream in Berwickshire in the Borders. The name is said to come from the family having cleared the area of wild boar and so were given the name, although it is more likely it is simply territorial (perhaps from the personal name 'Sween' or 'Swan', and 'ton', meaning 'settlement' or 'seat').

The family claim descent from the lords of Bamburgh in Northumberland. The Arbuthnotts were originally called Swinton in the twelfth century, but they changed their name to Arbuthnott (see that name) when they married an Oliphant heiress and acquired the lands of Arbuthnott in Kincardineshire.

Swinton House [NT 819471] is a classical mansion of two storeys, dating from 1800, but it stands on the site of a castle or old house, which was gutted by fire in 1797. The lands were held by the Swintons from the time of Malcolm Canmore in the eleventh century, although their first charter was dated 1140. Sir John Swinton was one of those instrumental in winning the Battle of Otterburn in 1388, although he was killed fighting the English at Homildon Hill in 1402.

Sir John Swinton, his son, is one of those reputed to have slain the Duke of Clarence, the brother of Henry V, at the Battle of Baugé in 1421, but he was himself slain at the Battle of Verneuil three years later.

John Swinton fought against Cromwell at the Battle of Worcester in 1651 and was captured; his brother was killed in the fighting. John later became part of the Cromwellian administration, and he was found guilty of treason at the Restoration and he was forfeited and imprisoned for six years. Another brother, Alexander, was also captured following the battle but went on to be an advocate and then a Lord of Session. The family recovered their lands after William and Mary came to the throne. John Swinton, twenty-seventh laird, was a member of the Supreme Court in 1782 and took the title Lord Swinton. The property had passed to the MacNabs by the nineteenth century, and the Swintons of that Ilk apparently now live in Montana in the USA.

The Swintons also held:
Cranshaws Castle [NT 681619], near Cranshaws, Borders; altered tower house.
> Held by the Swintons from 1400 to 1702, when it passed to the Douglases. This is one of the houses which is said to have had a brownie. This particular one used to gather and thresh corn, but a servant moaned that it had not been neatly stacked. The brownie was disgusted and immediately left, taking the grain with him and dumping it in the Whiteadder Water at Raven's Crag.

Kimmerghame House [NT 815514], near Duns, Borders; castle
replaced by mansion.
Held by the Morhams, by the Sinclairs, by the Homes and by
the Johnstones before passing to the Swintons (later Campbell-
Swinton) in the second half of the eighteenth century. The
mansion was damaged by fire around 1850, and was only partly
rebuilt.

Little Swinton [NT 825459], near Coldstream, Borders; site of
tower.
Held by the Swintons, but destroyed by the English in 1482.

Mersington Tower [NT 775443], near Greenlaw, Borders; site of
castle.
Held by the Kerrs and then by the Swintons, and was burned
by the English in 1545. Alexander Swinton, Lord Mersington,
was one of those who led an attack on the Chapel Royal at
Holyrood in 1688 during a Protestant riot.

Stevenson [NT 170430], near Peebles, Borders; site of tower house.
Held by the Swintons but passed by marriage to the Sinclairs
in the seventeenth century.

www.swintonfamilysociety.org
No. of castles/sites: 6
Rank: 212=/764

Sydserf

The name is territorial and
comes from the lands of
Sydserf, which are a
couple of miles south of
North Berwick in East
Lothian. The name may
come from 'St Serf', a
sixth-century holy man
who is associated with
Culross in Fife and an
island in Loch Leven, and the name is on record from
the end of the thirteenth century.

Sydserf [NT 542818] is an altered L-plan house, now
of two storeys, and probably dating from the
seventeenth century. There are shot-holes in one wall,
and the house is now part of a farm. The lands were
held by the family in 1577, and probably from the
thirteenth century or earlier. Thomas Sydserf was
Protestant Bishop of Brechin, and then of Galloway and
then of Orkney, and he died in 1663. Thomas, his son,
was a dramatist and also published news-sheets in the
1650s.

Ruchlaw House [NT 618741] is four miles south-west
of Dunbar, also in East Lothian. The building dates from
the seventeenth century or before, and is an L-plan
house of three storeys. The property was held by the
Sydserfs from 1617 or earlier until the middle of the
twentieth century, although they were latterly Buchan-
Sydserf. There is a burial enclosure for the family at
Whittinghame Parish Church.

No. of castles/sites: 2
Rank: 396=/764

Syme

The name is from a diminutive for Simon, and is on record in Scotland from the middle of the fifteenth century.

Northfield House [NT 389739], to the south of Prestonpans in East Lothian, is a substantial and atmospheric house, dating from the sixteenth century and L-plan in design. The building has a very steeply pitched roof, and turrets crown the corners. The property was owned by the Hamiltons, by the Marjoribanks and by the Nisbets before passing to the Symes. They held it until 1890 when it went to the MacNeils, and the house is still occupied and can be seen from the road.

No. of castles/sites: 1
Rank: 537=/764
Xrefs: Sim; Sime

Symmer

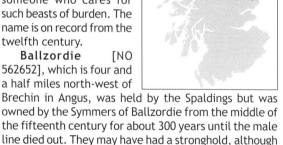

The name comes from 'sumpter', meaning a pack horse or mule, but also someone who cares for such beasts of burden. The name is on record from the twelfth century.

Ballzordie [NO 562652], which is four and a half miles north-west of Brechin in Angus, was held by the Spaldings but was owned by the Symmers of Ballzordie from the middle of the fifteenth century for about 300 years until the male line died out. They may have had a stronghold, although there are no remains except for name Castle of Ballzordie.

House of Mergie [NO 796887], four miles west and north of Stonehaven in Kincardineshire, is a tall T-plan tower house, dating from the seventeenth century and rising to three storeys. Mergie was owned by the Douglases, but passed to Paul Symmer, an officer in Cromwell's army. The property was sold to the Garioch family in 1772 and then to the Duffs; House of Mergie is now used as a farmhouse.

No. of castles/sites: 2
Rank: 396=/764
Xrefs: Summer; Somers

Symson

The name is from 'Simon's son', 'Sim' or 'Sym' being a diminutive for Simon, and the name is on record from the twelfth century. Symson, Simson and Simpson are variations in spellings. Sir James Young Simpson, born in Bathgate in 1811, was Professor of Midwifery at Edinburgh, and he experimented with various forms of anaesthesia, including chloroform in 1847. He was made a Baronet in 1866. Simpson Memorial Hospital (now amalgamated into the new Royal Infirmary) in Edinburgh was named after him.

Craighouse [NT 234709] lies to the south and west of Edinburgh, and is an altered tower house, dating from the sixteenth century. There is a long narrow block with a projecting stair tower and a later addition. The lands

Craighouse (M&R)

were held by the Symsons, and they built the castle. Craighouse passed to the Dicks in the seventeenth century and then to the Elphinstones. Craighouse was part of a psychiatric hospital but is now in the campus of Napier University; the building is used as offices.

Feddinch House [NO 485135], two miles south-west of St Andrews in Fife, is an elegant symmetrical mansion. The property was held by the Symsons in 1542, but passed to the Aytons and then to the Lindsays and to the Wedderburns. Accommodation is available (01334 470888; www.feddinch-house.com).

Nearby **Wilkieston** [NO 449120], four miles south-west of St Andrews, was held by the Symsons of Wilkieston in 1735.

No. of castles/sites: 3
Rank: 328=/764
Xrefs: Simson; Simpson

Tait

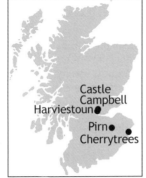

Tait is believed to originally have been a nickname, and it is derived from 'teitr' in Old Norse and means 'glad or cheerful'. The name is on record from the fourteenth century in Scotland, and the family held lands in the Borders and then much later in Clackmannan. Archibald Campbell Tait, who was born in Edinburgh in 1811, became Bishop of London in 1856 and then Archbishop in 1868; he died in 1882.

Pirn [NT 337370] is to the east of Innerleithen in the Borders, and there was a tower house, which was replaced by a mansion. The lands were long a property of the Taits, but the line ended in heiresses and Pirn went to the Horsburghs in the eighteenth century. The tower and house have been demolished, and the site is occupied by a school.

Cherrytrees [NT 810293], a mile or so north-west of Town Yetholm in the Borders near the English Border, is a symmetrical mansion of about 1800, but it replaced a tower or old house. Held by the Rutherfords in 1523, the property had passed to the Taits by 1605, but may have gone to the Kerrs in the same century.

One mile east of Tillicoultry in Clackmannan, **Harviestoun Castle** [NS 937978] was a castellated mansion of 1804 with later extensions, but it was blown up and demolished in 1970. There was an earlier house, perhaps from 1610, but this has also gone. The lands were held by the Taits in the seventeenth and eighteenth centuries, and they built the mansion. Their family mausoleum is on the A91 between Tillicoultry and Dollar. There are stories that the area is haunted, with apparitions of people and vehicles, some which have reputedly caused accidents.

Castle Campbell [NS 962994], half a mile or so north of Dollar, is a fine partly ruinous castle in a magnificent spot. As the name suggests, it was for generations occupied by the Campbells, but they sold the property to the Taits of nearby Harviestoun in 1807, and then later that century the property went to the Orrs. The castle was later put into the care of The National Trust

for Scotland in 1948, although managed by Historic Scotland, and it is open to the public (01259 742408).

Loudoun Hall [NS 337221], on New Bridge Street in Ayr, is a fine townhouse and dates from early in the sixteenth century. The hall was built by James Tait, a burgess of Ayr, but was sold to the Campbells of Loudoun (and hence the name) in 1530 and later went to the Chalmers family of Gadgirth. The hall is now used by various groups and societies for meetings and events.

www.the-taits.net
No. of castles/sites: 5
Rank: 240=/764

Tarrel

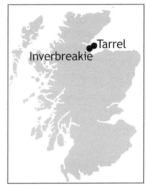

The name is territorial and comes from the lands of Tarrel, which are eight miles east of Tain in Ross and Cromarty. The family is on record from the middle of the fourteenth century but in the sixteenth century the property had gone to the MacCullochs. It is not clear whether the Tarrel family had a castle, but there is a stronghold at **Little Tarrel** [NH 911819], a restored sixteenth-century L-plan tower house, and there was another tower house at **Meikle Tarrel** [NH 900810], although this has gone; both of these were later held by the Munros. The main line of the family appears to have died out and the remaining members took the name Mackintosh.

The Tarrels also held lands in Strathfleet, Pittentrail and Doll in Sutherland at one time, and may have also been in possession of Inverbreakie, as a Janet Tarrel of Innerbrecky is mentioned in the sixteenth century. There was castle at **Inverbreakie** [NH 715700], just north-east of Invergordon also in Ross and Cromarty, once a substantial stronghold, although there are no traces. The property was held by the Innes family before being sold to the Gordons at the beginning of the eighteenth century.

No. of castles/sites: 3
Rank: 328=/764
Xref: Tarril

Castle Campbell 1904?

Taylor

The name comes from the occupation of 'tailor', a cutter of cloth; and the name is on record in Scotland from the thirteenth century. The name was descriptive to begin with, indicating occupation ('John le Taillur' or 'John the tailor'), but was later used as a surname.

Kirktonhill [NO 692659] is four and a half miles northwest of Montrose in Angus, and there was a castle or old house. This was replaced by Kirktonhill House, a symmetrical U-plan mansion, although the main block was demolished in the 1960s and only the wings remain. Possibly a property of the Keiths, Kirktonhill was held by the Taylors from the eighteenth century, who had made money from sugar plantations in Jamaica. Nearby is Kirktonhill Tower, a three-storey folly, which is octagonal at the base and round at the top.

No. of castles/sites: 1
Rank: 537=/764
Xref: Tailor

Telfer

The name comes from 'taillefer' from Norman French, and means 'cut iron', and may be descriptive of an occupation. The name is on record in Scotland from the thirteenth century.

Harecleuch [NT 003193] is three or so miles east and south of Crawford in Lanarkshire, and this may be the property that is on record as being held by the Telfers from 1369 for about 300 years. They may have had a tower or old house, although there was also a Harecleuch Sheel [NS 913215], further north and some two miles south-west of Abington.

Kimmerghame House [NT 815514], two and a half miles east of Duns in Berwickshire in the Borders, was a tall and grand castellated mansion, although it stands on or near the site of a castle or old house. The building was damaged by fire and was only partly rebuilt. Held by the Morhams, by the Sinclairs and by the Homes, it later passed to the Johnstones and then to the Swintons, but it was also latterly held by the Telfers.

No. of castles/sites: 2
Rank: 396=/764

Tennant

The name comes from 'tenere', which is Latin meaning 'to hold', and hence a tenant of a house or of lands. The name is on record in Scotland from 1296.

Cairns Tower [NT 091604] is six or so miles west and south of Balerno, and is a ruinous keep or tower, which rose to three storeys or more, and it dates from the fifteenth century. The property was held by the Cairns family and by the

Cairns Tower (M&R)

Crichtons, but passed to the Tennants in the middle of the sixteenth century; they owned the property for 150 years.

Linnhouse [NT 062630], two and a half miles east of West Calder in West Lothian, is an L-plan tower house, dating from the sixteenth century. To this was added another L-plan block in the next century, making the house E-plan. The tower was probably built by Francis Tennant, Provost of Edinburgh, in 1571, who was taken prisoner after fighting for Mary, Queen of Scots.

Linnhouse (M&R)

569

In later years the Tennants also held:

Glen [NT 298330], near Innerleithen, Borders; castle or old house replaced by mansion.

Held by the Glen family, but had passed to the Tennants by the nineteenth century. The family are Barons Glenconner, and they may still live here. Their residence, however, is given in *Burke's* as in St Lucia in the West Indies.

Innes House [NJ 278649], near Elgin, Moray; fine altered L-plan tower house.

Held by the Inneses, then later by the Duffs and by the Tennants.

Inverernan House [NJ 330110], near Strathdon, Aberdeenshire; castle replaced by mansion.

Held by the Forbeses, then much later went to the Wallaces and then to the Tennants.

No. of castles/sites: 5 / Rank: 240=/764

Thirlestane

The name is territorial and comes from the lands of Thirlestane (now Old Thirlestane), which are two miles east of Lauder in the Borders.

Old Thirlestane Castle [NT 564474] is now quite ruinous, but there was a tower and a courtyard.

The property was held by the Thirlestane family from the twelfth century, but the line ended in an heiress, and the lands passed by marriage to the Maitlands in the thirteenth century. They moved to Thirlestane Castle, near Lauder, about 1595.

No. of castles/sites: 1 / Rank: 537=/764

Thomas

The name was a common Anglo-Norman personal name, but Thomas was not used in Scotland as a surname until relatively late.

Cammo House [NT 174747] stood on the western outskirts of Edinburgh, but most of it has been demolished and it now stands in a country park. The lands were held by the Niddries, by the Menzies family and by others before coming to the Thomas family. Sir Mitchell Thomas of Cammo was Lord Provost of Edinburgh in the nineteenth century. The house was occupied until 1975, and was then given to The National Trust for Scotland. Cammo House was then set on fire several times and vandalised, and most of it has been demolished. The grounds are now a country park, and there is a visitor centre.

No. of castles/sites: 1 / Rank: 537=/764

Thomson

The name comes from 'Thom's son', as 'Thom' is a diminutive for Thomas, and the surname was relatively common in Scotland. The name is on record from the beginning of the fourteenth century. Robert William Thomson, born in Stonehaven in 1822, was an engineer and he took out patents for rubber tyres in 1845 and then the fountain pen four years later. He made improvements and advances in other fields, not least by using electric current to set off explosions. Alexander Thomson, born in Balfron in 1811, was an architect in Glasgow and designed his buildings with gothic and Greek classical influences, earning him his nickname 'Greek Thomson'.

The Thomsons held the following properties, most in the north-east of Scotland:

Arduthie [NO 868865], near Stonehaven, Kincardineshire; site of castle or old house.

Held by the Arbuthnotts but passed to the Thomsons of Arduthie, who held the property in the late seventeenth century. Arduthie was sold to the Barclays of Urie in 1759.

Beannachar [NJ 915024], Aberdeen; castle and house replaced by mansion.

Held by the Gardynes but passed to the Thomsons, who held the property in the nineteenth century. Now used as a school.

Castle of Fiddes [NO 825813], near Stonehaven, Kincardineshire; L-plan tower house.

Held by the Arbuthnotts, but sold to the Thomsons of Arduthie in the late seventeenth century. Now a farmhouse.

Disblair House [NJ 862197], near New Machar, Aberdeenshire; castle replaced by mansion.

Held by the Thomsons and then by the Setons in the sixteenth century, but passed to the Blairs and then to the Dyce family about 1750.

Dunino Den [NO 542113], near St Andrews, Fife; site of castle or fortified house.

Held by the Thomsons in the seventeenth century.

Keillour Castle [NN 979256], near Methven, Perthshire; tower house replaced by mansion.

Held by the Thomsons of Keillour in 1496, then possibly later by the Hays.

Pitmedden [NJ 863149], near Dyce, Aberdeenshire; castle replaced by mansion.

Held by the Thomsons in the nineteenth century. George Thompson was Provost of Aberdeen in 1847-50 and MP for Aberdeen, a member of the Liberal Party.

No. of castles/sites: 7
Rank: 182=/764
Xrefs: Thompson; MacTavish

Thorburn

The name comes from the Old English personal name 'Thurbrand', and it is on record in Scotland from the fourteenth century.

Ormiston Tower [NT 315378] stood a mile or so west of Innerleithen in the Borders, but was demolished around 1805 when Glenormiston House was built. This building, although extended in 1824 and 1846, was itself demolished in the 1950s. The lands were held by the Stewarts of Traquair, and possibly by the Dicksons, but were sold to William Chambers, author and publisher, and then were held by the Thorburns at the end of the nineteenth century.

No. of castles/sites: 1
Rank: 537=/764
Xref: Thurburn

Thornton

The name is territorial and comes from the lands of Thornton, which are a mile or so north-west of Laurencekirk in Kincardineshire; the name is on record from around the beginning of the thirteenth century.

Thornton Castle [NO 688718] is a plain L-plan tower house to which a modern mansion has been added. The tower dates from the sixteenth century, but there was a castle here, dating from 200 years earlier. Owned by the Thorntons from the thirteenth century or earlier, the property passed by marriage to the Strachans in 1309 and they held it until 1683. Thornton went to the Forbeses of Newton and then to others, and the castle is still occupied.

No. of castles/sites: 1
Rank: 537=/764

Threipland

The name is territorial and comes from the lands of **Thriepland** [NT 042354], which are one or so miles south of Biggar, just in the Borders. The family apparently held the lands in 1296, but the line ended in an heiress and she resigned the lands in favour of the Douglases. There was probably a later tower house here, and there are also places in Moray and in Ayrshire called Threipland, Thriepland or Threepland.

Fingask Castle [NO 228275] is some seven miles east and north of Perth, and is an L-plan tower house, which dates from 1594, but was altered down the centuries, and it is now T-plan. Held by the Dunbars and by the Bruces of Clackmannan, Fingask was bought by the Threiplands in 1672. Patrick Threipland, Provost of Perth, was knighted in 1674 after he had been successful in suppressing Covenanters, but died a prisoner in Stirling Castle two years later. His son was one of the first to join the Jacobite Rising of 1715. James VIII, the Old Pretender, stayed at Fingask twice in 1716, but the family was forfeited after the Rising, although they recovered the property. During the Jacobite Rising of 1745, the elder son was killed at the Battle of Prestonpans; and the family were forfeited again after its failure, and the castle was sacked and partially demolished in 1746. Sir Stewart Threipland, a younger son, escaped to France after helping Bonnie Prince Charlie and apparently securing for himself some of the Loch Arkaig Treasure. He returned to Edinburgh in 1747 and was able to buy back Fingask in 1783. The house was restored early in the twentieth century, and again in 1967, and the gardens are occasionally open to the public (www.gardensofscotland.org). There are stories here of a tunnel linking the castle to nearby Kinnaird, which was also owned by the Threiplands.

Kinnaird Castle [NO 242291] is about a mile and a

Kinnaird Castle (M&R)

half away further east and north of Perth. It is a tall and impressive keep or tower of four storeys, and it dates from the fifteenth century. Kinnaird was owned by the Threipland family, but passed to the Colvilles and then was bought back by the Threiplands, later of Fingask, in 1674. The building was abandoned and became ruinous, but was restored and recovered by the Threiplands. It is still occupied.

No. of castles/sites: 3 / Rank: 328=/764
Xref: Threepland; Thriepland

Tilliedaff

The name is territorial and comes from the barony and lands of Tilliedaff, which are two miles west and north of Echt in Aberdeenshire. The name is on record from the beginning of the fourteenth century, and the family held the lands of **Tilliedaff** (now **Tillydaff**) [NJ 715074] from 1317 or earlier until 1588 when the laird died leaving three daughters. William Tullidaff had been slain at the Battle of Harlaw in 1411. There may have been a castle or old house at Tillydaff, although the location is not certain. Tillydaff's Cairn stood a couple of miles northeast of Old Rayne also in Aberdeenshire, but the cairn has gone. This is said to be where Tillidaff, laird of Warthill, was killed in 1530. **Warthill** [NJ 710315] is the site of a castle, and was held by the Cruickshanks and the Leslies, although it does not appear to have been held by the Tilliedaff family.

No. of castles/sites: 1 / Rank: 537=/764
Xrefs: Tillydaff; Tuledaff

Tinsdale

The name may be from Tynedale in Northumberland in England, although the 's' is not usually found in that name. Tinsdale is on record in Scotland from the twelfth century.

Muiravonside [NS 965753] is a couple of miles west and south of Linlithgow in West Lothian. The house dated from the seventeenth century or earlier, but it has been demolished and nothing survives except foundations, a burial ground and an old doocot. The lands were held by a Reginald Tinsdale in the twelfth century, but passed to the Rosses in 1421, and then later went to the MacLeods and to the Stirlings, who held Muiravonside in the twentieth century. The grounds are now a country park.

No. of castles/sites: 1 / Rank: 537=/764

Tod

The name apparently comes from 'tod', a nickname for a fox, and is on record from the end of the thirteenth century. The Tods were found in the Borders and then in Edinburgh and elsewhere.

Sheriffhall [NT 320680] is one and a half miles south-east of Dalkeith in Midlothian, and there was a castle here, although most of it was demolished because of subsidence caused by mining and all that remains is a stair-turret. The Tods of Sheriffhall are on record at the end of the fifteenth century, although perhaps not for the most glorious of reasons: Thomas Tod of Sheriffhall, along with others, agreed to deliver the King of Scots (James IV) to Henry VII of England in 1491 in return for a loan. The property passed to the Scotts of Buccleuch and then to the Giffords in the sixteenth century.

There were also the Tods of Kirklands, who originally came from Musselburgh; the location of the lands of Kirklands have not been established.

No. of castles/sites: 1
Rank: 537=/764
Xref: Todd

Torthorwald

The name is territorial and comes from the lands of Torthorwald, which are four miles north-east of Dumfries. The family are on record from the thirteenth century.

Torthorwald Castle [NY 033783] consists of a ruinous rectangular keep which stands on a motte with ramparts and a ditch, and dates from the fourteenth century or earlier. The lands were held by the Torthorwalds, who are mentioned between 1215 and 1245. The property appears to have passed by marriage to the Kirkpatricks later that century, but the Torthorwalds still held land. They sided with the English in the Wars of Independence, and Sir James Torthorwald was slain at the Battle of Bannockburn in 1314. The family lost their remaining possessions, although they were compensated by Edward III of England in 1328. Torthorwald passed from the Kirkpatricks by marriage to the Carlyles in 1418. The property later went to the Douglases, who were made Lords Torthorwald, and the castle was occupied until about 1715.

No. of castles/sites: 1
Rank: 537=/764

Towers

The name probably comes from Walter Towers, a French merchant in Edinburgh in the fourteenth century, and the name is recorded as 'de Tours'. The family held lands near Leith and in East Lothian.

Inverleith House [NT 245753] dates from 1744 and is a plain mansion of three storeys with a bow front. It stands to the north of Edinburgh in what is now the Royal Botanic Garden. The lands were held by the Ramsays, but passed to the Towers family, who were in possession in the sixteenth and seventeenth centuries.

Wardie Tower [NT 243770] was apparently built near the sea to the north of Edinburgh to defend the coast, but its location is not certain. The lands were owned by the Towers family in 1504 when it was constructed, although it did not deter the English from landing at Newhaven, devastating the area, and torching Leith in 1544.

A mile or so to the north of Haddington in a rugged spot (for East Lothian) are the remains of **Garleton Castle** [NT 509767], which was long associated with the Lindsays. Garleton later passed to the Towers family of

Garleton Castle (M&R)

Inverleith, who sold the property to the Setons. The castle consisted of ranges around a courtyard within an enclosing wall, but only one block remains complete, while the other sides are ruinous or have been rebuilt as cottages.

No. of castles/sites: 3
Rank: 328=/764

Trail

The name may be local in origin, although from where has not been determined. One branch of the family held lands in Fife, while another became established in Orkney and Shetland in the sixteenth century and then at Castlehill and at Rattar in Caithness.

Blebo Hole [NO 423134] was three miles east of Cupar in Fife, but only slight remains, if any, now exist. The lands were held by the Trails of Blebo, and one of the family, Walter Trail, was Bishop of St Andrews in 1385 and ambassador to France six years later; he was responsible for the rebuilding of St Andrews Castle. The castle at Blebo Hole was besieged by the Learmonths of Dairsie in 1599, and the Trails sold the property to the Beatons in 1649. The Beatons moved their seat to **Blebo House** [NO 423145], which was later owned by the Lows and is still occupied.

No. of castles/sites: 1
Rank: 537=/764
Xref: Traill

Trent

The name may come from Trent in England, or it may be a shortened form of Tranent, a burgh in East Lothian. The name is on record from the middle of the fifteenth century.

Pitcullo Castle [NO 413196], three miles east and south of Leuchars in Fife, is an L-plan tower house with a corbelled-out stair-turret and the walls are whitewashed. Held by the Sibbalds and then by the Balfours in the sixteenth century, Pitcullo later passed to the Trents. The castle has been restored with some demolition and alteration, and won a Saltire Award in 1972.

No. of castles/sites: 1
Rank: 537=/764

Trotter

The name is thought to come from 'trottier', which (as it sounds) comes from the office of 'runner' or 'messenger'. The name is on record in Scotland from the fourteenth century, and the family held lands near Duns in the Borders and to the south of Edinburgh.

Bite-About Pele [NT 784467] is four or so miles south of Duns, and is now a very ruinous L-plan tower house, which dates from the sixteenth century. The tower is at **West Printonan** and the name 'Bite-About' is said to be derived from when the tower was being besieged by the English. The garrison was low in provisions, and had to share their food, each taking a 'bite about'. Printonan was held by the Trotters, and the head of the family was style 'of Prentannan'. It is not certain whether this was their tower or there was another building at nearby **Printonan** [NT 797470]. The Trotters are said to have followed the Homes on raids into England, and the head of the Trotter family was killed at the Battle of Flodden in 1513.

Charterhall (or earlier **Catchelraw**) [NT 763473], four and a half miles south and west of Duns, is a modern mansion on the site of an earlier house, and there was probably a castle or tower house. Catchelraw may have been the older name, or this may have referred to a nearby property. The lands were held by the Trotters from around the turn of the fifteenth century, and George Trotter of Charterhall presented two communion cups to the kirk at Fogo in 1662; the family had a laird's loft in the church. The Trotters of Mortonhall still apparently own Charterhall, and the grounds are occasionally open to the public and there is holiday accommodation on the estate (www.charterhall.net/ www.gardensofscotland.org).

Mortonhall [NT 262683] is one of the Trotter's properties which is to the south of Edinburgh. There was a castle, with a moat and drawbridge, which was owned by the Sinclairs, and then by the Ellis family. The lands were acquired by John Trotter, who was a successful merchant in Edinburgh, in 1635. His son, John, was fined for supporting the Marquis of Montrose. The castle was demolished, and the Trotters built a classical mansion in 1769. The house has been divided but is occupied, although the Trotters of Mortonhall still apparently own the lands. There is a caravan and camping site and houses can be rented on the estate (www.mortonhall.co.uk).

Morton House [NT 254679] is nearby, and is a tall plain mansion with later extensions, but it also included older work. The property was held by the Trotters of Charterhall at one time, and is still occupied. The family also owned two other houses in Edinburgh, but both

have been demolished. **Broomhill House** [NT 269674] replaced a castle with a wet moat and drawbridge, but was itself demolished in the twentieth century. Broomhill was held by the Hendersons of Fordell and the by Bairds of Newbyth before coming to the Trotters of Mortonhall in 1827.

Dreghorn Castle [NT 225684] was replaced by a castellated mansion, built by the Trotters after they had come into possession in 1820. The property had been held by the Murrays and by other families before being destroyed by the army in 1955 and the site is within the barracks.

Ballindean [NO 268299] is several miles west of Dundee in Perthshire. The present building dates from 1832, and is symmetrical classical mansion which replaced an earlier house. Held by the Fotheringhams, by the Starks and by the Ruthvens, Ballindean then passed to the Trotters, who held Ballindean until the 1960s. One of the family, Sir William Trotter, was Lord Provost of Edinburgh; and the wife of Robert Knox Trotter reputedly had an affair with Napoleon III of France.

www.trotterclan.com
No. of castles/sites: 7
Rank: 182=/764

Troup

The name is probably territorial and comes from the lands and barony of Troup, which are six or so miles west of Rosehearty in Aberdeenshire in the far north-east of the country. The family held the lands, but may also have had some land in Ayrshire. A later branch of the family, the Troups (formerly) of Dunbennan by Huntly, still live near the burgh.

Castle of Troup [NJ 838663] perches on cliffs on a promontory above the sea, but little survives of the courtyard castle, built with the ramparts of an Iron Age fort. It was held by Hamelin Troup, but may have been one of the Comyn strongholds destroyed by Robert the Bruce in 1307-08. Hamelin Troup added his seal to the Ragman Roll of 1296, and was accused of treason at the Black Parliament of Scone in 1320. The property may have passed by marriage to the Keith Earls Marischal, but was sold to the Gardynes of Troup in 1654. Troup House, a castellated building of 1897, stands on the site of a mansion designed by John Adam in 1760.

Findon Castle [NJ 795644] lies further along the coast to the west, but only earthworks survive from the fourteenth-century castle on an older site. Findon was also held by the Troups and passed to the Gardens, and is said to have been garrisoned in the tenth and eleventh centuries to guard against Viking raids.

No. of castles/sites: 2
Rank: 396=/764

Tulloch

The name comes from the lands of Tulloch, which are one mile north of Dingwall in Ross and Cromarty. The name is on record from the middle of the fourteenth century. The Tullochs held lands in Kincardineshire, but came to prominence on Orkney.

Tulloch Castle [NH 547605] mostly dates from the sixteenth century, although it probably has much older work. There is an altered keep or tower with a round stair-tower at one corner. There are later extensions, and the basement of the keep is vaulted. It is not clear whether the Tulloch family owned the castle or the lands, and it is mostly associated with the Bains and with the Davidsons. Tulloch Castle is said to be haunted by a Green Lady, and is now a hotel (01349 861325; www.tullochcastle.co.uk).

Noltland Castle [HY 430487] is on the north-east side of Westray in Orkney, and is a large ruinous Z-plan tower house, which rose to four storeys. The building

Noltland Castle (RWB)

dates from the sixteenth century, but an earlier stronghold was built by Thomas Tulloch in 1420. He was the Bishop of Orkney from 1420 to 1461, and he was succeeded as Bishop by William, his son, who held the position until 1477. Thomas was buried in St Magnus Cathedral in Kirkwall, but his tomb was destroyed by Cromwell's forces in the 1650s. Noltland Castle was besieged around the end of the fifteenth century, but later passed to the Balfours, who built the present castle. The building was abandoned around 1760, and is said to have been haunted by the Boky Hound, and also to have had a brownie which would clear roads and beach boats. Noltland is in the care of Historic Scotland and is open to the public (01856 841815).

Kirkwall Castle [HY 448109], on the mainland of Orkney, was south and east of the impressive cathedral, but nothing of the castle survives, the last remains being used to build the tolbooth and the town hall. The castle was held by the Sinclair Earls of Orkney but also by

Thomas Tulloch, Bishop of Orkney, in the fifteenth century. The earldom and the castle went to the Stewarts.

Bonnyton Castle [NO 657559] stood three and a half miles south-west of Montrose in Angus but nothing remains apart from some heraldic stones built into farm building. Bonnyton was held by the Tulloch family at the end of the fourteenth century, but had passed to the Woods of Bonnyton by 1493.

No. of castles/sites: 4
Rank: 278=/764

Turing

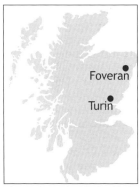

The name is probably from the lands and barony of Turin, which are a few miles east and north of Forfar in Angus. The name is on record from the fourteenth century.

Turin House [NO 545527] perhaps incorporates some of an old stronghold, and the property may have been held the Turin family. Turin passed to the Oliphants, who held the lands in the sixteenth century, then later went to the Carnegies of Lour and Turin.

Foveran Castle [NJ 990244] was four or so miles south-east of Ellon in Aberdeenshire, but it collapsed in 1720 and there are no remains. The castle dated from the twelfth or thirteenth century, and was held by the Turings from the next century. Sir John Turing was a Royalist and was made a Baronet of Nova Scotia in 1638. The family lost the lands soon afterwards, and Foveran had passed to Forbes of Tolquhon by about 1750. The line of the Turings of Foveran, Baronets, flourishes and they apparently live in St Albans in Herefordshire in England. One of Thomas the Rhymer's prophecies is: 'When Turing's Tower falls to the land, Gladsmuir shall be near at hand; When Turing's Tower falls to the sea, Gladsmuir the next year shall be'. This is said to perhaps refer to the Battle of Prestonpans in 1745, which is near Gladsmuir in East Lothian.

No. of castles/sites: 2
Rank: 396=/764
Xref: Turin

Turnbull

The name probably comes from the Old English personal name 'Trumbald', which means 'strongly bold', and the name was pronounced 'Trummell' or 'Trumel' in some parts of the Borders. The more fanciful story about its origin is the a fellow called Rule managed to turn a bull that was intent on goring the king. He was given the lands of Bedrule in reward and changed his name to Turnbull. The name is on record from the fourteenth century, and there are many different spellings. William Turnbull was Keeper of the Privy Seal in the 1440s and was made Bishop of Glasgow in 1447. He obtained permission from the Pope to found the University of Glasgow four years later.

Bedrule Castle [NT 598180] is a couple of miles east of Denholm in the Borders, but little now remains of a thirteenth-century courtyard castle, which once had five round towers and a strong gatehouse. Held by the Comyns and by the Douglases, Bedrule passed to the Turnbulls in the fifteenth century. The Turnbulls were apparently a turbulent lot and 200 of the family were brought before James IV in 1494 'with halters round their necks and naked swords in their hands'. James then hanged some of them for good measure.

The Turnbulls held the following castles and lands:

Airdrie House [NO 567084], near Crail, Fife; altered tower house.
　Held by the Dundemores and by the Lumsdens, but was bought by the Turnbulls of Pittencrieff in 1602. Airdrie was also held by the Prestons, by the Anstruthers and by the Erskine Earls of Kellie, and it is still occupied.

Balglassie [NO 538576], near Brechin, Angus; site of castle or old house.
　Held by the Dishingtons but passed to the Turnbulls and then to the Arbuthnotts.

Barnhills Tower [NT 589212], near Jedburgh, Borders; slight remains of tower house.
　Held by the Turnbulls, but torched by the English in 1545.

Fast Castle [NT 590190], near Denholm, Borders; site of castle.
　Held by the Turnbulls.

Fatlips Castle [NT 582209], near Jedburgh, Borders; tower house.
　Held by the Turnbulls, who were apparently rather full about the mouth and hence the name 'Fatlips'; another story is that they family were rather free with their kisses and the name come from the puckering up their lips. The property passed to the Stewarts in 1705 and then to the Elliots of Minto.

Fulton Tower [NT 605158], near Jedburgh, Borders; ruinous L-plan tower house.
　Held by the Homes of Cowdenknowes, but passed by marriage to the Turnbulls of Bedrule in 1570.

Hallrule [NT 593140], near Bonchester Bridge, Borders; site of tower house.
　Held by the Turnbulls but was destroyed by the English in 1545.

Houndwood House [NT 855630], near Granthouse, Borders; mansion incorporating tower house.
　Held by the Homes and by the Logans of Restalrig, but passed

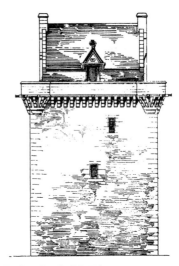

Fatlips Castle (M&R) – see previous column

to the Turnbulls in the eighteenth century, and then went to others. Said to be haunted by a ghost known as 'Chappie', and still occupied.

Hundleshope [NT 230364], near Peebles, Borders; site of tower or old house.
　Held by the Turnbulls from the fourteenth century, but later passed to the Murrays, to the Scotts and then to the Campbells.

Minto House [NT 573203], near Hawick, Borders; site of tower house and mansion.
　Held by the Turnbulls, but passed to the Scotts in the fourteenth century and then to the Elliots. The house was mostly demolished after a fire.

Newton Tower [NT 597205], near Jedburgh, Borders; site of tower house.
　Probably held by the Turnbulls.

Pittencrieff [NO 373159], near Cupar, Fife; site of castle or old house.
　Held by the Balfours and by the MacDuff Earls of Fife, but was owned by the Turnbulls in 1602.

Spittal Tower [NT 585175], near Jedburgh, Borders; site of tower house.
　Probably held by the Turnbulls.

Wauchope Tower [NT 580084], near Bonchester Bridge, Borders; site of tower house.
　Held by the Turnbulls and demolished in the nineteenth century.

www.turnbullclan.com
www.clanturnbull.com
www.members.optusnet.com.au
No. of castles/sites: 15
Rank: 94=/764
Xref: Trimble

Turner

The name comes from the occupation of 'turner' or lathe-worker, a skilful craft worker, and is on record from the fifteenth century. The name was found in Aberdeenshire an in Cowal in Argyll, as well as in Galloway. Sir James Turner served in Sweden with Gustave Adolphus in 1632 and then became a Covenanter. He was captured following the Battle of Preston in 1648, and then again after Worcester three years later. He joined Charles II and took action against the Covenanters. He was captured by them at Dumfries in 1666 but escaped following their defeat at Rullion Green the same year; he died in 1686.

Ardwall [NX 581547], which is one and a half miles south-west of Gatehouse of Fleet in Galloway, was a property of the MacCullochs from the sixteenth century or earlier, but appears to have been held by the Turners for several generations. There is a mansion, which dates from 1762 with later remodelling, and the house probably stands on the site of a castle or tower house.

No. of castles/sites: 1
Rank: 537=/764

Tweedie

The name is territorial and comes from the lands of Tweedie, which are a mile or so south-east of Strathaven in Lanarkshire. The more colourful story is that they were descended from a kelpie or water sprite which lived in the Tweed. They certainly held lands by the banks of the Tweed, and got a reputation as a war-like and aggressive lot.

Tweedie Castle [NS 727427] has gone and the site may be occupied by the present farm. The lands were a property of the Tweedies in the thirteenth and fourteenth centuries, but later passed to the Hamiltons of Silvertonhill, and they built Newton House at Cambuslang in 1602. Tweedie later passed to the Lockharts of Castlehill.

Drumelzier Castle [NT 124334] is three miles south and east of Broughton in the Borders and to the west of the Tweed. The ruins consist of an L-plan tower house of three storeys, dating from the sixteenth century but

Drumelzier 1910?

with older work. Drumelzier was a property of the Tweedies from the fourteenth century until 1632 when Drumelzier passed to the Hays of Yester. John Tweedie of Drumelzier – and others – assassinated John Fleming, Chancellor of Scotland, in 1524, while he was out hawking, starting a bloody feud. James Tweedie of Drumelzier was later pardoned for the murder of William Geddes in 1558 during another feud. The castle was abandoned in the eighteenth century for a new house.

Oliver Castle [NT 098248], further south of Broughton, was also a stronghold of the Tweedies after passing from the Frasers, but was razed to the ground. Thomas Tweedie of Oliver Castle was also involved in the murder of Lord Fleming in 1524.

The Tweedies also owned:
Bield Tower [NT 100248], Tweedsmuir, Borders; house on site of tower house.
Probably held by the Tweedies.

Castlehill Tower [NT 214354], near Peebles, Borders; ruinous tower house.
> Held by the Lowis family of Manor, then others until coming to the Tweedies of Quarter in 1838, and they had abandoned the tower within a few years.

Dreva Tower [NT 140359], near Drumelzier, Borders; site of tower house.
> Held by the Tweedies from the beginning of the fifteenth century.

Fruid Castle [NT 106180], near Tweedsmuir, Borders; site of castle.
> Held by the Frasers but passed to the Tweedies. John Tweedie of Fruid, and other family members, were accused of the cruel slaughter of William Geddes. They were fined and received warnings from the Privy Council. The lands passed to the Murrays of Stanhope and then to the Hay Lord Yester in the 1630s.

Halmyre House [NT 174496], near West Linton, Borders; mansion incorporating part of tower house.
> Held by the Tweedies of Drumelzier in the sixteenth and early seventeenth centuries, but passed to the Murrays of Stanhope, and then to the Gordons.

Kittlehall [NT 113337], near Biggar, Borders; site of tower house.
> Held by the Geddes family (who feuded with the Tweedies) but was sold to the Tweedies of Quarter in 1752, then later passed to the Marshall family.

Quarter House [NT 100334], near Broughton, Borders; tower house replaced by mansion.
> Held by the Livingstones and by the Murrays, but was bought by the Tweedies in 1741.

Rachan [NT 122345], near Biggar, Borders; castle replaced by mansions.
> Held by the Geddes family (who feuded with the Tweedies) but passed to the Tweedies in 1752 and then to the Marshalls.

Tinnis Castle [NT 141344], near Broughton, Borders; ruinous castle in Iron Age fort.
> Held by the Tweedies of Drumelzier, who were involved in the murder of John Fleming. The castle may have been destroyed by gunpowder as a result.

Wrae Tower [NT 115332], near Broughton, Borders; slight remains of tower.
> Held by the Tweedies of Wrae in the sixteenth and seventeenth centuries.

www.tweedie.org
No. of castles/sites: 13
Rank: 113=/764

Tyninghame

The name is territorial and comes from the lands of Tyninghame, which are three miles west and north of Dunbar in East Lothian. The family held the property as tenants of the Bishopric of St Andrews from the middle of the twelfth century or earlier, and are still on record at the end of the fourteenth century. **Tyninghame House** [NT 619798] is a fine mansion set in wooded grounds and dates from the sixteenth century or earlier. The property was held by the Lauders of the Bass by that time, and then by the Hamilton Earls of Haddington. The grounds are open to the public, as are occasionally the gardens (www.gardensofscotland.org).

No. of castles/sites: 1 / Rank: 537=/764

Tyrie

The name is local and probably comes from the place of the same name in Perthshire, although there was also a Tyrie in Aberdeenshire, a few miles south-west of Fraserburgh. There was a castle here, but it does not appear to have any connection with the Tyrie family. James Tyrie, who was a Jesuit, penned a 'Refutation' aimed at John Knox and publicly debated (and argued) with Andrew Melville in Paris in 1574.

Drumkilbo [NO 304449], which lies some six miles south and east of Coupar Angus, is a sprawling whitewashed building which includes part of an old stronghold. The lands were given to Maurice Tyrie by Robert the Bruce in the fourteenth century. Members of the family were buried in Kirkinch or Nevay [NO 312441] burial ground, and the Tyries held the property until Drumkilbo was sold to the Nairne family in 1650; then later it was held by other families. The house is available to rent on an exclusive basis (01828 640445; www.drumkilbo.com).

Dunnideer Castle [NJ 613282] is a mile west of Insch, but little of the buildings remain and it was constructed within the ramparts of an Iron Age fort. The castle may have been built by John Balliol about 1260, but was long held by the Tyries, who were still in possession in 1724. King Arthur is said to have held court here with Giric, King of Scots, at Dunnideer in the ninth century. The site of the castle is accessible.

No. of castles/sites: 2 / Rank: 396=/764

Tytler

The name was not common in Scotland, and it may be derived from 'titeler', which means 'tatler' from Middle English, although this is thought by some to be unlikely. The name is on record in Scotland from the eighteenth century.

James Tytler, who was born about 1747, studied medicine in Edinburgh and, although in the debtors' sanctuary in Holyrood, made a successful balloon flight in 1784. He also contributed to early editions of *Encyclopaedia Britannica*, and emigrated to the Americas, where he died in 1805.

Fulford Tower or **Woodhouselee** [NT 238645] stood two or so miles north of Penicuik in Midlothian, and there was a castle here, dating from the fourteenth century. This was incorporated into a mansion in the seventeenth century, and this was then rebuilt and remodelled down the years. The lands were held by the Purvis family, but later passed to the Tytlers. Alexander Fraser Tytler was a historian and writer, and his son Patrick was also an eminent historian, and the author of a history of Scotland, as well as other books. Sir Walter Scott visited the house, but it was completely demolished in 1965, except for the stables, and the site has been grassed over. There is at least one account of the house being haunted by the ghost of Lady Hamilton, who is more usually associated with Old Woodhouselee. This had the intriguing possibility that her ghost was brought here along with building materials from the older site in a renovation of 1665, although it is probably just a confusion.

No. of castles/sites: 1
Rank: 537=/764

Udny

The name is territorial and comes from the barony and lands of Udny, which are a few miles east of Oldmeldrum in Aberdeenshire. The family are on record from 1406, although they probably held their lands from before then.

Udny Castle [NJ 882268] is a large keep or tower with turrets and battlements, and it formerly had later ranges but these have been demolished. The lands were held by the Udnys from the fourteenth century, and the family supported Mary, Queen of Scots, and were then

Udny Castle (RWB)

Royalists in the seventeenth century. They moved to Knockhall Castle in 1634. Although Udny was abandoned in 1775, it was later restored and is said to be occupied by descendants of the Udny family.

Knockhall Castle [NJ 992265] is a ruinous L-plan tower house of four storeys and an attic, and stands one mile north-west of Newburgh in Fife. It dates from the sixteenth century but was altered and extended down the years. Knockhall was built by the Sinclairs but was bought by the Udnys in 1633. The castle was attacked and seized by Covenanters in 1639, and then again in the following year. It survived this but was accidentally gutted by fire in 1734, and the family were only saved from death by their fool (jester) Jamie Fleeman (or Fleming). The building was not restored.

Tillery [NJ 915229], four miles south and east of Pitmedden in Aberdeenshire, is the site of an castle or old house, which was replaced by Tillery House in 1788. This was remodelled in 1826 as a Greek-revival mansion, but was burnt out in the 1950s and is a ruinous shell. Tillery was held by the Udnys, but was sold in 1788 to John Chambers or Chalmers, who had been a plantation owner in the southern USA.

No. of castles/sites: 3
Rank: 328=/764

Urie

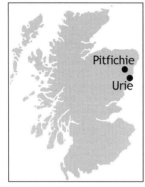

The name may be territorial and comes from the lands of Urie, which are one mile north and west of Stonehaven in Kincardineshire. The name is on record from the end of the thirteenth century, and variations in spelling include Hurry.

Urie House [NO 860877] is a large baronial mansion, but part of a Z-plan tower house is included in the fabric; the newer part is apparently derelict. The lands may have been held by the Uries at one time, but at an early date passed to the Frasers, then went by marriage to the Keith Earls Marischal, then to the Hays in 1415 and then to others.

Pitfichie Castle [NJ 677168], which is three or so miles west of Kemnay in Aberdeenshire, is a tower house with a round tower projecting from one corner. The building dates from the sixteenth century, and was built by the Uries after the property had passed to them from the Cheynes. One of the family was Sir John Urie, or Hurry, who led Covenanter armies that were defeated by the Marquis of Montrose at the battles of Auldearn and then at Alford, both in 1645. Urie went on to join Montrose and was with him when their forces were defeated at Carbisdale in 1650; Hurry was captured and executed. William Urie of Pitfichie, and others, raided the lands of Forbes of Forneidlie some five years later, mistreating the locals and driving off their cattle to Pitfichie, for which Urie was outlawed. The property went to the Forbeses of Monymusk in 1657 and was ruinous by 1796, but the castle has been restored and is occupied.

No. of castles/sites: 2
Rank: 396=/764
Xref: Hurry

Urquhart

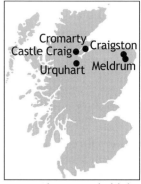

The name is territorial and comes from the lands of Urquhart, which are by Drumnadrochit on the shores of Loch Ness. **Urquhart Castle** [NH 531286] is a fine ruinous fortress, and it is from here that there have been many sightings of the Loch Ness Monster. The clan, however, do not appear to have ever held the old stronghold, and they became established in Ross and Cromarty and in Aberdeenshire.

Cromarty Castle [NH 794670], which stood in the burgh, was a strong L-plan tower house with work from the twelfth or thirteenth century. The castle was demolished in 1772 and Cromarty House, an impressive classical mansion, was built on the site. Cromarty was held by the Urquharts, and the stronghold was originally a royal castle. The Urquharts were hereditary sheriffs and defended the castle against the English around 1300. Thomas Urquhart of Urquhart was a prodigious (and busy) fellow, and is said to have fathered twenty-five sons, although seven of them are believed to have been killed at the Battle of Pinkie in 1547. Sir Thomas Urquhart of Cromarty was a Royalist and fought at Worcester in 1651, after which he was imprisoned in the Tower of London. The family fought for the Jacobites, and Colonel James Urquhart was badly wounded at the Battle of Sheriffmuir in 1715. The Urquharts, however, lost everything as predicted by the Brahan Seer, and the property was sold to the Murray Lord Elibank in 1763. Cromarty passed to the Rosses 1771, who demolished the castle and built the mansion. The line of the Urquharts of Urquhart continues, but they now apparently live in Louisiana in the USA.

The Urquharts also held:
Braelangwell [NH 696645], near Cromarty; castle replaced by mansion.
    Held by the Urquharts from the end of the seventeenth century or earlier, but the property was sold to the Frasers in 1839.
Castle Craig [NH 632638], near Dingwall, Ross and Cromarty; ruinous tower house on cliffs.
    Held by the Urquharts.
Craigston Castle [NJ 762550], near Turriff, Aberdeenshire; fine and tall tower house.
    Held by the Craigs but passed to the Urquharts. One of the family was Captain John Urquhart, known as 'The Pirate' and born in 1696. He may have amassed a fortune from captured ships after he joined the Spanish navy. He was a Jacobite and had a narrow escape from death at the Battle of Sheriffmuir in 1715. Craigston is still apparently owned by the Urquharts and can be visited (01888 551640).
Crombie Castle [NJ 591522], near Aberchirder, Aberdeenshire; altered L-plan tower house.
    Held by the Inneses but passed to the Urquharts in 1631, and then went to the Meldrums and to the Duffs. The castle is apparently not currently occupied.

Craigston Castle (M&R) – see previous page

Kinbeachie Castle [NH 634622], near Dingwall, Ross and Cromarty; site of castle.

Held by the Urquharts and a modern mansion was built nearby.

Meldrum House [NJ 812291], near Oldmeldrum, Aberdeenshire; mansion incorporating castle.

Held by the Meldrums and by the Setons, but went to the Urquharts in 1670, who were Jacobites although the chief did not take part in the 1745-46 Rising. The family held the property until the nineteenth century, the building is said to be haunted by a Green or White Lady, and it is now a hotel (01651 872294; www.meldrumhouse.co.uk).

www.clanurquhart.com
www.urquhart.org
No. of castles/sites: 7
Rank: 182=/764

Usher

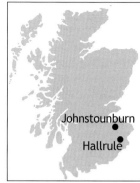

The name comes from the office of 'usher' or door-keeper, whose job it was to both guard the entrance into the king's chambers but also to know the rank and precedence of those who were to see the monarch (and many other courtly duties). The name is on record from the end of the thirteenth century.

Johnstounburn House [NT 460616] is several miles south-east of Dalkeith in Midlothian, and it is a fine old mansion, dating from the seventeenth century or earlier. Held by the Johnstones, by the Borthwicks and by the Browns, Johnstounburn was a property of the Ushers, noted whisky blenders, from 1884. The house was a hotel but this has shut.

Hallrule [NT 593140], a mile north of Bonchester Bridge in the Borders, is a modern mansion, but there was a tower house. The property was held by the Turnbulls and was destroyed by the English in 1545 after being torched in 1523 and in 1544. The property was latterly held by the Ushers, who were made Baronets in 1899 and they now apparently live in London in England.

No. of castles/sites: 2
Rank: 396=/764

Castle Craig (M&R) – see previous page

Vallance

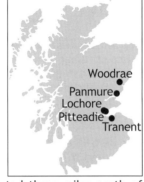

The name comes from several possible places in Normandy in France, and the family were established in Scotland from the twelfth century. **Lochore** or **Inchgall Castle** [NT 175959] is a ruinous fourteenth-century keep or tower on a motte formerly on an island in a loch. It is located three miles north of Cowdenbeath in Fife, and was also known as Inchgall, 'island of strangers'. The lands were held by the Val-

Lochore Castle (M&R)

lances from the fourteenth century and they built the keep. Lochore was described as one of the four strongest castles in Fife by the English in 1547. The property went to the Wardlaws of Torrie and then to the Malcolms of Balbedie, and loch was drained in the eighteenth century and the whole area was devastated by mining. The lands were landscaped and are now Lochore Country Park (01592 414300).

The Vallances also owned:

Panmure Castle [NO 546376], near Carnoustie, Angus; site of castle.
  Held by the Vallances, who had a castle, which was rhomboid in plan with corner towers, a hall, and a chapel. The property passed by marriage to the Maules around 1224, and was held by the English before being recovered by the Scots in 1306. The Maules became Earls of Panmure, and the castle was replaced by **Panmure House** [NO 537386], but this has been demolished.

Pitteadie Castle [NT 257891], near Burntisland, Fife; ruinous castle.
  Held by the Vallance family, who probably built the original keep. They held the lands until 1519 when Pitteadie went to the Sinclairs, and then to others.

Tranent Tower [NT 404729], Tranent, East Lothian; ruinous L-plan tower house.
  Held by the Setons but passed to the Vallance family in the seventeenth century.

Woodrae Castle [NO 518566], near Brechin, Angus; site of castle.
  Held by the Vallances (Vellums), but passed to the Lindsays and then to the Fletchers. The castle was very ruinous by the nineteenth century.

No. of castles/sites: 5 / Rank: 240=/764
Xrefs: Vallence; Vellum

Vaux

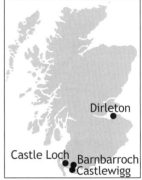

The name comes from 'vaux' or 'vaus', which is a Norman name and means 'valleys'. The family came to England with William the Conqueror, and held lands in Norfolk, in Suffolk and in Essex, and also in Cumberland. Probably because of a transcription or spelling mistake, the family also became recorded as Vans rather than Vaux.

Dirleton Castle [NT 518840], two miles west of North Berwick in East Lothian, is one of the best castles in Scotland. It is a magnificent ruin perched on a rock with a splendid gateway and ditch, a round drum tower with

Dirleton Castle (LF)

two hexagonal chambers, and other towers and ranges around a courtyard. The lands were held by the Congiltons in the twelfth century, but passed to the Vaux family. Dirleton Castle was attacked by the English in 1298 during the Wars of Independence, and there was a long and hard siege when the English used large engines of war. The garrison eventually surrendered, but were allowed to leave with their goods. The castle was recaptured by the Scots in 1311 and slighted, although it was rebuilt. The property passed to the Halyburtons in the second half of the fourteenth century, then went to the Ruthvens, and then to others. The castle is now in the care of Historic Scotland, has very fine gardens, and is open to the public (01620 850330).

Barnbarroch Castle [NX 398516], which is three miles south-east of Wigtown in Galloway, passed to the Vauxs of Dirleton around 1384. There was a castle, and John Vaux of Barnbarroch was killed at Pinkie in 1547. Sir Patrick Vaux of Barnbarroch was made ambassador to Denmark in 1587, and a Lord of Session as Lord Barnbarroch. The family married into the Agnews in 1747 and took their name, becoming Vans Agnew. The house was greatly altered in the nineteenth century, gutted by fire in 1941, and remains a ruin. The property was sold seven years later, and the family, having gone back to Vans of Barnbarroch, now apparently live in Gloucestershire in England.

The Vauxs also owned:

Airyolland [NX 308475], near Port William, Galloway; slight remains of castle or house.

Held by the Dunbars but passed to the Vaux family in 1583.

Balneil [NX 179639], near Glenluce, Galloway; site of castle.

Held by the Kennedy Earls of Cassillis, then by the Vauxs of Barnbarroch, then by the Rosses in the seventeenth century, and then by the Dalrymples of Stair.

Carscreugh Castle [NX 223599], near Glenluce, Galloway; ruinous castle and mansion.

Held by the Vaux family but passed to Rosses of Balneil, then to the Dalrymples of Stair.

Castle Loch Castle [NX 294541], near Glenluce, Galloway; ruinous castle on island.

Held by the Earls of March and by the Dunbars of Kilconquhar, but passed to the Vauxs of Barnbarroch in 1590 and it was used into the seventeenth century. The ruins were cleared and excavated in 1912 and again in 1950.

Castlewigg [NX 428432], near Whithorn, Galloway; site of castle and tower.

Held by the Vauxs, but sold to the Stewarts in 1584. Demolished

Castlewigg (M&R)

in the twentieth century.

Larg Castle [NX 167644], near Glenluce, Galloway; site of castle.

Held by the Vauxs of Barnbarroch and Longcastle, but passed to the Lynns in the seventeenth century.

Longcastle [NX 394469], near Whithorn, Galloway; slight remains of castle.

Held by the MacDowalls, but later passed to the Vaux family. The castle stood on an island in a loch but the loch has been drained.

No. of castles/sites: 9
Rank: 149=/764
Xrefs: Vans; Vaus

Veitch

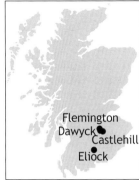

The name probably comes from 'Viche' in France, and the name is on record from the beginning of the thirteenth century. The family held lands in the Borders. William Veitch was a Presbyterian minister but he was outlawed in 1667 and was imprisoned on the Bass Rock after being captured at the Battle of Bothwell Brig in 1679. He escaped to Holland. His son, Samuel, served in the Dutch army and then accompanied William of Orange to England in 1688. He was an officer in the Cameronian forces who defended Dunkeld from the Jacobites the following year. Later he took part in the disastrous Darien Scheme to the isthmus of Panama, and he then went to America.

The Veitchs held the following properties:

Blyth [NT 132458], near West Linton, Borders; site of castle or old house.

Held by several families including by the Blyths and by the Lauders, but passed to the Veitchs of Dawyck in 1603, then went to the Stewarts of Traquair in 1635, then to the Geddeses and to the Carmichaels of Skirling.

Castlehill Tower [NT 214354], near Peebles, Borders; ruinous tower house.

Held by the Lowises of Manor but was bought by the Veitchs in 1637, then passed to the Baillies of Jerviswood in 1672, then went to others. Abandoned around 1840.

Dawyck House [NT 168352], near Peebles, Borders; castle or old house replaced by mansion.

Held by the Veitch family from the thirteenth century and they were in possession of Dawyck for about 400 years, but then passed to the Naesmiths, and then later to the Balfours.

Easter Dawyck [NT 191376], near Peebles, Borders; site of tower house.

Held by the Veitchs, but was demolished by Sir Walter Scott's father to build a steading.

Eliock House [NS 796074], near Sanquhar, Dumfriesshire; mansion including part of castle.

Held by the Dalziels, then by the Crichtons and by others, before being bought by the Veitchs, who held it in the nineteenth century. Part was burnt out in 1940 and remains ruinous.

Flemington Tower [NT 166451], near West Linton, Borders; ruinous tower house.

Held by the Hays but passed to the Veitchs. Occupied until the end of the nineteenth century.

Glenrath Tower [NT 218324], near Peebles, Borders; site of tower.

Held by the Veitchs in the sixteenth century, and then by the Murrays in the next century.

Lour Tower [NT 179356], near Broughton, Borders; slight remains of tower house.

Held by the Veitchs from the thirteenth century, but passed to the Naesmiths around the end of the eighteenth century. Inhabited until 1715 but ruinous sixty years later.

North Synton [NT 485237], near Selkirk, Borders; altered tower house.

Held by the Veitchs in 1407, who built the tower, but passed

Flemington Tower (M&R) – see previous page

to the Cunninghams by the end of the seventeenth century. Used as a farmhouse.

No. of castles/sites: 9
Rank: 149=/764

Vipont

The name comes from Vipont, near Lisieux in Normandy in France, and means 'old bridge'. The family held lands in England after the Norman conquest, and then also settled in Scotland and are on record from the twelfth century.

Blackness Castle [NT 056803] is a fine and foreboding castle, which is four miles east of Bo'ness in central Scotland. It stands by the sea and there is a tall keep or tower defended by a strong curtain wall and landward tower. The castle was used as a prison, but the lands were held by the Viponts in the twelfth century. Sir William Vipont was killed fighting for the Scots at the Battle of Bannockburn in 1314 and the line died out in the middle of the fourteenth century. Blackness was later held by the Crichtons, but was burnt in 1481 and was damaged when besieged and captured by Cromwell's forces in 1650. It was repaired, and is now in the care of Historic Scotland and is open to the public (01506 834807).

Carriden House [NT 026808] is nearer Bo'ness and is an altered tower house, dating from the sixteenth century but extended by a modern mansion. Again the lands were held by the Viponts from the twelfth century, but they passed by marriage to the Cockburns in 1357. Carriden was then owned by several different families and is still occupied. B&B accommodation is available and the house is suitable for weddings (01506 829811; www.carridenhouse.co.uk).

Langton Castle [NT 756534] has gone, but it dated from the fifteenth century and stood a couple of miles west of Duns in the Borders. The lands were held by the Viponts, but also passed to the Cockburns by marriage in the fourteenth century. Langton later went to the Gavin family and then to the Campbell Marquises of Breadalbane. They built a new mansion but this was demolished in the 1950s.

No. of castles/sites: 3
Rank: 328=/764

Walker

The name comes from the occupation of 'waulker', 'waulking' being a process which thickens woollen cloth, and it comes from the Old English 'wealcere'. The name is on record in Scotland from the fourteenth century.

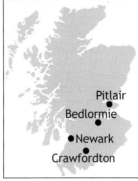

Pitlair [NO 319121] is three or so miles west and south of Cupar in Fife, and there is a modern mansion which replaced an earlier house or castle. The lands were held by the Walkers from the seventeenth century. The Walkers of Pitlair still flourish but now apparently live near Kinross, while the mansion is used as a nursing home.

Bedlormie [NS 874675], four miles west of Armadale in West Lothian, is an L-plan tower house, which dates from the seventeenth century. The property was owned by the Murrays of Ogilface, then by the Forresters of Corstorphine, and then by the Walkers in the sixteenth century. Bedlormie then passed by marriage to the Livingstone Earls of Linlithgow, who held it until 1853.

Crawfordton Tower [NX 796905], one mile east of Moniaive in Dumfries and Galloway, was replaced by a modern mansion, but there was a tower house. Held by the Crichtons and then by the Hays, the mansion was a property of the Walkers in the nineteenth century.

Lying three miles south of Ayr, **Newark Castle** [NS 324173] is an altered and extended tower house, which has work from the fifteenth century. The castle was built by the Kennedys of Bargany, then passed to the Crawfords of Camlarg and then to the Kennedy Earls of Cassillis. It is now apparently owned by the Walkers after being purchased by Archibald Walker of the Distillers company.

No. of castles/sites: 4
Rank: 278=/764

Walkinshaw

The name is territorial and comes from the lands of Walkinshaw, which are a couple of miles east of Renfrew in the west of Scotland. The name is on record from the thirteenth century. Perhaps the most famous of the name was Clementina Walkinshaw,

who met Bonnie Prince Charlie at Bannockburn House during the 1745-46 Jacobite Rising, and became his mistress. She followed him into exile and bore him a daughter, Charlotte, but the Bonnie Prince was less charming as he grew older and neglected and abused Clementina. She eventually left him but, when the French Revolution overtook her in Paris, she fled to Switzerland and died there in poverty.

Walkinshaw [NS 464667] was held by the family from 1235, and there was a tower house. It was replaced by a mansion at the end of the eighteenth century, but this was itself demolished in 1927. The family were hereditary foresters for the barony of Renfrew.

Bishopton House [NS 422717] is three miles north-east of Bridge of Weir also in Renfrewshire, and is a tall L-plan tower house, dating from the seventeenth century but with earlier work. The building was long associated with the Brisbanes, but it passed to the Walkinshaws about 1671. Bishopton then went to the Dunlops, to the Sempills and then to the Maxwells of Pollok. The building was used as a farmhouse, but is now part of a convent.

No. of castles/sites: 2
Rank: 396=/764
Xref: Walkingshaw

Wallace

The name is on record in Ayrshire from the twelfth century, and means a 'Welshman' or 'of the Welsh' (Middle English 'walshe', and means 'foreigner'; also see Walsh). In this case, it probably indicating that the family sprang from the Britons of Strathclyde, which was an ancient kingdom which occupied modern-day Clydesdale, Dunbartonshire, Ayrshire and Dumfriesshire. It has also been suggested that the family came from Shropshire near the Welsh border where they held lands, and then moved to Scotland in the twelfth century.

The most famous of the name is Sir William Wallace, renowned as a great patriot and freedom fighter in the Wars of Independence. He is thought to be the son of Malcolm Wallace of Elderslie. His father and elder brother were executed by the English, and his wife is also said to have been murdered by Hazelrig, the Sheriff of Lanark. His early career is not known in detail but, along with Andrew Moray, Wallace won a great victory against the English at Stirling Bridge in 1297, but was then defeated by Edward I of England at Falkirk the following year. Wallace continued the struggle but was betrayed and handed over to Edward in 1305. He was convicted of treason (although neither he nor his father had ever sworn allegiance to the English; his feudal superiors, the Stewarts, had, though) and brutally executed, being hanged, drawn and quartered, including being disembowelled and having his innards burnt before him. The different parts of his body were then put on display in towns in Scotland. There is no contemporary account of his life, and much comes from Blind Harry's poem, written for the Wallaces of Craigie in the second half of the fifteenth century, more than 150 years after the events. *Braveheart* has little to commend it for historical accuracy, not least that the Battle of Stirling Bridge had something vital omitted: the bridge. The implication also appears to be that Edward III of England was Wallace's son, a situation that would no doubt have appalled and startled the great man himself: Edward III was to be a bane to the Scots and, of course, Wallace never met the English queen.

Riccarton Castle [NS 427364] is to the south of Kilmarnock in Ayrshire, and the name 'Richard's town' is from Richard Wallace. The lands were held by the Wallaces from the thirteenth century or before, and they had a castle, although there are no remains. Malcolm Wallace, the famous William's father, is said to have been born here, and a plaque marks the site. The Wallaces of that Ilk now apparently live in Edinburgh, and represent this line, as well as the Wallaces of Craigie and of Elderslie.

In the village of **Elderslie** in Renfrewshire was **Wallace's Buildings** [NS 442630], and this is said to have been the birthplace of William Wallace, although other places have been suggested. Elderslie was a property of the Wallaces from the thirteenth century until about 1850. The buildings here, when they were demolished in the 1970s, dated from the seventeenth century. All that remains are grassy mounds and a monument.

Craigie Castle [NS 408317] is four miles to the south of Kilmarnock, and is a ruinous hall house and castle, which dates from the thirteenth century. The castle had

Craigie Castle (M&R)

two courtyards and was defended by ditches. Held by the Lindsays, Craigie then passed by marriage to the Wallaces of Riccarton in 1371. As mentioned above, they had Blind Harry collect and record stories about William Wallace. The castle was abandoned about 1600 when the Wallaces moved to Newton in Ayr. Hugh Wallace of Craigie was made a Baronet of Nova Scotia in 1669.

Craigie House [NS 352215] was built in Ayr and was held by the Wallaces of Craigie. The building dates from around 1730 and is a fine three-storey mansion with a bow-windowed front. This property went to the Campbells in 1782 and was sold to the local council in 1942. It is now used as a management centre for Paisley University and the grounds are open to the public.

The Wallaces also owned:

Auchans [NS 355346], near Troon, Ayrshire; mansion incorporating castle.

Held by the Wallaces, and one of the family was Colonel James Wallace, a Covenanter, who was one of the leaders of the disastrous Pentland Rising of 1666, which ended in defeat at Rullion Green. The lands passed to the Cochranes and then to the Montgomery Earls of Eglinton. The house is now ruinous.

Auchenbathie Castle [NS 397565], near Beith, Renfrewshire; slight remains of castle.

Held by the Wallaces of Elderslie.

Auchencruive Castle [NS 387235], near Ayr; castle replaced by mansion.

Held by the Wallaces but passed to the Cathcarts in 1374, and it became their principal seat. Much later Auchencruive went to the Murrays and then to the Oswalds, who called it Oswald Hall. Now part of the Scottish Agricultural College. The grounds are open to the public.

Auchinvole House [NS 714769], near Kilsyth; site of L-plan tower house.

Held by the Starks, then much later by the Wallaces.

Busbie Tower [NS 392409], near Kilmarnock, Ayrshire; castle replaced by mansion.

Held by the Mowats but later passed to the Wallaces.

Cairnhill House [NS 756641], near Airdrie, Lanarkshire; site of castle and mansion.

Held by the Wallaces and by the Mures (Mores) and then by the Nisbets, who now apparently live at the Drum. Demolished in 1991 except for the stables and a doocot.

Candacraig [NJ 339111], near Ballater, Aberdeenshire; castle replaced by mansion.

Held by the Andersons, who had a castle, but the property had gone to the Wallaces by 1900. Candacraig House was built in 1835, but the property later passed from the Wallaces. Candacraig was purchased by Billy Connolly in recent years and is still occupied. A cottage on the estate can be rented (www.candacraig.com).

Caprington Castle [NS 407363], near Kilmarnock, Ayrshire; mansion incorporating castle.

Held by the Wallaces of Sundrum, but passed to the Cunninghams by 1400. Still occupied.

Carnell [NS 467323], near Kilmarnock, Ayrshire; mansion incorporating castle.

Held by the Wallaces. William Wallace of Carnell was killed at the Battle of Flodden in 1513, and the property passed to the Cathcarts in the seventeenth century. The Wallaces later recovered the property, but it had been lost again by 1843. Carnell can be rented as holiday accommodation (01563 884236; www.carnellestates.com).

Cessnock Castle [NS 511355], near Galston, Ayrshire; castle and mansion.

Held by the Campbells, and then by others including by the Wallaces. Still occupied.

Cessnock Castle (M&R)

Cloncaird Castle [NS 359075], near Maybole, Ayrshire; altered tower house.

Held by the Mures, and then by others families including by the Wallaces. Still occupied.

Crosbie Castle [NS 217500], near West Kilbride, Ayrshire; tower house and mansion.

Held by the Wallaces and by the Crawfords of Auchenames. William Wallace sheltered here from the English in an earlier castle. The treacherous murder of his uncle led to the torching of the Barns of Ayr and the slaughter of many English men in revenge.

Ferguslie Castle [NS 467637], near Paisley, Renfrewshire; site of castle and mansion.

Held by the Hamiltons and later by the Wallaces.

Glassingall [NN 798045], near Dunblane, Stirlingshire; mansion on site of castle.

Held by the Chisholms of Glassingall but passed to the Smiths and then to the Wallaces in the nineteenth century.

Inverernan House [NJ 330110], near Strathdon, Aberdeenshire; castle replaced by mansion.

Held by the Forbeses of Inverernan, but later passed to the Wallaces and then to the Tennants.

Kelly House [NS 198685], near Inverkip, Renfrewshire; site of castle and mansion.

Held by the Bannatynes, but passed to the Wallaces in 1792 and they built a new house. The property passed to Sir James Young, pioneer of oil technology, and a later mansion was burned down in 1913, probably by suffragettes.

Kildonan [NX 227831], near Barrhill, Ayrshire; mansion on site of castle.

Held by the Eccles family and by the Chalmerses, then later by the Hamiltons and by the Wallaces, for whom the new mansion was built in the twentieth century.

Milliken [NS 418634], near Johnstone, Renfrewshire; site of castle or old house.

Held by the Wallaces of Elderslie and by the Houstons, but passed to the Millikens in 1733 and they built a new mansion, itself replaced by a new house in the 1920s.

Newton Castle [NS 339223], Newton on Ayr, site of castle.

Held by the Wallaces, then by the Hamiltons, and then by the Wallaces of Craigie in 1588. Site occupied by a car park.

Sundrum Castle [NS 410213], near Ayr; mansion incorporating castle.

Held by the Wallaces of Sundrum from 1373 or earlier, but passed to the Cathcarts and then to the Hamiltons. The building has been divided and can be rented (01530 244436; www.sundrumcastle.com).

Woolmet House [NT 309701], Danderhall, Edinburgh; site of tower and mansion.

Held by the Biggar family but had passed to the Wallaces by 1686. Demolished in 1950.

www.clanwallace.org
No. of castles/sites: 24
Rank: 56=/764
Xrefs: Wallis; Walls

Walsh

The name is from Middle English 'walshe', and means 'foreigner', although presumably it was the English speakers, being the incomers, who were the strangers and not the 'Welsh'. The name is on record in Scotland from the middle of the fourteenth century (also see Wallace).

Mossfennan [NT 117317] is a couple of miles southwest of Drumelzier, just west of the River Tweed, in the Borders. There was a tower house which was replaced by Mossfennan House, and the mansion dates from the eighteenth century. The property was sold to the Welsh family in 1753.

No. of castles/sites: 1
Rank: 537=/764
Xref: Welsh

Wardlaw

The name comes from several places in Scotland, and means 'guard hill'; the name is on record in Scotland from the fourteenth century.

Torrie Castle [NT 015867] has gone and the site is probably occupied by Torrie House, which lies five miles west and south of Dunfermline in Fife. The lands were held by the Wardlaws in the fourteenth century. Walter Wardlaw, Bishop of Glasgow, was made a Cardinal in 1381 and he is buried in Glasgow Cathedral. Henry Wardlaw, his nephew, was Bishop of St Andrews and he founded the University of St Andrews in 1413. The property appears also to have been held by the Bruces and by the Balfours at one time, but was in the possession of the Erskine-Wemyss family in the nineteenth century.

Balmule [NT 101913] is three miles to the north of Dunfermline, and the present house incorporates part of a tower house. A panel is dated 1605, and the tower was built by the Wardlaws of Balmule. Sir Henry Wardlaw of Balmule was Chamberlain to Anne of Denmark, wife of James VI, and the Wardlaws have a burial vault in Dunfermline Abbey. The family acquired Pitreavie; and Balmule is still occupied.

Pitreavie Castle [NT 117847] is to the south of Dunfermline, and is a U-plan tower house and mansion, dating from the seventeenth century but remodelled down the years. The castle was built by the Wardlaws of Balmule, who gained the lands in 1608, and Sir Cuthbert Wardlaw was made a Baronet of Nova Scotia in 1633. The Battle of Inverkeithing took place close by in 1651. A Royalist force, made up mostly of Highlanders, was routed by Cromwell's army. Some 1600 men were killed, and more than 1200 were captured. A group of MacLeans, many badly wounded, sought refuge in Pitreavie, but they were refused and the laird and his people cast missiles from the roof. Wardlaw and his family were cursed by the MacLeans: the laird of Pitreavie died within eighteen months, and the family had lost the property within fifty years. One of the ghost stories is also associated with this event: the apparition of a headless Highlander. The castle also had stories of both and Grey and a Green Lady, and other manifestations. The property was sold to the Primrose Lord Rosebery in 1703, and then passed to the Blackwoods and then to the Beveridge family before being used by the armed forces. The base has been closed and the castle was put up for sale. The line of the Wardlaws, Baronets, flourishes and they now apparently live in Victoria in Australia.

Lochore Castle [NT 175959], some three miles north of Cowdenbeath in Fife, is a ruinous keep and castle, dating from the fourteenth century. Lochore was held by the Vallance family, then by the Wardlaws of Torrie and by the Malcolms of Balbedie. The area was devastated by mining, but the land was reclaimed and landscaped and is now Lochore Country Park (01592 414300).

The Wardlaws also held property in and around Edinburgh. **Grange House** [NT 258718] was to the south of the city, and was a substantial L-plan tower house, although it was demolished in 1936. The property was held by the Wardlaws in the fourteenth century, but then passed to the Cants, to the Dicks and to the Lauders. **Baberton House** [NT 195696] is to the west of the city. The house incorporates an old tower house, and the lands were also held by the Wardlaws. Baberton was then owned by the Elphinstones in 1597 and then went to the Murrays, and the house is still occupied

No. of castles/sites: 6
Rank: 212=/764

Warrender

The name comes from the office of 'warrener', a person charged with managing a park or a warren of rabbits, and the name in on record from the middle of the thirteenth century.

Bruntsfield House [NT 252723] is in Edinburgh, and is an altered Z-plan tower house, which rises to three storeys and an attic, and dates from the sixteenth century. The property was held by the Lauders and then by the Fairlies of Braid, before coming to the Warrenders in 1695. Sir George Warrender was Lord Provost of Edinburgh 1715-22, and was made a Baronet in 1715. The house is now part of James Gillespie's School. A secret room was found in the early nineteenth century, when a count of the windows on the outside did not tally with those inside, and this is linked to the ghost story. The house is said to be haunted by a Green Lady, the spirit of a woman whose remains were found in the secret room.

No. of castles/sites: 1
Rank: 537=/764

Watson

The name is from 'Watt's son', 'Watt' being a diminutive for Walter, and the name is on record from the fourteenth century. George Watson, a merchant in Edinburgh and the first accountant for the Bank of Scotland, left money for the foundation of a hospital for the offspring of merchants who had fallen on hard times. The establishment became a school for boys in 1870, and a girls' school was opened the following year; George Watsons College is now a private school.

The Watsons held the following properties:

Aberdour Castle [NT 193854], Aberdour, Fife; partly ruinous E-plan castle.
  Held by the Mortimers and by the Douglas Earls of Morton, and one range of the old castle was occupied by Robert Watson of Muirhouse until his death in 1791. The castle has fine gardens, is in the care of Historic Scotland, and is open to the public (01383 860519).
Aithernie Castle [NO 379035], near Leven, Fife; slight remains of tower house.
  Held by the Lundin family, by the Carmichaels and by others, but was bought by the Watsons in 1670.
Cammo House [NT 174747], near Edinburgh; site of castle or old house.
  Held by the Niddrie family, then by the Menzies clan and by the Clerks, before passing to the Watsons of Saughton in 1741. Later it passed to the Thomases, was occupied until 1975, but then Cammo House was demolished after being vandalised and set on fire. The grounds are now a country park.
Pitcruvie Castle [NO 413046], near Lower Largo, Fife; ruined castle.
  Held by the Lindsays, but was bought by the Watsons in the seventeenth century.
Rothes Castle [NJ 277490], near Charlestown of Aberlour, Moray; ruinous castle.
  Held by the Pollocks but passed by marriage to the Watsons, then to the Leslies, who were made Earls of Rothes in 1457.
Saughton House [NT 205713], Edinburgh; site of tower house.
  Held by the Watsons, but passed to the Ellis family, and then to the Baillies and to the Bairds. Burned down in the 1950s and subsequently demolished. The grounds are a park.
Stenhouse [NS 879829], near Falkirk; site of tower house.
  Held by the Watsons in the fifteenth century, but had passed to the Bruces of Stenhouse by 1611, then later went to the Sheriffs of Carronvale. Demolished in the 1960s.

No. of castles/sites: 8
Rank: 160=/764

Watt

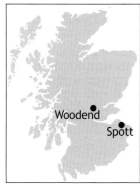

The name comes from 'Watt', a diminutive for Walter, and is on record as a surname from the end of the sixteenth century. The most famous person of the name is James Watt, who was born in Stewarton in 1774 and was a pioneer of steam engines, devising a separate condenser as well as a flywheel and governor. Also see Watson.

Woodend [NN 938221] is a few miles east of Crieff in Perthshire, and the present building dates from the end of the seventeenth century, although there was a castle or old house at or near Woodend. The lands were held by the Oliphants and by the Murrays, but were bought by the Watts around 1750. The house is still occupied.

Spott House [NT 679752], two or so miles south of Dunbar in East Lothian, incorporates work from an old castle. The property has had many owners down the centuries, including the Homes, but was held much later by the Watts. The parish of Spott is infamous for the number of witchcraft accusations, and many of those suspected were reputedly burned on Spott Loan.

No. of castles/sites: 2
Rank: 396=/764

Wauchope

The name comes from the lands of Wauchope, which are just to the south-west of Langholm in the far east of Dumfries and Galloway. There is a **Wauchope Castle** [NY 354840], although it appears to have only been held by the Lindsays and perhaps the Moffats, but not by the Wauchopes themselves. The name comes on record at the beginning of the fourteenth century.

Niddrie Marischal [NT 295715], to the south and east of Edinburgh, was a large castle and mansion, and was a rather grand place, but it was demolished and housing schemes were built at Niddrie. The lands were

Niddrie Marischal (M&R)

held by the Niddries and then by the Heriots, but in the fifteenth century passed to the Wauchopes. A castle here was burnt by an Edinburgh mob in the sixteenth century, and Mary, Queen of Scots, visited the castle several times. The Wauchopes were forfeited in 1587 because of their support for Francis Stewart, fifth Earl of Bothwell, and the property was acquired by the Sandilands family, before returning by marriage to the Wauchopes in 1608. Charles I was present at the christening of one of Sir John's Wauchope's sons, and gave the baby a gold and enamel chain. This was kept by the family and is now in the Museum of Edinburgh (Huntly House) in the Canongate. The house was occupied until the 1930s.

The Wauchopes also owned:
Cakemuir Castle [NT 413591], near Gorebridge, Midlothian; altered tower house.
   Held by the Wauchopes, one of whom was Adam Wauchope,

Cakemuir Castle (M&R)

an advocate who defended James Hepburn, fourth Earl of Bothwell, against the charge of murdering Darnley, the second husband of Mary, Queen of Scots. The hall is known as Queen Mary's room, because it was to Cakemuir that she came, disguised as a pageboy, after escaping from Borthwick Castle in 1567. The Wauchopes lost the property in 1794. The castle is still occupied and the gardens are occasionally open to the public (www.gardensofscotland.org).
Culter House [NJ 845013], Peterculter, Aberdeenshire; large mansion on site of older house and castle.
   Held by the Wauchopes but passed by marriage to the Cummings, and then much later to the Duffs. Used as the boarding house for a girls' school.
Edmonstone Castle [NT 304704], near Edinburgh; mansion on site of castle.
   Held by the Edmonstones and then by the Raits, but passed by marriage to the Wauchopes of Niddrie in 1671. One of the family was John Wauchope, Lord Edmonstone, who was a Lord of Session.
Newton [NT 332699], near Musselburgh, East Lothian; mansion incorporating castle.
   Held by the Newtons and by the Murrays, but may have passed to the Wauchope Lords Edmonstone in 1710. Still occupied.
Newton Don [NT 709372], near Kelso, Borders; castle replaced by mansion.
   Held by several families before coming to the Don family in 1648, and they were made Baronets in 1667. The Baronetcy is now held by the Don-Wauchopes of Edmondstone, who apparently live in South Africa.

No. of castles/sites: 6
Rank: 212=/764

Wedderburn

The name is territorial and comes from the lands of Wedderburn, which are a mile or so south-east of Duns in Berwickshire in the Borders. The family lost the original lands at an early date, but then held property around Dundee and in the north east.

Godfrey Wedderburn of Wedderhill is said to have been a Knight Templar who was based at the Preceptory at Maryculter. Godfrey went on crusade to the Holy Land, but was wounded and he was then helped by a Saracen woman. Years later the woman travelled to Scotland and found Godfrey at Maryculter. But the head of the Templars forced Godfrey to kill himself, believing that the innocent Godfrey had shamed the order. The lady also slew herself, but called down a curse; a lightning bolt struck the Templar, and killed him, leaving a hollow, the 'Thunder Hole', which can still be seen. It is said that Godfrey and the Saracen were buried side by side, but that his apparition returns to ride over the hill of Kingcausie while the ghost of the Saracen woman has been seen in the woods. Maryculter House, which stands on the site of the preceptory, is a hotel (01224 732124; www.maryculterhousehotel.com).

Wedderburn Castle [NT 809529] is a large castellated mansion, designed by Robert and James Adam and dating from the eighteenth century. It stands near the site of an old castle, and the property was held by the Wedderburns, but it later passed to the Homes, who still apparently own it. The mansion can be hired for exclusive use (01361 882190; www.wedderburn-castle.co.uk).

Wedderburn Castle or **Easter Powrie** [NO 435352], three or so miles north-east of Dundee, has been demolished, although it was mostly complete in 1704. Owned by the Douglases and by the Ogilvies, Wedderburn passed to the Scrymgeours at the end of the eighteenth century, who took the additional surname of Wedderburn, and are Earls of Dundee and Viscounts Dudhope: the heir of the family is also chief of the Wedderburns. The family owned Wedderburn into the twentieth century, and their seat is now apparently Birkhill.

The Wedderburns also owned:

Ballindean [NO 268299], near Dundee, Perthshire; mansion on site of castle.
  Held by the Fortheringhams, by the Starks and by the Ruthvens, Ballindean was also held by the Trotters, who were in possession to the 1960s. The Wedderburns of Ballindean are also on record in the eighteenth and nineteenth centuries, and they were made Baronets in 1775. The family, now Ogilvy-Wedderburn, Baronets, apparently lives near Blairgowrie in Perthshire.

Blackness Manor House [NO 370300], near Dundee; site of old house.
  Held by the Wedderburns. Sir John Wedderburn of Blackness

was the Clerk of Bills and was made a Baronet in 1704. The Wedderburns were Jacobites, and Sir John Wedderburn, who would have been the sixth Baronet, was captured after the Battle of Culloden in 1746 and was then executed for treason. The lands and title were forfeited. The house was demolished in 1939.

Feddinch House [NO 485135], near St Andrews, Fife; castle or old house replaced by mansion.
  Held by the Symsons, by the Aytons and by the Lindsays before going to the Wedderburns, who held the property in 1895. Accommodation is available (01334 470888; www.feddinch-house.com).

Kingennie [NO 477354], near Broughty Ferry, Angus; site of castle.
  Held by the Wedderburns. Alexander Wedderburn of Kingennie was one of the favourites of James VI, and was one of the signatories of the Act of Union of the Crowns in 1603.

Lindertis [NO 337515], near Kirriemuir, Angus; site of castle and mansion.
  Held by the Fletchers but was bought by the Wedderburns in 1780, and then later passed to the Munros. The mansion was demolished in 1955.

Pearsie [NO 366594], near St Andrews, Fife; castle or old house replaced by mansion.
  Held by the Edwards but passed by marriage to the Wedderburns in 1738.

No. of castles/sites: 8
Rank: 160=/764

Weir

The name could originate from one of several places in France, and comes from Norse and means a 'station' (such as a fishing station); it also means 'dam' in Old English. The name is on record from the twelfth century in Scotland when Ralph Ver, along with William the Lion, was captured by the English at Alnwick in 1174. Major Thomas Weir, who was born in Lanarkshire in 1600, served in Ulster and then was the leader of the City Guard in Edinburgh, and he was thought to be very pious. He did, however, confess to various crimes (of which witchcraft has been added in stories) including incest with this sister and blasphemy, and both he and his sister were executed. His ghost is then said to have haunted their house off Edinburgh's Royal Mile, although this building has since been demolished.

Blackwood House [NS 773433], four miles west of Lesmahagow in Lanarkshire, is the site of a castle but this was demolished to build a mansion, itself later demolished to build a smaller house. The property was held by the Weirs of Blackwood. James Weir of Blackwood was one of the supporters of Mary, Queen of Scots, and was one of those accused of the murder of Darnley. Blackwood passed to the Lawries, but was held by the Hope Veres (Weirs) at the end of the nineteenth century.

The family owned property in Lanarkshire, and held the following:
Auchtyfardle Castle [NS 826409], near Lesmahagow, Lanarkshire; site of castle.
Held by the Dowane family, but passed to the Weirs and then to the Kennedys.
Birkwood [NS 752417], near Strathaven, Lanarkshire; site of tower house.
May have been held by the Weirs.
Craigiehall House [NT 167754], near Edinburgh; castle replaced by mansion.
Held by several families and then latterly by the Hope Veres (Weirs) and then by the armed forces.
Dowane [NS 857422], near Lanark; probable site of castle.
Held by the Dowane family but passed to the Weirs.
Glenane [NS 812421], near Lesmahagow, Lanarkshire; tower house replaced by mansion.
Held by the Weirs in 1612.
Kirkton of Carluke [NS 844502], Carluke, Lanarkshire; site of castle and mansion.
Held by the Weirs of Stonebyres, but passed to Lockhart of The Lee in 1662. Demolished in the mid twentieth century.
Poneil [NS 840343], near Douglas, Lanarkshire; site of tower house.
Held by the Douglases and by the Folkertons, but passed to the Weirs, who were in possession in 1636.
Stonebyres House [NS 838433], near Lanark; site of castle and mansion.
Held by the Weirs, possibly from the thirteenth century to 1845, when it was sold to the Monteiths. Demolished in 1934 and only foundations survive.

Stonebyres House (M&R) – see previous column

Waygateshaw House [NS 825484], near Lanark; tower house and courtyard.
Held by the Murrays of Touchadam and by the Lockharts, but bought by the Weirs in 1720, then later passed to the Steels. Restored in the 1980s but later damaged by fire.

No. of castles/sites: 10
Rank: 140=/764
Xref: Vere

Wellwood

The name comes from the lands of Wellwood, which are to the north of Dunfermline in Fife, and the name is on record from the fifteenth century. William Wellwood was a professor of law and mathematics at St Andrews and died in 1622.

Garvock Hill [NT 105875] is to the east of Dunfermline, and there was a strong castle with a round tower and gunloops. Nothing remains, and the lands were held by the Wellwood family. The castle was abandoned in the middle of the seventeenth century, and the Wellwoods moved to a house in Maygate in Dunfermline. The family were provosts and officers of the regality for about 200 years. The family became Maconochie-Welwood of Garvock and Meadowbank, but Garvock was sold in 1920, and the family now apparently live at Kirknewton.

No. of castles/sites: 1
Rank: 537=/764

Wemyss

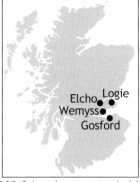

The name is territorial and comes from the lands of Wemyss, which are three miles north and east of Kirkcaldy in Fife. The name Wemyss comes from 'uamh' in Gaelic, which means 'cave', and there are many caves along the coast here.

Wemyss Castle [NT 329951] is a large stronghold and mansion, which may incorporate work from the thirteenth century or earlier. It was built around a courtyard and there was a rectangular keep or tower. Wemyss has long been a property of the Wemyss family. Sir Michael Wemyss was one of the ambassadors sent to bring Margaret, Maid of Norway, to Scotland at the end of the thirteenth century, and a silver basin, preserved

Wemyss Castle 1903?

at the castle, is said to have been given to Sir Michael by the King of Norway. The Wemyss family sided with Robert the Bruce and the castle was sacked by the English during the Wars of Independence. Sir David Wemyss added his seal to the Declaration of Arbroath in 1320, and another Sir David Wemyss was killed at the Battle of Flodden in 1513. Mary, Queen of Scots, first met Lord Darnley here in 1565, and the Wemyss family fought for her at the Battle of Langside in 1568. The family were made Earls of Wemyss in 1633, and Charles II visited in 1650 and 1651. The family were forfeited for their part in the Jacobite Rising of 1745-46, although the title was restored in 1826; the family now takes the name Charteris. They still apparently occupy the castle, and the building is said to be haunted by a Green Lady, who has reputedly been witnessed in all parts of the castle. She was described as 'tall and slim and entirely clad in green, with her visage hidden by the hood of her mantle' in the 1890s. The gardens at Wemyss are open on Thursdays from mid April to August (www.gardens ofscotland.org).

Elcho Castle [NO 165211], four miles east and south of Perth, is a very fine castle, and was both defensible and comfortable. There is a long main block with towers projecting from each side. It probably dates from the

Elcho Castle (RWB)

sixteenth century, although William Wallace is said to have sheltered here, and there may be earlier work. The Wemyss family owned Elcho from 1468, and were made Lords Elcho in 1633. David, Lord Elcho, fought and survived the Battle of Culloden on the Jacobite side in 1746, but had to flee to France, where he died in 1787. Elcho was abandoned as a residence soon afterwards, although it may have housed farm workers. The building is now in the care of Historic Scotland, there is the fine quarry garden, and the castle is open to the public (01738 639998).

The Wemyss family also owned:
Balgreggie [NT 222963], near Cowdenbeath, Fife; site of castle and mansion.
  Held by the Wemyss family, but passed to the Boswells at the end of the fourteenth century.
Carden Tower [NT 226937], near Cardenden, Fife; some remains of tower house.
  Held by the Martins, but passed to the Wemyss family in 1623, and then to others. The site is accessible to the public.
Drumry [NS 515710], near Duntocher, Glasgow; site of tower house.
  The lands were held by the Callendar family and then by the Wemyss family before passing to the Livingstones and then to others. The castle was demolished in 1959.
Dura House [NO 413141], near Cupar, Fife; mansion incorporating old work.
  Held by the Wemyss family in 1624.
Gosford House [NT 453786], near Longniddry, East Lothian; mansion.
  Built for the Earl of Wemyss (now Charteris) to designs of Robert Adam but rebuilt in 1890. The south wing is apparently the family home of the Earl of Wemyss and March, now represented by the Charteris family.
Lathockar House [NO 492106], near St Andrews, Fife; site of castle or old house.
  Held by the Wemyss family in the sixteenth and seventeenth centuries. The mansion is ruinous.
Leuchars Castle [NO 454219], near Leuchars, Fife; site of castle.
  Held by the Quincy family but passed to the Wemyss family in the fifteenth century, and there was a tower house, although this has been demolished. The parish church of St Athernase [NO 455215], a fine old building, dates from 1183 and is open to the public in the spring and summer.
Logie House [NO 408206], near Leuchars, Fife; mansion incorporating part of tower house.
  Held by the Logies and then by the Wemyss family in the fifteenth century or earlier. One of the lairds is the protagonist of the old ballad, 'The Laird of Logie'. The laird was imprisoned

in the tolbooth of Edinburgh, and was about to be executed by the king. Using a cunning plan, he was freed by his lover and together they escaped abroad.

MacDuff's Castle [NT 344972], East Wemyss, Fife; ruinous castle near shore.

Held by the MacDuffs, but passed to the Wemyss family, who built the castle, then went by marriage to the Livingstones,

MacDuff's Castle 1910?

to the Hamiltons and to the Colvilles, before returning to the Wemyss family, later Earls of Wemyss, in 1630. The castle is said to be haunted by a Grey Lady, the spirit of a woman who died as a result of a harsh punishment for thievery.

Pittencrieff House [NT 087873], Dunfermline, Fife; fine T-plan house.

Held by the Setons and then by the Wemyss family after the Reformation. John Wemyss of Pittencrieff was the suitor of Dorothy Ruthven towards the end of the sixteenth century. Dorothy made the 'Maiden's Leap' at Huntingtower Castle, and two later eloped. In 1612 John Wemyss of Pittencrieff was excommunicated for slaying his brother. The property passed to others, but was finally purchased by Andrew Carnegie and given to the people of Dunfermline. The grounds are a popular public park (01383 722935/313838; www.fifedirect.org/museums).

Rires Castle [NO 464046], near Elie, Fife; site of castle.

Held by the Wemyss family in the fourteenth century. The castle was besieged and captured by the Duke of Rothesay in 1402 using a wooden siege engine built at St Andrews.

Rossend Castle [NT 225859], Burntisland, Fife; restored E-plan tower house.

Held by the Duries and by the Melvilles, but later passed to the Wemyss family, who were made Lords Burntisland in 1672. Used as an office.

Rumgally House [NO 407149], near Cupar, Fife; mansion incorporating tower house.

Held by the Scotts of Balwearie and possibly by the Wemyss family, then by James MacGill, minister of Largo. It is still occupied and B&B accommodation is available (01334 653388; www.sol.co.uk/r/rumgally/).

Scotstarvit Tower [NO 370113], near Cupar, Fife; fine tall L-plan tower house.

Held by the Inglises, by the Scotts and by the Gourlays of Craigrothie, and then by the Wemyss family and by the Sharps. Given to The National Trust of Scotland and can be visited: key from Hill of Tarvit (01334 653127).

Torrie Castle [NT 015867], near Dunfermline, Fife; site of castle.

Held by the Wardlaws, then probably by the Bruces and by the Balfours, but was owned by the Erskine-Wemyss family in the nineteenth century.

West Wemyss [NT 319947], near Kirkcaldy, Fife; tower houses, one ruinous.

Held by the Wemyss family.

No. of castles/sites: 18
Rank: 76=/764

White

The name may come from a personal name from Old English or may be descriptive from hair colour (or lack of it) or complexion. The name is on record from the turn of the thirteenth century.

Barskimming [NS 482251] is a mile or so south-east of Mauchline in Ayrshire, and the present plain classical mansion replaced an old castle. Robert the Bruce gave a grant of the lands to the Whites at the beginning of the fourteenth century, but Barskimming was held by the Reids from 1375. The property later passed to the Stewarts, to the Millers and then to the Galbraiths.

Overtoun Castle or **House** [NS 424761] lies a mile and a half north-east of Dumbarton and is a large baronial mansion, which dates from the middle of the nineteenth century; it stands on the site of a castle. Held by the Colquhouns and by Laings, Overtoun was bought by James White in 1859. It is now used as a Christian Centre for Hope and Healing, and the estate around the house is open to the public with formal gardens and a nature trail (www.overtounhouse.com).

No. of castles/sites: 2
Rank: 396=/764
Xref: Whyte

Whitefoord

The name is territorial and comes from the lands of Whitefoord, which are to the south-east of Paisley in Renfrewshire. The name was usually spelt with a 'Qu', instead of a 'W', in the sixteenth and seventeenth centuries. Walter Whitefoord was made Bishop of Brechin in 1635 but only held the post for three years before being dethroned.

Whitefoord Tower [NS 505625] is no more than a site now, but the lands were long a property of the family. A warrior named Walter is said to have distinguished himself at the Battle of Largs in 1263, and Alexander III gave him the lands in reward. The Whitefoords held the lands until 1689.

The family also held:

Ballochmyle House [NS 521264], near Mauchline, Ayrshire; tower house replaced by mansion.
  Held by the Reids but passed to the Whitefoords, although they got into debt and it was sold to the Alexanders in 1723. Robert Burns was a visitor, and wrote 'Farewell to Ballochmyle', after he had witnessed the sadness of one of the Whitefoord ladies at leaving her old home. The building was later used as a hospital but this has now closed. The site is to be redeveloped, restoring the house, and luxury homes are to be built in the grounds.

Blairquhan [NS 367055], near Maybole, Ayrshire; castle replaced by mansion.
  Held by the MacWhurters and by the Kennedys, but passed to the Whitefoords in 1623. Charles Whitefoord of Blairquhan fought for the Hanoverians at the Battle of Culloden in 1746. The property passed to the Hunter Blairs, and they still apparently own it. The Whitefoords, formerly of Blairquhan, now live in Shropshire in England. Blairquhan is open to the public from July to mid August (01655 770239; www.blairquhan.co.uk).

Cloncaird Castle [NS 359075], near Maybole, Ayrshire; altered tower house.
  Held by the Mures, and then later by the Wallaces and by the Whitefoords. Still occupied and said to be haunted by the ghost of a man.

Dunduff Castle [NS 272164], near Maybole, Ayrshire; altered L-plan tower house.
  Held by the Stewarts, but passed to the Whitefoords in the seventeenth century. Restored and occupied.

No. of castles/sites: 5
Rank: 240=/764
Xrefs: Quhitefoord; Whiteford

Whitelaw

The name is territorial or local, and may come from the lands and barony of Whitelaw, three miles east and north of Selkirk in the Borders. There are, however, at least two other places with the name Whitelaw, which means 'white hill': one near Duns, one near Morebattle, both in the Borders. The name is on record from the end of the thirteenth century.

The Whitelaws owned:

Alderstone House [NT 044662], near Livingston, West Lothian; altered tower house.
  Held by the Kinlochs, by the Sandilands, by the Mitchells of Todhaugh and by the Bruces before passing to the Whitelaws in the twentieth century. One of the family was William Whitelaw, Viscount Whitelaw of Penrith, who was Secretary of State in the Thatcher government, and died in 1999. The house is currently used as company offices.

Fenton Tower [NT 543822], near North Berwick, East Lothian; restored L-plan tower house.
  Held by the Fentons, but passed by marriage to the Whitelaws, but they were forfeited in 1587, presumably because of their support for Francis Stewart, fifth Earl of Bothwell. Fenton passed to the Carmichaels, to the Erskines and to the Maxwells,

Fenton Tower (MC)

and then became ruinous. It was restored in the 1990s, starred in *Balamory* as Archie's Castle, and luxury accommodation is available (01620 890089; www.fentontower.co.uk).

Gartsherrie House [NS 726659], near Coatbridge, Lanarkshire; site of castle and mansion.
  Held by the Colts, but passed to the Whitelaws in the nineteenth century. The site is occupied by a container base.

Gartshore House [NS 692737], near Kirkintilloch; site of old mansion.
  Held by the Gartshore family, then by others, but came to the Whitelaws of Gartshore in the nineteenth century. The family now apparently live at Burton Agnes Hall in Yorkshire in England (which is open to the public and has one of the best ghost stories in Britain about Old Nance and her skull). One of the family was William Whitelaw, Viscount Whitelaw of Penrith, who was Secretary of State in the Thatcher government and died in 1999 (as mentioned above).

Tannochside House [NS 716620], near Coatbridge, Lanarkshire; site of castle or old house.

Held by the Raes, but passed to the Whitelaws in the eighteenth century, then went the Hosiers in 1840. Demolished about 1950 and the site is occupied by housing.

No. of castles/sites: 5
Rank: 240=/764
Xref: Whytelaw

Wilkie

The name is a diminutive of William, itself from Old German 'Willihelm', and the name is on record in Scotland from the beginning of the fourteenth century. The family were established by then at Ratho, as well as in Fife. Sir David Wilkie, born in Fife in 1785, was a well-known artist and portrait painter, and he was made King's Limner in Scotland in 1823.

Bonnington

Bonnington House [NT 111691] is two miles southwest of Ratho to the west of Edinburgh, and the two-storey house dates from 1622, although it was altered in the following centuries. Held by the Erskines, by the Foulis Lord Colinton, by the Durhams, and by the Cunninghams, Bonnington House was then a property of the Wilkies of Ormiston.

No. of castles/sites: 1
Rank: 537=/764

Williamson

The name is from 'William's son', from the Old German personal name 'Willihelm', and the name is on record from the middle of the fourteenth century. The family held lands near Peebles in the Borders and elsewhere, and there are the Williamson Barons Forres of Glenogil, a title created in 1922 although they now apparently live in Australia.

Murieston   Foulitch
Cardrona
Castle
Robert

The Williamsons owned:

Cardrona Tower [NT 300378], near Peebles, Borders; L-plan tower house.

Held by the Govans, but passed to the Williamsons in 1685, when the tower was abandoned.

Castle Robert [NS 804148], near Sanquhar, Dumfriesshire; site of castle.

Held by the Williamsons in the sixteenth and seventeenth centuries. The tower may have been destroyed by fire as melted lead, presumably from the roof, has been found at the site.

Chapelhill [NT 245422], near Peebles, Borders; altered tower house.

Held by the Pringles but later passed to the Williamsons, who owned it in the second half of the eighteenth century. Now a farmhouse.

Foulitch Tower [NT 256436], near Peebles, Borders; site of castle.

Held by the Caverhills, then by others, before passing to the Williamsons in the seventeenth century, and then went the Littles of Winkston.

Hutchinfield Tower [NT 255422], near Peebles, Borders; slight remains of tower house.

Held by the Horsburghs, but passed to the Williamsons in 1659.

Murieston Castle [NT 050636], near West Calder, West Lothian; ruinous tower house.

Held by the Sandilands and by the Cochranes, and then perhaps the Williamsons, but had passed to the Steels in 1903. Rebuilt as a folly in 1824.

No. of castles/sites: 6
Rank: 212=/764

Wilson

The name is from 'Will's son', Will being a diminutive for William, and the northern branch, part of the Gunns, comes from William, son of George Gunn, who lived in the fifteenth century.

The family owned the following properties:

Airdrie House [NS 749654], Airdrie, Lanarkshire; site of castle and mansion.

Held by several families, including by the Clellands and by the Hamiltons, but passed to the Wilsons in the nineteenth century and they were made Baronets in 1905. The house was then used as a maternity hospital, but was demolished in 1964, and Monklands General Hospital built. The Wilsons of Airdrie, Baronets, now apparently live in Buckinghamshire in England.

Balnakeilly House [NN 946598], near Pitlochry, Perthshire; mansion incorporating very old work.

Held by the Stewarts from the sixteenth century, and the family, now Stewart-Wilson, still apparently own the property. The gardens are occasionally open to the public (www.gardensofscotland.org).

Carbeth House [NS 524876], near Killearn, Stirlingshire; castle replaced by mansion.

Held by the Grahams and by the Buchanans, but passed to the Wilsons in the nineteenth century, and they were made Baronets in 1920, although they now apparently live in Surrey in England. The house is still occupied.

Chapelton [NX 798667], near Castle Douglas, Galloway; site of castle or old house.

Held by the Maxwells, then latter by the Biggars and by the Wilsons.

Craigend Castle [NS 545778], near Milngavie, Stirlingshire; site of castle and mansion.

Held by the Grahams, by the Smiths, by the Ingalises and by the Buchanans, before being bought by the Wilsons in the middle of the twentieth century. Craigend was used as a zoo before being abandoned and then demolished, and the stables now house a visitor centre for Mugdock Park (0141 956 6100; www.mugdock-country-park.org.uk).

Dinnet [NO 465982], near Ballater, Kincardineshire; site of castle.

Held by the Gordon Earls of Huntly, then by the Wilsons in the nineteenth century, who built a new house, and this later passed to the Humphreys.

Ferguslie Castle [NS 467637], Paisley, Renfrewshire; site of castle and mansion.

Held by the Hamiltons and by the Wallaces, then by the Wilsons in 1837.

Glengeith [NS 947166], near Elvanfoot, Lanarkshire; slight remains of tower house.

Held by the Wilsons, one of whom John Wilson was a noted Covenanter. He sheltered many hunted men here, including Donald Cargill, the ardent Covenanter who was eventually arrested and executed in 1681.

Thainstone House [NJ 759186], near Inverurie, Aberdeenshire; castle or old house replaced by mansion.

Held by the Forbeses and by the Mitchells, then by the Wilsons, one of whom, James Wilson, signed the American Declaration of Independence. The building is said to be haunted by a Green Lady, the ghost of a girl killed in a riding accident; an alternative version is that she was killed when the house was torched during the Jacobite Rising of 1745-46. Thainstone is now a hotel (01467 621643; www.macdonald-hotels.co.uk).

No. of castles/sites: 9 / Rank: 149=/764

Winram

The name is on record in Scotland from the fifteenth century, and the family held lands in Clydesdale. John Winram was a subprior of St Andrews but he had joined the Protestant reformers by 1560.

Wiston Place [NS 956320] lies three miles south-west of Symington in Lanarkshire, and was originally held by one Wice, probably a Fleming, and hence the name ('Wice ton'). The lands and barony were later held by the Winram family, who were in possession in the fifteenth century, and possibly later. There was a castle or old house, but there are no remains.

Inch House [NT 278709] is to the south-east of Edinburgh, and is an L-plan tower house of four storeys and garret, dating from the seventeenth century but incorporating older work. Inch was held by the Gilmours and also by the Winrams. James Winram of Nether Liberton was Keeper of the Great Seal in 1623. The house is now a community centre and stands in a public park.

No. of castles/sites: 2
Rank: 396=/764

Winton

The name is territorial and comes from the lands of Winton, which are three or so miles south-east of Tranent in East Lothian. The family are on record from the end of the twelfth century, but the property passed to the Quincy family and then to the Setons when the Quincys were forfeited by Robert the Bruce about 1320.

Winton House [NT 439696] is a magnificent Renaissance mansion dating from 1620 with later additions, although incorporating older work. Winton is now a property of the Ogilvys and is open to the public by guided tours while the gardens are also occasionally open (01875 340222; www.wintonhouse.co.uk).

There were also Wintons recorded in Ayrshire and in Aberdeenshire. Andrew Winton (or Wyntoun) was prior of Lochleven and was author of *Original Chronicle of Scotland*, an account of the history of Scotland which was compiled at the end of the fourteenth century.

No. of castles/sites: 1
Rank: 537=/764

Wishart

The name comes from 'guishard' or 'wishard' from Old French, and means 'prudent' or 'wise'. The name is on record in Scotland from around 1200. Robert Wishart was the Bishop of Glasgow in 1273 and was a Guardian of Scotland after the death of Alexander III. He was active against the English during the Wars of Independence and was imprisoned, but he officiated at the inauguration of Robert the Bruce in 1306. He was captured again and went blind in prison before being released after the English were defeated at Bannockburn in 1314.

Pittarrow Castle [NO 727751] stood three miles north and east of Laurencekirk in Kincardineshire, but all that survives of the castles is a date stone with 1599, other fragments, and an old doocot. The lands were long a property of the Wisharts, four of whom were bishops. Pittarrow was the birthplace of the Protestant martyr George Wishart, who was charged with heresy and fled to Germany and Switzerland, and then to Cambridge in England. He returned to Scotland in 1543, and preached widely, firstly in the west where he was sheltered by local lairds, but then in Leith. He was hunted down and arrested in East Lothian on the orders of Cardinal David Beaton, and burned alive at St Andrews in 1546 after being held for a month in the dungeon there. Sir John Wishart of Pitarrow was a reformer and was Collector General of Thirds, effectively a property tax to support the monarch and pay for ministers. Wishart was opposed to Mary, Queen of Scots. Pittarrow later passed to the Carnegies.

Logie House [NO 394521], a mile or so south of Kirriemuir in Angus, is a plain tower house with a round tower at one corner. It dates from the sixteenth century, although it has since been altered and extended. Held by the Wisharts, one of the family was George Wishart, chaplain to (and later biographer of) the Marquis of Montrose from 1644, and he followed him into exile. Montrose returned to Scotland in 1650 but he was executed; Wishart was perhaps wiser and waited until after the Restoration of 1661 before he came back, and was made Protestant Bishop of Edinburgh in 1662. He is buried in a lavish tomb in the church of Holyrood Abbey, now part of Holyroodhouse. Logie went to the Kinlochs of Kilrie, who held it until the twentieth century.

Clifton Hall [NT 109710] is two miles east of Broxburn in West Lothian, and the present mansion dates from 1850, although it replaced a castle or old house. The property was held by the Grahams of Abercorn, then by others, before coming to the Wisharts, who were made Baronets in 1706. The property was sold to the Gibsons of Pentland in 1761; the mansion is now used as a school.

www.wishart.org
No. of castles/sites: 3 / Rank: 328=/764

Wiston

The name is territorial and comes form the lands and barony of Wiston, which are three miles south-west of Symington in Lanarkshire. The name is from the personal name 'Wice' and his seat or 'ton', and the family are in record from the middle of the twelfth century.

Wiston Place [NS 956320] was an old castle or house, but nothing survives of the building. The property of Wiston passed from the family around 1300, and in the fifteenth century was being held by the Winrams.

No. of castles/sites: 1
Rank: 537=/764

Woddrop

The family held lands in Lanarkshire, and may be descended from one of the Border lairds who were charged with complicity in the murder of David Rizzio, the secretary of Mary, Queen of Scots, at Holyrood Palace.

Dalmarnock [NS 615628] lies to the south of Glasgow on the north side of the Clyde, and part of the lands were held by the Grays, and part by the Woddrops, who were in possession for many generations. The Woddrops held their lands into the nineteenth century, and the family had a castle or old house.

Elsrickle [NT 062435] is a few miles east of Carnwath in Lanarkshire, and there was a castle although there are no remains. The lands were held by the Hepburns, but had passed to the Woddrops of Dalmarnock by the eighteenth century.

Four miles north-east of Biggar, also on Lanarkshire, is **Edmonston Castle** [NT 070422], a ruinous castle of the fifteenth century. The property was held by the Edmonstone family, by the Douglases, by the Baillies of Walston and by the Browns before passing to the Woddrops of Elsrickle and Dalmarnock.

No. of castles/sites: 3
Rank: 328=/764

Wood

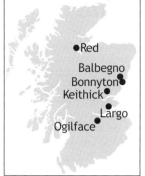

The name comes from one who had a residence by or in a wood, and the Norman name from Latin (which means the same) was 'de Bosco'. The name is on record from the end of the fourteenth century.

Largo Castle [NO 418034] was to the north of Lower Largo in Fife, but nothing survives of the building except one round tower with a conical roof.

Balbegno Castle (M&R)

Largo Castle (M&R)

The castle dated from the fifteenth century, and it was replaced by Largo House. This mansion was begun about 1750, but is now a ruinous shell. The property was held by Sir Andrew Wood from 1482, and he supported James III, who had employed him to defend Scottish ships against English pirates and privateers in his ship the *Yellow Carvel*. After the king was killed at Sauchieburn in 1488, Wood at first refused to treat with James IV. Wood continued to be instrumental in defeating English attacks on Scottish merchant men, and he then helped James IV in his campaign against the Lords of the Isles in the 1490s. He defeated an English fleet off Dundee in 1504, taking three of the ships as prizes, and he also commanded the massive warship the *Great Michael*. It was the largest ship of its day, although perhaps not all that practical as it was so slow. Sir Andrew was sent to France after the disastrous Battle of Flodden in 1513 to fetch the Duke of Albany to be Regent for the infant James V; Wood died in 1540. Largo went to the Blacks, to the Gibsons of Durie and then to the Durhams, who held the property into the nineteenth century.

The Woods also owned:

Balbegno Castle [NO 639730], near Fettercairn, Kincardineshire; altered L-plan tower house.

Held by the Woods, hereditary constables of Kincardine Castle, who were in possession of the lands in 1488 and built Balbegno Castle. The property was sold to the Middletons in 1687, then later passed by the Ogilvies and then to the Ramsays.

Bonnyton Castle [NO 657559], near Montrose, Angus; site of castle.

Held by the Woods of Bonnyton, who owned the property from 1493 to the eighteenth century.

Craig House [NO 704563], near Montrose, Angus; strong courtyard castle.

Held by the Woods, who built the castle, but passed to the Carnegie Earls of Southesk in 1617. Still occupied.

Geilston House [NS 339783], near Dumbarton; mansion incorporating old work.

Held by the Woods in the sixteenth century, who had a tower house, but had passed to the Henrys by the nineteenth century. The gardens are open to the public (01389 841867; www.nts.org.uk).

Keithick [NO 203385], near Coupar Angus, Perthshire; castle replaced by mansion.

Held by the Campbells, but latterly by the Collins Wood family.

Ogilface Castle [NS 927690], near Bathgate, West Lothian; site of castle.

Held by the De Boscos (Woods), then by the Murrays and by the Livingstone Earls of Linlithgow.

Red Castle [NH 584495], near Muir of Ord, Ross and Cromarty; large ruinous castle.

Held by the Bissets and then in 1278 by Sir Andrew de Bosco (Wood), and then to the Frasers and to other families.

No. of castles/sites: 8
Rank: 160=/764
Xref: Bosco

Craig House (M&R)

Wright

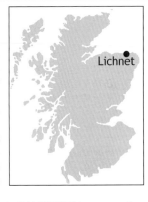

The name comes from 'wyrtha' from Old English and means a carpenter or worker, mostly in wood. The name is on record from the end of the thirteenth century, and it is believed that some members of the MacIntyre clan changed their names to Wright.

    Lichnet or **Lethnot Castle** [NJ 809653] is seven miles east of Macduff in Aberdeenshire, and there was a castle although there are no remains. Wright of Lethnot is on record in 1410.

No. of castles/sites: 1
Rank: 537=/764

Wylie

The name is derived from 'Willie', a diminutive of William, and is on record from the middle of the fifteenth century. Sir James Wylie, who was born in Kincardine in 1768, was a surgeon and a physician and he went to Russia where he was in the service of Czar Alexander I.

    Airleywight [NO 057365] is just north and west of Bankfoot in Perthshire, and the present symmetrical mansion of 1810, which has round towers flanking the entrance, replaced a castle or old house. The lands were held by the Wylies in the nineteenth century.

No. of castles/sites: 1
Rank: 537=/764

Young

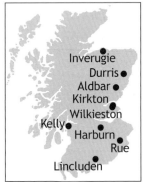

The name is derived from a simple designation that the person was younger, which is sometimes expressed now as 'the younger'. Gaelic uses a similar way to denote this, such as Angus Og, 'og' meaning 'young'. This was used because generations of men of noble houses had the same personal name. The name is on record as a surname from the fourteenth century. The Youngs of Partick, Baronets, still flourish, but this is a modern creation and was established in 1945.

The Youngs owned several properties around Scotland:
Aldbar Castle [NO 572577], near Brechin, Angus; castle and mansion.
    Held by several families, including by the Lyons, before latterly passing to the Youngs, and then to the Chalmers of Balnacraig, who held it in the twentieth century. The castle was demolished in 1965.
Durris House [NO 799968], near Banchory, Kincardineshire; altered L-plan tower house.
    Held by the Frasers, then by others, until it was bought by James 'Paraffin' Young in 1871. Divided but occupied.
Harburn Castle [NT 044608], near West Calder, West Lothian; castle replaced by mansion.
    The mansion was built for Alexander, father of James 'Paraffin' Young, in 1804, but later passed to the Barrs. Now a hotel and conference centre (01506 461818; www.harburnhouse.com).
Inverugie Castle [NJ 152687], near Elgin, Moray; site of castle.
    Held by the Youngs, but passed to the Mortimers, who built a mansion in 1864.
Kelly House [NS 198685], near Inverkip, Renfrewshire; site of castle and mansion.
    Held by the Bannatynes and by the Wallaces, who built a new mansion, and it was later owned by James 'Paraffin' Young. Young was born in 1811 and was involved in producing oil from shale in the Lothians from 1865. The house was rebuilt in 1890, but was burnt down twenty-three years later, probably by Suffragettes.
Kirkton [NO 447260], near Leuchars, Fife; ruinous mansion incorporating castle.
    Held by the Lockharts, then by the Balfours and by the Youngs, then by the Gillespies. The building has been partly restored.

Lincluden (TP) – see next page

Lincluden Collegiate Church [NX 967779], near Dumfries; remains of collegiate church and domestic buildings, later remodelled into a house.

Held by the Stewarts after the Reformation, then by the Douglases of Drumlanrig and by the Gordons of Lochinvar, but Lincluden was later held by the Youngs of Lincluden, who have a mausoleum at Holywood. They had a mansion called Youngfield and then later Lincluden House. This was gutted by fire in 1875, then was rebuilt, but the building was later demolished except for the stables.

Rue Castle [NT 613202], near Jedburgh, Borders; site of castle.

Held by the Youngs at one times, and was torched in 1513 and 1545 by the English.

Wilkieston [NO 449120], near St Andrews, Fife; site of castle or old house.

Held by the Youngs of Wilkieston in the seventeenth century, although it is possible this is a confusion with a place of the same name in West Lothian, and then by the Symsons in 1735.

www.clanyoung.tripod.com
No. of castles/sites: 9
Rank: 149=/764

Younger

The name probably means the same as Young, that the original holder of the name was younger than another member of the family with the same personal name; it has also been suggested that it might come from a Flemish personal name. The name is on record from the end of the fourteenth century.

Old Leckie House [NS 690946] is several miles west of Stirling near the village of Gargunnock. It is a T-plan tower house, dating from the sixteenth century and rising to three storeys. The lands were held by the Leckie family and by the Moirs, before passing to the Youngers, who had founded the brewing company George Younger and Son, and were made Viscounts Younger of Leckie in 1911.

Auchen Castle [NT 063035] is a couple of miles south-west of Moffat in Dumfriesshire, but little remains of the old castle. The property was held by the Kirkpatrick family and others, before passing to the Johnstones, who held Auchen in the nineteenth century, and then it passed by marriage to the Youngers. They were made Baronets in 1911 (as mentioned above), and now apparently live in London in England. A new **Auchen Castle** [NT 063047] had been built, about half a mile away from the old one, in 1849. This building is said to be haunted by the ghost of a child and is now a hotel (01683 300407; www.auchencastle.com).

No. of castles/sites: 2
Rank: 396=/764

Yuille

The name may come from one who was born on Christmas Day (Yule), but this has been discounted by some. The name is on record from the end of the fourteenth century.

Garleton Castle [NT 509767] is a mile or so north of Haddington in East Lothian and is a partly ruinous courtyard castle, dating from the sixteenth century. One block is still occupied, one part has been replaced by cottages, and one side is ruinous. The property may have been held by the Yuilles in 1400, but was long a property of the Lindsays, and then of the Towers family of Inverleith and of the Setons.

Darleith House [NS 345806], a couple of miles north of Cardross in Dunbartonshire, was a classical mansion, which incorporated an altered tower house, but the house is now ruinous. Held by the Darleith family, the property was bought by the Yuilles in 1670. It was later used as a seminary, but is now ruinous.

No. of castles/sites: 2
Rank: 396=/764
Xrefs: Yule; Yuill

The Development of the Castle

The main function of the castle was defensive, to protect the laird and his family from their enemies, in as comfortable surroundings as possible; but the castle also served as the centre of administration of the laird's lands, where tenure, economy and trade were controlled, where law was dispensed, wrong-doers punished, and taxes collected. The design of castles depended very much on the social organization, political climate, expense and building fashions of the time, but they were always a show of the lord's wealth, prestige and power, and a symbol of his authority. Most, however, were never intended as strategic fortresses and were fortified houses: strong enough to see off a raid or foray but vulnerable to attack by a determined army, especially with the increased use of effective artillery. Some do not feel that such buildings merit the term 'castle', although using 'chateau' hardly seems more accurate.

Introduction

The earliest fortified sites consist of hill forts, brochs and duns, dating from before recorded history. Some of these were occupied as late as the seventeenth century – and the sites of many others were reused for later fortresses. Hill forts are found all over Scotland, but brochs and duns tend to be concentrated in the north and west.

Motte and bailey castles were introduced to Scotland along with feudalism. They are unevenly distributed, however, being particularly numerous in Galloway, where there was unrest among the native population in the twelfth century, but with few surviving examples in Lothian. This form of defence was not used for long. Stone castles were already being used in Orkney and Norse-controlled areas from the twelfth century, and brochs and duns were modified or reused.

By the thirteenth century castles of enclosure (enceinte) were being built, where a site was surrounded by a strong stone wall encircling timber or stone buildings. These developed, in some cases, into large castles with strong keeps, gatehouses and towers.

Large stone castles were expensive to build and maintain, and in the late fourteenth and fifteenth centuries simple keeps were built, usually with a barmkin or courtyard. The keep evolved into the tower house, which was not as strong but more complex and had more regard to comfort. Hundreds of these towers were built in the sixteenth century. During the later sixteenth and seventeenth centuries the simple rectangular tower house developed into L- and Z-plan tower houses, which provided more accommodation and comfort as well as covering fire.

At the same time as nobles built and developed keeps and tower houses, the kings of Scots built or refurbished ornate royal palaces. These were often developed out of older strongholds, but during the fifteenth and sixteenth centuries they were remodelled in the Renaissance style to become comfortable residences.

As the need for defence decreased, many castles and tower houses were developed into mansion houses.

There is a great deal of overlap between the different types of stronghold, and often a new castle was built on the site of a previous one, and reused materials from the original or was simply built around, or out of, the existing building. There are also definite regional differences. In areas such as the Borders, feuds, reiving and warfare, and land ownership contributed to the building of a large number of simple tower houses, peel towers and bastles, although few of these survive intact. Whereas in Aberdeenshire there are a large number of seventeenth-century Z-plan tower houses. The topography of particular areas influenced the position and style of building: an island in a marsh was as good a site as a rocky promontory.

Hill Forts, Brochs and Duns

Hill forts may date from as early as the Neolithic period to about 500 BC, and some were used until medieval times. Ramparts of earth and stone walls, often laced with timber, or wooden palisades protected hilltops or other defensible sites. Some hill forts enclosed whole villages within their ramparts.

Brochs and duns date from about 200 BC or earlier, and a few were reused or occupied into the seventeenth century.

Brochs are round hollow towers, built of dry-stone masonry, with very thick walls. These walls were formed from two shells of masonry with a gallery running up inside the wall. The entrance was extremely narrow, allowing only one person at a time to enter, and a small guard chamber defended the entrance. There were often many buildings around the broch, with outer ditches

Dun Carloway – an Iron Age broch

and ramparts to defend the settlement. Brochs appear to have been concentrated in Orkney and Shetland, Caithness and Sutherland, and the Western Isles, but there are also examples in other parts of the country, including Lothian and Dumfries and Galloway.

The best remaining examples of brochs are Mousa and Clickhimin (Shetland), Dun Carloway (Lewis), Midhowe and Gurness (Orkney), Dun Dornaigil (Sutherland) the Glen Elg brochs (Lochaber) and Dun Beag (Skye).

Duns are also most widely distributed in the north and west. 'Dun' means hill or fortified place in Gaelic and is used for both duns and brochs in Gaelic-speaking areas. The general distribution of duns is similar to that of brochs, but duns were usually irregular in plan, following the contours of a rock, and vary in size from a small homestead to a hill fort. The building style was sometimes very similar to brochs, and some duns have galleried walls and small cells within the walls.

Motte and Bailey Castles (twelfth century)

During the twelfth century motte and bailey castles were introduced into Scotland along with feudalism, mostly into lowland areas, where the style was adopted and adapted by native lords. Motte and bailey castles are mostly concentrated in Clydesdale, Galloway and Grampian. There appear to have been few in central Scotland, the Lothians, the north-west and the Highlands.

Motte and bailey castles consisted of an earthen mound, known as a motte, and a courtyard, or bailey, enclosed by a wooden palisade and defended by a ditch. The plan of the motte was usually round, but some were also oval or rectangular and used existing defensive features such as ravines, spits of land between rivers, or cliff tops. At the base of the motte was a dry or wet ditch or moat.

A wooden tower was built on the motte, where the lord and his followers could shelter if attacked. The bailey contained many buildings, such as the hall, chapel, kitchen, bakehouse and stables. The motte and bailey were linked by a removable bridge which spanned the ditch.

Often all that remains today is evidence of the earthworks, some good examples of these being Motte of Urr (Galloway), Peel Ring of Lumphanan and Doune of Invernochty (both Aberdeenshire). Duffus Castle

(Moray) and Rothesay Castle (Bute) are two of the few examples where a stone keep was added as the earthen motte was often not strong enough to take a stone building. Other mottes and their surrounding earthworks were reused by later castle builders.

Wooden castles were not used for long, as they could be set alight, but had the advantage of being easy and quick to build. Most of the castles built by Edward I of England to control Scotland were built of wood; after his costly Welsh campaigns, which included the building of such massive castles as Caernarvon, he could afford little else.

Stone Castles of Enclosure or Enceinte (eleventh to thirteenth century)

Stone began to be used as a building material, because it was less vulnerable to attack by fire and because it was easily obtainable. Stone castles of enclosure were built as early as the eleventh or twelfth century, but most appeared in the thirteenth century. The simplest form was a wall enclosing a two-storey hall block of wood or stone. The entrance to the hall block was on the first floor, and was reached by a ladder, which could be removed easily during attack. The wall was usually surrounded by a ditch and rampart.

There are good examples of castles of enclosure on the western side of Scotland, including Castle Sween (Argyll), Castle Tioram (Morvern) and Mingary Castle (Ardnamurchan).

By the thirteenth century, walls were heightened and strengthened, enclosing a courtyard which contained both the hall and lord's chamber, as well as kitchens, bakeries, brewhouses, stables and storerooms. Corner towers were added to defend the castle. The walls were pierced by slits through which crossbows could be fired.

The weakest part of these castles was the entrance through the wall, and strong gatehouses were added with portcullises, drawbridges, iron-studded doors, and murder-holes. The curtain walls were given battlements for archers to shelter behind.

By the fourteenth century, large stone castles such as Bothwell Castle (Lanarkshire), Caerlaverock Castle (Dumfries) and Kildrummy Castle (Aberdeenshire) had been built. These castles had a keep – a large strong tower separate from the rest of the castle – as well as a gatehouse. The keep had a hall and chambers for the

Duffus Castle – originally a motte and bailey castle

Castle Sween – originally a simple castle of enclosure

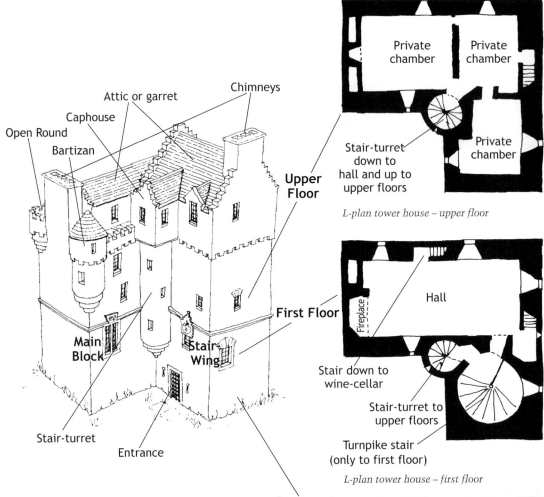

Open Round

Bartizan

Caphouse

Attic or garret

Chimneys

Upper Floor

Main Block

Stair Wing

First Floor

Stair-turret

Entrance

Basement

Private chamber

Private chamber

Private chamber

Stair-turret down to hall and up to upper floors

L-plan tower house – upper floor

Fireplace

Hall

Stair down to wine-cellar

Stair-turret to upper floors

Turnpike stair (only to first floor)

L-plan tower house – first floor

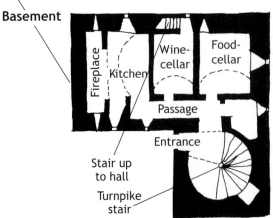

Fireplace

Kitchen

Wine-cellar

Food-cellar

Passage

Entrance

Stair up to hall

Turnpike stair

L-plan tower house – basement

Diagram of L-plan tower house, showing the three main floors

The basement contained the entrance (at the foot of the stair-wing and defended by a door and an iron yett) and was occupied by a kitchen, wine-cellar, and food-cellar. The main turnpike stair only climbed to the first-floor hall, while the upper floors were reached by a turnpike stair in the turret in the re-entrant angle. The lord's private chamber was on the floor above the hall, although there was little privacy for the rest of the household, as each room opened from the last. The upper floors and garret or attic housed guests or servants. The turret stair rose up to the parapet, and was crowned by a caphouse and watch-chamber.

The tower would have had a walled courtyard, or barmkin, enclosing ranges of buildings, including stabling, workshops, a brewhouse and more accommodation.

The walls of the tower were usually harled and whitewashed. The heraldic panel showed the arms of the lord and his wife, who used her own family name, and the date of building or alteration.

Dunnottar Castle – a large and spectacular fortress

lord. These castles also had thick curtain walls with round or square corner towers.

There are relatively few large castles left in Scotland, partly due to the expense of constructing and maintaining such large buildings, and partly because many were destroyed by the Scots during the Wars of Independence, so that they could not be reused by the English. However, some strong royal castles were maintained, including those at Edinburgh, Stirling, Roxburgh, Dumbarton and Dunbar, and a few of the most powerful families could also afford massive fortresses such as the Douglas strongholds of Tantallon (Lothian) and Threave (Galloway) and the Keith stronghold of Dunnottar (Aberdeenshire).

Simple Keeps (fourteenth/fifteenth century)

These consisted of a simple square or rectangular tower, usually with an adjoining courtyard. The walls of the keep were thick, and normally rose at least three storeys to a flush crenellated parapet with a projecting wooden gallery. The basement and first floor were

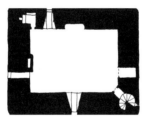

Plan of a keep

Alloa Tower – a simple keep

vaulted to increase the strength of the building. The size of the keep depended on the wealth of the builder.

The basement contained a cellar, often with no connection to the floor above. The hall was on the first floor, with a private chamber for the lord on the floor above, and a garret storey above this. The thick walls contained many mural chambers, either small bedrooms or garderobes. The entrance was at first-floor level, and was reached by an external timber stair, which could be removed during an attack. Stairs led up, within the walls, to each floor. The keep was roofed with stone slates, or slabs, to protect the keep against attack by fire.

The courtyard enclosed buildings such as a kitchen, stables, chapel, brewhouse, and was surrounded by a wall, often with a ditch and drawbridge.

Royal Palaces (fifteenth/sixteenth century)

The Stewart kings spent much of their energy acquiring wealth, usually by forfeiting unpopular subjects or appropriating church revenues and lands. They built or remodelled castles or royal palaces in the Renaissance style at Stirling Castle, Holyrood (Edinburgh), Edinburgh

Falkland Palace – a royal residence

Castle, Linlithgow (West Lothian) and Falkland (Fife), with elaborate ornamentation, larger windows and classical and religious carvings, as well as improved comfort and amenity.

Tower Houses (sixteenth century)

In 1535 an Act of Parliament declared that every man who owned land valued at £100 (Scots) was to build a castle to defend his property.

Although there is no clear divide, tower houses evolved from keeps. The walls became less thick, and the entrance was moved to the basement. Parapets were corbelled-out so that they would overhang the wall and missiles could be dropped on attackers below. The corners had open rounds, and the stair was crowned by a caphouse and watch-chamber. Gunloops and shot-holes replaced arrowslits. The walls were harled and often whitewashed to weatherproof the building. This would, however, make the castle stand out from – rather than blend into – the landscape.

Tower houses also underwent change and adaption in the sixteenth century. After the Reformation, with the increased wealth of Protestant landowners, and the increased availability of land, which had previously belonged to the Church, many examples of more comfort-

Smailholm Tower – a strong tower house

able tower houses were built. These were mostly in the north-east, the central belt and the south, including in the Borders and in Galloway.

The reduction in the need for defensive features meant that these later tower houses were more spacious and comfortable. The structures were still built vertically, and most continued to have one room on each floor. However, wings or towers were either incorporated into or added to the design. Good examples of tower houses can be found at Smailholm

Plan of a tower

Tower (Borders), Crathes Castle (Aberdeenshire) and Amisfield Tower (Dumfries and Galloway).

L-plan Tower Houses (from mid-sixteenth century)

The L-plan tower house had a stair-wing added to the main block. The stair was usually turnpike and climbed only to the hall on the first floor. The upper floors were reached by a turnpike stair in a small stair-turret corbelled out, above first-floor level, in the re-entrant angle. This stair was crowned by a caphouse and watch-chamber. In some cases, the wing contained a stair which climbed to all floors, and sometimes a separate stair-tower stood within the re-entrant angle, and the wing

contained chambers. Greenknowe Tower (Borders) is a fine ruined L-plan tower house while Craigievar (Grampian) is complete.

The defensive features became less obvious. Larger windows were still protected by iron yetts or grills, and gunloops became orna-mental. Open rounds were replaced by bartizans, with conical roofs, and parapets were covered. Decorative features, as well as heraldic panels, inscribed lintels, tempera painting and modelled plasterwork were introduced. These design features showed French and Italian influences. The tower usually had a

Plan of an L-plan tower

Craigievar Castle – an L-plan tower

courtyard with ranges of buildings, including a brew-house, stabling and more accommodation. There were formal and walled gardens, as well as orchards and parks.

The basement was vaulted and contained a kitchen with a large fireplace, a wine-cellar with a small stair to the hall above, and other cellars. The hall was on the first floor of the main block with private chambers on the floors above, and within the garret or attic storey.

Z-plan Tower Houses (late-sixteenth century)

A variation of the L-plan, a Z-plan tower house consisted of a main block, with two towers at diagonally opposite corners. One of the towers usually housed a stair, while the other provided more accommodation. Often further wings or ranges were added to the tower making it E-plan. Glenbuchat Castle (Aberdeenshire) is a fine example of a ruined Z-plan tower house, as is Drochil Castle (Borders), while Claypotts Castle (Angus) is still roofed.

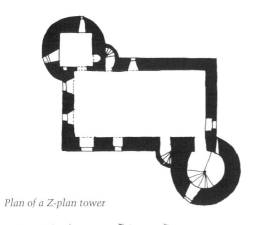

Plan of a Z-plan tower

Claypotts Castle – a Z-plan tower house

Forts (sixteenth to eighteenth century)

With the advent of more sophisticated artillery, the castle became increasingly redundant as a major defensive structure. As early as the 1540s, forts were being built to withstand attack by cannon. The English constructed forts during the invasion of Scotland in 1547-50, including those at Roxburgh (Borders), Eyemouth (Borders) and Haddington (Lothian), which consisted of ramparts and bastions of earth rather than high walls. In the 1650s Cromwell built forts known as citadels at Ayr, Leith (Lothian), Perth, Inverlochy (Highland), Inverness and Aberdeen. The Hanoverian Government built forts, barracks and roads after the Jacobite Risings of 1715 and 1745, including those at Fort George, Fort William, Fort Augustus and Ruthven Barracks (all Highland). Other castles such as Corgarff and Braemar (both Aberdeenshire) were given artillery defences, and were used as bases for campaigns against illicit whisky distilling in the late eighteenth century.

Castellated Mansion Houses (nineteenth century)

Even before the Jacobite Risings, most new houses had ceased to be fortified, and by the end of the seventeenth century the architect Sir William Bruce had built Kinross House, a fine symmetrical mansion. By the mid-eighteenth century, most new houses were built in a classical, Palladian or symmetrical style, designed by architects such as William Adam and his son Robert.

Armadale Castle – a castellated mansion

Many castles were abandoned at this time, because they were uncomfortable and unfashionable as dwellings – many landowners wishing to forget their unruly and barbaric past, and even that they were Scottish.

In the nineteenth century, baronial mansions came into fashion, incorporating or recreating mock castellated features such as towers and turrets, corbelling and machiolations. In many cases these were called castles, although they were certainly never fortified.

Castles, themselves, were reused, restored and reoccupied. Architects such as William Burn, James Gillespie Graham and David Bryce in the nineteenth century, and Sir Robert Lorimer in the twentieth century, designed these castellated mansions. Many of these large country houses did not survive use by the government in World War II, while some others have been used as hotels, schools and youth hostels. Others still remain the centre of estates, some still owned by the original families.

The fashion for restoring and living in many of the smaller towers and fortified houses has greatly increased in recent years, although some of these restorations have been far from successful, at least aesthetically.

Adapted from *The Castles of Scotland*, fourth edition, published by Birlinn in September 2006.

Glossary of Castle Terms

Arcade A series of arches supported by piers or columns. A blind arcade is built against a wall

Arch A self-supporting structure capable of carrying a superimposed load over an opening

Architrave A moulding surrounding, or framing, a doorway or window opening

Ashlar Masonry of worked stone blocks with even faces and squared edges

Astragal A bar in a window, often wooden, between the panes

Attic The top storey entirely within a gabled roof

Aumbry Originally almry, 'a place for alms'. A cupboard, usually in a stone wall, originally to hold sacred vessels for the Mass, but later for domestic use

Bailey A defensible area enclosed by a wall/palisade and a ditch

Balustrade Ornamental parapet of posts and railings

Barbican A building or enclosure, usually of modest size and defensive strength, to protect an entrance or gateway

Barmkin A walled courtyard, often of modest size and defensive strength

Bartizan A turret, corbelled out from a wall, usually crowning corners of a building

Basement The lowest storey of a building, sometimes below ground

Bastle house Small tower house with a living room over a byre

Batter A slight inward inclination or tilt of a wall from its base upwards, either to add strength or to make tunnelling by attacking forces more difficult

Battlement A crenellated parapet to shoot from between the solid sections, or merlons – the crenel being the space

Bay A section or compartment of a building

Bay window A window projecting from a building at ground level, either rectangular or polygonal, of one or more storeys. If it is corbelled out above ground level, it is an oriel window

Boss A knob or projection to cover the intersection of ribs in a vault

Bow window As bay window; but curved in plan

Brattice (Scots: bretasche) A projection from a wall-head, normally built of wood, providing machicolations

Broch (Scots) A round tower-like structure, open in the middle, the double wall of dry-stone masonry being linked by slabs to form internal galleries at varying levels. Found in north and west Scotland, most probably dating from the 1st century AD although some were in use until the 17th century

Buttress A vertical member projecting from a wall to stabilise it, or to resist the lateral thrust of an arch, roof or vault. A flying buttress transmits the thrust to a heavy abutment by an arch or half-arch

Cable moulding A Norman moulding carved like a length of rope

Caphouse A small watch-chamber at the top of a turnpike stair, often opening into the parapet walk and sometimes rising from within the parapet

Caponier A covered passage across a ditch of a castle from which to defend the bottom of the ditch from attack

Castle A fortified house or stronghold; the residence of a nobleman or landowner

Castellations Battlements and turrets

Chevron A Norman zig-zag decorative design based on an inverted V

Classic Revival of classical architectural styles used by the Greeks and Romans, characterized by columns, pediments and symmetrical designs

Close (Scots) A courtyard or passage giving access to a number of buildings

Colonnade A series of evenly spaced columns

Corbiestepped (Scots) Squared stones forming steps upon a gable

Corbel A projecting bracket supporting other stonework or timbers

Courtyard castle Usually a castle of some size and importance built around a central courtyard, normally with a tower or keep, gatehouse, and ranges of buildings such as a kitchen, bakehouse, stable and chapel

Crenellations Battlements made up of crenels and merlons

Crowstepped Squared stones forming steps upon a gable (corbiestepped)

Curtain wall A high enclosing stone wall around a bailey

Donjon The keep or central fortress in a castle

Doocot (Scots) A dovecot

Dormer window A window standing up vertically from a slope of a roof

Dressings Features such as quoins or string-courses made from smoothly worked stone

Drystane (Scots) Dry-stone construction without mortar

Dun, Dum An Iron Age fortified enclosure, built of dry-stone, often with galleried walls, dating from the first century or earlier although some were occupied until the sixteenth or seventeenth century or reused. Can be similar to brochs but not always round in plan

E-plan tower house Tower house with a main block and at least two wings at right angles, dating from the 16th and 17th centuries

Eave An overhanging edge of a roof

Embrasure A small splayed opening in the wall or battlement of a fortified building

Enceinte The line of the wall encircling a fortress

Entresol A low storey within two high ones (mezzanine)

Fore Structure protecting an entrance, as in forestair, forework

Fortalice (Scots) A medium-sized fortified building

Fosse A ditch

Fresco A painting done on wet plaster

Frieze A horizontal band of ornament

Gable A vertical wall or other vertical surface, frequently triangular, at the end of a pitched roof, often with a chimney. In Scotland often corbiestepped (crowstepped)

Gallery A balcony or passage, often with seats, usually overlooking a great hall or garden

Garderobe A medieval privy, usually built into the wall of a castle

Garret The top storey of a building within the roof; attic

Gothic Non-classical medieval architecture, distinguished by high-pitched roofs, sharp-pointed arches, and narrow windows, which progressively became less severe. Revived in its various forms by the Victorians, and seen in many 19th-century mansions

Groin The line of intersection of two vaults

Gunloop An opening for shooting firearms through with an external splay. See also shot-hole

Hall house Defensible usually two-storey building containing a hall, usually above a basement

Hammer-beam An elaborate type of roof used in Gothic and Tudor buildings. To avoid tie-beams across an imposing hall, short timber cantilevers (or hammer-beams) were used

Harling (Scots) Wet dash or roughcasting, hurled or dashed onto a rubble wall of a castle or house to give additional protection against the weather

Heraldic panel A stone panel with the arms and initials of a noble and his wife (using her maiden name). Often records the date, referring usually to the construction or modification of a building

Hill fort Fortified site, often on summit of a hill or coastal promontory, usually with series of ditches and ramparts, many with stone walls. Although most of these settlements were small, others were large towns. Date from Iron Age. Many later castles were built within these fortifications.

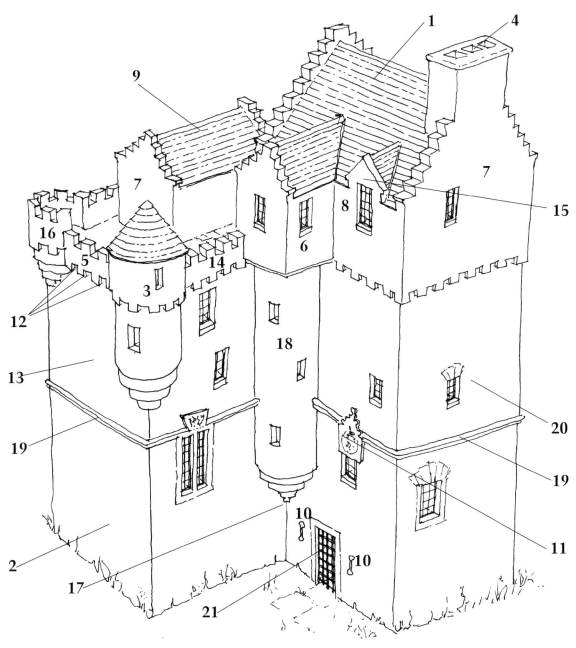

L-plan tower house showing common elements

KEY

1. Attic
2. Basement
3. Bartizan (with conical roof, corbelled out)
4. Chimney
5. Battlement
6. Caphouse (square)
7. Corbiestepped gable
8. Dormer window
9. Garret
10. Gunloops
11. Heraldic panel
12. Machicolations
13. Main block
14. Parapet
15. Pediment (triangular)
16. Round (open)
17. Re-entrant angle
18. Stair-turret (corbelled out)
19. String-course
20. Stair-wing
21. Yett (protecting entrance)

House A castle, tower or fortalice, especially where these have been extended or modified; also mansion, home or dwelling etc.

Jamb The side of a doorway, window, or other opening

Keep Strong stone tower. A citadel or ultimate strong point, normally with a vaulted basement, hall and additional storeys. Often with very thick walls, a flush parapet, and mural chambers. Dates from the fourteenth and fifteenth centuries. Originally called a donjon

L-plan tower house Distinctive Scottish form of the tower house in which a wing was added at right angles to the main tower block, thereby affording greater protection by covering fire and providing more accommodation. Dates from 1540 to 1680

Lancet window A slender pointed arch window

Lintel A horizontal beam of stone, bridging an opening

Loggia A covered open arcade

Loop A small opening to admit light or for the firing of weapons

Machicolation A slot out of which stones or missiles could be shot

Main block Principal part of a castle, usually containing the hall and lord's chamber

Merlon One of the solid tooth-like projections of a battlement

Mezzanine A low storey between two higher ones (entresol)

Moat A ditch, water filled or dry, around an enclosure

Motte A steep-sided flat-topped mound

Motte and bailey A defence system, Roman in origin, consisting of an earth motte (mound) carrying a wooden tower with a bailey (open court) with an enclosing ditch and palisade

Moulding An ornament of continuous section

Mullion A vertical dividing beam in a window

Murder-holes Openings in the roofs of passages, especially entrances, through which attackers could be ambushed

Newel The centre post in a turnpike or winding stair

Niche A vertical recess in a wall, often to take a statue

Ogee A double curve, bending one way then the other

Oratory A small private domestic chapel

Oriel A bay window projecting out from a wall above ground level

Palace An old Scottish term for a two-storey hall block

Pantile A roof-tile of curved S-shape section

Parapet A wall for protection at any sudden drop but defensive in a castle

Pediment A small gable over a doorway or window, especially a dormer

Peel/Pele Originally a palisaded court. Later a stone tower house

Pend (Scots) An open-ended passage through a building, at ground level

Pendant A suspended feature of a vault or ceiling, usually ending in a boss

Pepperpot turret A bartizan with conical or pyramidal roof

Pinnacle Small slender turret or spire

Piscina A basin with a drain for washing the Communion or Mass vessels, usually set in, or against, a wall

Pit-prison A dark prison only reached by a hatch in a vault

Pleasaunce, Pleasance A walled garden

Plinth The projecting base of a wall. It may be battered or stepped

Pointing Exposed mortar joints of masonry or brickwork

Portcullis A wooden and/or iron gate designed to rise and fall in vertical grooves

Postern A secondary gateway or doorway; a back entrance

Quatrefoil Like a four-petalled flower or leaf

Quoin Dressed (ie carefully shaped) stone at a corner of a building

Rampart A stone or earth wall surrounding a castle

Re-entrant angle Inside corner where two wings of a building meet when at right angles

Renaissance Rebirth; the rediscovery of classical architecture in Italy about 1420, which then spread throughout Europe, coming to Scotland somewhat later

Rib-vault A vault supported by ribs or decorated with them

Roll-and-hollow moulding Simple round edging formed at outside vertical corner of hewn stone at the side of door or window

Roll moulding Moulding of near-circular or semi-circular pattern

Romanesque (or **Norman**) Pre-Gothic style of medieval architecture characterised by round-headed arches

Round (Scots) A roofless bartizan

Roundel Round open turret

Royal castle A castle held by a keeper or constable for the monarch

Scale-and-platt Stair with short straight flights and turnings at landings

Screen A wall, wooden or stone, to divide an adjoining kitchen from the hall in a castle

Segmented Broken into segments of a circle

Sill The horizontal projection at the bottom of a window

Skew (Scots) Sloping or sloped stones finishing a gable higher than the roof

Shot-hole A small round hole in a wall through which weapons were fired

Slight To destroy a castle's defences to a greater or lesser extent

Solar (Literally, sun-room) Upper living-room of the lord in a medieval dwelling

Spring Level at which a vault or an arch rises

Squinch A small arch built obliquely across each internal angle of a square tower or other structure to carry a turret or tower

Steading (Scots) A group of farm buildings

Stoup A vessel for holy water

String-course Intermediate course, or moulding, projecting from the surface of a wall

Tempera Form of wall-painting directly on plaster or wood

Tower house Self-contained house with the main rooms stacked vertically usually with a hall over a vaulted basement with further storeys above. Normally in a small courtyard, or barmkin. Dating mainly from 1540 to about 1680

T-plan House or tower where the main (long) block has a wing or tower (usually for the stair) in the centre of one front

Transom Horizontal dividing beam in a window

Trefoil Like a three-petalled flower or leaf

Turnpike stair (Scots) Spiral stair around a newel or central post

Turret A small tower usually attached to a building

Vault An arched ceiling, most usually of stone. Tunnel- or barrel-vaulting, (the simplest kind) is, in effect, a continuous arch. Pointed tunnel-vaults are found occasionally in Scottish buildings. Groin-vaults have four curving triangular surfaces created by the intersection of two tunnel-vaults at right-angles. Also see Rib-vault

Yett A strong hinged gate made of interwoven iron bars

Wall-walk A walkway on top of a wall, protected by a parapet

Walled enclosure A simple castle, normally where a wall encloses a rock or island with a wooden hall and buildings. Dates from the 12th and 13th centuries (castle of enceinte, castle of enclosure)

Ward A defensive enclosure with a stone wall

Z-plan Distinctive Scottish form of the tower house whereby two corner towers were added to the main tower block at diagonally opposite corners, thereby affording greater protection by covering fire and providing more accommodation. Dates from the sixteenth and seventeenth centuries

Glossary of Titles and Offices

Abbot The head of an abbey, a religious house of higher standing than a priory.

Admiral of Scotland The office was held by the Earls of Bothwell from 1488 until 1567 and then from 1581 until 1595.

Advocate A person appearing in court to plead a case; a trained lawyer who can represent the Crown of defendants in court.

Archbishop A bishop of the highest rank; created in Scotland in 1472 (St Andrews), and then in 1492 (Glasgow).

Armour-bearer A person who carried the arms and armour of the king or other noble.

Banner-bearer for Scotland *see* **Standard Bearer**

Baron Originally a land-holding noble; now the second lowest rank of title in Great Britain.

Baronet The lowest rank of title in Great Britain; in Scotland many families were made Baronets of Nova Scotia (a colony in Canada) from 1625 until about 1714.

Bishop A clergyman having spiritual and administrative control over a diocese or area; in Scotland in medieval times there were bishops of St Andrews, Glasgow, Galloway, Dunblane, Dunkeld, Brechin, Aberdeen, Moray, the Isles, Caithness, and Orkney (also see **Archbishop** and **Cardinal**).

Butler Usually the head servant in a household, in charge of wines, food and the table.

Cardinal A member of the Sacred College of the Catholic Church, ranking next to the Pope; the most famous person holding the office in earlier times was Cardinal David Beaton, Archbishop of St Andrews, who was murdered in 1546.

Chamberlain The chief financial officer or administrative officer, and on record from the twelfth century; the office holder was a layman and duties included supervising royal burghs, but the financial duties were later divided between the **Treasurer** and the **Comptroller**; the importance of the office diminished from the fifteenth century although it continued until 1705.

Chancellor An office, first on record from the twelfth century, who was in charge of the Great Seal (also see **Keeper of the Great Seal**); until 1335 the Chancellor was a cleric; in the sixteenth and seventeenth centuries the head of the civil administration in Scotland under the monarch; also the head of a university.

Claviger *see* **Macer**

Clerk of the Rolls *see* **Clerk Register**

Clerk Registrar On record from the thirteenth century, and the office involved keeping the royal and national archives and records; in the sixteenth and seventeenth centuries was usually a trained lawyer; the office still continues but is now only ceremonial.

Commendator Originally a churchman appointed to administer (and use the revenues from) an abbey, priory, bishopric or other benefice that the holder was not qualified to hold; in the sixteenth century used by laymen to enjoy the revenues of Church property without performing any religious duties.

Comptroller 'Roller of Accounts' (or controller of royal finances), and on record from the thirteenth century; the office was responsible for financial control of the royal household and gathered rents from crown lands and shared responsibilities with those of the **Treasurer**.

Constable of Scotland The office is on record from the twelfth century; duties included organising the monarch's forces during times of war and keeping peace at court; long held by the Hay, Earls of Errol.

Countess The female equivalent or wife of an **Earl**.

Duke A noble of the highest rank, beneath the monarch; the first Dukedom in Scotland was created in 1398 for David, son of Robert III; the title is currently held by Prince Charles; **Marquis/Marquess** is the next title in descending order.

Earl A title equivalent to a count or mormaer (rulers or lesser kings of an area beneath the monarch or high king) or Norse Jarl; this became translated to the English Earl; reputedly there were originally seven earldoms or provinces in the early kingdom of Scots: Angus, Atholl, Strathearn, Fife, Mar, Moray and Caithness; others were created from the twelfth century onwards; in the British peerage the title is higher in rank than **Viscount** and lower than **Marquis/Marquess**; there is no female equivalent of Earl so the term **Countess** is used.

Great Steward of Scotland *see* **Steward**

High Steward *see* **Steward**

Justiciar The office is on record from the twelfth century, and the holder was the chief legal and political officer and supervised the work of the **Sheriffs** and heard any appeals; the office was eventually subsumed into that of the **Justice General.** There were two nobles holding the office, one for north of the Forth and one for the south of the Forth.

Justice Clerk The second in command to the Justice General and established in the seventeenth century.

Justice General The chief judge in criminal cases, and the office was held by several families until being held by the Campbells of Argyll from 1514 until 1628. After 1672 the office was held by a professional lawyer, and it was joined with **Lord President** in 1837.

Keeper of the Great Seal The Great Seal (a metal mould for producing wax seals) allowed charters to be ratified by the monarch without having to individually sign each document; the office of keeper was held by many different individuals down the centuries, but it is now held by the First Minister of the Scottish Parliament.

Keeper of the Privy Seal of Scotland The office is first on record from the fourteenth century. The office was held by many different individuals down the centuries but there has been no appointment since 1922.

King The ruler or head of an independent state; in Scotland the first recognised King of Scots was Kenneth MacAlpin, who came to power around 843, although the kingdoms of Scots and of Picts which he united had had one king on more than one occasion before then. Scotland remained an independent kingdom with its own monarchs for much of the following time (a notable exception being apart from the run up to the Wars of Independence after the death of Alexander III in 1290) until the crowns of Scotland and England were united by James VI, King of Scots, in 1603.

King's Advocate *see* **Lord Advocate**

Knight A gentleman invested by a king or high lord with the military and social standing of this rank; the person knighted used the title 'Sir'.

Lady-in-waiting A lady of the royal household who attends a queen or princess.

Laird Scot's word for lord, often used to denote a smaller landowner.

Lord A male member of the nobility or one who has power or ownership of land or some other office.

Lord Advocate The chief law office of the monarch who has discretion over prosecution and could give advice on legal matters; the office was established in 1478 and survives until this day, the holder now being the chief law officer to the Scottish Parliament.

Lord Chancellor *see* **Chancellor**

Lord Clerk Register (or **Registrar**) *see* **Clerk Register**

Lord High Admiral *see* **Admiral of Scotland**

Lord High Commissioner On record from the twelfth century and the representative of the monarch, who attended both the Scottish Parliament and the General Assembly of the Church of Scotland, although only this latter duty now applies. Some of the duties of the office were similar and at times taken over by the **Keeper of the Great Seal.** The office has not been filled since the eighteenth century, the last holder being James Ogilvie, Earl of Seafield, who died in 1730.

Lord High Constable *see* **Constable of Scotland**

Lord High Steward *see* **Steward**

Lord Justice Clerk *see* **Justice Clerk**

Lord Justice General *see* **Justice General**

Lord Lyon King of Arms *see* **Lyon King of Arms**

Lord of the Isles A title taken by the MacDonalds in the thirteenth century as they controlled much of the western seaboard of Scotland. It was not officially recognised by the kings of Scots until the fifteenth century, but James IV imprisoned the last Lord in 1493 and the title is now one of those held by the heir to the British throne, Prince Charles.

Lord President (of the Court of Session) The presiding judge of the Court of Session (the highest court in Scotland) since 1532 and still in existence. The office was originally only held by a cleric but this was abolished in 1579; the office was combined with that of the **Justice General** in 1837.

Lord of Session Originally one of the fifteen judges of the Court of Session (see **Lord President** above). Numbers were increased in recent times; the Lords of Session can also preside in the High Court.

Lyon King of Arms Office, first on record from the fourteenth century, which has ultimate jurisdiction for matters armorial and heraldic. There is a Public Register of all arms and bearings from 1672, and there are several Heralds and Pursuivants associated with the office.

Macer Office responsible for maintaining order at court.

Marischal Office, on record from the twelfth century, which was long held by the Keith family, Earls Marischal from 1458, although the Keiths were forfeited following the 1715 Jacobite Rising.

Marchioness The female equivalent or wife of a **Marquis/Marquess**.

Marquess The second highest rank of nobility in the British peerage, between a **Duke** and an **Earl. Equivalent** to the **Marquis** in the Scottish peerage.

Marquis The second highest rank of nobility in the Scottish peerage, between a **Duke** and an **Earl. Marquess** is equivalent in the British peerage; Marquis was used in Scotland, France and elsewhere.

Master Carver A member of the royal household in Scotland, long held by the Anstruthers, baronets of Balcaskie.

Master of the Household An important office, essentially combining the duties of the High Steward, Comptroller and Treasurer. Long held by the Dukes of Argyll in Scotland and created by James I in the fifteenth century.

Master of the Wardrobe A member of the royal household in Scotland and concerned with organising furniture and raiments for state occasions and visits.

Mormaer *see* **Earl**

Preceptor The head of a preceptory, the religious house of an order of holy knights. The Knights Templar were established in Scotland, but when they were suppressed by the Pope in 1320 their property went to the Knights of St John, who were based at Torphichen in central Scotland and the last of whom, before the Reformation, was Sir James Sandilands.

Prior The head of a priory, a religious house of less standing than (and dependant upon) an abbey or cathedral.

Queen The female equivalent of or wife of a King, The only woman to rule Scotland as an independent kingdom in her own right was Mary, Queen of Scots.

Sheriff Originally (from the twelfth century) the office was concerned with financial and civil administration of an area as well as the hearing of appeals from barony courts. From the later medieval period the office became hereditary but this was abolished in 1747. In Scotland Sheriff Courts have jurisdiction in most areas except for the most serious of crimes such as rape, murder and treason, which are tried at the High Court (of Justiciary), while appeals are held at the Court of Session.

Standard Bearer The holder had the privilege of bearing the Scottish standard into battle; hereditary office, held by the Scrymgeour family, later Earls of Dundee, from the time of William Wallace. This was disputed by the Earls of Lauderdale and a separate office was established for them in the nineteenth century called Bearer of the National Flag of Scotland.

Steward (of Scotland) Office held by Walter Fitzalan from the middle of the twelfth century and then by his descendants. Responsibilities included being the chief of the royal household, collecting taxes, administering justice and the High Steward was also next in power to the king during time of war. Robert, son of Walter the High Steward and Marjorie, daughter of Robert the Bruce, became Robert II, King of Scots, in 1371. The title of High Steward was given to the heir to the monarch and is currently one of the titles held by Prince Charles.

Thane The term was used in Scotland from the twelfth century, and was a landowner or head of a family, although of lesser rank than an **Earl** (or Mormaer).

Treasurer An office sharing financial administration of Scotland along with the **Comptroller**; responsibilities included managing crown expenses not involved with the royal household.

Viscount Rank of nobility between a **Baron** and an **Earl**.

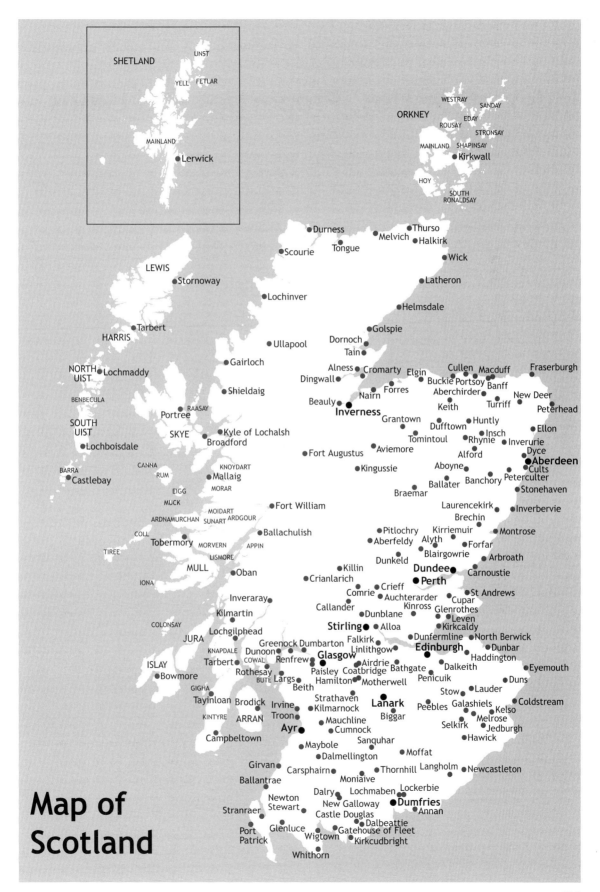

Map of
Scotland

Index of Castles, Properties and Lands

623

Selected Further Reading

Black, G F *The Surnames of Scotland* (New York Public Library, 1946)

Coe, G *The Heart and West of Fife* – Castle Touring Guide (Coecast, 1999)

Coe, G *Edinburgh and the Lothians* – Castle Touring Guide (Coecast, 2006)

Connachan-Holme, J R A *Country Houses of Scotland* (House of Lochar, 1995)

Council for Scottish Archeology *Discovery and Excavation in Scotland* (CSA, yearly)

Coventry, M *Haunted Castles and Houses of Scotland* (Goblinshead, 2004)

Coventry, M *Castles of Scotland*, fourth edn (Birlinn, 2006)

Cruden, S *The Scottish Castle*, third edn (HMSO, 1981)

Dewar, P B *Burke's Landed Gentry of Great Britain: The Kingdom in Scotland*, nineteenth edn (Burke's, 2001)

Donaldson, G and Morpeth, R S *A Dictionary of Scottish History* (John Donald, 1988)

Drahony, P & Drahony, D *Angus Castle Trails* (Finavon Print and Design, 2000)

Dunbar, J G *Scottish Royal Palaces* (Tuckwell Press, 1999)

Fawcett, R *Castles of Fife* (Fife Regional Council, 1993)

Fenwick *Scottish Baronial Houses* (Robert Hale, 1986)

Groome, F *Ordnance Gazetteer of Scotland*, five vols. (MacKenzie, c1890)

Hannan *Famous Scottish Houses* (Mercat Press, 1928)

Keay J and Keay J *Collins Encyclopedia of Scotland* (Collins, 1994)

Lindsay, M *The Castles of Scotland* (Constable, 1986)

MacGibbon, D & Ross, T *The Castellated and Domestic Architecture of Scotland*, five vols. (David Douglas, 1887-92)

McKean, C *The Scottish Chateau* (Sutton Publishing, 2001)

MacKenzie, W M *The Medieval Castle in Scotland* (Methuen, 1927)

Mason, G W *The Castles of Glasgow and the Clyde* (Goblinshead, 2000)

McKean, C (ed.) *Illustrated Architectural Guides* (RIAS, from 1985) *Series of books covering most of Scotland*

McNeill P G B & MacQueen H L *Historical Atlas of Scotland* (University of Edinburgh, 1996)

Miket, R and Roberts, D L *The Mediaeval Castles of Skye and Lochalsh* (MacLean Press, 1990)

Moncreiffe of that Ilk, Sir I *et al Clan Map* (Bartholomew, 1983)

Mosley, C (ed.) *Burke's Peerage, Baronetage and Knightage*, 107th edn (Burke's, 2003)

Ross, S *Scottish Castles* (House of Lochar, 1990)

Ross, S *The Castles of Scotland* (Chambers, 1987)

Salter, M *The Castles of Grampian and Angus* (Folly, 1995)

Salter, M *The Castles of the Heartland of Scotland* (Folly, 1994)

Salter, M *The Castles of Lothian and the Borders* (Folly, 1994)

Salter, M *The Castles of South-West Scotland* (Folly, 1993)

Salter, M *The Castles of Western and Northern Scotland* (Folly, 1995)

Smith, J S *North East Castles* (AUP, 1990)

Stone, J *Illustrated Maps of Scotland from Blaeu's Atlas Novus of the 17th century* (Studio Editions, 1991)

Tabraham, C *Scotland's Castles* (Batsford/ Historic Scotland, 1997)

Tales from Scottish Lairds (Jarrold, 1985)

Tranter, N *The Fortalices and Early Mansions of Southern Scotland* (Moray Press, 1954)

Tranter, N *The Fortified House in Scotland*, 5 vols. (James Thin/Mercat Press 1962-70)

Tranter, N *Tales and Traditions of Scottish Castles* (NWP, 1982)

Way, G & Squire, R *Scottish Clan & Family Encyclopedia* (Collins, 1994)

Guidebooks are available for most castles and mansions that are open to the public.